TimeOut

timeout.com/shopping

EDITION
11

C(

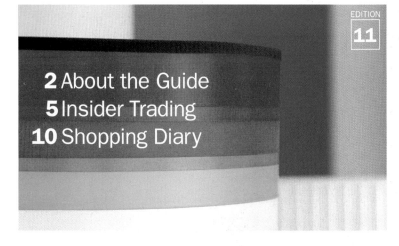

2 About the Guide
5 Insider Trading
10 Shopping Diary

About the Guide

No retail guide to a city of London's scale can be completely comprehensive; we have tried to select what we believe are the best of the capital's shops and services. If you feel we've missed somewhere exceptional or included a place that's gone downhill, please email us at guides@timeout.com.

Opening hours

Many of the shops, companies and individuals listed in this guide keep regular store hours; others are small concerns run from private addresses or workshops that have erratic opening hours, or are open by appointment only. In such cases, the times given are a guide as to when to phone, not when to visit.

The opening times were correct at the time of writing, but if you're going out of your way to visit a particular shop, always phone first to check (especially as stores are constantly launching and closing down in London). Many outlets extend their opening times in summer (to benefit from tourist traffic) and in the run-up to Christmas; others take their holidays in August and close altogether. Some are closed on bank holidays or have reduced opening times.

Credit cards

The following abbreviations are used: **AmEx**: American Express; **DC**: Diners Club; **MC**: MasterCard; **V**: Visa. Some larger shops and department stores also accept euros (€).

Disabled

We have indicated provisions for disabled shoppers where appropriate. *Disabled: lift* is self-explanatory; *toilet* indicates that there is a toilet adapted for disabled use somewhere on the premises. It's always worth phoning to check the specifics of such facilities if you're making a special trip.

Fashion

We have indicated whether shops that are listed in the fashion section sell menswear and/or womenswear with the letters **M** and **W** respectively. Childrenswear is represented by a **C**, babywear by a **B**.

Prices

Where prices are quoted, bear in mind that while they were accurate at the time of writing, they are subject to change.

Mail order

We consider that companies operate a mail-order service only if it is a formal, regular part of their business. Always use the full postcode when shopping by mail order or writing to an organisation for information, otherwise letters may be sent second class. Many more shops will send goods by post on an informal basis; it's always worth asking.

Branches

We have included listings for London branches in the A-Z index at the back of this Guide. For shops with branches throughout the city, please see the telephone directory for the location of your nearest. Note that different branches of a shop may have different opening times; it is therefore always advisable to call to check times before setting out.

Sponsors and advertisers

Published by
Time Out Guides Limited
Universal House
251 Tottenham Court Road
London W1T 7AB
Tel +44 (0)20 7813 3000
Fax +44 (0)20 7813 6001
email guides@timeout.com
www.timeout.com

Editorial
Editor Ismay Atkins
Deputy Editors Jan Fuscoe, Lisa Ritchie
Copy Editors Sally Davies, Dominic Earle
Researchers Jill Emeny, Holly Furneaux, Cathy Limb, Ben Machell
Proofer Sylvia Tombesi-Walton

Editorial/Managing Director Peter Fiennes
Series Editor Sarah Guy
Deputy Series Editor Cath Phillips
Business Manager Gareth Garner
Guides Co-ordinator Holly Pick
Accountant Kemi Olufuwa

Design
Art Director Scott Moore
Art Editor Tracey Ridgewell
Designer Josephine Spencer
Junior Designer Pete Ward
Digital Imaging Dan Conway
Advertising Designer Jenni Prichard

Picture Desk
Picture Editor Jael Marschner
Deputy Picture Editor Tracey Kerrigan
Picture Researcher Helen McFarland

Advertising
Sales Director & Sponsorship Mark Phillips
Sales Manager Alison Wallen
Advertising Sales Linda Hall, Ben Holt, Ali Lowry, Jason Trotman
Advertising Assistant Lucy Butle
Copy Controller Amy Nelson

Marketing
Marketing Director Mandy Martine
Marketing & Publicity Manager, US Rosella Albanese
Marketing Designer Simeon Greenaway

Production
Production Director Mark Lamond
Production Controller Marie Howell

Time Out Group
Chairman Tony Elliott
Managing Director Mike Hardwick
Group Financial Director Richard Waterlow
Group Commercial Director Lesley Gill
Group General Manager Nichola Coulthard
Group Art Director John Oake
Online Managing Director David Pepper
Group Production Director Steve Proctor
Group IT Director Simon Chappell
Group Circulation Director Jim Heinemann

Sections in this guide were written by:
Shopping Diary Natasha Polyviou. **One-stop** Department Stores Jan Fusc (*Eat, Drink, Shop* Christi Daugherty); **Markets** Jan Fuscoe (*Markets under threat* Rebecca Taylor); **Shopping Centres** Sue Webster, Anna Norman. **Fashion Designer** Maggie Davis; **Boutiques** Lisa Ritchie (*Hot jeans* Maggie Davis); **Womenswear** Lisa Ritchie; **Menswear** Alfred Tong; **Street** Andrew Staffell, Alfred Tong (*Trainerspotting* Andrew Staffell); **Bespoke** Tom Greatrex; **Retro & Second-hand** Jessica Ferguson (*Thrift solutions* Bay Garnett); **Weddings** Natasha Polyviou; **Maternity** Ronnie Haydon; **Fetish** Elise Rana; **Unusual Sizes** Jill Emeny; **Shoes** Jessica Ferguson; Lisa Ritch **Lingerie & Underwear** Kate Riordan (*Splash out* Lisa Ritchie); **Accessorie** Natasha Polyviou; Sue Webster; **Jewellery** Natasha Polyviou; **Dry-cleaning & Repairs** Cathy Limb; **Health & Beauty** Shops Lesley McCave (*Natural beauty* Ismay Atkins); **Services** various (*Bed & backrub* Lisa Ritchie); **Hairdressers** various (*Best for...* Lisa Ritchie); **Opticians** Jan Fuscoe; **Nail Accessories** Max Fraser; **Antiques** Lindsay Calder; **Bathrooms & Kitchen** Jan Fuscoe; **Design, Art & Crafts** Lindsay Calder; **Furniture** Max Fraser, Jan Fuscoe, Lisa Ritchie; **Gardens & Flowers** Jill Emeny, Holly Furneaux, Cathy Limb; **Interiors** Jan Fuscoe; **20th-century Design** Claire Fogg; *Leisu* **Books** Anna Norman; **CDs & Records** David Jenkins; **Electronics** Andrew Staffell (*Chic tech* David Phelan); **Entertaining** Ben Machell; **Gifts** Anna McIlreavy; **Hobbies & Crafts** Amy Bratley; **Magic & Games** Cathy Limb; **Music** Andrew Staffell; **Pets** Cathy Limb, Lisa Ritchie; **Photography** Lam Thuy Vo (*Picture this* Christi Daugherty); **Sport** Patrick Welch; **Stationery** Lam Thuy Vo; **Transport** Cathy Limb; *Food & Drink* **Food** Sejal Sukhadwa **Drink** James Aufenast; Lam Thuy Vo (*Cigars* Ben Machell); **Babies & Children** Ronnie Haydon; **Additional reviews written by** Ros Atkins, Simo Cropper, Christi Daugherty, Lily Dunn, Jill Emeny, Sarah Guy, Helen Hamb Ruth Jarvis, Kate Johnson, Cathy Limb, Julie Manniche, Anna McIlreavy, Mandy Martinez, Anna Norman, Sara Northey, Cath Phillips, Holly Pick, Natasha Polyviou, Lisa Ritchie, Ros Sales, Andrew Staffell, Rebecca Tayl Lam Thuy Vo. **Subject Index** Jackie Brind.

Thanks to: Maggie Davis, Katherine Hayes, Steve Proctor, Kate Riorda

Cover Photography by Chris Tubbs.

Openers Photography by Chris Tubbs. Styling by Nicki Peters.

Photography pages 2, 21, 30, 31, 68, 73, 91, 92, 93, 113, 149, 15 264 Alys Tomlinson; pages 5, 6, 9, 38, 89, 123, 196 Rob Greig; pag 5, 6 Rex Features; page 9 Topfoto; pages 13, 35, 40, 44, 57, 63, 74 79, 97, 102, 127, 141, 165, 179, 189, 200, 201, 214, 244, 245, 249, 252 Britta Jaschinski; pages 15, 47, 48, 50, 60, 80, 110, 111 158, 229, 265 Anthony Webb; pages 36, 84, 85, 161, 119, 120, 20 212, 217, 230 Ming Tang Evans; pages 54, 125, 183, 206, 226, 22 Sean Gallagher; pages 59, 129, 145, 176 Nicky Willcock; pages 65, 76, 132, 162, 168, 169 Gemma Day; pages 66, 222, 223 Magnus Andersson; page 75 Ed Marshall; pages 235 Tricia de Courcy Ling; pages 240, 256, 257, 259, 260, 261 Heloise Bergman.
The following images were provided by the featured establishments: pages 14, 27, 32, 53, 94, 105, 131, 138, 196, 203

Maps by JS Graphics – jsgraphics@wanadoo.fr.

Reprographics by Icon Reproduction, Crowne House, 56-58 Southwa Street, London SE1 1UN.

Printed and bound by Cooper Clegg Ltd, Shannon Way, Tewkesbury, Glos GL20 8HB.

Copyright © Time Out Group Limited 2005
ISBN 0 903446 67 7
Distributed by Seymour Ltd (020 7396 8000)
Distributed in USA by Publishers Group West

HACKETT

JUBILEE PLACE MALL

CORNEY & BARROW

MONTBLANC

WHISTLES

AREN MILLEN

L'OCCITANE

CANADA PLACE PARK

BANG & OLUFSEN

THOMAS PINK

CRABTREE & EVELYN

CRABTREE & EVELYN

BURRELLS INTERNATIONAL

REISS

CAFFÈ NERO

PLATEAU RESTAURANT BAR AND GRILL

ITSU

JUBILEE PARK

CANARY WHARF
SHOPS, CAFÉS, BARS & RESTAURANTS

CANARY WHARF OFFERS A GREAT DAY OUT WITH OVER 200 SHOPS, BARS AND RESTAURANTS OPEN SEVEN DAYS A WEEK. THIS UNIQUE AND THRIVING AREA OF LONDON IS EASY TO GET TO BY BUS, CAR, JUBILEE LINE OR ON FOOT.

FOR FURTHER INFORMATION VISIT MYCANARYWHARF.COM

www.korres.com

❷ Korres natural products

Athens
Dermatologically tested
Mineral oil free
Silicone free

With roots in the oldest homeopathic pharmacy in Athens, Korres' history is as rich as the gourmet body butters, nourishing creams, hair products and shaving preparations we create.

Let us remove Christmas shopping stress by taking care of your gift dilemmas: a variety of gift-boxes can be filled to order and posted direct to your door, simply by phoning the Korres Store for a brief chat with one of our consultants.

Alternatively, we look forward to seeing you at our Kings Road store where one of our team would be delighted to help you and pick out a range of samples to suit your needs.

Korres Flagship Store King's Road
124 King's Road, Chelsea, London, SW3 4TR
T 020 7581 6455 E info@korresstore.co.uk

Insider *Trading*

The best places to shop by those in the know.
Lindsay Calder gets some top tips.

PHOTOGRAPHY I MAGNUS ANDERSSON

Fashion

Fashion designer **Tracey Boyd** *lives in Chelsea.*

'I tend to walk everywhere in London, so the shops I like are near my home and work. My regular shopping track is from my house down the King's Road to Sloane Square, through Elizabeth Street – where my shop is – then up towards Bond Street. Something of an expensive route! **Manolo Blahnik** (*see p71*) is a firm favourite – I go for the really bright, mad high heels. I used to treat myself to one pair a season, but it's now one a year because they've become so expensive. I buy quite a few pairs of shoes over the year from **Miu Miu** (*see p30*) – the prices aren't bad and I love the bags and little jackets. There's also a gorgeous shop called **Austique** (*see p36*) on the King's Road – it has everything from clothes to really lovely underwear and bath things.

Out of my area, **aQuaint** (*see p35* **Ashley's Boutique**; *pictured above*) in Covent Garden is more exciting than the better-known

boutiques. I also go to the little shops on **Portobello Green** (*see p15* **Portobello Road Market**) under the flyover. I prefer the intimacy of small shops, but **Liberty** (*see p13*) manages to feel more like a boutique than a department store. It's not as sprawling as the big stores, which just make me feel exhausted.

On the high street I rate **Topshop** (*see p45*) and **H&M** (*see p44*). I've designed for the high street and I've also done a new range for *Empire* catalogue – you get the look for about a tenth of the price. I like being able to open up the field to people who can't afford my main line. My most recent high-street buy was a fantastic pair of boots from **Ravel** (184-188 Oxford Street, W1D 1NP, 7631 4135). I never buy cheap shoes, but these were so good I couldn't resist them. I saw a model wearing them on a shoot and thought they were Chloé. **Miss Selfridge** (*see p45*) is definitely worth a look too; it has some great shoes and accessories. I was about to buy some beads for the shop from a designer in Paris at £200 a row, when I discovered almost exactly the same thing in Miss Selfridge for a tenner – if you wear a few strands with a cashmere jumper they look really pricey.

If I'm buying vintage clothes for myself I go to the monthly vintage fashion fairs at Hammersmith Town Hall (for vintage fairs, *see p10* **Shopping Diary**). There's also a fine shop on Fulham High Street called **Circa** (*see p58*) that stocks lots of Ossie Clark. I don't ever shop for party dresses. If I'm going to a glitzy do, I always wear my own designs.'

For a review of Tracey Boyd's shop **BOYD**, *see p24*.

Food

Cookery writer **Nigella Lawson** *lives in Chelsea.*

'I have a far-flung shopping life. The food shop I go to most, which is a long way from me, is **Panzer's** (*see p238*) in St John's Wood. It's been around for about 50 years, and I remember going there with my grandmother. Not only does it have fruit and veg and fancy stuff, but it's also the only place outside Brick Lane where you can get a proper bagel rather than a soft bun with a hole in it. I don't have a car anymore, but they deliver, and I have them on speed dial on my mobile.

Having lived in Shepherd's Bush for a long time, I go back to **Sri Thai** (*see p244*) for Thai ingredients. I rather like strange, obsessive shops that just deal in one thing, like **Nut Case** (*see p242*) on Uxbridge Road. You can buy pistachios that have just been roasted – delicious.

If I'm buying meat, then I'll go to **Allen & Co** (*see p245*) in Mount Street. For fish I go to **Chalmers & Gray** (*see p246*). I had my first flat in Notting Hill and started shopping there then. I still haven't found anywhere else with better fish who will deliver.

I do shop locally. I have a gem-like **Waitrose** (www.waitrose.com) near me that stocks tins of giant marrowfat peas, which I love. I go there in the morning when I take my daughter to school, then I drop in at **Poilâne** (*see p233*) and pick up a loaf of bread. I sometimes go to **Jeroboams** (*see p233*) in Elizabeth Street for wine, but if I'm buying a lot I'm likely to phone up **John Armit** (*see p250*) and have it delivered.

Because I bake quite a lot, I don't think of going to a cake shop as a treat. My idea of indulgence is a visit to **La Fromagerie** (*see p233*; *pictured above*) in Marylebone – it's the most wonderful shop and eating cheese is the best way to get fat there is. You can sit there and order a plate of cheeses – they have a different selection each day. I often arrange to have meetings nearby, so I have an excuse to go in. **Selfridges** (*see p232*) has my favourite food hall, but if **Harvey Nichols** (*see p232*) could be persuaded to keep its food hall open as long as its restaurant, I would consider changing allegiances. For kitchen things I go to **Peter Jones** (*see p14*), **Divertimenti** (*see p135*), **Summerill & Bishop** (*see p124*) and **Mint** (*see p147*). If I need a cake tin in a particular size, I know that **Kitchen Ideas** (*see p124*) on Westbourne Grove will have one. It also has ridiculous things – I recently bought a £1.99 tea-bag squisher which everyone teases me about, but I love strong tea and it squeezes out every last drop.

The best thing I've bought recently is a dark wicker tray that's big enough to carry two vast dinner plates up to the bedroom. But I'd quite like to find a cigarette girl tray that I could wear…'

For Nigella Lawson's kitchenware collection, *see p124* **Living Kitchen**.

Beauty

Ruby Hammer, *co-owner of Ruby & Millie cosmetics, lives in Maida Vale.*

'In the old days I liked going to **Space NK** (*see p93*), but now I love the beauty hall in **Liberty** (*see p13*). It's got absolutely everything. I enjoy just going in there for a little sniff around. I love the small pharmacies and perfumeries you find in Spain and France. We don't really have anything like that in London, but nothing beats going to a good **Boots** (*see p88*) – you get all your basics in one go.

When it comes to beauty treatments, I go to **Tinya Yan** (07957 384068) – a wonderful Chinese lady in Hallam Street – for deep tissue massages; they are so heavy-duty that they almost verge on medical. If I could recommend one place for beauty in London, it would have to be **Vaishaly Patel** (*see p98*; pictured right) in Paddington Street. I have regular facials, which Vaishaly customises for me with massage, micro-dermabrasion or whatever she deems necessary depending on the damage. It's a great one-stop place; there's a very good manicurist, and there's John, who practises traditional Chinese medicine. I always feel very comfortable there – everyone knows me.'

Ruby & Millie cosmetics (www.rubyandmillie.com) are available at larger branches of Boots (*see p88*) throughout the capital.

Oxo Tower Wharf

A complete London riverside shopping experience under one roof

Innovative, one-off creations and objects of delight available all year round

33 designer-maker shops on 3 floors

Plus places to eat and drink and free exhibitions in the.gallery@oxo and Bargehouse

Visit www.oxotower.co.uk to find out about products, designers, exhibitions and events

Shops open Tues–Sun 11am-6pm, restaurants and bars open daily until late

10 minutes from Waterloo, Blackfriars and Southwark tubes; between the National Theatre and Tate Modern

Oxo Tower Wharf Bargehouse Street, South Bank, London SE1 9PH 24 hour information line 020 7401 2255

Beauty

Socialite **Tamara Beckwith** *lives in Chelsea.*

'I'm not the type to wander through a department store and try lots of different products – I go in knowing exactly what I want. If I'm on a job and someone uses a new cream or make-up on me I'll ask what it is and make a note of it. If I'm buying refills, I go to **Harrods** (*see p12*) because I have an account there and it stocks most of the products I use, such as Lancôme and La Prairie. For more chi-chi brands, I'll go to **Space NK** (*see p93*). It stocks Korner products – an Australian brand that I love. I'm also a mad fan of **Jo Malone** (*see p95*) and I panic if I can't get hold of her ginseng moisturiser. But I tend to order rather than go to the shop – otherwise I end up buying scented candles and things that I don't really need.

I'm not good at spending hours somewhere being pampered – I just lie there going stir-crazy – so I don't have facials regularly. But I was hugely impressed by the rehydration facial at the **Elemis Day Spa** (*see p99; pictured right*); it's a lovely place because it's not too spa-ish – there aren't lots of girls wandering around in dressing gowns.

I've had my nails done at the **Country Club** (*see p103*) in SW6 since I was 18 and I wouldn't dream of going anywhere else. Electra is the best manicurist in London – her acrylics look completely real. My father can't bear women with bad nails, and I think I grew up being conscious of that. My eyebrows are an obsession, too. **Arezoo Kaviani** (7584 6868, 07768 903 090) waxes them – she does all my waxing, including a Playboy

bikini (all off). I took my daughter Anouska, now 18, there for her first bikini wax, but I'm not sure that was a very maternal thing to do. **Charles Worthington** (*see p107*) cuts my hair twice a year, and for colour I go to Josh at **Realhair** (6-8 Cale Street, SW3 3QU, 7589 0877) in Chelsea – I don't trust anyone else. For a fake tan, I go to **St Tropez**'s private salon. I'm not obsessed with tanning, but my boyfriend, Giorgio Veroni, is Italian, so I look really ill next to him if I don't have a tan. But fake tans and nails are where it stops. I'm totally against things like Botox, and I tell friends who've had it that they look dreadful – they don't even know what they're putting into their faces. When it comes to your skin, it all depends – sometimes you drink like a monster and sometimes you're as good as gold.'

Books

Novelist **Sarah Waters** *lives in Kennington.*

'When I first moved to London I worked at the **Owl Bookshop** (*see p183*) in Kentish Town. It's expanded since then, but the staff have worked there for years and really know their stuff. If you get to know a small bookseller and trust their selections, you can end up reading things you wouldn't necessarily have gone for.

I tend to go to Charing Cross Road for books – I know it's a bit unimaginative, but I really like the second-hand bookshops. There's one in particular called **Any Amount of Books** (*see p187*) that has a fabulous basement full of obscure old novels – all very cheap. **Stephen Foster Books** (*see p189; pictured right*) on Bell Street is another top-notch second-hand bookshop. It's very Dickensian and higgledy-piggledy inside, so you find things unexpectedly. I also like **Foyles** (*see p182*), which now contains the women's-interest bookshop **Silver Moon** (*see p187*). If I'm buying a new book by a female author, I try to go there to support them. They have a very good stock of gender issue books. I also go to **Gay's the Word** (*see p185*), which has done really well considering that gay books are now in the mainstream.

I was dubious about the size of the Piccadilly **Waterstones** (*see p182*) before it opened as I thought it might be a bit soulless. But of all the big bookshops, that one really works. I love the layout and the sense of space – you can spend a long time in there. And it has a loo!

I don't tend to go to the posher antiquarian shops, like the places opposite the British Museum, but I was always hoping that I would

find somewhere like the erotica dealer in my novel *Fingersmith*. I thought if you went into one of those antiquarian shops and said the right thing to the man at the counter, they'd suddenly open up a door and you'd find this fantastic collection. But I was never brave enough to try it.'

Sarah Waters's latest novel, *The Night Watch*, is published by Virago in February 2006.

Shopping Diary

London's shopping scene is by no means restricted to the high street – there is always a specialist fair, sale, auction or open studio offering up niche items for the discerning shopper. A selection of the best is listed below, though, as there are scores of similar events in the capital, your best resource is the weekly *Time Out* magazine. If you have a specific interest, check other chapters of this guide, where we've listed relevant events. We advise you to check the date and venue nearer the time.

Antiques & collectibles

Alexandra Palace Antique & Collectors Fair
Great Hall, Alexandra Palace, Alexandra Palace Way, N22 7AY (8883 7061/www.pigandwhistle promotions.com). Wood Green tube then W3 bus or free shuttle bus. **Dates** 20 Nov 2005, 15 Jan, 12 Mar, 14 May, 17 Sept, 19 Nov 2006.
London's largest antiques fair, where you can browse a vast array of items, from jewellery and china to textiles and furniture.

Antiquarian Book Fair
Olympia Exhibition Halls, Hammersmith Road, W14 8UX (7439 3118/www.olympiabookfair.com). Kensington Olympia tube/rail. **Date** 8-11 June 2006.
Draws some 150 book dealers from around the world. Prices range from a few quid into the thousands.

Bloomsbury Auctions
24 Maddox Street, W1S 1PP (7833 2636/www.bloomsbury-book-auct.com). Oxford Circus tube. **Dates** check website for details.
Around 40 book, photograph and modern print sales are held each year.

Decorative Antiques & Textiles Fair
Battersea Park, SW11 4NJ (7624 5173/www.decorativefair.com). Sloane Square tube then free shuttle bus. **Dates** 24-29 Jan, Apr, Oct 2006.
Interior design fair showing around 100 dealers.

Grosvenor House Art & Antiques Fair
Le Meridien Grosvenor House Hotel, Park Lane, W1K 7TN (7399 8100/www.grosvenor-antiques fair.co.uk). Hyde Park Corner or Marble Arch tube. **Date** 15-21 June 2006.
Everything from antiquities to 20th-century iconic pieces is up for grabs at this show.

London ABC Show
Royal National Hotel, Bedford Way, WC1H 0DG (8768 0022/www.bookpalace.com). Russell Square tube. **Dates** check website for details.
This Art, Books & Comics show has annuals, pulp and paperback books, plus original comic artwork.

Olympia Fine Art & Antiques Fairs
Olympia Exhibition Halls, Hammersmith Road, W14 8UX (0870 126 1725/www.olympia-antiques. com). Kensington Olympia tube/rail. **Dates** 7-13 Nov 2005, 28 Feb-5 Mar, 8-18 June 2006.
A vast array of items from many periods; the summer fair is the biggest, with around 400 dealers.

Design, art & crafts

Affordable Art Fair
Battersea Park, SW11 4NJ (7371 8787/ticket hotline 0870 777 2255/www.affordableartfair.co.uk). Sloane Square tube then free shuttle bus. **Dates** 15-19 Mar, 18-22 Oct 2006.

The name says it all – a contemporary art fair with pieces ranging from £50 to £3,000.

The Chocolate Factory
Farleigh Place, N16 7SX (7503 6961/www.chocolatefactory.org.uk). Dalston Kingsland rail. **Dates** June, Nov.
Ceramics, paintings, sculptures, glassware, textiles and lighting from young designers. *See also p137.*

Cockpit Open Studios
www.cockpitarts.com. **Deptford** *18-22 Creekside, SE8 3DZ (8692 4463). Deptford or Greenwich rail.* **Holborn** *Cockpit Yard, Northington Street, WC1N 2NP (7419 1959). Chancery Lane tube.* **Dates** end May-mid June; 1st weekend Dec (Deptford), last weekend Nov (Holborn).
The largest designer-maker support network in London, with wares from jewellers, ceramicists, glass artists, textiles and interiors designers.

Collect
Victoria & Albert, Cromwell Road, SW7 2RL (recorded info 09013 310 035/bookings 0870 842 2208/www.craftscouncil.org.uk/collect). South Kensington tube. **Date** 9-13 Feb 2006.
International art fair for contemporary objects, presented by the Crafts Council, which also organises Chelsea Crafts Fair (see website for details).

Country Living Fair
Business Design Centre, 52 Upper Street, N1 0QH (ticket hotline 0870 126 1801/www.countryliving fair.com). Angel tube/Highbury & Islington tube/rail. **Dates** 9-13 Nov 2005, 15-19 Mar 2006.
High-quality rural products from small British businesses, including gifts, food and drink.

East London Design Show
Shoreditch Town Hall, 380 Old Street, EC1V 9LT (8510 9069/www.eastlondondesignshow.co.uk). Old Street tube/rail. **Dates** 1-4 Dec 2005.
Established names and recent graduates show, offering affordable interior and fashion design.

Hidden Art
7729 3800/www.hiddenart.com. **Date** 26-27 Nov, 3-4 Dec 2005.
Designers' studios are open to the public during these times; call for a map of participants.

London Art Fair
Business Design Centre, 52 Upper Street, N1 0QH (0870 126 1783/www.londonartfair.co.uk). Angel tube. **Date** 18-22 Jan 2006.
The biggest art fair in town, with dealers offering everything from traditional to cutting-edge works.

Made in Clerkenwell
Clerkenwell Green Association, Pennybank Chambers, 33-35 St John's Square, EC1M 4DS (7251 0276/www.cga.org.uk). Farringdon tube/rail. **Dates** 25-27 Nov 2005; early June 2006.
Buy jewellery, fashion, textiles, illustration, photography, ceramics and glass directly from the hottest new design talents.

20/21 British Art Fair
Royal College of Art, SW7 2EU (8742 1611/www.britishartfair.co.uk). South Kensington tube. **Dates** 13-17 Sept 2006.
This long-established fair specialises in art from 1900 to the present day.

Fashion

Alternative Fashion Week
Spitalfields Traders' Market, Brushfield Street, E1 6AA (7375 0441/www.alternativearts.co.uk). Liverpool Street tube/rail. **Dates** 20-24 Mar 2006.

London's hippest new design talents sell and exhibit their work. Catwalk shows start at 1.15pm.

British Designer Sale
Chelsea Old Town Hall, King's Road, SW3 5EE (7228 5314/bds@london83.freeserve.co.uk). Sloane Square tube. **Dates** Nov 2005, Feb, May, July (womenswear only), Sept, Nov 2006.
Mens- and womenswear from big-name designers. Members (£40/yr) can attend private viewings before the main sale.

Designer Sale UK
Studio 95, Old Truman Brewery, 95A Brick Lane, E1 6QL (mailing list 01273 470 880/during sale week 7247 8595/www.designersales.co.uk). Aldgate East tube. **Dates** Dec 2005; Feb, Apr, May, Sept, Oct 2006.
Orla Kiely, Fake London and Duffer regularly feature. Get on the mailing list for previews.

Designer Warehouse Sales
45 Balfe Street, N1 9EF (7837 3322/www.dws london.co.uk). King's Cross tube/rail. **Dates** Dec 2005, Feb, Mar, Apr, June, Sept, Oct 2006.
Both general mens- and womenswear sales are held, plus a Nicole Farhi sale twice a year and a Ghost sale in the summer.

London Fashion Weekend
Natural History Museum, Cromwell Road, SW7 5BD (ticket hotline 0870 890 0097/www.london fashionweek.co.uk). Sloane Square tube. **Dates** Feb, Sept (weekend after Fashion Week).
Tickets to Fashion Week are for trade only, but you can buy clothes and accessories at this event.

London Textiles, Vintage Fashion & Accessories Fair
Hammersmith Town Hall, King Street, W6 9JH (8543 5075/www.pa-antiques.co.uk). **Dates** every 5wks; call for dates.
Textiles and accessories from the 1800s to the 1980s. There's also a thrice-yearly London Antique Textiles, Tribal Art & Decorative Antiques Fair at the same venue (6 Nov 2005).

20th-Century Fashion Sale
Christie's, 85 Old Brompton Road, SW7 3LD (7930 6074/www.christies.com). South Kensington tube. **Date** 8 Mar, end Sept 2006.
Couture clothing from big names in design.

Food

Henrietta Green's Food Lovers' Market
The Piazza, WC2E 8RF (8206 6111/www.food loversbritain.com). Covent Garden, Embankment or Temple tube/Charing Cross tube/rail. **Dates** 4-6 Nov 2005.
Fresh produce from small British companies. Cooking demonstrations add to the fun.

Festive BBC Good Food Show
Earl's Court One, Warwick Road, SW5 9TA (0870 161 2148/www.festivebbcgoodfoodshow.com). Earl's Court tube/rail. **Dates** 2-4 Dec 2005.
Buy food and kitchen gadgets while watching demonstrations by celebrity chefs.

Homes & gardens

Daily Telegraph House & Garden Fair
Olympia Exhibition Halls, Hammersmith Road, W14 8UX (0870 121 2525/www.houseand gardenfair.co.uk). Kensington Olympia tube/rail. **Date** 29 June-2 July 2006.
The latest interior design and garden trends.

Ideal Home Show
Earl's Court Exhibition Centre, Warwick Road, SW5 9TA (ticket hotline 0870 606 6080/www.idealhomeshow.co.uk). Earl's Court tube. **Dates** 6-15 Oct 2006.
Show houses and interiors, as well as lots of advice from experts, feature at this big-budget affair.

One-stop

BUTTONS AND JAR FROM LOOP (7288 1160, WWW.LOOP.GB.COM). EVERYTHING ELSE FROM PORTOBELLO MARKET.

Department Stores

These days, one-stop shopping couldn't be easier. No longer the home of sad-sack T-shirts and polyester slacks, department stores now stock sensational designer ranges of everything from lingerie to homeware. Instead of bland cafeterias, some boast top-notch eateries (see p14 **Eat, drink, shop**). Sadly, the competition is too much for some. Over the years, the high streets have seen the closure of such names as Bourne & Hollingsworth, Swan & Edgar, Derry & Toms and Simpsons in the Strand. More recently, 2005 saw the demise of Allders' Oxford Street store, which proved to be too close to Marble Arch and too far from Bond Street to trade well. The biggest shock, however, was news that House of Fraser plans to close one of its best-known department stores, Regent Street's Dickins & Jones, which has been trading since 1803. Perhaps the competition from nearby Liberty and trendier openings like the Apple Store are a factor, but the most likely reason is swingeing rent increases – and the simple fact that D&J could no longer cut the mustard in a highly competitive environment.

Debenhams
334-348 Oxford Street, W1C 1JG (0844 561 6161/www.debenhams.com). Bond Street tube. **Open** 9.30am-8pm Mon, Tue, Fri, Sat; 10am-8pm Wed; 9.30am-9pm Thur; noon-6pm Sun. **Credit** AmEx, DC, MC, V.
Famous for its Designers at Debenhams concept of exclusive, cheap capsule ranges in every department from homeware to shoes, the store itself could do with a designer makeover. The utilitarian decor doesn't do the clothes justice, although matters have improved somewhat with a more spacious layout in the designer section and easy-to-navigate, trend-focused concessions, including Warehouse, Topshop and Jane Norman. The cosmetics hall stocks all the familiar upmarket brands; accessories include jewellery by the likes of funky Red Herring, Liz Claiborne, Erickson Beamon and Theo Fennell's Tomfoolery; bags by Jasper Conran and John Rocha, as well as Debenhams' own brand, Debut. There's also an eveningwear collection, Star, by Julien Macdonald, evening separates by GS by Gharani Strok, and dresses courtesy of BDL by Ben De Lisi. Newcomers include Elie Tahari's Elie New York and Betty Jackson's Black. Menswear includes designer rags by Hamnett and Quiksilver, polo shirts by Nigel Cabourn's utility and St George by Duffer, and shoes from Ben Sherman and Caterpillar. The homes department features yet more designer names, including *Grand Designs* guru Kevin McCloud (dinner sets and cushions). Children don't miss out either: on the third floor you'll find everything from nightwear (Conran's j junior) to bikes (Falcon, Nitrogen) to shoes (Pineapple, Tiger Lily). There is also a wedding gift service. The canteen-style restaurant on the second floor may look like something straight out of Heathrow Terminal 3, but the internet café on the third is definitely a nod to the 21st century.
Beauty salon. Cafés. Disabled: lift, toilet. Hair salon. Mail order (0845 605 5044). Nappy-changing facilities. Personal shopping Restaurant. Toilets.
For branches see index.

Fenwick
63 New Bond Street, W1A 3BS (7629 9161/www.fenwick.co.uk). Bond Street tube. **Open** 10am-6.30pm Mon-Wed, Fri, Sat; 10am-8pm Thur. **Credit** AmEx, MC, V.

Smaller and better-groomed than some of its competitors, Fenwick is a pleasant place to shop. All the stock is prudently chosen: the beauty hall boasts a big Chantecaille counter, and other lines include Paul & Joe, T LeClerc, Becca and Prada. In the renowned accessories department, the bag range includes hip names such as Jamin Puech and Orla Kiely, and there are accessories as well as clothes by boho-chic label Antik Batik. West End gals stock up on scarves by Missoni, Pucci and Cacharel, hats by Stephen Jones and Philip Treacy, and hosiery by Armani. Newcomers in the lingerie section include Aubade and Damaris diffusion line Mimi Holliday. On the next two levels, familiar names – Nicole Farhi, Armani and Joseph – mingle with funkier fare by the likes of Boyd, Issa and C&C California. The shoe department has been kicked into shape with a swanky new Kurt Geiger boutique showcasing designer footwear by the likes of Chloé, Marc Jacobs and Emma Hope among others. On the third floor, deluxe denim-hunters will find Seven, James and Sass & Bide jeans, while two top-notch beauty services are discreetly tucked away: John Gustafson's fabled personal beauty studio and the Chantecaille Healing Spa (see p96). For pit stops there's Joseph Bar Restaurant on the second floor or Carluccio's in the basement, also home to the small menswear department, which includes Earl, Wayne Cooper, Missoni Sport and Paul & Joe. Alongside menswear is a new department for Sue Walker home accessories: a mix of tableware, china, cushions, glass, ceramics, furniture and more.
Beauty salon. Café. Disabled: lift, toilet. Mail order. Nappy-changing facilities. Personal shopping Restaurant. Toilets.
For branch see index.

Fortnum & Mason
181 Piccadilly, W1A 1ER (7734 8040/www.fortnumandmason.co.uk). Green Park or Piccadilly Circus tube. **Open** 10am-6.30pm Mon-Sat; noon-6pm Sun (food hall only). **Credit** AmEx, MC, V.
In business for more than 300 years, F&M is most famous for its wonderfully over-the-top ground-floor food hall with marbled pillars, chandeliers and long rows of tea, coffee and chocolates (see p232). The elegant upper levels are blissfully quiet and make for very pleasant shopping too. Although the women's clothing department closed in July 2005, there are up-to-date accessories by the likes of Lulu Guinness (handbags and umbrellas), Philip Treacy (handbags), plus chic scarves by Pucci and Georgina von Etzdorf. Lingerie features Louis Feraud and New York label Jonquil, plus La Perla, Lise Charmel, Mary Jo and Prima Donna (for the fuller figure). There's also an excellent perfumery, home to the Clive Christian range (Harrods is the only other stockist in London). The basement now has a cook shop and Christmas department, while the third floor is a treasure trove of Limoges china and Ginori tableware. Peckish shoppers will need a wallet to match their appetite: formal lunch or afternoon tea at the St James's Restaurant, and light meals and teas at the Fountain and Patio restaurants don't come cheap.
Beauty salon. Disabled: lift, toilet. Hair salon. Mail order. Nappy-changing facilities. Personal shopping. Restaurants. Toilets.

Harrods
87-135 Brompton Road, SW1X 7XL (7730 1234/personal shopping 7893 8000/www.harrods.com). Knightsbridge tube. **Open** 10am-7pm daily. **Credit** AmEx, DC, MC, V.
With floor after floor of designer wares overseen by surprisingly friendly staff, Harrods is the mother of all upscale department stores. From the gift wrapping service on the lower ground floor to the

sports section on the fifth (where, among the stock, you'll find Prada Sport and a golf simulator), it's shoppers' paradise and, though the goods are uniformly expensive, it's fun to gawp at the over-the-top glitz that helped make the Harrods name. It costs nothing to soak up the ambience in the ground-floor Room of Luxury, showcasing accessories by the likes of Tina Tarantino (think Paris Hilton's chunky Day-Glo necklace), Gucci, Dior and Hermès; or browse designs by Joseph, Armani, Dolce & Gabbana and more. Fellas will be thrilled by gadgets and grooming options, as well as the British Tailoring Room, featuring designers such as Vivienne Westwood, Ozwald Boateng and Timothy Everest. The enormous cosmetics and skincare section has some affordable options too, so you can walk out of the store with a little something in a Harrods bag. If money is no object, make a beeline for the fifth floor, where the swanky Urban Retreat hairdressing and beauty salon (see p98) has a huge menu of services, including ultra-exclusive Crème de la Mer facials. But for us it's the legendary food halls that are the biggest draw (see p232). In summer 2005 Harrods launched a free personal shopping service called By Appointment, based on the first floor.
Beauty salon. Cafés. Disabled: lift, toilet. Hair salon. Mail order. Nappy-changing facilities. Personal shopping. Restaurants. Toilets.

Harvey Nichols
109-125 Knightsbridge, SW1X 7RJ (7235 5000/www.harveynichols.com). Knightsbridge tube. **Open** Store 10am-8pm Mon-Fri; 10am-7pm Sat; noon-6pm Sun. *Café* 10am-10pm Mon-Sat; 10am-6pm Sun. *Restaurant* 10am-11pm Mon-Sat; 10am-6pm Sun. **Credit** AmEx, DC, MC, V.
Harvey Nicks is an elegant one-stop shop for front-line fashion. New in womenswear for autumn 2005 are ready-to-wear collections by former Ungaro designer Giambattista Valli (tailored and sexy separates), Portuguese Francisco Rosas's series of below-the-knee dresses in burgundy, light grey and pink washed silk, and Luella's pussy-bow blouses and snaffle-print trenches. Menswear is equally eclectic, with Kris van Assche (double-breasted grey cashmere coats and trick-of-the-eye shirting) and Cloak (Russian-born Alexandre Plokhov's exaggerated sharp lines and military-style detailing). Casualwear includes Hammock's lumberjack shirts and Permanent Vacation's shirts for the post-T generation. The ground floor is a cosmetics junkie's paradise, featuring exclusives from Trish McEvoy, Sue Devitt Studio, Kevyn Aucoin and RMK. There is Poutlet – a mini Pout store that offers Quickies (mini makeovers) and Hand Jobs (manicures) – while QuickBliss offers treatments and cult Bliss products. The holistic Beyond Beauty area stocks hair- and skincare by the likes of mop, Dr Hauschka, Ole Henriksen, Cowshed, Hei Poa and This Works, alongside an organic juice bar. Accessories include bags by Alexander McQueen, Roberto Cavalli and Tanner Krolle; while the shoe department avoids designer ubiquity – fabulous finds include ultra-glam Italian high heels by René Caovilla and more understated offerings from British designer Jane Brown. For refreshment, head to the fifth floor, which houses the light-suffused café, bar and restaurant, plus the small, elegant food market.
Bar. Beauty salon. Café. Disabled: lift. Hair salon. Mail order. Nappy-changing facilities. Personal shopping. Restaurant. Toilets.

House of Fraser
318 Oxford Street, W1C 1HF (0870 160 7258/www.houseoffraser.co.uk). Bond Street or Oxford Circus tube. **Open** 10am-8pm Mon-Wed, Fri, Sat; 10am-9pm Thur; noon-6pm Sun. **Credit** AmEx, DC, MC, V.
House of Fraser packs a huge variety of brands into its six spacious floors. While some concessions are a little fusty (Country Casuals, Windsmoor, Planet), contemporary lines are found in Therapy (basement), House of Fraser's answer to Topshop; its well-made, eponymous young label is sold alongside brands such as Miss Sixty, Warehouse, Fornarina and Hooch. The boys can pick from

ONE-STOP

the likes of Valentino and Versace, with a few casualwear offerings from Diesel, French Connection and Paul & Shark; traditional looks come courtesy of Austin Reed and Crombie. The fourth floor is devoted to homeware brands, from Alessi to Yves Delorme, with designer-look towels, bedding and accessories by H of F's own label, Linea; furniture is on the fifth floor. The store also offers personal shopping services, good cafés, a Nails Inc manicure bar and a mini branch of the Walk-in Backrub. The slick 'boutique' House of Fraser branch in the City has a more exclusive selection of designer names – Moschino's Cheap & Chic, Roland Mouret, Jean Paul Gaultier and Marilyn Moore.

Beauty salon. Café. Disabled: lift, toilet. Mail order. Nappy-changing facilities. Personal shopping. Restaurants. Toilets.
For branches see index.

John Lewis

278-306 Oxford Street, W1A 1EX (7629 7711/ www.johnlewis.co.uk). Bond Street or Oxford Circus tube. **Open** 9.30am-7pm Mon-Wed, Fri, Sat; 9.30am-8pm Thur; noon-6pm Sun. **Credit** MC, V.
Knocking on for 150 years of trade, John Lewis represents the best of British middle-class consumer values with its 'never knowingly undersold' prices, customer perks such as free delivery (within a 30-mile radius) and services from lingerie fitting to dressmaking advice. What the store lacks in glamour it makes up for in choice: in the renowned basement cook shop you can get everything from an apple corer to a complete fitted kitchen. There are 2,500 different furnishing fabrics on the second floor, alongside a huge array of bedding and bath towels. The kids' department boasts highly trained, hugely patient staff and enough school uniforms and Start-Rite shoes to clothe virtually every classroom in the country. The skiwear selection is also impressive. Although clothes are predominantly conservative, there are attempts to keep abreast of younger fashions (with lines such as Coast, Joseph, Hobbs and Ted Baker for women; Ben Sherman, Missoni, Farhi and Kenzo for men). In furniture, the emphasis is also on solid bourgeois, while the spacious cosmetics hall includes the fabled Crème de la Mer, Sisley, Bobbi Brown make-up and mop hair and body products. At the peaceful restaurant on the third floor you can light-lunch while enjoying views of Cavendish Square. For a bit of culture on your way out, pause to gaze up at Barbara Hepworth's striking 1960s cast-aluminim *Winged Figure*, on the Holles Street side of the John Lewis building.
Beauty Salon (Clarins). Café. Disabled: lift, toilet. Mail order. Nappy-changing facilities. Personal shopping. Restaurant. Toilets.
For branches see index.

Liberty

210-220 Regent Street, W1B 5AH (7734 1234/ www.liberty.co.uk). Oxford Circus tube. **Open** 10am-7pm Mon-Wed, Fri, Sat; 10am-8pm Thur; noon-6pm Sun. **Credit** AmEx, DC, MC, V.
Its famous prints are coveted the world over, and you can get them here on fabrics, bags, scarves and notebooks. But there are other riches to be had. Made up of two interlinked buildings, the store can be tricky to navigate: in Regent House on Regent Street, key sections include lingerie (limited to the likes of Myla, Bodas and FrostFrench), menswear (newbies such as Nihilismus, Rushmore, La Rocka as well as older-school labels) and skincare and perfumery (Stila, E Coudray, Nars and perfumer Keiko Mecheri, among others). The original 1920s Tudor House on Great Marlborough Street contains the celebrated scarf hall, as well as womenswear (international, designer and contemporary collections). A host of designer names includes Ann Demeulemeester, Dries van Noten, Roland Mouret and Veronique Branquinho. There's a rich mix of accessories by the likes of Alexander McQueen, Pucci, Megan Park, Tait & Style and Stoned and Waisted. The fourth floor now houses a furniture department mixing vintage one-offs with 20th-century design classics, Arts and Crafts and modern pieces. There is a contemporary carpets section as well as a revamped furnishing fabrics department offering both contemporary and archive textiles. As we went to press, the fabulous Gift Room was about to be renovated and will now showcase travel and stationery products. The jewellery section includes a new Dinny Hall concession as well as collections by Sarah Pulvertaft, Patch NYC and Perle De Lune. Refreshment comes in the form of the Art Bar Café, an updated British tearoom and Arthur's Bar in the lower ground floor, named after the founder Arthur Lasenby Liberty.
Cafés. Disabled: lift, toilet. Mail order. Nappy-changing facilities. Personal shopping. Restaurant. Toilets.

Marks & Spencer

458 Oxford Street, W1C 1AP (7935 7954/www. marksandspencer.co.uk). Marble Arch tube. **Open** 9am-9pm Mon-Fri; 9am-8pm Sat; noon-6pm Sun. **Credit** AmEx, DC, MC, V.
In spite of fading fortunes and turning down the latest Philip Green billion-pound takeover offer, M&S is making the admirable efforts to improve and update its stock. Womenswear has started to have a more boutiquey feel: Limited Collection pieces are cut to flatter and run the gamut from casual to eveningwear, and the new Per Una accessories range, featuring semi-precious stones, has a retro appeal. Good-quality leather shoes and bags are also particularly strong, as well as chunky

ONE-STOP

Eat, drink, shop

Change is in the perfumed air at London's top department stores, where focus is shifting away from the traditional sales of clothes, cosmetics and accessories towards entertainment, food and other ways to keep you inside just that little bit longer. Upscale restaurants, fishmongers, butchers and DJs are pushing out haberdashery, embroidery and stuffy old cafeterias, and even the most stalwart of the city's department stores are taking notice.

At the forefront of the movement are, as ever, Harvey Nichols and Selfridges. For years those two sleek doyens of couture and cool have pushed the boundaries that defined what a department store really is. First they added lavish food halls and trendy cafés, then in-demand hair salons (Daniel Hersheson at Harvey Nicks, Cobella at Selfridges; for both, see p104), bars... Clothes can be an afterthought when people enter their swinging doors.

At Harvey Nicks, Modern European **Fifth Floor** (*pictured*) showed London that a department store could have a classy modern restaurant, and others soon followed. Selfridges has added über-trendy Moroccan **Momo** to its slate of offerings, while Peter Jones's recently renovated **Top Floor** restaurant continues to impress, as much for its lovely views over Chelsea as for its seared tuna steaks. Even the most traditional of London department stores, Fortnum & Mason, has three very different eating options – the elaborate

but laid-back **Fountain**, serving modern English food, the **Patio** overlooking the food hall and the marvellously stuffy **St James's Restaurant**, where you feel you ought to sit up straight over formal luncheons and afternoon teas. Not to be forgotten is lovely Liberty, which straddles the line between modern and traditional with its **Art Bar Café**, where the look is up to date, but the cake and tea on offer are comfortingly familiar.

Then, of course, there's Harrods. Not one to do anything by halves, it's packed itself with restaurants, doughnut shops, delis, sushi bars – you name it, it's here. Looking for halal Moroccan food? It's on the second floor at the lavish **Ishbilia**. A formal dining room serving traditional British cuisine? Head to the **Georgian Restaurant** on the fourth floor. An

American-style diner? Make your way to **Mo's** for burgers and milkshakes. Food for the kids? That'll be **Planet Harrods**. Or how about a light lunch outside on a sunny day? Head for the **Terrace Bar**.

Stores are constantly upping the ante, egging each other on to greater heights: Harrods had its fish counter and Sea Grill, now Harvey Nicks has a traditional fishmonger, and a butcher selling well-sourced British meats, as well as a branch of Mitch Tonks's **FishWorks** restaurant. Selfridges and Harvey Nichols have often featured DJs, live bands, and general entertainment, but the new Harvey Nicks in Dublin has a nightclub complete with dancefloor that stays open until 3am.

So, erm, where do we find the knitting yarn, then?

---

belts. The basics for which M&S is famous are still present and reliable – cotton T-shirts, everyday undies (although look out, too, for the Truly You Embroidery underwear range). Menswear has been beefed up with a new Autograph range, featuring collections by leading designers Timothy Everest and Nigel Hall. We were impressed by colourful cashmere sweaters, tailored suits and sexy leather jackets on a recent visit. M&S homewares feature lots of rich velvets, sexy satins, natural stone, and etched and coloured glassware; furniture includes elegant chaises longues. The new children's range is adorable: soft knits, cargo trousers and the cutest baby moccasins. The Oxford Street store could do with an interior facelift, but has a third-floor café, not to mention quality own-label beauty products and the well-loved food hall.
Bar. Cafés. Disabled: lift, toilets. Mail order. Nappy-changing facilities. Personal shopping. Toilets. **Branches**: throughout the city.

Peter Jones

Sloane Square, SW1W 8EL (7730 3434/ www.peterjones.co.uk). Sloane Square tube. **Open** 9.30am-7pm Mon-Sat; 11am-5pm Sun. **Credit** MC, V.
The £100-million refit can be admired as soon as you set foot on the ground floor and look up to see the impressive six tiers of curved glass balconies. While the shop keeps its traditional customers happy with extended china and soft furnishing sections, plus the usual haberdashery and hats, it's also aiming at a younger clientele with a sparkling new accessories section and some cool cosmetic brands like Fresh, Farmacia, Benefit, Perricone and mop, as well as new fashion brands Coast, Warehouse and Hobbs. The inventory of personal

services is endless, too: fitted kitchen planners, made-to-measure menswear, fashion advisers, bra fitting, schoolwear advice and more. Pampering comes courtesy of the first-floor Footopia clinic and Clarins Studio, where you can have all manner of treatments and massages. A slick café and cocktail bar affords wonderful views down over Sloane Square.
Beauty salon (Clarins). Disabled: lift, toilet. Mail order. Nappy-changing facilities. Personal shopping. Restaurants.

Selfridges

400 Oxford Street, W1A 1AB (0870 837 7377/www.selfridges.com). Bond Street or Marble Arch tube. **Open** 10am-8pm Mon-Fri; 9.30am-8pm Sat; noon-6pm Sun. **Credit** AmEx, DC, MC, V.
Combining comprehensive merchandising tactics with more than a dash of razzle-dazzle, Selfridges aims to be both all-embracing and exciting. Expensive names are big business here, and you could blow your budget within seconds of stepping in the door – that is, if you enter via the luxury fashion accessories department and fall under the spell of Miu Miu, Mulberry, Balenciaga, Prada, Burberry... At the centre of the ground floor is a heaving cosmetics and fragrance marketplace where you can't swing a Fendi bag without bumping into a display for Stila, MAC, Christian Dior, Bobbi Brown, Aveda, Nars, Benefit and more. There are not one, but two brow bars (at Estée Lauder and Bobbi Brown). The layout isn't always logical (some of the homewares concessions, such as Skandium, sit in the basement, while others, including SCP – good for British designers such as Matthew Hilton, Andrew Stafford and Tom Dixon – are up on the fourth

floor). Likewise, the beauty offerings are divided, with REN, St Tropez and other cult lines out on a limb by the luxury chocolates. But, weird layout aside, it's all here.

Younger women have the run of the vast ground-floor Spirit section, home to concessions of Topshop, Diesel, Warehouse, Karen Millen and more; the second floor houses the major designers, plus of-the-moment labels like Jonathan Saunders, People Tree and La Petite Salope. Also on this floor, the idea of shopping as an 'experience' (espoused by pioneering former chief executive Vittorio Radice) continues with the Superbrands section, dedicated to eight top designers (including Balenciaga and Marni). If you need to get into the mood for shopping, there's a new Moët champagne bar overlooking the women's accessories; to refuel afterwards there are several cafés and restaurants, including an offshoot of Momo. Men have a vast range of accessories on the ground floor, and clothes on the first. The recently launched Superbrands for Men features cult luminaries as McQueen, Helmut Lang and Yves Saint Laurent, and jewellery by the likes of Shaun Leane and Ben Day, plus the Lonsdale Bar for lads' refreshments. On the third floor, you can lose yourself in the excellent lingerie department (complete with a lavish Agent Provocateur concession). Frenetic ground-floor, disjointed layout and wallet-busting opportunities aside, there's no denying that for sheer selection Selfridges is top of the heap. As if that wasn't enough, it stages regular store-wide extravaganzas, featuring entertainers, art displays and events.
Beauty salon. Bar. Cafés. Disabled: lift, toilet. Hair salon. Mail order. Nappy-changing facilities. Personal shopping. Restaurants. Toilets.

Markets

For flower markets, *see chapter* **Gardens & Flowers**. For antiques markets, such as Bermondsey Market and Alfie's Antique Market, *see chapter* **Antiques** and **20th-century Design**. For information on the London car boot scene consult www.carbootcalendar.com for listings (a fee applies); for sales in north London, as well as Cambridgeshire, Essex and Hertfordshire, visit www.countrysidepromotions.co.uk.

East London's **Chrisp Street Market** (*see p19*) holds regular summer 'Super Saturdays' (0845 262 0846, www.chrispstreet.org.uk), mixing street performers with stallholders selling everything from handmade jewellery, vintage fashion and organic beauty products to food and antiques. It also holds a Christmas Victorian Market, complete with old barrows, street theatre and roasted chestnuts.

General

Berwick Street Market

Berwick Street, Rupert Street, W1. Piccadilly Circus or Tottenham Court Road tube. **Open** 9am-6pm Mon-Sat.
Don't bother rising with the lark to catch the best Saturday bargains at this traditional fruit and veg market in the seedy heart of Soho. Like the rest of Soho, Berwick Street Market doesn't get going until a bit later. Fresh produce is seasonal and ranges from vine tomatoes, new potatoes and strawberries to mangoes, passion fruit, avocados and watermelons. Other stalls sell flowers, nuts, CDs, electric toothbrushes, sweets, knickers and socks. South beyond Walker's Court a few stalls offer trendy jackets, combat gear and accessories.

Camden Market

Camden Market *Camden High Street, junction with Buck Street, NW1 (7485 3459/www.camden lock.net).* **Open** 9.30am-5.30pm daily.
Camden Canal Market *off Chalk Farm Road, south of junction with Castlehaven Road, NW1 9XJ (7485 8355/www.camdenlock.net).* **Open** 9am-6.30pm Fri-Sun.
Camden Lock *Camden Lock Place, off Chalk Farm Road, NW1 8AF (7485 3459/www.camden lockmarket.com).* **Open** 10am-6pm daily.
Electric Ballroom *184 Camden High Street, NW1 8QP (7485 9006/www.electric-ballroom.co.uk).* **Open** 10am-6pm Sat, Sun; *record & film fairs* occasional Sats throughout the year.
Stables *off Chalk Farm Road, opposite junction with Hartland Road, NW1 8AH (7485 5511/ www.stablesmarket.com).* **Open** 10am-6pm daily (reduced stalls Mon-Fri).
All *Camden Town tube.*
Despite the tourist scrum that Camden market has become on the weekends, it still occupies a special place in the heart of most Londoners. It's one of the few shopping areas in the capital that has resisted the might of the developers, and it boasts a veritable smörgåsbord of street culture, where hippies, goths, punks, rockabillies and metallers rub elbows and eye each other warily over their smoothies. In recent years the market has also had a facelift resulting in a cleaner, less crushed shopping experience and a more distinctive identity for different areas of the market.
The first stalls you hit are at the Buck Street market, to the right of Camden Town station. Here you can pick up cheap fashion items, clubber's clothing and retro T-shirts with 'Chopper' and 'Bagpuss' on the front. But the most interesting part of the market is at Camden Lock, which features original designers with beautifully laid out boutiques and workshops, as well as great food

stalls serving everything from Japanese octopus dumplings to Filipino stir-fries. The Market Hall, just behind the lock, is a Victorian building housing two floors of arts and crafts, such as leather-bound books, pressed flower lanterns and original jewellery. Further down, along Chalk Farm Road, the clothes get trendier at the Stables market. Here fashionistas stock up on bodices so tight you need breathing apparatus, and enough PVC, plastic and quilted outfits to keep even the hardiest of clubbers happy. Retro clothes shops selling 1960s Afghan coats and '70s kaftans also abound. Proud Galleries, which exhibits contemporary photography exhibitions, is a recent addition.
The Horse Hospital (where horses injured pulling barges on the canal were cared for) is vintage heaven. Pop memorabilia, old *Jackie* annuals, '50s telephones, maps and books, as well as classic 1960s furniture such as bubble chairs and Verner Panton lights spill (stylishly) from the storefronts. Of the other smaller markets, the Electric Ballroom is the place for decadent velvet goth jackets and the like, while Inverness Street market sells cheap fruit and veg, cut-price electrical gods, kids' toys and London memorabilia. There are also some good late-night Spanish-style bars here.

Leadenhall Market

Whittington Avenue, off Gracechurch Street, EC3. Bank tube/DLR. **Open** 7am-4pm Mon-Fri.
More historic building than market, Leadenhall is worth visiting simply to admire its Victorian good looks. Designed by the architect Horace Jones in 1881, it combines a glass roof and ornate ironwork with rich cream, green and maroon paintwork to produce an arcaded masterpiece. The market oozes history, standing on the site of a Roman forum and being home to food markets since the Middle Ages. Its City location means that it has become more of a retail centre, packed with upmarket shops, trendy cafés and bars, but every Friday (10am-4pm) there is a food market where you can pick up choice cheeses, pastries, honey, meat, fruit and vegetables.

Petticoat Lane Market

Middlesex Street, Goulston Street, New Goulston Street, Toynbee Street, Wentworth Street, Bell Lane, Cobb Street, Leyden Street, Strype Street, *Old Castle Street, Cutler Street, E1. Liverpool Street tube/rail.* **Information** 7364 1717 **Open** 8am-2pm Mon; 8am-4pm Tue-Fri; 9am-2pm Sun.
Selling mainly tat (though new, rather than old), toys and electronic goods, Petticoat Lane is the destination for the odd one-off bargain like Miss Selfridge or River Island skirts or trousers for a fiver, leather jackets, Tomy Hilfigger (sic) shirts, or 4 pairs of socks for a quid. There are plenty of cheap shoes and designer rip-off bags, beauty products you've never heard of, bedlinen, textiles and, in particular, towels, plus a couple of cheap fruit stalls. But its proximity to Spitalfields Market (*see p17*) means it may not be a wasted journey after all.

Portobello Road Market

Portobello Road, W10, W11; Golborne Road, W10. Ladbroke Grove, Notting Hill Gate or Westbourne Park tube. **Open** *General* 8am-6pm Mon-Wed; 9am-1pm Thur; 7am-7pm Fri, Sat. *Antiques* 4am-6pm Sat.
Portobello Road is several markets rolled into one. Starting at the Notting Hill end are mainly antiques stalls (*see p127*) selling silverware, medals, old maps, vases, bric-a-brac and general Victoriana. Further up, you come to the food stalls, packed with everything from traditional fruit and veg to tasty cheeses, stuffed olives, organic biscuits and crackers, bratwurst and crêpes. Next up come clothes and jewellery, ranging from cheap trendy club- and casualwear to delightful craft bracelets and earrings. The cafés under the Westway are a good place to rest before plunging into the next section – new designers' clothes and vintage items at the cutting edge of fashion along the walkway to Ladbroke Grove, while on the right-hand side are fairly random selections of bric-a-brac, including antique military uniforms and old photographs, typewriters and gardening tools.

Roman Road Market

Roman Road (between Parnell Road & St Stephen's Road), E3. Bethnal Green, Bow Road or Mile End tube/8, S2 bus. **Open** 8am-2pm Tue, Thur; 8am-6pm Sat.
Established in 1843 to meet the food and clothing demands of the booming East End, the Roman Road Market is now a place to spot trends and labels before they hit the high street. Expect to find everything from underwear (practical and glam) to shoes and cheap and cheerful renditions of catwalk pieces, as well as bedlinen and plenty of fruit and veg. The stretch of Roman Road further towards Bethnal Green tube is also worth investigating, with organic shops such as Friends Organic (No.83, 8980 1843) and interiors shop Evolution (Nos.59-61, 8981 7219), plus ceramics, art and furniture at

Brick Lane Market. See p19.

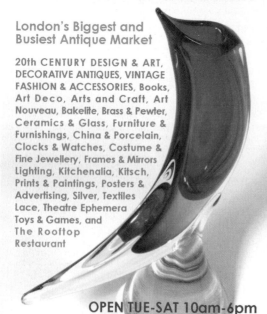

Budge & Coward (No.67, 8980 8837), which is run by two Royal College of Art graduates. For top-notch seafood and fish, head to Winkles (No.238, 8880 7450) further up the Roman Road.

Spitalfields Market

Commercial Street, between Lamb Street & Brushfield Street, E1 (7247 8556/www.visit spitalfields.com). Liverpool Street tube/rail. **Open** *Antiques fair* 8am-3.30pm Thur. *General market* 10am-4pm Mon-Fri; 9am-5pm Sun. *Food market* 10am-4pm Wed. *Fashion market* 10am-4pm Fri. *Record market* 10am-4pm 1st and 3rd Wed of mth.

In that little bit of East End that is being rapidly bulldozed and developed into the bright shiny buildings of the expanding City, the Spitalfields indoor market is thriving. It's surrounded by cool shops selling rare movie posters and second-hand books, and old-fashioned confectioners selling humbugs and pear drops. Inside, stalls offer anything from dyed sheepskin rugs and cushions to craft jewellery, aromatherapy products, flowers, plus CDs, books and handmade cards. Fashion offerings vary from brightly coloured, unusual creations by up-and-coming designers to second-hand glad rags. There are also cake and bread stalls and, around the edge, stands selling grub from all over the world at bargain prices. There is a food market every Wednesday, plus a record market on the first and third Wednesday of every month. The weekly fashion market (Fridays, 10am-4pm) is an opportunity to buy your gear directly from London's creative young designers.

Books

Riverside Walk Market

Outside the National Film Theatre, under Waterloo Bridge, SE1 9PX. Waterloo tube/rail. **Open** 10am-7pm irregular weekdays, Sat, Sun.

Located in front of the National Film Theatre, Riverside Walk Market gets bigger as the weather gets better. There are rows of trestle tables stacked with books, maps and old prints from all over Britain. There's plenty to browse through, from hardback picture volumes, first editions and weighty academic tomes to hundreds of Penguin paperbacks, sci-fi thrillers and trashy romances. There's usually lots on offer for art, film and theatre buffs, including plays, scripts and cut-price glossy art books. But don't expect rock-bottom prices – these books are a better-quality selection than at some bargain basements and prices reflect that.

Crafts & handmade goods

Apple Market

The Piazza, Covent Garden, WC2E 8RF (0870 780 5001/www.coventgardenmarket.co.uk). Covent Garden or Embankment tube/Charing Cross tube/rail. **Open** *Arts & crafts* 10.30am-6.30pm Tue-Sun. *Antiques & collectibles* 10.30am-6.30pm Mon.

These few rows of Victorian-style wooden stalls inside Covent Garden's old market building sell mainly cottage-industry handicrafts aimed at tourists and gift buyers: hand-knitted jumpers, paper lampshades, chunky jewellery, hand-printed baby clothes, fork sculptures and the like. Stalls change regularly (over 100 traders are registered with the market). The antiques stalls – selling mainly Victoriana – on Monday may be of interest to collectors.

Jubilee Market

1 Tavistock Court, The Piazza, Covent Garden, WC2E 8BD (www.jmh.company.org.uk). Covent Garden or Embankment tube/Charing Cross tube/rail. **Open** *Antiques* 5am-4pm Mon. *General goods* 10am-5pm Tue-Fri. *Arts & crafts* 10am-5pm Sat, Sun.

On the southern edge of Covent Garden, Jubilee Market has a wider range of gear than neighbouring Apple Market, selling knitwear, leather goods (bags, belts and wallets), velvet scarves, silver and gold jewellery, photography (including découpage), wooden toys and Japanese papercraft. On Mondays the antiques stalls sell porcelain, silverware, objets d'art and jewellery.

Merton Abbey Mills

Watermill Way, opposite Sainsbury's, off Merantun Way, SW19 2RD (8543 9608/www.mertonabbeymills.com). Colliers Wood or South Wimbledon tube/57, 200, 219, 493 bus. **Open** *Antiques & collectibles* 7am-noon Thur. *Crafts, foodstuffs & farmers' market* 10am-5pm Sat, Sun, bank holidays.

Divided into outdoor stalls, a huge barn devoted to crafts and a little food court, Merton Abbey Mills is a great place for gifts, ornaments and an excellent range of good food. There are organic eggs and bacon, vegetables and meat, as well as home-made cakes, or hot food from vans selling everything from the exotic (Thai, Indonesian and more) to the domestic (full English breakfasts). The watermill, with its potter's wheel powered by the River Wandle, is also well worth a visit.

St James's Piccadilly Market

Courtyard of St James's Church, 197 Piccadilly, W1J 9LL (7734 4511/www.st-james-piccadilly.org). Green Park or Piccadilly Circus tube. **Open** *Antiques & collectibles* 10am-6pm Tue. *Arts & crafts* 10am-6pm Wed-Sat.

Owing to its location in the centre of town, just off busy Piccadilly, this market housed in a little leafy church courtyard offers a combination of tourist tat and tasteful crafts. There are African sculptures, Chinese dresses, Roman coins, books, pictures, Murano glass, traditional Aran wool jumpers and, naturally, an array of souvenirs such as postcards, tea towels and baseball caps. The café – which has outside seating – is a pleasant place to rest before heading back out into the crowded streets.

Farmers' markets

If you want to cook according to the seasons (after the winter root vegetables, it's the turn of asparagus, peas and broad beans, then summer fruits and veg take centre stage), as well as be sure that the food on your plate hasn't travelled more than you have this year, head to a farmers' market near you. Strict regulations ensure that all products sold have been grown, reared, caught, pickled, baked, smoked or processed by the stallholder. All produce at London farmers' markets is grown within 100 miles of the M25, and the markets bring the industry a welcome £3 million a year. As well as fresh fruit and vegetables, farmers' markets sell cheeses, meats, fish, bread and eggs, plus honey, cider, wine and juices.

As we went to press, a weekday trial market was taking off at Paddington Central (Sheldon Square, near the Bishop's Bridge project, noon-6pm Thur). Follow signs to 'Waterside' from Paddington Station. The market is located between Little Venice and Paddington, next to the canal.

The following is the current line-up, although farmers' markets do sometimes relocate, while others open up elsewhere. For further information, get in touch with the **National Association of Farmers' Markets** (0845 458 8420, www.farmersmarkets.net), which is the umbrella organisation for farmers' markets across the country. **London Farmers' Markets** (7704 9659, www.lfm.org.uk) covers all the capital's markets, except for Stoke Newington.

Blackheath

Blackheath railway station car park, Blackheath Village, SE3 0TX (7704 9659/www.lfm.org.uk). Blackheath rail. **Open** 10am-2pm Sun.

Ealing

Leeland Road, W13 9HH (7704 9659/www.lfm. org.uk). West Ealing rail. **Open** 9am-1pm Sat.

Islington

Essex Road, opposite Islington Green, N1 8EA (7704 9659/www.lfm.org.uk). Angel tube. **Open** 10am-2pm Sun.

Marylebone

Cramer Street car park, off Marylebone High Street, W1U 4EA (7704 9659/www.lfm.org.uk). Bond Street or Baker Street tube. **Open** 10am-2pm Sun.

Notting Hill

Car park behind Waterstone's, access via Kensington Place, W8 7PR (7704 9659/www.lfm.org.uk). Notting Hill Gate tube. **Open** 9am-1pm Sat.

Peckham

Peckham Square, Peckham High Street, SE15 5QN (7704 9659/www.lfm.org.uk). Peckham Rye or Queens Road rail. **Open** 9.30am-1.30pm Sun.

Pimlico Road

Orange Square, corner of Pimlico Road & Ebury Street, SW1W 0NZ (7704 9659/www.lfm.org.uk). Sloane Square tube/11, 211, 239 bus. **Open** 9am-1pm Sat.

Richmond

Heron Square, off Hill Street, Richmond, Surrey TW9 (8878 5132). Richmond rail. **Open** 11am-3pm Sat.

Stoke Newington

The Old Fire Station, 61 Leswin Road, N16 7NX (7502 7588/www.growingcommunities.org). Stoke Newington rail/73, 393 bus. **Open** 10am-2.30pm Sat.

Swiss Cottage

O2 Centre car park, Finchley Road, NW3 6LU (7704 9659/www.lfm.org.uk). Finchley Road tube. **Open** 10am-3pm Wed.

Twickenham

Car park, Holly Road, Twickenham, Middx TW1 4EA (7704 9659/www.lfm.org.uk). Twickenham rail. **Open** 9am-1pm Sat.

Wimbledon Park

Wimbledon Park First School, Havana Road, SW19 8EJ (7704 9659/www.lfm.org.uk). Wimbledon Park tube/Earlsfield rail. **Open** 9am-1pm Sat.

Global

Brixton Market

Electric Avenue, Pope's Road, Brixton Station Road, Atlantic Road, SW9 8JX. Brixton tube/rail. **Open** 8am-6pm Mon, Tue, Thur-Sat; 8am-3pm Wed.

One of the buzziest markets in London, Brixton is a real experience. Electric Avenue is packed with stalls that are piled high with exotic fruit and veg – yams, plantains, mangoes, papayas and much more – as well as fresh tomatoes, courgettes, carrots and other staples. Opposite the stalls are stores crammed with halal meats and an incredible variety of fish. As the market moves into Atlantic Road, it turns more towards clothes, towels and cheap wallets, and on Saturdays a few stalls of rather jumbly second-hand clothes appear along Brixton Station Road. What was once the Granville Arcade has been given a bit of a spruce-up over the past few year to become Brixton Village, with brightly painted signs at the Pope's Road, Atlantic Road and Coldharbour Lane entrances. Inside are African and Caribbean food stores, household goods, books, crafts and specialist hair and wig shops. One newcomer worth looking out for is the compact but very well-stocked hip hop specialist HQ (88 Brixton Village, Coldharbour Lane, SW9 8PS, 7274 4664). Here you'll discover new hip hop on CD and vinyl, personalised belt buckles and a range of street art supplies (serious aerosol artists should note that there are over 250 shades of Molotow Premium and Spanish Montana).

Markets under threat

On a fruit stall of dazzling colours, a white stallholder shouts out 'Oi, oi, juicy bananas, we're almost givin' them away!' Behind him, next to a stall selling beans from Sierra Leone and a storefront selling Nigerian *dashikis* (shirts), sits a young Asian trader with audio tapes blaring out the teachings of the *Koran*. This is **Queen's Market** in Newham, which for more than a century has reflected the changing face of the metropolis. Or, as the posters put it: 'Sixty shops, 80 stalls – one unique market'. As successive waves of immigrants have gravitated towards the east of London, each has left an imprint on one of the most culturally diverse shopping precincts in Britain: descendants of cockneys shop and trade with Indians, Pakistanis, Africans, West Indians and Eastern Europeans, and British cabbages sell alongside okra, green bananas, catfish and spices.

But the traders in Queen's Market face challenges ahead, and ones that aren't unique – as the market infrastructure decays, it is being threatened by property development. The Newham site is hugely attractive to developer St Mowden and the supermarket giant Asda and, if the current £50 million proposals go ahead, the market will be demolished, and an Asda will occupy the site, along with 130 new homes.

Other local markets across London are facing similar problems, as formerly run-down areas are targeted for regeneration. At **Deptford Market**, plantains, yams, okra and *tindola* (a type of Indian gourd) sell alongside live eels and electrical goods. But its multicultural brew is being threatened by nearby property developments, where houses are breaking the £1 million barrier. Deptford High Street is fighting fiercely to retain its identity, but as the locals who use the stalls are increasingly priced out of the area, the market is under threat, as chain stores and coffee bars try to move in. Similarly, **Queen's Crescent Market** in Kentish Town, which caters to the large Somali community in the area, has a history of resisting the big supermarket chains who regularly apply to set up shop there.

Back in Newham, traders have set up a campaign to fight the development, to which poet Benjamin Zephaniah lends his support. He has lived in Newham for 20 years and, a regular customer at the market, he says, 'The development proposals aren't appropriate to the people who live here. There's something very wonderful about a traditional English market with influences from West India and Asia. This is true multiculture.'

Deptford Market *High Street, SE8.* **Open** 9am-5pm Wed, Fri, Sat.
Queen's Crescent Market *Queen's Crescent, NW5.* **Open** 9am-5pm Thur, Sat.
Queen's Market *Green Street, E13.* **Open** 8am-noon Tue; 8am-5pm Thur-Sat.

everything from Iberian acorn-fed ham to free-range chicken – and on Saturday lunchtime lengthy queues wait patiently for a famous barbecued chorizo and rocket roll from the stall selling Spanish goods from Brindisa (which also has its own shop in Exmouth Market; *see p244*). Add to this fresh fruit and veg, organic goods (cakes, breads), exotic teas, olive oils, dairy (cheeses, yoghurts), fish, beers, ciders and wines and you've got the makings of a feast. Many stalls offer tasters, so you can try before you buy. Quality is high, and prices match that. If you want to sample the delights but can't make it down here, order from the Borough Market selection from delivery company Food Ferry (www.foodferry.com).

Brick Lane Market

Brick Lane – north of railway bridge, Cygnet Street, Sclater Street, E1; Bacon Street, Cheshire Street, Chilton Street, E2. Aldgate East or Shoreditch tube/Liverpool Street tube/rail. **Information** 7364 1717 **Open** daybreak-2pm Sun.
Once a traditional flea market, Brick Lane still has the odd stall selling cheap soaps and razors, second-hand clothes and old furniture, and catering-size bags of fruit and veg, along with bagel shops and seafood stalls. But these days the market is much more about the trendy clothes boutiques and expensive home accessories shops that line the narrow streets off Brick Lane, such as Dray Walk and Cheshire Street. In 2004 the Truman Brewery (off Hanbury Street) opened its doors to a collection of new and exciting traders selling clothes and shoes (vintage and new), handmade handbags, art, contemporary lighting, homewares, accessories, jewellery, greeting cards, food and drink. Feeling peckish? The market is lined with curry houses, and the Brick Lane Beigel Bake (159 Brick Lane, 7729 0616) has the best bagels in London.

Broadway Market

Between Regent's Row/Andrews Road & Westgate Street, E8 (www.broadwaymarket.co.uk). London Fields rail/236, 394 bus. **Information** 07709 311 869. **Open** 8am-5pm Sat.
The revival of one of London's oldest chartered markets, which runs between Regent's Canal and London Fields, is nowadays a Saturday farmers'-style market (plenty of goods are organic). Stalls sell great cheeses (British, French, Italian), breads, meats, chocolate treats, luscious fruit tarts and cakes, plus more than one coffee barrow. There is also a string of boutiquey shops, cafés and galleries – try Black Truffle (No.74, 7923 9450, www.prescottandmackay.co.uk) for handmade designer shoes or Mac Black (No.47, 8376 5205) for retro furniture. La Vie Boutique (No.18, 7254 5864) sells fab vintage fashion, from jewelled bags (from £12) to pretty floaty fairy dresses (from £45). There are several galleries: for contemporary art have a look at Seven Seven (No.77, 0780 816 6215, www.sevenseven.org.uk) or Gallery (No.69, 7275 7473, www.flaca.co.uk). When you're shopped out, there are plenty of places to revive: Armadillo (No.41, 7249 3633) serves excellent Argentinian food, the Cat & Mutton (No.76, 7254 5599) serves great lunches, the Dove pub (No.24-28, 7275 7617) has over 100 Belgian beers, or you could stock up at the superb deli L'Eau à la Bouche (No.49, 7923 0600) and have a picnic in nearby London Fields. The latest addition is Rebel Rebel (*see p163*), selling inspirational flowers and beauty products.

Greenwich Market

General enquiries 8293 3110/www.greenwichmarket.net. Greenwich rail/Cutty Sark DLR. Antiques & collectibles 8.30am-5.30pm Thur, Fri. *Village Market Stockwell Street,* 8am-5pm Sat, Sun. *Arts & crafts* 9.30am-5.30pm Thur-Sun. *Food court* 9.30am-5.30pm Sat, Sun.
Greenwich Market has been trading since 1700 and it's packed out every weekend. It has three markets, with the smallest – the Weekend Market – situated nearest Greenwich DLR. It's mostly bric-a-brac and junk, though you'll also find retro pottery and ceramics. Next along is the Village Market, where a second-hand clothes flea market mingles with

Ridley Road Market

Ridley Road, off Kingsland High Street, E8. Dalston Kingsland rail/30, 38, 56, 67, 76, 149, 236, 242, 243, 277 bus. **Open** 8.30am-5.30pm Mon-Sat.
As diverse as the community it serves, Ridley Road Market sells everything from domestic and exotic fruit and veg (Turkish, Jewish, Asian, Cockney, African and Caribbean) to cheap clothes, home furnishings and toys. But more interesting are the permanent stalls in buildings lining the market – here Ghanaian music, African clothes and sari fabrics sit next to butchers selling goat necks, boiler chickens and cows' feet; fishmongers selling everything from bream to barracuda; and other traders selling bundles of dried, whole fish with price tags ranging from £6 to £50.

Shepherd's Bush Market

East side of the railway viaduct, off Goldhawk Road, W12. Goldhawk Road or Shepherd's Bush tube. **Open** 9am-5pm Mon-Wed, Fri, Sat; 9am-1pm Thur.
This super local market, running between Uxbridge Road and Goldhawk Road, has a little bit of everything: excellent fruit, vegetables, meat and fish, with stalls selling sweet potatoes, yams, coconuts, dudi, cassava, okra, falafel, rice, mangoes and other foodstuffs, as well as a good selection of clothing and fabrics. There are clothes for men, women and children – smart and casual, under-, night- and footwear, African and Indian styles, saris and textiles – plus watches, jewellery, scarves and hats. There are also plenty of home furnishings; among them you'll find bedclothes, blankets, duvets, pillows, bath mats and rugs. Add to all that kitchenware, toys, tools and

electronic equipment, cheap soaps, perfumes, snacks, sweets, CDs and DVDs, not to mention a stall selling reggae music and luggage, and you'd be hard-pressed to ask for more.

Southall Market

The Cattle Market, High Street, opposite North Road, Southall, Middx, UB1 3DG (8574 1611). Southall rail. **Open** *General* 9am-5pm Sat. *Poultry* 10am-noon Tue. *Horses* 8am-5pm Wed. *Furniture* 6am-noon Fri.
Housed in a scruffy yard behind the high street, Southall Market on a Saturday is a cross between a traditional working market and a visit to India. The range of goods is massive: fresh fruit and veg (including all types of chillies), lentils, eggs and fish sit alongside sari fabrics and clothes. Then there are hair accessories, costume jewellery, kitchenware, haberdashery, cheap pants… and a stall selling bibles and gospels. The market is also unusual in that it varies from day to day: on Tuesdays it's a poultry market, where you can buy live birds for the pot; Wednesday is devoted to the buying and selling of horses (really); Friday will remind you of *Steptoe & Son*; and Saturday is when the whole glorious mess comes together and looks like downtown Delhi.

Weekend

Borough Market

8 Southwark Street, SE1 1TL (7407 1002/www.boroughmarket.org.uk). London Bridge tube/rail. **Open** noon-6pm Fri; 9am-4pm Sat.
Our favourite market, and endorsed by many a celebrity chef, Borough offers a wonderfully rich mix of excellent foods. Meat encompasses

Chinese silk dresses, home furnishings and lighting, cheap trendy clothes, ethnic ornaments, CDs and more. Passing the food court you come to the covered Crafts Market, which is full of designers selling handicrafts, jewellery, home furnishings and clothes for all ages; it's also ideal for gifts (wooden toys, model ships and plenty of accessories). There are lots of restaurants, cafés, bars and pubs in and around the market, and it's hard to resist in the central hub of stalls, where you'll find a delicious range of foods including breads, cakes, cheeses, olives, honeys, juices and jams.

Northcote Road Market

Northcote Road, SW11 (8871 6384). Clapham Junction rail. **Open** 9am-5pm Mon-Sat.
This is a superb opportunity for the locals of 'Nappy Valley' to buy the freshest fruit and vegetables, as well as flowers, ceramics, vintage ladies' clothes, handbags, exotic homeware and photographic prints. There is also an excellent selection of independent shops along Northcote Road, including Kelly's Organic Foods (No.46, 7207 3967), Hamish Johnston (*see p233*) for cheeses, A Dove & Son (*see p246*) for organic meat and the Hive Honey Shop (*see p237*) for all things bee-centric. The Antiques Market (No.155A, 7228 6850, 10am-6pm Mon-Sat, noon-5pm Sun) has 40 dealers (in a 3,000sq ft space) offering antique furniture, china, glass, silver, jewellery, cutlery, lighting, prints and pictures. There are also plenty of decent eateries if all that shopping has worked up an appetite.

Local markets

See also p18 Markets under threat.

Central

Earlham Street Market *Earlham Street, WC2.* **Open** 9am-5pm Mon-Sat. **Leather Lane Market** *Leather Lane, EC1.* **Open** 10am-2.30pm Mon-Fri.

North

Chalton Street Market *Chalton Street, NW1.* **Open** 9am-5pm Fri. **Church Street Market** *Church Street, NW8. Bell Street, NW1.* **Open** *Church Street* 9am-5pm Mon-Sat. *Bell Street* 9am-5pm Sat. **Inverness Street Market** *Inverness Street, NW1.* **Open** 9am-5pm daily. **Nag's Head Market** *Seven Sisters Road (junction with Enkel Street), N7.* **Open** *General* 6am-5pm Mon, Tue, Thur. *Second-hand & antiques* 6am-3.30pm Wed. *New goods* 6am-5pm Fri; 6am-5.30pm Sat. *Flea market* 7am-2pm Sun. **Plender Street Market** *Plender Street, NW1.* **Open** 9am-5pm Mon-Sat. **Swiss Cottage Market** *College Crescent, NW3.* **Open** 9am-4pm Fri, Sat.

North-east

Walthamstow Market *Walthamstow High Street, E17.* **Open** 8am-6pm Mon-Sat.

East

Bethnal Green Road Market *Bethnal Green Road, E2.* **Open** 8am-6pm Mon-Sat. **Chrisp Street Market** *Chrisp Street, E14.* **Open** 10am-4pm Mon-Sat. **Hoxton Street Market** *Hoxton Street, N1.* **Open** 9am-5pm Mon-Sat. **Queen's Market** *off the junction of Green Street & Queen's Road, E13.* **Open** 8am-noon Tue; 8am-5pm Thur-Sat. **Roman Road Square Market** *Roman Road Square, E2.* **Open** 8.30am-6pm Mon-Sat. **Watney Street Market** *Watney Street, E1.* **Open** 8am-6pm Tue-Sat. **Well Street Market** *Well Street (Morning Lane to Valentine Road), E9.* **Open** 8.30am-5pm Mon-Sat. **Whitechapel Market** *Whitechapel Road (Vallance Road to Cambridge Heath Road), E1.* **Open** 8am-6pm Mon-Sat.

South-east

Catford Market *Catford Broadway, SE6.* **Open** 9am-4pm Mon, Thur-Sat. **Choumert Road Market** *Choumert Road, SE15.* **Open** 8am-5pm Mon-Sat. **Collyer Place Market** *Collyer Place, SE15.* **Open** 8am-2pm Sun. **Deptford Market** *Douglas Way & Deptford High Street, SE8.* **Open** 9am-5pm Wed, Fri, Sat. **East Street Market** *East Street, SE17.* **Open** 8am-5pm Tue-Fri; 8am-6.30pm Sat; 8am-2pm Sun. **Lewisham Market** *Lewisham High Street, SE14.* **Open** 9am-4pm Mon-Sat; 9am-2pm Sun. **Lower Marsh Market** *Lower Marsh (Westminster Bridge Road to Baylis Road), SE1.* **Open** 8am-6pm Mon, Tue, Thur, Sat; 8am-3pm Wed; 8am-7pm Fri. **North Cross Road Market** *North Cross Road, SE22.* **Open** 8am-5pm Fri, Sat. **Woolwich Market** *Beresford Square, SE18.* **Open** 9am-4pm Mon-Wed; 9am-1pm Thur; 9am-4.30pm Fri, Sat.

South

Hildreth Street Market *Hildreth Street, SW12.* **Open** 8am-6pm Mon-Sat. **Nine Elms Market** *New Covent Garden Market, Nine Elms Lane, SW8.* **Open** 8am-2pm Sun. **Tooting's Markets** *Broadway Market & Tooting Market, Upper Tooting Road, SW17.* **Open** 9am-5.30pm Mon, Tue, Thur-Sat; 9am-1pm Wed. **Wimbledon Stadium Market** *Plough Lane, SW17.* **Open** 9am-2pm Sun.

South-west

North End Road Market *North End Road (Walham Grove to Lillie Road), SW6.* **Open** 9am-6pm Mon-Sat.

North-west

Kilburn Square Market *off Kilburn High Road, NW6.* **Open** 9am-5pm Thur-Sat. **Queen's Crescent Market** *Queen's Crescent (Grafton Road to Malden Road), NW5.* **Open** 9am-5pm Thur, Sat. **Wembley Market** *Stadium Way, Wembley, Middx.* **Open** 9am-3pm Sun. **Willesden Market** *White Hart High Street, NW10.* **Open** 9am-5.30pm Wed, Sat.

Shopping Centres

While there are many retail outlets calling themselves shopping centres in London, some are really only a small collection of shops contained within the same area. We've covered what we consider to be the pick of the bunch. Full listings of shops and services for most centres can be found on their websites. Note that cinemas and restaurants within the complexes often stay open later than the shops themselves. For **Bicester Village Outlet Shopping**, see p34.

Central

Covent Garden Market
Between King Street & Henrietta Street, WC2E 8RF (7836 9136/www.coventgardenmarket.co.uk). Covent Garden, Embankment or Temple tube/ Charing Cross tube/rail. **Open** 10am-8pm Mon-Sat; 11am-6pm Sun.
Although it's a London institution, Covent Garden Market is too commercial and crowded to provide the characterful retail experience visitors might expect – the area north of the actual market, including Floral Street and Neal Street, is more interesting. The colonnaded 19th-century building, with its cast-iron-and-glass roof, is made up of two halls and two piazzas (usually full of street performers). The North Hall houses the Apple Market, where individual stalls sell crafts and jewellery, while the South Hall is home to the two most authentic independent shops here, the atmospheric Segar & Snuff Parlour and Benjamin Pollock's Toy Shop (selling model theatres and traditional toys). Among the chain stores, highlights include L'Occitane and jewellers Argenteus; there's a Crabtree & Evelyn, Whittard teas and Thorntons chocs, and on the fashion front Hobbs, Monsoon and Whistles. Below ground level (accessed via the stairs in the South Hall) there's even more of a touristy, gift-shop vibe; it's the place to go for a caricature. On the south (Strand) side, Jubilee Market hosts antiques dealers on Monday and crafts at the weekend, but the rest of the week sells mainly cheap clothes and tourist tat. Chez Gérard on the East Piazza is your best bet over the uninspiring eateries in a pizza and crêpe vein.
Cafés. Restaurants. Toilets.

Duke of York Square
King's Road, between Sloane Square & Cheltenham Terrace, SW3 4LY (7823 5577). Sloane Square tube. **Open** times vary.
Behind the King's Road, this is the first new public square to be created in west London for over a century. The former military barracks is now a tastefully landscaped, tree-lined retail and pedestrian area. A combination of listed and new buildings houses a selection of high-end, high-street clothes stores, including All Saints, Ted Baker, GAS, Agnès b and – in the modern glass-walled pavilion in the centre – Joseph, Myla lingerie and Suede menswear. There's a line-up of good shoe shops – Kate Kuba, LK Bennett and Pied à Terre – while other highlights include Space NK, Yves Delorme for luxury French linens and a large Jigsaw in the Grade II listed former chapel. Celebrity hairdresser Richard Ward has opened his swanky new flagship salon here, and a lovely branch of Pâtisserie Valerie sits beside restaurant Manicomio; both have lots of outdoor tables and are great people-watching spots.
Cafés. Disabled: toilets. Nappy-changing facilities.

Kingly Court
Carnaby Street, opposite Broadwick Street, W1B 5PW (www.carnaby.co.uk). Oxford Circus tube. **Open** 11am-7pm Mon-Sat; noon-6pm Sun.

Tucked behind Carnaby Street, this haven of independent boutiques epitomises all that is good about the modern shopping centre. It was developed from a three-storey Victorian building with an internal courtyard (which doubles as an alfresco café in summer), and the open architecture and attractive balconies make strolling about here a pleasure. Retailers tend to be offbeat on the upper levels, while a sporty, branded atmosphere dominates at ground level (Henri Lloyd, Puma and Sweaty Betty). Vintage clothes hounds will find rich pickings at Marshmallow Mountain, Sam Greenberg and – biggest of all and selling homewares as well as clothing – Twinkled. Boutiques such as Harriet's Muse have a flowery, vagabond look, while there are oceans of affordable sparkle at designer Wing Sze Tsoi's boutique, Siren. There's the Nail Lounge at ground level, and eating opportunities include a juice bar, plus popular wine bar Shampers.
Cafés. Disabled: toilets. Nappy-changing facilities.

Plaza Shopping Centre
120 Oxford Street, W1D 1LT (7637 8811/ www.plaza-oxfordst.com). Oxford Circus tube. **Open** 10am-7pm Mon-Wed, Fri, Sat; 10am-8pm Thur; noon-6pm Sun.
This small, standard-issue shopping centre amid the chaos of Oxford Street contains a few inexpensive boutiques alongside well-known names. You'll find Dune, Warehouse, Oasis, cheap Japanese outfitters Uniqlo and the new Evans flagship store. There's also a fairly large WH Smith – one of the newsagent's only central London branches and a Supercuts hair salon. Food choices are hardly gourmet (McDonalds, KFC), but the first-floor food court also includes a branch of reliably good Pizza Express and outlets selling Singaporean and Indian food, plus fresh juices. There are useful health facilities in the shape of Medicentre walk-in docs and a Holmes Place health club on the second floor.
Disabled: lift, toilets. Nappy-changing facilities. Restaurants. Toilets.

Thomas Neal Centre
29-41 Earlham Street, WC2H 9LD (7240 4741). Covent Garden tube. **Open** 10am-7pm Mon-Sat; noon-6pm Sun.
This small shopping complex in a converted warehouse off Neal Street is calmer than the rest of Covent Garden. There's a quick turnover of shops (and often a few empty retail units), which are mainly young with a 'street' vibe, without being right at the cutting edge. There's an obvious skate/surfwear slant: Quiksilver, Mooks and Fat Face dominate the space, while Rusty vs Freerider and Superdry (selling lots of clothing from Bench) are located downstairs. Other highlights are Lambretta, Paul Frank, Luomo menswear and Moda Moda. There's also a branch of Space NK and jewellery from Silverworks. Food options (on the lower level) are above average, with a Progreso Fairtrade coffee bar in the main 'square' and the Bünker Bierhall & Kitchen tucked behind the stairs.
Cafés. Disabled: lift, toilets. Nappy-changing facilities. Restaurants. Toilets.

Local

Bentall Centre
Wood Street, Kingston-upon-Thames, Surrey KT1 1TP (8541 5066/www.thebentallcentre-shopping.com). Kingston-upon-Thames rail. **Open** 9.30am-6pm Mon-Wed, Fri, Sat; 9.30am-9pm Thur; 11am-5pm Sun.
With a façade inspired by Hampton Court, a soaring atrium and galleries illuminated with glinting fibre-optic lights, the Bentall Centre is pretty classy for a shopping mall. Yet, despite the

upmarket image, most of the 85-plus shops are mainstream (Aldo, Sole Trader, Esprit, The Pier, Waterstones and, of course, Bentalls department store). At the upper end, there are branches of Austin Reed, crystal specialist Swarovski and Holmes Place Health Club. Food is standard fare: TGI Friday's and a food court with everything from fish and chips to ice-cream. The centre is very community-oriented, supporting charities and hosting family activities, plus the twice-yearly animatronics events, when it's taken over for more than a month by 6ft, all-singing, all-dancing bears.
Cafés. Car park. Crèche. Disabled: lift, toilets. Nappy-changing facilities. Restaurants. Toilets.

Brent Cross Shopping Centre
NW4 3FP (8202 8095/www.brentcross.co.uk). Brent Cross tube then 210 bus/Hendon Central tube then 143, 186 bus. **Open** 10am-8pm Mon-Fri; 9am-7pm Sat; 11am-5pm Sun.
Brent Cross was the first large, enclosed shopping centre in the UK and, although the external design is beginning to look dated, it doesn't detract from the quality of the experience. In recent years, the centre has been promoting a more fashion-led image, introducing 30 additional stores. Alongside classics like John Lewis, Fenwick, Russell & Bromley and Marks & Spencer, Brent Cross is keeping pace with central London for quality fashion chains: Massimo Dutti, Reiss, Hobbs, Hugo Boss, H&M, Tommy Hilfiger, Jigsaw and Kew, to name but a few. Recent openings include Timberland, Levi's and, in autumn 2005, Office and the White Company; an Apple Store will open in early 2006. Carluccio's café and Wagamama provide sustenance. Families are well catered for, in terms of both shops and services. There's a new Monsoon Children to enhance the existing Gap Kids, Mothercare and Buckle My Shoe. Child-friendly perks include free pushchair loan and Boobaloo shopping trolley-cum-play mobiles (£2.50/hr), plus funhouse Topsey Turvey World.
Cafés. Car park. Crèche. Disabled: lift, toilets. Nappy-changing facilities. Restaurants. Toilets.

Canary Wharf Shopping Centres
Canada Place & Cabot Place, E14 5AB. Jubilee Place, E14 5AB (7477 1477/www.mycanary wharf.com). Canary Wharf tube/DLR. **Open** 9am-7pm Mon-Fri; 10am-6pm Sat; noon-6pm Sun.
Like the offices that surround them, Canary Wharf's enclosed shopping centres are all spotless chrome and glass, creating a smart yet rather soulless atmosphere. There are three main malls (all linked): Cabot Place (divided into East and West), Canada Place (below street level) and, on the other side of the square (but also accessed underground), the newer Jubilee Place. While they all feature mainstream stores, Canada Place has the highest proportion of high-street staples (including a Topshop, Next, Accessorize, JD Sports, HMV, Toni & Guy and Nails Inc, plus a large Waitrose Food & Home), while Jubilee Place houses the majority of the higher-end units, such as Fiorelli, Molton Brown, Reiss and LK Bennett. Some more upmarket stores and brands are also in evidence: Space NK, Ackermans Chocolates; Church's (shoes), Fish Brothers (jewellery) and Sweaty Betty (women's sportswear) in Cabot Place; Mont Blanc and TM Lewin (men's shirts) in Canada Place. In terms of food, there's a smattering of Prets and Coffee Republics, plus two branches of Itsu for sushi, a Pizza Express, a Wagamama and, above Waitrose in Canada Place, Conran's modern French restaurant, Plateau.
Cafés. Car park. Cinema. Disabled: lift, toilets. Nappy-changing facilities. Restaurants. Toilets.

Centre Court Shopping Centre
4 Queens Road, SW19 8YA (8944 8323/ www.centrecourt.uk.net). Wimbledon tube/rail. **Open** 9.30am-7pm Mon-Wed, Fri; 9.30am-8pm Thur; 9am-6pm Sat; 11am-5pm Sun.
Developed on the site of Wimbledon's old town hall and courthouse in 1992, Centre Court houses 70-odd retailers, including Debenhams, Gap, River Island, Morgan and Oliver Bonas. Higher-end

Thomas Neal Centre

fashion is available at Colors, which sells a wide range of designer labels for men and women, including Moschino, Versace, D&G and Patrick Cox. The food court isn't particularly exciting, so your best bet is Marks & Spencer's Simply Food. There are children's workshops during school holidays and various festivities at Christmas.
Cafés. Car park. Crèche. Disabled: toilets. Nappy-changing facilities. Restaurants. Toilets.

N1 Islington
21 Parkfield Street, N1 0PS (7359 2674/www. n1islington.co.uk). Angel tube. **Open** 10am-7pm Mon-Sat; 11am-5pm Sun.
This newish centre in the Angel is marked by a metal 'wings' sculpture (geddit?) at the Parkfield Street entrance, where you'll also find florist Angel Flowers. Shops here, as with most shopping malls, are of the high-street variety, with French Connection, Gap, Karen Millen, HMV, Borders and Next all featuring. Marginally less ubiquitous stores include trendy sneakers and sportwear shop size?, L'Occitane and Mambo. Eating options are mainly on the upper level: Wagamama and Yo! Sushi are still present and correct, along with a number of mediocre pub-style options, while entertainment is in the form of Carling Bar Academy and the Vue nine-screen cinema. The car park is below.
Cafés. Car park. Cinema. Disabled: lift, toilets. Nappy-changing facilities. Restaurants. Toilets.

Putney Exchange Shopping Centre
High Street, SW15 1TW (8780 1056/www. theexchangesw15.com). East Putney or Putney Bridge tube/Putney rail. **Open** 9am-6pm Mon-Wed, Fri, Sat; 9am-8pm Thur; 11am-5pm Sun.
This pleasant centre is more in the 'quick dash to the shops' category than the place for a full-scale spending spree. It's great for kids' clothes and toys, there are shops like Gap, Next, Argos and Carphone for clothes and home basics, and Waitrose for groceries. There's also a nail bar, beauty salon, fitness centre, florist and several café options.
Cafés. Car park. Disabled: lift, toilets. Nappy-changing facilities. Restaurants. Toilets.

Whiteleys
151 Queensway, W2 4YN (7229 8844/ www.whiteleys.com). Bayswater or Queensway (station closed until May 2006) tube. **Open** 10am-8pm Mon-Sat; noon-6pm Sun.
With its original Edwardian decor (in particular the iron 'La Scala' staircase), glass dome and marble flooring throughout, four-floored Whiteleys is the grandest and most atmospheric of London's shopping centres, and it is deservedly popular. With over 70 units, there's room for a few slightly lesser-

known shops to supplement the usual high-street chains (Accessorize, Books Etc, the Body Shop, French Connection, M&S, JD Sports, HMV, Nine West and various well-known mobile phone names are all here). Doucereux, on the first floor, stocks Italian designer menswear labels, Beauty Base sells discounted cosmetics and perfumes, while Dr & Herbs is the place for alternative remedies. Other stores include La Senza lingerie and L'Occitane and there's also an eight-screen cinema, a Soho gym, a Vidal Sassoon, an Enzo Trevi beauty salon, a rooftop car park and a plethora of (mainly chain) eateries on the second floor.
Cafés. Car park. Car valet. Cinema. Disabled: lift, toilets. Nappy-changing facilities. Restaurants. Toilets.

Out of town

Bluewater
Greenhithe, Kent DA9 9ST (0870 777 0252/ www.bluewater.co.uk). Greenhithe rail. **Open** 10am-9pm Mon-Fri; 9am-8pm Sat; 11am-5pm Sun.
Covering 53 acres, this immense shopping centre has so many facilities you could practically live here. Four travel agents, two hairdressers, over 40 eating and drinking options, a cinema… You can even fit in a bit of fishing, rock climbing or perhaps a few rounds on the putting green (from £3). And that's before you get to the shopping. But, of course, if you've come for retail therapy, it's here in spades – from department stores like House of Fraser to fashion chains spanning the price/style spectrum (New Look, Coast, Miss Sixty, Fred Perry, Pringle, Diesel, Joseph), via homewares, electronics, books, cosmetics and more. But if that all sounds too much like hard work, offload the kids in the Nestlé All Stars Active Zone (that is, a play area), and book yourself into the Molton Brown Day Spa.
Cafés. Car park. Car valet. Cinema. Crèche. Disabled: lift, toilets. Nappy-changing facilities. Restaurants. Toilets. Wheelchair hire.

thecentre:mk
24 Silbury Arcade, Milton Keynes, Bucks MK9 3ES (01908 678 641/www.thecentremk.com). Milton Keynes rail then bus. **Open** 9am-6pm Mon-Wed, Sat; 9am-8pm Thur, Fri; 11am-5pm Sun.
Given Milton Keynes's American-influenced urban design – grid-like street planning, modern glass and concrete buildings – it makes sense that it's the home of the UK's most authentic shopping 'mall'. With three miles of shopfronts, you'd better get your walking shoes on if you're going to cover this extensive retail ground (luckily there are free buggies or Kiddy Cabs to hire at £2.50/hr to save little legs). The emphasis is mainly on the big names, but alongside Dorothy Perkins, John Lewis,

Marks & Spencer, HMV and French Connection are less ubiquitous stores such as Pineapple dancewear and Boros luggage and leather goods, stocking such upmarket brands as Mulberry and Coccinelle. There's a separate food centre, a general market five days out of seven just outside and events throughout the year (see website for details). Disabled services are excellent, including Shop and See escorts for the visually impaired (01908 282 282) and a Hearing Induction Loop.
Cafés. Car park. Cinema. Crèche. Disabled: lift, toilets. Nappy-changing facilities. Restaurants. Toilets.

Lakeside
West Thurrock, Grays, Essex RM20 2ZP (01708 869933/www.lakeside.uk.com). Chafford Hundred rail. **Open** 10am-10pm Mon-Fri; 9am-7.30pm Sat; 11am-5pm Sun.
While it's been somewhat overshadowed by its rival Bluewater, Lakeside got a glossy £30 million makeover in summer 2004, including a spectacular glass ceiling, state-of-the-art lifts, revamped loos and comfortable seating areas for weary shoppers. The place packs in nearly 300 retailers, ranging from high-street names such as French Connection, Mikey, H&M, River Island and Morgan to staples such as pet shops, stationers and opticians, plus department stores House of Fraser and Debenhams. The food hall includes a Häagen-Dazs café and Fresh Italy, which dishes up freshly cooked pasta. In the unlikely event of boredom setting in there's a seven-screen cinema and a packed calendar of events, including biannual fashion shows and kids' holiday activities. Visit the website or sign up to the text-message service (07797 882 288) for news.
Cafés. Car park. Car valet. Crèche. Cinema. Disabled: lift, toilets. Nappy-changing facilities. Restaurants. Toilets. Wheelchair hire.

McArthur Glen Designer Outlet
Kimberly Way, Ashford, Kent TN24 0SD (01233 895 900/www.mcarthurglen.com). Ashford rail then shuttlebus. **Open** 10am-6pm Mon-Wed, Fri; 10am-8pm Thur; 10am-7pm Sat; 10.30am-5pm Sun.
Designed by Millennium Dome architect Lord Richard Rogers, this award-winning centre is part of a Europe-wide chain. It has over 70 shops under a huge tented roof, all offering discounts of up to 50% off typical retail prices (goods are excess or end-of-season). Though it's billed as a designer outlet, it's more of a catch-all shopping centre, stocking mid-range high-street labels, such as M&S, Oasis and Miss Sixty, as well as accessories, homewares, china and crystal. Further attractions include restaurants, cafés and a range of seasonal activities, from children's workshops to jazz bands.
Cafés. Car park. Disabled: toilets. Nappy-changing facilities. Restaurants. Toilets. Wheelchair hire.

ONE-STOP

Fashion

ALL FROM MATCHES (7221 0255,
WWW.MATCHES.CO.UK).

Designer

We've listed designers' stand-alone stores where they exist, but department stores, in particular **Harrods**, **Selfridges** and **Harvey Nichols**, also carry many of the labels listed in this chapter (for all, *see chapter* **Department Stores**). Other stockists are reviewed in the **Boutiques**, **Menswear** and **Street** chapters of this guide. 2005 has seen lots of exciting new additions to the fold, including up-and-coming designers like **Ashish** and **Basso & Brooke**, and the newly revamped **Rochas**, injecting yet more style into London's eclectic designer scene.

Alberta Ferretti
205-206 Sloane Street, SW1X 9QX (7235 2349/ www.aeffe.com). Knightsbridge tube. **Open** 10am-6pm Mon, Tue, Thur-Sat; 10am-7pm Wed. **Credit** AmEx, DC, MC, V. **Sells** W.
Italian designer Alberta Ferretti has made frothy, girlie chiffon dresses her forte for the past decade (although she actually established her label in 1980), and has a fiercely loyal following including Anna Friel, Beyoncé Knowles and Kim Cattrall. Her newest offerings take a slightly slicker direction, with neat felt pea coats featuring astrakhan collars, printed dirndl skirts and elegant knee-high suede boots – but, don't worry, there are still plenty of those signature floaty frocks to be found. The light and friendly two-floor Sloane Street store is one of the more inviting shops in the area.

Alexander McQueen
4-5 Old Bond Street, W1S 4PD (7355 0088/ www.alexandermcqueen.com). Green Park tube. **Open** 10am-6pm Mon-Wed, Fri, Sat; 10am-7pm Thur. **Credit** AmEx, DC, MC, V. **Sells** M, W.
Alexander McQueen has grown up somewhat since he launched his label with his daring graduate collection in 1994. Since being taken on by the Gucci Group in 2000, McQueen has toned down his notorious bad boy image (both in his private life and on the catwalk) and that's reflected in his new collection – the most wearable to date. Taking inspiration from the 1960s mod look and muses Tippi Hedren and Marilyn Monroe, he combines his deft Savile Row-acquired tailoring skills with elegant Parisian couture in the form of devilishly glamorous cinch-waisted evening gowns with sculpted fishtails. For daytime, there are more wearable neat, tailored jackets, pencil skirts and a few very saleable Navaho Indian ponchos with pompoms thrown into the mix. Men can choose from sharply cut suits and luxurious fur-trimmed parka jackets for autumn/winter 2005/6. All of this can be found in the designer's modern two-floor Bond Street store. McQueen has also recently collaborated with Puma on a new range of trainers.

Ann Demeulemeester
Sells M, W. **Available at** Browns, Feathers, Harvey Nichols, Liberty, Selfridges.
When all the other designers in the world become obsessed with colour and prints, you can rely on Belgian designer Ann Demeulemeester to be whipping up a vision in black, black and more black. For she is the mistress of all things *noir*, and her subtle, sophisticated tailored clothes in pared-down shapes have an obsessive fan base. Her latest designs include diaphanous layered chiffon dresses in black and cream, chunky biker boots and well-cut redingotes. Menswear is a real strength: slim, precisely cut and highly wearable.

Antoni & Alison
43 Rosebery Avenue, EC1R 4SH (7833 2002/ www.antoniandalison.co.uk). Farringdon tube/ rail/19, 38, 341 bus. **Open** 10.30am-6.30pm Mon-Fri. **Credit** AmEx, MC, V. **Sells** W.
Design duo Antoni Burakowski and Alison Roberts launched their quirky label 15 years ago. Their tongue-in-cheek slogan T-shirts were an overnight hit with hip young models and trendy urbanites. Since then, Antoni & Alison has grown into a fully fledged fashion label. For autumn/winter 2005/6, the emphasis is on cute separates and funky accessories, including the irresistible Manchester bag. But there are still plenty of the good old cheeky Ts – some with historical references inspired by the designers' recently acquired 1820s studio in Bermondsey (go for a virtual guided tour via their new online catalogue, launching late autumn 2005). The pair continue to design a range for Debenhams, for whom they are currently developing a kids' collection.

Antonio Berardi
Enquiries 7287 9890/www.antonioberardi.com. **Sells** W. **Available at** Feathers.
When Antonio Berardi launched his design career in London nearly a decade ago, he was the toast of London Fashion Week, with Kate Moss starring in his show and celebrities lining the front row, who all adored his intricately embellished frocks. Then he took off to Milan to establish the business side of things and now he's just moved a little closer back home to Paris, where his elegant, ultra-feminine signature style seems to have landed in its natural home. His figure-hugging, intricately detailed frocks and finely sculpted jackets should be worn with high heels and a lot of sass.

Ashish
Enquiries www.ashish.co.uk. **Sells** M, W. **Available at** Browns Focus, Diverse, Selfridges, Sixty 6.
The charmingly upbeat designs of Indian designer Ashish Gupta have been gaining a cult following since he launched his label in London a few years back. He initially made a name for himself with a range of sequin-scattered bomber jackets, which remained an insider secret among models and the hip Notting Hill set. Now you can buy similarly decorative full skirts and vest tops alongside more wearable sweatshirts scattered with sequins, many of which are lovingly handbeaded in his homeland.

Balenciaga
Enquiries www.balenciaga.com. **Sells** M, W. **Available at** Harrods, Harvey Nichols, Joseph, Selfridges.
The creative director of this Parisian house, the hugely talented Nicolas Ghesquière, is top of the design league in the eyes of the world's fashion experts. The concession in Selfridges Superbrands section continues to please his trendy fans with satisfying helpings of delectable military-inspired woollen coats, cropped jackets and skinny-cut trousers, sold alongside the hugely covetable bag range, including the internationally bestselling tassel leather style, beloved of Kate Moss. Two new, well-priced basics ranges, Balenciaga Knits and Balenciaga Pants, starting from just £80, are available at Selfridges and Harvey Nichols, but tipped to sell out fast.

Basso & Brooke
Enquiries www.bassoandbrooke.com. **Sells** W. **Available at** Browns, Harrods.
Just when you thought all London's big designer names – and greatest talents – had long decamped to Paris, Milan and New York, Bruno Basso and Christopher Brooke burst on to the London scene to introduce some much-needed buzz and glamour. After winning the first Fashion Fringe award in 2005 and scooping a rather helpful £100,000, the pair, now backed by Aeffe fashion group, have become known for their dazzling computer-generated prints (initially of a naughty sexual nature, now more socially acceptable chains, faces and harlequin checks) and tightly tailored silhouettes. Not the kind of clothes to wear top to toe, but that's not the idea: one of Basso & Brooke's chain-print jackets for autumn/winter 2005/6 would liven up a pair of skinny jeans a treat.

Blaak
Sells W. **Available at** Selfridges.
Sachiko Okada and Aaron Sharif, the duo behind Blaak, design hip, wearable clothes with attitude. They've picked up quite a following with their street-inspired designs, which for autumn/winter 2005/6 come in a subdued colour palette of pale grey, yellow and black. The cool, well-cut urban jackets and slouchy, menswear-inspired tailored trousers are the things to look out for this season.

Boudicca
Enquiries www.platform13.com. **Sells** W. **Available at** Browns, Focus, Dover Street Market. Named after the warrior queen of the Iceni tribe, this uncompromising (read: not the easiest to wear) label has been going since 1997. Still, Zowie Broach and Brian Kirby have pursued an independent route that has earned them a devout following who adore their ultra-sharp tailoring; the autumn/winter 2005/6 collection includes strictly cut jackets and skirts embroidered with the words of Visconti.

BOYD
42 Elizabeth Street, SW1W 9NZ (7730 3939/www. traceyboyd.com). Sloane Square tube. **Open** 10am-6pm Mon-Fri. **Credit** AmEx, MC, V. **Sells** W.
When former fashion illustrator Tracey Boyd launched her womenswear label ten years ago, the utterly English combination of wearable, feminine styles with a dash of witty individuality was an instant hit. Her clothes are still highly desirable. For autumn/winter 2005, you'll find demure, wispy frocks embellished with beading or embroidery, or in a folksy patchwork print, stripy knits, and fitted tweed jackets sexed up with a leopard-print skirt or splashed with large embroidered flowers. Spring/summer 2006 is even more indulgent, being inspired by Monet and dominated by gorgeous tulle, georgette and cotton lawn dresses, some in lovely, hand-painted floral prints designed by Boyd. At her shop, the clothes, as well as her recently launched bags and shoes, are displayed alongside home items reflecting the designer's cosy, yet quirky, tastes, such as cushions featuring her prints, embroidered tea cosies, quilts, furniture, hand-painted picture frames – even some of her own artworks.

Celine
160 New Bond Street, W1S 2UE (7297 4999/ www.celine.com). Bond Street or Green Park tube. **Open** 10am-6pm Mon-Wed, Fri, Sat; 10am-6.30pm Thur. **Credit** AmEx, DC, MC, V. **Sells** W.
Part of the exclusive LVMH (Louis Vuitton Moët Hennessy) luxury goods conglomerate, which also owns Vuitton and Dior, Celine is more of a niche label appealing to the chic, jet-setting woman who can afford to take holidays on exclusive Caribbean islands every February. Now under the design direction of Roberto Menichetti (formerly at Burberry), the label continues to trade off that slick style of low-key luxe, epitomised in autumn/winter 2005/6 by just-right tailored cashmere trousers, sumptuous rollnecks and oversized tortoiseshell shades. The cashmere coats are particularly desirable and of the highest quality. The range of bags – enamelled chain-link shoulder bags and doctor-style holdalls embellished with tiny buckled straps – will no doubt be highly sought after among the ladies who lunch. *Mail order.*

Chanel
278-280 Brompton Road, SW3 2AB (7581 8620/ www.chanel.com). South Kensington tube. **Open** 10am-6pm Mon-Sat; 1-5pm Sun. **Credit** AmEx, DC, MC, V. **Sells** W.
He of the white ponytail and black sunglasses, Chanel's highly talented creative director Karl Lagerfeld has got the formula right. Inspired by

FASHION

the kooky 1960s model Penelope Tree for autumn/winter 2005/6, he has created a monochromatic collection of A-line minidresses, neat little bouclé jackets and skinny cropped trousers. A more affordable way to buy into the label is to pick up an item from the ever-growing accessory lines, whether one of the new quilted wallets or a woollen beanie hat. The star item this winter, however, is the latest take on that classic quilted bag – a highly covetable distressed leather version.

Chenpascual
www.oki-ni.com/chenpascual.htm. **Sells** M, W. **Available at** oki-ni.
London-based designer Maria Pascual (née Chen) has cut out a niche for herself, creating cool, urban and conceptual clothes that appeal equally to men and women. This season sees more of her gentle but cutting-edge designs in a muted colour palette.

Chloé
152-153 Sloane Street, SW1X 9BX (7823 5348/ www.chloe.com). Sloane Square tube. **Open** 6pm Mon, Tue, Thur-Sat; 10am-7pm Wed. **Credit** AmEx, DC, MC, V. **Sells** W.
Since taking over from Stella McCartney as creative director in 2002, hip and sassy London gal Phoebe Philo has been injecting more of her cool, laid-back urban sense of style into the label each season. Philo manages to hit the right note every time, balancing good-quality classics (those high-waisted, wide-leg trousers) with a dash of humour (remember the iconic banana-print tops?). The autumn/winter 2005/6 collection – expertly designed by her team while she was off on maternity leave – includes some very desirable cropped trousers rolled up on the calf and neat little Victorian-style jackets. Add to that an ever-growing accessory line, including the 'it' bag of the moment, the Chloé Paddington, and you have one of the grooviest designer labels in town.
Mail order.

Christian Dior
31 Sloane Street, SW1X 9NR (7245 1300/ www.dior.com). Knightsbridge tube. **Open** 10am-6.30pm Mon, Tue, Thur-Sat; 10am-7pm Wed; noon-5pm Sun. **Credit** AmEx, DC, MC, V. **Sells** W.
Usually you can bank on John Galliano to whip up some crazy and colourful creations that splice cultural influences and break all the rules, but he's gone all grown-up and serious for autumn/winter 2005/6, with a collection largely in black and white that takes its inspiration from the modish look of the 1960s. He's worked in some luxurious belted sheepskin coats and jackets (which have only a slight whiff of Del Boy about them), a very fine new Aviator bag and wicked statement sunglasses. Don't worry, there are some highly glam fishtail dresses to keep the glitzy red-carpet contingent happy. Menswear is designed by the celebrated perfectionist Hedi Slimane, whose slimline suits for Dior Homme are a hit with women (including Kate Moss and Madonna) as well as men (Chanel's Karl Lagerfeld famously lost weight to fit into his designs).
Mail order.

Clements Ribeiro
Sells M, W, C. **Available at** Diverse, Harvey Nichols, House of Fraser, Koh Samui, The Cross.
Known and loved for their colourful cashmere knits and abundant use of colour and print, husband-and-wife team Suzanne Clements and Inacio Ribeiro design clothes for men, women and children. This autumn, they are inspired by Frida Kahlo, with many floral, vintage-look frocks and little tweed jackets appliquéd with flowers. The ever-growing accessory line includes butterfly-decorated wedge sandals and leather granny-style handbags.

Comme des Garçons
Dover Street Market, 17-18 Dover Street, W1S 4LT (7491 8460). **Open** 11am-6pm Mon-Wed, Fri, Sat; 11am-7pm Thur. **Credit** AmEx, MC, V. **Sells** M, W.
Japanese designer Rei Kawakubo, one of the most progressive and influential designers living today, is a woman who sticks to her design principles.

Queen of the deconstructed look, whereby clothes, their seams and linings take on new dimensions and meanings, she strives to push boundaries, but doesn't create a radically different collection each season; it's more like a quiet step forward. Dover Street Market has been successfully exhibiting the clothes in what is now their natural London home. Here, along with other selected designer labels, you'll find Kawakubo's current collection of whimsical, romantic, Victorian-spirited clothes, featuring leg-of-mutton sleeves, patchworks of fan pleating, tulle and satin.

Diane von Furstenberg
83 Ledbury Road, W11 2AG (7221 1120/www. dvflondon.com). Notting Hill Gate tube. **Open** 10am-6pm Mon-Sat; noon-6pm Sun. **Credit** AmEx, DC, MC, V. **Sells** W.
It was over 30 years ago (1972, to be precise) that New York-based designer Diane von Furstenberg came up with the simple but brilliant concept for the now iconic wrap dress. You can buy a huge variety of them in all sorts of colourways at this pleasant Notting Hill store. She has added subtle military details to the classic design, and spun out a glamorous line of cocktail dresses appliquéd with gold sequins for those looking for some extra evening sass.
Mail order.

Dolce & Gabbana
6-8 Old Bond Street, W1S 4PH (7659 9000/ www.dolcegabbana.it). Green Park tube. **Open** 10am-6pm Mon-Wed, Fri, Sat; 10am-7pm Thur. **Credit** AmEx, DC, MC, V. **Sells** M, W.
No one else (except perhaps Roberto Cavalli) designs clothes that simply ooze sexiness like Domenico Dolce and Stefano Gabbana. In Italian it's called *molto sexy* and that pretty much sums up the spirit of the duo's latest offerings: slick little maxi-dresses and miniskirts pared with boxy jackets, Beatles caps and furry hats in a collection they say is inspired by *La Dolce Vita* meets swinging London'. Menswear ranges from sexy, sophisticated Italian suits through to casually frayed, embroidered jeans. D&G, the street-influenced diffusion line, has its own dedicated store on New Bond Street.
For branch see index.

Donna Karan
19 New Bond Street, W1S 2RD (7495 3100/ www.donnakaran.com). Bond Street tube. **Open** 10am-6pm Mon-Wed, Fri, Sat; 10am-7pm Thur. **Credit** AmEx, DC, MC, V. **Sells** W.
Donna Karan is a mighty force in the fashion world. She is, after all, the woman who invented the 'body' back in the early 1990s and purveyed a new relaxed but smart way of dressing for 'real' women. autumn/winter 2005/6, a collection she has called Manhattan Rush, includes many of her signature fluid, tailored pieces, including a delectable pinstripe suit, as well as sumptuous wool coats and full-skirted taffeta ball gowns. For dressed-down – and more affordable – clothing look to the DKNY diffusion range (27 Old Bond Street, 7499 6238), which this season includes pretty tiered skirts, fitted jackets and shearling coats.

Dries Van Noten
Enquiries *www.driesvannoten.be.* **Sells** M, W. **Available at** Browns, Harvey Nichols, Liberty, Selfridges (accessories).
Dries Van Noten was king of the boho look way before everyone jumped on the bandwagon. He's been rolling out a sophisticated, layered look – which this season includes cropped military-style jackets, rolled-up men's trousers and platform shoes. Van Noten is an expert at mixing up colours and pattern in his womenswear collection (these clothes guarantee compliments), while his menswear line is luxurious and sophisticated too.

Duro Olowu
Enquiries 8960 7570. **Sells** W. **Available at** A La Mode, Browns.
Raised in Lagos, educated and settled in London, Duro Olowu designs clothes that combine English tailoring traditions with African vibrancy. And, since fashion's recent love affair with Africa, his time

has come. In winter 2004 Olowu's signature V-neck, Empire-line silk dress, inspired by 1970s Nigerian style, was declared the dress of the season by American *Vogue.* Made in specially printed fabrics, with vivid, contrasting trims, it's still a staple of his latest collection, which also features a bold floral silk-satin wrap dress; a dramatic, melton swing coat with sunflower-yellow piping; and a sexy skirt suit fit for a film noir seductress. The label is stocked in Browns and A La Mode (*see p35*), but the full range is available at Olowu's cool studio/boutique, OG2 (open by appointment only), alongside own-label bags, handmade by Genevieve Round, large-scale chain-and-gem necklaces by former Chanel couture jewellery designer Taher Chemirik and other unusual items picked up on Olowu's travels.

Eley Kishimoto
40 Snowsfields, SE1 3SU (7357 0037/www.eley kishimoto.com). **Open** 10.30am-6.30pm Thur-Sat; also by appointment. **Credit** AmEx, MC, V. **Sells** W. **Available at** b Store, Browns, Harvey Nichols, Hoxton Boutique, Koh Samui, Liberty.
Mark Eley and Wakako Kishimoto, the hugely talented British design duo who have made wacky prints their forte, have gone all subdued for their most recent collection. New prints include subtle, flame-printed dresses and modern renditions on the tartan check, plus some clothes (like a navy belted blazer with scalloped collar) with no prints at all. The pair are introducing a hip menswear line in autumn 2005, plus there's more of the desirable homeware, luggage, shoes and sunglasses, as well as a cute, retro-chic sportswear range for Ellesse.

Elspeth Gibson
7 Pont Street, SW1X 9EJ (7235 0601/www. elspethgibson.com). Knightsbridge or Sloane Square tube. **Open** by appointment Mon-Fri. **Credit** AmEx, DC, MC, V. **Sells** W.
Like Collette Dinnigan and Alice Temperley, Elspeth Gibson sticks to a formula of ultra-pretty, feminine design. At her London boutique, everything is made to measure. Eveningwear comprises drop-waisted, 1920s-style lace dresses, silk numbers with swishy skirts and glamorous LBDs. Daywear includes embroidered dresses, cropped trousers and sparkly necked jumpers.

Emanuel Ungaro
150 New Bond Street, W1S 2TT (7629 0550/ www.emanuelungaro.com). Bond Street or Green Park tube. **Open** 10am-6pm Mon-Wed, Fri, Sat; 10am-7pm Thur. **Credit** AmEx, DC, MC, V. **Sells** W, M.
A new designer, Vincent Darré, formerly at Balenciaga, is now at the helm of this traditionally feminine and quirky French label. His first collection somehow lacks the *joie de vivre* the label had in the past, but there are some perfectly lovely pared-down shearling coats, 1960s-style A-line skirt suits and dresses in bold primary colours to be snapped up from the bright and beautiful Bond Street store.

Emma Cook
Enquiries 7242 5483/*www.emmacook.co.uk.* **Sells** W. **Available at** Harrods, Liberty, Selfridges.
Emma Cook, who established her label in 2002, is a typically British designer, in that she fuses quirky sensibilities with handmade craftsmanship. Recent hits include her cool draped jersey dresses, neat cropped jackets and flower-strewn cotton separates. Charmingly offbeat.

Emporio Armani
51-52 New Bond Street, W1S 1DQ (7491 8080/ www.emporioarmani.co.uk). Bond Street tube. **Open** 10am-6pm Mon-Wed, Fri; 10am-7pm Thur; 10am-6.30pm Sat; noon-6pm Sun. **Credit** AmEx, DC, MC, V. **Sells** M, W.
Emporio Armani is, on the whole, a more youthful range than the main collection, with garments like moleskin safari jackets, leather blazers and gently tailored eveningwear featuring in the autumn/winter 2005/6 collection. Styling is classic enough to last a few seasons, with luxury fabrics and sleek tailoring providing that unmistakable Italian finish.
Mail order.
For branch see index.

Pucci. See p30.

Etro

14 Old Bond Street, W1X 3DB (7495 5767/ www.etro.it). Green Park tube. **Open** 10am-6pm Mon-Sat. **Credit** AmEx, DC, MC, V. **Sells** M, W.
While every other design house in the world is dishing out clothes in black, you can rely on Italian label Etro to whip up some toxic-coloured swirls and modern renditions of paisley. Yet again, the label has hit the right spot, with Dadaist prints with splashes of geranium red, and some more subtle rose prints in luxury fabrics, such as velvet, silk, cashmere and linen. Luscious accessories include jewel-bright scarves, ties and bags to complete the look. The men's print shirts have a cult following for good reason – they are modern collectibles. *Mail order.*

Fendi

20-22 Sloane Street, SW1X 9NE (7838 6280/ www.fendi.com). Knightsbridge tube. **Open** 10.30am-6.30pm Mon-Sat; noon-5pm Sun. **Credit** AmEx, DC, MC, V. **Sells** M, W.
If you oppose fur, then Fendi is definitely a label to avoid – it positively relishes animal skins of all kinds and the autumn/winter 2005/6 collection is even bigger and more ostentatious than usual. However, the label, designed by the multi-talented Karl Lagerfeld, also offers sumptuous slim-cut military coats, pencil skirts and trim, wasp-waisted jackets in deep shades, including aubergine, bottle green and brown. And, of course, there are bags galore: new takes on the Fendi baguette along with elegant bejewelled clutches – all of which are housed in the sumptuous Sloane Street store. *Mail order.*

Gharani Strok

Enquiries *8749 5909/www.gharanistrok.co.uk.* **Sells** W. **Available at** The Cross, Harrods, Koh Samui, Matches, Mimi, Selfridges.
Nargess Gharani and Vanja Strok have become known for designing clothes for the Ibiza-going party girl. Barely there eveningwear and skimpy swimwear for summer, and sexy cream coats (that look like they could be from Morgan at a glance), fur hats and a sultry boho look

(waistcoats worn over floaty chiffon dresses) for winter. Still, they know what their customers want and they deliver it each season. The pair also design a capsule collection, GS by Gharani Strok, for Debenhams and a maternity range that is sold at Blossom Mother & Child (164 Walton Street, SW3 2JL, 7589 7500).

Ghost

14 Hinde Street, W1U 3BG (7486 0239/ www.ghost.co.uk). Bond Street tube. **Open** 10am-6pm Mon-Wed, Fri, Sat; 10am-7pm Thur. **Credit** AmEx, MC, V. **Sells** W, C.
Ghost designer Tanya Sarne has a huge following thanks to her winning formula of bias-cut, machine-washable dresses. They're made in a special viscose fabric that has been washed for a delicate antique appearance. The newest collection includes a subdued colour palette of forest green, orange and maroon, and some unexpected floaty chiffon dresses too.
For branch see index.

Giles by Giles Deacon

Sells W. **Available at** Harvey Nichols, Liberty, Selfridges.
Giles Deacon is still the hottest name on the London fashion scene since he launched his own line in 2004 (having previously designed womenswear for Italian luxury-goods label Bottega Veneta), generating a huge buzz. The Central Saint Martin's-trained designer seems to peddle in a special saucy, but ardently sophisticated, blend of ladylike chic. His autumn/winter 2005/6 collection is a case in point: grown-up, impeccably tailored riding jackets, cinch-waist pencil skirts and opulent opera coats, all lovingly finished with superior attention to detail. Buying a Giles piece is an investment.

Giorgio Armani

37 Sloane Street, SW1X 9LP (7235 6232/ www.giorgioarmani.com). Knightsbridge tube. **Open** 10am-6pm Mon, Tue, Thur-Sat; 10am-7pm Wed. **Credit** AmEx, DC, MC, V. **Sells** M, W.
It's 30 years since the silver-haired, perma-tanned Giorgio Armani made the tailored trouser suit a staple for the working woman's wardrobe, and what

an achievement it was. These days, his beautifully tailored jackets are still in evidence in the collection alongside more frivolous garments like kooky bloomers and Bermuda shorts with fluted frills.

Gucci

18 Sloane Street, SW1X 9NE (7235 6707/ www.gucci.com). Knightsbridge tube. **Open** 10am-6pm Mon, Tue, Thur-Sat; 10am-7pm Wed. **Credit** AmEx, DC, MC, V. **Sells** M, W.
This is the second season without Tom Ford, and Gucci fans and the fashion world still miss him madly. That said, his replacements, Alessandra Facchinetti on the women's side and John Ray on menswear (both of whom worked under Ford on the label), have done a sterling job at maintaining the high-octane sense of glamour and sex appeal for which Ford's Gucci was known and loved. There are plenty of balloon-sleeve taffeta blouson shirts, sexy LBDs and skintight pants in the women's collection, while men can select from well-cut classic tailoring with a suave Italian twist. *Mail order.*

Helmut Lang

Enquiries *www.helmutlang.com.* **Sells** M, W. **Available at** Harrods, Harvey Nichols, Liberty, Selfridges.
Lang's experimental use of techno fabrics and his sportswear-inspired, stripped-down silhouette for both sexes made him one of the most influential designers of the 1990s. His fans still love him for his directional, brilliantly cut separates – skinny trousers, hard-wearing jeans, T-shirts, complicated-looking strappy jersey tops and no-frills jackets. For a more directional alternative to classic evening-wear, look out for intricate silk dresses with strategic chiffon cut-outs.

Hussein Chalayan

Enquiries *7287 9890.* **Sells** M, W. **Available at** Browns, Diverse, Harrods, Liberty, Selfridges.
Hussein Chalayan has been designing clothes for a decade now and his focus has changed: once the master of uncompromising conceptual fashion, he has now – five years on from bankruptcy – accepted that more commercial (although still beautifully

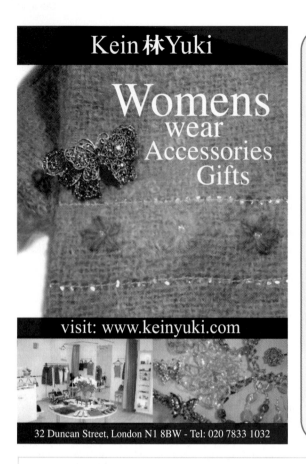

constructed) garments may be the way forward. His current collection includes well-made belted raincoats with voluminous backs and slim-fitting wool cocktail dresses for night-time glamour.

Issey Miyake

52 Conduit Street, W1S 2YX (7851 4620/www.isseymiyake.com). Oxford Circus tube. **Open** 10am-6pm Mon-Sat. **Credit** AmEx, MC, V. **Sells** M, W.
Issey Miyake is known for pioneering innovative fabrics, but that doesn't mean he doesn't make lovely, wearable clothes. His current collection – mainly in black and cream – includes sharply cut trench coats and shapely draped dresses. Besides his own-name label (currently designed by Naoki Takizawa), he has a stand-alone boutique at 20 Brook Street housing Pleats Please, his line of practical clothing made from a wrinkle-free pleated fabric – handy for holidays. Other projects include A-POC (which stands for A Piece of Cloth), an innovative way of constructing clothes using a 3D 'tube' of cloth, which can be trimmed down to size as required. It's a process that sounds complex on paper but that is beautifully simple in practice – see for yourself at the Conduit Street flagship store. **For branches (including Pleats Please) see index.**

Jean Paul Gaultier Boutique

171-175 Draycott Avenue, SW3 3AJ (7584 4648/www.jpgaultier.com). South Kensington tube. **Open** 10am-6pm Mon, Tue, Thur-Sat; 10am-7pm Wed. **Credit** AmEx, DC, MC, V. **Sells** M, W.
Jean Paul Gaultier, once the *enfant terrible* of the Paris fashion scene, now perfectly fuses couture training with a punk spirit and a large dose of humour. For autumn/winter 2005/6, he has delivered some characteristically risqué but adorable clothes inspired by Ziggy Stardust – from silver sequinned leggings to neat brocade-print trousers and some clever reworks of the classic duffel and trench coats.
Mail order.

John Galliano

Enquiries *www.johngalliano.com*. **Sells** W. **Available at** Browns, Harrods, Harvey Nichols, Liberty, Selfridges.
Despite the fact he's been showing in Paris for years, John Galliano remains one of London's greatest living designers. Gloriously eccentric and decadent, he favours dramatic tailoring, vibrant colour and kaleidoscopic prints, which he mixes up like some kind of fashion conjuror. For autumn/winter 2005/6, he's produced some *Great Gatsby*-esque swishy 1920s dresses that drip with silver-screen glamour, while for day there are some lovely slouchy blazers and wide-leg trousers.

Jonathan Saunders

Enquiries *7331 1433*. **Sells** M, W. **Available at** Ashley's Boutique, Harrods, Harvey Nichols, Liberty, Selfridges.
Jonathan Saunders graduated from Central St Martins in 2003 and since then he's won acclaim in the fashion world for his dazzling array of colourful prints, frequently compared to pattern-master Pucci. His autumn/winter 2005/6 collection includes more vibrant prints inspired by Inuit, Japanese and African designs in a slightly more subdued colour palette than usual: dark oranges, muted yellows and reds worn contrasted with grey. He also designs a capsule collection for Topshop.

Joseph

77 Fulham Road, SW3 6RE (7823 9500). South Kensington tube. **Open** *Winter* 10am-6.30pm Mon, Tue, Thur-Sat; 10am-7pm Wed; noon-5pm Sun. *Summer* 10am-6.30pm Mon, Tue, Thur-Sat; 10am-7pm Wed; 1-6pm Sun. **Credit** AmEx, DC, MC, V. **Sells** M, W.
Joseph Ettedgui's luxe separates are popular with men and women of all ages. Subtly stylish rather than cutting-edge, his long-legged trousers, tuxedo-inspired suits, flattering tops and chunky knitwear are updated just enough to tempt loyal customers back for more each season. The Brompton Cross flagship is the best of the London stores if you're after designer names: as well as the Joseph main line, you'll find a selection of clothing and accessories by desirable, high-end labels such as Prada and Marni.
Mail order.
Branches: throughout the city.

Julien Macdonald

Enquiries *7730 1234*. **Sells** W. **Available at** Harrods.
Welshman Julien Macdonald isn't the kind of designer who does things quietly. He likes glitz, glamour and heaps of bling (who cares if it's not trendy any more?). Luckily, so do his fans, who will no doubt be asking to borrow his glittery evening dresses and silk bias-cut 1930s-inspired evening gowns for numerous C-list red carpets events. The trashy fur coats pulled in at the waist with Swarovski crystal belts can stay in the closet, though.

Junya Watanabe

Sells M, W. **Available at** Browns, Dover Street Market.
Part of the new generation of Japanese designers, Junya Watanabe is a protégé of Rei Kawakubo of Comme des Garçons, but his clothes tend to be more colourful and commercial than his mentor's. He often uses technical or functional fabrics. For autumn/winter 2005/6, he's played around with one of his favourite fabrics, tartan, putting it on neat ruched jackets with high open collars. For men, there is more conceptual, brilliant clothing along similar lines.

Kenzo

70 Sloane Avenue, SW3 3DD (7225 1960/www.kenzo.com). South Kensington tube **Open** *Winter* 10am-6.30pm Mon, Tue, Thur-Sat; 10am-7pm Wed; noon-5pm Sun. *Summer* 10am-6.30pm Mon, Tue, Thur-Sat; 10am-7pm Wed; 1-6pm Sun. **Credit** AmEx, MC, V. **Sells** M, W.
It's the third season for the Sardinian designer Antonio Marras, who's been busy adding his eclectic vision into the French-owned Japanese label. Expect bold tartan trousers, floral appliquéd jackets and grand floral-print chiffon dresses in vibrant colours. Menswear, which is also available in-store, has been given a similarly eclectic design ethic.
Mail order.
For branch see index.

Lanvin

Sells W. **Available at** A La Mode, Harrods, Harvey Nichols, Joseph, Liberty, Selfridges (accessories).
Moroccan-born Alber Elbaz, the highly talented designer formerly at Yves Saint Laurent, has been injecting his innate sense of chic into this elegant French fashion house since he arrived a couple of years back, propelling it back to the top spot as one of Paris's most desirable fashion labels. He excels at just-perfect LBDs. The collection also includes some sleek belted coats and pencil skirts. All highly desirable, though expensive, stuff.

Louis Vuitton

190-192 Sloane Street, SW1X 9QX (7399 4050/www.vuitton.com). Knightsbridge or Sloane Square tube. **Open** 10am-6.30pm Mon-Sat; noon-5pm Sun. **Credit** AmEx, DC, MC, V. **Sells** M, W.
While Marc Jacobs continues to do a fine old job designing the ready-to-wear collection for Louis Vuitton, it's really the embossed ultra-luxe luggage and accessory lines that keep the label buoyant. Both the huge Sloane Street premises and its Bond Street counterpart boast entire floors dedicated to leather goods and accessories. Expect efficient service from one of the many petite, black-clad shop assistants.
For branches see index.

Luella

Enquiries *7808 8188/www.luella.com*. **Sells** W. **Available at** Browns, Harvey Nichols, Harrods, Joseph, Liberty, Matches, Mimi.
Former fashion journalist-turned-surfer chick/designer Luella Bartley provides rock-solid proof of her professional credibility in autumn/winter 2005/6, with a collection of properly chic and grown-up clothes, including chocolate suede belted coats and prim high-collared secretary blouses, which she pared on the runway with skinny trousers and thin yellow belts. Add to that an even more than usually gorgeous range of her chunky, buckle-strewn bags, and you have her strongest collection to date.

Maison Martin Margiela

1-9 Bruton Place, W1J 6NE (7629 2682). Bond Street or Green Park tube. **Open** 10am-6.30pm Mon-Wed, Fri, Sat; 10am-7pm Thur. **Credit** AmEx, MC, V. **Sells** M, W.
This reclusive Belgian designer recently opened his first London store. With its white-painted floorboards and exposed pipes, the industrial space tucked away in a quiet mews couldn't be more different from the glitz of nearby Bond Street – even the sign outside has been scribbled on a piece of masking tape and stuck to the door frame. Margiela – often dubbed the fashion designer's fashion designer – is a master at making deconstructed clothing elegant. His expertly tailored pieces exude quiet luxury and are loaded with quirky details, like buttons that fasten the wrong way round. His four lines are differentiated by number: 1 is the women's main line, 4 is a more classic collection, 6 is a cheaper, urban line and 10 is menswear. An 0 on the label indicates that the piece has been deconstructed and remodelled by hand.

Marc Jacobs

Enquiries *www.marcjacobs.com*. **Sells** M, W. **Available at** A La Mode, Browns, Harvey Nichols, Liberty, Matches, Selfridges.
Marc Jacobs is one of the most copied designers on the high street. He shows something on the catwalk and, just a few weeks later, you can guarantee you'll see something remarkably similar in Topshop. Of course, the Marc Jacobs line wins in terms of quality and finish, and Jacobs always seems to keep pushing his label ahead of any competition. His collection includes lots of black, neat cropped slacks and some rather glamorous silk evening skirts in jewel tones. There's also a particularly desirable cropped cream double-breasted jacket that has 'bestseller' written all over it.

Marni

26 Sloane Street, SW1X 9NH (7245 9520/www.marni.com). Knightsbridge tube. **Open** 10am-6pm Mon, Tue, Thur-Sat; 10am-7pm Wed. **Credit** AmEx, DC, MC, V. **Sells** M, W, C.
Designer Consuelo Castiglioni was doing hippy-dippy boho-chic way before last summer's infuriating mania. Naturally she's had to move things on a little to stay ahead of the game. She's done that succinctly by ditching the girlie brights and designing her latest collection almost entirely in black, brown, beige and grey, but don't worry – all her usual charmingly naïve shapes are still there, along with some great accessories, including some yummy slingback platforms. All can be found in the wonderfully curvy, space-age shop that still feels more like a gallery space than a fashion boutique.
Mail order.

Matthew Williamson

28 Bruton Street, W1J 6QH (7629 6200/www.matthewwilliamson.com). Green Park tube. **Open** 10am-6pm Mon-Sat **Credit** AmEx, MC, V. **Sells** W.
Matthew Williamson has grown into a nice mature London label with a high-profile celebrity following, including the likes of the designer's muses Sienna Miller and stylist Bay Garnett. Williamson has made pretty, whimsical clothes with a gypsy vibe his thing, and the autumn/winter 2005/6 collection includes cashmere turtlenecks with epaulettes, Empire-line mini-dresses and smartly tailored trousers.

MaxMara

19-21 Old Bond Street, W1S 4PX (7499 7902). Green Park tube. **Open** 10am-6pm Mon-Wed, Fri, Sat; 10am-7pm Thur. **Credit** AmEx, DC, MC, V. **Sells** W.
If there's one thing MaxMara does well it's coats. Not particularly directional, but certainly not

frumpy, they are simply good-quality classics: belted macs in luxe fabrics (the softest cashmere and the finest lambswool) and easy fluid shapes. For autumn/winter 2005/6 the focus is on a colour palette of cream, black, beige and grey, and the silhouette is a little more voluminous than usual. *Mail order.*

Miu Miu
123 New Bond Street, W1S 1AJ (7409 0900). Bond Street or Oxford Circus tube. **Open** 10am-6pm Mon-Wed, Fri, Sat; 10am-7pm Thur. **Credit** AmEx, DC, MC, V. **Sells** W.
If Prada is for the grown-up, sophisticated glamourpuss, Miu Miu is for her sassier little sister. Thankfully, the Italian label's sibling is also more affordable. Clearly inspired by the beatnik generation, Miuccia Prada has designed some funky checked capes, trim A-line and patchwork skirts for the current collection, which is sold alongside the slightly rustic, and ever popular, accessories in the unintimidating Bond Street store.

Moschino
28-29 Conduit Street, W1S 2YB (7318 0555/ www.aeffe.com). Bond Street tube. **Open** 10am-6pm Mon-Wed, Fri, Sat; 10am-7pm Thur. **Credit** AmEx, DC, MC, V. **Sells** W.
The playful Italian label loved by Kylie, Moschino usually reveals its love of quirky details, cute prints and bright colour, but it's gone a little off kilter in autumn/winter 2005/6, with a collection of mainly black scalloped-neck leather minidresses and dodgy leather blazers. Still, in the lively Conduit Street store, you'll be able to find a range of unexpectedly desirable bags and shoes. Moschino Cheap and Chic is the diffusion range and offers similarly maximalist clothing – but beware, cheap it is not. *Mail order.*

Paul & Joe
39-41 Ledbury Road, W11 2AA (7243 5510/ www.paulandjoe.com). Notting Hill Gate tube. **Open** 10.30am-6.30pm Mon-Fri; 10.30am-7pm Sat; 12.30-5.30pm Sun. **Credit** AmEx, MC, V. **Sells** M, W.
Sophie Albou designs this feminine label, which has been gaining fans since it launched six years ago. Albou, who named the label after her sons and now has four airy London shops, has a knack of mixing cute boyish ideas (such as tangerine tailored shorts and mini-dungarees) with utterly girlie garments (sweet strapless dresses and delicately printed chiffon tops). She's also good at designing well-cut, sexy jeans for ladies. Menswear, including suits, floral-print shirts and easy-to-wear separates, has a similarly quirky, romantic feel. *Mail order.*
For branches see index.

Paul Smith
Westbourne House, 120 & 122 Kensington Park Road, W11 2EP (7727 3553/www.paulsmith. co.uk). Notting Hill Gate tube. **Open** 10am-6pm Mon-Fri; 10am-6.30pm Sat. **Credit** AmEx, DC, MC, V. **Sells** M, W, C.
While other British designers are known for pushing the boundaries, Paul Smith is quietly focused, with a businesslike approach. He takes a little bit of the current trend (the 1960s vibe 2005/6) and mixes it up with classic British subtlety and a little of his own English eccentricity. Small wonder that he's the most commercially successful designer working in London today. His current collection includes Sherlock Holmes-style capes, tartan minidresses and huge velvet kaftans for a dash of opulent, bohemian London glamour. Menswear is a strong point, with an abundance of lively print shirts, lovely scarves and smart cufflinks. *Mail order.*
For branches see index.

Prada
16-18 Old Bond Street, W1X 3DA (7647 5000/ www.prada.com). Green Park tube. **Open** 10am-6pm Mon-Wed, Fri, Sat; 10am-7pm Thur. **Credit** AmEx, DC, MC, V. **Sells** M, W, C.
The London stores have the air of a luxe boudoir (all rose-coloured carpets and mint-hued walls) with a wonderfully enticing accessory and shoe

Stella McCartney. See p32.

section. Miuccia Prada upholds a more demure dress code than the majority of her fellow Italian designers. This year, she has continued to play with 1940s and '50s silhouettes to produce a collection that contrasts feminine full skirts and prim tweed suits. Menswear includes classic suiting and colourful casualwear. There are also concessions in Harrods and Selfridges. *Mail order.*
For branches see index.

Preen
5 Portobello Green, 281 Portobello Road, W10 5TZ (8968 1542). Ladbroke Grove tube. **Open** 11am-6pm Thur, Fri; 10am-6pm Sat. **Credit** MC, V. **Sells** M, W.
This London-based design company has been in business for nearly ten years. Designers Justin Thornton and Thea Bregazzi are skilled at deconstructing, then reconstructing clothing, so that what looks like a muddle of twists, straps and ragged hems on the hanger really works on the body. In addition to women's and men's clothes, they also have a successful accessory line of bags, belts, purses and scarves. There are also concessions at Selfridges and Liberty.

Pucci
170 Sloane Street, SW1X 9QG (7201 8171/ www.pucci.com). Knightsbridge tube. **Open** 10am-6pm Mon, Tue, Thur-Sat; 10am-7pm Wed. **Credit** AmEx, DC, MC, V. **Sells** M, W.
Eccentric French designer Christian Lacroix continues to take the Italian print label forward with style, verve and a lot of wit. The latest collection includes – shock, horror – plain black dresses and voluminous frocks in just one colour. But fear not, the signature swirly prints, for which the label is adored, are still in place for autumn/winter 2005/6, in the form of a dynamic pink, red, purple and orange colourway. Plus, there's a dazzling flame-orange and black print for the super daring. The Sloane Street shop features bikinis, make-up bags and a selection of the hip homeware line too. *Mail order.*

Robert Cary-Williams
Enquiries *7439 9888.* **Sells** M, W. **Available at** Concrete (W), Harrods (M), Hoxton Boutique (W).
Robert Cary-Williams's clothes are often dismantled, distressed and tattered, resulting in original, experimental pieces. Not to everyone's taste but interesting nevertheless, his collection includes

FASHION

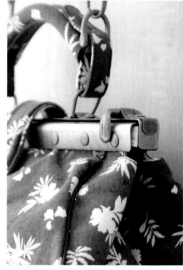

strange and sometimes beautiful garments, from military cropped jackets held together with belts to delicate chiffon dresses embellished with crystals.

Roberto Cavalli

181-182 Sloane Street, SW1X 9QP (7823 1879/ www.robertocavalli.com). Knightsbridge tube. **Open** 10am-6pm Mon-Sat. **Credit** AmEx, MC, V. **Sells** M, W.
Like many other Italian designers, Cavalli doesn't know the meaning of the words subtle or demure. His clothes are highly charged and ultra-sexy. For 2005/6, he takes inspiration from *Dynasty*-style 1980s glamour, with figure-hugging evening dresses and some glitzy boho chiffon ones nipped in tightly at the waist. With fans like Cindy Crawford, Cavalli will rule the catwalks of Milan for some time yet. *Mail order.*

Rochas

Sells W. **Available at** A La Mode, Harrods, Joseph.
Newly revived after years of obscurity, Rochas has suddenly become one of the most exciting fashion labels going. That's thanks to the remarkable talents of 28-year-old designer Olivier

Theyskens, who has been at the French house for the past two years injeting subtle glamour (namely the killer fitted frocks, and some mighty fine accessories) into the label. His latest collection includes an elegant Edwardian-style silhouette with long, slim skirts and dresses that simply exude style.

Roland Mouret

Enquiries *7376 5762*. **Sells** W. **Available at** Browns, Harrods, Harvey Nichols, Liberty, Matches, MiMi, Net-a-Porter, Selfridges, Sixty 6.
Mouret creates eveningwear to die for. He is a master cutter and his dresses drape and flatter the contours of the body to perfection. Although French, he launched his career in London before taking his business to New York last year in order to expand. His autumn/winter 2005/6 collection includes enough sexy dresses to keep his fans happy, along with pencil skirts, cashmere polo-necks, neat jackets and belted coats – all very Hitchcock heroine.

Ronit Zilkha

34 Brook Street, W1K 5DN (7499 3707/ www.ronitzilkha.com). Bond Street tube. **Open**

10am-7pm Mon-Wed, Fri, Sat; 10am-7.30pm Thur; 11.30am-5.30pm Sun. **Credit** AmEx, DC, MC, V. **Sells** W.
With several stand-alone shops in London, as well as concessions in major department stores, including Harrods, Harvey Nichols and Selfridges, Ronit Zilkha is positioned halfway between a designer brand and a high-street chain. Although not cutting-edge, her clothes are always pretty and wearable, and take into account most women's need for stylish work clothes, as well as partywear. Her focus is on colour, fabric detail and flattering cuts, so, for example, nubbly tweed jackets are trimmed with velvet ribbon or lace, and luxury knitwear is decorated with a colourful cross stitch.
For branches see index.

Selina Blow

1 Ellis Street, SW1X 9AL (7730 2077/www. selinablow.com). Sloane Square tube. **Open** 10am-6pm Mon-Fri; 11am-6pm Sat. **Credit** AmEx, MC, V. **Sells** M, W, C.
London-based designer Selina Blow favours flamboyant textiles (often oriental in style) but employs traditional English tailoring techniques. She opened this retail space in October 2003 to

Modern classics

Never considered popping into Daks when you were looking for a cool cropped jacket? You thought Austin Reed was a stuffy old place full of boring grey suits? And that Burberry was only really for Japanese tourists? Think again, for the times they are a-changing. Granted, only a few years ago the thought of being able to buy a truly fashionable designer outfit in one of the capital's long-established fashion houses was quite ludicrous. Sure, you could find a fantastic rain mac, argyle knit or cashmere twin set. But a natty Empire-line dress, cool brass buttoned military-inspired jacket or sumptuous leather it-bag? Forget about it. Fast forward to 2005/6 and those very same labels suddenly have serious appeal for the most stylish twenty- and thirtysomething urbanite, thanks to a new breed of talented forward-thinking designers who have been simultaneously enlisted to bring the labels into the 21st century.

The new stars? **Stuart Vevers**, recently enlisted as creative director of Mulberry, who has been injecting a little rock 'n' roll cool into the traditional leather bag line, which is already giving Hermès and Gucci a run for their money. Then there's the eminently talented **Christopher Bailey** at Burberry, who's been recreating classics

like the pea coat, trench and cashmere knits in vibrant new colour combinations and modern shapes to international acclaim. Over at Aquascutum (*see p39*), **Michael Herz** and **Graeme Fidler** have enlivened the 155-year-old brand with new takes on old classics like the 'Imperium' trench coat (luscious bottle-green corduroy), knits in acid colours and classic check over-dyed in Prussian blue. Pringle of Scotland, currently celebrating its 190th birthday, has enlisted new talent in the form of Royal College of Art graduate **Claire Waight Keller**, formerly of Calvin Klein and Ralph Lauren, to breath new life into the fashion side of things, while **Simona Ciacchi**, formerly of Gucci, will be taking care of accessories.

As for Daks (*pictured*), **Anthony Cuthbertson** and **Bruce Montgomery** play on the upper-crust British heritage while adding modern style and wit. Even Austin Reed is a credible place to hang out these days thanks to a groovy art deco grooming salon, **Equilibrium** (*see p97*); laid-back, luxurious changing rooms; and affordable but slick ready-to-wear suits. So, forget Paris. Who needs Milan? These are exciting and progressive times in London, on whose streets some of the most luxurious and innovative labels can currently be found.

FASHION

showcase her vibrant women's and men's separates, and shares it with fellow womenswear designer Ann-Louise Roswald and the Jackson twins. The neon-pink exterior points to Blow's love of colour before you even enter the store.

Sonia Rykiel

27-29 Brook Street, W1K 4HE (7493 5255/ www.soniarykiel.com). Bond Street tube. **Open** 10am-6.30pm Mon-Wed, Fri, Sat; 10am-7pm Thur. **Credit** AmEx, DC, MC, V. **Sells** M, W, C.

Sonia Rykiel is loved for her signature rainbow-striped knits, which are often imitated on the high street. She's been gaining an increasingly strong presence in the UK over the last few years, thanks to her fabulously affordable diffusion line, Sonia, which flies off the rails of boutiques and department stores across the capital (from Diverse (*see p36*) to Selfridges (*see p14*)). Her inviting, two-floor shop stocks a good selection of her main womenswear collection, menswear and her adorable kids' range (think shrunken versions of those great stripy knits). Menswear for autumn/winter 2005/6 includes sumptuous blends of fabrics: slim-cut tweed jackets and multi-coloured striped shirts with dashes of military and a little rock 'n' roll attitude. All very desirable. *Mail order.*

Sophia Kokosalaki

Enquiries 7704 8866. **Sells** W. **Available at** Browns, Harrods, Liberty.

Decamped from London to Paris, Sophia Kokosalaki continues to impress with her signature knotting, twisting and draping. Rather than reinvent her look each season, she takes a subtle step closer to perfection. Her collection includes smart, wide-cut trousers, neat cropped leather jackets, slim pencil skirts and, naturally, more of the glorious draped dresses for which the Greek designer goddess is known. Kokosalaki is currently expanding her accessory line of belts, bags and shoes, and also designs a capsule collection for Topshop.

Stella McCartney

30 Bruton Street, W1J 6LG (7518 3100/www. stellamccartney.co.uk). Bond Street or Green Park tube. **Open** 10am-6pm Mon-Wed, Fri, Sat; 10am-7pm Thur. **Credit** AmEx, DC, MC, V. **Sells** M, W.

Just days after giving birth to her firstborn, son Miller, Stella McCartney showed her strongest collection to date, with a lovely fluid, voluminous silhouette and some sassy military jackets, sumptuous knits and desirably cool slouchy, masculine tailored trousers – worn with heels, natch. All of this is housed in her wonderful four-storey Georgian townhouse shop in Bruton Street. With its fireplaces and panelling, it feels like someone's laid-back yet undeniably chic house rather than an intimidating designer boutique. Also in-store are the shoes, bags, fragrance and a bespoke tailoring service for men. Stella McCartney is outspoken on the subject of animal rights and doesn't use any leather or fur in her clothes. *Mail order.*

Temperley

6-10 Colville Mews, Lonsdale Road, W11 2DA (7229 7957/www.temperleylondon.com). Notting Hill Gate tube. **Open** by appointment 9.30am-5.30pm Mon-Fri; noon-5.30pm Sat. **Credit** AmEx, MC, V. **Sells** W.

Sienna Miller might have been crowned the queen of boho, but perhaps that title should have gone to west London designer Alice Temperley. Having launched her label in 2000, she has quickly established her own brand of femininity, which involves floral-print, Empire-line dresses, full-length chiffon evening gowns and flouncy, girlie skirts, all of which are embellished with an intricate network of sequins or beads (a bit too much, in some cases). Some women adore it and others find it sickeningly sweet. Of course it's all simply a matter of taste.

Veronique Branquinho

Sells M, W. **Available at** Browns, Harvey Nichols, Liberty.

Veronique Branquinho is a serious kind of person. Her collections are almost entirely in black and the

mood is always sombre – somewhat funereal, in fact – but that doesn't mean she's boring. Far from it. Her fluid tailoring and use of sober colours give an edgy elegance to the wearer. Alongside minimalist black separates, you will find ultra-fine jerseys, sheer chiffon dresses and the occasional splash of colour – in autumn/winter 2005/6's striped knitwear, for example. Her menswear line, characterised by strong tailoring and dark fabrics, is available from Browns.

Versace

183-184 Sloane Street, SW1X 9QP (7259 5700/ www.versace.com). Knightsbridge tube. **Open** 10am-6.30pm Mon, Tue, Thur-Sat; 10am-7pm Wed. **Credit** AmEx, DC, MC, V. **Sells** M, W.

Bling might not be in, but that doesn't stop Donatella Versace. Figure-hugging dresses, the skinniest black satin trousers known to woman, toxic lime-green leather jackets, and lashings of fur and gold – you could be forgiven for thinking you'd stepped on to the set of *Dynasty* rather than entered a designer boutique. Still, Donatella knows what Versace women (J Lo and Liz Hurley among them) want, and for all the glitz there are wearable, luxuriously made clothes to be found here, from cream cashmere coats to perfectly cut black trousers. Made-to-measure haute couture is also available.

Viktor & Rolf

Enquiries *00 31 20 41 96 188/www.viktor-rolf.nl.* **Sells** M, W. **Available at** Browns, Homme Plus, Joseph, Liberty (M), Selfridges, Souvenir (W).

Dutch designers Viktor Horsting and Rolf Snoeren are a quirky but ardently dedicated duo, whose latest collection arrives entirely in black and cream, and took inspiration from the fairy tale *Sleeping Beauty*. That might all sound a bit obscure, but there are plenty of wonderful, wearable clothes in the collection. Womenswear ranges from the eccentric (cotton shirts with oversized pleated collars, which take their cue from bed linen details) to the utterly wearable. For autumn/winter 2005/6, they've done the best cropped jackets in the world, some of them slightly quilted, all of them masterfully structured. There are also some simple white shirts printed with 'I love you' in elegant black typography. Menswear, too, is the result of a surrealist vision combined with impeccable tailoring skills.

Vivienne Westwood

44 Conduit Street, W1S 2YL (7439 1109/ www.viviennewestwood.com). Oxford Circus tube. **Open** 10am-6pm Mon-Wed, Fri, Sat; 10am-7pm Thur. **Credit** AmEx, DC, MC, V. **Sells** M, W.
Vivienne Westwood has been designing clothes for well over 30 years and, my, what a lot she has achieved. Since pioneering the punk look all those years ago, she's now one of Britain's most revered designers. Her designs are recognisable for their voluminous use of fabric – frequently in her trademark tartan – and range from the outré to the wearable. She might not lead the fashion game these days but she merrily does her thing, making statements and, of course, those signature bias-cut gowns that look just right on curvy women like Nigella Lawson and Agent Provocateur's Serena Rees. The Conduit Street flagship houses the women's Gold Label main line, two diffusion ranges – Red Label and the more casual Anglomania – as well as menswear. The original King's Road premises carries a smaller selection of clothing but, on the plus side, often has special-edition pieces, which are exclusive to the store. The small Davies Street salon stocks only the Gold Label and also provides a couture service.
Mail order.
For branches (including Worlds End) see index.

Yohji Yamamoto

14-15 Conduit Street, W1S 2XJ (7491 4129/ www.yohjiyamamoto.co.jp). Oxford Circus or Piccadilly Circus tube. **Open** 10am-6pm Mon-Wed, Fri, Sat; 10am-7pm Thur. **Credit** AmEx, MC, V. **Sells** M, W.
Yohji Yamamoto's designs are characterised by a sense of functionality, which in his latest collection can be seen in his wide belted trench coats and sexy tuxedo trousers. Although mainly in black, the collection features unexpected splashes of colour like fuchsia and canary yellow. For a more relaxed, wearable look (no wraparound skirts for blokes here), check out the Y's diffusion lines for men and women, available from Selfridges. The department store also stocks Y3, a sportswear range created in collaboration with Adidas.

Yves Saint Laurent: Rive Gauche

33 Old Bond Street, W1X 4HH (7493 1800/ www.ysl.com). Green Park tube. **Open** 10am-6pm Mon-Wed, Fri, Sat; 10am-7pm Thur. **Credit** AmEx, DC, MC, V. **Sells** M, W.
Following Tom Ford's departure, the role of creative director of Gucci's second-biggest brand was handed to his deputy, Stefano Pilati, who has now designed two collections for the house. Yves Saint Laurent himself, who is said to have disapproved of Ford's handling of the Rive Gauche heritage, has signalled his support for the new director, who has so far taken it in a slightly more grown-up and demure direction, with high-collared jackets, neat pencil skirts, dresses and coats, belted primly high on the waist. Some will miss Ford's immense sense of luxe and sexiness, while others will welcome the new look.
For branch see index.

Zac Posen

Enquiries *00 1 212 925 1263/www.zacposen. com.* **Sells** W. **Available at** Harvey Nichols, Matches.
Zac Posen, the precocious, curly-haired designer who has been courting New York's hot young party scene for the last couple of years, has already got a reputation for his expertly draped evening dresses. In just a handful of seasons, this young New York-based upstart has built a reputation for himself based on his ability to make a mean dress.

Numbers such as an emerald-green strapless silk evening dress (look out for it at the Oscars) and amazing chiffon gowns fit for a goddess make you understand why chicks like Scarlett Johansson and Natalie Portman love him so much. Casual yet luxurious daywear completes the collection.

Zandra Rhodes

81 Bermondsey Street, SE1 3XF (7403 5333/ www.zandrarhodes.com). London Bridge tube/rail. **Open** by appointment Mon-Fri. **No credit cards. Sells** W.
Zandra Rhodes's heyday may have been the 1970s, when her fluid, kaftan-like shapes and flamboyant patterns were the height of fashion, but she continues to have an important presence on the London fashion scene thanks to her labour-of-love project: Bermondsey's worthwhile and enlightening Fashion and Textile Museum. Whatever the season, you'll find lots of loose, asymmetric dresses and tops in bird-of-paradise coloured chiffons in the designer's collection.

Classic

Amanda Wakeley

80 Fulham Road, SW3 6HR (7590 9105/ www.amandawakeley.com). South Kensington tube. **Open** 10am-6pm Mon, Tue, Thur-Sat; 10am-7pm Wed. **Credit** AmEx, DC, MC, V. **Sells** W.
Amanda Wakeley designs elegant eveningwear and stylish daywear in classic shapes and muted neutral tones to perfection. Her clothes aren't pushing the boundaries of fashion design – they are just nice, smart, simple clothes that well-heeled women find utterly desirable. Her collection includes sharply cut daywear (beige skirt suits, trumpet skirts) and her usual helping of glamorous evening gowns, including a striking bias-cut design in gold silk and a diaphanous silver sheath dress. Sposa, her ready-to-wear bridal range, is also available in-store, with dresses ranging from simple strapless silk sheaths to full-on gowns. Wakeley has recently added a glamorous jewellery range and shoe collection to her main line, and continues to design a capsule collection for Littlewoods catalogue.
Mail order.

Ben de Lisi

40 Elizabeth Street, SW1W 9NZ (7730 2994/ www.bendelisi.com). Sloane Square tube/Victoria tube/rail. **Open** 10am-6pm Mon-Fri; noon-5pm Sat; also by appointment (bridalwear). **Credit** AmEx, MC, V. **Sells** W.
Although this American-born, London-based designer has been well established in this country since 1995, he was catapulted into the limelight a few years back when Kate Winslet wore his scarlet, floral-strapped dress to the Oscars. Classic, ultra-elegant red-carpet gowns are what he does best. For autumn/winter, they arrive in gold, black and a most eye-catching crimson shade. Inside his chic Elizabeth Street store you'll also find a selection of daywear, including pretty blouses, skintight trousers and a made-to-order bridal service. De Lisi also continues to design a hugely successful range for Debenhams.

Betty Jackson

311 Brompton Road, SW3 2DY (7589 7884/ www.bettyjackson.com). South Kensington tube. **Open** 10.30am-6.30pm Mon-Fri; 10am-6pm Sat; noon-5pm Sun. **Credit** AmEx, DC, MC, V. **Sells** W.
An affectionately held British designer, Betty Jackson has been designing clothes in the capital for over 20 years and is a regular fixture at London Fashion Week. Her aesthetic is unmistakably English and very feminine. Characteristically prim clothes with a twist include beige toggle-fastened knits, chocolate leather belted macs and beautifully tailored cropped jackets. Jackson is renowned for her well-cut skirts in all manner of shapes and styles and good-quality coats.

Bruce Oldfield

27 Beauchamp Place, SW3 1NJ (7584 1363/ www.bruceoldfield.com). Knightsbridge tube. **Open** 9.30am-6pm Mon-Fri; 11am-5pm Sat. **Credit** AmEx, DC, MC, V. **Sells** W.

The ultimate rags-to-riches story, this couturier, who spent many years of his childhood in care, has been selling his elaborately designed frocks to the rich and famous since 1975. His glamorous eveningwear ranges from simple jersey shapes cut on the bias to full-blown taffeta gowns – all big-event designs. In addition to couture, Oldfield has also relaunched his ready-to-wear line, which includes casual daywear as well as evening dresses.

Burberry

21-23 New Bond Street, W1S 2RE (7839 5222/ www.burberry.com). Bond Street tube. **Open** 10am-7pm Mon-Sat; noon-6pm Sun. **Credit** AmEx, DC, MC, V. **Sells** M, W, C.
Chav connotations aside (get that image of Danniella Westbrook with the buggy out of your head once and for all), Burberry is finally getting its credibility back at a rapid rate. The reason? Christopher Bailey, the hugely talented British designer who is bringing style and glamour into Burberry's Prorsum collection with sharp tailoring and cool British sensibilities. Inspired by Marianne Faithfull in her 1960s heyday, Bailey's current collection includes eloquent flared pea coats, tweedy plaids, desirable updates on the classic Burberry trench and fun pompom-strewn scarves. The equally smart menswear collection includes streamlined tailoring and some big checked woollen coats.
For branches see index.

Caroline Charles

56-57 Beauchamp Place, SW3 1NY (7225 3197/ www.carolinecharles.co.uk). Knightsbridge or South Kensington tube. **Open** 10am-6pm Mon-Sat. **Credit** AmEx, DC, MC, V. **Sells** W.
Back in the 1960s, Caroline Charles dressed people like Lulu, Mick Jagger and Queen Muna of Jordan, so with that decade's icons inspiring many of the international collections, it may well be her moment to make a comeback. She is, after all, the one who knows how to do the look best. Her most recent collection includes elegant, floaty clothes with a distinctly bohemian vibe, such as floral-print blouses and gypsy skirts. There are currently three collections available in-store: at the top end is the luxurious Studio line, designed for special events; businesswomen rely on the London collection for timeless suits and co-ordinating accessories; while the Caroline collection features casual separates, which cater to a younger but equally elegantly turned-out clientele.
Mail order.
For branches see index.

Daks

10 Old Bond Street, W1S 4PS (7409 4040/ www.daks.com). Bond Street or Green Park tube. **Open** 10am-6pm Mon-Wed, Fri, Sat; 10am-7pm Thur. **Credit** AmEx, DC, MC, V. **Sells** M, W.
Established in 1894, this label has renewed appeal thanks to the injection of two British design talents: Anthony Cuthbertson on womenswear and Bruce Montgomery on menswear. Both have been playing on the brand's super-crust British heritage while infusing it with modern style and wit – the current collection includes smart new takes on great British classics from the rain mac to the blazer. There's also a vast array of quality accessories, from fine leather driving gloves to stylish work bags (for men and women), many of which are in Daks signature black, brown and cream check.
Mail order.

Jacques Azagury

50 Knightsbridge, SW1X 7JN (7245 1216). Knightsbridge tube. **Open** 9.30am-5.30pm Mon-Fri; 10am-5.30pm Sat. **Credit** AmEx, MC, V. **Sells** W.
Couturier Jacques Azagury was a favourite of Princess Diana, and has also dressed the likes of Cherie Blair and pop star Sophie Ellis-Bextor. His Knightsbridge salon caters to a loyal clientele of SW1 ladies who come in search of classic elegance, either from the luxurious ready-to-wear collection or made to order.

Jean Muir

48 Conduit Street, W1S 2YR (7434 9077/ www.jeanmuir.co.uk). Oxford Circus tube. **Open** 10am-6pm Mon-Sat. **Credit** AmEx, MC, V. **Sells** W.

It's over ten years since Jean Muir's death, but her label lives on, remaining in the very capable hands of a team of designers she trained. Muir, who described her job as 'engineering in cloth', had a very practical approach to designing clothes, and her team has stayed true to her principles. The current collection includes refined, polished and precisely cut trousers cropped at the knee, sleek little black dresses and smart tailored daywear in a colour palette of browns and greys. The emphasis is always on cut, quality and wearability. In the airy and modern white shop in Conduit Street, you'll also find elegant coats and quality cashmere knits.

Jil Sander

7 Burlington Gardens, W1S 3ES (7758 1000). Green Park tube. **Open** 10am-6pm Mon-Wed, Fri, Sat; 10am-7pm Thur. **Credit** AmEx, DC, MC, V. **Sells** M, W.

Jil Sander resigned halfway through designing the autumn/winter collection in 2005, leaving her team to take over, so it's hard to tell exactly how much in the enormous Mayfair store is actually her own work. Still, the clothes stay true to her minimalist, perfectionist vision: clean-lined dresses, coats and jackets, in mainly black and white. Menswear is strong and desirable, featuring the same impeccable cuts and luxurious fabrics.

Loewe

130 New Bond Street, W1S 2TA (7493 3914/ www.loewe.com). Bond Street tube. **Open** 10am-6pm Mon-Sat. **Credit** AmEx, DC, MC, V. **Sells** M, W.

Founded in Madrid in 1846, Enrique Loewe's leather company is still known for its fine luggage and leather clothing, which falls with the fluidity of a much lighter fabric. It's a great starting place if you are on the hunt for a classic, high-quality leather handbag. Men's and women's clothing, accessories and shoes are predominantly crafted in nappa leather and suede, with cashmeres and quality tailoring providing the finishing touches. *Mail order.*

Margaret Howell

34 Wigmore Street, W1U 2RS (7009 9009/ www.margarethowell.co.uk). Bond Street tube. **Open** 10am-6pm Mon-Wed, Fri, Sat; 10am-7pm Thur. **Credit** AmEx, DC, MC, V. **Sells** M, W.

In the last couple of years, Margaret Howell's label has become highly desirable as her cool, crisp English aesthetic has reached the height of cool. In fact, her deftly tailored trousers, neatly cropped jackets and crisp white shirts, which she does to utter perfection, have recently become wardrobe staples for London's fashion insiders. Her shirts, trousers, jackets and jumpers are all timeless classics and have a soft, lived-in appeal that improves with age. She also produces a denim line in collaboration with Japanese label Edwin Jeans, and MHL, a range of sturdy, workwear-inspired clothing. The Wigmore Street shop houses the full collection, including homewares, and also acts as an occasional exhibition space for 20th-century art and design. *Mail order.*
For branch see index.

Mulberry

41-42 New Bond Street, W1S 2RY (7491 3900/ www.mulberry.com). Bond Street tube. **Open** 10am-6pm Mon-Wed, Fri, Sat; 10am-7pm Thur. **Credit** AmEx, DC, MC, V. **Sells** M, W.

Since Mulberry won the British Fashion Council's Accessory Designer of the Year award in 2004, bags have been at the forefront of the brand, with the delightful Phoebe and Tyler joining the already cult Bayswater and Roxanne. The men's accessory collection includes the new bestselling Woody bag. The clothes are interesting too. Stuart Vevers has recently been appointed design director, and there is a variety of luxe tweeds, soft velvets and military-style jackets and coats in a collection that draws inspiration from romanticism and Russia. Menswear fuses dandyism with cosy British must-haves; sharp woollen trench coats and chunky knits feature in the mix. A new bespoke bag service (from £995) is being introduced in the Westbourne Grove and Bond Street stores from November. *Mail order.*
For branches see index.

Nicole Farhi

158 New Bond Street, W1S 2UB (7499 8368/ www.nicolefarhi.com). Green Park tube. **Open** 10am-6pm Mon-Wed, Fri; 10am-7pm Thur; 10am-6.30pm Sat; 11am-5pm Sun. **Credit** AmEx, DC, MC, V. **Sells** M, W.

Nicole Farhi's fans rely on her for stylish, comfortable classics, such as her light, airy linens in washed-out colours, cosy knitwear and luxurious sheepskin jackets. There have lately been a few more racy pieces such as cheeky cropped culottes and belted coats. The flagship store on Bond Street, complete with chic restaurant, is pleasantly laid-back yet refined. As well as clothes for both sexes, there is a selection of home accessories, but the full interiors range is available around the corner at Nicole Farhi Home (*see p119*). *Mail order.*
For branches see index.

Pringle of Scotland

112 New Bond Street, W1S 1DP (7297 4580/ www.pringlescotland.co.uk). Bond Street tube. **Open** 10am-6.30pm Mon-Wed, Fri, Sat; 10am-7.30pm Thur. **Credit** AmEx, MC, V. **Sells** M, W.

Designer Stuart Stockdale helped propel this label into the 21st century by updating its golfing heritage with style and verve. Now he's been replaced by talented Royal College of Art graduate Clare Waight Keller, but Stockdale's designs will be available in-store until autumn 2006. For autumn/winter 2005/6, the signature diamond pattern is reproduced on super-soft cashmere cardigans (with a silk ribbon to fasten them at the waist), while sumptuous cashmere turtlenecks – in both the men's and women's collections – feature vibrant floral prints that work surprisingly well. Simona Ciacchi has also recently been appointed accessory designer and she'll be working on a new range due to launch in summer 2006. *Mail order.*
For branch see index.

Ralph Lauren

1 New Bond Street, W1S 3RL (7535 4600/ www.polo.com). Green Park tube. **Open** 10am-6pm Mon-Wed, Fri, Sat; 10am-7pm Thur; noon-5pm Sun. **Credit** AmEx, DC, MC, V. **Sells** M, W, C.

Ralph Lauren continues to deliver his smart-casual preppy style for men and women with an increasing focus on sportswear – he recently designed a tennis range and limited-edition polo shirts. Stepping into his enormous, American colonial-style flagship on Bond Street is an experience in itself, as you are whisked into a *Great Gatsby* world of East Coast affluence. It houses the full quota of Lauren's labels, from men's suiting through to the casual Polo range and homewares. Childrenswear has a dedicated shop down the road at No.143.
For branches see index.

Valentino

174 Sloane Street, SW1X 9QG (7235 5855/ www.valentino.it). Knightsbridge tube. **Open** 10am-6pm Mon-Fri; 10.30am-6pm Sat. **Credit** AmEx, DC, MC, V. **Sells** M, W.

As he's known for his divinely glamorous evening dresses, it's no surprise that veteran Paris catwalk designer Valentino has a loyal celebrity following among women who adore his flattering creations: Claudia Schiffer, Jennifer Lopez and Elle Macpherson are all fans. He loves red – and each season you can guarantee some show-stopping, beautifully fitted evening dresses in the colour, as well as neat skirt suits for power lunching. The latest collection is no exception, including luscious full-length, figure-hugging crimson dresses. He also imparts his innate sense of glamour to smart daywear – for example, in narrow jeans with python-embellished pockets and sable-trimmed bomber jackets. His tailored menswear line can be found in the basement of the store.

Net-a-porter

www.net-a-porter.com. **Credit** AmEx, MC, V. **Sells** W.

Set up by Natalie Massenet in 2000, the award-winning Net-a-porter is still one of the best online designer boutiques. It's all down to vast selection of labels, which have been edited perfectly: niche names such as Ashish, Meli Melo and Proenza Schouler are sold alongside international designer brands like Marni and Marc Jacobs. The accessory collection is diverse and inspiring too, and includes Jimmy Choo shoes, Chloé bags and Erickson Beamon jewellery. Londoners can also enjoy a next-day delivery service.

See also chapter **Shopping Diary**. For McArthur Glen Designer Outlet, *see chapter* **Shopping Centres**.

Bicester Village Outlet Shopping

Junction 9 off M40, Bicester, Oxon OX26 6WD (01869 323 200/www.bicestervillage.com). **Open** 10am-6pm Mon-Fri, Sun; 9.30am-7pm Sat. **Credit** AmEx, MC, V. **Sells** M, W, C.

An hour's drive outside London, this ten-year-old shopping 'village' is like a very clean, sanitised version of a traditional British high street with a weird assortment of designer and mid-range labels. At the end of every season, most major fashion brands are left with excess stock, which some choose to sell off through discount outlets. International fashion names such as Christian Lacroix, Burberry, DKNY, Christian Dior, Earl Jean, MaxMara, Ralph Lauren Polo, TSE cashmere and Versace all feature, with discounts of up to 60%. There are amazing bargains on high-street lines such as Monsoon and French Connection.

Browns Labels for Less

50 South Molton Street, W1K 5RD (7514 0052/www.brownsfashion.com). Bond Street tube. **Open** 10am-6.30pm Mon-Wed, Fri, Sat; 10am-7pm Thur. **Credit** AmEx, MC, V. **Sells** M, W.

Just over the road from its mother boutique Browns, this sale shop is worth a visit if you crave designer labels but lack the funds to support your addiction. Here you'll find end-of-season lines by names such as Missoni, Lanvin, Marc Jacobs and Jil Sander at 30%-70% off. There is a good selection of both men's and women's clothing and some accessories. *Mail order.*

Burberry Factory Shop

29-53 Chatham Place, E9 6LP (8328 4287). Hackney Central rail. **Open** 11am-6pm Mon-Fri; 10am-4pm Sat; 11am-4pm Sun. **Credit** AmEx, DC, MC, V. **Sells** M, W, C.

This is an excellent place to find classic Burberry pieces, from macs to checked bags, at hugely discounted prices – sometimes 50% off. But it's hit or miss. On one visit, there may be lots of fabulous bargains to be had; on another nothing but a house-check wallet or umbrella. Persistence may be rewarded by something from Christopher Bailey's highly desirable Prorsum collection.

Paul Smith Sale Shop

23 Avery Row, W1X 9HB (7493 1287/ www.paulsmith.co.uk). Bond Street tube. **Open** 10am-6pm Mon-Wed, Fri, Sat; 10am-7pm Thur; 1-5pm Sun. **Credit** AmEx, DC, MC, V. **Sells** M.

This place is great for menswear. On ground level you'll find a selection of T-shirts and casualwear, while discounted suits and accessories can be found upstairs. Ladieswear is more limited, but there are usually good accessories, from gloves to scarves.

Boutiques

As shop categories often cross over, *see also* chapter **Street** for cutting-edge boutiques.

Aimé
32 Ledbury Road, W11 2AB (7221 7070/ www.aimelondon.com). Notting Hill Gate tube. **Open** 10.30am-7pm Mon-Sat. **Credit** AmEx, MC, V. **Sells** W.
Truffaut film posters set the mood in this airy, two-floor shop. French-Cambodian sisters Val and Vanda Heng Vong bring a slice of understated Parisian cool to Notting Hill, showcasing designers such as Isabel Marant and Claudie Pierlot. Aimé is the main London stockist of chic French basics line APC, and sells the sweet Repetto ballet flats (£100) sported by Brigitte Bardot. There are also delicately packaged bath products and home accessories for the perfect Rive Gauche pad.
Mail order.

A La Mode
10 Symons Street, SW3 2TJ (7730 7180). Sloane Square tube. **Open** 10am-6pm Mon-Sat. **Credit** AmEx, MC, V. **Sells** W.
Liberally sprinkled in the fashion credits of *Vogue*, A La Mode stocks big-league designers such as Lanvin, Rochas, Marc Jacobs, Missoni and Marni, and the must-have accessories to complete each season's look. New for autumn/winter 2005/6 is the dramatic eponymous collection by recently appointed Givenchy designer Riccardo Tisci.
Mail order.

Anna
126 Regent's Park Road, NW1 8XL (7483 0411/ www.shopatanna.co.uk). Chalk Farm tube. **Open** 10am-6pm Mon-Sat; noon-6pm Sun. **Credit** AmEx, MC, V. **Sells** W.

Coco Ribbon

Anna Park's laid-back Primrose Hill shop (part of a mini chain with branches in the King's Road, Norfolk and Suffolk) manages to pull off generation-spanning appeal – Jules Oliver and Marianne Faithfull are both fans. But despite the celebrity following, much of the pricing is down-to-earth, with mid-range labels (Rützou, Noa Noa, Saltwater) amid the more expensive designer fare (Issa, Betty Jackson). There is also an excellent selection of top-drawer jeans by labels such as Paige Premium Denim, Rogan and Salt Works, plus posh T-shirts from C&C California and Velvet to go with them. Park is also co-owner of Anna and Victoria (590 King's Road, SW6 2DX, 7731 7300).
Mail order.

Ashley's Boutique
18 Conduit Street, W1S 2XN (7499 9658). Bond Street or Oxford Circus tube. **Open** 10am-6pm Mon-Sat. **Credit** AmEx, V. **Sells** W.
This swish boutique is the second venture of designer Ashley Isham, who opened diminutive aQuaint in Covent Garden a few years ago. Isham's own glamorous, red-carpet creations (he was official womenswear designer for the 2004 BAFTAs) hang alongside designs by such high-profile peers as Sophia Kokosalaki, Jonathan Saunders and Temperley, plus specially selected vintage pieces by Ossie Clark, Pierre Cardin and Yves Saint Laurent. At aQuaint Isham's own label rubs shoulders with a slightly different mix, including Roland Mouret, Hussein Chalayan, Milla, Boyd and Betty Jackson. All this and he's still several years shy of 30.
For branch (aQuaint) see index.

Austique
330 King's Road, SW3 5UR (7376 3663/ www.austique.co.uk). Bus 11, 22. **Open** 10.30am-6.30pm Mon-Sat; noon-5pm Sun. **Credit** AmEx, MC, V. **Sells** W.
This place gets glamour kittens purring. Austique's laid-back, girlie atmosphere was inspired by boutiques in Australia; the light, two-floor space brings together a super-feminine collection of clothes, lingerie and accessories. Key designers from down under include Alannah Hill (whose glam, sequinned party dresses are among the shop's bestsellers), Zimmermann and Leona Edmiston. But not all of the stock hails from Oz: there are skirts and dresses in specially designed fabrics by New Zealander Trelise Cooper and simple, sexy pieces by hot New York newcomer Doo Ri. The shop is also a great source of jeans from not-yet-ubiquitous US labels such as Salt Works, Grass and 575 Denim. Upstairs you'll find everything for the boudoir: well-priced S.P.A.N.K. silk knickers, Julianne French silk and lace negligees and wispy Kalito chiffon knickers, embroidered with the slogan of your choice, plus pretty natural bath ranges.
Mail order.

Browns
23-27 South Molton Street, W1K 5RD (7514 0000/www.brownsfashion.com). Bond Street tube. **Open** 10am-6.30pm Mon-Wed, Fri, Sat; 10am-7pm Thur. **Credit** AmEx, DC, MC, V. **Sells** M, W.
Joan Burstein's venerable store has reigned supreme over London's boutiques for over 35 years. Among the 100-odd designers jostling for attention in its five interconnecting shops are Diane von Furstenberg, Marc Jacobs, Chloé and Sophia Kokosalaki; there is an entire floor devoted to Jil Sander. New for 2005/6 are Michael Kors and former Ungaro designer Giambattista Valli. As well as the catwalk superstars, you'll find lesser-known treasures such as Diane De Clercq's quirky patterned knitwear and former costume designer

Barbara Tfank's 1950s-style coats and dresses in bold vintage fabrics. Across the road, Browns Focus is younger and edgier – think Marc by Marc Jacobs, Boudicca, Vanessa Bruno and Erotokritos, with accessories from Lara Bohinc 107. At No.50, there's also a sale shop called Browns Labels for Less (*see p34*). For the men's collections, *see p46*.
Mail order.
For branch see index.

Bunka
4 Dartmouth Road, SE23 3XU (8291 4499/ www.bunka.co.uk). Forest Hill rail. **Open** 10am-7pm Mon-Sat. **Credit** MC, V. **Sells** W.
Forest Hill's one and only funky clothes shop is strong on accessories: there's a wide range of pretty jewellery, starting from just £4, from Indian-inspired drop earrings to modern charm bracelets, and the back of the shop has been expanded to accommodate the shoe 'boudoir', showcasing diverse footwear from Birkenstock, Miss Sixty and Gola. As for the clothes, well-known streetwear brands such as Freesoul, Miss Sixty and Boxfresh are supplemented by exclusive, up-and-coming labels from Denmark, Argentina and Brazil. As we went to press, there were plans for a second boutique in Balham.
Mail order.

Clusaz
56 Cross Street, N1 2BA (7359 5596/ www.clusaz.co.uk). Angel tube. **Open** 10.30am-6.30pm Mon-Sat; 1-5.30pm Sun. **Credit** AmEx, DC, MC, V. **Sells** W.
It's testimony to the eclectic range of clothes and prices that Clusaz has been leading Cross Street's style revolution for 18 years. The rails are groaning with a something-for-everyone mélange of Chine, Omnia, Tara Jarmon and Betty Jackson. The store's ethos is to edit stock constantly, and new pieces are introduced weekly to keep regulars interested. Notable newcomers for 2005/6 include Issa dresses and Bi La Li knitwear and jersey pieces.

Coco Ribbon
133 Sloane Street, SW1X 9AX (7730 8555/ www.cocoribbon.com). Sloane Square tube. **Open** 10am-6.30pm Mon-Fri; 10am-6pm Sat; noon-5pm Sun. **Credit** AmEx, MC, V. **Sells** W.
While Coco Ribbon's original Notting Hill store is a shabby-chic paean to girliness, this extravagant new Chelsea shop is like a 1930s starlet's boudoir: creamy chaise longue, feather-trimmed satin drapes concealing the changing rooms and reproduction Venetian chandeliers, mirrors and dressing tables (all for sale). The stock is equally glamorous; when we last visited, we were dazzled by long, vintage-inspired sequinned and beaded chiffon gowns by Collette Dinnigan and Temperley, delicate Esther Franklin sequinned jackets and Yes Master chiffon bra and French knicker sets fit for Marcel-waved pin-ups. It's also a great place to pick up presents for the girl who has everything: there are gorgeously packaged candles and bath products, Dishya's fabulous retro embroidered fan cushions (£145), Tea Lights candles in vintage china cups (£35), books with titles like *The Lazy Girl's Guide to Beauty* and the ever-popular butterfly garlands (£10).
Mail order.
For branch see index.

Comfort & Joy
109 Essex Road, N1 2SL (7359 3898). Angel tube. **Open** 10.30am-6pm Mon-Sat. **Credit** AmEx, MC, V. **Sells** W.
A great source of unusual, high-quality clothes at high-street prices. Many of the unique garments are made by partners Ruth and Anthony Wilson, others are bought in small numbers from other independent designers, such as Blue Stone, Dress Up, Lumi and Korean label ODD, which does affordable Japanese-style designs. On our latest visit, the collection was colourful and eclectic, with lots of prints (from paisley to vintage sari silk) and influences ranging from kaftans to 1930s tea dresses, but stock changes frequently.

FASHION

The Cross

141 Portland Road, W11 4LR (7727 6760).
Holland Park tube. **Open** 11am-5.30pm Mon-Sat.
Credit AmEx, MC, V. **Sells** M, W, C.
With consistently good collections and choice
accessories, not to mention the A-list following, the
Cross remains one of London's most successful
boutiques. The eclectic compilation of designers
takes in Easton Pearson, Missoni, Betty Jackson,
Gharani Strok and Clements Ribeiro. American
imports include New York designer Jane Mayle
and environmentally friendly celeb-fave Dosa from
LA. New for 2005/6 is eveningwear by British
designers Jenny Dyer and Alice Lee – the latter's
long, printed knits have a Missoni feel. There's also
casualwear from Ella Moss, Juicy Couture and
Splendid, and great sweaters from Tania and the
shop's own luscious cashmere, from £280. Cross
The Road – at No.139 – sells homewares.
Mail order.

Diverse

294 Upper Street, N1 2TU (7359 8877/
www.diverseclothing.com). Angel tube. **Open**
10.30am-6.30pm Mon-Wed, Fri, Sat; 10.30am-
7.30pm Thur; 12.30-6pm Sun. **Credit** AmEx,
DC, MC, V. **Sells** W, C.
The shop lives up to its name, with an excellent
selection of luxe labels. Expect the likes of Marc by
Marc Jacobs, Matthew Williamson, Chloé, Rick
Owens and Missoni. There's also a healthy stock of
hip jeans from Paper Denim & Cloth, Rogan,
Earnest Sewn and Notify. Diverse children's
clothing is at 46 Cross Street (N1 2BA, 7226 6863).

Feathers

176 Westbourne Grove, W11 2RW (7243 8800).
Notting Hill Gate tube. **Open** 10am-6pm Mon-
Sat; noon-5pm Sun. **Credit** AmEx, DC, V.
Sells W.
This spacious boutique is a browser's paradise,
with friendly staff and a huge mix of unusual
pieces. The globe-spanning stock includes
tailoring by Italian Maurizio Pecoraro, delicate
beaded dresses by Australian Megan Park and
extravagant knitted fur jackets by Paris-based
Adam Jones. The joy of the place is the fact that
lesser-known lines, such as the Japanese-
influenced designs of Indian/Danish duo Peachoo
and Krejberg, sit alongside big-league pieces by
Pucci and Etro, by way of new-generation stars
Sophia Kokosalaki and Alexander McQueen.
Accessories are strong – Gianni Barbato's high-
button cracked leather boots (£455) and Patricia
Viera's delicate, fringed suede shawls are tipped
to be the objects of desire for 2005/6. It's also a
good place for one-step-ahead-of-the-pack denim,
such as Khozo jeans from Japan, made from such
unlikely materials as bamboo leaf and cannabis
(around £200). Devotees will want to hop
from Notting Hill to the recently reopened
Knightsbridge branch to compare stock.
For branch see index.

Gigi

124 Draycott Avenue, SW3 3AH (7584 1252).
South Kensington tube. **Open** 10am-6.30pm Mon,
Tue, Thur-Sat; 10am-7pm Wed; 1-6pm Sun.
Credit AmEx, DC, MC, V. **Sells** W.

Forming part of Joseph's Brompton Cross empire,
which also includes Joe's Café, the designer's
Essentials shop and grand flagship store across
the street, this small boutique stocks a selection of
hip young labels. On our last visit, the tills were
ringing to the tune of Prada Sport, Marc by Marc
Jacobs, Miu Miu and Diane von Furstenberg.

Hoxton Boutique

2 Hoxton Street, N1 6NG (7684 2083/www.
hoxtonboutique.co.uk). Old Street tube/rail.
Open 10am-6pm Mon-Fri; 11am-6pm Sat.
Credit MC, V. **Sells** W.
The West End branch didn't last, but the original,
just beyond Hoxton Square, is still going strong.
The house style here tends to reflects what the
area's arty denizens are sporting on the street.
Designers include nonconformists such as Vivienne
Westwood, Robert Cary Williams, Eley Kishimoto,
Martelo Toledo and Hussein Chalayan. In summer
2006, the shop's own Boutique line will be expanded
and revitalised as HOBO, a young, directional label
with an emphasis on individualism.

Hub

49 & 88 Stoke Newington Church Street, N16
0AR (7254 4494). Bus 73. **Open** 10.30am-
6.30pm Mon-Sat; noon-5pm Sun. **Credit** MC,
V. **Sells** M, W.
The London outpost of Manchester indie boutique
Hub is thriving – so much so it's expanded into a
second shop across the street. Now there is more
room for the interesting mix of fashion, taking in
designer names such as Cacharel and Sonia by

Labour of Love

Sonia Rykiel, mid-priced brands such as Rützou and Hoss, and small labels from London, Scandinavia and Australia. Look out for co-owner Beth Graham's charming, clean-lined collection (£45-£180); for autumn 2005 it features Harris-tweed jackets, dance-inspired jersey dresses and tie-front Liberty-print shirts. Men get a look-in too, with cool, casual clothes by 6876, John Smedley and Edwin Jeans from Japan. More changes were afoot as we went to press: the larger corner premises at No.49 will focus on higher-end womenswear and menswear, while No.88 will house less expensive women's labels.

Iris

73 Salusbury Road, NW6 6NJ (7372 1777). Queen's Park tube. **Open** 9am-7pm Mon-Fri; 10am-6pm Sat; 11.30am-5.30pm Sun. **Credit** AmEx, MC, V. **Sells** W, C.

In an area teeming with trendy young mums, this girlie boutique stocks hip labels alongside a range of cool kids' clothes, including some made by local mothers. Soft colours, sequins and sparkles define the look. Feminine clothes by the likes of Malene Birger, Day Birger et Mikkelsen and Orla Kiely, jeans to suit all pockets from Lee (£60) to Blue Cult (£160), Elle Macpherson underwear and Paul & Joe cosmetics are all temptations.

JW Beeton

48-50 Ledbury Road, W11 2AJ (7229 8874). Notting Hill Gate tube. **Open** 10.30am-6pm Mon-Fri; 11am-6pm Sat; noon-5pm Sun. **Credit** AmEx, MC, V. **Sells** M, W.

It may not have the big designer names of some of its sprawling neighbours in this densely boutique-populated patch, but JW Beeton's quirky charm appeals to a wide cross-section of shoppers. Owner Debbie Potts's strategy is to buy small amounts from numerous labels. Delicate, beaded evening tops, sequinned skirts and crocheted capes by Somi (£100-£200), cushions by Fake London and understated jackets and trousers from Italian label Transit (£115-£150) are just some of the highlights for 2005/6.

Koh Samui

65-67 Monmouth Street, WC2H 9DG (7240 4280/www.kohsamui.co.uk). Covent Garden tube. **Open** 10am-6.30pm Mon, Sat; 10.30am-6.30pm Tue, Wed, Fri; 10.30am-7pm Thur. **Credit** AmEx, DC, MC, V. **Sells** W.

This store's reputation as one of the capital's premier cutting-edge clothes emporia precedes it – and we've yet to be disappointed. On a recent visit, we were bowled over by the sheer variety of gorgeous items from elite designers and new talent mixed in with vintage finds. Choice pieces by Chloé, Marc by Marc Jacobs, Balenciaga and Missoni rub shoulders with independents exclusive to the shop, such as Victim's reworked 1940s frocks, Ada's sweet handknitted, customised cardigans (around £200) and Misconception's dresses in stunning vintage fabrics. Accessories are another joy – jewellery by more than 70 designers from around the world is displayed in large glass units. We were especially struck by Central Saint Martin's grad Katherine Kwan's dramatic necklaces made from enormous pink plastic 'crystals' (£198). Balenciaga and Marc by Marc Jacobs bags, jeans by Chloé, James and Seven For All Mankind are predictably hot sellers.

Kokon To Zai

57 Greek Street, W1D 3DX (7434 1316/ www.kokontozai.co.uk). Leicester Square or Tottenham Court Road tube. **Open** 11am-7.30pm Mon-Sat; noon-6pm Sun. **Credit** AmEx, MC, V. **Sells** M, W.

Surely a contender for London's most avant-garde boutique, on account of Liz Neal's porno-orgy ceiling mural and the eccentric clothes on the rails, dominated by designs by the shop's creative director Marjan Pejoski. Expect such weird and wonderful pieces as a knitted admiral's jacket and a jersey dress with a spider-web pattern made of delicate silver chains. Björk is a fan – she sports his swan dress on her 2001 *Vespertine* album cover and often pops in. Other featured labels include Bernhard Willhelm, Jessica Odgen, Raf Simons and Antonio Ciutto, and the shop also sells the electro tunes that form the soundtrack to a browse here.
Mail order.

Labour of Love

193 Upper Street, N1 1RQ (7354 9333/ www.labour-of-love.co.uk). Highbury & Islington tube/rail. **Open** 10.30am-6.30pm Mon-Wed, Fri, Sat; 10.30am-7pm Thur; 12.30-5.30pm Sun. **Credit** MC, V. **Sells** W.

Designer Francesca Forcolini's boutique is a beguiling mix of cutting-edge and cute. Designers include avant-gardists such as Peter Jensen, Karen Walker and Laura Lees Label, whose pretty print tea dresses are embroidered with subversive motifs such as skulls and crossbones or razor blades. New for the autumn/winter 2005/6 collection is Forcolini's range of knitwear based on an inherited cache of 1930s and '40s patterns and knitted by a team of grannies – from pom-pom hairbands and sweet mini berets to cardies. There are lots of great accessories, such as Porselli ballet shoes (£49), Miss Budd's screen-printed metallic leather bags and jewellery by Australian designer KT, made of deconstructed Victorian necklaces, lockets and fob watches (£35-£250). Handpicked CDs, books and chocs with sequinned wrappers add to the mix.

Matches

60-64 & 85 Ledbury Road, W11 2AJ (7221 0255/www.matches.co.uk). Notting Hill Gate tube. **Open** 10am-6pm Mon-Sat; noon-6pm Sun. **Credit** AmEx, DC, MC, V. **Sells** M, W.

After taking over a large swathe of Wimbledon Village with no fewer than five shops on the high street, Matches brought its precedent-setting formula of posher-than-average wares in refreshingly non-intimidating surroundings to Notting Hill. The main shop at 60 Ledbury Road sells heavyweights such as Balenciaga, Lanvin, Missoni, Prada and Marc Jacobs, and all the fabulous accessories created to accompany the clothes (menswear is downstairs), while across the street are the diffusion lines (Miu Miu, Marc by Marc Jacobs), piles of premium jeans and other hip pieces, such as modern tailoring from 3.1 by Philip Lim (formerly of US label Development), chic Peruvian knitwear by Mario's sis Giuliana Testino and bags designed by Sudanese supermodel Alek Wek. The dedicated Diane von Furstenberg store at No.83 is also part of the empire.
For branches see index.

Mimi

309 King's Road, SW3 5EP (7349 9699/ www.mimilondon.co.uk). Sloane Square tube/ 11, 19, 22 bus. **Open** 10.30am-6.30pm Mon-Sat; 1-6pm Sun. **Credit** AmEx, MC, V. **Sells** W.

Catering to the Chelsea party set, even in winter, Mimi is a rich mix of diaphanous, patterned and embellished tops and dresses from the likes of Antik Batik, Rebecca Taylor, Matthew Williamson, Issa and Collette Dinnigan. It's also a good place to stock up on hip jeans (Rock & Republic, True Religion) and T-shirts (Velvet, C&C California). Citrine's delicate gold-and-precious-stone jewellery from LA is a hot seller.
Mail order.

Musa

31 Holland Street, W8 4NA (7937 6282/ www.musalondon.com). High Street Kensington tube. **Open** 11am-6pm Tue-Sat. **Credit** MC, V. **Sells** W.

This bijou boudoir combines cool labels such as Sass & Bide, Gharani Strok, Megan Park, Ann-Louise Roswald and Clements Ribeiro with specially selected vintage pieces that capture the season's fashion zeitgeist (pristine embroidered linen Japanese kabayahs last summer, for example, and lots of black lace for autumn/winter 2005/6). Also in the mix is vintage jewellery and unique accessories by local designers, such as Iam Mai's roomy metallic leather cube bags (£185-£300). Musa's own glamorous resort label, in-store throughout the year, features delicate, hand-embroidered kaftans and tops, and dresses in vintage floral prints (from £125), with co-ordinating sandals with Swarovski crystals (from £85).
Mail order.

no-one

1 Kingsland Road, E2 8AA (7613 5314/ www.no-one.co.uk). Old Street tube/rail. **Open** 11am-8pm Mon-Sat; noon-6pm Sun. **Credit** AmEx, MC, V. **Sells** M, W.

Owned by the style-setting siblings behind hip bar dreambagsjaguarshoes across the road, Teresa and Nick Letchford's boutique showcases local talent, directional labels like Peter Jensen, Galibardy, Merlin, Karen Walker and PPQ, a smattering of vintage, plus original artworks. The store has an upbeat, friendly vibe aided and abetted by the adjoining coffee shop and über-cool but amicable staff.
Mail order.

The Pineal Eye

49 Broadwick Street, W1F 9QR (7434 2567). Piccadilly Circus tube. **Open** 11am-7pm Mon-Fri; noon-6pm Sat. **Credit** MC, V. **Sells** M, W.

The life-sized chicken-wire figures hanging by their necks in the window are a tip-off that the stock here is hardly mainstream. The Pineal Eye wears its deconstructivist heart on its sleeve. Staff are achingly trendy; stock-wise, you'll find Kim Jones, Beca Lipscombe, Bernhard Willhelm and Raf Simons, although a Dior Homme capsule collection offers a rare concession to big catwalk names.

Press

3 Erskine Road, NW3 3AJ (7449 0081). Chalk Farm tube. **Open** 10am-6.30pm Mon-Wed, Fri, Sat; 10am-7pm Thur; noon-6pm Sun. **Credit** MC, V. **Sells** W.

This is where hip Primrose Hill chicks come for not-trying-too-hard chic: effortlessly cool casuals by Ella Moss, coats and dresses by Vanessa Bruno, Indian-inspired patchwork print pieces by Ana-Mika and cult Belstaff jackets, interspersed with striking vintage pieces and Splendid T-shirts. Chloé bags, Missoni scarves and Belstaff high-heeled boots will be snapped up before you can say 'Meet me in the Lansdowne.'

Question Air

229 Westbourne Grove, W11 3SE (7221 8163/ www.question-air.com). Notting Hill Gate tube. **Open** 10.30am-6pm Mon-Wed; 10.30am-6.30pm Thur-Sat; 1-5.30pm Sun. **Credit** AmEx, MC, V. **Sells** W.

Question Air was one of the first boutiques to stock Shirin Guild's ethnic-influenced separates and, later, now-ubiquitous American labels such as Juicy Couture and Seven For All Mankind. This spacious, three-floor branch of the five-strong boutique chain still has an excellent selection of the above lines in the eclectic mix, which also includes Vivienne Westwood, Ella Moss and Plenty, but trailblazing owner Dylan Ross is always on the lookout for new sources of unusual, affordable stock. Recently, Scandinavia has come up trumps with Danish label Stella Nova and Hunky Dory from Sweden. Elaborately printed, embroidered and dyed hippie-chic pieces by Dutch company People of the Labyrinth are a long-standing feature, while newer recruit London-based Poppy Pills has been giving Issa a run for its money with jersey wrap dresses in quirky retro prints for around £195. The range of premium jeans here is among the most exhaustive in town.
For branches see index.

Relax Garden

40 Kingsland Road, E2 8DA (7033 1881/ www.relaxgarden.com). Bus 55, 67, 149, 242. **Open** 1-7pm Mon-Fri; noon-6pm Sat. **Credit** MC, V. **Sells** M, W.

Shinya Abe's compact shop is a showcase for fresh young fashion designers from Tokyo, Hong Kong and Korea. Buyer Eriko Nagata co-designs the shop's own label, which for autumn brings luxurious fabrics to its signature simple lines: draped tunic tops in gold, soft blue or silvery

FASHION

Hot jeans

The jeans revolution began when LA brand Earl Jean launched its simple but brilliant straight-legged Style 55 jean in London back in 1998. Eight years on, and a new designer jeans brand is launched practically every week. Indeed, there are now jeans out there to suit any shape, occasion and mood. For girls, there are **True Religion** for when you're feeling like a laid-back groupie, **Blue Cult** for when you want to show off those curves (both at **YDUK**, 82 Heath Street, NW3 1DN, 7431 9242), **Lee** drainpipes for when you're 21 and want to work the electro Brit-rock fan look (sold at the Lee flagship, 13-14 Carnaby Street, W1F 9PL, 7434 0732) and **Acne** and **Superfine** if you're seriously skinny and want to look like Kate Moss (both at Browns Focus; *see p35*). Then, for the moments when you just want a good everyday pair of flattering, wearable jeans, there's **Seven for All Mankind** (although they can lose shape after a while) and **Citizens for Humanity** (all in all, the most flattering and practical shape). Both are available at Harvey Nicks (*see p12*). Purists will plump for **Earnest Sewn**, the super-luxe brand created by Paper, Denim & Cloth co-founder Scott Morrison, who has made limited-edition denim his speciality. **Rag & Bone** are Kentucky-made jeans, originally intended for men but adopted by women, including Sienna Miller. Both are available at Start (*see below*). LA brands **Serfontaine** and **Juicy Couture** (at Selfridges, *see p14*) offer a bit of Jessica Simpson sass.

And for guys? The coolest jeans have got to be **Rogan** (at Start; *see below*), made from a nice thick, quality Japanese denim in the most flattering of cuts: slightly baggy but not hanging around your arse. There are the ultra-stylish **Paper Denim** (at Selfridges, *see p14*) and Levi's new rendition of the 501 (at the Levi's Store, *see p54*). Turkish brand **Mavi** (available at Urban Outfitters; *see p55*) are also a good buy, as they have designer looks without the hefty price tag.

Buying jeans can be bewildering, so if you're going into a department store (Harvey Nicks and Selfridges have the best ranges) do ask the shop assistants for advice – they know the products inside out and which styles will suit your shape. Selfridges still offers its magical Bodymetrics measuring machine, which scans your body and helps ascertain which styles will fit you perfectly (we've had good results in the past). Boutiques are also good places to buy jeans as they tend to offer a more personalised service. **Start** in Shoreditch is excellent. Co-owner Brix Smith is a jeans genius and can find you the perfect pair in three attempts. **Browns Focus**, **Diverse** in Islington and **YDUK** (*see above*) in Hampstead also offer a good selection and excellent service.

Pictured left to right: **True Religion**, Billy, £159.50; **Superfine**, Harry, £135; **Rag & Bone**, RBW2-1, £199; **Earnest Sewn**, Hefner, £169.50. All these styles are available at Start (*see below*).

---

grey faux suede and jersey, say, or a bold multicoloured tweed cape. Her solo line, East Meets East, features one-off tunics and simple dresses in striking vintage fabrics. The store wins on price points – most pieces are around £30-£60.

Saloon
23 Arlington Way, EC1R 1UY (7278 4497/ www.saloonshop.co.uk). Angel tube. **Open** 11am-7pm Mon, Wed-Fri; 11am-6pm Tue; noon-6pm Sat. **Credit** AmEx, MC, V. **Sells** M, W.
Tucked down a villagey street behind Sadler's Wells Theatre, Keiko Kim-Hindley's little shop combines fashion with interior items, stationery and a bit of art. Her excellent eye for pieces that are original but wearable takes in established names like Ginka by Neisha Crosland, Erotokritos, Peter Jensen and Jo Gordon, but also less familiar finds such as Finnish label Ivana Helsinki, London-based Milena's hand-dyed raw silk dresses and Parisian chic for men and women courtesy of Bali Barret, exclusively stocked by Saloon in the UK. Many items fascinate or amuse – such as Tara Holmes's jewellery amalgamating found objects such as buttons, old belt buckles and vintage costume jewellery (around £70 for a necklace, £80 for a brooch), or Donna Wilson's handknitted figures, which combine homely craft with creepy subtexts, such as her Canibdoll, whose mouth is stuffed with another creature (£42).

Sixty 6
66 Marylebone High Street, W1U 5JF (7224 6066). Baker Street tube. **Open** 10.30am-6.30pm Mon-Fri; 10am-6pm Sat; 1-5pm Sun. **Credit** AmEx, MC, V. **Sells** W.
This tiny Marylebone gem makes use of every available space to offer customers a wide choice of gorgeous pieces from numerous labels. Owner Jane Collins has a knack for choosing clothes that are eye-catching and feminine without being showy; many items feature interesting trimmings or embellishment, and Collins often works with designers to bring exclusive pieces into the shop, such as the one-off beaded wrap skirts created in collaboration with textile designer Samson Soboye (£500-£600), or Gianni Barbato boots made to her own specifications. Clothes by Megan Park, Roland Mouret, Temperley, Ashish, Chine and Just in Case are displayed in complete outfits you might not have thought of, providing inspiration. Accessories include beautiful gold and semi-precious stone jewellery and decorative Jamin Puech bags.

Souvenir
53 Brewer Street, W1F 9UY (7287 8708/ www.souvenirboutique.co.uk). Piccadilly Circus tube. **Open** 11am-7pm Mon-Wed, Fri, Sat; 11am-7.30pm Thur; noon-6pm Sun. **Credit** AmEx, MC, V. **Sells** W.
Anna Namiki and Anthony Meynell's brace of Souvenir boutiques are within convenient walking distance, so you can easily check out both. The newer Brewer Street shop, opened in 2003, is more high fashion, showcasing dramatic pieces by catwalk stars such as Hussein Chalayan, Vivienne Westwood and Viktor & Rolf. Accessories are an irresistible mix of big league (John Galliano shoes, Westwood purses) and affordable, cultish items such as Leona Baker's Lady Luck Rules OK rock-themed jewellery made from retro novelty charms (around £35 for a bracelet). The Lexington Street branch is younger and more casual in outlook, featuring feminine designs by APC (including clothes, shoes and bags), Anna Sui, Paul & Joe, Ella Moss and Tocca. **For branch see index.**

Start
42-44 Rivington Street, EC2A 3BN (7729 3334/ www.start-london.com). Old Street tube/rail. **Open** 10.30am-6.30pm Mon-Fri; 11am-6pm Sat; 1-5pm Sun. **Credit** AmEx, DC, MC, V. **Sells** M, W.
This spacious new boutique – opened by Woodhouse founder Philip Start and his rock-chick wife Brix Smith – has a slick New York feel. Across the road from the original premises, which now houses menswear, the two-level double shopfront is like a mini department store. The ground floor is devoted to daywear and an excellent range of premium jeans – Superfine, Earnest Sewn, True Religion and the ingenious Radcliffe with its adjustable hems, to name but a few. In the next room is a Becca cosmetics counter, where you can have a free makeover, and striking accessories – Scott Stephen's jewellery features intricate handmade baubles that look like mini Tiffany eggs (bracelets £235). Downstairs, in a modern 'boudoir' decked out with velvet couches and a huge illuminated red heart, are carefully selected pieces by Cacharel, Alberta Ferretti and Miu Miu.

Sublime
99 Lauriston Road, E9 7HJ (8986 7243). Mile End tube then 277 bus. **Open** 10am-6pm Mon-Sat; 11am-4pm Sun. **Credit** MC, V. **Sells** M, W.
This appealing boutique plays to its Victoria Park demography. On the ground floor is a mix of fun accessories, such as Kate Sheridan's printed handbags (from £65), pretty, inexpensive home items such as coloured glasses and funky shower caps, and a selection of soaps, body products and fragrances from the likes of Neal's Yard Remedies and Miller Harris. Downstairs are feminine, mid-range clothes from Ann-Louise Roswald, Noa Noa, Day Birger et Mikkelsen and Hoss. *Mail order.*

FASHION

Womenswear

High-street shoppers have never had it so good. Since the recent democratisation of 'designer' fashion, which has seen major catwalk names lending their talents to chain-store collections, and an influx of excellent European brands, London is now a cornucopia of inexpensive, high-quality, up-to-the-minute clothes. It's also worth visiting department stores (*see p12*) for labels that don't have their own boutiques, such as **Coast** (available at Debenhams and House of Fraser to name but two), which offers simple yet contemporary dresses, suits and strappy tops. House of Fraser's (*see p12*) own label, **Linea**, is great for purse-friendly, fashion-conscious dresses and casual basics.

Mid-range

Adolfo Domínguez
129 Regent Street, W1B 7HT (7494 3395/ www.adolfodominguez.com). Oxford Circus or Piccadilly Circus tube. **Open** 10am-7pm Mon-Fri; 10am-8pm Sat; noon-6pm Sun. **Credit** AmEx, MC, V. **Sells** M, W.
Spanish designer Adolfo Dominguez creates chic, thoroughly contemporary clothes without kowtowing to the vagaries of catwalk fashion. New stock arrives weekly, and there's a wide range of clothing for all occasions, from casuals to grown-up suits that are smart without being severe. It's a good place to come if you're looking for something unusual at a reasonable price; this highly creative designer has a penchant for subtle yet striking details and innovative fabrics, such as a crinkled shell top, or a sleeveless ribbed wool sweater with strips of rabbit fur woven into its cowl neck. Prices are surprisingly reasonable given the high quality – expect to pay between £50 and £100 for a top, and around £75 for trousers. There are also accessories – including some neat, Prada-esque functional bags from around £40 – and menswear. The Covent Garden store carries the younger, funkier U range.
For branch see index.

Agnès b
111 Fulham Road, SW3 6RL (7225 3477/ www.agnesb.fr). South Kensington tube. **Open** 11am-6pm Mon; 10am-6pm Tue, Thur, Fri; 10am-7pm Wed; 10am-6.30pm Sat; noon-5pm Sun. **Credit** AmEx, DC, MC, V. **Sells** M, W, C.
The low-key French designer's beautifully finished clothes exude a slightly retro Left Bank chic: bold print dresses (from £95), classic trench-coats (£450), even the odd Gallic stripy top (£70). The range of fine cotton camisoles, pullovers and cardigans (from £30) – core items since day one – make great wardrobe staples, and the signature heavy-cotton snap-front cardie has just been given a new fitted shape (£75). The T-shirt des Artistes series is an ongoing project reflecting Agnès b's support of young artists; the latest design is by Wadall, from the Ivory Coast (£70). There is also a maternity range, accessories and more unusual fashion-led pieces each season. Not all branches sell menswear and childrenswear, so call before making a special trip.
For branches see index.

Anne Fontaine
151 Fulham Road, SW3 6SN (7584 7703/ www.annefontaine.com). South Kensington tube. **Open** 10am-6.30pm Mon-Sat; noon-6pm Sun. **Credit** AmEx, DC, MC, V. **Sells** W.
Young, Brazilian-born Fontaine has built up an impressive worldwide retail empire since opening her first shop in Paris over a decade ago. Her concept is simple and saleable: to offer every imaginable variation on the white shirt – wrapped, ruched, ruffle-fronted or appliquéd. Most designs are in cotton poplin or cotton/Lycra, but there are also linen, jersey, lace and organza designs, depending on season, and a small selection in other colours, including black. The exquisitely crafted shirts aren't cheap (from around £100), but they do come with a mini pot-pourri sachet.

Aquascutum
100 Regent Street, W1B 5SR (7675 8200/ www.aquascutum.co.uk). Piccadilly Circus tube. **Open** 10am-6.30pm Mon-Wed, Fri, Sat; 10am-7pm Thur; noon-5pm Sun. **Credit** AmEx, MC, V. **Sells** M, W.
Along with the recent revamp of its 115-year-old flagship, Aquascutum has also had an image overhaul. Second only to Burberry as a bastion of British style – Churchill himself wore it, as did Edmund Hillary on his hike up Everest – the label has been sexed up like its rival in check. The main womenswear collection has been given more modern lines (while retaining its classic English air), three new raincoat styles – including the military-tinged Imperium – have been introduced for autumn 2005 and the accessory range has been expanded. Prices are lower than you might expect: from £129 for a cashmere sweater, although the coats come in at £395-£895. But the biggest news is the debut of a second line – the first in 150 years. Called Aquascutum (the main line is officially Aquascutum London), it is more expensive and has a younger, high-fashion feel, including borrowed-from-the-boys shirts and trousers, vividly hued PVC raincoats, feminine lace and tulle dresses – even corset tops. Churchill would be shocked.

Benetton
255-259 Regent Street, W1B 2ER (7647 4200/ www.benetton.com). Oxford Circus tube. **Open** 10am-8pm Mon-Sat; noon-6pm Sun. **Credit** AmEx, DC, MC, V. **Sells** M, W, C.
Benetton's continuing global expansion is proof that the 1980s knitwear giant is going strong. The famous sweaters (the classic shapes have been joined by a cute angora shrug) and T-shirts in a rainbow of colours are still in store. The collection for 2005/6 sees an influx of bright, cropped trousers and shrunken blazers, duffel coats and Euro-preppy schoolgirl flannel skirts, long shorts and crisp tailored blouses – which will probably appeal to younger shoppers. Lambswool pullovers (from £27) and tailored blouses (from £17) are good quality given the price tags. The Undercolors of Benetton includes lingerie, loungewear and sleepwear, while the Sisley range offers more sophisticated designs in finer fabrics, at slightly higher prices.
Branches: throughout the city.

East
105 King's Road, SW3 4PA (7376 3161/ www.east.co.uk). Sloane Square tube. **Open** 10am-6.30pm Mon, Tue, Thur-Sat; 10am-7pm Wed; noon-6pm Sun. **Credit** AmEx, MC, V. **Sells** W.
Since former M&S womenswear supremo Yasmin Yusuf was appointed chief executive, the ethnic overtones of this globally influenced brand have been toned down in favour of a subtle Eastern flavour – she's hoping to make East an oasis for discerning over-40s in the youth-obsessed high street. While what we've seen so far is quite nice, it doesn't rock this 40-year-old's world. Expect vividly hued sequinned wrap tops, beaded, Indian-print tunics and silk gypsy skirts mixed up with English country elements such as suede blazers, rose-print tea dresses and cropped tweed trousers. Prices range from around £30 for a top

(more for silk or intricately embellished styles), from £80 for a jacket, £50 for trousers and skirts. The company also supports a disabled children's charity in Rajasthan, India where much of its stock is manufactured.
Branches: throughout the city.

Esprit
178-182 Regent Street, W1B 5DF (7025 7700/ www.esprit.com). Oxford Circus or Piccadilly Circus tube. **Open** 10am-7pm Mon-Wed, Fri, Sat; 10am-8pm Thur; noon-6pm Sun. **Credit** AmEx, DC, MC, V. **Sells** M, W, C.
This global brand has made its presence felt over the past year with four new shops in the capital. The image is contemporary yet wholesome, and womenswear is divided into three lines: the main collection is the most sophisticated and catwalk-led (we like 2005's sharp little Jacquard jacket); the Casual range comprises fashionably cut, relaxed trousers, denim, knitwear and cool outerwear from capes to corduroy trench coats; EDC is younger, with street-influenced styles. The vast Regent Street store also showcases a full complement of accessories, children's and men's clothes, and the expanded Bodywear lingerie line. The high quality belies the low prices: from around £10 for a T-shirt, £38 for trousers, £57 for a jacket and from a mere £30 for a dress.
Mail order.
For branches see index.

Fenn Wright Manson
95 Marylebone High Street, W1U 4RQ (7486 6040/www.fennwrightmanson.com). Baker Street or Bond Street tube. **Open** 10am-6.30pm Mon-Wed, Fri, Sat; 10am-7.30pm Thur; 11.30am-5.30pm Sun. **Credit** AmEx, DC, MC, V. **Sells** W.
While we started out as fans of this feminine, mid-range label, for the past couple of seasons it seems to have hit a bum note. Maybe it's us, but we find autumn/winter 2005/6's large-scale 'silver birch' and 'Japanese flower' prints on satin devoré dresses and skirts a bit too loud, while bland neutral trousers and tops seem at the other extreme, blending into the background. There are still some pretty dresses to be found, however, such as a silk georgette strappy style gathered at hip level with a corsage, and prices are reasonable for the quality and materials (about £150). Well-priced yet luxurious knitwear is another highlight (£55 for a simple, cashmere-blend square-necked top; £65 for an angora shrug).
Mail order.
For branches see index.

French Connection
396 Oxford Street, W1C 7JX (7629 7766/www.frenchconnection.com). Bond Street tube. **Open** 10am-8pm Mon-Wed, Fri; 10am-9pm Thur; 9.30am-7pm Sat; noon-6pm Sun. **Credit** AmEx, MC, V. **Sells** M, W.
Forget the cheeky double-take slogan T-shirts – French Connection still produces some irresistibly elegant clothes. Flattering jersey dresses (bold floral wraps and a fitted, posy-print style) for just £65, demure silk blouses for £60 and a dapper tweed riding jacket for £95 are just some of the great pieces in-store as we went to press, alongside the young, predominantly casual menswear. It's good to see this good-quality label back on form. Nightwear, accessories, home and beauty ranges are also sold. The branch (curiously unmarked) at 191 Westbourne Grove, W11 2SB (7229 8325) showcases clothes, shoes and make-up alongside a cool café stocked with a library of style mags.
Mail order.
Branches: throughout the city.

Full Circle
13-15 Floral Street, WC2 (7395 9420/www.full circleuk.com). Covent Garden tube. **Open** 10am-6.30pm Mon-Wed, Fri, Sat; 11.30am-6pm Sun. **Credit** MC, V. **Sells** M, W.
This hip young British label, previously found in boutiques and upmarket department stores, recently got its own spacious shop, housing the men's and women's lines, as well as Cult of Denim,

a jeans range for both sexes. The look for womenswear is gently experimental without being cutting-edge: a sweater made of strips that cross over at the back; a layered skirt incorporating three different patterned fabrics. There are some fine pieces for autumn/winter 2005/6 in a rich, muted colour palette of purple, nutmeg and green, such as draped jersey dresses in several different styles, pretty ruffled or back-tied sleeveless silk tops and fitted, rugged cotton jackets. While it exudes a designer air, prices are more in line with the high street: dresses and jackets from £65; skirts and trousers from £40. The Covent Garden store, designed by the company behind Comme des Garçons in Paris and Men's Superbrands in Selfridges, incorporates 'architectural animation', so if you think you see a mirror move of its own accord, you really did.

Hobbs
84-88 King's Road, SW3 4TZ (7581 2914/ www.hobbs.co.uk). Sloane Square tube. **Open** 10am-7pm Mon, Tue, Thur, Fri; 10am-7.30pm Wed; 10am-6.30pm Sat; noon-6pm Sun **Credit** AmEx, DC, MC, V. **Sells** W.
Known for its contemporary and slightly quirky take on classic clothes, Hobbs has recently become more trend-led without losing its identity. Its collection is strong and versatile enough to have broad appeal – as well as taking in more conservative items such as long tweed or devoré skirts, there are such covetable 'of the moment' pieces as a Diane von Furstenberg-esque wrap dress in a retro graphic pattern (£115) and some neat little nipped-waist 1940s-flavour jackets (from £159), paired with fluid knee-length skirts. There

is also an array of smart, short coats (from £229) in a variety of materials, and the good-quality co-ordinating knitwear and cotton tops (from £19) are a perennial feature. The spacious, triple-fronted King's Road store has an entire room devoted to the smart, solidly constructed shoe collection by former Mulberry designer Michaela Wenkert. **Branches**: throughout the city.

Jaeger
200-206 Regent Street, W1R 6BN (7200 4000/ www.jaeger.co.uk). Oxford Circus tube. **Open** 10am-6.30pm Mon-Wed, Fri; 10am-8pm Thur; 10am-7pm Sat; noon-6pm Sun. **Credit** AmEx, DC, MC, V. **Sells** M, W.
Famous for its wool tailoring, knitwear and coats (which kept early 20th-century explorers Scott and Shackleton warm on their Antarctic expeditions), Jaeger has been trying to boost its fashion credibility for several years now; first there was the range designed by Bella Freud, then the company brought in celeb model Laura Bailey as its 'face' in 2003. As we went to press, a new trend-led collection that also draws on the company's archives, Jaeger London, was about to be launched, with a campaign starring Erin O'Connor. But don't overlook the main line, which gives conservative a contemporary gloss, and features limited-edition capsule ranges. We spotted some highly desirable pieces for autumn/winter: a brown python-print silk wrap dress (£199), a herringbone pencil skirt that buttons up at the front (£140), little pastel cashmere camis and cardies starting at just £75, and, of course, some luxuriously soft, shawl-collared wrap coats (£399).
For branches see index.

Jesiré
28 James Street, WC2E 8PA (7420 4450). Covent Garden tube. **Open** 10am-7pm Mon-Wed; 10am-8pm Thur, Fri; 10am-7.30pm Sat; noon-6pm Sun. **Credit** AmEx, DC, MC, V. **Sells** W.
After a slightly dodgy patch last year, when both the clothes and the Covent Garden flagship were looking a bit trashy, Jesiré is back on form with a shop refurb planned for spring 2006 and a tasteful collection, including some lovely dresses, which have always been its forte. Styles range from a simple, subtly beaded variation on a flapper dress to 1950s-inspired silk and satin frocks in vintage-look floral prints with net underskirts. The label mixes the season's looks to create an eclectic collection that covers both casual and smart options. Other highlights include ladylike tweeds with a youthful edge and interesting skirts, from Russian-accented dirndls to a fab oversized-rose-motif puffball. Knitwear costs from £35 up to £200, dresses around £120-£175, jackets and coats from around £100 to £240.
For branch see index.

Jigsaw
126-127 New Bond Street, W1A 9AF (7491 4484/www.jigsaw-online.com). Bond Street tube. **Open** 10am-6.30pm Mon-Wed, Fri, Sat; 10am-7.30pm Thur; noon-6pm Sun. **Credit** AmEx, MC, V. **Sells** W, C.
High-quality fabrics, flattering styles and a rich yet subdued colour palette have made Jigsaw justifiably popular. Shapes are fashionable without being enslaved to catwalk trends, and the use of pretty trimmings and patterns is striking without going overboard. Women of all ages rely on the

Reiss. See p43.

stylish perennials, including deep-hued jersey tops (£18-£44), feminine dresses (£98 for silk organza) and tailoring (from around £100 for a jacket). Jigsaw Beyond is a new capsule collection of more unusual pieces in special fabrics, available in some branches. At the stunning Duke of York Square branch (6 Duke of York Square, King's Road, SW3, 7730 4404), housed in a former chapel, the sweeping double staircase leads to shoes, accessories and Jigsaw Junior – trendy, scaled-down versions of the adult designs at nearly grown-up prices. There's also a stand-alone Jigsaw accessories store on South Molton Street.
Mail order.
Branches: throughout the city.

Karen Millen

247 Regent Street, W1B 2EW. (7629 1901/ www.karenmillen.com). Oxford Circus tube. **Open** 10am-8pm Mon-Fri; 10am-7pm Sat; 11am-6pm Sun. **Credit** AmEx, DC, MC, V. **Sells** W.
This British designer made her name in the late 1980s with sharp, sexy trouser suits – the kind that demand to be worn with high heels. There are still some smart fitted jackets (from around £165) and trousers (around £110) to be had, and lots of slinky camisoles and bustier tops to go underneath (including a striking one with appliquéd net-and-diamanté flowers, £120), but the range now encompasses a wide variety of catwalk-influenced clothes. The mood is ladylike for 2005/6, including vintagey silk dresses and lots of shrunken cashmere-mix beaded cardies and pastel angora shrugs, paired with pencil skirts. The flagship has moved to a spacious, glam new shop on the opposite side of Regent Street.
Branches: throughout the city.

Kein Yuki

32 Duncan Street, N1 8BW (7833 1032). Angel tube. **Open** 11am-7pm Tue-Sat; 11am-4pm Sun. **Credit** MC, V. **Sells** W, C.
If you want to break free from identikit high-street looks, you might investigate this little shop in an unprepossessing building down an Islington side street. The simple, feminine clothes are enhanced by subtle, girlie touches. When we last stopped by, we saw A-line skirts embellished with beaded butterflies, ribbons and crocheted flowers from £65, and silk floral dresses for under £200. Downstairs is a variety of similarly decorated purses and bags (£8-£20), plus inexpensive bead jewellery and cute knitted baby hats and mittens.

Kew

10-12 James Street, W1M 5HM (7495 4646/ www.kew-online.com). Bond Street tube. **Open** 10.30am-7pm Mon-Wed, Fri; 10am-8pm Thur; noon-6pm Sun. **Credit** MC, V. **Sells** W.
A spacious new West End outpost of this cheaper Jigsaw (*see p40*) offshoot proves the concept is a success. Kew has many similar styles to its sister store, in the same colour palette of rich aubergines, muted greens and putty (in some cases, items are practically identical), but the prices are on average 25% to 30% cheaper. The catch? The materials and finishes, while perfectly good in their own right, are not a patch on Jigsaw's quality. Still, the store is a boon for women of all ages who long for the more expensive label's feminine floral dresses, long skirts, subtly trimmed tops and classic tailoring. Expect to pay around £15 for a lace-trim cotton camisole, from £35 for knitwear and from around £50 for a dress. Shoes and accessories are equally good value.
Mail order.
Branches: throughout the city.

Kookaï

257-259 Oxford Street, W1R 2DD (7408 2391/ www.kookai.co.uk). Oxford Circus tube. **Open** 10am-7pm Mon-Wed; 10am-8pm Thur-Sat, noon-6pm Sun. **Credit** AmEx, DC, MC, V. **Sells** W.
Ooh là là! The shapes and detailing may change with the catwalk trends, but Kookaï's slinky, strappy tops and figure-skimming dresses exude Parisian sex appeal. Autumn/winter 2005/6 has an antique boudoir feel, featuring such seductive pieces as a flimsy, ruched-front corset, flirty tiered

skirts, and tight, Victorian-inspired jackets. Quality is good for the prices, which start from around £20 for a top and £45 for trousers; £60 and up for a jacket or dress.
Branches: throughout the city.

Madeleine Press

90 Marylebone High Street, W1U 4QZ (7935 9301/www.mpress.com). Baker Street or Bond Street tube. **Open** 10.30am-6.30pm Mon-Wed, Fri, Sat; 10.30am-7pm Thur; noon-5pm Sun. **Credit** AmEx, DC, MC, V. **Sells** W.
Madeleine Press's small but perfectly formed collection reflects her attention to detail – a deceptively simple jacket may be made of 35 pieces for a precise fit. There are only a few styles hanging in the minimalist shop each season; typical items include delicate camisoles, strappy A-line dresses (in glamorous chiffon from £294), tailored jackets and Press's signature creased jeans in various rinses. Gwyneth Paltrow and Dido are among the fans of her low-key yet immaculate pieces. Tops start at £78, jeans at £110 and jackets at £340. Also sold at Harvey Nichols (*see p12*), Liberty (*see p13*) and Clusaz (*see p X*).
Mail order.

Massimo Dutti

156 Regent Street, W1B 5LB (7851 1280/ www.massimodutti.com). Oxford Circus or Piccadilly Circus tube. **Open** 10am-7pm Mon-Wed, Fri, Sat; 10am-8pm Thur; noon-6pm Sun. **Credit** AmEx, DC, MC, V. **Sells** M, W.
Massimo Dutti's grand Regent Street store, with casually posed mannequins in the large picture windows, has the air of a European Ralph Lauren. Inside, the illusion of exclusivity continues. In the airy cream and black interior, leather armchairs are grouped around coffee tables stacked with glossy art books, and the clothes exude preppy glamour. The surprise comes when you turn over the price tags: smart wool blazers for £100, well-cut, mannish trousers for £50, crisp cotton shirts for under £30, rugged leather jackets for just over £200. The fabulous, catwalk-savvy shoes (around £60), loungewear (£12 for a pretty vest) and menswear have the same sleek, expensive look. It's no surprise, then, that MD is part of the massive Spanish fashion group Inditex, owner of Zara.
Mail order.
For branches see index.

Mexx

112-115 Long Acre, WC2E 9NT (7836 9661/ www.mexx.com). Covent Garden or Leicester Square tube. **Open** 11am-7.30pm Mon-Wed, Fri; 11.30am-8pm Thur; 10am-7.30pm Sat; 12.30-6.30pm Sun. **Credit** AmEx, MC, V. **Sells** M, W.
A great resource for stylish workwear, Mexx has trend-conscious suits and shirts at very reasonable prices (from just £80 for a short, fitted jacket, £25 for a shirt). The casual clothes (T-shirts, cargo pants) and dresses are also superb value – we spotted a retro-inspired print silk dress for just £55 for autumn 2005. There are some duds, however: some of the synthetic prints give away their low price tags. XX by Mexx, with a more streetwise edge, caters to teens and early twentysomethings, and there are also ranges for men and kids. As we went to press a new flagship was due to open on Oxford Street.
For branches see index.

Monsoon

5-6 James Street, WC2E 8BH (7379 3623/ www.monsoon.co.uk). Covent Garden tube. **Open** 10am-8pm Mon-Sat; 10am-7pm Sun. **Credit** AmEx, DC, MC, V. **Sells** W, C, B.
The first to bring hippie chic to the high street, Monsoon has never strayed far from its roots, mixing boho looks and current trends to create an eclectic collection with broad appeal. The 2005/6 collection is especially vibrant and sumptuous: floaty dip-dyed dresses, diaphanous patterned kaftans, delicate silk camisoles and cobwebby knits paired with tweeds. Prices won't break the bank (from around £35 for a top; £50 for a skirt). The eveningwear line is still going strong, with a variety of styles, including stunning full-length

Best for...

Luxe looks on a budget
From the interior decor to the effortless Euro-chic clothes, **Massimo Dutti** (*see above*) exudes class – but the price tags are delightfully downmarket.

Fresh-off-the-catwalk trends
Topshop (*see p45*) has its finger on the pulse, with capsule collections by hot names such as Sophia Kokosalaki and regular injections of talent through its New Generation programme, which supports promising young designers.

Brilliant basics
Japanese lifestyle company **Muji** (*see p43*) is great for tasteful knits and simple, heavy cotton pieces, while for essential white shirts and skinny jeans, it pays to mind the **Gap** (*see p44*). For more upmarket tastes, **Agnès b**'s fine cotton camis and cardis look good for years (*see p39*).

Great British style
No longer just for Japanese tourists and county matrons, **Aquascutum** (*see p39*) has hipped up its image with a revitalised main line and a new catwalk collection.

Pretty dresses
Saltwater's simple frocks in delicate, exclusive prints have fresh, feminine appeal (*see p43*).

Well-priced workwear
Suits you, madam – **Mexx** (*see below*) and **Next** (*see p43*) both knock out modern tailoring for ridiculously cheap prices. The latter's machine-washable options will save you a fortune in dry-cleaning.

Minimalist perfection
The queen of precision fit, **Madeleine Press** (*see below*) creates deceptively simple designs that are masterpieces of understatement.

Maximalist glamour
Beaded, appliquéd, beribboned, sumptuously patterned, richly hued... **Whistles** (*see p43*) mixes it all up in its inimitable eclectic style.

red-carpet numbers (around £150). There are also bridal and kids' collections, home accessories and now menswear in some branches.
Mail order.
Branches: throughout the city.

Morgan

270 Oxford Street, W1C 1DT (7491 1883/ www.morgandetoi.com). Oxford Circus tube. **Open** 10am-7.30pm Mon-Wed, Sat; 11am-8pm Thur, Fri; noon-6pm Sun. **Credit** AmEx, DC, MC, V. **Sells** W.
The flirty French label still offers plenty of sexy camisoles and halter-neck tops (even the odd fully fledged Moulin Rouge-style silk bustier), slinky dresses and flouncy miniskirts, but there are also more demure, catwalk-led items tapping into autumn/winter Victorian and military trends. These include below-the-knee skirts in tartan, rich floral and paisley, and fitted velvet and Jacquard

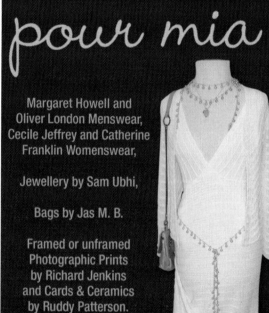

jackets. Jeans and casual tops, a girlie nightwear range, shoes and accessories are also in store. Prices are slightly higher than for comparable young brands: you'll pay around £30 for a top, £50 for trousers and £70 for a dress.
Mail order.
Branches: throughout the city.

Muji

135 Long Acre, WC2E 9AD (7379 0820/ www.muji.co.uk). Covent Garden or Leicester Square tube. **Open** 10.30am-7.30pm Mon-Wed, Fri, Sat; 10.30am-8pm Thur; noon-6pm Sun. **Credit** AmEx, DC, MC, V. **Sells** M, W.
The Japanese lifestyle store celebrated its 25th birthday in 2005, and remains true to its founding mission to provide inexpensive, simple yet stylish products for everyday urban life. Budget-conscious Londoners already know Muji is a goldmine for functional basics in durable natural fabrics (autumn/winter 2005's great military trench for just £69, or a minimalist kimono jacket that could pass for designer for £49). A muted colour palette, precision of cut and attention to detail elevate the clothes above mainstream high-street offerings. The womenswear now includes pieces in luxurious fabrics – some very reasonably priced silk-satin wrap tops (£39) and skirts (£45).
Mail order.
Branches: throughout the city.

Next

15-17 Long Acre, WC2E 9LD (7420 8280/ www.next.co.uk). Covent Garden, Holborn or Leicester Square tube. **Open** 10am-8pm Mon-Wed, Sat; 10am-9pm Thur; 11am-8pm Sat; 11.30am-6pm Sun. **Credit** AmEx, DC, MC, V. **Sells** M, W, C.
It's been a long time since the Next chain caused a stir, but women across the country rely on its safe yet stylish office, evening and casual clothes – all of better quality than some of its trendier competitors. There's a wide range of streamlined suits (some of which are even machine-washable) from around £100, basic knitwear from a mere £9.99, jersey tops in a plethora of styles, and some great fashion items for autumn/winter, such as a belted herringbone trench for under £80 and an elegant mink-coloured angora-mix brooch-fastened cardigan for under £40. Most of the styles can be found in Next Directory, along with lingerie, accessories, homeware and children's and men's clothes.
Mail order (0845 600 7000).
Branches: throughout the city.

Noa Noa

14 Gees Court, St Christopher's Place (7495 8777/www.noa-noa.com). Bond Street tube. **Open** 10am-6.30pm Mon-Wed, Fri, Sat; 10am-7pm Thur; noon-5pm Sun. **Credit** AmEx, MC, V. **Sells** W.
First we had the Spanish invasion. Now the Scandinavians are impressing us with well-priced, tasteful designs that have an air of individualism. This Danish company's clothes are floaty and feminine, in natural fabrics – a delicate vintage quality is crossed with Eastern-accented shapes and patterns. They're also a steal: tops start at just £8, skirts and dresses from £35 – although some cost considerably more. Expect oriental brocade jackets, beaded silk 1920s-inspired tea dresses and Tibetan-style knitwear for autumn/winter 2005/6. The London shops are all individually owned franchises – the new West End branch, about to open at 14 Gee's Court as we went to press, will no doubt raise the label's profile in the UK.
Mail order.
For branches see index.

Reiss

51 South Molton Street, W1K 5SD (7491 2208/ www.reiss.co.uk). Oxford Circus tube. **Open** 10am-7pm Mon-Wed, Fri, Sat; 10am-8pm Thur; noon-6pm Sun. **Credit** AmEx, DC, MC, V. **Sells** M, W.
The popularity of Reiss's female offshoot was cemented by the launch of this stand-alone womenswear store in spring 2005. The clothes have a designer feel: full or pleated skirts with unusual stitching details, or abstract 'patterns' in the weave, cotton tops in contemporary blouson

shapes, modern tailoring, and understated draped, ruched or wrapped dresses that are sexy but never slutty. It all looks expensive, but prices start at £59 for knitwear, £69 for skirts and trousers and £125 for jackets.
Branches: throughout the city.

Ross+Bute by Anonymous

57 Ledbury Road, W11 2AA (7727 7400/ www.anonymousclothing.com). Notting Hill Gate tube. **Open** 10am-6pm Mon-Sat; 11am-5pm Sun. **Credit** MC, V. **Sells** W.
Ever wonder who was behind the Anonymous line of dyed lace-trim thermal vests and cardigans? Well, the secret's out – it was former stylists Lindy Ross and Serena Bute, who could be credited with popularising the continuing craze for underwear as outerwear. The duo now have this chic little shop in Notting Hill. As well as the signature camis and cardies, with a variety of seasonally changing trimmings (£45 plus for a vest; from around £95 for a cardigan), stock for 2005/6 includes fitted 1940s-inspired cardigans with lace collars or sequins and a line of bright satin skirts and dresses with black lace overlay. Loungewear and accessories are also sold.
Mail order.

Saltwater

98 Marylebone Lane, W1U 2QB (7935 3336/ www.saltwater.net). Bond Street tube. **Open** 10am-6pm Mon-Sat; noon-5pm Sun. **Credit** AmEx, MC, V. **Sells** W.
There's a lovely, sunny seaside vibe in this spacious shop tucked behind chicified Marylebone High Street – which falls into place when you learn that the label's designer, Laura Watson, comes from Cornwall. Many of the clothes, in delicate fabrics with subtle, washed-effect patterns (all designed in house), from floral prints to muted stripes and paisleys, have an appealingly worn feel. Shapes are simple and vaguely nostalgic without tipping into full period garb, such as apron and kaftan dresses and full, gathered or pintuck skirts. Autumn/winter 2005/6 brings items in heavy, utilitarian cottons, simple knits and neat wool coats with a 1940s flavour. Prices are at the high end of high-street: dresses and skirts start from £79, tops average around £55 (£75-£165 for knitwear), while coats cost around £300. Canvas bags in the delectable house prints (£65-£75), loungewear and statement jewellery (some exclusive to the shop) are also sold. Saltwater is also available at Fenwick (*see p12*), and boutiques Anna (*see p35*) and The Cross (*see p36*).
Mail order.

Shoon

94 Marylebone High Street, W1U 4RG (7487 3001/www.shoon.com). Baker Street or Bond Street tube. **Open** 10am-6.30pm Mon-Sat; 11am-5pm Sun. **Credit** MC, V. **Sells** M, W, C.
This Bath export is hard to categorise, but adventure and exploration are linking themes. In the spacious, red-walled shop, travel books, neoprene bottle coolers and an antique African harp are displayed next to piles of jumpers. Shoon initially focused on activewear, and still stocks outdoor gear by excellent American brands such as Patagonia and Columbia. The non-technical clothes for both sexes are mainly European, with a casual, outdoorsy feel. Womenswear includes loose, heavy linen or boiled-wool pieces from German brand Oska, chunky knits and cotton separates from Dutch company Sandwich and delicate wrap cardigans from Irish label Anthology by Avoca (from around £95). Recently introduced labels include Wax from Belgium and Marc O'Polo. Prices start at around £29 for a T-shirt and go up to around £285 for a skirt by Austrian-based Turkish designer Ischiko. Downstairs is devoted to footwear, with a huge choice of brands and styles, from proper walking boots to stylish yet comfortable shoes from the likes of Birkenstock, Arche, Think!, Thierry Rabotin and Ecco. There are also other accessories and baby clothes and gifts.
Mail order.

Ted Baker

9-10 Floral Street, WC2E 9HW (7836 7808/ www.tedbaker.co.uk). Covent Garden tube. **Open** 10am-7pm Mon-Wed, Fri, Sat; 10am-8pm Thur; noon-6pm Sun. **Credit** AmEx, MC, V. **Sells** M, W, C.
Ted Baker categorises itself as a 'lifestyle' brand, with a home collection, as well as ranges for men, women and kids, plus shoes, eyewear, watches and a fragrance. We're just not quite sure what sort of lifestyle Ted represents. Certainly, there's a zany, clubby air about the former Glasgow shirtmaker's Floral Street warehouse premises, with its exposed brick, larky handwritten signage and blaring disco beat, and this is the guy who brought us the liquid-resistant Party Animal suit for men. But the womenswear is on the mainstream side of the street – body-conscious tops, jeans, slinky silk dresses and a few of the well-cut shirts on which Baker founded his business. While a lot of it looks like any other young fashion label, there are some unusual prints and styles to be found. Prices are from around £40 for a jersey top, £80 for trousers and £90 for a dress.
Mail order.
Branches: throughout the city.

Wall

1 Denbigh Road, W11 2SJ (7243 4623/www. wall-london.com). Notting Hill Gate tube. **Open** 10.30am-6.30pm Mon-Fri; 10am-6pm Sat; noon-5pm Sun. **Credit** AmEx, MC, V. **Sells** W.
Unapologetically aimed at those among us whose proportions are more ample than waif-like, Wall offers simple 'forgiving' designs in luxurious fabrics – hand-picked Peruvian Pima cotton, baby alpaca, Irish linen, silk and cashmere – and the clothes have a loyal following among a well-heeled, older, creative crowd. Many styles – draping cardigans, fluid skirts and loose trousers – have a Japanese feel, although there are some fitted styles, notably Wall's excellent-quality T-shirts (from around £30). Prices start at £115 for knitwear, trousers and skirts. Sumptuous accessories include fluffy alpaca hats and slippers (from £85) and, exclusive to the UK, scarves and wraps made from the protected llama-like creatures known as *vicuñas* (£550-£980) – but don't worry, the animals died of natural causes, hence the high price tags.
Mail order (0870 350 7373).

Whistles

12 St Christopher's Place, W1U 1NQ (7487 4484/www.whistles.co.uk). Bond Street tube. **Open** 10am-6pm Mon-Wed, Fri, Sat; 10am-7pm Thur; noon-5pm Sun. **Credit** AmEx, MC, V. **Sells** W.
'Eclectic' best sums up the style of this well-loved label, which manages to interpret catwalk trends without losing its distinctive identity. Window mannequins are often dressed in quirkily layered items and clashing patterns. While signature mainstays include hand-finished tailoring, intricately beaded, appliquéd and embroidered tops and dresses, influences span Victoriana to 1970s boho, by way of the 1940s and '50s. Price-wise, you're looking at around £50 for a top, £99 for trousers, £165 for a jacket and £120 for a dress. The airy St Christopher's Place store stocks a constantly changing selection of designer pieces alongside its own label – current lines include Antik Batik, Italian label Twinset, T-shirts by Michael Stars and Velvet, and jeans courtesy of Paige Premium Denim (as well as Whistles' own), plus fab own-label shoes, bags and other accessories.
Branches: throughout the city.

Budget

True bargain-seekers may want to venture to **Primark** in Hammersmith (Kings Mall, King Street, W6 0PZ, 8748 7119, www.primark. co.uk), where you can find seasonal trends reproduced at cheaper-than-charity-shop prices (military jackets for just £12, for example, or a beaded bolero for a tenner), but as you might imagine, items sell out fast, and you have to pick over the tat to find a prize. While you're in the neighbourhood, it's worth checking out **TK Maxx** (57 King Street, W6 9HW, 8563 9200, www.tkmaxx.co.uk), which offers branded merchandise at up to 60 per cent off the recommended retail price. If you fancy a road trip, some large suburban branches of **Tesco** (0800 505 555, www.tesco.com) sell the cheap 'n' chic catwalk-copycat Florence+Fred line, while **Asda** fashion range George has a stand-alone store in Greater London (42-46 North End, Croydon, 8603 0000, www.asda.co.uk).

Dorothy Perkins

189 Oxford Street, W1D 2JY (7494 3769/ www.dorothyperkins.co.uk). Oxford Circus tube. **Open** 9am-8pm Mon-Wed, Fri, Sat; 9am-9pm Thur; noon-6pm Sun. **Credit** AmEx, DC, MC, V. **Sells** W.
The name lets it down – not very sexy, is it? But among the rather dull office suits and acres of denim, Dorothy Perkins has some surprisingly trendy pieces. When we last visited, we saw a huge array of delicate angora and crocheted shrugs, and a fashionably fitted velvet jacket that you can even throw in the washing machine (£45). But star of the autumn/winter season has got to be the beige suede military-style jacket for just £60.
Branches: throughout the city.

Gap

376-384 Oxford Street, W1C 1JY (7408 4500/ www.gap.com). Bond Street tube. **Open** 9.30am-9pm Mon-Sat; 11.30am-6pm Sun. **Credit** AmEx, MC, V. **Sells** M, W, C.
The American giant is going from strength to strength, with Pina Ferlisi, who helped create Marc by Marc Jacobs, at the design helm. The new Skinny Jeans (from £45), available in several washes, have tapped into autumn/winter 2005/6's fashion zeitgeist and there are fab cords in the same cut in a range of colours including purple, charcoal and teal blue. Pair them with several variations on the white shirt, the new range of cashmere sweaters (from £68), velvet blazers and wool pea-coats for a perfect modern-preppy look. Cute metallic-leather ballet flats (£25) and great bags by former Marc Jacobs accessory designer Emma Hill (£19-£65), such as big-buttoned retro-vibe totes, are covetable extras.
Branches: throughout the city.

H&M

261-271 Regent Street, W1B 2ES (7493 4004/ www.hm.com). Oxford Circus tube. **Open** 10am-8pm Mon-Wed, Fri, Sat; 10am-9pm Thur; noon-6pm Sun. **Credit** AmEx, MC, V. **Sells** M, W.
The Swedish stalwart's fashion cachet has been boosted in the past few years – in 2004 the catwalk king himself, Karl Lagerfeld, designed a capsule collection for the store, while Stella McCartney's eagerly awaited range is due to hit the rails in November 2005. In the main collection, there are some remarkably cheap directional items for autumn/winter 2005/6, such as tweed capes, strappy empire-line dresses and little lace-trimmed, antiquey fine cotton camisoles for just £9.99. A new jeans line, &denim, was about to hit stores as we went to press. For those who find the mighty Oxford Circus flagship a bit too frenetic, the newish, elegant Knightsbridge branch stocks clothes for men, women and teens, plus cosmetics, accessories and lingerie.
Branches: throughout the city.

Mango

233 Oxford Street, W1D 2LP (7534 3505/ www.mango.com). Oxford Circus tube. **Open** 10am-8.30pm Mon-Wed, Fri; 10am-9pm Thur; 11am-6pm Sun. **Credit** AmEx, MC, V. **Sells** W.
Its 2005/6 collection was slavered over by a broadsheet style section – and we can understand why. Among the wide range of jeans and little strappy tops (patterned, beaded, lacy) the sassy Spanish label does so well are some on-the-button catwalk-inspired pieces: a viscose dress in a Cavalli-esque python-floral print for just £35 and some fabulous fitted jackets (with either tux or military overtones) for around £40. The Exclusive

Saltwater. See p43.

Edition capsule line features more elaborate, special items in luxury materials – for example, a flamboyant purple feather shrug for £85.
Branches: throughout the city.

Miss Selfridge

36-38 Great Castle Street, W1W 8LG (7927 0218/www.missselfridge.co.uk). Oxford Circus tube. **Open** 9am-8pm Mon-Wed, Fri, Sat; 9am-9pm Thur; noon-6pm Sun. **Credit** AmEx, DC, MC, V. **Sells** W.

Although somewhat in the shadow of its big sis Topshop, with which it shares the Oxford Circus flagship premises, Miss Selfridge produces an exciting collection for young trendsters, including lots of urban shorts (from around £22), tiny jackets and pretty chiffon dresses (£45). The Miss Vintage range is strong on hip thrift-store accessories, while Terry de Havilland's diffusion shoe collection, D-Havz, and the new Bella collection by Bella Freud, which mixes masculine tailoring with a dash of 1970s Biba, are generating a buzz in fashion circles.
Branches: throughout the city.

New Look

500-502 Oxford Street, W1C 7HL (7290 7860/ www.newlook.co.uk). Bond Street or Marble Arch tube. **Open** 10am-9pm Mon-Sat; noon-6pm Sun. **Credit** MC, V. **Sells** M, W, C.

Once the prepubescent's favourite fashion store, New Look reinvented itself a few years back. There's something vaguely theme park about its futuristic flagship, with its sweeping chrome staircase, space-age trolleys equipped with hanging rails for easy shopping, and a corner where bored boyfriends can lounge on metallic banquettes and listen to the latest club sounds on headphones. As for the clothes, although some of the stock is, frankly, shocking (polyester trousers, synthetic jumpers), there are still many goodies to be had. Much of the autumn/winter 2005/6 stock carries on summer's boho obsession with peasanty patchwork skirts and floaty ethnic tops, but we liked the soft, washed-effect fitted velvet jackets for a mere £25, a chunky-knit zip gilet for £20 and Ossie Clark-esque print dresses for £30. There were also cool leather jackets for £50, suede skirts at an astonishing £35 and a huge selection of shoes (fabric round-toed flatties for just £12) and lingerie.
Branches: throughout the city.

Oasis

12-14 Argyll Street, W1F 7NT (7434 1799/ www.oasis-stores.com). Oxford Circus tube. **Open** 10am-7pam Mon-Wed, Fri, Sat; 10am-8pm Thur; noon-6pm Sun. **Credit** AmEx, MC, V. **Sells** W.

Stock varies here – while some items are great value, others betray their price bracket. The prevailing style is quite ladylike compared to some of the racier high-street brands. Gems we spotted as we went to press include a range of sweet, hand-crocheted shrugs (around £30-£40), funky 'washed' leather jackets, including a blazer and Victorian style (£120), and pristine short tweed coats from as little as £75. The Love Rosa collection, featuring designer Anne-Louise Roswald's distinctive prints (on tops, dresses and bags), pretty Odille lingerie and the New Vintage collection, which reproduces such sought-after pieces as flapper dresses and Victorian jackets, are well worth a look.
Branches: throughout the city.

Principles

260 Regent Street, W1B 3AG (7287 3365/ www.principles.co.uk). Oxford Circus tube. **Open** 10am-7pm Mon-Wed, Fri, Sat; 10am-8pm Thur; noon-6pm Sun. **Credit** AmEx, MC, V. **Sells** W.

For years it was associated with boring, officey clothes, but suddenly Principles has brought out a very fashion-savvy collection, and at excellent prices too. There's an array of sharp, military-detail jackets from around £40, Victorian black lace tops, embroidered Russian-style waistcoats, antique-look camisoles for under £20 and even some high-quality jeans (£37) with stitching details that look remarkably similar to a certain ubiquitous premium label. Let's hope the brand keeps up the good work for the next season.

River Island

301-309 Oxford Street, W1C 2DZ (7493 1431/ www.riverisland.com). Bond Street or Oxford Circus tube. **Open** 10am-8pm Mon-Fri; 10am-7pm Sat; noon-6pm Sun. **Credit** AmEx, MC, V. **Sells** M, W.

For would-be R&B divas on a budget, this place oozes bling. But once you get past the jeans and denim minis splashed with glitter and dripping with diamanté, there are less flashy, and excellent quality, finds. Among the items that have caught our eye are tasteful beaded mesh shrugs for under £40, expensive-looking, deep-dyed T-shirts for £9.99 and heavy-cotton, sashed full skirts in rich colours such as purple and sage green (around £40) – we're not naming names, but we have seen a very similar style by an independent designer in one of the capital's top boutiques for considerably more.
Branches: throughout the city.

Topshop

36-38 Great Castle Street, W1W 8LG (7636 7700/ www.topshop.co.uk). Oxford Circus tube. **Open** 9am-8pm Mon-Wed, Fri, Sat; 9am-9pm Thur; noon-6pm Sun. **Credit** AmEx, MC, V. **Sells** W.

The 'world's largest fashion store' just got bigger. The high-street darling of the fashion pack, which has worked hard to build up its undisputed supremacy (starry customers include trendsetters Scarlett Johansson and Kate Moss), shows no signs of resting on its laurels. As we went to press, Topshop was poised to spread out into the former Evans premises alongside, to accommodate its expanded, trend-led maternity range. The denim department is also getting a boost with a fitting area. The vintage section is still going strong, while the vast, up-to-the-minute accessory range is being topped off with a new hat line. Long known for nurturing young talent, Topshop continues to feature ranges by recent graduates alongside established names in its Boutique – this year's stable includes Peter Jensen, Jonathan Saunders and Sophia Kokosalaki. Other exciting developments include collaborations with Laura Lees, known for her sweetly subversive rock-chick dresses, and hip shoemaker Adele Clarke. As if all that wasn't enough of a draw, there is also a team of personal style advisers who will guide you through the myriad choices in-store, or even come to your house with a selection of clothes; both services are free of charge and there is no obligation to buy. What are you waiting for?

Warehouse

19-21 Argyll Street, W1F 7TR (7437 7101/ www.warehousefashion.com). Oxford Circus tube. **Open** 10am-7pm Mon-Wed, Fri, Sat; 10am-8pm Thur; noon-6pm Sun. **Credit** AmEx, DC, MC, V. **Sells** W.

As we went to press, Warehouse was preparing to unveil its revamped flagship, which will showcase special pieces exclusive to the branch alongside the main collection. The brand's eclectic range covers the main trends of each season, and the quality is good for the price – autumn/winter 2005/6's essential military-inspired coats and jackets are around £90 and £65 respectively, and we love the cute puffball minis for £35. Lavish embroidered and appliquéd items are on the agenda later in the season.
Branches: throughout the city.

Zara

79-81 Brompton Road, SW3 1DB (7590 6990/ www.zara.com). Knightsbridge tube. **Open** 10am-7pm Mon-Sat; noon-6pm Sun. **Credit** AmEx, MC, V. **Sells** M, W, C.

For convincing catwalk copies, it's hard to beat this Spanish success story. If you don't mind the odd loose thread, the styles and fabrics are spot on, and the choice is staggering. There's a dizzying stock turnover, but on a recent visit the rails were dominated by military, ladylike and Victorian trends. We were impressed by delicate, real silk blouses for around £35, countless variations on the military jacket from around £40, and some fab trench-coats at around £100. T-shirts are as little

as £4. Womenswear falls into three categories: Zara Woman is the main catwalk-inspired collection, Basic includes cheaper everyday pieces, while TRF is young and funky, incuding denim. The Knightsbridge branch also sells menswear, kids' clothes and Zara Home, which brings the company's cheaper-than-it-looks ethos to interior accessories.
Branches: throughout the city.

Knitwear

For **Pringle Scotland**, *see p34*. **Ballantyne** (*see p46*) and **John Smedley** (*see p48*), listed in **Menswear**, do knitwear in a similar vein for women. For luxury on a budget, **Gap** has a new line of cashmere sweaters (*see p44*).

Belinda Robertson

4 West Halkin Street, SW1X 8JA (7235 0519/ www.belindarobertson.com). Hyde Park Corner or Knightsbridge tube. **Open** 10.30am-6.30pm Mon-Fri; 10am-6pm Sat; (summer only) noon-5pm Sun. **Credit** AmEx, DC, MC, V. **Sells** M, W, B.

Scottish lass Belinda Robertson is known for her cashmere sweaters in modern shapes and a dazzling range of 120 colours; you can have any current style made up in the colour of your choice, at no extra cost, in about four weeks. Prices start at £165 for a camisole, and fashion-conscious styles include a baby bolero, ballet wrap and some glam evening options such as a Swarovski crystal-trimmed halter-neck (£415) and matching bolero (£395). The new White Label is a cheaper line (around £100) made in the Far East.
Mail order.

Brora

344 King's Road, SW3 5UR (7352 3697/ www.brora.co.uk). Sloane Square tube/11, 19, 22 bus. **Open** 10am-6pm Mon-Sat; noon-5pm Sun. **Credit** AmEx, MC, V. **Sells** M, W, C, B.

Contemporary Scottish cashmere company Brora offers some unusual designs each season alongside its range of updated basics, such as lacy knits, wrap styles and zip hoodies. Colours are unusual too – including nude pink, rich burgundy and slate for autumn/winter. Most sweaters are around the £150 mark. Blankets, scarves, socks and hats and adorable baby cashmere are also sold.
Mail order (7736 9944).
For branches see index.

Marilyn Moore

7 Elgin Crescent, W11 2JA (7727 5577). Notting Hill Gate tube. **Open** 10am-6pm Mon-Sat; noon-5pm Sun. **Credit** AmEx, DC, MC, V. **Sells** W.

She honed her craft at Jaeger, so it's hardly surprising Marilyn Moore creates variations on classic English knitwear. The selection includes fine cashmere-silk shrugs and cardigans in fitted shapes that evoke the 1940s, in an understated 'vintage-washed' colour palette including beige, mink brown and mossy green. Some feature subtle, contrasting trimmings. Matching camisoles start at £80; sweaters are around £160. Co-ordinating A-line tweed skirts, nostalgic dresses and tops are also for sale in the appealing Notting Hill shop.
Mail order.

N Peal

37 & 71-72 Burlington Arcade, W1J 0QD (7493 5378/www.npeal.com). Green Park or Piccadilly Circus tube. **Open** 9.30am-6pm Mon-Sat. **Credit** AmEx, DC, MC, V. **Sells** M, W.

Burlington Arcade stalwart N Peal has been in business since 1936, but contemporary styles are displayed alongside the classics. This is the place to come for luxurious pieces, such as a nine-ply cableknit rollneck in a delicious shade of pecan (£650). Simpler pullovers and cardies can be had for around £175-£210. The cheaper npealworks range, for both men and women, offers fresh, funky styles in pastels, brights or stripes, or featuring cute motifs (from around £90). There's a wide array of scarves and pashminas, and sumptuous cashmere dressing gowns (around £900).
Mail order.

Menswear

Several of London's department stores have excellent menswear departments. **Selfridges** (*see p14*), **Harvey Nichols** (*see p12*) and **Liberty** (*see p13*) all stock original and interesting labels. Further clothes shops are covered in the **Womenswear**, **Bespoke**, **Street** and **Designer** chapters.

APC

Selfridges, 400 Oxford Street, W1A 1AB (0870 837 7377/www.apc.fr). Bond Street or Marble Arch tube. **Open** 9.30am-8pm Mon-Wed, Fri, Sat; 9.30am-9pm Thur; noon-6pm Sun. **Credit** AmEx, DC, MC, V. **Sells** M, W.

APC designs clothes in the manner of a rather expensive Muji or Gap: military-style coats, elegantly cut denim, hard-wearing sweatshirts and stripy tops complemented by a line of simple accessories. In short, good, solid basics for those who like to express their style with a sly wink and a nod. Casual but never scruffy, smart but never fussy, APC's clothes are full of the kind of subtle nuances that your average Gap wearer will never quite get, which is probably why the label is a perennial favourite among fashion editors and designers, architects and graphic designers. The APC inky blue straight-leg jeans in particular never fail to flatter skinny physiques, which is why Dior Homme's Hedi Slimane can often be seen in a pair. Not that he'd ever want you to know, of course. *Mail order.*

Aquascutum

100 Regent Street, W1B 5SR (7675 8200/ www.aquascutum.co.uk). Piccadilly Circus tube. **Open** 10am-6.30pm Mon-Wed, Fri, Sat; 10am-7pm Thur; noon-5pm Sun. **Credit** AmEx, DC, MC, V. **Sells** M, W.

There was once a danger that Aquascutum might get mistaken for a poor man's Burberry. Both were labels with a grand military heritage that needed reinventing. While Burberry went the high-octane fashion route, Aquascutum fell back on the central qualities of authenticity and quality that make traditional British clothing so desirable. The refit of the Regent Street store is beautiful and the new tailoring collections have an air of quiet luxury about them. However, for the men, it's the classics that matter most, such as the single-breasted raglan-sleeve gabardine raincoat favoured by Mayor Ken Livingstone.

Bailey

9-11 Shorts Gardens, WC2H 9AZ (7836 6097). Covent Garden or Leicester Square tube. **Open** 10.30am-7pm Mon-Wed, Fri, Sat; 10.30am-7.30pm Thur; 12.30-5.30pm Sun. **Credit** MC, V. **Sells** M.

Here's a shop for guys who are over the street thing and looking for something smarter. Newly opened Bailey straddles the middle ground between Zara and Paul Smith, offering stylish, well cut gear at non-outlandish prices. The latest venture from Chris Bailey, the former creative director of Uth, Jigsaw's men's range, the shop offers all the benefits of a boutique – styles you're not going to see everywhere – but with the regular stock turnaround of the high street. So what's on the rails? Quality Italian-made cashmere coats for £295, cashmere sweaters in funky tangerine, mustard yellow or dusky pink for £120 and statement shirts. There's also art on the walls, and an exhibition space upstairs that will soon be available for small events. Impressive.

Ballantyne

303 Westbourne Grove, W11 2QA (7493 4718/ www.ballantyne.it). Notting Hill Gate tube. **Open** 10am-6pm Mon-Sat. **Credit** AmEx, DC, MC, V. **Sells** M, W.

Ballantyne was originally one of Scotland's most traditional cashmere manufacturers, sourcing fibres from goats in Mongolia to make super-luxurious, hand-finished cashmere jumpers that your grandad might like. Not any more. Central to its reinvention has been the use of colour, both in collections and in the incredible shop interior. Every wall is lined with kaleidoscopic wallpaper, designed in the '40s by Viennese architect Joseph Frank, the fruit and flower motif giving the place a uniquely mind-bending character. The clothes are a flamboyant fusion of cool Italian style and traditional Scottish craftsmanship. As well as classic crew and V-necks, rendered in vivid shades of turquoise, cherry red, sunflower yellow and lime green, are staples of casual Italian style, such as high-necked zip-up cardies and two-buttoned cotton polo shirts. Beware the prices, though: the hand-finished cashmeres cost a whopping £800. *Mail order.*
For branch see index.

Browns

23-27 South Molton Street, W1K 5RD (7514 0038/www.brownsfashion.com). Bond Street tube. **Open** 10am-6.30pm Mon-Wed, Fri, Sat; 10am-7pm Thur. **Credit** AmEx, DC, MC, V. **Sells** M, W.

Not the biggest menswear store in London, but what Browns lacks in size it most definitely makes up for in quality. Much has been said about the fact that its founder Joan Burstein has been credited with giving the likes of John Galliano and Hussein Chalayan their big breaks, but that is only half the story. The shop's current buyer, Bernie Thomas, is just as intuitive and has brought Junya Watanabe, Dior Homme and Belgium's latest darling, Kris Van Assche, into the fold. It's less frantic than Selfridges and staff are certainly better informed and far more attentive. Its sale is worth waiting for. *Mail order.*

A Butcher of Distinction

11 Dray Walk, Old Truman Brewery, E1 6QL (7770 6111). Aldgate East tube/Liverpool Street tube/rail. **Open** 10am-7pm daily. **Credit** AmEx, MC, V. **Sells** M.

The problem with the whole Shoreditch-Brick Lane fashion explosion is that it has never really lived up to all the hype. All that 'fashion' – odd-looking barnets, ripped denim of a Bros persuasion and 'ironic' T-shirts – but nowhere to buy any decent clobber. The arrival of A Butcher of Distinction, based in the heart of the Truman Brewery, could not have come soon enough. Not only does it have an impressive interior (based loosely on a butcher's shop and freezer, geddit?), its range of smart casualwear and footwear from the likes of 6876, Milkcrate Athletic, Ralph Lauren and Tricker's is more than ample reason to avoid the tortures of shopping in the West End. Preppy with an edge.

Cordings

19 Piccadilly, W1J 0LA (7734 0830/www.cordings. co.uk). Piccadilly Circus tube. **Open** 9.30am-6.30pm Mon-Wed, Fri; 10am-7pm Thur; 10am-6pm Sat. **Credit** AmEx, DC, MC, V. **Sells** M, W.

In the frenzy to reinvent traditional British menswear brands, Cordings remains unashamedly fusty and old-fashioned. Its core countryside fan base would never countenance such changes to their glorious 165-year-old institution, now owned by Eric Clapton. Typical stock includes candy-coloured cords and moleskin trousers to go with hard-wearing and equally brightly coloured Macintosh raincoats. Cordings also makes some of the best three-quarter-length covert coats, certainly the finest tweed and also the original tattersall-check shirts. *Mail order.*

Designworks

42-44 Broadwick Street, W1F 7AF (7434 1968/ www.abahouse.co.jp). Oxford Circus tube. **Open** 10.30am-7pm Mon-Fri; 11am-6pm Sat. **Credit** AmEx, MC, V. **Sells** M.

Japanese directional fashion brand Designworks is truly a cut above when it comes to blending innovative materials with understated design. The shop, which opened in 2001, boasts the sort of slick and elegant designs many British brands can only dream of. As well as a selection of unusual gifts and lifestyle items, such as chairs by Graf, it is the clothes, shoes (by Alfredo Bannister) and accessories that really do the talking. Expect loads of techno fabrics, slick styling and finishes from the autumn collection, which includes silk macs and unusually buckled jackets – dare we say, modern classics with a twist? And with prices for a jacket starting at around £200, you can't go wrong. In addition, it has the best-dressed staff in the West End. *Mail order.*

Duffer of St George

29 Shorts Gardens, WC2H 9AP (7379 4660/ www.thedufferofstgeorge.com). Covent Garden tube. **Open** 10.30am-7pm Mon-Wed; 10.30am-6.30pm Sat; 1-5pm Sun. **Credit** AmEx, MC, V. **Sells** M.

When the history of menswear gets written, Duffer of St George will surely be central to any chapter about London in the 1980s and '90s. During these decades, founder 'Fast' Eddie Prendergast would be busy unearthing dead-stock vintage trainers and obscure labels that effortlessly appealed to many of London's disparate style tribes. Football hooligans, acid house ravers and decadent dandies all made Saturday afternoons at Duffer a rather lively place to hang out. The shop consistently has a knack of making what were considered fuddy-duddy labels relevant again. John Smedley, Clarks, Macintosh and Tricker's all got a second lease of life here. In recent years the shop had been looking rather busy, with too many T-shirt labels no one cares about, but that's all been sorted out with some judicious editing. What you'll find now are the boiled-down essentials a boy needs to look cool: wearable Comme des Garçons, Stone Island jackets, Ralph Lauren tops in colours you won't even find in the designer's flagship, a few obscure workwear labels from America and quality premium denim brands. *Mail order.*
For branch see index.

Dunhill

48 Jermyn Street, SW1Y 6LX (7290 8622/ www.dunhill.com). Green Park tube. **Open** 9.30am-6.30pm Mon-Wed, Fri, Sat; 9.30am-7pm Thur. **Credit** AmEx, DC, MC, V. **Sells** M.

Another heritage brand and yet another facelift to bring it up to date. More than a century ago, Alfred Dunhill created one of the quintessential British luxury brands around an automotive theme, offering discerning gents 'everything but the motor'. Once known for innovations such as the Unique, the first lighter that could be held and operated with one hand in 1924, the firm has seen some patchy times, finding a market among Japanese businessmen, although the wonderful boys' toys remain as desirable as ever. However, the inspired decision to hire Richard James (suiting), Nick Ashley (motoring clothing), Bill Amberg (leather accessories) and Tom Bolt (watches) has given the new collection a fresh, modern edge, without compromising the brawny elegance that made Dunhill great in the first place. *Mail order.*

Ermenegildo Zegna

37-38 New Bond Street, W1S 2RU (7518 2700/ www.zegna.com). Bond Street or Green Park tube. **Open** 10am-6pm Mon-Wed, Fri, Sat; 10am-7pm Thur. **Credit** AmEx, DC, MC, V. **Sells** M.

When it comes to crisp, understated Italian menswear, Zegna (pronounced Zenya) is the thinking man's Armani. Fabrics and clever technical innovations are the family-owned firm's

A Butcher of Distinction

strong points. With mills based in Trivero, in the industrial heartland of northern Italy, Zegna was a pioneer in the development of lightweight wools that were more suited to the demands of the modern workplace than those of its Scottish counterparts. While big Italian labels like Armani and Dolce & Gabbana continue to court tacky celebrity endorsements, you're more likely to find the likes of concert pianist Peter Cincotti and Oscar-winning actor Adrien Brody wearing Zegna. The Z line is inspired by yachting clothes, while the made-to-measure and sartorial lines have found an audience in sophisticated boardrooms worldwide. *Mail order.*

Etro

14 Old Bond Street, W1X 3DB (7495 5767/ www.etro.it). Green Park tube. **Open** 10am-6pm Mon-Sat. **Credit** AmEx, DC, MC, V. **Sells** M, W.
Etro is the antithesis of Armani, eschewing quiet good taste in favour of riotous colour and patterns. It's a shame that the label isn't more popular among men in London; chic Upper East Side New Yorkers swear by the striped, checked and paisley shirts, and butter-soft tweed and corduroy jackets. This is also a good place for accessories – paisley-printed silk and wool scarves form the backbone of the family-owned company.
Mail order.

G.room

46 Carnaby Street, W1F 9PS (7734 5994/www. theg-room.com). Oxford Circus tube. **Open** 10am-7pm Mon-Wed, Fri, Sat; 10am-8pm Thur; noon-6pm Sun. **Credit** AmEx, MC, V. **Sells** M.
Michael Pike, founder of this recently opened lifestyle shop for men, has taken grooming back to basics: top-to-toe elegance, from shaving soap to shoes, via the suit. Perfect for men who don't need the security blanket of buying into one brand and have the confidence to cherry pick, G.room takes a lot of the hard work out, with a heavily edited and ever-evolving collection. The shelves are a contrasting mix of trendy utilitarian and old-fashioned genteel. So there are skin products from Prince Charles' favourite, Geo F Trumper, and David Beckham's choice, NV Perricone. Similarly, clothes run from Jermyn Street formal to Tonic T-shirts and casual Belstaff leather jackets. You'll also find Burton snowboards, a selection of CDs (rap, electro, indie), coffee-table books, wallets, Gola trainers, scarves and cufflinks – plenty here to keep the discerning men of Soho happy.

Hackett

137-138 Sloane Street, SW1X 9AY (7730 3331/ www.hackett.co.uk). Sloane Square tube. **Open** 9.30am-6.30pm Mon, Tue, Fri, Sat; 9.30am-7pm Wed, Thur; 11am-5pm Sun. **Credit** AmEx, DC, MC, V. **Sells** M, W.
The self-styled 'Essential British Kit' has long been a uniform for the capital's rugger buggers and tally-ho toffs. It is a bit of a shame, as quite a lot of the stock of suits, tailoring, knits and ties is rather nice, but the association might put some off. Hackett celebrated its 21st birthday by revamping its flagship shop in Sloane Street, which reopened in September 2004 to a very positive reaction from customers. The shop represents Britishness with a combination of new and old, including an eclectic selection of found objects. Recent additions to the Hackett range include slick grooming products and eyewear – further reasons to get over a stereotype. *Mail order.*
Branches: throughout the city.

Ilk

24 All Saints Road, W11 1HG (7221 5033). Ladbroke Grove tube. **Open** 10am-6pm Tue, Wed, Sat; 10am-8pm Thur, Fri; noon-4pm Sun. **Credit** MC, V. **Sells** M.
Hip shops fusing clothing, furniture and a dash of culture are usually located in Hoxton side streets, so it's refreshing to find one out west. Especially when the emphasis is on the chaps, for a change. Owner Phil Lawrence has chosen menswear pieces with a relaxed-but-slick style. Something for the weekend? A brown and pink (it works, trust us) jumper by Geeson is well priced at £80 and looks

FASHION

FASHION

good with the Nudie cross-hatch jeans (£110) and a Marshall Artist toffee-coloured jacket (£130). The bookshelves are stacked with arty titles by Phaidon and Taschen. A one-stop style shop for boys in the know.

Interno 8

19 Conduit Street, W1S 2QR (7529 2788/ www.interno8.net). Bond Street or Green Park tube. **Open** 10am-7pm Mon-Sat; 1-6pm Sun. **Credit** AmEx, MC, V. **Sells** M, W, C.

Every once in a while even the most tasteful, soberly suited devotee of Savile Row and Jermyn Street fancies something more flamboyant. Paul Smith aside, it's the Italians who subvert traditional tailoring with the most flair, and banker-turned-designer Angelo Galasso, with his trademark high-collared shirts, is one of the best. Collars are doubled up and feature two – maybe even three – buttons. Perhaps Galasso's most brilliant conceit is the Polso Orologio, a double cuff with a hole cut into it, allowing you to show off your Breitling or Rolex. The style is a homage to the late playboy Gianni Agnelli of the Fiat empire, who often wore his watch over his cuff – which is apt, because wearing one of Interno 8's shirts makes you feel, quite simply, rich. No wonder everyone from Thierry Henry to Roger Moore can be spotted in them. *Mail order.*

For branches see index.

J Simons

2 Russell Street, WC2B 5JD (7379 7353/http:// j.simons.mysite.freeserve.com). Covent Garden tube. **Open** 10am-6.30pm Mon-Thur; 10am-6pm Fri; 10am-5.30pm Sat; noon-5pm Sun. **Credit** AmEx, MC, V. **Sells** M.

The preppy look may come in and out of fashion, but this shop has built up enough of a following of devotees to keep selling the Harrington jackets, half-lined suits, chinos and loafers so beloved of the

East Coast American establishment. If you've ever harboured an ambition to look like an off-duty JFK, Miles Davis or Steve McQueen (let's face it, what man hasn't?), then this is where you can pick up the few remaining labels they actually wore. Shoes are particularly strong, with an authentic selection of Red Wing, Sebago, Bass and Mack James. *Mail order.*

John Smedley

24 Brook Street, W1K 5DG (7495 2222/ www.john-smedley.com). Bond Street tube. **Open** 10am-6pm Mon-Wed, Fri, Sat; 10am-7pm Thur. **Credit** AmEx, MC, V. **Sells** M, W.

Quite possibly the best producer of knitwear in the world, John Smedley was founded in 1784 in Matlock, Derbyshire, as a company specialising in the production of muslin and spinning cotton. Today its fine-gauge knits are sold to over 35 countries. The small shop stocks the full range of sweaters, cardigans and even knitted T-shirts. While simplicity is a defining characteristic, Smedley always retains a fashion edge – a recent collaboration with long-time fan Vivienne Westwood (to celebrate the company's 220th anniversary) has resulted in a collection of knitted underwear. *Mail order.*

The Library

268 Brompton Road, SW3 2AS (7589 6569). South Kensington tube. **Open** 10am-6.30pm Mon, Tue, Thur-Sat; 10am-7pm Wed; 12.30-5.30pm Sun. **Credit** AmEx, DC, MC, V. **Sells** M, W.

This is much more than a clothing emporium that sells books. Some have dismissed the Library over the years for being a little drab on the decor front and a little obvious on the book front. But in terms of the labels it carries, it's a razor-sharp one-stop shop for lovers of exquisite purist brands. Buyer Peter Sidell is considered to have one of the best eyes in the business for spotting and nurturing hot

talent. Stock comes from a virtual *Who's Who* of hip menswear, including Scaglione knitwear, Martin Margiela, Comme des Garçons and Junya Watanabe, YMC, Dirk Bikkemberg, alongside scents by Creed and one of the best selections of Maharishi outside its Covent Garden flagship store. And, even better, the staff are right on the money in terms of looks and knowledge. *Mail order.*

Maison Martin Margiela

1-9 Bruton Place, W1J 6NE (7629 2682). Bond Street or Green Park tube. **Open** 10am-6.30pm Mon-Wed, Fri, Sat; 10am-7pm Thur. **Credit** AmEx, MC, V. **Sells** M, W.

While Bond Street's designer environments continue down the boringly minimalist route, Maison Martin Margiela is thrillingly offkilter. Down a Mayfair mews, the former stable (which also served as a studio to Francis Bacon and Lucien Freud) is a refined exercise in shabby chic. What's more, Margiela's men's clothes are just as cleverly cut and interesting as his girls' stuff. Some are straight-up replicas of interesting vintage finds like American Air Force leather jackets and even donkey jackets of the type a bin man might wear. Others generally have a vintage artisan quality to them, in fabrics and colours that are slightly washed out, creating the effect of an old favourite. Even when they're breaking conventional rules of good taste – pairing mismatched patterns and colours on the same jacket, for example – his clothes are always surprisingly flattering and never make a man look like he's trying too hard. *Mail order.*

Old Hat

66 Fulham High Street, SW6 3LQ (7610 6558). Putney Bridge tube. **Open** 10.30am-6.30pm Mon-Sat; 1.30-7pm Sun. **Credit** MC, V. **Sells** M.

For the decadent dandy with an abundance of taste and a lack of a trust fund, Old Hat is a smelly treasure trove of vintage men's clothing where – if you're eagle-eyed – you can pick up a really smart suit or coat from a grand Savile Row tailor for as little £125. All the gentlemanly prerequisites can be found here: tweed, an extensive selection of top hats and trilbies, Burberry coats and silk scarves. All of which is brought to you by David Saxby, the tea-quaffing fashion editor of *The Chap*.

Palmer

711 Fulham Road, SW6 5HA (7384 2044). Parsons Green tube. **Open** 10am-6pm Mon-Sat; evenings by appointment. **Credit** AmEx, MC, V. **Sells** M.

The trouble with a shop that offers sublime service and unusually sourced clothing and that treats you like an old friend as soon as you walk through the door is that you want to keep it all to yourself. And without the obligatory website to promote itself, Palmer seems to keep itself to itself too. Shame, really, as it sells some of the most interesting, well-considered and stylish menswear around. Based both in the Fulham Road and in Barnes, it sells handmade shirts from Del Siena, unstructured tailoring from Cord and knitwear by Italian brand Baldassari, as well as the more familiar Sebago, Alfred Sergeant and Crockett & Jones footwear. The clothes here aren't flashy, nor are they ridiculously expensive, but they will make you look and feel like a millionaire.
For branch see index.

Paul Smith

122 Kensington Park Road, W11 2EP (7727 3553/www.paulsmith.co.uk). Notting Hill Gate tube. **Open** 10am-6pm Mon-Fri; 10am-6.30pm Sat. **Credit** AmEx, DC, MC, V. **Sells** M, W, C.
Paul Smith's popularity as the doyen of British style shows little sign of waning, and this comes as no surprise. Free from the constraints of his wood-panelled Floral Street shop, this converted Notting Hill double-fronted Victorian house offers menswear shopping at its best. The collections – which also comprise women's, kids', accessories and even furniture – are spread over four floors of what feels like a quirky residence. The place is dotted with Sir Paul's collection of art and other objects, providing a fascinating insight into the vision behind his colourful yet refined suits, tailoring, luxe knits, preppy casualwear and outerwear.
Mail order.
For branches see index.

Per Lui

The Chimes Shopping Centre, 196-197 Uxbridge High Street, UB8 1LD (01895 810 066/www.per lui.co.uk). Uxbridge tube. **Open** 9am-6pm Mon-Wed, Fri, Sat; 9am-8pm Thur; 11am-5pm Sun. **Credit** AmEx, MC, V. **Sells** M, W.
With shops in Uxbridge, Enfield and further afield, Per Lui has been successfully mixing up designer brands, footwear, casualwear and accessories for over 35 years. And it's got plenty of life in it still. Although the stock is a little on the laddish side of menswear, the staff's knowledge and service are as good as you will find anywhere across London. The brands stocked aren't bad, either. Ted Baker, G-Star, Pringle, Tommy Hilfiger, Thomas Burberry, Paul Smith and JC de Castelbajac are but a few, and each is well represented.
For branch see index.

Reiss

Kent House, 14-17 Market Place, W1H 7AJ (7637 9112/www.reiss.co.uk). Oxford Circus tube. **Open** 10am-6.30pm Mon-Wed, Fri, Sat; 10am-7.30pm Thur; noon-6pm Sun. **Credit** AmEx, MC, V. **Sells** M, W.
Established in London back in the 1970s, Reiss continues to set the standards for high-street menswear. The thinking behind it is simple – to provide good-quality, aspirational own-label ranges at affordable prices for a target audience aged 18 to 40. No stone is left unturned. The exceptional choice of basics, such as denim, T-shirts and casual shirts, mixes seamlessly with slightly more formal offerings and sharp suiting. Considering the quality of the designs, prices are reasonable. There's a superb women's collection too (*see p43*).

Stone Island + CP Company

46 Beak Street, W1F 9RJ (7287 7734/www.stone island.co.uk & www.cpcompany.co.uk). Oxford Circus tube. **Open** 10am-6pm Mon-Wed, Fri, Sat; 10am-7pm Thur. **Credit** AmEx, MC, V. **Sells** M.
Whether for sport or work, all the best men's clothing – the sweatshirt, jeans, the suit – had at some point a practical function. Italian brands Stone Island and CP company continue this grand tradition in the most progressive manner, transferring the practicality of workwear and the excellent detailing of classic tailoring to everyday clothing. As with all the great Italian brands, fabric innovation has been the key to their success. They can be considered modern-day alchemists of the field, fusing the best natural fibres with cutting-edge synthetics to create high-performance garments. The archive includes such way-out items as a rain cloak that transforms into a tent and a jacket that becomes an inflatable chair. This is the kind of clothing that will one day be displayed in design museums.

TM Lewin

106-108 Jermyn Street, SW1 6EQ (7930 4291/www.tmlewin.co.uk). Piccadilly Circus tube. **Open** 9.30am-6pm Mon, Tue, Fri, Sat; 10am-6pm Wed; 10am-7pm Thur; 11am-5pm Sun. **Credit** AmEx, MC, V. **Sells** M, W.
For a decent shirt, there's no better place in the world than Jermyn Street. TM Lewin prides itself on being one of the UK's most highly respected shirtmakers on the street. Shirts are made the traditional way from 33 separate components that require 47 different processes to assemble. The top-notch shirts, knitwear, cufflinks, casual basics and the recently introduced suits offer even the most reluctant menswear buyer exceptional value for money. The best thing is that they almost always seem to be on sale.

Topman

36-38 Great Castle Street, W1W 8LG (7636 7700/www.topman.co.uk). Oxford Circus tube. **Open** 9am-8pm Mon-Wed, Fri, Sat; 9am-9pm Thur; noon-6pm Sun. **Credit** AmEx, DC, MC, V. **Sells** M.
On the whole, the British high street isn't the place for men of discerning taste. Topman used to epitomise this. But in order to keep up with its cooler, more fashion-conscious sister Topshop, it has had to step up its game. Gone are the horrible, shiny four-button suits that screamed 'Young offender on his way to court', to be replaced by well-cut numbers in tasteful patterns and fabrics (even classic tweed), good enough for a graduate on the way to his first job interview. Collaborations with bright young talent such as Kim Jones, Markus Lupfer and Lebanese-born artist Ziad Garnem make it the most fashion-forward of all the high street menswear offerings. And the Sam Greenberg vintage concession is good for classic Ralph Lauren and Lacoste polo tops.
Mail order.

21 The Green

21 The Green, Winchmore Hill, N21 3NL (8882 4298). Winchmore Hill rail. **Open** 10am-6.30pm Mon-Sat; 11am-1.30pm Sun. **Credit** AmEx, MC, V.
This might not seem like the most obvious fashion destination, but with footballers aplenty flocking to the area and some of the capital's biggest houses, 21 The Green is sitting pretty. Mixing up Italian suiting by the likes of Corneliani with top-end casualwear from CP Company, Armani Jeans and Nigel Hall, plus footwear provided by Oliver Sweeney and Emporio Armani, this store really offers something for everyone. Hugo Boss and Stone Island are being brought into the brand mix this autumn. If 21 The Green's beautiful location fails to impress you, its clothing selection certainly will.

William Hunt

41 Savile Row, WIS 3QQ (7439 1921/www.williamhunt-savilerow.com). Green Park tube. **Open** 10am-6pm Mon-Sat. **Credit** AmEx, MC, V. **Sells** M.
At the vanguard of the New Romantic look in the 1980s, William Hunt dressed the likes of Spandau Ballet and Heaven 17. And his look is still 100% modern dandy; signature styles include brightly coloured tailoring, elaborate frock coats and slick trouser silhouettes. These are clothes for those who demand to stand out from the crowd – no surprise, then, that his client list reads like the contents page of *Hello!*.

Best for...

Brilliant basics

Attention to detail and sturdy fabrics elevate **APC**'s (*see p46*) simple, well-cut sweatshirts and jeans above standard high-street staples.

English understatement

A triumvirate of robust British talent is leading **Dunhill** (*see p46*) into the 21st century, while Sir **Paul Smith** (*see above*) is fashion's undisputed knight of immaculate tailoring with a twist.

Getting kitted out under one roof

Take a leaf out of buyer Peter Sidell's book at the **Library** (*see p48*), where knowledgeable staff will guide you through the inspired collection of hip menswear. North Londoners will find a sharp mix of tailoring and casualwear at **21 The Green** (*see below*).

Hot designers

The men's domain of Joan Burstein's sprawling boutique, **Browns** (*see p46*), draws the A list for its well-edited compilation of labels currently in the fashion spotlight.

Innovative gear

For the ultimate in high-performance garments, **Stone Island + CP Company**'s (*see above*) outerwear is made from hard-working hybrid fabrics – including one that is 100% water-, wind- and oil-proof. And it even manages to be stylish.

Looking the business on a budget

Young job-seekers can get suited and booted at **Topman** (*see below*), or bag a vintage Savile Row ensemble at **Old Hat** (*see p48*) – just make sure you factor in the bill for a superior dry cleaner.

Sweaters

Ballantyne's (*see p46*) bold cashmeres will make you stand out from the crowd (and last a lifetime), while **John Smedley**'s (*see p48*) muted pullovers are quieter classics.

Italian flash

Show off your Rolex through a special cut-out cuff on one of **Interno 8**'s (*see p48*) clever shirt styles, or go for all-out peacock pattern-play at **Etro** (*see p47*).

Street

Since mainstream and designer clothes have become more street-influenced and vice versa, you may find other shops of interest in the **Boutiques**, **Womenswear** and **Menswear** chapters. Crossovers include **Bunka** (*see p35*), **no-one** (*see p37*), the **Pineal Eye** (*see p37*) and **Full Circle** (*see p39*). **Miss Sixty** (31 Great Marlborough Street, W1V 1HA, 7434 3060, www.misssixty.com) has an extensive range of denim and young, fashion-led clothes for women; also in-store is the casual men's range **Energie**. The company's higher-end men's line, **Sixty** (available at House of Fraser, *see p12*), has launched reversible jeans (£95-£115) for autumn/winter 2005/6, giving you a choice of two finishes for the price of one (call 0870 751 6040 for stockist information). **Diesel** (43 Earlham Street, WC2H 9LX, 7497 5543, www. diesel.com) has subversive ad campaigns but they tend to be more controversial than its clothes; its low-slung, slim-fitting jeans (for both sexes) have legions of devotees.

*A Bathing Ape 'Busy Workshop'

4 Upper James Street, W1F 9DG (7494 4924). Piccadilly Circus tube. **Open** 11am-7pm Mon-Fri; 11am-6.30pm Sat. **Credit** AmEx, MC, V. **Sells** M, C.
From selling T-shirts out of a duffel bag at hip hop parties in Harajuku in Tokyo, Japanese DJ Nigo has turned *A Bathing Ape into a global phenomenon, even getting himself on the cover of *Time* magazine. His tees (from £50) and sweatshirts (from £130), produced in limited quantities and always featuring some variation of the famous simian motif, are a badge of street cred the world over. Accessories are also hot property, and there are jeans and footwear too. Stock doesn't arrive on a seasonal basis, but rather as and when it's ready. Clever graphic innovation, epitomised by the Warhol-esque camouflage ape print, ensures that everyone from Jay-Z to skinny record-shop nerds are in constant thrall to *A Bathing Ape.
Mail order.

Adidas Originals Store

9 Earlham Street, WC2H 9LL (7379 4042/ www.adidas.co.uk). Covent Garden tube.
Open 10.30am-7pm Mon-Sat; noon-6pm Sun.
Credit AmEx, MC, V. **Sells** M, W.
The Adidas Originals Store aims to capitalise specifically on the enormous retrospective value of the Adidas brand: few companies can continue to reproduce old designs and ideas with quite the same success. Here you'll find (remakes of) classic footwear (*see also p53* **Trainerspotting**), T-shirts, zip-ups and accessories. For autumn/winter 2005/6, the 1980s are as productive an influence as ever, inspiring branded hip hop jackets, loud puffer coats in red, orange, yellow and blue, and zip-ups in retro colourways like orange/dark brown, even gold. As always, there's a vast range of sneakers.

All Saints

57-59 Long Acre, WC2E 9JL (7836 0801). Covent Garden tube. **Open** 10am-7pm Mon-Wed, Fri, Sat; 10am-8pm Thur; noon-6pm Sun.
Credit AmEx, MC, V. **Sells** M, W.
An insistence on pseudo-Christian iconography (highly stylised crucifixes) as a corporate identity mars some otherwise sterling collections at All Saints. Forgetting the T-shirts and other garments thus affected, the brand turns out a wide range of top-quality, well-made and seriously stylish threads, available at an increasing number of shops across the capital. Original, funky urban tees, sweats, sharp jackets and distressed jeans sit alongside smarter items like superbly cut shirts and original suits (for parties rather than the office). All Saints is reasonable rather than cheap, though catch the sales and you'll be laughing.
For branches see index.

American Apparel

2-4 Carnaby Street, W1F 9DW (7734 4477/ www.americanapparel.net). Oxford Circus tube.
Open 10am-7pm Mon-Fri; 10am-8pm Sat; noon-8pm Sun. **Credit** DC, MC, V. **Sells** M, W, C.
American Apparel makes simple, high-quality essentials in an infinite array of colours and cuts. Its slogan 'Made in Downtown LA' is designed to point out that the clothes aren't made in sweat-shop

conditions, but while socially responsible firms often like to make a thing of their underdog status, you can tell these guys are gunning for Gap. T-shirts, polos, tank tops, track jackets, shorts and underwear are inexpensive (tees are around £10, nothing exceeds £40), comfortable and cool.

American Classics

398 King's Road, SW10 0LJ (7352 2853). Sloane Square tube/11, 19, 22 bus. **Open** 10.30am-6.30pm Mon-Sat; noon-5pm Sun.
Credit AmEx, MC, V. **Sells** M.
Sadly, it no longer holds the original vintage Americana that catapulted it into the public's fashion consciousness 25 years ago, but American Classics remains one of the most influential retailers of denim in the UK, if not the world. There's also a good mix of footwear (for example, Red Wing logger boots and Sperry deck shoes), as well as some great Hawaiian shirts and printed tees. But the mainstay is undoubtedly premium denim sourced from across the globe. As well as limited-edition, vintage-style Levi's (£120), there's a great selection of Lee, Wrangler and Japanese (not European) Evisu.
For branch see index.

Antipodium

5A Carlisle Street, W1D 3BH (7287 3841/ www.antipodium.com). Oxford Circus or Tottenham Court Road tube. **Open** 10am-7pm Mon-Fri; 10am-6pm Sat. **Credit** AmEx, MC, V. **Sells** M, W.
London's principal (if not only) outpost for cutting-edge Australasian fashions recently relocated from Shoreditch to Soho, and its escape from the increasingly hackneyed (no pun intended) 'alternative' enclave into more mainstream territory tells of a shop that is growing up. Now smarter and more compact, Antipodium has exclusive imports for both sexes, from new and established designers, all based on the other side of the planet – and for the most part unknown on these shores. In autumn/winter 2005/6, look out for Akira Red's ethereal wispy tops, Gail Sorronda's chic modern eveningwear, Mjolk's contemporary menswear and much more. Colourful, funky Elke jewellery, and LIFEwithBIRD urban bags for men are among the classy accessories.

b Store

6 Conduit Street, W1S 2XE (7499 6628/ www.buddhahood.co.uk). Oxford Circus tube.
Open 10.30am-6.30pm Mon-Sat. **Credit** AmEx, MC, V. **Sells** M, W.
A little bit of Hoxton edginess in venerable Mayfair. The latest addition to b Store's diverse stock is from Pelican Avenue, whose one-off, beautifully colourful stylised bibs for women start at £200. Not everything commands this sort of price tag, though – Peter Jensen sweatshirts begin at £60 and accessories like brooches start from as little as £15. b Store is the exclusive stockist for Bernhard Willhelm; young, original menswear designers Carola Euler, whose rapier-sharp tailoring is embellished with intricate layering; and Deepti, whose pieces are also grounded in careful tailoring, but feature exaggerated silhouettes and big, bright blocks of colour. b Store also has the monopoly on Judy Blame accessories and her T-shirts, each one unique. An original Blitz Club kid and stylist for *i-D* during the '80s, Blame is a genuine legend, so this is quite a coup. There's also a constant flow of Eley Kishimoto, Siv Stodal and many other cutting-edge designers. Also check out its own-brand Buddhahood footwear.
Mail order.

Belstaff

12-13 Conduit Street, W1S 2XQ (7495 5897/ www.belstaff.com). Oxford Circus or Piccadilly Circus tube. **Open** 10am-6pm Mon-Sat. **Credit** AmEx, MC, V. **Sells** M, W.
Belstaff, alongside Barbour, was one of the first companies to develop totally waterproof waxed-cotton jackets. But, while Barbour became part of the countryside uniform, Belstaff went the slightly racier route by specialising in high-performance

Adidas Originals Store

gear for motorcyclists, and in latter years it has received a healthy continental influence from new Italian owner Franco Malenotti, a dedicated motorcycle enthusiast. This newly opened flagship store right in the heart of Mayfair houses the exclusive Aviator by Belstaff collection (jackets from £80 to £700), inspired by original archive pieces from the 1930s and '40s, as worn by Leonardo DiCaprio in the Martin Scorsese film *The Aviator*. There are also jackets for women and kids, plus Belstaff accessories.
Mail order.

Bond International

17 Newburgh Street, W1F 7RZ (7437 0079/ www.bondinternational.com). Oxford Circus tube. **Open** 10.30am-6.30pm Mon-Sat; noon-5pm Sun. **Credit** AmEx, MC, V. **Sells** M.
Established in 1987, Bond International was one of the first stores in London to specialise in cult hip hop threads. Graffiti still adorns the walls of this shop and break beats boom out of the speakers. Stock includes clothing from BI's own label, as well as Silas, Stüssy and Alife. The best efforts from the staff's doodle book eventually make their way on to the own-label tees at £27. BI is also good for obscure T-shirt brands such as Answer, which features exclusive prints from the cult comic-book artist Vaughn Bode.
Mail order.

Boxfresh

13 Shorts Gardens, WC2H 9AT (7240 4742/ www.boxfresh.co.uk). Covent Garden tube. **Open** 10.30am-7pm Mon-Sat; noon-6pm Sun. **Credit** AmEx, MC, V. **Sells** M, W.
The continued use of the slogan 'We Are You', appropriated from the Zapatista guerrilla movement, is a little crass in these politically troubled times, and the drug-inspired theme of a recent collection (slogans include 'Drop Acid not Bombs') is just embarrassing. But the less self-conscious items from Boxfresh – baggy trousers, polo tops, Harrington jackets – remain reliable, and prices are manageable: jackets from £80, jeans £60, T-shirts from £25.
Mail order.

Bread & Honey

205 Whitecross Street, EC1Y 8QP (7253 4455/ www.breadnhoney.com). Barbican tube. **Open** 10am-6.30pm Mon-Wed, Fri; 10am-7pm Thur; 11am-5pm Sat. **Credit** AmEx, MC, V. **Sells** M, W.
Owned and run by Laurent Roure (buyer and expert on urbanwear) and Laurent Chaumet (nightclub promoter), this little gem houses an eclectic collection of funky T-shirts and internationally sourced streetwear labels. The store's stock is all hand-picked, upscale streetwear, mixing familiar labels like Stüssy and Lee Jeans with younger contenders such as MHI and Peruvian brand Misericordia. Recent additions include menswear brands Umbro by Kim Jones, Carhartt, Merlin and Duffer; for women there's now Religion, French label Sessùn, and Blood & Glitter jeans. There are also bags from Ollie & Nic, shoes from Swear, Block headwear, plus extras like toys and publications.
Mail order.

Carhartt

15-17 Earlham Street, WC2H 9LL (7836 1551/ www.carhartt-europe.com). Covent Garden or Tottenham Court Road tube. **Open** 11am-6.30pm Mon-Wed, Fri, Sat; 11am-7pm Thur; noon-5.30pm Sun. **Credit** MC, V. **Sells** M, W.
For 115 years, intuitive design and exceptional standards of durability and comfort have defined Carhartt's 'workwear' – high-quality products for both on and off the job. The American range is now complemented by urban designs from the European division. The jeans – available for both men and women in a variety of styles (£45-£70) – remain perennial favourites for rangy models, skaters and those in the creative industries. There are also some well-crafted, functional separates, plus shirts, sweatshirts, jackets and accessories – all uncomplicated, good looking and fairly priced.
For branches see index.

Cinch

5 Newburgh Street, W1V 1LH (7287 4941). Oxford Circus tube. **Open** 10.30am-6.30pm Mon-Sat. **Credit** MC, V. **Sells** M, W.
Shunning the pile-'em-high attitude of some denim retailers, Cinch is the hyper-cool testing ground for much of Levi's bleeding-edge product launches. Don't expect to find excessive bleaching, 'cat's whiskering' or any other shabby denim finishes here – Cinch is about offering purists the best in denim. It stocks the exclusive and pricier Levi's Red and Vintage lines (from £125 upwards), tees (around £35) by independent designers like Passarella Death Squad, Horace and the Failing Zebra, and some sweaters and jackets.
Mail order.

The Dispensary

200 Kensington Park Road, W11 1NR (7727 8797). Ladbroke Grove or Notting Hill Gate tube. **Open** 10.30am-6.30pm Mon-Sat; noon-5pm Sun. **Credit** AmEx, MC, V. **Sells** M, W, C.
The long-established Dispensary continues to offer an upfront selection of consistently good labels from around the world. Men's brands include favourites John Smedley, Oliver Spencer, Without Prejudice and Duffer, plus other obscure denim and T-shirt brands. The huge range of womenswear includes Citizens of Humanity jeans (£145), Only Hearts underwear, and Finnish brands Ivana Helsinki and Nanso. Mavi jeans for both sexes begin at £65 a pair. The Dispensary also sells its own tees, all at £18.
Mail order.
For branch see index.

DPMHI

2-3 Great Pulteney Street, W1F 9LY (0871 218 0260/www.dpmhi.com). Oxford Circus tube. **Open** 10am-7pm Mon-Sat; noon-5pm Sun. **Credit** AmEx, MC, V. **Sells** M, W.
The offshoot of the hip, military-inspired fashion label Maharishi (*see p54*), DPMHI stocks men's and women's clothes by sub-brand MHI, which takes a more urban and graphics-oriented approach to the basic Maharishi theme. Previous ranges have been designed in collaboration with graffiti artists; this season's clothes are inspired by Stanley Kubrick, with designs from films like *A Clockwork Orange* and *2001: A Space Odyssey* appearing on T-shirts (£35), hoodies, sweats and more. The shop also sells founder Hardy Blechman and Alex Newman's tome, *DPM: Disruptive Pattern Material; An Encyclopedia of Camouflage: Nature – Military – Culture*, as well as other art and fashion books, sought-after vinyl toys and sneakers. Designed by French architect François Scali, the industrial space is surprisingly relaxed, with an emphasis on street culture.
Mail order.

Evisu

9 Savile Row, W1F 3PF (7292 0500/ www.evisu.com). Green Park or Piccadilly Circus tube. **Open** 10am-6pm Mon-Wed, Fri, Sat; 10am-7pm Thur. **Credit** AmEx, MC, V. **Sells** M, W.
It's sure to ruffle a few elegant feathers, but premium denim brand Evisu has now set up permanent residence on Savile Row, the mecca of traditional tailoring. It offers a comprehensive range of Evisu's premium denim, with Heritage Denim jeans from £145 and tops from £65. There are also Evisu Deluxe suits (from £650), shirts (from £145) and a steady flow of limited-edition pieces from Japan. Evisu is also doing its bit to keep traditional tailoring alive, by offering a fully bespoke tailoring service in collaboration with the long-established Airey & Wheeler tailors, the former occupants of the shop.
Mail order.

Fenchurch

36 Earlham Street, WC2H 9LA (7240 7847/ www.fenchurchclothing.com). Covent Garden or Leicester Square tube. **Open** 10am-7pm Mon-Sat; noon-6pm Sun. **Credit** AmEx, MC, V. **Sells** M, W.
This clean-cut urban fashion brand, previously only available in scattered outlets across the capital, has finally opened its own flagship in the

fashion hive of Seven Dials. Exposed brickwork, good lighting and a sensibly compact range make for an enjoyable browsing experience. For autumn/ winter 2005/6, there are stripy knits in muted colours for men (£60) and slightly brighter ones for women (£55); simple jackets and duffel coats; a range of branded and design T-shirts (from £20); jeans in a variety of colours and washes (from £45); and lots of accessories, of which we particularly liked the aurora belt for girls (£45) and men's caps (£19). The current Kid Acne collection of tees adapts the Fenchurch 'rail tracks' logo into a variety of fun invented scenes: birds flying around a fountain, say, or pirates on a ship.
Mail order.

Firetrap

21 Earlham Street, WC2H 9LL (7395 1830/ www.firetrap.net). Covent Garden tube. **Open** 10am-7pm Mon-Wed, Fri, Sat. 10am-7.30pm Thur; noon-6pm Sun. **Credit** MC, V. **Sells** M, W.
This self-styled 'premium fashion jeanswear brand' launched in 1993 and opened this spacious flagship store in Covent Garden's trendy Seven Dials a little over a decade later. For autumn/winter 2005/6 men can find the usual range of well-cut jeans, plus branded retro track tops, stylised blazers, detailed shirts and funky leather jackets; women are equally well served by a selection of originally cut jackets, sweaters and skirts. Firetrap introduced its new Black Seal 50 Premium line in late 2004. Developed from the 'heavy slub' of Japanese Kurabo denim and inspired by the biker gangs of the 1950s, the jeans (from £80) are heavily distressed – they're not just stonewashed, but rather (seemingly) oil-stained or driven over – an indication of Firetrap's continuing dedication to 'interesting' new uses of fabric.

Fred Perry

Unit 6-7 Thomas Neal Centre, Seven Dials, WC2H 9LD (7836 4513/www.fredperry.com). Covent Garden tube. **Open** 10.30am-7pm Mon-Sat; noon-5pm Sun. **Credit** MC, V. **Sells** M, W.
One of the most recognisable brands in the world, Fred Perry manages to mix up its heritage with a dose of cutting-edge cool in its Covent Garden store. Standard-range shirts, jumpers and track tops are all here (from £60), plus some impressive clothing collaborations with the likes of Comme des Garçons (*see p26*), Mrs Jones and, more recently, Vinti Andrews, who has taken the classic polo shirt and decorated and distressed it in varied ways (£90). If that's not enough to coax you, there's also a bespoke shirt service (£75) and even a back room housing limited-edition imports and original collectable slim-fit polo shirts (from £55). The Newburgh Street branch is smaller, with a more boutiquey approach; the main Covent Garden store is better for sportswear.
For branches see index.

Griffin Concept Store

297 Portobello Road, W10 5TD (8960 9607/ www.griffin-studio.com). Ladbroke Grove tube. **Open** 10am-6.30pm Tue-Sat. **Credit** MC, V. **Sells** M, W.
This imaginative British urban label has built up an obsessive international following – apparently there are regular queues of up to 200 people outside the store in Japan. Founder and designer Jeff Griffin reinvents military-inspired clothing with unexpected shapes, textures and innovative details. Knitwear is heavy and distressed, jackets look as though they've been turned inside out, and trousers have zips along the seams. But although the label's slogan is 'Combat Tailoring', not everything connotes warfare – there are T-shirts with original prints (from £20) and plain-coloured sweats (from £45). Griffin also undertakes collaborations with oki-ni (*see p54*).
Mail order.

Hope & Glory

30 Shorts Garden, WC2H 9PX (7240 3713/ www.hopeandgloryclothing.com). Covent Garden tube. **Open** 10am-6.30pm Mon-Wed, Fri; 10am-7pm Thur, Sat; noon-5pm Sun. **Credit** MC, V. **Sells** M.

Trainerspotting

Why are trainers such big business? These days you can scarcely group them under the broader heading of fashion, as they've become a global industry in their own right. And we're pretty sure that the huge demand has little to do with, er, training. Sneaker culture, particularly the new limited-edition fad, cunningly taps into every bloke's – and it does seem to be a predominantly, though not exclusively, male thing – innate tendencies towards obsessiveness and competitiveness. There is even a book on the subject: *Sneakers: The Complete Collectors' Guide* (Thames & Hudson, £16.95).

The number of London shops that are given over mainly, or entirely, to trainers continues to grow. The latest contender is the **Onitsuka Tiger UK** flagship store (*pictured*), which opened in May 2005. Tiger illustrates the other curious thing about the sneaker business: in no other sphere do old products and designs enjoy such continual currency. At the new store you'll find an array of remakes of classic Onitsuka designs like the Mexico 66 and Javelin 75, alongside brand-new designs (retro-influenced, of course) such as the Gantrai Challenger Limited Edition (£80) and Mexico 2K5 (£70).

In the same mould are other brand flagships like the **Adidas Originals Store** (*see p50*). From here Adidas sells its inexhaustible ranges of retro and reinvented sneaks, plus other 'originals' like classic zip-ups, T-shirts and bags. One of the newest ranges is Adidas Oddity: five designs in impossibly strange colourways that somehow manage to work (from £65). Other classics, like the Trimm Trabb and Gazelle, are frequently remade. Hardened Adidas fans should, however, cut through Soho to **oki-ni** (*see p54*), where exclusive and highly original Adidas collaborations are purveyed.

Nike is the other huge brand trading on its heritage, and its trainers; everything from basketball boots to proper running shoes is available from the flagship store, **Nike Town** (*see p224*). Other big brands also have London flagships – **Puma** and **Vans** are neighbours in the Carnaby Street vicinity, while **RbK**, the Reebok spin-off, is over in Covent Garden.

If you haven't already invested your loyalty in a particular brand, and want to see a selection of the newest designs on offer, you could investigate one of the chain or independent trainer boutiques that pepper the city. Of the chains, **Size?** is a clear favourite; staff are experts and there's an up-to-the-minute selection of shoes from the big brands (Adidas, Nike, Puma), but also less predictable ones such as Lacoste and Gravis & Hurley. Also recommended is **Offspring**, which has Vans, Converse and Dunlop's Green Flash (in its myriad non-green varieties, of course).

But if you really want to indulge in a sport of one-upmanship, head to one of the independents. **Gloria's** has sneakers sourced from stockists in Hong Kong, Japan, New York and Europe, while **Meteor Sports & Leisure** is a cult sneak boutique known to attract celebrities with its limited editions from Nike, Rocafella and others. **Kazmattazz** also does a fine line in accessible rarities; owner Kayzar Dunasia has been collecting trainers since he was 13. Compact **Foot Patrol** boasts a very well-edited collection of current trainers; not far away is **Slammin' Kicks**, which selects hip hop-oriented Nike, New Balance, QMK and Adidas models. Another great independent is **my trainers**, which has K-Swiss, Gola and Dunlop, and staff will also track down genuine originals (rather than remakes). It also sells a collection of Japanese and American imports.

Foot Patrol

16A St Anne's Court, W1F 0BG (7734 6625/www.foot-patrol.com). Oxford Circus tube. **Open** 11am-7pm Mon-Fri; 11am-6.30pm Sat. **Credit** AmEx, MC, V.

Gloria's

6 Dray Walk, E1 6QL (7770 6024/ www.superdeluxe.net). Liverpool Street tube/rail. **Open** 10am-7pm daily. **Credit** AmEx, MC, V.

Kazmattazz

38-39 Hoxton Square, N1 6NN (7739 4133). Old Street tube/rail. **Open** 10.30am-6.30pm Mon-Thur; 10.30am-11pm Fri, Sat; 10am-5.30pm Sun. **Credit** MC, V.

Meteor Sports & Leisure

408-410 Bethnal Green Road, E2 0DJ (7739 0707). Bethnal Green tube/rail. **Open** 10.30am-6pm Mon-Thur; 10.30am-1pm, 2-7pm Fri; 10.30am-7pm Sat. **Credit** MC, V.

my trainers

3 Brixton Station Road, SW9 8PA (7274 0022/www.mytrainers.com). Brixton tube/rail. **Open** 10am-6pm Mon-Sat; noon-5pm Sun. **Credit** AmEx, MC, V.

Offspring

60 Neal Street, WC2H 9PA (7497 2463/ www.offspring.co.uk). Covent Garden tube. **Open** 10.30am-7.30pm Mon-Wed, Fri; 10.30am-8pm Thur; 10.30am-7pm Sat. **Credit** AmEx, MC, V. **For branches see index.**

Onitsuka Tiger

15 Newburgh Street, W1T 7RX (7287 7480/www.onitsukatiger.co.uk). Oxford Circus tube. **Open** 11am-7pm Mon-Wed, Fri; 11am-7.30pm Thur; noon-5pm Sat. **Credit** MC, V.

Puma

52 Carnaby Street, W1F 9QE (7439 0221/www.puma.com). Oxford Circus tube. **Open** 10am-7pm Mon-Sat; noon-6pm Sun. **Credit** AmEx, MC, V.

RbK

51 Neal Street, WC2H 9PQ (7240 8689/www.rbk.com). Covent Garden tube. **Open** 10am-7pm Mon-Sat; noon-6pm Sun. **Credit** AmEx, MC, V.

Size?

17-19 Neal Street, WC2H 9PU (7379 7853). Covent Garden tube. **Open** 9.30am-7.30pm Mon-Wed, Fri, Sat; 9.30am-8pm Thur; noon-6pm Sun. **Credit** AmEx, MC, V. **For branches see index.**

Slammin' Kicks

37 Beak Street, W1F 9RZ (7439 0180/www.slamminkicks.com). Oxford Circus or Piccadilly Circus tube. **Open** 10.30am-7pm Mon-Sat. **Credit** MC, V.

Vans Footwear Ltd

47 Carnaby Street (7287 9235). Oxford Circus tube. **Open** 10am-7pm Mon-Wed, Fri, Sat; 10am-8pm Thur; noon-6pm Sun. **Credit** AmEx, MC, V.

FASHION

Nowadays Hope & Glory never really hits the headlines, like it did as a small, original brand sold in Hyper Hyper back in early 1990s, but its simple, classic styles are just as strong. Knits, tees, jeans and jackets are straightforward slices of urban cool. For autumn/winter 2005/6, there are T-shirts with Victoriana-inspired prints (from £25), stripy knits (from £50) and, as always, a strong selection of jackets. Casual jackets in materials such as moleskin and tweed start at £140; these sit alongside more formal tailored jackets. Hope & Glory has also launched its first range of jeans: there are three washes available in loose and narrow fits, and prices are reasonable, at around £60. Also stocked is a select range of footwear by brands like Onitsuka Tiger and Converse. *Mail order.*
For branch see index.

Interstate
17 Endell Street, WC2H 9BJ (7836 0421). Covent Garden tube. **Open** 11am-6.45pm Mon-Fri; 10.30am-6.30pm Sat; noon-6pm Sun. **Credit** MC, V. **Sells** M.
One of the first UK stockists of Carhartt, Interstate remains one of the best places in London to pick up American workwear and related urban threads. Highlights include iconic Hanes tees (as worn by Marlon Brando in *A Streetcar Named Desire*), still widely regarded as the best white T-shirt money can buy, as well as clothes by G-Star, Woolrich, Penfield, jeans by Japanese brand Edwin, and heavy-duty jackets by New York company Spiewak (from £180). Eastpak bags are stocked in every shape and colour imaginable.

Levi's Store
174-176 Regent Street, W1R 5DF (7439 2014/ www.eu.levi.com). Oxford Circus tube. **Open** 10am-7pm Mon-Wed, Fri, Sat; 10am-8pm Thur; noon-6pm Sun. **Credit** AmEx, MC, V. **Sells** M, W, C.
Like Hoover was to vacuum cleaners, there was a time when the name Levi's was synonymous with all things denim. With so many other firms trying to get a piece of the pie, this flagship is designed to reassert the brand's supremacy. Taking its cues from theme parks – with a record shop, films, gallery space and opportunities to see the latest DJ or hot band – the shop aims to immerse you in the Levi's world. While all the plasma screens, flashing lights and MTV might weary more weathered shoppers, for younger generations this is a wonderland. It stocks all the key Levi's lines including Sta-Prest, Red Tab and 100%, all of which are made in a wide array of cuts, fits and washes. The jeans are complemented by a range of straightforward T-shirts, shirts and knits. *Mail order.*
For branches see index.

Mambo
39 Shelton Street, WC2H 9HJ (7438 9800/ www.mambo.com.au). Covent Garden tube. **Open** 10am-7pm Mon-Sat; 11.30am-5.30pm Sun. **Credit** AmEx, MC, V. **Sells** M, W.
Started by a couple of Aussie surf and graffiti addicts, Mambo has gone from strength to strength, churning out easily identifiable collections that are bright, bold and cheerful. Despite the obvious association with surfing, many of the clothes are much more street than beach. Quietly funky graphics adorn well-cut T-shirts, sweatshirts and skirts; the more beachy clothes, including swimwear, are louder. The women's range is more extensive than the men's, with feminine hoodies, skirts, strappy tops and dresses aplenty. A brand for both urban busybodies and beach bums.
For branches see index.

Maharishi
19A Floral Street, WC2E 9HL (7836 3860/ www.emaharishi.com). Covent Garden tube. **Open** 10am-7pm Mon-Sat; noon-5pm Sun. **Credit** AmEx, MC, V. Sells M, W, C.
In 1994, Hardy Blechman began Maharishi with the intention of reintroducing hemp into clothing on the grounds that it is more durable and environmentally friendly than cotton. His patterned

combat trousers became a late 1990s essential, and the brand has continued to grow in stature, even spawning sub-brand MHI, available at DPMHI (*see p52*). The clothes, especially the jackets, are based on simple military shapes, with subtly tweaked camouflage patterns and embroidery. Eastern mysticism is also key, so care labels on the garments also contain positive messages dedicated

to the wearer. The design of the shop merges Eastern influences with a raw industrial edge – further proof that trendy shops don't have to be boringly minimalist. *Mail order.*

Mash
73 Oxford Street, W1D 2EP (7434 9609/ www.mashclothing.com). Tottenham Court Road tube. **Open** 10am-7pm Mon-Wed, Fri, Sat; 10am-8pm Thur; 11am-6pm Sun. **Credit** AmEx, MC, V. **Sells** M, W.
Mash may not be in the sartorial epicentre of Covent Garden and the choice of labels might not be the most directional or exclusive, but there's certainly plenty to choose from on two floors. Expect to see skate- and street-influenced fashions from the likes of G-Star, Custard, Bench, Hooch, Million Dollar, Soochi and Komodo, to name but a few. Accessorise with baseball caps, Stone Roses-esque hats, trainers and rucksacks. *Mail order.*

Microzine
3-4A Little Portland Street, W1W 7JB (7704 6667/www.microzine.co.uk). Oxford Circus tube. **Open** 11am-6pm Mon-Fri; 10am-7pm Sat; noon-6pm Sun. **Credit** AmEx, MC, V. **Sells** M.
The original store in Angel had the air of a walk-in magazine. It sold the kind of exclusive clothes you see in men's mags like *GQ* and *Arena*, with the stock changing each month. Typical items include hard-to-find Adidas running shoes and the bizarre Brionvega Cuboglass – a crystal, cube-shaped TV. As we went to press, Microzine was in the process of moving to a new, smaller site in Little Portland Street, where the company intends to simmer down its stock by turning up the exclusivity even further. At the new, more boutiquey store, instead of stocking whole ranges, buyers will pick and choose the best single item from a range. And for limited periods the shop will be given over to a particular brand or product for a launch or showcase. *Mail order.*

oki-ni
25 Savile Row, W1F 3PR (7494 1716/www.oki-ni.com). Oxford Circus tube. **Open** 10am-6pm Mon-Wed, Fri, Sat; 10am-7pm Thur. **Credit** AmEx, MC, V. **Sells** M, W.
Oki-ni pioneered the idea of brand collaboration, and this Savile Row showroom continues to bring discerning consumers some of the most interesting and covetable products in the world. The oki-ni philosophy is more about reinventing classics than producing high fashions, hence collaborations with brands such as Adidas, 6876, Duffer of St George and Aquascutum. Current highlights include the Aquascutum reversible Harrington jacket (£450) – discreet black on the outside, a mayhem of colour on the inside – and a striking remake of the Adidas APS trainer in pink, burnt orange and dappled black and white (£125). *Mail order.*

Pepe
309 Portobello Road, W10 5TD (8960 7001/ www.pepejeans.com). Ladbroke Grove tube. **Open** 10am-6pm Mon-Sat. **Credit** AmEx, MC, V. **Sells** M, W.
Despite the fact that for some time now Pepe has been lagging behind other denim specialists – notably Levi's and Diesel – it finally seems to be making inroads with some significantly improved men's and women's clothes, friendly and intimate shops and great prices. The Notting Hill shop stocks a wide range of five-pocket Westerns and more contemporary styles, along with some covetable casualwear basics, T-shirts and a bespoke jeans service.

Quiksilver
Units 1 & 23, Thomas Neal Centre, Earlham Street, WC2H 9LD (7836 5371/www.quiksilver.com). Covent Garden tube. **Open** 10am-5pm Mon-Sat; noon-6pm Sun. **Credit** AmEx, MC, V. **Sells** M, W.
As well as being one of the most popular surf labels on the block, Quiksilver is one of the best

Stüssy

places to get snowboarding gear. The designs of its clothes – board shorts, T-shirts, cargo pants and baggy jumpers for the boys, micro-skirts, floral dresses and slinky bikinis for the girls – can border on the garish. There's a wide selection of accessories, including heavily branded hats, caps, key rings, wallets and watches, while surf gear includes boards, board bags, wetsuits and wax.
For branches see index.

Slam City Skates
16 Neal's Yard, WC2H 9DP (7240 0928/ www.slamcity.com). Covent Garden tube. **Open** 10am-6.30pm Mon-Sat; noon-5pm Sun. **Credit** AmEx, MC, V. **Sells** M, W.
An institution among the younger generation of skate kids desperate to tackle the complexities of a half-pipe rather then the mind-numbing boredom of an Xbox. It offers a wide range of skateboards, and some snowboards in winter, plus clothing and accessories, and even a delivery service. The label choice is exemplary – if you're into skating, at least – including We, Silas, Volcom, Fresh Jive, Stüssy and New Era, and footwear from Vans, Etnies, Emerica, DVS and Lakai. Jeans start at about £100, T-shirts at £25 and footwear at £50.
Mail order.

Stüssy
19 Earlham Street, WC2H 9LL (7836 9418/ www.stussystore.co.uk). Covent Garden tube. **Open** 11am-7pm Mon-Sat; 1-5.30pm Sun. **Credit** AmEx, MC, V. **Sells** M, W.
Twenty-five years old and still one of the finest streetwear labels around. Today, the shop is a more grown-up affair, with the minimalist interior lending the clothes a more designer feel. The baggy T-shirts, sweatshirts and combat-style parachute pants do a sterling job of mixing hip hop iconography with a collegiate sensibility, and prices remain palatable. There's little to tempt the ladies, but there is a nice line of accessories taking in everything from jewellery to umbrellas.
Mail order.

Urban Outfitters
200 Oxford Street, W1D 1NU (7907 0800/ www.urbanoutfitters.com). Oxford Circus tube. **Open** 10am-8pm Mon-Wed, Fri, Sat; 10am-9pm Thur; noon-6pm Sun. **Credit** AmEx, MC, V. **Sells** M, W.
You'll find everything you need for cool city living at this aptly named American emporium, which recently opened a huge flagship store on Oxford Street. After kitting out your flat with retro posters, Perspex chandeliers, vintage furniture from the Found Furniture range or various toys and games, you can peruse the extensive range of hip clothing for both sexes, including vintage pieces. Girls will find items from FrostFrench, Sonia by Sonia Rykiel and Fornarina, alongside a host of household names like Lee and more esoteric designers. Men will find clothes from Full Count, Gravis, Smedley and others. Prices often stretch the budget, and not everything is good value, but there are some superb one-off finds. It also has a branch of Carbon, the record shop and label that started off in the original High Street Kensington store.
Mail order.
For branches see index.

The World According To
4 Brewer Street, W1F 0SB (7437 1259). Leicester Square, Piccadilly Circus or Tottenham Court Road tube. **Open** 11am-6.30pm Mon-Sat. **Credit** AmEx, MC, V. **Sells** W.
Formerly called Shop, this Soho basement boutique opened in 1995 and has been a favourite with savvy Londoners ever since, on account of its high-end streetwear for women. It's the biggest UK stockist of Silas, including the upmarket offshoot Silas Babette, which has classier, more feminine clothes in superior fabrics (dresses from £230). There's also Anglomania from Westwood, Sonia by Sonia Rykiel, H by Hussein Chalayan and Tonite T-shirts. It also has Westwood jewellery and Cacharel perfumes, and is the exclusive UK stockist for Anna Sui cosmetics.
Mail order.

Bespoke

Tailors

Since a new generation of hip young tailors shook up fusty Savile Row in the 1990s, a wider section of the population has discovered the joys of individually made garments. While we haven't listed every tailor here, we've included noteworthy traditionalists, as well as those who are breathing new life into the craft. In general, a bespoke suit costs upwards of £2,000, requires several fittings and is completely hand-stitched, often on the premises, while made-to-measure is usually assembled in a factory, then hand-finished. However, these terms are not strictly adhered to, so it's best to consult your tailor about your requirements.

Savile Row W1

Gieves & Hawkes
1 Savile Row, W1S 3JR (7434 2001/www.gieves andhawkes.com). Green Park or Piccadilly Circus tube. **Open** 9.30am-6.30pm Mon-Thur; 9am-6pm Fri; 10am-6pm Sat. **Credit** AmEx, DC, MC, V.
It's fitting, really, that Gieves & Hawkes has occupied the prized Savile Row address – No.1 – for over 90 years. For bespoke tailoring it really is exemplary, offering superlative service, second-to-none knowledge of made-to-order (everything from military uniforms to ties and T-shirts), and sublime cut, finish and fabrication. The premises are spacious and airy and, under creative director James Whishaw (formerly of Calvin Klein), the company has been working hard to broaden its appeal to both men and women. As well as the classic Gieves & Hawkes ready-to-wear collection, a second label, Gieves, was launched in 2003, bringing Savile Row craftsmanship to an utterly contemporary, design-led collection. A bespoke suit starts at £2,750, made-to-measure £695 and ready-to-wear £550. Gieves & Hawkes is also available at Selfridges, Harvey Nichols, House of Fraser's City branch, Harrods and Selfridges. For something a bit different, opt for a pair of its bespoke jeans resplendent with military insignia.
For branch see index.

Henry Poole & Co
15 Savile Row, W1S 3PJ (7734 5985/www.henry poole.com). Green Park or Piccadilly Circus tube. **Open** 9am-5.15pm Mon-Fri. **Credit** AmEx, MC, V.
Credited with inventing the tuxedo, Henry Poole, whose shop was founded in 1806, was the first tailor on Savile Row. The shop is looking a little tired, but splash out £2,200 on a bespoke suit, and you're guaranteed to look smart. You'll also be in famous company – such disparate characters as Napoleon, Winston Churchill and 'Buffalo Bill' Cody have been on the client list. The suits really are a cut above the rest, using the finest Huddersfield worsteds, tweeds from the lowlands of Scotland and flannels from the west of England.

H Huntsman & Sons
11 Savile Row, W1S 3PF (7734 7441/www.h-huntsman.com). Green Park or Piccadilly Circus tube. **Open** 10am-6pm Mon-Fri; 10am-5pm Sat. **Credit** AmEx, MC, V.
H Huntsman & Sons prides itself on producing a bespoke suit that will last a lifetime. Just as well, really, given the prices – expect to shell out over £3,000 for a suit handmade on the premises, though ready-to-wear versions are available from £1,000. Its jackets are typified by a close fit, high shoulders and a very fitted waist. Huntsman also produces its own fabrics, introducing new tweeds

each year and resurrecting designs from the archives. True to its name, the former sporting tailor also makes dashing riding and hunting jackets. Despite its traditional image and over 150 years of history, the tailor has the stamp of fashion approval: Anderson & Sheppard-trained bad boy designer Alexander McQueen selected Huntsman to make his range of bespoke suits, available at his Old Bond Street shop (*see p24*). As well as suits, the Huntsman collection now incorporates sports coats and overcoats.

James & James
38 Savile Row, W1S 3QE (7734 1748/www.james james.co.uk). Green Park or Piccadilly Circus tube. **Open** 9am-5.30pm Mon-Fri. **Credit** AmEx, MC, V.
Mr James Jnr, trained by his founder father, is still at the helm here. J&J was the preferred tailor of the dapper Duke of Windsor, and one of his suits is displayed in the window. Though it now stocks some made-to-measure laser-cut shirts and suits from £750 (you can even do the measuring yourself and order online), its bespoke hand-stitched suits (from £2,200) and shirts are still much sought after, particularly among broader men. In addition, few tailors can cut a suit in denim better.

Kilgour
8 Savile Row, W1S 3PE (7734 6905/www.8savile row.com). Green Park or Piccadilly Circus tube. **Open** 9am-6pm Mon-Wed, Fri; 9am-7pm Thur; 10.30am-6pm Sat. **Credit** AmEx, DC, MC, V.
Arguably the film stars' favourite tailor, this distinguished outfitters has dressed leading men from Cary Grant to Hugh Grant. Its modern tailors have also attracted the likes of Noel Gallagher and Johnny Vaughan. The convergence of old and new is illustrated by the division of the premises into a classic English-style entrance and a contemporary Philippe Starck-furnished shop. The cut is characterised by structured lean shoulders and clean chest definition. Bespoke suits start at £1,400 (made abroad with one fitting) or from £2,800 (made on the premises with as many fittings as required), while hand-cut, off-the-peg suits start at a more affordable £750. The ready-to-wear collection includes cashmere sweaters, coats and understated shirts; a small selection is also sold at Liberty. Kilgour's sister company, equestrian clothier Bernard Weatherill, is based at the same address, where George Roden is the last man in the business to make riding breeches to measure. But keeping up with the times and responding to the demand for ultra-lightweight clothing, Kilgour has reconstructed its classic suit to make it 25% lighter, by quarter-lining the jacket and removing some of the trimmings.

Richard Anderson
Sherborne House, 13 Savile Row, W1S 3PH (7734 0001/www.richardandersonltd.com). **Open** 9am-5pm Mon-Fri; by appointment only Sat. **Credit** AmEx, MC, V.
One of the nicest men on Savile Row, Richard Anderson takes the pomp and stuffiness out of a visit to the tailor. The showroom is bright, comfortable and beautifully furnished, with a luxurious sofa covered in his signature fabric. The Anderson Line is the unique style – long and flattering to the body and cut high in the armholes to ensure that the jacket doesn't ride up – developed by the man himself. Never one to shy away from colour, Anderson's suits come in a palette that includes mid blue, orange, green and yellow. He is also credited for producing the first bespoke duffel coat on the Row, cut in the finest cashmere (from £2,700).

Richard James

29 Savile Row, W1S 2EY (7434 0605/www. richardjames.co.uk). Green Park or Piccadilly Circus tube. **Open** 10am-6pm Mon-Wed, Fri; 10am-7pm Thur; 11am-6pm Sat. **Credit** AmEx, DC, MC, V.

When Richard James was founded in 1992 by Richard James and Sean Dixon, many of the traditional tailors on Savile Row didn't think it would last more than a couple of years. But the company has now been credited with pioneering the 'modern classic' approach for Savile Row, and is very much here to stay. In line with the modern approach, the airy premises have polished beech floors, white-painted walls and contemporary displays more akin to those of a fashion designer. The signature (one-, two- or three-buttoned) single-breasted suit – heavily weighted with deep side vents in unusual fabrics, including camouflage, soft denim, rich velvets and jewel-coloured mohair – have attracted customers from the worlds of music, movies and politics. Bespoke prices start at £2,290, while off-the-peg suits range from £575 to £1,150. A made-to-measure, factory-produced option has recently been introduced from £1,100. As well as offering some slick luxury sports garb and denim, James has just launched some training shoes, developed in collaboration with cult Swedish brand Tretorn.
Mail order.
For branch see index.

Soho W1

Eddie Kerr

52 Berwick Street, W1F 8SL (7437 3727/ www.eddiekerr.co.uk). Oxford Circus tube. **Open** 8am-5.30pm Mon-Fri; 8.30am-1pm Sat. **No credit cards.**

Ever wonder where Graham Norton gets his outrageously flamboyant jackets? The talented Eddie Kerr and his son Chris operate from behind an understated green shopfront in Soho, but there's nothing subtle about many of their clients. However, in addition to ostentatious styles, such as velvet frock-coated suits, they create more traditional tuxedos, blazers and shooting jackets. Two-piece bespoke suits start at £850.

John Pearse

6 Meard Street, W1F 0EG (7434 0738/www.john pearse.co.uk). Piccadilly Circus tube. **Open** 10am-7pm Mon-Fri; noon-7pm Sat. **Credit** AmEx, MC, V.

Hailed by many as the godfather of new British tailoring, John Pearse combines a playful eccentricity with rock-solid tailoring credentials. After a traditional apprenticeship at Hawes & Curtis, he opened the legendary Granny Takes A Trip boutique in the 1960s, kitting out the likes of Cream, Jimi Hendrix and Mick Jagger in pony-skin shirts and frock coats. Sir Mick is still a customer, and has been joined by such snappy celebrity dressers as George Clooney, Brad Pitt and Jack Nicholson. At Pearse's laid-back Soho salon, ready-to-wear suits and coats are displayed in gothic wardrobes. There's also a selection of shirts (from £150) and some very naughty hand-painted silk ties, and an online shirt service is in the pipeline. Bespoke suits start at just over £1,760, and materials run the gamut from classic wools and tweeds to natty pinstriped denims and flamboyant floral prints. Pearse also sources vintage fabrics, which imbue his creations with an air of authenticity. Women are also catered for.

Mark Powell

12 Brewer Street, W1R 3FS (7287 5498/ www.markpowellbespoke.co.uk). Piccadilly Circus tube. **Open** by appointment only Mon-Sat. **No credit cards.**

Self-taught tailor Mark Powell draws freely on the Edwardian and Regency periods – an elongated silhouette here, a high-buttoned coat there – as well as on the styles of the 1960s and '70s. Widely known for his encyclopaedic knowledge of men's dress, he has successfully combined old-school fitting traditions and modern fashion sensibilities to create

suits with a dash of raffish attitude. He cites the cuts of the 1920s and '30s as a major influence (along with the late Tommy Nutter), and there's more than a touch of mob swagger to some styles – appropriate, given he's probably best known for tailoring a visiting-hours ensemble for banged-up East End gangster Ronnie Kray. Clients these days include traditional gents, as well as celebs like Naomi Campbell and George Michael. Bespoke suits start at £1,400, but there's also a ready-to-wear collection in the studio, from £750 for a suit, £120 for a shirt. His Brewer Street premises, with their dark woodwork and original yellow walls, have the feel of an Edwardian gentleman's club.
Mail order.

Elsewhere

Charlie Allen

1 Cooper's Yard, N1 1RQ (7359 0883/www. charlieallen.co.uk). Angel tube/Highbury & Islington tube/rail. **Open** by appointment only 9.30am-7pm Mon-Sat. **Credit** AmEx, MC, V.
Charlie Allen was head of menswear at the Royal College of Art, so not only does he turn out top-notch bespoke suits, he pays due attention to the whole outfit. The shirt, cufflinks, belt, even the socks are taken into consideration, and after-sales pressing and mending are also included in the £1,200-plus price tag. Allen dresses women as well as men, and has just expanded his business by adding an Italian-made ready-to-wear line that includes more casual pieces. His latest service, available at his Islington premises, allows you to design your own cloth – colour, weight and pattern.

Douglas Hayward

95 Mount Street, W1K 2TA (7499 5574). Bond Street or Green Park tube. **Open** 9am-5.30pm Mon-Fri. **Credit** AmEx, DC, MC, V.
Douglas Hayward is known for suits with a sleek silhouette – said to make the wearer look taller and slimmer – which have attracted such smoothies as Roger Moore, Hugh Grant and Michael Caine. Despite the lofty clientele and prices – from £2,000 for a bespoke suit – the atmosphere at his Mayfair premises is relaxed and informal. A selection of shirts and ties is available to pull the look together.

Imtaz

7 The Walk, Independent Place, Shacklewell Lane, E8 2HE (7503 3537/www.imtaz.com). Dalston Kingsland rail. **Open** 9am-5.30pm Mon-Fri; by appointment only Sat. **No credit cards.**
Trained at the London College of Fashion, qualified tailor and designer Imtaz Khaliq has designed for both business clients and a few stars, including supermodel Tatjana Patitz, Michelle Pfeiffer and Dina Caroll. She sketches designs, provides swatches and makes up suits for men and women. Prices start at £650 for a skirt suit and £750 for a trouser suit made from basic wool from Yorkshire. She also makes weddings dresses. Imtaz also offers exclusive tailoring classes at £27.50 an hour.

Jonathan Quearney

3 Windmill Street, W1T 2HY (7631 5132). **Open** 9am-5.30pm Mon-Fri; by appointment only Sat. **Credit** AmEx, MC, V.
Jonathan perfected his contemporary tailoring in Savile Row before starting his own business, which now retails from this plush shop in Fitzrovia. His made-to measure suits (from £700) have taken a back seat, as his more luxurious bespoke service moves to centre stage (prices from around £1,500 for a suit). There an in-house shirt-maker (from £125) and a tailoring-inspired ladies range (designed with his girlfriend), which can be found at no-one (see p37).

Nick Tentis

14 Hampden House, 2 Weymouth Street, W1W 5BT (7355 3399/www.nicktentis.com). Great Portland Street tube. **Open** by appointment only. **Credit** AmEx, MC, V.
Though not a tailor himself, Tentis employs a team of ex-Savile Row stitchers to create fully bespoke suits and a ready-to-wear collection with a modern

twist. The classic Tentis look marries a soft shoulder with defined waist and narrow lapel for a pared-down 1960s feel. Unlike the stiffer Savile Row outfitters, at Nick Tentis English tailoring is given an Italian accent to create a relaxed yet sharp signature style. The ready-to-wear range, which includes knitwear and accessories, as well as suits, has been expanded, but the bespoke service remains central to the business. Clients can opt for made-to-measure from £1,500 or full bespoke for £2,000. The latter is completely hand-stitched and, as a result, takes longer to produce.

Susannah Hall

110 Clerkenwell Road, EC1M 5SA (7253 4055/ www.susannahhall.co.uk). Farringdon tube/rail. **Open** 10am-6pm Mon-Wed, Fri; 10am-7pm Thur; by appointment Sat. **Credit** MC, V.
Individually created suits in traditional and innovative fabrics – including funky tweed – have won business and celebrity clients of both sexes. Prices are very reasonable – from just £500 for a suit, from £80 for a shirt – and the atmosphere in the shop is relaxed yet efficient, though you can have the tailor come to you. There is also a selection of exclusive ties and cufflinks.

Timothy Everest

32 Elder Street, E1 6BT (7377 5770/www. timothyeverest.co.uk). Liverpool Street tube/rail. **Open** 9am-6pm Mon-Fri; 9am-4pm every other Sat. **Credit** AmEx, MC, V.
What do Jarvis Cocker, Tom Cruise and David Beckham have in common? A fondness for handmade suits by the charming Timothy Everest. Former apprentice of Tommy Nutter, Everest is one of the shining stars in the cast of next-generation London tailors. He rejects the rigidity of more conventionally 'classic' cuts for easier styles of suit, often with a higher notch on the lapels and in a range of softer fabrics such as mohair. Bespoke two-pieces start at £1,595, but a made-to-measure suit can cost as little as £695.
Mail order.

Shirtmakers

Quality shirt chain **Pink** (85 Jermyn Street, SW1Y 6JD, 7930 6364, www.thomaspink.co.uk) has a made-to-order shirt service, with a choice of over 100 fabrics (from £125). As many traditionally tailored shirts require cufflinks, modern dandies looking for more interesting fastenings should check out **Duchamp** (75 Ledbury Road, W11 2AG, 8743 5999, www.duchamp.co.uk), which has a vast array of patterned enamel and jewelled options. For the maker of Jon Snow's eyecatching ties, *see p142* **Victoria Richards**. Those with quieter tastes might prefer some subtle silver cylinders or ovals from **Links of London** (*see p81*).

Budd

1A Piccadilly Arcade, SW1Y 6NH (7493 0139). Piccadilly Circus tube. **Open** 9am-5.30pm Mon-Thur; 9am-5pm Fri; 10am-5pm Sat. **Credit** AmEx, DC, MC, V.
Budd is the only family-owned bespoke shirtmaker in London that will still make shirts in its own workrooms. For four generations they have gathered knowledge and expertise to provide unrivalled service. Budd's dress shirts can include unusual details such as riding tails, and detachable cuffs and collars. Its evening shirts have appeared on the silver screen in films such as *The English Patient* and *Eyes Wide Shut*. Bespoke shirts cost from £125, in a choice of more than 1,000 fabrics; ready-made styles from £65; nightshirts and silk pyjamas are also available.
Mail order.

Emma Willis

66 Jermyn Street, SW1Y 6NY (7930 9980/ www.emmawillis.com). Green Park tube. **Open** 10am-6pm Mon-Sat. **Credit** AmEx, MC, V.
One of the few women among London's largely male shirtmaking fraternity, Emma Willis is less traditional than most Jermyn Street stalwarts.

Her trademark Swiss cotton shirts are available for men and women (from £190 bespoke, £120 ready to wear), with female clients particularly well catered for in the downstairs salon. Here, there are bespoke skirts, dresses and jackets in a range of eye-catching but irresistibly English colours and fabrics. If that's not enough to satisfy, it is one of the few companies left still offering a bespoke sock service, with each foot measured individually.
Mail order.

Harvie & Hudson
97 Jermyn Street, SW1Y 6JE (7839 3578/ www.harvieandhudson.com). Green Park or Piccadilly Circus tube. **Open** 9am-5.30pm Mon-Sat. **Credit** AmEx, DC, MC, V.
While most of the so-called 'family' shirtmakers were long ago snapped up by bigger companies, this establishment is still run by just two sorts of people: Harvies and Hudsons. The interior may be looking a little rough around the edges, but it's just another sign that nothing has really changed since the business was founded in 1949. Shirts are still cut in the back and made in H&H's London

workroom, whether semi-bespoke 'stock specials', adjusted to fit from existing patterns (from £99), or fully custom-made numbers in a full range of cut, shapes and styles (from £145 each), with Kent cut-away collars. For bespoke shirts, there is a minimum order of four, though you will be asked to wear and wash one first to make sure you're happy with it. Though known particularly for its bold business stripes, H&H has hundreds of other fabrics to choose from. It's quite a small-scale operation, so the process takes about 12 weeks. Ready-made options start at £50. Online ordering services are now available.
For branches see index.

Thresher & Glenny
50 Gresham Street, EC2V 7AY (7606 7451). Moorgate tube/rail. **Open** 9am-5.30pm Mon-Fri. **Credit** AmEx, DC, MC, V.
While gents can be completely outfitted by Thresher & Glenny, the company speciality is shirts. Its first royal warrant was granted by George III in 1783, and renewed by every succeeding monarch since, so the company has been exposed to more than its fair share of good

breeding – but, having also made suits for Lord Nelson and Garibaldi, it can claim to know something about the tough guys too. Shirts start at £59.50 off the peg, made to measure from £95.
For branch see index.

Turnbull & Asser
71-72 Jermyn Street, SW1Y 6PF (7808 3000/ www.turnbullandasser.co.uk). Green Park tube. **Open** 9am-6pm Mon-Fri; 9.30am-6pm Sat. **Credit** AmEx, DC, MC, V.
The original Jermyn Street shirtmaker (established 1885) may have shops in New York and Beverly Hills these days, but its London shop – complete with heavy wood panelling and grandfather clocks – has retained an old-fashioned character. The appeal is partly historic but, more importantly, it's the shirts that people (Prince Charles and Al Pacino) come back for. Immaculately cut from a choice of 1,000 fabrics, bespoke designs start at £145 (minimum of six – after wearing and washing one to ensure it still fits perfectly). But you can be in eminent sartorial company for less – ready-to-wear shirts start from £60. Ties, tailoring and womenswear are also sold.

Bespoke on a budget
If you frequent Savile Row, you can expect to shell out thousands for a bespoke suit, but go for a small-name local tailor and the prices are substantially more affordable. **Bertie Wooster** (*see p58*) also offers an extensive traditional English tailoring service at reasonable prices.

George's Tailors
50 Wightman Road, N4 1RU (8341 3614). Manor House tube. **Open** 8am-7pm Mon-Sat. **No credit cards.**
George Christodoulou, a Savile Row-trained tailor, uses his expertise in his own family-run business. He is known for his sharp mod suits and keen eye for detail. His handmade two-piece suits range from £450 up to £550 depending on the fabric chosen; he can also recreate styles from magazine pictures (from about £350 for a jacket).

Luke's Ladies and Gent's Tailors
348 Barking Road, E13 8HL (7476 5956). Canning Town tube. **Open** 9.30am-5.30pm Mon-Fri; 10am-5pm Sat. **No credit cards.**
This 30-year-old family business specialises in tailoring for weddings, and boasts City men and women, lawyers and a top-ranking judge among its clients. A basic made-to-measure suit comes in at a competitive £450. It can also replicate tailored garments from magazines or your wardrobe – as long as they are classics.

Norton & Townsend
3rd Floor, 111 Cannon Street, EC4N 5AR (7929 5662/www.nortonandtownsend.co.uk). Cannon Street tube/rail. **Open** by appointment only 9am-5.30pm Mon-Fri. **Credit** MC, V.
This shop will send someone to your home or office to get you measured up. The affordable prices are down to the company buying wool in bulk direct from cloth mills – therefore a two-piece suit is priced from a reasonable £525. It also offers made-to-measure shirts from just £60 and trousers from £180. A secret among City slickers.

Threadneedleman Bespoke Tailors
187 Walworth Road, SE17 7RW (7701 9181/ www.threadneedlemantailors.co.uk) Elephant & Castle tube/rail. **Open** 10am-6pm Mon-Sat. **No credit cards.**
George Dyer has been in business for the past 30 years, cutting suits for every smart British youth cult you care to imagine – he's now concentrating on mods, but has done teddy boys and skinheads in the past. He can also do a respectable City suit (from £550) and sharp ladies' suits, skirts and slacks from £150. George will happily visit disabled customers in their homes on request.

Kilgour. See p55.

Retro & Second-hand

Some shops in the **20th-century Design** chapter, notably **Ooh-La-La**, **Past Caring** and **Radio Days**, are worth a rummage for retro and vintage items, as is **Story** in the **Design, Art & Crafts** chapter. For specialists in vintage fancy dress, *see chapter* **Entertaining**. The Oxford Street branches of **Urban Outfitters**, **Topshop** and **Miss Selfridge** (conveniently located next door to each other) all now have vintage clothing sections too.

Vintage

Admiral Vernon Antiques Market

141-149 Portobello Road, W11 2DY (7727 5242/ www.portobello-antiques.co.uk). Notting Hill Gate tube. **Open** 5am-5pm Sat (outside stalls also open 10am-6pm Fri, Sun). **Credit** varies. **Sells** M, W, C.
Portobello Road Antiques Market can seem like a daunting jumble of stalls and arcades on Saturdays, but for vintage clothes hunters, the best place to start is Admiral Vernon. It's easily identified by the distinctive blue flags hanging outside and houses more than 180 stalls selling everything from antique lace and costume jewellery to tribal artefacts. Lyn Munro has an intriguing selection of baby clothes, lace collars and paisley throws, while Linda Bee offers an eclectic selection of costume jewellery. Sadie Ead (of *Vintage Modes, see p60*) sells a carefully selected range of vintage clothing. Outside the building, Jacquie Allmond's mini Portobello outpost of Gadjo Dilo (*see below*) is well worth a visit for gorgeous 1960s prints, beaded textiles and tribal clothing. Prices range from a few pounds into the thousands, but bargaining is possible.

Annie's Vintage Clothes

12 Camden Passage, N1 8ED (7359 0796). Angel tube. **Open** 11am-6pm Mon, Tue, Thur, Fri; 9am-6pm Wed, Sat. **Credit** AmEx, MC, V. **Sells** W, C.
In the 30 years she has been in business, Annie Moss has built up a solid reputation and a loyal following. Her shop is airy, pretty and feminine, full of fluttering chiffon and lace. The focus here is mainly on clothes from the 1920s and '30s. Beaded flapper dresses sell for anything from £400 to £900, while those with less cash to splash could pick up a cashmere cardigan for £48. There is a great selection of 1930s tea dresses, bias-cut silk nighties and vintage wedding dresses starting from around £250.

The Antique Clothing Shop

282 Portobello Road, W10 5TE (8964 4830/ 8993 4162). Ladbroke Grove tube. **Open** 9am-6pm Fri, Sat; also by appointment. **Credit** AmEx. **Sells** M, W, C.
A wonderful patchwork quilt of shop, packed from floor to ceiling with gorgeous antique dresses, silks, shawls, pencil scarves and petticoats. You could happily spend days here, sifting through the vast range of clothes and accessories dating from the 1890s to the 1970s. Flapper dresses cost from £250 to £800, 1940s and '50s daywear starts from around £50. It's a good place for menswear too, with a whole section of the shop dedicated to blazers, old school scarves, shoes and ties.
For branch (The Vintage Home Store) see index.

Appleby

95 Westbourne Park Villas, W2 5ED (7229 7772/ www.applebyvintage.com). Westbourne Park tube. **Open** 11am-6pm Mon-Sat. **Credit** AmEx, MC, V. **Sells** W.
Only the most immaculate pieces make it on to the rails of Jane Appleby-Deen's shop – a favourite among film and TV wardrobe scouts. Her stock is an interesting mix of pieces from the early 1920s through to the 1980s. Most customers come here if they are looking for something special; at the time of writing there were some great 1970s Ossie Clark designs, starting at £230 for a shirt. While the bulk of the clothes are over £80, cheaper items have been introduced. Appleby-Deen also supplies the Vintage Princess range to Topshop.

Bertie Wooster

284 Fulham Road, SW10 9EW (7352 5662/ www.bertie-wooster.co.uk). Earl's Court or Fulham Broadway tube. **Open** 10am-6pm Mon-Fri; 10am-5pm Sat. **Credit** MC, V. **Sells** M.
Any man looking for sharp tailoring on a budget will be pleased to hear about this well-kept secret, a hit with dapper City boys. Bertie Wooster also specialises in top-quality second-hand suits, handmade leather shoes and hats. You can find a beautiful Savile Row suit here for around £120 for the jacket and £45 for the trousers. There are also some very gentlemanly cufflinks, as well as hunting and fishing gear, including plus fours.

Biba Lives

Alfie's Antique Market, 13-25 Church Street, NW8 8DT (7258 7999/www.bibalives.com). Edgware Road tube/Marylebone tube/rail. **Open** 10am-6pm Tue-Sat. **Credit** AmEx, MC, V. **Sells** M, W, C.
While you can find the occasional Biba item here, that's not where this stall gets its name; owner Sonia Smith-Hughes has been nicknamed Biba since her school days. All of the pieces, which date from the 1930s to the '80s, are in excellent condition and have a Biba Lives label sewn inside. Prices for dresses range from £40 to £500 for a full-length gown. Men's shirts and jackets sell from £20 upwards. You may stumble across a designer item, but clothes are chosen more on the basis of individual appeal than the label.

Blackout II

51 Endell Street, WC2H 9HJ (7240 5006/ www.blackout2.com). Covent Garden or Tottenham Court Road tube. **Open** 11am-7pm Mon-Fri; 11.30am-6.30pm Sat. **Credit** AmEx, MC, V. **Sells** M, W.
A small shop crammed full of goodies ranging from the 1920s to '70s, with a few items from the '80s. Items are arranged beneath chronological labels, which makes for easier, as well as more interesting, browsing. Blackout II is a great destination for unusual and flamboyant one-off pieces. We found a stunning red and white wide-check 1940s dress for £60, but dress prices start at £24. Sparkly evening bags line a shelf just above the ceiling, and there is a good selection of multicoloured shoes in the basement.

Butler & Wilson

189 Fulham Road, SW3 6JN (7352 8255/ www.butlerandwilson.co.uk). South Kensington tube. **Open** 10am-6pm Mon, Tue, Thur-Sat; 10am-7pm Wed; noon-6pm Sun. **Credit** AmEx, MC, V. **Sells** W.
Fans of costume jewellery have been snapping up Simon Wilson's flamboyant baubles for 25 years; less well known is the fact that Butler & Wilson's Fulham Road shop has a treasure trove of vintage clothes upstairs. The era-spanning stock includes Victorian crocheted tops and shawls, sequinned 1920s dresses and 1960s mini dresses. There is also antique jewellery, including some beautiful Victorian black jet pieces. Prices start from about £100 for sequinned shawls and bolero tops, going up to £2,000. Jewellery prices start at around £258 for a brooch. The room is often shut around lunchtime, so it is probably wise to time your visit for before noon or after 3pm.
Mail order.
For branch see index.

Circa Vintage Clothes

8 Fulham High Street, SW6 3LQ (7736 5038/ www.circavintage.com). Putney Bridge tube. **Open** 10am-6pm Mon-Fri; 11am-5pm Sat; also by appointment. **Credit** AmEx, MC, V. **Sells** W.
This vintage boutique, with plush red sofas and trompe l'oeil walls, houses a hand-picked collection of clothes dating from 1920s (sequin and beaded dresses and boleros) through to 1970s pieces by Ossie Clark, Zandra Rhodes and Missoni. At the time of writing, Clark was very much in evidence, with pieces from around £250. The Circa Back to Life collection comprises rejuvenated vintage items.

Cloud Cuckoo Land

6 Charlton Place, Camden Passage, N1 8AJ (7354 3141). Angel tube. **Open** 11am-5.30pm Mon-Sat. **No credit cards. Sells** W.
This tiny shop competes with nearby Annie's to offer the most beautifully delicate, feminine pieces. While the stock covers wide ground, from Victorian times to the 1960s, the focus is on the 1920s, '30s and '40s, including day dresses for around £50-£60. More unique pieces command higher prices, such as a beautiful Chinese turn-of-the-20th-century hand-embroidered skirt we spotted for £185. Kitsch 1950s handbags decorated with diamanté, poodles or shells are ever popular.

Cornucopia

12 Upper Tachbrook Street, SW1V 1SH (7828 5752). Pimlico tube/Victoria tube/rail. **Open** 11am-6pm Mon-Sat. **Credit** MC, V. **Sells** M, W.
An old-fashioned place that has been in business for about 30 years, housing a huge, overflowing selection of clothes from the Victorian period up to the present day. Owner Jerry Richards and his colleague Ralph are happy to guide you through the overwhelming selection of stock. Most of it falls into the 1920s-1970s category and many items cost around £25. Womenswear is very strong (especially long evening gowns).

Gadjo Dilo

531 Battersea Park Road, SW11 3BL (7585 1770). Sloane Square tube then 319 bus/44, 344 bus. **Open** 2-6pm Mon-Fri; noon-6pm Sat. **Credit** MC, V. **Sells** W.
Not your run-of-the-mill vintage emporium, this shop in a quiet Battersea backwater, which brims with vivid colours, beading and gorgeous patterns, is a boon for boho fashion fans. Owner Jacquie Allmond is a former stylist and chooses her clothes for their texture, colour and craftsmanship, sourcing pieces from far-flung places such as Peru, India and the Far East. Most garments range from the early 1900s to the '80s and prices are reasonable (from around £28). We lusted after Allmond's selection of long dresses (£65-£125), including bold-patterned, old Hollywood halter-neck styles picked up in Palm Springs, and heavily beaded and embroidered numbers from Pakistan. Sara Sanskara's vintage-inspired textiles are also for sale. Highly recommended.

Gallery of Antique Costume & Textiles

9 Connaught Street, W2 2AY (0845 207 9981/ www.gact.co.uk). Marble Arch tube. **Open** by appointment 10.30am-6pm Tue-Sat. **Credit** AmEx, MC, V. **Sells** W.

More like a museum than a shop in its historical scope, the Gallery sells antique clothing dating back to the 17th century, all in immaculate condition. And indeed, the shop has supplied pieces to museums; it's also a source of inspiration for fashion designers. But it's not all crinolines and breeches – it's a great place to find 1930s bias-cut evening gowns, '40s day dresses, '50s skirt suits and 1960s coats. There are also some exceptional antique textiles, including heavily embroidered Middle Eastern fabrics and 18th-century damask. As you might expect, prices are high for the more unusual and older clothing: expect to pay between £295 and £895 for a 1930s evening dress. But not everything in here is prohibitively expensive; prices for daywear start from around £50.

The Girl Can't Help It
Alfie's Antique Market, 13-25 Church Street, NW8 8DT (7724 8984/www.thegirlcanthelpit. com). Edgware Road tube/Marylebone tube/rail. **Open** 10am-6pm Tue-Sat. **Credit** AmEx, MC, V. **Sells** M, W.
Sparkle Moore and Cad van Swankster's sprawling stalls overflow with bygone glamour and more than a dash of kitsch. Blonde bombshell Moore's lingerie from the 1940s and '50s is fit for a pin-up; it's sourced from America, where quality is superior to the British equivalent. There are also Joan Crawford-esque evening dresses and a selection of spectacular, Mexican hand-painted circle skirts (from £150), plus eye-catching bags and shoes. Van Swankster's selection of suave Hollywood-style menswear is of a similar vintage. The ex-mixologist also has a collection of cocktail shakers, tiki mugs and risqué bar accessories.

Hilary Proctor: Advintage
Shop E20, Lower Gallery, Grays Antique Markets, South Molton Lane, W1K 5AB (7499 7001/ www.graysantiques.com). Bond Street tube. **Open** 10.30am-6pm Mon-Fri. **Credit** MC, V. **Sells** W.
If you want to stand out from the crowd, pay a visit to Hilary Proctor, who was a personal shopper at Fenwick for ten years. Highlights at her quirky little stall include wonderful antique kimonos and 1930s bias-cut dresses. On a recent visit, we unearthed a beautiful '60s navy linen Biba coat for £185. Proctor is well known for her fabulously unusual bags. For label hunters, she also sells some unusual arm candy by Gucci, Christian Dior and Louis Vuitton, mostly at her smaller stall in Admiral Vernon Antiques Market (*see above*).

Hurwundeki
98 Commercial Street, E1 6LZ (7392 9194/ www.hurwundeki.com). Liverpool Street tube. **Open** 10am-7pm Mon-Sat; 11am-7pm Sun. **Credit** MC, V. **Sells** W, M.
Browsing in this murky, wood-beamed basement feels like rooting around in someone's cellar, well-stocked with fabulous finds. Clothes range from Victorian costumes to 20th-century evening dresses. You can pick up American 1950s daywear from as little as £15 for a skirt, or splash out on a Valentino number for £450. There is also a rich cache of accessories: you could pick up anything from a vintage identity bracelet to a delicately carved hand mirror. There are tonnes of unique shoes, plus handbags by heavyweight designers, which tend to be around the £200 mark.

Mary Moore
5 Clarendon Cross W11 4AP (7229 5678/ www.marymoorevintage.com). Holland Park tube. **Open** 11am-6pm Tue-Sat. **Credit** AmEx, MC, V. **Sells** W.
With its exotic vermilion wallpaper and kaleidoscopic clothes collection, Mary Moore's new Holland Park vintage shop stands out from its low-key neighbours. Moore, a flamboyant former theatre designer and daughter of the sculptor Henry Moore, has been an avid collector of top-notch vintage clothing for the past 40 years. In that time she's picked up some real treasures, from immaculate 1940s tweed coats to sculptural '80s cocktail dresses, via '60s Jackie O-style skirt suits. The shop is an edited selection of some of her 1,000-strong collection. What makes Moore's shop

Virginia. See p60.

different to other vintage shops across London is the fact it has such a unique personal style: bold, bright and slightly eccentric. More expensive than your average vintage shop – but the quality and condition are so much better.

One of a Kind Too
259 Portobello Road, W11 1LR (7792 5853/ www.oneofakind.co.uk). Ladbroke Grove tube. **Open** 11am-6pm Mon-Thur; 10am-6.30pm Fri, Sat; 10am-5pm Sun. **Credit** MC, V. **Sells** M, W, C.
Clothes hang from every available surface in this stylish shop, including the ceiling, creating an Aladdin's Cave atmosphere. There are interesting and covetable clothes from every era, from Victorian times onwards. Unusual pieces by designers such as Chanel, Pucci, Gucci and Vivienne Westwood attract local celebrities. Prices start at around £25 for accessories, going up into the thousands for a spectacular evening dress (the sister shop sited a few doors along, open by appointment only, has even more expensive confections). The shoe room at the back is well worth checking out.
For branch (One of a Kind) see index.

Orsini Gallery
76 Earl's Court Road, W8 6EQ (7937 2903/ www.orsini-vintage.co.uk). Earl's Court or High Street Kensington tube. **Open** noon-6.30pm Mon-Sat. **Credit** AmEx, MC, V. **Sells** W.
A long-standing feature of Earl's Court, the Orsini Gallery was taken over a couple of years ago by Sophie Bulley, who has introduced more wearable

stock and a glamorous, fresher feel. Stock spans most of the last century, with particular emphasis on the 1920s to the 1950s. There is also a fine selection of beaded bags (£35-£80) and an impressive selection of hats (£45-£60).

Palette London
21 Canonbury Lane, N1 2AS (7288 7428/ www.palette-london.com). Highbury & Islington tube/rail. **Open** noon-6.30pm daily. **Credit** MC, V. **Sells** M, W.
Mark Ellis's stylish 'lifestyle boutique' combines carefully selected vintage pieces with more contemporary clothing and furniture. He introduces two themed collections a year: the latest fuses the structure of the 1940s with the glamour of the '70s. Items are sourced from America, the Far East and Europe, and all the vintage clothing is in pristine condition. Expect to find original and individual gems from designers such as Ossie Clark, Pucci, Jean Varon and Oscar de la Renta; prices range from around £125 to £900. Ellis also runs a vintage sourcing service. Look out for his menswear shop, due to launch in Hoxton towards the end of 2005.

Persiflage
Alfie's Antique Market, 13-25 Church Street, NW8 8DT (7724 7366). Edgware Road tube/rail. **Open** 10.30am-6pm Tue-Sat. **Credit** AmEx. **Sells** M, W.
This top-floor shop in Alfie's Antique Market packs masses of character into a tiny space. It's the place to come for trimmings: sift through

sequins, buttons, beads, cottons, laces, silks and other luscious bits and bobs. Many of the beads and sequins here come from the remaining stock from the famous Hartnell beading atelier, and over 2,000 knitting patterns are sold. Prices are low.

Rellik
8 Golborne Road, W10 5NW (8962 0089/ www.relliklondon.co.uk). Westbourne Park tube. **Open** 10am-6pm Tue-Sat. **Credit** AmEx, DC, MC, V. **Sells** M, W.
Arguably the trendiest of London's retro shops, Rellik (located across the street from the love-hate landmark Trellick Tower) counts models, designers and fashion journalists among its loyal customers. It was set up by three stallholders from Portobello Road Antiques Market, who pooled their individual specialities to ensure a diverse mix. Clothes range from the 1920s to the 1980s, taking in pieces by Vivienne Westwood, Pucci, Yves Saint Laurent, Bill Gibb, Ossie Clark and Zandra Rhodes among many others.

Sheila Cook
184 Westbourne Grove, W11 2RH (7792 8001/ www.sheilacook.co.uk). Notting Hill Gate tube. **Open** by appointment only. **Credit** AmEx, MC, V. **Sells** W.
Sheila Cook's shop can be visited only by appointment, which does not deter her fan base of serious collectors and fashion devotees. Cook's thoughtfully selected collection of antique clothes, costumes and textiles ranges from the late 1700s to the 1970s, and her discerning eye is the result of around three decades of experience. Clothes can be either bought or hired, and the collection includes a good range of trimmings, ribbons, fabrics and lace.

Shikasuki
67 Gloucester Avenue, NW1 8LD (7722 4442/ www.shikasuki.com). Camden Town or Chalk Farm tube. **Open** 11am-7pm Mon-Sat; noon-6pm Sun. **Credit** AmEx, MC, V. **Sells** M, W.
Shikasuki is a delightful dressing-up box of a shop, brimming with vintage gems for men and women. There are too-good-to-take-out handbags, like a show-stopping 1950s gold clasp covered in multi-coloured stones (£85), plus vintage jewellery. Downstairs are separate men's and women's vintage clothing boutiques and an enticing mirror-tiled changing room. The carefully edited selection encompasses everything from shoes, wedding and party dresses, to kilts, shirts and suits (a men's black and white check suit comes in at £150). The service is personal and the collection irresistible.

Steinberg & Tolkien
193 King's Road, SW3 5EB (7376 3660). Sloane Square tube/11, 19, 22, 49, 319 bus. **Open** 11am-6.30pm Tue-Sat; noon-6pm Sun. **Credit** AmEx, DC, MC, V. **Sells** W.
Reputedly housing London's largest collection of vintage clothing, Steinberg & Tolkien is something of a London legend, the haunt of *Vogue* fashion staff and supermodels. Prices start at £10 and rocket into the thousands. The clothes, spanning 1890 to 1990, are a mixed bag: you could find beautifully preserved Pucci, Westwood or Clark, but there are also mounds of damaged or dirty clothes with inflated price tags. Certainly worth a visit, but since the rise of the trend, there are many worthy competitors for its crown.

Still
61D Lancaster Road, W11 1QG (7243 2932). Ladbroke Grove tube. **Open** 11am-6pm Mon-Sat; noon-4pm Sun. **Credit** DC, MC, V. **Sells** W.
A zingy selection of hand-picked vintage pieces, housed in a refreshingly bright and colourful shop. On a recent visit we found a couple of fantastic handbags: one was wicker and covered in seashells (£125), the other was a 1940s tapestry bag in the shape of a house (£145). There were also some delicious oversized '70s sunglasses and chiffon gloves, as well as fur jackets. Vintage stock is complemented by the shop's own retro-inspired label, which starts at £65 and includes hand-embroidered, hand-woven and organic items.

Tin Tin Collectables
Alfie's Antique Market, 13-25 Church Street, NW8 8DT (7258 1305/www.tintincollectables. com). Edgware Road tube/Marylebone tube/rail. **Open** 10am-6pm Tue-Sat. **Credit** AmEx, MC, V. **Sells** W, C.
Fans of the Belgian comic-book hero will be disappointed. You won't find him here, but you will find a specialist selection of period clothing from 1900 to 1930. The well-loved stall is a staple of costume researchers for period films, and it also sells to museums. Aspiring flappers, in particular, are well catered for, with an excellent selection of beaded dresses at around £200-£300. There are also some items from later decades, such as a brocade Hardy Amies coat from the 1930s, or a Biba dress from the 1960s (around £250).

Vintage Modes
Grays Antique Markets, 1-7 Davies Mews, W1K 5AB (7409 0400/www.vintagemodes. co.uk). Bond Street tube. **Open** 10am-6pm Mon-Fri. **Credit** MC, V. **Sells** W.
Vintage Modes only opened a couple of years ago, but has quickly become a popular (and award-winning) landmark on the vintage scene. Seven dealers operate from the premises, the red velvet and gilt decor which gives it a 'basement boudoir' feel. Between them, they offer a diverse overview of fashion from 1890 to 1980. Prices are sane, and designer names include such leading lights as Jean Muir, Chanel, Pucci, Mary Quant and Biba.

Virginia
98 Portland Road, W11 4LQ (7727 9908). Holland Park tube. **Open** 11am-6pm Mon-Fri; by appointment only Sat. **Credit** AmEx, DC, MC, V. **Sells** W.
This is easily the most beautiful vintage clothing shop in London, and worth a visit for the ambience alone. In contrast to the strip lighting and incessant pop music of high-street stores, the calm recalls another era. A beaded curtain leads out to a small garden, while the basement is a pale cloud of floaty petticoats, chiffons and laces. Virgina Bates selects exquisite pieces from Victorian times through the 1940s and everything is in pristine condition. Prices are not cheap, but quality is reliably impeccable, making Virginia a favourite haunt of fashion A-listers, including John Galliano, who uses it as a research source. Prices range from around £350 for a Victorian petticoat to £3,000 for a beaded 1920s flapper dress.

What the Butler Wore
131 Lower Marsh, SE1 7AE (7261 1353/ www.whatthebutlerwore.co.uk). Lambeth North tube/Waterloo tube/rail. **Open** 11am-6pm Mon-Sat. **No credit cards**. **Sells** M, W.
Murals of Rita Tushingham and Paul Weller gaze down at you as you browse this intimate shop's well-chosen selection of British clothes. A few pieces are from the 1940s and '80s, more are from the 1950s, but the biggest selection is from the 1960s and '70s, including Biba and Mary Quant rarities. Shoes are a forte here (£20-£80), dresses start at £15 and suits are priced at £60 upwards. Vinyl junkies should head downstairs, where record shop Downbeat specialises in reggae oldies.

Retro & contemporary

Absolute Vintage
15 Hanbury Street, E1 6QR (7247 3883/ www.absolutevintage.co.uk). Liverpool Street tube/rail. **Open** by appointment only Mon; noon-7pm Tue-Sat; 11am-7pm Sun. **Credit** AmEx, MC, V. **Sells** M, W.
If you're after a pair of second-hand shoes or boots, look no further. If you can't find them here, you can't have looked hard enough: this big warehouse space is packed to bursting point with slips-ons, heels, stilettos and cowboy boots in all the colours of the rainbow. This shop is more about style and individuality than designer labels (although we did find a tasty pair of Manolos for £85). There is also a huge selection of dresses, particularly long-sleeved '70s styles. Prices are reasonable.

Beyond Retro

Bang Bang

21 Goodge Street, W1T 2PJ (7631 4191). Goodge Street tube. **Open** 10am-6.30pm Mon-Fri; 11am-6pm Sat. **Credit** MC, V. **Sells** W.

Bang Bang rocks. The shop is full of eccentric, original and stylish clothes, with something for everyone. If you want rich-bitch labels, they're here (we recently saw Marc Jacobs patent leather stilettos for £150 and a Pucci dress at around £1,000). But it isn't all about designer finds: you may spot a psychedelic-print dress from the '60s, a silk kimono or a crushed-velvet bed jacket, and many items are under a tenner. Accessories are a highlight, with quirky bags and a fantastic selection of big, bold earrings. Fancy selling your own cast-offs? If they pass the rigorous inspection, you'll get 30% of the potential price tag in cash, or 50% in merchandise.

Beyond Retro

112 Cheshire Street, E2 6EJ (7613 3636/ www.beyondretro.com). Liverpool Street tube/rail. **Open** 10am-6pm Mon-Sat; 11am-7pm Sun. **Credit** MC, V. **Sells** M, W.

On a Brick Lane side street, this is a great one-stop shop for fashion-conscious retro clothing at palatable prices. The vast, yellow-walled warehouse space has rails and rails of vintage wardrobe staples, including denim, tutus and leather jackets. You'll also find flight bags, old skool trainers and much, much more. There is a wide selection of very reasonably priced dresses, and when we last popped in, we bagged a stunning pale silk kimono for £45.

Cenci

4 Nettlefold Place, SE27 0JW (8766 8564/ www.cenci.co.uk). West Norwood rail. **Open** 11am-6pm Tue, Wed, 1st wknd of month; also by appointment. **Credit** AmEx, DC, MC, V. **Sells** M, W, C.

This purveyor of American and Italian clothing from the 1940s to the 1980s used to be something of an institution in Covent Garden, where it had been based since 1985. Last year, the owners relocated to their wholesale warehouse, which they have turned into a vast shop on two floors. Clothing now covers broader ground – from the 1930s to contemporary – but the majority is from the 1960s. The larger premises allows more room for accessories, such as hats, bags, cases, cufflinks, ties, jewellery, brooches and even old pens, pencils and cigarette cases. Italian 1960s tailor-made suits can be snapped up for £75, while '40s and '50s handbags range from £67 to £145.

Dolly Diamond

51 Pembridge Road, W11 3HG (7792 2479/ www.dollydiamond.com). Notting Hill Gate tube. **Open** 10.30am-6.30pm Mon-Fri; 9.30am-6.30pm Sat; noon-6pm Sun. **Credit** AmEx, MC, V. **Sells** M ,W, C.

A recommended haunt for fans of post-war chic, Dolly Diamond sells vintage clothes from the 1920s to the '70s, mostly focused on the '40s and '50s. Bridalwear is also a speciality. There are lots of chiffon dresses and gloves, beaded evening accessories and some original Liberty-print dresses from £145. Designer names are not the shop's main interest, but the odd big-name pieces do turn up.

The Emporium

330-332 Creek Road, SE10 9SW (8305 1670). Cutty Sark DLR. **Open** 10.30am-6pm Wed-Sun. **Credit** MC, V. **Sells** M, W.

For vintage fans, the main attraction in Greenwich is neither the Observatory nor the Cutty Sark, but this shop, where prices are more reasonable than in central London. The emphasis is slightly more on menswear than womenswear (though there's a good range of eveningwear for women, with dresses from £50, and most items are from the 1950s, '60s and '70s. The Emporium is famous for its vintage sunglasses, with a strong selection of sought-after '70s designer styles (from £45).

Episode

26 Chalk Farm Road, NW1 8AG (7485 9927). Camden Town or Chalk Farm tube. **Open** 11am-7pm daily. **Credit** MC, V. **Sells** M, W.

Although fairly new on the Camden scene, Episode has been luring customers away from the Stables Market opposite with very reasonable prices and the high quality of its stock. Most items are from the 1970s, '80s and '90s, but there are some '60s pieces too. There are separate menswear and womenswear sections, while the upper level is dedicated to accessories. Adidas tracksuit jackets from the 1970s sell for £45, while '70s and '80s dresses go for around £20. Episode also sells an interesting collection of clothing made from recycled second-hand clothes (for example, a dress made out of two or three old vintage frocks) for around £33.

Evil Cathedral

29 Grimsby Street, E2 6ES (07932 439 050). Liverpool Street or Shoreditch tube. **Open** 1-7pm Wed-Sat; 10am-7pm Sun. **Credit** AmEx, DC, MC, V. **Sells** M, W.

In a cavernous railway arch just off Brick Lane, a man named Dexter lurks in this lair, surrounded by crammed rails of vintage clothing. Dexter has possibly the longest dreadlocks of any man in London, stretching straight down past his waist, which he sometimes wears in pigtails. With dungarees. And red plastic sunglasses. Dexter doesn't like these sorts of guides and has expertly dodged inclusion – until now. This is a fantastic, dank place, selling all sorts of odd stuff from the 1960s through the '90s, including unusual denim, old high-tops, back issues of *The Face*, chopper bikes, records and rollerboots. Prices are cheap, and the punk sensibility is a defiant two fingers in the face of the Shoreditch pretentiousness.

Junky Styling

12 Dray Walk, The Old Truman Brewery, 91-95 Brick Lane, E1 6RF (7247 1883/www. junkystyling.co.uk). Liverpool Street tube/rail. **Open** 10am-6.30pm daily. **Credit** AmEx, MC, V. **Sells** M, W.

Junky Styling is a whole new take on second-hand clothing. The formula is simple: owners Kerry Seager and Anni Saunders take two or more items of formal clothing (a pinstripe suit, a men's shirt and a tweed jacket, for example) and recycle them into an entirely new garment (skirts £50-£200; jackets £120-£350), always sharply tailored, usually with a hint of grunge. Alternatively, you can bring your own clothes to the shop's 'Wardrobe Surgery' to be transformed into a new garment of your choice in two to four weeks. There is also a range of bags, most of which are also made from recycled menswear, from £15 to £120.

Loewy

21 Earlham Street, WC2H 9NN (7836 3440). Covent Garden tube. **Open** 11am-7pm Mon-Wed; 11am-8pm Thur-Sat; noon-6pm Sun. **Credit** MC, V. **Sells** M, W.

A new addition to Covent's Garden retro shops, Loewy is also a welcome one for its comprehensive, well-laid-out and reasonably priced stock, most from the 1950s to the '80s. Both the menswear and womenswear are strong here, with a collection of leather jackets, military wear, T-shirts, denim, sports tops (£20-£60) and some very striking dresses. This shop's real trump card, however, is found downstairs: a room entirely dedicated to accessories. There's a floor-to-ceiling display of sunglasses (all a reasonable £15 each), row upon row of shoes and a whole wall of belts.

ModernAge Vintage Clothing

65 Chalk Farm Road, NW1 8AN (7482 3787/ www.modern-age.co.uk). Chalk Farm tube. **Open** 10.30am-6pm daily. **Credit** MC, V. **Sells** M, W.

Away from the crowds of Camden Market, this small shop usually comes up trumps. Clothes range from the 1940s to the 1970s; the menswear is particularly splendid, including leather jackets, trousers, corduroy blazers, suit jackets and ties. ModernAge also sells its own popular line of vintage-inspired, frill-fronted tuxedo shirts, which come in a choice of nine colours (£39). For women, there is a good selection of dresses from the 1950s to the '70s, starting at around £15. Unusually, there is a range of retro swimsuits. The shop also runs

Movietone Frocks, a warehouse open by appointment only that hires clothes (7482 1066, www.movietonefrocks.co.uk).
Mail order.

The 1920s-70s Crazy Clothes Connection

134 Lancaster Road, W11 1QU (7221 3989). Ladbroke Grove tube. **Open** 11am-7pm Tue-Sat. **Credit** AmEx, DC, MC, V. **Sells** M, W.

This is just as every vintage shop should be: an eccentric, unpredictable jumble of everything from plastic ski goggles to a pair of stunning '70s platforms. The shoe room at the back is also packed with treasures. Prices are as unpretentious as the shop itself: we found a striking cheesecloth shirt with hand-stitched details for £10. Shopping here is a bit of an adventure – like rummaging through a school drama cupboard. The friendly owner's enthusiasm is infectious.

Pop Boutique

6 Monmouth Street, WC2H 9HB (7497 5262/ www.pop-boutique.com). Covent Garden tube. **Open** 11am-7pm Mon-Sat; 1-6pm Sun. **Credit** AmEx, MC, V. **Sells** M, W.

A hit with younger shoppers for its low prices and the speedy turnover of its goods. Most of the stock is from the 1950s and the 1980s, including printed dresses, tracksuit tops, T-shirts and vintage jeans. Pop Boutique also sells its own inexpensive vintage-inspired range of clothes; a bag made from original '70s curtain fabric is around £15, while the own-label jeans and skinny canvas trousers for men and women (both £25) have long been a cult favourite among vintage-style aficionados.

Retro Man/Retro Woman

16, 20, 28, 32 & 34 Pembridge Road, W11 3HL (7792 1715/7221 2055/www.mveshops.co.uk). Notting Hill Gate tube. **Open** 10am-8pm daily. **Credit** AmEx, MC, V. **Sells** M, W.

This cluster of shops is a familiar Notting Hill landmark. They are run on an exchange basis and stock comes from the general public. On the whole, buyers get a pretty good deal, but be careful about selling here: you may not always get the best price. The shops are heavy on labels, and on a recent visit we found a Vivienne Westwood corset for £160. In the menswear shops, there is a lot of vintage sportswear; Adidas tracksuit tops sell for about £30. There are also Savile Row suits (£200-£300).

Ribbons & Taylor

157 Stoke Newington Church Street, N16 0UD (7254 4735). Stoke Newington rail/73 bus. **Open** 11am-6pm Tue, Wed, Fri, Sat; 11am-7.30pm Thur; noon-5pm Sun. **Credit** MC, V. **Sells** M, W.

Catering to Stoke Newington's vintage lovers, this place is worth a bus trip if you're not local. Prices are sane, and there's good range of skirts and dresses from the 1950s to the '70s. Menswear is also good, with a strong selection of leather jackets (£27-£40). New stock arrives regularly and items are priced down according to how long they have been in the shop.

Rokit

42 Shelton Street, WC2 9HZ (7836 6547/ www.rokit.co.uk). Covent Garden tube. **Open** 10am-7pm daily. **Credit** AmEx, MC, V. **Sells** M, W.

From its humble roots in Camden, Rokit has expanded, with a flagship store in Covent Garden and two shops of Brick Lane. Each has a slightly different focus. In the main Covent Garden shop there is a comprehensive selection of second-hand clothing, including dresses, skirts, tutus, military wear, leather jackets and denim (prices from £10). There is also a good selection of accessories and shoes including cowboy boots and trainers (£35-£50). Stock in the Camden store is similar, with clothes packed into much smaller, two-floor premises. The shops in Brick Lane specialise in Americana and have a slightly more cutting-edge vibe. For guys, there is a good selection of old sportswear including team T-shirts and vests (from £12), and Hawaiian shirts (around £50). For the ladies, there is a wide choice of shoes and cowboy boots in good condition, as well as 1950s

FASHION

Thrift solutions

Fashion stylist **Bay Garnett** on buying vintage designer.

One of the most satisfying things about thrifting is finding fabulous classic designer labels at low prices. Nothing beats the thrill of uncovering an old Chanel handbag or an original 1970s Yves Saint Laurent pussy-bow shirt for just a few quid in a dusty corner of a charity shop. These things might sound dated and grannyish, but they can easily be updated and worked into a modern wardrobe, lending it a quirky twist.

New designer items are prohibitively expensive, but with a little effort it's possible to find them for a fraction of the price in charity shops. The trick is to know precisely which charity shops to target – you don't want to be sifting through last season's H&M, after all. To find the classics, you have to target areas that have been wealthy for decades, such as Chelsea and Belgravia, rather than recently rich places like Islington and Notting Hill.

The **British Red Cross** in Chelsea has superb old designer pickings, including 1960s Biba dresses and 1980s Versace and Armani. I usually find a Krizia jacket or some Chanel pumps, and it has great accessories too, such as Gucci wallets and designer handbags. Regular designer and vintage evenings are also held, when the shop's newest and best stock is showcased.

Oxfam on the King's Road is also a safe bet for designer classics at low prices, while Kensington Church Street has several stand-out charity shops, including the **Notting Hill Housing Trust** and **Trinity Hospice Shop**. Among all the bric-a-brac at these places, you can usually find an old Yves Saint Laurent cashmere jumper, say, or a Burberry trench. The **Red Cross Shop** on Ebury Street is another of my favourites. The last time I dropped by, I happened upon the most wonderful Chanel coat, which was dramatically cheaper than it would have been in Steinberg & Tolkien (see p60). Here you can also find old Hermès belts, and one of my all-time favourite things: a 1980s gilt Chanel belt.

British Red Cross Shop
67 Old Church Street, SW3 5BS (7351 3206). Sloane Square tube. **Open** 10am-5.30pm Mon-Wed, Fri; 10am-7pm Thur; 10am-6pm Sat. **Credit** MC, V.

The Notting Hill Housing Trust
57 Kensington Church Street, W8 4BA (7937 5274). High Street Kensington tube. **Open** 10am-6pm Mon-Sat; 1-6pm Sun. **Credit** MC, V.

Oxfam
123A King's Road, Shawfield Street, SW3 4PL (7351 7979). Sloane Square tube. **Open** 10am-5pm Mon-Sat. **Credit** MC, V.

Red Cross
81 Ebury Street, SW1 W9QU (7730 2235). Victoria tube/rail. **Open** 10am-5.30pm Mon-Fri; 10am-4pm Sat. **Credit** MC, V.

Trinity Hospice Shop
31 Kensington Church Street, W8 4LL (7376 1098). High Street Kensington tube. **Open** 10am-4.45pm Mon-Sat; 11am-5pm Sun. **Credit** MC, V.

worn. Because of the area, prices tend to be fairly high. There is a good selection of Jimmy Choo shoes, many unworn.

The Dress Box
8 Cheval Place, SW7 1ES (7589 2240). Knightsbridge or South Kensington tube. **Open** 10am-6pm Mon-Fri; 10.30am-6pm Sat, Sun. **Credit** AmEx, DC, MC, V. **Sells** M, W.
Made up of two adjoining shops, this is the oldest and most established of the Cheval Place agencies. The Dress Box is heavy on rich-bitch labels such as Dior, Gucci, Louis Vuitton, Chanel and Hermès – one room is devoted to the latter two labels.

The Dresser
10 Porchester Place, W2 2BS (7724 7212/ www.thedresseronline.co.uk). Marble Arch tube. **Open** 11am-6pm Mon-Fri; 11am-5pm Sat. **Credit** MC, V. **Sells** M, W.
The Dresser focuses on contemporary labels (including couture) and sells to a younger, trendier market than many of London's dress agencies. Often stylists and celebrities drop off unwanted clothes here, which means there is usually a very fine selection of goodies by labels such as Marc Jacobs, Gucci and Missoni.

Frock Market
50 Lower Richmond Road, SW15 1JT (8788 7748). Putney Bridge tube. **Open** 10.30am-6pm Mon-Sat. **Credit** AmEx, MC, V. **Sells** W.
The owner of this shop looks out for items with 'wow' factor, making it a great place to pick up a quirky bargain. Most of the stock is less than two years old, by designers such as Voyage and Prada, though there is also a vintage presence.

L'Homme Designer Exchange
50 Blandford Street, W1H 3HD (7224 3266). Baker Street tube/Marylebone tube/rail. **Open** 11am-5pm Mon-Thur, Sat; 11.30am-5pm Fri. **Credit** AmEx, DC, MC, V. **Sells** M.
Unusually, this one is just for the boys, selling designer clothes only. Much of the clothing is nearly new couture, which has been worn once in a film, a television advert or a magazine shoot. All the top names are here.

Pandora
16-22 Cheval Place, SW7 1ES (7589 5289/ www.pandoradressagency.com). Knightsbridge or South Kensington tube. **Open** 10am-7pm Mon-Sat; noon-6pm Sun. **Credit** AmEx, MC, V. **Sells** W.
The biggest of the Cheval Place dress agencies, Pandora boasts a good collection of Chanel suits (£500-£2,000) and bags by designers such as Dior, plus a cabinet full of Swarovski crystal pieces.

Salou
6 Cheval Place, SW7 1ES (7581 2380). South Kensington or Knightsbridge tube. **Open** 10am-5pm Mon-Sat. **Credit** MC, V. **Sells** W.
Salou is dominated with rows and rows of *Sex and the City*-esque heels by much-coveted labels such as Manolo Blahnik and Jimmy Choo. Bags and sunglasses are further strengths. Salou also sells clothing, ranging from Joseph up to Chanel.

floral skirts and punky 1980s ball gowns; No.107 has more expensive, specially selected items and unusual one-off pieces. Vintage homeware has recently been introduced.
For branches see index.

The Shop
3 Cheshire Street, E2 6ED (7739 5631). Liverpool Street tube/rail. **Open** noon-6pm Thur; 9am-3pm Sun. **No credit cards. Sells** M, W, C.
This well-kept Shoreditch secret is open only for a very short period each week, and regulars queue outside the door to be the first in. The wait is amply rewarded with great prices for high-quality clothing. Most of the stock is from the 1950s to the '70s, and is lovingly ironed and repaired. Space is also given over to vintage textiles such as curtain and dress fabrics from the '40s to the '70s, and some delicious buttons and bits and bobs. Silk scarves by Hermès and Chanel can be found here for as little as £1. The Shop also has a large selection of handbags, almost all under £15.

Wow Retro
10-16 Mercer Street, WC2H 9QE (7379 5334). Covent Garden tube. **Open** 11.30am-6.30pm Mon-Fri; 11am-7pm Sat; noon-5pm Sun. **Credit** MC, V. **Sells** M, W.
Wow Retro comprises two big shops: one for women and one for the gentlemen. The men's shop has a good selection of old skool trainers (from £15

to £250 for pristine Air Jordans) and Adidas sports bags (from £20). It is also a popular destination with the pink pound for leather wear. Over in womenswear, there is a sprinkling of designer names supplementing a base of quirky, non-brand pieces, mostly from the '60s to the '80s. There is a good selection of psychedelic-print dresses, unusual ponchos and a wide range of corsets.

Dress agencies

Bertie Golightly
48 Beauchamp Place, SW3 1NX (7584 7270/ www.bertiego.co.uk). Knightsbridge or South Kensington tube. **Open** 10am-6pm Mon, Tue, Thur-Sat; 10am-7pm Wed; noon-5pm Sun. **Credit** AmEx, MC, V. **Sells** W.
Former stunt girl Roberta Gibbs started this shop, which specialises in new, nearly new and second-hand evening wear, in the early '80s. There's a comprehensive selection of ball gowns, with prices starting at £250, and accessories are a strong point.

Designer Bargains
29 Kensington Church Street, W8 4LL (7795 6777). High Street Kensington tube. **Open** 10am-6pm Mon-Sat. **Credit** AmEx, MC, V. **Sells** W.
The lunching ladies of Kensington keep Designer Bargains freshly stocked with the very top end of the designer spectrum (Gucci, Chanel, Prada), often bringing in items that have never been

Charity shops

Travel to Kensington, Chelsea, Notting Hill and Marylebone for designer cast-offs from wealthy local residents (the Oxfam shop on Gloucester Road is especially good). If you want to locate your nearest charity shops, consult the **Association of Charity Shops** (7255 4470, www.charityshops.org.uk), which has a shop locator on its website. You can also visit the sites of individual charities, such as **Oxfam** (www.oxfam.org.uk) and **Salvation Army Charity Shops** (www.salvationarmy.org.uk). The Brixton branch of **Traid** (2 Acre Lane, SW2 5SG, 7326 4330, www.traid.org.uk) has a great selection, including its own customised second-hand clothes. Some dress agencies also act as charity fundraisers, notably the **Dresser** (see above). See also above **Thrift solutions**.

Weddings

The average cost of a wedding now stands at a colossal £17,000, and a good place to start deciding how to spend all that money is the twice-yearly (February and October 2006) **National Wedding Show**, held over three days at either Earl's Court or Olympia (tickets 0870 730 0064, www.nationalweddingshow. co.uk). More exclusively upmarket is the **Designer Wedding Show** in Battersea Park in November (box office 0870 190 9098, www.designerweddingshow.co.uk), where bridal fashion comes courtesy of the likes of top designers Vera Wang and Carolina Herrera. From 2006 the show will be held in February and October.

For stand-alone hat shops, *see chapter* **Fashion Accessories**, and for rings and big-day accessories, *see chapter* **Jewellery**. If you're looking for a party organiser or professional videographer, *see chapter* **Entertaining**.

One-stop

Confetti

80-81 Tottenham Court Road, W1T 4TE (0870 774 7177/www.confetti.co.uk). Goodge Street tube. **Open** 10am-6.30pm Mon-Wed, Fri, Sat; 10am-8pm Thur; noon-6pm Sun. **Credit** MC, V.
The Confetti website, rather than the shop, should be your first port of call upon starting the mammoth organisational task of wedding planning. Advice and suggestions on themes, etiquette, readings and insurance are all clearly laid out, and there's a wedding dress guide that lets you search by style and price (you're referred to the designer when it comes to the actual purchase). The shop offers budget-conscious items like stationery, candles, wedding music compilation CDs, balloons and an inexplicable pick 'n' mix counter. The wedding planning folder (£29.99) should prove a useful purchase.
Mail order (0870 840 6060).

Bridal shops

Department stores are a good place to set off on your quest for the perfect dress, as they provide an idea of the styles and fabrics on the market. For exclusivity, head to the Wedding Shop at **Liberty** (*see p13*), while affordability is **Debenhams** (*see p12*) domain, with its Designers at Debenhams lines. High-street chains are also worth keeping in mind for both adult and child bridesmaids' outfits – in particular, **Monsoon** (*see p41*), which offers perfectly respectable wedding gowns for a couple of hundred pounds.

Basia Zarzycka

52 Sloane Square, SW1W 8AX (7730 1660/www.basias.com). Knightsbridge or Sloane Square tube. **Open** 10am-6pm Mon-Sat. **Credit** MC, V.
Effervescent designer Basia Zarzycka specialises in realising dreams of fairy-tale wedding gowns. Intricacy and quality craftsmanship are key attributes of her designs, which are all bespoke and sewn up by a staff of 20. Fabric flowers, embroidery and beading all feature heavily on the £5,500-plus creations, while easy finishes like zips are anathema. Tiaras and accessories start at £150, theatrical costume jewellery is from around £45. During the dress fitting, the charming staff will also include a styling session to give a clearer picture of the final look.
Mail order.

Browns Bride

59 Brook Street, W1K 4HS (7514 0056/www. brownsfashion.com). Bond Street tube. **Open** by appointment 11am-6pm Mon-Sat. **Credit** MC, V.
This dedicated bridal outpost of Browns' finger-on-the-pulse fashion boutiques (*see p35*) is the place to come for prestigious and hard-to-find labels. Alberta Ferretti, Emanuel Ungaro and Badgley Mischka are all stocked alongside lesser-known but equally impressive designers. Monique Lhuillier's dresses, particularly the multi-tiered numbers, are truly spectacular, with elaborate detailing and evident craftsmanship. In general, prices aren't as steep as you might expect (starting at under £1,000 and moving up to £7,000), and these are catwalk-quality gowns to treasure.

By Storm

11 Chiltern Street, W1U 7PF (7224 7888/ www.bystorm.co.uk). Baker Street tube. **Open** 10am-6pm Tue-Sat. **Credit** MC, V.
This shop's USP is a collection of outfits specially designed for weddings abroad. They're lightweight, easily transportable and include some truly original ideas, such as a delicate lace jacket teamed with wide-legged organza trousers. There's a good choice of traditional dresses, some with pretty pink or gold detailing (£1,000-£3,000), plus an imaginative range of gowns incorporating tartan, if you'd like to co-ordinate with a kilt-wearing groom.

Caroline Castigliano

62 Berners Street, W1T 3NN (7636 8212/ www.carolinecastigliano.co.uk). Oxford Circus tube. **Open** 10am-6.30pm Mon-Wed, Fri, Sat; 10am-8pm Thur. **Credit** MC, V.
Castigliano is a big name in British bridalwear, and it's down to the simplicity and excellent quality of her gowns. One of the key looks is the structured bodice, which can be combined with a variety of skirt styles. Shrugs also feature frequently and are a pretty addition. A selection of pieces by other designers is also available; particularly impressive is a halter-neck number by Endrius, which leaves the back bare. Expect to pay an average of £2,500, though some styles are available at £1,800.

Christiana Couture

53 Moreton Street, SW1V 2NY (7976 5252/ www.christianacouture.com). Pimlico tube. **Open** by appointment only. **Credit** MC, V.
Christina Marty's designs are all about delicate femininity – she's a past winner of the 'Full Romantic' British Bridal Award. A starting budget of £2,900 is required, but this does get you a personally tailored couture service. Options range from slinky bias cuts to modern versions of fuller skirts, with key detailing like crystal trims and vintage-look lace trains added on. If you fall in love with what you see but can't quite stretch the budget that far, an off-the-rack range in sizes 8-18 is available at Caroline Castigliano (*see p63*).

Johanna Hehir

10-12 Chiltern Street, W1U 7PR (7486 2760/ www.johanna-hehir.com). Baker Street tube. **Open** by appointment 11.30am-7pm Mon-Fri; 10am-6pm Sat. **Credit** MC, V.
Designers and business partners Johanna Hehir and Paul O'Donoghue are taking a stand against the meringue. Instead, their tailor-made dresses are about making an impression without being over the top. They still do the full-skirted look, just in a lighter and less cumbersome way – one dress in this category has a two-tiered silk hem over a sleek tulle skirt for £3,050. Or go for a grown-up prom-dress style featuring a pink flower print and ribbon on a calf-length dress (£1,900).
Mail order.

Morgan Davies

62 Cross Street, N1 2BA (7354 3414/www. morgandavieslondon.co.uk). Angel or Highbury & Islington tube. **Open** by appointment 10am-6pm Mon-Sat. **Credit** MC, V.
There's a tastefully selected medley of designers to choose from here. For unfettered glamour, make a beeline for Jenny Packham's gowns. A-listers such as Helena Christensen and Kristin Davis love her eveningwear, and the bridal collection radiates the same appeal. The Alan Hannah range is replete with architectural ruching and handpainted details. Reem Acra specialises in dramatic designs embellished with embroidery or beading. All dresses range from £1,500 to £4,500.

Pronuptia

95 Hatton Garden, EC1N 8NX (7419 9014/ www.pronuptia.co.uk). Chancery Lane tube. **Open** 9.30am-5.30pm Mon-Wed, Fri, Sat; 9.30am-8pm Thur; 11am-4pm Sun. **Credit** MC, V.
With several branches in the London area and more nationwide, Pronuptia is as close as you'll get to a bridalwear chain. The big lure is the reasonably priced designs – a simple column dress is available for just under £400. The range of gowns on offer is huge and encompasses some surprisingly stylish styles for the prices. For an outfit that eschews tradition, consider the Intuition ensemble, with a corset top and trousers overlaid with a diaphanous skirt (£595). Headdresses, veils, shoes, bridesmaids' dresses and men's outfits (for sale or hire) are also stocked. **For branches see index.**

Ritva Westenius

28 Connaught Street, W2 2AS (7706 0708/ www.ritvawestenius.com). Marble Arch tube. **Open** by appointment 9am-6pm Mon-Sat. **Credit** AmEx, MC, V.
For guaranteed quality, head for this Finnish-born designer's boutique. Ritva Westenius won the prize for Outstanding Contribution to the Bridal Industry 2005 and has nearly 30 years' experience in the wedding business. Dresses are awash with beautifully original details, such as a garland of fabric roses around the waist or luxurious draping with a sexy side split. Prices start at £1,500 and climb far higher for the full couture service.

Basia Zarzycka

Sarah Owen

3 Junction Mews, W2 1PN (7262 4086/
www.sarahowenlondon.co.uk). Edgware Road tube.
Open by appointment 10am-7pm Mon-Fri; 10am-
5pm Sat. **Credit** MC, V.

Despite her small collection, Sarah Owen seems to
have a dress to suit every occasion. From her
signature look (an A-line, duchesse satin affair) to a
pleated 1920s-style slip dress and a bias-cut crêpe
gown with plunging cowl back, each is exquisitely
designed and carefully made. Owen carries out
fittings in person and her honest approach will help
you choose what's best for you. An off-the-peg dress
goes for between £1,500 and £2,500, while bespoke
designs start at £3,000. A pretty (but unremarkable)
range of tiaras is available, as well as gorgeous
shoes by Jean-Claude Bidi, starting at £250. Allow
a minimum of six months for your order.

Stewart Parvin

14 Motcomb Street, SW1X 8LB (7235 1125/
www.stewartparvin.com). Hyde Park Corner or
Knightsbridge tube. **Open** by appointment 10am-
6pm Mon-Sat. **Credit** AmEx, MC, V.

For those with serious money to spend, Stewart
Parvin's couture designs are a safe bet, costing
between £3,500 and £12,000. Following a two-hour
viewing with the welcoming staff, you can create
your own version of the designer's substantial
dresses, featuring made-to-measure corsetry, A-lines
and fishtails. The structured designs are great for
bigger sizes. The diffusion line at the Wedding Dress
Shop (*see below*) is more affordable (£1,250-£2,600).

Suzanne Neville

29 Beauchamp Place, SW3 1NJ (7823 9107/
www.suzanneneville.com). Knightsbridge tube.
Open by appointment 10am-6pm Mon-Sat.
Credit AmEx, MC, V.

Suzanne Neville's designs are award-winning, and
the quality of her work is plain to see. Dresses are
handmade and high-end – expect to pay upwards
of £1,500, with many hovering around the £2,000
mark. The range is extensive and runs through an
assortment of styles. Even the modestly named
Classic collection is awash with imaginative
detailing. Gowns are dressed up with draping, lace,
organza, smatterings of feathers or pearls… the
list is seemingly endless. If you have a style in
mind, Neville probably has it covered. If not, this
is the place to come for inspiration.

The Wedding Dress

First floor, Harrods, Brompton Road, SW1X 7XL
(7225 5933/www.harrods.com). Knightsbridge
tube. **Open** by appointment 10am-7pm Mon-Sat;
noon-6pm Sun. **Credit** AmEx, DC, MC, V.

A modest collection of dresses by seven designers
is housed in this corner of Harrods. The gowns are
mostly quite traditional affairs – you won't find
anything ground-breaking here. Prices range from
£2,500 to £8,000 for dresses, and there's a shoe
collection too. A few dresses by the well-known
Caroline Castigliano (*see p63*) are available, with
some nice details like a marabou stole. Atelier Aimée
dresses feature a lot of beadwork, while those by
Max Chaoul come in lilac or mint green tulle.

The Wedding Dress Shop

174 Arthur Road, SW19 8AQ (8605 9008/
www.theweddingdressshop.co.uk). Wimbledon Park
tube. **Open** by appointment 10am-5pm Mon-Sat.
Credit AmEx, MC, V.

A high-quality collection of ready-to-wear and
custom-made dresses (£950-£2,200) is available
here. Blue by Angela Pitcher features understated,
flattering dresses in silk, with lovely details like
covered buttons down the back (that's what your
guests will be looking at during the ceremony).
Emilie Costa's designs feature lace overlays and
interestingly structured trains, while Watters &
Watters do bridesmaids' dresses you'd consider
wearing for other occasions too.

The Wedding Shop

171 Fulham Road, SW3 6JW (7838 0171/
www.weddingshop.com). South Kensington tube.
Open by appointment 10am-6pm Mon-Sat. **Credit**
AmEx, DC, MC, V.

The Wedding Shop's dress department is the only
place you can go for a much-coveted Vera Wang
gown. You can also buy dresses by Elie Saab, whose
designs have appeared on many a red carpet. Factor
in the recently acquired exclusive stockist status for
Carolina Herrera (responsible for several of Renée
Zellweger's outfits for the Oscars), and you've got one
exceedingly glamorous shop. Prices begin at around
£2,500 and rocket from there. The Wedding Shop
has an excellent wedding list service (*see below*) and
also owns the bridal room at Liberty (7573 9922).
Mail order.

Shoes

Both high-street and designer shoe shops are
keen for their slice of the lucrative wedding
market, so plenty cater for brides. Among the
best are Anello & Davide, Office, Emma Hope
and Jimmy Choo (for all, *see chapter* **Shoes**).

Baboucha

218 High Street, High Barnet, Herts EN5 5SZ
(8441 3788/www.baboucha.com). High Barnet
tube. **Open** 10am-5pm Mon-Sat. **Credit** MC, V.

You may not be thrilled with Baboucha's location
at the far end of the Northern Line, but do have a
look at this third-generation shoemaker's well laid-
out website. The range of shoes is staggering, and
the client list includes the likes of Nicole Kidman
and Sophie Wessex. Despite this, prices remain
affordable, with plenty of styles below the £100
mark. There's also a bespoke service, and a shoe-
covering option if you want to wear a tried-and-
tested pair of heels for the big day.
Mail order.

Emmy

65 Cross Street, N1 2BB (7704 0012/www.emmy
shoes.co.uk). Highbury & Islington tube/rail. **Open**
by appointment 10.30am-6.30pm Tue-Sat. **Credit**
MC, V.

Emmy Scarterfield puts her experience working for
brands such as Giorgio Armani and Mulberry to
impeccable use in her sophisticated bridal shoe
designs. The made-to-measure footwear is based
on a choice of elegant styles in various fabrics and
heel sizes, with a range of detailing options such
as brooches and feathers. Prices begin at £245.

Hanna Goldman

Studio 4, 10-13 Hollybush Place, E2 9QX (7739
2690/www.hannagoldman.com). Bethnal Green
tube. **Open** by appointment 11am-7pm Mon-Sat.
No credit cards.

This workshop is filled with silk and satin samples,
bows, buckles and beading – make an appointment
to discuss your bespoke bridal footwear, and be
assured that while designs may not be the most
contemporary, this is old-fashioned craftsmanship
at its best. Prices start at £240; allow six to eight
weeks for a pair of handmade shoes. Helen Tonkin's
beautiful tiaras start at £75. Call for a brochure (£3).

Hire shops

Lipman & Sons

22 Charing Cross Road, WC2H 0HR (7240 2310).
Leicester Square tube. **Open** 9am-6pm Mon-Wed,
Fri, Sat; 9am-8pm Thur. **Credit** AmEx, DC, MC, V.

A traditional selection of smart suits is on offer here.
A three-piece morning suit costs £31.95 (an imprint
of your credit card will be taken for £250 as an
insurance). If you want to go for the full top-hat look,
they're available too, as are ex-rental purchases.
Branches: throughout the city.

Moss Bros Hire

27-28 King Street, WC2E 8JD (7632 9700/
www.mossbros.co.uk). Covent Garden tube. **Open**
9am-6pm Mon-Wed, Fri, Sat; 9am-7pm Thur;
11am-5pm Sun. **Credit** AmEx, MC, V.

Moss Bros has been around for upwards of 150
years and has all the menswear hire categories
covered. Affordability is the main draw – a dinner
suit with cummerbund can be rented for under
£50, while morning suits complete with shirts and
cravats range from £65 to £129.
Branches: throughout the city.

Young's Hire at Suits You

372 Oxford Street, W1T 9HB (7499 3154/
www.youngs-hire.co.uk). Bond Street tube. **Open**
9am-7pm Mon-Wed, Fri, Sat; 9am-8pm Thur;
11am-5pm Sun. **Credit** AmEx, MC, V.

All the usual staples such as frock coats and
morning jackets are stocked, with a notable
collection of patterned waistcoats. You can even
hire shoes, if you can face the thought, and cute
suits for the younger male members of the
wedding party. A morning suit with plain
waistcoat costs £49.95 for three-day hire, plus
£4.95 insurance and £50 deposit, or you can opt
for a fancier waistcoat for an extra £12.95.
Branches: throughout the city.

Services

For an extensive list of wedding services,
covering everything from marquee and classic
car hire to caterers and printers, see www.guides
forbrides.co.uk and www.weduk.com. For
more on organising special events, *see chapter*
Entertaining.

Wedding invitations

Cinnamon Cards

8870 1389/www.cinnamon-cards.co.uk.

Beautiful handmade invitations featuring tasteful
monochrome images or original touches such as
feathers and fabric flowers. Prices start at £2.25
per card. Allow at least five weeks for delivery as
these creations are a labour of love.
Mail order.

Oh So Inviting

42 Rasper Road, N20 0LZ (0845 458 2771/
www.invitin.com). **Phone enquiries** 9.30am-5pm
Mon-Fri. **Credit** MC, V.

A huge range of wedding and hen party
invitations, plus post-event thank-you cards. Prices
range from £2.30 to £6 per card. There are reams
of contemporary or classic designs to choose from,
with touches such as stitching on cards or scroll-
type invites contained in a silk purse.
Mail order.

Wedding lists

All major department stores offer wedding list
services: *see chapter* **Department Stores**.
John Lewis (www.johnlewisgiftlist.com) is a
reliable favourite, while **Selfridges** lets
guests pledge money that you spend as you
like (0870 121 2187). Many other shops,
including **Heal's** and the **Conran Shop**, offer
a similar service so it's worth asking.
Alternatively, you can ask your guests to make
a charity donation in your name at
www.thealternativeweddinglist.co.uk.

The **Wedding Shop** (*see above*) allows
you to construct your wedding list from an
extensive array of products by 250 companies,
following a meeting at the showroom; your
guests can then order online or in person. The
products available range from the highly
traditional, such as Wedgwood and Royal
Doulton china, to the modern, such as Alessi
kitchenware and Samsonite luggage. The
Wedding Shop's dress department (*see above*)
is also top-notch.

Wrapit

89 Great Titchfield Street, W1W 6RN (7307
8660/www.wrapit.co.uk). Oxford Circus tube.
Open by appointment 10.30am-6pm Mon-Sat.
Credit MC, V.

Wrapit seems to have every angle of the gift
list covered for starry-eyed couples and their
guests, from king-size beds to Missoni bathrobes.
The breadth of choice is amazing, and everything
is linked by stylishness and good taste, with prices
to suit all pockets. There are also unusual options,
such as a weekend of Harley-Davidson motorbike
rental or a case of fine wine.

Maternity

Several high-street chains now have stylish sidelines in maternity, including **H&M** and **Agnès b**, but **Topshop** is our favourite, with an expanded trend-led range, which now includes nightwear and lingerie, on the ground floor. For all three, *see chapter* **Womenswear**. Dedicated lingerie shop **Rosa** (3 Stoke Newington Church Street, N16 0NX, 7254 3467) has an expert maternity/nursing bra-fitting service. Many of the shops listed below also sell baby clothes and gifts, and offer mail order.

Blooming Marvellous
725 Fulham Road, SW6 5UL (7371 0500/mail order 0870 751 8944/www.bloomingmarvellous. co.uk). Parsons Green tube. **Open** 9am-6pm Mon-Sat; 11am-5pm Sun. **Credit** AmEx, MC, V.
Offering a wide choice and great value for money, BM's 20 years in the bump business make it a sensible first stop for pregnancy wear. There are low-key basics, such as T-shirts, sedate, relaxed workwear, and adapted fashion favourites such as wrapover dresses (£34.99) and jeans, plus lingerie, nightwear and swimwear. None of it is spectacularly trendy, but all of it is useful.
For branches see index.

Bumpsville
33 Kensington Park Road, W11 2EU (7727 1213/www.bumpsville.com). Ladbroke Grove tube. **Open** 10.30am-6.30pm Mon-Fri; 10am-6pm Sat; noon-5pm Sun. **Credit** MC, V.
The funky, colourful look of the West Village womenswear is adapted in the Bumpsville range, which has the signature strident print shirt-dresses in a more expansive form (£189). The simple Soos jersey dress (£99) is perfect to wear over jeans, and the converted vintage 501s are Bumpsville's jeans of choice (£129). Our favourite thing, though, is the pretty lace nursing bra (£48).

La Conception
46 Webbs Road, SW11 6SF (7228 7498/www.la conception.com). Clapham Junction rail. **Open** 10am-5.30pm Mon-Sat. **Credit** MC, V.
La Conception's ever-growing range, sourced from all over the world, currently features lovely items from the likes of Arabella B, Veronique Delachaux and Melissa Odabash. Bestselling pieces include the long vest in a variety of colours (£22.50) and

9London

the beautiful Empire-line Parker dress (£166). There are also designer maternity jeans from the crème de la crème, including Juicy Couture (£150).

Elias & Grace
158 Regent's Park Road, NW1 8XN (7449 0574/ www.eliasandgrace.com). Chalk Farm tube. **Open** 10am-6pm Mon-Sat; noon-6pm Sun. **Credit** MC, V.
Gorgeousness is the name of the game in this new shop for the young, loaded and pregnant, stocking the likes of Sonia Rykiel, Vivienne Westwood, See by Chloé and Matthew Williamson. Not everything is maternity wear, but much is suitably adaptable. If you're planning multiple pregnancies, you may consider investing in Citizens of Humanity pregnancy jeans (£199). Underwear is by Elle Macpherson and pampering comes courtesy of E&G's bespoke organic products.

Formes
33 Brook Street, W1K 4HG (7493 2783/mail order 8689 1133/www.formes.com). Bond Street tube. **Open** 10am-6pm Mon-Wed; 10am-7pm Thur; 10am-6.30pm Fri, Sat. **Credit** AmEx, MC, V.
Formes was at the forefront, as it were, of making maternity wear remotely trendy. It blew sack-like pregnancy smocks out of the water with sleek tailored trousers and bump-celebrating bandeaux. Twenty years on, the look combines classics with contemporary styles – soft black trousers and layered skirts (from £69) to dress up with flouncy camis or down with wraparound cardies.
For branches see index.

JoJo Maman Bébé
3 Ashbourne Parade, 1259 Finchley Road, NW11 0AD (8731 8961/mail order 0870 241 0560/ www.jojomamanbebe.co.uk). Golders Green tube. **Open** 9.30am-5.30pm Mon-Sat; 11am-5pm Sun. **Credit** MC, V.
Affordable and practical, with occasional flashes of French chic, JoJo is one of the most useful maternity ranges around. Although the pieces don't make you faint with desire, there are some fantastic bargains (bestsellers include under-bump jeans for a mere £29 and side-ruched tops for £25). There's a range of everyday utility wear (T-shirts £17), swimwear and multistyle underwear.
For branches see index.

The Maternity Co
42 Chiswick Lane, W4 2JQ (8995 4455/www.the maternityco.com). Turnham Green tube. **Open** 10am-5.30pm Mon-Sat. **Credit** AmEx, MC, V.
A great find for the modish mother look without spending a fortune. Clothes are mainly by European designers and cover all bases, including special occasions (a stretch-cotton party dress is £69.95), slouching about (hipster jeans from £61.95) and business (a jersey suit is £119). There's also lingerie and a maternity bra-fitting service, as well as toilets and free parking.

Merry Go Round
21 Half Moon Lane, SE24 9JU (7737 6452). Herne Hill rail. **Open** 9.15am-5pm Mon-Fri; 10am-4pm Sat. **No credit cards**.
This smartly appointed shop's speciality is previously owned and new, discounted end-of-line maternity wear, including must-have designers like Noppies, Fragile and Arabella B, as well as choice high-street maternity wear by Topshop and H&M. Stock changes frequently, so you never know what treasures you might find.

Mums 2 Be
3 Mortlake Terrace, Mortlake Road, Kew, Surrey TW9 3DT (8332 6506/www.mums-2-be.co.uk). Kew Gardens tube/rail. **Open** 10am-5.30pm Mon-Sat. **Credit** MC, V.

Friendly staff defy any pregnant jeans lover not to find a pair to suit here. There's a wide range of Noppies and Valia denims, with under/over bump waists and all manner of styles. Apart from jeans, there are smart casual lines from Sara, Menonove, Essere, Atessa and Blooming, plus a large range of underwear. A sister company, Larger Than Life, provides plus-size fashion to fit up to size 26. There's also a designer eveningwear hire service.
For branches see index.

9London
8 Hollywood Road, SW10 9HY (7352 7600/ www.9london.co.uk). Earl's Court tube. **Open** 10am-6pm Mon-Sat. **Credit** MC, V.
Co-owners Adela King and Emily Evans reckon that being pregnant shouldn't spoil your fashion fun. And so say a host of celeb clients. The duo approached their favourite designers, who adapted their collections. Highlights are Diane von Furstenberg's maternity line (tops from £155, dresses from £250), Juicy Couture's, Sitting Pretty's sexy tops and Melissa Odabash's swimwear.

1 et 1 font 3
54 Ledbury Road, W11 2AJ (7229 6088). Westbourne Park tube. **Open** 10am-1.30pm, 2-6pm Mon-Sat; noon-5pm Sun. **Credit** AmEx, MC, V.
Chic French fashions to celebrate a form that's busting out all over. Svelte jersey dresses (from £118) with singular prints skim the bump but don't swamp the figure. Hand-smocked blouses and floral frocks are worn over cord jeans (£80), and the beautiful, clinging, long lace dresses are strictly for those wanting to show off the cargo (£146).

Pretty Pregnant
102 Northcote Road, SW11 6QW (7924 4850/ www.prettypregnant.co.uk). Clapham Junction rail. **Open** 10am-6pm Mon-Sat; noon-4pm Sun. **Credit** MC, V.
The look is young and cool and the atmosphere is welcoming, but it's the labels that really count. From Noppies there are jeans (£65), cardies, sweats, jackets and the full underwear range. Fragile provides delightful wrap dresses (£81), swirly skirts and soft knits. Cache Cache does strappy dresses and vests, plus neat daywear. There's an unusually sexy collection of maternity underwear.

Push
9 Theberton Street, N1 0QY (7359 2003/ www.pushmaternity.com). Angel tube. **Open** 10.30am-6pm Mon-Wed, Fri, Sat; 10.30am-7pm Thur; noon-5pm Sun. **Credit** MC, V.
An oasis of calm for expectant glamour pusses, Push has exclusive fashions in fine fabrics. We loved a handbeaded silk camisole top by Cadeau (£137), but gulped at the price tags on this and a gorgeous print dress by Leona Edmiston (£255). Another push-the-boat-out item is the now-famous Earl jeans (£156). Zita West's therapeutic products include Precondition Down Under oil for the all-important perineal area. Let's not forget why you're here, after all.

Mail order & internet
If you can't face schlepping your bump to the shops, there are some excellent home-shopping options. **Isabella Oliver** (www.isabellaoliver. com) offers a contemporary collection sported by Trinny Woodall during her gestation period. **Harry Duley**'s (0870 075 2142, www.harry duley.co.uk) stylish tops, trousers and skirts stretch over an expanding tummy, but bounce back afterwards for extended wear. **Crave** maternity (0870 240 5476, www.businessbump. co.uk) does a neat line in tailored suits, among other things. **Mothernature** (01782 824 242, www.mothernaturebras.co.uk) has a vast range of nursing and maternity bras and swimwear. The **National Childbirth Trust** (0870 112 1120, www.nctsales.co.uk) is a trustworthy source of pregnancy essentials. For a bit more glamour, try **Figleaves** (*see p76*).

Fetish

Although Soho remains the capital's sex shop hub, and fetish designers continue to colonise Holloway Road, London's fetish shops are scattered far and wide. Those wishing to plug into the growing scene should head to Covent Garden's **Coffee, Cake and Kink** (61 Endell Street, WC2H 9AJ, 7419 2996) and pick up a copy of the *London Fetish Map*. If you're in the market for a new kink or dedicated to the one you have, join fellow fetishists from around the country at the monthly **London Fetish Fair**, (www.londonfetishfair.co.uk) for the latest information. The UK's longest-running event of its kind, it's the last word in fetish fashion, dungeon design and everything in between, from erotic photography to ponycarting weekends. It's also one of the few fetish events that permits street clothes. If footwear is your thing, head to **Leatherworks** (77-79 Southgate Road, N1 3JS, 7359 9778, www. leatherworks.co.uk), where you can browse the 700-odd styles in stock to find the seven-inch platform boots of your dreams or join the ranks of past customers Vivienne Westwood and Prince and have something made to order.

Shops

Breathless

Unit 38B, The Stables Market, Chalk Farm Road, N1 8AH (7267 3705/www.breathless. uk.com). Camden Town or Chalk Farm tube. **Open** 11am-7pm Mon-Fri; 10am-7pm Sat, Sun. **Credit** AmEx, MC, V.
Bar the Velda Lauder corsets and the odd piece from the likes of House of Harlot and Inner Sanctum, the fashions at Breathless are mostly the work of owner and designer Dolenta. She aims to provide more affordable options than are generally available on the scene, and her colourful latex designs attract cybergoth clubbers, as well as fetishists. Miniskirts and men's T-shirts start at around £30. Particularly fab are the riding jackets, military-style peaked caps and cute rubber ties.
Mail order.

Clone Zone

64 Old Compton Street, W1D 4UQ (7287 3530/www.clonezone.co.uk). Leicester Square or Tottenham Court Road tube. **Open** 11am-9pm Mon-Sat; noon-8pm Sun. **Credit** AmEx, DC, MC, V.
Gay-owned, Clone Zone Soho is a bright, busy, compact space with greeting cards, CDs, accessories and clothing (T-shirts, muscle tops, underwear and a few dashing numbers from Guilty Kilts) on the ground floor, leading to more businesslike fare downstairs. Alongside the wide range of videos, DVDs, magazines and books, a reasonable selection of sex toys and fetish props includes douches, gags and vinyl gas masks, with Colt leather accessories ranging from bicep straps to cock restraints.
Mail order (0800 783 7953).
For branches see index.

Expectations

75 Great Eastern Street, EC2A 3RY (7739 0292/ www.expectations.co.uk). Old Street tube/rail. **Open** 11am-7pm Mon-Fri; 11am-8pm Sat; noon-5pm Sun. **Credit** AmEx, MC, V.
With its neon sign and pumping music, there's a clubby vibe to Expectations – a glance around at the Tom of Finland imagery, and you're in no doubt what kind of club. Get kitted out with latex briefs from £13.99 or a pair of leather rear-zip jeans at £169, or stock up on hardware from the range of restraints, harnesses and slings – there's also a particularly wide range of hoods and masks. In a nook under the stairs, glass cabinets house a preponderance of steel rings, speculums, dildos and butt plugs that range in size from modest to eye-watering.
Mail order.

Fettered Pleasures

90 Holloway Road, N7 8JG (7619 9333/ www.fetteredpleasures.com). Holloway Road tube/Highbury & Islington tube/rail. **Open** 11am-7pm Mon-Sat; noon-5pm Sun. **Credit** MC, V.
From the moment you're buzzed in, it's clear that there are few kinks this friendly fetish superstore hasn't thought of. Chain and rope by the metre lead into a thorough display of whips, canes, floggers and paddles, beyond which lies a veritable sea of bondage gear, from clothing and restraints to contraptions to make your dungeon the envy of all. Womenswear includes chastity harnesses, hobble dresses and some high-class corsetry, while niche lines include medical kits, clear plastic worship pants, puppy masks and mitts.
Mail order.

Harmony

167 Charing Cross Road, WC2H 0EN (7439 6261). **Open** 9am-midnight Mon-Fri; 10am-midnight Sat; 11am-11pm Sun. **Credit** AmEx, MC, V.
The three floors of Harmony's Charing Cross flagship house a comprehensive stock ranging from hen party novelties to specialist mags, books and DVDs. Sex dolls and toys are on the first floor, with the top floor devoted to lingerie, footwear and entry-level fetish outfits. Developing the sex department store concept, the new Oxford Street branch is distinctly female-friendly, featuring an ingenious vibrator demo area.
For branches see index.

Honour

86 Lower Marsh, SE1 7AB (7401 8219/ www.honour.co.uk). Waterloo tube/rail. **Open** 10.30am-7pm Mon-Fri; 11.30am-5pm Sat. **Credit** AmEx, MC, V.
Feeding your fetish can be a costly business, but this one-stop shop offers a good range of products to suit all budgets, with clothing from under £30. PVC fashion rules the ground floor, with maid, police and nurse uniforms alongside classic catsuits and corsets, available up to size 26. Upstairs in the 'bondage attic' are sex toys, cuffs, restraints and clamps, rubber stockings and gloves, and a range of unisex tops, briefs and dresses in waterproof clear plastic. There are wigs, hosiery and shoes (up to size 12) to complete the look.
Mail order (8450 6877).
For branch see index.

House of Harlot

90 Holloway Road, N7 8JG (7700 1441/ www.house-of-harlot.com). Holloway Road tube/Highbury & Islington tube/rail. **Open** 10am-6pm Mon-Fri; 11am-7pm Sat. **Credit** MC, V.
Fashion designers and pop stylists looking for a sartorial wonder in sheet rubber know this is the place to come to. House of Harlot's creations range from basic T-shirts and trousers to bumless ball gowns, men's three-piece suits and fabulously kinked-up uniforms from air hostess to French maid. Prices are consistent with the workmanship involved, but service is friendly and professional, and garments can be cut to measure at no extra cost – browse the catalogue for inspiration (or just for a perve at the delectable Dita Von Teese). The shop also stocks jewellery by Prong and excellently kooky shoes from Natasha Marro.
Mail order.

Liberation

49 Shelton Street, WC2H 9HE (7836 5894/ www.liberationlondon.com). Covent Garden tube. **Open** 11am-7pm Mon-Sat; also by appointment. **Credit** MC, V.
Opened in October 2004, the flagship store for latex couturiers Libidex has already established itself as the coolest kink boutique in town. Stockists of House of Harlot, Inner Sanctum, Jack the Rubber and Torture Garden, Liberation also features its own couture, which ranges from Leigh Bowery-esque fantasy to a new sewn-rubber line geared towards straight males who don't fancy the harness and jockstrap look. The real delights, however, are the one-off fetish antiques and pervy collectibles dotted about the place – why settle for the same old paraphernalia when you can spice up your role play with a Victorian bridle and spurs or an antique holy communion set?
Mail order.

Paradiso Bodyworks

60 Dean Street, W1D 6AW (7287 6913). Tottenham Court Road tube. **Open** 11am-7.30pm Mon-Sat. **Credit** AmEx, MC, V.
More glamorous than your average Soho fetish bunker, Paradiso Bodyworks operates out of two adjacent shops. Enter via Old Compton Street for leather, rubber and PVC fetish fashion and footwear, plus a rather lovely line in leather collars, leads and masks, including a sheepskin-lined blindfold at £75. As the window display suggests, next door on Dean Street the focus is on boudoir chic, with girlie silk, satin and lace lingerie, vintage-look corsets and sequinned nipple tassels (from £35).
Mail order.
For branch see index.

Regulation

17A St Alban's Place, N1 0NX (7226 0665/ www.regulation-london.co.uk). Angel tube. **Open** 10.30am-6.30pm Mon-Sat; noon-5pm Sun. **Credit** AmEx, MC, V.

Liberation

Catering mostly to the gay market, Regulation is dedicated to the art of control. New additions to the toy department include leather spankers and Plexiglas paddles, while rubber and leather clothing for clubbing or home entertainment ranges from shorts, tops and sailor-front jeans to caps, straps, harnesses and hoods. The more adventurous should check out the Exposing Vac Rack (£279.95) or perhaps splash out on the new piss tent at £549.95.
Mail order.

RoB London
24 Wells Street, W1T 3PH (7735 7893/ www.rob.nl). Oxford Circus tube. **Open** 10.30am-6.30pm Mon-Sat; noon-5pm Sun. **Credit** AmEx, MC, V.
The tamer-end BDSM accessories draw in a few kinky straights, but RoB London's core clientele is a gay, clearly defined (in both senses) bunch who make no bones about their lust for leather, rubber and lots of it. The legendary Dutch company's central London outlet is a no-frills, no-nonsense hardware store, stocking everything from leather and rubber hoods and gloves to restraints, slings, made-to-order body bags and some brutal stainless-steel sex toys.
Mail order.

sh!
57 Hoxton Square, N1 6HD (7613 5458/www. sh-womenstore.com). Old Street tube/rail. **Open** 10am-8pm Mon-Sat; noon-7pm Sun. **Credit** MC, V.
Men may only pass through the hallowed pink portals of London's only female-oriented sex shop with a woman, though lesbians and straight gal pals make up the usual clientele anyway. Books, accessories and gifts are displayed alongside strap-on harnesses and a sex toy demo desk on which the colourful clitoral pump (£30) remains a hot favourite. Clothing ranges from corsetry and skimpy lace to rubber, leather and PVC lady-cop outfits from Insinuate. Most romantic is the silk sweetheart thong in a jar from Hackney-based lingerie label Buttress & Snatch (£42). Cotton shorts and vests remain popular – make your talents (and your intentions) clear with the slogan 'dive mistress'.
Mail order.

Showgirls
64 Holloway Road, N7 8JL (7697 9072/ www.showgirls.uk.com). Holloway Road tube/ Highbury & Islington tube/rail. **Open** 10.30am-6.30pm Mon-Thur; 10.30am-7pm Fri, Sat. **Credit** AmEx, MC, V.
Latex couture is the order of the day at this small but stylish fetish boutique featuring pieces from Ectomorph, Murray & Vern and Inner Sanctum. Start with a £15 thong or splash out on a slinky Vampirella dress at £230 – opt for fail-safe black or go superhero in red and gold. For retro-fetishists, particularly stylish are the jacket and pencil skirt ensembles from Atsuko Kudo in her trademark lace print, complete with a delicate veiled pill-box hat to match (£250). Choose from a range of towering Perspex heels to complete your outfit.
Mail order.

Zeitgeist
66 Holloway Road, N7 8JL (7607 2977/ www.fetishcentral.net). Highbury & Islington tube/rail. **Open** 10am-6pm Mon-Thur; 10am-7pm Fri; 11am-7pm Sat. **Credit** AmEx, MC, V.
From latex heaven next door at Showgirls, slip through to the PVC equivalent at Zeitgeist. More wallet-friendly than most fetish materials, it's made into everything from simple trousers to nurses' uniforms. Clothing starts at around £30. Stilettos, knee-high and thigh boots in classic red or black are stocked up to size 12 (from around £40, though sale bargains can often be had). Magazines, videos and a good selection of rubber hoods also feature. In the basement, paddles, whips and restraints are displayed in a dungeon area along with metal chairs, harnesses, stocks and a solid aluminium St Andrew's Cross at £275.
Mail order.

Unusual Sizes

Finally, the high street is responding to the fact that people come in all shapes and sizes. **New Look** (*see p45*) has a line, Inspire, for sizes 16-28, **Miss Selfridge** (*see p45*) has introduced an up-to-the-minute range for trendy petites, while **Dorothy Perkins** (*see p44*) caters for both small and tall girls. **Principles** (*see p45*) has a petite range for women who are 5ft 3in and under (in sizes 6-16); there's a concession in **Debenhams** (*see p12*). The department store also has a branch of **Elvi's** (www.elvi.co.uk), which is aimed at the over-40s, with stock ranging from casual daywear and smart suits to special-occasion outfits in sizes 16-26. Elvi's has concessions in Bentalls, Allders and Bluewater.

Ann Harvey
266 Oxford Street, W1N 9DC (7408 1131). Oxford Circus tube. **Open** 10am-7pm Mon-Wed, Fri, Sat; 10am-8pm Thur; noon-6pm Sun. **Credit** AmEx, MC, V. **Sells** W.
Well-cut, good-value classics aimed at the mature woman, from evening dresses and separates to swimwear, in sizes 16-28. Accessories include both jewellery and footwear.
Branches: throughout the city.

Base
55 Monmouth Street, WC2H 9DG (7240 8914/ www.base-fashions.co.uk). Covent Garden tube. **Open** 10am-6pm Mon-Sat. **Credit** AmEx, MC, V. **Sells** W.
Upmarket, continental designerwear in sizes 16-28. You'll find luxurious silks and velvets by Cocoon, bold ethnic prints from Ischiko and easy linens by Ppep and Wille. New ranges are added each season.

Beige
8 Hallswelle Parade, NW11 0DL (8455 1122/ www.beigeplus.com). Golders Green tube. **Open** 9.30am-5.30pm Mon-Sat; 10.30am-4pm Sun. **Credit** AmEx, DC, MC, V. **Sells** W.
Selling upmarket plus-size clothing (16-26) and aimed at women over 35, the boutique stocks casual and formal attire as well as accessories. Sourced from Italian, French and Spanish designers, labels include Oui, Hucke Women, NP and Elena Miro.

Evans
538-540 Oxford Street, W1C 1LS (7499 0434/ www.evans.ltd.uk). Marble Arch tube. **Open** 10am-7pm Mon-Wed, Fri, Sat; 10am-8pm Thur; 11am-5pm Sun. **Credit** AmEx, MC, V. **Sells** W.
A high-street favourite for fashionable women, offering flattering interpretations of current trends in sizes 14-32. Prices are good: dresses are around £35, jeans £10-£30, and lightweight jackets £35-£45. There are also petite (5ft 3in and under) and tall (5ft 10in and above) ranges.
Mail order (0870 606 9666).
Branches: throughout the city.

Frank Usher
Stockists 7629 9696/www.frankusher.co.uk. **Phone enquiries** 9am-5pm Mon-Fri. **Sells** W.
Elegant styles for day and evening from Dusk (in sizes 8-18), Frank Usher, Coterie (both in sizes 10-22) and Quintesse (sizes 16-26). Clothes are feminine and cut to flatter, although they come at a price: a dramatic Quintesse 'feather jacket' in the autumn/winter 2005/6 collection is £185, the matching skirt £120.

High & Mighty
145-147 Edgware Road, W2 2HR (7723 8754/ www.highandmighty.co.uk). Edgware Road tube. **Open** 10am-6pm Mon; 9am-6pm Tue, Wed, Fri, Sat; 9am-7pm Thur. **Credit** MC, V. **Sells** M.

A good mix of formal and casualwear for men. Most lines cater for those over 6ft 2in, with a 17in-21in collar size, 44in-60in chest, and 32in-60in waist. Shoes go up to size 19. Underwear and pyjamas are also sold.
Mail order (08456 010 212).
For branches see index.

Ken Smith Designs
6 Charlotte Place, W1T 1SG (7631 3341). Goodge Street tube. **Open** 10am-6pm Mon-Fri; 10am-2pm Sat; occasional Sun (call to check). **Credit** AmEx, DC, MC, V. **Sells** W.
An upmarket women's boutique stocking an assortment of continental labels (up to size 34) including Doris Streich, Anna Scholz and Annikki Karvinen. There's a wide assortment of smart occasionwear, casual outfits and eveningwear. Phone orders welcomed.
Mail order.

Long Tall Sally
19-25 Chiltern Street, W1U 7PH (7487 3370/ www.longtallsally.co.uk). Baker Street tube. **Open** 9.30am-5.30pm Mon-Wed, Fri, Sat; 10am-7pm Thur. **Credit** AmEx, DC, MC, V. **Sells** W.
Contemporary designs for women 5ft 9in and over include formal and casual outfits, swimwear, nightwear and maternity clothes in sizes 10-20. The Tall Zone is a young, trendy range (sizes 8-18). Jeans and jackets start from around £45, dresses from around £35. An LTS concession can also be found in Allders, 2 North End, Croydon (8686 9336).
Mail order (0870 990 6885).

Marina Rinaldi
39 Old Bond Street, W1S 4QP (7629 4454). Green Park tube. **Open** 10am-6pm Mon-Wed, Fri, Sat; 10am-7pm Thur. **Credit** AmEx, MC, V. **Sells** W.
Part of the MaxMara fashion group, Rinaldi's designer clothes (up to size 28) are expensive, but the quality is good. Shoes, handbags, scarves and belts are also included in the range. There are concessions in Selfridges and Harrods.

Rochester Big & Tall
90 Brompton Road, SW3 1ER (7838 0018/ www.rochesterclothing.com). Knightsbridge tube. **Open** 9.30am-6pm Mon, Tue, Thur-Sat; 9.30am-7pm Wed. **Credit** AmEx, DC, MC, V. **Sells** M.
This shop caters for men from 6ft 1in tall, who take large sizes (chest 42in-74in, waist 36in-72in). Names stocked include Versace, Zegna, Ralph Lauren, Kenneth Cole and Wrangler. Shoes go up to size 15.
Mail order.

Sixteen 47
www.sixteen47.com. **Credit** MC, V. **Sells** W.
Dawn French and Helen Teague's womenswear range catering for sizes 16-47 (hence the name) is now only available online. The pricier collection of garments by French & Teague has merged with the more affordable Sixteen 47 range, now covering great-quality basics such as jersey tunics (around £42) and jackets from £48. A bespoke service for wedding dresses and formalwear is also available.
Mail order.

Vivace
2 Bridge Street, Richmond, Surrey TW9 1TQ (8948 7840/www.vivace.co.uk). Richmond tube/rail. **Open** 10am-5.30pm Tue-Sat; noon-5pm Sun. **Credit** MC, V. **Sells** W.
Women's designer fashions in sizes 16-22, from suits and casuals to party outfits, in comfortable, natural fabrics. Expect to see labels such as Persona, Elena Miro, Gerry Weber, Basler and Laurie. Accessories are limited to costume jewellery and a small selection of bags and belts.
Mail order (online).

Shoes

London's strong shoemaking tradition, coupled with its status as a cutting-edge fashion capital, makes it a fertile hunting ground for footwear. Some streets are literally lined with shoe shops – South Molton Street is 'Mid-range Chain Row', while the area around Seven Dials, notably Neal Street, is brimming with sneaker specialists. In addition, practically every big high-street clothing retailer sells footwear. Harvey Nichols, Liberty and Selfridges have good designer departments (for all, *see chapter* **Department Stores**), while you can often find unusual lines in boutiques; former Hussein Chalayan footwear designer Adele Clarke's shoes are available at **Matches** (*see p37*), while Victor & Rolf's new shoe line is at **Souvenir** (*see p38*).

Aldo

3-7 Neal Street, WC2H 9PU (7836 7692/ www.aldoshoes.com). Covent Garden or Leicester Square tube. **Open** 10am-8pm Mon-Sat; noon-6pm Sun. **Credit** AmEx, MC, V. **Sells** M, W, C.

This Canadian shoe emporium is hard to beat for sheer choice, boasting a dizzying array of styles for men and women, at surprisingly cheap prices. For women, all the latest trends are covered, from cork-soled wedge platforms and ballet shoes to metallic strappy sandals and cowboy boots. Most of the prices are around the £50 mark, with a range of designer-lookalike handbags at around £30. For the boys, some of the trainer styles have a slightly orthopaedic air; this aside, there is a good selection of modern-looking loafers, lace-ups and boots, mainly around the £60 mark. A small selection of men's accessories includes watches and identity bracelets. There is also a sale shop in Camden Town (231-233 Camden High Street, NW1 7BU, 7284 1982), offering some of the wackier styles at slashed prices.
Branches: throughout the city.

Anello & Davide

20-21 St Christopher's Place, W1U 1NZ (7935 7959/www.handmadeshoes.co.uk). Bond Street tube. **Open** 10am-6pm Mon-Wed, Fri, Sat; 11am-7pm Thur; noon-4pm Sun. **Credit** MC, V. **Sells** M, W.

Founded in 1922 as a dance and theatrical shoe company by two Italian brothers, Anello and Davide has earned a place in the footwear hall of fame. Not only did the duo make Dorothy's ruby slippers for *The Wizard of Oz*, they also designed the Beatle boot for the Fab Four. Neo-mods can still pick up the original cuban-heeled boots here (from £225 for both men's and women's styles). For boys with less flashy tastes, there is a range of traditional and contemporary shoes, from finely detailed brogues to sleek loafers and Chelsea boots, designed in-house and made in Italy (£150-£495). The women's A&D range is updated every four to six weeks and encompasses everything from plain courts and pumps to more elaborate beaded styles. While shapes are based on current trends, the details don't trot meekly after the fashion pack, so styles will appeal to individualists rather than catwalk queens. The Kensington branch houses the bridal collection (prices range from £75 to a jaw-dropping £10,000), and a bespoke service is also available.
For branch see index.

Audley

72 Duke of York Square, King's Road, SW3 4LY (7730 2902/www.audley.com). Sloane Square tube. **Open** 10am-6pm Mon, Tue, Thur-Sat; 10am-7pm Wed; noon-5pm Sun. **Credit** AmEx, MC, V. **Sells** W.

Audley started out as a bespoke shoemaker, which is reflected in the artful lines and fine detailing of these well-made shoes. Although prices are in line

Kurt Geiger

FASHION

with upper-end high-street chains (around £100 for shoes, £190 for boots), the shoes look more expensive. Styles change seasonally in response to trends, but the ladylike shoes tend to be characterised by architectural toe and heel shapes combined with unusual colours. The autumn/winter 2005/6 collection has a folkloric, hand-crafted feel and features embossed and burnished leather and blanket-edged stitching. For an extra £75 you can have a pair of shoes made up in a different colour to match an outfit (good news for brides), and there is a range of matching handbags. Audley is planning to introduce a 'handmade to order' service in 2006.
Mail order.

Bertie

36 South Molton Street, W1K 5RH (7493 5033/ www.theshoestudio.com). Bond Street tube. **Open** 10am-7pm Mon-Wed, Fri, Sat; 10am-8pm Thur; noon-6pm Sun. **Credit** AmEx, MC, V. **Sells** W.
Hot on the heels of the catwalk, Bertie offers up-to-the-minute shoes at affordable prices. From pointy high-heeled courts to chunky wedges, if it's trendy, it's here. Bertie's characteristically creative use of colours and trimmings, however, makes the label more than a bland catwalk ape. The prices are slightly higher than high-street competitors (shoes hover around the £70 mark, with boots from £100 upwards), but quality is also significantly better, making Bertie popular with a slightly older crowd than Faith, Office and Shelly's.
Mail order.
For branch see index.

Birkenstock

70 Neal Street, WC2H 9PR (7240 2783/www. birkenstock.co.uk). Covent Garden or Leicester Square tube. **Open** 10.30am-7pm Mon-Wed, Fri, Sat; 10.30am-8pm Thur; noon-6pm Sun. **Credit** AmEx, MC, V. **Sells** M, W, C.
This is the UK's only shop entirely dedicated to Birkenstock, easily identifiable by the queue outside, particularly in the summer season. You'll find the full range of the famous ergonomic sandals (plus a few clogs, shoes and boots), from the bestselling single-strap Madrid (£29.95) to a funky line styled by supermodel Heidi Klum (think metallic leathers, studs, rhinestones and animal prints). Prices top £190 for a pair of zebra-print boots. If you want to avoid the crowds, then head down the road to parent shop The Natural Shoe Store (*see p70*), which stocks a smaller selection of the brand.
Mail order (0800 132194).

Black Truffle

74 Broadway Market, E8 4QJ (7923 9450/ www.blacktruffle.com). Bus 26, 48, 55. **Open** 11am-6pm Tue-Fri; 10am-6pm Sat; noon-6pm Sun. **Credit** AmEx, MC, V. **Sells** M, W, C.
Shoemaker Melissa Needham opened this shop in 2003 as a showcase for her own Prescott & Mackay label, as well as for shoes and accessories by other leading designers and new talents. The fairly high prices are in line with the quality of both materials and design; for example, a pair of 'hair-on-hide' men's trainers by Joco Momola sells for £130. Highlights for 2005/6 include calfskin, crêpe-soled pumps by Momola (from £75) and chocolate sheepskin boots by Neet (from £80). Prescott & Mackay also runs a range of shoe-making and other courses in central London – see the website for more details.
Mail order.

The British Boot Company

5 Kentish Town Road, NW1 8NH (7485 8505/ www.britboot.co.uk). Camden Town tube. **Open** 9.30am-6pm Mon-Fri; 9am-7pm Sat, Sun. **Credit** AmEx, DC, MC, V. **Sells** M, W, C.
A Camden institution, the BBC was the first shop to sell Doc Martens. It's also a little slice of rock 'n' roll history: the walls are plastered with posters signed by famous customers – Damon Albarn, Morrissey and Madness (Suggs and the boys used to live in the flat upstairs), to name a few. Stacked to the ceiling with shoeboxes, the shop is still the main London stockist for DMs, from the original

metal-toed stomping boot to floral-patterned styles. It's also the only UK stockist of Grinders and Gladiator. Prices start at around £50 and, if you're lucky, might include an anecdote about the old Camden scene from affable owner Nick Holt, whose drummer father started the shop in 1958.
Mail order.

Camper

8-11 Royal Arcade, 28 Old Bond Street, W1S 4SQ (7629 2722/www.camper.com). Green Park tube. **Open** 10am-6pm Mon-Wed, Fri, Sat; 10am-6.30pm Thur. **Credit** AmEx, MC, V. **Sells** M, W.
While this Mallorcan company has expanded worldwide, it hasn't sold out its ideals and retains a strong ethical conscience. Camper is committed to using environmentally friendly materials in the manufacture of its comfortable, round-toed shoes, and the Old Bond Street premises is an 'info-shop', its walls dedicated to a campaign to save the endangered Somera donkey. Bestselling styles are the bowling shoe (£90) and the Twins range (featuring fun decorative variations on left and right). Camper also has a range of comfortable, rubber-heeled shoes for girls in fruity, Toytown colours (the Sofia and Minie ranges). New for 2005/6 are Stuart riding boots for both sexes, and the Peu wide-topped, soft-leather shoe for men. Prices range from £60 to £260, but sit mainly around the £100 mark.
Mail order.
For branches see index.

Church's Shoes

201 Regent Street, W1B 4NA (7734 2438). Oxford Circus tube. **Open** 10am-6.30pm Mon-Wed, Sat; 10am-7pm Thur, Fri; noon-6pm Sun. **Credit** AmEx, MC, V. **Sells** M, W.
A combination of classic construction techniques – the shoes have been made in Northamptonshire since 1873 – and an old-fashioned sense of style makes this one of London's best-loved shoe labels, and the imposing marble interior at Church's provides a fittingly grand setting. Dapper brogues, Oxfords and loafers can all be found here, with prices starting at £250 for calf's leather and rising to £1,815 for crocodile skin. The slightly cheaper subsidiary brand, Cheaney, starts at £170. There are also old-fashioned leather slippers (£70) and a range of belts, ties and luggage.
Branches: throughout the city.

Clarks

476 Oxford Street, W1C 1LD (7629 9609/ www.clarks.co.uk). Marble Arch tube. **Open** 10am-8pm Mon-Fri; 10am-7pm Sat; noon-7pm Sun. **Credit** AmEx, MC, V. **Sells** M, W.
With a reputation that's more frumpy than funky, Clarks has some styles that undeniably tread on the dowdier side of sensible, but this is no reason to write it off. Careful hunting can turn up some surprising fashion jewels – for example, sequinned peep-toe ankle-strapped evening shoes (£35) and kitten-heeled Victorian-style maroon lace-up ankle boots (£55). The Mulberry-esque handbags are also worth looking out for, and the Originals range, including the famous Desert Boot and the nerdy-cool Wallabee, is reputed to have some rock-star fans. A slick new men's collection in collaboration with designer Oliver Sweeney (*see p71*) launches in November; prices start from £70.
Branches: throughout the city.

Dune

18 South Molton Street, W1Y 1DD (7491 3626/ www.dune.co.uk). Bond Street tube. **Open** 10am-7pm Mon-Wed, Fri, Sat; 10am-8pm Thur; noon-6pm Sun. **Credit** AmEx, MC, V. **Sells** W.
Dune makes subtly sexy shoes that appeal to women who shy away from the edgier end of fashion footwear. High-heeled courts, slinky slingbacks and strappy sandals are typical styles, but Dune also picks up on seasonal trends. Characteristic touches include girlie details such as corsages and beading, and prices are reasonable (around £50-£70 for shoes). There is a small selection of men's shoes in some stores (around £90 for loafers).
For branches see index.

Faith

192-194 Oxford Street, W1A 1DG (7580 9561/ www.faith.co.uk). Oxford Circus tube. **Open** 10am-8pm Mon-Sat; noon-6pm Sun. **Credit** MC, V. **Sells** W.
Faith was one of the first shoe shops to produce affordable copies of designer looks as soon as they'd stepped off the catwalk. Now that central London is a hive of similar shoe shops, with New Look, Shelly's, Faith and Office all scrambling to get the latest styles on the shelves (not to mention foreign contenders Aldo and Zara), it's no longer such a unique fashionista hotspot. That said, its collection features bold, adventurous takes on key styles, with details inspired by vintage shoes such as intricate leather lattice-work, chunky wooden soles and unusually shaped heels, capturing the look of the moment in an idiosyncratic and exciting way. Shoes in the main range are around £40, while the higher-quality Solo range is a bit more expensive. There are plans to feature quirky one-off styles in the basement, which formerly housed vintage shoes.
Mail order (0800 289297).
For branches see index.

Kate Kuba

22 Duke of York Square, King's Road, SW3 4LY (7259 0011/www.katekuba.co.uk). Sloane Square tube. **Open** 10am-6.30pm Mon-Sat; noon-6pm Sun. **Credit** AmEx, MC, V. **Sells** M, W.
This airy branch of the award-winning British shoe retailer has a wide range of stock and friendly staff to help you choose. Shapes, patterns and trimmings are unusual, attracting celebrity clients such as Beyoncé and Rachel Stevens. There are lots of equestrian-style boots, sexy, bejewelled high-heeled sandals and smart daywear heels that can double as eveningwear. Prices start at £45 (but expect to pay around £100 for most structured styles). The more exclusive Kuba Kouture label, featuring such extravagant styles as heavily gold-studded slingbacks and snakeskin cork wedges, starts at £195. New in 2005 is the Otto & Moi collection of vintage-style shoes, mostly medium heels with intricate detailing and studding, and some sumptuous almond-toed ruched leather boots (prices are around £125-£165). Other brands covered here include the likes of Diesel Style Lab, Ugg and Camper, and there is a small collection of men's shoes.
For branches see index.

Kurt Geiger

65 South Molton Street, W1K 5SU (7758 8020/ www.kurtgeiger.com). Bond Street tube. **Open** 10am-7pm Mon-Wed, Fri, Sat; 10am-8pm Thur; noon-6pm Sun. **Credit** AmEx, MC, V. **Sells** M, W.
Having shaken off the last vestiges of its staid department-store image, Kurt Geiger now has its finger firmly on the fashion pulse, with a variety of fresh-off-the-runway styles. Women's shoes are often a quirky and flamboyant take on current fashion, featuring embellishment and decorative detailing. Prices average around £140 for shoes, and £200 for boots. The younger, edgier kg range is less expensive – most shoes are around £65. Patent ballet pumps (£79) come in an array of tempting colours. For men, the Kurt Geiger 7 range offers a different classic shoe for each day of the week (around £150), and there are also shoes in interesting materials, such as goatskin and real snakeskin.
Mail order.
For branches see index.

LK Bennett

130 Long Acre, WC2E 9AA (7379 1710/ www.lkbennett.com). Covent Garden tube. **Open** 10.30am-7.30pm Mon-Wed, Fri, Sat; 10.30am-8pm Thur; noon-6pm Sun. **Credit** AmEx, MC, V. **Sells** W.
These elegant, feminine shoes have a nostalgic air. LK Bennett is moving away from its signature kitten-heel style to focus on stack heels, wedges and round toes (although for diehard fans there will still be some kitten heels in stock). The latest collection has strong Russian and Victorian

influences, featuring rich, jewel-coloured velvets and satins, sequins and chiffon trimmings. Prices start at £100 for shoes, while most of the boots hover around the £200 mark.
Mail order (7491 3005).
Branches: throughout the city.

Men's Traditional Shoes

171 Camberwell Road, SE5 0HB (7703 4179). Bus 12, 35, 40, 45, 68, 171, 176. **Open** 9am-5pm Mon-Sat. **Credit** DC, MC, V. **Sells** M.
A reputable, old-fashioned shop that has been in business since 1861, during which time it has had only three owners. A trip here pays off, as the out-of-the-way location means the shop can sell stylish brogues, Oxfords and loafers for around £30-£50 less than you would expect to pay in the West End (prices are around £80-£200). Labels include Trickers, Benson's, Church's and, especially, Loakes. The shop also sells industrial steel-capped work boots and DMs.

The Natural Shoe Store

21 Neal Street, WC2H 9PU (7836 5254/ www.thenaturalshoestore.com). Covent Garden tube. **Open** 10am-6pm Mon, Tue; 10am-7pm Wed, Fri; 10am-8pm Thur; 10am-6.30pm Sat; noon-5.30pm Sun. **Credit** AmEx, DC, MC, V. **Sells** M, W.
The small parent shop of the slick Birkenstock store down the road has been in business for more than 30 years and was the first to introduce the German sandal brand to the UK. Although it now stocks only a few styles, the shop's low-key, earthy atmosphere provides a refuge from the hype of the often-crowded Birkie flagship down the road. The Natural Shoe Store is dedicated to selling comfortable shoes by brands such as Trippen, Think! and Arche (£30-£130), and has branches in Chelsea and Westbourne Grove – the latter is especially chic and spacious.
Mail order.
For branches see index.

Office

57 Neal Street, WC2H 4NP (7379 1896/ www.office.co.uk). Covent Garden tube. **Open** 10.30am-7.30pm Mon-Wed, Fri; 10.30am-8pm Thur; 10.30am-7pm Sat; noon-6pm Sun. **Credit** AmEx, DC, MC, V. **Sells** M, W.
Office's takes on catwalk looks are among the most daring and successful of the high street chains in this price bracket (around £50 for shoes, £80-plus for boots). Office is unafraid to explore the edgiest and wildest trends – anything from metallic gladiator sandals to platform wedge espadrilles and clog boots. Capsule collections, such as the much-loved Office Vintage range, which recreates bygone styles, often with a modern twist, keep things interesting. For men there are sensible brogues and loafers, but also quirky styles such as bright plimsolls (shades of *Miami Vice*) in the Ask the Missus collection, and high-fashion pastel leather shoes with side lacing by Three Little Pigs. Boys and girls can both choose from a selection of trendy trainer labels like Converse, Adidas and Nike. Quality, especially on women's heels, is occasionally less than perfect, but this doesn't pose too much of a problem as most customers come here for a cheap fashion fix to wear for one season.
Mail order (0845 058 0777).
Branches: throughout the city.

The Old Curiosity Shop

13-14 Portsmouth Street, WC2A 2ES (7405 9891). Holborn tube. **Open** noon-6pm Mon-Fri; noon-5pm Sat. **Credit** MC, V. **Sells** M, W.
This quirky little cubby hole of a shop is purported to have spurred Charles Dickens into writing the eponymous novel. Whether that holds or not, the oft-seen tourists snapping away seem content to buy into the story, and the shop's off-kilter charm alone warrants a visit. Inside there's a small and decidedly eclectic collection of shoes, clothes and leather accessories handmade by Daiko Kimura in his workshop downstairs. Unisex footwear prices span £200-£300 and include such oddities as two-piece leather sandals (£120). The second designer selling here is George Cox, whose

'brothel creeper' shoes (£100) were favoured by the Sex Pistols. Alternatively, go for an idiosyncratic pair of silver winkle pickers (£88).

Pied à Terre

19 South Molton Street, W1K 5QX (7629 1362/www.piedaterre.com). Bond Street tube. **Open** 10am-7pm Mon-Wed, Fri, Sat; 10am-8pm Thur; noon-6pm Sun. **Credit** AmEx, MC, V. **Sells** W.
This once-innovative label may not be as ground-breaking as it used to be, but the quality is still good and there are some interesting details among the mainstream styles, such as stitching and embellishment on knee-high boots, or an oversized bow on a court shoe. Prices hover around the £110 mark for shoes, with boots at around £225.
Mail order.
For branch see index.

Poste

10 South Molton Street, W1K 5QJ (7499 8002). Bond Street tube. **Open** 10am-7pm Mon-Wed, Fri, Sat; 10am-8pm Thur; noon-6pm Sun. **Credit** AmEx, MC, V. **Sells** M.
Poste (and its sister shop Poste Mistress; *see below*) is the quirky, upmarket offshoot of the Office chain. The interior gives an ironic nod to the ambience of a gentlemen's club, with a chesterfield sofa, scattered glossy lads' mags and even a cravat-wearing skeleton. Poste's own label (around £100 for shoes), which has a 1970s rock vibe for autumn/winter 2005/6, is mixed in with hip labels such as Miu Miu, Patrick Cox and Jeffery-West. There are also unusual finds, such as Mr Boots Spanish handmade boots, recalling '70s glam rock styles (from £108). There is an 'out-Poste' in Harvey Nichols.
Mail order (08450 580 777).

Poste Mistress

61-63 Monmouth Street, WC2H 9EP (7379 4040). Covent Garden tube. **Open** 10am-7pm Mon-Wed, Fri, Sat; 10am-8pm Thur; 11.30am-6.30pm Sun. **Credit** AmEx, MC, V. **Sells** W.
Floral wallpaper straight out of the '70s, burgundy velvet pouffes and retro paintings of doe-eyed Spanish girls give this place the atmosphere of a kitsch boudoir, which goes well with the über-cool designer shoes. Creations from Vivienne Westwood, Dries van Noten and Miu Miu sit beside such finds as Spanish designer Chie Mihara's vintagey designs with snakeskin and embroidered details (£150), in dusky pinks and emerald greens, and cult ballet flats from Repetto (around £100). Poste Mistress's own label (from about £95) covers the season's basics – flat pumps, mid-heel dancing shoes – with a few eccentricities like Perspex wedge heels thrown in. A range of jewellery by Tatty Devine and Vivienne Westwood is also available (from £45), and there is a concession in Harvey Nichols.
Mail order (8747 7142).

R Soles

109A King's Road, SW3 4PA (7351 5520/ www.rsolesboots.com). Sloane Square tube. **Open** 10am-7pm Mon-Sat; noon-6pm Sun. **Credit** AmEx, MC, V. **Sells** M, W, C.
R Soles – geddit? More stylish than the brash name would suggest, this shop is world-famous for its cowboy boots designed by Judy Rothchild, which have attracted a host of celebrities including Madonna, Arnold Schwarzenegger and Victoria Beckham. The interior is lined with an amazing array of boots for cowboys, cowgirls and even cowkids in a variety of exotic colours and skins (snake, ostrich, crocodile, stingray), or featuring colourful floral embroidery or jewels. Cowboy boots start at £195, going up to £800 for hand-tooled designs. There are also a few other styles, such as biker and ankle boots (prices from £140).
Mail order.

Russell & Bromley

24-25 New Bond Street, W1S 2PS (7629 6903/ www.russellandbromley.co.uk). Bond Street tube. **Open** 10am-6.30pm Mon-Wed, Fri, Sat; 10am-7.30pm Thur; 11am-5pm Sun. **Credit** AmEx, DC, MC, V. **Sells** M, W.

R&B is popular with an older age bracket than many of the high-street shops included in this section, mainly because of the quality of the shoes and their somewhat conservative interpretation of current trends. The emphasis as we went to press was on equestrian-style boots, platform court shoes and stack-heeled slouch boots, with some metallic leathers spicing things up across the store. Prices are fairly middle-of-the-road (from about £100), but high-quality materials lend these shoes a luxurious look. DKNY trainers (for men and women) are sold here, and glitzy American designers Beverly Feldman and Stuart Weitzman produce exclusive women's collections for the shop. For men, there are well-made options from R&B's own label, plus shoes by Barker, Church's and Moreschi. Covetable handbags and an excellent repair service are further plus points.
Mail order.
For branches see index.

Schuh

200 Oxford Street, W1 (7467 8970/www. schuhstore.co.uk). Open 9.30am-8pm Mon-Wed, Fri; 9.30am-9pm Thur; 10am-8pm Sat; noon-6pm Sun. **Credit** AmEx, MC, V. **Sells** M, W, C.
A legend in its native Scotland, Schuh had a virtual monopoly on Edinburgh's trendy footwear market for years after it launched back in the 1980s. It opened a London store in summer 2004 and it is holding its own against other Oxford Street giants, with a strong selection of branded fashion footwear for men and women. Women's shoes are in hot pursuit of catwalk trends, ranging from high heels, bold boots, strappy sandals and quirkier styles from labels such as Irregular Choice, to trainers by the likes of Adidas and Acupuncture. For men, there are plenty of loafers, brogues and trainers from brands such as Camper, Base and Converse. Schuh also sells some cute baby shoes, and a small range of trendy, sportswear-inflected bags.

Shelly's

266-270 Regent Street, W1B 3AH (7287 0939/ www.shellys.co.uk). Oxford Circus tube. **Open** 10am-8pm Mon-Wed, Fri, Sat; 10am-8.30pm Thur; noon-6pm Sun. **Credit** AmEx, MC, V. **Sells** M, W.
Shelly's can be a bit hit or miss. As we went to press the offerings were mixed, with some slightly off-key women's styles (misplaced animal prints and clashing colours) and some unconvincing fake-snake pointy brogues for men. However, there are a few gems, such as the vintage-inspired black-and-gold platforms for £70, or a pair of two-tone Mary Janes for £80; there are also some quite stylish men's Chelsea boots. And on the plus side, quality tends to be good for the price (£30-£80 for shoes; £60-£125 for boots).
Mail order.
For branches see index.

Shipton & Heneage

117 Queenstown Road, SW8 3RH (7738 8484/ www.shipton.com). Queenstown Road rail/137 bus. **Open** 9am-6pm Mon-Fri; 10am-4pm Sat. **Credit** AmEx, MC, V. **Sells** M, W.
This purveyor of traditional, bench-made shoes uses the same Northamptonshire factories as many of the more celebrated shodders, but sells footwear for considerably cheaper (around a quarter less). The catch? You have to come down to Battersea and might have to wait a few days for your order. All the classic styles are here: Oxfords, Derbys, brogues, loafers and Chelsea boots, plus deck shoes and gentlemanly velvet slippers. Shoes come in three different quality categories: premium (mostly £185), select (mostly £155) and grade (mostly £110). There are also sensible loafers and deck shoes for women.
Mail order.

Sole

72 Neal Street, WC2H 9PA (7836 6777/www. sole.co.uk). Covent Garden tube. **Open** 10.30am-7pm Mon-Wed, Fri, Sat; 10.30am-8pm Thur; noon-6pm Sun. **Credit** AmEx, MC, V. **Sells** M, W, C.

FASHION

This upmarket central London outpost of the Soletrader chain draws in label-loving lads from all over town. The futuristic, curvaceous shelves are stocked with an impressive array of branded footwear. There are trendy, edgy trainers from the more boutiquey end of the sportswear brands, such as Neil Barrett's Puma ranges and Y3 by Adidas, as well as niche brands like Camper. Dressier shoes come courtesy of Oliver Sweeney, Buddhahood and Patrick Cox. Sole also makes its own range of brogues and loafers (from £69). There is a smaller selection of shoes for women from the likes of Diesel, Adidas and Converse. **For branch (Soletrader) see index.**

Swear
22 Carnaby Street, W1F 7DB (7734 1690/ www.swear-net.net). Oxford Circus tube. **Open** 11am-7pm Mon-Sat; 1-6pm Sun. **Credit** AmEx, MC, V. **Sells** M, W.
Swear sells playful shoes in wacky colours with a slightly punky flavour. For women, there's a wide range of round-toed kitten-heeled court shoes in a variety of bold patterns and rainbow-hued strappy sandals. Men's styles are equally quirky, with a new black-and-white version of Swear's popular Fun brogue style and lots of jazzy takes on the loafer (including velcro strips and stitching). Prices hover around £70-£75 for shoes, and around £100 for women's boots.
Mail order.

Designer

Beatrix Ong
117 Regent's Park Road, NW1 8UR (7499 0480/ www.beatrixong.com). Chalk Farm tube. **Open** 10am-6pm Mon-Sat; noon-6pm Sun. **Credit** MC, V. **Sells** W.
Young ex-Jimmy Choo designer Beatrix Ong doesn't believe you should have to suffer for fashion. Her aim is to create shoes that are comfortable enough for everyday wear, yet special enough to take you into the evening. This versatility is evidenced in her round-toed suede style with a detachable pearl-and-Swarovski-crystal cluster and, especially, by glittery, velvet-trimmed ballet flats in collaboration with Holistic Silk, featuring removable massaging and magnetic insoles to aid circulation and wellbeing (£115, perfect for chic jet-setters). At Ong's Primrose Hill shop, shoe shapes span the trend spectrum, from round-toed courts to pointy flatties (by way of more unusual styles such as a streamlined version of men's dress lace-ups), in materials from stingray and patent to glitter. Most shoes are over the £200 mark; boots start at £300.
Mail order.

Christian Louboutin
23 Motcomb Street, SW1X 8LB (7245 6510). Knightsbridge tube. **Open** 10am-6pm Mon-Fri; 11am-6pm Sat. **Credit** AmEx, MC, V. **Sells** W.
The French designer has upped the glam factor in the recent revamp of his small Knightsbridge shop, with characteristic wit – a selection of shoes is displayed behind antique gilt frames, and the semi-circular black velvet buttoned sofa evokes a 19th-century bordello. Louboutin mixes a hint of kink (skyscraper heels, curvy-calved boots) with a nostalgic sensibility expressed in his signature red soles and styles, such as peep-toe satin high heels decorated with a crystal rosette, complete with matching clutch – utterly 1940s debutante. There are also adorable Audrey Hepburn-esque flatties. Prepare to part with around £350 for shoes, £800 for boots. There is also a small collection of bags.

Emma Hope
53 Sloane Square, SW1W 8AX (7259 9566/ www.emmahope.co.uk). Sloane Square tube. **Open** 10am-6.30pm Mon, Tue, Thur-Sat; 10am-7pm Wed; noon-5pm Sun. **Credit** AmEx, MC, V. **Sells** M, W.
Best known for her beautifully embroidered and beaded mules, slingbacks and ballet slippers, Emma Hope has recently introduced funkier styles into her oeuvre, such as Converse-inspired

sneakers and high tops for men and women in unusual materials, including animal-print ponyskin, python and velvet (from around £170). There are also plainer, ladylike designs in calf and suede and more fashion-led styles such as the new season's very Puss-in-Boots gunmetal nappa-leather thigh-highs (£629). Shapes are sleek and contemporary, and the craftsmanship doesn't come cheap: most of the structured shoes are around £250, or £300-plus for intricately embellished designs. There are also some elegant satin and kid bridal shoes.
Mail order.
For branches see index.

Georgina Goodman
12-14 Shepherd Street, W1J 7JF (7499 8599/ www.georginagoodman.com). Green Park tube. **Open** 10am-6pm Mon-Sat. **Credit** AmEx, DC, MC, V. **Sells** M, W, C.
Georgina Goodman's unique, sculptural shoes are like wearable works of art, so it's fitting that her shop resembles a gallery, decorated with the designer's own footwear-themed mobiles. Made to measure on the premises to the customer's requirements, the couture shoes are created from one piece of untreated leather, which is hand-stitched and moulded to shape, then painted if required. Prices reflect the craftsmanship and individual attention – from £600 for women's shoes and £1,000 for men's. The women's ready-to-wear collection (from £100) is more colourful, in materials from hand-painted satin to python, featuring Goodman's signature shapes and details such as brushstroke-effect stripy wooden heels. The 2005/6 autumn/winter collection sees some chunky platform styles and delectable gold-striped suede ballet pumps in five colours (£100). There are also adorable children's shoes and a line of chic bags. The ready-to-wear footwear is available at Harrods and Matches, as well as the Mayfair shop.
Mail order.

Gina
189 Sloane Street, SW1X 9QR (7235 2932/ www.ginashoes.com). Knightsbridge tube. **Open** 10am-6pm Mon, Tue, Thur-Sat; 10am-7pm Wed. **Credit** AmEx, MC, V. **Sells** W.
Appealing to Chelsea socialites and footballers' wives alike, Gina's towering sandals dripping with diamanté are pure bling; there are also flat flip-flops and variations in opulent jewel colours. There are other, slightly less dazzling styles each season with the ostentatious glamour befitting the label's namesake Gina Lollobrigida, such as metallic python open-toed courts and stilettos combining leopard and snake. You'll have to raid the trust fund for the mainly £300-plus price tags.
Mail order.
For branch see index.

Jimmy Choo
32 Sloane Street, SW1X 9NR (7823 1051/ www.jimmychoo.com). Sloane Square tube. **Open** 10am-6pm Mon, Tue, Thur-Sat; 10am-7pm Wed; noon-5pm Sun. **Credit** AmEx, MC, V. **Sells** W.
The fave footwear brand of the lunch-and-pedicure set continues to expand apace – this luxurious store, its largest worldwide, opened in spring 2005, complete with a VIP room for celeb (or merely filthy-rich) clients. With two stand-alone stores in the capital, plus mini-salons in Harvey Nicks, Harrods and Selfridges, the label doesn't feel quite as exclusive as it used to, yet there seems to be no sign of Choo fatigue, with eager buyers splashing out around £300 on each exquisitely made pair, and the equally popular bags to match. Shapes are sleek, ladylike and impeccably crafted. The House Collection comprises core staples in tasteful neutrals, subtle metallics and black, while each season brings a crop of flamboyant, fashion-led seasonal designs, such as bright suede courts and boots. There are spectacular evening shoes, such as satin peep-toes ornamented with a large Swarovski-crystal flower (£650) or sandals hung with chains, charms or gems. If only the best will do on your big day, check out the bridal range.
Mail order.
For branch see index.

Lollipop London
114 Islington High Street, N1 8EG (7226 4005). Angel tube. **Open** 11am-7pm Mon-Sat; noon-5pm Sun. **Credit** MC, V. **Sells** W.
Laura Allnatt's pretty little footwear boutique is a goldmine of gorgeous shoes by hard-to-find independent British and European designers, including Victoria Fox, Beatrix Ong, Chie Mihara and, exclusive to the shop, Alexa Wagner and Avril Gau. Wagner's real python peep-toes and Gau's military-edged knee boots in leather and suede are the stars for autumn/winter 2005/6. Covetable accessories are thrown into the mix, including Heba Nouman's roomy handmade leather shoulder bags, vintage handbags sourced from the US, and jewellery, including chunky charm pieces by Millie and Me. Prices for shoes start at £50 and go up to around £400. It's worth getting on the mailing list to be notified of the shop's monthly 'pink champagne and pedicure' day, when customers are pampered with a 25-minute pedicure, champers and fairy cakes.

Manolo Blahnik
49-51 Old Church Street, SW3 5BS (7352 3863). Sloane Square tube then 11, 19, 22 bus. **Open** 10am-5.30pm Mon-Fri; 10.30am-5pm Sat. **Credit** AmEx, MC, V. **Sells** W.
While his *Sex and the City* rival Jimmy Choo has gone for high-profile expansion, Blahnik prefers to stay out of the limelight. For such a globally celebrated designer, this small salon on a Chelsea backstreet is remarkably low-key; it's even partially hidden by creeper. Blahnik has occupied the same address for over 30 years and has a fiercely loyal clientele across the generations, including numerous (undisclosed) celebs. Flattering, feminine heels are the speciality, in striking materials such as contrasting skins or vibrant brocades, or flaunting ultra-luxe trimmings such as crystal gems on a sandal or a chinchilla 'rose' on a satin mule. Shapes are on the whole quite classic, which is just as well: when you're spending over £350 on a pair of Manolos you don't want them to look dated next season. It's the craftsmanship and materials that dazzle – when we visited, a high-heeled ankle boot featured alternating strips of astrakhan, patent, crocodile and ponyskin, all in black (£1,700).

Mootich
34 Elizabeth Street, SW1 9NZ (7824 8113/ www.mootich.com). Sloane Square tube. **Open** 10am-6pm Mon-Sat. **Credit** AmEx, MC, V. **Sells** W.
Award-winning Belgrade-born footwear designer Katarina Mutic has traded edgy Portobello Road for chi-chi Belgravia. In her demure little shop, shoes are displayed in deconstructed antique commodes. Made in small quantities in an artisanal factory in Italy, they display whimsical touches such as feather and fur trims, layered effects using different skins and unusual heels such as stacked horn discs. Prices start at around £275 rising to £400 for boots. Mootich is also available at Poste Mistress (*see p70*).

Oliver Sweeney
29 King's Road, SW3 4RP (7730 3666/ www.oliversweeney.com). Sloane Square tube. **Open** 10am-7pm Mon, Tue, Thur-Sat; 10am-8pm Wed; noon-6pm Sun. **Credit** AmEx, MC, V. **Sells** M.
A host of sport, pop and movie stars – from David Beckham to Will Smith – like Oliver Sweeney's sleek takes on classic gents' footwear. Not only do the shoes look cool, Sweeney's innovative Anatomical Last, which simulates the natural arch of the foot, apparently eliminates the 'breaking in' period. Styles range from slightly left of traditional brogues, loafers and ankle boots in a variety of skins (from high-shine calf to stingray) and finishes to smart trainer-inspired leather casuals with natty details like go-faster stripes and Velcroed straps. Prices start at around £155. There's a range of leather jackets and accessories, and a repair service.
Mail order.
For branch see index.

Olivia Morris

355 Portobello Road, W10 5SA (8962 0353/ www.oliviamorrisshoes.com). Ladbroke Grove tube. **Open** by appointment Mon, Tue; 11am-6pm Wed, Thur; 10am-6pm Fri, Sat. **Credit** AmEx, MC, V. Sells W.

Morris seems to have mellowed since she brought in such radical concepts as 'paint-your-own' blank canvas shoes a few years back – although clip-on patent bows and chandelier-inspired crystal shoe jewellery carry on the customisation theme. Her latest collection, inspired by upholstery fabrics, is understated, with a few eccentric touches, such as an oversized tassel decorating an emerald-green velvet boot, a vibrant paisley print on a silk court shoe and a giant wooden button punctuating a velvet peep-toe. The queen of the retro court, Morris features both round and pointy toes, as well as stiletto, kitten, flat and stacked heels for 2005/6. Expect to pay over £250 for shoes; around £400-£700 for boots. Morris's shoes are also sold at Harrods and The Cross (see p36).
Mail order.

Patrick Cox

129 Sloane Street, SW1X 9AT (7730 8886/ www.patrickcox.co.uk). Sloane Square tube. **Open** 10am-6pm Mon, Tue, Thur-Sat; 10am-7pm Wed; noon-5pm Sun. **Credit** AmEx, MC, V. Sells M, W.

The Canadian designer celebrates 20 years in shoe biz this autumn and, after a two-year stint as creative director of Charles Jourdan (which seems to have all but disappeared from the London retail scene), has turned his attention to his own label with renewed vigour. The formerly faded flagship store has been given a long-overdue revamp; in the slick, walnut-floored premises classic films play in a gilt-framed plasma screen above the travertine cash desk. In previous seasons, Cox has seemed stuck in a 1990s time warp, but the latest collection is bang on the current mood: vintage-look stilettos in antiqued mock croc, for example, or almond-toed, stacked heel calfskin boots – luxuriously lined in rabbit fur. Russian-style hand-embroidered gold thigh-highs are show-stoppers (£900). Designs sometimes dip their toes into flash trash – Ana Matronic is said to like the sandals that dangle a mini chandelier behind their wedge heels (around £350), while only the most flamboyant dandy would dare sport the men's black military boot emblazoned with a prominent bejewelled cross (£900). The new steel-capped, round-toed sneaker in plain or faux skin-stamped leathers is more understated (from £195) and a semi-bespoke range of mix-and-match classic styles and colours in French calf will appeal to men of refined tastes (from £300). Although the Wannabe range has been axed, shoes start from as little as £125.
Mail order.

Robert Clergerie

67 Wigmore Street, W1U 1PY (7935 3601/ www.robertclergerie.com). Bond Street tube. **Open** 10.30am-6pm Mon-Wed, Fri, Sat; 10.30am-7pm Thur. **Credit** AmEx, DC, MC, V. Sells W.

After a brief retirement, during which he entrusted design to Michel Vivien, Robert Clergerie is back at the helm of his 25-year-old label. To his loyal customers worldwide, however, these transitions have been seamless. The shoes, which are handmade in France, have a strikingly unique style rather than being governed by passing trends, and are comfortable as well as chic, with supple leather linings and padded insoles. However, by a twist of fashion fate, the signature styles – wedge-heeled knee boots in suede, leather or stretch fabric, and organic clog-shaped shoes with lightweight, Latex-like soles – are in sync with the catwalk. Given the craftsmanship, prices are reasonable (from around £155 to £410 for boots). Most styles are limited to two pairs in each size – although they can be ordered – so you won't see them all over town.
For branch see index.

Rupert Sanderson

33 Bruton Place, W1J 6NP (0870 750 9181/ www.rupertsanderson.co.uk). Bond Street or Green Park tube. **Open** 10am-6pm Mon-Fri; 11am-6pm Sat. **Credit** AmEx, DC, MC, V. Sells W.

Although Rupert Sanderson perfected his craft working for Sergio Rossi and Bruno Magli in Italy, there is something quintessentially English about his understated designs (reinforced by this quietly tasteful shop, tucked down a Mayfair mews). Ladylike yet thoroughly modern, they feature fine Italian leathers, graceful heels, refined details such as subtle cut-outs and slender, criss-crossing straps and sometimes surprising colours (bright blue suede or pale pink python, for example). Such quality comes at a price – most shoes are over £300. The 2005/6 autumn/winter collection fuses 1940s and '70s influences, executed in rich velvets, suede, ponyskin and corduroy. Sanderson also designs a range of nostalgic pigskin luggage fit for a Cunard cruise, made in your choice of trim in six to eight weeks (£600-£2,200).

Terry de Havilland

www.terrydehavilland.com. **Available at** *Liberty and Selfridges.*

His King's Road shop, Cobblers to the World, was a 1970s sensation, but after his glam-rock heyday, platform king de Havilland had been quietly making one-off shoes for private clients, from drag queens to pop stars such as Christina Aguilera – until last year's copycat designs on the catwalk prompted him to step back into the spotlight. His collection pays homage to his archive shapes – the chunky platform peep-toes and ankle-strap shoes that are very much in vogue – in vividly hued snakeskin, suede and metallic leather. Shoes cost around £250. There are also killer stiletto ankle and knee boots (£400-£700) and courts. A diffusion line, D-HAVZ, is sold in Miss Selfridge (from £65-£85 for shoes; £80-£120 for boots).
Mail order.

Tod's

35-36 Sloane Street, SW1X 9LP (7235 1321/ www.tods.com). Knightsbridge tube. **Open** 10am-6pm Mon-Fri; 10.30am-6pm Sat. **Credit** AmEx, MC, V. Sells M, W.

Best known for its driving moccasins in a variety of materials from calf to exotic skins (more prevalent in the summer months), luxury Italian label Tod's also offers elegant sandals and structured shoes and boots. Most women's styles still feature the signature rubber heel studs, essential to protect them from scuff marks when braking suddenly in your Ferrari. Prices for shoes are usually around the £200 mark; £400 for boots. There is also a classy bag collection and, for men, a range of Italian-accented brogues and loafers. Down the road, sister shop Hogan (10 Sloane Street, SW1X 9LE, 7245 6363), has a younger, urban feel, offering sleek interpretations of trainers such as the Interactive and the Olympia in eye-catching combinations of colourful suede, fabric and metallic leathers (from £165), alongside leather shoes, boots and bags.
For branches see index.

Tracey Neuls

29 Marylebone Lane, W1U 2NQ (7935 0039/ www.tn29.com). Bond Street tube. **Open** 11am-6.30pm Mon-Wed, Fri; 11am-8.30pm Thur; noon-5pm Sat. **Credit** AmEx, MC, V. Sells W.

Tracey Neuls is giving footwear clichés a kick in the kitten heels. After scooping up a string of prestigious awards at Cordwainers, the Canadian designer launched her inventive TN_29 label, which has been quietly amassing devotees from Seattle to Sydney over the past five years. Her first stand-alone shop is refreshingly unfashiony, adorned with Erica Akerlund's impish illustrations and eight-month-old daughter Viola's toys – there are even plans to serve customers coffee and freshly baked bread. Shoes dangle on ribbons suspended from the ceiling and a shelf displays a collection of objects, from old spectacles to a creepy vintage hairnet, that have provided inspiration. Neuls's fascination with detail, playful curiosity and refusal to follow the fashion pack are reflected in her designs (£120-£300). Heels range from totally flat to an organic wedge-Louis hybrid, and there are unexpected cut-outs and surprising trimmings, such as net. The 2005/6 collection has a slightly louche Edwardian feel with furry

insoles providing private pleasure. Highlights include a teal nappa-leather round-toed court with an integrated black mesh 'stocking' and lace-up boots with cut-out calves, so they fit everyone – including one satisfied customer, a sturdy-legged Russian gymnast.

Bespoke

If you have hard-to-fit feet or simply want a unique style made up, there is no shortage of bespoke shoemakers in the capital. Not only are made-to-measure shoes more comfortable, they will last longer as they can be repaired many times over. It can take between three and eight months for the first pair to be made, because a last (the wooden model of your foot) is made for each customer, but as this is kept for you, subsequent orders are quicker.

Caroline Groves

37 Chiltern Street, W1U 7PW (7935 2329/ www.carolinegroves.co.uk). Baker Street tube. **Open** by appointment 10am-7.30pm Tue-Fri. **Credit** MC, V. Sells W.

Specialist in nostalgic women's styles, recalling the 1920s through to the '50s, such as platform mock-croc peep-toes and lace-up ankle boots – all very 'now'. Prices start at £850 for a first pair.

George Cleverley

13 The Royal Arcade, 28 Old Bond Street, W1S 4SL (7493 0443/www.gjcleverley.co.uk). Bond Street tube. **Open** 9am-5.30pm Mon-Fri; 10am-4pm Sat. **Credit** AmEx, MC, V. Sells M.

Prices may be lower (£1,600) than at John Lobb, but the clientele is almost as lofty, with Laurence Olivier and Winston Churchill among the famous feet to be immortalised in wood. There is also a ready-to-wear collection starting at a rather more palatable £300.

James Taylor & Son

4 Paddington Street, W1U 5QE (7935 4149/ www.taylormadeshoes.co.uk). Baker Street tube. **Open** 9am-5.30pm Mon-Fri; 10am-1pm Sat. **Credit** MC, V. Sells M, W.

James Taylor caters to both men and women at its old-fashioned shop. As well as a bespoke service (from around £1,290), it offers orthopaedic options, 'elevator' shoes and Birkenstocks.

John Lobb

9 St James's Street, SW1A 1EF (7930 3664/ www.johnlobbltd.co.uk). Green Park tube. **Open** 9am-5.30pm Mon-Fri; 9am-4.30pm Sat. **Credit** AmEx, MC, V. Sells M, W.

London's most famous shodder bears the name of the Cornish farmboy turned bootmaker to King Edward VII. At this traditional wood-panelled establishment, a pair of made-to-measure leather shoes will set you back over £2,300.

Dance

Dancia International

187 Drury Lane, WC2B 5QD (7831 9483/ www.dancia.co.uk). Covent Garden or Holborn tube. **Open** 10am-6pm Mon-Sat; 11am-4pm Sun. **Credit** AmEx, MC, V. Sells M, W, C.

Footwear for every discipline is available here, from long-lasting, foot-friendly plastic Gaynor Minden pointe shoes and modern jazz sneakers, to sparkly ballroom T-bars and flamenco shoes from Spain. Dance clothing and accessories are also sold.
Mail order.
For branch see index.

Freed of London

94 St Martins Lane, WC2N 4AT (7240 0432/ www.freedoflondon.com). Leicester Square tube. **Open** 9.30am-5.30pm Mon-Fri; 9am-3.30pm Sat. **Credit** AmEx, MC, V. Sells M, W, C.

The undisputed king of the pointe shoe, Freed of London has been fitting dancers' feet since the late 1920s and supplies the crème de la crème of the dance world, including the Royal Ballet. Aspiring ballerinas can have a pair made up for as little as

£30. Freed also caters to ballroom dancers and musical theatre, and moves with the times, introducing innovations and up-to-date styles such as the Urban Trainer.

Unusual sizes

Crispins

28-30 Chiltern Street, W1U 7QG (7486 8924/ www.crispinsshoes.com). Baker Street tube. **Open** 10am-6pm Mon-Wed, Fri, Sat; 10am-7pm Thur. **Credit** MC, V. **Sells** W.
This shop sells chic shoes for sizes 6 to 10 in narrow AA, and 8½ to 12 in standard width (C). It's the sole UK supplier of large-size footwear by quality American label Stuart Weitzman. Prices range from £60 to £150.
Mail order.

Elephant Feet

8 Chiltern Street, W1U 8PU (7346 8916/www. elephantfeet.com). Baker Street tube. **Open** 10am-6pm Mon-Wed, Fri, Sat; 10am-7pm Thur. **Credit** MC, V. **Sells** W.
Women's styles in sizes 8-12 are refreshingly fashion-led – including stylish boots – and prices start at about £40. The men's range, sported by the likes of Lennox Lewis and covering sizes 13-18, is only available in the Brixton outlet.
Mail order.
For branch see index.

The Little Shoe Shop

71 York Street, W1H 1BJ (7723 5321/www.the littleshoeshop.com). Baker Street tube. **Open** 10am-5pm Mon-Wed, Fri, Sat; 10am-7pm Thur. **Credit** MC, V. **Sells** W.
This small-size specialist sells its own range in sizes 12½ to 3, in C and D widths.
Mail order.

Repairs

In addition to the recommended shops below, **Timpson** (www.timpson.co.uk) is a well-regarded chain with branches around town. *See also p70* **Russell & Bromley.**

Fifth Avenue Shoe Repairers

41 Goodge Street, W1T 2PY (7636 6705). Goodge Street tube. **Open** 8am-6.30pm Mon-Fri; 10am-6pm Sat. **Credit** (£20 min) AmEx, MC, V.
This efficient operation can repair heels while you wait – we were out of the door in about five minutes (from £5.95 for a ladies' rubber reheel). As well as offering the full range of repair services (bags too), Fifth Avenue sells traditional bench-made men's shoes by the likes of Church's, Loakes and Cheaney, plus an extensive array of polishes, cleaners and sprays.

KG Shoes

253 Eversholt Street, NW1 1BA (7387 2234/ www.cobbler.co.uk). Mornington Crescent tube. **Open** 8am-6pm Mon-Fri; 9am-1pm Sat. **No credit cards.**
Master mender George Zorlakkis is at the helm of this 50-year-old family business. The shop is entrusted with repairs for 35 of London's swankiest stores, yet reheeling costs from just £6. KG will also stretch or tighten boots and repair leather bags and jackets.
Mail order.

Michael's Shoe Care

4 Procter Street, WC1V 6NX (7405 7436) Holborn tube. **Open** 8am-6.30pm Mon-Fri. **Credit** AmEx, MC, V.
A reheel starts at £4.95 and a rubber half-sole at £11.95 at this friendly shop. Stretching and tightening (boots only) are also undertaken.
For branches see index.

Sole-Man

1 White Horse Street, W1Y 7LA (7355 2553). Green Park tube. **Open** 8am-6pm Mon-Fri; 9am-3pm Sat. **No credit cards.**
Recommended by top shoe shops, H Suleyman has 25 years' experience. Reheels start from £4.95.

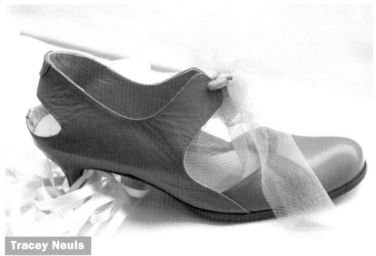

Tracey Neuls

Lingerie & Underwear

Aware

Hosiery

Note that almost all the shops listed below offer a mail order service.

Fogal
3A Sloane Street, SW1X 9LA (7235 3115/ www.fogal.com). Knightsbridge tube. **Open** 10am-6.30pm Mon, Tue, Thur-Sat; 10am-7.30pm Wed; noon-5pm Sun. **Credit** AmEx, DC, MC, V. **Sells** M, W, C.
This high-quality hosiery specialist has come a long way since Léon Fogal opened his first shop in 1923, selling (and mending) stockings for Zurich flappers; there are now outlets worldwide. Stock includes socks, stockings and, of course, tights (which start at £11) in a mind-boggling array of colours, designs and patterns. DNA-like swirls, muted blue checks, delicate antique-pink flowers and vibrant olive-coloured hold-ups are just some of the styles on offer. Men and children aren't neglected: the former get a range of luxury socks and kids get 'froggies' – non-slip socks they can pad around the house in.

Tabio
94 King's Road, SW3 4TZ (7591 1960/www. tabio.co.uk). Sloane Square tube. **Open** 10am-7pm Mon-Sat; noon-6pm Sun. **Credit** AmEx, MC, V. **Sells** M, W, C.
This Japanese company sells a huge range of socks for men, women and children in a clearly laid-out shop with staff keen to help you choose. Every kind of (innocent) foot fetish is catered to, from toe socks to bright stripy jobs. Tabio's women's range includes tights, stockings and that 1980s staple, leg warmers. Go for the quirky styles and shapes here over elegance and understatement.
For branch see index.

Wolford
3 South Molton Street, W1K 5QB (7499 2549/ www.wolfordboutiquelondon.co.uk). Bond Street tube. **Open** 10am-6pm Mon-Wed, Fri, Sat; 10am-7pm Thur. **Credit** AmEx, DC, MC, V. **Sells** W.
Synonymous with quality, Wolford is still producing a varied selection of tights, stockings and hold-ups. You won't find a kaleidoscope of bright colours supplied by the Wolford shop – this classy brand is much more suited to the elegant woman than the experimenting teenager (not least because the prices start at £12 for a basic pair of tights). There's also a good selection of bodywear available here, such as sheer all-in-ones and seamless bras. Label lovers will lap up the collaborations with Lagerfeld, Vivienne Westwood and Pucci.

Lingerie & underwear

London's leading department stores sell a wide selection of lingerie, hosiery, sleepwear and swimwear – **Harrods**, **Fenwick** and **Harvey Nichols** are all strong on designer labels, but **Selfridges** surpasses them all with a lingerie department that boasts mini Myla and Agent Provocateur boutiques. **Liberty** is also worth a look, particularly for the original label Frankly Darling.

These days, in addition to reliable but not wildly exciting underwear chains such as **Knickerbox** (which now has a concession in Ann Summers; *see below*), most of the high-street fashion chains have sidelines in lingerie: **French Connection**, **Dorothy Perkins**, **Gap**, **H&M** and particularly **Oasis**, with its pretty, vintage-inspired Odille range, all sell inexpensive, decent-quality smalls. The underwear section of **Topshop**'s Oxford Circus flagship store has grown dramatically and, as well as its own range – spanning functional to fancy – stocks Calvin Klein and Aussie brand Bonds.

For details of the above stores, *see chapters* **Department Stores** and **Womenswear**. Many boutiques also sell lingerie, notably **Austique** and **Coco Ribbon**; for both, *see chapter* **Boutiques**.

Agent Provocateur
6 Broadwick Street, W1V 1FH (7439 0229/mail order 0870 600 0229/www.agentprovocateur. com). Oxford Circus or Tottenham Court Road tube. **Open** 11am-7pm Mon-Wed, Fri, Sat; 11am-8pm Thur. **Credit** AmEx, DC, MC, V. **Sells** W.
Agent Provocateur serves up decadent sauciness without descending into sleaze. The distinctive retro-glamour of the shops' pink and black decor is extended to the staff, who are kitted out in cleavage-enhancing pink nurses' uniforms with lacy black bras peeping out provocatively (natch). As a brand, it's a well-executed and well-oiled machine – from the packaging and perfume (no prizes for guessing the colour scheme) to the lingerie itself, but with its deserved success has come a vague but discernible air of smug satisfaction. Bras, from 32A to 38F, cost from £70 up to over £200, and many are beautiful, such as a gorgeous aqua satin demi-cup bra trimmed with chocolate lace (£98): perhaps slightly ambitiously priced given the growing high-street competition.
For branches see index.

Alice & Astrid
30 Artesian Road, W2 5DD (7985 0888/ www.aliceandastrid.com). Royal Oak tube. **Open** 11am-6pm daily. **Credit** AmEx, DC, MC, V. **Sells** W.
Walking into this tiny, light-filled treasure trove, which opened in 2004, feels like stumbling across a local's secret. Although it's just off boutique-heavy Ledbury Road, you're unlikely to encounter many others while you browse, which makes for very civilised shopping, and the laid-back interior has the air of someone's private, rather girlie boudoir. Stock ranges from pretty briefs in cotton, chiffon or silk (£36-£61) to delicate vintage-inspired silk slip nighties (around £125) and patterned kimonos (£175). New for autumn/ winter 2005 are delicate baby alpaca knits (a shrug is £120; a longer 'cardigown' £250) to complement the nightwear and loungewear. Candles, bath products and jewellery – all great gift ideas – are also sold.

Ann Summers
95 Oxford Street, W1D 2HB (08700 534 042/ www.annsummers.co.uk). Oxford Circus or Tottenham Court Road tube. **Open** 10am-7pm Mon-Wed, Sat; 10am-9pm Thur; 10am-8pm Fri; noon-6pm Sun. **Credit** MC, V. **Sells** W.
Stock up here for booze-fuelled hen nights on cheap and brightly hued tights and hold-ups (from a fiver). The Ann Summers range of underwear will prove too tacky for some, with lashings of black and pink satin, as well as racy favourites like basques and crotchless knickers. Party pieces are plentiful, fun and cheap, from feather boas (£10) to edible thongs (£6). The Knickerbox corner, characterised by pretty pastels and decent prices, comes as sensory relief, with items such as comfy Palazzo pants for lounging in (£20) and bras trimmed with 'luxury French lace' (£12).
Branches: throughout the city.

Aware
25 Old Compton Street, W1D 5JN (7287 3789/ www.awareunderwear.co.uk). Leicester Square or Tottenham Court Road tube. **Open** 11am-8pm Mon-Sat; 1-7pm Sun. **Credit** AmEx, MC, V. **Sells** M.
This diminutive shop sells a comprehensive collection of men's designer labels to the Old Compton Street crowd of image-conscious and well-honed young men. Expect to find boxers and briefs by Puma, Dolce & Gabbana, Hom, Calvin Klein and, from December 2005, Versace, among others. A simple pair of Calvins start at £13. Swimwear, close-fitting T-shirts and beachwear are also available. There are also other two branches for women. Called Amelie's Follies, they cater to yummy mummies looking for labels such as Aubade, Lejaby and Simone Perele, and provide a good fitting service.
For branches (Amelie's Follies) see index.

Bodas

38B Ledbury Road, W11 2AB (7229 4464/mail order 0870 333 0411/www.bodas.co.uk). Notting Hill Gate tube. **Open** 10am-6pm Mon-Sat; noon-4pm Sun. **Credit** AmEx, MC, V. **Sells** W.

In this glass-fronted, minimalist shop, high comfort takes precedence over glamour and detail. The range is simple but versatile: bras come in soft-cup, underwired, seam-free, padded and strapless styles, and knickers can be mixed and matched – from a hipster thong (£9) to a full brief (£11). Simple white cotton is the cheapest, but the same styles are also available for a bit more money in 'smooth Tactel' (for no VPL) and lace. Bra sizes range from 32A to 38D (and up to 38E in selected ranges), and the cheapest is the soft bra in 'silky toile' at just £15. A range of simple white cotton pyjamas and nighties is also worth a look.

Bravissimo

28 High Street, W5 5DB (8579 6866/mail order 01926 459859/www.bravissimo.com). Ealing Broadway tube/rail. **Open** 10am-5.45pm Mon-Sat; 11am-5pm Sun. **Credit** MC, V. **Sells** W.

Applauded by the well-endowed for providing style and femininity in bigger bra sizes, Bravissimo also welcomes the more petite woman. In fact, the shop's speciality is fitting comfortable bras on those with small backs and large cup sizes – the 28Ds of this world. For the broader-backed, sizes go up to 40HH. The lingerie comes courtesy of such established brands as Panache (the cheapest, starting at £21 for a bra), Kalyani, Fantasy and Freya. Bravissimo also sells a range of own-label clothing, featuring suits (trousers/skirts £40;

jackets £75) and strappy tops with inbuilt bras (£30) – very useful for the large-busted among us as they avoid double-strap syndrome. **For branch see index**.

Calvin Klein

65 New Bond Street, W1F 1RN (7495 2916/ www.ck.com). Bond Street tube. **Open** 10am-6.30pm Mon-Wed, Fri, Sat; 10am-7pm Thur; noon-5pm Sun. **Credit** AmEx, MC, V. **Sells** M, W.

Don't go to Calvin Klein expecting a plunging cleavage and full-on sex appeal, or if your cup size exceeds a D. What you will get, though, is well-made, subtly stylish underwear free of fuss and frills. Designs are prettier and less utilitarian than they used to be, but graphic patterns, clever touches (such as neat buttons rather than bows) and muted colours (burgundy spruced up with pink piping, for example) maintain the label's cool. Mix and match bras (from £22), vests (from £19) and thongs or briefs (from £9) in the same fetching patterns. Men's briefs – of larger-than-life billboard fame – start at £18.50. **For branch see index**.

Coco de Mer

23 Monmouth Street, WC2H 9DD (7836 8882/ www.coco-de-mer.co.uk). Covent Garden tube. **Open** 11am-7pm Mon-Wed, Fri, Sat; 11am-8pm Thur. **Credit** AmEx, MC, V. **Sells** W.

Coco de Mer does sex in a risqué, vaguely Victorian and rather intellectual way. So, towards the back of this sumptuous shop, you'll find erotic literature among the beautifully crafted ticklers, wooden spankers and other assorted tools of the boudoir.

The lingerie collection, towards the front of the shop, is small but well edited, with the sort of flimsy and flirty items that manage to leave something to the imagination without sacrificing any eroticism. Prices are steep but fair for what's on offer, from a Chloé bikini for £115 to a sorbet-toned half-cup bra for £72. However, given all the heat Coco de Mer hopes to ignite in the bedroom, it seems a shame that the staff are on the glacial side.

Eda

132 King's Road, SW3 4TR (7584 5937/mail order 7584 0435/www.eda-lingerie.com). Sloane Square tube. **Open** 10am-6.30pm Mon, Tue, Thur-Sat; 10am-7pm Wed; noon-6pm Sun. **Credit** AmEx, DC, MC, V. **Sells** W.

Set up 20 years ago, this family-run company uses top-notch lace and embroidery sourced from France and Switzerland – Leavers lace is heavily employed – to adorn its ultra-feminine designs. Such detail doesn't come cheap – while bras start at around £30, some elaborate designs are four times that sum. Styles include balconette, push-up and padded, and sizes go from 32A up to 38F. Silk nighties and camisoles are also sold (from £100) and you can order from the website.

Exotica Brazil

15 Gloucester Arcade, 128 Gloucester Road, SW7 4SF (7835 0669/www.exotica.co.uk). Gloucester Road tube. **Open** 11am-7pm Mon-Sat. **Credit** AmEx, DC, MC, V. **Sells** W, C.

No one pulls off unswerving self-confidence in next to nothing like the Brazilians, and with its vibrant range of lingerie and swimwear this shop pays

Splash out

Tracking down a decent bikini in London used to be a bit like looking for a nice jumper on a Greek island. Hunting grounds were confined to department stores or, in summer, high street chains – pickings were slim if you were jetting off to the Caribbean in January. Heidi Gosman and Penny Klein changed all that a few years ago when they opened **Heidi Klein** (174 Westbourne Grove, W11 2RW, 7243 5665, www.heidi klein.com), a year-round, one-stop shop for swimwear and holiday chic. In the summery Westbourne Grove shop, complete with palm trees and sand, expertly trained staff are on hand to advise on the best styles for your shape, and there's a salon in the back for those essential preparations before you bare. As well as gorgeous own-label and designer bikinis (including Melissa Odabash and, exlusive to Heidi Klein, LA line TNA, beloved of jet-setters such as Jemima Kahn), there are beaded Apsara kaftans, Kristina Ti and Tocca dresses, plus Havaiana flip-flops and beachy bead jewellery to complete the resort-chic look. Children aren't forgotten and there are bold Vilebrequin shorts for big and small boys. Business is booming – at press time, there were plans to expand the Chelsea branch, introducing treatment rooms and a new floor for children and men.

Smaller but with a similar glam beach-hut vibe, **Pistol Panties** (75 Westbourne Park Road, W2 5QH, 7229 5286, www.pistolpanties.com) opened in summer 2005 and is already a hit with hip London beach bunnies. The bright bikinis by Paris-born, Miami-

raised designer Deborah Fleming have a retro feel, with frills, bows and patterns such as polka dots and abstract floral prints (from £79). Lara Bohinc sunglasses, kitsch straw beach bags, exotic shell jewellery and a sprinkling of vintage items are also sold here.

If, like most of us, your top doesn't match your bottom, newcomer **Biondi** (55B Old Church Street, SW3 5BS, 7349 1111) offers a bespoke bikini service (from £150) alongside other jet-set essentials such as cashmere flight blankets, eye masks and resortwear.

Once you've been measured and had a consultation with designer Jennifer Murphy, you can choose from about a dozen styles (or have one custom-created) and select your fabric and trimmings – you can even have it monogrammed. A toile bikini is then whipped up to ensure a flawless fit before the swimsuit is made on the premises. The service takes between ten days and three weeks.

Barely there bikinis are also the stock in trade at **Exotica Brazil** (*see above*).

Pistol Panties

homage to that sassy attitude. The bikinis are predictably teeny-weeny, but if you've got the nerve, the comprehensive range comes in appealing aquas, oranges and hot pinks. The simplest styles are £60 and many are £80, which is pricey for such a small amount of material. Still, the fit is very good, and the all-important Lycra of superior quality. On the lingerie front, lace abounds (for around £40 on a bra) but there are also plain, seamfree styles with transparent silicone straps (£35). Some styles don't go beyond a C cup but there is the odd E cup to be found. Childrenswear also sold.
For branch see index.

Janet Reger
2 Beauchamp Place, SW3 1NG (7584 9368/ www.janetreger.com). Knightsbridge tube. **Open** 10am-6pm Mon-Sat. **Credit** AmEx, DC, MC, V. **Sells** W.
High glamour, intricate embroidery and a propensity for black silk add up to a range of lingerie that is beautiful but, dare we say it, a touch dated. The prices are on the frightening side for briefs and bras (you'd do well to get change out of £50 for a pair of knickers, lovingly designed as they are), but the basques, if that's what you're after, seem reasonable by comparison (from £75).

Marks & Spencer
458 Oxford Street, W1C 1AP (7935 7954/ www.marksandspencer.com). Marble Arch tube. **Open** 9am-9pm Mon-Fri; 9am-8pm Sat; noon-6pm Sun. **Credit** AmEx, DC, MC, V. **Sells** M, W.
For sheer choice, you can't beat good old M&S these days (though men don't get anywhere near the variety women enjoy). Whether you're after a pair of plain white cotton briefs or something more sensual, the Marble Arch flagship has it all. For feminine prettiness, seek out the Adored range, available in soft, muted tones of rose, coffee and duck's egg and trimmed with cream lace. A basic bra costs a mere £12, going up to £20 for a more robust balcony style. Matching camis are £18, while briefs are £4. The Truly You collection turns the temperature up with Italian-style ostentation, but for every day, there's a huge range for every possible need: backless, strapless, seamless, nude-coloured… Huge changing rooms are also a big plus.
Branches: throughout the city.

Miss Lala's Boudoir
144 Gloucester Avenue, NW1 8JA (7483 1888). Chalk Farm tube. **Open** 10.30am-6.30pm Mon-Wed, Fri, Sat; 10.30am-6.30pm Thur; 1-5pm Sun. **Credit** DC, MC, V. **Sells** W.
Fine Rees's pretty little boutique bills itself as a 'dressing-up shop for grown-up girls', and cheeky lingerie labels are its stock in trade. Current showstoppers include the Burlesque Collection by East London label Buttress & Snatch – the frilled taffeta knickers à la Moulin Rouge and Hollywood-style bras with huge bows were originally designed for postmodern burlesque star Immodesty Blaise. Less extravagant are beribboned undies embroidered with each day of the week – in French, of course (£18) – and bright Peachy Keen broderie anglaise boy shorts (£18). But it's not all sexy nothings – campy Miss Lala T-shirts embellished with sequins, Swarovski crystals and glitter (£79) and the shop's signature tutu skirts are typical beyond-the-bedroom buys. Stock changes rapidly.

Myla
74 Duke of York Square, King's Road, SW3 3LY (7730 0700/mail order 0870 745 5003/ www.myla.com). Sloane Square tube. **Open** 10am-6pm Mon-Sat; noon-5pm Sun. **Credit** AmEx, DC, MC, V. **Sells** W.
Myla manages to be both light-hearted and sexy, maybe because it's more geared towards women buying for themselves than men buying into a fantasy on behalf of the lady in their life. This branch is bigger and more pleasant to shop in than the original Notting Hill store. Upstairs, away from prying eyes, a good bra-fitting service is available, in addition to an advice service. Many items are very lovely but they're not cheap: G-strings are

around £30, while bras are closer to £100 (and go from A to E cup). For those on a tighter budget, diffusion line My by Myla offers simpler designs at more affordable prices (around £50 for a bra). Designer sex toys are another (ahem) pull.
For branches see index.

La Perla
163 Sloane Street, SW1X 9QB (7245 0527/ www.laperla.com). Knightsbridge tube. **Open** 10am-6pm Mon, Tue, Thur-Sat; 10am-7pm Wed. **Credit** AmEx, DC, MC, V. **Sells** M, W.
This world-renowned Italian luxury label sells underwear, swimwear, nightwear, a clothing line and accessories. As beautiful as many of the designs are, the brand could be accused of some complacency because, with so much competition at more palatable prices, the price tags seem more than a bit steep. Be warned also: haughty staff used to dealing with wealthy ladies might make you feel a bit like a pre-makeover Julia Roberts in *Pretty Woman*.

Rigby & Peller
22A Conduit Street, W1S 2XT (7491 2200/ www.rigbyandpeller.com). Oxford Circus tube. **Open** 9.30am-6pm Mon-Wed, Fri, Sat; 9.30am-7pm Thur. **Credit** AmEx, MC, V. **Sells** W.
Her Majesty's corsetière of choice has been measuring busts since 1939. The company prides itself on its free expert fitting service – highly trained and down-to-earth staff can often accurately guess your size by sight. Ready-to-wear bras are available in sizes from 30A to 40E, but you can have them made to measure (which, of course, will cost more). Styles tend to be ultra-feminine, with prices to match the quality (from around £50 for a ready-to-wear bra, £30 for thongs and briefs). Bespoke bras start at £250. There's also a small but impressive swimsuit section, plus some nightwear.
For branch see index.

La Senza
162 Oxford Street, W1N 9DL (7580 3559/www.la senza.co.uk). Oxford Circus tube. **Open** 10am-7pm Mon-Wed, Fri, Sat; 10am-8pm Thur; noon-6pm Sun. **Credit** AmEx, DC, MC, V. **Sells** W.
La Senza spoils the overall look of its shops with tacky cartoon-emblazoned nightwear. This aside, however, you'll find a well-priced selection of seamless-cupped plunge bras, elegant and expensive-looking silk sets for around £28, and white cotton waffle-weave dressing gowns for £25. It may be worth branching out from M&S for your smalls: you can bag five pairs of knickers here for just £12. The Dreamshapers range found behind the counter is great for those who love barely there clothes but don't want to go braless. As well as that Oscars ceremony essential, 'tit tape', there are strapless, backless cups that you literally stick on to your chest, for £20.
Branches: throughout the city.

Tallulah Lingerie
65 Cross Street, N1 2BB (7704 0066/www. tallulahlingerie.co.uk). Angel tube. **Open** 11am-6.30pm Mon-Fri; 10.30am-6.30pm Sat; 12.30-4.30pm Sun. **Credit** MC, V. **Sells** W.
Vivid red walls, antique furniture and dark wood create a boudoir backdrop for labels such as Pleasure State, Aubade, Lejaby and Fleur T at this well-edited lingerie boutique the fan base of which extends from teens at one end of the spectrum to the owner's grandmother at the other. Brides-to-be might like the bestselling pearl thong (£59).

VPL
61A Ledbury Road, W11 2AA (7221 6644/ www.vpl-london.co.uk). Notting Hill Gate tube. **Open** 10am-6pm Mon-Sat; noon 5pm Sun. **Credit** AmEx, DC, MC, V. **Sells** W.
The clever name is apt, as much of the wares in this new boutique are meant to be seen. Owner Aimee Goring, who believes lingerie should be shown off, is promoting a new genre of clothing: 'after wear', as in something to lounge around in after work, after a bath, after the gym and so on. Gimmicky, but we like the stock, which includes pretty silk camisoles by Mary Green and Khurana, simple but flirty knickers by Cosabella and cashmere lounge suits by Nude. Prices are reasonable too – starting at £20 for a camisole and £35 for a bra.

Mail order & internet

Figleaves
0870 499 9000/www.figleaves.com. **Phone enquiries** 8.30am-11pm Mon-Fri; 9am-5.30pm Sat. **Credit** AmEx, MC, V. **Sells** M, W.
Figleaves claims to be the world's largest online retailer of branded underwear for both sexes. New labels joining established favourites include Madame V, Fayreform and UK brand Miss Manderlay – the latter two have bras rising to a G cup. In the large sleepwear section, DKNY's intricate patterns and vivid colours stand out, and the prices aren't too ruinous given the designer tag: a pansy-print vest costs £24. Expectant mums will also find a large section devoted to their needs – new additions include Amoralia luxury maternity lingerie, created by a designer from the Agent Provocateur stable, and Blossom Mother & Child. Both delivery and returns are free within the UK.

Ultimodirect
0845 130 3232/www.ultimodirect.com. **Phone enquiries** 9am-6pm Mon-Fri. **Credit** AmEx, MC, V. **Sells** W.
This company is best known for bras with removable liquid silicone gel pads. These magic little sacs can transform a modest décolletage into the ample cleavage of the brand's model, Rachel Hunter. There are some useful styles, such as halterneck bras, available without gels. Bras start at around £24; thongs at £10.

Eda. See p75.

Accessories

Many of the names listed within the **Designer** chapter of this guide also produce high-end accessories, while independent fashion shops (*see chapter* **Boutiques**) are often a rich source of shoes, bags, jewellery and scarves. Among the high-street chains, **Topshop** and **Zara** are good for inexpensive wardrobe-updating extras, and **Gap**'s handbag designer has an impressive pedigree (for all three, *see chapter* **Womenswear**). For a catalogue of designer brands under one roof, try upmarket department stores, such as **Fenwick**, **Harvey Nichols** or **Selfridges**. For all, *see chapter* **Department Stores**.

As we went to press, **Orla Kiely**'s flagship (31 Monmouth Street, WC2H 9DD, 7240 4022, www.orlakiely.com) was about to open its doors. The designer's full collection of clothing and accessories will now be under one roof, including delectable bags in a wide range of materials, from her famous graphic prints to richly hued leather and ponyskin (from £90 for laminated fabric), plus scarves, hats, wellies, luggage and, new for 2005, cushions and blankets.

General

Accessorize
22 The Market, Covent Garden, WC2H 8HB (7240 2107/www.accessorize.co.uk). Covent Garden tube. **Open** 9am-8pm Mon-Fri; 10am-8pm Sat; 11am-7pm Sun. **Credit** AmEx, DC, MC, V.
This high-street accessories chain is an offshoot of Monsoon (*see p41*), which accounts for the subtle ethnic flavour of many of its ranges – historically the company sourced products in Asia and the Far East. The shops are heaven for fans of boho or sheer glitz, with acres of satin and beads incorporated into slippers, purses, scarves and so on. Accessories are regularly updated, yet the overall formula never seems to change much: woolly hats, striped scarves, bags and jewellery crop up each winter; flip-flops and beach hats join the bags and jewellery for summer. That's not meant as a criticism: whether you're dressing for a wedding or the beach, you can rely on finding the necessary extras in pretty styles and a vast array of colours – at affordable prices.
Branches: throughout the city.

Anya Hindmarch
15-17 Pont Street, SW1X 9EH (7838 9177/ www.anyahindmarch.com). Sloane Square tube. **Open** 10am-6pm Mon, Tue, Thur-Sat; 10am-7pm Wed. **Credit** AmEx, MC, V.
Hindmarch excels as a designer of bags that make a statement, be it verbal or textural. 'How to Avoid Having Sex on the First Date' is neatly picked out in sequins on a bag that appears to be a book, but most pieces are less jokey, involving, say, gold python skin with plaited handles and ruched pockets, or the signature bow motif in many different colours. Prices hover around the £500 mark. The Bespoke Ebury range (£895-£6,500), geared towards gift-buyers, allows the buyer to choose from a range of colours and shapes, and have a message embossed in their own handwriting on the inside. The Be A Bag series, popular with celebs, enables you to have a personal image printed on to a bag (£75 for a wash bag); it's one of the less expensive ways to own a Hindmarch design. In addition to clothing, shoes and handbags, there's luggage, key rings, iPod covers and passport holders.

Claire's Accessories
108 Oxford Street, W1D 1LP (7580 5504/ www.claires.co.uk). Oxford Circus tube. **Open** 9am-7pm Mon-Wed, Fri, Sat; 9am-9pm Thur; 11.30am-5.30pm Sun. **Credit** MC, V.
All the sparkly delights a girl could ever hope for are here, from chandelier earrings to glittering Alice bands, via stick-on body gems. Prices are low and, even if the quality is sometimes poor, how long could you be in love with a rhinestone tiara incorporating the words 'Birthday Girl', or a set of lip glosses with fuzzy animals on the lids? Exactly. On a practical note, you can also find just about every type of hair grasp you can think of – all at pocket money prices.
Branches: throughout the city.

Comfort Station
22 Cheshire Street, E2 6EH (7033 9099/www. comfortstation.co.uk). Liverpool Street tube/rail. **Open** by appointment only 11am-6pm Mon-Thur; 11am-6pm Fri-Sun. **Credit** AmEx, MC, V.
This is the sort of cult boutique that any serious shopaholic loves to stumble across. It has a dismantled piano and vintage leather suitcases for shelves, and a floor painted in vertiginous monochrome stripes. The wares are just as wacky; the 'clam bag', for example, is made of solid oak covered in wavy pleats, and opens to reveal printed birds on the lining. Earrings feature Houdini suspended in silver chains, Alice in Wonderland or 1920s swimmers. Neck scarves and fabric belts also have vintage hints, while being ultra-modern. It's all just the ticket for Brick Lane style slaves.

Doors by Jas MB
8 Ganton Street, W1F 7PQ (7494 2288/www. doorsbyjasmb.com). Oxford Circus tube. **Open** 11am-7pm Mon-Sat; 1-5pm Sun. **Credit** MC, V.
An intoxicating smell of leather greets visitors to this small boutique. The titular salvaged doors lining the shop are almost obscured by racks of own-label leather jackets and an intriguing range of bags based on pre-war English workwear. This means lots of crackled leather, brown suede, ponyskin and rope handles – wholesome relief for shoppers jaded by too many girlie accessories and sequins. There are sturdy overnight bags, rucksacks (canvas version for impecunious students, £70) and travellers (£490) made to last and last. As well as leather goods, the shop sells designer clothing for men and women by the likes of Martin Margiela (*see p29*) and Carpe Diem. Men's jewellery by Rust, in dull silver with 1920s coins and medals, is another unusual feature – an attractive alternative to bling.

Ginka
137 Fulham Road, SW3 6SD (7589 4866/www. neishacrosland.com). South Kensington tube. **Open** 10am-6pm Mon-Sat; noon-5pm Sun. **Credit** AmEx, MC, V.
A tiny boutique with an entrance so narrow you could easily miss it, the original home of Neisha Crosland's textile design business has been dedicated to her beautifully patterned accessories since 2004; the interiors side of the business can now be found in her eponymous second shop. Her designs – which change each season – often have a retro flavour, with big flowers or geometrics in vivid colours. Her fans snap up bags, hats and belts to match bold silk dresses and cunning, one-size wrap-around skirts. A big silk floppy hat – good for weddings or the beach – costs in region of £50, while a large fabric overnight bag will set you back £189. Some embroidery has crept into Crosland's designs lately, such as wool scarves beautifully adorned with chain-stitch flowers and leaves.
For branch (Neisha Crosland) see index.

Hermès
179 Sloane Street, SW1X 9QP (7823 1014/ www.hermes.com). Knightsbridge tube. **Open** 10am-6pm Mon-Sat. **Credit** AmEx, DC, MC, V.
The brand may be firmly associated in the modern mind with big, expensive silk squares, but Hermès began as a saddler, and its leather goods remain among the best in the world. Such luxe naturally comes at a price, so it's not surprising the perfectly stitched £600-plus wallets are kept in a locked glass display case. There are none of the famous Birkin bags on show – despite the cost (over £4,000), there's still a waiting list. To own a little of the cachet without breaking the bank, you could splash out on a cute animal bookmark (£70) or a Twilly (£60), a strip of printed silk (about 2in wide) that you can tie around your neck, wrist or handbag – preferably with the label showing.
Mail order.

Hide All
9 Greenwich Market, SE10 9HZ (8858 6104/ www.hideall.co.uk). Greenwich rail/DLR. **Open** 10am-5.30pm Mon-Fri; 10am-6pm Sat, Sun. **Credit** AmEx, DC, MC, V.
On the edge of Greenwich Market, this is an exemplary local bag shop offering a wide range of useful styles and sizes from brands that don't cost the earth. No wonder Hide All has a loyal clientele. Leather holdalls and briefcases are likely to be by Hidesign, while Tula takes care of the soft, often brightly coloured, small leathers such as wallets and key cases. There's also cool design from Radley, plus whimsical and more expensive items by Orla Kiely, Amano, Noa Noa and Barbour.
Mail order.
For branch see index.

The Jacksons
5 All Saints Road, W11 1HA (7792 8336/ www.thejacksons.co.uk). Notting Hill Gate tube. **Open** 10am-6pm Mon-Fri; 11.30am-6.30pm Sat. **Credit** AmEx, DC, MC, V.
Twins Louise and Joey Jackson's boutique is piled high with accessories ranging from shoes, bags and hats to brightly coloured collars for trendy dogs (from £24). Boots in worn-looking leather are stylish but understated (£195), or go for a flapper-style pair of round-toed high heels at £135. One of the most eye-catching bags is a cowskin style with multicoloured beaded handles, but there are plainer styles to choose from too.
Mail order.

Jigsaw Accessories
49 South Molton Street, W1K 5HL (7499 3385/ www.jigsaw-online.com). Bond Street tube. **Open** 10am-6.30pm Mon-Wed, Fri, Sat; 10am-7.30pm Thur; noon-6pm Sun. **Credit** AmEx, MC, V.
Although a varying selection of accessories is available in Jigsaw womenswear stores (*see p40*), this devoted shop, which opened in autumn 2004, showcases the full range. In a muted colour palette and featuring tasteful embellishment, Jigsaw accessories carry on the label's understated yet individualistic style. The shoes are the stars – in rich shades of suede and velvet or antiqued faux skins, they are often enhanced with embroidery or jewels. Nostalgic T-bar or ankle-strap styles are a mainstay, and prices for autumn/winter 2005/6 are mostly around £90-£190. There are also gorgeous beaded shawls, unusual belts, chunky leather bags for under £100 and a sensible yet sexy underwear range, featuring camisoles and proper knickers.

Lotus
11 Pont Street, SW1X 9EH (7235 3550/ www.lotuslondon.com). Sloane Square tube. **Open** 9.30am-6pm Mon-Sat. **Credit** AmEx, DC, MC, V.
Mother-and-daughter team Selina and Fee Craig have expanded their stock at this smart new premises. The rich cache of accessories includes charming jewellery sourced from India (where the Craigs used to live), with characteristic chandelier shapes and milky semi-precious stones (£30-£800), pumps by Jaime Mascaró (£52-£98) and printed

canvas bags embroidered with sequins – a snip at £35. There is also a new range of beautiful evening bags decorated with Swarovski crystals for £95-£220. As well as the signature jewelled kaftans (£120), there are skirts (£60-£100 for cotton; £220 for suede) and covetable cashmere twinsets (£220) linked with an elegant silk bow.
Mail order.
For branch see index.

Lulu Guinness
3 Ellis Street, SW1X 9AL (7823 4828/www.lulu guinness.com). Sloane Square tube. **Open** 10am-6pm Mon-Fri; 11am-6pm Sat. **Credit** AmEx, MC, V.
Lulu Guinness continues to reinvent the handbag, investing it with female wit and wisdom. 'Gardening is Good for the Soul' is the motto on clutches covered with rose bushes and watering cans. Lips, shoes, fishnets and lilac stripes – other well-known Guinness motifs – can be found on affordable make-up bags (£25), but if you admire the style, it will only be a matter of time before you start coveting one of her exquisite limited-edition works of portable art. You might be tempted by a flower-pot bag topped by silk roses (£265), or one in the shape of a box of chocolates (£300) or a birdcage (£395). The new 'pebble pouch', covered with pearls (£250) like some gorgeous underwater treasure, makes a fabulous evening bag. Guinness also designs slightly cartoonesque shoes, scarves, umbrellas and sunglasses.
Mail order.
For branch see index.

Octopus
28 Carnaby Street, W1F 7DQ (7287 3916). Oxford Circus tube. **Open** 10am-7pm Mon-Sat; noon-6pm Sun. **Credit** AmEx, DC, MC, V.
A playful tendency to turn everyday objects into toys characterises the appeal of this growing chain, which sells both fashion and home accessories. UV-sensitive necklaces are fun for clubbers, while 'moving eyeball' bracelets and rings full of liquid are more appealing than they sound. If you fancy bringing a bit of humour into your kitchen (or boudoir), check out the dolly-shaped cheese graters, which double as earring hangers, or the cuckoo clocks the chimes of which are a series of different animals trumpeting their own farmyard sounds.
Mail order.
Branches: throughout city.

Pavane
162 Archway Road, N6 5BB (8341 2799/ www.pavanehighgate.co.uk). Highgate tube. **Open** 10am-6pm Mon-Fri; 10am-5.30pm Sat. **Credit** MC, V.
A 'lifestyle' shop with a curious mixture of home accessories and personal adornment, Pavane is a breath of fresh air on the thunderous Archway Road. There are colourful pashmina wraps (£65), stretchy silk patchwork scarves (a snip at £35) and suede belts with Celtic-influenced buckles at around £49.50. But it's the jewellery that is most intriguing, with Brazilian resin necklaces aptly called 'liquorice allsorts' (from £37) and rings and cufflinks made of Murano glass (£25). On the home front are silk cushions incorporating Japanese obi fabric (from £55), Afghani rugs, mohair throws and contemporary candelabra, among other items.

Pickett
32-33 & 41 Burlington Arcade, W1J OPZ (7493 8939/www.pickett.co.uk). Green Park tube. **Open** 9am-6pm Mon-Fri; 10am-6pm Sat. **Credit** AmEx, DC, MC, V.
Partly a lesson in how to cram an extraordinary amount of stock into a tiny space, Pickett is the place to come if you would be likely to own, say, a matching pink purse, gloves, wallet and pashmina. Everything here can be co-ordinated. An upstairs showroom has antique games and newly designed backgammon sets in vividly coloured leather. Photo albums get the same luxurious treatment. A bespoke service offers to copy irreplaceable items, and classics like kilim-covered slippers (£95) are

reassuringly available all year round. Semi-precious jewellery is stunning, arranged in drawers of different colours from amethyst to rose quartz – ask to see them for a visual feast.
Mail order (7626 3636).
For branches see index.

Swaine Adeney Brigg
54 St James's Street, SW1A 1JT (7409 7277/ www.swaineadeney.co.uk). Green Park tube. **Open** 10am-6pm Mon-Sat. **Credit** AmEx, DC, MC, V.
Nothing ever seems to change at the posh person's brolly store – though you do have to wonder how long Swaine Adeney Brigg will be able to sustain a business that relies on big hats for Ascot, tweed jackets and breeches for the shooting season and picnic hampers (around £8,000) that are so heavy two footmen are required to carry them from the car. Meanwhile, check out the walking length umbrellas for gentlemen with their malacca, hickory or cherry handles (from £175), the panama hats complete with private club or military ribbons, the polo gear, glossy Aigle riding boots, hefty leather luggage and bespoke millinery. SAB is also the last remaining equestrian outfitter in the West End – an essential stop for Rotten Row riders.
Mail order.

Tatty Devine
57B Brewer Street W1 (7739 9009/www.tatty devine.com). Piccadilly Circus tube. **Open** 11am-7pm Mon-Sat. **Credit** AmEx, MC, V.
Increasingly known for their laser-cut Perspex necklaces (you can order one with your own name for £25), Rosie Wolfenden and Harriet Vine have many other – largely kitsch – strings to their bow. At this one-year-old boutique in a passageway, feast your eyes on charm bracelets made of plectrums (£21) and earrings in the form of tiny vinyl records. A recent collaboration with Basso & Brooke (*see p24*) has resulted in a collection of earrings, belts and sashes incorporating shields, swords, pennants and erotic fantasy creatures.
Mail order.
For branches see index.

Topshop
36-38 Great Castle Street, W1W 8LG (7636 7700/www.topshop.co.uk). Oxford Circus tube. **Open** 9am-8pm Mon-Wed, Fri, Sat; 9am-9pm Thur; noon-6pm Sun. **Credit** AmEx, DC, MC, V.
Topshop is still at the forefront when it comes to aping catwalk trends at high-street prices, and little islands of style go some way towards helping new customers navigate the maelstrom that is its ground floor. 'Road to Marrakesh', for example, may have sparkly harem slippers (£15), while another display is devoted to beaded and fringed American Indian-style bags. Other lines are simply glitz: metallic leather bags (£60), belts with diamanté buckles (£45), teen make-up and even synthetic hairpieces. A Jelly Bean Centre makes the point that most of our desires for such fripperies are infantile, and blends seamlessly with the irresistible carnival colours of Mikey jewellery.
Branches: throughout the city.

Belts, buttons & trims

For **MacCulloch & Wallis** and the **Bead Shop**, *see chapter* **Hobbies & Crafts**.

Button Queen
19 Marylebone Lane, W1U 2NF (7935 1505). Bond Street tube. **Open** 10am-5pm Mon-Wed; 10am-6pm Thur, Fri; 10am-4pm Sat. **Credit** MC, V.
Packed into these small Marylebone premises are buttons in all shapes and sizes, at prices to suit any budget. There are modern buttons in plastic, glass and diamanté, plus antique buttons from the 1920s, '30s and the Victorian era. Cufflinks, blazer buttons and horn buttons for suits are also sold.
Mail order.

Elliot Rhodes
79 Long Acre, WC2E 9NG (7379 8544/ www.elliotrhodes.com). Covent Garden tube. **Open** 10am-7.30pm Mon-Sat; noon-5pm Sun. **Credit** AmEx, MC, V.

Justin Rhodes is on a mission to elevate the humble belt to a wearable art form. Inspired by his inability to find one he wanted, he realised others must be facing the same frustrations. That's all in the past, thanks to his unique store, which specialises in this largely overlooked accessory. Belt straps and buckles are sold separately, so you can mix and match for exactly the right combination. You can also buy multiple buckles to change the look of one strap – a brilliant idea. Belts are individually displayed, gallery-style, rather than hung in an unidentifiable mass. Straps (from £50) range from plain calfskin to exotic reptile skins, by way of suede and textured leather. Buckles range from £10 for a basic style to £400 for a sterling silver design embellished with semi-precious stones.
Mail order.

JT Morgan
128 Railway Arches, behind Macfarlane Road, W12 7LA (8222 6711). Shepherd's Bush tube. **Open** by appointment 1-5pm Mon-Fri.
No credit cards.
JT Morgan caters to the trade and public with over 19,000 lines of stock, so it's worth keeping in mind if you've had no luck finding a very specific item elsewhere. He can deal with nearly all your dressmaking requirements as long as you provide the fabric. He can cover buttons (10p-£1) and is happy to tackle jobs such as repairing zips, turning up hems and so on.
Mail order.

Taylor's Buttons
22 Cleveland Street, W1T 4JB (7436 9988). Goodge Street tube. **Open** 11am-4pm Mon-Fri.
No credit cards.
Were it not for the fading, handwritten sign in the window asking you to ring for entry, you'd be forgiven for thinking that Taylor's Buttons had shut up shop years ago. However, once inside, you can find all manner of vintage and contemporary buttons. Belts, buckles and buttons can be covered, and buttons can be dyed to order.
Mail order.

VV Rouleaux
6 Marylebone High Street, W1U 4NJ (7224 5179/ www.vvrouleaux.com). Bond Street tube. **Open** 9.30am-6pm Mon, Tue, Thur-Sat; 10.30am-6pm Wed. **Credit** AmEx, MC, V.
VV Rouleaux has become an established name within the fashion industry, and you'll often see the company's handmade accessories, such as glittery butterflies, in glossy magazines. A complete range of traditional haberdashery is also available – particularly ribbons, which are a speciality here. There's a good range of Christmas products, such as wreaths and garlands, and a huge selection of fabric flowers.
Mail order.
For branch see index.

Hats

Swaine Adeney Brigg (*see above*) sells hats by Herbert Johnson.

Bates the Hatter
21A Jermyn Street, SW1Y 6HP (7734 2722/ www.bates-hats.co.uk). Piccadilly Circus tube. **Open** 9am-5.15pm Mon-Fri; 9.30am-4pm Sat. **Credit** AmEx, DC, MC, V.
Bates bills itself as a 'gentleman's hatter', and no wonder: it has supplied stylish hats and caps to discerning gents since the early 20th century. Classic panama hats (from £62), bowlers (£167) and fedoras (£139.50) are straight out of a BBC period drama. If you fancy yourself as Mr Darcy or Sherlock Holmes, this is your place.
Mail order.

Cozmo Jenks
21 New Quebec Street, W1H 7SA (7258 0111/ www.cozmojenks.co.uk). Marble Arch tube. **Open** by appointment 10am-5pm Mon-Fri.
Credit MC, V.
Couture milliner Cozmo Jenks recently opened this Marylebone-based boutique, where you can buy ready-to-wear and made-to-measure designs. The

Doors by Jas MB. See p77.

former (at around £200) span berets, flat caps, trilbies and fur caps, while the couture collection includes more elaborate creations and bridal headwear. Selected pieces from the range are also stocked at Selfridges, Harvey Nichols and Coco Ribbon (*see p35*).
Mail order.

Edwina Ibbotson
45 Queenstown Road, SW8 3RG (7498 5390). Battersea Park or Clapham Junction rail/77, 77A, 137 bus. **Open** by appointment 10am-6.30pm Mon-Sat. **No credit cards.**
Edwina Ibbotson shop caters to the smart set, offering soignée Ascot hats alongside glamorous beaded headpieces and a range of bridal headwear. Expect diminutive hats that perch decoratively on the head for autumn/winter 2005/6, while come spring/summer 2006, Italian braided straw hats will feature. Everything is made to order for a perfect fit. Prices start at £300. Ibbotson also creates bags to match.

Fred Bare
118 Columbia Road, E2 7RG (7729 6962). Old Street tube/rail/26, 48, 55 bus. **Open** 9am-2pm Sun. **Credit** AmEx, MC, V.
Anita Evagora and Carolyn Pekkam, the duo behind Fred Bare headwear, have relocated the business up north to Yorkshire. However, on Sunday mornings they continue to open the Columbia Road store, where you can peruse their huge range of eccentric yet wearable headwear. In winter 2005/6 there'll be wool hats with chunky embroidery, sequinned berets and cashmere beanies. Some styles are accompanied by matching scarves – crochet is set to feature strongly – and prices span £25 to £100. Fred Bare hats can also be found in Harvey Nichols and Fenwick.

Gabriela Ligenza
5 Ellis Street, SW1X 9AL (7730 2200). Sloane Square tube. **Open** 10am-6pm Mon-Sat. **Credit** AmEx, MC, V.
For pretty, feminine head candy of excellent quality, pay a visit to milliner Gabriela Ligenza's shop. For autumn/winter 2005/6, 1940s-inspired shapes come to the fore; grey-blue and plum are key colours. Interesting three-colour medleys are also found in wintry hues, and soft felt is used in several designs. The C'est Ala Bank range (from £59) features beautifully printed, woven fabrics. Jewellery, shawls and umbrellas are also available.
Mail order.

Hectic Hat Hire
242 Munster Road, SW6 6BA (7381 5127). Hammersmith or Parsons Green tube. **Open** 10am-5pm Mon, Tue, Thur, Fri; 10am-1pm Wed, Sat; also by appointment. **Credit** MC, V.
Hectic Hat Hire is packed with an eclectic range of styles that will add the glamorous finishing touch to an outfit. It costs from £30 to hire a hat for the weekend, and owner Rosie Bloom is also happy to customise styles with details like butterflies or flowers in a colour to match your outfit. Recent hits include the sculptural feather headpieces.

Hepsibah Hats
112 Brackenbury Road, W6 0BD (8741 0025/ www.hepsibah.freeserve.co.uk). Goldhawk Road tube. **Open** by appointment only. **No credit cards.**
Jayne Hepsibah Sullivan's millinery would impress even the most discerning hat aficionado. Lately the designer has taken to incorporating architectural influences in her work, and the wired pieces enhanced with various materials and straws are sure to impress. Vintage fabrics (from the late 19th

century to the 1930s) are another passion; used as trims, sequinned embroidery or birds-of-paradise prints add an element of luxury. Made-to-order hats range from £180 to £400; hat hire costs £55 for a weekend.

Lock & Co
6 St James's Street, SW1A 1EF (men's 7930 8874/women's 7930 2421/www.lockhatters.co.uk). Green Park tube. **Open** 9am-5.30pm Mon-Fri; 9.30am-5pm Sat. **Credit** AmEx, DC, MC, V.
Lock & Co has a hefty British heritage, as well as a couple of royal warrants. Founded in 1672, it is one of the oldest family businesses in the world. The hats themselves are based on classic shapes but many – fashion being the renewable creature it is – have come back into vogue. Tweed caps can be had for as little as £59, while a pork-pie hat is £105. Women can opt for styles ranging from floppy, wide-brimmed beach hats (£79) to outlandish couture designs by Sylvia Fletcher.
Mail order.

Philip Somerville
38 Chiltern Street, W1U 7QL (7224 1517). Baker Street tube. **Open** 9am-5.30pm Mon-Fri. **Credit** AmEx, MC, V.
As milliner to the Queen, Philip Somerville is very much part of the traditional hat-making establishment; his designs are now collectors' items. He works to commission, but the shop also stocks a large selection of off-the-peg hats for women, which typically cost from £150 to £700.

Philip Treacy
69 Elizabeth Street, SW1W 9PJ (7730 3992/ www.philiptreacy.co.uk). Sloane Square tube. **Open** 10am-6pm Mon-Fri; 11am-5pm Sat. **Credit** AmEx, MC, V.
The leading man of millinery continues to innovate and impress with each season's designs. This winter sees the arrival of extravagant creations adorned with ostrich feathers and veiling, plus velour designs in seasonal colours like taupe, berry and olive. Look out for the Folding Topper, with animal influences such as alligator trim – Treacy hopes this style will become established as one of his new signature pieces. For everyday hats, look to the Street Wear collection – it features berets, military-style caps and mini trilbies, in fabrics like angora and tweed. On the accessories side, high-glam bags in metallic colours are sure to be popular. Some items are also available at Selfridges, Fenwick and Harvey Nichols.

Pip Hackett
Studio 19, Great Western Studios, The Lost Goods Building, Great Western Road, W9 3NY (7266 4667). Westbourne Park tube. **Open** by appointment only. **No credit cards.**
Glamorous hats for special occasions. From her studio space, Pip Hackett works mainly to order (prices from £200) but also stocks a selection of ready-to-wear designs, from small hair accessories to Ascot-worthy numbers.

Siggi Hats
48 Fulham High Street, SW6 3LU (7736 2030/ www.siggihats.co.uk). Putney Bridge tube. **Open** 9am-5.30pm Mon-Fri. **Credit** MC, V.
Designer Siegfried Hesbacher caters to the Ascot-bound but also has a large range of hats and headpieces for other special occasions. His range of 'fascinators' aren't quite hats, they are more decorative headbands with feathers or flowers (£56-£300). Expect to see designs such as a monochrome beribboned toque (£150) in winter 2005, plus berets adorned with lace butterflies or velvet roses. A bespoke service is also available.
Mail order.

Stephen Jones
36 Great Queen Street, WC2B 5AA (7242 0770/ www.stephenjonesmillinery.com). Holborn tube. **Open** 11am-6pm Tue, Wed, Fri; 11am-7pm Thur. **Credit** AmEx, MC, V.
Stephen Jones has been designing millinery for a quarter of a century, and in that time has worked with big-name fashion designers John Galliano and

Christian Dior, as well as newcomer Giles Deacon. Prices range from £90 to £1,500, as a couture service is available alongside the ready-to-wear Miss Jones and Jones Boy lines. For everyday headwear, search within these diffusion lines. Even a bobble hat ends up looking like a luxury purchase, while other styles are elevated to the designer realm with elements such as fine ruching or a vogueish distressed look. There's a consultation service for brides (from £200), and other commissions are also undertaken.

Tit Fer Tat
5 Paved Court, Richmond, Surrey TW9 1LZ (8332 1189/www.titfertathats.co.uk). Richmond tube/rail. **Open** 10.30am-6pm Mon-Sat; noon-5pm Sun. **Credit** MC, V.
In addition to stocking hats by designers such as Philip Treacy and Frederick Fox, this company will make a hat to your requirements (for around £200), or dye one you already have to match a specific outfit. An eclectic range of accessories takes in Lulu Guinness's nattily designed bags, plus elbow-length evening gloves and feather headpieces. Tit Fer Tat will also organise a hat party for you and a few friends.

Leather goods

Other shops in this chapter that sell leather goods include **Anya Hindmarch** and **Doors by Jas MB** (for both, *see p77*).

Bill Amberg
21-22 Chepstow Corner, W2 4XE (7727 3560/ www.billamberg.com). Notting Hill Gate tube. **Open** 10am-6pm Mon-Wed, Fri, Sat; 10am-7pm Thur. **Credit** AmEx, MC, V.
This new flagship store for the established Bill Amberg brand is as grand as the designer's reputation. The range of products spans old-school doctor's bags (from £390) and briefcases to the most up-to-date women's bags and accessories, such as a metallic python-skin purse at £110. An extensive collection for babies includes nappy bags, bootees and the celebrity-endorsed papoose (£295). A small home collection features luxurious leather storage boxes, from £115.
Mail order.

Bottega Veneta
33 Sloane Street, SW1X 9NR (7838 9394/ www.bottegaveneta.com). Knightsbridge tube. **Open** 10am-6pm Mon, Tue, Thur-Sat; 10am-7pm Wed. **Credit** AmEx, DC, MC, V.
BV operates in serious designer territory, with prices to match. This season it's back to black, with creative touches such as relief flowers, beading and ruching on bags. The company's classic bags in woven leather are still going strong, while one of the more affordable handbags is the Campania Boston style at £685. There are plenty of accessories to choose from, such as suede gloves

at £400, and a range of jewellery and shoes complements the clothing line for which the company is equally well known.
For branch see index.

Connolly
32 Grosvenor Crescent Mews, SW1X 7EX (7235 3883). Hyde Park Corner tube. **Open** 10am-6pm Mon-Fri. **Credit** AmEx, MC, V.
Connolly's Belgravia store, which reopened in 2004, is located in the former Belgravia Riding School. This seriously luxurious label built its reputation by producing motor upholstery for the likes of Rolls-Royce and Maserati. Today it taps into that heritage with items like driving shoes (from £175), driving jackets (£1,000) and a portable espresso coffee set that plugs into the car lighter socket. Luggage, designed by Ross Lovegrove, evokes the fascia of a 1960s sports car with polished burr walnut frames and aluminium fittings. Cashmere suits, leather-bound stationery and a new homeware collection provide customers with additional ways to spend a fortune.
For branch see index.

Custom Leather
Unit 72, Camden Lock, Chalk Farm Road, NW1 8AF (7482 1407/www.htleather.co.uk). Camden Town tube. **Open** noon-5.30pm Wed-Fri; 11am-6pm Sat, Sun. **Credit** MC, V.
Henry Tomkins' range of hard-wearing bags and leather accessories is based on classic styles and built to last a lifetime. Simple satchels start at £95, with shoppers priced from £70. A bespoke service is also available.
Mail order.

J&M Davidson
42 Ledbury Road, W11 2AB (7313 9532/www. jandmdavidson.com). Notting Hill Gate tube. **Open** 10am-6pm Mon-Sat; noon-5pm Sun. **Credit** AmEx, MC, V.
As well as modern, unshowy bags and wallets, the Davidson duo design a wide range of belts, both classic and with interesting studs and buckles – a woman's belt with turquoise buckle is £210. There's also a luxurious women's (non-leather) clothing range, plus a selection of homewares. If you don't have hundreds to spend, check out the compact mirrors with leather holders at £45.
Mail order.

Matt Fothergill
01588 640 908/www.mattfothergill.com. **Phone enquiries** 10am-6pm Mon-Fri. **Credit** MC, V.
The Fothergill collection includes specialised cases such as music bags, gym bags or a classy overnight bag in a choice of smooth- or grain-finish leather (£259). The usual suspects, like briefcases and wallets, are joined by home accessories like beanbags (£395) and a range of jackets. Fothergill's work is also available at Selfridges and the Conran Shop, as well as online.
Mail order.

Osprey
11 St Christopher's Place, W1U 1NG (7935 2824/www.ospreylondon.com). Bond Street tube. **Open** 10.30am-6pm Tue, Wed, Fri, Sat; 10.30am-7pm Thur. **Credit** AmEx, MC, V.
Osprey's leather bags combine classic styling with a sense of fun. For autumn/winter 2005/6, they're in line with catwalk fashion, with the focus on more muted colours like chocolate, black and neutrals. A few items have subtle details in pink or racing green, so they won't overpower your outfit. Prices start at £25 for a coin purse, and go from £95 to £495 for bags.
Mail order.

Tanner Krolle
3 Burlington Gardens, W1S 3EW (7287 5121/ www.tannerkrolle.co.uk). Green Park tube. **Open** 10am-6.30pm Mon-Sat. **Credit** AmEx, MC, V.
Despite being in business for 150 years, TK produces some of the most fashion-conscious bags around. Covetable designs include the roomy, slouchy yet undeniably chic Money Bag (£495-£895), which comes in various colours and sizes. The traditional products on which the company's reputation was built are still around and feature briefcases, washbags and folios for men. There is also a small but perfectly formed collection of women's shoes, plus accessories such as luggage tags, frames or a heart-shaped mouse pad (£60).
Mail order.
For branches see index.

Texier
6 New Cavendish Street, W1G 8UH (7935 0215/ www.texier.fr). Bond Street tube. **Open** 9.30am-5.30pm Tue-Sat. **Credit** AmEx, MC, V.
This French family business, founded by Monsieur and Madame Texier in the 1950s, is the place to come for leather bags that are stylish without making an overt fashion statement. As well as designs in traditional muted colours, women can choose from bags in pretty pastels, brights or flower prints. For men there are briefcases galore, plus modern rucksacks. Well-made wallets and simple leather belts complete the collection.
Mail order.

Scarves, shawls & ties

Many other shops in this chapter sell a wide range of scarves, in particular **Ginka** and **Hermès** (for both, *see p77*).

Georgina von Etzdorf
4 Ellis Street, off Sloane Street, SW1X 9AL (7259 9715/www.gve.co.uk). Sloane Square tube. **Open** 10am-6pm Mon-Sat. **Credit** AmEx, DC, MC, V.
This textile designer creates accessories and clothes for women who have the means to indulge their taste for high-quality fabrics and exquisite craftsmanship. She is best known for her vibrant, handprinted scarves in silk and velvet, which she has been producing for over two decades. More recently the collection has expanded to include clothing in luxurious fabrics. The starting price for scarves is £99.
Mail order.

Umbrellas

See also p78 **Swaine Adeney Brigg**.

James Smith & Sons
53 New Oxford Street, WC1A 1BL (7836 4731/ www.james-smith.co.uk). Holborn or Tottenham Court Road tube. **Open** 9.30am-5.25pm Mon-Fri; 10am-5.25pm Sat. **Credit** AmEx, MC, V.
This family-owned business, with a 170-year history, offers clues as to what the shopping experience might have been like before the advent of identikit high streets. Staff are impeccably polite and can help you find the umbrella, walking stick or cane you want among the dozens of high-quality models. Some antiques are stocked, and prices start at £15 for umbrellas and sticks. There's also a repair and re-covering service – but only for umbrellas bought from the shop.
Mail order.

Ginka. See p77.

Jewellery

For other shops selling jewellery, *see chapter* **Accessories**.

Classic

Asprey

167 New Bond Street, W1S 4AR (7493 6767/ www.asprey.com). Bond Street or Green Park tube. **Open** 10am-6pm Mon-Sat. **Credit** AmEx, DC, MC, V.

This imposingly grand flagship, extensively and expensively overhauled by Norman Foster in 2004, has cabinets filled with all the aristocratic-chic jewellery you would expect from this long-standing brand. The white-gold, diamond-heavy Swirl necklace, for example, goes for a gasp-worthy £39,000. For those with shallower pockets, a pendant from the same range is £2,300. More modern in style is an 18ct white-gold pendant with a cut-out heart, for £600. Asprey also sells high-end leather accessories, timepieces, tableware and the recently launched Purple Water fragrance. *Mail order.*

Boodles

1 Sloane Street, SW1X 9LA (7235 0111/ www.boodles.co.uk). Knightsbridge tube. **Open** 10am-6pm Mon-Sat. **Credit** AmEx, DC, MC, V.

Formerly known as Boodle & Dunthorne, 107-year-old Boodles is today run by the sixth generation of the same family. The designs, worn by a plethora of celebrities, range from dainty dragonflies in the new Angel's Garland line to the fluid, elegant lines of the established Amare collection. The Pop Pearl necklace on coloured plastic is a fun buy (£450) or you could go all out with the Dive Deep double-row necklet at £49,500. **For branches see index.**

Cartier

175-176 New Bond Street, W1S 4RN (7408 5700/www.cartier.com). Green Park tube. **Open** 10am-6pm Mon-Fri; 10am-5pm Sat. **Credit** AmEx, DC, MC, V.

There are few more luxurious places than Cartier for those with a predilection for diamonds. Many of the pieces are 'price on application', for which read: if you have to ask, you can't afford it. Ranges to look at if you can, however, include the geometric China collection and the Lace range, which lives up to its suggestion of intricacy. The Santos watch is still popular 100 years after its inception: a version in high-shine steel costs between £1,550 and £13,000. *Mail order (8080 0330).* **For branches see index.**

Fred

174 New Bond Street, W1S 4RG (7495 6303/ www.fred.com). **Open** 10am-6pm Mon-Sat. **Credit** AmEx, DC, MC, V.

It's refreshing to see some new ideas joining the jewellery old guard on Bond Street. Fred has been in quiet residence for three years, but that's not to say it doesn't have a pedigree – it was established in Paris back in 1936. The Serpentine collection is based on a slinky, sensuous design; a pendant on a red silk cord is £720. There is also an original engagement and wedding collection, starting at £3,000, and an *haute joaillerie* range that gets off the starting blocks at £100,000.

Garrard

24 Albemarle Street, W1Y 4HT (7758 8520/ www.garrard.com). Bond Street or Green Park tube. **Open** 10am-6pm Mon-Fri; 10am-5pm Sat. **Credit** AmEx, MC, V.

Jade Jagger's input as creative director at the crown jewellers continues to rejuvenate the prestigious company season by season. The popular Superstyle range has diamond charms starting at £1,000 or modern enamel pendants from £650. If you'd like to treat yourself to a bit of sparkle, the My First Diamond line begins at £220. Traditional tastes are still catered for, with stratospheric prices for some of Garrard's classic diamond jewellery. *Mail order.*

Georg Jensen

15 New Bond Street, W1S 3ST (7499 6541/ www.georgjensen.com). Bond Street tube. **Open** 10am-6pm Mon-Sat. **Credit** AmEx, DC, MC, V.

Georg Jensen recently celebrated its centenary, yet you wouldn't know it from the super-contemporary designs on offer. Smooth, fluid shapes unify the elegant ranges. The new Droplet range by Kim Buck has edible-looking rings with rose or smoky quartz (£175), or for the same price you could choose Nana Ditzel's wave-like Surf earclips in sterling silver. *Mail order.*

Links of London

24 Lime Street, EC3M 7HF (7623 3101/ www.linksoflondon.com). Monument tube/DLR. **Open** 9.30am-6pm Mon-Fri. **Credit** AmEx, DC, MC, V.

Links, a specialist in sterling silver, is a fine example of a traditional firm that successfully modernises its ranges. The collections are forever being updated, with one of the newest ideas being a pink leather box filled with silver beads, semi-precious stones in several shades, plus silk string for you to compose your own jewellery (£95). The Objets Trouvés collection adds colour by way of jade, turquoise and scarlet coral. *Mail order (7404 9899).* **For branches see index.**

Mikimoto

179 New Bond Street, W1S 4RJ (7629 5300/ www.mikimoto.co.uk). Green Park tube. **Open** 10am-5.30pm Mon-Fri; 10am-5pm Sat. **Credit** AmEx, DC, MC, V.

Mikimoto's focus, and unique selling point, is pearls. This is the place to come to for unusual specimens, such as black- and silver-lipped cultured pearls, or captivating pink conch pearls. Of the new pieces available, the Fire collection is the most striking, combining pink sapphires with black South Sea pearls (the necklace is £8,300). Or go for an Infinity Heart pendant (£1,700-£3,000 depending on the pearl).

Swarovski

137-139 Regent Street, W1B 4JA (7434 2500/ www.swarovski.co.uk). Oxford Circus or Piccadilly Circus tube. **Open** 10am-7pm Mon-Wed, Fri, Sat; 10am-8pm Thur; noon-6pm Sun. **Credit** AmEx, DC, MC, V.

A good place to get glam without breaking the bank. The famous crystals come in cute animal shapes from £17, while a peach-and-rose-coloured swan charm for your mobile phone is £27. Bling belts go for £75. *Mail order.* **For branches see index.**

Theo Fennell

169 Fulham Road, SW3 6ST (7591 5000/ www.theofennell.com). South Kensington tube. **Open** 10am-6pm Mon-Sat. **Credit** AmEx, DC, MC, V.

For all-out sophistication, Theo Fennell is hard to beat. There's a quirky, playful sensibility at work too – silver covers for everyday consumables can

be made for anything you care to request, from a Marmite jar to your favourite booze bottle (from £95). As for jewellery, sunset-coloured citrine and pink tourmaline drop earrings are dazzling at £945. The Lief line plays with combinations of yellow gold, green tourmaline, amethyst and diamonds – a key-shaped pendant is £1,315. *Mail order.* **For branch see index.**

Tiffany & Co

25 Old Bond Street, W1S 4QB (7409 2790/ www.tiffany.com/uk). Green Park tube. **Open** 10am-6pm Mon-Fri; 10am-5.30pm Sat. **Credit** AmEx, MC, V.

An aura of Audrey Hepburn glamour will always linger around the legendary Tiffany's. You can even get a droll silver ring proclaiming 'Please return to Tiffany & Co'. At £105 it's one of the more affordable items; the highly coveted diamond engagement rings are priced from around £800 to a staggering £965,000. Though famous for its diamonds, the company also has other ranges – an arresting, Elsa Peretti-designed, black lacquer and hardwood bangle is £205. In addition to jewellery, Tiffany sells accessories, bridal gifts (including china, silverware and crystal) and tableware. *Mail order.* **For branch see index.**

Designers

@work

156 Brick Lane, E1 6RU (7377 0597/ www.atworkgallery.com). Aldgate East tube/ Liverpool Street tube/rail. **Open** 11am-6pm Mon-Sat; 10am-6pm Sun. **Credit** MC, V.

This little workshop and gallery is a great place to come looking for quirky, notice-me jewellery. The extensive, ever-changing collection – featuring the works of around 50 designers – means prices vary dramatically but, once you account for the commissioning charge, you're looking at prices from £25 to many thousands of pounds for bespoke items. Interesting work comes from the likes of Rhonda Khulman, who can make something beautiful out of recycled materials, and Ofra Shelef, who melds silver, wire, gems and pearls. The gallery was founded by Jo Butler, Amy Madge and Adele Tipler, who also show their own work in the shop. *Mail order.* **For branch see index.**

Angela Hale

5 Royal Arcade, 28 Old Bond Street, W1S 4SE (7495 1920/www.angela-hale.co.uk). Green Park tube. **Open** 10am-6pm Mon-Sat. **Credit** AmEx, MC, V.

The romantic, whimsical aesthetics of Angela Hale's designs will make any girl swoon. This little boutique is awash with costume jewellery in any colour you care to name. The handmade creations are based on hypo-allergenic bronze, and set with Swarovski crystals. All manner of accessories are also available to jazz up a feminine outfit, while the shop itself is a boudoir of flowers, antique picture frames and ornate textiles. The bridal room houses handmade necklaces (from £75), earrings (from £40) and tiaras (from £75) with a vintage feel, some with Edwardian or art deco influences. *Mail order.*

Aurum

8 Avery Row, W1K 4AL (7586 8656/ www.aurumgallery.com). Bond Street tube. **Open** 10.30am-6pm Tue-Sat. **Credit** MC, V.

Aurum showcases designs by some 50 designers, including Scott Wilson, Tina Engell and Shaun Leane. Leane's celeb fans include David Bowie and Liv Tyler, and his distinctive designs can be yours from £100. Lily Gardner's unusual work comprises Perspex cuffs inlaid with Victorian lace, and Johnny Rocket's ray gun and robot charms help explain his popularity with catwalk designers and music video producers. A bespoke service

is available, and exhibitions featuring established names and new talents are held regularly. *Mail order.*
For branch see index.

Autrum Gallery
7 New Cavendish Street, W1G 8UY (7486 8695/ www.autrumgallery.co.uk). Bond Street tube. **Open** 10.30am-6pm Tue-Fri; 10.30am-5pm Sat. **Credit** AmEx, MC, V.
If you're in search of a bespoke piece of jewellery with an unusual stone, look no further than Marion Autrum's workshop. The Context and Spirit cuts are used to give diamonds a clean, contemporary look. A sophisticated brown Spirit cut diamond on a rose-gold ring is £1,850, and you can also browse further collections from guest goldsmiths.

Ben Day
18 Hanbury Street, E1 6QR (7247 9977/ www.benday.co.uk). Liverpool Street tube/rail. **Open** 11am-6pm Tue-Fri; 11am-5pm Sat, Sun. **Credit** AmEx, MC, V.
Ben Day's beautiful shop near Spitalfields Market is a great introduction to his designs, which he creates in the workshop downstairs. The decor – all chandeliers and antique mirrors – is as impressive as the statement-making jewellery he crafts around different types of stones. Striking signet rings are a popular choice, with prices starting just under the £300 mark. This is also the place to come for style-conscious male accessories, as there's also a cool range of luxury cufflinks. Commissions are undertaken – bespoke wedding and engagement bands start at £300.

Clerkenwell Green Association
Pennybank Chambers, 33-35 St John's Square, EC1M 4DS (7251 0276/www.cga.org.uk). Farringdon tube/rail. **Open** by appointment only 9am-5pm Mon-Fri. **No credit cards.**
A good way of picking up hot new jewellery at a fraction of the shop price is to head for workshop

sales where the designers sell direct to the public. Look out for the Clerkenwell Green Association's twice-yearly Clerkenwell Dressed open days, where you can view and buy designs by around 50 on-site craftspeople (*see p10* **Shopping Diary**). You might choose something by Alison Ibbs, who uses the 5,000-year-old forging, or hammering technique (prices £30-£1,000). Daisy Choi combines porcelain stone-shaped beads, silver and 24ct gold-plated silver components to create unusual pieces priced from £30 to £400. Also unconventional is Tina Lilienthal's work, which mixes plastics and fabrics with the more usual silver, gold and pearls for a contemporary feel (£40-£250).

Cockpit Arts
Cockpit Yard, Northington Street, WC1N 2NP (7419 1959/www.cockpitarts.com). Chancery Lane tube. **Open** by appointment only. **Credit** MC, V.
Cockpit Arts houses designers from a variety of disciplines. Two exhibitions take place each year (*see p10* **Shopping Diary**), where you can see and buy work by all the designers. Check the website for more details and to get an idea of the variety of work available. Allison Wiffen's ideas are particularly striking, engaging as they do with the urban environment. Using images from digital photographs, she has created a range of unusual ceramic jewellery featuring graffiti, flowers and even railings that caught her attention. Maxine V Wareham's Karrat jewellery uses enamel, precious metals and more uncommon assorted materials; the results make for a bright, fun range of jewellery.
For branch see index.

Cox & Power
31C Marylebone High Street, W1U 4QA (7935 3530/www.coxandpower.com). South Kensington tube. **Open** 10am-6pm Mon-Wed, Fri, Sat; 11am-7pm Thur. **Credit** AmEx, DC, MC, V.
C&P works with all sorts of metals and stones, but the results are invariably dazzling. There are prices to suit most pockets, as exemplified by the

elliptical Metamorphic rings, which go for £120-£1,850. One collection is inspired by all things berry-sweet – among the temptations are the Loganberry ring (£825) and the cherry-red Maraschino necklace (£4,500). Some of the designs are stocked at Liberty (*see p13*), and a bespoke service is also available. *Mail order.*

Dinny Hall
200 Westbourne Grove, W11 2RH (7792 3913/ www.dinnyhall.com). Notting Hill Gate tube. **Open** 10am-6pm Mon-Wed, Fri, Sat; 11am-7pm Thur. **Credit** AmEx, MC, V.
Hall's graceful designs have clean, unfussy lines that stand the test of time. These are evident in the Curved Tear or Almond stud earrings, neither of which will break the bank at £31 and £21. A girlier sensibility emerges in pieces like the briolette necklaces in pretty colours (from £245). There's a bespoke service for wedding and engagement rings, with much of the work done with precious gemstones set in 18ct gold or platinum. *Mail order.*
For branch see index.

Dower & Hall
60 Beauchamp Place, SW3 1NZ (7589 8474/ www.dowerandhall.com). Knightsbridge tube. **Open** 10.30am-6.15pm Mon-Sat. **Credit** AmEx, DC, MC, V.
Since starting work together in 1990, Dan Dower and Diane Hall have made quite a name for themselves. Their ranges are contemporary and superbly crafted – bold tastes are catered for with a set of cuffs (£250 in hammered silver, or go all out with yellow gold at £2,500). The Rose range has an updated Victorian charm; a small silver ring is £195. For those about to pop the question, you could make use of D&H's service that allows you to use a generic ring to propose, then return and exchange it for one that the receiver designs to their own taste. *Mail order.*

ec one

41 Exmouth Market, EC1R 4QL (7713 6185/ www.econe.co.uk). Farringdon tube/rail. **Open** 10am-6pm Mon-Fri; 10.30am-6pm Sat. **Credit** AmEx, MC, V.

The two branches of this contemporary shop are ones to note if you are searching out truly modern designs. Alexis Bittar's resin bangles, for example, have a strokeable texture and come in wintry shades of plum, burgundy and bronze (£40). Natasha Dahlberg's bracelets are loaded with coral, chalcedony (a kind of quartz) and mother-of-pearl charms, in pretty flower, fish and leaf shapes (from £225). Engagement rings by Niessing have tension-set diamonds seemingly suspended between the edges of C-shaped rings (from £895). Make sure you don't overlook Jos Skeates's super-luxurious collection of cocktail rings – the Dragonfly version with beryl, morganite and white diamonds is £5,130.
Mail order.
For branch see index.

Efva Attling

8 Foubert's Place, W1F 7PD (7287 9885/ www.efvaattlingstockholm.com). Oxford Circus tube. **Open** 11am-6.30pm Mon-Wed, Fri, Sat; 11am-7pm Thur. **Credit** AmEx, MC, V.

The Scandinavian aesthetics of clean, uncluttered lines are in evidence in Attling's work. Celeb support comes from the likes of Kylie – who has the Kisses necklace (£115 in silver, £660 in yellow gold or £700 in white gold), if you have copycat tendencies. If you choose the Cross bracelet (£140) or Angels pendant (£80) some of the profits support Red Cross work in Cambodia and survivors of 2004's tsunami respectively.
Mail order.

Electrum Gallery

21 South Molton Street, W1K 5QZ (7629 6325). Bond Street tube. **Open** 10am-6pm Mon-Fri; 10am-5pm Sat. **Credit** AmEx, DC, MC, V.

Electrum gives exposure to fashion-forward, highly original designers. Nina Bukvic, for example, has developed a technique for knitting fine wire with pale grey freshwater pearls (complex bangles from £850). Angie Boothroyd crafts delicate linked disc or square necklaces and bracelets in a variety of gold and silver, while Catherine Mannheim uses gold and multicoloured gemstones. Gerda Flöckinger and Wendy Ramshaw, both CBEs, also show here.
Mail order.

Erickson Beamon

38 Elizabeth Street, SW1W 9NZ (7259 0202/ www.ericksonbeamon.com). Sloane Square tube/ Victoria tube/rail. **Open** 10am-6pm Mon-Fri; 11am-5pm Sat. **Credit** AmEx, MC, V.

Erickson Beamon is a partnership between Karen Erickson and Vicki Sarge, and given their history of designing catwalk jewellery for big names, you can expect to see some seriously stylish jewellery here. The own-range is mostly costume pieces, priced from £150 to £600. The autumn/winter collection includes ranges inspired by iconic women. The Venus range is classically oriented and uses pearl and turquoise on gold plate. Twentieth-century muse Edie Sedgwick is honoured with the '60s-style Edie collection, with black diamonds and Swarovski crystals on antique silver.
Mail order.

gill wing

182 Upper Street, N1 1RQ (7359 4378). Angel tube/Highbury & Islington tube/rail. **Open** 10am-6pm Mon-Sat; noon-5pm Sun. **Credit** MC, V.

If you're checking out contemporary jewellery designers, this is one to keep in mind. Many of the jewellers on show have studios at Clerkenwell Green and Cockpit Arts, so you can be assured of finds from the cream of young craftspeople. Among the notable names based here are Annette Warham, Sarah Stafford and Sophie Harley, who uses the heart motif with a bit of attitude – winged heart earrings go from around £65.

Horace

312 Portobello Road, W10 5RU (8968 1188/ www.horacedesign.com). Ladbroke Grove tube. **Open** 11am-6pm Tue-Sat. **Credit** AmEx, MC, V.

Horace deals in solid silver and satisfyingly solid designs. The jewellery is intended to be unisex, and it's easy to see how the simple, graphic lines of the pieces would work equally well on either sex. The Stripi rings, for instance, come in various thicknesses to suit your finger (£35-£65). For pure bling check out the Fatboy Five chain at a hefty 1.3kg (£1,000). If you take a shine to the designs but would prefer them in a different metal, gold and platinum commissions are undertaken. The shop is easily spotted thanks to the huge ring graffitied on its side wall.
Mail order.

Jess James

3 Newburgh Street, W1F 7RE (7437 0199/ www.jessjames.com). Oxford Circus or Piccadilly Circus tube. **Open** 11am-6.30pm Mon-Wed, Fri; 11am-7pm Thur; 11am-6pm Sat. **Credit** AmEx, MC, V.

The aquarium around which designs are showcased should give you a hint that convention is not one of this shop's concerns. Jess James gives space to off-the-wall work by both established designers and the young guns hot on their heels. Names to note include Shaun Leane, Sarah Jordan, Suzy Telling and Carol Mather, who all possess idiosyncratic styles. In the way of engagement rings, it would be hard to go wrong with James's own collection – a platinum band with diagonally set diamonds is particularly impressive (£3,575).
Mail order.

Jewel

16 Camden Passage, N1 8ED (7226 2065/ www.jewellondon.co.uk). Angel tube. **Open** 11am-6pm Tue-Fri; 10am-6pm Sat; noon-4pm Sun. **Credit** AmEx, MC, V.

Adding a dash of shine and sparkle to Islington's Camden Passage is a new jewellery shop, aptly named Jewel. Revered London-based designers Kirt Holmes and Lesley Vik Waddell have joined forces to create an elegant space with dark wooden floors, antique cabinets and jewellery-draped deer antlers. Their intimate, elegant shop works perfectly – Waddell's spindly feminine designs, including lattice rings and chokers, complement Holmes's bolder, rock-strewn bracelets, necklaces and oversized cluster rings. But what makes this shop stand out are the affordable prices – rings start at just £40 and earrings at around £50.

Lara Bohinc 107

51 Hoxton Square, N1 6NU (7684 1465/ www.larabohinc107.co.uk). Old Street tube/rail. **Open** 10am-6pm Mon-Fri. **Credit** AmEx, MC, V.

Bohinc has designed catwalk jewellery for Julien McDonald and Gucci, which gives you an idea of her style – think high-end glamour with an ultra-modernist edge. Celebs with tastes as diverse as Tori Amos and Mary J Blige are devotees. Her underground gallery on Hoxton Square displays the jewellery under futuristic space bubbles, or you can buy a selection from Browns, Harrods and Selfridges. The architecturally influenced Wrap Around ring is plated with black gold and costs £138, or you could splash out on a double-stranded Delay choker, in rose-gold plated brass, at £540.
Mail order.

Lesley Craze Gallery

33-35A Clerkenwell Green, EC1R 0DU (7608 0393/www.lesleycrazegallery.co.uk). Farringdon tube/rail. **Open** 10am-5.30pm Tue-Sat. **Credit** AmEx, DC, MC, V.

Diamonds aren't the focus here, but jewellery at Lesley Craze is certainly cutting-edge. Over 100 designers are showcased, and exhibitions regularly held, focusing not just on precious metals but imaginative mixed media. The avant-garde jewellery is destined to be a talking point. Fiona Book's work, for instance, is made up of outsized, outlandish pieces, while Jenny Deans's designs are as intricate as spiderwebs. Herman Hemsen's

work, meanwhile, uses digital images in original ways (such as the picture book-style bracelet). Men's designs are available, and some of Joel Degen's designs could be interpreted as unisex.

Mikala Djørup

2 Gabriel's Wharf, 56 Upper Ground, SE1 9PP (7021 0011/www.djorup.net). Waterloo tube/rail. **Open** 11am-4.30pm Tue, Wed; 11am-6pm Thur-Sat. **Credit** AmEx, MC, V.

Nestled unassumingly in the cute environs of Gabriel's Wharf on the South Bank is this Danish designer's jewellery shop. Like the highest-end boutiques, the collection is laid out in elegant sparsity, but it's bursting with creative ideas. The detailing on Djørup's solid rings resembles a crop of miniature woodland mushrooms. The work is mostly silver-based, coaxed into original shapes and put together in dazzling but unfussy designs.

Les Néréides

166 King's Road, SW3 4UP (7376 6270/ www.lesnereides.com). Sloane Square tube. **Open** 10am-6.30pm Mon-Thur; 10am-7pm Fri, Sat; noon-5pm Sun. **Credit** AmEx, MC, V.

Ambience is everything at this family-run French boutique, the proprietors of which take the trouble to change the shop design regularly. But whenever you visit, it's always enchanting, in line with the fairy tale jewellery. The jewellery is dainty and romantic, based on whimsical motifs such as birds, bees and flowers. Prices start at £18 for delicate earrings, and rise to £275 for elaborate necklaces. Les Néréides also produces natural perfumes (£10-£30), which come beautifully wrapped in fairytale crêpe paper, ribbon and feathers.
For branch see index.

Nicholas James

16-18 Hatton Garden, EC1N 8AT (7242 8000/ www.nicholasjames.com). Chancery Lane tube or Farringdon tube/rail. **Open** 10am-5.30pm Mon-Fri; 10am-5pm Sat. **Credit** AmEx, MC, V.

Nick Fitch (James is his middle name) creates tasteful high-end jewellery. The extensive line of eternity rings includes a classically influenced Roman ring in 18ct yellow gold with diamonds (from £995). A multi-stranded choker with pavé-set diamond pendant is pricier at £2,695. Fluid, feminine engagement and wedding rings are designed to fit together. The clean aesthetics of the jewellery are reflected in this minimalist new shop, which is characterised by clean lines and decked out in unfussy white and glass showcases.

Nude Contemporary Jewellery

36 Shepherd Market, W1J 7QR (7629 8999/ www.nudejewellery.co.uk). Green Park tube. **Open** 11am-7pm Mon-Fri; 11am-6pm Sat. **Credit** AmEx, DC, MC, V.

Located in a quaint, well-hidden corner of Mayfair, this little shop is well worth nosing out. Designer Nikki Galloway has gathered work from a prestigious and innovative collection of designers, which she sells alongside her own bespoke creations. Galloway can work with a budget as small as £50 for a tailor-made creation, and in a wide range of materials. Look out for Kathryn Marchbank's truly original bracelets in silver, enamelled steel and Perspex – they snake up the arm and are priced between £74 and £270. Masculine pieces include rings by UrbanMetal, in reflective or matt titanium (from £29).
Mail order.

Ruby Red

Dudley House, 169 Piccadilly, W1J 9EH (7499 9177/www.rubyred.co.uk). Open by appointment only 10am-6pm Mon-Fri. No credit cards.

Whatever your taste in jewellery, RR's designers have pretty much every angle covered. Samantha Salmons caters to the earth mother in you, considering pressure points when creating her organic, stone-based jewellery. Lucy Goldman's work is graphic and more hip than hippie – the Mod-like Target collection starts at £300. Although traditionally trained, the designers offer a bespoke service specialising in funky, unusual designs. As with all commissions, prices vary hugely

FASHION

(from £100 to £15,000). The ready-to-wear range includes contemporary charms like palm trees and lipsticks (£15). The designers can also remodel jewellery with a sentimental value to your taste. *Mail order.*

Slim Barrett
7624 2221/www.slimbarrett.com. **Open** by appointment only Mon-Fri. **Credit** MC, V.
Irish-born Slim Barrett's designs have graced the catwalks of Chanel and Ungaro, snapped up by Lenny Kravitz and Christina Ricci, and are permanently on show at the V&A. A little bit of that prestige can be yours for £600, for which you can pick out a necklace with your star sign in the shape of its heavenly constellation. Barrett's work has a Celtic influence, most evident in the crowns and coronets for which he's famed. The Celtic Swirl design, with mirror crystals to ensure maximum attention-grabbing, is £450. The bespoke service starts at £600, but can soar into thousands. As we went to press, Slim Barrett was in the process of moving premises; consult the website for details.
Mail order.

Solange Azagury-Partridge
171 Westbourne Grove, W11 2RS (7792 0197/ www.solangeazagurypartridge.com). Notting Hill Gate tube. **Open** 10.30am-6pm Mon-Sat. **Credit** AmEx, MC, V.
If you're looking for extrovert, luxury statement pieces, you can stop the search at this striking shop. Fusing precious metals with less prestigious but colour-soaked gems and modern materials, the resulting designs scream fun and games. There's the Ball Crusher drop earrings, a feisty fusion of 18ct yellow gold, yellow pearls, rubies and enamel (£7,400). The Adam and Eve ring comes with serpent, apple and fig leaf, as well as a temptation-testing mix of onyx, coral, emerald and ruby (£9,800).

Stephen Einhorn
210 Upper Street, N1 1RL (7359 4977/ www.stepheneinhorn.co.uk). Highbury & Islington tube. **Open** 10am-6pm Mon-Sat. **Credit** AmEx, DC, MC, V.
There's no end to the original ideas Stephen Einhorn successfully realises in this little shop. Heard of the material that's rarer than diamonds? Well, here you can buy a ring made from 2,000-year-old historic oak excavated by the Museum of London, set in silver, gold, titanium or platinum, from £197 (for silver). Or how about one of the greetings cards with detachable items to keep? The Christmas Card with a stainless steel snowflake for the tree is £2.95. Purchases can be sealed in a heart-shaped box, which is cleverly designed so the receiver actually has to break it open. Commissions are a big part of the business, and Einhorn will undertake anything from wedding bands (or his new range of commitment rings for gay couples) to key rings and men's chains.
Mail order.

Stephen Webster Boutique
1A Duke Street, W1U 3EB (7486 6576/ www.stephenwebster.com). Bond Street tube. **Open** 10am-6pm Mon-Fri. **Credit** MC, V.
Webster's work is a favourite of fashion types, and you only have to set eyes on a few of his designs to work out why. They're extravagant, they make a firm statement and – of course – they're very 'now'. The Buffer rings, for example, come set with a big gem across the centre and a smattering of smaller ones on the rest of the ring for extra sparkle. Possible combinations include the purple and green of amethyst and tsavorites, or the more subtle smoky quartz and brown diamonds.
Mail order.

William Prophet Gallery
11 Lower Marsh, SE1 7RJ (7928 7123/www. williamprophet.co.uk). Waterloo tube/rail. **Open** 9.30am-6pm Mon-Sat. **Credit** AmEx, DC, MC, V.
William Prophet's unconventional designs could be termed 'jewellery for clubbers'. Signature pieces are stainless-steel rings, bangles and pendants inset

with glow-in-the-dark acrylics. Bracelets start at around £100, rings from £40, and all pieces come in a choice of bright colours. Prophet's range of 'functional jewellery' is made from Allen keys and screwdrivers, and intended for use with sporting equipment such as skateboards and mountain bikes. Lisa Hendry also shows her precious metal designs here, and both designers also work on commission. *Mail order.*

Wint & Kidd
237 Westbourne Grove, W11 2SE (7908 9990/ www.wintandkidd.com). Notting Hill Gate tube. **Open** 10.30am-5.30pm Mon-Wed, Fri, Sat; 10.30am-6.30pm Thur. **Credit** AmEx, MC, V.
Named after the villains in *Diamonds Are Forever*, Wint & Kidd deals only in diamonds, specialising in rare coloured specimens. Its mainstay is an excellent bespoke service, where you can even choose a loose diamond as a present, and let the receiver design a piece of jewellery to their taste. Prices begin at £1,000, but there is a ready-to-wear collection with earrings starting just shy of £300. The Matthew Williams-designed store is a pleasure to shop in, with a Bond-like glamour and pretty chandeliers.
For branch see index.

Wright & Teague
1A Grafton Street, W1S 4EB (7629 2777/ www.wrightandteague.com). Green Park tube. **Open** 10am-6pm Mon-Wed, Fri; 10am-7pm Thur; 10am-5pm Sat. **Credit** AmEx, MC, V.
Husband and wife Gary Wright and Sheila Teague have been creating enchanting jewellery together for 25 years. There's a folksy feel to a lot of their work – stackable silver bangles come with charms like the Star of Hope or the Walk on the Wild Side disk for a glamorous hippie look. Many ranges come in a choice of silver, 18ct gold or platinum – the Cybele pendants, for example, which run from £80 to £3,350.
Mail order.

Antique & vintage

In addition to the shops below, note that Thursday at **Spitalfields Market** (*see p17*) is antiques day.

Berganza
88-90 Hatton Garden (entrance in Greville Street), EC1N 8PN (7404 2336/www.berganza.com). Chancery Lane tube/Farringdon tube/rail. **Open** 10am-5.30pm Mon-Sat. **Credit** AmEx, MC, V.
The main specialist periods represented here are Victorian (look out for black enamel camellias), Edwardian, flouncy art nouveau and monochrome art deco. A deco diamond hairclip on sale recently was £1,250. There are four workshops where antique restoration is carried out, and wedding and engagement rings are also made.
Mail order.

Eclectica
2 Charlton Place, N1 8AJ (7226 5625/www. eclectica.biz). Angel tube. **Open** 11am-6pm Mon, Tue, Thur, Fri; 10am-6pm Wed, Sat. **Credit** AmEx, MC, V.
Eclectica, true to its name, is a pick 'n' mix kind of shop selling fun costume jewellery. Think Opal Fruits colours and materials like resin, enamel and lucite. This is a good place to look for one-off wedding jewellery – staff are experienced in this field. In addition, there are vintage bags for sale. Prices – from £12 to £250 – are affordable.

Merola
195 Fulham Road, SW3 6JL (7351 9338/ www.merola.co.uk). South Kensington tube. **Open** 10am-6pm Mon, Tue, Thur-Sat; 10am-7pm Wed; 2-6pm Sun. **Credit** AmEx, DC, MC, V.
Merola has vintage jewellery spanning a huge price range – starting around the £65 mark and going into thousands. The works of sought-after designers like Miriam Haskell and Trifari are stocked, plus there is a range of contemporary jewellery by Kenneth Lane.
Mail order.

Lara Bohinc 107. See p83.

Mail order & internet

Diana Porter
0117 909 0225/www.dianaporter.co.uk.
Credit MC, V.
Former UK Jewellery Designer of the Year, Bristol-based Diana Porter is still creating clean-lined, impeccably crafted contemporary jewellery. Best known are her rings etched with the phrase 'on and on' in relief – a silver version costs £101. Unisex pins in silver with 18ct gold details cost £30-£70, and there's a full range of necklaces, earrings, bracelets and cufflinks. A selection of Porter's work is stocked in @work (*see p82*) and Jess James (*see p83*). If you want to add your own touch, commissions are also undertaken.

Engraving

ACS Engraving Limited
Basement, 49 Maddox Street, W1S 2PQ (7629 2660). Oxford Circus tube. **Open** 9am-5pm Mon-Fri. **No credit cards.**
Expect impeccable service from ACS, which undertakes both hand- and machine-engraving. Prices for a first name start at £4 by machine or £9 by hand.

Bennett & Thorogood
Grays Antique Market, 58 Davies Street, W1K 5LP (7408 1880). Bond Street tube. **Open** 10am-4.30pm Mon-Fri. **No credit cards.**
Look to B&T for careful hand-engraving on precious jewellery, metal and glass. Prices reflect the quality and begin at around £7 per initial.

Gem matching/ bespoke

R Holt & Co
98 Hatton Garden, EC1N 8NX (7405 5286/ www.rholt.co.uk). Chancery Lane tube/Farringdon tube/rail. **Open** 9.30am-5.30pm Mon-Fri; occasional Sat. **Credit** AmEx, DC, MC, V.
For DIY jewellery enthusiasts, Holt is a step up from string-them-together bead shops. It offers a treasure trove of real gems, such as opals, peridots, emeralds, rubies and lapis lazuli, with prices starting at under £1. Helpful staff can advise on setting individual stones in necklaces, rings or earrings. There is a jewellery school downstairs and ready-made pieces are also available; a pair of blood-red garnet studs is £260.
Mail order.

Watches & clocks

Frosts of Clerkenwell
60-62 Clerkenwell Road, EC1M 5PX (7253 0315/www.frostsofclerkenwell.co.uk). Barbican tube. **Open** 9.30am-5.30pm Mon-Fri; 1-4pm Sat. **Credit** MC, V.
Established in the 1930s, Frosts buys, sells and restores antique timepieces. Prices vary, as most pieces are one-offs, but range from £150 to £15,000. It's good for unusual items such as lantern clocks or second-hand pocket watches.

P Cyrlin & Co
Bond Street Antiques Centre, 124 New Bond Street, W1S 1DX (7629 0133/www.cyrlin.co.uk). Bond Street tube. **Open** 10am-5pm Mon-Sat. **Credit** AmEx, MC, V.
Head to Stand 17 in the Bond Street Antiques Centre for vintage watches by Rolex, Cartier, Audemars Piguet and Jaeger-LeCoultre. Many pieces are hard-to-find limited editions so prices are fairly steep (£2,000-£5,500). For glamour that's hard to find these days look into Patek Philippe models; a recent find was a green and gold detailed ladies' wristwatch at £2,500.
Mail order.

Russell Callow
7 Sunbury Workshops, Swanfield Street, E2 7LF (7729 1211/www.russellcallowclocks.com). Old Street tube/rail. **Open** by appointment only 10am-6pm daily. **Credit** MC, V.
Russell Callow's one-man workshop sells 20th-century timepieces. Though collecting and repairing these is his speciality – we recently saw a 1970s graphic wall clock at a bargain £35 – he also has a selection of traditional clocks around the £200 mark. Eco-friendly cleaning products are used in restoration, as far as is practically possible. Check Russell's website for details of exhibitions.
Mail order.

Watches of Switzerland
16 New Bond Street, W1S 3SU (7493 5916/ www.watches-of-switzerland.co.uk). Bond Street or Green Park tube. **Open** 10am-6pm Mon-Sat. **Credit** AmEx, DC, MC, V.
Luxury is the watchword here. From Breitling and Chanel to Longines and Chopard, you're looking at four-figure prices.
Mail order.
For branches see index.

Repairs

City Clocks
31 Amwell Street, EC1R 1UN (7278 1154/ www.cityclocks.co.uk). Angel tube. **Open** 9am-5pm Tue-Sat. **Credit** AmEx, MC, V.
The third-generation horologists at City Clocks are happy to have a go at repairs to most watches and clocks. They sell an extensive range of hand-crafted and antique clocks, as well as traditional barometers (from £115). The website has a link to www.chronotrac.com, where the company sells Avia and Junghans watches, plus a selection of jewellery, such as cute charms from £70.
Mail order (0800 783 4587).

The Clock Clinic
85 Lower Richmond Road, SW15 1EU (8788 1407/www.clockclinic.co.uk). Putney Bridge tube. **Open** 9am-6pm Tue-Fri; 9am-1pm Sat. **Credit** AmEx, DC, MC, V.
The qualified clockmakers of this family-run company carry out repairs, cleaning and free valuations. If it's antiques you want, there's a range of 18th- and 19th-century clocks and barometers.

Watch Service Centre
60 Clerkenwell Road, EC1M 5PX (7253 4925). Barbican tube/Farringdon tube/rail. **Open** 8.30am-4pm Mon-Fri. **No credit cards.**
John Lloyd is at the top of his field in timepiece repair with over 40 years' experience, and he's very friendly with it, too.
Mail order.

Useful contacts

British Horological Institute
Upton Hall, Upton, Newark, Notts NG23 5TE (01636 813 795/www.bhi.co.uk). **Phone enquiries** 9am-5pm Mon-Fri.
The BHI offers free referrals if you're in search of a qualified craftsperson to repair a watch, clock, barometer or chronograph.

Gemmological Association
27 Greville Street, EC1N 8TN (7404 3334/www. gagtl.ac.uk). Farringdon tube/rail. **Open** 9am-5pm Mon-Fri. **Credit** AmEx, MC, V.
The association sells specialist books and instruments, and offers courses in gemology (the study of precious stones) at a professional level.

National Association of Goldsmiths
78A Luke Street, EC2A 4XG (7613 4445/ www.jewellers-online.org). Old Street tube/rail. **Phone enquiries** 9am-5pm Mon-Fri.
A long-standing association that can provide details of goldsmiths, plus information on hallmarks and commissioning.

World Gold Council
55 Old Broad Street, EC2M 1RX (7826 4700/ www.gold.org). Liverpool Street tube. **Phone enquiries** 9am-5pm Mon-Fri.
The WGC is a good resource for information on gold, hallmarks, design and valuation.

FASHION

Cleaning & Repairs

Dry-cleaners

Blossom & Browne's Sycamore

*73A Clarendon Road, W11 4JF (7727 2635/
www.blossomandbrowne.co.uk). Holland Park
tube.* **Open** 8.30am-5.30pm Mon-Wed, Fri; 8.30am-
4.30pm Thur; 8.30am-3pm Sat. **Credit** MC, V.
Popular with celebs, this venerable launderer and
dry-cleaner also caters to the Queen. Rates start at
£12 for a two-piece suit, or £40 for an evening dress.
The 'jet set' service for travellers cleans and repacks
the contents of a suitcase (cost varies). Alterations
and repairs are undertaken, and delivery is free.
For branch see index.

Celebrity Cleaners

*9 Greens Court, W1F 0HJ (7437 5324). Piccadilly
Circus tube.* **Open** 8.30am-6.30pm Mon-Fri. **No
credit cards.**
Dry-cleaner to West End theatres and the ENO,
Celebrity offers good all-round cleaning (a two-piece
suit costs from £10.90; a cotton shirt, £2.50), plus an
alteration and repair service.

Fresh Collection

*Great Portland Street tube station, W1N 5DA
(7631 0847). Great Portland Street tube.* **Open**
8am-6pm Mon-Fri. **Credit** AmEx, MC, V.
As well as dry-cleaning services (a two-piece suit
costs a reasonable £9.99), shirt laundering (£2.20) is
offered. Shoe and garment repairs are undertaken.
Branches: throughout the city.

Jeeves of Belgravia

*8-10 Pont Street, SW1X 9EL (7235 1101/
collection & delivery service 8809 3232/www.
jeevesofbelgravia.co.uk). Knightsbridge or Sloane
Square tube.* **Open** 8.30am-7pm Mon-Fri;
8.30am-6pm Sat. **Credit** AmEx, MC, V.
Jeeves's new free delivery service is well worth a
try – just phone to arrange van collection. Items
are returned in a week (two weeks for leather and
suede). An environmentally friendly non-toxic
cleaning process is used, and results are
impressive. Skirts or trousers are cleaned from
£11.50; shirts are laundered for £4.90.
Branches: throughout the city.

Lewis & Wayne

*13-15 Elystan Street, SW3 3NT (7589 5075).
South Kensington tube.* **Open** 8am-5pm Mon-Fri;
8.30am-12.30pm Sat. **Credit** MC, V.
Most cleaning needs are catered for at Lewis &
Wayne. Shirts and linens can be laundered from
£4.50, while dry-cleaning a skirt or a pair of
trousers starts at £9.50. The speciality is wedding
dresses, from £90 to £150. Repairs are also offered.
For branch see index.

Lilliman & Cox

*34 Bruton Place, W1X 8LD (7629 4555). Bond
Street or Oxford Circus tube.* **Open** 8.30am-
5.30pm Mon-Fri. **Credit** AmEx, MC, V.
This respected cleaners offers laundering (shirts,
£4.90) and dry-cleaning (suits from £22); suede and
leather cleaning (from £65) and coat waxing are also
available. Wedding dresses can be vacuum-packed.
A pick-up/delivery service is available.

Master Cleaners

*189 Haverstock Hill, NW3 4QG (7431 3725).
Belsize Park tube.* **Open** 8am-7pm Mon-Wed, Fri;
8am-5pm Thur; 8am-6pm Sat; 10am-4pm Sun.
Credit AmEx, MC, V.
Using an eco-friendly hydrocarbon wash, this
company specialises in cleaning designer and
bespoke garments. Expect to pay at least £15.95 for
a two-piece suit. Repairs or alterations are handled
by a Savile Row tailor.

Toggs

*484 Fulham Road, SW6 5NH (7386 8545/
www.shirtstream.com). Fulham Broadway tube.*
Open 7.30am-7.30pm Mon-Fri; 9am-5pm Sat.
Credit MC, V.
Toggs uses eco- and textile-friendly products. A
two-piece suit can be dry-cleaned for £8.50, a dress
from £6.99, trousers from £4.75. Shirt laundering
starts at £1.90.
For branches see index.

Washington Dry Cleaners

*18 Half Moon Street, W1J 7BF (7499 3711).
Green Park tube.* **Open** 8am-6pm Mon-Fri; 9am-
1pm Sat. **No credit cards.**
Friendly Trevor and George run this competitively
priced dry-cleaner. A suit costs from £10, while
laundered shirts are £2. Repairs and alterations are
also carried out – on suede and leather too.

Laundries

Danish Express

*16 Hinde Street, W1U 2BB (7935 6306). Bond
Street tube.* **Open** 8am-7pm Mon-Fri; 9am-3pm Sat.
Credit AmEx, DC, MC, V.
This long-standing Marylebone fixture launders
everything from sheets to shirts (£2.45; less in
bulk). It also provides a 'bag wash' service, charged
at around £7.50 for 6kg.
**For branches (White Rose Laundry) see
index.**

The Mayfair Laundry

*Stirling Road, W3 8DJ (8992 3041/www.mayfair
laundry.co.uk). Acton Town tube.* **Open** 8am-
4.30pm Mon-Thur; 8am-3.30pm Fri. **Credit** MC, V.
In business since 1860, the Mayfair Laundry is a
fine resource for those who value traditional
starched collars and cuffs (£4 for shirts finished
by hand). The company also deals with domestic
laundry, from sheets and duvets to curtains.

Repairs & alterations

British Invisible Mending Service

*32 Thayer Street, W1U 2QT (7935 2487/
www.invisible-mending.co.uk). Bond Street tube.*
Open 8.30am-5.30pm Mon-Fri; 10am-1pm Sat.
No credit cards.
This family-run business has been perfecting its
trade for over 50 years. Reweaving starts at around
£38 and takes three or four days, though there's
also a more expensive 24-hour service.

Designer House

*1st Floor, 18 Great Portland Street, W1W 8QR
(7323 6792). Oxford Circus tube.* **Open** 10am-
6pm Mon-Sat. **No credit cards.**
Rates start at £8 for shortening trousers (staff are
a dab hand at reproducing stitched hems on jeans).
Designer House also tackles major jobs – for
example, reducing a jacket by one size – and
making clothes to measure.

First Tailored Alterations

*85 Lower Sloane Street, SW1W 8DA (7730 1400).
Sloane Square tube.* **Open** 9am-6pm Mon-Sat.
Credit MC, V.
With a combined tailoring experience of 400 years,
this team of bespoke tailors and couturiers offers
a highly professional service. Alterations start at
£15 for hemming, rising to £400 to recut a jacket.

KS Tailoring Services

*Lower Ground Floor, 13 Savile Row, W1S 3NE
(7437 9345). Green Park tube.* **Open** 9.30am-
5.30pm Mon-Fri; 10am-2pm Sat. **No credit cards.**

Staff here can deal with most remodelling, repair
and alteration jobs (from £9.50 for hemming), but
prefer to steer clear of delicate fabrics.

Maurice Alteration Service

*2nd Floor, 5B Monmouth Street, 3 Nottingham
Court, WC2H 9AY (7836 9401). Covent Garden
tube.* **Open** 10am-7pm Mon-Fri. **No credit cards.**
A high standard of repairs and alterations is
offered here. Simple jobs, such as trouser-
shortening, start at £9.

Stitchcraft

*3rd Floor, 7 South Molton Street, W1K 1QG
(7629 7919). Bond Street tube.* **Open** 9am-5pm
Mon-Fri; 10am-4pm Sat. **No credit cards.**
A full repair and alteration service, covering suede,
leather and delicate or beaded garments, as well as
everyday clothing. From £15 for trouser-hemming.

Specialists

Cashmere

Cashmere Clinic

*Flat 5, 53 Redcliffe Gardens, SW10 9JJ (7584
9806). South Kensington tube.* **Open** by
appointment only Mon-Fri. **No credit cards.**
Your sweater will be sent to Scotland to be cleaned,
reconditioned and debobbled at a cost of £20.
Small holes can be fixed from £10.

Dyers

Chalfont Dyers & Cleaners

*222 Baker Street, NW1 5RT (7935 7316). Baker
Street tube.* **Open** 8.30am-5.30pm Mon-Fri; 9am-
1pm Sat. **Credit** AmEx, MC, V.
Chalfont can restore a faded garment to its former
glory in a few weeks, but doesn't deal with leather,
suede or sheepskin. Dyeing knitwear costs £40 for
a shirt or trousers, or £67.50 for coats.

Embroiderers

Hand & Lock

*86 Margaret Street, W1W 8TE (7388 4994/
www.handembroidery.com). Oxford Circus tube.*
Open 9am-5pm Mon-Fri. **Credit** AmEx, MC, V.
An authority on all forms of fabric decoration and
adornment, H&L works with bridalwear designers
to create bespoke dresses and shoes; hand-
embroidered couture eveningwear, chokers and
handbags are also specialities.

Leather & suede

General Leather Company

*56 Chiltern Street, W1U 7QY (7935 1041/
www.generalleather.co.uk). Baker Street tube.*
Open 10am-6pm Mon-Fri; 10am-5pm Sat. **Credit**
AmEx, MC, V.
Primarily a top-end retailer and manufacturer of
high-quality leathers, GLC also offers made-to-
measure tailoring and repairs.

Peters & Falla

*281 New King's Road, SW6 4RD (7731 3255).
Parsons Green tube.* **Open** 8.30am-6.15pm Mon-
Fri; 9.30am-2pm Sat. **No credit cards.**
As well as dry-cleaning and laundry, this long-
established cleaner can spruce up leather and suede
(from £39.50 for a jacket). Items can be altered, tears
repaired and buttons or linings replaced.
For branch see index.

Useful contact

Textile Services Association (TSA)/Dry-Cleaning Information Bureau

*7 Churchill Court, 58 Station Road, North Harrow,
Middx HA2 7SA (8863 7755/www.tsa-uk.org).*
Phone enquiries 8am-6pm Mon-Fri.
For details of reputable launderers in your area and
help with complaints about TSA dry cleaners.

Health
& Beauty

BEAUTY PRODUCTS FROM SPACE NK (7299 4999, WWW.SPACENK.CO.UK). NECKLACE FROM
LOOP (7288 1160, WWW.LOOP.GB.COM). PHILIPPE STARCK DUMBELL FROM CONRAN (7589
7401, WWW.CONRAN.COM).

Health & Beauty Shops

Department stores where the beauty halls transcend the usual selection of big names include the almighty **Selfridges**, **Liberty** and **Fenwick**; the latter, though small, boasts niche brands such as Chantecaille, Becca and T LeClerc. **Harvey Nichols** is strong on make-up artists' lines, such as Trish McEvoy, Sue Devitt Studio, Kevyn Aucoin and RMK. As we went to press, **Benefit**'s first stand-alone UK shop was opening on Westbourne Grove (No.227, W11 2SE, 7243 7800); the retro-kitsch beauty boutique stocks a full range of products, as well as offering waxing, brow shaping, and eyelash and brow tints.

Cosmetics & healthcare

Aveda Lifestyle Institute
174 High Holborn, WC1V 7AA (7759 7355/ www.aveda.com). Holborn tube. **Open** 9.30am-7pm Mon-Fri; 9am-6.30pm Sat. **Credit** AmEx, MC, V.
Since Aveda was founded by the fabulously monikered Horst Rechelbacher in 1978 – with just one shampoo – it has flown the flag for environmentally sound beauty products: the packaging uses post-recycled content, and the company is committed to the long-term goal of 100% organic ingredients (though it is currently some way from achieving it). What's more, the goods here – hair- and bodycare, make-up, teas, vitamins and more – are a real pleasure to use. The haircare range is excellent, particularly the Rosemary Mint and Shampure ranges, plus the rich Cherry Almond Bark Conditioning Treatment (£19). On the face and body front, we like the super-effective Hand Relief (£13) and the divine-smelling Caribbean Therapy range, with mango, lime and aloe. The Aveda Experience Centre, opening in Kensington in October 2005, offers express hair treatments alongside the full range of products.
Mail order.
For branches see index.

Becca
91A Pelham Street, SW7 2NJ (7225 2501/www. beccacosmetics.com). South Kensington Steel. **Open** 10am-6pm Mon-Sat. **Credit** AmEx, MC, V.
More than just a make-up shop, though not quite a full-on beauty parlour, Aussie cosmetics brand Becca's first outlet is divine decadence set over three floors. Step inside to a world of unashamed indulgence, with mocha-coloured walls, deep-pile carpets, velvet curtains and comfy suede sofas. Rebecca Morrice Williams started the company in her quest for the perfect foundation, and the products, in sexy chocolate-brown packaging, aim for an 'unmade-up' look. A variety of primers and perfectors prepare the skin for barely there Luminous Skin Colour (£28) or a stick foundation (£26) that's used only where you need it; both come in an impressive range of skin tones. The bestselling Creme Blush (£18) imparts a dewy, natural-looking glow. The recently launched Jewel Dust (£18) for eyes is a sparkling powder in a cool crystal cube, and comes in 16 shades. It's a bit messy to use, but gives glam results with careful application. Expert make-up artists are on hand in-store to dispense advice or give you a revamp (from £30 for a 'natural' makeover), and a private VIP area is available downstairs. Amid the make-up is a tempting array of jewellery, skincare and lingerie.
Mail order.

The Body Shop
374 Oxford Street, W1N 9HB (7409 7868/www .bodyshop.co.uk). Bond Street tube. **Open** 9.30am-8pm Mon-Sat; 11am-6.30pm Sun. **Credit** AmEx, MC, V.
With its dedication to good causes and use of natural ingredients, the Body Shop was a pioneer when it was founded nearly three decades ago. These days, however, newer, trendier companies have stolen its crown, and we're more likely just to pop in for a product that truly stands out. Take, for instance, the bestselling body butters – thick, glossy creams, all with matching body scrub (tip: mango is the most natural-smelling, coconut is a bit overpowering). On the other hand, the Peppermint Foot Lotion and Elderflower Eye Gel have been around so long, they seem almost quaint. But it's good to see that the Body Shop is keen to stay up to date, while staying true to its principles: look out for the Kinetin skincare treatment range – the key ingredient is a gentle, natural antioxidant said to smooth and tone skin. The make-up range, too, is good for no-nonsense neutrals. Some branches, including the one on Long Acre, also offer on-site treatments in the Green Room (7379 9600, www.thegreen-room.co.uk).
Branches: throughout the city.

Boots
75 Queensway, W2 4QH (7229 9266/www. boots.com). Bayswater tube. **Open** 9am-10pm Mon-Sat; noon-10pm Sun. **Credit** AmEx, MC, V.
Boots may be the place to stock up on such workaday staples as cotton wool and toothpaste, but its domination of the high-street toiletries market doesn't end there. Whoever's in charge of buying is certainly earning their keep: in addition to well-known perfume and skincare brands such as Clarins, Clinique and Lancôme, larger stores are now also stocking Nails Inc products (as well as the varnishes), Naked 97% natural toiletries, Jemma Kidd make-up brushes, Karmatherapy (exclusive to Boots, from the people behind the calmia spa, *see p96*), plus a wide selection of men's ranges, from Aramis Lab Series to Zirh. And if Boots' own Shapers sarnies and snacks haven't worked miracles on your love handles, then maybe Elle Macpherson's affordable range of body products or renowned aromatherapist Danièle Ryman's PhytoSlender line will do the trick. The generous loyalty scheme and frequent special offers also keep us coming back for more.
Mail order.
Branches: throughout the city.

Cosmetics à la Carte
19B Motcomb Street, SW1X 8LB (7235 0596/ www.cosmeticsalacarte.com). Knightsbridge tube. **Open** 10am-6pm Mon-Sat. **Credit** AmEx, MC, V.
This small, well-designed shop offers a huge range of make-up and skincare for all ages and skin types. Gone are the days of buying an eyeshadow trio because you like two of the shades. Cosmetics à la Carte's click-in Colourbox system allows you to fill up a palette with whatever you fancy (eye, lip and cheek colours cost between £10 and £25). Having trouble finding your perfect foundation? If one of the ready-made shades (£30) doesn't match your complexion perfectly, you can have one specially mixed for £40. Make-up artists are on hand to give advice, even if you don't opt for one of renowned make-up lessons (£40-£150).
Mail order (7622 2318).

Crabtree & Evelyn
6 Kensington Church Street, W8 4EP (7937 9335/www.crabtree-evelyn.co.uk). High Street Kensington tube. **Open** 10am-6pm Mon-Wed, Fri, Sat; 10am-7pm Thur; 11am-5pm Sun. **Credit** AmEx, MC, V.
Sitting firmly in the upper middle class of the toiletries world, C&E still appeals to the twinset-and-pearls brigade but also has a dedicated following for its younger, trendier, results-led lines. Chief among these is the highly successful 60-Second Fix kits (Hand Recovery Scrub and Hand Therapy Cream), available in various fragrances, as well as mini versions. In general, give the Lily of the Valley and Gardenia a miss and stick to Aloe Vera, Jojoba or Goatmilk – all fresh-smelling ranges that look great on the bathroom shelf. Or, for something bang up to date, the La Source collection, which now includes a peel-off mask that's billed, somewhat dramatically, as a 'mini facial' (messy to mix, but fun to remove). The new Nursery Tails range of toiletries for children is as cute as a button. There are also gift items – teas, biscuits, jams and the Gardeners range of products.
Branches: throughout the city.

Fresh
92 Marylebone High Street, W1U 4RD (7486 4100/www.fresh.com). Baker Street tube. **Open** 10am-7pm Mon-Wed, Fri, Sat; 10am-8pm Thur; noon-5pm Sun. **Credit** AmEx, DC, MC, V.
This high-end American range of skin-, body- and haircare was set up in Boston in 1991. The products aren't just lovely to look at, but with ingredients such as soy, milk, rice and sugar, they smell good enough to eat. The Index fragrances – gentle scents with such mouth-watering names as Pear Cassis and Fig Apricot – are also popular. The new range, V-Tonic, is designed to nourish the skin by replacing nutrients lost through stress and exercise. As with the rest of Fresh's products, it doesn't come cheap (Foaming Shea Butter is £34, Body Cream £28), but the quality is clearly high. The new In-Flight Kit includes an in-flight mask and a post-flight serum but, at £97.50, it may end up costing more than your airfare. If that's outside your budget, book yourself in for a mini treatment (facials from £65, make-up lesson £85) – the cost is redeemable against products. Fresh is also sold at some department stores, including Harrods, Liberty and Selfridges.
Mail order.

HQ hair & beautystore
2 New Burlington Street, W1S 2JE (0871 220 4141/www.hqhair.com). Oxford Circus tube. **Open** 10am-6pm Mon, Sat; 10am-7pm Tue, Fri; 10am-8pm Wed, Thur. **Credit** AmEx, MC, V.
HQ began life as a humble hair salon on Queensway (which is still going strong), before opening this one-stop salon and beauty shop a few years ago. We like it for its huge roster of cult names, from hair- and skincare to make-up, via perfumes, accessories and tools of the trade. The collection is too extensive to list here, but current highlights include Mario Badescu and Joey skincare, Comptoir Sud Pacifique and Carthusia perfumes, Joico and Terax hair products, DuWop and Jelly Pong Pong make-up, and fun accessories such as South Beach Rocks jewellery and Cleavage Cupcakes (gel inserts for the bra: 'pop them in and they'll leave you perfectly risen'). Recent additions include Prawduct (from celeb LA hairstylist Robert Hallowell), Hei Poa (rich hair, body and sun products containing coconut oil from Tahiti) and the Japonesque range of make-up brushes and tools, but the selection is continually being updated, and there's even more on the exhaustive website (backed up by an excellent delivery service). As well as hairdressing, the salon offers services such as Dermalogica facials, Aromatherapy Associates massages, waxing, Barielle manicures and pedicures, Fantasy Tans and more. Highly recommended.
Mail order.
For branch (HQ hair) see index.

Kiehl's

29 Monmouth Street, WC2H 9DD (7240 2411/ www.kiehls.com). Covent Garden, Embankment or Leicester Square tube/Charing Cross tube/rail. **Open** 10.30am-7pm Mon-Sat; noon-5pm Sun. **Credit** AmEx, MC, V.

It's not every company that has a line of products designed specifically for horses. But then, Kiehl's has had plenty of time to develop its range since it began life as a humble pharmacy in New York way back in 1851. And develop it does. The Cryste Marine range is the latest addition to the family – a cream, firming face serum and firming eye treatment made with criste marine, 'an unusual botanical found aside the Mediterranean sea', designed to improve firmness and soften the appearance of lines. Will it be the contender to the crown currently held by the Abyssine line, last year's must-have (a little overrated, in our opinion)? Who knows. We're sticking to our long-standing, tried-and-trusted faves, such as the rich, gooey lip balms (£6.50-£10/15ml) and the subtle fragrances (musk, cucumber). Fans of the highly popular Crème de Corps range take note: there is now a

Natural beauty

The increasing number of column inches warning of the potential (though not yet proven) health threat of 'nasties' in cosmetics has done nothing for the beauty industry's glossy image. Among the prime suspects are parabens (a widely used preservative that has been linked to breast cancer), sodium lauryl sulphate (a harsh detergent and foaming agent) and many more chemicals with frightening names. Alarmingly, 60 per cent of what we put on our skin is absorbed into our bloodstream. And since 'natural' and 'organic' became the buzzwords *du jour* in the food industry (the organic food trade is worth a whopping £1.2 billion a year in the UK), it was only a matter of time before the beauty industry caught on. Naturally sourced cosmetics, once the preserve of an alternative-minded minority, are now penetrating the mainstream in force, gracing the pages of the glossies and making their way on to supermarket shelves. And the good news is that it's not all home-made cucumber deodorants and oatmeal scrubs either.

Categorisation of organic and natural beauty products is still very much in its infancy, and regulation is non-existent, so the onus is on the consumers to do their homework – no easy task when faced with misleading labels, a long list of ingredients with impenetrable names, and much bickering between companies over what constitutes 'organic'. But things are slowly changing. Health and beauty standards were introduced in 2002 by the Soil Association in the UK, so products displaying its stamp of approval are at least 95 per cent organic. But since organic beauty companies are sprouting up around the globe without any standard classification, the only real way to be sure of the facts is to investigate yourself. And, as with organic food, brace yourself for high prices and small bottles.

Spiezia makes its products from a farm in Cornwall and is one of the most passionately organic beauty companies we have come across – in fact, it's the first and only company in the UK to produce a 100 per cent organic range. Though steeply priced, the products are rich and beautiful – the Floral Skin Toner (£16.50; *pictured*) is one of our favourites.

Another company with impeccable credentials is New Zealand-based **Living Nature**, which uses no synthetic ingredients whatsoever in its extensive skincare range. In fact, its products are so 'alive' (hence the name) that they have a sell-by date. Much of the range is based on manuka honey, which is said to have anti-inflammatory and antibacterial qualities, and we love the fresh-smelling Manuka Shower Gel (£7).

The prize for luxe and good looks, though, has to go to the upmarket New York-based hair and skin range **John Masters Organics** (www.johnmasters.com). Go for the edible-smelling Blood Orange and Vanilla Body Milk (£18) or the Honey and Hibiscus Shampoo (£26; *pictured*).

You won't find any trendy packaging at **Dr Hauschka**, but you will find some of the most effective skincare products around, certified natural by Germany's BDIH, similar to the UK's Soil Association. The German brand has been around since the 1920s, but over the past few years it has developed something of a cult following in the UK, endorsed by many a celebrity. Do believe the hype: the Rose Day Cream (£16) is one of the richest, most effective moisturisers we've used, and the Lemon Body Oil (£16) is exquisite.

There are other well-established organic heavyweights on the scene: **Green People** offers a vast, accessible range of products for men and women; **Lavera** has an ultra-gentle range designed for users with neurodermatitis but good for everyone (including 100 per cent natural sun protection); 80-year-old Swiss company **Weleda** employs biodynamic farming techniques to produce the ingredients for its vast collection of hair and skin products, among them gems like the 100 per cent natural Wild Rose Deodorant (£6.95) and the new, sweet-smelling Sea Buckthorn range (£3.60-£6.95); Austrian **Jurlique** uses its fine products at its day spa in Chiswick (*see p101*); and the lovely **Neal's Yard Remedies** (*see p91*) is one of the UK's favourite organic brands (Rose Water, £4.75; *pictured*).

Other ranges with a strong natural agenda include America's **Burt's Bees**, with its fun, fruity and affordable range (we love the Carrot Day Cream, £10.95, and the good-enough-to-eat Lemon Cuticle Butter, £3.95), and British **REN** (*see p92*); though not certified organic, REN (which means 'clean' in Swedish) makes a fantastic range of hair and skin products (try the Moringa Seed Micro Protein Universal Shampoo, £16.50; *pictured*), which contain no artificial preservatives, colours or fragrances.

The main stockists of natural beauty products in London are **Farmacia** (*see p102*), the **Organic Pharmacy** (96 Kings Road, SW10 0LN, 7351 2232, www.theorganicpharmacy.com), **Fresh & Wild** (*see p246*) and **Planet Organic** (*see p246*), though **Harrods**, **Selfridges** and **Harvey Nichols** (for all, *see chapter Department Stores*) also stock choice ranges. New website **So organic.com** stocks organic brands.

Burt's Bees (01225 461 049, www.myburtsbees.co.uk).
Dr Hauschka (01386 791 022, www.drhauschka.co.uk).
Green People (01403 740 350, www.greenpeople.co.uk).
John Masters Organics (www.johnmasters.com).
Jurlique (www.jurlique.co.uk).
Lavera (01557 870 203, www.lavera.co.uk).
Living Nature (www.livingnature.co.uk).
Spiezia (0870 850 8851, www.spiezia.co.uk).
Weleda (0115 944 8200, www.weleda.co.uk).

lighter version (Light-Weight Body Lotion, £20) and a Crème de Corps Nurturing Body Washing Cream (£15), which makes an useful summer alternative to the original thick-as-custard formula. Kiehl's products are also sold at Harrods, Liberty, Selfridges and Space NK (*see p93*). *Mail order.*

Korres

124 King's Road, SW3 4TR (7581 6455/www. korres.com). Sloane Square tube. **Open** 10am-7pm Mon-Sat; noon-6pm Sun. **Credit** AmEx, DC, MC, V. Set up nearly a decade ago, this Athens-based company produces a line of gorgeous products based on kitchen ingredients such as coriander, lemon, nutmeg and vanilla, and avoiding mineral oils (thought to clog the skin and prevent the elimination of toxins), silicones or propylene glycol. The range is wide, with face, body, hair, sun and men's lines, and continually expanding. True to the company's Greek roots, the Yogurt range (made with real yoghurt rather than the powdered stuff) now includes a face cream and a mask (both £16/40ml) that target oily yet dehydrated skin. There's an anti-cellulite soap and cream-gel, and the Multivitamin Skin Shield has been garnering lots of positive press for the wonders it works on fine lines, skin discoloration and ageing. We're also pleased by the prospect of a new make-up range, which kicks off with eye, lip and brow pencils. *Mail order.*

Lush

Unit 11, The Piazza, Covent Garden, WC2E 8RB (7240 4570/www.lush.com). Covent Garden tube. **Open** 10am-7pm Mon-Sat; 11am-6pm Sun. **Credit** AmEx, MC, V. Celebrating its tenth birthday in 2005, Lush now has an impressive 325-plus shops in 35 countries. With their deli-style packaging (complete with use-by dates) and ludicrous names (Buffy the Backside Slayer Body Butter, anyone?), the products might not attract the more conservative shopper, but there are some gems in there too. Fans of the Ultra Bland Cleanser (£4.35/45g) swear it's as good as Eve Lom's legendary cleansing balm and, while the Ocean Salt Scrub might be too harsh for the gentlest of skins, it leaves normal or oily skin baby-bottom soft. The new Shower Jellies (£1.75-£2.50/100g) and Butter Creams (£1.75-£3.45/100g) are great straight out of the fridge on a hot day, and their gentle suds are a reminder of Lush's principles: it doesn't use harsh foaming agents and chemicals, but as many fresh, organic ingredients as possible, such as clays, herbs, flowers, butters and oils. There's even a vegan hair conditioner. *Mail order (01202 668 545).* **Branches:** throughout the city.

MAC Cosmetics

109 King's Road, SW3 4PA (7349 0022/ www.maccosmetics.com). Sloane Square tube. **Open** 10am-6.30pm Mon-Sat; noon-5.30pm Sun. **Credit** AmEx, MC, V. This Canadian company is renowned for its bright, long-lasting make-up. It's serious stuff but it has a fun edge – ranges are designed to mix and match and perfect for experimenting with a variety of dramatic looks. New for autumn 2005 is the Rebelrock collection, with aptly named shades: Punkin', a bluey-pink lipstick; Anti-Establishment, a metallic-grey eyeshadow; and Non-Conformist, a purple shade of the Fluidline gel liner range. If you've overdone it, fear not – you can take it all off using MAC's skincare: eye make-up removers, cleansers and easy-off wipes. Don't be put off by an in-store atmosphere that's as loud and brash as the make-up – staff are always friendly and full of tips. *Mail order (7534 9222).* **For branches see index.**

Molton Brown

18 Russell Street, WC2B 5HP (7240 8383/ www.moltonbrown.co.uk). Covent Garden tube. **Open** 10am-7pm Mon-Fri; 10am-6pm Sat; noon-5pm Sun. **Credit** AmEx, MC, V. Containing such exotic ingredients as Himalayan wild indigo and Madagascan ylang-ylang, Molton Brown products are an international byword for luxury. Shower gels are a forte – good old Vitamin AB+C gives the body a wake-up call in the morning, while Blissful Templetree soothes sun-parched skin in summer. Matching body lotions complete the indulgence. The Celestial Maracuja range has recently been expanded to include a Bathing Nectar and Body Cloud (£45), a barely there finishing powder in a compact. MB's skincare is also worth a look: the Recover Eyes Firmlift and Wonder Lips Booster (both £24) continue to make waves, while, over in make-up, limited editions in sexy hues keep things bang up to date. Compared with other travel kits on the market, the New Age Traveller set (available for men or women), containing ten decent-size products in a smart leather bag, seems positively reasonable at £69. *Mail order (7625 6550).* **Branches:** throughout the city.

Neal's Yard Remedies

15 Neal's Yard, WC2H 9DP (7379 7222/ www.nealsyardremedies.com). Covent Garden or Leicester Square tube. **Open** 10am-7pm Mon-Sat; 11am-6pm Sun. **Credit** AmEx, MC, V. Still going strong after more than two decades, Neal's Yard Remedies continues to stand by its commitment to creating natural remedies and toiletries. No artificial preservatives, chemical derivatives or synthetic aromas are used. While the company's claim that it 'doesn't sell anything it feels won't genuinely give benefit to other people's lives' is ambitious, the products, with their smart dark blue packaging (recyclable), are undeniably popular. Bestsellers include the Frankincense Nourishing Cream (£10.50/40g), Wild Rose Beauty Balm (£20/40g), Rose Facial Oil (£11.75/50ml) and Honey and Orange Scrub (£7.85/60g), while more recent hits include the White Tea Eye Gel (£16). Check out the Plant Therapy line – tinctures and creams for common ailments such as skin,

Ormonde Jayne. See p95.

HEALTH & BEAUTY

circulation and digestion problems (from £4.50 for loose tea). The Neal's Yard Therapy Rooms offer a wide range of therapies, including various types of massage, plus acupuncture, counselling and cranio-sacral therapy. Prices are reasonable, especially if you attend the low-cost clinic on Sundays (10am-5.30pm), when you can choose a therapy at the cost of just £25 with a newly qualified practitioner. *Mail order (0845 262 3145).* **For branches see index.**

L'Occitane

149 Regent Street, W1B 4JD (7494 0467/ www.loccitane.com). Oxford Circus or Piccadilly Circus tube. **Open** 10am-7pm Mon-Wed, Fri, Sat; 10am-8pm Thur; 11am-5pm Sun. **Credit** MC, V.
Inspired by the South of France, L'Occitane's products tap into the natural goodness of ingredients such as almonds, oranges, olives and honey. Packaging is thoroughly attractive and, while products aren't especially cheap, there are some interesting finds among the day-to-day soaps and shower gels. The Almond Shaping Gel, for instance, does seem to smooth lumpy, bumpy skin – as well it might for £28. We're also fans of the Honey Harvest and Shea Butter ranges (the latter has just expanded to include a Magic Eye Balm, £16/15ml, designed to reduce puffiness and dark circles). The Green Tea collection has also had a boost; among the new products in the line are a Light Body Gel (£17.50/250ml), great in summer; fans of florals, meanwhile, might like the new Eau des 4 Reines Eau de Toilette (£26/125ml), with four types of rose.
Mail order (7907 0301).
Branches: throughout the city.

Origins

42 Neal Street, WC2H 9PS (7836 9603/www. origins.com). Covent Garden tube. **Open** 10am-6.30pm Mon-Wed, Fri, Sat; 10am-7pm Thur; noon-6pm Sun. **Credit** AmEx, MC, V.
Yet another naturally inspired collection, with yet more wacky names, but this Estée Lauder-owned company, which just celebrated its tenth anniversary, straddles the line between natural and high-tech beauty. The Peace of Mind range (£3.50-£20) of de-stressing potions contains basil, peppermint and eucalyptus essential oils, while A Perfect World (£12.50-£36.50) has beauty editors going gaga due to the inclusion of white tea, known for its antioxidant properties (the Skin Guardian does make skin look smoother, we admit). But there's some more light-hearted items in here too – Incredible Spreadable scrubs, Gloomaway Grapefruit Body Wash and Soufflé (£20/200ml), and, new for autumn 2005, the Ginger with a Twist body line (£15-£25), with ginger, lime, mandarin

and grapefruit. The incredibly minty Modern Friction (£27.50/125ml), a face exfoliator, is another naturally inspired favourite. Origins' make-up (lip glosses, mascaras, bases) takes a back seat but is worth a rummage for its gentle neutral shades.
Mail order.

Pixi

22A Foubert's Place, W1F 7PW (7287 7211/ www.pixibeauty.com). Oxford Circus tube. **Open** 11am-7pm Mon-Sat; noon-5pm Sun. **Credit** MC, V.
As the name suggests, Pixi puts the fun back into make-up. There are no drab browns and greys here, just unashamedly girlie hues and shades in all formats – glitters, glosses, brushes and pens. It's clear that the three Swedish sisters behind the brand understand we have trouble fitting everything in our handbags; there are cute, dinky kits (the eyeshadow/concealer ones include some highly wearable shades) and multi-use products such as Lip Boosters (£14, a brush and gloss in one; applying them feels rather like running a highlighter pen over your lips) and Hydrotint Duos (£26) – tubes of sheer tinted moisturiser that contain a co-ordinating shade of blusher/lip stain in a bullet-tipped applicator in the lid. The new Lip Blushes (£14) are matt lip stains in the shape of a felt-tip marker, offering the precision of a lip liner (shine addicts will have to add gloss on top). Don't overlook the own-brand skincare based on herbal and botanical ingredients, the highlight of which is a rich, thick, glide-on serum – pricey at £36, but you only need a dab. Also new is the subtle fragrance and candle line, El Jardin de las Higueras, meaning fig tree orchard.
Mail order.

Pout

32 Shelton Street, WC2H 9JE (7379 0379/ www.pout.co.uk). Covent Garden tube. **Open** 10.30am-7pm Mon-Wed, Fri, Sat; 10.30am-8pm Thur; noon-6pm Sun. **Credit** MC, V.
Still going strong after four years, Pout is a make-up maven's dream come true. Stock covers several hard-to-find industry favourites, among them Cargo, Lola and Mister Mascara, but we prefer Pout's own products, in their pretty turquoise packaging. The hugely successful range of Pout Plump lip glosses has been expanded with two new ultra-sexy shades (Bubblegum and Caramel) and, while the blurb may sound too good to be true ('after one month of continuous treatment, lip volume is proven to increase by 40%'), the sales speak for themselves. Also bound to make its mark is the new own-brand Twinset & Pearls collection, with English Rose-inspired shades of eyeshadow, blushes, lipslicks and eyeslicks. Skin- and bodycare get a look-in too: there's REN, Fake Bake tanning products, Ole

Henriksen (LA-based celeb facialist) and much-hyped B Kamins. If all that shopping leaves you inspired, you can also get a mini treatment such as eyebrow shaping, a manicure or makeover (for you or your make-up bag). There are 'Poutlets' at Harvey Nicks and House of Fraser, and the products are sold at HQ hair & beautystore (*see p88*).
Mail order.

REN

40 Liverpool Street, EC2M 7QN (7618 5353/ www.renskincare.com). Liverpool Street tube/rail. **Open** noon-3pm, 4-7pm Mon; 11am-3pm, 4-7pm Tue-Fri. **Credit** AmEx, MC, V.
Another company focusing on natural ingredients, REN is bold in its aim: to come up with a line of products that are 100% plant- and mineral-derived. Refreshingly, the company is upfront with its claims, admitting it's still 3% off target so far. Ingredients include herbs, minerals and flowers; among our favourites are the Moroccan Rose Otto Bath Oil (£22.50/150ml) and Neroli and Grapefruit Shower Wash (£15/250ml). We've also been impressed by the shampoos, conditioners and body creams, as well as the Frankincense and Boswellia Serrata Repair Cream (£25/50ml), which lives up to expectations, helping to regenerate ravaged skin – proof, if it were needed, that you don't need a skinful of chemicals to get results.
Mail order (0845 225 5600).
For branch see index.

Screenface

48 Monmouth Street, WC2H 9EP (7836 3955/ www.screenface.com). Leicester Square tube. **Open** 10.30am-6.30pm Mon-Sat; noon-5pm Sun. **Credit** AmEx, MC, V.
Fancy yourself as a film goddess? Then this is the place for you. Make-up artists seek out Screenface for high-quality, long-lasting make-up and tools of the trade. Only the tried and trusted make it on to the shelves: Fardel face and body paints, Lord & Berry eye and lip liners, plus Screenface's own range of make-up, foundation and powder compacts (from £6.95). Haircare is of a similar calibre (Joico, Fudge, Phyto), as are the make-up brushes and other tools. Special effects are also big business – fake blood, adhesives and removers, and all types of facial hair, from handlebar moustaches to mutton chops.
Mail order (7221 8289).
For branch see index.

Shu Uemura

55 Neal Street, WC2H 9PJ (7240 7635/ www.shuuemura.com). Covent Garden tube. **Open** 10.30am-7pm Mon-Sat; noon-5pm Sun. **Credit** AmEx, DC, MC, V.

Space NK

You practically need sunglasses to enter Shu Uemura's bright, futuristic shop, which stocks the company's high-quality make-up, skincare and accessories. While there's every shade you could imagine, Shu Uemura's forte is loud and bright colours – even the new Fiber Xtension Mascara (£15) is available in green and blue, as well as good old black. Many products are designed to get results, such as Principe Eye Zone Complex and Lash Repair. The Moisture Recovery Nanowater (£19.50/150ml), a pre-moisturiser treatment in the Depsea Therapy range, even contains tiny 'nano-emollients' that penetrate quickly to quench dry skin. Fans of the famous cleansing oil take note: there's now a new, lighter Fresh version (from £20/150ml). Make-up artists also flock here for the high-quality brushes and tools. A further bonus: staff run make-up lessons and makeovers: they're not redeemable against products but are reasonably priced (£20 for a 45-minute makeover, £30 for a 90-minute make-up lesson).
Mail order.

South Molton Drug Store
583 Roman Road, E3 5EL (8981 5040). Bethnal Green tube then 8 bus. **Open** 10am-5.30pm Mon, Wed, Fri; 9.30am-5.30pm Tue, Thur; 9.30am-6pm Sat. **Credit** AmEx, MC, V.
The remaining branch of this bargain beauty store is still doing a brisk trade in cut-price cosmetics. Expect to find, at less than half price, brands like Clarins, Christian Dior, Revlon, Lancaster and Benefit – for instance, Elizabeth Arden lipsticks go for £3.99, and blushers for £4.99. Special offers change regularly, so if you're not local, phone before you make a special trip.
Mail order.

Space NK
8 Broadwick Street, W1F 8HW (7287 2667/ www.spacenk.com). Piccadilly Circus or Tottenham Court Road tube. **Open** 10am-7pm Mon-Wed, Fri, Sat; 10am-8pm Thur. **Credit** AmEx, MC, V.
After 12 years and with more than 30 stores in its portfolio, Space NK is showing no signs of slowing down. On the contrary: it has just opened a new men's shop in Soho, stocking fresh-from-the-lab lines such as MenScience Androceuticals, SKINethics, 4th_Floor and Space NK Men's Blue fragrance (don't worry, ladies, it sells our favourite stuff too in the adjoining women's wing). It's no wonder it's such a success story: stocking a roster of high-class cult lines, Space NK is a magnet for anyone who's serious about skincare and cosmetics. Only the best make the grade, but it's reassuring to see the old faves – Diptyque and L'Artisan Parfumeur candles, Eve Lom skincare (albeit in its expanded and sexily repackaged

form), Nars and Laura Mercier make-up – sharing shelf space with newer, high-tech additions (Freeze 24-7 and Dr Sebagh, both of which aim to reduce the signs of ageing). Staff are helpful but not pushy, and give free makeovers at quieter times.
Mail order.
Branches: throughout the city.

This Works
18 Cale Street, SW3 3QU (7584 1887/www.this works.com). Sloane Square tube. **Open** 10am-6pm Mon-Sat. **Credit** MC, V.
The brainchild of ex-*Vogue* health and beauty director Kathy Phillips and Geraldine Howard and Sue Beechey of Aromatherapy Associates, this sleek, white haven stocks a range of sleek, white This Works products. The choice isn't huge, but that's not necessarily a bad thing when the quality is this good. For instance, bath and body oils and burning essences are made with 100% natural plant oils, and the bath oils are blended at a concentration of 30% (unusually high in retail products). New for 2005 is the rich, nourishing Stretch Mark Oil (£30) and the Orla Kiely-designed travel kit (£70) is still on our wish list. The small treatment area now offers a Post Pregnancy Treatment plus aromatherapy facials and massages. This Works is also sold at Harvey Nichols and Harrods.
Mail order (0845 2300 499).

Verde
75 Northcote Road, SW11 6PJ (7223 2095/ www.verde.co.uk). Clapham Junction rail/35, 37, 319 bus. **Open** 9.30am-6pm Mon-Sat; 11am-4pm Sun. **Credit** MC, V.
Set up in 1988 by ex-Neals Yard-er Ruby Cook, Verde uses only high-quality botanical ingredients and oils, and is resolutely against animal testing. The products, in their distinctive, straightforward packaging, are old-fashioned, yes, but a pleasure to use: Lavender and Myrrh Mouthwash (£6.80), Brazilian Lime and Organic Lavender Sea Salt Scrub (£10.40) and Italian Lemon Hand Cream (£8.20) sound (and smell) good enough to eat, while the new Rose and Vanilla Body Cream (£20) sinks in straight away.
Mail order (7585 2926).
For branch see index.

Zarvis
4 Portobello Green, W10 5TZ (8968 5435/ www.zarvis.com). Ladbroke Grove tube. **Open** noon-6pm Wed-Sat; by appointment Mon, Tue. **Credit** AmEx, MC, V.
Vivian Zarvis's herb- and essential oil- based lotions, potions and remedies continue to attract an army of fans, 30 years after she set up in

business. The packaging (silver tins, clear glass bottles with cork stoppers) is smart enough to liven up the drabbest of bathrooms. Some products are aimed at the modern city-dwelling sloth (Executive Stress Tea, Flabby Flesh Bath Herbs), while others sound delightfully archaic (Patchouli Bath Crystals, £19.95, and the new Oil of Jerusalem Anointing Oil, £34.50, possibly of limited use in 21st-century London). But there's no arguing with the quality of the ingredients, and the lack of pomp makes a welcome change.
Mail order.

Afro

Afro Hair & Beauty, an annual exhibition, is held in May at Alexandra Palace. For information and tickets, phone 7498 1795 or visit www.afrohairshow.com.

AfroEuro Hair & Beauty
209 Uxbridge Road, W13 9AA (8579 9595). West Ealing rail/207 bus. **Open** 9am-6pm Mon-Sat; 11am-5pm Sun. **Credit** MC, V.
There's a wide choice of Afro and European hair and beauty products up for grabs here. Expect to find the Dermalogica skincare range, and haircare by Matrix, Nioxin (recommended for thinning hair), Fudge and Joico. T LeClerc make-up – rarely available in London – is also sold. Upstairs, there's now a beauty and hair salon offering facials, manicures, pedicures and waxing.
Mail order.

Pak Cosmetic Centre
25-27 Stroud Green Road, N4 3ES (7263 2088). Finsbury Park tube/rail. **Open** 9am-8pm Mon-Sat; 10am-6pm Sun. **Credit** MC, V.
A great local source for black hair and skincare products, with familiar brands (Ponds, Olay) through to organic treatments for Afro hair. The hairdresser's (for all types of hair) at Nos.34-36 is run by the same people.
Mail order.
For branches see index.

Sade Bodycare
28-30 Kingsland High Street, E8 2JP (7254 1313). Dalston Kingsland rail/67, 76, 149, 243 bus. **Open** 10am-6.30pm Mon-Fri; 9am-7pm Sat. **Credit** MC, V.
The huge selection of Afro beauty products for sale at Sade Bodycare includes a wide choice of wigs and hair extensions. Among the haircare items you'll find Dark & Lovely and Designer Touch, while cosmetics feature Sleek and LA Girl (for white as well as black skins).
Mail order.

HEALTH & BEAUTY

Mail order & internet

Many shops within this chapter have their own websites with online shopping facilities (**HQ hair and beautystore**'s is particularly extensive; *see p88*). Shop-shy blokes may want to check out **Mankind** (www.mankind.co.uk), which has an impressive range of men's goods.

Materia Aromatica

7 Penrhyn Crescent, SW14 7PF (8392 9868/ www.materia-aromatica.com). **Phone enquiries** 9am-7pm Mon-Fri. **Credit** MC, V.
This supplier of essential oils and skincare products is certified by the Soil Association. The company deals only with small, family producers, and ingredients are organic wherever possible.

Herbalists

AcuMedic Centre

101-105 Camden High Street, NW1 7JN (7388 5783/www.acumedic.com). Camden Town tube. **Open** 9am-6pm Mon-Sat; 11am-4pm Sun. **Credit** AmEx, MC, V.
A serene, wooden-floored shop championing Chinese medicine and herbal remedies. It's a brilliant resource, with a huge choice of books on everything from cranio-sacral therapy and homeopathy to nutrition and Chinese medicine. Also sold are own-brand acupuncture needles, holistic medicine and lots of teas (in bags and loose). The range of toiletries is limited, but well chosen; Shou Wu shampoo is great for hair loss, apparently. The clinic on the other side of the shop offers treatments such as acupuncture, reflexology and massage, and in between is a Chinalife tea house serving tea, herbal tonics and healthy snacks. The website is highly informative.
Mail order.

Ainsworths

36 New Cavendish Street, W1G 8UF (7935 5330/www.ainsworths.com). Bond Street tube. **Open** 8.30am-6.30pm Mon-Fri; 9am-4pm Sat. **Credit** MC, V.

The front of this store is tiny; the real action goes on out the back, where men and women in white coats work busily. Ainsworths has been making traditional homeopathic medicines for more than 25 years and currently manufactures around 3,300 remedies for humans and animals. A selection of books and Bach flower remedies is also stocked.
Mail order.

DR Harris & Co

29 St James's Street, SW1A 1HB (7930 3915/ www.drharris.co.uk). Green Park or Piccadilly Circus tube. **Open** 8.30am-6pm Mon-Fri; 9.30am-5pm Sat. **Credit** AmEx, MC, V.
A delightfully old-fashioned chemist's, with two royal warrants. The shelves and cabinets are filled with hair-, clothes- and shaving-brushes, razors, loofahs and modern brands of perfume and soap. But it's Harris's own ranges of bath- and bodycare, eaux de toilette and essential oils that take pride of place. The packaging is gorgeously retro. Products boast mouth-watering names such as Lemon Cream Shampoo (£7.30), Bay Rum Aftershave (£14.95) and Almond Oil Skin-Food (£10.25). But Harris & Co still moves with the times – its Crystal Eye Gel (£7.50) is a cult favourite.
Mail order.

G Baldwin & Co

171-173 Walworth Road, SE17 1RW (7703 5550/ www.baldwins.co.uk). Elephant & Castle tube/rail. **Open** 9am-5.30pm Mon-Sat. **Credit** AmEx, MC, V.
Established in 1844 and operating on this site for more than 35 years, this family business flies the flag for natural and homeopathic products, selling all manner of books, herbs, teas, tinctures and oils. Products include Weleda, Australian Bush flower essences and Bach flower remedies; Baldwin's own Synergy range of essential oils is well worth a look too. The excellent website is now also in Japanese.
Mail order.

Napiers

44 Goodge Street, W1T 2AD (7637 1610/ www.napiers.net). Goodge Street tube. **Open** 9am-7pm Mon-Wed, Fri; 9am-8pm Thur; 10am-6pm Sat; 11am-5pm Sun. **Credit** MC, V.

Founded in 1860, Napiers is a natural health shop and treatment centre rolled into one. Toiletries include natural and organic ranges such as Dr Hauschka, Burt's Bees and its own brand, including the children's line, Napiers Bébé. Hypochondriacs are well catered for, with all manner of supplements, tinctures and homeopathic herbs and tablets (by Napiers and the likes of Weleda and Quest). If you're uneasy about self-diagnosing, ask at the dispensary for tinctures and dried herbs. The downstairs rooms provide a host of treatments, from massage to reiki, counselling to cranio-sacral therapy. If you're not feeling quite yourself, phone for a 40-minute appointment with the resident medical herbalist (first visit £30, subsequent 20min visits £20). There's also a herbal advice line (0906 802 0117; calls cost 60p a minute) running from 9am to 1pm Monday to Friday.
Mail order (0131 343 6683).
For branch see index.

Perfumeries

If you want your abode to smell as gorgeous as you, head for **Terre d'Oc**. The Provençal home fragrance brand launched a two-pronged attack on London in 2004, opening two stand-alone branches: one on the King's Road (No.184, SW3 5XP, 7349 8291), the other on Marylebone High Street (No.26, W1U 4PJ, 7486 0496, www.terredoccreations.com). The company's signature fragrance collections, such as Travel Diaries and Fresh Waters come in various forms, including room sprays (from £6.90/40ml), oils, incense cones (from £3.90/20) and even scented pencils.

Angela Flanders

96 Columbia Road, E2 7QB (7739 7555/www. angelaflanders-perfumer.com). Bus 26, 48, 55. **Open** 9am-2.30pm Sun; also by appointment. **Credit** AmEx, MC, V.
Fittingly set within the Sunday flower market at Columbia Road, this perfumery is awash with its own unique scents. All perfumes are created in-house, including bespoke ones that moneyed individualists can order for £500. Less pricey are her signature fragrances (eau de toilette costs £24.95/100ml), including Seville, with hints of bergamot and lemon, and Millefleurs, with violet and iris. Also available are candles, room essences, bodycare products and linen water to spray on clothes before ironing. Also useful are the moth bags made of French herbs (£6.95).
Mail order.

L'Artisan Parfumeur

36 Marylebone High Street, W1U 4QD (7486 3435/www.artisanparfumeur.com). Baker Street tube. **Open** 10am-6.30pm Mon-Sat; noon-5pm Sun. **Credit** AmEx, MC, V.
This impressive boutique has recently opened a chic flagship in Marylebone High Street, complete with Swarovski chandelier and a perfume bar where you can sniff its exquisite scents from glass goblets. Among the range of perfumes, candles and bodycare products available are several with unusual ingredients that work surprisingly well. Méchant Loup features woody notes combined with hazelnut, while Premier Figuier Extrême is redolent with figs and comes in a beautiful tenth-anniversary, leaf-decorated bottle. Fleur d'Oranger (£140) is a limited-edition luxury buy created by perfumer Anne Flip. A range of jewellery by French designer Gaz is also available (a charm bracelet costs £48). Those with more than a passing interest in perfumery can browse the books on the subject in-store or sign up for the one-day perfume workshop available.
Mail order (7352 4196).
For branch see index.

Diptyque

195 Westbourne Grove, W11 2SB (7727 8673/ www.diptyqueparis.com). Notting Hill Gate tube. **Open** 10am-6pm Mon-Sat; noon-5pm Sun. **Credit** AmEx, MC, V.

This Works. See p93.

Fashion fiends salivate over Diptyque products, and it's no wonder as they have that uniquely Parisian air of sophisticated luxury. The candles are chief among the desirables, in countless varieties, including Baies (blackcurrant leaves and Bulgarian rose) and Chèvrefeuille (honeysuckle). The candles are great for creating a specific atmosphere – at Christmas time, say – and you can tailor-make a mood by burning a couple at a time. Perfumes include Jardin Clos eau de toilette, with musk and hyacinth, while the combined hair and body washes come in dreamy combinations, such as Olene, with wisteria and narcissus. Room fragrances and prettily packaged soaps are also sold.
Mail order.

Farmacia Santa Maria Novella

117 Walton Street, SW3 2HP (7460 6600). South Kensington tube. **Open** 10am-6pm Mon, Tue, Thur-Sat; 10am-7pm Wed. **Credit** AmEx, MC, V.
This diminutive outpost of an Italian pharmacy founded way back in 1612 by Dominican friars is a wonderful address to keep in mind for charming gifts with an old-world feel. Its monastic history is evident in herbal recipes used for everything from teas and tanning oil (containing walnut and almond oil, SPF3, £22) to sugar-free jams and liqueurs with healing properties (try the digestif Elisir d'Edimburgo, from £20). The newest cologne available is Città di Kyoto, created to mark the 40th anniversary of Florence's twinning with Kyoto. It combines the typical Tuscan scent of iris with oriental lotus flower. Classy gifts for men include old-fashioned shaving sets with ceramic mug and brush, or a bottle of Aceto da Toilette – a cosmetic vinegar with myriad uses, including aftershave and mouthwash.
Mail order.

Floris

89 Jermyn Street, SW1Y 6JH (7930 2885/ www.florislondon.co.uk). Green Park tube. **Open** 9.30am-6pm Mon-Fri; 10am-6pm Sat. **Credit** AmEx, DC, MC, V.
Among the few remaining traditional British perfume brands, Floris champions the old guard. One corner of the shop expounds on its history, with handwritten explanations of customs such as change being presented to the customer on a tray, for example. The perfumes and room fragrances use conservative but reliable scents such as lavender, gardenia and white rose. The Santal range for men is as modern-looking as it gets in here, though the red-and-black packaging conceals classically designed bottles. Prices for the range start at £5.50 for a bath soap. There's an extensive array of gifts, including brushes (which can be engraved), or a wooden bowl containing an impressively hefty semi-spherical soap with an old-fashioned application brush (£65).
Mail order (0845 702 3239).

Jo Malone

150 Sloane Street, SW1X 9BX (7730 2100/ www.jomalone.co.uk). Sloane Square tube. **Open** 9.30am-6pm Mon, Tue, Sat; 9.30am-7pm Wed-Fri; noon-5pm Sun. **Credit** AmEx, MC, V.
In the 11 years since Jo Malone launched her luxurious fragrance brand, the business has been a runaway success, with three London shops, plus stockists around the globe. At the swanky Sloane Street flagship, there is a sleek 'tasting bar', where you can sample specially mixed-up potions as part of a free hand and arm massage, and be initiated into the art of fragrance combining. Malone's coveted range of scents, candles, skincare and bodycare is sleekly packaged, mainly in glass bottles or jars with simple cream-and-black labels. Fragrances are subtle and authentic (the grapefruit range is one of our all-time favourites), and many products smell good enough to eat (the recently launched White Nectarine Blossom & Honey Cologne, Body Crème and Shower Gel, for example, from £28). New products include autumn 2005's Pomegranate Noir cologne, a sexy, sweet, smoky scent combining raspberry, plum and pomegranate with patchouli, frankincense and spicy wood notes (from £30/30ml); and the Tea Collection set of three

travel candles – Eau de Cologne Tea, Parma Violets Tea and Sweet Almond Macaroon Tea (£54). Pricing can seem unnecessarily steep (£20 for a tube of Vitamin E Lip Conditioner, albeit one of the chicest lip balms on the market), and the concept of buying multiple fragrances to layer, while tempting, may be detrimental to your financial health. The Scent Surround Cube and Travel Scent Surround kits (containing candle and linen spray, £54), encouraging you to 'scent your world' are certainly aspirational, but no less the lovely for it. Jo Malone's facials, incorporating her acclaimed massage techniques, are also available (£125).
Mail order (7720 0202).
For branches see index.

Miller Harris

21 Bruton Street, W1J 6QD (7629 7750/ www.millerharris.com). Bond Street or Green Park tube. **Open** 10am-6pm Mon-Sat. **Credit** AmEx, DC, MC, V.
Over the past five years Lyn Harris has built a reputation as one of the industry's most highly regarded 'noses', and in 2004 she opened this sleekly designed second store. She still operates her sought-after bespoke fragrance creation service from the original W11 premises (though this will set you back £4,000), but, luckily for those of us whose budget doesn't stretch that far, she continues to develop her range of off-the-peg perfumes, soaps, body washes, body lotions, body oils, candles and room sprays. From fruity to floral to masculine, they are aimed at different tastes but all are packed with rich natural extracts and oils, so their fragrance lasts for ages. Among the most exquisite are Noix de Tubéreuse, a deep, sensuous perfect-for-winter fragrance, and the salty, summery Figue Amère, both of which are now available as body lotions and candles. The shower range has also been expanded to include Tangerine Vert (fruity) and Fleur du Matin (floral). Liberty, Harrods and Fortnum & Mason stock the Classic Line, and Selfridges now has a concession in its beauty hall, with free consultations.
Mail order.
For branch see index.

Ormonde Jayne

12 The Royal Arcade, 28 Old Bond Street, W1S 4SL (7499 1100/www.ormondejayne.com). Green Park tube. **Open** 10am-6pm Mon-Sat. **Credit** AmEx, DC, MC, V.
Linda Pilkington's gorgeous little shop is perfectly placed in one of London's prettiest old arcades. Ingredients reflect her time spent travelling in the Far East and Africa – the range of eight perfumes includes Sampaquita (the national flower of the Philippines) and Ta'if (named after a rose and a town in Saudi Arabia); an eau de parfum spray costs £54, while perfume in a hand-blown glass bottle is £78. The new Parfum d'Or Naturel (£43) is a concentrated gold perfume purée in a base of natural sugars; smoothed over the décolletage and shoulders, it adds a subtle shimmer as well as fragrance (available in Tolu, Ta'if or Ormonde Woman). There are also attractively packaged candles (£35 for a large one; £45 for four smaller ones), bath and body requisites. Prices are on the high side, but ingredients are luxurious, and a little goes a long way.
Mail order.

Parfums de Nicolaï

101A Fulham Road, SW3 6RH (7581 0922/ www.pnicolai.com). South Kensington tube. **Open** 10am-1pm, 1.30-6pm Mon-Sat. **Credit** AmEx, MC, V.
This corner shop may be tiny, but company founder Patricia de Nicolaï has a distinguished history, coming, as she does, from the Guerlain family. Fragrances, including the bestselling New-York eau de toilette (£36/100ml), are produced in the company's Orléans factory. For women, the award-winning Number One perfume has notes of jasmine, tuberose and white flowers (from £43/50ml). Gifts can be had for as little as £5 for a mini candle – or go all out with a fragrance lamp decorated with gold leaf at £159.
Mail order.

Penhaligon's

41 Wellington Street, WC2E 7BN (7836 2150/ www.penhaligons.co.uk). Covent Garden tube. **Open** 10am-6pm Mon-Wed, Fri, Sat; 10am-7pm Thur; 11am-5pm Sun. **Credit** AmEx, DC, MC, V.
Penhaligon's pedigree stretches back to 1870, but the company's shops have a feel of modern luxury. The traditional fragrance and toiletries ranges are still popular, and include such striking scents as the colonial-influenced Malabah, a sultry mix of amber, cardamom and ginger (eau de toilette from £45/50ml). Staff can help you pick a perfume by asking some simple questions about your tastes – our 'scent mapping' was fun and yielded a fragrance we instantly fell in love with. The packaging of some products makes them reasonably priced gifts for discerning mums – for example, the Lily of the Valley talcum powder comes in a decorated retro tin (£9). The brand was given a contemporay boost recently with the introduction of a travel accessories range by Alice Temperley, hand-embroidered in pink and purple (from £22.50 for a key fob).
Mail order (0800 716 108).
For branches see index.

Roja Dove Haute Parfumerie

Urban Retreat, 5th Floor, Harrods, 87-135 Brompton Road, SW1X 7XL (7893 8797/ www.urbanretreat.co.uk). Knightsbridge tube. **Open** 10am-7pm Mon-Sat; noon-6pm Sun. **Credit** AmEx, DC, MC, V.
An exclusive perfumery, where renowned fragrance expert Roja Dove holds consultations (as part of his, ahem, 'Odour Profiling') to find clients' signature fragrance from among those available here. We're talking crème de la crème: expect the day-to-day (Bulgari, Penhaligon's), the historical (Caron, Creed) and the obscure (Jean Charles Brosseau, Piver); Dove has even had several defunct 'fumes revived exclusively to sell here – among them, Le Dix by Balenciaga. Fans of Diptyque candles, meanwhile, will be in their element, as the whole range is here. The setting is suitably dark and sumptuous, with black lacquered furnishings and glass cabinets displaying vintage perfume bottles (also for sale). A one-hour consultation with the man himself is £200 (not redeemable against products); with a member of the team it's £50 (and redeemable).
Mail order.

Scent Systems

11 Newburgh Street, W1F 7RW (7434 1166/ www.scent-systems.com). Oxford Circus tube. **Open** 11am-6.30pm Mon-Sat; 1-5pm Sun. **Credit** AmEx, MC, V.
Scent Systems founder Hiram Green is ushering in the new wave of fragrance buying from his miniature boutique, by sourcing independently produced perfumes you'd be hard pressed to find anywhere else. The idiosyncratically named U4EAHH! By Yosh, for instance, aims to induce feelings of euphoria with pear, pomegranate and refreshing cucumber. Men could go for Mr Hulot's Holiday, which is meant to be reminiscent of sea air and old suitcase leather. Green has recently introduced a bespoke perfume service – following a discussion and smelling session, your own personal perfume can be ready in as little as a day. It costs £150 for 30ml of concentrated scent, and the recipe is kept on file for reorders.
Mail order.

Les Senteurs

71 Elizabeth Street, SW1W 9PJ (7730 2322/ www.lessenteurs.com). Sloane Square tube/ Victoria tube/rail. **Open** 10am-6pm Mon-Sat. **Credit** AmEx, DC, MC, V.
Celebrating its 21st anniversary in 2005, this refined perfumery has introduced a crystal scent fountain for refilling bottles of exclusive Caron perfumes. Men can be indulged with a matt metallic travel holder for Frédéric Malle scents. New products in-store include the hyper-luxurious Jasmine de Nuit fragrance (£84.50) and a skincare range by Circaroma. Also sold are room sprays, candles and skincare products by Darphin and South African Environ. Facials are also available.
Mail order.

Health & Beauty Services

Hairdressers are offering an ever-growing list of beauty treatments (*see chapter* **Hairdressers**), while skincare companies have also caught on to the benefits of offering treatments in-store. At **Fresh**, you can redeem the cost of your treatment against products. **Jo Malone** facials (£125) are available in her shops. Those on a tighter budget may want to try the **Body Shop**'s Green Room. For all, *see chapter* **Health & Beauty Shops**.

While many places in this chapter offer a variety of massages, specialists include the **Energy Clinic** (132 Commercial Street, E1 6NG, 7247 8464, www.energyclinic.com), **Relax** (65-67 Brewer Street, W1F 9UP, 7494 3333, www.relax.org.uk) and the **Walk-in Backrub** (14 Neal's Yard, WC2H 9DP, 7836 9111); the latter is great for stressed-out city folk who need some quick TLC but don't fancy stripping off.

Salons

Ark Health & Beauty

339 Putney Bridge Road, SW15 2PG (8788 8888/ www.arkhealthandbeauty.com). Putney Bridge tube/Putney rail. **Open** 10am-7pm Mon, Fri; 10am-8pm Tue-Thur; 9.30am-6pm Sat; 11am-5pm Sun. **Credit** MC, V.
Treatments: body treatments, facials, hot stone therapy, manicures, massages, pedicures, reflexology, reiki, self-tanning treatments, waxing.
This is a beautifully presented salon, with warm tones, smart staff and the soothing trickle of a water feature creating the right atmosphere. Treatments for 'mind, body and soul' are performed by friendly and well-trained therapists in apricot-shaded rooms. The Ark Facial (£68/75mins) includes a consultation that is more in-depth than the norm. Aromatherapy massage (from £69/75mins), reiki (£55/1hr) and hot stone massage (£85/90mins) also feature. Beauty essentials and a wide range of men's treatments are also available. Prices are at the upper end, but standards are high.
For branches see index.

Beautyworkswest

8-9 Lambton Place, W11 2SH (7221 2248. www.beautyworkswest.com). Notting Hill Gate tube. **Open** 10am-8pm Mon-Fri; 10am-6pm Sat; noon-6pm Sun. **Credit** MC, V.
Treatments: body treatments, Endermologie, facials, IPL hair removal, manicures, massage, non-surgical facelifts, pedicures, waxing.
Beautyworkswest opened in spring 2005 with the catchphrase 'Blending beauty and science' – the science comes courtesy of anti-ageing expert Dr Daniel Sister, who relocated from his Harley Street clinic to offer treatments such as hormone therapy, 'age management' and 'injectables'. For those who prefer pampering to procedures, there's plenty of that too, albeit still with a high-tech bent. The most popular is the Oxygen Plasma and Ultra-sound Ling Facial, an 85-minute treatment that is rather like a seven-course gourmet meal – it just keeps on coming. There's exfoliation, steaming, extraction, several masks and an ultrasound probe, which moves across the Oxygen Plasma mask to stimulate collagen. It's not cheap at £100, but with so much activity you feel you've got your money's worth. Nail

treatments have snappy names like the Clickety Split express manicure (£25), and you won't get bored while having your toenails tended – there are individual screens and a library of DVDs including, of course, *Sex and the City*.

Bharti Vyas Holistic Therapy & Beauty Centre

24 Chiltern Street, W1U 7QE (7935 5312/ www.bharti-vyas.com). Baker Street tube. **Open** 9am-6pm Mon, Tue, Thur, Sat; 9am-7pm Wed, Fri. **Credit** MC, V.
Treatments: alternative therapies, anti-cellulite treatments, body treatments, body wraps, electrolysis, eyebrow tinting & shaping, eyelash tinting, facials, holistic beauty therapies, laser hair treatment; lymphatic drainage, massages, reflexology, self-tanning treatments, threading, waxing.
While this isn't the most glamorous salon in the world (the treatment rooms are fairly basic), Bharti and her daughter Shailu have built up a high-profile reputation for holistic beauty. In addition to her numerous TV appearances, books and a range of products for Tesco, Bharti is set to break new ground as the Bharti Vyas Method becomes part of a foundation degree in Holistic Beauty Therapy at Buckinghamshire Chiltern University. Her signature Ultimate Harmonising Treatment (£120/90mins) begins with a diagnosis of the general type and state of the body; Bharti was spot-on with us, noticing that we have a tendency to put on weight. The treatment might not be everyone's cup of tea: we found the massage (a combo of friction, acupressure and lymphatic drainage) hard-going, but there's relaxation too, in the form of hand and foot masks, and even some fun, as you get to wear inflatable Flowtron Lymphatic Boots, which apparently boost circulation.

Calmia

52-54 Marylebone High Street, W1U 5HR (7224 3585/www.calmia.com). Baker Street tube. **Open** *Spa* 9am-9pm Mon-Sat; 10am-7pm Sun. *Store* 10am-7pm Mon-Sat; 10am-6pm Sun. **Credit** AmEx, MC, V.
Treatments: body treatments, facials, massages.
Calmia is part spa, part store. On the ground floor, beauty and health products, clothes, books, and yoga mats and accessories – all high-end stuff – are alluringly displayed alongside a green tea and 'herbal elixir' bar. Calmia's aim is to provide its customers with a holistic lifestyle 'by fusing the ancient wisdom and spiritual philosophies of the East with modern Western science and technology', and regardless of whether you buy into this or not, it's certainly a calming place to have a treatment. These take place in the basement. There's not much room down there, which will disappoint anyone looking for a spa experience, but the treatments are worth having. The Complete Stress Release (£70/60mins) involved essential oils in a back, foot and head massage, and while it could never have provided the promised 'long-lasting peace', it certainly made a positive impact. Small caveats – we weren't offered a shower afterwards (even though we were covered in oils) and the inevitable product soft sell counterbalances any feelings of spirituality you might be experiencing. Still, warmly recommended for anyone wanting to go more than skin-deep with their spa treatment.

Chantecaille Healing Spa

3rd Floor, Fenwick, 63 New Bond Street, W1A 3BS (7409 9870/www.fenwick.co.uk). Bond Street tube. **Open** 10am-6.30pm Mon-Wed, Fri, Sat; 10am-8pm Thur. **Credit** AmEx, MC, V.
Treatments: facials, massages.
It may not be London's biggest 'spa', but this calm, white-curtained room on the top floor of Fenwick is one of the few places in the world where you can experience treatments using Sylvie Chantecaille's gorgeous products. The French-born New Yorker launched her make-up line and Aromacologie plant-based skincare (sold in the cosmetics hall) after conceiving the Prescriptives make-up range. Yet this major beauty player maintains involvement in the treatments through regular contact with the two therapists – and the attention to detail shows. In the Healing Facial (£125/90mins), your face, shoulders and décolletage are massaged with organic flower oils before the application of a custom-blended mask. A Magnetic Lift machine employs magnetic and electrical pulses to improve lymphatic flow, tone facial muscles and aid absorption. It's hard to believe sponge attachments gently pressed on your face can have any effect, but afterwards our face looked visibly lifted and skin was peachy-smooth – or was that just tension draining away? Those who shy away from machinery can opt for the hour-long Flower Facial (£85), comprising manual massage and a mask garnished with fresh rose petals. A body massage (£85/60mins) has been added to the brief menu.

C2 Clinic

11 Heath Street, NW3 6TP (7435 1554/ www.caci-international.co.uk). Hampstead tube. **Open** 9am-6pm Mon; 9am-7pm Tue-Fri; 8.30am-4pm Sat. **Credit** MC, V.
Treatments: anti-cellulite treatments, body treatments, bust treatments, Endermologie, facials, Futur-Tec, IPL hair removal, non-surgical facelifts.
The flagship for the CACI non-surgical facelifts looks as high-tech as the treatments on offer, albeit with a luxury spa slant. Instead of waxing, it offers IPL – intense pulsed light – a more permanent and expensive option. But the majority of customers come for CACI, which uses micro-currents to 're-educate' the facial muscles (£55/hr). The skin-rejuvenating Futur-Tec – a four-step treatment combining ultrasound, micro-current, laser and vacuum suction – is the same price. While it's suitable for all skin types, it's especially beneficial for acne, wrinkles and scarring. For those who live in fear of bingo wings and a saggy bottom, the Endermologie cellulite treatment claims to smooth out lumps and bumps. It feels rather like a once-over with a vacuum cleaner and a minimum of ten treatments is recommended – which at £55/35mins a go takes a lot of faith.

Elizabeth Arden Red Door Spa

29 Davies Street, W1K 4LW (7629 4488/ www.reddoorspas.com). Bond Street tube. **Open** 10am-7pm Mon; 9am-7pm Tue, Sat; 9am-8pm Wed-Fri; 11am-5pm Sun. **Credit** AmEx, DC, MC, V.
Treatments: acne treatments, acrylic nail extensions, anti-cellulite treatments, aromatherapy, body treatments, body wraps, electrolysis, facials, hairdressing, makeovers, manicures, massages, microdermabrasion, non-surgical facelifts, pedicures, pigmentation treatments, reflexology, scar treatments, self-tanning treatments, waxing.
London's original Elizabeth Arden salon was the preserve of high society and royalty when it opened in Bond Street in 1921, but today's Red Door Spa is not quite as luxurious as you might expect. Still, the treatment rooms are calming, with dim lights and flickering candles, and any shortcomings in the decor soon fall by the wayside when it comes to the treatments: a signature facial (£67/50mins) was professional and soothing. The salon is also well regarded for its microdermabrasion and CACI facials, glycolic peels and waxing (woossies are treated with the utmost sympathy), and tempting day and half-day packages. There's also a hair salon and make-up studio.

Equilibrium

Lower Ground Floor, Austin Reed, 103 Regent Street, W1B 4HL (7534 7719/www.re-aqua. co.uk). Piccadilly Circus tube. **Open** 9.30am-7pm Mon-Wed, Fri, Sat; 9.30-8pm Thur. **Credit** AmEx, MC, V.

Treatments: aromatherapy, body wraps, electrolysis, facials, hairdressing, manicures, massages, non-surgical facelifts, pedicures, Swedish massages, tanning, waxing.

Run by the large beauty salon chain re-aqua, Equilibrium is the reincarnation of Austin Reed's former barber's, set in the store's 1920s art deco basement. The most popular treatment here is the highly effective Guinot Hydradermie facial (*see below*); you'll pay up to £70 for it, but it's cheaper here than at some other salons. And with experienced staff, you can feel confident that you'll walk out with a clearer complexion. Other highlights include, from a large number of available treatments, L'Elixir and Thalgo facials, body wraps, polishing and massage. There's also a hairdresser's on site, and plenty of treatments for men. Hen parties can be arranged.

Groom

49 Beauchamp Place, SW3 1NY (7581 1248/ www.groomlondon.com). Knightsbridge tube. **Open** 10am-6pm Tue, Fri; 11am-7pm Wed; noon-8pm Thur; 9am-6pm Sat. **Credit** AmEx, DC, MC, V.

Treatments: facials, manicures, massages.

Despite its location, slap bang in Hoorah Henry territory, this salon is run by a down-to-earth crew. In the two years since she opened the salon, owner Susie Baddeley has built up a gang of highly trained staff, ready to whip you into shape. The motto is 'One chair, two therapists, one hour'; while the salon now offers à la carte treatments, the original concept was to present them in time-saving packages. It's more of a salon than a total retreat, consisting of one room with curtained-off treatment areas. But on our most recent visit a Combined Power Hour (including a Crystal Clear Microdermabrasion and Oxygen Facial, brow tidy, mini mani and pedi; £175) left us surprisingly chilled out. Although you can hear clients in the next treatment area, the super-comfy leather chairs tilt back properly, and having two therapists working on you in tandem feels highly indulgent. And you certainly can't complain about the results: our pedicure lasted several weeks. A concession is due to launch in Selfridges in early 2006.

Guinot

17 Albemarle Street, W1S 4HP (7491 9971/ www.rrobson.co.uk). Green Park tube. **Open** 9.30am-6.30pm Mon, Tue, Fri; 9.30am-8pm Wed, Thur; 9.30am-5.30pm Sat. **Credit** AmEx, MC, V.

Treatments: body treatments, facials, prenatal treatments, self-tanning treatments.

Sometimes the old ones are the best: the Guinot Hydradermie Facial (formerly Cathiodermie) has been getting clear results since it was developed in 1965; it's the signature treatment at the French skincare company's elegant flagship salon. Although it employs mild electrotherapy, it's far more relaxing than it sounds. After cleansing, plant-based products are applied, then Hydraderm rollers are guided over the face, emitting a galvanic current to aid deep penetration; this is followed by a ball-like high-frequency instrument, which apparently has an oxygenating, antibacterial effect. There is a buzzing noise, but you feel nothing more than a slight tingling and metallic sensation in your mouth. For mature skin, the Hydraderm machine now has a third string to its bow – a microcurrent massage to drain toxins and stimulate the facial muscles, producing a 'lift' effect (Hydradermie Lift Deluxe, £75). The new techniSPA body-contouring treatment (£68) harnesses the same draining and lifting technology to attack cellulite. If all that sounds a bit technical, there are also non-machine-based facials and body treatments.

Parlour

3 Ravey Street, EC2A 4QP (7729 6969/ www.theparlouruk.com). Old Street or Liverpool Street tube/rail. **Open** 10am-8pm Mon-Thur;

10am-7pm Fri; 10am-5pm Sat. **Credit** MC, V.

Treatments: body polishing, detox treatments, facials, hairdressing, make-up, manicures, massages, pedicures, threading, waxing.

More urban glam than go-for-broke luxury, this friendly boutique salon in Shoreditch is a cosy beauty pit stop. Downstairs in the hair salon, among the chandeliers and fresh blooms, you'll find bespoke solutions to city-scotched tresses. Upstairs, the beauty experts, armed with the industrious Dermalogica range, will fine-tune the rest. Special date? Book an hour and choose four mini treatments from the 'Beauty Bonsai' menu (£65/60mins), which includes manicure, pedicure, make-up, neck and shoulder massage and hair finishing. There is even a resident cosmetic dermatologist providing in-house Botox and expert medical advice. The emphasis here is on individually tailored treatments, which goes some way towards explaining the high prices.

Skin & Tonic

604 Roman Road, E3 2RW (8980 5492/ www.skinandtonicuk.com). Bow Road tube/ Bow Church DLR/8 bus. **Open** 10am-8pm Tue, Thur; 10am-5pm Wed; 10am-6pm Fri; 9am-5pm Sat. **No credit cards**.

Treatments: body treatments, Botox, collagen clinic, eyebrow shaping & tinting, eyelash

tinting, facials, makeovers, massages, non-surgical facelifts, pedicures, self-tanning treatments, steam treatments, sunbeds, tattooing, waxing.

Following a recent refurb, this East End beauty salon is no longer as 'no frills' as it once was: now it's all pale walls with Venetian etched mirrors. Familiar features remain, though: some of the cheapest beauty treatments in London and a friendly, chatty atmosphere. Don't be surprised if one of the beauticians occasionally pops her head round the curtain to natter to the girl who's got your leg cocked in the air to put the finishing touches to your Brazilian (£15). Waxing is definitely not on the wane here, with an average of two or three Hollywoods (all off, £20) performed daily. The usual facials, manicures and pedicures are available, as well as more specialised fare: Botox, thread vein removal and the new DiamondTome skin resurfacing (£30). The most popular procedure here, though, has to be the St Tropez booth for an all-over year-round tan.

Space.NK

8 Broadwick Street, W1F 8HW (7287 2667/ www.spacenk.com). Piccadilly Circus or Tottenham Court Road tube. **Open** 10am-7pm Mon-Wed, Fri, Sat; 10am-8pm Thur. **Credit** AmEx, MC, V.

Urban Retreat. See p98.

HEALTH & BEAUTY

Treatments: body treatments, body wraps, detox treatments, facials, lymphatic drainage, massages, waxing.

Spa.NK on Westbourne Grove is still going strong, but if you're more centrally based and don't want to schlep all the way to W11, the new Soho Space NK also has a treatment room; just the one for now, but luxurious it is, offering a select repertoire of massages, facials, waxing and tinting. We opted for an Aromatherapy Indulgence (from £70/60mins), using Aromatherapy Associates' gorgeous oils. After filling out a detailed questionnaire (always a good sign that they're looking after you), the therapist talked us through the different choices of oils. Being wimps, we requested a light massage, and that's exactly what we got. There's no escaping the fact you're in central London, so a bit of background noise creeps in. Spa.NK in W11 has a dedicated chill-out area and a wider range of treatments, including tanning, waxing and facials (Eve Lom, Darphin, Jurlique, Peter Thomas Roth, oxygen facials), with more treats in the pipeline.
Branches: throughout the city.

Urban Retreat

5th Floor, Harrods, 87-135 Brompton Road, SW1X 7XL (7893 8333/www.harrods.com). Knightsbridge tube. **Open** 10am-7pm Mon-Sat; noon-6pm Sun. **Credit** AmEx, DC, MC, V.
Treatments: anti-cellulite treatments, body wraps, Botox, chiropody, electrolysis, laser treatments, makeovers, manicures, massages, microdermabrasion, nail extensions, non-surgical facelifts, pedicures, reflexology, self-tanning treatments, semi-permanent make-up, waxing.

It's as if the aptly named Urban Retreat has been positioned on the top (fifth) floor of Harrods as a reward for making it past all the shuffling tourists. While the stark design may not be to everyone's taste (the corridors and waiting area are a bit '80s, with dark glass and mirrors), there's no denying the pedigree of the treatments. Our La Prairie facial (from £90/90mins) was heavenly: it seemed to last forever (in a good way), and the therapist could spot problems a mile off. Other facials and massages are by Aveda, Elemis, Crème de la Mer, Guinot, Thalgo and more, and all these products are sold in the retail area on the same floor. But the *Who's Who* of services doesn't end there: highlights include natural-looking Bali Sun airbrush tans, a Bobbi Brown Make-up Studio, expert eyebrow shaping by Shavata, nails by Leighton Denny (*see p103*), the Roja Dove Haute Perfumerie (*see p95*) and a swanky hair salon. Fellas in need of TLC will have to hotfoot it to the mini version of men's spa The Refinery (*see p99*) in the basement.

Vaishaly Patel

51 Paddington Street, W1U 4HR (7224 6088/ www.vaishaly.com). Bond Street tube. **Open** 9am-6pm Mon-Sat. **Credit** AmEx, MC, V.
Treatments: eyelash tinting, facials, lymphatic drainage, manicures, massages, pedicures, threading.

One look at Vaishaly's glowing complexion and you'll understand why she has a client list as long as your arm. Celebrity client list, that is, including professional 'faces' (and bodies) Elle Macpherson and Sophie Dahl. Behind what looks like an unremarkable Marylebone shopfront is a clutch of serene treatment rooms, where Vaishaly gets down to business. Her signature facial (£100/hr) includes lymphatic stimulation, extraction and microdermabrasion (using what feels like a mini vacuum cleaner), which gets rid of the layer of gunk that sits on top of the skin. Rather than provide a full-on pamper-fest, her facials focus on results, but Vaishaly really knows her stuff and gives tons of useful tips. While you're here, get Vaishaly or one of her assistants to sort your eyebrows out with threading (£20-£35), an Eastern technique using nothing but a length of cotton. Also based here are John-Yiannis Tsagaris, for traditional Chinese medicine, and Nonie R Crème, known for her manicures and pedicures.

Men only

Many hair salons and barber shops also offer men's treatments (*see chapter* **Hairdressers**).

Gentlemen's Tonic

31A Bruton Place, W1J 6NN (7297 4343/ www.gentlemenstonic.com). Bond Street or Green Park tube. **Open** 10am-7pm Mon, Fri; 10am-8pm Tue, Wed; 10am-9pm Thur; 10am-6pm Sat; 11am-6pm Sun. **Credit** AmEx, DC, MC, V.
Treatments: body treatments, facials, hairdressing, manicures, massages, pedicures, waxing, wet shaves.

How do you sell beauty to red-blooded males without encroaching on their virility? This discreet Mayfair grooming salon dispatches the problem with aplomb. It's a bastion of assured masculinity, crossing ocean liner elegance with the clean lines of an old-fashioned butcher's shop. Haircuts, colouring and wet shaves all take place on the first floor in tiled booths equipped with plasma screens and leather barbers' chairs. Downstairs, in swanky treatment rooms, a fleet of masseurs, osteopaths, reflexologists and beauty therapists is on hand for facials, hand treatments, waxing and teeth-whitening, plus several types of massage. Prices are surprisingly reasonable: a wet shave is £25, while a 30-minute Swedish massage clocks in at £35. But the real beauty is the privacy. A speakeasy hush pervades, while each treatment room has an adjoining private shower room.

Men's Salon at Selfridges

1st Floor, 400 Oxford Street, W1A 1AB (7318 3709/www.selfridges.com). Bond Street tube. **Open** 9.30am-8pm Mon-Wed, Thur, Sat; 9.30am-9pm Fri; 11.30am-6pm Sun. **Credit** AmEx, DC, MC, V.
Treatments: back cleansing, electrolysis, facials, manicures, massages, pedicures, waxing.

This small salon in Selfridges is a boon for guys too shy to venture into a unisex environment. Three treatment rooms are tucked behind a

Bed & backrub

If you're badly in need of a tonic, but don't have the time or money for a full-scale spa break, London's luxury hotels are a valuable stress-busting resource. Book in for a soothing post-work treatment and have a steam or sauna before ordering room service, hanging up the 'do not disturb' sign and kicking back on fluffy white pillows. The room rates at these classy establishments aren't cheap, but seasonal deals are often available online. Forget minibreaks – welcome to the microbreak.

The flamboyantly opulent **Dorchester** (*see p99*; double rooms £476-£582) is home to the grande dame of London hotel spas, with its art deco reception area and traditional spa treatments; note that it will be closed for refurbishment from January to May 2006. If you fancy pretending you're in Miami, take a chance on the weather and opt for the **Berkeley** (*see p99*; double rooms £356-£563) in summer, which is crowned by a (quite small) pool with retractable roof – guests get a reduced entry fee of £9.75. The spa menu includes such relaxing treatments as LaStone therapy (£90/75mins) and Balinese body massage. More serious swimmers may prefer **One Aldwych** (1 Aldwych, WC2B 4RH, 7300 1000, www.onealdwych.co.uk; double rooms £335-£464), which has an 18m pool (with soothing underwater music), plus a high-tech gym, sauna, steam room and treatments courtesy of Aveda and Carita.

But for oriental chic, it doesn't come much better than the **Mandarin Oriental**'s celebrated spa (*see p101*; double rooms £382-£440). You can indulge in a Life Enhancing Ritual (£435/3hrs 45mins) – a 'holistic journey', including reflexology, body scrub, wrap, Lifedance (shiatsu-inspired) massage or Ama Releasing Abhyanga (an Ayurvedic massage treatment) and an intensive facial. New Age puff aside, we reckon spending a day in this gorgeous facility, complete with hyrdrotherapy pool and steam room, is pretty life-enhancing in itself. The Urban Spa Escape package for two, available until end of December 2005, includes accommodation in a deluxe room and one hour of treatment time per person for £504 per night. Swathed in white curtains and dotted with snowy Louis XVI-style chairs, **Agua** (*see p99*; double rooms £310-£500) feels more like a glamorous beauty salon than a total retreat, though there's hydrotherapy and algae body wraps, alongside Aromatherapy Associates and Eve Lom treatments.

Less style-conscious, **Zest!**, the health spa of venerable Pimlico apartment/hotel complex Dolphin Square (Chichester Street, SW1V 3LX, 7834 3800, www.dolphinsquare hotel.co.uk; studio rooms £175), boasts excellent facilities. You may, however, need a full weekend to take advantage of the 18m pool, sauna and steam rooms, gym, squash courts, outdoor Thames-side tennis court – even a croquet lawn. The extensive menu of Decléor and Carita treatments is undertaken in six treatment rooms. The accommodation itself is blandly comfortable.

The centrepiece of lavish boutique hotel the Bentley Kempinski's classical spa Le Kalon (Harrington Gardens, SW7 4JX, 7244 5371, www.thebentley-hotel.com; double rooms £199-£326) is a full-size Turkish Hammam. Treatments include Karin Herzog facials, reiki and reflexology. Although the **COMO Shambhala Urban Escape** at the Metropolitan (Old Park Lane, W1K 1LB, 7447 5750, www.metropolitan.como. bz; double rooms £250-£390) is a rather grand way of describing two treatment rooms, this retreat offers a variety of relaxing and rebalancing treatments, including massage, acupuncture and even 'intuitive counselling' (£95/60mins). A package deal for two, available until the end of December 2005, includes an hour-long COMO Shambhala massage and a goody bag, from £295 per night in a king room.

frosted-glass wall in a slick barbershop off the men's department – perhaps so blokes can pretend they're going in for a short back and sides instead of a facial. As a result, it's perhaps better suited to essential maintenance than utter relaxation – despite soothing music in the treatment room, noise does seep through the barrier. That aside, facials using Guinot and MD Formulations products (from £35 for a mini facial) are luxurious, and the therapists highly professional. Chaps can be waxed (from £18 for shoulders), have their eyelashes and brows tinted (£25 for both), nails tended to (from £20) or indulge in an aromatherapy massage (£55/90mins).

The Refinery

60 Brook Street, W1K 5DU (7409 2001/www.the-refinery.com). Bond Street tube. **Open** 10am-7pm Mon, Tue; 10am-9pm Wed-Fri; 9am-6pm Sat; 11am-5pm Sun. **Credit** MC, V.
Treatments: acupuncture, aromatherapy, barbering, body treatments, electrolysis, eye treatments, facials, hot stone therapy, laser treatment, manicures, massages, pedicures, reflexology, salt scrub, self-tanning treatments, waxing, wet shaves.
This salon, set within an impressive Mayfair townhouse, is designed entirely for men – and it shows. A world away from the pastel shades offered by women's and unisex salons, the Refinery aims for a 'clubby' feel and prides itself on keeping to the client's timetable – if you have half an hour for a haircut, then you'll be out the door within 30 minutes. The expert staff cater to the likes of Pierce Brosnan, Sasha Baron Cohen (Ali G's beard was created here) and Rio Ferdinand, as well as a loyal following of businessmen and travellers – some of whom discover it during stays at Claridge's, across the street. Treatments range from LaStone Therapy (£115/90mins) to sports massages (£83/60mins). There is also a concession in Harrods.
For branches see index.

Spas

The distinction between spas and beauty salons, which are increasingly offering holistic and relaxing treatments, has become blurred. While spas traditionally have facilities such as steam rooms and saunas, this is no longer always the case. However, they do tend to offer more body treatments and hydrotherapy than salons, and generally have a dedicated room for pre- and post-treatment chilling.

Agua

Sanderson Hotel, 50 Berners Street, W1T 3NG (7300 1414). Oxford Circus or Tottenham Court Road tube. **Open** 9am-9pm daily. **Credit** AmEx, DC, MC, V.
Treatments: aromatherapy, body treatments, facials, hydrotherapy, manicures, massages, pedicures, personal training, Shiatsu, waxing.
For a spa housed in the theatrically modern Sanderson Hotel, Agua is fittingly big on aesthetics. It has an unusually dreamy feel (compared to the more common spa minimalism), with double-height flowy white curtains in all directions, white-clad staff and a lovely, calm atmosphere. Less calming for some, perhaps, will be the fact that there is nothing but the floaty curtains separating the therapy rooms, so you can hear everything in the next cubicle – and being starkers within speaking distance of an American businessman can be a tad disconcerting. That said, it's a place you must experience at least once if you're a keen spa-goer. Treatments are generally of a high standard – the legendary Eve Lom facial is wonderful (£110/90mins), as is the spa's signature Synchronised Milk and Honey massage (£73/55mins), and there are a variety of Aromatherapy Associates body treatments, such as the pampering Bed of Roses (£70/55mins). To get your money's worth, arrive early and take some time to relax in the communal chill-out area, which has plenty of chaise longues, glossy mags and fresh fruit. Our final verdict? Agua may not

be as cool as it was when it opened in 2000, to a chorus of celebrity approval, but it still has the wow factor.

The Berkeley Spa

The Berkeley, Wilton Place, SW1X 7RL (7201 1699/www.the-berkeley.com). Knightsbridge tube. **Open** 6.30am-10pm Mon-Fri; 8am-8pm Sat, Sun. **Credit** AmEx, DC, MC, V.
Treatments: facials, manicures, massages, pedicures.
The Berkeley Spa's crowning glory is its rooftop pool, which is open to the elements in good weather. It's not huge but it's rarely busy, and there are loungers aplenty, plus a fridge stocked with freshly squeezed juices. The treatments are also pretty special. The Dramatic Radiance facial (£95/90mins), using dermatologist-endorsed product line DDF, was one of the most thorough and professional we've experienced and includes a paraffin wax hand treatment. Staff are as you'd expect in a luxury hotel: not too coldly efficient but never sycophantic. If you want a more vigorous experience than the lapping waters upstairs or the Balinese massage (£90) below, there's always the gym. A day pass, including the gym, pool, sauna and steam room, costs £60.

Bliss London

60 Sloane Avenue, SW3 3DD (7584 3888/www.blissworld.com). South Kensington tube. **Open** 9.30am-8pm Mon-Fri (12.30-8pm alternate Wed); 9.30am-6.30pm Sat; noon-6pm Sun. **Credit** AmEx, MC, V.
Treatments: body treatments, eyelash tinting, facials, manicures, massages, microdermabrasion, self-tanning treatments, pedicures, waxing.
This South Kensington branch of the New York spa offers the usual range of face, nail and body treatments, but often with a twist. The delicious Double Choc pedicure (£65) includes a chocolate milk skin soak and sugar scrub accompanied by a cup of creamy cocoa (to drink). Request a customised treatment for specific problems, or indulge in a Bliss signature treatment such as the Triple Oxygen (or, for men, the Homme Improvement), a divine 85-minute facial with a cooling blast of 'vitaminised oxygen' to finish (£130). Although you 'check in' on the ground floor, where the shop (selling the covetable Bliss beauty products) and nail stations are located, the serious relaxation happens downstairs. Arrive early to nibble on the complimentary fruit and brownies in the waiting area. When you're ready, slip between crisp cotton sheets in the tranquil treatment rooms and try not to drift off and miss the bliss.

Body Experience

50 Hill Rise, Richmond, Surrey TW10 6UB (8334 9999/www.bodyexperience.co.uk). Richmond tube/rail. **Open** 9am-6.30pm Mon; 9am-8.30pm Tue-Thur; 9am-7.30pm Fri, Sat; 10am-6.30pm Sun. **Credit** AmEx, MC, V.
Treatments: body treatments, body wraps, facials, makeovers, manicures, massages, pedicures, personal training, reflexology, self-tanning treatments, waxing.
Body Experience has proved a big hit with Richmond residents since opening in spring 2004. The narrow, glass-fronted entrance gives no hint of the warren of rooms within this upmarket health spa – though trickling water features and sleek grey-and-purple decor set a reassuring tone. The extensive range of treatments covers facials (Thalgo, Elemis and LaTherapie), wraps, massages, steams, scrubs, anti-ageing and detox sessions. Short of time? Then pick one of the 'interludes': express treatments in the room next to the shop. For full-on pampering, try the Frangipani Delight wrap (£72/60mins), which involves a scrub, dry float, head and neck massage and being doused in fantastic-smelling lotions, or a Kiradjee massage (£140/120mins), based on Aboriginal techniques. Treatments come with a free fruit salad and herbal tea; alcohol and light meals are also available to buy. There's also a small, light-filled fitness studio with personal trainers, and Pilates courses.

The Dorchester Spa

Dorchester Hotel, Park Lane, W1A 2HJ (7495 7335/www.dorchesterhotel.com). Green Park or Hyde Park Corner tube. **Open** 8am-8pm daily. **Credit** AmEx, DC, MC, V.
Treatments: body treatments, eyebrow shaping, facials, hydrotherapy, lymphatic drainage, manicures, massages, pedicures, reflexology, self-tanning treatments, waxing.
The Dorchester's striking art deco spa is set to undergo major refurbishment to add new facilities, principally a relaxation room. While it's closed (Jan-May 2006), a limited selection of treatments will be available in a set of guest rooms. The full spa menu covers, among other things, Eve Lom facials and luxurious body treatments. We tried the Slim & Sculpt (£135/105mins) – a combination of massage with 'slimming' and firming creams and wraps by Thalgo. The treatment's USP is its dual action, and clients can pick what they want doing and where. We started with exfoliation, followed by a shower and sauna, then massage, which was pretty firm, Russian style, but we knew we were in good hands with our empathetic therapist. A quick turn in the shower and sauna, and it was time for creams and wraps: the chocolate-scented slimming wrap is made with cocoa pods and dries to a hard shell; firming products have a gorgeous ginger scent. Our skin texture seemed to improve – but our state of mind undoubtedly did.

Elemis Day Spa

2-3 Lancashire Court, W1S 1EX (7499 4995/www.elemis.com). Bond Street tube. **Open** 9am-9pm Mon-Thur; 9am-8pm Fri, Sat; 10am-6pm Sun. **Credit** AmEx, MC, V.
Treatments: body treatments, detox treatments, facials, manicures, massages, mud & steam treatments, pedicures, prenatal treatments, self-tanning treatments.
Tucked away down a quiet cobbled courtyard off Brook Street, this day spa offers relaxing, luxurious treatments inspired by exotic locations such as Thailand, India and Morocco. Prices start at £45 and end where your pampering imagination stops. Top treatments include the full body Exotic Frangipani Body Nourish Float (£75): brushed skin is slathered in rehydrating Frangipani Monoi Oil, followed by a weightless dry float, combined with a foot massage and a final layer of Exotic Island Flower Body Balm; as well as being blissfully relaxing, it leaves skin smooth and glowing. The Visible Brilliance facial (£115) is designed to combat the signs of ageing, and the pampering Hawaiian Wave Four Hands massage (£140) speaks for itself. The gorgeous skincare and spa therapy range (including one for men) will tide you over until your next visit.

Halo City

8 Eagle Court, EC1M 5QD (7253 0400/www.halocity.com). Farringdon tube. **Open** 6.30am-9pm Mon-Fri; 9.30am-6pm Sat. **Credit** MC, V.
Treatments: facials, massages, St Tropez fake-tanning, manicures, pedicures, brow and lash tinting, alternative therapies, counselling, far infra-red sauna, yoga, pilates.
Former City worker Sam Jones was spurred on to set up this spa because of her own difficulties finding a suitable centre in the area. As well as spacious pilates and yoga studios (considering the upper limit of 12 people per class), there are five rooms dedicated to treatments spanning specialist massage, Ayurveda, acupuncture, nutrition consultations, osteopathy and hypnotherapy. As a dreamy end to a stressful day, go for the Very Special Treat, a two-hour indulgence incorporating Dermalogica Face Mapping and relaxing massage (£150). Our therapist was professional and thorough in tailoring the facial to specific dermatological issues and afterwards, our problem skin looked clearer and fresher than it had in ages.

Ironmonger Row Baths

1-11 Ironmonger Row, EC1V 3QF (7253 4011/www.aquaterra.org/irb.htm). Old Street tube/rail. **Open** 6.30am-9.30pm Mon-Fri; 9am-6pm Sat; 10am-6pm Sun. *Sauna Mixed* 8am-8pm Mon-Fri; 9am-5pm Sat; noon-5pm Sun. *Turkish Baths*

sameday doctor +

Fully confidential Sexual Health Clinic in Harley Street W1
Sameday Appointments -
Sameday HIV results
+
General Medical & Psychological Consultations

114 Harley Street, London W1G 7JJ
www.samedaydoctor.co.uk
0207 935 0113

Men only 9am-9.30pm Tue, Thur; 9am-6.30pm Sat. *Women only* 9am-9.30pm Wed, Fri; 10am-6.30pm Sun. *Mixed* 2-9.30pm Mon.
Treatments: body scrubs, massages, reflexology, reiki.

Even those strapped for cash can indulge in some quality spa time at this 1930s Turkish bath. A day's use of the hot rooms, steam room, plunge pool and swimming pool costs just £6.70 before noon Mon-Fri (£11.50 thereafter and all day at weekends). Tea, toast and snacks can be munched in front of the TV or ferried to your bed in the relaxation room. Treatments, which must be booked in advance, include Turkish body scrubs (from £5), massages and reflexology (both from £18/30mins).

Jurlique Day Spa & Sanctuary

300-302 Chiswick High Road, W4 1NP (8995 2293/www.apotheke20-20.co.uk). Chiswick Park or Turnham Green tube. **Open** 10am-8pm Mon-Fri; 9.30am-6pm Sat; 10am-6pm Sun. **Credit** AmEx, MC, V.
Treatments: aromatherapy, body treatments, detox treatments, facials, hydrotherapy, manicures, massages, naturopathy, pedicures, reflexology, waxing.

Discreetly situated above a posh chemist in leafy Chiswick, the Jurlique spa announces itself with the heady scent of aromatherapy oils. This is a laid-back place for people who want the treatments but without all the fuss. There's no fancy chill-out room here – you do your chilling on the massage table – which probably helps keep the prices down (the Anti-Stress Facial is only £35), and staff are friendly and efficient. We tried a new treatment that seemed to promise the impossible: the Deluxe Rejuvanessence Facial (£99.50), billed as a 'natural facelift'. The two-hour relaxation bonanza started with cleansing, exfoliation and steam combined with a shoulder, neck and scalp massage. Then lightly scented oils were applied to our face, and a gentle treatment ensued for nearly an hour. It involved little more than fingertips pressed at key points on the face and neck, but the therapists encourage you to look in a mirror at the beginning, middle and end of the process, and there was a visible difference. We're believers now.

May Fair Spa

Radisson Edwardian May Fair Hotel, Stratton Street, W1A 2AN (7915 2826/ www.mayfairspa.com). Green Park tube. **Open** 9am-9pm Mon-Thur; 9am-8pm Fri-Sun. Times may vary, call ahead to check. **Credit** AmEx, MC, V.
Treatments: body treatments, body wraps, facials, manicures, massage, pedicures, sauna, steam room, tanning studio.

This striking new spa in the basement of the Radisson Edwardian May Fair Hotel has been designed to appeal to both sexes, being luxurious but unfussy, with state-of-the-art equipment and a small gym. The pampering options include the Cleopatra Bathing Experience – a mud bath and steam room combo that you can experience alone (£50/45mins) or with a friend (£80/45mins). There are body treatments, such as the Detox Aromatic Seaweed Wrap Therapy (£90, or £15 more if you opt to have this on the hammam table), and massages and other beauty treatments, plus day packages and 'executive hour' deals (in which you're worked on by more than one therapist so that several treatments can be packed in). Arrive at least an hour before your treatment (as they advise), in order to enjoy the herbal sauna, aromatic steam room and relaxation room. Staff are personable and the place is spotless; we were impressed.

Molton Brown Day Spa

Upper Floor, Bluewater, Kent DA9 9SE (01322 383 382/www.moltonbrown.co.uk). Greenhithe rail. **Open** 10am-8pm Mon-Fri; 9am-5pm Sat, Sun. **Credit** AmEx, MC, V.
Treatments: aromatherapy, body treatments, body wraps, crystal stone therapy, eyebrow shaping & tinting, eyelash tinting, facials, manicures, massages, pedicures, waxing.

In a corner of Bluewater shopping centre, the Molton Brown Day Spa is a fine retreat from the retail bustle. The surroundings have a distinctly modern Japanese feel – all dark wood, dim lighting, exotic plants and mood music, and staff and therapists are clad in chic black. We opted for a Mirror of Life facial (from £65/60mins); our therapist was a master of his craft, asking questions about our lifestyle to tailor the treatment to our needs. Before long, our face was cleansed, hydrated, nourished, oxygenated and massaged. But there was more to come – a head, foot and hand massage, which sent us to sleep. At the end of the treatment, just when we thought it couldn't get any better, we were given a delicious raspberry sorbet.

The Porchester Spa

The Porchester Centre, Queensway, W2 5HS (7792 3980). Bayswater tube. **Open** *Women only* 10am-10pm Tue, Thur, Fri; 10am-4pm Sun. *Men only* 10am-10pm Mon, Wed, Sat. *Mixed couples* 4-10pm Sun. Last admissions 2hrs before closing. **Credit** MC, V.
Treatments: body scrubs, body wraps, eyebrow shaping & tinting, eyelash tinting, facials, manicures, massages, pedicures, waxing.

The Porchester is quite unlike any other spa you'll visit. Forget air-conditioning and tinkly music. In here, the climate is that of a municipal swimming pool: hot, balmy and smelling of chlorine, but with some original art deco architectural touches. At first glance, the clientele seems to be made up chiefly of large, topless middle-aged ladies having a relaxing cigarette in the smoking area of the spa (there are women's, men's and mixed days). But if all this is beginning to sound rather off-putting, it shouldn't. It's a friendly sort of place, and the therapies are as good as many of those costing three times as much in more luxurious surroundings. At £32 for a basic full-body massage (£36/60mins aromatherapy massage), mere mortals on average salaries can afford it. Our massage took place in a warm, dimly lit, subterranean room, a world away from some of the sumptuous therapy rooms in the capital. But, once your eyes are closed, it doesn't make any difference.

The Sanctuary

12 Floral Street, WC2E 9DH (0870 063 0300/ www.thesanctuary.co.uk). Covent Garden tube. **Open** 9.30am-6pm Mon, Tue; 9.30am-10pm Wed-Fri; 10am-8pm Sat, Sun. **Credit** AmEx, DC, MC, V.
Treatments: aromatherapy, body treatments, body wraps, dry flotation, facials, heat treatments, hot stone therapy, manicures, massages, pedicures, reflexology.

The only London spa with bona fide chill-out areas, the Sanctuary is still going strong after nearly three decades. The koi carp lounge is our favourite zone – we could spend all day here, were there not so many other attractions (two pools at different temperatures, a sauna, a hammam, two whirlpools, to name but a few). And that's before you've had any treatments, of which there's a good, accessibly priced selection. We opted for the Mande Lular treatment (£59/55mins), which involves exfoliation, Balinese massage and rich moisturising; it was thoroughly relaxing (if not exactly transformational) and left our skin super-soft. There's still some room for improvement with the food, especially given that the prices aren't exactly low (over £10 for a plate of pan-oriental nibbles, £3.50 for the cheapest glass of wine). We love the beauty products testing bar, where you get to try the entire range of Sanctuary lotions and potions. The decor looks a little dated in parts, and the changing rooms can get very crowded, but judging by the champagne corks popping when we were last here, this place is as popular as ever (with gals, that is: it's women only). And we're still hoping someone will buy us an annual membership.

Spa Illuminata

63 South Audley Street, W1K 2QS (7499 7777/www.spailluminata.com). Bond Street or Green Park tube. **Open** 10am-9pm Mon-Fri; 10am-6.30pm Sat. **Credit** AmEx, DC, MC, V.
Treatments: body treatments, body wraps, facials, hot stone therapy, makeovers, massages, self-tanning treatments, steam treatments, waxing.

This sophisticated, marble-clad Mayfair haven offers a range of treatments using French brands Decléor and Carita. We sampled a Decléor Aromatic facial (£75/60mins) and reckon it's one of the most pleasant treatments we've had. Therapists start off by giving you a diagnostic back massage, which allows them to get a full picture of your skin and overall health. With Decléor's high quotient of essential oils, it's no surprise that our skin felt plumper, cleaner and more radiant after the treatment. But it was the level of relaxation that made the biggest impression: the beds are motorised, so you are lulled back to earth gently (although we were in such a deep state of bliss we still had to be helped to our feet). Other indulgences at Spa Illuminata include purifying clay and salt treatments in an aromatic steam room and four-hand massages. Well worth a splurge.

The Spa at Mandarin Oriental

The Mandarin Oriental Hyde Park, 66 Knightsbridge, SW1X 7LA (7838 9888/ www.mandarinoriental.com). Knightsbridge tube. **Open** 7am-10pm daily. **Credit** AmEx, DC, MC, V.
Treatments: aromatherapy, Ayurveda treatments, body treatments, body wraps, facials, hot stone therapy, jet lag revival treatments, manicures, massages, pedicures, prenatal treatments, reflexology.

From the uniformed doorman that ushers you into the opulent hotel to the oriental-style minimalism of the spa area, the multi-award-winning Spa at the Mandarin Oriental is a luxury pampering experience that beats others hands down. One of the best features of the spa is the fact that you are booked 'time', rather than a pre-chosen treatment, which means you can tailor your session to your mood. We were impressed at how quickly the therapist adapted the treatment to our needs: a massage for the areas of the body that harbour stress (the back and shoulders), combined with a facial. We weren't asked how hard we wanted the massage, but all was forgiven when our therapist Matt delivered a phenomenal deep-tissue massage, kneading out knots of tension, followed by a exquisite facial and scalp massage. But most of all, we liked the way we left feeling invigorated rather than dozy. The attention to detail is impressive throughout the spa experience – from the fresh orchid on the tray with your slippers to the inhalation of eucalyptus during the treatment. The public areas are blissfully uncrowded (the prices see to that; £210/2hrs), and we advise arriving 40 minutes in advance to make the most of the body-pummeling jet pool, sauna and Amethyst (steam) Room and the beautiful relaxation area. Lemongrass-perfumed Espá products in the changing area are the icing on the cake. Highly recommended.

Temple Spa at FACE Smile & Skin Spa

38 Knightsbridge, SW1X 7JN (7245 6979 www.facebylundosler.com). Hyde Park or Knightbridge tube. **Open** 9am-6pm Mon-Fri. **Credit** AmEx, MC, V.
Upmarket Knightsbridge dentist's Lund Osler, co-owned by celebrity dentist and *Ten Years Younger* consultant Surinder Hundle, opened this salon a few doors up the road in summer 2005. It's billed as a 'one-stop spa that marries dermal and dental treatments for whole image beauty couture' – what that actually means is that, as well as getting your teeth sorted out, you can also get a massage or facial, using Temple Spa's lovely aromatherapy products. The massage tables have warmed water mattresses to get you in the mood, and we found the Prescriptive Facial (£73/75mins) excellent – the therapist seemed to pick up on what was going on with our whole body, not just our face. There's the odd faint rumble from passing tube trains, but you really hardly notice as you are cleansed, exfoliated and massaged. There are also shorter treatments, though you'd do well to spend a few minutes in the candlelit pre- and post-treatment chill-out area before heading back into the cold light of day.

Clinics

As most complementary therapy clinics offer a broad range of treatments – some medical, some for well-being and many requiring multiple visits – it's tricky to assess a clinic based on an isolated experience. In light of this, we have listed those that have been recommended to us, and the services they offer, below. For **Napiers** and **AcuMedic Centre**, *see chapter* **Health & Beauty Shops**. More clinics and therapies are covered in the new *Time Out Health & Fitness Guide*, published in January 2006.

Ashlins Natural Health

181 Hoe Street, E17 3AP (8520 5268/www. ashlins.co.uk). Walthamstow Central tube/rail. **Open** 9am-9pm Mon-Fri; 9am-7pm Sat. **No credit cards.**
Treatments: acupuncture, Alexander technique, aromatherapy, Bach flower remedies, chiropody, chiropractic treatments, counselling, homeopathy, Hopi ear candle treatments, hypnotherapy, kinesiology, massages, psychotherapy, reflexology, reiki, sports massages, Thai yoga, yoga.

Balance the Clinic

250 King's Road, SW3 5UE (7565 0333/ www.balancetheclinic.com). Sloane Square tube. **Open** 9am-7pm Mon, Tue, Fri; 9am-8pm Wed, Thur; 9am-6pm Sat; 10am-4pm Sun. **Credit** MC, V.
Treatments: acupuncture, anti-cellulite treatments, body treatments, chiropody, colonic

hydrotherapy, detox treatments, electrolysis, eyebrow tinting & shaping, eyelash tinting & perming, facials, homeopathy, lymphatic drainage, manicures, massages, nutritional advice, osteopathy, reflexology, semi-permanent make-up, tanning treatments, waxing.

Bliss Creative Health Centre

333 Portobello Road, W10 5SA (8969 3331/ www.bliss.me.uk). Ladbroke Grove or Notting Hill Gate tube. **Open** 9am-9pm Mon-Fri; 9am-6pm Sat; 11am-7pm Sun. **Credit** MC, V.
Treatments: acupressure, acupuncture, aromatherapy, counselling, cranio-sacral therapy, electro-diagnosis, homeopathy, hypnotherapy, iridology, lymphatic drainage, massages, naturopathy, osteopathy, oxidation therapy, physiotherapy, Pilates, reflexology, reiki, shiatsu, yoga.

Bodywise

119 Roman Road, E2 0QN (8981 6938/ www.bodywisehealth.org). Bethnal Green tube/rail. **Open** 9am-8pm Mon-Fri; 9am-1pm Sat. **Credit** AmEx, DC, MC, V.
Treatments: acupuncture, Alexander technique, counselling, cranial osteopathy, herbal medicine, homeopathy, hypnotherapy, kinesiology, massages, naturopathy, nutritional advice, osteopathy, Pilates, psychotherapy, reflexology, reiki, shiatsu, t'ai chi, yoga.

Brackenbury Natural Health Clinic

30 Brackenbury Road, W6 0BA (8741 9264/ www.brackenburyclinic.com). Goldhawk Road tube. **Open** 9am-6pm Mon-Sat; 10am-4pm Sun. **No credit cards.**

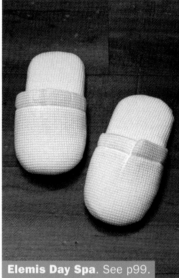

Elemis Day Spa. See p99.

Treatments: acupuncture, Alexander technique, allergy testing, aromatherapy, Chinese medicine, chiropody and podiatry, colonic hydrotherapy, counselling, homeopathy, hypnotherapy, life coaching, massages, nutritional advice, osteopathy, psychotherapy, reflexology, shiatsu.

Common Sense

7A Clapham Common Southside, SW4 7AA (7720 8817/www.southlondonnaturalhealth centre.com). Clapham Common tube. **Open** 9.30am-9.45pm Mon-Fri; 9.30am-6.30pm Sat; 10am-4pm Sun. **Credit** (not health centre) MC, V.
Treatments: acupuncture, aromatherapy, chiropractic treatments, colonic hydrotherapy, counselling, cranial osteopathy, cranio-sacral therapy, flotation, herbal medicine, homeopathy, hypnotherapy, life coaching, lymphatic drainage, massages, metamorphic technique, nutritional therapy, osteopathy, reflexology, reiki, rolfing, shiatsu, Thai yoga.

Complete Health Care Centre

160 City Road, EC1V 2NP (7336 0466/ www.completehealthcare.co.uk). Old Street tube/rail. **Open** 8am-8pm Mon-Fri; by appointment Sat. **No credit cards.**
Treatments: acupuncture, allergy testing, aromatherapy, hypnotherapy, life coaching, lymphatic drainage, massages, nutrition, osteopathy, personal training, reflexology, reiki, shiatsu, well-woman clinic.

Farmacia

4th Floor, Selfridges, 400 Oxford Street, W1A 1AA (7318 2365/www.farmacia123.com). Bond Street tube. **Open** 10am-8pm Mon-Sat; noon-6pm Sun. **Credit** AmEx, DC, MC, V.
Treatments: allergy testing, aromatherapy, body treatments, diagnostic testing, facials, health screening, herbal medicine, homeopathy, manicures, massages, nutritional advice and screening, pedicures, reflexology.

Hale Clinic

7 Park Crescent, W1B 1PF (7631 0156/ www.haleclinic.com). Great Portland Street or Regent's Park tube. **Open** 8.30am-8.30pm Mon-Fri; 9am-5pm Sat. **No credit cards.**
Treatments: acupressure, acupuncture, Alexander technique, alternative therapies, aromatherapy, chiropody, chiropractic treatments, colonic hydrotherapy, counselling, hypnotherapy, kinesiology, lymphatic drainage, massages, non-surgical facelifts, osteopathy, physiotherapy, psychotherapy, reflexology, reiki, shiatsu, spiritual healing, trichology.

The Happiness Centre

204 Uxbridge Road, W12 7JD (8749 3792/ www.thehappinesscentre.com). Goldhawk Road or Shepherd's Bush tube. **Open** 8am-8pm Mon-Fri; by appointment only Sat, Sun. **No credit cards.**
Treatments: acupuncture, aromatherapy, Buteyko method, counselling, couples coaching, cranio-sacral therapy, homeopathy, hypnotherapy, massages, osteopathy, Pilates, psychotherapy, reflexology, reiki, yoga.

The Life Centre

15 Edge Street, W8 7PN (7221 4602/www. thelifecentre.com). Notting Hill Gate tube. **Open** 6.30am-10pm Mon-Fri; 8.45am-7.30pm Sat; 9am-7.30pm Sun. **Credit** (classes only) MC, V.
Treatments: acupressure, acupuncture, Alexander technique, alternative therapies, aromatherapy, chiropractic treatments, cranio-sacral therapy, healing, homeopathy, hypnotherapy, kinesiology, life coaching, lymphatic drainage, massages, nutritional advice, osteopathy, Pilates, psychotherapy, reflexology, reiki, shiatsu, yoga.

Panakeia

44 Pimlico Road, SW1W 8LP (7730 9977/ www.panakeia.co.uk). Sloane Square tube/ Victoria tube/rail. **Open** 10am-8pm Mon-Fri; 10am-6pm Sat. **Credit** MC, V.
Treatments: acupuncture, aromatherapy, cranio-sacral therapy, facials, gel nails, hot stone therapy, lymphatic drainage, manicures, massages, osteopathy, pedicures, reflexology, reiki, self-tanning treatments, waxing.

Specialists

Body art

Into You

144 St John Street, EC1V 4UA (7253 5085/ www.into-you.co.uk). Farringdon tube/rail. **Open** noon-7pm Mon-Sat. **Credit** (jewellery & piercings only) MC, V.

Now in its 11th year, Into You has produced some of the most beautiful, intricate tattoos we've ever seen. You'd be unlucky to find a design that one of the eight highly trained artists can't manage, which is probably why Britney Spears, Will Smith and members of the Red Hot Chili Peppers have all gone under the needle here. Piercing is also available (£30 for navel, ear or nose, including basic titanium jewellery), along with custom-made gold body jewellery, clothing and books. Tattoos (from £60) are by appointment only, although a limited walk-in service is available on Saturday.

Lasercare Clinic

c/o The London Medical Centre, 144 Harley Street, W1G 7LD (7224 0988/www.lasercare-clinics.co.uk). Regent's Park tube. **Open** 9am-8pm Mon, Wed; 9am-7pm Tue-Fri; 9am-4pm Sat. **Credit** AmEx, DC, MC, V.

Whether you want to expunge an old lover's name or simply want ink-free skin again, Lasercare offers the latest tattoo removal technology. The consultation is free, but a test patch costs £35. The cost of the procedure depends on the size and colour of the tattoo; each session is from £60, and it can take from five to 12 treatments, with a break of three months between each, to remove the tattoo fully. Lasercare also offers hair removal, skin resurfacing for acne scars and wrinkles, and thread vein removal. Skin peels, microdermabrasion and Botox are also offered at this clinic. Note that only this branch of the chain carries out tattoo removal. **For branches see index.**

New Wave Tattoo

157 Sydney Road, N10 2NL (8444 8779/ www.newwavetattoo.co.uk). Bounds Green or Highgate tube/33, 134 bus. **Open** by appointment only 10.30am-5.30pm Mon-Fri; 10am-5pm Sat. **No credit cards.**

This friendly, long-established parlour is a popular haunt for tattoo aficionados, not to mention Marc Almond, Patsy Kensit and Sean Pertwee – just some of the celebs who have had work done here. Prices start at £45; you can choose from the many displayed samples or opt for customised artwork from your own design. In addition to its four permanent tattooists, New Wave hosts occasional international guest artists. A Saturday drop-in service is available (arrive early or you could face a long wait), but advance booking is preferred.

Diet

Many general clinics also offer nutritional advice (*see p102*).

The Food Doctor

76-78 Holland Park Avenue, W11 3RB (7792 6700/www.thefooddoctor.com). Holland Park tube. **Open** 9am-6pm Mon-Fri; also by appointment. **Credit** MC, V.

Ian Marber first got interested in nutrition when he started to suffer from coeliac disease (gluten intolerance). Since then, he has dedicated his life to learning about food – what to eat, what to avoid and how to fit his nutritional advice into a busy life. Clients may have intolerances or simply want to shed pounds. His Personal Weight Loss Plan costs £99 and includes 100 days of food advice, as well as a copy of his *Food Doctor Everyday Diet* book (usually £12.99). New clients provide a three-day food diary and some hair (taken from the nape of the neck). The clinic looks for eating patterns (when tired, stressed, hungover) and performs a hair mineral analysis test to check for deficiencies. A personal diet is then created and,

for those who need a little more motivation, personal coaching is also available (£60/four 15min sessions).

Feet

The Foot Pad

30 Lamb's Conduit Street, WC1N 3LE (7404 6942/www.footpad.co.uk). Holborn or Russell Square tube. **Open** 10.30am-7pm Mon-Thur; 10.30am-6pm Fri. **Credit** MC, V.

A member of the Institute of Chiropodists and Podiatrists since 1994, Charles Goldman takes a holistic approach to foot problems; he looks at possible causes rather than just prescribing a quick fix, and offers no-nonsense advice. His high-tech Biogun (which, mercifully, only produces a slight tingling sensation) zaps nasty nail fungi with ions and promises a 60%-65% success rate (the same, Goldman stresses, as drug treatments, which can have serious side effects). A basic chiropody session tends to nails, corns and calluses and culminates in a foot-cream massage (£35/30mins).

Scholl Footcare Centre

40 Upper Street, N1 0PN (7226 3781/www. scholl.co.uk). Angel tube/Highbury & Islington tube/rail. **Open** 9am-7pm Mon-Fri; 9am-6pm Sat; 11am-5pm Sun. **Credit** MC, V.

This high-street shop combines a shoe shop with a chiropodist's. Every footcare product you can think of is stocked, from custom-made insoles (£19-£65) to foot sprays, and you can have a free foot assessment from a shop attendant. Treatments are conducted by qualified chiropodists on the first floor. A basic session, including a foot bath, hard-skin and corn removal, ingrowing toenail treatment and half-leg massage, costs £35. A bio-mechanical assessment (£65) examines not just your feet but your knees and the way you walk.
For branch see index.

Make-up lessons & makeovers

Many cosmetics shops, including **Becca, Cosmetics à la Carte, MAC Cosmetics** and **Molton Brown** (for all, *see chapter* **Health & Beauty Shops**), have make-up artists on hand to dispense advice, and offer makeovers for an extra charge. Beauty guru **John Gustafson** does consultations three days a week on the third floor of Fenwick (*see p12*). The fee is reasonable (£100, of which £50 can be redeemed against products), which partly explains the waiting list of up to four years. If you want to join the queue, call 7409 9823.

James Miller

8455 0696. **Phone enquiries** 10am-8pm daily. **No credit cards.**

Personable yet professional, James Miller has 15 years' experience, and has turned his hand to fashion and TV. As well as a celebrity portfolio, he caters to private clients who want to look gorgeous for a special occasion – especially brides – or just update their image. Miller excels at transforming you into an enhanced yet natural-looking version of yourself. He airbrushes away your flaws with the latest foundation technology from the US, custom-blended for a perfect match. Glamourpusses can be assured he is equally expert at dramatic evening looks. Miller arrives with his kit and charges £120. If your look is stuck in the last decade, book a make-up lesson (£150/90mins-2hrs).

Mathew Alexander

Nyumba, 6-7 Mount Street, W1K 3EH (7408 1489/www.nyumbasalon.com). Green Park tube. **Open** 9am-6pm Tue, Wed, Fri, Sat; 9am-8pm Thur. **Credit** AmEx, MC, V.

Though he works on shoots with many a famous face, Mathew Alexander lives in the real world. We had scary visions of him telling us to throw our

entire make-up collection in the bin, but it soon became apparent that his aim is to make the most of your features, without having to resort to buying hundreds of pounds' worth of new products. Sure, his bag of tricks includes all the latest shades from all the luxury brands (Givenchy currently has some particularly hot new shades), but he's equally keen for you to carry on using items you already own, if they work for you. By the end of our consultation (£80/30-40mins), he had enhanced our looks using things we never would have considered (deep purple mascara, for one), but that worked amazingly well (he even found our cheekbones!). The results were subtle yet noticeable. Mathew also does longer sessions for £150, and make-up lessons (£250/120mins).

Nails

Although a mini boom of nail-bar chains a few years back brought manicures into the mainstream, they're still pricey in London – most places charge at least £20 for a full manicure (considerably more than you would pay in New York). At first glance, **Nails Inc** (now 'the largest nail bar chain in the world') seems to be the cheapest option (a shape and paint starts at a tenner), but this shoots up to £25 for a very basic 15-minute manicure. Its main selling point is convenience, with outposts in department stores, as well as stand-alone branches like the one at 41 South Molton Street, W1Y 1HB (7499 8333, www.nailsinc.com). Main competitor **NYNC** (17 South Molton Street, W1K 5QT, 7409 3332, www.newyorknail company.com) has far fewer outposts but is a better bet; you'll pay more for shape and paint (£14 hands), but staff spend an extra ten minutes on the job.

Chic newcomer the **Nail Lounge** (1 Kingly Court, Kingly Street, W1B 5PW, 7287 1847, www.thenaillounge.com) brings new meaning to the term 'nail bar' – clients are served complimentary wine (or non-alcoholic options) while their talons are tended. Prices compare well to the chains (£23/30min manicure; £29/45mins). Going more upmarket, well-groomed socialites have long relied on the talents of Electra Sawbridge and her team at one-stop shop the **Country Club** (101 Moore Park Road, SW6 2DA, 7731 4346), which also offers beauty treatments and hair styling; manicures start at £30. **The Chelsea Nail Studio** (5 Pond Place, SW3 6QR, 7225 3889), with its kitsch basement pedicure room, is another long-standing favourite (£25 manicure).

For the full luxury experience, award-winning nail guru **Leighton Denny** – who counts Jade Jagger and Rachel Stevens among his clients – heads the nail bar at Harrods' **Urban Retreat** (*see p98*). Famous for his ultra-natural-looking acrylic nails, Leighton also creates fabulous jewel-encrusted fingertip accessories, and now has his own range of nail products. Manicures with the man himself start at £80, or £30 with a member of his team.

Problem skin

Helen Sher Water Therapy

30 New Bond Street, W1S 2RN (7499 4022/ www.sher.co.uk). Bond Street tube. **Open** 9am-5.30pm Mon-Fri. **Credit** AmEx, MC, V.

If you've got problem skin, look no further. Helen Sher has run this office-cum-studio on Bond Street for nearly 15 years, sorting out all manner of skin conditions, from acne (both teenage and adult) to rosacea, by using the Sher System. As part of her 'working from the inside out' philosophy, Helen (who looks a good deal younger than her 70 years) believes that water is the key – both drinking lots of it and using loads to splash off your cleanser.

During a consultation (£75 for Helen; £50 for teenage acne specialist Anita), you're talked through the products and encouraged to try them out; our hormone-addled skin was – no lie – already looking less ravaged by the time we left, and continued to improve with the use of the cleansing gel, liquid colloidal silver (a natural antibiotic), rinse-off cleanser and skin serum. The products aren't cheap, but they last for ages. A month later, our skin was looking better than it had in years. You can also order products via the website. We can't recommend this place highly enough.

Waxing

Otylia Roberts at Greenhouse
142 Wigmore Street, W1U 3SH (7486 5537/ www.otyliaroberts.co.uk). Bond Street tube. **Open** 10am-6pm Mon; 10am-7pm Tue-Thur; 10am-5.30pm Fri; 9.30am-4.30pm Sat. **Credit** MC, V.
Recent beauty features have proclaimed that 'the bush is back', but you wouldn't know it at this ever-popular salon. Brazilians are the speciality here, and Otylia Roberts has deforested some of the most famous nether regions in Britain, and stars flock to her as she's one of the fastest waxers in the West. But don't fret if you can't get an appointment with Otylia herself – the rest of the staff here are excellent. Cassie, Caroline and Nicola are fastidious – not a single hair escapes them. They matter-of-factly guide you into the positions needed for such an intimate procedure and, like good doctors, they up the conversation just before an 'ouch' moment. The hot wax method – the salon melts kilos of the stuff every day – is used here: the wax is smeared on, left to set, then whipped off. It's less painful on sensitive areas than strip wax. Brazilians start at £45 and a half-leg wax is £34.

Strip
112 Talbot Road, W11 1JR (7727 2754/ www.2strip.com). Notting Hill Gate tube. **Open** 10am-8pm Mon-Thur; 10am-6pm Fri, Sat; noon-5pm Sun. **Credit** MC, V
Who says you have to suffer for beauty? Strip aims to make waxing as painless as possible. The ground-floor lingerie shop stocks a selection of wispy nothings by the likes of Damaris and S.P.A.N.K. to get you in the mood. Downstairs, behind the pink padded doors of the four treatment rooms, there are flat-screen TVs to distract you, and the popular Chocolate-Hazelnut wax (in either strip or hot form) smells good enough to eat. The quality Lycon waxes come from Australia – beach-babe country – and there is one for every need. The pale pink Rosette hot wax, containing soothing rose and chamomile, is gentle on sensitive areas such as the face and underarms, while Lycojet Lavender hot wax grips shorter hairs. Unusually, a pre-wax oil is applied to protect the skin. And because waxing is all they do here, the staff are experts. Depending on which wax you choose, it doesn't necessarily work out more expensive than other London salons (upper lip from £8; half-leg from £20; £40-£45 for a Brazilian), and it's about as near to a treat as waxing can get.

Unlisted London
59 Egerton Gardens, SW3 2DA (0870 225 5007/ www.unlistedlondon.com). **Phone enquiries** 9am-9pm daily. **Credit** AmEx, MC, V.
If you can't be bothered to leave the house, Unlisted will bring the total spa experience to your home. Staff arrive with all the equipment they need, including massage table and scented candles if you book a rubdown. Treatments run the gamut: Brazilian wax, St Tropez self-tan, hair (cut, colour, extensions), facials using Dermalogica and Dr Hauschka products, makeovers – even 'cosmetic clean-out and personal shopping' (£650). There are deals for multiple bookings and, if you prefer, you can visit the spa studio in Knightsbridge.

Hairdressers

In a highly competitive market, many salons have bumped up their beauty menus. **Richard Ward** (*see p105*) has an in-salon spa, as does **Daniel Hersheson** (*see below*) in his Harvey Nichols outpost, to name but a few. For the **Urban Retreat** at Harrods, *see chapter* Health & Beauty Services.

Andrew Jose
1 Charlotte Street, W1T 1RB (7323 4679/ www.andrewjose.com). Tottenham Court Road tube. **Open** 9am-6pm Mon; 9am-7pm Tue, Wed; 9am-9pm Thur, Fri; 9am-5pm Sat. **Credit** AmEx, MC, V.
One of three Andrew Jose salons (the other two are in Leicester and Prague), this attractive split-level salon occupies a prime corner spot on restaurant hot spot Charlotte Street. Being coiffed by the much-lauded Andrew may force you to dip into the rent money (£150) but fortunately for most of us the other stylists are wonderfully able and much cheaper (prices start at £37); on our latest visit we were pleased with a warmer colour broken up by ultra-subtle highlights (£50-£65 for a full head tint; highlights £75-£89) and a new yet unintimidating twist to our usual hairstyle. We also liked the efficient speed of the experience – which isn't to say that it felt rushed, just that the staff got straight down to business. Jose runs a training school in Prague, where most of the staff are trained. Students and under-12s get 20% off all hairdressing services.

Cobella AC
3rd Floor, Selfridges, 400 Oxford Street, W1A 1AB (0870 900 0440/www.cobella.co.uk). Bond Street or Marble Arch tube. **Open** 10am-8pm Mon-Fri; 10am-9pm Thur; 9.30am-8pm Sat; 11.30am-6pm Sun. **Credit** AmEx, DC, MC, V.
Selfridges is arguably London's top department store, so you'd expect it to have a top hairdressing salon – and it has. On the third floor, the funky, contemporary interior is divided into specialist 'zones', including the Colour Zone, VIP Express Zone and Shiatsu Zone, which gives you some idea of the services on offer. The high-tech environment doesn't make the experience any less relaxing – time and care was taken. Having discussed the length and condition of this indecisive client's hair, senior stylist Richard was reassuringly friendly yet professional, and proceeded to transform us with a sharp yet wearable cut. Cuts start at £45 (£85 for the art director), plus £10 for a restyle. Colour starts at £45 for semi-permanent on short hair, while foil colour starts at £58 (hairline and parting), rising to £115 for a full head. The Beauty Zone offers treatments for every need, from ageing hands (£40) to cellulite (£65).
For branch see index.

Daniel Hersheson
Harvey Nichols, 109-125 Knightsbridge, SW1X 7RJ (7235 5000/www.danielhersheson.com). Knightsbridge tube. **Open** 10am-8pm Mon-Fri; 10am-7pm Sat; noon-5pm Sun. **Credit** AmEx, MC, V.
Up on Harvey Nichols's fourth floor is a new pampering experience. As sleekly decked out as a spaceship, this desirable salon is matt grey, with recessed lights, rounded edges and mirrors stretching along its entire length. In keeping with the salon's ultra-trendy appearance, Daniel Hersheson specialises in bang up-to-date, fashion-led hair styling. Daniel and his son Luke (co-owners of the salons) are hot talents on the hairdressing scene, and both give inspiring cuts

– the transformation will cost you a daunting £250 (though fortunately you can get a cut with another capable stylist from a more digestable £65). Another key draw here is the revered colourist Gary Richardson, who decided to swap the heady world of session styling for ad campaigns, editorial shoots and catwalk shows to provide highlights to lowly beings like us. You wouldn't know he's used to tending the locks of Kate Moss for Missoni and J-Lo for Louis Vuitton, mind – like the rest of the staff, he's down-to-earth and as keen to please you as he would be an A-list diva. Colour is a strong point at Daniel Hersheson – on our latest visit, we were thrilled with a colour from Senior Colour Technician James Foward (£110). There's also a chance to indulge in a Kerastase ritual (conditioning treatment; from £15) and, hair aside, there are classy beauty treatment rooms, a nail bar and even a food menu. The original salon on Conduit Street, founded in 1994, is still going strong, and the salons sell their own range of hair tools called Smooth Groove.
For branch see index.

Errol Douglas
18 Motcomb Street, SW1X 8LB (7235 0110/ www.erroldouglas.com). Knightsbridge tube/ Victoria tube/rail. **Open** 9am-6pm Mon; 9am-7pm Tue-Sat. **Credit** AmEx, MC, V.
Despite a shelf-full of awards and a swanky Knightsbridge address, the atmosphere here is welcoming, bustling and pretension-free. Granted, the clientele is dominated by moneyed locals (prices for a cut and blow-dry with Errol himself start at £127), but the staff are bright young things, some sporting tattoos and blue fringes. Errol clearly enjoys huge popularity, chatting familiarly with clients and even posing for photos, and naturally his coterie of stylists and colourists consists of talented individuals. We went for highlights and we weren't disappointed – they were of the subtle sort you can only get at a high-calibre salon like this. Service was attentive, and if you're having a lengthy restyle, such as extensions (they looked amazingly natural on another customer), you can have lunch brought to you or watch TV on one of the mini monitors by the styling stations. A range of ED-branded electrical styling tools, including straightening irons, has recently been launched, and products by KMS, Phytologie and Dermalogica are sold.
Mail order.

John Frieda
75 New Cavendish Street, W1W 6XA (7636 1401/www.johnfrieda.com). Oxford Circus tube. **Open** 9am-5pm Mon-Sat. **Credit** MC, V.
This energetic little salon is all business. From the moment you walk in, staff swoop down to take your particulars, find you a robe, get you a drink, show you around... It's high energy and high quality. Our fading highlights were a disaster when we walked in, but Gary figured out how to fix them and, using a mixture of blonde and brown tints (and no foils), he redesigned our hair strand by strand, separating the layers of colour with cotton wool and creating a soft, polished look. When he washed it all out, we felt reborn. Then Joel did a magnificent dry cut – blow-drying our thick, unruly mane before reinventing it as a classy, tousled 'do. You could easily spend an afternoon here – there's an in-house chef making sandwiches and salads, and Evian is served in frosted glasses by runners. You'll pay for all this professionalism – tints start at £55, rising to £200 and beyond for a full head of highlights – but if you can swing the fees, you'll look gorgeous.
For branch see index.

HEALTH & BEAUTY

Lee Stafford

*155A Wardour Street, W1F 8WG (7494 1777/
www.leestafford.com). Oxford Circus or Tottenham
Court Road tube.* **Open** 10am-8pm Mon, Wed-Fri;
10am-6pm Tue, Sat. **Credit** AmEx, MC, V.
A session at Lee Stafford is not just about getting
your hair done – it's a total experience. The salon
shouts 'attitude' from the moment you walk in to
be greeted by staff in bubblegum-pink
cheongsam. The upper level is pure *Barbarella*:
space-shuttle white with neon-pink fittings;
downstairs it's more Peter Greenaway, with candy-
coloured 18th-century French dressers and
clusters of antique chandeliers. Even the staff are
appropriately theatrical: at the initial consultation,
head stylist Janice tutted disapprovingly over our
less-than-groomed bedhead, before whisking the
offending bird's nest off to be 'properly washed'.
This is a salon for people who take hair very
seriously indeed, and it's no surprise to hear that,
apart from a slew of regular TV appearances (not
to mention his own fly-on-the-wall TV series, *The
Hairdresser*) and awards, Stafford is also
hairdresser *du jour* to numerous pop stars and
film types. If you want to experiment, this is
probably a good bet, but it's also excellent for the
basics. Cuts range from £45 with a stylist up to
£150 with the man himself; highlights begin at
£60 for a quarter of a head's worth. As for the
bedhead? We went in grunge and came out glam
– what more could a girl want?

Nicky Clarke

*130 Mount Street, W1K 3NY (7491 4700/
www.nickyclarke.co.uk). Bond Street tube.* **Open**
9am-5pm Tue-Sat. **Credit** AmEx, MC, V.
Movie stars, TV presenters and socialites rely on
him to make them look gorgeous but uncontrived.
Nicky Clarke is known for sexy, wearable styles –
and the walls of his light, airy salon are plastered
with *Elle* and *Vogue* covers to prove it. The
atmosphere is upbeat and unintimidating; even the
golden-maned one himself, who was cutting a
client's hair with great flourish on our last visit, is
remarkably attitude-free. But then, when you're
charging new clients £425 for a woman's cut and
blow-dry (£260 thereafter; £350/£250 for men), it
pays to be friendly. Those who don't want to be
preened centre stage can retreat to the mirrored VIP
room. Thankfully, prices dip dramatically for the
rest of the staff. We had the attentions of talented
managing director Ian Denson (£150 for a cut and
blow-dry), but a cut by one of the other highly
trained stylists starts at £50. The focus is very much
on the individual rather than the latest trends –
although, of course, staff are up to speed. Ian gently
guided us away from a style that required more
maintenance, and the resulting cut was flattering
and, as promised, easy to look after. Colour is
undertaken in the basement (a half head of
highlights starts at £132). Perricone facials and
high-tech treatments are available in the Beautiful
Body Company's in-salon studio.

Nyumba/Michael Charalambous

*6-7 Mount Street, W1K 3EH (7408 1489/
www.nyumbasalon.com). Bond Street or Green
Park tube.* **Open** 9am-6pm Wed, Fri, Sat;
9am-8pm Thur. **Credit** AmEx, MC, V.
Michael Charalambous is not backwards at
coming forwards. He'll tell you straight (but
politely) if your current haircut doesn't suit you
(mine made my face look too round, apparently),
and he'll name-drop anyone famous whose tresses
he has tended (from Charlize Theron to Queen
Rania of Jordan, since you ask). But it's a testament
to the success of his two-year-old salon (the name
of which means 'home' in Swahili; Michael was
raised in Africa) that he needs no PR. Word of
mouth keeps this place fully booked and buzzing.
And it's hard not to like or trust him – he knows
what he's talking about and will devote his full
attention to you. Colour is also a strong point: we
were talked into going darker by Julia, and didn't
regret it. In fact, anything you have here is
guaranteed to be highly professional, as Michael
has built up a real dream team. Additional services
include eyebrow threading, waxing and facials;
reiki, holistic treatments and Japanese facial
massages; reflexology; and manicures and
pedicures with long-lasting results. Mathew
Alexander, meanwhile, is make-up man (*see p103*).
Cuts start at £60, but you'll have to fork out £250
for Michael himself.

Richard Ward

*82 Duke of York Square, SW3 4LY (7730
1222/www.richardward.co.uk). Sloane Square
tube.* **Open** 9am-7pm Mon-Sat. **Credit** MC, V.
Trinny and Susannah's official hairdresser and the
preferred snipper of a slew of celebs, Richard
Ward has turned a humdrum trip to the salon into
a far more exciting experience. His new 5,000sq ft
flagship is a show-stopper, combining the services
of a luxury hotel (a doorman to feed your parking
meter and internet access, to name a couple) with
top-notch hairdressing and beauty treatments.
Everything in the light, loft-style space is slick,
stylish and geared towards relaxation, from the
ultra-comfortable, electronic shampoo chairs in the
Cleansing Zone to the chic licenced bar, where you
can sip champagne or have a bite from the on-site
kitchen (food and drink costs extra). At one of the
Philippe Starck-designed workstations in the
Colour Zone, you can zone out in front of your
personal mini TV. Prices for a cut and finish start
from £45 (£30 for men) up to £165 with Richard
himself; colour is from £30 up to £175 for the
technical director. The talented Huseyin (£80 for a
cut and blow-dry) temporarily transformed our
unruly curls into a sleek, straight curtain (which
fell nicely into shape when washed at home).
The Metrospa offers exclusive Jan Marini
Cosmeceuticals facials, waxing for both sexes,
massage and other holistic treatments, plus
numerous packages, from full-day pampering
sessions to fast-track multitasking.

Trevor Sorbie

*27 Floral Street, WC2E 9DP (7379 6901/www.
trevorsorbie.com). Covent Garden tube.* **Open**
9am-7pm Mon, Tue; 9am-8pm Wed; 9am-8.30pm
Thur, Fri; 9am-6pm Sat. **Credit** AmEx, MC, V.
Four-time winner of British Hairdresser of the Year,
Sorbie counts Helen Mirren and Julian Clary among
his celebrity clients, but more impressive is his
straightforward philosophy of 'real hair for real
people'. Colouring is a particular strength; book a
complimentary (and comprehensive) consultation
and skin test to discuss your ideas. We were
delighted with the results of our natural-looking tint
and highlights, and stylist Bree transformed our
tired look into something more edgy yet wearable.
The entire experience felt relaxed, indulgent and
unaffected. Given the level of expertise and the
Covent Garden location, prices are surprisingly
affordable – from £33.50 for semi-permanent colour,
rising to £210 for a full head of highlights, while
cuts range from £35 to £111. A cut and blow-dry
with Sorbie himself will set you back £200 – though
he has a one-year waiting list.

Daniel Hersheson

HEALTH & BEAUTY

Chains

Charles Worthington

7 Percy Street, W1T 7DQ (7631 1370/ www.cwlondon.com). Goodge Street tube. **Open** 8am-8pm Mon-Thur; 10.15am-7pm Fri; 9.15am-6pm Sat; 10am-5pm Sun. **Credit** AmEx, MC, V.
The cool, calm Percy Street flagship salon, housed within a listed Georgian terrace, is deceptively large inside. The lower ground level is given over entirely to colouring, with the well-respected Carolyn Newman at the helm (a half head of highlights starts at £87). Her new Colour Clinics let you play around with wigs and hairpieces before you commit to a colour; there is a charge of £20, which is redeemable if you book. On the two upper floors, black T-shirted stylists scurry around the white and glass space, providing head massages, free champagne if you fancy it, and – above all – some great cutting. Of all the 'big name' salons, this is one of the least complacent about client loyalty, cutting out snobbery without stinting on any of the luxury extras you'd expect at a high-end salon. A cut and blow-dry starts from a reasonable £49.
For branches see index.

Essensuals

10 Berkeley Street, W1J 8DP (7499 4222/ www.essensuals.co.uk). Green Park tube. **Open** 9.30am-6.30pm Mon, Tue; 9.30am-8pm Wed-Fri. **Credit** AmEx, DC, MC, V.
Essensuals offers Toni & Guy stylists a chance to run their own salon under the umbrella of the mother company. Top stylist Beverly Cobella has recently joined as creative director for the diffusion brand, so it will be interesting to see if it takes its own trajectory. This particular branch is small yet light with the feel of a young, friendly local salon – albeit in Covent Garden. A thorough consultation with charming, no-nonsense Kara resulted in a good cut, plus lots of advice on how to care for those misbehaving tresses. Prices are reasonable (a cut and blow-dry starts at £36 for women, £28 for men). Colour prices start from £35 for a tint, £55 for a half head of highlights and from £75 for a full head. While many Essensuals salons offer beauty services, this one is hair-only, probably due to space restrictions. A reliable choice.
Branches: throughout the city.

Headmasters

11-12 Hanover Street, W1S 1YQ (7408 1000/ www.hmhair.co.uk). Oxford Circus tube. **Open** 9am-9pm Mon-Fri; 9am-6pm Sat, Sun. **Credit** MC, V.
Headmasters used to be a bit of a south-west London secret, but with the opening of its flagship salon at Hanover Square, this looks set to change. Prices are mid-range, with women's cuts ranging from £33 to £74 (men's from £25). The emphasis here is on getting the right style for you, rather than a beautiful salon creation that disappears after one wash. Stylists are clued up about the new colour trends and techniques, but you won't automatically get the latest high-fashion cut (unless, of course, you ask for it). Clients are given practical tips on how to maintain a style (blow-drying lessons are occasionally offered for those wanting to recreate a polished look at home). The salons are stylish without being intimidatingly fancy, and a good balance of male and female stylists ensures that men feel welcome too.
Branches: throughout the city.

Mr Topper's

13A Great Russell Street, WC1B 3NH (7631 3233). Tottenham Court Road tube. **Open** 9am-6.30pm Mon-Sat; 11am-5.30pm Sun. **No credit cards**.
The large sign advertising cuts for £6 draws in a steady stream of traffic, but, as you'd expect, there are no luxury extras in this no-nonsense establishment. The majority of customers are men, but women are welcome too (though they have to pay an extra £4). The cutting is competent, the staff are friendly and for these prices, what more could you ask for?
For branches see index.

Best for...

Colour

London's undisputed queen of highlights, **Jo Hansford** (*see p109*) was entrusted with Camilla's crowning glory before her big day in spring 2005. Colour Clinics at **Charles Worthington** (*see left*) allow you to experiment with coloured wigs and hairpieces before you commit, while **Anita Cox** (*see below*) has won British Colour Technician of the Year, not once but twice.

Dramatic looks

Session work for the likes of *i-D* and *Dazed & Confused* keeps the creative juices flowing among the staff at **Tommy Guns** (*see p110*), and reality-TV hairdresser **Lee Stafford**'s funky salon (*see p105*) is a good place to cut loose. But if you really want to stand out from the crowd, seek out the (expensive) services of Angelo Seminara at **Trevor Sorbie** (*see p105*), who won Avant Garde Hairdresser of the Year in both the 2003 and 2004 British Hairdressing Awards.

A complete overhaul

Book in for a four-hour Total Transformation at **Richard Ward** (*see p105*): for £265, you get an in-depth consultation and cut from the official *What Not to Wear* hairdresser, plus a mini-facial and manicure, a touch of make-up, and light lunch and champagne in the bar; at **Nyumba** (*see p105*), there's a team of experts on hand to relax and reinvent you, including an in-house make-up artist.

Cheap 'n' chic chops

Railway station barber's **Cut** (*see p111*) will give you a super-quick style for a snip, while **Mr Topper's** (*see below*) offers cut-price cuts for men and women.

Attitude-free atmosphere

The mood is laid-back and family-friendly at **Guy Parsons Hairdressing** (*see p109*), which offers reduced rates for kids' cuts two days a week, while at **Cello** (*see p108*), in Marylebone, the emphasis is on building stylist-client relationships.

Taming or creating curls

Fed up with unruly waves? Turn to **James Lee Tsang** (*see p109*), London pioneer of the Japanese JL Ionic Hair Retexturising Treatment. Black and white customers alike rely on **Pacific Hair Artists'** (*see p110*) curl-handling skills, while **Windle** (*see p109*) offers a freestyle perm (£200), as well as being renowned for hair straightening.

Saks Hair & Beauty

4-10 Tower Street, WC2H 9NP (7379 1188/ www.sakshairandbeauty.com). Covent Garden tube. **Open** 9am-9pm Thur, Fri; 9am-6pm Sat. **Credit** MC, V.
With several branches in and around London – and indeed outposts all over the world – Saks is a convenient and reliable chain. As well as great cuts (from £35 for a junior stylist to £75 for the creative director; colour from £70), the Covent Garden salon has expanded its beauty offerings beyond the usual list of massages, facials (using Elemis products) and nail treatments. In the treatment rooms that surround the light and airy hairdressing area, you can have anything from an anti-ageing Oxygenator facial (£85) to something a little more permanent, such as Botox. There's even a clinical team to deal with problem feet, a teeth-whitening clinic, mist-on tanning booths and more holistic treatments such as reiki and Indian head massage.
Branches: throughout the city.

Toni & Guy

28 Kensington Church Street, W8 4EP (7937 0030/www.toniandguy.co.uk). High Street Kensington tube. **Open** 9am-8pm Mon-Fri; 9am-6.30pm Sat; 11am-6pm Sun. **Credit** AmEx, MC, V.
With a plethora of awards under their belt (including L'Oréal's Next Generation and London Regional Winners Awards in 2005), the young staff at this branch of the Toni & Guy hairdressing empire stand out for their personal approach and technical expertise. The colour team is especially strong here (as at all Toni & Guy salons, a compulsory skin test must be undertaken 48 hours before a colour appointment), but we were also impressed by the directional styling. High-tech back-massaging chairs make the shampooing even more relaxing than usual. A half head of highlights/lowlights starts at £85, while cuts start at £45, rising to £70 for a cut by multi-award winners Gary or Kirsten France (to whom the branch is franchised).
Branches: throughout the city.

Central London

Anita Cox Hair & Beauty

62 Britton Street, EC1M 5UY (7251 8220/ www.anitacox.co.uk). Farringdon tube/rail. **Open** 9am-8pm Mon-Fri; 10am-6pm Sat. **Credit** MC, V.
Anita Cox snapped up her Clerkenwell salon in the 1990s before you could say 'loft apartment'. Twice winner of the British Hairdressing Awards Colour Technician of the Year (and a finalist in 2005's awards), she counts brunette Anna Friel and Kerry Katona among her clients. Her own dark, glossy tresses and her easy manner inspire confidence. Our hair was both sun-damaged and badly highlighted; she pointed out what had gone wrong and talked through a solution. The result was classy – rather than brassy – blonde, finished off by a sassy cut. A half head of highlights costs from £87 to £127, depending on the technician. Colour with Anita is 'price on application', but she charges £76.50 for a cut and blow-dry. The salon also offers beauty treatments such as Hot Stone Therapy (from £40). A Chelsea branch opened in summer 2005.
For branch see index.

Brooks & Brooks

13-15 Sicilian Avenue, WC1A 2QH (7405 8111/ www.brooksandbrooks.co.uk). Holborn tube. **Open** 9am-7pm Mon, Tue; 9am-8pm Wed-Fri; 10am-5.30pm Sat. **Credit** MC, V.
This light and bright salon has an air of relaxed sophistication, with walls in mushroom tones and polished wood floors reflecting the light from the huge front window. Sally Brooks, former international artistic director for Trevor Sorbie, set up Brooks & Brooks with her husband Jamie four years ago; since then they've won a shelf-full of awards, including London Hairdresser of the Year (twice). Sally's expertise is paired with a friendly, relaxed manner that put us right at ease, and the cut was just what we needed. Our highlights were sorted by Marc, who used foils and a semi-permanent colour for a more natural look. Carefully chosen staff pays dividends in the form of an easy-going, pleasant atmosphere.

Cello

92 York Street, W1H 1QX (7723 7447/ www.cellohair.com). Baker Street tube. **Open** 9am-9pm Mon-Fri; 9am-6pm Sat. **Credit** DC, MC, V.
Sick of slick style salons? This place is all about mellow music, comfy leather sofas and, above all, friendly staff. Customers don't just come here for a great haircut – they also come to chat and chill out. A sense of community prevails: the walls are covered with the work of local artists, and the aim is to make customers feel special. One stylist is devoted to you from shampooing to colouring and cutting, which, according to owner Dino Houtas, produces better results. We were impressed with the attentiveness and the final look, and would definitely go back. In spite of the area, prices are reasonable: men's cuts start from £25, women's from £45, while colour starts from £40 for tints, £65 for a half head of highlights and £70 for a full head.

Fish

30 D'Arblay Street, W1F 8ER (7494 2398/ www.fishweb.co.uk). Leicester Square tube. **Open** 10am-7pm Mon-Wed, Fri; 10am-8pm Thur; 10am-5pm Sat. **Credit** MC, V.
Those who prefer a more informal atmosphere than the sleek sterility of many upmarket hair salons should come here. The feel is breezy and genial – though, make no mistake, the service is ultra-professional. The dexterous stylist took copious care over our simple cut, ensuring it would pretty much style itself when we were left to our own devices. A cut and blow-dry costs £38 (£32 for men), a permanent tint is £40 and a half head of highlights £75-£80. The myriad hip postcards (Brigitte Bardot, Patti Smith) lining the mirrors provide a focal point as you get snipped. Highly recommended.

Fordham White

47 Greek Street, W1D 4EE (7287 8484/ www.fordhamwhite.com). Tottenham Court Road tube. **Open** 10am-7pm Mon, Tue; 10am-8pm Wed-Fri; 10am-6pm Sat. **Credit** AmEx, MC, V.

This Soho salon is buzzing with a varied clientele – you are as likely to see a glamorous blonde topping up her highlights as a young office worker in for a quick lunchtime trim. The salon is refreshingly unpretentious and relaxed (if a little shambolic), which may surprise you after passing through the swanky entrance area. There's plenty of enthusiasm among the stylists for those wanting a change. Men will pay between £30 and £55 for a cut and finish, ladies from £40 to £75, while colour starts from £40 (semi-permanent) up to £110 for a full head of highlights by the colour director. Downstairs there's a beauty salon with treatments for both sexes, including facials, waxing, manicures, pedicures – even Botox. All services are accompanied by a glass of wine or beer and, on alternate Thursdays, a DJ.

4th Floor

3rd & 4th Floors, 4 Northington Street, WC1N 2JG (7405 6011). Chancery Lane tube. **Open** 9am-7pm Mon-Fri; 9am-6pm Sat. **Credit** AmEx, MC, V.
On two spacious and light-filled levels (nope, not just the fourth), just above design guru Tom Dixon's headquarters, is a hair-snipping emporium quite unlike any other. 4th Floor is hidden away down a backstreet off Gray's Inn Road, identified only by a small, unobtrusive buzzer. As you'd expect from its Clerkenwell location, its clients are a well-heeled, varied mix, from hip lawyers to style-savvy media types. But despite the trendy industrial feel, retro barber's chairs and a minimalist-looking own product line, the staff are distinctly frost-free. As the mood is unisex (leaning towards masculine) rather than girlie, it's the kind of place to go for a good-quality cut rather than a pre-Saturday-night blow-dry. Women's cuts start at £40; men's at £35.

Haringtons

14 Great Marlborough Street, W1F 7HP (7292 2890/www.haringtons.com). Oxford Circus tube. **Open** 10.30am-6.30pm Mon-Wed, Fri; 11.30am-7.30pm Thur; 9.30am-5.30pm Sat. **Credit** MC, V.

Haringtons stands out for its friendly, laid-back vibe, and it has a solid reputation behind it and several awards in the bag (including Artistic Team of the Year). On our last visit, we were pleasantly surprised by the soundtrack of smooth jazz instead of the intrusively loud music in many salons. This, combined with a cool, minimalist – but not blindingly bright – interior, made for a relaxing experience. Stylists are quick to understand what you're after, but perhaps on this occasion a bit too quick to finish, as the cut could have been better rounded off. A cut and finish starts at £40.50 for a stylist, going up to £79 for a salon director (£35-£59 for men). A whole head of highlights costs between £95 and £124.

HOB

60 Baker Street, W1U 7DE (7935 5883/6775). Baker Street tube. **Open** 9am-6pm Mon; 9am-8pm Tue-Fri; 8.30am-6pm Sat; 11am-5pm Sun. **Credit** AmEx, DC, MC, V.
This London- and Hertfordshire-based chain goes from strength to strength, and now has ten outlets in total. But the big news is the opening of this flagship hair and beauty salon in autumn 2005. The new premises boasts super-duper massaging shampoo chairs, plasma screens for when you're *Vogue*-d out, and a dedicated beauty area for St Tropez tans, waxing, massages, and hand, feet, face and body treatments, including Karin Herzog Oxygen Facials. But it's the staff who deserve the attention: they're a talented bunch, who have picked up a clutch of awards over the years. Artistic director Akin Konizi, in particular, is one to watch; renowned for his cutting techniques, he holds the Most Wanted Look of 2005 trophy as part of the Creative HEAD Awards and has been nominated for London Hairdresser of the Year (2005) for the third year running. Colour is also a strong point (ask for Linda). Prices in the central London salon start at £50 for a cut and £85 for a half head of highlights; the out-of-town branches are cheaper.

James Lee Tsang

49 Eastcastle Street, W1W 8DZ (7580 0071).
Oxford Circus tube. **Open** 9am-8pm Mon-Fri;
10am-7pm Sat. **Credit** MC, V.
Entering the recently opened JLT, you might feel as
if you've walked on to the set of *The Salon* – the
reality TV show that showed us some inspiring
places to trade the mullet – it has that shiny, futuristic
feel, and a batch of trendy staff (with compellingly
trendy haircuts) for added entertainment. But that's
not to say it's all hot air. Cutting-edge cuts are JLT's
forte, as well as extensions and permanent
straightening (JLT is the British pioneer of the JL
Ionic Hair Retexturising Treatment from Japan), but
this is also a good place for a plain old trim and half-
head of highlights. With about 50 years of expertise
between them, directors Pierre, Tom and Lisa make
an impressive team – add to this an airy and relaxed
space, Alterna products (from the US) and possibly
the most comfortable basins in London (complete
with head rest). Book yourself in with Tom (for a
reasonable £65 if you can and ask him to tell you
about 'texture'.

Jo Hansford

19 Mount Street, W1K 2RN (7495 7774/
www.johansford.com). Bond Street or Green
Park tube. **Open** 8.30am-6pm Tue-Sat. **Credit**
MC, V.
Given that Jo Hansford is one of the country's best
colourists, and her salon is in the heart of Mayfair,
the easy atmosphere here comes as a surprise. Staff
are friendly without being sychophantic.
Unusually – and this is probably part of its secret
– the salon stocks four different brands of colour,
which are mixed and matched, rather than being
bound to one manufacturer. Jo herself still works
three days a week and charges £225 for a half
head of highlights. Booking Taylor or Amy will
cost a more affordable £125. Tints are from £65
and all new customers must go along for a
consultation beforehand (£20 or £50 for Jo). This
is redeemed against the first appointment (unless
you're seeing Jo or one of her top four colourists).

Karine Jackson

24 Litchfield Street, WC2H 9NU (7836 0300/
www.karinejackson.co.uk). Leicester Square tube.
Open 10am-7pm Mon, Fri; 10am-8pm Tue; 11am-
8pm Wed; 11am-9pm Thur; 9am-6pm Sat. **Credit**
AmEx, MC, V.
A bubble of calm in the mayhem around Cambridge
Circus, this small but perfectly formed salon, a few
doors down from the Ivy, is a pleasure to visit. Staff
are super-attentive with the complimentary
refreshments – the bubbly was flowing freely on the
Saturday afternoon we visited – but also, and more
importantly, with the hair-cutting and beauty
treatments. Each customer is treated to an
unusually in-depth consultation (with questions like
'What do you like and dislike about your current
hairstyle?', 'Do you want a big change or an
update?') before the scissors come near your hair –
which makes a change from hairdressers who do
what *they* want, rather than what *you* want. Best of
all, the price/results ratio puts other central London
hairdressers to shame; no wonder the chatty
regulars seemed so pleased with their secret. A cut
and finish starts at a reasonable £32, rising to £60
for Karine herself, and a half head of highlights
starts at £50. There are also beauty treatments
along the lines of manicures (£18-£20), facials (£30-
£75) and massages (£30-£45).

Mahogany

17 St George Street, W1S 1FJ (7629 3121/
www.mahoganyhair.co.uk). Oxford Circus tube.
Open 9am-6.15pm Mon, Fri; 10am-7.45pm Tue-
Thur; 10am-4.45pm Sat. **Credit** AmEx, MC, V.
The emphasis at this relaxed and friendly Mayfair
salon, tucked behind Oxford Street, is on bringing
your locks back to their optimum condition. So, hair
is left natural and healthy rather than sleek and
coiffed. Ours was pinned and left to dry into gentle
waves by itself, which made a pleasant change from
the usual straightening irons. In keeping with this
preference for all things natural, the products used
are from Aveda's botanically based range. Cutting
is good and, crucially, you get exactly what you ask

for. Stylist Robyn clearly explained the options well
before any snipping began – which is great when
you're nervous. A cut and finish is from £47, and the
Yuko straightening system is also available.

Michaeljohn

25 Albemarle Street, W1S 4HU (7629 6969/
www.michaeljohn.co.uk). Green Park tube.
Open 8am-6.30pm Mon, Sat; 8am-8pm Tue-Fri.
Credit MC, V.
Still holding its own after all these years in the face
of stiff competition, this smart supersalon was
doing a roaring trade on the weekday we visited.
The selling point? Highly skilled staff who are
more interested in individual style than fashion-led
uniform cuts. Our hair was styled by one the salon's
senior artistic directors (£110), who was genuinely
passionate about hair and took precision cutting to
a new level – we were asked to stand up so he could
check that the ends were completely level. The
results were impressive and transformational – we
left with a new look, and a spring in our step. On
the colour front, a half head of highlights costs
£150, a full head £180 and tints start at £70. The
Ragdale Clinic downstairs is a hive of activity,
offering all the basics (manicure £32, pedicure £45,
facials from £60), as well as more high-tech
treatments such as IPL hair removal (from £60).
Considering its location (within striking distance of
Bond Street) and its pedigree, Michaeljohn stands
out for keeping its feet firmly on the ground.

Sejour

3-5 Bray Place, SW3 3LL (7589 1100/
www.sejour.co.uk). Sloane Square tube. **Open**
10am-4.30pm Mon; 8.30am-8pm Tue-Fri; 10am-
6pm Sat. **Credit** MC, V.
The owners of this salon wanted to create a setting
redolent of a chic, decadent boudoir to reflect their
luxurious haircare service. With alternating deep-
red and opulent Osborne & Little-papered walls,
candles, and shampoo recliners with a remote-
controlled back-massage facility (enhancing the
manual head massage), we reckon they have
succeeded. If you can find the place, tucked away
in a mews house on a peaceful Chelsea street, you'll
discover it offers substance as well as style. Co-
owner Carl Dawson, from the Nicky Clarke stable,
is a whizz with the foils and highlights, while chirpy
new boy Dwight is a demon blow-dryer. Upstairs,
Jade does extensions, using the Connect system.
Cuts start at £75 and rise to £140 for a top stylist.

Windle

41-45 Shorts Gardens, WC2H 9AP (7497 2393/
www.windlehair.com). Covent Garden or Leicester
Square tube. **Open** 10am-6pm Tue; 10am-7.15pm
Wed, Thur; 10.30am-7.15pm Fri; 9.30am-6pm Sat.
Credit MC, V.
For somewhere that straightens Orlando Bloom's
hair and curls up Katie Melua's, Windle is enjoyably
un-self-conscious. A team of rated cutters and
technicians works together (sometimes literally)
with an evident rapport, easy in their chat, secure
in their skills and sound on advice. It's a big, broad
two-level place done out in an understated
boutiquey style, heavy on leather and red accents,
with a shampooing room (Bumble and Bumble
products) softened by a pebble floor, scented candles
and super-comfortable recliners. As well as the
standard range of colour options (vegetable dye
included), there's a short list of texture treatments,
including a collagen and keratin repair system (£50)
and a freestyle perm (£200); Windle is known for its
hair straightening, to the extent that it sells its own-
brand iron (£100), with more electricals due to be
released in 2006. Also new is the appearance by
session supremo Neil Moodie, who is expected to
bring more celebs in. We can't see them demanding
special treatment; it's a bit too democratic-chic for
that. Cuts go from £40, up to £90 for Paul Windle.

Diverse Hair

280 Upper Street, N1 2TZ (7704 6842). Angel
tube/Highbury & Islington tube/rail. **Open** 11am-
7pm Mon-Fri; 10am-5pm Sat; other times by prior
arrangement. **Credit** AmEx, MC, V.

Part of an Islington mini-empire that also includes
men's and women's fashion boutiques (*see p36*) and
a trendy kid's outlet, Diverse Hair is a friendly local
salon providing top-notch cutting and colouring at
prices that won't make your hair stand on end.
Clients range from fashionable mums with small
babies (who appreciate that the music, while
eclectic, is unlikely to wake their offspring up with
a start) to groovy young men, all looking for
professionally snipped, eminently wearable barnets
and a relaxing atmosphere. Staff are used to the
quirks of their regulars, so if you don't want to gas
about your forthcoming holiday, you can zone out
with a mag and plentiful refreshments. Prices are a
big plus here: a cut and blow-dry costs £38, tints
£38, and a half head of highlights from £75.

Gina Conway Salon

62 Westbourne Grove, W2 5SH (7229 6644/
www.ginaconway.co.uk). Bayswater or Notting Hill
Gate tube. **Open** 10am-5pm Mon, Sun; 9am-7pm
Tue, Sat; 9am-9pm Wed-Fri. **Credit** MC, V.
Following her success in Fulham Road, Californian
Gina Conway has stridden into chic Westbourne
Grove, hand in hand with Aveda. With artfully
placed mirrors and delicate cornicing on super-
high ceilings, the salon is incredibly calming and
elegant – a bit like Gina herself. She heads a young
team from all over the place, which contributes to
the international feel. Staff are sweet and attentive,
taking time to talk through options, and giving a
shiatsu-style shoulder and scalp massage before
kicking in with the shampoo. Specialist colour
work is noteworthy, particularly as the salon
majors in natural colour products such as Aveda.
Expert cutting starts at £55 for women (£40 for
the fellas), up to £95 and £70 respectively for the
John Frieda-trained Gina. A full head of highlights
starts at £110 and a semi-permanent dye from £60.
Yuko straightening system, and scalp and hair
conditioning treatments are also available (from
£25). Downstairs, the Urban Oasis offers masses
of customised Ayurvedic face and body treatments
and other exotic indulgences such as Lava Stone
Massage (£70 an hour).
For branch see index.

Guy Parsons Hairdressing

243 Westbourne Grove, W11 2SE (7243 0939).
Notting Hill Gate tube. **Open** 10am-7pm Mon-Fri;
9am-6pm Sat. **Credit** AmEx, DC, MC, V.
Husband-and-wife team Guy and Nicola Parsons
have been running their laid-back, split-level
Westbourne Grove salon for 12 years and boast
many loyal customers – one family even flies down
from Scotland. Staff are super-friendly, there are
comfy, old-style barbers' chairs to sit on, funky
music on the stereo, even a handy newspaper kiosk
that opens on to the street. Far from banishing
brats, the salon positively welcomes them, offering
reduced-rate kids' trims on Mondays and Tuesdays.
Cuts start at £52 (£42 for men), rising to £70 for
Guy – you might recognise him from his age-
defying transformations on Channel 4's *Ten Years
Younger*. Prices for colour start at £50 for tints and
highlights, and a range of treatments from plant-
based range Phytologie is also available. In 2006
beauty services will be added to the salon menu.
We were impressed with the high level of personal
care and attention, often absent from busy central
London chains.

Kell Skött Haircare

*93 Golborne Road, W10 5NL (8964 3004/www.
kellskotthaircare.com). Ladbroke Grove tube.* **Open**
10am-6pm Mon; 9am-6pm Tue; 9am-8pm Wed,
Thur; 9am-7pm Fri; 8am-6pm Sat. **Credit** MC, V.
Kell Skött's friendly salon is a calming sanctuary
on edgy-chic Golborne Road. As you slip into one
of the plush shampoo chairs (imported from
Japan), you'll automatically gaze up at the rotating
display of photographs by Kell and local artists. If
your hair's a bit frazzled, opt for a session under the
Japanese MicroMist machine, which emits an ultra-
fine steam that helps conditioning treatments to
penetrate the hair (£25). The salon uses the
excellent plant-based Phytologie products, which
are also available to buy. Prices are very reasonable:
£28 to £55 for women (£25-£50 men), with colour

at £30 to £40 for an all-over tint or £60 to £100 for a full head of highlights. The DIY manicure bar is a great way to pass the time while you're waiting for your colour to take. A real find.

The Klinik
65 Exmouth Market, EC1R 4QL (7837 3771/ www.theklinik.com). Angel tube/Farringdon tube/rail. **Open** 9am-8pm Mon-Fri; 9am-6pm Sat. **Credit** MC, V.
Situated in bustling Exmouth Market, this small, minimalist salon mixes a trendy atmosphere with a warm welcome, which has earned it a devoted clientele. In the hands of former make-up artist Anna Forsling and her trusty team, customers are treated to friendly, personal and high-quality haircare. Technical innovations set the salon apart from the crowd – customers can watch their hair being cut on the mini screens at their feet. Cuts start at £41, colour from £56, or you can pop in for a complimentary consultation. A hair-styling workshop is held on Sundays to help regulars brush up on DIY techniques.

Tommy Guns
49 Charlotte Road, EC2A 3QT (7739 2244/ www.tommyguns.com). Old Street tube/rail. **Open** 11am-8pm Mon-Fri; 10.30am-6pm Sat. **Credit** AmEx, DC, MC, V.
Occupying a spacious studio well served by natural daylight, this popular salon continues to fire on all cylinders. With such celebrity clients as Kate Moss and the Darkness, and eclectic background music delivering the likes of Peaches and the Breeders, there's a low-key rock 'n' roll edge to the place – though the floor-to-ceiling mirrors, old-fashioned barbers' chairs and brushed-steel cabinets keep things crisp and practical. At once aspirational (copies of *Wallpaper**, *Pop* and *Condé Nast Traveller* keep you occupied) and friendly, the salon employs only highly trained stylists – some have defected from Toni & Guy or Vidal Sassoon – so there is one rate for everyone. A woman's cut and finish costs £45, men's £35; tints start at £44, and a full head of highlights is £120. Staff also take on session work, which means more directional cuts are a forte. Tommy Guns is a sure shot.
For branch see index.

Willie Smarts
11 Pavement, Clapham Common, SW4 0HY (7498 7771/www.williesmarts.com). **Open** 11am-8pm Mon-Fri; 9.30am-6pm Sat; 12.30-6.30pm Sun.
A hit with the hip young folk of SW4 for 15 years, and it's easy to see why. A stone's throw from the Common, this no-frills salon oozes a relaxed vibe; stylists are friendly without being OTT, and it offers decent value for money (haircuts start from £27.50; colours from £25). The salon itself had a successful makeover in 2004 and now feels fresh and fashionable. White decor dominates, with a few splashes of colour courtesy of handmade flowers and hearts. Pre-treatment discussion was thorough, and the resulting colour achieved the desired hue – and glossy to boot. Willie Smarts only uses Aveda products – for washing, styling and colouring. Don't be put off by the dentist-style shampoo chairs – just kick back, get horizontal and relax.

Afro

Aquarius
9 Stroud Green Road, N4 2DQ (7263 2483). Finsbury Park tube/rail. **Open** 9.30am-5pm Mon, Tue, Fri; 9.30am-6pm Thur; 8.30am-4pm Sat. **Credit** MC, V.
This award-winning family business is very popular with a trendy, young black crowd, as well as older regulars. Staff are friendly but have a no-nonsense approach – they need to as some of the styles (extensions, bonding, weaving) take several hours. As clients' friends tend to stop by, this neat little place can feel more like a social gathering than a hair salon. Prices are extremely reasonable, with a basic cut for men from £8 to £10 (starting at £14.95 for women). Singles (plaited extensions) start from £105 and 'virgin' (first-time) perms from £49.95; cornrows go from £54.95 with extensions, or £24.95 without. Manicures and pedicures are available in the basement (from £11.95).

Back to Eden
14 Westmoreland Road, SE17 2AY (7703 3173). Elephant & Castle tube/rail. **Open** 10.30am-6.30pm Tue-Sat. **No credit cards**.
True to its name, Back to Eden puts the emphasis on natural hairstyling, which is why there's no cutting, perming or weaving on offer. The speciality is dreadlocks, although styles for hair in its natural Afro state – such as double twists, china bumps and cornrows – are also available. Most customers with 'locks opt for a deep-moisturising steam treatment, followed by retwisting and manipulation into a variety of styles. Prices start from £15 for cornrows or £25 for a retwist. A full treatment, including wash, steam, scalp massage and twists, starts from £35; you can add a scalp massage for a tenner. Non-chemical hair dyes and own-brand natural hair products are also sold if you want to continue the experience at home. Service is friendly and energetic.

Burnett Forbes
15 Wells Street, W1P 3FP (7580 5006). Oxford Circus tube. **Open** 10am-6pm Mon, Wed; 10am-8pm Tue, Thur, Fri; 9am-6pm Sat. **Credit** MC, V.
Burnett Forbes has a varied client base and attends to both European and Afro hair, and customers come from all over the country to have their hair relaxed, plaited and permed at this beautifully designed salon. The emphasis is on healthy hair, so harsh products are avoided and conditioning treatments are a forte. An intensive protein mask treatment (£53, including a massage and blow-dry) is well worth splurging on. Cuts are £55, weaving is £10 a row and plaiting starts at around £65 (£150 with extensions). Those on tighter budgets can attend training sessions on Mondays and Wednesdays, when you can get a cut with a junior member of staff for £15.

Pacific Hair Artists
80-82 Regent Street, 13 Quadrant Arcade, W1B 5RP (7584 5565). Piccadilly Circus tube. **Open** 9.30am-6.30pm Mon, Tue, Fri, Sat; 9.30am-9pm Wed, Thur. **Credit** AmEx, MC, V.
This salon caters to both black and white customers looking to have their short hair lengthened with extensions, or their curly hair tamed. A well-heeled and celebrity clientele (Laurence Fishburne has been groomed here, Ms Dynamite is a regular) is attracted by the impeccable service. Cuts start at £42.50, hair relaxing is from £71.50 and extensions cost from £49.50 per section.

Barbers

Old-fashioned barbers abound in every corner of the city, but these are some of the most exceptional. *See also p107* **Mr Topper's**.

Cut
Nr Platform 1, Euston Station, NW1 2HS (7388 8500/www.cutbarbers.com). Euston tube/rail. **Open** 8am-8pm Mon-Fri; 9am-6pm Sat. **No credit cards**.
No ordinary chop shop, Cut throws in some 21st-century trimmings with its £8 haircuts (£15 for women, £3 each for beard or fringe trims). Based on a concept pioneered in Japan, it's a concourse-based operation whereby barbers work to a ten-minute timer from the moment you sit down in the chair. Pre-chair waiting times are also logged on a large digital stopwatch, which is automatically activated when punters take a seat at one of the four waiting stations. Equipment is meticulously sterilised, a Cut Hair Removal System ensures you'll head off on your business without an itchy neck, and an

Sejour. See p109.

automated ticket-dispenser takes all the hassle out of payment. Oh, and by the way, the haircuts are as good as you'd get at twice the price elsewhere.

Flittner

86 Moorgate, EC2M 6SE (7606 4750). Moorgate tube/rail. **Open** 8am-6pm Mon-Wed, Fri; 8am-6.30pm Thur. **Credit** AmEx, MC, V.

When the 'new' proprietor has been in charge for three decades, you can be confident you're in safe hands: Chris Christodoulou took over Flittner's from his dad way back in 1973. The company celebrated its 100th anniversary in June 2004, and you get the feeling that not much has changed since it first opened: this is a magnificently old-fashioned gentlemen's hairdressers, right down to the barbers' pole and frosted glass front, and Edwardian mahogany and long mirrors within. Even the leather-upholstered swivel chairs date back to the '50s. Haircuts cost from £14.50 (up to £22 for wash and cut), but the hot-towel shave (£19.50) is the thing. More like a massage than the demonic blade-stropping of legend, it's the beauty treatment men were made for. No wonder businessmen and lawyers keep returning, some of them long after they've retired and moved out of town. Admirably unstuffy, unobtrusively chatty, calmingly professional.

Geo F Trumper

9 Curzon Street, W1J 5HQ (7499 1850/www.trumpers.com). Green Park tube. **Open** 9am-5.30pm Mon-Fri; 9am-1pm Sat. **Credit** AmEx, DC, MC, V.

Every man should have an open-razor shave at least once in his life, and this traditional Mayfair barber's (founded in 1875) is amply qualified to do the honours. With its abundance of wood panelling and basement booths equipped with ancient sinks and vintage leather chairs, Trumper's looks every inch the Victorian barber shop, yet it does a brisk trade with modern metrosexuals as well as old-school gents. The shave is a relaxing half-hour affair of hot towels, massage, pre-blade 'skin food' lotion and shaving cream in such admirably un-macho varieties as rose and violet. Trumper's also does haircuts, manicures and pedicures, and its ground floor – loads of glass cabinets full of colognes, skin products, badger-hair brushes, manicure sets and silvered handles fitted to take Gillette Mach 3 heads – has plenty of gift ideas for the men in your life.

Pankhurst at Alfred Dunhill

48 Jermyn Street, SW1Y 6LX (7290 8636). Green Park or Piccadilly Circus tube. **Open** 9.30am-6.30pm Mon-Fri; 10am-6.30pm Sat. **Credit** AmEx, MC, V.

Upmarket barber shop Pankhurst invites high expectations: it resides within the rarefied St James's headquarters of menswear supremo Alfred Dunhill, boasts a celebrity clientele, and has a price list to match: £45 for a cut, £35 for a wet shave. Thankfully, the price tags are justified both by the overall service and the quality of individual treatments. On a recent visit, an excellent complimentary espresso set the tone for an hour of refined comfort. A haircut was slower than you'd expect in a regular high-street barber's, but also much more accomplished – and in any case, the unhurried approach is part of the luxury ethos espoused by owner Brent Pankhurst, former head artistic director for Vidal Sassoon. His vision was to create a gentlemen's grooming parlour that combined the informality of a barber shop with the ambience of a gentleman's club. So expect good, leisurely conversation – as well as a skilful cut or shave – from a visit. Other treatments available include manicures (£20), head massage (£20) and a hot-towel facial (£40).

Sadlers Wells Barber Shop

110 Rosebery Avenue, EC1R 4TL (7833 0556). Angel tube. **Open** 8am-6pm Mon-Sat. **No credit cards.**

An old-fashioned gem, this little barber's sits right opposite the Sadlers Wells Theatre. Prices here seem fixed in the '70s: from £7.50 for your basic cut, rising to the dizzy heights of £10.50 for the works (wash, cut and blow-dry). A trad wet shave (with hot towel) costs £8, or just £4.50 for OAPs.

Salon:1

11 Barons Court Road, W14 9DP (7385 6622/www.salon-1.co.uk). West Kensington tube. **Open** 10am-7.30pm Mon-Wed; 10am-8pm Thur; 10am-7pm Fri; 8.30am-5.30pm Sat; 11am-4pm Sun. **Credit** MC, V.

Developed by chef-turned-barber Frank Bertorelli, Salon:1 aims to combine a clubby vibe with thoroughly modern surroundings and service. So, chaps, as well as a bit of beard-trimming, a hot-towel shave or a decent clipper cut, you get a state-of-the-art chair, a proper head massage, a cappuccino and a flat-screen TV to watch the cricket on. The contemporary styling (walnut panelling, Philippe Starck basins, American Crew products) means it's masculine yet modern, but pricing's also on the acceptable side – a wet cut costs £23.50, a scented hot-towel wet shave is from £18.50 and back waxes £22.

Truefitt & Hill

71 St James's Street, SW1A 1PH (7493 2961/www.truefittandhill.com). Green Park tube. **Open** 8.30am-5.30pm Mon-Fri; 8.30am-4.30pm Sat. **Credit** AmEx, MC, V.

Tradition goes a long way. In the case of Truefitt & Hill, founded in 1805, it goes all the way to Las Vegas, where there's an outpost of the London original inside Caesar's Palace. The increased marketing presence, though, means little to the St James's old-timers who make up the core clientele at this splendid shop (the company relocated here from nearby Old Bond Street in 1994). The cuts (£30) are traditional and immaculate, the atmosphere gloriously hushed and wonderfully unhurried. The truly decadent indulge themselves further with a wet shave, complete with hot towels (£35), before stocking up on toiletries and shaving accoutrements from the firm's own range.

Hairdressing schools

L'Oréal Technical Centre

255 Hammersmith Road, W6 8AZ (8762 4200/www.loreal.com). Hammersmith tube. **Open** 9am-5pm Mon-Fri. **Credit** MC, V.

If you're over 16, open-minded and prepared to hang around for a while, then you will be well suited as a model at this established academy. Willing participants must register and have a skin test 48 hours before their appointment, but it's worth it as the first session is free. Subsequent trips will set you back from £8 for an up-for-

anything cut (£15 with colour) and £13 for more conventional colouring. Perms and straightening systems are £13, while hair-ups, blow-dries and consultations are free. All sessions are supervised and all trainees are qualified.

Toni & Guy Academy

71-75 New Oxford Street, WC1A 1DG (7836 0606/www.toniandguy.co.uk). Tottenham Court Road tube. **Open** call for details. **Credit** AmEx, DC, MC, V.

Want a trendy haircut but on a tight budget? The Toni & Guy Academy will welcome you with open arms as long as you are reasonably open-minded and have at least two hours free for the session. The cuts only cost a fiver, while those wanting a new colour (£10 glossing, £15 for full head or tints, £20 for highlights) can visit the Colour Academy at 58-60 Stamford Street, SE1 9LK (7921 9100). You will need to have a sensitivity test at least 48 hours prior to a colour appointment.

Vidal Sassoon's Advanced Academy

19-20 Grosvenor Street, W1K 4QH (7491 0030/www.vidalsassoon.co.uk). Bond Street tube. **Open** appointments 1.30pm Tue-Thur. **Credit** AmEx, MC, V.

Not for the faint-hearted – models at this academy should be prepared for a potentially dramatic change of style, although if you take pictures of your preferred look, it should be taken into account. Cuts cost £11 (or £6.50 for students) and can sometimes include free colouring if the mood takes them. Alternatively, the school at 56 Davies Mews, W1K 5AA (7318 5205) offers a similar service catering for more classic style requests. You may need to book two or three weeks in advance for an appointment.

Problem hair

London Centre of Trichology

74 Wigmore Street, W1U 2SQ (7935 1935/www.londontricho.com). Bond Street tube. **Open** 9.30am-7pm Mon-Fri; 9am-1pm Sat. **Credit** AmEx, DC, MC, V.

This trichology centre focuses mainly on the problem of thinning hair (in both men and women), and advises on suitable treatments, weaving or, in some cases, surgery. Scalp disorders are also treated. Prices start at £14 for a shampoo, going up to a couple of grand for surgery.
Mail order.

Philip Kingsley

54 Green Street, W1K 6RU (7629 4004/www.philipkingsley.co.uk). Bond Street or Marble Arch tube. **Open** 8.30am-6pm Mon, Tue, Thur, Fri; 8.30am-8pm Wed; 8.30am-2.30pm Sat. **Credit** MC, V.

Philip Kingsley has been in the business for over 40 years and is a leading authority on hair health. While the company sells its own range of hair products, it is keen to stress the role nutrition and diet play in preventing hair problems. Consultations cost between £110 and £150, treatments are £55, and products start at £9.95. An appointment with Philip himself is £150. There's also a Philip Kingsley treatment centre in Harrods' Urban Retreat (*see p98*).
Mail order.

Scalp & Hair Clinic

108 St John's Hill, SW11 1SY (7924 2195/www.scalp-hair.co.uk). Clapham Junction rail. **Open** 9am-6pm Thur, Fri; 8.30am-2pm Sat. **No credit cards.**

The scalp experts at this clinic are all members of the Institute of Trichologists and are particularly sympathetic to the distress that conditions such as hair loss can cause. Along with treatments, advice is offered on haircare and medical scalp conditions, including damage caused by hairdressing chemicals such as those used in relaxants. An initial consultation costs £45, dry treatments are £22 and wet treatments £28.
Mail order.

HEALTH & BEAUTY

Opticians

The selection of designer frames – whether for spectacles or sunglasses – is expanding all the time. Look out for **Miss Sixty** glasses (colourful and funky), **Stella McCartney** (boho-esque), **Persol** (studded with Swarovski crystals), **Nike Interchange** (removable lens system), **Krizia** (think *Club Tropicana* mirrored shades) or **Salvatore Ferragamo** (we love the Picnic collection with raffia woven into the frames). Then there's Digital Music Eyewear, courtesy of **Oakley**: the Thump is an entire music system (including speakers) attached to an eyewear frame.

If you're on a tight budget but still want to make a statement, there are thankfully still plenty of options: you can pick up some vintage eyewear from **www.klasik.org** or buy direct from the stall in Spitalfields market (*see p17*), where you'll find a huge selection of cool American, French and Italian frames from the 1940s, '50s, '60s and '70s; your prescription can be fitted for an additional £35 (single tint £45, graduated tint £55). **Topshop** (*see p45*) is a good option for sunglasses, with prices from £12 and a decent selection. **Fabris Lane** (available in most department stores) has a huge selection of shades at budget prices. Going more upmarket, **Selfridges** (*see p14*) stocks an swank range (Gucci, Givenchy, Diesel, D&G, Stella McCartney and Lulu Guinness, among others).

A word of warning – we have had reports of some fairly cursory free eye tests, so check how thorough the appointment will be first.

Arthur Morrice
11 Beauchamp Place, SW3 1NQ (7584 4661). Knightsbridge tube. **Open** 10am-6.30pm Mon-Sat. **Credit** AmEx, DC, MC, V.
Stock includes vintage frames (some in tortoiseshell) dating back as far as the 1920s. Prices start at around £150 and go up to £2,000 for solid gold frames. The shop also has a wide selection of designer brands, including Chrome Hearts, Paul Smith, Oliver Peoples, ic! berlin, Philippe Starck and Freudenhaus. Service is friendly.

Auerbach & Steele
129 King's Road, SW3 4PW (7349 0001/ www.auerbach-steele.com). Sloane Square tube. **Open** 10am-6.30pm Mon-Fri; 10am-6pm Sat; noon-5pm Sun. **Credit** AmEx, DC, MC, V.
Frames start at about £70 for standard metal, and rise to £300 for Lindberg Air Titaniums. The store tends to carry mostly chic labels, such as Beausoleil, Alain Mikli and Maui Jim (Hawaiian sunglasses with polarised lenses). A&S's stylish own-brand frames cost around £99 to £125. Contact lenses include Vistakon, Bausch & Lomb and CIBA Vision.

Boots Opticians
22 Wigmore Street, W1U 2RH (7491 9644/ www.boots.com/opticians). Bond Street tube. **Open** 8am-9pm Mon-Sat; noon-7pm Sun. **Credit** MC, V.
There are usually plenty of in-store offers here, such as 25% off selected designer frames, free contact lens trials or free glasses for under-16s. Boots's own-brand range (clip-ons, half-eyes, reading glasses, plastic and rimless) starts at around £39 (frame and lenses). More exciting styles encompass a decent selection of high-street regulars (Oasis, Silhouette, FCUK and Police). The own-brand contact lenses range covers most prescriptions; monthly disposables cost around £27 for a month's supply. **Branches**: throughout the city.

Bromptons
202A Kensington High Street, W8 7RG (7937 5500). High Street Kensington tube. **Open** 9.30am-6.30pm Mon-Wed, Fri; 9.30am-7.30pm Thur; 9.30am-6pm Sat; 11am-6pm Sun. **Credit** AmEx, MC, V.
Open seven days a week (and performing eye tests every day), this cheerful, funky store attracts lots of local trendies looking for titanium frames by Lindberg and Silhouette (both from £219), or designs by Philippe Starck (£250 and upwards). The shop also sells designer sunglasses, including German brand ic! berlin and Oliver Peoples (from £125). There's a 12-month, interest-free payment option on purchases over £300.
Mail order.

Crawford Street Opticians
37 Crawford Street, 7A Wyndham Place, W1H 1PN (7724 8033/www.crawfordstreetopticians. com). Baker Street tube/Marylebone tube/rail. **Open** 10am-5.30pm Tue-Fri; 10am-4pm Sat. **Credit** AmEx, MC, V.
This contemporary shop in a quiet stretch of Marylebone stocks a range of stylish sunglasses and frames from the likes of Face à Face, Kata and LA Eyeworks. Frames cost from around £99 to £220. A wide choice of contact lenses from all the major suppliers is also available.
Mail order.

Cutler & Gross
16 Knightsbridge Green, SW1X 7QL (7581 2250/www.cutlerandgross.com). Knightsbridge tube. **Open** 9.30am-6pm Mon-Sat. **Credit** AmEx, DC, MC, V.
This flagship store was completely renovated at the beginning of 2005 and the result is an airy, modern and luxurious interior with plenty of chrome and acid green to provide the backdrop for C&G's stock of handmade frames. Looking for a pair of iconic 1960s specs? Then check out Tony

Gross's Vintage store at No.7, showcasing a selection of rare collectibles from names such as Pierre Cardin, YSL and Porsche. C&G's range of glasses with crystal frames and rose-pink lenses, created in conjunction with fashion label Comme des Garçons, is available at Dover Street Market (*see also p26* Comme des Garçons).
Mail order.

David Clulow
185 King's Road, SW3 5EB (7376 5733/ www.davidclulow.com). Sloane Square tube. **Open** 10am-6.30pm Mon-Sat; 11am-5pm Sun. **Credit** AmEx, DC, MC, V.
During the summer, DC usually halves the price of its designer frames (including top brands such as Paul Smith, Prada, Face à Face and Dior), and those who join its Privilege Club will be the first to hear about the sale. The wide selection of sunglasses ranges from £150 for a pair of funky Ray-Bans to £1,000 for lavish Cartier styles. Marc Jacobs fans will be pleased to see his sunglasses range in store. Those with more minimal tastes are also looked after – DC offers the latest technology for the thinnest lenses and lightest frames around. A number of stores have an express service, where spectacles can be made up within the hour. There are concessions in Selfridges and Harrods.
Mail order.
Branches: throughout the city.

Dollond & Aitchison
90-92 Oxford Street, W1D 1BY (7255 3896/ www.danda.co.uk). Oxford Circus or Tottenham Court Road tube. **Open** 10am-6.30pm Mon-Sat. **Credit** AmEx, MC, V.
D&A's 'Computereyes' service makes choosing the right specs much easier: it takes a photo of you and shows how a selection of frames look on screen (it works especially well for kids). The shop is strong on rimless styles, such as the astonishingly featherweight Lozza Superlights. Men's designer styles start at around £120 and include distinctive Hugo Boss, Police and Lacoste, plus trad sunglasses from Timberland. Frames for women include subtle numbers from Fila, Karen Millen and French Connection (also from around £120). A mail-order contact lens service is also available. Half-price eye tests and an extra 10% off glasses are up for grabs when you book online.
Branches: throughout the city.

The Eye Company
159 Wardour Street, W1F 8WH (7434 0988/ www.eye-company.co.uk). Oxford Circus or Tottenham Court Road tube. **Open** 10.30am-6.30pm Mon-Wed, Fri; 10.30am-7.30pm Thur; 10.30am-6pm Sat. **Credit** AmEx, DC, MC, V.
A big range of contemporary eyewear is available at this achingly hip little store in the heart of Soho. There are colourful designs by LA Eyeworks, cool metal frames from ic! berlin, funky, reasonably priced (around £105) sunglasses by Paul Frank, and more understated styles from Minima and Paul Smith. Frances Klein's frames are particularly beautiful. Titaniums will set you back around £160-£250, while the decent sunglasses selection includes Paul Smith and Beausoleil. The shop also stocks vintage frames, mainly from the 1950s and '60s – though some date back as far as the 19th century. A bespoke service is available.

Eye Level Opticians
37 Upper Street, N1 0PN (7354 9277/ www.eyelevelopticians.co.uk). Angel tube. **Open** 10am-6pm Mon-Fri; 10am-5pm Sat; 11am-4pm Sun. **Credit** MC, V.
This independent Islington store offers a selection of distinctive frames. Moving away from heavyweight designers such as Chanel and Gucci, Eye Level focuses on more unusual ranges. There are some wacky options from Oliver Peoples and Kirk Originals, plus edgy laser-cut (no screws or hinges) glasses from Germany's ic! berlin. The sunglasses range includes Face à Face and Beausoleil. Daily disposable lenses by Bausch & Lomb cost £1 a pair.
Mail order.

20/20 Optical Store. See p115.

Eye to Eye

3A Montpelier Street, SW7 1EX (7581 8828/ www.eyetoeyeopticians.co.uk). Knightsbridge tube. **Open** noon-6pm Mon; 10am-6pm Tue-Fri; 10am-5.30pm Sat. **Credit** AmEx, MC, V.

Though it sells such luxe eyewear as diamond-encrusted Cartier glasses (prices start at a cool £5,000), this slick Knightsbridge store also has a good selection of more affordable specs. Armanis cost about £125, Miklis £150, Starcks £225 and Flexon titanium £150. Contact lenses and handmade frames (including horn) are also sold (starting at around £400). Oh, and there are more basic Cartier styles from a slightly less jaw-dropping £200.

Kirk Originals

29 Floral Street, WC2E 9DP (7240 5055/www.kirk originals.com). Covent Garden tube. **Open** 11am-7pm Mon-Sat; 1-5pm Sun. **Credit** MC, V.

Kirk Originals started life in the early 1990s, when Jason Kirk came across some glasses made by his uncle 70 years earlier. These days, the shop is a byword for cool, with colourful, chunky retro-inspired frames. The Kirk Heroes range has six styles and six colourways (for example, purple/blue and chocolate/olive). The store also hosts art exhibitions.
Mail order.

Michel Guillon Eye Boutique

35 Duke of York Square, SW3 4LY (7730 2142/www.michelguillon.com). Sloane Square tube. **Open** 10am-7pm Mon-Sat; noon-6pm Sun. **Credit** AmEx, MC, V.

One of the UK's leading experts in cornea and contact lens research, Guillon specialises in issues such as dry eyes and is currently developing bespoke contact lenses for people who can't usually wear them. The company also offers bespoke spectacles. Eye examinations start from £45. The range of designer frames (including sunglasses) includes Robert Marc, Bugatti and Danish brand ProDesign, as well as Prada and YSL, and customers can be expertly fitted with the use of the video spectacle selector.
Mail order.
For branch see index.

Opera Opera

98 Long Acre, WC2E 9NR (7836 9246). Covent Garden tube. **Open** 10am-6pm Mon-Sat. **Credit** MC, V.

If you're after something a bit different, Opera Opera is the place to head. As well as providing specs for the theatre (most recently *Chitty Chitty Bang Bang*), it can also make bespoke spectacles (even from a picture) – pairs of 'Johnny Depps' are selling well. Bespoke prices start at around £225. The store has been operating since 1984 and its own brand, Harpers (from £140), is strong on retro-NHS styles. It also stocks a great range of Lindberg titanium frames (including Air, Strip and Spirit), from £219, and a small array of designer offerings (expect to pay £250 for a pair of Alain Miklis).

Optical Express

316-318 Regent Street, W1R 5AF (0870 220 2020/www.opticalexpress.com). Oxford Circus tube. **Open** 9am-5.30pm Mon-Sat. **Credit** AmEx, MC, V.

This chain has some good-value offers – at press time there were designer frames from £79; a free second pair (including bifocal and varifocal) when you spend £100 or more on specs; and contact lenses for £9 per month (including free trial, solutions, aftercare and home delivery). Expect smart designer styles galore, including Calvin Klein, Giorgio Armani, Dolce & Gabbana, Gucci, Versace and Diesel. Prices start from £25 for a pair of simple frames, rising to over £200. The I-design range allows you to create your own rimless glasses. Sunnies cover the usual designer suspects, plus Oakley, Police and Ray-Ban, from £55. The Shaftesbury Avenue branch (7379 3979) offers laser eye correction (from £395 per eye) if you want to ditch the glasses altogether.
Mail order.
Branches: throughout the city.

Paris Miki London

69 Regent Street, W1B 4ED (7437 4770/ www.paris-miki.com). Piccadilly Circus tube. **Open** 10am-7pm Mon-Sat. **Credit** AmEx, DC, MC, V.

This shop goes a step further than offering the standard selection of frames and services. Firstly, there's a computer system that analyses your facial features and recommends the most suitable frames. Then there are the innovative frames: Mikissimes Nature is a new collection that incorporates natural materials such as wood, leather and bamboo; the Gum Metal range is made from a lightweight, flexible titanium alloy material; Microvision reading glasses fit in a working pen case that slips into a breast pocket.

Schuller Opticians

44 Lamb's Conduit Street, WC1N 3LB (7404 2002). Holborn tube. **Open** 9.30am-5.30pm Mon-Fri; 9.30am-1pm Sat. **Credit** AmEx, MC, V.

Mr Schuller is a well-known specialist in contact lenses, and his shop has a faithful fan base. Inside, it's smart and spacious, with a broad choice of chic and wearable frames such as La Fonts for £139, J Freys for £169 and a large range of the rarely seen Munich-based Freudenhaus brand for £189. Schuller also stocks Beausoleil, Belgium's Theo and Lindberg Air Titanium rimless (from £269).
For branch see index.

Specsavers

Unit 6, 6-17 Tottenham Court Road, W1T 1BG (7580 5115/www.specsavers.com). Tottenham Court Road tube. **Open** 10am-8pm Mon-Fri; 10am-7pm Sat; 11am-7.30pm Sun. **Credit** AmEx, MC, V.

While some say 'you should have gone to Specsavers', others aren't so sure. We like it for the friendly, efficient service and low prices, but it won't appeal to those in search of cutting-edge frames and stylish surroundings. But with prices starting at £30 for plastic frames (albeit rather unremarkable ones), who's arguing? If you want something a little more exciting, you'll have to pay more (the £75 range is the starting point for one of the many 'two for one' offers). Designer glasses from the likes of Boss, Red or Dead and Quiksilver are on offer at £99. Bifocal lenses start from £35. For contact lens wearers, all-in packages start from £8; daily disposables from £59.88 (three months' supply).
Branches: throughout the city.

Spex in the City

1 Shorts Gardens, WC2H 9AT (7240 0243/ www.spexinthecity.com). Covent Garden or Leicester Square tube. **Open** 11am-6.30pm Mon-Sat; 1-5pm Sun. **Credit** AmEx, MC, V.

Sale stock can dip as low as £25 at this funky, independent optician. The idiosyncratic array of styles ranges from the quirky to the sophisticated, with Alain Mikli, Philippe Starck and Porsche, as well as Brit designers Booth & Bruce and Japanese Yellows Plus. Full-price frames start at around £100 and go up to £379. Mention the website and you can get an eye test for a relatively cheap £20.

Sunglass Hut

141 Oxford Street, W1R 1PD (7287 5273/ www.sunglasshut-europe.com). Oxford Circus or Tottenham Court Road tube. **Open** 10am-7pm Mon-Wed, Fri, Sat; 10am-8pm Thur; noon-6pm Sun. **Credit** AmEx, MC, V.

In the designer section of this cool little Italian-owned chain, expect to find stylish designs by the likes of Miu Miu, Givenchy, Dior, Gucci, plus Danish Skägen, New York's Kenneth Cole, futuristic Oakleys and funky offerings from Kahuna and Maui Jim.
Branches: throughout the city.

20/20 Optical Store

216-217 Tottenham Court Road, W1T 7PT (7596 2020/www.20-20.co.uk). Goodge Street or Tottenham Court Road tube. **Open** 9am-8pm Mon-Fri; 9am-7pm Sat; 11.30am-6pm Sun. **Credit** AmEx, MC, V.

This spacious store gets a mixed response. While some speak of the great range and helpful service (sourcing glasses not in stock, for example), others dislike the heavy sales pitch. That said, eye tests

are extensive, the contact lens service is very good (12 months' interest-free credit) and there are plenty of discounts. Frame designers include the varied likes of Anna Sui, Fred, John Richmond and Nike. There are also shades from the latter two, as well as Oakley, Persol and others. It's one of only a few clinics to use an Optomap retinal camera to examine the back of the eye when carrying out sight tests, and an on-site branch of Ultralase (0808 144 2020) offers laser eye correction.
Mail order.

University Vision

University of London Union Building, Malet Street, WC1E 7HY (7636 8925). Euston Square or Goodge Street tube. **Open** 9am-5.30pm Mon-Fri; 10am-2pm Sat. **Credit** AmEx, DC, MC, V.

Short-sighted students don't have to look far to find this cheap and cheerful store, based in the University of London students' union building. But it's also open to the general public. Eye tests are just £15 for students and staff, or £20 for others. Designer frames – including Ray-Ban, Burberry, Calvin Klein, Emporio Armani, Gucci and Moschino – are priced at around £100. Single vision glasses start at around £49.
For branches (Neil Hershman Opticians and Pitman & Risner) see index.

Vision Express

263-265 Oxford Street, W1C 2DF (7409 7880/ www.visionexpress.com). Oxford Circus tube. **Open** 9.30am-8pm Mon-Sat; noon-6pm Sun. **Credit** AmEx, MC, V.

Fed up with broken specs? Vision Express calls its Memoform frames 'life-proof'; made from titanium alloy for strength and flexibility, they're perfect for active types (from £99). Regular offers include a pair of selected designer glasses and prescription sunnies for £99. The chain sells various designer labels (Chanel, Prada, Karen Millen) from around £139, as well as its own brand, which starts at just £29. On the contact lens front, Proclear monthly disposables cost £19.50 per month.
Branches: throughout the city.

Get Lenses

0800 652 5569/www.getlenses.com. **Phone enquiries** 9am-6pm Mon-Fri; 10am-4pm Sat. **Credit** MC, V.

This company sends contact lenses to any address in the UK, with free postage, providing you supply a proper contact lens prescription (as opposed to just an eye-test result). Choose from a wide range of disposable lenses, from daily to monthly, including Acuvue, Focus, CIBA Vision and Bausch & Lomb. A three-month supply of Focus Dailies disposable lenses costs £69; a six-month stash of Johnson & Johnson Surevue is just £29.50. A good range of solutions and accessories is also available. You can order online if you prefer.

Iris Optical

6 Maguire Street, SE1 2NQ (7407 7951/ www.irisoptical.co.uk). Tower Hill tube/London Bridge tube/rail. **Open** 9am-7pm Mon-Fri. **Credit** DC, MC, V.

Although Iris Optical has a walk-in showroom, mail order is the mainstay of the business. If it's specs you're after, the company will courier any pairs you fancy trying on (there's a £10 fee if you decide not to buy). There are frames by Gucci, Nike Flexon, Philippe Starck and Alain Mikli, among others. The range of contact lenses is enormous, from 1-Day Acuvue by Johnson & Johnson to Freshlook Colours (available in blue, sapphire, green, hazel, misty grey and violet at £11.49 a pair, minimum order six boxes). A three-month supply of Focus Dailies costs £69.

Sunglassesuk.com

www.sunglassesuk.com. **Credit** AmEx, MC, V.

The UK's biggest online sunglasses retailer has over 8,000 styles from all major designers (at up to 30% off high-street prices). Brands include Fendi, Bollé, Oakley, Prada and Gucci.

HEALTH & BEAUTY

Home

Accessories

Many shops in the **Furniture** chapter of this guide also sell attractive home accessories, in particular **Skandium** and **Mint**, as well as large stores **Habitat**, **Heal's** and the **Conran Shop**. Of the department stores, **Selfridges** and **Harvey Nichols** have particularly interesting homeware concessions, while **Debenhams** boasts a range by *Grand Designs* guru Kevin McCloud (for all three, *see chapter* **Department Stores**).

All rounders

Argos

80-110 New Oxford Street, WC1A 1HB (0845 165 7023/www.argos.co.uk). Tottenham Court Road tube. **Open** *10am-6pm Mon; 10am-7pm Tue-Fri; 10am-6.30pm Sat; noon-6pm Sun.* **Credit** AmEx, MC, V.

Argos is not known for offering an enjoyable customer experience, nor is that its mission. The payment/collection system – whereby you wait for your number to be called as staff bring the goods out of the warehouse – can be reminiscent of a cattle market or a bingo hall, but for low prices and fairly efficient catalogue system you'd be hard-pressed to find an equal. The selection of items on sale is immense, ranging from lawnmowers to sofas, jewellery to electronics, clothes to kettles, and even clothes. With stores across the city, this is a convenient place to buy cheap essentials at competitive prices.

Mail order (0870 600 2020).
Branches: throughout the city.

Contemporary

Alessi

22 Brook Street, W1K 5DF (7518 9091/ www.alessi.com). Bond Street tube. **Open** *10am-6.30pm Mon, Wed, Fri, Sat; 10am-7pm Thur.* **Credit** MC, V.

Founded in 1921, this giant, iconic Italian tableware brand is now world-famous for its products created by some of the leading design luminaries of the 20th century – Ettore Sottsass, Richard Sapper, Achille Castiglioni, Alessandro Mendini, Aldo Rossi, Michael Graves, Philippe Starck... the list goes on. Always driven by quality, and often with an injection of wit, the collections in metal, glass, ceramics and plastics are sold in many authorised dealers, but the largest selection is here in the flagship store. For autumn/winter 2005/6, Jean Nouvel's sleek Tea and Coffee Set (£45) caught our eye, as did the Mediterraneo fruit bowl (small bowl £54, large bowl £70) by Emma Silvestris.
Mail order.

Aria

295-297 Upper Street, N1 2TU (7704 1999/ www.aria-shop.co.uk). Angel tube/Highbury & Islington tube/rail. **Open** *10am-7pm Mon-Fri; 10am-6.30pm Sat; noon-5pm Sun.* **Credit** AmEx, MC, V.

Aria is a good one-stop shop for stylish contemporary home accessories, lighting and furniture. Always rammed full of gorgeous offerings, the store brings in the big names of the design world, such as Philippe Starck, Jasper Morrison and Ron Arad. It also boasts a decent-sized Alessi concession. Whether you succumb to a dish for £15, a Starck light for £99 or a linear Chair One by Konstantin Grcic for £155, you're unlikely to leave empty-handed. The sister store across the road (No.133) sells smaller items, such as watches, bags and picture frames.
Mail order.
For branch see index.

Babylon

301 Fulham Road, SW10 9QH (7376 7255/ www.babylonlondon.com). South Kensington tube. **Open** *10am-6pm Mon-Sat.* **Credit** AmEx, DC, MC, V.

Partners Birgit Israel and Peter Wylly launched this shop in 1999, having run a successful design consultancy. The aim was to showcase their own range of products to an affluent audience, while mixing it in with other complementary designs, both new and vintage. The result is a rather unique fusion of styles. Stunning antique chandeliers illuminate smaller items such as Orrefors glass vases, Danish rosewood cutlery sets or a Raymond Loewy-designed tea set, all sitting on top of a Danish sideboard. Prices are high, but so is the quality of the selection, backed up by knowledgeable staff who can source items for you.
Mail order.

Bodum

24 Neal Street, WC2H 9QW (7240 9176/ www.bodum.com). Covent Garden tube. **Open** *11am-7pm Mon; 10am-7pm Tue, Wed, Fri; 10am-7.30pm Thur, Sat; noon-6pm Sun.* **Credit** AmEx, MC, V.

A good source of sleek, modern and affordable items for the kitchen, in particular coffee and tea accessories. The cafetières – Bodum's signature pieces – come in an array of sizes, styles and colours, from classic glass (from £19.99) to the curvy, chrome Columbia model (from £34.99). The shop also sells everything else you might need to make a perfect brew, such as electric milk frothers, and sugar and cream sets. Other kitchenware includes smart storage jars, plates, chopping boards and transparent butter dishes – all designed to be simple yet effective.
Mail order.

Carden Cunietti

81-83 Westbourne Park Road, W2 5QH (7229 8630/www.carden-cunietti.com). Royal Oak or Westbourne Park tube. **Open** *10am-6pm Mon-Sat.* **Credit** AmEx, MC, V.

Audrey Carden and Elenora Cunietti are the names behind this quirky Notting Hill shop. The interior design duo decided to bring together an eclectic array of objects sourced from around the world, with one-off period pieces rubbing shoulders with modern items. Stock is constantly changing, but you might see stunning Murano glass lamps, Asian lacquered furniture, and throws in various fabrics, from fleece to silk. Prices vary considerably, but you can find items for as little as £10 (for a seashell cupboard door handle, say) and as much as £2,000 for a sofa or a cabinet.
Mail order.

Cho Cho San

9 Camden Passage, N1 8EA (7359 6000/ www.chochosan.co.uk). Angel tube. **Open** *noon-6pm Wed-Sat; noon-4pm Sun; also by appointment.* **Credit** AmEx, MC, V.

Part gallery, part shop, part showroom, this rather sexy little space makes a refreshing break from the surrounding antiques stores. Interior designer Clare Gardner uses her displays – a chair and a daybed combined with a light fixture, say – to exhibit art and artisanal objects for various interior spaces, such as dressing room, bedroom, cocktail bar, lounge. Gardner offers a consulting service and has a large collection of handmade textiles, architectural glass, lighting, felt flooring, vases and tiles to choose from. The space embodies the mood of the moment in design, with a contemporary, eclectic feel. Gardner is a great supporter of emerging young designers.
Mail order.

Design Museum Shop

Shad Thames, SE1 2YD (7940 8753/ www.designmuseum.org). Tower Hill tube/ London Bridge tube/rail. **Open** *10am-5.45pm daily.* **Credit** AmEx, MC, V.

Although a trip to the Design Museum is going to be your primary reason for a visit to this riverside location, the accompanying shop reveals some wonders of its own. Small items prevail, such as the Vitra miniature chair range (around £100), vases from Rosenthal, Pigeon lights by Ed Carpenter (£55) and an array of functional design classics, current and future. Plenty of coffee-table books will keep the imagination ticking. *See also p203* **Museum shops.**
Mail order.

Ella Doran Design

46 Cheshire Street, E2 6EH (7613 0782/ www.elladoran.co.uk). Bethnal Green tube/ Liverpool Street tube/rail/Shoreditch rail. **Open** *10am-6pm Mon-Fri (by appointment only); noon-5pm Sat; 10am-5pm Sun.* **Credit** AmEx, MC, V.

These days, Cheshire Street is something of a hotspot for quirky interiors shops – Ella Doran has joined Labour & Wait (*see p120*) and Mar Co (*see p125*) with her first retail outlet. As it's part showroom, part studio, customers can speak directly to Ella about commissions and pick up rare and occasionally exclusive pieces, as well as her iconic place mats featuring striking photographic images (a kiwi fruit, artichokes, shells or a Tokyo street scene). Her home accessory collection includes blinds (made to measure only), cushions, tableware and stationery. Fast becoming a contemporary classic, her Meadow Melamine Picnic Ware range, inspired by the Eden Project, features a lush image of grasses and wild flowers; as well as beakers, plates and a tray (from £2.95), the range includes a limited-edition bag (£35). Doran's famous photo designs are available on handmade cushions, journals, purses and bags in limited editions.
Mail order.

Espadrille

32 Parsons Green Lane, SW6 4HS (7736 5454/ www.espadrille.co.uk). Parsons Green tube. **Open** *10am-6pm Mon-Sat.* **Credit** MC, V.

The story of Basque linen dates back to the 14th century, when it was used to make 'coats' for cows for protection from the sun and flies in south-west France. The seven stripes printed on to unbleached linen were used to identify the cows' origins and were later interpreted by linen factories into designs for household textiles. The attractive designs are sold here as aprons, napkins, table runners and oven gloves, as well as straight off the roll – minimum width is 150cm and prices start at £20/m. With vivid reds, shocking pinks, soft whites or fresh blues – there's a colour scheme to appeal to most tastes. Fabrics are suitable for upholstery, blinds and curtains.
Mail order.

Freud

198 Shaftesbury Avenue, WC2H 8JL (7831 1071/www.freudliving.com). Covent Garden or Leicester Square tube. **Open** *11am-7pm Mon-Fri; 11am-6pm Sat; noon-5pm Sun.* **Credit** MC, V.

Freud stocks a decent selection of own-brand products, aiming at a modern yet classic way of living, which are supplied to retailers across the world. The small, unassuming store above a basement bar of the same name plays host to a range of solid-wood picture frames (from £10.95 to £29.95), candle holders, china mugs (£7.50-£14.95), glassware, coffee makers and crockery. In addition, there is some furniture, plenty of vases and the iconic metal-grill Cinni fans (from £75 for a table model, or from £175 for a free-standing floor fan).
Mail order.

Graham & Green

4 & 10 Elgin Crescent, W11 2HX (7727 4594/ www.grahamandgreen.co.uk). Ladbroke Grove tube. **Open** *10am-6pm Mon-Sat; 11.30am-5.30pm Sun.* **Credit** AmEx, MC, V.

Home to a varied mix of furniture and accessories with a comforting yet trendy feel. Classic, simple garden furniture is displayed outside; inside you can peruse myriad unique delights in various cultural styles: silver lanterns, fabulous Venetian mirrors, Moroccan tea sets, silk kaftans in pastel hues, Indian semi-precious jewellery and Mongolian cushions and throws. There are also some excellent retro toys. Well worth a visit. *Mail order (0845 130 6622).*
For branches see index.

Indish
16 Broadway Parade, N8 9DE (8342 9496/ www.indish.co.uk). Finsbury Park tube/rail then W3, W7 bus. **Open** 10.30am-5.30pm Mon-Sat. **Credit** AmEx, MC, V.
A Crouch End favourite, Indish sells a nicely edited selection of new designs and more established creations from names such as Alessi, Guzzini, Magis and Kartell. Pick up some gorgeous stripy ceramic bowls by iittala (from £9), quirky accessories by Suck UK or a practical but stylish Dish Doctor drying rack by Marc Newson (£35), perfect for adding drying space to small kitchens. *Mail order.*

Maisonette
79 Chamberlayne Road, NW10 3ND (8964 8444/ www.maisonette.uk.com). Queen's Park tube/rail/ Kensal Rise rail. **Open** 11am-6pm Tue-Sat. **Credit** AmEx, MC, V.
A gem of a shop hidden away in Kensal Rise, selling both vintage and contemporary glass, ceramics, furniture and lighting alongside shaggy sheepskin rugs and the popular paint-it-yourself canvas kits; the latter contain canvas, paints and instructions to create stylish, large-format artworks (from £85). Other lifestyle items are sold, such as fragrances, CDs, books and Maisonette's own cotton voile bedlinen (double duvet cover, £168; oxford pillowcases, £50 per pair).

Nicole Farhi Home
17 Clifford Street, W1X 3RQ (7494 9051/ www.nicolefarhi.com). Green Park or Piccadilly Circus tube. **Open** 10am-6pm Mon-Wed, Fri, Sat; 10am-7pm Thur. **Credit** AmEx, DC, MC, V.
This small shop is adorned with an array of simple yet eminently luxurious ceramics, glass, tableware, candles and furniture, in the laid-back, natural hues that characterise the designer's clothing collections (*see p34*). One-off antiques, gathered from Farhi's travels around the world, are also here, as well as cushions covered in various materials, from handwoven fabrics to brightly dyed cowskin. It's the antithesis of mass-produced designer ranges – many pieces are sourced from small rural workshops. Prices are generally reasonable. *Mail order.*
For branch (202) see index.

Zara Home
79-83 Brompton Road, SW3 1DB (7590 6990/ www.zarahome.com). Knightsbridge tube. **Open** 10am-7pm Mon-Sat; noon-6pm Sun. **Credit** AmEx, DC, MC, V.
Applying Zara's affordable policy to interior fashions, the home section in the Knightsbridge branch offers everything from tableware to bedlinen and cushions in a range of vibrant colours and with a surprising attention to detail. Plates start at around £2.50 and place mats are £3 each. Bedlinen features plenty of deep, rich hues and stripes (a cotton double duvet cover starts from £19). Glassware, towels, candles and a children's home accessories range are also sold. *Mail order.*

Traditional

Blue Door Yard
74 Church Road, SW13 0DQ (8748 9785/ www.bluedoorbarnes.co.uk). Hammersmith tube then 33, 72, 209 bus/Barnes Bridge rail. **Open** 10am-5pm Mon-Sat. **Credit** AmEx, MC, V.
This charming shop, with a display of garden furniture in its attractive courtyard, specialises in furniture, fabrics and accessories in the light,

elegant Gustavian style. Everything exudes classic Swedish simplicity. As well as hand-painted furniture, there are pretty handmade fabric lampshades (£59-£115) and cushions (£16-£60) in fresh prints, chandeliers, mirrors and wonderful handpainted Swedish clocks (around £1,800 for antique; £1,600 for reproduction).

Cath Kidston
8 Clarendon Cross, W11 4AP (7221 4000/ www.cathkidston.co.uk). Holland Park tube. **Open** 10am-6pm Mon-Sat; noon-5pm Sun. **Credit** AmEx, MC, V.
Cath Kidston has developed a loyal, mainly female, following over recent years with her adorable polka dots, stripes and floral prints. Bedlinen, cushions, washbags, lamps and numerous other accessories are girlie and cute, with a 1950s vintage feel. *Mail order (7229 8000).*
For branches see index.

Grand Illusions
41 Crown Road, Twickenham, Middx TW1 3EJ (8607 9446/www.grandillusions.co.uk). St Margarets rail. **Open** 10am-5pm Mon, Sat; 10am-6pm Tue-Fri. **Credit** AmEx, MC, V.
Primarily a mail-order company, Grand Illusions also displays its rustic, artisan-made furniture in this showroom. Unusual and one-off pieces make

up the collection of French-inspired cupboards, tables and chairs. Accessories include iron candlesticks, baroque sconces and Valencian chandeliers. Paint for wood surfaces is also sold. *Mail order.*

Irish Linen Co
35-36 Burlington Arcade, W1J 0QB (7493 8949). Green Park or Piccadilly Circus tube. **Open** 9.30am-5.45pm Mon-Fri; 10am-4.30pm Sat. **Credit** AmEx, DC, MC, V.
This delectable little store in the venerable Burlington Arcade has been supplying the best in delicate, hand-embroidered Irish linen to discerning customers – including royalty – for years. Simple and traditional designs are to be found on handkerchiefs, napkins and bedlinen, with the odd floral motif here and a masculine naval stripe there. Prices may be a little high (from £15 for a guest towel, from £165 for a damask linen tablecloth), but the quality is higher and staff are knowledgeable and courteous. *Mail order.*

Joanna Wood
48A Pimlico Road, SW1W 8LP (7730 5064/ www.joannawood.co.uk). Sloane Square or Victoria tube. **Open** 10am-6pm Mon-Fri; 10am-4pm Sat. **Credit** MC, V.

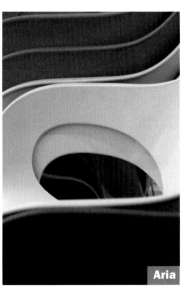

Aria

Conservative accessories, with a contemporary twist, can be found here for the 'well-dressed house'. Lighting, furniture, cushions, blankets and Limoges tableware are sold, as well as quirky gift items. The bright decorative watering cans are original and fun (if rather expensive at £88 upwards). The signature Joanna Wood slippers made from Lewis & Wood Chelsea check (£77.50) are sold here, as well as a collection of fabrics and wallpapers to order. *Mail order.*

Labour & Wait

18 Cheshire Street, E2 6EH (7729 6253/ www.labourandwait.co.uk). Liverpool Street tube/ rail. **Open** 10am-5pm Sat, Sun; by appointment Fri. **Credit** AmEx, MC, V.
This little street off Brick Lane comes alive at the weekend, with a line-up of interesting shops. Labour & Wait's collection of English goods for home and garden pulls off the trick of being both traditional and utterly contemporary. There is an emphasis on quality and functionality, and everything displays a simple, honest approach to design. Items include a white enamelled colander (£15) and ladle set (£32), ostrich feather dusters (£18) and dinky children's watering cans (£15). *Mail order.*

Nina Campbell

9 Walton Street, SW3 2JD (7225 1011/ www.ninacampbell.com). Knightsbridge or Sloane Square tube. **Open** 10am-6pm Mon-Sat. **Credit** AmEx, MC, V.
Nina Campbell has developed a reputation as one of London's leading interior designers. Her shop is a showcase for her sumptuous collection of fabrics and wallpapers for Osborne & Little (*see p173*), as well as rugs, tableware, lighting, furniture and accessories. The wares are pretty eclectic: there are hand-painted glass tulip bowls, fabric trays, tortoiseshell soap dishes, and a classic range of shoe bags and signature candles. Superb antiques and original pieces come and go. *Mail order.*

Tobias & the Angel

68 White Hart Lane, SW13 0PZ (8878 8902/ www.tobiasandtheangel.com). Hammersmith tube then 209 bus/Barnes Bridge rail. **Open** 10am-6pm Mon-Sat. **Credit** AmEx, MC, V.
This long-standing shop sells own-made and antique furniture, pottery and vintage textiles. Top-quality dusters, dish cloths and balls of string sit next to antique Staffordshire jugs and old wooden carving boards. The passion for good workmanship and design is evident in the range of furniture, Christmas decorations, soft furnishings and block-printed fabrics. *Mail order.*

Bedlinen

Austrian Bedding Company

205 Belsize Road, NW6 4AA (7372 3121). Kilburn Park tube. **Open** 10am-5.30pm Mon-Fri; 10am-5pm Sat. **Credit** MC, V.
For a fabulous selection of duvets of all fills and thicknesses, in both continental and UK sizes, this shop has it well covered. There is also high-quality European bedlinen, with sheets in seven sizes, plus a bespoke service on duvets, pillows and quilt covers. The friendly staff also offer a cleaning and re-covering service. *Mail order.*

Cabbages & Roses

3 Langton Street, SW10 0JL (7352 7333/ www.cabbagesandroses.com). Sloane Square tube then 22 bus. **Open** 9.30am-5.30pm Mon-Sat. **Credit** MC, V.
This well-presented shop displays a selection of rustic-chic home accessories, including beautiful cushions, towels, linen blinds, fabrics, duvets, tablecloths and wallpaper adorned with the signature Cabbages & Roses repeat flower design. Clothes are also sold, as well as candles and books. *Mail order.*
For branch see index.

Ella Doran Design. See p118.

Cologne & Cotton

39 Kensington Church Street, W8 4LL (7376 0324/www.cologneandcotton.com). High Street Kensington tube. **Open** 10am-7pm Mon-Sat; noon-5pm Sun. **Credit** AmEx, MC, V.
Cologne & Cotton aims to corner the market in pure cotton bedlinen and towels. Sheets are made from Egyptian cotton or linen and come in classic white, ivory, muted blues, pinks and purples. Pick some hard-wearing white cotton sheets for £19.95 or push the boat out with a hand-embroidered linen double duvet cover for £165. A good selection of blankets, bedspreads and quilts is available, as well as plenty of super-soft towels and his 'n' hers towelling robes. Luxurious toiletries add to the allure: scented candles from Diptyque, beautifully packaged products from Côté Bastide and fragrances from D'Orsay and Molinard. *Mail order.*
For branches see index.

Couverture

310 King's Road, SW3 5UH (7795 1200/ www.couverture.co.uk). Sloane Square tube. **Open** 10am-6pm Mon-Sat. **Credit** AmEx, MC, V.
Designer Emily Dyson's store is popular with local parents, drawn to the originality, humour and charm of the place. It sells everything from one-off designer pieces for the home and fashion for women to charming knitted toys. Dyson's soft lambswool throws (£495) and cushions (£75) may be expensive, but they are wonderfully homely and tactile. Children's knitwear, sold alongside traditional toys, tea sets and vintage pieces, completes the unique stock. *Mail order.*

Damask

10 Sullivan Enterprise Centre, Sullivan Road, SW6 3DJ (7731 3470/www.damask.co.uk). Parsons Green tube. **Open** 9.30am-5pm Mon-Fri. **Credit** AmEx, MC, V.
Founded by Carolyn Dunn in 1987, Damask has grown steadily, selling a selection of contemporary classics with a feminine feel, like bedlinen, quilts and nightwear. The range oozes comfortable and affluent country living, with light pastels, floral patterns and vintage-tinged satins creating an aura of familiarity and cosiness. Prices are high (£110 for a double duvet cover in the signature Naples Egyptian cotton Jacquard), but not necessarily unreasonable considering the use of natural materials and traditional handicraft. The Sweet Dreams range of children's nightwear and bedlinen includes pretty patchwork sleeping bags (also available in baby sizes). *Mail order.*

Descamps

197 Sloane Street, SW1X 9QX (7235 6957/ www.descamps.com). Knightsbridge tube. **Open** 10am-6.30pm Mon, Tue, Thur-Sat; 10am-7.30pm Wed; noon-6pm Sun. **Credit** AmEx, MC, V.
Since 1888 Descamps has led the way in the world of French linen, and has grown into a highly desirable global brand. Look past the snooty service and you will find bright and cheerful striped Allure bedlinen or the bold flower prints of the Diva range. Towels, quilts, loungewear, toiletries and a cute children's range complete the expensive picture. There is also a bespoke service for towels and bedlinen. *Mail order.*
For branch see index.

The Linen Mill

103 Wandsworth Bridge Road, SW6 2TE (7731 3262/www.thelinenmill.com). Fulham Broadway tube. **Open** 10am-6pm Mon-Sat. **Credit** AmEx, MC, V.
The high-quality pure linen bedding at the Linen Mill comes in a range of natural hues, including white, ivory and herringbone (double duvet covers start at £120), while pillows and duvets are stuffed with soft, Siberian grey-goose down, and underblankets are made of natural spun wool. Knitted linen throws (from £100) and cushions (from £20) are also stocked, as are sauna towels, table linen and tea towels. Linen can be bought by

HOME

the metre (from £7/m), and used for the company's line of clothing and curtain panels. A bespoke service is available, and leather beds are also sold. *Mail order.*

Peacock Blue
201 New King's Road, SW6 4SR (7384 3400/ www.peacockblue.co.uk). Parsons Green tube. **Open** 9am-6pm Mon-Fri; 10am-5pm Sat. **Credit** MC, V.
In an area in which linen shops abound, Peacock Blue stands out by placing an emphasis on check and gingham patterns across its range of simple, traditional bedlinen and delicate home accessories, such as bedspreads, quilts and lampshades. New England-style stripes and florals are also prevalent. Prices are reasonable – a 100% cotton woven gingham double duvet cover, available in a range of colours, costs just £45.
Mail order (0870 333 1555).

The White Company
12 Marylebone High Street, W1U 4NR (7935 7879/www.thewhitecompany.com). Baker Street or Bond Street tube. **Open** 9am-7pm Mon-Sat; 11am-5pm Sun. **Credit** MC, V.
As the name suggests, this store specialises in home accessories in the purest of colours. Why white? Founder Christian Rucker identified it as a gap in the market when he launched the company in 1993. Today, there are 11 branches, plus a significant mail-order division producing eight brochures every year. Its success comes down to its high-quality and highly covetable selection of bedlinen, towels, napkins, duvets, pillows, blankets, bathrobes, nightwear and bathroom accessories geared towards mid-range budgets.
Mail order (0870 900 9555).
For branches see index.

Candles

Gifts on the Green
50 New King's Road, SW6 4LS (7736 0740/ www.candlesontheweb.co.uk). Parsons Green tube. **Open** 10am-6pm Mon-Sat. **Credit** MC, V.
Formerly called the Candle Shop, this general card and gift shop still has a vast portfolio of candles in numerous colours and shapes. Should you be looking to bulk-buy, or can't find what you're looking for, talk to the staff, who really know their products. Handmade, beeswax, church, feng shui, scented, gel wax, aromatherapy candles… you name it, chances are it's here. There's an even bigger selection on the company's website.
Mail order.

Price's
100 York Road, SW11 3RD (7924 6336/ www.prices-candles.co.uk). Clapham Junction rail. **Open** 9.30am-5.30pm Mon-Sat; 11am-5pm Sun. **Credit** AmEx, MC, V.
If you're planning on getting in the supplies for an approaching bar mitzvah or wedding, this is the place to come. Set on a busy main road, Price's is more a factory outlet than a gift shop, and bulk buying is encouraged. Every type of candle is stocked, from church varieties (£1.10 for two) to anti-tobacco scented tea lights (£1.99 for six). There are some great deals (a pack of ten dinner candles for £3.15) and a wide range of candle holders, from simple to highly decorative designs.

Ceramics

Bodo Sperlein
Unit 105, Oxo Tower Wharf, Barge House Street, SE1 9PH (7633 9413/www.bodosperlein.com). Blackfriars tube/rail. **Open** 10am-6pm Mon-Fri; 1-5pm Sat, Sun. **Credit** AmEx, DC, MC, V.
A highlight of the Oxo Tower's hotbed of design and craft studios and shops, Bodo Sperlein creates smooth, sculptural ceramics. The delicately crafted items – including dishes, teapots, trays and vases – are mostly white with a stripe of colour here and a spattering of red berries there. Original, often organic shapes and understated motifs give the pieces a contemporary slant. We liked the 'dented' white carafe and beaker (£30 and £12 respectively)

and the curved Bilbao salt and pepper set in red or black berry (£25). There is also dramatic lighting, made to commission.
Mail order.

Lamps & lighting

Many shops in this chapter sell lighting; **Aria** (*see p118*) and **Bodo Sperlein** (*see above*) feature striking modern designs. For specialist lighting shops, *see chapter* **Interiors**; for vintage lamps and lights, *see chapter* **20th-century Design**.

Gallop Workshop
198 Deptford High Street, SE8 3PR (8694 8601/www.gallop.co.uk). Deptford rail. **Open** by appointment Mon-Fri. **No credit cards.**
Husband-and-wife design duo Harry Richardson and Clare Page produce their fabulous Kebab floor lamps in this studio/gallery in Deptford. Each is a one-off – a tall, totem pole-like base composed of found objects and antique crockery (toy cars, teapots, figurines, a travel iron), topped with a trad shade. These cutting-edge, unique designs don't come cheap – prices start at £2,500.

Mathmos
22-24 Old Street, EC1V 9AP (7549 2700/www.mathmos.com). Barbican tube or Old Street tube/rail. **Open** 9.30am-6pm Mon-Sat. **Credit** MC, V.
Mathmos is the manufacturer of the original lava lamp. The retail shop is below head office, so staff are well placed to give you advice and information about the 30 or so designs available. Among them is the Space Projector light (£68), which casts psychedelic patterns on the wall, or the clever, sensor-controlled Airswitch tc (£48): to change the intensity of the light, all you need to do is move your hand through the air above the switch.
Mail order.
For branch see index.

Mail order & internet

Completely Modern
7240 4260/www.completelymodern.com. **Credit** AmEx, MC, V.
This website has a huge offering of accessories for the home, office and garden, steering towards the contemporary end of the market, as its name suggests. Expect plenty of big, respected brands such as Dyson vacuum cleaners, Guzzini kitchen products, Magimix food processors and iittala tableware. In the lower price range, you can pick up beautiful sky-blue Kivi tea-light holders for £8, Sombrero buffet dishes (from £29.99) or a cheese-knife set for £29.99.

Dibor
0870 013 3666/www.dibor.co.uk. **Credit** MC, V.
This online business sells 'beautiful things for the home – direct'. By which it means traditional, high-quality (and accordingly pricey) furniture, and plenty of smaller and more accessible products for the kitchen, bathroom, bedroom and garden. The Wild Rabbit clock (£34.95) and the wicker furniture would suit a country home.

Dutch by Design
0870 744 6478/www.dutchbydesign.com. **Credit** MC, V.
The Dutch are internationally recognised for their design prowess through an ability to merge beauty and timelessness with a sense of humour and irony. Brands Moooi and Droog excel in this field, with such pieces as the epoxy-finished burnt Smoke chandelier (£485) by Maarten Baas, Tejo Remy's chandelier made from recycled milk bottles (£575) and the Egg Vase (£99) by Marcel Wanders – made by stuffing a condom with eggs, then casting its form in ceramic. The website is great.

DWCD
8964 2002/www.dwcd.co.uk. **Credit** MC, V.
Themes like 'cosy home', 'tea time' and 'gorgeous' feature heavily on this home accessories website, where products are apparently 'made with love'.

Hearts, flowers and all things sweet and feminine, such as scented sachets, vintage canvas doorstops and the dog-shaped Buster (a 'suede-feel cuddler'), take centre stage. The product selection does, however, sometimes seem a little random.

Ede & Nia
7602 8229/www.edeandnia.co.uk. **Credit** MC, V.
Products – be it a merino wool and cashmere throw, embroidered silk cushions, a leather wallet or a cashmere handbag – are selected to add 'a little luxury to everyday life'. Prices at Ede & Nia vary massively to suit most budgets – you could spend a tenner on some hand-painted tea lights, £34 on a ribbed cotton tablecloth, or splash out £80 on a leather-bound personal organiser. A stunning raspberry-coloured felted wool throw with red suede fringe costs a respectable £124.

Found
0870 166 8131/www.foundat.co.uk. **Credit** MC, V.
Found specialises in home accessories, gifts and old-fashioned toys, made according to traditional techniques, with an emphasis on natural, organic materials where appropriate. Check out the Regency candlesticks, hand-blown glassware and wooden nativity scenes with knitted animals.

The Holding Company
8445 2888/www.theholdingcompany.co.uk. **Credit** MC, V.
Effective storage is the key to an uncluttered existence, especially if you are the sort of person who can't bring themselves to throw anything away. Clear Perspex boxes for shoes and shirts don't appear intrusive in your bedroom, while tall video and CD towers deal with your vast collections. The stacking recycling bins for the kitchen are particularly clever (£23.95 each).

Iggloo
0845 257 1659/www.iggloo.co.uk. **Credit** MC, V.
This website is bright, cheerful and very easy to navigate, with sections for lighting, furniture, accessories, kitchen, bath, tableware, 'kitsch' and so on. Both contemporary and retro pieces are sold, many at prices lower than the manufacturers' recommended retail price. The Flowerpot pendant light by Verner Panton is £105 instead of £110, a retro bird-print cushion £55 instead of £70.

Manufactum
0800 096 0937/www.manufactum.co.uk. **Credit** MC, V.
This range of practical, stylish goods is pricey, but items are of a high quality, traditionally crafted from durable materials. The sturdy cookware, furniture, innovative camping gear and garden utensils should last long enough to pass on to your progeny. A range of toys that includes table football, wooden puzzle kits, steel kazoos, and a crossbow and rubber arrows will keep them busy.

Melin Tregwynt
01348 891 644/www.melintregwynt.co.uk. **Credit** MC, V.
Traditional methods are used to make the cosy accessories sold by this family-owned Welsh firm. A pure new wool plaid blanket, available in pinks, reds, grey and blues (£80-£200), is perfect for a winter. There is an increasing number of contemporary designs, featuring bold stripes, funky colours and retro patterns. Prices for throws start at £108; a cushion with multicoloured spots costs £31.50. Classic slippers come in various colours, and hot-water bottle covers (£35) and cute teddies (£19) make for perfect presents.

Mulberry Hall
01904 620 736/www.mulberryhall.co.uk. **Credit** AmEx, DC, MC, V.
A superb website selling tableware from the leading brands on the market: think Alessi, Royal Doulton, Eva Solo, Royal Worcester, Georg Jensen, Baccarat, Salviati, Wedgwood and so on. Cutlery, porcelain, delicate little figurines and bold contemporary statements are all available. You could spend hours browsing this site – and you won't knock over a thing.

HOME

The Natural Collection

0870 331 3333/www.naturalcollection.com.
Credit MC, V.
At last, a business that is wholeheartedly supporting a move to environmentally friendly products, sustainability and responsible use of products. There's a solar-powered garden light (£29.95), a recycled glass set (£29.75 for six) and a kilim cushion cover that supports traditional village crafts in India (£15.95).

Plümo

0870 241 3590/www.plumo.com. **Credit** MC, V.
Colourful, decorated accessories aimed at the thirtysomething female market. Small items for 'living' are offered alongside clothes, shoes, bags, jewellery and even festive decorations. It's a good site for gifts – pick up a set of six charming Grandma cups and saucers for £59, or some Moroccan tea-light holders for £7.95 each. Other items include Japanese bowls and lamps, Venetian wine goblets and silk cushions.

RE

01434 634 567/www.re-foundobjects.com.
Credit MC, V.
Ever wished your house looked like it belonged to a seasoned traveller? Now you can get the look and save the airfare with a selection of items from former fashion designers Simon Young and Jenny Vaughan's mail-order business. They identify fashionable, functional homeware – all of it globally sourced and much of it recycled or made by locals. The silk Memento cushions (from £35), glass cakestands (from £28) and stunning striped French deckchairs (£60) all caught our eye.

Traidcraft

0870 443 1018/www.traidcraftshop.co.uk.
Credit MC, V.
Everything sold on this online site is fairly traded, and details of the suppliers are provided. There's an Indian double duvet cover for £40, or a Log Cabin cotton patchwork throw for £75. Cheaper gift ideas include orange- and ginger-scented candles for £10, or four blue Bolivian glasses for only £8. Other items include kitchen accessories, stationery, tea, coffee, wine, chocolate and snacks.

Whites of London

0800 915 9445/www.whitesoflondon.co.uk.
Credit MC, V.
Whites of London sells a comprehensive, traditional range of bedlinen, duvets, pillows, towels, bedspreads and bathrobes, as well as photo frames, mirrors, paintings and laundry baskets.

Mirrors & frames

Creative Picture Framing

81 Baker Street, W1U 6RQ (7935 7794/ www.creativepictureframing.co.uk). Baker Street tube. **Open** 9.30am-6pm Mon-Fri; 10am-5pm Sat. **Credit** AmEx, MC, V.
Once part of the Frame Express chain, this shop is now a successful independent. In addition to its excellent bespoke service, there's a 2,000-strong collection of prints, plus a few ready-made frames.

Fix-a-Frame

280 Old Brompton Road, SW5 9HR (7370 4189). Earl's Court tube. **Open** 10am-6.30pm Tue-Sat. **Credit** MC, V.
This well-established framer offers a bespoke service, with both contemporary and traditional tastes catered for. A range of services, from canvas stretching to restoration, is offered too. Fix-a-Frame also sells a do-it-yourself framing pack.

Frame

137 Portobello Road, W11 2DY (7792 1272). Notting Hill Gate tube. **Open** 10am-6pm Mon-Sat. **Credit** MC, V.
An upmarket, contemporary framing shop specialising in a full bespoke service. Conservation framing and canvas stretching are available too. It also sells a selection of striking, individually printed Cuban film posters (£39.99). Popular this

year are canvas-printed A-Z maps centred on a postcode of your choice, which make good gifts for London friends. Staff are very friendly.

Frame Emporium

123-129 Pancras Road, NW1 1UN (7387 6039). King's Cross tube/rail. **Open** 9.30am-6pm Mon-Fri; 9.30am-5.30pm Sat. **Credit** AmEx, MC, V.
Situated behind a massive building site in King's Cross, the Frame Emporium is popular with artists and galleries. It's home to a huge collection of frames and specialises in framing large artworks, but staff will happily cater for all sizes. The shop offers an ever-popular series of impressive screen prints of film and sporting legends: Paul Newman, Muhammad Ali, Michael Caine and the like (from £95). Or you can opt for a family picture to be converted to a screen print. The company also holds a large range of repro Regency, Victorian and contemporary mirrors. Well worth a look.
For branch see index.

Frame Factory

20 Cross Street, N1 2BG (7226 6266). Angel tube. **Open** 9.30am-5.30pm Mon-Fri; 10am-5.30pm Sat. **Credit** MC, V.
Occupying an arty atmospheric warehouse space, Frame Factory offers a bespoke service with finishing expertise. The friendly staff will take on work at short notice, and the service is popular with local businesses. An impressive collection of art posters from the likes of Warhol, O'Keefe and Kandinsky is for sale, along with vintage posters, photographic prints and other frame fillers.

Frame, Set & Match

113 Notting Hill Gate, W11 3LB (7229 7444/ www.framesetandmatch.com). Notting Hill Gate tube. **Open** 9.15am-6pm Mon-Wed, Fri, Sat; 9.15am-7.30pm Thur. **Credit** MC, V.
This laid-back shop has an extensive choice of frames, in both hand-finished natural woods and contemporary metal styles. Staff can offer Denglass, UV filters and reflection control. The selection of framed prints includes impressive black-and-white London panoramas, cartoon prints and 18th-century antique prints. Other services include repairing scratched glass, dry-mounting, oil-painting restoration and box-framing football shirts.
For branch see index.

House of Mirrors

597 King's Road, SW6 2EL (7736 5885/ www.houseofmirrors.co.uk). Fulham Broadway tube. **Open** 10am-6pm Mon-Fri; 10am-4pm Sat. **No credit cards.**
As well as the superior collection of 19th-century English antique mirrors here, you'll also find a selection of exquisite gilded furniture and Edwardian giltwood chandeliers. Mirrors range from elegantly simple designs to the flamboyantly rococo, scaling grand proportions. A mirror restoration service is also available.

London Picture Centre

287-289 Hackney Road, E2 8NA (7739 6624). Liverpool Street tube/rail then 26, 48 bus. **Open** 7am-5pm Mon-Fri; 8am-4pm Sat; 10am-2pm Sun. **Credit** MC, V.
A reliable local store, popular for its reasonably priced bespoke framing service. Oil paintings, mirrors and repro posters are also sold.
For branches see index.

Overmantels

66 Battersea Bridge Road, SW11 3AG (7223 8151/www.overmantels.co.uk). Bus 45A, 49, 319. **Open** 9.30am-5.30pm Mon-Sat. **Credit** MC, V.
Overmantels is at the top of its trade, housing one of London's largest collections of mirrors. Antique and period reproduction pieces are the forte. Mirrors start at £425 and go into thousands of pounds. The Irish oval mirrors, with black ebonised frames and cut-glass beads (£1,100), are gorgeous. There's an in-house team of experts, so expect contemporary designs and high-quality finishes, including rusted aluminium and wood. Bespoke work is undertaken.

Art framers

Alec Drew

5-7 Cale Street, SW3 3QT (7352 8716/ www.alec-drew.co.uk). Sloane Square tube. **Open** 9am-6pm Mon-Fri; 9.30am-1.30pm Sat. **Credit** AmEx, DC, MC, V.
This local Chelsea favourite offers a wide choice of frames, ranging from aluminium and plain wood finishes to a selection of hand-made, gessoed and gilded mouldings in traditional and modern finishes. A variety of mount-boards and museum-quality, non-reflective and UV reflective glass is also available, as well as mouldings for mirrors made to size.

Art & Soul

Unit G14, Belgravia Workshops, 157 Marlborough Road, N19 4NF (7263 0421/www.artandsoul frames.com). Archway tube. **Open** 9am-5pm Tue-Fri; by appointment Sat. **No credit cards.**
A workshop-based shop, Art & Soul offers a framing service to designers, photographers and artists, as well as the general public. Care is taken when framing by using conservation techniques. Window mounts or box frames are available. Mouldings come in various styles, including silver, gilt, matt and lacquer; plain woods can be stained, waxed or limed. Ready-made frames start at £4.

Darbyshire Framemakers

19-23 White Lion Street, N1 9PW (7812 1200/ www.darbyshire.co.uk). Angel tube. **Open** 9am-5.30pm Mon-Fri. **Credit** MC, V.
This prestigious firm has a host of high-profile, Brit Art clients, including Damien Hirst, Tracey Emin and Sam Taylor-Wood. It has collaborated in numerous framing projects over the past decade with galleries such as White Cube, Saatchi's County Hall and the Royal Academy – which bodes well for the framing service. Bespoke furniture for specific spaces is also made, with a minimalist and contemporary slant. Appointments are advised.

Framework

5-9 Creekside, SE8 4SA (8691 5140/www.frame workgallery.co.uk). Deptford rail. **Open** 9.30am-6pm Mon-Fri; 9.30am-1pm Sat. **Credit** MC, V.
This Deptford framer, popular with local artists, doubles as a contemporary art gallery. A bespoke service is available, and prices are good for the quality. There's a huge range of mouldings, as well as conservation framing, mount-cutting and an assortment of fittings. Startlingly original mirrors are on display, including the Eclectica range of overmantel mirrors with traditional, swept and contemporary frames. Other services include mirror cutting and tapestry stretching. Posters and prints are also sold.
Mail order.

John Jones Art Centre

2 Morris Place, off Stroud Green Road, N4 3JG (7281 5439/www.johnjones.co.uk). Finsbury Park tube/rail. **Open** 9.30am-6pm Mon-Fri; 10am-5pm Sat. **Credit** MC, V.
Consisting of four warehouses, the Centre offers an array of framing services, plus a well-stocked art materials shop. Various materials can be used for bespoke framing, including timber, welded metal and Perspex boxes. Conservation work is a forte. There's also a fine art photographic service.
Mail order.

Special Photographers Company

236 Westbourne Park Road, W11 1EL (7221 3489/www.specialphotographers.com). Ladbroke Grove tube. **Open** 10am-5.30pm Mon-Fri; 11am-5.30pm Sat. **Credit** AmEx, MC, V.
This trendy framer's and gallery space has a host of exciting exhibitions, mixed shows and classic prints. Black and white celebrity portraits are a speciality, with exclusive prints of icons like Hendrix, Marley and Bowie (from £400). There's an impressive Jazz Legends series, with portraits of giants such as Count Basie and Charlie Parker. Sets of 'elitist' art books are also sold.
Mail order.

Posters & prints

Artcadia Lifestyle
108 Commercial Street, E1 6LZ (7426 0733/ www.artcadia.co.uk). Liverpool Street tube/rail. **Open** 10am-6pm Mon-Fri; 11am-4pm Sat; 10am-6pm Sun. **Credit** AmEx, MC, V.
Artcadia is a digital-design studio and gallery. The in-house team of designers and production staff create, print and mount vibrant, trendy and psychedelic images on to virtually any material. It's all very bright and abstract; prints are filled with stripes, geometrics and other mind-whirling patterns. The designers operate a bespoke service and will print canvases of any size (from £35). *Mail order.*

Cine Art Gallery
759 Fulham Road, SW6 5UU (7384 0728/ www.cineartgallery.com). Parsons Green tube. **Open** 11am-6.30pm Mon-Fri; 11am-6pm Sat. **Credit** AmEx, MC, V.
A leading light in the world of cinema art, this shop holds a wide choice of film posters and lobby cards, from classic Hollywood to recent blockbusters. Bond films are a speciality; an original British *Dr No* costs £4,500, and there are posters of the silent era, Hammer Horror and classic foreign films (*La Dolce Vita* for £1,650). Prices start at around £10 for a *Spiderman* poster, and reach a staggering £10,000 for a 1920s poster of *Dr Jekyll and Mr Hyde*. Staff are down-to-earth, welcoming collectors and novices alike. *Mail order.*

55max
105 Boundary Road, NW8 8RG (7625 3774/ www.55max.com). St John's Wood tube. **Open** 10am-6pm Mon-Fri; 11am-6pm Sat. **Credit** MC, V.
The premise of 55max is to sell the works of photographers from the worlds of fashion, journalism and design to the public at fair prices, with a 20in x 16in framed photograph costing a maximum of £55 (hence the name). Clients include Jack Nicholson, Elton John and Michael Caine. Bestselling prints from contemporary snappers include *Trannies in Laundrette* by Jeanette Jones, Toby Green's shots of the London Eye, and striking reportage prints by Fiona Campbell (from £25). A bespoke service is offered: particularly popular is the personal photo montage (from £40), and staff will also print your own snaps on to blinds, wallpaper, tiles and canvas. As we went to press, 55max had plans to relocate in February 2006; consult the website for further details. *Mail order.*

Flashbacks
6 Silver Place, W1F 0JS (7437 8562/ www.dacre.org). Piccadilly Circus tube. **Open** 10.30am-7pm Mon-Sat. **Credit** AmEx, MC, V.
This tiny, idiosyncratic closet of a shop is a delight for anyone with an interest in film. Boxes of files are piled high throughout. There's plenty to please both collectors and movie-goers; one standout is an Italian Marx Brothers festival poster priced at £25. Postcards cost 50p; black and white star portraits are £2.50. Prices depend on the rare and collectable nature of the pieces. *Mail order.*

The Reel Poster Gallery
72 Westbourne Grove, W2 5SH (7727 4488/ www.reelposter.com). Bayswater or Queensway tube. **Open** 11am-7pm Mon-Fri; noon-6pm Sat. **Credit** AmEx, MC, V.
This roomy, airy gallery space holds a great display of original vintage film posters, as well as an extensive collection on file. There's an emphasis on classics, European and art films, with attention paid to the designer of the posters. Among the eye-catching originals are the renowned *The Man With the Golden Arm*, designed by Saul Bass (£2,800); a fantastic Italian edition of *Sweet Smell of Success* (£1,800); and *Twelve Angry Men* (£750). Very few items fall under £250, but a rare poster for *Being John Malkovich* – rare because it is an alternative design not widely used – costs £150. *Mail order.*

Visions on china

Until recently, the only people with matching dishes and plates were married couples. Cool urbanites shunned the dinner service, preferring to express their identity through casual crockery that could be disposed of whenever interiors took some fashionable new turn. But now the cunning involvement of big-name fashion designers in traditional companies, such as Wedgwood and Royal Albert, is making new converts to the art of the table.

Jasper Conran's Colours range has added ultra-modern shades (tangerine, mint, chartreuse) to **Wedgwood** cups and plates, while his Chinoiserie collection is an irresistible millennial reinterpretation of 18th-century Chinese ornamental design (£30; *pictured right*). Fashion designer Zandra Rhodes has captured the ubiquitous boho motif – the butterfly – and painted it on a **Royal Albert** tea set (which includes a butterfly-shaped cake plate) in vivid pinks and purples. Better known for frock designs – bold prints and fab florals – **Cacharel** has produced a covetable paisley-patterned dinner service as part of its Seven Seas homeware range. But all this seems positively muted compared to **Missoni**'s Margherita bone china, which is a tropical cocktail of pink, lime, orange, blue, cerise and lemon. More striking still is Missoni's wonderfully dramatic monochrome Bianconero (£14; *pictured right*).

Thanks to a renaissance of the 'high tea', smart eateries such as the Ritz, the Wolseley and Sketch are also bringing out their best china; at the Berkeley, for instance, tea is served on **Paul Smith**'s signature Stripes tableware (designed exclusively for Mayfair's Thomas Goode & Co, *see p124*). A good budget option is **Maxwell & Williams**'s (www.maxwellandwilliams.co.uk) distinctly retro Rose Bud cup, saucer and plate sets from its bone china Chintz range, costing a mere £15 each.

Ironically, just as British potteries are embracing the avant-garde, a parallel trend for 'vintage' designs is also blossoming, to the extent that those same manufacturers are encouraging customers to mix 'n' match designs – Conran's Chinoiserie with his other ranges, say – to create an individual flea-market look.

For fabulous one-offs, check out the work of young designers Hannah Dipper and Robin Farquhar at **People Will Always Need Plates** (www.peoplewillalways needplates.co.uk); their unusual plates have established something of a cult following. We particularly like the graphic images of 1930s Modernist London Homes; the Me Old China range features beautiful two- and three-tier cake stands made from the sort of dinner service odds and ends usually found in charity shops. People Will Always Need Plates products are available through trendy style outlets **Vessel** (*see p137*) and **SCP** (*see p150*), but can also be ordered from the website.

To get an idea of what's hot, tour the new Fine Dining area in the basement at **Selfridges** (*see p14*), which is completely dedicated to glamorous tableware. You'll find collections by Missoni, Wedgwood, Royal Albert, Cacharel and Kenzo, among others. You'll also find the quirkier work of **Polly George**, who embellishes white china with sculptures of roses or butterflies – look out for her cake stand, a witty tower of two cups and saucers. At the hushed emporium of **Thomas Goode & Co** (*see p124*), you'll find an unrivalled collection of names and designs of fine china and porcelain – fear not, friendly staff are just as helpful to non-millionaires. The **General Trading Company** (2 Symons Street, SW3 2TJ, 7730 0411, www.general-trading.co.uk) also stocks a super-chic selection of china, and **Heal's** (*see p147*) sells practical ranges that won't break the bank (including **Maxwell & Williams** and the **Tabletop Company**).

HOME

Tate Britain Shop

Tate Britain, Millbank, SW1P 4RG (7887 8876/ www.tate.org.uk). Pimlico tube. **Open** 10am-17.40pm daily. **Credit** AmEx, MC, V.
Fantastic for browsers, the Tate's shop contains an unrivalled collection of art books, as well as art-house DVDs, stationery, magazines and postcards. The wide range of stock is supplemented by products that complement current exhibitions. Posters reflect the works held by the Tate, with repros from all the big names in modern and British art, including Picasso, Dali, Chagall and Patrick Heron, plus more recent prints from photographers such as Martin Parr. Posters start at £7, but can hit triple figures.
Mail order (7887 8869).

Vertigo

22 Wellington Street, WC2E 7DD (7836 9252/ www.vertigogalleries.com). Covent Garden tube/ Charing Cross tube/rail. **Open** 10am-6pm Mon-Thur; 10am-7pm Fri, Sat. **Credit** AmEx, MC, V.
Swanky Vertigo is one of the leading dealers in original vintage movie posters and lobby cards. All the classic posters are here, including vintage prints like a scarce 50th-anniversary *Casablanca* poster (£395), and a large collection from the Bond movies, *Carry On* films and *Star Wars* episodes. Recent releases are generally lower in price, with a series of *Bridget Jones* lobby cards costing £40. The shop now offers a range of autographs from stars such as Audrey Hepburn (£1,350), Stanley Kubrick and Johnny Depp.
Mail order.

Vintage Magazine Store

39-43 Brewer Street, W1F 9UD (7439 8525/ www.vinmag.com). Piccadilly Circus tube. **Open** 10am-8pm Mon-Thur; 10am-10pm Fri, Sat; noon-8pm Sun. **Credit** MC, V.
Although it's the vintage magazines for which this Soho institution is renowned, all manner of memorabilia from popular culture can be found, from Che Guevara ashtrays to a quirky range of retro robots based on 1940s and '50s designs. As well as some original movie posters, there is a huge range of reproductions, mostly priced at £8.99 (including an Italian version of *The Hustler*). The vintage magazine stock covers a broad spectrum of 20th-century life, from pre-war issues of *Vogue* to 1960s issues of *Playboy* and a Mod special edition of *Melody Maker*. It all makes for superb browsing territory.
Mail order.

Tableware

Nigella Lawson's **Living Kitchen** range (01789 400 077, www.blisshome.co.uk) has a classic, 1950s feel to it, with duck-egg blue measuring cups, cream-coloured bread bins and glass storage jars; her products are also available from the **Royal Doulton** website (www.royaldoulton.com). Jamie Oliver's **Easy Entertaining** line of Royal Worcester tableware (01905 746 000, www.royalworcester. com) is a bit like the man himself: simple and unpretentious. The look is plain, white and chunky, and it's available from **John Lewis**. In fact, china is so fashionable that even fashion designers are getting in on the act (*see p123* **Visions on china**).

The **Delia Collection**, available from her website (www.deliasmith.co.uk), comprises her recommended kitchenware and appliances, ranging from Panasonic bread bakers and SKK pans to Gaggia ice-cream makers. And **Antony Worrall Thompson** has teamed up with Breville (0800 525 089, www.breville.co.uk) to make a series of stylish appliances, such as juicers, blenders and healthy grills.

For beautiful pieces of classic tableware, try the 'Cutlery King', **David Mellor** (4 Sloane Square, SW1W 8EE, 7730 4259, www.david mellordesign.co.uk), or the **Gill Wing Cook Shop** (190 Upper Street, N1 1RQ, 7226 5392).

Style aficionados should head to **Oggetti** (135 Fulham Road, SW3 6RT, 7581 8088) for its selection of sleek modernist classics. Shrines to modern design include **Aria** (*see p118*), **Estilo Kitchen Shop** (87 High Street, SW19 5EG, 8944 6868), the **Kitchenware Co** (36 Hill Street, Richmond, Surrey TW9 1TW, 8332 3030) and **Bodum** (*see p118*). For a complete change of pace, **Summerill & Bishop** (100 Portland Road, W11 4LN, 7221 4566) sells tableware with a rustic Provençal look. **Richard Dare** (93 Regent's Park Road, NW1 8UR, 7722 9428) – a favourite of Moro restaurant's Sam Clark – has chic international crockery and cookware.

Local shops such as the **Cookery Nook** (32 Montpelier Vale, SE3 0TA, 8297 2422), **La Cuisinière** (81-83 & 91 Northcote Road, SW11 6PJ, 7223 4409, www.la-cuisiniere.co.uk), **Kitchen Ideas** (70 Westbourne Grove, W2 5SH, 7229 3388), **Kooks Unlimited** (2-4 Eton Street, Richmond, Surrey TW9 1EE, 8332 3030), **Rhode Design** (137-139 Essex Road, N1 2NR, 7354 9933, www.rhodedesign.co.uk) and the **Scullery** (123 Muswell Hill Broadway, N10 3RS, 8444 5236) all offer top-quality goods. For classic cutlery, try **Sheffield Metal Company** (5 Cavendish Place, W1G 0QA, 7637 9888).

For more on kitchens, *see also chapter* **Bathrooms & Kitchens**.

Ceramica Blue

10 Blenheim Crescent, W11 1NN (7727 0288/ www.ceramicablue.co.uk). Ladbroke Grove or Notting Hill Gate tube. **Open** 11am-5pm Mon; 10am-6.30pm Tue-Sat. **Credit** MC, V.
This strikingly colourful store, just off Portobello Road, stocks a truly eclectic collection of ceramics. The ceramics, textiles and glass hail from around the world, and many of the pieces are hand-finished. Simple but arresting glass tableware is a popular line; it comes in an array of vibrant colours (dinner plate, £14). Another highlight is a delicate cup with petal saucer (£13). Staff are friendly.
Mail order.

Emma Bridgewater

739 Fulham Road, SW6 5UL (7371 5264/ www.bridgewaterpottery.co.uk). Parsons Green tube. **Open** 10am-6pm Mon-Sat; 11am-4pm Sun. **Credit** AmEx, MC, V.
Emma's designs are all apple-pie sweetness and sentimentalism, but her shop is good for gifts (there are lots of Thank You Teacher and Grandma-type mugs at around £15). The quality of the materials is high, with products made using traditional methods. The plethora of flowers, hearts and cats might make you slightly queasy – and the children's Ducklings are Fluffy range should certainly be avoided by the weak of stomach – but humorous numbers, like an I Love You More Than Elvis mug (£19.95), create a balance, and there are also classic designs including creamware and polka dots.
Mail order (7371 5489).
For branch see index.

Reject China Shop

183 Brompton Road, SW3 1NU (7581 0739/ www.tableware.uk.com). Knightsbridge tube. **Open** 9am-6pm Mon, Tue, Thur-Sat; 9am-7pm Wed; noon-6pm Sun. **Credit** AmEx, DC, MC, V.
Chintzy is the operative word in this shop, which is chock-full of crockery sporting the Queen's head, and figurines aplenty. What lures customers in from all over the world (it's one stop down the road from Harrods) is the marked-down seconds of high-quality brand tableware from names like Royal Worcester, Wedgwood and Royal Doulton. There are also some original, if not cutting-edge, comic art ornaments by Guillermo Forchino – characters on motorcycles, golf carts and taxis (£60-£750).
Mail order.

Reject Pot Shop

56 Chalk Farm Road, NW1 8AN (7485 2326). Chalk Farm tube. **Open** 11am-5.30pm Tue-Sun. **Credit** AmEx, MC, V.
A local shop selling classic basics for the kitchen, at low prices because they are mostly factory seconds or end-of-line products. There's a mass of stock with lots of white porcelain mugs and crockery from names like Royal Stafford and Churchill. Among the kitchen essentials are a line of fairly priced terracotta cookware, venetian blinds, Bodum cafetières and various utensils.

Thomas Goode & Co

19 South Audley Street, W1K 2BN (7499 2823/ www.thomasgoode.co.uk). Bond Street or Green Park tube. **Open** 10am-6pm Mon-Sat. **Credit** AmEx, DC, MC, V.
A colossal store that plays host to all the big names in tableware, including Wedgwood, Royal Worcester and Royal Copenhagen, as well as Thomas Goode's own designs. If a Leures-style jewelled blue ground porcelain tea set (original filled case, circa 1880) with a kitsch design is your thing – and within your budget, at a cool £32,000 – you'll love Goode's. More understated items include contemporary tableware lines from Bodo Sperlein and Paul Smith (dinner plate, £48). You'll also find porcelain vases, Lalique crystal, Georg Jensen cutlery and hand-embroidered Irish linen by Gayle Warwick. Bespoke work is undertaken.
Mail order.

Villeroy & Boch Factory Shop

267 Merton Road, SW18 5JS (8875 6006). Southfields tube. **Open** 10am-6pm Mon-Sat; 11am-5pm Sun. **Credit** AmEx, MC, V.
If you don't mind the trek to suburban Southfields – and people do travel here from abroad – then the discontinued lines make this place worth a visit. The tableware gets here six to 18 months after reaching Harrods, but discounts range from 25% to 90%. Among the discontinued patterns, you can find Foglia tableware (30% off) and the classic-white modern patterns of the City Life collection. There's also a line of top-quality glassware from Luigi Bormioli (four flutes for £13.95), plus napkins and trays. Staff are informed and helpful.

Repair/replacement

China Repairers

The Old Coach House, King Street Mews, off King Street, N2 8DY (8444 3030). East Finchley tube. **Open** 10am-4pm Mon-Thur.
No credit cards.
Specialist repairers of broken glassware, porcelain and pottery – antique and modern.

Tablewhere

4 Queen's Parade Close, N11 3FY (8361 6111/ www.tablewhere.co.uk). Bounds Green tube then 221 bus. **Open** 9am-5.30pm Mon-Fri; 9.30am-4pm Sat. **Credit** AmEx, MC, V.
Tablewhere specialises in finding that elusive tea cup or dinner plate lost or smashed from your favourite set. Its London warehouse holds over a million pieces, but if what you're looking for isn't there, the team of specialists will happily search elsewhere. Regularly requested patterns include designs from Wedgwood and Royal Doulton. No fee is charged for placing a requirement. The firm is keen to buy discontinued tableware and will offer valuations for your china.
Mail order.

Wilkinson

1 Grafton Street, W1S 4EA (7495 2477/ repairs 8314 1080/www.wilkinson-plc.com). Green Park tube. **Open** 9.30am-5pm Mon-Fri.
No credit cards.
If you've damaged chandeliers or glass, come to Wilkinson's. The restoration and glass-repair business can restore chandeliers and light fittings of all shapes, from Georgian to continental styles. The firm manufactures its own metal frames and components for crystal chandeliers and has millions of replacement drops and buttons.
For branch see index.

Global style

Chloe Alberry

84 Portobello Road, W11 2QD (7727 0707).
Notting Hill Gate tube. **Open** 9am-6pm Mon-Sat;
11am-6pm Sun. **Credit** MC, V.
This fantastic store is packed full of diverse and
distinctive treasures from around the globe. Pieces
range from 18th-century Manchurian to 1930s art
deco designs, including Edwardian Mackintosh
tiles from 1910 (£18 each), 1930s Kioto tiles (£15-
£24) and a selection of rare kitchen enamelware
from the 1920s and '30s. There's also a huge
collection of doorknobs (including pieces in crystal
and bone), mirrors of all sizes, Buddhas, old bells
and much more. Staff are friendly and helpful.
Mail order.

Ganesha

3-4 Gabriel's Wharf, 56 Upper Ground, SE1 9PP
(7928 3444/www.ganesha.co.uk). Waterloo tube/
rail. **Open** 11.30am-6pm Tue-Fri; noon-6pm Sat,
Sun. **Credit** AmEx, DC, MC, V.
Everything at this colourful little shop is fairly
traded, and many items are made from recycled
goods. Ganesha has recently branched out, and
now includes two neighbouring shops selling
homewares, as well as personal accessories and
clothes. Among the beautiful stock are papier
mâché bowls (from £7.99) produced by the Wola
Nani project in Cape Town, which gives an income
to women living with HIV, and mats from Dakar,
Senegal, woven from recycled plastic (£10-£30).
Also for sale are colourful hats, bedlinen,
Bollywood CDs and notebooks made of recycled
carrier-bag covers.
Mail order.

Joss Graham Oriental Textiles

10 Eccleston Street, SW1W 9LT (7730 4370).
Victoria tube/rail. **Open** 10am-6pm Mon-Sat.
Credit AmEx, MC, V.
This shop doubles up as a gallery space, with
temporary exhibitions reflecting the company's
current trend. Joss Graham regularly travels the
globe to seek out individual pieces, with Asia and
Africa being paid special attention. Among the
unique objects we found were woven-raffia wall
hangings from Congo decorated with abstract
geometric patterns in earthy tones (£150-£3,500),
and Indian fabrics (delicately embroidered silk
phulkaris in golden yellows and pink, £2,000-
£4,000). The collection also includes traditional
costumes, bags, rugs, cushions and tiles, plus
smaller items such as beads and jewellery.

Mar Mar Co

16 Cheshire Street, E2 6EH (7729 1494/
www.marmarco.com). Aldgate East tube/Liverpool
Street tube/rail. **Open** by appointment 11am-5pm
Mon-Fri; 1-5pm Sat; 11am-5pm Sun. **Credit**
AmEx, MC, V.
This small, elegant shop is something of a
blueprint for minimalist Scandinavian design.
Each stylish piece is prominently displayed.
Cutting-edge pieces include a Copenhagen carafe
with tumblers (£31), a flower-patterned dish by
Melene Helbak (£17.50), Arne Jacobsen cutlery and
an Ole Jensen rubber washing-up bowl (£39.50).
Mar Mar Co also carries Georg Jensen ceramics
and a small but sophisticated lighting range (lamp
with mouth-blown glass shade, £70).
Mail order.

Minh Mang

182 Battersea Park Road, SW11 4ND
(7223 6030/www.minhmang.co.uk). Battersea
Park or Queenstown Road rail. **Open** 10am-
5.30pm Mon-Fri; 10am-5pm Sat. **Credit** MC, V.
Named after the Emperor of Vietnam, Minh Mang
specialises in chic, ethnic accessories in luxurious
fabrics. The label is popular for its handbags;
clients include Yasmin Le Bon and Elle
Macpherson. The current range includes crushed
velvet cloche bags with ribbon detail and metal
clasp (£48) and floral-embroidered totes. An
elegant footstool with silk cushion and lacquered
feet costs £85; girlie rose fairy lights are £75. The
Lotus hand-painted glasses (£10 a pair) and

Cambodian silk wallets (£15) make ideal gifts.
Colourful, and richly decorated, silk brocade (£25
a metre) is also sold.
Mail order.

Mô Tearoom

23 Heddon Street, W1B 4BH (7734 3999/
www.momoresto.com). Oxford Circus or Piccadilly
Circus tube. **Open** 11am-11pm Mon-Wed; noon-
midnight Thur-Sat. **Credit** AmEx, DC, MC, V.
This North African tearoom-cum-bazaar, popular
with chic professionals, is situated next to the
celebrated Momo restaurant. Most items displayed
in the tearoom are for sale, including the glittering
array of glass lamps hanging from the ceiling, and
the elaborate mirrors. While sipping your mint tea
you can view the authentic pots, lamps, books,
rugs, clothing and jewellery. But watch your back,
as even the chairs and tables you're sitting on are
for sale. Prices are surprisingly reasonable.
Mail order.

Tann-Rokka

123 Regent's Park Road, NW1 8BE (7722 3999/
www.tannrokka.com). Chalk Farm tube. **Open**
10am-6pm daily. **Credit** AmEx, MC, V.
Oriental and vintage homewares are the fortes of
this laid-back, ultra-stylish shop, housed in what
was once Primrose Hill rail station. Notable
accessories include a carved wooden smoking
Buddha (£50), lucite desk lamps (from £500) and
Thai silk cushions. The firm carries out hand-
printing on its own range of fabrics; Romany
Delight cloth is the current bestseller (£60/m).
Mail order.

Tribal Gathering London

1 Westbourne Grove Mews, W11 2RU
(7221 6650/www.tribalgatheringlondon.com).
Notting Hill Gate or Westbourne Park tube.
Open noon-6pm Mon; 10.30am-6.30pm Tue-Sat.
Credit AmEx, MC, V.
Set on a tiny backstreet, and filled with artefacts
from around Eastern and Central Africa, this store
is a one-off. Owner Bryan Reeves is as much
anthropologist as businessman, constantly
seeking authentic pieces from his trips around
Africa. Currently on display are a Tanzanian
beaded women's ceremonial skirt (from £1,600), a
late 19th-century Ethiopian coffee bench (£1,400)
and a Zulu woman's hat (£680).
Mail order.

Utsuwa-No-Yakata

Oriental City, 399 Edgware Road, NW9 0JJ
(8201 3002). Colindale tube/32, 142, 204, 292,
303 bus. **Open** 10am-6.30pm Mon-Fri; 10.30am-
7.30pm Sat; 11am-6.30pm Sun. **Credit** MC, V.
Japanese tableware is stacked high at this oriental
shopping centre in the depths of suburbia. The
owners travel to Japan several times a year to
bring back piles of teacups, bowls, dishes and
teapots. Many pieces come in great-value sets, and
make good gifts (an opulent bowl set costs around
£25). Staff don't speak much English.

Antiques

As one dealer told us: as in fashion, antique trends are always changing. Last year, we were dazzled by white painted furniture – it's still around, of course, but less overwhelming. Now art deco seems to have come to the fore, with many shops displaying elegant glass and mirrored pieces. And there is a place in our hearts for 'home sweet home' nostalgia, particularly when it comes to kitchenalia – perhaps in an attempt to live out domestic goddess (or god) fantasies. What makes London great for antiques hunters is its convenient shop clusters and excellent arcades, where unusual bric-a-brac and museum-quality pieces are within convenient striking distance.

Arcades & markets

Alfie's Antique Market

13-25 Church Street, NW8 8DT (7723 6066/ www.alfiesantiques.com). Edgware Road tube/ Marylebone tube/rail. **Open** 10am-6pm Tue-Sat. **Credit** varies.

Alfie's higgledy-piggledy levels can be confusing for the first-time visitor. One dealer, who's been there for years, admits that she still gets lost sometimes. Dealers come and go here, and there are grumbles about changes and unfair rents, but there is always enough variety to ensure you'll find something of interest. Vintage fashion is a draw and the market is a must for unusual lighting. The charming Vincenzo Caffarella specialises in 20th-century Italian lights and furniture, and passionately declares 1950s and '60s Italian lighting is simply the best. His empire extends over the ground floor and takes up much of the first floor, where his displays are like 1960s Bond movie sets: you almost expect to see an evil genius with a purring cat beside one of the huge chrome lights. Beautiful Murano-glass linked chandeliers by big names such as Angelo Mangiarotti drip like cascades of icicles (from £1,500). We spotted impressive ceiling lights from an Italian bank, back when such places were showy and elegant. If you want to add a touch of *la dolce vita* to your home, a pair of '60s chandeliers from a Lugano hotel should do the trick. Caffarella does most of his business at the expensive end – New Yorkers are big fans of the serious stuff. But there are lower-priced items too: 1950s desk lamps for £350 and slightly fetishistic hand moulds from a 1928 rubber-glove factory (£100).

Don't miss Dodo Posters on the first floor, where Liz Farrow has a huge collection of advertisements from the 1920s and 1930s. Most posters are very affordable (from £50), while large French food and drink adverts for brands such as Pastis start from around £400. To complete the Parisian chic, check out Christopher Hall. We spotted metal park chairs worthy of the Tuileries and wonderfully elaborate china oyster plates. On the same level, Louise Verber deals in mirrored and glass decorative antiques and accessories. Chic glass lamp bases start at £75. Verber also specialises in silvered mercury glass. For all things silver, stop off at Goldsmith and Perris on the ground floor. Ideal for christening or anniversary gifts such as enamel-backed dressing table sets (from £150) or silver-backed powder compacts (from £150).

Antiquarius

131-141 King's Road, SW3 5EB (7351 5353/ www.antiquarius.co.uk). Sloane Square tube then 11, 19, 22 bus. **Open** 10am-6pm Mon-Sat. **Credit** varies.

Although this arcade can sometimes seem a little sleepy, it houses some noteworthy specialists. Robin Haydock deals in rare antique textiles from 1500 to 1850 with the emphasis on pre-industrial handspun, handdyed and stitched pieces. On our last visit we saw a stunning embroidered duchesse-satin table runner that had belonged to the last tsarina. Jasmin Cameron specialises in drinking glasses and decanters 1750-1910. Sets of Victorian glasses are priced £300-£600 and decanters start at £95. Look out for 1830s wine rinsers – these mini glass buckets would have been part of every place setting, so that you could rinse your glass between vintages (£340 a pair). Don't miss the 19th-century stationery boxes at Gerald Mathias: these wonderful wood desk organisers are the Victorian equivalent of the laptop (from £350). Fox hunting is not dead at Ferguson Fine Art, which specialises in field sports and equestrian antiques such as hunters' talismans and foxy cufflinks. Check out XS Baggage for piles of vintage Louis Vuitton trunks, as well as hatboxes and humidors should you need them.

Bermondsey (New Caledonian) Market

Corner of Bermondsey Street & Long Lane, SE1 4QB (7525 5000/www.southwark.gov.uk). London Bridge tube/rail/1, 42, 47, 78, 188 bus. **Open** 4am-2pm Fri. **No credit cards**.

There used to be tales of people having valuable antique furniture stolen from their homes, only to find them by torchlight at Bermondsey at 4am on a Friday. Apocryphal perhaps, but there's not much furniture here at all these days. The open-air market with its trestle tables of silver and china looks rather like a well-off great aunt's car-boot sale. Comparing it to the other markets mentioned in this section, you might wonder why you bothered getting up so early. That said, if you want bundles of silver-plated cutlery, there's plenty to choose from and people come to one particular stall to match up sets. Victorian cups and saucers start at £25, and most stands have single pieces of pretty Victorian china. You may find a bargain here, but prices tend to be on the high side, so haggle. If you walk up Bermondsey Street, you'll come to Celia Foley Antiques (No.142, 7234 0651), who has reasonably priced Victorian and Edwardian furniture (dining chairs from £30; desks from £150).

Camden Passage

Camden Passage, off Upper Street, N1 5ED (7359 0190/www.antiquesnews.co.uk/camden passage). Angel tube. **Open** *General market* 7am-4pm Wed; 7am-5pm Sat. *Book market* 8.30am-6pm Thur. **Credit** varies.

Set back from the busy artery of Islington's Upper Street, Camden Passage provides an interesting mix of quality and price, from tatty pavement bric-a-brac to antique-shop perfection. The Angel Arcade is home to Turn On Lighting (7359 7616), which specialises in English lighting from 1850 to 1950. Prices start at £300 for overhead pendants and £450 for substantial 1940s chromium-plated brass desk lamps. Val Cooper (7226 4901) deals in early Victorian papier mâché trays and furniture painted with dog portraits. Trays start at around £200 – terriers and spaniels are popular. The feel here is predominantly English domestic, with shell-work objects, tapestries and brassware. Don't miss the pleasant little passage of Pierrepont Arcade. Here, cheery Kay Leyshon (7226 8955) specialises in silver-plated flatware, and her stock is of lovely quality and very keenly priced. A full canteen of cutlery with 45 pieces starts at around £140. Or if you need extra cutlery to bulk up an existing set, we spotted large bundles of good-quality silver-plated dessert spoons for £25. Elegant cathedral-shaped 1930s toast racks make pretty gifts at around £20. Back on Camden Passage itself, Charlton House provides a touch of art deco splendour in the form of stylish chrome desk sets,

lighting and furniture. Further along, Provence spills out on to the passage at Rosemary Conquest (No.27, 7359 0616), where sets of French white metal garden furniture start at £400. Inside we spotted glam and girlie wall chandeliers (£250 a pair) and 19th-century ceiling chandeliers from £350. This is a good spot for large, French gilt and painted mirrors. Vintage 18 (No.18) is where old shop fittings come to rest. The result is quite surreal – from a giant pharmacy pestle and mortar to rows of wooden racks from shoe factories. Industrial lighting is a particular favourite here – huge film-set lights that make you want to shout 'Action!' (£300-£1,000). Antlers from German hunting lodges (from £60) are strangely popular.

The shops housed in the Georgian Arcade at the end of the Passage are good for collectable glass, china and silver. Van Den Bosch has stunning examples of Arts and Crafts-era silver by such important makers as Omar Ramsden, AE James and Liberty. Christopher Pearce (7359 4560) deals in collectable glass from the past three centuries and has everything from 18th-century dwarf ale glasses to Victorian champagne flutes. We spotted a small Victorian decanter for just £49. Jonathan's Kitchenware (7359 4560) feels like a wartime kitchen, enhanced by the 1940s music playing softly in the background. If you want ration-book chic at home, pick up some enamel utensils or commemorative mugs. We saw an Edward VIII Coronation mug (£25), imbued with added collectors' cachet because he abdicated and was never actually crowned.

Grays Antique Markets & Grays in the Mews

58 Davies Street, W1K 5LP & 1-7 Davies Mews, W1K 5AB (7629 7034/www.graysantiques.com). Bond Street tube. **Open** 10am-6pm Mon-Fri. **Credit** varies.

Grays is just moments away from the chain-store anywheresville of Oxford Street, yet decades apart. Stalls at the entrance are mostly dedicated to jewellery and watches, but keep going and more unusual delights await. Evonne has elegant silver cocktail ephemera, stylish clocks and photograph frames. The window of ZMS is full of enticing gift-sized objects such as silver boxes and exquisite pink, deep-blue and jade-green enamel dressing table sets. Downstairs, stop off at Britannia for commemorative china and interesting majolica dishes. In the Mews section of Grays, don't miss the fascinating Michael's Boxes. China boxes from the 1780s inscribed with such messages as 'A trifle from an admirer' or 'A trifle from Ramsgate' may look like cute little pill boxes, but were in fact used to carry decorative patches to cover up smallpox marks (hence the mirror inside the lid). An insulting gift by modern standards, perhaps, but an interesting piece of history from around £200. The long-established doll dealer Sandra Fellner is also here – look out for wax-faced war dolls and itsy-bitsy dolls' furniture. For yesteryear glamour from the 19th century onwards visit Vintage Modes (*see p60*).

Northcote Road Antiques Market

155A Northcote Road, SW11 6QB (7228 6850). Annexe at 70 Chatham Road, SW11 6HG (7738 2896). Clapham Junction rail then 319 bus. **Open** 10am-6pm Mon-Sat; noon-5pm Sun. **Credit** AmEx, MC, V.

This is the heart of Clapham's nappy valley, with its pricey children's shops, organic food stores and trendy, child-friendly cafés. The antiques market is small, but has a good mix. Notable is a dealer specialising in collectable china such as Clarice Cliff. Another stall has lots of neatly stacked silver cutlery. Prices seem reasonable – we spotted church chairs (£35) and a Victorian chaise longue (£480). Old pine wall cabinets had been painted white and backed with Cath Kidston material to appeal to SW11 yummy mummies. Carey B Antiques (149 Northcote Road, 7924 7257) has very good Victorian tables and chests of drawers, as well as china and glassware. The smell of polish will lead you to the shop – the owner's husband restores the furniture.

Henry Gregory at **Portobello Road Antiques Market**

HOME

Portobello Road Antiques Market

Portobello Road, W10 & W11 (7229 8354/ www.portobelloroad.co.uk). Ladbroke Grove or Notting Hill Gate tube. **Open** 8am-5pm Sat. **Credit** varies.

Be patient and grit your teeth as you battle through the tourist crowds on Portobello Road. Then duck inside the shops and arcades, as that's where the goodies are. Lipka is one of the most interesting and varied arcades. On its two levels you'll find everything from toy soldiers, 19th-century weather vanes, tribal art, porcelain and oil paintings. On the ground floor, Marringdean Antiques is a good stop for reasonably priced Staffordshire figures and the distinctive pairs of spaniels and poodles. Downstairs, Pedigree Collectables always has items with a tale attached. We spotted German wartime radios made specially so they couldn't pick up foreign stations (now you can get medium wave on them) from £225. Also here, Natural History has stuffed creatures by noted Victorian taxidermists such as Rowland Ward. There are such un-PC items as a bespectacled monkey dressed up as a fisherman. Opposite Lipka, the 20th Century Theatre is good hunting ground for

homey nostalgia such as Victorian jelly moulds, stitched samplers, and stone bottles and jars. There's also antique fishing paraphernalia for nostalgic JR Hartley types. Admiral Vernon is another large arcade with a variety of specialities including vintage sporting photographs, clocks and watches and armour. Henry Gregory (No.82) has antique silver, vintage sporting equipment and luggage. As a result, the shop feels rather like below stairs at *Gosford Park*. If you are gift-hunting, don't miss Atlam (No.111) for an excellent selection of small silver and glass objects, such as 18th-century coral baby rattles and pomade bottles (from £150). When you start hearing shouts of 'Two avocados for a pound!' it means you've come to the end of the antiques section of the market.

Architectural

SALVO (8761 2316, www.salvo.co.uk) produces lists of architectural salvage dealers in London, the UK and France.

The House Hospital

14 Winders Road, SW11 3HE (7223 3179/ www.thehousehospital.com). Clapham Junction rail. **Open** 10am-5pm Tue-Sat. **No credit cards.**

This Battersea institution deals in all types of architectural salvage from brass doorknobs to fireplaces. So if your feature-stripped Victorian house needs a bit of TLC, this is the place to come. Victorian roll-top baths start at £300 – a bargain when you compare them to new plastic baths. The ornate Victorian radiators are objects of beauty and can be supplied blasted and pressure tested. You'll find every detail to restore your home to its original state – even 19th-century drainpipes.

LASSCo/Westland London

LASSCo, St Michael's Church, Mark Street, off Paul Street, EC2A 4ER (7749 9944/ www.lassco.co.uk). Old Street tube/rail. **Open** 10am-5pm Mon-Sat. **Credit** AmEx, MC, V. *Westland London, St Michael's Church, Leonard Street, EC2A 4ER (7739 8094/www.west land.co.uk). Old Street tube/rail.* **Open** 9am-6pm Mon-Fri; 10am-5pm Sat. **Credit** MC, V.

A visit to LASSCo never fails to inspire a childlike wonder. As you walk through the lofty aisles of the former St Michael's church, you never know what wonderful piece of historic salvage you'll bump into. We spotted a 16th-century Florentine stone entranceway, reconstructed panelled rooms, Victorian display cabinets from the V&A and a

huge stained-glass nave window from a 19th-century church. All scarce and unusual and, as a result, price tags are hefty. You won't find a bargain here, but you might discover that continental wrought-iron balcony (£3,042) your house has been crying out for. Look out for very good replica door furniture such as an ebonised beehive mortice set (£76). Westland & Co, also at this site, has the cream of period fireplaces. There are wonderfully elaborate ones from Italian palazzos and English country houses – all with serious prices to match. In May 2005, LASSCo's reclaimed flooring and bathroom site moved to a large 18th-century mansion in Vauxhall (Brunswick House, 30 Wandsworth Road, SW8 2LG, 7394 2124). It had been invaded by squatters for years and is being – appropriately – restored by LASSCo.
For branch (LASSCo) see index.
Mail order.

Willesden Green Architectural Salvage

189 High Road, NW10 2SD (8459 2947). Willesden Green tube. **Open** 9am-6pm Mon-Sat. **No credit cards**.
Willesden Green concentrates on small-scale domestic salvage rather than the fancy talking-point stuff. Fireplaces are the most popular buy, with Victorian bedroom fireplaces starting at £300. Choose from stacks of cast-iron radiators from £50 and find a Victorian door to fit (from £50). Upstairs on the roof you'll discover stained-glass windows and panels – again from Victorian and Edwardian houses rather than churches (from £20). The BBC and Channel 4 often turn up looking for butlers' sinks and fireplaces for interiors programmes.

Fireplaces

All the good salvage shops have fireplaces. Other reliable places to look include **Chesneys** (734-736 Holloway Road, N19 3JF, 7272 7462, www.chesneys.co.uk), which has superb reproduction fireplaces; **Better Hearth** (109 Holloway Road, N7 8LT; 7609 3245, www.the betterhearth.com); and also the **Edwardian Fireplace Company** (Former All Saints Church School, Armoury Way, SW18 1HX, 8995 2554, www.edwardianfires.com).

Antiques shops

Decorative

The Dining Room Shop

62-64 White Hart Lane, SW13 0PZ (8878 1020/ www.thediningroomshop.co.uk). Hammersmith tube/Barnes Bridge rail. **Open** 10am-5.30pm Mon-Sat. **Credit** AmEx, DC, MC, V.
According to recent surveys, sit-down family dinners are a thing of the past. But if you need any encouragement to chow down *en famille*, this is the place to come. The stylish shop was started 20 years ago by a former deputy editor of *World of Interiors* magazine and it has become dining-room central, with everything you need, from the table itself to napkins. You can choose from formal Georgian dining tables (from £4,000) or use the shop's bespoke service and select the wood and dimensions. Glassware, dinner services and silver complete the dining experience. Victorian dinner services start at £300, single wine glasses from £30 and vintage damask napkins from £10 each. Meat plates, cake stands and Georgian decanters all hark back to the time when dinner was more than pricking a cellophane wrapper and pressing 'start'. *Mail order.*

Filippa & Co

51 Kinnerton Street, SW1X 8ED (7235 1722/ www.filippaandco.com). Hyde Park Corner tube. **Open** 10am-5.30pm Mon-Fri; by appointment Sat. **Credit** MC, V.
Filippa Naess has been called the 'queen of Gustavian style', and her shop is a palace of that icy and elegant Swedish look. Antique painted day beds sell for around £2,700, gate-leg tables for

£2,200. Naess goes back to her homeland on regular buying trips, and she recently cast a bust of one of her ancestors to make a range of quirky painted plaster lamp bases (£850). She also has her own range of linen and voiles, which look like they could have come from your Swedish granny's linen chest. *Mail order.*

The Floral Hall

Crouch Hill & Haringey Park, N8 9DX (8348 7309). Finsbury Park tube/rail then W7 bus/41, 91 bus. **Open** 10am-5pm Tue-Sat; also by appointment. **No credit cards**.
The Floral Hall continues to be popular in affluent Crouch End. The owner regularly travels to fairs in France to source furniture and, as a result, the shop floor creaks with faded French grandeur. Gilt overmantel mirrors may not be in the top-notch nick you'll find in the West End, but they are much cheaper (from around £350) if you don't mind the slightly battered look. Look out for white wrought-iron garden furniture sets to create an *au terrasse* atmosphere at home. Call before visiting in August, as, in true French style, the shop sometimes closes.

Josephine Ryan Antiques & Interiors

63 Abbeville Road, SW4 9JW (8675 3900/ www.josephineryanantiques.co.uk). Clapham Common tube. **Open** 10am-6pm Mon-Sat; noon-5pm Sun. **Credit** MC, V.
'Effortless chic' best describes Josephine Ryan's Clapham shop. A clever combination of periods creates a timeless yet contemporary look. French 19th-century armchairs are a speciality, sympathetically reupholstered in neutral fabrics (from £600). Italian 18th-century painted candlesticks make lovely wedding gifts (from £195). Among the more unusual items, we saw a 19th-century stone crown from a gate (£295) and table lamps made from reclaimed French oak (£495).

The French House

Unit A, Parsons Green Depot, Parsons Green Lane, SW6 4HH (7371 7573/www.thefrench house.co.uk). Parsons Green tube. **Open** 10am-6pm Mon-Sat. **Credit** MC, V.
Francophiles will appreciate finding Ricard glasses and enamelware *allumette* boxes (£48) in the general clutter here. It's more warehouse than shop, and you'll have to edge your way round various bits of furniture to see what's on offer. The look is chateau shabby chic, in some cases very shabby indeed, as most items of furniture are unrestored. The idea is that the client decides what finish and upholstery they like and pieces are then restored on site – so you do need a bit of imagination. On our last visit, we saw interesting caned occasional chairs, 19th-century Louis XVI-style beds (from £1,100), armoires, marble-topped tables and tall pier mirrors. The owners go on buying trips to France once a month and also have a shop in York.

Judy Greenwood Antiques

657-659 Fulham Road, SW6 5PY (7736 6037/ www.judygreenwoodantiques.co.uk). Fulham Broadway tube/14 bus. **Open** 10am-5.30pm Mon-Fri; 10am-5pm Sat. **Credit** MC, V.
Judy Greenwood has a very good eye for the sort of elegant yet affordable French antique furniture people want in their homes. Her gilt crested mirrors are in immaculate condition – although some have new glass, which lessens the value – and are very reasonably priced. We spotted a very good 19th-century 5ft x 3ft overmantel for £890. The basement here could tell a tale or two – it's heaving with antique French beds (from £690 for a double). Greenwood also has her own range of reproduction Louis XVI painted bedroom furniture. Thought has gone into everything, down to the antique linen napkins tied with ribbon (£120 for a set of 12).

Furniture

La Maison

107-108 Shoreditch High Street, E1 6JN (7729 4646/www.atlamaison.com). Liverpool Street tube/rail/26, 48, 149, 242 bus. **Open** 10am-6pm Mon-Fri; 10.30am-6pm Sat. **Credit** AmEx, MC, V.

If you need to add a little romance to your boudoir, then head to La Maison. The beds here are the stuff of French costume dramas and perfect for any *liaisons dangereuses*. If you don't know your Louis XVI from your Louis Philippe, the charming French staff will guide you through bedroom history. Don't be put off by the rather cramped dimensions of the antique doubles (smaller than today's beds): La Maison provides an extension service and the result is seamless. Single Louis XVI beds go for £500 and doubles from £800. The shop also sells its own range of reproduction beds – expect to pay around £2,000 for a simple Louis XV-style double. Even hardened rockers such as Liam Gallagher, Charlie Watts and David Gilmour have succumbed to La Maison's romantic charms.

The Old Cinema

160 Chiswick High Road, W4 1PR (8995 4166/ www.theoldcinema.co.uk). Turnham Green tube. **Open** 10am-6pm Mon-Sat; noon-5pm Sun. **Credit** MC, V.
Over three floors of this former 1890s 'picture palace', you can find everything from Arts and Crafts movement to oriental furniture, but the bulk of the stock is Victorian and Edwardian, typified by vast mahogany dining-room tables and corpulent cabinets. Among the more interesting items, we saw a 1930s saucer-mirrored dressing table and stool (£1,150), an early 20th-century Globe Wernicke roll-top desk (£1,300) and a Victorian library chair (£895).

Glass & ceramics

See also p126 Antiquarius.

Andrew Lineham Fine Glass

Van Arcade, 105 Portobello Road, London, W11 2QB (01243 576 241/www.antiquecoloured glass.com). Notting Hill Gate tube. **Open** 8am-3pm Sat. **Credit** AmEx, MC, V.
Andrew Lineham specialises in beautifully crafted English and European coloured glass from 1820 to 1950, which was valuable from the start, especially engraved glassware and cameo scent bottles by Stourbridge firms Thomas Webb and Stevens & Williams, and sumptuously hued Bohemian glass. This is a rich repository of unusual items, such as a Webb cameo perfume bottle in the shape of a fish (which will set you back a cool £10,000), exquisite turn-of-the-20th-century Heckert floral liqueur glasses with green stamen stems (£200 each), or, for shallower pockets, a deep-red Bohemian eyebath (£75). Antique Moser and Mary Gregory are always in stock. There are also Victorian fairy lamps, sporting-themed items and a small selection of pottery and porcelain.

Jeanette Hayhurst

32A Kensington Church Street, W8 4HA (7938 1539/www.antiqueglasslondon.co.uk). High Street Kensington tube. **Open** 10am-5pm Mon-Fri; noon-5pm Sat. **Credit** AmEx, MC, V.
Jeanette Hayhurst has been a glass specialist for 25 years and known as 'the decanter lady' because of her well-stocked window. Decanters make reliable wedding gifts: Victorian ones start at £70 and 18th-century examples go for £300. Her other main speciality is 18th-century English drinking glasses. Single dwarf ale glasses start at £50, but for something really special and collectable, like an 18th-century engraved colour twist glass, you can pay as much as £5,000.

Mark J West

Cobb Antiques, 39B High Street, SW19 5BY (8946 2811/www.markwest-glass.com). Wimbledon tube/rail then 93 bus. **Open** 10am-5pm Mon-Sat. **Credit** AmEx, DC, MC, V.
This Wimbledon shop is dazzling. A large Victorian dining table heaves with decanters – there are always about 500 in stock, with prices starting at £160. Look out for unusual pieces – we spotted an English 1840s olive-green decanter (£480) and a French 1860s midnight-blue one (£248). Considering the typical breakage rate at home, it seems amazing that glasses can survive for 300 years. They come at a price, of course –

Andrew Nebbet Antiques at Church Street. See p130.

around £3,000 for a 1710 English baluster wine glass. Sets of anything earlier than Victorian rarely exist these days, but you can pick up six large 1830s Bristol green wine glasses for £600 and Georgian flute champagne glasses from £50 each.

Medical & scientific

Curious Science

307 Lillie Road, SW6 7LL (7610 1175/07956 834 094/www.curiousscience.com). West Brompton tube then 74 bus. **Open** 11am-5pm Mon-Sat (phone to check). **Credit** MC, V.
David Burns's shop has moved a few doors down to bigger premises, all the better to display his fascinating stock. There's now room for larger, quite baffling 19th-century scientific machines, as well as wall charts and natural-history prints. Not only does it attract collectors, the shop is a magnet for prop scouts (*see p130* **Prop culture**), particularly for horror films, and this section of the business is located downstairs. You can still pick up a turn-of-the-20th-century glass eye for £25 and all manner of pickled and wall-mounted critters. Be prepared for the unexpected – what looked like an instrument of torture was in fact a 1920s beauty-salon hairdryer. Nestling in a smart wooden box was a phallic-shaped object stamped 'The Comforter' – a Victorian euphemism for a dildo. Designed for 'medical purposes', comforters were used to relieve women who were suffering from 'hysteria'. Antiques are never dull at Curious Science. Note that it's always best to phone ahead to check that the shop is open.
Mail order.

Silverware

See also p126 for **Bermondsey (New Caledonian) Market** and **Camden Passage**.

London Silver Vaults

Chancery House, 53-64 Chancery Lane, WC2A 1QT (7242 3844/4863). Chancery Lane tube. **Open** 9am-5.30pm Mon-Fri; 9am-1pm Sat. **Credit** AmEx, MC, V.
This underground vault was originally the Chancery Lane Safe Deposit, where London toffs stored their valuables in guarded strongrooms. Gradually, silver dealers began to trade on the premises and the current building (rebuilt in 1953) houses around 30 dealers – many of whom have been here for three generations. Not all that sparkles is sterling silver – silver plate and Sheffield plate is on sale here too – but all dealers are part of an accredited association, which means stock must be accurately described. You'll see monumental silver table centrepieces, such as a 2ft silver boat (£18,500) and huge tureens worthy of a royal banquet. But don't be put off by the grandeur of some displays. You can pick up smaller, more affordable items too. Stephen Kalms (vault 13-15) has bowls brimming with early 20th-century silver-plated napkin rings from £30 – an added bonus if you find one monogrammed with a godchild's initials. At Langfords (vault 8-10), we spotted a pair of George III silver ladles made in 1804 (£245) and a Victorian basket-effect silver hip flask (£450). Other affordable items to look out for include grape scissors, cocktail shakers and card cases.

20th century/ Arts and Crafts

Antique Trader @ The Millinery Works

85-87 Southgate Road, N1 3JS (7359 2019/ www.millineryworks.co.uk). Old Street tube/rail then 76, 141 bus. **Open** 11am-6pm Tue-Sat; noon-5pm Sun. **Credit** MC, V.
This discreet Victorian terrace is a tardis of an antiques shop. The large showroom, on two levels, is packed with Arts and Crafts and Aesthetic Movement furniture and objects. Simple, well-made pieces can still be picked up for reasonable prices. Even the most basic dining tables and chairs are sturdy and of good quality – expect to pay £1,200 for an oak Arts and Crafts table and four chairs by an unknown maker. Specialised pieces that you wouldn't be surprised to see in the V&A are a real draw for fans of this period and some are strictly POA. On a recent visit we saw a Gothic Pugin-esque wardrobe, similar to furniture found in the Palace of Westminster (£12,000). If you have an enormous family to seat for dinner and dream of matching chairs, you'll find them here. Sets of ten or 12 are not uncommon, and we even saw a set of 24 oak slatted chairs (£6,000). Look out too for smaller items in the cabinets, such as Liberty & Co dressing-table sets. There are regular monthly exhibitions as well as excellent Arts and Crafts shows twice a year in June and November with furniture sourced from Voysey, Morris & Co, Liberty, Goodyer of Regent Street and Heal's.

Prop culture

Whether it's silverware for a dining scene in a period drama or instruments of torture in a horror film, the props all have to come from somewhere. The following shops – reviewed in this chapter – are particularly fertile hunting grounds.

Curious Science

Horror-film props people swear by this place for its stuffed animals and creatures in formaldehyde, but Curious Science also hires and sells props to other productions, such as *Around the World in 80 Days* with Steve Coogan (scientific instruments), and *Charlie and the Chocolate Factory* (dental tools and teeth moulds). *See p130.*

Graham Kirkland

Kirkland specialises in late Victorian Catholic or high Church of England objects and furniture – a boon for filmmakers recreating religious scenes. Everything from rosaries to chalices were sourced here for the 2002 film *The Magdalene Sisters*. Kirkland has also provided props for such diverse television programmes as *Messiah*, *Murphy's Law*, *Casualty* and *Holby City*. *See p130* **Lillie Road**.

Lacquer Chest

About 40% of its business is prop work – for anything from films to cookery books and fashion shoots (Mario Testino's stylist is a big fan). The Lacquer Chest provided the furniture for the maids' rooms in *Gosford Park*, as well as the dressing table sets for Kristin Scott Thomas and the other ladies. The knives that were counted out after the stabbing came from here too, although not the weapon itself. Copper pots and furniture in 2005's Crusade epic *Kingdom of Heaven* were sourced here. Other films that have used Lacquer Chest props include *About a Boy* and Woody Allen's latest starring Scarlett Johansson. *See p130* **Kensington Church Street**.

LASSCo

Remember the door brackets in *Mission Impossible*? Thought not, but anyway, they came from LASSCo, as did the doorknobs in *101 Dalmatians*. A good deal of York stone was also bought here for *Rob Roy*. One of the shop's oddest sales was a bust worth several hundred pounds – bought by a film company to be blown up. *See p127.*

Art Furniture

158 Camden Street, NW1 9PA (7267 4324/ www.artfurniture.co.uk). Camden Town tube. **Open** noon-5pm daily. **Credit** MC, V.
This large space is a one-stop shop for Arts and Crafts items. You'll find furniture by all the main firms such as Liberty & Co, Shapland & Petter, Heal's, Harris Lebus and Wylie & Lochhead. You can buy substantial items by named makers and firms for around £2,000 – on a recent visit we saw an oak Liberty & Co dresser (£2,800) and a large 1905 wardrobe by East End manufacturer Harris Lebus (£1,850). A three-figure budget will still bag you a named piece, such as a 1905 child's chair from Heal's (£280) or a Liberty & Co smoker's cabinet (£220). Furniture by unnamed makers is cheaper – we spotted a set of four oak chairs with a distinctive Arts and Crafts pierced heart design that seemed well priced at £850. Check the website for daily updates on new stock.

Liberty

210-220 Regent Street, W1B 5AH (7734 1234/ www.acfc.co.uk). Oxford Circus or Piccadilly Circus tube. **Open** 10am-7pm Mon-Wed, Fri, Sat; 10am-8pm Thur; noon-6pm Sun. **Credit** AmEx, DC, MC, V.
Liberty items that have had several lifetimes in various houses return to the place where they were first sold, only to depart to yet another family and future. The antique furniture department always has a good selection of Liberty and other Arts and Crafts makers such as William Birch, Morris & Co, Shapland & Petter and the Glasgow School, but Liberty's annual summer exhibition pulls in collectors from all over the world. At last summer's show we saw an 1890 Liberty Thebes oak sofa (£2,400), a pair of Morris & Co Sussex armchairs (£1,450) and an 1895 green-stained oak bedroom suite attributed to CR Ashbee's Guild of Handicraft (£9,500). Look out, too, for silver Cymric bowls and pewter Tudric clocks and inkwells (designed by Archibald Knox and others) and Clutha glass and Cordofan candlesticks designed by Christopher Dresser, but prices aren't cheap. Hold your breath before asking the 'on application' price of Liberty silver, particularly clocks.

Shop clusters

Church Street, NW8

Edgware Road tube/Marylebone tube/rail.
Opening times here tend to match those of Alfie's Antique Market. The theme on the street is predominantly art deco, but another trend creeping in of late is quirky industrial chic. Andrew Nebbett Antiques (Nos.35-37, 7723 2303) has a careful mix of 'the decorative and unexpected'. On our last visit we saw a 1930s operating-theatre lamp converted into a table (£1,000) and a stack of floor mats made from old gymnasium leather. The overall feel is quite spartan, which is why 1900's oak refectory tables work with 1950s Danish furniture. It's the perfect hunting ground for loft dwellers. The new kid on the block is James Worrall Antiques at Joe's Confectionery Stores (No.28, 7563 7181). The small shop has a slightly baffling mixture of objects: a Fry's Chocolate display cabinet (£235), a dentist's lamp and a bison-skin bin were among the items that jostled for space when we last visited. You might leave thinking 'Hmm...', but it's worth a peek as you never know what you'll find.

A visit to the lovely Cristobal (No.26, 7724 7230) feels rather like snooping round an absent diva's boudoir. The shop specialises in period costume jewellery by the likes of Haskell and Hugler, as well as furniture. Swedish chaises and mirrored deco bedroom furniture complete the glam look. Susie Cooper Ceramics (No.18, 7723 1555) is a must for deco enthusiasts and has recently added quality Arts and Crafts-era silver by names such as Liberty and Archibald Knox to its repertoire. This is the place to come for silver or chrome deco photograph frames, nostalgically filled with pictures of silver-screen stars like Grant and Garbo (from £80).

Kensington Church Street, W8

Kensington High Street or Notting Hill Gate tube.
You won't feel as though you've stumbled across a bargain on this smart west London street, especially if you've come via nearby Portobello Road – it's not really rummaging territory. Instead, you'll find established speciality shops and quality antiques with 'better sleep on it' price tags. Paul

---

Reeves (No.32B, 7937 1594) deals in museum-quality furniture and artefacts from 1860 to 1960, with emphasis on Arts and Crafts and the Aesthetic Movement, including big names such as Godwin and Rennie Mackintosh. Clients include The British Museum, the V&A and the Metropolitan Museum of Art in New York.

Pruskin Gallery (No.73, 7937 1994) concentrates on important art deco furniture and objects by the likes of Lalique. Jonathan Horne (No.66C, 7221 5658, www.jonathanhorne.co.uk) specialises in early English pottery: medieval earthenware, 17th- and 18th-century Delftware, stoneware and Staffordshire figures, among other rare pottery. Just off Kensington Church Street, Roderick Antique Clocks (23 Vicarage Gate, 7937 8517) is a clock-watcher's dream, ticking away with a wonderful selection of long-case, carriage, bracket and decorative French clocks. Attractive 19th-century circular wall clocks by London makers start at about £600, and fine grandfather clocks start at £4,500. At the Lacquer Chest and the Lacquer Chest Too (Nos.71 & 75, 7937 1306), the ordered clutter of the 18th- and early 19th-century household antiques creates a more intimate atmosphere than the shop's smarter neighbours. Think William Morris rush chairs, Welsh milking stools and early 19th-century samplers. Prices aren't scary – you can pick up individual pieces of early 19th-century china for around £30.

Don't miss Hope & Glory (No.131A, 7727 8424), specialists in commemorative ceramics. The fascinating selection spans two centuries of royal and other historic events. Prices range from £20 to £2,500 depending on date, maker and rarity. A good Queen Victoria jubilee mug costs around £125. When we last visited, the bestsellers were what could be described as 'future collectables' – Charles and Camilla wedding mugs with the wrong date (£30); a mug with the revised date was £10 cheaper.

Lillie Road, SW6

West Brompton tube then 74 bus.
This quirky enclave has a relaxed, slightly bohemian feel. Dealers dip in and out of each other's shops for coffee, or share lunch in the little gardens out back. It's very quiet during the week, but as shops tend to be small and rather cluttered, it's a pleasant time to visit. Nimmo & Spooner (No.277, 7385 2724) has lighting, mirrors and 18th-20th century painted and contemporary furniture. The feel is fresh and breezy – more seaside simplicity than faded grandeur. You'll find elegant, decorative antiques at Hindley (No.281, 7385 0706), such as girlie trefoil-mirror dressing tables (from £450). For more masculine appeal, head to Stephen Sprake (No.283, 7381 3209), where stock tends to be large and unusual. We saw the head of a noble steed (stuffed and wall-mounted, £550), and on the same theme a surprisingly beautiful 1900s blacksmith's sign/gate. Otherwise, expect to see large 1960s lights and oversized statuary. Andrew Bewick (No.287, 7385 9025) does a good line in convex gilt mirrors (from £380). The chic basement, scented with Diptique candles, is home to classy pieces of furniture. We spotted a pair of 1900s French gilt armchairs reupholstered in pale linen (£1,680). At No.297, Lorraine Plummer and Katherine Pole share a space (7386 1888). Look out for cushions made from antique French linen and ribbons (from £30) from the latter and quirky items like an Indian monkey cage and Victorian garden cloches from Plummer.

Haven't been to church lately? Then step inside Graham Kirkland Religious Art & Antiques (No.271, 7381 3195). Modernising vicars flog off the old stuff here, while traditionalists come to buy replacements. Life-size plaster-of-Paris Virgin Marys are popular (from £800). When we last visited, a large crucifix was being hired out for an episode of *Casualty*. Everything you see here is late Victorian, either Catholic or high Church of England. Chapel chairs are a good buy at £25 each. Paul Williams (No.275, 7386 7382) specialises in high-quality Perspex lamps and furniture, mainly 1970s and '80s and sourced from Florida. Not antique, but we mention the shop here because, being see-through, Perspex works well with any period of furniture, avoiding nasty clashes. Lamps sell for around £500 a pair.

Bathrooms & Kitchens

For advice and information, the website for the **Bathroom Manufacturers Association** (Federation House, Station Road, Stoke-on-Trent, Staffs ST4 2RT, 01782 747 123, www.bathroom-association.org) has downloadable fact sheets on everything from spa baths to saving water and special-needs equipment. The **Kitchen Bathroom Bedroom Specialists Association** (12 Top Barn Business Centre, Holt Heath, Worcester WR6 6NH, 01905 726 066, www.ksa.co.uk) can direct you to your nearest design specialist (all have been vetted and follow an approved code of practice). The association also offers an interactive planning questionnaire and advice on installation.

All-rounders

For everything from serious appliances – ovens and fridge-freezers – to kettles and toasters, crockery, cutlery, bins, pots and pans, **Argos** (*see p118*) stocks well-known brands such as Brabantia, Kenwood and Brita. It also has a good selection of bathroom hardware, including electric showers (Triton), taps and accessories such as bathroom scales (Salter), shower curtains, laundry hampers and loo seats.

Alternative Plans
4 Hester Road, SW11 4AN (7228 6460/ www.alternative-plans.co.uk). Sloane Square tube. **Open** 9am-5.30pm Mon-Fri; 10am-4pm Sat. **Credit** MC, V.
Designed by Piero Lissoni, this dedicated Boffi showroom is a stylish mix of dark-grey walls, Pral artificial stone and resin flooring. Advice is available on everything from choosing taps to lighting options. In the bathrooms section, highlights include Claudio Silvestrin's beautifully sculpted Po bath in solid limestone (the larger of the range is £19,870, excluding VAT). At the Notting Hill branch, names represented include Agape, Vola, Nito and Fantini. Look out for the Agape Woodline bath (around £6,000): a 'chaise longue in a box', it has a sloped interior for supremely lazy soaking. Kitchens (from £35,000, including appliances) have a clean, modern feel with such features as liquid lacquer-coated kitchen doors (for extra shine), slatted aluminium wall units and multi-ply oak worktops.
For branch see index.

Bisque
244 Belsize Road, NW6 4BT (7328 2225/ www.bisque.co.uk). Kilburn Park tube. **Open** 9am-5pm Mon-Fri; 10am-4pm Sat. **Credit** AmEx, MC, V.
Using Swiss and Italian manufacturers, the English design team at Bisque creates radiators that emanate style as well as heat. The latest is Vamp, a sleek, wall-mounted model in chrome-plated copper and brass, which can be used on any central heating or hot-water system. The website includes a virtual showroom and all the technical information necessary for choosing and installing radiators. There are many playful designs, including the Hollywood (from £1,426), a tubular art deco-style radiator set around a mirror, but the more traditional styles are still the most popular. Paul Priestman's much-praised, circular Hot Hoops is a further example of Bisque's innovative approach.
Mail order.

Charles Collinge Architectural Ironmongery
9-11 Cottage Green, SE5 7ST (7787 0007/ www.charlescollinge.co.uk). Denmark Hill rail/343 bus. **Open** 8.30am-5pm Mon-Fri. **Credit** MC, V.
This ironmonger specialises in all types of door furniture, particularly locks, hinges and latches; its patented hinges have been in use since before the Battle of Waterloo. Modern and traditional fittings come in a range of materials, including bronze, chrome, polished brass and stainless steel. Bathroom accessories include towel rails, mirrors and loo-roll holders.
Mail order.

CP Hart
Newnham Terrace, Hercules Road, SE1 7DR (7902 1000/www.cphart.co.uk). Lambeth North tube. **Open** 9am-5.30pm Mon-Sat. **Credit** MC, V.

Edwins. See p133.

CP Hart shows the best in high-class, innovative kitchen and bathroom design and has an impressive portfolio – from Foster and Alessi to Citterio and Starck. It's always expanding its range of products, but expect to see Aquavision TVs for shower rooms, bespoke frameless shower enclosures, glass radiators and Kohler products – including the Sok bath with hydrotherapy and chromatherapy, and basins and baths made from glass and corian (a non-porous blend of natural minerals and acrylic resin that can be cut and shaped just like wood). The Primrose Hill branch is due for a full refurb, and many of these products will be on display for the first time, including the new Starck X (for Duravit) range of ceramics and taps: a ceramic basin with incorporated yellow shelf area costs £727 (chrome stand £271). CP Hart is now part of the Nobia group, which also owns the renowned Poggenpohl kitchen range, and the SE1 branch has the largest display of Poggenpohl products anywhere in Europe, including the +Dimension 75 systems with extra-deep base units (prices start at £20,000). Accessories include chrome shelves, soap dishes and towel rings.
Mail order (0845 600 1950)
For branch see index.

General Supplies
465A Caledonian Road, N7 9BA (7609 6111). Caledonian Road or Holloway Road tube. **Open** 7.30am-5pm Mon-Fri; 8am-2pm Sat. **Credit** MC, V.
In business for over 20 years, this family outfit sells plumbing supplies galore, as well as bathroom and kitchen fittings. Prices are competitive, staff are friendly and helpful, and there's a delivery service. There is also a fully stocked bathroom showroom, with styles, products and prices across the board. Names include Grohe, Bristan, Twyfords and Mira; the shop is also the main dealer for the Radiator Company (based in Somerset).

Holloways of Ludlow
121 Shepherd's Bush Road, W6 7LP (7602 5757/ www.hollowaysofludlow.com). Hammersmith or Shepherd's Bush tube. **Open** 9.30am-6pm Mon-Sat; 11am-4pm Sun. **Credit** MC, V.
Holloways specialises in complete kitchens and bathrooms, using 1930s washbasins, brass taps, cast-iron baths, Victorian servants' bells, retro-looking lighting and Roberts radios as props. Although the shop can source anything from gorgeous Napoleonic baths to well-worn marble tiles, many of its commissions are utterly modern, including wet-rooms. The appliances, so it's claimed, are among the cheapest in the UK.
Mail order.

In Design
Kiran House, 53 Park Royal Road, NW10 7LQ (8963 5841/www.indesignuk.co.uk). Harlesden tube. **Open** 9.30am-5.30pm Mon-Fri; 10am-4pm Sat. **Credit** MC, V.
Measuring more than 10,000sq ft, and with more than 50 displays (often with working features), In Design is London's largest dedicated Siematic and Villeroy & Boch showroom. The kitchen and bathroom layouts allow customers to see how the products will fit in with their lifestyle.
Mail order.

John Lewis of Hungerford
156-158 Wandsworth Bridge Road, SW6 2UH (7371 5603/www.john-lewis.co.uk). **Open** 9am-6pm Mon-Wed; 9am-7pm Thur, Fri; 9am-5.30pm Sat; 10am-4pm Sun. **Credit** MC, V.
Established over 30 years ago, John Lewis of Hungerford has pioneered beautifully crafted kitchens, freestanding furniture and now a new range of simple, practical, made-to-measure bathroom cabinetry. Kitchens and bathrooms are renowned for their affordability, good looks, craftsmanship and simple designs that will stand the test of time. This flagship showroom in Fulham showcases the new Crème de la Crème retro-inspired kitchen, which is available in four different high-gloss paint colours – sugar candy pink, minty leaf green, sweet almond cream and ocean island blue. Prices start at £15,000.
For branch see index.

London Plumbing & Heating Supplies

322 Hackney Road, E2 7AX (7739 8883). Bus 26, 48, 55. **Open** 7am-5pm Mon-Fri; 8am-3pm Sat. **Credit** MC, V.

This plumbers' merchant sells central heating and plumbing goods at discount prices, as well as sanitary, kitchen and bathroom wares from the likes of Bristan. Stock includes boilers, taps, showers and fittings. Any make or model not on show can be ordered, but the most attractive feature is the 25% discount off the usual catalogue prices.

For branch see index.

Mark Wilkinson Furniture

126 Holland Park Avenue, W11 4UA (7727 5814/ www.mwf.com). Holland Park tube. **Open** 9am-5.30pm Mon-Fri; 10am-5pm Sat. **Credit** MC, V.

Wilkinson has been designing domestic furniture for kitchens, bathrooms and bedrooms since 1976, and there is a distinct *Country Living* style to his work – think Provençal 'distressed' finishes and trompe l'oeil effects. Materials are of the highest quality: stones and natural woods (two trees are planted for every client's furniture order), as well as stainless steel and glass. MWF's National Trust kitchen (with its 'intelligent' storage of plate racks, labelled drawers and sliding cupboards) costs from £25,000. The service includes design from flooring to appliances – computers and TVs embedded in refrigerator doors, for instance.

For branch see index.

MFI

398-400 Chiswick High Road, W4 5TF (8996 0590/www.mfi.co.uk). Chiswick Park tube. **Open** 10am-6pm Mon-Wed, Fri, Sat; 10am-8pm Thur; 10am-4pm Sun. **Credit** AmEx, MC, V.

No longer the purveyor of cheap MDF cabinets, MFI is a good place to start to get ideas for your new kitchen or bathroom. The London-wide stores stock a great range of kitchen and bathroom suites, accessories, flooring and appliances. Brands sold include Bosch, Diplomat, Rangemaster and Stoves. Stores sell on a delivery-only basis. The website has an online design service.

Branches: throughout the city.

Nicholas Anthony

44-48 Wigmore Street, W1U 2RY (7935 0177/ www.nicholas-anthony.co.uk). Bond Street tube. **Open** 9.30am-6pm Mon-Fri; 10am-4.30pm Sat. **Credit** MC, V.

This family business has been going since 1963 and produces bespoke kitchens and bathrooms that fall somewhere between classic and contemporary. Expect plenty of cream walls and wood mixed with dark ceramic or metal surfaces in the kitchens, and pretty white ceramic sink bowls in the bathrooms. The kitchen furniture is designed by Anthony and manufactured in Germany. Poggenpohl is stocked at the Knightsbridge branch, while appliances are by the likes of Gaggenau, Siemens, Neff and Hansgrohe. On the bathroom front, Italian designer Antonio Lupi has produced style-led concoctions of zebrano wood, limestone and marble tiles.

For branch see index.

Nu-line

305-317 Westbourne Park Road, W11 1EF (7727 7748/www.nu-line.net). Ladbroke Grove or Westbourne Park tube. **Open** 7.30am-5.30pm Mon-Fri; 8am-1pm Sat. **Credit** MC, V.

In business since 1965, this huge, family-run builders' merchant, spanning eight shops, sells around 20,000 lines connected with painting and decorating, plumbing, ironmongery, lighting, kitchen accessories, electrical goods and tools. There's even a timber yard around the corner (8 Malton Road, W10 5UP, 8968 1002). The refurbished bathroom centre provides baths, showers and steam units from brands such as Vola, Duravit, Roca, Laufen, Hansgrohe, Keramag and Inda. Bisque's gorgeous coiled-steel radiators are a particular highlight (from around £120).

Plumbcraft

Unit 2, Ellerslie Square, SW2 5DZ (7274 0174/ www.plumbcraft.co.uk). Clapham North tube/137 bus. **Open** 8am-5.30pm Mon-Fri; 8.30am-12.30pm Sat. **Credit** MC, V.

Brixton's one-stop shop for fitted kitchens and bathrooms, appliances, heating and plumbing needs. Names are good – Smeg, Bosch, Neff and Baumatic – and staff can map out a kitchen (including hob, sink and shelving) for you. Bathroom products include everything from corner baths to roll-tops. Service is good value, with bathroom designs starting at £300.

Tsunami

27 Wigmore Street, W1U 1PN (7408 2230/ www.tsunamiuk.com). Bond Street tube. **Open** 9.30am-5.30pm Mon-Fri; 10am-4pm Sat. **Credit** AmEx, MC, V.

Minimalist sums up Tsunami's aesthetic; lines are clean, crisp and streamlined. For kitchens, a key addition this season will be textured wooden Tebe kitchen doors topped with stainless steel. Minotti, creator of chic wooden kitchens, is still a major player here. Appliances include Gaggenau, Miele, Siemens and Dacor. For bathrooms, Tsunami offers its own design service and also carries products by Karol, Milldue, Toscoquattro, Teuco and Minotti.

Bathrooms

From accessories to walk-in showers, online **Bathroom Heaven** (www.bathroomheaven. com) is a useful resource; recent finds include a Bronte slipper bath (£515) with cast-iron ball-and-claw feet (£110). Old stalwart **Ideal Standard** (01482 346 461, www.ideal-standard. co.uk) is constantly updating its range, which now includes Pearson Lloyd's Serenis rain showers (the wet-room version starts at £1,145 excluding shower valve and kit). Wet-room fans should contact **Alfix UK** (01462 686 611, www.alfix.co.uk) for a free booklet, 'Creating the Perfect Wet Room'.

For antique and salvage bathtubs, radiators, fixtures and fittings, try **LASSCo RBK** (Brunswick House, 30 Wandsworth Road, SW8 2LG, 7394 2102, www.lassco.co.uk) or **Water Monopoly** (16-18 Lonsdale Road, NW6 6RD, 7624 2636, www.watermonopoly.com), which has a good spread of original antique bathroom fittings, complemented by a full range of reproduction pieces.

Modernists will swoon at the basins and tubs on display at the **Limestone Gallery** (Arch 47, South Lambeth Road, SW8 1SS, 7735 8555, www.limestonegallery.co.uk), such as the ivory stone Ellipse bath carved from Italian limestone (£16,540). Prices start from £560 for a basin.

The **Conran Shop** (*see p143*) has revamped its bath shop and now has an eclectic range of bathroom furniture and accessories from around the world. **Habitat** (*see p145*) also has a range, Spa, featuring bathroom storage and sink consoles in clean, simple lines of oak and marble. For **Fired Earth** (bathroom furniture as well as tiles) and **European Heritage** (for stone basins), *see chapter* **Interiors**.

For suitable bathroom flooring, *see p164-75*.

Aston Matthews

141-147A Essex Road, N1 2SN (7226 7220/ www.astonmatthews.co.uk). Angel tube/38, 56, 73, 341 bus. **Open** 8.30am-5pm Mon-Fri; 9.30am-5pm Sat. **Credit** AmEx, MC, V.

With more than 2,000 lines of contemporary and traditional bathroom products, this venerable operation (around since 1823) is one of London's

HOME

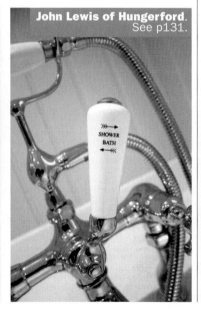

John Lewis of Hungerford. See p131.

finest purveyors of all things to do with bathing. Tubs are its forte: the selection of cast-iron models is the largest in Britain. Styles include free-standing repro roll-tops, double-ended, corner, extra deep and sitz; hydrotherapy systems can also be fitted. If space is at a premium, the Ergo fits a corner loo and basin on a 1m wall. There is also a large range of heated towel warmers and bathroom radiators. Accessories, such as soap dishes, bathroom mirrors and loo-roll holders, are also available, and featured names include Starck, Vola and Hansgrohe.
Mail order.

Bathroom Discount Centre

297 Munster Road, SW6 6BW (7381 4222/ www.bathroomdiscount.co.uk). Hammersmith tube/rail. **Open** 8am-6pm Mon-Fri; 9am-5pm Sat, Sun. **Credit** MC, V.
Incredibly, prices haven't changed at all at this large west London showroom, where discounted, non-designer bathroom gear is the order of the day. There are usually some great deals to be had instore, such as on bathtubs – a cast-iron, double-ended roll-top for £390, say, or a luxury six-jet whirlpool bath for £375. Cash-strapped playboys will find no shortage of sunken baths either. Catering for both traditional and modern tastes, there are trendy glass bowl sinks (sand-blasted models at £183) alongside Victorian-style bathroom suites.
Mail order.

Bathrooms International

4 Pont Street, SW1X 9EL (7838 7788/www.bath roomsint.com). Knightsbridge or Sloane Square tube. **Open** mid May-mid Sept 10am-6pm Mon-Fri. *Mid Sept-mid May* 10am-6pm Mon-Fri; 10am-4pm Sat. **Credit** MC, V.
If luxurious spas and whirlpool baths are your thing, Bathrooms International, providers of bathrooms to luxury hotels (including Dubai's Burj Al Arab), is your place. Its exclusivity starts at the front door, where you have to buzz to gain entry. Mirrored glass-panelled baths, waterfall spouts, surround-jet showers, watering-can shower heads, and baths and basins made in ceralite (a lightweight concrete, starting from £415) are all available, as well as bathroom styles from art deco to Russian palace, created by top London designers such as Nina Campbell and Joanna Wood. Simple taps start at £110, but if you want something really special, such as Lalique or Baccarat taps in crystal, silver or gold, prices go through the roof. Colour-matching is a big feature – to put, say, a faux-limestone finish on a white bath – with prices starting at £430 to colour-match a basin. Top-notch brands include JCD, Max Pike and Kallista.

Bathstore.com

62-82 Commercial Road, E1 1NU (7702 9898/ www.bathstore.com). Aldgate East or Whitechapel tube. **Open** 9am-6pm Mon-Fri; 9am-5pm Sat; 10am-4pm Sun. **Credit** MC, V.
With over 6,000sq ft of showroom displays, Bathstore is one of the largest bathroom shops around. It has ten branches in London, with plenty more around the country. The website is a good starting point, with a great selection of baths, showers, sanitaryware and accessories, including cabinets, mirrors, radiators and light fittings.
Branches: throughout the city.

Burge & Gunson

13-27 High Street, SW19 2JE (8543 5166/ www.burgeandgunson.co.uk). Colliers Wood tube. **Open** 8am-5.30pm Mon-Fri; 8am-4pm Sat. **Credit** MC, V.
If you want to watch *EastEnders* while soaking in the bath, head to Burge & Gunson: the Aquavision unit has a heated TV screen, so it won't steam up even if you do. Mirrors, towel rails and cabinets are also available, along with baths, showers and furniture from the likes of BC Designs (free-standing bateau baths), Bette (clean-lined steel baths), Ideal Standard, Kaldewei, Sottini and Villeroy & Boch. Check out the ultrasound whirlpools and high-tech wet rooms.

Catchpole & Rye

Saracens Dairy, Jobbs Lane, Pluckley, Kent TN27 0SA (01233 840 840/www.crye.co.uk). **Open** preferably by appointment 9am-5pm Mon-Fri; 10am-3pm Sat. **Credit** MC, V.
For good old-fashioned ablutions, Catchpole & Rye is a good port of call, selling original (and repro) baths – from the bohemian (copper) to the decadent (the Bateau Grande is big enough for two). Water closet options include the fabulous Catchpole & Rye cistern (the Deluge) – a high-level cistern with copper finish and brackets, silver nickel flush pipe and lever arm, and a crackle-glazed pull. You can also get French pillar taps with 'Froid' and 'Chaud' inserts. Accessories include bath racks, towel rails, ceramic cistern pulls and shaving mirrors.
Mail order.

Colourwash

63-65 Fulham High Street, SW6 3JJ (7371 0911/ www.colourwash.co.uk). Putney Bridge tube. **Open** 9am-5.30pm Mon-Fri; 10am-5pm Sat. **Credit** AmEx, MC, V.
Colourwash offers bathrooms for all tastes: minimalist, boldly contemporary, traditional and downright wacky: the glass Foozball Fun Basin (£934) features table football so you can have a game, presumably, while brushing your teeth. The equivalent of a 'little black dress' for your bathroom is the Liquid Basin made of black and matt silver resin. Or how about a waterproof TV (including ceiling-mounted speakers and a waterpoof floating remote control, for £1,874) or a freestanding oval bath with two headrests (£2,941). Colourwash stocks a decent cross-section of brands, from Duravit, Starck and Dornbracht to Bisque and Vola.
Mail order.
For branches see index.

Czech & Speake

39C Jermyn Street, SW1Y 6DN (7439 0216/ www.czechspeake.com). Green Park tube. **Open** 9.30am-6pm Mon-Fri; 10am-5pm Sat. **Credit** AmEx, MC, V.
As you'd expect on Jermyn Street, this well-turned-out boutique is a niche supplier of traditional bathrooms but also stocks contemporary styles – including a sleek range by David Chipperfield Architects and a few art deco/cubist designs. Made and designed in-house with superior materials such as ingot brass, porcelain and bone china, this is classy stuff. Clients include the Savoy hotel and Steven Spielberg – which should give you an idea of the prices. Look out for the claw-foot bathtub with brass taps (£3,500) and 12in-rose shower heads (£250). C&S also does a limited range of kitchen taps. If you can't afford the hardware, you can always opt for something from the elegant range of toiletries and fragrances.
Mail order (0800 919 728).

Edwins

17, 19 & 26 All Saints Road, W11 1HE (7221 3550/www.edwinsbathrooms.co.uk). Ladbroke Grove tube. **Open** 8am-5pm Mon-Fri; by appointment 9am-1pm Sat. **Credit** MC, V.
Plumbing, heating and bathroom sales are the name of the game at Edwins, which has been trading for more than two decades. The company consists of two halves: a blokey plumbers' merchant (No.17) and a stylish showroom at No.19, which has recently been extended. Edwins is now a main dealer for Kohler products, including its chromatherapy (effervescent bubbles) and colour-therapy (mood-enhancing coloration) systems. Other baths, showers and basins fashioned in sleek, modern forms are by reputed designers such as Villeroy & Boch, Vola and Ritmonio. Starck fans will find his bathroom line here. For the best results, book an appointment (Saturdays) for a member of staff to take you round the premises. The showroom at No.26 is devoted almost exclusively to sanitaryware.

Godwin Bathrooms

426-432 Watford Way, Mill Hill, NW7 2QJ (8203 6789/www.godwinbathrooms.com). Hendon Central tube. **Open** 8am-5pm Mon-Fri; 9am-1pm Sat. **Credit** MC, V.

With over 35 years' experience, this large Mill Hill showroom displays bathrooms, showers and sanitaryware by all the top brands (Aqualisa, Hudson Reed, Pom d'Or, Samuel Heath, Grohe, Hansgrohe, Kaldewei and Twyfords, among others). Its porcelain tile range (RAK Ceramics) is also very popular, with numerous colours and patterns. Design help comes courtesy of a virtual-reality environment for you to visualise before you buy.

Heated Mirror Company

01666 840 003/www.heated-mirrors.com. **Phone enquiries** 9am-6pm Mon-Fri. **No credit cards.**
In 1988 Malcolm Syme came up with the nifty idea of heated mirrors, which are designed not to steam up. The mirrors have enjoyed success the world over, particularly in hotels, from Barbados (Sandy Lane) to Brighton (Grand Hotel). They're all made to order, in a range of sizes, styles and materials, from pink to acid-etched glass. Prices range from £200 to £2,000. The company is based in Wiltshire.

Jeff Bell

299 Haggerston Road, E8 4EN (7275 8481/ www.glasscasts.co.uk). Liverpool Street tube/rail then 26, 48 bus. **Open** by appointment 9am-6pm Mon-Fri. **No credit cards.**
Jeff Bell produces beautiful, contemporary, hand-cast bathtubs, basins and shower screens from raw glass sheets, each with a different luminosity and texture. His award-winning talents don't come cheap – prices start at about £6,500 plus VAT for a bath – but the craftsmanship is impressive.

Locks & Handles

4-8 Exhibition Road, SW7 2HF (7581 2401/ www.doorhandles.co.uk). South Kensington tube. **Open** 9am-5pm Mon-Fri; 9am-3.30pm Sat. **Credit** AmEx, DC, MC, V.
A long-established, friendly hardware store with a decent selection of bathroom fittings and accessories. It's particularly good for towel rails, mirrors, loo-roll holders and good-quality loo seats.
Mail order.

M&O Bathrooms

174-176 Goswell Road, EC1V 7DT (7608 0111). Barbican tube. **Open** 9am-5pm Mon, Tue, Fri; 9am-2pm Wed; 9am-7pm Thur; 9am-1pm Sat. **Credit** MC, V.
This no-nonsense builders' merchant has a showroom that offers a decent range of bathroom equipment. Most of the big-name manufacturers are represented, including Laufen, Vitra, Heritage, Saneu, Grohe and Hansgrohe. Tap prices start at £40 (a single mixer costs £100-£240); basin and loo sets go from £140 to £3,000; while baths start at £70 rising to £10,000 (for a whirlpool system that cleans and dries itself).
Mail order.

Original Bathrooms

143-145 Kew Road, Richmond, Surrey TW9 2PN (8940 7554/www.original-bathrooms.co.uk). Richmond tube/rail. **Open** 9am-5.30pm Mon-Fri; 10am-5pm Sat. **Credit** MC, V.
In business for well over a century, this family-run venture stocks all the leading mainstream names, as well as a selection of Italian imports, including Cesame, Fantini, Falpa and Agape. The popular Flaminia sanitaryware range includes the rounded Flaminia IO inset basin (£340), which contrasts well with a geometric shelf or vanity top (wood or coloured lacquer finish from £482). OB also offers a free design consultation service at the store and can recommend installers. Costs for a complete bathroom start at around £2,000-£3,000 and go up to £23,000.
Mail order.

Pipe Dreams

72 Gloucester Road, SW7 4QT (7225 3978/ www.pipedreams.co.uk). Gloucester Road tube. **Open** 10am-5.30pm Mon-Fri; 11am-4pm Sat. **Credit** AmEx, MC, V.
Aiming at the contemporary end of the market, Pipe Dreams' newly refurbished showroom highlights modern materials, including glass, clean white ceramics and African wenge wood. The in-house design team offers a bespoke service that can include hand-painting with butterflies,

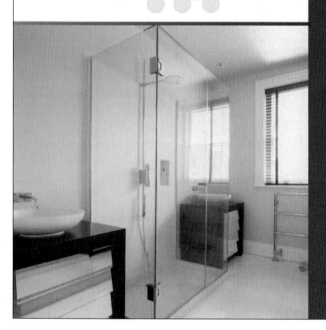

ladybirds and flowers. Wet rooms and steam rooms are strong points too. Traditionalists will be pleased to learn that Victorian, Edwardian and art deco bathrooms are still available (a Regent en-suite – hand-painted vanity and storage cupboards finished in polished blue stone with an eau de nil effect – starts at £23,500), as are claw-foot bathtubs and toilets with pull chains.
Mail order.

Sitting Pretty
122 Dawes Road, SW6 7EG (7381 0049/ www.sittingprettybathrooms.co.uk). Parsons Green tube. **Open** 10am-5pm Mon-Fri; by appointment Sat. **Credit** MC, V.
Handmade wooden toilet seats – carved from mahogany and oak – are the main draw here. And good-looking they are too, with their Victorian and Georgian designs and brass fittings. Prices start at £135 for a standard seat, while polyester-coated seats are £395 and the angular Thunderbox model starts at £395. The shop also does basins and fittings, including the Berkeley Suite (a classic design based on those found at the Berkeley hotel).
Mail order.

West One Bathrooms
45-46 South Audley Street, W1K 2PY (7499 1845/www.westonebathrooms.com). Bond Street tube. **Open** 9.30am-6.30pm Mon-Fri; 10am-6pm Sat. **Credit** AmEx, MC, V.
Established in 1978, West One Bathrooms stocks ornate taps and accessories in full over-the-top splendour. Think pink marble tubs, statues of naked women, and basins in gold, platinum and elaborate hand-painted designs. Downstairs, there is more contemporary, minimalist fare using resin, Carrara marble, wood, natural stone, ceramic, glass and granite. The Mem Lifestyle 'rain-sky' shower system starts from around £4,200. The shop also has an excellent selection of bathroom scales.
For branches see index.

Repairs

The Lab
16-18 Lonsdale Road, NW6 6RD (8964 9955). **Phone enquiries** 9am-6pm Mon-Thur; 9am-5pm Fri. **No credit cards.**
If your bathroom is looking a little grotty, this company (sister to salvage outfit Water Monopoly; *see p132*) will put you in touch with its nationwide network of bathroom repairmen, who will restore antique bathtubs (from £240 to resurface a bath in situ), mend chipped basins (from £60) or resurface damaged tiles. Phone enquiries only; there's an answer machine at weekends.

Kitchens

For an incentive to do the washing-up, check out the enamelled sinks by US company, Kohler, which are sold at **Elon** (12 Silver Road, W12 7SG, 8932 3000, www.elon.co.uk or www.kitchensinks.co.uk) – also known for its classic fired-clay sinks and handmade terracotta floor tiles. For those who value substance over style, **Davies Kitchens & Appliances** (17-19 Mill Lane, Woodford Green, Essex IG8 OUN, 8505 5616, www.davies-electrics.co.uk) sells huge American fridges and range cookers. Those on a tighter budget should take a trip to **Buyers & Sellers** (120 Ladbroke Grove, W10 5NE, 7229 1947, www.buyersandsellersonline. co.uk). The shop is crammed full of competitively priced fridges, dishwashers and cookers, from top-name brands such as AEG, Bosch and Miele.
Traditionalists might want to opt for the invention of a blind, Nobel Prize-winning Swede back in 1869: for more on the 'range of ranges', call **Aga** (0845 712 5207, www.aga-web.co.uk) or head for the **Aga Shop** (5 Beauchamp Place, SW3 1NG, 7589 6379) in Knightsbridge, which can offer advice on these old-fashioned design icons. Technology-lovers

will be more impressed with an IceBox entertainment system by **Kitchen Vision** (01932 252 458, www.kitchenvision.co.uk), which includes a flip-down TV, DVD and CD player, as well as a waterproof keypad.
For further inspiration, *see chapters* **Home Accessories**, **20th-century Design**, **Department Stores** and **Interiors**. For tableware, *see chapter* **Home Accessories**.

Bulthaup
37 Wigmore Street, W1U 1PP (7495 3663/ www.bulthaup.com). Bond Street tube. **Open** 9.30am-5.30pm Mon-Thur; 9.30am-4.30pm Fri; 10am-4pm Sat. **No credit cards.**
Founded in Bavaria in 1949, Bulthaup specialises in sleek, contemporary styles. The bespoke kitchen service emphasises aesthetics and ergonomics. Work surfaces are available in laminate, granite, beech and maple; snazzy glass shelves and state-of-the-art drawers are further strengths. Bulthaup is also known for its high-performance air-extraction systems. New in 2005 was the 'revolutionary' b3 kitchen; technically advanced and designed for flexibility, the system is cantilevered from a steel framework attached to the wall, so that base and wall cabinets and applicances can be fitted at any height to suit the user. Minimalist kitchens start from £25,000 to £35,000 (excluding appliances).
For branch see index.

Chalon
The Plaza, 535 King's Road, SW10 0SZ (7351 0008/www.chalon.com). Fulham Broadway tube. **Open** 9am-5.30pm Mon-Fri; 9am-5pm Sat. **Credit** AmEx, MC, V.
Chalon creates furniture inspired by 18th- and 19th-century English and European designs, with French country house and Georgian being particular specialities. Handmade by craftsmen in Somerset, the free-standing furniture – fashioned from pine, teak, maple and oak – comes painted, stained or distressed. Highlights include an oiled pine chopping table (£1,020), a pine Chelsea housekeeper's cupboard (from £5,999) and a period pine corner cupboard (£2,585). Chalon's kitchen design service (£250 for the first room, £100 thereafter) incorporates appliances from Miele, Amana and Britannia, as well as recommending flooring, wall paint, tiles and fabrics. Bathrooms and bedrooms are available too, in a similarly traditional style.

Divertimenti
33-34 Marylebone High Street, W1U 4PT (7935 0689/www.divertimenti.co.uk). Bond Street tube. **Open** 9.30am-6pm Mon-Wed, Fri; 9.30am-7pm Thur; 10am-6pm Sat; 11am-5pm Sun. **Credit** AmEx, DC, MC, V.
Divertimenti boasts well-chosen kitchen- and tableware, cooking utensils, pots and pans, glasses and electrical appliances. Knife-sharpening is available every other Wednesday (£2.50 per knife; knives must be at the shop by the previous day's close of business). You can even have your copper pans retinned. Cookery classes are run on subjects such as 'Ice Cream and Beyond' or 'Simple French Entertaining' and include guests such as chef Alastair Little. Wedding lists are also available. The new branch in South Kensington also has a great café.
Mail order.
For branch see index.

Furniture Craft International
Rays House, North Circular Road, NW10 7XP (8961 7780/www.fci.uk.com). Hanger Lane tube. **Open** 10am-6pm Mon-Sat; 11am-5pm Sun. **Credit** MC, V.
The latest creations from venerable Italian company Snaidero are displayed in this huge showroom. Designs run from cottage chic to more contemporary styles, give or take a few extravagances. The most reasonable kitchen costs £15,000 (excluding appliances). Look out for sales too – the £40,000 Gioconda kitchen was recently knocked down to half price.
Mail order.
For branch see index.

Greenwich Wood Works
Friendly Place, Lewisham Road, SE13 7QS (8694 8449/www.greenwichwoodworks.co.uk). Lewisham rail/DLR. **Open** by appointment Mon-Sat. **No credit cards.**
Since 1981 Greenwich Wood Works has been creating bespoke, handcrafted wooden furniture in maple, oak, ash, cherry or walnut; pieces can also be painted. The shop is well known for traditional kitchens in styles such as Arts and Crafts, Shaker, Georgian and deco, but more contemporary stuff is available too. The average cost for a complete kitchen, without appliances, is £20,000 to £25,000.

Harvey Jones
57 New King's Road, SW6 4SE (7731 3302/ www.harveyjones.com). Fulham Broadway tube. **Open** 9.30am-6pm Mon-Fri; 10am-5pm Sat. **Credit** MC, V.
Harvey Jones offers handmade customised kitchens. The most popular style is Shaker, made from tulip wood, which is given a hand-painted finish in any colour (if required) after installation. Kitchens cost from £7,000 to £13,000, excluding appliances (Bosch, Miele, Neff) or installation.
For branches see index.

Kitchen Central
19 Carnwath Road, SW6 3HR (7736 6458/ www.kitchencentral.co.uk). Parsons Green tube. **Open** 9.30am-6pm Mon-Fri; 10am-4pm Sat. **No credit cards.**
Claiming to be where 'architecture meets food', Kitchen Central has undergone a recent refit with plenty of new ideas and concepts on display. The planning and design area has also been refurbished and now displays attractive, contemporary kitchens by Italian firms ABC and Comprex, plus the Spanish brand Santos. The design team sees the process right through to installation. Prices start from £10,000 and go up into six figures.

Kitchens Italiana
72B George Lane, E18 1JJ (8518 8411). South Woodford tube. **Open** 9.30am-5.30pm Mon-Fri; 9.30am-4pm Sat. **No credit cards.**
As the name suggests, this is an emporium of Italian (and French) designed kitchens. Its main import is Comprex, a range of mid-market, contemporary kitchen furniture. The company also represents Mobalpa, Linear Quattro and Scavolini. Planning and installation services are another feature. Prices are slightly more expensive than at the likes of MFI, but competitively priced for quality imported ranges.

Living in Style
162 Coles Green Road, NW2 7HW (8450 9555/ www.livinginstyle.co.uk). Brent Cross tube. **Open** 9.30am-5.30pm Mon-Fri; 10am-4pm Sat. **Credit** MC, V.
Daring and way-out kitchens can be found at Living in Style. From conceptual design through to installation, a full service is offered by this company, which draws its inspiration from Italian design houses. At the cutting edge is Giemmegi's curvaceous Americana kitchen: pale yellow satin lacquer-painted units are teamed with stainless-steel worksurfaces (£20,000) to give the ultimate in futuristic style.

Roundhouse
25 Chalk Farm Road, NW1 8AG (7428 9955/ www.roundhousedesign.com). Camden Town or Chalk Farm tube. **Open** 9.30am-6pm Mon-Fri; 11am-5pm Sat. **Credit** MC, V.
This partnership of architects and designers makes beautiful customised furniture in wood (oak, cherry, maple, beech, American black walnut) and other materials (glass, concrete, granite and stainless steel). Cabinet styles range from Classic (panelled) via Shaker through to streamlined contemporary looks such as Urbo (minimalist glossy acrylic). Initial planning and design is free of charge, and kitchens start at around £18,000. Roundhouse also designs living and bedroom furniture.
For branches see index.

HOME

Design, Art & Crafts

Design & craft outlets

Inhale that heady mix of oils and turps. Yes, painting is back. Even installation king Charles Saatchi cast aside his dirty bed linen and pickled animals for the three-part 'The Triumph of Painting' exhibition at the Saatchi Gallery (until May 2006) and, whether consciously or not, the effect seems to have rippled through to studios and galleries. That is bound to change, of course, but for the time being 'painterly' is the new buzzword. Design and craft are strong in London, with the more sophisticated showcase galleries exhibiting the cream of the craft world, and smaller outlets focusing on more affordable and functional objects – you'll find everything from a large contemporary glass sculpture that's simply for staring at to an espresso cup that can go in the dishwasher.

Artemidorus

27B Half Moon Lane, SE24 9JU (7737 7747). Herne Hill rail. **Open** *Jan-Nov* 10.30am-7pm Tue-Fri; 10am-6pm Sat. *Dec* 10.30am-7pm Mon-Fri; 10am-6pm Sat; 11-5pm Sun. **Credit** MC, V.
Artemidorus has regular exhibitions in the first-floor gallery, while the ground floor has a good stock of applied arts, with everything from quirky toys to striking textiles. Jo Butler's pleated and wired wraps make dramatic sculptural accessories in deep colours such as burnt orange and purple; scarves start at £50 and large wraps are £180. Meryl Till's large cylindrical porcelain lights are stippled with small round or square holes to cast a dreamy glow. They come in three different sizes, starting from £98; candle covers are £38. Look out for Sarah-Jane Brown's unusual woven metal sculptures of animals, sometimes mounted on little wheels and trollies (£25-£98). Jewellery is a strong point here. Scottish designer Colin Duncan fuses metals at high temperatures to create his slender necklets, but anything that's next to the skin is silver (from £60).

Barrett Marsden Gallery

17-18 Great Sutton Street, EC1V 0DN (7336 6396/www.bmgallery.co.uk). Barbican tube. **Open** 11am-6pm Tue-Fri; 11am-4pm Sat. **Credit** AmEx, MC, V.
The gallery aims to give an overview of the best of contemporary applied arts in the UK, and you'll find some exceptional examples here. The cool, minimalist space on the ground floor hosts six solo or two-person exhibitions a year, while a changing display by other artists is downstairs. Large focal-point pieces are particularly striking, such as Steven Newell's one-off glass bowls and platters with bold figurative scenes (from £3,000). Other gallery artists include Carol McNicoll, whose sculptural yet functional ceramics incorporate 3-D figures. Look out for cast-glass vessels by former Jerwood Prize-winner Tessa Clegg, and Nicholas Rena's imposing modernist ceramics. Solo shows in 2006 include ceramicists Richard Slee and Philip Eglin, and Caroline Broadhead, with her ghostly tulle garments.

Cecilia Colman Gallery

67 St John's Wood High Street, NW8 7NL (7722 0686/www.ceciliacolmangallery.com). St John's Wood tube. **Open** 10am-5.30pm Mon-Fri; 2-5pm Sat. **Credit** MC, V.

After 28 years, Cecilia Colman's gallery is practically an institution in prosperous St John's Wood. NW8 newlyweds can usually count on at least one gift being chosen here. Decorative, rather than functional, glass and ceramics are popular. When we last visited, Colman was showing work by ceramicist Laurel Keeley, whose flat dishes in pale sea blues with shell-like motifs are inspired by her Cornish home. Ceramicist Rob Whelpton also uses a seaside theme, but in a different way; his lidded containers and vases (£60-£300) have brightly painted images of boats and fishermen and often incorporate gold leaf. South African ceramicist Henni Meyer makes unusual pots and jugs in rustic colours, decorated with geometric designs (from £33). Look out, too, for Will Shakespeare's colourful hand-blown glass vessels and platters. His perfume bottles make affordable gifts from around £30.

Contemporary Applied Arts

2 Percy Street, W1T 1DD (7436 2344/www.caa.org.uk). Goodge Street or Tottenham Court Road tube. **Open** 10.30am-5.30pm Mon-Sat. **Credit** AmEx, MC, V.
CAA is undoubtedly the best central London location to see leading contemporary craft. The award-winning gallery holds regular exhibitions on the upper level, showing top names such as ceramicist Rupert Spira. His pale, delicate bowls and cylinders have a pure, almost spiritual, beauty. His last exhibition centred on prayer bowls with incised texts (from £80) and large cylindrical vessels embossed with poems (£4,800 a pair). Museum and gallery curators buy and commission through CAA, and the gallery also arranges commissions of everything from furniture to jewellery for individuals. The bespoke engagement and wedding ring service is particularly popular. The basement area has a wide selection of crafts for sale in all price ranges. You'll find inexpensive functional ceramics such as cups and saucers, as well as large one-off studio pieces. Glass is always exceptional here, with makers such as Ronald Pennell and Joanne Ballard. Look out for Colin Reid's sculptural kiln-cut glass – large, irregular hunks that look like organic material hewn from another world.

Contemporary Ceramics

William Blake House, 7 Marshall Street, W1F 7EH (7437 7605/www.cpaceramics.com). Oxford Circus or Piccadilly Circus tube. **Open** 10.30am-6pm Mon-Wed, Fri, Sat; 10.30am-7pm Thur. **Credit** AmEx, MC, V.
The Craft Potters Association, established in 1958, owns and runs this gallery, where members show and sell their work. New talent is encouraged, with an annual 'Setting Out' exhibition for new graduates every February. You can buy attractive, functional ceramics here – some are even dishwasher-proof – but look out for more unusual decorative pieces too. Jack Doherty uses thrown porcelain to create textural effects, so a dish might look ripped or moth-eaten and a vase might appear dimpled (from £20 for a mug). Jane Perryman is inspired by African and early Celtic pots. Her items look like beautiful pieces of wood, but are, of course, ceramics, burnished and fired in sawdust (from £100). Ashraf Hanna's use of the Japanese technique of raku to smoke-fire her natural and spontaneous ceramics brings results that are truly spectacular.
Mail order.

Cosa

7 Ledbury Mews North, W11 2AF (7727 0398/www.cosalondon.com). Notting Hill Gate tube. **Open** by appointment only. **Credit** AmEx, MC, V.
Cosa shows both painting and craft in tandem in this studio-style space. The mainly urban, edgy landscapes and often deconstructed, textural ceramics work well together. Simon Carroll's thrown and hand-built ceramic vessels are battered and uneven. Inspired by the unruliness of nature, they are the antithesis of minimalist chic (from £750). James Evans creates organic forms in monochrome metallic ceramics – the works resemble unidentifiable body parts, strangled pillows or large blobs of matter. The effect is intriguing, as soft, changeable objects are rendered solid and permanent (from £950). Ceramicist Andy Shaw and glassmaker Noel Hart also show here.

Crafts Council

44A Pentonville Road, N1 9BY (7806 2559/www.craftscouncil.org.uk). Angel tube. **Open** 11am-5.45pm Tue-Sat; 2-5.45pm Sun. **Credit** AmEx, MC, V.
If you want to commission something special, make this your first online stop. The Craft Council's extensive database of over 50,000 images of quality crafts was previously only accessible in its reference library, but now you can search for the maker of your dreams at home. There are links from the Crafts Council website, or you can go directly to www.photostore.org.uk. Access was free at the time of launch, but users will eventually be charged an annual £10 subscription to cover administration costs. The site is, fittingly, very well designed and categories cover every imaginable object, such as altar vestments, body sculpture and fountains. At the Islington premises, in addition to the exhibition space, there is a shop with an excellent selection of smaller pieces, usually by four selected artists. When we last popped in, we saw Disa Allsopp's jewellery (from £81 for a silver coiled ring) and Kate Blee's colourful body-wrap scarves inspired by South African townships (from £220). The shop has an extensive range of craft-related books, magazines and postcards (there's also an outlet at the V&A). Since 2004, the Crafts Council has organised Collect, an international art fair for contemporary objects at the V&A (9-13 February in 2006).
Mail order.

Flow

1-5 Needham Road, W11 2RP (7243 0782/www.flowgallery.co.uk). Notting Hill Gate tube. **Open** 11am-6pm Mon-Sat. **Credit** AmEx, DC, MC, V.
Now in its seventh year, Flow has an impressive exhibition programme, featuring a sophisticated smörgåsbord of international crafts. Past shows have focused on Czechoslovakian, Danish, Swedish and Polish crafts and jewellery. In January 2006 the focus is closer to home: '100% Proof' showcases silversmithing and jewellery from Scotland. This is followed in March by an exhibition of contemporary Japanese crafts. Gallery artists include ceramicist Zoë Whiteside, who creates porcelain animals without a hint of the tweeness you might expect from animal art. A white goat or a polar bear look wistful and contemplative (from £275). Glassmaker Jon Lewis creates 'wisps' shaped like teardrops or squat bottles with very elongated necks in a spectrum of colours (from £200). Papier mâché artist Julie Arkell shows her nostalgic doll-like figures here. Moving back to the Scandinavian theme, Finnish metal artist Maria Jauhianen's delicate, brass veined-leaf bowls are photo-etched then powder-coated red (from £375). They are so unusual and impressive that both the V&A and the Museum of Scotland have snapped them up for their collections. Note that there's no garden crafts 'Inside Out' show in summer 2006.
Mail order.

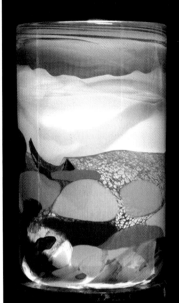

Anthony Stern. See p140.

Frivoli

7A Devonshire Road, W4 2EU (8742 3255).
Turnham Green tube. **Open** 10am-6pm Mon-Sat.
Credit MC, V.

Hazel Peiser's West London gallery is an excellent
source of good-quality, often very affordable
crafts, ranging from clothes to jewellery. Terry
Macey uses linen that's been grown, spun and dyed
in Ireland for his handmade clothing. Pieces are
either one-offs or made in very small quantities in
subtle and strong colours (from £125). Ceramicist
Lilia Umana Clark creates free-standing stoneware
for the garden, such as a hare bird bath (exterior
pieces start at £350). Her smaller items in white
porcelain have a touch of humour – a winged
bonbon dish, for example, or a butter dish
featuring a little cow. They aren't at all naff, but
subtle and charming (from £25). Amanda
Brisbane's heavy sand-cast glassware is dramatic
– her butterfly vases are made from free-flowing
clear glass with colours running through them
(£59), and her large free-standing fish are bold and
sculptural (£150-£400).
Mail order.

Lesley Craze Gallery

34-35A Clerkenwell Green, EC1R 0DU (7608
0393/www.lesleycrazegallery.co.uk). Farringdon
tube/rail. **Open** 10am-5.30pm Tue-Sat. **Credit**
AmEx, DC, MC, V.

Lesley Craze is firmly established as one of the main
players in the crafts world. The gallery is best known
for contemporary jewellery in both precious metals
and mixed media, but also concentrates on
silverware, textiles and accessories. More than 40
textile designers are represented here, and it's a great
place to find unique scarves and quirky handbags
you won't see on everyone's arm, such as Edson
Raupp's sexy bags made from recycled suits and
shimmering buttons (around £245). There is always
a good selection of craft on display, in addition to the
regular 'spotlight' exhibitions showcasing one maker,
and the gallery's annual international show. Recently
featured was Betty Pepper, who uses charity-shop
books to house her textile jewellery, inspired by the
adage 'never judge a book by its cover'. In June 2006
look out for the Architectural Biennale show,
featuring jewellery, metalwork and textiles inspired
by architectural stimuli. *See also chapter* **Jewellery**.

Story

4 Wilkes Street, E1 6QF (7377 0313). Aldgate
East tube/Liverpool Street tube/rail. **Open** 1-7pm
daily. **Credit** AmEx, MC, V.

You never know just what you'll find in this
contemporary Spitalfields space. The stock is
constantly changing, depending on what Lee
Hollingworth and his partner Anne Shore have
sourced. Heavy rustic driftwood-like furniture is a
continuing theme, whether in the form of an
Indian charpoy or an 18th-century French dairy
table. In contrast, girlie vintage fabrics and
costume jewellery are another staple, such as
1940s silk scarves or prom dresses (£150).
Contemporary paintings and photography also
feature from time to time. The shop smells
fantastic thanks to Story's own 100% botanical-oil
incense sticks. Shore and Hollingworth are
committed to respecting the environment and the
ethos here is 'recycled', reclaimed, ethically traded
and organically sound. They've recently expanded
their organic and biodynamic beauty range (£7-
£20). Story's classy and eclectic mix of art and
artefacts attracts chic interiors magazines, and
Donna Karan is a fan. Call first to make sure
they're open.

Studio Fusion

Unit 106, Oxo Tower Wharf, Bargehouse
Street, SE1 9PH (7928 3600/www.studiofusion
gallery.co.uk). Blackfriars or Waterloo tube/rail.
Open 11am-6pm Tue-Sun. **Credit** MC, V.

Studio Fusion is a collaboration by six award-
winning designer-enamelists including Tamar de
Vries Winter and Alexandra Raphael. As well as
displaying their work, the gallery holds special
shows every six weeks or so; some introduce new
artists in individual showcase exhibitions, others
feature new work by established artists. Enamelling
is a highly specialised technique that commands
serious prices. The intricacy of Alexandra
Raphael's plique-à-jour bowls is quite breathtaking.
Little wonder they feature in European and US
museum collections.

Themes & Variations

231 Westbourne Grove, W11 2SE (7727 5531/
www.themesandvariations.com). Notting Hill Gate
tube. **Open** 10am-1pm, 2-6pm Mon-Fri; 10am-6pm
Sat. **Credit** AmEx, MC, V.

Liliane Fawcett brought style to Notting Hill long
before the area became a byword for trendy living.
In her enduringly chic gallery, there is a strong
focus on Scandinavian and Italian decorative arts
and furniture. It takes its name from celebrated
Italian designer Piero Fornasetti's eponymous
series and is the exclusive agent for the Fornasetti
studio. Plates from the series, featuring a woman's

head in one of 365 positions, are £55. Stylish post-
war and contemporary furniture is a speciality, and
the gallery has excellent lighting. The handmade
nickel-and-glass chandeliers of Mark Brazier-Jones
are both beautiful and dramatic (from £3,000). Tord
Boontje's colour-burst chandeliers in silk and
embroidered cotton are bound to soothe SAD
symptoms (£1,900). Look out too for interesting
glass – a recent exhibition showcased work by
Yoichi Ohira, a Japanese artist based in Venice. The
exhibition of post-war design every September/
October is a diary must.

Vessel

114 Kensington Park Road, W11 2PW (7727
8001/www.vesselgallery.com). Notting Hill Gate
tube. **Open** 10am-6pm Mon-Sat. **Credit** AmEx,
MC, V.

Vessel is not a vast shop, but it's the place to find
the best of contemporary table accessories and
design – as customers such as Mario Testino and
Liz Hurley have discovered. Vessel's owner, Nadia
Demetriou Ladas, insures that everything is top
quality – not even a teaspoon is mediocre – and
her ethos is that functional can be beautiful too.
The mix is Italian and Scandinavian, with the
cream of British design. Classics from large
companies, such as Hackmann's superb stainless-
steel pots and cutlery, sit comfortably beside
major one-off pieces by individuals. Look out for
Swedish designer Lena Bergstrom's dynamic,
sculptural glass pieces. The pure, round shapes,
sliced at the top, look as though they might have
landed from outer space (from £1,000). Vessel
commissioned a series of 15 glass 'chairs' from
designer Thomas Heatherwick – comprised of
three large glass bubbles, they're sculptures rather
than functional seating although you can use the
recess as a vase (£7,500). If you're getting married,
have loaded friends and don't fancy piles of run-
of-the-mill department store offerings, use Vessel's
wedding list service.
Mail order.

Mail order & internet

Commissionacraftsman.com

7921 9708/www.commissionacraftsman.com.
Credit V.

This buying and commissioning service
was set up by Gregory Page-Turner, a former
Christie's expert, who is also the brains behind
Commissionaportrait.com (*see p139*). The

comprehensive and easy-to-use website represents a selection of British craftspeople working in all manner of disciplines, from jewellery and ceramics to furniture. You can buy specific pieces that are featured on the site or find a maker you like and start off the commissioning process. The site gives biographical details on each designer and shows several examples of their work. If you want to see work in the flesh, studio or workshop visits can be arranged. The online part is really just an introduction. Thereafter, you discuss your idea with staff over the phone or in person and will be put in touch with the maker. Payment for commissions is in two parts: half before work starts and the remainder on completion. A wedding list service is available, and the company can create a special web page with its own address so your guests can access the list.

Design Nation

7435 4348/www.designnation.co.uk. **Credit** V.
Design Nation is part of the Design Trust, a registered charity that was established to promote the excellence of British design, so it doesn't take commission on sales or orders. Around 130 designers are members and, each year, a panel nominates new additions. Members include jeweller Disa Allsopp, glass designer Aline Johnson and hip Glasgow wallpaper designers Timorous Beasties. Phone numbers and email addresses of designers are listed on the site, so you can make direct contact. You can order a printed copy of the catalogue if you prefer off-line browsing (£8 including UK delivery). *Mail order (01736 333 333).*

Hidden Art

7729 3301/www.hiddenart.com.
Hidden Art is a not-for-profit organisation, set up to promote the work of designer-makers. Its co-ordinated open studio events used to be limited to the East End, but are now pan-London. These are usually held the last weekend in November, but consult the website for details. Hidden Art currently has 300 members represented on its website, which you can search according to discipline. Each designer's entry includes a statement, images of their work with prices, direct contact details and information about their open studios. An excellent facility.

Mixed spaces

Open studio weekends are a great introduction to the capital's designers. Every year you'll discover something different as new designers move into the spaces and others start working on different projects. These events tend to have a relaxed end-of-term feel, with wine corks popping and designers' friends and family dropping in to say hello. Work is displayed for sale in the hastily tidied-up spaces. Designers are happy to talk about their work and most will accept commissions. Many supply to shops, but prices here are often considerably lower. Alternatively, you can phone individual designers to make an appointment to visit.

The Chocolate Factory

Farleigh Place, N16 7SX (7503 6961/ www.chocolatefactory.org.uk). Dalston Kingsland rail/67, 76, 149, 243 bus. **Open** by appointment only. **Credit** varies.
The Chocolate Factory (formerly exactly that) is set to double in size this year with the addition of a further 16 studios. Tucked away in a cobbled yard, the studios currently house 21 designer-makers specialising in ceramics, fashion, lighting, through to painting, fine art, photography and sculpture. Look out for lampshade designer Helen Rawlinson (*see p139*), womenswear designer Kate Clarkson, ceramicists Susan Nemeth and Sophie MacCarty and painter Keith Ashley. Many designers based here sell their work through leading galleries and outlets such as Heal's, the Conran Shop, the Cross, Koh Samui and Harrods. Open weekends are at the end of November and around the summer solstice.

The Chocolate Factory

Clarendon Road, N22 6XJ (8365 7500). Wood Green tube/W3 bus. **Open** by appointment only. **Credit** varies.
Another ex-confectionery building – the former headquarters of the Barratts sweet company – but no relation to the N16 studios of the same name. Collage Arts (formerly Haringey Arts Council) provides subsidised studios for artists and makers, and the rest of the space is taken up with creative businesses. Painting is strong here – artists include Andy Burgess, Marcus Nisbet and the printmaker Lara Harwood. Look out for glass painter and gilder Alexandra Abraham, who combines dyes and gilding metals to decorate glass bowls, mirrors and wall panels – a technique characteristic of Russian icon painting (items from £35). The open studios event is held every November.

Cockpit Arts

Cockpit Yard, Northington Street, WC1N 2NP (7419 1959/www.cockpitarts.com). Chancery Lane tube. **Open** by appointment only. **Credit** varies.
The variety of disciplines and wealth of talent at Cockpit mean the open weekends are a craft buyer's dream. There are 100 designer-makers working here and a further 65 at Cockpit's Deptford studios. On our last visit we loved Liz Emtage's porcelain lighting – delicate, luminescent cylinders that look almost organic, as if they've been created from shell or even moon dust. Extra-large lamps are £280, but we spotted pretty night lights for £24. Timea Sido's 'Tangled Web' ceramics are crisply delicate, like coral or lace (£24), while May Luk's transfer-printed plates have a sense of humour (small plates from £10).
Textiles are another Cockpit strength – look out for Alpa Mistry's hand-woven textiles in rich colours (from £120). Embroidery artist Lissie Baldwin's collages ooze retro kitsch. She incorporates vintage fabrics and beads to create bikini-clad beach girls or saucy waitresses (£350). More whimsical are Claire Coles's Girls dressed up in wallpaper: collages of layered vintage wallpaper, fabric and stitching. Small panels start at £75. Coles's own wallpaper is handmade to commission at £500 a length. Natasha Kerr's fine-art textiles are scrapbook-like tributes to a person or family and are often commissioned for special birthdays or anniversaries. Old black-and-white family photos are transferred or printed on to fabric and combined with anything from maps to Post-it notes that mean something to the individual. The result is a contemporary heirloom that is very touching to receive (around £1,000). Aline Johnson's candy-striped glass plates look like enormous sweeties; her 'wave' salad servers are fun (£49) and large fused-glass chandeliers are also striking (£550). As well as a series of open studio weekends (June/July and November/December), Cockpit runs a programme of creative courses.
For branch see index.

Great Western Studios

The Lost Goods Building, Great Western Road, W9 3NY (7221 0100/www.greatwestern studios.com). Westbourne Park tube. **Open** by appointment only. **No credit cards.**
A former British Rail building in the shadow of the Westway might seem an unlikely location for a hotbed of creativity, but the 140 artists and designers who work here don't seem to mind the sounds of buses, trains and automobiles. On our last visit the whiff of turps in the corridors confirmed that painting is thriving at GWS. Established abstract painter Martyn Brewster has a studio here. Looking at home in the location are Justin Hibbs's urban landscapes of stairwells and power stations; their slightly eery quality has echoes of De Chirico. Prices range from £200 for a print to £7,000 for a large oil. If you prefer a sunnier palette, look out for Penelope Anstice's luminous paintings of India. There are many other disciplines represented here too, including furniture designer Alex Henebury, milliner Pip Hackett, fashion designer Zakee Shariff, mosaicist Catherine Parkinson and stone carver Belinda Eade. Open studios are during the first weekends of June and December.

Oxo Tower & Gabriel's Wharf

Oxo Tower Wharf, Bargehouse Street, SE1 9PH & 56 Upper Ground, SE1 9PP (7401 2255/www.oxotower.co.uk). Waterloo tube/rail. **Open** 11am-6pm Tue-Sun. **Credit** varies.
The Oxo Tower isn't just a chic eaterie, it also houses a complex of small but interesting design shops and studios. Work ranges from ceramics to textiles, and prices always seem reasonable. Bodo Sperlein continues to produce his popular Japanese-inspired red-berry-pattern porcelain, as well as one-off pieces and bespoke dinner services. His white, stylised porcelain is particularly attractive – prices start at £12, and there are often seconds for sale, so look out for bargains. Michele Oberdieck hand-prints and dyes clothes, scarves and fabrics in her studio – you can often see her at work. Her silk wrap tops (from £130) are inspired by Japanese obi shirts; cushions cost £60-£125. She also takes interiors commissions. Ceramicist Caterina Fadda's organic-shaped bowls and plates (from £26.50) use a 1950s-kitchenware palette of pale blue and green – she also collaborates with big-name companies such as Thomas Rosenthal.

Designers & makers

Bookbinders

Wyvern Bindery

56-58 Clerkenwell Road, EC1M 5PX (7490 7899/ www.wyvernbindery.com). Farringdon tube/rail. **Open** 9am-5pm Mon-Fri. **No credit cards.**
If you've had the good fortune to select from the wine list at the Fat Duck in Bray, you'll have handled a Wyvern creation. Other commissions include props for the latest Harry Potter film. As well as bookbinding and restoring battered tomes, the team can bind theses and create boxes, photo albums and notebooks using a wide range of materials, both traditional and contemporary. Enticing leather choices include goatskin, buckram and morocco. Photograph albums start from £140 for buckram and from £320 for full goatskin binding.

Ceramics & ceramic artists

Annabel Faraday

Unit 5, 73-75 Shacklewell Lane, E8 2EB (07876 746 823/www.annabelfaraday.co.uk). **Open** by appointment only. **No credit cards.**
Faraday prints maps on to raw clay, then builds from the printed slabs. Pots, bottles and platters can be commissioned (from £75) using the A-Z or Ordnance Survey maps and are a perfect memento of a much-loved street or area. You simply select the shape, the colour and then the postcode or location you fancy. Recently she has developed this theme further and her new work is based on street art of particular areas, with a map on the inside and images based on graffiti from the neighbourhood on the outside. Her most popular commissions are the A-Z map pots, but Faraday can print any text or line drawings on to clay. *Mail order.*

Chris Keenan & Carina Ciscato

Unit 7C, Vanguard Court, rear of 36-38 Peckham Road, SE5 8QT (7701 2940). Oval tube then 36 bus/Elephant & Castle tube/rail then 12, 171 bus. **Open** by appointment only 10am-5pm Mon-Fri. **No credit cards.**
Trained by Edmund de Waal, one of the country's leading ceramicists, Keenan specialises in hand-thrown porcelain using celadon and temoku (dark brown) glazes. Prices start from £20. Ciscato's celadon-glazed white porcelain is fluid and delicate, with uneven rims and distorted shapes. An espresso cup costs £20 and large one-off pieces go up to £1,000. The duo have an open studio weekend in late November/early December – call for dates.

Cosmo China

11 Cosmo Place, WC1N 3AP (7278 3374/ www.cosmochina.co.uk). Holborn tube. **Open** 10am-6pm Mon-Sat. **Credit** MC, V.
For 20 years now, Cosmo China has been a godsend for those who want customised gifts, but don't fancy an afternoon in a paint-your-own-ceramics café. The 17-strong team of artists create fun and quirky plates for birthdays, anniversaries and weddings – ideal if you want to go off-list. A specially commissioned dinner plate costs from £60, plus about £10 for the inscription. The shop also has a stock of painted china by artists such as Josie and Charlotte Firmin. Last April, Charlotte Firmin's humorous Charles and Camilla wedding mugs were so popular that there was a queue outside the shop for the first time ever.
Mail order.

The Pottery Workshop

77A Lauriston Road, E9 7HA (8986 9585/ www.carolinebousfield.co.uk). Mile End tube/26, 277, 388 bus. **Open** 10.30am-5.30pm Tue, Wed, Fri, Sat; also by appointment. **Credit** MC, V.
This is Caroline Bousfield-Gregory's 30th year at the Pottery Workshop. She's now such a local institution that she's 'head gardener' at the public roundabout outside the Victoria Park Village premises. Her cheerful ceramics, with bulbous shapes and bold patterns, yearn to be used. Ideally they should be heaving with food for a large alfresco lunch. Unsurprisingly, she loves cooking and the shapes of her functional pieces are often influenced by food. Prices start at £8 for a small dish and go up to £90 for a bird bath. Platters and casserole dishes are very good value at around £40. She takes commissions of all sorts. Past requests have included replacement lids for favourite teapots and dummy eggs for broody pigeons, but more often she's asked to make commemorative pieces for weddings and christenings. The commissions usually take three to four weeks.

Glass & glassworkers

Anthony Stern

205 Avro House, Havelock Terrace, SW8 4AL (7622 9463/www.anthonysternglass.com). Battersea Park rail/137 bus. **Open** 10am-5pm Mon-Fri. **Credit** MC, V.
Anthony Stern thrives on the ritual of glassmaking, so much so that he calls describes it as his 'first language'. His Battersea studio turns out everything from unique wine glasses to massive chandeliers. His Seascape bowls are particularly stunning and look as if they've been scooped from the ocean (£200-£2,000). Stern thinks of them as abstract paintings and as a result they're his most personal pieces. Lighting commissions are very popular. If you want to see a commission in situ, drop into Jigsaw on the King's Road and admire the vibrantly coloured, 4.5m spiral chandelier. Stern also creates smaller domestic lighting, such as sleek lamp bases and individual hanging pendants (both from £650). Look out for his clear wine goblets (£50 each) – the stunning simple shapes recall ancient Rome and are lovely to hold. At the biannual open weekends (at the beginning of July and the end of November), you can pick up seconds.
Mail order.

London Glassblowing/ Glass Art Gallery

7 The Leathermarket, Weston Street, SE1 3ER (7403 2800/www.londonglassblowing.co.uk). London Bridge tube/rail. **Open** 10am-5pm Mon-Fri. **Credit** AmEx, MC, V.
Glass guru Peter Layton celebrates his studio's 30th anniversary in 2006 with a new book *Glass Art* and a travelling exhibition. A changing team of glassblowers work in the former leather exchange, which houses the furnace, as well as a large gallery area displaying works for sale. Prices range from £90 to £3,500, depending on design and scale. The current team includes Anthony Scala, Louis Thompson, Marie Holm and Layne Rowe. Scala's sleek, sculptural clear-glass pieces are exceptional and very different from Layton's highly coloured work. Look out for the summer open weekend and sale, where you can watch glassblowing demonstrations. If you'd like to learn the technique yourself, the workshop offers introductory classes. It is £200 for one day's tuition, but the class is restricted to four students taught by two teachers.

Lettering & sculpture

Belinda Eade

Studio 70, Great Western Studios, The Lost Goods Building, Great Western Road, W9 3NY (7266 0328/www.belindaeade.com). Westbourne Park tube. **Open** by appointment only. **No credit cards**.
Belinda Eade's carved inscriptions on stone are rather like tattoos – they can be viewed by others, but have a very special meaning for the owner. She has made gravestones for pets as well as all sorts of occasion-marking plaques. If you worry that commissioning a piece for a living person may be like giving them an early gravestone, fear not. Eade makes small-scale stone pieces as well as sundials (around £1,500). You select the type of stone, the size, the look (rough or smooth) and, of course, the inscription. Photo albums of past commissions will provide inspiration if you are a bit stuck. Eade and her studio team also design and build elaborate grottoes decorated with stones and shells for both private gardens and public spaces.

Richard Kindersley

40 Cardigan Street, SE11 5PF (7735 9374/ www.kindersleystudio.co.uk). Oval tube. **Open** by appointment only. **No credit cards**.
It's 40 years since Kindersley set up his London studio, and he is now one of the best-known stone carvers working in the UK. His history of commissions is impressive, spanning a host of well-known public buildings, from Westminster Abbey to Tower Bridge. You can also see his exquisite work on the Blitz memorial stone outside St Paul's Cathedral. Carved from a three-ton block of Irish limestone, the large circular memorial bears the inscription 'Remember before God the people of London'. His tall, slender standing stones in Caithness stone and Welsh slate are particularly beautiful and are sought after for private commissions. These start at £5,000, but prices vary depending on the work involved and the stone used. His busy studio has four full-time assistants and welcomes visitors as long as they phone ahead.

Lighting

Anna Perring

07774 626 536/www.lunalighting.co.uk. **No credit cards**.
Perring's Luna lights have a magical feel. Light scatters through a pattern of tiny holes, so that they twinkle like fireflies or fairy lights (Perring admits that she always hated taking down her fairy lights after Christmas). Her aim was to create organic, feminine lighting that would look right in a modern space. Lights are individually hand-built in stoneware and fired with a creamy white semi-matt glaze, or scraped for a textured, sculptural look then varnished. Stoneware lights are frost-proof so they can be used outside. Luna 'Snowballs' start at £99 and tall cylinders go up to £299. Her porcelain range includes mini individual tea-light holders (£12) and pyramid-shaped tea-light triangles (£35). Perring takes part in Hidden Art open studios (*see p138*) and shows at Frivoli (*see p137*).

Helen Rawlinson

Unit 5, First Floor, The Chocolate Factory, Farleigh Place, N16 7SX (7503 5839/www.helen rawlinson.com). Dalston Kingsland rail/67, 76, 149, 243 bus. **Open** by appointment only. **No credit cards**.
Rawlinson brings out a new range of lampshades each year. Her latest collection has a Moroccan twist using a luminous Mediterranean palette. The lampshades are hand-printed using silk-screen techniques and finished with stitched details. Rawlinson also undertakes commissions for turned wooden lamp bases. Small drum shades start at £31, but at the open studio weekends (*see p138* The Chocolate Factory) samples and seconds of shades and bases are sold at 50% of the usual prices.
Mail order.

Portrait painters

The annual **BP Portrait Award** is held every summer at the National Portrait Gallery (St Martin's Place, WC2H 0HE, 7312 2463, www.npg.org.uk) and is one of Britain's most prestigious and lucrative art prizes – the winner of the award receives £25,000 and a £3,000 commission. Around 50 portraits for exhibition are chosen from over 1,000 entries, making the show a great place to see the best of contemporary portraiture.

Commissionaportrait.com

7921 9708/www.commissionaportrait.com. **No credit cards**.
This comprehensive website is a great introduction if you are thinking of commissioning a portrait. It caters for all tastes and there is a section showing examples for under £1,000 – mostly drawings and works on paper. The service also covers sculpture, photography and caricature. If you don't fancy the look of your own family, you can buy a copy of a famous portrait. There are good examples of work by each artist – often portraits of public figures. Once you have chosen an artist and a contract has been signed through Commissionaportrait.com, you either go for sittings in a studio or the artist will come to you. Some will paint from a photograph and you can even commission a portrait of your cat, horse or country pile. Chief executive Gregory Page-Turner is a former Christie's watercolour expert who is also behind Commissionacraftsman.com (*see p137*).

Fine Art Commissions Ltd

79 Walton Street, SW3 2HP (7589 4111/ www.fineartcommissions.com). South Kensington tube. **Open** 10am-6pm Mon-Fri. **Credit** MC, V.
This website works rather like a property site: you type in your budget, then see what you can afford. Prices depend on artist and medium, but charcoals start at around £400, single portrait oils at £1,200 and 'conversation' (group) portraits from £5,600. You can flick through the artists' portfolios in the office, or staff can send you a tailor-made mini portfolio or CD-Rom. As is often the nature of portraiture, the set-up is pretty posh – the site makes gift suggestions such as commissioning 'wine labels for private parties' or a 'watercolour of a friend's first flat'. Many artists have impressive lists of starry sitters, including royals; for example, Theo Platt painted Princess Diana, and Julian Barrow has immortalised six members of the Royal Family, including the Queen. The gallery in Walton Street also has a changing exhibition programme.

Royal Society of Portrait Painters

17 Carlton House Terrace, SW1Y 5BD (7930 6844/www.mallgalleries.org.uk/www.therp.co.uk). Charing Cross tube/rail. **Open** 10am-5pm daily. **Credit** AmEx, MC, V.
Whistler and Millais were among the original members of the Royal Society of Portrait Painters, which began in 1891. Current members include Richard Foster, Michael Reynolds and Peter Kuhfeld. The annual spring exhibition at the Mall Galleries shows a variety of portrait work in different styles. A commissions consultant can put you in touch with members. Oils start at £4,000 and charcoal/pencil sketches from £1,000, depending on the artist. Call first to check they're open.

Rugs

For additional rug and carpet companies, *see* chapter **Interiors**.

Deirdre Dyson Contemporary Carpets

331 King's Road, SW3 5ES (7795 0122/ www.deirdredyson.com). Sloane Square tube. **Open** 10am-6pm Mon-Fri; 10am-5pm Sat. **Credit** AmEx, DC, MC, V.
Deirdre Dyson, who's fittingly married to James of vacuum-cleaner fame, designs all the handmade carpets here. Using her personalised design service, you can have a truly bespoke rug made to any size or shape in a choice of over 1,500 colours using pure wool or silk. All carpets are made to order in Scotland or Spain (tufted) or Nepal (hand-knotted). Prices start at £290/sq m. Last year Dyson was commissioned by the V&A to design a rug to accompany its Arts and Crafts exhibition.

Textile designers

Cecilie Telle

98C Tollington Park, N4 3RB (7272 1335/ www.cecilietelle.com). Finsbury Park tube/rail. **Open** by appointment Mon-Fri. **No credit cards.**
Telle continues to create her cosy and charming knitted garments and accessories, and has recently started recycling wool in collaboration with the Norwegian Salvation Army. Her circle-pattern Elvish Bonnets will be adored by young children (£26), while adults will be amused by her hoof-like Tabi Toe slippers with non-slip soles (£52). Last year she took part in Extreme North, a touring exhibition of Norwegian design and architecture. Her work is also sold at Dover Street Market (*see p26* Commes des Garçons).
Mail order.

Claire O'Hea

Great Western Studios, The Lost Goods Building, Great Western Road, W9 3NY (8964 3664/ www.ohea.co.uk). Westbourne Park tube. **Open** by appointment only. **No credit cards.**
Claire O'Hea has cut down on her lighting range this year and instead has turned her focus to wall panels: the textile equivalent of abstract paintings. Silk or jersey Lycra is used to create a rich sheen, and vibrant colours, such as burnt orange and jade, are layered to enhance positive feelings and well-being. Panels range from £190 to £1,500. O'Hea's delectable cushions are also in stunning colours such as fresh greens and sea blues (from £30). Lighting is still available, with small drum shades starting at around £30. You can pick up bargains at the open weekends.
Mail order.

Clarissa Hulse

132 Cavell Exchange, Cavell Street, E1 2JA (7375 1456/www.clarissahulse.com). Whitechapel tube. **Open** by appointment only. **Credit** MC, V.
Hulse's silk interiors range changes every year but always oozes elegance. Her latest collection is divided into four palettes. Pampas features neutral shades such as honey and bronze. Purple Haze is feminine without being girlie, and Modern Orient has an East-meets-West look combining rich reds and chocolate. Despite the current vogue for neutrals, the Brighton Rock palette of vibrant and neon colours has been a bestseller. Silk cushions start at £39 and lampshades at £59.
Mail order.

Fabrications

7 Broadway Market, E8 4PH (7275 8043/ www.fabrications1.co.uk). Bus 26, 48, 55. **Open** noon-5pm Tue-Sat; also by appointment. **No credit cards.**
Barley Massey's studio/shop is an outlet for her own designs as well as those of other textile designers such as Buttress + Snatch. Her work focuses on recycled materials, such as rubber rugs made from bicycle inner tubes (from £75) and cushions made from old shirts and ties (£40). She also creates costumes for theatre and film, and undertakes commissions for one-off interior pieces.

Expect to see anything from large wall hangings to underwear in the shop. Fabrications now boasts 'The Hagedashery', an area stocking quality and unusual knitting and sewing supplies.
Mail order.

Hikaru Noguchi

Unit E4, Cockpit Workshops, Cockpit Yard, WC1N 2NP (7813 1227/www.hikarunoguchi.com). Holborn tube. **Open** by appointment only. **Credit** V.
This Japanese knitwear designer has been working in London for 14 years. Her accessories are a contemporary take on traditional British knits – for example, Fair Isle hat-and-scarf sets come in colourways such as berry and glitter, and classic pullovers incorporate graphic motifs, such as owls. Hats start at £55 and scarves at £75. She also makes capes and other accessories such as bags. Her designs are sold in Selfridges and Harvey Nichols as well as boutiques such as Anna (*see p36*) and The Cross (*see p36*).

Victoria Richards

Clockwork Studios, 38 Southwell Road, SE5 9PG (7737 8009/www.victoriarichards.com). Brixton tube/rail/Loughborough Junction rail. **Open** by appointment only. **No credit cards.**
You've probably seen Richards's work on the news. Channel 4 News presenter Jon Snow is a big fan of her vibrant, hand-painted silk ties (£50) and she gets lots of orders as a result. In fact, the television station has been so inundated with people asking where to buy them, there's now a link to Richards on its website. However, ties are not the designer's main interest. Look out for her rich velvet dressing gowns (£450) and silk scarves (£42-£200).
Mail order.

Tiles & mosaics

Catherine Parkinson

Studio 66, Great Western Studios, The Lost Goods Building, Great Western Road, W9 3NY (7221 0100/www.greatwesternstudios.com). Westbourne Park tube. **Open** by appointment only. **No credit cards.**
Catherine Parkinson makes mosaics for kitchens, bathrooms, floors and gardens. Look through her album of past commissions to see how stunning they are in situ – you'd feel like you had your very own Roman villa. A circular floor in a shower will set you back around £2,500.

Dominic Crinson

15 Redchurch Street, E2 7DJ (7613 2783/ www.crinson.com). Liverpool Street tube/rail/ 8, 26, 48, 242 bus. **Open** by appointment Mon-Fri. **No credit cards.**
Dominic Crinson's Digitiles blow traditional tile design out of the water. Don't expect twee little shell motifs; Crinson thinks big and bold. His Bodywall range is just that – a wall of multiple nudes that can be made to any scale. His Incredible Edibles range will give wow factor to the dreariest kitchen. You can have giant slices of lime, kiwis or cabbages throughout the kitchen or one enormous slice all the way across the wall. New designs are released every six months and images can be scaled to the required size or repeated as patterns. Crinson has expanded his repertoire to cover wall and floor tiles, carpet and wallpaper. Prices start from £130/sq m for carpet, £245/sq m for wall tiles and £28/m for wallpaper.
Mail order.

Mosaik

10 Kensington Square, W8 5EP (7795 6253). High Street Kensington tube. **Open** noon-6.30pm Mon-Fri; 11am-6pm Sat; also by appointment. **No credit cards.**
Architect Pierre Mesguich has been moving more towards marble mosaic, but his elegant glass mosaics still attract those in search of bespoke bathrooms and hallways. White-on-white works with soft, textured effects are currently very popular. Colourful Venetian glass mosaics make vivid interior design features (from £80/sq ft). Simple bathroom designs start at around £1,000.

Almost every area of London has a commercial gallery worth visiting, but the numerous art fairs now provide a one-stop taster of the London arts scene and beyond. The **London Art Fair** (www.londonartfair.co.uk), **artLONDON** (www.artlondon.net) and the **20/21 British Art Fair** (www.britishartfair.co.uk) are excellent hunting grounds. Most fairs are sociable affairs with well-stocked bars, so you can wander at leisure with a glass of wine. Other gallery clusters often have special evenings and events, such as **Art Fortnight** (www.artfortnightlondon.com) and **Asian Art Week** (www.asianartinlondon.com).

A&D

51 Chiltern Street, W1U 6LY (7486 0534/www.a-and-d.co.uk). Baker Street tube. **Open** 10.30am-7pm Mon-Sat. **Credit** AmEx, MC, V.
There's a camp, kitsch atmosphere here – as you might expect with a stable including mixed-media artist Nancyboy, glamour photographer Ben Westwood (Vivienne's son) and 'English eccentric' Andrew Logan. The latter's large, mirrored mosaic brooches (from £100) have the ultimate fashion validation – Samantha wore one in the final series of *Sex and the City*. But it's not all glitter and glam. There are six solo shows and six group exhibitions each year, plus a good selection of prints by leading artists such as Roy Lichtenstein, Andy Warhol, Helmut Newton and Joseph Beuys. A&D stands for 'amusing and delightful', and the gallery certainly lives up to its name.

Andrew Mummery Gallery

Studio 1.04, The Tea Building, 56 Shoreditch High Street (entrance on Bethnal Green Road), E1 6JJ (7729 9399/www.andrewmummery.com). Liverpool Street tube/rail. **Open** noon-6pm Wed-Sat. **No credit cards.**
Andrew Mummery was the first gallery to move into the Tea Building, which now also houses the Hales Gallery and Rocket. He continues to concentrate on new developments in painting and also shows photography and mixed-media work. Gallery artists include Dutch painter Philip Akkerman, whose sole preoccupation is the self-portrait – he has vowed to paint one every day for the rest of his life. Look out for Scottish photographer Wendy McMurdo's slightly surreal shots of people. On our latest visit we saw an exhibition by painter Graeme Todd, from a period when he lived and worked in Osaka.

Blue Gallery

15 Great Sutton Street, EC1V 0BX (7490 3833/ www.thebluegallery.co.uk). Barbican tube/ Farringdon tube/rail. **Open** 10am-6pm Mon-Fri; 11am-3pm Sat. **No credit cards.**
Contemporary art world insiders rate Blue Gallery very highly, and it's easy to see why. Exhibitions show innovative work in a variety of media. Gallery artists include Oliver Marsden, Paul Riley and Jerwood Prize-winning photographer Veronica Bailey. A recent addition to the stable is Emily Allchurch, who recreates Old Master paintings using montages of photographs of London. Her unusual works are very popular – be they in the style of Turner or Giorgione (£2,500-£4,500).

Chinese Contemporary Gallery

21 Dering Street, W1S 1AL (7499 8898/ www.chinesecontemporary.com). Bond Street or Oxford Circus tube. **Open** 10am-6pm Mon-Fri; 11am-4pm Sat. **No credit cards.**
This is the only gallery in the UK devoted to contemporary Chinese art, specifically post-1989 avant-garde. The gallery, which also has a branch in Beijing, was set up ten years ago with the aim of showcasing artists living and working in mainland China. Big names such as leading Cynical Realist Fang Lijun, figurative painter Yue Minjun and Zhang Xiaogang – whose work is also in the Guggenheim in New York – show here. Prices start at around £1,000 for small works by young artists and go up to about £100,000 for major pieces.

Cockpit Arts. See p139.

Clapham Art Gallery

Unit 2, 40-48 Bromell's Road, SW4 0BG (7720 0955/www.claphamartgallery.com). Clapham Common tube. **Open** 11am-6pm Tue-Sat. **Credit** AmEx, MC, V.

The gallery has moved from its Venn Street space to its larger unit round the corner, where it continues to show the work of emerging artists as well as its regulars. One of the gallery's best-known artists is photorealist painter Dan McDermott, who focuses on Americana. Jo Barrett also paints 'I can't believe it's not a photo' still lifes and landscapes. Linocut artist Paul Catherall chooses iconic buildings as his subjects, such as the Oxo Tower, the Gherkin and the London Eye – his clean, sharp palette gives his work a retro quality (from around £300). *Mail order.*

Danielle Arnaud

123 Kennington Road, SE11 6SF (7735 8292/ www.daniellearnaud.com). Lambeth North tube. **Open** 2-6pm Fri-Sun; also by appointment. **Credit** AmEx, MC, V.

Danielle Arnaud's elegant Georgian home makes a striking backdrop for the exhibitions of contemporary video art and photography held here. Arnaud puts on six shows a year, featuring young international artists, such as Mr and Mrs Ivan Morison, who observe, collect and record things they come into contact with – for one project, Ivan made a short film of himself gardening in the nude. Video artists include Susan Morris, Paulette Phillips, and Marie-France and Patricia Martin. Arnaud also collaborates on an annual exhibition at the Museum of Garden History. *Mail order.*

Eagle Gallery – Emma Hill Fine Art

159 Farringdon Road, EC1R 3AL (7833 2674/www.emmahilleagle.com). Farringdon tube/rail. **Open** 11am-6pm Wed-Fri; 11am-4pm Sat. **Credit** MC, V.

The Eagle Gallery was established by Emma Hill in 1991 and promotes the work of a number of contemporary British artists, as well as showing more established names such as Basil Beattie and Prunella Clough. Regulars include Tom Hammick, whose figurative lithographs have both a nostalgic and imaginative quality. Zara Matthews's photorealistic portrait paintings on linen take on the genre anew. The gallery is particularly well known for publishing limited-edition artists' books and has a good selection of attractive and well-priced graphics. *Mail order.*

England & Co

216 Westbourne Grove, W11 2RH (7221 0417). Notting Hill Gate tube. **Open** 11am-6pm Mon-Sat. **Credit** AmEx, MC, V.

Jane England mainly focuses on contemporary artists, but there are usually a couple of historic exhibitions each year. Thematic shows are a speciality – for example, contemporary art inspired by maps. In 2006 look out for a one-man show by Jason Wallis-Johnson, who works in a variety of media. Prices range from £100 to £10,000.

Eyestorm

18 Maddox Street, W1S 1PL (7659 0860/ www.eyestorm.com). Oxford Circus tube. **Open** 10am-6pm Mon-Fri; 11am-5pm Sat. **Credit** AmEx, MC, V.

As well as gallery space in Maddox Street, Eyestorm has showrooms in Newcastle, Warwick and New York. The online gallery sells limited-edition art by contemporary artists and seems to have sourced something by everyone who is anyone in the art world. We spotted Martin Parr photographs (from £480), a Jenny Saville lithograph (£5,875) and a silkscreen by Chris Ofili (£1,300). If the work you like is over your budget, there is an online facility to email a 'reasonable' offer – which will be accepted or rejected within a day. The sister website www.britart.com is another decent resource photography, installations, sculptures, even gifts.

Flowers East

82 Kingsland Road, E2 8DP (7920 7777/www. flowerseast.com). Old Street tube/rail. **Open** 10am-6pm Tue-Sat; 11am-5pm Sun. **Credit** AmEx, MC, V.

Flowers has blossomed over the years – in addition to its East End base and Flowers Central in Cork Street, there are US branches in New York and Santa Monica. It's undoubtedly one of the sleekest, yet still accessible, contemporary galleries around, representing big-name painters such as Peter Howson and Tai-Shan Schierenberg. Don't miss Patrick Hughes's amazing spatial illusions – his rooms and landscapes seem to move as you walk past them (prices from £2,000). Flowers Central's ambitious summer 'Artist of the Day' exhibition invites respected British artists (such as Allen Jones in 2005) to select a less fêted artist to be showcased for a day – it's a great way to find out who the big boys rate. At Flowers East, make sure you venture upstairs to the graphics department, where you'll find fine prints in very small editions (25 on average). Peter Howson's etchings start at around £400.

For branch (Flowers Central) see index.

Greenwich Printmakers

1A Greenwich Market, SE10 9HZ (8858 1569/ www.greenwich-printmakers.org.uk). Greenwich rail/DLR. **Open** 11am-6pm daily. **Credit** MC, V.

This small gallery in bustling Greenwich Market is a co-operative, administered and run by the members who exhibit here. Prices are very affordable (£40-£300) and shows change regularly. As well as framed exhibition works, the stands of unframed prints are always worth browsing through. Sonia Rollo's etchings are enchanting, particularly her sparring hares and gentle dogs. Theresa Pateman's dreamy Chagall-like figures are placed in urban settings such as taxis.

Hales Gallery

The Tea Building, 7 Bethnal Green Road, E1 6LA (7033 1938/www.halesgallery.com). Liverpool Street tube/rail. **Open** noon-6pm Thur-Sat; also by appointment. **Credit** AmEx, DC, MC, V.

Installation work is prominent in this gallery, which features artists such as Hans Op de Beeck. A show is planned for 2006 with Tomoko Takahashi, who was shortlisted for the Turner Prize in 2000. She recently exhibited at the Serpentine Gallery, where her installation 'My Play-station' was made from 7,600 pieces of rubbish that she'd collected from skips and car-boot sales. Look out too for surrealist LA landscape painter Adam Ross and collage paintings by Kirsten Glass. Photographer Spencer Tunick, who photographs groups of nudes in incongruous urban settings, shows here.

Jill George Gallery

38 Lexington Street, W1F 0LL (7439 7319/ www.jillgeorgegallery.co.uk). Oxford Circus or Piccadilly Circus tube. **Open** 10am-6pm Mon-Wed, Fri; 10am-8pm Thur; 11am-5pm Sat; by appointment only Sun. **Credit** MC, V.

Jill George has been in Soho for 18 years and maintains a consistent and interesting stable of artists. The mix of abstract and figurative painting makes for a balanced exhibition programme. Figurative painters include BP Portrait Award-winner Tomas Watson and Alison Lambert. Vibrant abstract painter Martyn Brewster and 3-D artists David Mach and Mark Firth show their work here. There is a good selection of limited-edition prints, and George displays the work of recent graduates every 18 months. The gallery also exhibits at international fairs in Toronto, San Francisco and Chicago. *Mail order.*

Plus One Gallery

91 Pimlico Road, SW1W 8PH (7724 7304/ www.plusonegallery.com). Sloane Square tube. **Open** 10.30am-6.30pm Mon-Fri; 11am-3pm Sat. **Credit** MC, V.

Realism is very much the speciality here, and the gallery's contemporary artists prove the genre is alive and well and not to be sniffed at. Elena Molinari's oil paintings of empty fizzy-drink cans give a strange beauty to items we normally trash or recycle. Another realist, Andrew Holmes, draws pick-up trucks and cardiac arrest-inducing deli counters with the exacting eye of a camera lens. In January 2006, look out for the group exhibition, aptly named 'Exactitude'. Individual shows for the year include Steve Smulka. Keep your eyes open for Beth Carter's strange bronze and resin figures of minotaurs sleeping or reading books.

Rebecca Hossack Gallery

35 Windmill Street, W1T 2JS (7436 4899/ www.r-h-g.co.uk). Goodge Street tube. **Open** 11 0am-6pm Mon-Sat. **Credit** MC, V.

Rebecca Hossack pioneered the introduction of Aboriginal art to the UK and she continues to be passionate about it, feeling that in comparison, much Western art lacks soul. The gallery plays host to a dedicated Songlines season of Aboriginal art every summer and has a range of stock from all the major Aboriginal communities, such as Fitzroy Crossing and Haasts Bluff. But Hossack also looks closer to home, with a particular emphasis on contemporary Scottish painters like Helen Flockhart. Sculpture, mixed-media work and jewellery are also shown here, so there is always something fresh and surprising. The nearby Charlotte Street Gallery (28 Charlotte Street, W1T 2NA, 7255 2828) is under the same ownership.

Rocket Gallery

Unit G04, Tea Building, 56 Shoreditch High Street, E1 6JJ (7729 7594/www.rocketgallery. com). Liverpool Street or Old Street tube/rail. **Open** 10am-6pm Tue-Fri; noon-6pm Sat, Sun. **Credit** AmEx, MC, V.

Formerly in the Cork Street area, the gallery has moved from the West End to premises in this vast Shoreditch warehouse, alongside Andrew Mummery and the Hales Gallery. Rocket shows abstract, design-influenced art and photography and represents renowned British photographer Martin Parr – he had his sixth show with the gallery last spring/summer. Artists' books are another speciality. *Mail order.*

Will's Art Warehouse

Unit 3, Heathmans Road, SW6 4TJ (7371 8787/ www.wills-art.com). Parsons Green tube. **Open** 10.30am-6pm daily. **Credit** MC, V.

It would be hard to find a more unashamedly commercial art gallery. All work for sale is priced between £50 and £3,000. Affordability is key, so much so that owner Will Ramsay went on to set up the Affordable Art Fair. The gallery is open seven days a week, offers a wedding list and even sells gift vouchers. We can't imagine any other gallery owner describing himself as 'the Oddbins of the art world'. You might think the commercial thing has gone too far when the website invites you to select colours and dimensions – it's more like buying made-to-measure blinds than a painting. A combination of 'pink', 'oils' and 'any artist' lands you a painting of black fish against a fuchsia background by Celia Wilkinson (£495). *Mail order.*

Wolseley Fine Arts

12 Needham Road, W11 2RP (7792 2788/ www.wolseleyfinearts.com). Notting Hill Gate or Westbourne Park tube. **Open** 11am-6pm Wed-Fri; 11am-5pm Sat. **Credit** AmEx, MC, V.

Rupert Otten specialises in 20th-century British and French works on paper, and holds about eight exhibitions a year in his small but charming gallery. This is the place to come for prints, drawings and watercolours by David Jones, Eric Gill, Edward Ardizzone and John Buckland Wright. Shows here are always interesting and Otten manages to find lovely small examples by names such as Vuillard and Bonnard (from about £3,000). The gallery also shows sculpture of the period, and the annual summer garden sculpture exhibition is displayed in the garden at the back. Carved lettering on stone is another speciality and includes the artists Richard Kindersley and Martin Cook. *Mail order.*

Furniture

Department stores are constantly increasing their repertoire of furniture. **Selfridges** houses concessions of **Viaduct** (*see p152*), **SCP** (*see p150*) and **Skandium** (*see p150*). Designer **Paul Smith** (*see p49*) has opened his first stand-alone furniture and antique shop in Mayfair, while Kevin McCloud, presenter of Channel 4's *Grand Designs*, has set up a mail-order venture, Place (0870 443 9391, placeto.co.uk), with an emphasis on sustainability and fair trade.

Alexander Miles
39 Wigmore Street, W1U 1AL (7486 4545/ www.alexandermiles.co.uk). Bond Street or Oxford Circus tube. **Open** 10am-6pm Mon-Sat. **Credit** MC, V.
This store, formerly called Defy Interiors, sells its own collection of contemporary bedroom, living-room and occasional furniture. The style is unobtrusive, elegant and not prey to fast-moving trends. The wooden-framed beds are particularly appealing, such as the Corsini bed in walnut (from £1,510), which is bound to stand the test of time, as is the fuss-free, handleless Ferra sideboard (from £2,595). The rich texture and durability of the woods – beech, oak and walnut – are enhanced by the precision of the craftsmanship. If nothing in the range quite hits the mark, discuss the bespoke service with the friendly staff.

Aram
110 Drury Lane, WC2B 5SG (7557 7557/ www.aram.co.uk). Covent Garden tube. **Open** 10am-6pm Mon-Wed, Fri, Sat; 10am-7pm Thur. **Credit** AmEx, MC, V.
Aram is a family-run business that has been selling contemporary furniture designs since the 1960s. This five-storey Covent Garden showroom, opened by Zeev Aram and his children Daniel and Ruth, houses some of the best contemporary European furniture, lighting and accessories. The store offers classic pieces by well-known designers, such as Eileen Gray, Alvar Aalto, Arne Jacobsen and the Eameses, alongside current masters Jasper Morrison, Ron Arad and Philippe Starck, plus occasional newcomers. It's particularly strong on sofas, with more than 20 different models on display, from Bauhaus classics to the latest designs from Milan. Sofas start at about £1,500, while coffee tables start at a respectable £150 and chairs at £50. Beds by Italian company Flou are now available here. The Duetto (with a second mattress stored beneath it) costs £1,500. *Mail order.*

Aria
295-297 Upper Street, N1 2TU (7704 1999/ www.ariashop.co.uk). Angel tube. **Open** 10am-7pm Mon-Fri; 10am-6.30pm Sat; noon-5pm Sun. **Credit** AmEx, DC, MC, V.
Aria manages to appeal to the everyday furniture buyer, avoiding the intimidating atmosphere of the 'design elite' yet remaining thoroughly stylish. The shop is home to a good selection of accessible furniture, such as colourful plastic chairs and tables from Italian brands Driade, Kartell and Magis, which start at a respectable £45. There's also a sizeable range of other interior items, such as lighting and tableware.

B&B Italia
250 Brompton Road, SW3 2AS (7591 8111/ www.bebitalia.it). South Kensington tube. **Open** 10am-6pm Mon-Sat; noon-5pm Sun. **Credit** AmEx, MC, V.
At leading furniture brand B&B Italia's gorgeous cathedral-like showroom, designs are displayed in stunning room sets. This is the place to come for the clean-lined, timeless quality one would expect from Italy, but it doesn't come cheap. This hasn't deterred a huge customer base looking for inspirational pieces for the living room, bedroom and kitchen. New for 2005 is Antonio Citterio's modular Arne sofa (from £3,195). Patricia Urquiola has also been busy with the unusual, stylish Digitable – an aluminium, laser-cut side table (£832) – and the Tufty-Time modular sofa system, her review of the classic chesterfield and capitonné. *Mail order.*

BoConcept
158 Tottenham Court Road, W1T 7NH (7388 2447/www.boconcept.co.uk). Goodge Street or Warren Street tube. **Open** 10am-6pm Mon-Wed, Fri, Sat; 10am-8pm Thur; noon-6pm Sun. **Credit** MC, V.
A clean, modern aesthetic is practised at BoConcept, providing a lifestyle package that can only be described as 'nice'. You won't find many cutting-edge designs, but what you will find is an affordable, non-obtrusive modern look. Bedroom furniture lines are reasonably strong, with a range of beds starting at only £335. Elsewhere, pick up a simple three-seater sofa for around £1,000 or a good-looking lounging Sharp chair for £329.
For branch see index.

Chair
98 Westbourne Grove, W2 5RU (7985 7460/ www.chair-london.com). Bayswater or Notting Hill Gate tube. **Open** 10am-6.30pm Mon-Sat; 11am-5pm Sun. **Credit** AmEx, DC, MC, V.
Ever sat in a restaurant and wanted to buy the chair you're sitting on or the plate you're eating from? Well, you can in this new shop/restaurant, opened by Andrew Cussins, the man who introduced Sofa Workshop. You can enjoy a meal of seasonal organic British food at ground level, or head straight to the shop in the basement, where you'll find a selection of furniture, lighting, soft furnishings, ceramics and glass. New and established British and international names include Tom Dixon, the Campana brothers and Committee. Prices are mid to high end.

The Chair Company
82-84 Parsons Green Lane, SW6 4HU (7736 5478/www.thechair.co.uk). Parsons Green tube. **Open** 10am-6pm Mon-Wed, Fri, Sat; 10am-7pm Thur; 11am-5pm Sun. **Credit** MC, V.
The range of chairs here is extensive and includes wood, plastic, leather and upholstered models in many shapes and sizes. There are chairs suitable for home and office use, and all styles are contemporary and fresh. Alongside big-name designers like Mies van der Rohe and Le Corbusier are several reinterpretations of classic designs. Well-known reproductions include the Eames chair in moulded rosewood-effect plywood and leather (£1,645) and the Barcelona chair (£1,195).
For branches see index.

Chaplins
17-18 Berners Street, W1T 3LN (7323 6552/ www.chaplins.co.uk). Goodge Street or Oxford Circus tube. **Open** 10am-6pm Mon-Sat; 10am-8pm Thur. **Credit** AmEx, MC, V.
If you're on the lookout for contemporary design pieces and have some money to spend, check out Chaplins. Leading Italian brands Cappellini, Zanotta, Edra and Cassina are among the high-end collections on display. Expect many avant-garde creations straight from the Milan exhibitions, alongside less garish sofas, chairs, tables, cabinets,

and beds. You can also pick up some gorgeous 'future classic' home additions from Jasper Morrison, Tom Dixon, the Bouroullec brothers and Patricia Urquiola in this slick showroom.
For branch see index.

Charles Page
61 Fairfax Road, NW6 4EE (7328 9851/ www.charlespage.co.uk). Finchley Road tube/31 bus. **Open** 9.30am-5.30pm Mon-Fri; 10am-6pm Sat. **Credit** MC, V.
If you're keen to adopt a contemporary style within your home but can't quite stomach some of the more avant-garde, and sometimes garish, offerings available elsewhere, Charles Page reckons it can sort you out with 'furniture you can live with'. Top-quality pieces are chosen by a well-informed staff group of interior designers, who can advise on the best solution for your particular needs. The lower ground floor is now given over to Ligne Roset, while the ground floor is predominantly Molteni furniture, such as the Reversi (a modular sofa with an adjustable back, £2,500). Staff will happily talk you through the portfolio of other items available to order from their extensive list of suppliers.

The Conran Shop
Michelin House, 81 Fulham Road, SW3 6RD (7589 7401/www.conran.com). South Kensington tube. **Open** 10am-6pm Mon, Tue, Fri; 10am-7pm Wed, Thur; 10am-6.30pm Sat; noon-6pm Sun. **Credit** AmEx, MC, V.
The Conran Shop was one of the first retailers to embody the term 'lifestyle' by introducing cosmopolitan shoppers to the notion of buying everything for their home from one place – from foodstuffs and furniture to style books and accessories. The company is careful to hand-pick pieces that are already, or destined to become, design classics, although it's not afraid to throw in newer, more eye-catching items. There is something for everyone's budget, be it a ceramic vase for £20, a Norm 69 pendant light for £75 or a Baby Elephant sofa with movable ears, each part of an audio system that can be connected to an iPod or CD player (£3,000; non-audio £1,995). *Mail order.*
For branches see index.

Couch Potato Company
23 Hampton Road, Twickenham, Surrey TW2 5QE (8894 1333/www.couchpotatocompany.com). Strawberry Hill train. **Open** 9.30am-5.30pm Tue-Fri; 10am-5.30pm Sat. **Credit** MC, V.
As the name suggests, the Couch Potato Company sells comfy seating, such as the Soho three-seater leather sofa (£1,295) and the chunky Gothenburg chocolate-brown leather armchair (£859). Large, leather-upholstered furniture displays are livened up with more recognisable and colourful items such as Eames plastic chairs (£143) and many other 1950s and '60s classic reissues.

De La Espada
60 Sloane Avenue, SW3 3DD (7581 4474/ www.delaespada.com). Sloane Square or South Kensington tube. **Open** 10am-6pm Mon, Tue, Thur-Sat; 10am-7pm Wed; noon-5pm Sun. **Credit** AmEx, MC, V.
De La Espada sells a refined collection of understated sofas, chairs, dining and coffee tables, desks, beds, cabinets and wardrobes, using timeless and durable materials such as solid oak and walnut. Most upholstery is limited to earthy tones such as chocolate, beige, cream, white and grey. Prices aren't low – the Minimal dining table for eight is £2,375, the Weekend long sofa is £6,055 and the Luna dining chair is £875 – but you do pay for lasting quality, high craftsmanship and solid wood. There is also a bespoke service. *Mail order.*

Dwell
264 Balham High Road, SW17 7AN (0870 241 8653/www.dwell.co.uk). Balham tube. **Open** 10am-7pm Mon-Sat; 11am-5pm Sun. **Credit** AmEx, DC, MC, V.

HOME

Founded in 2003 by the ex-CEO of Ocean (*see p149*), Dwell caters for those after modern furniture and interior items at very affordable prices – straight-back leather dining chairs are £69, a corner sofa is £795 and an oak dining table seating eight to ten is £459. The collection offers reasonable quality and is a useful source for busy people who want to achieve a contemporary look without having to shop around. Lighting and accessories are other areas of the business. A new addition is the DwellBaby range – traditional cribs with retro-style brushed-cotton crib sets. *Mail order.*

Espacio

82 Tottenham Court Road, W1T 4TF (7637 1932/www.espacio.co.uk). Goodge Street or Tottenham Court Road tube. **Open** 10am-6.30pm Mon-Wed, Fri, Sat; 10am-7pm Thur; noon-5pm Sun. **Credit** MC, V.

Espacio stocks an impressive choice of contemporary sofas, tables, chairs, lighting, storage and bedroom furniture from leading European manufacturing brands, including Zanotta, Magis, Kartell and Tacchini. Prices vary, so you can go easy with a slick sofa for around £1,000 or climb the ladder to £3,000-plus. The colourful stackable plastic Air Chair by Jasper Morrison is a bargain at £43, and the more garish Easy chair by Jerszy Seymour is only £53. *Mail order.*
For branch see index.

European Design Centre

77 Margaret Street, W1W 8SY (7323 3233/ www.edcplc.com). Oxford Circus tube. **Open** 9am-5.30pm Mon-Fri; noon-5pm Sat. **Credit** AmEx, MC, V.

Up until 2004, EDC operated as a trade showroom before seeing the benefits of opening its doors to the public. Immense top-quality sofas by leading brand Minotti will burn a hole in pocket, but stools, tables and chairs from the more colourful collection by Segis might be easier to bear. EDC also imports products from Casamilano, Holland-based Arco and Finnish makers Inno.

Furniture Craft International

Rays House, North Circular Road (east of Hanger Lane roundabout), NW10 7XP (0870 770 2964/ www.fci.uk.com). Hanger Lane tube. **Open** 10am-6pm Mon-Sat; 11am-5pm Sun. **Credit** MC, V.

In business for over 20 years, FCI sells traditional and modern furniture. The family-run showrooms operate from two immense premises in less-than-desirable locations. But if it's choice you're after, it's worth the trip. You mightn't like everything, but if you put in the time browsing you're likely to hit on various options that appeal for bedroom, living room, kitchen or home office. There's plenty of derivative and safe modern design, enlivened by the odd intriguing piece.
For branches see index.

The Furniture Union

65A Hopton Street, SE1 9LR (7928 5155/ www.thefurnitureunion.co.uk). Southwark tube/ rail. **Open** 10am-6pm Mon-Fri. **Credit** MC, V.

Because of its location behind the Tate Modern, the Furniture Union benefits from a captive audience passing its decent-sized showroom each day. The open-plan space, which can seem cluttered or disjointed depending on its stock, displays sofas, chairs, office furniture, wardrobes, beds and tables. Expect to find a strong collection of seating, with several sleek and expansive sofas dominating floor space. Alongside the contemporary pickings are some big-name classics, including a Mies van der Rohe daybed (around £1,995) and plenty of Philippe Starck accessories. There's also a full design service.
For branch see index.

Geoffrey Drayton

85 Hampstead Road, NW1 2PL (7387 5840/ www.geoffreydrayton.com). Warren Street tube. **Open** 10am-6pm Mon-Sat. **Credit** DC, MC, V.

Geoffrey Drayton was one of the first retailers to introduce modern furniture and lighting design to London over 40 years ago, and has developed a firm following and a loyal clientele. While selling high-end and often pricey interior items, the shop somehow manages to remove the pretentiousness often associated with 'designer' brands with welcoming, if somewhat cluttered, displays. You could be tempted to blow up to £6,000 for a corner unit by Cassina or B&B Italia. A Montis Loge chair with ottoman, covered in hard-wearing Highland leather in a range of colours, starts at £1,725. Rest assured that professionalism, knowledge and good service will steer you towards the right decision for your budget. More affordable pieces include contemporary plastic chairs around the £50 mark, such as Jasper Morrison's stackable Air Chairs.

Habitat

196 Tottenham Court Road, W1T 7LG (7631 3880/www.habitat.co.uk). Goodge Street tube. **Open** 10am-6.30pm Mon-Wed, Fri; 10am-8pm Thur; 9.30am-6.30pm Sat; noon-6pm Sun. **Credit** AmEx, MC, V.

Chair. See p143.

It's been over 40 years since Sir Terence Conran opened the first Habitat store in Fulham, and since then the company has expanded dramatically, with branches in most UK cities, as well as in France, Germany and Spain. The draw? Good-quality contemporary interior goods at high-street prices, but a cut above the IKEA approach. Habitat works with leading designers, including Tord Boontje, Robin Day, Simon Pengelly and Bethan Gray, as well as some less-expected partnerships. The VIP collection boasts Philip Treacy's bright, funky armchairs (£899) and Louis de Bernière's portable bookshelf (£189). There is enough choice within each product category, enabling customers to pop in for a quick accessory gift or an entire fit-out.
For branches see index.

Harmer

253 New King's Road, SW6 4RB (7736 5111/www.harmer.uk.com). Parsons Green tube. **Open** 10am-6.30pm Mon-Thur; 10am-6pm Fri, Sat; noon-5pm Sun. **Credit** MC, V.

Live beautifully.

FACETT. Design: Ronan and Erwan Bouroullec.
The magic of Facett will touch all those who
desire purity without compromising on comfort.
For further inspiration call in to our showroom at
23/25 Mortimer Street, London W1 visit the
website at **www.ligne-roset-westend.co.uk**

ligne rose

Harmer is a relatively new and well-run independent retailer of cutting-edge furniture and lighting designs, allowing customers to step on to the ladder of contemporary living. Styling is important and clearly selected by a well-trained eye while paying attention to the lasting appeal of a design. That said, the buying team always throws in a few slightly out-of-place pieces that have caught their imagination. Recent designs include the Hasta storage column (six glass boxes suspended from an extendable aluminium vertical rod, £1,335-£1,375) and the Kontiki night table topped by a lit-glass surface (£395). The showroom is clearly laid out and easy to navigate. As well as designs by the big names, there are also items from smaller independent designers to shake up the collection.

Heal's

196 Tottenham Court Road, W1T 7LQ (7636 1666/www.heals.co.uk). Goodge Street tube. **Open** 10am-6pm Mon-Wed; 10am-8pm Thur; 10am-6.30pm Fri; 9.30am-6.30pm Sat; noon-6pm Sun. **Credit** AmEx, MC, V.

Heal's continues to hold a firm list of loyal customers who trust the integrity of the store and its buyers. Such a heritage could easily see the company slip into complacency. However, a recent rebranding has breathed new life into the store. This has been backed up by the introduction of several ranges of interior goods created by leading young British talent, such as the Louis black lacquer console table (£495), designed by 24-year-old John Reeves. We also like the Italian-designed Gigolo stool (£259) in chrome with gas-lift height adjustment. Living, dining, and bedroom furniture, soft furnishings and accessories are spread over several expansive floors, and room displays are tastefully arranged. Arguably the most dramatic display is on the ground floor, which is given over to eye-catching accessories, furniture and lighting. Glassware and kitchenware are particularly fine, and won't break the bank.
Mail order.
For branches see index.

IKEA

Brent Park, 2 Drury Way, North Circular Road, NW10 0TH (0845 355 1141/www.ikea.co.uk). Neasden tube/92, 112, 206, 232, 316, PR2 bus. **Open** 10am-midnight Mon-Fri; 9am-10pm Sat; 11am-5pm Sun. **Credit** MC, V.

With 216 stores in 33 countries, the IKEA empire expands apace: the cheap Swedish blond-wood aesthetic is a mainstay of homes worldwide. Basic displays of a wide range of well-designed products, coupled with rock-bottom prices, are crucial elements to the warehouse retailer's turnover. Bed frames start from £37.60, armchairs from £19.99, and sofas from £120 (leather from £355). Quality is variable, so don't expect items to last forever. Style-wise, products are plain yet clean-lined, which means that, if considered carefully, they combine well with more upmarket pieces. Trudge through the windowless departments and stock up on essentials, such as cheap light bulbs, batteries, glasses, pans, storage… the list goes on, which explains your heaped trolley by the time you finish the marathon to check out. It's no surprise that IKEA ticks all the right boxes for students, first-time buyers, or anyone needing basic updates. Check the website for details of big discounts.
For branches see index.

Interni

51-53 Fairfax Road, NW6 4EL (7624 4040/www.interni.co.uk). Finchley Road tube. **Open** 10am-6.30pm Mon-Sat. **Credit** DC, MC, V.

This 400sq m showroom in Swiss Cottage offers a fine selection of furniture design exuding Italian style – quality, simplicity and comfort combined with sharp elegance – from reputable suppliers, such as Presotto (beds, cabinets, storage systems and built-in wardrobes), Cattelan Italia (sophisticated dining tables and chairs) and Arketipo (cutting-edge soft furnishings), as well as its own-label bespoke kitchen range, Cesar. Interni is a good place to invest in some solid pieces that will stand the test of time, both in terms of durability and looks.

Isokon Plus

Turnham Green Terrace Mews, W4 1QU (8994 0636/www.isokonplus.com). Turnham Green tube. **Open** 10.30am-5.30pm Tue-Fri; 10am-6pm Sat. **Credit** MC, V.

This furniture company was founded in 1935 and laid its foundations with top designs from Bauhaus master Walter Gropius, who oversaw the brand's design direction. Design master Marcel Breuer pushed bent-plywood furniture to new levels pioneering high-quality, hand-finished pieces, such as the much-imitated Isokon Long Chair. Nowadays the intriguing Isokon Plus workshop produces re-editions of these classic pieces in its workshops next door, while its owners continue to progress design development with new-generation ranges created by the likes of Barber Osgerby, Michael Sodeau, Simon Pengelly, and Shin and Tomoko Azumi. This beautiful showroom houses complementing designs from other manufacturers, and the experience is topped off by knowledgeable and friendly staff.
Mail order.

Kelly Hoppen

175-177 Fulham Road, SW3 6JW (7351 1910/www.kellyhoppen.com). South Kensington tube. **Open** 10am-6pm Mon-Sat. **Credit** AmEx, DC, MC, V.

Once described as the 'Madonna of decoration', Kelly Hoppen is a world-renowned interior designer behind luxe hotel interiors, fabric collections, and even paint colours (also stocked at B&Q). Fusing East and West, this is the place to go for a simple but opulent style. Objects from antiques to photography are sourced from around the globe to make up this lifestyle environment. Hoppen also produces her own line, with Century Furniture, of well-thought-out, clean-lined, high-quality accessories and furniture. Her latest venture is a rug collection by Transocean, in burnt oranges and neutrals, with flowing lines, geometric patterns and hand-knotted details (from £150).

Key London

92 Wimpole Street, W1G 0EG (7499 9461/www.key-london.com). Bond Street tube. **Open** 10am-6pm Mon-Sat. **Credit** AmEx, MC, V.

Here is a store that oozes individual charm within the realm of high-end design. Charismatic owner Lethwin Kuwana presents a personal selection of furniture, lighting, ceramics, glass and artwork from around the world in her light and airy West End showroom. Pieces are new, fresh and unique – even to more jaded customers. The selection from talented designers will elicit mixed reactions, but this is not a 'one-look' lifestyle store, and Kuwana's imaginative buying has won a loyal following. Pick up a glass sculpture for around £60 or a glass cabinet with three walnut drawers for £3,870.
Mail order.

Ligne Roset

23-25 Mortimer Street, W1T 3JE (7323 1248/www.ligne-roset-westend.co.uk). Goodge Street tube. **Open** 10am-6pm Mon-Wed, Fri, Sat; 10am-8pm Thur. **Credit** AmEx, MC, V.

This massive French interiors brand continues to embrace an increasing variety of talented designers for its collections. Although the Europeans on display here are not the usual headliners, they are no less worthy for it. The contemporary collections are elegant and easy to live with, such as Arik Levy's bed settee (in a range of colours and fabrics, £2,348-£2,879) and Ligne Roset's extendable dining table in anthracite and ebony oak (from £1,390). Elsewhere, modular shelving systems, storage, lighting, beds, rugs and table-top accessories are just as impressive. Prices are mid to high end. A new showroom opens in Swiss Cottage in October 2005.
Mail order.
For branches see index.

Linley

60 Pimlico Road, SW1W 8LP (7730 7300/www.davidlinley.com). Sloane Square tube. **Open** 10am-6pm Mon-Thur; 10am-5pm Fri, Sat.

Linley has been trading for over 20 years and has become a fixture on Pimlico Road. Reputation is all-important at this high end of the market, and

detail is key to the discerning clientele searching for the highest-quality handmade furniture. The service is very much bespoke, and traditional pieces are skilfully reworked using interesting woods, marquetry effects and even perspex. New for 2005 is the Slipmatch Collection; the range is delicate and feminine in its design, using sycamore with an inlaid figured angre top and bubinga stringing. Prices – a low table (£3,750), console (£4,500) and desk (£5,900) – can seem high. Chesterfield sofas start from £3,590 (three-seater) and £4,090 (four-seater). There is a more affordable range of accessories, encompassing picture frames, candle holders and wooden dice.
Mail order.

Living Space

36 Cross Street, N1 2BG (7359 3950/www.livingspaceuk.com). Angel tube/Highbury & Islington tube/rail. **Open** 10.30am-6pm Mon, Wed-Fri; 10am-6pm Sat; noon-5pm Sun. **Credit** AmEx, MC, V.

This fresh, white-walled showroom off Upper Street stocks high-end European furniture and lighting. Its clientele is made up of well-informed architects, interior designers and individuals who are looking for lasting interior items not easily found in London. In other words, big brands and big designers aren't the mainstay here, but rather the quality of the product – in terms of design and construction. High-gloss storage systems, slick beds, beautifully proportioned sofas and comfortable seating are some of the items on display. The amazing Floating bed (in the Fulham showroom) costs £1,713; the Ziggy chaise longue (fabric or leather) starts from £1,511. Staff seem keen to help and can arrange a free, no-obligation home visit to advise. As you might expect for such good quality, prices can be high, although there are regular promotions offering discounts on showroom stock.
For branch see index.

Mandala

The Old Truman Brewery, Gallery 6, 91 Brick Lane, E1 6QL (7684 4883/www.mandala furniture.com). Liverpool Street tube/rail. **Open** 11am-7pm Tue-Fri; 10.30am-6.30pm Sat, Sun. **Credit** MC, V.

The symbol of the mandala is widely recognised as a positive unifying force that brings about tranquillity, order, balance and calm within people's lives. These are attributes Mandala strives to bring about in its range of furniture and homewares. The company works with master craftsmen in Asia to bring traditional skills to European contemporary design. The store is rich with textures and tones – for example, there are clean-lined sofas made from water-hyacinth weave (dried stems of an aquatic plant) or chairs made from bamboo and resin. Prices are reasonable – £745 for a three-seater weave sofa and £225 for a fantastic low-level spiral weave chair.

Mint

70 Wigmore Street, W1U 2SF (7224 4406). Bond Street tube. **Open** 10.30am-6.30pm Mon-Wed, Fri, Sat; 10.30am-7.30pm Thur. **Credit** AmEx, MC, V.

Bored by our obsession with classics and labels, Mint's owner, Lina Kanafani, showcases an inspiring collection of globally sourced one-off or production pieces to her growing band of loyal customers. The ever-changing array of furniture, lighting, ceramics, glass, tableware and textiles, by both big-boy designers and new talent, is housed in a cosy space over two floors. Look out for eclectic pieces like Neringa Dervinyte's Romance table (£450). Mint is great for unusual gifts around the £10-£50 mark, as well as statement pieces well into the thousands.
Mail order.

Modus

88 Great Portland Street, W1W 7NS (7631 4886/www.modusfurniture.co.uk). Oxford Circus tube. **Open** 10am-6pm Mon-Fri. **Credit** MC, V.

Modus manufactures a growing collection of sofas, chairs, tables, shelving and cabinets, selling its own goods alongside a few other choice accompaniments

from the Illizi brand to both trade and consumers. The contemporary, British-made range can boast collaborations with leading designers such as Simon Pengelly, Michael Sodeau and Pearson Lloyd. More recently, top Swedish designers have helped steer this company further into the top league. The London sideboard (veneered walnut with a solid ash edging) by Morph and Sam Johnson starts at £795. Pearson Lloyd's Lolo chair (timber arms and upholstered seat, on a stainless steel tube base) costs £1,130 (£1,210 for leather).
Mail order.

Mufti

789 Fulham Road, SW6 5HD (7610 9123/ www.mufti.co.uk). Parsons Green tube. **Open** 10am-6.30pm Mon-Sat. **Credit** DC, MC, V.
Plenty of customers are drawn through the doors of former advertising exec Michael D'Souza's shop – a light, airy and sophisticated backdrop for the earthy tones of 'casual colonial' furniture, lighting and accessories that seem to have been lifted from a bygone era and adjusted for modern living. Mufti aims to keep traditional craft skills alive, and designs are handmade using natural, tactile materials such as dark woods, leather and linen. The Shikari bench with a rope seat (£480) is typical. Items can also be customised or commissioned from scratch. Mufti is also now available at Harvey Nichols (*see p12*).
Mail order.

Ocean

201-207 Lavender Hill, SW11 5TB (7228 3671/ www.oceanuk.com). Clapham Junction rail. **Open** 10am-6pm Mon-Fri; 10am-5pm Sat; 11am-4pm Sun. **Credit** MC, V.
Ocean started out as a mail-order company before opening up three London stores, one in Lavender Hill, the other in Kentish Town. The Tooting branch closed last year. Furniture is essentially modern but quite bland, comprising rather anonymous and predictable items characterised by blond-wood veneers, chromed legs and frosted-glass tops. This store would appeal to the individual who hates spending time shopping and wants to buy into an all-of-a-piece modern look, without making a personal statement. Beds start from £495, chairs are generally around £80-£275 (the ubiquitous Barcelona chair and footstool leaps to £695, however) and sofas go for between £1,000 and £2,000. There is plenty of storage to choose from, as well as lighting and accessories. Simple, elegant and affordable maybe, imaginative no.
Mail order (0870 242 6283).
For branch see index.

Places and Spaces

30 Old Town, SW4 0LB (7498 0998/ www.placesandspaces.com). Clapham Common tube. **Open** 10.30am-6pm Mon-Sat; noon-4pm Sun. **Credit** MC, V.
Places and Spaces occupies tiny premises, but what it lacks in space it makes up for with one of the most interesting and best-edited selections of furniture, lighting and accessories in London. The shop has built up a loyal following for its iconic pieces and future classics. Chat to the friendly staff about your requirements, and they will help to identify a suitable product from their impressive portfolio or source it specially. Mixing new talent with the more established, this place is solely about quality products and the promotion of contemporary design across various budgets. Find Jerszy Seymour's colourful stackable chairs (£54), Dot cushions (£170) and Magis' plastic Puppy seat (£39). Launched at this year's Maison & Objet in Paris was Mark Cox's Proud lamp (turned solid walnut, or white or black gloss, from £490).

Poliform

278 King's Road, SW3 5AW (7368 7600/ www.poliform.it). South Kensington tube. **Open** 10am-6pm Mon-Sat. **Credit** AmEx, DC, MC, V.
This impressive 8,000sq ft flagship store showcases the Italian brand's entire collection of understated sofas, chairs, storage, tables and beds. The ultra-minimalist environment provides the perfect setting for room sets displaying the slick

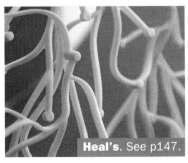

Heal's. See p147.

ranges, although such pristine presentation seems somewhat irrelevant to the actualities of one's home. Don't feel intimidated by this – browsing is encouraged throughout the store. As well as furniture from Poliform, you can also purchase items from its sister brands Flexform (famous for its comfy sofas) or Varenna (kitchens) – its Minimal kitchen won the Design & Decoration Award for Kitchen Product Design. Expect high prices throughout.

Pop UK

278 Upper Richmond Road, SW15 6TQ (8788 8811/www.popuk.com). East Putney tube/Putney rail. **Open** 10am-6pm Mon-Sat; noon-5pm Sun. **Credit** AmEx, DC, MC, V.
The owners of this store have cleverly targeted the wealthier areas in south London to sell high-end contemporary furniture, lighting and accessories from top European brands. Expect some classics by Eames, Le Corbusier, Panton and Jacobsen, and more cutting-edge releases from Matthew Hilton, Starck, Arad, Dixon and Morrison. The various showrooms are all well presented and house the right balance of items, so they feel neither cluttered nor sparse. This clean display approach gives appropriate pride of place to items such as Arne Jacobsen's Egg chair (£2,250), the classic Costes chair by Philippe Starck (£495) or Terence Woodgate's comfortable contemporary three-seater sofa (£2,590).
Mail order.
For branch see index.

Purves & Purves

220-224 Tottenham Court Road, W1T 7PZ (7580 8223/www.purves.co.uk). Goodge Street tube. **Open** 10am-6pm Mon-Wed, Fri; 10am-7.30pm Thur; 9.30am-6pm Sat; 11.30am-5.30pm Sun. **Credit** AmEx, DC, MC, V.
The huge windows on Tottenham Court Road are an excellent, and always colourful, clue to what lies in store at leading contemporary design retailer Purves & Purves, where both affordable and high-end furniture is sold, along with lighting, kitchenware, rugs and accessories. Top European brands like Alessi, Driade, Kartell, Magis and MDF Italia grace the large showroom spread across two floors. P&P manages to strike a good balance between smaller impulse purchases and more considered long-term investment pieces, such as sofas and chairs. Good buys include Erik Jorgensen's Rondo stackable laminated-beech chairs (from £89) in a rainbow of shades, and the Magis Puppy chair, designed by Eero Aarnio and seen on *Big Brother* (£26). Cool kids' furnishings that fit in with the modern design philosophy are also available. Most budgets are catered for, so ask a member of staff for advice on anything from a single stool to a complete interior fit-out.
Mail order.

Rabih Hage

69-71 Sloane Avenue, SW3 3DH (7823 8288/ www.rabih-hage.com). South Kensington tube. **Open** 10am-6pm Mon-Sat. **Credit** AmEx, MC, V.
Winner of 2004's idFX BIDA Interior Designer of the Year, French-Lebanese Rabih el Hage brings together some of his own furniture and product designs with high-specification, expertly crafted interior objects by other designers such as Christophe Côme, Mark Harvey, Johnny Swing and Christian Tortu. The premises, spread across two floors, house an ever-changing selection of one-off or limited designs. The exhibition on our latest visit merged furniture made from reclaimed wood by Piet Hein Eek with recycled-glass objects by Tord Boontje. Come here for special items that fuse top craftsmanship with a rich diversity of materials, techniques and styles. Also on offer are bespoke interior design and architectural services.

RJM Furniture

Gainsborough Studios, 213-215 New North Road, N1 6SU (0800 0015 888/www.rjmfurniture.com). Old Street tube. **Open** 9am-7pm Mon-Fri; 11am-5pm Sat, Sun. **Credit** MC, V.

HOME

RJM Furniture has moved away from Kentish Town, opting for larger premises with a car park. This means its contemporary sofas, armchairs, beds, chairs, tables and storage are usually in stock, so you don't have to wait the standard eight to ten weeks for delivery, and indeed many orders are delivered on the same day. An L-shaped River sofa is a snip at £1,395, while the York sofa oozes contemporary classic style and starts at only £995. The store also runs regular special offers. *Mail order.*

Sasha Waddell

269 Wandsworth Bridge Road, SW6 2TX (7736 0766/www.sashawaddell.com). Fulham Broadway tube. **Open** 10am-6pm Mon-Fri; 10am-4pm Sat. **Credit** MC, V.
Drawing inspiration from Swedish furniture of the 18th and 19th centuries, and ornate French classical decoration, well-known designer Sasha Waddell creates a beautiful range of bedroom, living-room, office and kitchen furniture, combining decoration with simplicity, elegance and functionality. Traditional styles, tapered legs and good-quality wood left plain or washed with pale colours define the look. *Mail order.*

SCP

135-139 Curtain Road, EC2A 3BX (7739 1869/ www.scp.co.uk). Old Street tube/rail. **Open** 9.30am-6pm Mon-Sat; 11am-5pm Sun. **Credit** MC, V.
SCP has become one of London's leading design stores for expertly sourced contemporary furniture, lighting, ceramics, glass, accessories and textiles,

plus some excellent design books. Owner Sheridan Coakley manages to transcend fashionable, fly-by-night furniture – these are the timeless design investments for the future. The shop features a clutch of respected designers, including Terence Woodgate, Jasper Morrison, Michael Sodeau and Matthew Hilton. New designs worth a special mention are the Slow sofa by Terence Woodgate (£1,595) and Matthew Hilton's Wing armchair (£1,170). There is also an SCP on the fourth floor of Selfridges (*see p14*). *Mail order.*

Skandium

86 Marylebone High Street, W1U 4QS (7935 2077/www.skandium.com). Baker Street or Bond Street tube. **Open** 10am-6.30pm Mon-Wed, 10am-7pm Thur; Fri, Sat; 11am-5pm Sun. **Credit** AmEx, DC, MC, V.
Skandium's bustling store houses a large selection of interior products from Scandinavian designers and manufacturers. The light and airy space spread across two floors displays a mix of familiar classic designs, such as Thomas Bergström's Gobble floor stand (£354), Verner Panton's 1960's classic chair (£597) and Gunilla Allard's Trolley Chicago I with three shelves (glass, £432; leather, £1,012). Gorgeous, well-proportioned and top-quality contemporary chairs, cabinets and tables from current designers such as Thomas Sandell, Claesson, Koivisto & Rune and Björn Dahlström are accompanied by lighting from the likes of Louis Poulsen and Le Klint, rugs by Asplund and a plethora of gorgeous table-top items from reputable brands including iittala, Orrefors, Boda Nova and Stelton. Skandium also offers an interior-design service.

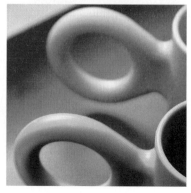

Thorsten van Elten

Thorsten van Elten

22 Warren Street, W1T 5LU (7388 8008/www. thorstenvanelten.com). Warren Street tube. **Open** 10.30am-6.30pm Mon-Sat. **Credit** AmEx, MC, V.
The design industry needs more people like Thorsten van Elten, with passion, conviction and a strong vision. He's been building up a successful reputation as manufacturer of products by young, London-based designers for the last few years. The full collection is on show at his central London shop. Highlights of his own lines include the Antlers coat hanger by Alex Taylor, Pigeon lights by Ed Carpenter, Plant Cup by Gitta Gschwendtner, and Keith's Console by Richard Shed. Alongside these are products by companies van Elten represents as agent and distributor, such as furniture by Kaether & Weise and Derin, lighting by Tronconi and home accessories and other quirky one-off items that are good for gifts.

Tisettanta

34 Bruton Street, W1J 6QX (7491 2044/ www.tisettanta.com). Bond Street or Green Park tube. **Open** 9am-6pm Mon-Fri; 10am-5pm Sat. **Credit** AmEx, DC, MC, V.
The top-notch Italian brand Tisettanta produces a sizeable range of modern storage and shelving systems of a rather masculine aesthetic. As its location on swanky Bruton Street might suggest, the collection doesn't come cheap – beds start at around £2,000, while prices for wardrobe and dressing-room systems vary depending on the size, finishes and extras. New for 2005 are the simple metal-framed Flide chair, upholstered in leather (around £452), and the stylish Atena cabinet, with a solid wood structure and tempered-glass top (from £3,455). The showroom also deals with sister brands Halifax (furniture and accessories), Elam and Citterio Cucine (kitchens) and Mixel (children's furniture).

Twentytwentyone

274 Upper Street, N1 2UA (7288 1996/ www.twentytwentyone.com). Angel tube/Highbury & Islington tube/rail. **Open** 10am-6pm Mon-Fri; 10am-5.30pm Sat. **Credit** AmEx, MC, V.
There are few shops we visit where pretty much everything on offer appeals. Twentytwentyone is one of those places. While most of their pieces are new, there are a few old vintage gems thrown into the eclectic mix. Find Poul Kjærholm's beautiful PK61 coffee table (slate top, stainless-steel base, £1,250) and Joe Colombo's vintage plastic desk lamp (£225) alongside cutting-edge furniture creations: Ron Arad's Little Albert plastic chair (£141) and Jasper Morrison's Hi-Pad stool (£394-£422), as well as lighting and accessories. There is more space for larger furniture at the warehouse down the road. **For branch see index.**

Unto This Last

230 Brick Lane, E2 7EB (7613 0882/www.unto thislast.co.uk). Liverpool Street or Old Street tube/rail. **Open** 10am-6pm daily. **Credit** MC, V.
'Affordable' and 'innovative' are rarely adjectives used in the same sentence, but the French furniture maker who owns this shop has achieved both. He cleverly brings the tradition of fine furniture into the 21st century, combining the best of old-school carpentry with up-to-date computer-assisted design to create interesting plywood pieces. The quality is top-notch and the prices are reasonably low. Shapes have a slight biomorphic appearance controlled through digital computer manipulation, such as the undulating slatted Wavy chair (£450) and table (£480). Modular shelving systems start from £60 (a circular 600-CD rack costs £145), while some dining chairs come in at around £70. Lighting and accessories are also available, such as flower lampshade by Gregory Epps made from a single strip of bent aeroply (£45) or plastic (£30). This store is about quality, simplicity and efficiency – with plenty of unpretentious charm. *Mail order.*

Viaduct

1-10 Summers Street, EC1R 5BD (7278 8456/ www.viaduct.co.uk). Farringdon tube/rail. **Open** 9.30am-6pm Mon-Fri; 10.30am-4pm Sat. **Credit** MC, V.

...alluringly different!

Viaduct's beautiful Clerkenwell showroom is filled with exciting new furniture and lighting from Europe's coolest designers. The collection is seductive, with colours to make you melt, super-sensory fabrics and interesting materials, from sleek aluminium to glossy glass. All areas are covered: upholstery, storage, kitchen, living, dining, bedroom and office. The friendly and helpful team offers expertise in room planning and storage solutions, helping to sift through the difficult selection process, from the practical (will it fit through the door?) to the aesthetic (will it go with the designer door handles?). Great for striking seating, such as Frank Gehry's Wiggle chair (£726) and the funky Butterfly Kiss by Christian Ghion for Sawaya & Moroni (£2,900). *Mail order.*

Vitra
30 Clerkenwell Road, EC1M 5PG (7608 6200/ www.vitra.com). Farringdon tube/rail. **Open** 9am-5.30pm Mon-Thur; 9am-5pm Fri. **Credit** MC, V.
Vitra is one of the leading furniture brands to come out of Germany. Its expansive, iconic collections can be viewed in this light-filled, David Chipperfield-designed showroom. Designs are often as well known as their creators, such as the iconic Eames chair (from £2,350). The newer Vitra Home collection steers the brand further into the domestic market, with stunning new additions from Jasper Morrison (Park two-seater sofa, £2,844) and the Bouroullec Brothers (zip rugs, £499 per segment). The atmosphere can be rather intimidating and businesslike, but once you start looking at the designs on display, this will fade into the background. If you can't stretch to a piece of furniture, invest in one of Vitra's miniatures – you can pick up a dinky Le Corbusier chaise for around £240, or a Panton chair for £75.

Mail order & internet

BeansBeans
0845 130 4546/www.beansbeans.co.uk. **Credit** MC, V.
It's beanbags galore here, and who can deny that they are the ultimate comfort when it comes to lounging around? As well as the usual 'chair' size (£99), there's a large and surprisingly suave sofa beanbag (£149), a kids' version and a bean cube. Antique brown, black and cream come as standard; allow six to eight weeks for other colours. *Mail order.*

BowWow
Chapel Barton House, High Street, Bruton, Somerset BA10 0AE (01749 812 500/ www.bowwow.co.uk). **Phone enquiries** 9am-5pm Mon-Sat. **No credit cards.**
If you're looking for restrained, impeccably styled handmade furniture that combines simple forms with natural colours and tactile materials, this a good place to start. Expect pieces such as coffee or dining tables, benches and seating in wood (some of which is reclaimed), leather, concrete, bronze, zinc and steel. Ahmed Sidki can also design for site-specific projects. Prices reflect the time and quality materials that go into each piece, but service is always impeccable. *Mail order.*

Cadira
233 Sandycombe Road, Kew, Richmond, Surrey TW9 2EW (08700 414 180/www.cadira.co.uk). **Phone enquiries** 9am-7pm daily. **Credit** MC, V.
There is a definite bias towards leather in Cadira's selection of pieces for living, dining, office and bedroom. A four-seater red leather sofa (£1,895) or a rotating coffee table/footstool (£675) are high-quality examples. There's also a showroom in Kew. *Mail order.*

Europe By Net
7734 3100/www.europebynet.com. **Phone enquiries** Mon-Fri 9am-8pm. **Credit** MC, V.
For those wanting to order everything via the internet and save a buck while you're at it, check out Europe By Net for reduced prices on European designer furniture. Pick up the ultimate B&B Italia Charles Large sofa for £5,387 instead of the RRP

£6,840, or a Bombo swivel chair for £243 instead of £320. A huge repertoire of products is featured and split into categories to facilitate your search. *Mail order.*

Find that Chair
0151 285 0975/www.findthatchair.com. **Phone enquiries** 9.30am-5pm Mon-Fri. **Credit** MC, V.
Does everything its name would suggest. There is a choice of furniture online from leading brands including Driade, Kartell, Frighetto, sphaus and Magis, with most chairs falling between £50 and £200. There are also tables, accessories, outdoor furniture and designer classics, such as black leather Eileen Gray armchairs. If you still can't find the right piece, use the product-sourcing service. *Mail order.*

Home Frenzy
0870 720 0098/www.homefrenzy.com. **Phone enquiries** 9.30am-5pm Mon-Fri. **Credit** AmEx, MC, V.
An impressive selection of modern furniture, lighting and accessories tends to steer towards plastics and colour. Plenty of choice and an easy-to-navigate site make buying such items as the Louis Ghost chair by Philippe Starck (£128) or the Air Chair by Jasper Morrison (£55) a breeze. Prices can be higher than those of traditional retailers. *Mail order.*

Interior Internet
01277 622 909/www.interiorinternet.com. **Phone enquiries** 9.30am-6.30pm Mon-Fri. **Credit** AmEx, MC, V.
An immense range of interior options, from seating, tables, lighting, storage and beds to tiles, carpets, wall hangings, mirrors and screens. Samples and swatches are provided on request. The range is eclectic and satisfies diverse tastes. *Mail order.*

lionwitchwardrobe
8318 2070/www.lionwitchwardrobe.co.uk. **Phone enquiries** 9.30am-5.30pm Mon-Fri. **Credit** MC, V.
Beautiful, solid modern furniture for the whole family (including the kids), with minimal designs in natural materials such as oak and soft leather. Check out the solid oak Bridge bed (£1,695) and the equally good-looking single bed version (£880), as well as storage, chairs, tables, mirrors and rugs. *Mail order.*

Tables Designed 4 You
8510 3346/www.tablesdesigned4you.co.uk. **Phone enquiries** 9am-5pm Mon-Fri; 9am-noon Sat. **Credit** MC, V.
This company will make a table to any design to fit any space you desire. The website provides an overview of what is possible in terms of materials, as well as offering some pre-made designs, should they miraculously suit. *Mail order.*

thisisfurniture.com
23-31 Hampstead Road, NW1 3JA (08456 446 675/www.thisisfurniture.com) Warren Street tube. **Open** 10am-7pm Mon-Sat; noon-6pm Sun. **Credit** AmEx, MC, V.
As well as operating two showrooms in London, thisisfurniture.com also sells a large amount of furniture and interior goods via its website, where one can track down well-known contemporary design pieces by Starck, such as his Ploof sofa (£403) or his Dr No chair (£95). It also sells cheap reproductions of classic 20th-century design icons such as the Diamond chair by Harry Bertoia (£370) or a Le Corbusier chaise longue (£345). Selection is a bit hit-or-miss at times. *Mail order.*
For branch see index.

Specialist

Beds

If you're after an antique bed, **La Maison** (*see chapter* **Antiques**) and **Les Couilles du Chien** (*see chapter* **20th-century Design**) are

well worth considering. **The French House** (7371 7573, www.thefrenchhouse.co.uk) provides a handy service for the owners of such beds; usefully, it has developed a technique for lengthening and widening narrow beds to accommodate modern bodies.

Alphabeds
92 Tottenham Court Road, W1T 4TL (7636 6840/www.alphabeds.co.uk). Warren Street tube. **Open** 10am-6pm Mon-Wed, Fri, Sat; 10am-7pm Thur; 11am-5pm Sun. **Credit** MC, V.
Alphabeds produces a huge range of self-assembly beds. For most styles, there are several size options, as well as a choice of materials. A simple treated-pine D Frame with slatted headboard costs £225 for a double, excluding mattress. Futon mattresses (bases are not sold) start at £175; other mattresses (including some with organic-cotton covers and wool filling) go from £375 single, £590 double. You'll also find under-bed storage and bunks, and a toddler's cot that converts to a bed when your child gets older (from £300, including mattress). Custom sizes and designs are possible as well. *Mail order.*

Amazing Emporium
347-349 King's Road, SW3 5ES (7351 0511/ www.amazingemporium.com). Sloane Square tube. **Open** 10am-6.30pm Mon-Sat; 11am-6pm Sun. **Credit** MC, V.
A competent yet unprepossessing range, including forged-iron and metal beds (from £849), and smart wooden sofabeds and daybeds. Classy designs include the Mau leather beds (from £2,169), and the limed-oak Barca bed (from £1,819), reflecting the elegant lines of a gondola. For the ultimate in comfortable mattresses, check out the heat-sensitive body-moulding Tempur range (single mattresses from £479); pillows are also sold. *Mail order.*

And So To Bed
15 Orchard Street, W1H 6HG (7935 0225/ www.andsotobed.co.uk). Bond Street or Oxford Circus tube. **Open** 10am-6pm Mon-Sat; noon-5pm Sun. **Credit** AmEx, DC, MC, V.
Roomy and opulent wooden, brass, cast- and forged-iron beds in mainly traditional styles, including half-testers and four-posters. The Brodsworth *lit bateau* (£5,995 for a six-footer) embraces maximalism, with intricate carving and gold-leaf overlay. Bedroom furniture, linen and accessories round things off. **For branch see index.**

Big Table
56 Great Western Road, W9 3BT (7221 5058/ www.bigtable.co.uk). Westbourne Park tube. **Open** 10am-6pm Mon-Wed, Fri, Sat; 10am-10pm Thur; noon-5pm Sun. **Credit** MC, V.
Despite the name, this shop specialises in pine beds and handmade mattresses. Frames are inexpensive but somewhat unimaginative (doubles £150-£320) and come in various finishes and styles. Beds and mattresses can be mixed and matched to suit. Under-bed storage boxes and bunks are also sold. *Mail order.*

City Beds
17-39 Gibbins Road, E15 1HU (8534 3097/ www.citybeds.co.uk). Stratford tube/rail/DLR. **Open** 8.30am-5pm Mon-Sat. **Credit** MC, V.
Founded more than 20 years ago, City Beds is still one of the capital's most keenly priced bed outlets, selling 'from budget to best' divans, storage beds, blow-up overnight beds, bunks, futons and all types of mattress. Prices for a double (including mattress) start at a very competitive £99, though regular special offers mean you can snap up even better bargains. See website for details.

Daniel Spring
158 Columbia Road, E2 7RG (7923 3033/ www.springmetalbeds.com). Liverpool Street or Old Street tube/rail. **Open** 10am-2.30pm Sun; also by appointment. **No credit cards.**
Spring's steel beds are stylish, sturdy and minimalist. The unfussy designs use straight lines and neat shapes that complement the finishes well.

All models are handmade and have detachable head and foot ends. Prices range from around £550 to £900, and alterations can be made.

Eclectic Furniture

86 Wandsworth Bridge Road, SW6 2TF (7371 8476). Fulham Broadway tube. **Open** 10am-5.30pm Mon-Sat. **Credit** MC, V.
Made-to-order classical French bed frames in beech or cherry, from leather *lits bateaux* to Louis XVI-style four-posters. The choice of finishes ranges from 'slightly antiqued' to 'heavily distressed' for the full-on period feel. For a king size, prices start from £1,500. Divans and mattresses are also sold.

Feather & Black

83 Tottenham Court Road, W1P 9HD (7436 7707/www.ironbed.com). Goodge Street or Warren Street tube. **Open** 10am-6pm Mon-Wed; 10am-8pm Thur; 10am-6.30pm Fri; 9.30am-6.30pm Sat; noon-6pm Sun. **Credit** MC, V.
Formerly the Iron Bed Company, this store sells beds in both metal and wood. Styles run the gauntlet from the curvy, metallic lines of the Rossetti (four-poster from £699) to the elegant, handcrafted walnut Navarra (from £799). Bedroom furniture, mattresses and bedlinen are also in-store. *Mail order.*
For branches see index.

Harlands London Wall Bed Company

430 Chiswick High Road, W4 5TF (8742 8200/www.wallbed.co.uk). Chiswick Park tube. **Open** 9.30am-5.30pm Mon-Fri; 10am-5pm Sat. **Credit** AmEx, DC, MC, V.
The perfect solution for an urban shoebox flat – all of these beds tuck away discreetly into the wall. The company will design and install a bed to fit your room and budget. Wall-bed frames cost from £435 (excluding mattress) for a single; double 'sofa' wall beds are from around £3,500, excluding delivery and fitting. Standard beds are available too, including the Neroa range by Lepanto. *Mail order.*

The Leather Bed Company

103 Wandsworth Bridge Road, SW6 2TE (7731 3262/www.theleatherbedcompany.com). Parsons Green tube. **Open** 10am-6pm Mon-Sat. **Credit** AmEx, DC, MC, V.
Its name is a giveaway. Leather lovers should check out this showroom's rich pickings; the range is also available in faux suede. A classic Chesterfield bed with footboard costs £4,250 for king size; the more modern Sleigh bed is £2,500 (king size). Bedroom furniture such as cabinets, bedside tables, ottomans and cubes, as well as linen from the Linen Mill (*see p120*), are also sold. *Mail order.*

Litvinoff & Fawcett

281 Hackney Road, E2 8NA (7739 3480/www.litvinoffandfawcett.co.uk). Bethnal Green tube/Old Street tube/rail. **Open** 10am-6pm Mon-Fri; 10am-5pm Sat; 10.30am-2.30pm Sun. **Credit** MC, V.
The wooden beds here are solid rather than dainty. Styles are largely low-key contemporary, designed to blend into a bedroom rather than be the main feature. There are some inexpensive designs – the bestselling Platform bed is £150 for a standard double, while the largest minimalist Manhattan bed peaks at £600 (super king size). A bespoke service can modify any style in your desired size. All of the beds and mattresses are hand-made and come with a lifetime structural guarantee. *Mail order.*

Marshall & Stewart

99 Crawford Street, W1H 2HN (7723 2925/www.marshallandstewart.com). Baker Street tube. **Open** 9.30am-5.30pm Mon-Sat. **Credit** AmEx, MC, V.
If you're happy with the look of your bed but need a new mattress, this specialist can guide you through the options: traditional, foam or water bed mattress. Our favourite has to be the Vi-Spring range for comfort and support. Elite mattress costs £440 for a double; lottery winners can stash their cash under an emperor-size Sublime Supreme – the ultimate in luxurious comfort – at £8,776.

Savoir Beds

104 Wigmore Street, W1U 3RN (7486 2222/www.savoirbeds.co.uk). Bond Street tube. **Open** 10am-6pm Mon-Sat. **Credit** MC, V.
Savoir Beds has been handmaking beds to exact specifications for a century. The company takes its craft very seriously and likes to remind you that you sleep for about a third of your life. Upholstered beds, four-posters, *lits bateaux*, or more contemporary designs cost from £3,337 for a single, or from £5,264 for a double.

Simon Horn Furniture

117-121 Wandsworth Bridge Road, SW6 2TP (7731 1279/www.simonhorn.com). Fulham Broadway tube. **Open** 9.30am-5.30pm Mon-Sat. **Credit** AmEx, MC, V.
Simon Horn's designs are drawn from French and classical wooden beds. All styles are luxurious – a popular choice is the contemporary cherry-wood Florence *lit bateau* (£2,575 double). Horn also manages to team opulence with modern needs; a daybed that pulls out to convert to a full-size double (from £1,710) is a great investment. *Mail order.*

Také

715 Fulham Road, SW6 5UN (7736 7031). Parsons Green tube. **Open** 10am-6pm Mon-Sat; 11am-5pm Sun. **Credit** AmEx, MC, V.
Formerly a futon specialist, Také now splits its between European-style beds and futons in a variety of materials. Styles range from traditional to modern minimalist – even futon bunk beds (from £199).
For branches see index.

Taurus Pine Beds & Mattresses

167 Finchley Road, NW3 6LB (7624 3024/www.taurusbeds.com). Swiss Cottage tube. **Open** 10am-6pm Mon-Sat; 11am-4pm Sun. **Credit** MC, V.
Taurus offers mostly pine beds alongside a range of mattresses and some other furniture. Prices are low: the Standard bed with a split headboard is £179 for a double, the Nexus with a straight headboard is £269. For compact bedrooms, the Kyoto bed (designed and sold exclusively at Taurus) is a worthwhile space saver and only £259 for a double.

Warren Evans

158A Camden Street, NW1 9PA (7284 1132/www.warrenevans.com). Camden Town tube. **Open** 9am-6pm Mon, Tue, Thur-Sun; 9am-9pm Wed. **Credit** MC, V.
Adaptable contemporary beds in a wide range of finishes (pale beech to black satin) at affordable prices. For a small charge (around £10-£15), the company will take away your old bed and mattress on delivery. The cheapest double platform bed costs from £165, excluding mattress. *Mail order.*
For branch see index.

Leather, suede & wood

Alma Home

8 Vigo Street, W1S 3HJ (7439 0925/www.almahome.co.uk). Piccadilly Circus tube. **Open** 10am-6pm Mon-Sat. **Credit** MC, V.
Alma is the name behind some of the best contemporary leather furniture seen in other showrooms around town. As well as sleek sofas upholstered in an array of leather finishes – including pony-skin – and a rainbow of colours, there are some unusual finds, including luxe daybeds and ottomans, plus a wide variety of cushions. Prices on the whole are competitive, despite the lavish W1 showroom location. Alma also has a concession in Selfridges (*see chapter* **Department Stores**).

Chest of Drawers

281 Upper Street, N1 2TZ (7359 5909/www.chestofdrawers.co.uk). Angel tube/Highbury & Islington tube/rail. **Open** 10am-6pm daily. **Credit** AmEx, MC, V.
Who can resist the visual and tactile qualities of a beautifully crafted, well-made, solid oak dining table? Chest of Drawers is one of the best independent places in town to go for excellent-quality wooden furniture. Many types and finishes are available – the classic oak range is particularly strong and timeless – but a made-to-measure service is also available should you not find exactly what you're looking for. A modern sideboard or a dining table costs in the region of £650-£1,500. There's also a range of comfortable leather sofas, sofabeds and chairs, plus attractive accessories, including a classic oak table lamp at £53.

New Heights

285-289 Cricklewood Broadway, NW2 6NX (8452 1500/www.new-heights.co.uk). Kilburn tube. **Open** 10am-6pm Mon-Sat; 11am-5pm Sun. **Credit** MC, V.
New Heights offers a diverse collection of solid wood and leather furniture for the bedroom, dining room, living room and home office. It has handcrafted designs for both traditional and contemporary rooms at surprisingly good prices, such as the Harbour bed (£895 king size), leather Oscar armchair (£695) and the Quadrant large solid oak dining table (£995).
For branches see index.

One Deko

111-113 Commercial Street, E1 6BG (7375 3289/www.onedeko.co.uk). Liverpool Street tube/rail. **Open** 10.30am-6pm Mon-Fri; noon-5pm Sat; 10.30am-5.30pm Sun. **Credit** MC, V.
A good range of leather furniture feeds the demand from the plethora of open-plan loft apartments in the surrounding area. The Georgia three-seater sofa in mustang leather is a mere £1,600, while the more cubist-inspired Holbrook range of armchairs and sofas starts at £750. All pieces are made to order and can be adjusted to specific measurements. Artwork, lighting and accessories complement the collections. *Mail order.*

Succession

84 Pimlico Road, SW1W 8PL (7259 9888/www.succession.uk.com). Sloane Square tube. **Open** 11am-5pm Wed-Sat. **Credit** AmEx, MC, V.
The furniture here looks high quality – and it is. There's plenty of leather seating to choose from in big, comfortable styles, including the much-imitated Coco (starting at £1,200) and the chunky Garvey armchair (from £1,200). Other notable pieces are slick leather coffee tables (£1,750) and fabric lamps (£90). Succession also stocks Carl Hensen chairs, a range of natural solvent free paints and award-winning wooden shelving from Avad (from £420). *Mail order.*

Tablemakers

153 St John's Hill, SW11 1TQ (7223 2075/www.individuallymade.com). Clapham Junction rail. **Open** 9.30am-5.30pm Mon-Fri; 9.30am-5pm Sat. **Credit** MC, V.
This light and airy showroom displays a selection of Tablemakers' handmade solid wood furniture. You can specify virtually any size and finish, combining various timbers with glass table-tops or metal legs. The aesthetic steers towards a timeless, understated, geometric modernism. Prices on application. *Mail order.*

Oriental style

The Futon Company

169 Tottenham Court Road, W1T 7NP (7636 9984/www.futoncompany.co.uk). Warren Street tube. **Open** 10am-7pm Mon-Sat; 11am-5pm Sun. **Credit** MC, V.
If any company has a hold on the futon market, it's this place. Prices start at £269 for a double frame and mattress. The Switch Three (£699) is a good space-saving option, with plumped-up cushions and easy conversion from bed to sofa. The store also sells guest solutions like the Polywool Pop Out bed, which converts from a floor cushion (£55).
For branches see index.

Lombok

204-208 Tottenham Court Road, W1T 7PL
(7580 0800/www.lombok.co.uk). Goodge Street
tube. **Open** 10am-6pm Mon-Wed, Fri, Sat; 10am-
8pm Thur; noon-5pm Sun. **Credit** MC, V.
Lombok's penchant for Indonesian teak means the
simple furniture has a dark, colonial look. The range
covers most rooms of the house. Beds are generally
sturdy, especially the Nirvana four-poster (from
£1,395). Dining chairs (from £130) are elegant, with
tapered legs and upholstered seats. Accessories are
also strong, with a range of attractive, well-priced
lacquered lamps (£80-£100) and linens.
Mail order (accessories).
Branches: throughout the city.

The Nine Schools

81 Haverstock Hill, NW3 4SL (7586 0444/
www.thenineschools.com). Belsize Park or Chalk
Farm tube. **Open** 10am-6pm Mon-Sat. **Credit**
AmEx, MC, V.
The Nine Schools is an importer of Chinese
antiques and accessories. These are showcased in
the Hampstead gallery alongside the company's
own range of modern, high-quality, Ming-inspired
furniture, with prices starting from £300 for a
bedside cabinet. The firm also has a concession in
Selfridges (*see chapter* **Department Stores**).

Orthopaedic

The Back Shop

14 New Cavendish Street, W1G 8UW (7935
9120/www.thebackshop.co.uk). Baker Street or
Bond Street tube. **Open** 10am-5.30pm Mon-Fri;
10.30am-5pm Sat. **Credit** AmEx, MC, V.
Ever looked at a chair with admiration but cursed
its distinct lack of comfort? As the name suggests,
the Back Shop specialises in ergonomic solutions
that address the issue of comfort and posture
when sitting and working. Options include
workstations customised to your height and needs
– some are motorised to accommodate both
standing and sitting positions. Soft leather
armchairs and swivel chairs can be adapted to fit
your own shape. There's also a range of electronic
massage chairs (from £2,900). Staff are helpful.
Mail order.

Back 2

28 Wigmore Street, W1U 2RN (7935 0351/0800
587 9000/www.back2.co.uk). Bond Street tube.
Open 9am-6pm Mon-Fri; 10am-6pm Sat. **Credit**
AmEx, MC, V.
Furniture's purpose is to support the body, and
Back 2 sells a variety of ergonomic chairs, sofas
and mattresses that do it best. The range may not
look particularly stylish, but it's a boon for those
suffering from back problems. Staff are extremely
knowledgeable, and prices cover most budgets.
Mail order.

Upholstery

Dudgeons

Brompton Place, SW3 1QE (7589 0322/www.dud
geonsofas.com). Knightsbridge tube. **Open** 9.30am-
5.30pm Mon-Fri; 10am-5pm Sat. **Credit** MC, V.
The majority of sofas here are of the traditional
fat, country-house variety. Comfort and quality
rank highly – all sofas are handmade. Every style
is available in an extensive range of fabrics by the
likes of Osborne & Little, Nina Campbell and
Colefax & Fowler. There's also a line of hand-
carved French chairs.

George Smith

587-589 King's Road, SW6 2EH (7384 1004/
www.georgesmith.co.uk). Fulham Broadway tube.
Open 9.30am-5.30pm Mon-Fri; 10am-5pm Sat.
Credit AmEx, MC, V.
George Smith's classic furniture designs include
scroll armchairs (from £1,729) and sofas (starting
at £2,520) in various patterns, including co-
ordinating stripes, checks and woven damasks, as
well as more luxe fabrics. Other designs include
chesterfields, ottoman sofas and chaises. Prices are
exclusive of fabric.
Mail order.

Highly Sprung

185-186 Tottenham Court Road, W1T 7PG
(7631 1424/www.highlysprung.co.uk). Goodge
Street tube. **Open** 9.30am-6pm Mon-Fri; 10am-
6pm Sat; noon-5pm Sun. **Credit** AmEx, MC, V.
Simple and uncluttered styles, either contemporary
or drawn from traditional designs, are Highly
Sprung's speciality. All sofas are available as two-
and-a-half- and three-seaters. Sofa beds (from
£899) and stools (from £285) are also sold.
For branch see index.

Kingcome Sofas

114 Fulham Road, SW3 6HU (7351 3998/
www.kingcomesofas.co.uk). South Kensington tube.
Open 9.30am-5.30pm Mon-Fri; 10am-5pm Sat.
Credit MC, V.
Kingcome Sofas now has a fresh base to showcase
its modernised furniture collection. Three recently
added lines – Soho, Texas and Manhattan – reflect
the new direction and a step away from the
traditional. Three-seater sofas start at around
£3,000, excluding fabric.

Roche-Bobois

419-425 Finchley Road, NW3 6HG (7431 1411/
www.roche-bobois.com). Finchley Road tube. **Open**
10am-6.30pm Mon-Sat. **Credit** MC, V.
Roche-Bobois's chic furniture comprises three
ranges: Les Contemporains (sleek, directional), Les
Voyages (contemporary, comfortable), and Les
Provinciales (cultured rusticity). A three/four-seater
leather sofa costs around £2,800. A new, bigger
branch opens in Wandsworth in December 2006.
Mail order.

Sofa Workshop

84 Tottenham Court Road, W1T 4TG (7580
6839/www.sofaworkshop.com). Goodge Street tube.
Open 9.30am-6pm Mon-Wed, Fri, Sat; 9.30am-
7.30pm Thur; noon-6pm Sun. **Credit** AmEx, MC, V.
Sofa Workshop has gained a fine reputation over
the years for its extensive range, excellent advice
and good aftercare. The popular made-to-measure
service offers its own styles tailored to customers'
individual specifications. Contemporary styles are
typically modern and boxy, such as the Braque
chaise (£1,195 excluding fabric), while the Casual
range favours softer, more sumptuous styles. The
Classic sofas (around £1,349 excluding fabric)
display details like rolled arms and turned legs.
Mail order.
Branches: throughout the city.

Wawa

3 Ezra Street, E2 7RH (7729 6768/www.wawa.co.
uk). Liverpool Street tube/rail then 26, 48 bus.
Open 10am-2.30pm Sun; by appointment only
Mon-Fri. **Credit** MC, V.
With bold colours, exaggerated curlicues, eccentric
arcs and etiolated legs, this is statement furniture
in a class of its own. Quality and comfort are as
important as innovation, hence the beech frames,
feather cushions and hand-tied springs. The Yasmin
range of modular, flexible seating systems includes
loungers and solo units that can be pushed together
to form an overnight bed. The most popular small
sofas are priced from £880, and three-seaters from
£1,800. Rugs can be made in your choice of colours.

Repairs

Capital Crispin Veneer

Unit 12, Bow Industrial Park, Carpenters Road,
E15 2DZ (8525 0300/www.jcrispinandsons.co.uk).
Stratford tube/rail/DLR. **Open** 8.30am-1pm, 2-
5pm Mon-Fri. **Credit** MC, V.
Part of the centuries-old East End furniture
tradition, CCV sells hundreds of veneers and inlays
in most woods, both traditional and exotic.
Mail order.

E&A Wates

82-84 Mitcham Lane, SW16 6NR (8769 2205).
Streatham Common rail/57, 133 bus. **Open** 9am-
6pm Mon-Wed, Fri, Sat; 9am-7pm Thur. **Credit**
AmEx, MC, V.

Antique restoration, french polishing, reupholstery
and repairs. Covers, carpets and curtains are sold,
and cabinets can be made.

Fens Restoration & Sales

46 Lots Road, SW10 0QF (7352 9883). Sloane
Square tube then 11, 22 bus. **Open** 9am-5.30pm
Mon-Fri; by appointment only Sat. **Credit** MC, V.
Furniture repaired, stripped and restored.

Hope & Piaget

12-13 Burmarsh Workshops, Marsden Street,
NW5 3JA (7267 6040/www.hope-piaget.co.uk).
Chalk Farm tube. **Open** 9.30am-5.30pm Mon-Fri.
No credit cards.
All furniture, even the fine stuff, undergoes
everyday scuffing and damage. This company of
skilled craftspeople will lovingly restore it.

JS Polishing

366 City Road, EC1V 2PY (7278 6803). Angel
tube. **Phone enquiries** 9am-5pm Mon-Fri. **No
credit cards.**
This french-polishing service can remedy fine
scratches or more serious damage. Phone to arrange
a call-out; items are assessed and polished in situ.

K Restorations

PO Box 20514, NW8 6ZT (7722 2869/
www.antiqueleathers.com). **Phone enquiries**
8.30am-5.30pm Mon-Fri. **Credit** MC, V.
Leather restoration work is undertaken, and seven
colours of leather linings for DIY desk and table
restoration are also available.

M&D

269 Putney Bridge Road, SW15 2PT (8789 3022/
www.putneypine.co.uk). East Putney tube/Putney
rail. **Open** 9.30am-5.30pm Mon-Fri; 9.30am-5pm
Sat. **No credit cards.**
As well as selling some pine and oak furniture (fire
surrounds and inserts), M&D strips pine doors by
dipping them in caustic tanks. Interior doors cost
£25; front doors start from £60.

William Fountain & Co

68A Cobden Road, E11 3PE (8558 3464/
www.williamfountain.co.uk). Leytonstone tube.
Open 8am-6pm Mon-Fri. **No credit cards.**
Alongside its furniture and carpet design, this
family business offers reupholstery, french
polishing, and restoration of antique furniture.

Reupholstery

David Scotcher Interiors

285 Upper Street, N1 2TZ (7354 4111). Angel
tube/Highbury & Islington tube/rail. **Open**
10.30am-6.30pm Tue-Sat. **No credit cards.**
This shop takes on reupholstery and restoration of
antique furniture. There are also sofas, chairs,
covers and fabrics for soft furnishings for sale.

Fineline Upholstery

63 New King's Road, SW6 4SE (7371 7073/
www.finelineupholstery.co.uk). Fulham Broadway
tube. **Open** 10.30am-5.30pm Mon-Fri; 10.30am-
4pm Sat. **Credit** MC, V.
A bespoke upholstery service for all furniture
shapes, sizes and ages. Repairs to most damage
and wear and tear.

Pilgrim Payne & Company

290-294 Latimer Road, W10 6QU (8960 5656).
Latimer Road or White City tube. **Open** 8am-6pm
Mon-Fri; 8am-1pm Sat. **Credit** MC, V.
Alongside reupholstery, the company offers a
professional on- or off-site carpet, curtain and
tapestry cleaning service.

Urban Sprawl

Unit W11, Metropolitan Business Centre, Enfield
Road, N1 5AZ (7923 2292/www.urbansprawl.co.
uk). Dalston Kingsland rail. **Open** by appointment
only; phone to arrange a home visit. **Credit** MC, V.
This Enfield company can provide tailored
removable covers for sofas and chairs, as well as
foam, feather and fibre cushions in any shape or
size. Bedspreads, bean bags, curtains and Roman
blinds are also made.

Gardens & Flowers

Gardens

Garden centres & nurseries

Camden Garden Centre
2 Barker Drive, NW1 0JW (7387 7080/ www.camdengardencentre.co.uk). Camden Town tube. **Open** *Apr-Sept* 9am-5.30pm Mon, Tue, Fri, Sat; 9am-7pm Wed, Thur; 11am-5pm Sun. *Oct-Mar* 9am-5pm Mon-Sat; 10am-4pm Sun. **Credit** AmEx, DC, MC, V.
This award-winning garden centre is also a charitable organisation, set up in 1982 to provide training and employment to disadvantaged Londoners – and the fair prices and friendly staff reflect its commitment to good service. Worldwide culinary herbs are found alongside a large range of Mediterranean plants and shrubs, making for rather an interesting shopping environment. Inside is everything you need for outdoor entertaining, including barbecues and lanterns, as well as colourful cacti, house plants, seeds and tools. Expect the biggest and best selection of trees for the Christmas season (up to 20ft high) and some great gift ideas for garden-loving relatives.

Capital Gardens
Alexandra Palace, Alexandra Palace Way, N22 4BB (8444 2555/www.capitalgardens. co.uk). Wood Green tube/Alexandra Palace rail. **Open** 9am-6pm Mon-Sat; 10.30am-4.30pm Sun. **Credit** MC, V.
Sheltered from blustery winds by Alexandra Palace, Capital Gardens has a well-deserved reputation as one of the capital's best garden centres. It's certainly one of the biggest, comprehensively stocked with a vibrant and healthy array of plants, from seasonal bedding plants to dramatic osteospermums, herbs, trees and shrubs. There's also a wide selection of garden furniture and water features, and the indoor area is full of succulents, gardening sundries and gifts. The website features an online service run by qualified horticulturalists, who will answer your gardening queries for free. The adjoining café, with a conservatory and terrace seating, sells own-made cakes. Overall, a real treat.
Mail order.
For branches (Highgate Garden Centre, Morden Hall Garden Centre, Woods of Berkhamsted, Temple Fortune Garden Centre, Neal's Nurseries) see index.

The Chelsea Gardener
125 Sydney Street, SW3 6NR (7352 5656/ www.chelseagardener.com). South Kensington tube/49 bus. **Open** 10am-6pm Mon-Fri; 9am-6pm Sat; noon-6pm Sun. **Credit** AmEx, MC, V.
At the Chelsea Gardener it's hard to imagine that gardening has anything to do with getting down and dirty. Top-of-the-range garden furniture, including elegant wooden sun loungers, barbecues and contemporary ceramic planters, can be found inside, while outside there are large architectural and specimen plants at higher-than-average prices. Informative labels make it an ideal place to swot up on plant care, and there's a wealth of detail about succulents in the mirrored greenhouse area, where lush dracaenas line the aisles. For what to wear among your blooms, check out Barbour's range of waterproof outdoor clothing and accessories.
For branch see index.

Clifton Nurseries
5A Clifton Villas, W9 2PH (7289 6851/ www.clifton.co.uk). Warwick Avenue tube. **Open** 8.30am-6pm Mon, Tue, Thur-Sat; 8.30am-8pm Wed; 10.30am-4.30pm Sun. **Credit** AmEx, MC, V.
This charming and distinguished nursery can be found among the stucco villas on the edge of Little Venice. Discerning London gardeners head here in search of contemporary mirror-finish pyramids (£225-£795), burnt terracotta urns (£3.95-£225), classical figures and limited-edition metal panels. Topiary lines the way to reception, while the enchanting conservatory is a haven of well-established ferns and bird of paradise flowers. With offerings of freshly cut flowers, French café furniture in every colour and an alluring giftshop, it's certainly worth having a nose around.

C Rassell
80 Earl's Court Road, W8 6EQ (7937 0481). Earl's Court or High Street Kensington tube. **Open** *Jan-Mar, mid July-Sept* 9am-5.30pm Mon-Wed, Fri, Sat; 9am-6.30pm Thur. *Apr-mid July, Oct-Dec* 9am-5.30pm Mon-Wed, Fri, Sat; 9am-6.30pm Thur; 11am-5.30pm Sun. **Credit** MC, V.
Founded in 1904, Rassell's has a reassuringly old-fashioned air, with painted notices on wooden boards giving gardeners seasonal advice. You'll find everything you need, from fertilisers to tools, by strolling round to the back entrance and entering the secret garden of narrow aisles tumbling with every kind of seasonal plant, tree and shrub imaginable. As far as containers go, there's a great terracotta, fibreglass and glazed pottery selection.

Dulwich Garden Centre
20-22 Grove Vale, SE22 8EF (8299 1089). East Dulwich rail. **Open** 9am-5.30pm Mon-Sat; 10am-2pm Sun. **Credit** AmEx, MC, V.
Running alongside the railway tracks, the terraces of Dulwich Garden Centre are lined with Tuscan citrus and olive trees, climbers, roses, young and mature trees, plus a vast range of bulbs, pots, containers, compost bins and bamboo. Inside, there are plenty of bird houses, food and treats to keep garden wildlife chirpy, and an enormous selection of rakes, spades, shears and watering cans. Few of the tools and garden sundries are limited to one brand, and it's great to see such a wide choice.

Fulham Palace Garden Centre
Bishop's Avenue, SW6 6EE (7736 2640/ www.fulhamgardencentre.com). Putney Bridge tube. **Open** 9.30am-5.30pm Mon-Thur; 9.30am-6pm Fri, Sat; 10am-5pm Sun. **Credit** AmEx, DC, MC, V.
Fulham Palace Garden Centre's distinctive tall greenhouse is a local landmark. The entrance welcomes customers with a display of topiary and classical statues. Plants and flowers have been placed in their natural environments, but look around, and you'll see the wallflowers aren't just sitting pretty – they're labelled with prices and information. There's a refreshingly tasteful selection of water features, hard-to-find tin laundry buckets and pails for use as containers, along with folding wigwams for climbing plants and sturdy garden furniture. All profits from the centre go to the Fairbridge charity, which supports disadvantaged inner-city youth.

Ginkgo Garden Centre
Ravenscourt Avenue, off King Street, W6 0SL (8563 7112/www.ginkgogardens.com). Ravenscourt Park tube. **Open** *Apr-Aug* 9am-8pm Mon-Fri; 9am-6pm Sat; 10am-6pm Sun. *Sept-Mar* 9am-6pm Mon-Sat; 10am-6pm Sun. **Credit** AmEx, MC, V.
There are many reasons to visit this garden centre, snuggled beneath railway arches in Ravenscourt Park. Firstly, Ginkgo specialises in larger plants and trees and is one of a few centres in London selling mature trees that will also deliver and plant them; call for an estimate. You can also peruse the splendid water garden, cactus greenhouse, natural fencing and topiary available. You'll also find plenty of contemporary garden furniture, including ornate metal folding tables and chairs from King Easton. Ginkgo's staff are experts on landscape, irrigation and garden design, and they offer a garden tidy-up service to sort out in one day what may take the amateur gardener two or three.

Growing Concerns
2 Wick Lane (corner with Cadogan Terrace), E3 2NA (8985 3222/www.growingconcerns.org). Bow Road tube/DLR then S2 bus. **Open** *Summer* 10am-4pm Tue; 10am-6pm Wed-Sun. *Winter* 9am-dusk Tue-Sun. **Credit** AmEx, MC, V.
Situated right next to the canal, this friendly community organisation – run by a team of knowledgeable locals – offers a decent range of shrubs and exotic plants at reasonable prices. Expect to find the likes of palms, cannas, bananas, bamboos and ornamental shrubs. The company also runs a successful garden design and maintenance business. Tea and cakes are served under the gazebo at weekends.

North One Garden Centre
The Old Button Factory, 25A Englefield Road, N1 4EU (7923 3553). Essex Road rail/76, 141 bus. **Open** *Summer* 9.30am-6pm Mon-Wed, Fri-Sun; 9.30am-7pm Thur. *Winter* 9.30am-6pm Mon-Wed, Fri-Sun; 9.30am-6pm Thur. **Credit** MC, V.
It may be in north London, but that doesn't stop gardeners from the east making this place their main port of call during the week, when there's no Columbia Road Market (*see p163*). Bedding plants colour the entrance, and although the main outdoor area is smaller than in other garden centres, it holds a plentiful range that stretches to herbaceous plants, ferns, grasses, bamboos and unusual phormiums. Indoors, you'll find garden furniture, barbecues, galvanised pots, candles and a selection of garden-inspired gifts, including children's tools.

The Palm Centre
Ham Central Nursery (opposite Riverside Drive), Ham Street, Ham, Richmond, Surrey TW10 7HA (8255 6191/www.thepalmcentre.co.uk). Richmond tube/rail then 371 bus. **Open** 9am-5pm daily. **Credit** MC, V.
This mecca of enchanting greenhouses and exotic delights, including palms, hardy bananas, tree ferns and bamboos, merits a visit even if you're not buying. Every week plants arrive from all corners of the globe, and more than 300 species, at all levels of maturity, are stocked, with prices ranging from £2.50 to £3,000. Owner Martin Gibbons's passion is tangible and, in addition to all the wonderful hardy exotics, there is an impressive range of indoor and conservatory plants housed in the tropical house. Plants can also be hired out for special occasions – just visit two to three weeks before the event and let them know what you want.
Mail order.

Patio
100 Tooting Bec Road, SW17 8BG (8672 2251). Tooting Bec tube. **Open** 9.30am-5.30pm daily. **Credit** MC, V.
Established some 200 years ago, Patio specialises in Mediterranean-style plants and a wonderful range of mainly terracotta pots from places such as Tuscany and Crete. There's an abundance of olive trees, palms and ferns.

Petersham Nurseries
Church Lane, off Petersham Road, Petersham, Richmond, Surrey TW10 7AG (8940 5230/ www.petershamnurseries.com). Richmond tube/rail. **Open** 11am-5pm Mon, Sun; 9am-5pm Tue-Sat. **Credit** MC, V.
Here, traditional greenhouses have been beautifully renovated and filled with high-quality garden tools, antique garden furniture and statuary – much of it from France and India. The nursery holds a comprehensive range of plants, including many hard-to-find perennials, old roses and rare Chinese peonies. The café, run by *Vogue's* consultant food writer Skye Gyngell and winner of *Time Out's* Best Alfresco Dining Award in 2005, is well worth a visit.

HOME

Secret Garden

*70 Westow Street, SE19 3AF (8771 8200/
www.thesecretgardencentre.com). Crystal Palace or
Gipsy Hill rail.* **Open** *Mar-Oct* 9am-6pm Mon-Sat;
10am-5pm Sun. *Nov-Feb* 9am-5pm Mon-Sat; 10am-
4pm Sun. **Credit** AmEx, MC, V.

Despite the name, you shouldn't have any trouble
finding this garden centre, as there are signposts
all over the neighbourhood. The Secret Garden
cascades down a hillside behind a large
supermarket – the large forecourt of bedding and
herbaceous plants leads to terraced levels
showcasing climbers, clematis, bamboos, pond
plants, parasols and garden furniture – all set
against the soothing backdrop of a waterfall
feature. A selection of garden sundries, gifts, house
plants and bird feeders is sold in the shed reception.

Tendercare Nurseries

*Southlands Road, Denham, Uxbridge, Middx
UB9 4HD (01895 835 544/www.tendercare.
co.uk). Uxbridge tube then 300, 331, 724 bus.*
Open 10am-6pm Mon-Sat. **Credit** MC, V.

Formerly wholesale only, this vast nursery just off
the M40 is now happy to cater to the general public.
Specialising in serious-sized mature and specimen
trees and shrubs, the nursery covers more than 18
acres. But don't be put off by the scale of things –
driving around in a golf buggy to select your
plants takes some beating for garden lovers.

Wyevale Garden Centre

*Syon Park, Brentford, Middx TW8 8JG (8568
0134/www.wyevale.co.uk). Gunnersbury tube/
rail/Syon Park rail/267 bus.* **Open** 9am-6pm Mon-
Sat; 10.30am-4pm Sun. **Credit** AmEx, MC, V.

After an inspirational trip to elegant Syon Park,
pay a visit to this conveniently placed garden
centre if you want to get cracking with big, green
ideas. You won't find anything particularly
revolutionary (it's part of the Wyevale chain), but
it's reliable for everything from alpines, herbs and
heathers to lawn-care products, wellies, watering
cans and summer houses. Plus, there are always
bargain buys to look out for and regular discount
shopping on Tuesdays. Maidenhead Aquatics has
a branch here, with everything you need to set up
a new home for your koi carp. When you're done,
head to the nearby butterfly house or for a relaxing
cuppa at the centre's coffee shop.
For branches see index.

Mail order

Two excellent, user-friendly websites for
gardeners are **Dig-it.co.uk** (0870 754 1823,
www.dig-it.co.uk) – which covers everything

from garden furniture, sculptures and lighting
to wheelbarrows and barbecues – and **Crocus**
(0870 000 1057, www.crocus.co.uk), which is
good for plants, with advice from Titchmarsh,
no less. Also recommended is the **Natural
Collection** (0870 331 3333, www.natural
collection.co.uk), selling eco-friendly garden
goodies. *See also chapter* **Home Accessories**.

Architectural Plants

*Cooks Farm, Nuthurst, Horsham, West Sussex
RH13 6LH (01403 891 772/www.architectural
plants.com).* **Open** 9am-5pm Mon-Sat. **Credit**
AmEx, MC, V.

If you are too impatient to nurture a sapling to
maturity, then head to this Sussex nursery for its
specialist range of unusual and dramatic plants.
Depending on what you have in mind, staff can
direct you to plants for specific purposes (such as
masking unscenic views quickly), or with certain
characteristics, like 'soft and fluffy' or 'jungly and
tropical'. Agaves, yuccas, epiphytes, palms, trailers
and hangers can sometimes be hard to propagate,
but Architectural Plants has selected the hardiest
forms and offers year-round advice on how to keep
your long and leafies looking splendid.
Mail order.

Beth Chatto Gardens

*Elmstead Market, Colchester, Essex CO7 7DB
(01206 822 007/www.bethchatto.co.uk).* **Open**
Mar-Oct 9am-5pm Mon-Sat. *Nov-Feb* 9am-4pm
Mon-Fri. **Credit** MC, V.

Highly regarded plantswoman Beth Chatto's
nursery stocks over 2,000 different types of top-
quality plants, predominantly herbaceous
perennials and bulbs, together with a good selection
of shrubs and climbers. Plants are divided into
various categories, such as 'plants for shade',
'plants for damp' and 'seasonal plants', and many
of them are propagated from those found in the
outstanding display gardens alongside the nursery.
Mail order.

The Big Grass Company

*Hookhill Plantation, Woolfardisworthy East, Black
Dog, nr Crediton, Devon EX17 4RX (01363 866
146/www.big-grass.com).* **Open** by appointment
only. **No credit cards**.

Specialist grass growers Alison and Scott Evans
boast a vast range of grasses and related plants,
such as restios, rushes and sedges, from all over the
world. All plants are grown from seed collected on
their regular international travels. They regularly
publish updated plant lists, and it's worth
contacting them if you are after something specific.
Mail order.

Edrom Nurseries

*Coldingham, Eyemouth, Berwickshire, Scotland
TD14 5TZ (01890 771 386/www.edrom
nurseries.co.uk).* **Open** *Mar-Sept* 9am-5pm daily.
Oct-Feb by appointment only. **Credit** MC, V.

Renowned for its fine collection of woodland
plants, including trillium, arisaema, primula and
anemone, Edrom Nurseries also stocks a select
range of quality alpines, bulbous plants and ferns.
Its informative, extensive online catalogue is
constantly updated, with new plants added on a
regular basis.
Mail order.

Four Seasons

*Forncett St Mary, Norwich, Norfolk NR16 1JT
(01508 488 344/www.fourseasonsplants.co.uk).*
Phone enquiries 9am-5pm Mon-Fri. **Credit**
MC, V.

Gardeners' heaven, this mail-order-only nursery
stocks a superb selection of hardy perennials,
including euphorbia, heleniums, hostas, irises and
geraniums. Four Seasons mainly supply plants in
9cm pots or specimens are dug up from the field
and supplied bare-rooted.
Mail order.

Great Dixter Nurseries

*Northiam, Rye, East Sussex TN31 6PH (01797
253 107/www.greatdixter.co.uk).* **Open** *Apr-Oct*
9am-12.30pm, 1.30-5pm Mon-Fri; 9am-noon,
2-5pm Sat, Sun. *Nov-Mar* 9am-12.30pm, 1.30-5pm
Mon-Fri; 9am-noon-Sat. **Credit** MC, V.

Venerable plantsman and writer Christopher
Lloyd's garden is an inspiration in how to keep
your outdoor space looking knock-out throughout
the season. Hard work, enthusiasm and years of
knowledge have made this one of the UK's most
famous and highly visited gardens. The small
nursery stocks a selection of plants grown in the
garden, so be prepared to spend a good time
pottering and making notes.
Mail order.

PMA Plant Specialities

*Junker's Nursery, Lower Mead, West Hatch,
Taunton, Somerset TA3 5RN (01823 480 774/
www.junker.co.uk).* **Open** by appointment only.
No credit cards.

These specialist growers of choice hardy and
unusual shrubs and trees propagate the majority
of plants themselves, so get in there quick because
once they've sold out (which they do), there's no
fresh supply until the next season. Reserve orders
are accepted. The small nursery is well worth a
visit for its woodland walk (make an appointment
before you go).
Mail order.

The Chelsea Gardener. See p157.

Special Plants

Hill Farm Barn, Greenways Lane, Cold Ashton, Chippenham, Wilts SN14 8LA (01225 891 686/ www.specialplants.net). **Open** *Mar-Oct* 11am-5pm daily. *Nov-Feb* phone to check times. **Credit** MC, V.
Derry Watkins's nursery specialises in tender perennials, such as salvia, pelargoniums, hardy geraniums, grasses and umbels. She also stocks several new introductions such as pennisetum purple majesty, an annual black grass from America, flowering schizanthus from Chile and silver-leafed shrubs with large yellow daisies from Tenerife. Many varieties are propagated in small numbers.
Mail order.

Woottens of Wenhaston

Wenhaston, Blackheath, Haleworth, Suffolk IP19 9HD (01502 478 258/www.woottensplants.co.uk). **Open** 9.30am-5pm daily. **Credit** AmEx, MC, V.
Michael Loftus's annually updated catalogue entitled the *Plantsman's Handbook* (available from the website for £4.90) is an utter delight. Alongside the extensive plant listings (highlights include a range of over 250 pelargoniums, 200 varieties of bearded irises and 2,000 varieties of herbaceous hardy perennials) are witty little anecdotes and line drawings to enchant gardeners. The website is updated on a monthly basis and has an easy-to-use plant-search facility.
Mail order.

Bulb specialists

Avon Bulbs

Burnt House Farm, Mid Lambrook, South Petherton, Somerset TA13 5HE (01460 242 177/ www.avonbulbs.com). **Phone enquiries** 9am-5pm Mon-Fri. **Credit** MC, V.
A friendly, family-run business specialising in a wide range of unusual and garden-worthy bulbs and related plants. The comprehensive online catalogue contains over 700 items, and you can also send off for the company's annually updated brochures (enclose four second-class stamps).
Mail order.

Broadleigh Gardens

Broadleigh Gardens, Bishops Hull, Taunton, Somerset TA4 1AE (01823 286 231/www.broad leighbulbs.co.uk). **Open** (viewing only) 9am-4pm Mon-Fri. **Credit** MC, V.
Based in Somerset, Broadleigh produces two illustrated catalogues a year – one for spring and the other for summer and autumn dispatches – send two first-class stamps to cover postage. Over 30 years old, the company offers an excellent range of cyclamens, snowdrops, crocuses and tulips, as well as herbaceous plants such as hellebores and exotic Pacific Coast irises.
Mail order.

Jacques Amand

The Nurseries, 145 Clamp Hill, Stanmore, Middx HA7 3JS (8420 7110/www.jacquesamand.co.uk). **Open** 9am-5pm Mon-Fri; 10am-4pm occasional Sat. **Credit** MC, V.
Specialists in bulbs for rare and unusual species, including lesser-known tulip varieties, fritillaria, arisaema and trillium.
Mail order.

Herbs

Jekka's Herb Farm

Rose Cottage, Shellards Lane, Alveston, Bristol BS35 3SY (01454 418 878/www.jekkasherb farm.com). **Open** by appointment only. **Credit** MC, V.
A fantastic selection of organic, culinary, medicinal and decorative herbs grown by herb guru Jekka McVicar. Regularly winning awards for its herb displays at the Chelsea Flower Show and Hampton Court, Jekka's supplies both herbs and culinary plants to the public via its website and catalogue, which feature more than 400 plants. Come and have a look for yourself at its open days and workshops; call for details.
Mail order.

Poyntzfield Herb Nursery

Nr Balblair, Black Isle, Dingwall, Ross & Cromarty, Highland, Scotland IV7 8LX (01381 610 352/www.poyntzfieldherbs.co.uk). **Open** *Mar, Apr, Sept* 1-5pm Mon-Sat. *May-Aug* 1-5pm Mon-Sat; 1-5pm Sun. **Credit** MC, V.
Duncan Ross's specialist herb nursery stocks over 400 types of popular and rare medicinal, culinary and ornamental herbs, all grown biodynamically.
Mail order.

Seed suppliers

Chiltern Seeds

Bortree Stile, Ulverston, Cumbria LA12 7PB (01229 581 137/www.chilternseeds.co.uk). **Phone enquiries** 9am-5pm Mon-Fri. **Credit** AmEx, MC, V.
Around 5,000 species and varieties of seeds are sold here, including succulents, house plants, cacti, exotic and organic ranges. There is also a section for wild flowers, herbs and vegetables. Check the website for half-price special offers (updated daily).
Mail order.

Mr Fothergill's Seeds

Gazely Road, Kentford, Newmarket, Suffolk CB8 7QB (01638 552512/www.mr-fothergills.co.uk). **Phone enquiries** *Jan-Apr* 8.30am-7pm Mon-Thur; 8.30am-5pm Fri; 10am-4pm Sat. *May-Dec* 8.30am-5pm Mon-Fri. **Credit** MC, V.
A mail order company with a large selection of seeds for herbs, fruit plants, flowers and vegetables, as well as a range of garden accessories.
Mail order.

Organic Gardening Catalogue

Riverdene Business Park, Molesey Road, Hersham, Surrey KT12 4RG (0845 130 1304/ www.organiccatalog.com). **Phone enquiries** 9am-5pm Mon-Fri. **Credit** MC, V.
This definitive collection of organic plants and gardening products is put together by the Henry Doubleday Research Association (*see p163*), in association with Chase Organics. The seed range is huge, covering vegetables, herbs and flower seeds, including wild and oriental varieties. Also featured are products for green gardeners, including biological pest-control products, soil improvers, compost bins and solar-powered fountains.
Mail order.

Sarah Raven's Cutting Garden

Perch Hill Farm, Brightling, Robertsbridge, East Sussex TN32 5HP (01424 838 000/ www.thecuttinggarden.com). **Open** *Gardens* by appointment only. *Shop* 9am-5pm Mon-Fri. **Phone enquiries** 9am-5pm Mon-Fri. **Credit** MC, V.
It's all about bringing the wonders of the garden into the home at Sarah Raven's Cutting Garden. Full of wonderful scents and fantastic colour combinations, the garden is open only on select days; however, you can get a taste of the good life by attending one of Raven's many short courses or purchasing seeds, plants, tools and gardening sundries from her extensive online catalogue.
Mail order.

Suttons

Woodview Road, Paignton, Devon TQ4 7NG (0870 220 0606/www.suttons.co.uk). **Phone enquiries** 24hrs daily. **Credit** MC, V.
One of the oldest seed companies in the UK, Suttons holds a royal warrant, but that doesn't mean it's stuck in the past. On the contrary, it develops new flowers each year and supplies organic vegetable seeds, as well as a Throw and Grow range of bio-coated seeds for easy germination and Soweasy kits for starting vegetables indoors.
Mail order.

Thomas Etty

45 Forde Avenue, Bromley, Kent BR1 3EU (8466 6785/www.thomasetty.co.uk). **Phone enquiries** 24hrs daily. **No credit cards.**
Quirky, mail-order supplier of heritage seeds with a wonderful range of hard-to-find vegetables, flowers and bulbs for the period garden. Phone for a catalogue or download one online.
Mail order.

Thompson & Morgan

Poplar Lane, Ipswich, Suffolk IP8 3BU (01473 688 821/www.thompson-morgan.com). **Phone enquiries** *Apr-Aug* 9am-5pm Mon-Fri. *Sept-Mar* 9am-8pm Mon-Fri; 10am-4pm Sat, Sun. **Credit** MC, V.
Specialist potato grower Thompson & Morgan loves its spuds, but it also has a range of edible flowers, ornamental fruit and unusual seeds from around the world.
Mail order.

Trees

Both the **Aboricultural Association** (01794 368 717, www.trees.org.uk) and the **Tree Council** (7407 9992, www.treecouncil.org.uk) are useful contacts. If you're in need of a tree surgeon, make sure you contact one that is registered with the Aboricultural Association. Many landscapers will also provide advice.

Bluebell Nursery & Arboretum

Annwell Lane, Smisby, Ashby-de-la-Zouch, Leics LE65 2TA (01530 413 700/www.bluebellnursery. com). **Open** *Mar-Oct* 9am-5pm Mon-Sat; 10.30am-4.30pm Sun. *Nov-Feb* 9am-4pm Mon-Sat. **Credit** MC, V.
Gardeners from all over the country flock here in search of rare trees and shrubs, as well as woodland, hedgerow and conservation plants, all sold by knowledgeable staff. Make sure to visit the display garden and arboretum.
Mail order.

Keepers Nursery

Gallants Court, East Farleigh, Maidstone, Kent ME15 0LE (01622 726 465/www.keepers-nursery.co.uk). **Open** by appointment only. **Credit** MC, V.
A highly respected nursery dealing in specialist fruit and nut trees, with over 600 varieties, including unusual trees such as quince, medlar and mulberry.
Mail order.

Reads Nursery

Hales Hall, Loddon, Norfolk NR14 6QW (01508 548 395/www.readsnursery.co.uk). **Open** *Oct-Easter* 10am-4.30pm Mon-Sat; 11am-4pm Sun; also by appointment. **Credit** MC, V.
This family-run business is now in its sixth generation. Alongside the National Collections of citrus trees, figs and vines are an outstanding selection of unusual fruit and nut trees, scented hardy plants, box and yew hedging and topiary.
Mail order.

Thornhayes Nursery

St Andrew's Wood, Dulford, Cullompton, Devon EX15 2DF (01884 266 746/www.thornhayes-nursery.co.uk). **Open** 8am-4pm Mon-Fri.
No credit cards.
Tree expert Kevin Croucher stocks a superb range of ornamental and fruit trees – both common and rare – at his 33-acre nursery. Worth a visit, but as many trees are field-grown, take your wellies.
Mail order.

Water gardening

East Ham Aquatics (146 High Street South, E6 3RW, 8470 3600, www.easthamaquatics.com), **One Stop Aquatics** (Wyevale Garden Centre, 89 Waddon Way, Croydon, Surrey CR0 4HY, 8681 3132, www.onestopaquatics.co.uk) and **Wildwoods Water Gardens** (Theobalds Park Road, Crews Hill, Enfield, Middx EN2 9BP, 8366 0243, www.wildwoods.co.uk).

Buildings & conservatories

Bartholomew Conservatories

Rakers Yard, Rake Road, Milland, West Sussex GU30 7JS (01428 742 800/www.bartholomew-conservatories.co.uk). **Open** 9am-5pm Mon-Fri; by appointment only Sat. **Credit** MC, V.

HOME

Stunning bespoke designs. All manner of projects can be undertaken – from conservatories to kitchen extensions and pool houses.
Mail order.

Glass Houses
41C Barnsbury Street, N1 1PW (7607 6071/ www.glass-houses.com). Highbury & Islington tube/rail. **Open** by appointment 9am-6pm Mon-Fri. **No credit cards.**
With a passion for period architecture, Glass Houses crafts ornate floor grilles and joinery to complement its specialist conservatories, orangeries and other glass structures. And don't worry about finding blinds to fit your glass walls – it makes them too.

Marston & Langinger
190-192 Ebury Street, SW1W 8UP (7881 5717/ www.marston-and-langinger.com). Sloane Square tube. **Open** 10am-6pm Mon-Fri; 10am-5pm Sat. **Credit** MC, V.
Though it's best known for its made-to-order conservatories, Marston & Langinger now also sells architectural fittings, natural floors (and under-floor heating), bespoke woodwork and doors, sash windows and own-brand paints.
Mail order.

Containers & statuary

Amphora
340 Fulham Road, SW10 9UH (7376 4808). Fulham Broadway tube. **Open** 9.30am-5pm Mon-Thur, Sat, Sun. **No credit cards.**
Pots in all shapes and sizes can be found at great prices in this two-storey Fulham shop. Stock invariably has 50% off marked price, so sidle between the towers of ceramic, terracotta and galvanised-zinc pots and wind your way through figurines and busts, and pick up a bargain.

H Crowther
5 Chiswick High Road, W4 2ND (8994 2326/ www.hcrowther.com). Stamford Brook tube. **Open** 7.30am-4.30pm Mon-Fri. **No credit cards.**
Specialists in handmade lead garden ornaments, H Crowther produces a fine selection of planters, fountains, statues, cisterns and bird baths – all reproduced using traditional methods. There has been a foundry here since 1908, and today you'll see one of the most comprehensive ranges of ornamental leadwork on permanent display.

Lucy Smith Ceramic Garden Sculpture
2A Richmond Road, E11 4BA (8558 4734/ www.lucysmith.org.uk). Leytonstone tube. **Open** by appointment only. **Credit** AmEx, DC, MC, V.
Artist Lucy Smith's range of handmade water features and garden ornaments, adorned with lizards and frogs, in glazed ceramic is a delight to behold. And if you want something unique, she's more than happy to take on commissions for individual pieces.
Mail order.

S&B Evans
7A Ezra Street, E2 7RH (7729 6635/www.sandb evansandsons.com). Bus 26, 48, 55. **Open** 9am-5pm Fri; 9am-1.30pm Sun; also by appointment. **Credit** MC, V.
While visiting Columbia Road Market (*see p163*), many people make a beeline for this excellent pot shop nearby. The staff are experts in city gardens and have a beautifully planted yard, where urban dwellers with even the smallest concrete patio can be inspired. The skilled craftsmen take commissions and have a client list that includes Kew Gardens.

Furniture & accessories

In addition to the shops listed below, the **Conran Shop** has a pretty extensive range of garden accessories, and **Purves & Purves** is good for stylish sun loungers and hammocks. It's also worth checking out **IKEA**, **Habitat** (for all, *see chapter* **Furniture**) and **John Lewis** (*see chapter* **Department Stores**).

David Harber Sundials
Valley Farm, Bix, Henley-on-Thames, Oxon RG9 6BW (01491 576 956/www.davidharbersun dials.com). **Open** by appointment 9am-5pm Mon-Fri. **Credit** MC, V.
David Harber makes extraordinary handcrafted sundials in contemporary and classical designs. He believes in working closely with clients to come up with unique designs. Using materials such as semi-reflective glass, stainless steel, copper, brass and slate, the sundials can be personalised in a variety of ways.

Hortus
26 Blackheath Village, SE3 9SY (8297 9439/ www.hortus-blackheath.co.uk). Blackheath rail. **Open** 9.30am-6pm Mon-Sat; 11am-5pm Sun. **Credit** MC, V.
Co-owned by garden designer Joanna Herald and landscape contractor Brian Hamilton, this tasteful garden and interiors shop sells an interesting selection of trees, shrubs, grasses, herbaceous perennials and annuals, together with unusual indoor plants. It also stocks a great range of garden furniture and accessories, including contemporary pots, quality tools and water features. Hortus also offers a design, build and maintenance service.
Mail order.

Judy Green's Garden Store
11 Flask Walk, NW3 1HJ (7435 3832). Hampstead tube. **Open** 10am-6pm Mon-Sat; 11.30am-6pm Sun. **Credit** AmEx, MC, V.
Tucked away down a cobbled side street, Judy Green's Garden Store is relaxed and stylish – and ideal for unique and inspiring one-off purchases. Garden equipment and accessories include Burgon & Ball shears, Le Chameau wellies, restored antique tools and Cath Kidston tablecloths. There's also a lovely selection of orchids, potted plants such as succulents in delicate pots, and sapling olive and fig trees.
Mail order.

The Modern Garden Company
Millars 3, Southmill Road, Bishops Stortford, Herts CM23 3DH (01279 653 200/www.modern garden.co.uk). **Open** 9.30am-5.30pm Mon-Fri. **No credit cards.**
Selling everything from funky loungers to minimalist canopies, the Modern Garden Company selects its contemporary outdoor furniture range on the basis of both design excellence and quality.

RK Alliston
173 New King's Road, SW6 4SW (7731 8100/ www.rkalliston.com). Parsons Green tube. **Open** 9.30am-6pm Mon-Fri; 10am-6pm Sat. **Credit** AmEx, DC, MC, V.
This stylish shop stocks beautiful luxury gardening goods, all carefully chosen by owner and garden designer Harriet Scott. For the garden there's a select range of high-quality tools, rubber trugs and nickel-plated watering cans. Garden apparel includes Hunter wellies, panama hats and suede aprons. Scott also runs her own garden design and maintenance business from the shop.
Mail order (0845 130 5577).

The Truggery
Coopers Croft, Herstmonceux, Hailsham, East Sussex BN27 1QL (01323 832 314/www.trug gery.co.uk). **Open** 10am-5pm Tue-Fri; 10am-1pm Sat. **Credit** AmEx, MC, V.
Settle for nothing less than the beautiful trugs sold here, which are handcrafted from sweet chestnut and cricket bat willow using traditional methods. Prices range from £15 to £55.
Mail order.

Landscaping

Designers

English Gardening School
66 Royal Hospital Road, SW3 4HS (7352 4347/ www.englishgardeningschool.co.uk). Sloane Square tube. **Open** 9am-5pm Mon-Thur; 9am-4pm Fri. **Credit** MC, V.

Based at the Chelsea Physic Garden, the English Gardening School can put you in touch with its graduates (who include a number of celebrity gardeners such as Joe Swift), who take on any number of projects.

Society of Garden Designers
Katepwa House, Ashfield Park Avenue, Ross-on-Wye, Herefordshire HR9 5AX (01989 566 695/ www.sgd.org.uk). **Phone enquiries** 9am-5pm Mon-Fri. **Credit** MC, V.
Most good-quality designers are registered with the Society of Garden Designers. It's affiliated to the Royal Horticultural Society and closely vets all its members.

Landscape materials

CED
728 London Road, West Thurrock, Grays, Essex RM20 3LU (01708 867 237/www.ced.ltd.uk). Purfleet rail then 20min walk. **Open** 8am-5pm Mon-Fri. **Credit** MC, V.
The beauty of natural stone is hard to beat, and CED is one of the few suppliers with a huge range of stone, gravel and aggregates – everything from usual fare such as York stone to the more hard to find, such as Indian sandstone in shades of pink or green. CED has been supplying both trade and private buyers since 1978, and its knowledgeable staff are happy to help with questions about design and home delivery. The head office is based in West Thurrock; however, CED also has smaller depots in Scotland (01324 841 321), Nottinghamshire (01773 769 916) and Middlesex (01895 422 411).

Naybur Bros
Potters Bar Brick & Paving Centre, The Ridgeway, Potters Bar, Herts EN6 5QS (01707 658 444/www.nayburbros.co.uk). Cockfosters tube then 298 bus/Potters Bar rail. **Open** 8am-5pm daily. **Credit** MC, V.
If you fancy changing the surfaces around your garden, you'll find everything you need here. As well as a good line in ready-to-lay wooden decking, there are lots of different types of stone and bricks for paths. Fresh new turf is also available.
For branch see index.

Thompsons
Lindale Nursery, Cattlegate Road, Crews Hill, Enfield, Middx EN2 9DP (8363 1383/ www.thompsonsofcrewshill.com). Crews Hill rail. **Open** 8am-6pm daily. **No credit cards.**
Thompsons sells everything from rockery stones to chimney pots, cobbles, pebbles and sleepers. Soil, fertilisers and mulches are only from green field loams and may be bought in small bags or by bulk.

Flowers

The **Flowers & Plants Association** (7738 8044, www.flowers.org.uk) is an excellent source of information and advice on flowers and house plants, from plant and flower care to recommended florists and suppliers. The following are our favourite florist; most deliver in London, with rates charged according to the postal code. Some will send flowers further afield.

Absolute Flowers
14 Clifton Road, W9 1SS (7286 1155). Warwick Avenue tube. **Open** 8am-7pm Mon-Sat. **Credit** AmEx, MC, V.
This is one hell of a stylish florist; the entrance is decked in magnificent Polynesian umbrellas and huge Chinese lanterns showing off the 5ft-high quirky dahlias (summer only). Flowers are set against a backdrop of black Perspex, allowing your eye to easily pick out the stems. Once you've made your choice, the imaginative creations are then set in retro containers and stylishly wrapped, echoing the rich and decadent feel of the shop. Absolute Flowers is currently working on its own range of scented candles, to be launched in 2006, but until then you can choose between the Miller Harris and Geodesis ranges.
Mail order.
For branch see index.

HOME

Angel Flowers

60 Upper Street, N1 0NY (7704 6312/www.angel-flowers.co.uk). Angel tube. **Open** 9am-7pm Mon-Sat; 11am-5pm Sun. **Credit** AmEx, MC, V.
Angel Flowers already enjoys a well-deserved reputation as one of north London quality florists, and it has expanded by opening a sister shop only a few minutes away: the Wings concentrates on potted outdoor plants and a larger collection of succulents. Marco and his partner David have a passion for exotic and tropical blooms, and they continue to create edgy and bold floral arrangements using diverse textures. Ready-made hand ties start at £30, but with more hard cash you can expect to find exotic foreign imports dominating your bouquet. *Mail order.*
For branch (Angel Flowers The Wings) see index.

Black Tulip

28 Exmouth Market, EC1R 4QEW (7689 0068/www.theblacktulip.co.uk). Farringdon tube. **Open** by appointment Mon, Tue; 10.30am-6.30pm Wed-Sat. **Credit** MC, V.
Stepping into Exmouth Market's newly opened Black Tulip – inspired by Alexandre Dumas's 17th-century tale of tulip-bulb mania – will give some idea of what's on offer here. With an aim to 'precipitate an aesthetic renaissance', Fiona Mackenzie-Jenkin has created a stylish interior with smoky black mirrored walls etched providing the backdrop to beautiful floral arrangements: expect to see Extase (the world's most scented red rose) or Lady Slipper orchids. The hand-picked collection includes hand-blown Venetian and Portuguese glassware, home scents by New York's Tocca and perfume from Carthusia, the world's smallest perfume laboratory in Capri. Everything in the boutique, including the furniture (lacquered antique-style tables, Marten Baas's burnt and resin-impregnated Smoke chairs) is for sale. Black Tulip also offers a diary service: flowers, plants and gifts can be delivered throughout central London for loved ones' special days.

Bloomsbury Flowers

29 Great Queen Street, WC2B 5BB (7242 2840/www.bloomsburyflowers.co.uk). Covent Garden tube. **Open** 9.30am-5pm Mon; 9.30am-5.30pm Tue-Fri. **Credit** AmEx, MC, V.
Bloomsbury Flowers is considered to be at the cutting edge of floral design. The stunning window displays are a theatrical mix of colour, illustrating the artistic flair of Stephen Wicks, Mark Welford and the rest of their expert floral designers. Unique designs can be prepared for your favourite container, or you can simply pick up a number of modern and stylish pieces in the shop. For any bride-to-be, a consultation with Mark is highly recommended, as he will design exclusively to your requirements with the utmost attention to detail. This year's special Valentine creation, Hot Lips, shunned traditional red in favour of a lip-smacking mix of pinks and oranges (bunch from £40).

Cottage Garden

132 Northcote Road, SW11 6QZ (7924 3238). Clapham Junction rail. **Open** 9am-6pm Mon-Sat. **Credit** MC, V.
Dip into the wonderfully eclectic collection of the Cottage Garden, with its quaint white-washed brick interior, mirrored walls and profusion of zinc buckets. Filled with top-quality fresh blooms, the effect is stunning and leaves you in a gloriously perfumed daze. *Mail order.*

Detta Phillips Floral Design

18 Redburn Street, SW3 4BX (7498 2728/www.dettaphillips.com). **Phone enquiries** 9am-5pm Mon-Fri. **No credit cards.**
Fancy something a little bit different for your next corporate function? Detta Phillips and her designers are at the top of their league when it comes to decking out venues. Memorable events include transforming the British Museum into an Egyptian palace, complete with 20ft-tall gold mosaic palm trees, bespoke mosaic jewel boxes

and enticing handcrafted bejewelled snakes. Another unforgettable display was the Art of the Garden exhibition at Tate Britain in 2004. Bespoke arrangements can be commissioned for private dinner parties, and a portfolio of classic and modern designs can be found on the website.

Fifi at The Chelsea Gardener

125 Sydney Street, SW3 6NR (7351 9611). Sloane Square tube. **Open** 10am-6pm Mon-Fri; 9am-6pm Sat; noon-6pm Sun. **Credit** AmEx, MC, V.
Fiona Barnett is renowned for upstaging the actors with her flowers for Cameron Mackintosh's *Mary Poppins*, as well as with her opening night bouquets. A simple hand tie of Fifi's Chocolate Cosmos creates a sexy, stylish arrangement for any fashion-conscious individual (bouquets from £30). The usual array of succulents is set against black slate, and there's a fine selection of Sarracenia hybrids.

Flower Store

Ground floor, Oxo Tower, Barge House Street, SE1 9PH (7928 7400/www.flowerstore.co.uk). Southwark tube/Waterloo tube/rail. **Open** 9am-6pm Mon-Sat. **Credit** AmEx, MC, V.
If your pennies don't stretch to dinner at the Oxo Tower, then head to the ground floor and pick up a bunch of beautifully wrapped summer sweet peas as a treat. Amala Shah's beautifully designed shop features a stunning mosaic wall as a backdrop to an incredible display of tightly packed, hand-tied bouquets and potted succulents. The Flower Store has concessions at a number of rail stations. *Mail order.*
For branch see index.

Harper & Tom's

73 Clarendon Road, W11 4JF (7792 8510). Holland Park tube. **Open** 9am-6pm Mon-Fri. **Credit** AmEx, MC, V.
These slightly eccentric florists take flowers very seriously, with a tendency for seasonal English blooms. Subtle, delicate combinations of pastels like lavender, pink and cream recreate a 'cottage garden' in a hand tie. Delicate rose bombes are one of the shop's fortes, from £50.
For branch see index.

Rebel Rebel. See p162.

In Water

70-76 Bell Street, NW1 6TB (7724 9985/www.inwater.uk.com). **Phone enquiries** 9am-5.30pm Mon-Fri. **Credit** MC, V.
Flower arranging gets a contemporary new twist, and this year's look is softer, more luxurious, but still with a great deal of imagination. Specialising in events and contracts, directors Robert Hornsey and Claire Garabedian continue to meet the demands of many swanky sites, such as the Metropolitan Hotel Park Lane and the National Gallery. In Water offers such delights as twisted, cascading arum lilies arranged in Perspex containers. Continuously on the hunt for innovative receptacles, In Water also carries a range of shiny nickel vases. Check the comprehensive website for the latest designs and home fragrances. Bouquets start at £50. *Mail order.*

Jane Packer Flowers

32-34 New Cavendish Street, W1G 8UE (7935 2673/www.janepacker.com). Bond Street tube. **Open** 9am-6pm Mon-Sat. **Credit** AmEx, MC, V.
Some might think that the celebrity florist would lose her touch with such an ever-expanding empire, but even with a client list as long as her arm; 11 books under her belt; her own diffusion collection for Designer Debenhams; styling the Selfridges stores with weekly innovative arrangements; and a list of her own schools/branches around the globe, there seems to be no evidence of this. For a fresh approach to flower arranging, we'd recommend any budding florist to view the window displays at the New Cavendish Street store. When it comes to Valentine's Day, have the bouquet of your choice wrapped in black lace, decorated with butterflies, or with some romantic diamanté words nestling among the flower heads. The company also produces a strong line of own-brand lifestyle goods; needless to say, the design of the range uses plants and flowers as the inspiration. Home furnishings, candles, fragrances and flower-based bodycare products can also be found in Packer's stores.

JW Flowers

Unit E8, Westminster Business Square,1-45 Durham Street, SE11 5JH (7735 7771/www.jwflowers.com). **Phone enquiries** 8.30am-5.30pm Mon-Fri. **Credit** AmEx, MC, V.
Husband-and-wife team Jane Wadham and Paul Ballard use the freshest seasonal flowers for their bright, contemporary arrangements. Browse through the website and you will discover pretty bouquets and exquisite arrangements that can be on your desk the next working day. Choose from a large blowsy arrangement of marshmallow-like pink peonies and alchemilla mollis, or a wild woodland-style bouquet of blue delphiniums, 'fat boy' lavender, deep-blue larkspur and double purple lisianthus. Prices start at £49. Call for a personal consultation for corporate events and weddings. *Mail order.*

Kenneth Turner

Harrods, Knightsbridge SW1X 7XL (7225 6665/www.kennethturner.com). Knightsbridge tube. **Open** 10am-7pm Mon-Sat; noon-6pm Sun. **Credit** AmEx, DC, MC, V.
Kenneth Turner has a distinctively English country-house style about it. Whether you're looking for single blooms or a planted floral shrub, Turner has the most enchanting selection (bouquets from £27). His vision doesn't stop there. Using flowers as his inspiration, he has created sophisticated room scents (for which he has been awarded a royal warrant) and a body collection called Nature/Nurture. There's nothing stuffy about his designs, as most of his presentations are daringly modern. Famed for using natural organic materials, he uses driftwood, shells and fruit, transforming dried arrangements into sumptuous works of art. For a preserved eucalyptus tree one can expect to pay from £375 upwards – pricey but everlasting. *Mail order.*

McQueens

126 St John Street, EC1V 4JS (7251 5505/www.mcqueens.co.uk). Barbican tube. **Open** 8.30am-6pm Mon-Fri; 9am-3pm Sat. **Credit** MC, V.

Ercole Moroni is the creative force behind one of London's most stylish florists, with a celeb-studded client list that includes Louis Vuitton, Graham Norton and Alexander McQueen. Specialising in bold sculptural arrangements, the shop is filled to the brim with monochromatic, textural flourishes of modern floral concoctions along with some cool vases too. The alluring window displays can be a mix of organic vegetables one week and a mass of dahlias the next. In the winter you can expect to find organic hedgerow wreaths, known as the Secret Garden, to flaunt on your front door. Hand-tied bouquets concentrate on one flower or a neutral effect to put emphasis on the flower's individuality, from £35. Candles and toiletries are also on offer, and are all based on white flowers, the most popular being peony.
Mail order.

Michael Pooley Flowers
21 Arlington Way, EC1R 1UY (7833 5599/ www.michael-pooley-flowers.co.uk). Angel tube. **Open** by appointment Tue-Fri. **Credit** MC, V.
Trained by Jane Packer, Michael Pooley is known for providing blooms to fashion designer Alexander McQueen. His Clerkenwell flower shop is stylishy well dressed, with metal buckets adorning unfussy floral displays.
Mail order.

Moyses Stevens
157-158 Sloane Street, SW1X 9BT (7259 9303/ www.moyses-stevens.co.uk). Sloane Square tube. **Open** 8.30am-6pm Mon-Sat. **Credit** AmEx, MC, V.
Moyses Stevens is one of the oldest and most established florist's in London. Founded in 1869, the flagship store can be found in the heart of Chelsea, with a concession just around the corner at Peter Jones (*see p14*). Now an owner of a double royal warrant, its service remains impeccable – so if that special someone deserves a luxury bouquet of a dozen Grand Prix long-stemmed roses, swathed in catkins and ivy trails, at £75, love will certainly blossom. This gracious store also stocks dried arrangements.
Mail order.
For branch see index.

Orlando Hamilton Flowers
59 St Helen's Gardens, W10 6LN (8962 8944). Ladbroke Grove tube. **Open** 9.30am-5.30pm Mon-Fri; 10am-3pm Sat. **Credit** MC, V.
If you're always on the lookout for unusual blooms and gorgeous arrangements, look no further than this Notting Hill boutique. Expect to find herbs, fruit and flowers as you've never seen them before. Orlando counts Madonna among his top clients and can turn his hand to anything, from a spectacular eyeball-searing combination of purples, reds and oranges to a gentle collection of old-fashioned white and cream roses for the devoted traditionalist. There is now an online range available at Sainsbury's.

Paula Pryke Flowers
The Flower House, Cynthia Street, N1 9JF (7837 7336/www.paula-pryke-flowers.com). Angel tube. **Open** 8am-6pm Mon-Sat. **Credit** AmEx, MC, V.
Paula Pryke's fine-tuned sense for wild and wonderful colour mixes keeps her arrangements thoroughly modern. She's renowned for her innovative use of containers and fabric, and for £50 you can select a rose and amaranthus set in a cabbage, ideal for a dinner party. Bouquets can be wrapped in cool Japanese paper or stylishly boxed. Cate Blanchett, Delia Smith, Terence Conran and Dido all come to her for whimsical arrangements that play with a multitude of textures and arresting colours. You may have spotted Paula working with a rather different clientele (of ex-cons) on Channel 4's recent series *Going Straight.* Concessions can be found at Michelin House (81 Fulham Road, SW3 6RD, 7589 4986) and Liberty (*see p13*), among others.

Pemizett Flowers
115 Parkway, NW1 7PS (7388 4466). Camden Town tube. **Open** 8am-7pm Mon-Sat. **Credit** AmEx, MC, V.

Head to the busy junction on Parkway and feast your eyes on the bold contrasting colours of Pemizett's sophisticated hand-tied arrangements. Whether you want something breathtakingly beautiful, stunningly simple or decidedly quirky, a visit here will provide. Pot plants – including some tall sculptural specimens – and seasonal blooms are also sold. There is a concession at gourmet foodstore Villandry (*see p239*).
Mail order.

Pesh
31-31A Denmark Hill, SE5 8RS (7703 9124). Denmark Hill rail. **Open** 7.30am-5pm Mon; 8am-5.30pm Tue-Fri; 8am-5pm Sat. **Credit** MC, V.
With the use of dramatic-looking proteas and seasonal British flowers, Pesh has proved a firm favourite among south Londoners. The highly unusual arrangements mix country style with fashionable contemporary foliage, such as curly bamboo, woven twigs and aromatic herbs. The deliciously scented blooms in contrasting rich shades are exquisitely wrapped at a digestible price (from £25).

Phillo
59 Chepstow Road, W2 5BP (freephone 0808 155 3578/www.philloflowers.com). **Open** 9.30am-8pm Mon-Sat; 11am-5pm Sun. **Credit** AmEx, MC, V.
Offering a wide variety of traditional and unusual flowers from all corners of the world, Phillo also presents a large collection of containers, vases and low-maintenance indoor or outdoor plants. A skilled team of florists and stylists works from this spacious, modern base to supply flowers and accessories for weddings, fashion shoots and personal celebrations. Attention to detail, good value and an understanding of clients' requirements are the key factors to Phillo's success.
Mail order.

The Real Flower Company @ Harvey Nichols
109-125 Knightsbridge, SW1X 7RJ (7235 5000/ 0870 403 6548/www.realflowers.co.uk). Knightsbridge tube. **Open** 10am-8pm Mon-Fri; 10am-7pm Sat; noon-6pm Sun. **Phone enquiries** 8.30am-5.30pm Mon-Fri. **Credit** MC, V.
The Real Flower Company prides itself on the small-scale production of the finest flowers, plants and herbs, and has now teamed up with Harvey Nichols to provide a home delivery service. The divine roses are grown and hand-picked in a rose garden in Hampshire and can be at your door within 24 hours. You can also find them at farmer's markets throughout London in the summer (phone for details). For a hand-tied arrangement of scented garden roses with aromatic herbs, expect to pay from £30.
Mail order.

Rebel Rebel
5 Broadway Market, E8 4PH (7254 4487/ www.rebelrebel.co.uk). London Fields rail. **Open** 10am-6pm Tue-Fri; 10am-5pm Sat. **Credit** AmEx, MC, V.
Opened in 2005 by event designers Athena Duncan and Mairead Curtin, Rebel Rebel is as much a showcase as a shop. Floral creations that have impressed high-profile clients such as Christian Dior, the Natural History Museum, Channel 4 and Lancôme are now available to east Londoners. The beautiful shop sells a veritable A to Z of flowers chosen for their freshness, colour, beauty and inspirational qualities. On our visit vases were filled with wonderful displays of lipstick-pink anemones, cherry blossoms, roses, delphiniums, hyacinth, blowsy pink peonies, orange poppies and French lavender. The shop also stocks a large range of Manuel Canovas candles, as well as vases, and tealight holders. Naturally, the team also offers bespoke event organising, arranging everything from design, lighting, sound, catering and entertainment – and, of course, flowers.

Rococo
7 Nelson Road, SE10 9JB (8293 3191). Greenwich rail/Cutty Sark DLR. **Open** 9.30am-5.30pm daily. **Credit** MC, V.

The Palm Centre. See p157.

Kym Hatala has been well established in SE10 for over 11 years. Her team of six trained florists specialises in offering the ultimate wedding package. Bouquets can be lavishly wrapped in leather, leopard-skin prints or whatever the client requests. Designs have appeared in the BBC adaptation of *The Canterbury Tales* and film director Jane Campion's productions. You can also pick up some very stylish black suede vases and Venetian-style mirrors to complete the look. *Mail order.*

Wild at Heart
49A Ledbury Road, W11 2AA (7727 3095/ www.wildatheart.com). Notting Hill Gate or Westbourne Park tube. **Open** 8am-7pm Mon-Sat. **Credit** AmEx, MC, V.
Over ten years have passed since Nikki Tibbles swapped the advertising world for a florist's apron, and she's still wooing fashionable customers with her styles. The upmarket emporium continues to stand out from the rest, with the emphasis on modern colours to capture the exuberance of an English country garden in full bloom (including peonies, sweet peas, cornflowers and roses, with splashes of lavender and thyme). For a personal consultation, call in at the shop; for the best of the day's blooms, head to Wild at Heart's island stall at 222 Westbourne Grove (no phone, W11 2RJ) and the lobby of the Great Eastern Hotel in Liverpool Street. If you're forgetful, check out the helpful reminder service on the website.

Wild Bunch
17-22 Earlham Street, WC2H 9LL (7497 1200). Covent Garden or Leicester Square tube. **Open** 9.30am-7pm Mon-Sat. **Credit** AmEx, MC, V.
Wild Bunch is a visual treat, screaming urban sophistication, at reasonable prices. Dominating the corner of Earlham Street off Seven Dials, the stalls display yellow kangaroo paw, ornamental cabbages, purple celosia and striking birds of paradise. You name it, they've got it – a great deal more than you'd expect even from a designer florist. Bouquets are beautifully wrapped within minutes, or you can pick from the ready-made collection from £20.

Woodhams
One Aldwych Hotel, 1 Aldwych, WC2R 4BZ (7300 0777/www.woodhams.co.uk). Covent Garden tube/Charing Cross tube/rail. **Open** 10am-6pm Mon-Fri. **Credit** AmEx, MC, V.
If you're in the vicinity, it's well worth dropping by the achingly cool shop situated alongside One Aldwych Hotel. Famed for his landscaping trends, Stephen Woodham is the king of floral fantasy and a firm favourite for all kinds of high-society events. Modern arrangements of seasonal flowers, orchids and architectural floral sculptures adorn this tiny shop, and you can choose from a collection of containers in galvanised metal, bone-coloured ceramics or clear glass (£15-£30). Bouquets are arranged in the company's trademark black plastic box tied with red ribbon, costing from £40. *Mail order.*
For branch see index.

The best of the rest
Barbara's Florist *63 Amwell Street, EC1R 1UR (7837 9500).*
Beryl Williams *71 Heath Street, NW3 6UG (7794 6853/www.lambertsflorist.co.uk).*
Chelsea Flowers *502 King's Road, SW10 0LD (7823 3410/www.flowers4events.com).*
Chiltern Flowers *Marylebone station, Melcombe Place, NW1 6JJ (7723 3034).*
Drake Algar *1B St John's Wood High Street, NW8 7NG (7722 4491).*
Dunn's *26-30 Lavender Hill, SW11 5RN (7350 2375).*
Earthworks *23 Marylebone High Street, W1U 4PF (7486 4914/www.earthworksflorist.com).*
Fabulous Flowers @ Relax *Ground Floor, 65-67 Brewer Street, W1F 9UP (7494 3333).*
Fast Flowers *609 Fulham Road, SW6 5UA (7381 6422/www.fastflowers.co.uk).*
Fitzroy's Floral Designers & Lifestyle *77 Regent's Park Road, NW1 8UY (7722 1066).*

Flowercity *40 City Road, EC1Y 2AN (7336 6337/www.flowercity.co.uk).*
Flowerdays *269 Caledonian Road, N1 1EE (7607 6868).*
The Flower Shop *Heal's Building, 196 Tottenham Court Road, W1T 7LQ (7323 9373/www.londonflorists.co.uk).*
Flowerstalk *210 Haverstock Hill, NW3 2AG (7433 1800).*
Flower Station *Rossmore Court, 55 Park Road, NW1 6XU (7724 7525).*
Galton Flowers *75 Golders Green Road, NW11 8EN (8455 5704/www.galtonflowers.com).*
Gardenia of London *10A High Street, SW19 5DX (8944 0942/www.gardeniaoflondon.co.uk).*
Green *125 Shepherd's Bush Road, W6 7LP (7603 0414).*
Inverblooms *20 Royal Exchange, EC3V 3LP (7623 0225/www.inverblooms.co.uk.).*
Lesley Telling Floral Design @ The Grosvenor House Hotel *Park Lane, W1K 7TN (7399 8141).*
Longmans *Bath House, Holborn Viaduct, EC1A 2FD (7248 2828/www.longmans.co.uk).*
Molly Blooms *787 Fulham Road, SW6 5HD (7731 1212/www.mollyblooms.co.uk).*
Paul Thomas *The Greenery, 4 Shepherd Street, W1J 7JD (7499 6889/www.paulthomas flowers.co.uk).*
Pollen Nation *303 Chiswick High Road, W4 4HH (8987 8533/www.pollen-nation.co.uk).*
Pot Pourri *255 Chiswick High Road, W4 4PU (8994 2404/www.potpourriflowers.co.uk).*
Salmon Florists *192 Haverstock Hill, NW3 2AJ (7794 3115).*
Seasons Florists *253 Coombe Lane, SW20 0RH (8947 6654/www.seasonsflorists.co.uk).*
Sells Florists *19-20 Crystal Palace Parade, SE19 1UA (8670 2453).*
SuperStems at Simon Harris Living *94 Holland Park Avenue, W11 3RB (7229 8788/www.superstems.com).*
Verdant Flower Design *138 Crouch Hill, N8 9DX (8340 9456).*
Wild Things *47 Davies Street, W1K 4LZ (7495 3030).*
William Hayford *Aldermary House, 15 Queen Street, EC4N 1TX (7248 5312/www.william-hayford.co.uk).*

Artificial flowers

Fake Landscapes
164 Old Brompton Road, SW5 0BA (7835 1500/ www.fake.com). South Kensington tube. **Open** 10am-6pm Mon-Sat. **Credit** AmEx, MC, V.
If your plants are looking a little worse for wear or you just don't have green fingers, take a trip to Fake Landscapes. This small shop provides endless amounts of lush green artificial plants to dress up your garden or home. The plastic labrador-sized topiary dog with amusingly cocked leg might be an extravagant purchase at £595, but it would certainly attract attention to your garden. For an artificial window box, look no further than topiary balls at £49, or lavender bushes at £25.

Markets

Columbia Road Flower Market
Columbia Road, between Gosset Street & Royal Oak pub, E2 (no phone). Bus 26, 48, 55. **Open** 8am-2pm Sun. **No credit cards.**
Follow the trail of people balancing colourful wraps of flowers and plants, and you'll come to agree that this is one market well worth dragging yourself out of bed for on a Sunday morning. Whether you're planning a garden makeover or just refreshing a window box, you'll discover all manner of shrubs, fresh-cut flowers, bulbs, trees and accessories at wholesale prices. With charming, charismatic stall holders, the odd café or two and increasingly idiosyncratic shops, Columbia Road is a treat for all.

New Covent Garden Market
Covent Garden Market Authority, Covent House, SW8 5NX (7720 2211/www.cgma.gov.uk). Vauxhall tube/rail. **Open** 3-11am Mon-Fri; 4-10am Sat. **Credit** varies.

Normally the public aren't welcome at wholesalers' markets. However, New Covent Garden Market is the exception to the rule. The climate-controlled warehouse covers three-and-a-half acres and sells blooms in bulk from all over the world. Use the entrance on Nine Elms Lane and park in the underground car park. The best days to go are Monday and Thursday; aim to arrive early, though. This isn't a family day out – the atmosphere is industrial, and being one of the last bastions of male Britain, things can get quite rowdy. But don't be put off – it's an excellent place to stock up on flowers before a party or special occasion at considerably less than retail price. Note that you can only purchase flowers in large bundles or trays, for example ten or 20 rose stems, 50 fuchsias or 300 daffodils, and none of the prices include VAT, so remember to calculate that into the cost. Also, be wary and shop around for quality as it can vary from stall to stall. And don't expect beautiful handties and bouquets – the creative stuff is up to you.

Schools
Jane Packer *32-34 New Cavendish Street, W1G 8UE (7935 2673/www.janepacker.com).*
Judith Blacklock Flower School *4-5 Kinnerton Place South, SW1X 8EH (7235 6235/www.judithblacklock.com).*
Kenneth Turner Flower School *Hall Road, Hemel Hempstead, Herts HP2 7BH (01442 838 181/www.kenturnerflowerschool.com).*
McQueens *130 Lauriston Road, E9 7LH (8510 0123/www.mcqueens.co.uk).*
Out of The Bloom *89-91 Bayham Street, NW1 0AG (7482 3301/www.outofthebloom.com).*
Paula Pryke *The Flower House, Cynthia Street, off Pentonville Road, N1 9JF (7837 7373/www.paula-pryke-flowers.co.uk).*
Sarah Raven *Perch Hill Farm, Willingford Lane, nr Brightling, Kent TN32 5HP (0845 050 4849/www.thecuttinggarden.com).*

Organisations

Henry Doubleday Research Association
Ryton Organic Gardens, Coventry, Warks CV8 3LG (02476 303 517/www.hdra.org.uk). **Open** 9am-5pm daily (closed 25 Dec-1 Jan). **Admission** £4.50; £4 concessions; £2 5-15s; free under-5s. **Credit** Shop MC, V.
For anyone interested in organic gardening, becoming a member of the HDRA is a must. The HDRA is Europe's largest organic society and is dedicated to researching and promoting organic gardening, farming and food. It has three stunning display gardens, a Heritage Seed Library and an extensive *Organic Gardening Catalogue* with a huge selection of seeds, books and garden sundries. *Mail order (Chase Organics 01932 253 666).*

National Society of Allotment & Leisure Gardeners
O'Dell House, Hunters Road, Corby, Northants NN17 5JE (01536 266576/www.nsalg.org.uk). **Open** 9am-4.30pm Mon-Fri. **No credit cards.**
For an annual cost of £15 (individual membership) you'll get free expert advice about obtaining and running an allotment. You can also join a nationwide seed-saving scheme.

Royal Horticultural Society
80 Vincent Square, SW1P 2PE (7834 4333/ membership 7821 3000/www.rhs.org.uk). **Open** *Library* 9.30am-5.30pm Mon-Fri. *Membership enquiries* 9am-5.30pm Mon-Fri. **Credit** AmEx, MC, V.
Founded in 1804, the RHS is today the world's leading horticultural organisation and is responsible for a range of top-notch flower shows, including the Chelsea Flower Show, display gardens and over 1,000 lectures and demos throughout the UK. Annual subscription costs £40; alternatively, you can opt for lifetime membership at £975. Members are entitled to free entry to RHS gardens and 120 partner gardens across the UK, France and Belgium; a monthly magazine, *The Garden*; plus seeds, gardening advice and information.

HOME

Interiors

Air conditioning

JS Air & Water Centre
Artex Avenue, Rustington, Littlehampton, West Sussex BN16 3LN (01903 858 657/ www.airandwatercentre.com). **Phone enquiries** 8.30am-5.30pm Mon-Thur; 8.30am-4.30pm Fri. **Credit** MC, V.
When this company took over the Air Improvement Centre last year, it became the UK's leading humidification and air conditioning specialist for both domestic and industrial use. Products range from air-purifiers, fans and humidifiers to ice makers, water filters and softeners. Visit the website for the full range. *Mail order.*

Building work

Choosing a plumber, electrician or builder doesn't have to be a lottery. Personal recommendations are generally the best bet, but there's also a host of helpful associations to guide you. However you find someone, it's preferable to employ a member of a trade association, which demands adherence to a strict code of practice. Most associations will give details of members, either by phone or website – usually free of charge.
If you'd prefer a female for the job, phone **Women & Manual Trades** (7251 9192, www.wamt.org). If you have legal concerns, contact the **Office of Fair Trading** (08457 224 499, www.oft.gov.uk), or consult the OFT's *A Buyer's Guide*, which explains consumer legal rights and advises on registering a complaint.

Architects & surveyors

Architectural Association
36 Bedford Square, WC1B 3ES (7887 4000/ bookshop 7631 1381/www.aaschool.ac.uk). Tottenham Court Road tube. **Open** *Bookshop* 10am-6pm Mon-Fri (during term time).
Open to the public for a series of free exhibitions, events and lectures. The bookshop stocks many useful journals and design books.

Association of Building Engineers
Lutyens House, Billing Brook Road, Northampton, NN3 8NW (01604 404 121/www.abe.org.uk). **Phone enquiries** 9am-5pm Mon-Fri.
Call the ABE with queries on all aspects of planning and building. It can put you in touch with builders, surveyors and structural designers, all of them qualified members of the association.

Royal Institute of British Architects
66 Portland Place, W1B 1AD (7580 5533/ www.architecture.com). Great Portland Street or Regent's Park tube. **Open** *Exhibitions* 10am-6pm Mon-Fri; 10am-5pm Sat.
The café, bookshop and exhibitions are all open to the public. To find a registered architect, search the website or phone RIBA Client Services (7307 3700).

Royal Institution of Chartered Surveyors
12 Great George Street, SW1P 3AD (0870 333 1600/www.rics.org). **Phone enquiries** 8.30am-5.30pm Mon-Fri.
The highly trained advisers at this independent, non-profit-making institution can help you find a surveyor (or a professional in a related field) from their directory. Members of RICS must adhere to strict ethical rules, and consumers using the service are protected by a formal complaints procedure.

Asbestos removal

Asbestos Removal Contractors Association
ARCA House, 237 Branston Road, Burton-upon-Trent, Staffs DE14 3BT (01283 531 126/ www.arca.org.uk). **Phone enquiries** 8.30am-5pm Mon-Fri.
A registered trade association that can put you in touch with a competent contractor.

Damp & rot

British Wood Preserving & Damp-proofing Association
1 Gleneagles House, Vernon Gate, Derby, Derbys DE1 1UP (01332 225 100/www.property-care.org). **Phone enquiries** 8.30am-5pm Mon-Thur; 8.30am-4pm Fri.
If the BWPDA's website doesn't answer your query relating to damp rot or woodworm, note that it also has an online list of members.

Decorators

British Interior Design Association
3-18 Chelsea Harbour Design Centre, SW10 0XE (7349 0800/www.bida.org). Fulham Broadway tube. **Open** 9am-5pm Mon-Fri.
If you lack interior decorating inspiration, use this website to search for a designer.

Painting & Decorating Association
32 Coten Road, Nuneaton, Warks CV11 5TW (024 7635 3776/www.paintingdecorating association.co.uk). **Phone enquiries** 9am-5pm Mon-Fri.
The Painting & Decorating Association will post you lists of approved painters and decorators; it can offer an arbitration service should any problems arise within six months of using any of its 2,500 members.

Electricians

Electrical Contractors' Association
ESCA House, 34 Palace Court, W2 4HY (7313 4800/www.eca.co.uk). **Phone enquiries** 9am-5pm Mon-Fri.
Contact the association for a list of contractors.

National Inspection Council for Electrical Installation Contracting (NICEIC)
Vintage House, 37 Albert Embankment, SE1 7UJ (0870 013 0431/www.niceic.org.uk). **Phone enquiries** 9am-5pm Mon-Fri.
All 10,500 members of this regulatory body must adhere to its strict rules, making it a valuable resource for finding a reliable electrician.

Plasterwork & mouldings

Butcher Plasterworks
Chalcot Yard, 8 Fitzroy Road, NW1 8TX (7722 9771/www.butcherplasterworks.com). Chalk Farm tube. **Open** 8am-5pm Mon-Fri. **No credit cards.**
This company of master plasterers can carry out lime plastering, freehand plastering and fix-only plastering, as well as matching existing plasterwork and creating contemporary clay and stone fabrications.

Thomas & Wilson
903 Fulham Road, SW6 5HU (7384 0111/www. thomasandwilson.com). Parsons Green tube. **Open** 9am-6pm Mon-Fri; 10am-4pm Sat. **Credit** MC, V.
T&W offers a huge range of panels, ceiling centres, corbels and brackets, niches and over-door panels. Cornices are particularly impressive, with a score of designs running from plain to Gothic. The material used is almost exclusively plaster.

Winther Browne
75 Bilton Way, Enfield, EN3 7ER (8344 9050/ www.wintherbrowne.co.uk). Brimsdown rail. **Open** 8.30am-4.45pm Mon-Fri; 8.30am-12.30pm Sat. **Credit** MC, V.
This firm has been making fine wood carvings and mouldings (including bespoke items) in pine, oak, beech, lime, obeche and ramin for over a century. Cornices, dados, picture rails, roses, skirtings, radiator cabinets and fire surrounds are its fortes.

Plumbing & heating

For antique radiators, check out some of the architectural reclaim firms listed under **Fireplaces** (*see p167*). If you can't face the restoration involved, get the **Old Radiator Company** (01233 813 355, www.theold radiatorcompany.co.uk) to do the work for you – from £145. Or – buy new: **B&Q's** Acova range (0845 222 1000, www.diy.com) is based on the timeless column radiators (from £91 for a 812mm rad). Hot towel radiators start at around £239.
For underfloor heating, the electric Devimat from **Devi Underfloor Heating** (01359 243 514, www.devi.co.uk) is an easy-to-use self-adhesive option and can be used under most flooring (£77.74 plus VAT for a 2m x 50cm roll, excluding control, which cost from £49.95 plus VAT).
For insulation advice, contact the **Draught Proofing Advisory Association** (PO Box 12, Haslemere, Surrey GU27 3AH, 01428 654 011), which can provide information on draught-proofing products and installation. The **Insulated Render & Cladding Association** (www.inca-ltd.org.uk) and the **National Insulation Association** (www.insulationassociation.org.uk) are also on this number.
The **Energy Saving Trust** (0845 727 7200, www.est.org.uk), a non-profit-making body, deals with all aspects of energy conservation. Visit the website or phone the hotline for an action pack, or details of grants for energy-saving heating, insulation or solar measures. For further advice, phone 0800 512 012 to find your nearest **Energy Efficiency Advice Centre**. *See also chapter* **Bathrooms & Kitchens**.

Association of Plumbing & Heating Contractors
14 Ensign House, Ensign Business Centre, Westwood Way, Coventry, Warks CV4 8JA (024 7647 0626/www.aphc.co.uk). **Phone enquiries** 9am-5pm Mon-Fri.
Phone for details of contractors in your area.

Council for Registered Gas Installers (CORGI)
1 Elmwood, Chineham Park, Crockford Lane, Basingstoke, Hants RG24 8WG (01256 372 200/www.corgi-group.com). **Phone enquiries** 9am-5.30pm Mon-Thur; 9am-5pm Fri.
All contractors should be registered with CORGI by law, but if you're in doubt, check them out by calling the above number. Staff here can give advice on gas safety and help you find a local installer. They can also deal with any complaints.

The Floor Warming Company

2 School Parade, High Street, Harefield, Middx UB9 6BT (01895 825 288/www.floorwarming company.co.uk). **Open** 9am-5pm Mon-Fri. **Credit** MC, V.

Providing alternatives to central heating, electrical underfloor heating systems can replace radiators, and are particularly useful under naturally cold surfaces like stone, marble and slate.

Heating & Ventilating Contractors' Association

ESCA House, 34 Palace Court, W2 4JG (7313 4900/www.hvca.org.uk). **Phone enquiries** 9am-5pm Mon-Fri.

The association can post you a list of registered contractors or refer you members over the phone.

Scaffolding

National Access & Scaffolding Confederation

Carthusian Court, 12 Carthusian Street, EC1M 6EZ (7397 8120/www.nasc.org.uk). **Phone enquiries** 9am-5.15pm Mon-Fri.

Advice and contact details for access and scaffolding services.

Stonemasons

Stone Federation Great Britain

Channel Business Centre, Ingles Manor, Castlehill Avenue, Folkestone, Kent CT20 2RD (01303 856 123/www.stone-federationgb.org.uk). **Phone enquiries** 9.30am-5pm Mon-Fri.

Obtain details of members (suppliers or a memorial stonemason) on the website or by phone.

Timber & builders' merchants

To find an outlet near you, contact the **Builders Merchants Federation** (0870 901 3380, www.bmf.org.uk).

AW Champion

2 Hartfield Crescent, SW19 3SD (8542 1606/www.championtimber.com). Wimbledon tube/rail. **Open** 8am-5.30pm Mon-Fri; 8am-5pm Sat. **Credit** MC, V.

This family-owned company really knows its stuff. All manner of raw materials are available here, including timber, sheet materials like plywood and MDF, plus decking, roofing and flooring. *Mail order.*

General Woodwork Supplies

76-80 Stoke Newington High Street, N16 7PA (7254 6052). Stoke Newington rail. **Open** 8am-5.30pm Mon-Wed, Fri; 8am-4pm Thur; 9am-5.30pm Sat. **Credit** AmEx, MC, V.

GWS sells, and cuts to size, timber and board materials, including plywood, MDF, laminates and decorative panels. *Mail order.*

Jewson

Baltic Sawmills, Carnwath Road, SW6 3DS (7736 5511/www.jewson.co.uk). Parsons Green tube. **Open** 7.30am-5pm Mon-Fri; 8am-noon Sat. **Credit** MC, V.

The UK's biggest timber and builders' merchant offers masses of timber products at low prices. The firm also sells bathrooms, kitchens, DIY tools and accessories. Staff are knowledgeable. *Mail order.* **Branches:** throughout the city.

W Sitch & Co. See p173.

HOME

Keyline
Cody Business Centre, South Crescent, off Cody Road, E16 4SR (7511 5171/www.keyline.co.uk). Canning Town tube/rail/DLR. **Open** 7.30am-5pm Mon-Fri; 8am-noon Sat. **Credit** MC, V.
This building chain offers everything from heavy construction materials to tool hire and decorating supplies, including timber.
For branches see index.

Moss & Co
Dimes Place, 104 King Street, W6 0QW (8748 8251/www.mosstimber.co.uk). Hammersmith tube. **Open** 8am-noon, 1-5pm Mon-Fri; 8-11.30am Sat. **Credit** MC, V.
With over 100 years of experience, Moss is a leader in the timber world. Sheet materials, hardwoods and softwoods are stocked.

Travis Perkins
763 Harrow Road, NW10 5NY (8969 2000/ www.travisperkins.co.uk). Kensal Green tube. **Open** 7.30am-5pm Mon-Fri; 8am-noon Sat. **Credit** MC, V.
A no-frills chain of builders' merchants used to dealing with DIYers.
Branches: throughout the city.

Tools
Buck & Ryan (Unit 4, Victorian House, Southampton Row, WC1B 4DA, 7430 9898, www.buckandryan.co.uk) has an excellent range of well-priced power tools; sanders start at £34.99, while Black & Decker cordless drills cost between £39.99 and £380. **Grizard** (84A,B&C Lillie Road, SW6 1TL, 7385 5109, www.grizard.co.uk) sells all manner of hand and power tools, including those for the garden; its website is excellent. With almost 40 outlets in the London area, you're never far from **HSS Hire** (www.hss.com); from wallpaper strippers to heavy-duty welding gear, HSS caters for DIY jobs large or small. A floor sander costs £37 a day, while a full hire pack (which also includes a floor-edging sander) is £55 a day. Equipment can be rented online or via the catalogue. The **London Power Tool Centre** (188-190 Lower Road, SE16 2UN, 7237 9884) is a handy one-stop shop selling both power tools and fixings.

Woodwork

British Woodworking Federation
55 Tufton Street, SW1W 3QL (0870 458 6939/ www.bwf.org.uk). **Phone enquiries** 9.30am-5.30pm Mon-Fri.
Use the online search to locate a joiner suitable for your needs, or call for a list.

Timber Decking Association
CIRCE Building, Wheldon Road, Castleford, West Yorks WF10 2JT (01977 712 718/ www.tda.org.uk). **Phone enquiries** 9am-5pm Mon-Fri.
Visit the website for a full list of members (including deck designers and installers, and related manufacturers), plus general information.

DIY
The big DIY chains have come a long way; these days their stores are usually user-friendly, well staffed and stocked with design-conscious collections. Some even offer an in-store or website-based designing service. *See also p165* **Timber & builders' merchants** and **Tools**, and for paints and wallpaper, *see also p175* **Wallcovering**.

DIY (big fish)
As well as B&Q and Wickes, **Robert Dyas** (123 Tottenham Court Road, W1T 5AR, 7388 0183, www.robertdyas.co.uk) is a good one-stop shop for anything from decorating equipment to hand and power tools to security; visit the website for your nearest. Other big fish include **Fads** (76-78 Church Street, Croydon, Surrey CR0 1RB, 8681 0713, www.fads.co.uk); **Focus Do It All** (149 Homesdale Road, Bromley, Kent BR1 2UE, 8460 9969, www.focusdiy.co.uk); and **Homebase** (195 Warwick Road, W14 8PU, 7603 6397, www.homebase.co.uk).

B&Q
Tottenham Hale Retail Park, Broad Lane, N15 4QD (8365 1699/www.diy.com). Tottenham Hale tube/rail. **Open** 7am-9pm Mon-Sat; 10am-4pm Sun. **Credit** AmEx, MC, V.
Leading the way with sleek urban kitchens and bathrooms, and contemporary Shaker-style bedroom furniture, B&Q also offers a design service. A wide choice of paints is sold, as well as garden furniture, sheds and gardening equipment.
Branches: throughout the city.

Wickes
317 Cricklewood Broadway, NW2 6JN (8450 9025/www.wickes.co.uk). Kilburn tube. **Open** 7am-9pm Mon-Fri; 7am-8pm Sat; 10am-4pm Sun. **Credit** MC, V.
DIY essentials are sold here at rock-bottom prices, with knowledgeable staff on hand. As well as garden equipment, Wickes also offers kitchens, appliances and conservatories, as well as a planning service and advice on how to build a patio or a pond.
Branches: throughout the city.

DIY (smaller fry)
The following all sell the nuts and bolts of DIY at decent prices. Phone or check the websites for your nearest branch and mail-order details.
Clerkenwell Screws *109 Clerkenwell Road, EC1R 5BY (7405 1215). Chancery Lane tube/Farringdon tube/rail.* **Open** 8.30am-5.30pm Mon-Fri; 9am-1pm Sat. **Credit** MC, V.
FW Collins & Son *14 Earlham Street, WC2H 9LN (7836 3964). Covent Garden or Tottenham Court Road tube.* **Open** 8am-5pm Mon-Fri; 11am-5pm Sat. **Credit** AmEx, MC, V.
Decorator's Mate *76-80 Streatham Hill, SW2 4RD (8671 3643). Streatham Hill rail.* **Open** 7.30am-5.30pm Mon-Fri; 8am-5.30pm Sat; 10am-4pm Sun. **Credit** AmEx, MC, V.
Romany's *104 Arlington Road, NW1 7HP (7424 0349). Camden Town tube.* **Open** 8am-5pm Mon-Fri; 9am-5pm Sat. **Credit** MC, V.
Spratt & Sons *618-620 Fulham Road, SW6 5RP (7736 3577). Parsons Green tube.* **Open** 8am-5pm Mon-Fri; 8am-1pm Sat. **Credit** MC, V.
WS Bartlett *249-253 Cambridge Heath Road, E2 0EL (7613 3689). Bethnal Green tube.* **Open** 7am-8am Mon-Fri; 8am-4pm Sat. **Credit** MC, V.

Doors, fittings & ironmongery
As well as at the shops listed below, you can pick up basic interior doors at some builders' merchants and DIY stores. For more suppliers, *see also p165* **Timber & builders' merchants** *and above* **DIY**. For ironmongery, the following supply, make or design gates, railings and staircases: **B Levy & Co (Patterns)** (37 Churton Street, SW1V 2LT, 7834 1073, www.metalstaircases.com) and **Metalcraft Tottenham** (6-40 Durnford Street, N15 5NQ, 8802 1715, www.making metalwork.com). For qualified locksmiths, as well as useful contacts for security and alarm-system companies, get in touch with the **Master Locksmiths' Association** (5D Great Central Way, Daventry, Northants NN11 3PZ, 01327 262 255, www.locksmiths.co.uk). **Clayton Munroe** (132-134 Lots Road, SW10 0RJ, 01803 865 700, www.claytonmunroe.com) is also worth contacting for fine door furniture.

Allgood
297 Euston Road, NW1 3AQ (7255 9321/ www.allgood.co.uk). Warren Street tube. **Open** 8.30am-5pm Mon-Fri. **Credit** AmEx, MC, V.
This architectural ironmonger's specialises in streamlined minimalist accessories. Brands include Philippe Starck's designs for FSB and BioCote's antibacterial coating. There are door handles, hinges, coat hooks and doorstops, plus bathroom accessories, letter plates and signs.

Cotswood
5 Hampden Way, N14 5DJ (8368 1664/www. cotswood-doors.co.uk). Southgate tube. **Open** 9am-5.30pm Mon-Fri; 9am-4pm Sat. **Credit** MC, V.
Cotswood offers a wide variety of internal and external doors using materials from sustainable sources. Products include weather excluders, door seals and door furniture.

Haute Déco
556 King's Road, SW6 2DZ (7736 7171/ www.doorknobshop.com). Fulham Broadway tube. **Open** 10am-6pm Mon-Sat. **Credit** MC, V.
Christian Migeon has been designing Poignée's eye-catching knobs, handles and drawer pulls since 1997 using materials including resin and solid cast stainless steel. A popular choice is the internal doorknob Florence in pumice (60mm) for £67.
Mail order.

Knobs & Knockers
567 King's Road, SW6 2EB (7384 2884/ www.knobs-and-knockers.com). Fulham Broadway tube. **Open** 10am-5.30pm Mon-Fri; 10am-6pm Sat. **Credit** AmEx, MC, V.
Door pulls, bell pushes, latch pulls and keyhole covers, as well as knobs and knockers in shapes ranging from a snail to a leaf are sold here. Most products are brass; other materials include leather, chrome, acrylic, nickel, wood and glass. A polished chrome centre doorknob (76mm) costs £27.95.
Mail order.

London Door Company
155 St John's Hill, SW11 1TQ (7801 0877/ www.individuallymade.com). Clapham Junction rail. **Open** 9.30am-5pm Mon-Sat. **Credit** MC, V.
The LDC's elegant period doors – external, internal and garden, plus fitted room dividers – can be tailored to specifications. Skilled joiners and various glass insets are also sold. Next door at No.153, LDC also has a tablemaker's.
Mail order.

Fireplaces
The **National Fireplace Association** (0121 200 1310, www.nfa.org.uk) publishes the annual *Fireplace Yearbook* (£4), which offers a 'comprehensive guide to all that is best in the world of fire and fireplaces'. It produces leaflets giving advice on installation too. Period fireplaces can also be obtained through architectural salvage dealers (*see chapter* **Antiques**). For a list of reclamation dealers in England or France, contact **Salvo WEB** (8400 6222, www.salvoweb.com).
To get chimneys swept, tested or lined, contact Andrew Taylor, secretary of the **Guild of Master Sweeps** (01733 330 449, www.guild-of-master-sweeps.co.uk). Or contact the **National Association of Chimney Sweeps** (0800 833 464, www.nacs.org.uk); ypou could also check the association's website for details of registered members in your area. **HG Lockey & Son** (8 Halton Cross Street, N1 2ET, 7226 7044) delivers smokeless coal, kindling and firelighters around London.

Amazing Grates
61-63 High Road, N2 8AB (8883 9590). East Finchley tube. **Open** 10am-5.30pm Mon-Thur, Sat. **Credit** MC, V.
Solid stone and marble are used to make impressive mantelpieces at Amazing Grates. Prices

HOME

are fair, with wooden mantels starting at just £150. Modern and retro hole-in-the-wall fireplaces, as well as various accessories, can also be found here. *Mail order.*

Arbon Interiors
80 Golborne Road, W10 5PS (8960 9787/ www.arboninteriors.com). Ladbroke Grove tube. **Open** 9am-5pm Mon-Sat. **No credit cards.**
Antique and repro fireplace surrounds, grates and inserts are Arbon's forte. Every style, from Regency marble to modern wood, is covered. The company's own pine surrounds start at £250.

CVO Firevault
36 Great Titchfield Street, W1W 8BQ (7580 5333/www.cvo.co.uk). Oxford Circus tube. **Open** 9.30am-6pm Mon-Fri; noon-6pm Sat. **Credit** AmEx, DC, MC, V.
The husband-and-wife team behind CVO works closely with architects and interior designers. CVO products are sexy, stunning and dramatic, in styles far removed from traditional mantels and surrounds, such as concrete fire bowls. CVO also has a range of homeware including furniture, painted fireplaces and accessories.

Original Features
155 Tottenham Lane, N8 9BT (8348 5155/ www.originalfeatures.co.uk). Turnpike Lane tube/ 41 bus. **Open** 9am-5pm Mon-Wed, Fri, Sat; 9am-1pm Thur. **Credit** AmEx, MC, V.
This firm sources Victorian fireplaces and spare parts such as grates, front bars and ash pan covers. It also offers an excellent restoration service, as well as cleaning and laying period geometric floors. *Mail order.*

Platonic Fireplace Company
Phoenix Wharf, Eel Pie Island, Twickenham, Middx TW1 3DY (8891 5904/www.platonic fireplaces.co.uk). Twickenham rail. **Open** 9am-5pm Mon-Fri; 10am-2pm Sat. **Credit** MC, V.
Architect Henry Harrison's Geolog Fire was the first gas fire designed for modern interiors – and he's the man behind Platonic. Expect sleek, modern designs, executed in materials such as stainless steel and concrete. If you think coal is a little passé, how about fire driftwood, pebbles, standing stones or even Corinthian capitals? *Mail order.*

Renaissance
193-195 City Road, EC1V 1JN (7251 8844/www. renaissancelondon.com). Old Street tube/rail. **Open** 9am-5pm Mon-Fri; 10am-5pm Sat. **Credit** MC, V.
Georgian marble fireplaces start from around £800 in this Aladdin's cave of antique and reproduction mantels. All styles, from cast-iron Victorian and slick art deco to fanciful French and Italian marble models, are here. Also sold are antique pieces: gilded mirrors, chandeliers and cast-iron radiators.

Flooring

Carpet, cork, tile & vinyl
The **Carpet Foundation** (01562 755 568, www.comebacktocarpet.com) can provide information on carpets and their care. To find a local cleaner, contact the **National Carpet Cleaners' Association** (0116 271 9550, www.ncca.co.uk). The **National Institute of Carpet & Floorlayers** (0115 958 3077, www.nicfltd.org.uk) has lists of approved fitters. *See also p174* **Tiles & mosaics.**

Abbott's
470-480 Roman Road, E3 5LU (0800 716 783/ www.abbottscarpets.co.uk). Bethnal Green tube. **Open** 8.30am-5.30pm Mon-Fri; 8.30am-5pm Sat. **Credit** MC, V.
This family business offers a massive range of carpets, vinyl and laminate flooring at excellent prices – look out for bargains such as the large remnants. There are also funkier options, like the Dalsouple rubber flooring (around £40/sq m) and Pergo Original, the world's first laminate flooring. A selection of curtains and blinds is also available.

Allied Carpets
389 Holloway Road, N7 0RY (7609 4143/ www.alliedcarpets.com). Holloway Road tube. **Open** 9am-5.30pm Mon-Fri; 9am-6pm Sat; 10am-4pm Sun. **Credit** AmEx, MC, V.
This is the grandaddy of carpet and hard-flooring retailers. Brands include Brintons, Kosset, Wilton Royal and Axminster. The carpets are undramatic, but prices are low. Despite the name, there are also many rugs, vinyl, laminate and hardwood coverings – even beds.
Branches: throughout the city.

Amtico Studio
233-235 Business Design Centre, 52 Upper Street, N1 0QH (0870 350 4080/www.amtico.com). Angel tube. **Open** 9.30am-5.30pm Mon-Fri; 10am-5pm Sat. **No credit cards.**
There is over 1,000sq m of showroom here, plus the full Amtico range, either on boards or on the floor. A design service is available; purchases can then be made through recommended retailers.

The Carpet Man
7A Putney Bridge Road, SW18 1HX (8875 0232/ www.carpetman.co.uk). Wandsworth Town rail. **Open** 8am-6pm Mon-Thur, Sat; 8am-5pm Fri. **Credit** AmEx, MC, V.

One of the best warehouses for bargain carpets. Carpets come as 100% wool, 80% wool, naturals, twists and berber. The Carpet Man also holds vinyls, seagrass (£11.95/sq m), coir (£11.95/sq m), laminate and wood.

First Floor
174 Wandsworth Bridge Road, SW6 2UQ (7736 1123/www.firstfloor.uk.com). Fulham Broadway or Parsons Green tube. **Open** 10am-5.30pm Mon-Fri; 10am-2pm Sat. **Credit** MC, V.
Specialising in contemporary floor coverings, First Floor sells ranges by Amtico and Marmoleum, plus vinyl tiles. Most eye-catching are the designs by rubber flooring company Dalsouple, which come in 60 hip colours and in smooth finishes and textures, terrazzo or marbled. Cork flooring and carpet can also be sourced here. *Mail order.*

Harvey Maria
17 Riverside Business Park, Lyon Road, SW19 2RL (8542 0088/www.harveymaria.co.uk). **Phone enquiries** 9am-5.30pm Mon-Fri. **Credit** MC, V.
Vinyl floor tiles with a splash of creativity and colour are the aim here. Harvey Maria's tiles are printed with ambient contemporary designs, such

Osborne & Little. See p173.

as pebbles, petals, grass, feathers and flowers like gerberas and daisies. You can view and order online. Packs cost £39.95 (inc VAT) for 11 tiles, which cover about one square metre.
Mail order.

S&M Myers
100-106 Mackenzie Road, N7 8RG (7609 0091/ www.myerscarpets.co.uk). Caledonian Road tube. **Open** 8am-5.30pm Mon, Wed, Fri; 8am-5pm Tue, Thur; 9.30am-2pm Sat. **Credit** MC, V.
S&M sells wool carpets, naturals, modern berbers plus vinyl and rugs – at bargain prices. The New Hampshire Twistpile range starts at £13.75/sq m.
For branch see index.

Sinclair Till
791-793 Wandsworth Road, SW8 3JQ (7720 0031/www.sinclairtill.co.uk). Wandsworth Road rail. **Open** 9.30am-5.30pm Mon-Fri. **Credit** MC, V.
Purveyors and fitters of stylish floor coverings for almost 20 years, Sinclair Till can offer a staggering range of colours (neutral, strong) and textures. Runners and rugs are a speciality. There's also wool carpet (from around £30/sq m, plus VAT), designs by Kasthall (from £80/sq m, plus VAT), vinyl, cork, rubber, sisal, wood and laminate flooring.

West End Carpets
1E Baker Street, W1U 8ED (7224 6635/ www.westendcarpets.co.uk). Baker Street or Marble Arch tube. **Open** 9am-5.30pm Mon-Fri. **Credit** MC, V.
West End Carpets claims to deliver and fit any standard carpet within 48 hours of the order being placed. As well as quality ready-to-lay and bespoke carpets, it also sells wood and laminate flooring, Amtico vinyl, tartan carpets and Persian rugs.
For branch see index.

Ceramic, marble, resin, rubber & stone

For details on resin flooring, contact **Altro** (01300 320 620, www.altro.co.uk). For a resin 'look' try **Amtico** (*see p168*) or **Sinclair Till** (*see above*). For advice and recommendations on using concrete for flooring, contact the **Concrete Society** (www.concrete.org.uk).

Absolute Floors
57 Poland Street, W1F 7NB (7439 0203/ www.absolutefloors.co.uk). Oxford Circus tube. **Open** by appointment 10am-5.30pm Mon-Fri. **Credit** MC, V.

Absolute manufactures and installs seamless resin-based flooring. Its Absolutely Stoned range is a carpet of small stones (in a huge range of colours including metallic) sealed with resin or polyurethane. Absolutely Calm is a concrete and resin floor, pigment-dyed in a wide choice of colours. It's not cheap, but then the process involves hand-pouring the resin then oiling and waxing for a beautiful finish.

European Heritage
48-54 Dawes Road, SW6 7EN (7381 6063/ www.europeanheritage.co.uk). Fulham Broadway tube. **Open** 8am-5pm Mon-Fri; 9am-5pm Sat. **Credit** AmEx, MC, V.
One of the largest importers of natural products used in walling and flooring. You'll find everything here from marble, porcelain, oak, limestone to other materials needed such as Mapre products (adhesives and grout) and Marmox concrete boards.
For branches see index.

Fired Earth
117-119 Fulham Road, SW3 6RL (7589 0489/ www.firedearth.com). South Kensington tube. **Open** 9.30am-6pm Mon, Tue, Thur-Sat; 10am-6pm Wed; noon-5.30pm Sun. **Credit** MC, V.
It started out making fired terracotta tiles, but Fired Earth has grown into an interiors empire. The emphasis is on natural products; the sustainable materials used for the tiles include marble, limestone, slate, terracotta and kiln-fired stoneware. Also stocked are pebbled flooring and glass mosaic tiles. The Fired Earth Home Collection covers furniture, fabric, flooring and paints. There's also a design service for every room in the house.
Branches: throughout the city.

Limestone Gallery
Arch 47, South Lambeth Road, SW8 1SS (7735 8555/www.limestonegallery.co.uk). Vauxhall tube/ rail. **Open** 8.30am-5.30pm Mon-Fri; 10am-4pm Sat. **Credit** MC, V.
All products are hewn from limestone. As well as tiles for walls, floors and stairs, you'll find bathroom basins, baths and vanity tops, kitchen sink surrounds and fireplaces – in stunning designs.

Paris Ceramics
583 King's Road, SW6 2EH (7371 7778/ www.parisceramics.co.uk). Fulham Broadway tube. **Open** 10am-5pm Mon-Fri. **Credit** MC, V.
The design studio here creates bespoke mosaics and murals for clients. Rare and antique materials are sourced from around the world. Other lines include natural stone flooring and decorative wall tiles. Paris Ceramics has launched a collection of French, English and Italian reproductions of carved stone chimney pieces, staircases, columns and fireplaces.
Mail order.

Stone Age
Unit 3, Parsons Green Depot, Parsons Green Lane, SW6 4HH (7384 9090/www.estone.co.uk). Parsons Green tube. **Open** 9am-5.30pm Mon-Fri; 10am-4pm Sat. **Credit** MC, V.
Trading from a large showroom, Stone Age offers over 100 limestones and sandstones, as well as basalt, slate, granite and marble, for interior and exterior use.

Stonell
521-525 Battersea Park Road, SW11 3BN (7738 0606/www.stonelldirect.com). Clapham Junction rail. **Open** 9.30am-5.30pm Mon-Fri; 9.30am-5pm Sat. **Credit** MC, V.
This firm sells a wide variety of natural stone, marble, limestone, travertine and granite, plus an impressive array of slate. The mosaics are a draw, as are bathroom vanity tops and kitchen worktops.

Terra Firma Tiles
70 Chalk Farm Road, NW1 8AN (7485 7227/ www.terrafirmatiles.co.uk). Chalk Farm tube. **Open** 10am-5pm Mon-Sat. **Credit** MC, V.
Among the terracotta, stone, slate and Moroccan tiles here are several unusual styles, especially the iridescent and stainless-steel mosaic tiles. There are

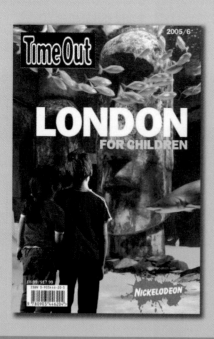

also several patterned options, including Moorish floor tiles and colourful Mexican designs. Limestone tiles start at £36/sq m.
Mail order.

Natural flooring

Crucial Trading
79 Westbourne Park Road, W2 5QH (7221 9000/ www.crucial-trading.com). Royal Oak tube. **Open** 10am-5.30pm Tue-Sat. **Credit** MC, V.
Now under friendly, new management, Crucial Trading has a huge range of natural floor coverings, including jute, coir, sisal (from £24.40/sq m), seagrass, wool, paper (surprisingly hard-wearing) and bamboo. New wool (from £20.45/sq m) ranges are also available. Samples and brochures can be sent out speedily upon request.

Reeve Flooring
Valley Farm, Brancaster Staithe, King's Lynn, PE31 8DB (0800 917 1016/www.reeveflooring. com). **Phone enquiries** 9am-5pm Mon-Fri. **Credit** MC, V.
Natural flooring company Reeve can match its coir, jute, sisal and seagrass to both the traditional or modern minimalist home. Hardwood flooring and decking are also available.

Rugs & mats

For **Deirdre Dyson Contemporary Carpets**, *see p142. See also* **Designers Guild** (*see p174*), the **Conran Shop** (*see p143*), **Habitat** (*see p145*) and **Purves & Purves** (*see p149*). For funky patchwork cowhide rugs, visit the Knightsbridge branch of **Zara** (*see p45*).

Charlotte Gaskell Oriental Carpets
183 Trinity Road, Wandsworth Common, SW17 7HL (8672 3224/www.charlotte gaskell.com). Tooting Bec tube/Wandsworth Common rail. **Open** by appointment only. **No credit cards**.
The Persian, Afghan and Turkish oriental rugs here are hand-woven from pure wool or wool/silk; designs range from the traditional to the contemporary. Rugs can be borrowed overnight to be tested in situ; contemporary designs can be commissioned in different colours; and copies of a favourite rug can be made. Prices start at £150.

Richard Morant
27 Chepstow Corner, W2 4XE (7727 2566/ www.david-black.com). Notting Hill Gate tube. **Open** 11am-5pm Tue-Sat. **No credit cards**.
After over 40 years in the business, David Black will be retiring, leaving his partner Richard Morant at the helm. The majority of products here are loomed vegetable-dyed pile carpets, kilims and silk embroideries. Custom-made kilims are the focus (from £480/sq m). Services include cleaning, moth-proofing and repair work, plus design consultancy.

Roger Oates Design
1 Monro Terrace, Riley Street, SW10 0DL (7351 2288/www.rogeroates.com). South Kensington tube. **Open** 10am-5pm Mon-Sat. **Credit** MC, V.
Refreshingly modern, Roger Oates's rugs come in wool, cotton, coir and abaca. The 100% wool range (from £75/m) has a masculine feel, with English seaside stripes. A flat-weave runner for a flight of straight stairs with 13 steps costs around £550 (£750 with plain metal stair rods). Linen fabrics for upholstery and curtaining (from £69/m) come in a range of neutral hues.

The Rug Company
124 Holland Park Avenue, W11 4UE (7229 5148/www.therugcompany.info). Holland Park tube. **Open** 10am-6pm Mon-Sat. **Credit** MC, V.
The Designer Collection at the Rug Company boasts collaborations with impressive names such as Vivienne Westwood, Diane von Furstenberg and Matthew Williamson. There's also a contemporary collection of hand-woven designs and animal hides sourced from around the world.
Mail order (7467 0690).

Wood

Listone Giordano (www.listonegiordano. com/uk) is a specialist in timber flooring and has produced a range suitable for bathroom use (hardwood backed with a base of marine ply birch) that is immune to changes in temperature and humidity. *See also p165* **Timber & builders' merchants** *and p167* **Woodwork**.

Campbell Marson
573 King's Road, SW6 2EB (7371 5001/ www.campbellmarson.com). Fulham Broadway tube. **Open** 10am-12.30pm, 1.15-4.30pm Mon-Fri; 10.30am-12.30pm, 1.15-4pm Sat. **Credit** MC, V.
Campbell Marson is a supplier of hardwood flooring from strip and boards to engineered floors. As well as installation and refurbishment, the company also designs parquet flooring.
For branch see index.

Hardwood Flooring Company
31-35 Fortune Green Road, NW6 1DU (7328 8481/www.hardwoodflooringcompany.com). West Hampstead tube/rail. **Open** 8.30am-5.30pm Mon-Fri; 10am-4pm Sat. **Credit** AmEx, MC, V.
All the flooring here, and there's plenty of it, is taken from sustainable sources. Woods include white oak, maple, walnut, cherry, larch, teak and mahogany. Choose from finished or unfinished flooring, from woodblocks or traditional boards.

Natural Wood Flooring Company
20 Smugglers Way, SW18 1EG (8871 9771/ www.naturalwoodfloor.co.uk). Wandsworth Town rail. **Open** 9am-6pm Mon-Fri; 9am-4pm Sat. **Credit** MC, V.
Sustainably sourced flooring (strip, boards, laminate, decking, pre-finished and parquet woodblock) comes in a wide range of timbers. The company also offers 3m block worktops (£180-£350) in oak, beech and maple.

Solid Floor
53 Pembridge Road, W11 3HG (7221 9166/ www.solidfloor.co.uk). Notting Hill Gate tube. **Open** 10.30am-6pm Mon-Fri; 10.30am-5pm Sat. **Credit** MC, V.
Claiming to have the largest choice in town, Solid Floor stocks non-branded, sustainably managed solid timber (light, mid, dark tones), produced to the customer's requirements. Options include the rare, traditional Versailles panels and 50cm-wide oak planks (£39-£159/sq m).
For branches see index.

Victorian Wood Works
54 River Road, Creek Mouth, Barking, Essex IG11 0DW (8534 1000/www.victorianwood works.co.uk). Barking tube/rail. **Open** 8.30am-5.30pm Mon-Fri; 9am-3pm Sat. **Credit** MC, V.
Parquet flooring is created from reclaimed antique woods (some 300 years old) sourced from French manors, chateaux and barns. Designs range from the simple and contemporary to the highly intricate. The firm also works with new woods.
For branch (Flooring Studio) see index.

Glass & windows

Check out the **Glass & Glazing Federation** website (www.ggf.org.uk) for a list of local glaziers who supply and fit glass panels. The **Classic Window Company** (8275 0770, www.classicwindow.co.uk) specialises in overhauling and repairing sash windows, while the **Original Box Sash Window Company** (0800 783 4053, www.boxsash.com) can adjust sashes to exclude draughts, as well as making traditional box sash windows in hardwood timber. **The Sash Window Workshop** (Unit 8-9, Brickfields Industrial Park, Kiln Lane, Bracknell, Berks RG12 1NQ, 0500 652 653, www.sashwindow.com) can also restore, replace, draught seal, double glaze, soundproof and generally overhaul sash windows. *See also p167* **The London Door Company**.

Edco Shotblasters
131A Clifton Road, SE25 6QA (8653 4730). Selhurst rail. **Open** 8am-5pm Tue-Fri; 8am-1pm Sat. **No credit cards**.
Edco undertakes glass sandblasting and etching, as well as the stripping of metal and wooden furniture. Architectural salvage goods are sold too.

T&W Ide
Glasshouse Fields, E1W 3JA (7790 2333/ www.twigroup.co.uk). Limehouse rail/DLR. **Open** 8.30am-4.30pm Mon-Fri. **Credit** MC, V.
Glass processing has taken place on this site for over 400 years and T&W Ide has continued the tradition since 1830, offering predominantly fireglass and glazing systems.

James Hetley & Co
Unit 9, Lyon Way, Greenford, Middx, UB6 0BN (8578 5788/www.hetleys.co.uk). Greenford tube/rail. **Open** 9am-4.15pm Mon-Thur; 9am-3.15pm Fri; 9am-12.15pm Sat. **Credit** MC, V.
Hetley's (now part of Pearsons Glass) is the biggest distributor of coloured glass in the country, and also sells tools and accessories. It can refer you to local artists to commission. There's a wealth of information and a gallery of designs with artists' details on the website.
Mail order.

Kate Maestri
Unit 2.11, Oxo Tower Wharf, Bargehouse Street, SE1 9PH (7620 0330/www.katemaestri.com). Southwark tube. **Open** by appointment 9am-6pm Mon-Fri. **No credit cards**.
Brightly coloured contemporary stained-glass designs are developed using modern technology without the lead frame. Maestri undertakes both domestic and commercial commissions. All sizes are covered, including floor and ceiling panels, screens, room dividers and windows.

Luxcrete
Premier House, Disraeli Road, NW10 7BT (8965 7292/www.luxcrete.co.uk). Harlesden tube/rail. **Open** 9am-5pm Mon-Fri. **Credit** AmEx, MC, V.
Find a glittering array of glass blocks in various sizes here, including etched, coloured and sandblasted designs suitable for wall, floor and roof-lighting. Luxcrete also makes industrial products, such as pavement lights and reinforced glass for police cells.
Mail order.

100% Glass
Unit 5, 172 Stoke Newington Church Street, N16 0JL (7249 4911/www.100percentglass.com). Bus 73. **Open** 9am-5pm Mon-Fri; by appointment Sat. **No credit cards**.
Glass specialists Didier Avignon and Marc Ballam create shower screens, mirrors, art installations, stained glass, room partitions, decorative window and door panels, splashbacks and table tops. The designs on view at 100% Glass include bright bubbles of colours suspended in sheets of glass and crackled panes.

Philip Bradbury Glass
83 Blackstock Road, N4 2JW (7226 2919/ www.philipbradburyglass.co.uk). Finsbury Park tube/rail. **Open** 9.30am-5.30pm Mon-Fri; 10am-2pm Sat. **Credit** AmEx, MC, V.
Victorian and Edwardian glass reproduction is Bradbury's speciality, including etched glass and leaded lights. A basic door panel costs from £75. You can also have a suitable work of art recreated on a glass table top, screen or mirror.

Stained Glass Shop
62 Fairfield Street, SW18 1DY (8874 8822/ www.stainedglassguild.co.uk). Wandsworth Town rail. **Open** 9am-5pm Mon-Fri; 10am-2pm Sat. **No credit cards**.
Primarily traditional designs – drawn from Victorian, Edwardian, art deco and art nouveau styles – are created at the Stained Glass Shop. Other designs include religious imagery and a series inspired by Charles Rennie Mackintosh. Staff can also restore cracked or more seriously damaged stained-glass panels.

Lighting & security

Chandeliers are being reinvented by everyone from top designers – Tom Dixon's crystal ball designs are available at **Swarovski** (£12,000, *see p81*) – to **Habitat** (Garland chandelier, £15, *see p145*). For funkier or contemporary lights, **Mathmos** (*see chapter* **Home Accessories**), **Skandium** (*see p150*), **Purves & Purves** (*see p149*) and **SCP** (*see p150*) are worth a look. *See also chapter* **20th-century Design**.

For details on recommended installers of security systems and burglar alarms, contact the **National Approval Council for Security Systems** (Sentinel House, 5 Reform Road, Maidenhead, Berks SL6 8BY, 0870 205 0000, www.nsi.org.uk).

Artemide
92A Great Portland Street, W1W 7JY (7291 9314/www.artemide.com). Oxford Circus tube. **Open** 10am-6pm Mon-Wed, Fri; 10am-7pm Thur; 10.30am-5pm Sat. **Credit** MC, V.
Italian lighting specialist Artemide creates indoor and outdoor designs that are unobtrusive but stylish: sleek constructions of opaque white satin-finish blown glass and metal. Popular lines on view at the store include the semi-recessed ceiling Elipse (from £195) and the outdoor Reed lights – slim luminous stems with a white LED illuminating the upper part – that move with the slightest breeze (from £312).

Christopher Wray
591-593 King's Road, SW6 2YW (7751 8701/ www.christopherwray.com). Fulham Broadway tube. **Open** 9.30am-6pm Mon-Sat. **Credit** AmEx, MC, V.
With over 3,000 lighting designs, covering all areas from bathroom to garden, and chandeliers to desk lamps, Christopher Wray has plenty to offer. Styles extend from traditional to modern (the Covent Garden and 600 King's Road branches both focus on contemporary styles), yet there's nothing especially cutting-edge. The King's Road shop also has an antique lighting repair service.
Mail order.
For branches see index.

Forbes & Lomax
205A St John's Hill, SW11 1TH (7738 0202/ www.forbesandlomax.co.uk). Clapham Junction rail. **Open** 9am-5pm Mon-Fri; 9am-1pm Sat. **Credit** MC, V.
For those looking for light switches and wall plates that blend into their surroundings, Forbes & Lomax supplies the alternative to ugly electrical fittings. Finishes include antique bronze, stainless steel, unlacquered brass, and plates and switches primed to be painted.
Mail order.

John Cullen Lighting
585 King's Road, SW6 2EH (7371 5400/ www.johncullenlighting.co.uk). Fulham Broadway tube. **Open** 9.30am-5.30pm Mon-Fri; 10am-4pm Sat. **Credit** MC, V.
Floating beds (lit from below), uplighters, downlighters, dimmers, garden and exterior lighting can all be found at Cullen's. Want to make a feature of a painting or vase, even door handles? A design service for those looking to light one room costs £100 (plus VAT).

The Lighting Store
779-781 Finchley Road, NW11 8DN (8201 8628/ www.thelightingstore.co.uk). Golders Green tube. **Open** 9am-5.30pm Mon-Fri; 10am-5.30pm Sat. **Credit** AmEx, MC, V.
Lighting up London since 1947, this store sources both traditional and contemporary European styles, with new products arriving each week. Modern technology and design come together in the low voltage 'spray' lights, while traditional wares include hand-forged, rustic styles and crystal chandeliers by Baccarat and Waterford.
For branch see index.

The Light Store
11 Clifton Road, W9 1SZ (7286 0233/www.the lightstore.co.uk). Warwick Avenue tube. **Open** 9am-6pm Mon-Fri; 10am-5pm Sat. **Credit** MC, V.
A quick look at its extensive online catalogue will give a clue as to how extensive the range is at the Light Store. Designs by Philippe Starck and Jasper Morrison, Artemide and Egoluce can be found alongside bathroom lighting, under-unit display lights, spotlights and masses of switches and sockets.
Mail order.

Mr Light
279 King's Road, SW3 5EW (7352 8398/ www.mrlight.co.uk). Bus 11, 19, 22. **Open** 10.30am-6pm Mon-Sat. **Credit** MC, V.
'Luminaires' since 1974, Mr Light has all your needs covered: floor, ceiling, spots and uplights, but it's the wall lights that stand out; whether it's a star-shaped plaster light (£85) or the cool, contemporary frosted-glass-with-chrome Landis (£149.99).
Mail order.
For branch see index.

W Sitch & Co
48 Berwick Street, W1F 8JD (7437 3776/www. wsitch.co.uk). Oxford Circus tube. **Open** 7am-7pm Mon-Sat. **No credit cards.**
Established in 1776, Sitch's buys, sells, restores and converts period lighting (including Bakelite, as well as non-halogen lighting) for modern use. Chandeliers are reproduced from original patterns.

SKK
34 Lexington Street, W1F 0LH (7434 4095/ www.skk.net). Oxford Circus tube. **Open** 10am-6.30pm Mon-Fri; 11am-6.30pm Sat. **Credit** AmEx, MC, V.
SKK produces some ultra-cute fairy light chains. Cheap and cheerful, they come in numerous styles (£19-£29): trees, cubes, hearts, flags or seasonal variations, such as ghosts and Christmas trees. Other items include a kitsch gorilla table lamp (£65-£79) with 5% of sales going to save the gorilla charities. The firm's more serious side is in commercial interior design lighting including LED, bare-wire and suspension fittings.
Mail order.

Organisation, removal & storage

For information on members of the professional moving industry in your area (storage, removals and shipping), contact the British Association of Removers (Tangent House, 62 Exchange Road, Watford, WD18 0TG, 01923 699 480, www.removers.org.uk). Hiring an average-sized skip (about six cubic yards) costs around £130 for up to a week. If the skip is to be left in the road you'll need a council permit (the fee depends on the borough, either you or the firm supplying the skip applies for it). **Site Compaction Services** (0800 294 0175) can provide skips – phone for rates.

California Closets
Unit 8, Staples Corner Business Park, 1000 North Circular Road, NW2 7JP (8208 4544/ http://calclosets.com). Kilburn tube then 32 bus. **Open** 9am-5pm Mon-Fri. **Credit** MC, V.
Storage solutions for every room: bespoke walk-in storage closets, home offices, as well as options for kitchens, bedrooms and garages. For smaller and cheaper solutions, check out the range of nifty accessories, which includes shoe storage, kitchen 'pantry' shelving and wine racks.

The Holding Company
241-245 King's Road, SW3 5EL (7352 1600/ www.theholdingcompany.co.uk). Bus 11, 19, 22, 49, 319. **Open** 10am-6pm Mon, Tue, Thur, Fri; 10am-7pm Wed, Sat; noon-6pm Sun. **Credit** AmEx, MC, V.

Good-looking, quality storage solutions come in all sizes here: sock boxes (holding nine pairs, £10.95) and stackable Perspex shoe boxes (£9.45 per box). For true clutterbucks, how about a classic school locker (£225) or zinc cabinet with wire mesh doors (£159)?
Mail order (8445 2888).

Screwdriver
0800 454 828/www.screwdriver-homework.com. **Phone enquiries** 9am-5pm Mon-Fri. **No credit cards.**
We can't all get the *Changing Rooms* team in to fix up our cupboards, but the biggest national home assembly company in the UK can arrange for retired handymen to assemble flatpack furniture in your home within two to three days of your phone call. Prices start at £42 for the first hour, then £36/hr.

Soft furnishings

For second-hand curtains, *see chapter* **20th-century Design**. For a list of local upholsterers, contact the **Association of Master Upholsterers & Soft Furnishers** (01633 215 454, www.upholsterers.co.uk).

Classic

Beaumont & Fletcher
261 Fulham Road, SW3 6HY (7352 5594/ www.beaumontandfletcher.com). South Kensington tube. **Open** 9.30am-5.30pm Mon-Fri; 10.30am-5.30pm Sat. **Credit** AmEx, MC, V.
All the fabrics and wallpapers here are based on 18th- and 19th-century designs, and reproduced in mellowed and faded hues, and there are hand-embroidered silks based on 17th-century botanical drawings. The company also makes traditional upholstered sofas and chairs, and 18th- and 19th-century reproduction lights and mirrors.

George Spencer
33 Elyston Street, SW3 3NT (7584 3003/ www.georgespencer.com). Sloane Square tube. **Open** 9.30am-5.30pm Mon-Fri. **Credit** AmEx, MC, V.
Fabrics, trimmings and wallpapers here are in an excellent range of understated classic fabrics such as cotton and antique linen. Many designs are taken from mid 19th- and early 20th-century originals, such as Spencer Rose, a pink-and-blue block print originally designed in the 1850s. More contemporary stripes are also available. The hand-blocked wallpaper collection includes designs in the style of early European papers, which date back to the 17th century. An extensive range of trimmings is also available.

Mrs Monro
Jubilee House, 70 Cadogan Place, SW1X 9AH (7235 0326/www.mrsmonro.co.uk). Sloane Square tube. **Open** 9.30am-5.30pm Mon-Thur; 9.30am-5pm Fri. **Credit** MC, V.
Founded in 1926, Mrs Monro may be the country's longest-established interior design company. Its look is definitely English country house chintz cotton (around £40/m) covered in pinks, sweet peas, peonies and cherubs. Antiques, ceramics and wallpaper are also sold. A landscape design service has been added to link indoors and outdoors.

Osborne & Little
304-308 King's Road, SW3 5UH (7352 1456/ www.osborneandlittle.com). Sloane Square tube then 11, 19, 22. **Open** 10am-6pm Mon-Sat. **Credit** AmEx, DC, MC, V.
O&L's wallpapers and fabrics are English patterns given a modern rework by the use of oversized motifs and contemporary colours. Textures and colours are combined, inspired by European (linens, flowers), African (chromatic yellows and oranges) and Japanese (opulent satins, woven silk) cultures. Fabrics are all complemented by the award-winning wallpapers. Look out for Nina Campbell's romantic Madame Bovary floral prints, as well as Michael Reeves' furniture (modern day beds, sofas and ottomans) and Liberty Furnishings.

HOME

Pierre Frey

251-253 Fulham Road, SW3 6HY (7376 5599/ www.pierrefrey.com). South Kensington tube. **Open** 9.30am-6pm Mon-Fri; 10.30am-5.30pm Sat. **Credit** AmEx, MC, V.

The name behind a host of fabrics, home accessories, tableware and lamps, Pierre Frey is synonymous with high-end furnishing. Having acquired European companies Braquenié, Lauer, and Boussac-Fadini Borghi, the collections now include specialist textiles and materials (damask, taffeta, velvet, sheer, some even fire-retardant). Traditional prints and jacquards of roses, cockerels and milkmaids now lie alongside more up-to-the-minute stripes, abstract shapes and velours.

Contemporary

Celia Birtwell

71 Westbourne Park Road, W2 5QH (7221 0877). Notting Hill Gate or Royal Oak tube. **Open** 10am-1pm, 2-5pm Tue-Fri. **Credit** AmEx, MC, V.

Apart from a small selection of scarves, interior fabrics are the mainstay here. Designs are considered classics, with animals, stripes and roses among the bestsellers.

Designers Guild

267-271 & 275-277 King's Road, SW3 5EN (7351 5775/www.designersguild.com). Sloane Square tube then 11, 19, 22 bus. **Open** Homestore (267-271) 10am-6pm Mon-Sat; noon-5pm Sun. Showroom (275-277) 10am-6pm Mon-Sat. **Credit** AmEx, MC, V.

This place is a must for anyone looking for bright, contemporary fabrics and prints. One of the latest collections is Samarkand: seven designs in 29 colourways inspired by the Silk Route (think rich, luxurious fabrics the colour of precious stones). Then there is Ralph Lauren's tailored stripes and tartans; Cath Kidson's much-imitated nostalgic prints of roses and cowboys, and printed ticking; and delicate neutrals by Emily Todhunter. The company also stocks wallpaper, paint, carpets and rugs, as well as furniture (including kids'), and bed and bathroom accessories. *Mail order.*

Marimekko

16-17 St Christopher's Place, W1U 1NZ (7486 6454/www.marimekko.co.uk). Bond Street tube. **Open** 10am-6.30pm Mon-Wed, Fri, Sat; 10am-7pm Thur; noon-5pm Sun. **Credit** AmEx, MC, V.

Finnish textile firm Marimekko is famous for the bold, brightly coloured floral prints that it has been producing since 1951. Fabrics can be used to create wall-hangings, bags, cushions, even towels and umbrellas.

Monkwell

227 King's Road, SW3 5EJ (7823 3294/ www.monkwell.com/www.crowsonfabrics.com). Sloane Square or South Kensington tube. **Open** 10am-6pm Mon-Sat. **Credit** MC, V.

With the oldest shopfront on the King's Road, Monkwell (along with sister firm Crowson, trading from the same site) offers over 12,000 furnishing fabrics and wallpapers. The latest designs include rich textured chenilles and plush faux furs. There's also a made-to-measure service available for curtains and blinds.

Sally Bourne Interiors

10 Middle Lane, N8 8PL (8340 3333/www.sallybourneinteriors.co.uk). Finsbury Park tube/rail then W7 bus. **Open** 10am-6pm Mon-Sat; noon-5pm Sun. **Credit** MC, V.

This extensive collection of home and garden wares encompasses fabrics, scented candles, flower pots and a decent choice of paints by the likes of Farrow & Ball, Morris & Co and Designers Guild. Also available are beautiful, subtle handmade tiles. Styles are inspired by nature and range from plain tiles in colours such as cornflower, limestone and driftwood to detailed designs with feather and fossil intaglios. Prices start at £1.18 a tile. *Mail order.*

Curtains, poles, blinds & shutters

The first port of call for blinds or shutters should be the **British Blind & Shutter Association** (01827 52337, www.bbsa.org.uk). Search the online database, which lists over 350 vetted firms offering everything from venetian, roman or roller blinds for the home to office window dressings, conservatory awnings and skylight blinds. The **Association of Master Upholsterers & Soft Furnishers** (*see p173* **Soft Furnishings**) also lists a number of curtain and blind suppliers. The **Curtain Exchange** (7731 8316, www.thecurtainexchange.co.uk) sells new, second-hand and made-to-measure curtains.

American Shutters

8876 5905/www.americanshutters.co.uk. **Phone enquiries** 9am-5.30pm Mon-Fri. **Credit** AmEx, MC, V.

The solid pine bespoke shutters produced by this firm are of a high quality and favoured by many interior designers. Louvres are adjustable and shutters can be stained or paint-matched at no extra cost. Special designs with curved louvred tops can accommodate arched windows very well.

City Blinds

273 Hackney Road, E2 8NA (7739 6206/ www.cityblinds.co.uk). Bus 26, 48, 55. **Open** 9.30am-5.30pm Mon-Fri; 10am-5pm Sat; 10am-3pm Sun. **Credit** MC, V.

An excellent selection of high-quality roller and venetian blinds, both ready-made and made to measure. Standard polyester roller blinds (2ft) cost from £14.

The Curtain Workshop

39 Amwell Street, EC1R 1UR (7278 4990). Angel tube. **Open** 9am-6pm Mon-Fri. **No credit cards.**

A professional making-up service for curtains and other soft furnishings; there are some cottons and silks here, or you can bring your own fabrics.

Eclectics

01843 608 789/www.eclectics.co.uk. **Phone enquiries** 9am-5.15pm Mon-Fri. **Credit** AmEx, MC, V.

Dedicated to uncluttered living, Eclectics offers a superb range of blinds – including roller, bottom up, roman, metal and wood venetians as well as Kyoto sliding panels and curtains. All the blinds sold by the firm are offered in a variety of different fabrics and finishes. *Mail order.*

Plantation Shutters

131 Putney Bridge Road, SW15 2PA (8871 9333/www.plantation-shutters.co.uk). East Putney tube. **Open** 9am-5.30pm Mon-Fri. **Credit** AmEx, MC, V.

Traditional custom-made slatted wooden shutters are available in a good range of styles (£175-£250/sq m). The firm also produces venetian and roller blinds, all custom-made from high-quality renewable wood. The MDF shutters are heavier, but they're also cheaper. *Mail order.*

Discount

Fabric World

287-289 High Street, Sutton, Surrey SM1 1LL (8643 5127/www.fabricworldlondon.co.uk). Morden tube/Sutton rail. **Open** 9am-5.30pm Mon-Sat. **Credit** MC, V.

With two shops in Surrey, Fabric World stocks at least 4,000 rolls of fabric suitable for curtains, soft furnishings and upholstery. Among the myriad designers, look out for Cath Kidston, Liberty and Colefax & Fowler. There are make-up, fitting and interior design services (£50 design fee, refunded if you spend over £500). **For branch see index.**

South London Fabric Warehouse

Unit F2, Felnex Trading Estate, 190 London Road, Hackbridge, Surrey SM6 7EL (8647 3313/www.fabricwarehouse.co.uk). Hackbridge rail. **Open** 9am-5pm Mon-Sat; 10am-4pm Sun. **Credit** MC, V.

Thousands of discount fabrics are kept here. There are no big designers, but quality is high, and prices low. Blinds and curtains can be made to order.

Wall to Wall

549 Battersea Park Road, SW11 3BL (7585 3335). Clapham Junction rail. **Open** 10am-5pm Mon-Sat. **Credit** MC, V.

A good range of designer end-of-line, seconds and discounted fabrics, starting at around £9.95/m. Some fabrics are repeatable and reorderable.

Naturals

Ian Mankin Fabrics

109 Regent's Park Road, NW1 8UR (7722 0997). Chalk Farm tube. **Open** 10am-5.30pm Mon-Fri; 10am-4pm Sat. **No credit cards.**

All fabrics here are natural – either 100% cotton, linen or cotton/linen mix. Prices start at around £3.90/m for muslin, rising to £24.50/m for linen. *Mail order.* **For branch see index.**

Warris Vianni

85 Golborne Road, W10 5NL (8964 0069/ www.warrisvianni.com). Ladbroke Grove tube. **Open** 10am-5pm Mon-Sat. **Credit** MC, V.

A beautiful range of unusual and luxurious natural fabrics, such as patterned silk organza (from £8.95/m), linens (from £10.95) and shot silk in around 40 subtle colours (£18.95/m). *Mail order.*

Tiles & mosaics

For designer tiles, it's worth checking out the delicate, ice-cream coloured tiles of Shropshire-based **Kenneth Clark** (01952 505 085, www.kennethclarkceramics.co.uk); **Andrew Tanner's** quirky 'knitted' and 'wooden' tiles (01273 818 811, www.andrewtannerdesign.co.uk) and the handmade tiles at **Sally Bourne Interiors** (*see above*). For marble, limestone and granite mosaic (from £108/sq m), contact **Roma Marble** (Unit 1A, The Ringway, Bounds Green Industrial Estate, N11 2UD, 8361 7544). Italian tile merchant **Bisazza** (8640 7994, www.bisazza.com) specialises in colourful mosaic tiles and slabs.

Criterion Tiles

196 Wandsworth Bridge Road, SW6 2UF (7736 9610/www.criterion-tiles.co.uk). Fulham Broadway tube then 295 bus. **Open** 9.30am-5.30pm Mon-Fri; 9.30am-5pm Sat. **Credit** MC, V.

The range of tiles here includes classics like Mezzo, for institution-chic eau de nil (£38.26/sq m), and monochrome combinations and decorative tiles. The branch at 178 Wandsworth Bridge Road (7731 6098) is also worth a visit. Most of its tiles are only slight seconds, and are otherwise exclusive to upmarket shops. It holds regular clearance sales. **For branches see index.**

Elon

12 Silver Road, W12 7SG (7460 4600/www.elon.co.uk). White City tube. **Open** 9am-5pm Mon-Fri. **Credit** MC, V.

Imported wall and floor tiles with a Mediterranean feel. Terracotta and natural tones predominate.

Reed Harris

27 Carnwath Road, SW6 3HR (7736 7511/ www.reedharris.co.uk). Parsons Green or Putney Bridge tube. **Open** 8am-5.30pm Mon-Fri; 9am-5.30pm Sat. **Credit** AmEx, MC, V.

Ceramic, glass, mosaic and stone tiles in muted tones or sophisticated contrasting colours. Prices for porcelain ceramic mosaics start at £24.30/sq m. High-end pure-glass tiles cost from £173.90/sq m. **For branch see index.**

Stone & Ceramic Warehouse

*51-55 Stirling Road, W3 8DJ (8993 5545/
www.stoneandceramicwarehouse.co.uk). Acton
Town tube.* **Open** 8.30am-5.30pm Mon-Fri;
10am-5pm Sat; 11am-3pm Sun. **Credit** MC, V.
Stones are imported from across the world for
these wall and floor tiles. Stones sourced from the
Middle East, such as the Bethlehem Gold aged
limestone, will set you back £85/sq m (plus VAT).
For branch see index.

World's End Tiles

*British Rail Yard, Silverthorne Road, SW8 3HE
(7819 2100/www.worldsendtiles.co.uk). Battersea
Park or Queenstown Road rail.* **Open** 8.30am-
5.30pm Mon-Wed, Fri, Sat; 8.30am-7pm Thur;
11am-5pm Sun. **Credit** MC, V.
A vast selection of tiles is offered here, including
ceramic, porcelain, mosaic and natural stone, with
prices from £68.88/sq m up to £127.64/sq m for
limestone. The showroom has a kids' area.

Wallcovering

Now that wallpaper has made a comeback, it
shows no sign of disappearing any time soon.
Habitat (*see 145*) has got designer **Matthew
Williamson** on board (£25/10m roll), as well
as **Barbara Hulanicki** of cult '60s shop Biba
(£22/roll). Or you could literally do it yourself
with wallpaper-by-numbers by **Jenny
Wilkinson** (01895 822 856, www.paint-by-
numbers.co.uk): you buy the paint with the
outline drawings on the paper and the end
result is entirely up to you (£35/roll, £60 with
kit of paints); look out for her lovely Venus
Flutterby. Always worth a look is paper
by **absolute zero degrees** at Places and
Spaces (*see p149*): Bees is a lovely clay and
lacquer print effect of a honeycomb structure
that morphs into bees and butterflies (£60/roll).
For those on a '70s tip, an excellent resource is
the German online company **Wallpaper from
the 70s** (www.wallpaperfromthe70s.com).

Why not jazz up your garden space too with
outdoor wallpaper by **Susan Bradley**
(www.susanbradley.co.uk), which can be used
as a garden trellis, screening or simply as a
decorative feature or installation. It's available
in a range of sizes, designs and finishes,
including stainless steel, aluminium and
powder-coated steel (in most colours), as well
as acrylic and wood.

For paints and wallpaper ranges (including
designer), *see also p167* **DIY**.

Paint & wallpaper

Cole & Son

*G10 Chelsea Harbour Design Centre, Lots Road,
SW10 0XE (7376 4628/www.cole-and-son.com).
Sloane Square tube.* **Open** 9am-5.30pm Mon-Fri.
Credit MC, V.
Making handprinted wallpapers since 1875, Cole
& Son has a staggering range of wallpaper and
paints – from Regency stripes to the award-
winning the Woods from the New Contemporary
Collection: sketches of trees in a unique repeat, in
shades of grey-blue and white, shaded purple, gold
and terracotta and dark brown on silver foil
(£38/roll). Metallics are hand-gilded papers using
painted copper and silver leaf or sumptuous flocks
on foil. A couple of rolls should cover the average
chimney breast. You can even create your own
block-print design or choose your own stripes for
a unique wallpaper.

Discount Decorating

*157-159 Rye Lane, SE15 4TL (7732 3986).
Peckham Rye rail.* **Open** 8am-5.30pm Mon-Fri;
9am-5.30pm Sat. **Credit** MC, V.
You may not find state-of-the-art decoration at
Discount Decorating, but you can save a packet on
cut-price Dulux paints, discontinued wallpapers
and accessories.

Farrow & Ball

*249 Fulham Road, SW3 6HY (7351 0273/
www.farrow-ball.com). South Kensington tube.*
Open 8.30am-5.30pm Mon-Fri; 10am-5pm Sat.
Credit AmEx, MC, V.
Paints and wallpapers are made using traditional
techniques. Many paints are recreations of shades
used in Georgian and Regency properties – though
you may need to apply more coats than usual. The
firm also produces one of the most extensive
ranges of whites and off-whites. Wallpaper is made
using block-printing methods; striped designs are
their forte (from £35.99/roll). Minimum order for
wallpaper is three rolls.
Mail order (01202 876 141).

Francesca's Lime Wash

*34 Battersea Business Centre, 99-109 Lavender
Hill, SW11 5QL (7228 7694/www.francescas
paint.com). Clapham Junction rail.* **Open** by
appointment 10am-5pm Mon-Fri. **Credit** MC, V.
Offering over 160 colours, this shop has one of the
largest limewash (for interior and exterior
application) collections around. Colours are matched
by eye, and they are soft and natural. Francesca's
knowledge of traditional paint finishes has been
gleaned from her extensive research trips – Mexico,
Namibia, Brazil, Australia, India – and is reflected
in the shades, which range from pale to vibrant.
Prices start at £25/2.5 litres (depending on depth of
colour) for eggshell, £29-£40 limewash and £17.92-
£25 emulsion. Colour consultation costs £200.
Mail order.

Hamilton Weston

*18 St Mary's Grove, Richmond, Surrey TW9
1UY (8940 4850/www.hamiltonweston.com).
Richmond tube/rail.* **Open** 9.30am-6pm Tue-Fri;
10am-4pm Sat. **Credit** MC, V.
Specialising in the reproduction of historical
wallpapers, Hamilton Weston recreates machine-
and handprinted designs dating from 1690, but
also sells modern lines. As well as having all the
wallpaper libraries, the shop runs an interior
design service and has access to furniture and
carpets. The retro handprinted paper (On The
Edge) that was recreated for *Bridget Jones: Edge
of Reason* costs £138/roll (minimum ten rolls).
Mail order.

Jocelyn Warner

*19-20 Sunbury Workshop, Swanfield Street,
E2 7LF (7613 4773/www.jocelynwarner.com).*
Phone enquiries 10am-6pm Mon-Fri.
No credit cards.
These original, sophisticated wallpaper designs are
loosely handpainted from natural forms – often in
striking and unusual colourways. New designs
include Leaf (repeats of outlines of oversized
leaves), which comes in ten contrasting colourways,
including gold on turquoise or black. Scribble is
retro-looking squiggles in five colourways, such as
blue with lilac, and jade with lime. Prices start at
£59/roll. Warner also designs simple lighting based
on her own wallpaper designs.

John Oliver

*33 Pembridge Road, W11 3HG (7221 6466/
www.johnoliver.co.uk). Notting Hill Gate tube.*
Open 9am-5.30pm Mon-Fri; 9am-5pm Sat.
Credit AmEx, MC, V.
Paints here are known for their clarity and strength
of colour. The palette spans the spectrum, and
includes muted shades, bold contemporary colours
(Russian Red) and historic options (Wedgwood
Blue), some of which have adorned the likes of
Babington House and Scotland's Dean Centre Art
Gallery. Matt emulsion costs £23.21/2.5 litres
(eggshell £28.31). In-house designers Inder Jamwal
and Marco Rizla are on hand to help customers
choose paint schemes, wallpapers, cushions and
fabrics. September 2005 saw the launch of Interior
Couture by DF Bean (www.dfbean.com), a recent
Central St Martin's graduate whose work includes
textiles, wallpaper and cushions covered in her
iconic Handbag design, as well as the latest Bird
and Chandelier collection, which was inspired by
a fire at her Primrose Hill house in April.
Mail order.

Malabar

*31-33 South Bank Business Centre, Ponton
Road, SW8 5BL (7501 4200/www.malabar.co.uk).
Vauxhall tube/rail.* **Open** 9am-5pm Mon-Fri.
Credit MC, V.
The Paintworks company has recently handed the
paint part of the business over to Malabar, hence
losing a few of its old lines (colourwashes in
particular) and workshops along the way. However,
there is now an expanded range of historical and
contemporary colours including 105 water-based
matt emulsions and satins, suitable for a variety
of surfaces.
Mail order.

Paint & Paper Library

*5 Elystan Street, SW3 3NT (7823 7755/
www.paintlibrary.co.uk). Sloane Square tube.*
Open 9am-5pm Mon-Fri; 10am-4pm Sat.
Credit MC, V.
P&PL specialises in cutting-edge colours and paint
finishes. Wallpaper lines include designs by David
Oliver, Allegra Hicks and Emily Todhunter. Silver
Fans wallpaper costs £45/10m roll.
Mail order.

The Paint House

*52 Northcote Road, SW11 1PA (7924 5118).
Clapham Junction rail.* **Open** 9am-5.30pm Mon-
Fri; 10am-5.30pm Sat. **Credit** MC, V.
Around 4,000 paint colours, plus eco paints, tiles
and mosaics, fabric and wallpapers are kept here.
Decorating services, including tiling, upholstery
and interior styling, can also be arranged.

Pickwick Papers & Fabrics

*6 Nelson Road, SE10 9JB (8858 1205/
www.pickwickpapers.co.uk). Cutty Sark DLR.*
Open 9.30am-5pm Mon-Wed, Fri, Sat; 9.30am-
3pm Thur. **Credit** MC, V.
Pickwick Papers & Fabrics has one of London's
largest choices of wallpaper and fabric. The
wallpapers available here include those by Neisha
Crosland's, as well as unique finds like David
Oliver's (of Paint & Paper Library, *see above*)
glam glitter designs and Zoffany's traditional
styles. In terms of fabric, there's everything from
Andrew Martin to Osborne & Little and Malabar.
A recent addition to the store is the shagpile and
rug showroom in the basement. Helpful staff are
on hand.

The Stencil Library

*Stocksfield Hall, Stocksfield, Northumberland
NE43 7TN (01661 844 844/www.stencil-
library.com).* **Phone enquiries** 9am-5.30pm
Mon-Sat. **Credit** AmEx, MC, V.
Thousands of stencil designs (suitable for wall and
floor) are kept here, from art deco flowers or
Japanese cherry blossoms (from £15.95) to
fabulous Doric columns (£43.95-£66.96), even
proverbs and quotations. Ordering can be done
online, where the website also has a useful 'As seen
in…' magazine feature. Accessories and painting
tools are also available.
Mail order.

Tracy Kendall

7640 9071/www.tracykendall.com. **Phone
enquiries** 9am-5pm Mon-Fri. **No credit cards.**
Tracy Kendall's trademark floral designs on
contrasting backgrounds are now joined by
digitally produced images of stacks of magazines,
books or plates. Other themes include feathers,
sequins and giant silver-service cutlery. All designs
can be printed in any colour. Panels cost around
£100 each, while the computer generated designs
are £120/sq m.
Mail order.

Wallpaper History Society

*c/o Mr D Burton, 49 Glenpark Drive, Southport,
Merseyside PR9 9FA (01704 225 429).* **Phone
enquiries** 9am-5pm Mon-Fri.
A valuable resource for anyone who wants to date
or trace period wallpaper, the Wallpaper History
Society also arranges visits, lectures and
conferences, and encourages the preservation of
period decorations.

20th-century Design

Accessories

Boom! Interiors

115-117 Regent's Park Road, NW1 8UR (7722 6622/www.boominteriors.com). Chalk Farm tube. **Open** noon-6pm Mon, Wed-Sun. **Credit** MC, V.
Since opening this smart store in 1998, Phil Cowan has expanded from 1950s, '60s and '70s design to embrace a broader period. For example, alongside a 1955 Thomas Appleby two-tone satinwood cabinet on a raised A-frame (£850), you'll now find older pieces such as an early Victorian child's chair with an ebony wood frame and gilt decoration (£750), Ernest Race's 1945 BA3 chairs (£350 each) or a streamlined art deco desk lamp (£335). Murano glass lights (£800-£3,500) are always popular, as are rosewood sideboards (£800-£3,500). Spread across three floors, everything is displayed in tasteful room settings, giving ample inspiration for anyone doing up their home. In the basement, which is laid out like a living room, we recently saw an iconic space-age Aphelion TV (from 1981, but adapted for satellite and cable, £1,750) and some well-chosen limited-edition silk-screen prints from 1960s op art pioneer Victor Vasarely (from £295). Prices are reasonable considering the chi-chi location, and Cowan also offers an interior design service. *Mail order.*

Caira Mandaglio

31 Pembridge Road, W11 3HG (7727 5496/www. cairamandaglio.co.uk). Notting Hill Gate tube. **Open** 11am-5pm Wed-Fri; 10.30am-5.30pm Sat; other times by appointment. **Credit** AmEx, MC, V.
This bijou shop champions the clean lines of 1930s-'50s French and Italian design, throwing in a few English and Scandinavian pieces for good measure. When we last stopped by, a large '30s art deco mirror was £950, while a gilded French sun mirror with exaggerated spikes came in at £330. Fulham Pottery vases are a mainstay, most frequently in black (£175-£350) or glazed white (£195-£395). Costlier items included a magnificent maple-topped 1950s Italian sideboard with red and black Formica side panels (£1,900) and a set of eight Dutch Friso Kramer dining chairs (£1,000). Stock is limited but changes frequently, and staff will try to source specific requests.

Century

68 Marylebone High Street, W1U 5JH (7487 5100). Baker Street tube. **Open** 10am-6pm Tue-Sat; by appointment Mon, Sun. **Credit** AmEx, MC, V.
This immaculate shop is divided into two distinct domains. On the ground floor, Norma Holland (trading under the name of Noho) continues to offer a decorative look, stocking repro mirrored chests of drawers (from £450) and cabinets, a handful of

antique French salon chairs, art deco mirrors and fabulous Italian ceiling lights from the 1930s to the '70s, often composed of cascading discs of opalescent glass. Andrew Weaving is master of the basement, concentrating on utilitarian mid-century accessories such as sideboards, desk lamps, vintage cushions and modernist reference books. The store also offers a well-regarded interior design service.

Fandango

50 Cross Street, N1 2BA (7226 1777/www.fan dango.uk.com). Angel tube/Highbury & Islington tube/rail. **Open** 1-4pm Tue-Fri; 11am-6pm Sat; other times by appointment. **Credit** AmEx, MC, V.
A smart shop for a classy street, Fandango keeps things stylish and simple, showcasing a relatively small number of top-quality pieces at any one time. Italian lighting is a key line, but visual interest takes priority over big names so, while you will find Murano glass and some rare Italian lighting at up to £1,800, most pieces are from non-standard names and are in the hundreds rather than the thousands as a result. Elsewhere, a wooden-framed 1950s English mirror was £95, a Cuban film print £180 and French mercury glass candlesticks £180. Memorable pieces of furniture were a leather De Sede swivel chair (£550) and a Haslev rosewood low coffee table (£465). *Très chic.*

Gary Grant Choice Pieces

18 Arlington Way, EC1R 1UY (7713 1122). Angel tube. **Open** 10.30am-6.30pm Tue-Sat. **Credit** AmEx, DC, MC, V.
Gary Grant always contextualises his ceramics, approaching them first and foremost from a design point of view. One 'selling exhibition' is staged each year and, when we last visited, 1950s Rye pottery was given pride of place, its gaily coloured glazed butter dishes (£25-£55) and vases (up to £550) illustrating how this small studio captured the imagination of a newly optimistic post-war Britain. In between such month-long shows, Grant stocks mid 20th-century names he considers to be significant design innovators. Expect to find

Jones Lighting

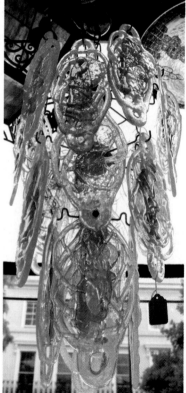

ceramics from Poole, Midwinter, Hornsey and Parkinson, as well as glass by Whitefriars and Alexander Hardie Williamson, among others. Also on sale are some textiles and design books.

The Lifestyle Company

17 Lamb Street, E1 6EA (7247 3503). Liverpool Street tube/rail. **Open** noon-6pm daily. **Credit** MC, V.

Stock here is more stripped down and less bling than of old, with plenty of tinted glass, brushed aluminium and chrome – most visibly in the Castiglioni-style arc floor lamps (around £300) that curve gracefully over glass tables and magazine racks throughout the front room of the store. Any one of a number of tile-topped tables can be yours for a reasonable sum, and a dinky side table may cost as little as £45, but this dealer certainly knows his market and, if he can get it, will charge it: the 1960s Eames chocolate-brown leather armchair in pride of place in the window lately was a purse-busting £1,500. Recent months have also seen a diversification into 1970s and '80s gadgets, toys and retro paraphernalia, everything from a duck-shaped hairdryer to chunky Aiwa ghetto blasters (£100-£150) and – for a cool retro 2012 accessory – a 1972 Munich Olympics holdall (£35).

Origin Modernism

25 Camden Passage, N1 8EA (7704 1326/ www.origin101.co.uk). Angel tube. **Open** 10am-6pm Wed, Sat; noon-6pm Fri, Sat.
No credit cards.

Try not to use the word 'retro' in David Tatham's chic little shrine to modernism, for, as he says, 'one looks forward, the other back'. Items here are Scandinavian, American or British and made between the 1930s and '50s; you'll often see Bruno Mathsson three-quarter chaise longues from the 1940s with their characteristic hemp webbing and, though there are some Hans J Wegner or Finn Juhl chairs in solid wood, Origin specialises in plywood (its bent forms epitomise this era), in particular the laminated wood and plywood furniture designed by the famous Finnish architect Alvar Aalto. Prices range from £50 for Scandinavian glass to £5,000 for a rare plywood chair of sound provenance. There are also British paintings (£300-£2,500) from some of the lesser-known artists of the '50s.

Planet Bazaar

397 St John Street, EC1V 4LD (7278 7793/ www.planetbazaar.co.uk). Angel Tube. **Open** 11.30am-6pm Mon-Sat; other times by appointment. **Credit** MC, V.

Pop art is the speciality at Maureen Silverman's vibrant two-floor store, which is awash with brightly coloured objects from the 1950s and '60s. Original and limited-edition artwork is always available: Jamie Reid (of Sex Pistols graphic design fame), Banksy, Peter Blake, Logue & Bouchier lithographs, James Cauty and Annabel de Vetten are among those usually featured. To get the complete pop look, pick up a vintage 700 Series red phone (£65) or, for your coffee table, a 1970 transcript of David Bailey's Andy Warhol documentary. Chairs include Harry Bertoia's large chrome mesh Diamond design, a white folding Garden Egg chair and the pod-like Kenny (£1,650). The extensive lighting stock includes a rare anglepoise desk lamp by Herbert Terry & Sons (£175). Increasingly popular are Italian Memphis ceramics – Sottsass-designed, from £175 – and the occasional '80s item, such as a Keith Haring inflatable baby.
Mail order.

two columbia road

2 Columbia Road, E2 7NN (7729 9933/www.two columbiaroad.com). Old Street tube/rail/26, 48, 55 bus. **Open** noon-7pm Tue-Fri; noon-5pm Sat; 10am-2pm Sun. **Credit** MC, V.

An enviable corner site gives eagle-eyed customers the chance to assess two columbia road's stock before moving inside to nail a bargain. Up close, the wares don't disappoint. After all, this stylish store belongs to the celebrated Tommy Roberts, who owned cult interiors shop Kleptomania on Carnaby Street in the 1960s and, later, Tom Tom. He still appears on Wednesdays, but otherwise his son

Keith runs the show, selling books on art, design and pop culture, and the best selection of 1950s and '60s Danish furniture we've seen. Arne Jacobsen Series 7 chairs with signs of wear are £120 each, a pair of immaculate Hans J Wegner wishbone chairs £900 and a rosewood pedestal desk £850. Vast, six-seater, low-slung corner sofas with their original leather are around the £2,300 mark. Stock rotates, so on another visit you could expect to find a wider spread of European and US post-war furniture.

Vincenzo Caffarella

Ground floor, Alfie's Antique Market, 13-25 Church Street, NW8 8DT (7724 3701/www.vinca. co.uk). Edgware Road tube/Marylebone tube/rail. **Open** 10am-6pm Tue-Sat. **Credit** AmEx, MC, V.

Continuing to go from strength to strength, Vincenzo Caffarella has expanded to include virtually all of the top floor of Alfie's, as well as its previous street-level stalls. Owners Monica Glerean and Vincenzo himself are passionate about colour and this is reflected in their vibrant Italian lamps and furniture, primarily from the 1950s to the '70s. Giò Ponti, Fontana Arte, Vistosi and Arteluce all feature prominently, but lesser finds are also deemed important, providing they are unequivocally fabulous, like the six '50s Italian chairs in complementary rainbow shades from an unknown designer (£1,800 for the set). Pieces aren't cheap, but this is *the* place for striking sculptural lamps (around £1,300) and glass disc chandeliers (available in white, yellow or blue, around £1,000 each), and the shop numbers Hugh Grant and Madonna among its celebrity browsers.

Budget

Ooh-La-La!

147 Holloway Road, N7 8LX (7609 0455). Highbury & Islington tube/rail. **Open** 11am-5pm Mon-Thur; 11am-6pm Sat. **No credit cards**.

Navigating this overcrowded emporium is all part of the fun. If you're up for a treasure-hunting challenge, you'll love diving behind three layers of furniture to try to discover what lurks at the back of the shop. Well-worn leather (and vinyl) chesterfields are a mainstay (three-seater £350, two-seater £250), as are armchairs (£100); the rest is cheap 'n' cheerful bric-a-brac, including old Penguin paperbacks, a 1980s black Bakelite phone (as seen, £15), porcelain, cutlery and a manual typewriter or two. Nestled behind all this is vintage men's and women's clothing, mainly from the 1970s and '80s; much of it with a burlesque flavour. An antique boned corset might hit £50, but other than that, it's flea-market prices all the way.

Past Caring

76 Essex Road, N1 8LT (no phone). Angel tube. **Open** noon-6pm Mon-Sat. **No credit cards**.

Cluttered to the point of chaos, Past Caring has the feel of a jumble sale: prices are dirt cheap, everything is jammed on to the shelves in one frantic muddle and you take your chances as to what gem or unloveable piece of junk you're likely to discover on the day. Truth be known, it's the kind of place that dealers leap on, but it might well take a professional eye to locate the beautiful white tablecloth in among the crocheted doilies and chairbacks, or the groovy 1960s mini dress nestling on a rail of nasty nylon. We found velvet curtains (around £50), a '70s quilted maxi skirt (£8), a Native American statue (£12), a tiered wooden sewing box (£15), a multicoloured round wicker table (£25) and a battered Ercol armchair (£40), not to mention badges, blankets, handbags, shot glasses, hat stands, endless piggy banks, '80s executive desk toys, floor-standing ashtrays and ceramic skulls. Well, you know what they say: one person's junk is another person's knowingly ironic gift.

Collectibles & curios

Back in Time

93 Holloway Road, N7 8LT (7700 0744/ www.backintimeuk.com). Highbury & Islington tube/rail. **Open** 10am-6pm Mon-Sat. **Credit** AmEx, DC, MC, V.

For the last 11 years, people who fancy N1 style at N7 prices have been popping in here for Panton lights and Jacobsen Swan, Egg and Ball chairs. Most of the shop floor is dedicated to 1950s, '60s and '70s furniture and accessories, with arc lights (£250-£500), a giant '60s bathroom cabinet (£700), a simple Eames round table (£95), a Le Corbusier glass dining table (£700) and brown leather sofas (£450-£2,000). That said, the chain-smoking proprietor can't disguise his real passion: he designs bespoke aluminium-and-Perspex Freeslide shelving systems, which can readily accommodate a plasma TV screen (neatly hiding the wires at the back) and cost about £450 for a two-shelf cabinet. More stock is housed in a warehouse, which can be viewed by appointment.
Mail order.

Les Couilles du Chien

65 Golborne Road, W10 5NP (8968 0099/ www.lescouillesduchien.co.uk). Ladbroke Grove tube. **Open** 9.30am-5.30pm Mon-Fri; 9am-5.30pm Sat. **Credit** AmEx, MC, V.

Once you spot the proudly displayed giant moose head (not for sale), you'll recognise this chaotic little shop for what it is: a charming bastion of eccentricity. Owner Jerome has run this ramshackle store for 16 years, indulging his passion for natural history and entomology and keeping switched on to the more bizarre market trends. Amid the anarchy there's a slightly ghoulish element: witness the framed bugs and beetles (£19-£40) often bought as kids' presents, or the eye-catching Damien Hirst-esque 1930s and '40s anatomical charts (£45-£180). You might think the 1970s hand-blown Murano glass ball (£280) or the Daum crystal clock (£100) would suit most people's tastes, but you'd be surprised: custom-made plaster-cast mutts are being snapped up at £3,500. Customers think they're the (eponymous) dog's bollocks.

Lighting

The Facade

99 Lisson Grove, NW1 6UP (7258 2017/www. thefacade.co.uk). Edgware Road or Marylebone tube. **Open** 10.30am-5pm Tue-Sat. **Credit** AmEx, MC, V.

Since relocating from Westbourne Grove in March 2005, the Facade has continued in precisely the same successful vein. Prepare to be dazzled: chandeliers are, quite simply, everywhere, sometimes hanging a hair's breadth from your barnet. All shapes and sizes are available, many boast coloured drops in aqua or peach, or take the typically Italian form of flower shapes. Bargain-seekers will be pleased that many are from the 1940s and '50s, and therefore are more budget-friendly than their Georgian and Victorian antecedents. Prices start at £120 and top £2,000, with most around £400 or £500. Repairs and rewiring are done in-store. Also available are humble bits of garden furniture, and impressive mirrors with organic-looking freeform frames of entwined driftwood (£780 for a 4ft x 6ft version).

Jones Lighting

194 Westbourne Grove, W11 2RH (7229 6866/ www.jonesantiquelighting.com). Notting Hill Gate tube. **Open** 9.30am-5pm Mon-Sat. **Credit** AmEx, MC, V.

Since our previous visit, Jones has branched out into costume jewellery (£5-£170), its glittering display adding to the immeasurable sparkle of the hundreds of lights already adorning this split-level store. Virtually everything here is original, so while prices aren't cheap, the pieces have a sound provenance and are highly individualistic, with items (such as a uranium light, £2,500) that are simply never going to be reproduced. The earliest lights are Victorian (generally English), converted to electricity, but the majority of stock is French art deco (table lamps £350-£1,500, ceiling lights £750-£4,500). Look up and you see a shimmering sea of elaborate shades – perhaps in the form of petals, or featuring opalescent or Vaseline glass. Kitsch-seekers should scour the back room for Pierrot lamps and a wealth of French 1900s spelter cherubs (£375-£1,300). All the lights, as you'd hope, are fully restored and rewired. One tip: don't go hunting any crystal droplet chandeliers, they're seldom available because most are reproductions.

Markets

Established in 1976 and housed in the rambling premises of a former Edwardian department store, **Alfie's Antique Market** (*see p126*) is a labyrinth of stalls representing over 100 different dealers. As well as the vibrant lights of Vincenzo Caffarella's newly expanded outlet (*see p177*), you'll find Arne Jacobsen chairs, puppet sets, Susie Cooper ceramics, chrome cocktail shakers and shot glasses, vintage fabrics and curtain panels, Poole pottery, tapestry cushions, reupholstered sofas and much more. When you've sated your vintage needs, nip along to the rooftop café.

Stables Market
Off Chalk Farm Road, opposite junction with Hartland Road, NW1 8AH (7485 5511/ www.camdenlock.net). Chalk Farm tube. **Open** 10am-6pm Sat, Sun. **Credit** varies.
Built in 1836 to care for beasts injured pulling canal barges, Camden's former Horse Hospital is now an eclectic agglomeration of market stalls. Rubbing shoulders with the vintage clothing and nostalgic toy traders are a handful of dealers focusing on 20th-century furniture and accessories. Of particular note is **Out of Time**, specialist in 1930s to '60s European and American furniture and accessories. There is plenty of kitsch, such as the 1950s Britvic table lamp with a pineapple-shaped base (£75) and animal-print bar stools (£75 each), but it also stocks a wealth of more utilitarian pieces: notably Ercol (a red low, two-seater sofa, £350, plus matching armchairs) and teak furniture by G-Plan (vanity desk with mirror, £350). For an even wider choice, visit the Out of Time warehouse in Islington (110-116 Sander House, Elmore Street, N1, 7354 5755). Elsewhere, **Mark Parrish** (Unit 33, 07957 300 848) concentrates on decorative design from the 1950s to the '80s; stand-outs include '60s rosewood sideboards (£500-£1,100) and Bakelite phones (£65-£185).
Stables Market extends under the vast railway arches, too, where you'll find a few more 20th-century dealers. A supplier to the interiors trade, **Sergio Guazzelli** can be relied upon for three-seater leather sofas (£700) and Murano glass disc chandeliers (£450 for a fine turquoise and pink example). If you're seeking something a little unusual, try **Arckiv** at Unit 90 – besides shelves of vintage sunglasses, it has rare (and accordingly costly) 1970s and '80s pieces, such as a white 1970 modular table, one of only ten produced by Fabio Lenci for Benini (price on request), and Ettore Sottsass's totem pole-like 1981 Casablanca cabinet (£4,500).

Nearly antiques

Bazar
82 Golborne Road, W10 5PS (8969 6262). Ladbroke Grove or Westbourne Park tube. **Open** 10am-5pm Tue-Thur; 9.30am-5.30pm Fri, Sat. **No credit cards.**
Stock can run low at this popular shop specialising in 1850s-1950s French decorative rustic furniture, and such was the case when we visited, though the owner assured us everything is replenished weekly. Alongside pretty painted wardrobes (from £750) and simple Victorian armchairs reupholstered in neutral shades of calico or Swedish linen (£500-£550 a pair) is collectable kitchenalia, such as an egg timer in a tiny wooden case. The store also does a nice line in industrial-looking, sand-blasted steel lighting and furniture, of which Kylie is apparently a fan.

Ben Southgate
4 The Courtyard, Ezra Street, E2 7RH (07905 960 792/www.bsouthgate.co.uk). Old Street tube/rail/26, 48, 55 bus. **Open** 9am-2.30pm Sun. **Credit** MC, V.

It's only two years old, but Ben Southgate is one of the more consistently interesting shops in this pretty little retail enclave just off Columbia Road. Bright and well organised, the shop floor is home to two main lines: restored 20th-century oak furniture for office and home, and the kind of metal medical furniture that will set your pulse racing if you're a fan of practical homeware with a twist. Furniture starts around the £75 mark for a varnished oak folding chair; more expensive pieces might include a polished steel medical cabinet (£850) or a 1900 oak pedestal desk with a new leather insert (£1,150). There are also adorable kitchen accessories, such as tea tins and French glass storage jars, as well as some nostalgic children's toys.

Castle Gibson
106A Upper Street, N1 1QN (7704 0927/ www.castlegibson.com). Angel tube. **Open** 10am-5.30pm Mon-Fri; 10am-6pm Sat; noon-5pm Sun. **Credit** MC, V.
A functional look, which is entirely in keeping with much of the stock, predominates at this four-storey shop: you can find good storage pieces here, such as old wooden trolleys (to be used as shelving), steel-and-glass display cabinets (£750), steel lockers and the odd 1940s polished metal four-drawer chest (£595). There are also distressed 19th-century painted bed frames (£495), large oak-framed mirrors (£275), 1940s brown leather armchairs (£895), the ubiquitous church chairs (£48 each) and, on a recent visit, we saw a simple, round Eames table (£235). A few oddities are usually tucked among the bulkier pieces: we spotted a vintage X-ray illuminator and a 1930s optician's apparatus lamp (£295), while a cute sky-blue garden set comprising two metal chairs and a dainty round table with heart motif (£195) sat on the pavement out front.

D&A Binder
34 Church Street, NW8 8EP (7723 0542/ www.dandabinder.co.uk). Edgware Road tube. **Open** 10am-6pm Tue-Sat. **Credit** MC, V.
With two London branches, D&A Binder has cornered the market in such traditional shop fittings as counters, cabinets, shirt units, mannequins and vitrines. The Holloway Road premises is a dingy, rambling, warehouse of a shop, with a workshop area at the back where cabinets are stripped, polished and made good, sometimes for prestigious clients such as Paul Smith. The Church Street premises, by contrast, is where you'll find finished items. Prices vary according to condition and individual requirements (clients might request a mirrored back or bottom, or extra shelves). Haberdashery cabinets (£700-£2,500) and counters (£200-£900) are always in demand; smaller items make good home storage units. Rarities and accessories might include a Fry & Sons chocolate cabinet (£700) or a brass suit and coat hanger to screw on a door (£35). Some *Star Wars* figurines (£3.50-£30) make a jolly addition to the Holloway store. **For branch see index.**

Harold's Place
148 South Ealing Road, W5 4QJ (8579 4825). South Ealing tube. **Open** 10am-5pm Mon, Tue, Thur-Sat. **No credit cards.**
You wouldn't think a store called Harold's Place would be a particularly inspiring place to pick up something as quintessentially girlie as a vase. You shouldn't judge this friendly shop by its name, though, as it's big on the kind of large crystal vases that would suit a giant bunch of roses. Designer names are few and far between, but no matter – it's the bargains that fuel trade here: vases are usually £15-£30, while most decanters go for £10-£25. More recently the shop has also started doing a mix of basic second-hand furniture (£10-£50) and framed prints of old masters (£12-£25, 16in x 20in).

Myriad Antiques
131 Portland Road, W11 4LW (7229 1709). Holland Park tube. **Open** 11am-6pm Tue-Sat. **Credit** MC, V.

Myriad is an apt name for this expansive shop; it makes full use of a conservatory-style extension and basement of nooks and crannies to display artfully a plethora of painted, mahogany and maple-framed mirrors, reupholstered Edwardian and Victorian armchairs, throws and Welsh blankets, coat hooks, peg rails and more. Fun items such as the antler shelving and mirrors (£250-£550) are popular among the well-to-do customers who want to accessorise their Alpine or Scottish piles. Bamboo mirrors, while costly (around £450), can be hard to source elsewhere. This shop is in Clarendon Cross, an undeniably smart spot, and prices reflect this, with quilts going for several hundred pounds and simple French metal garden furniture approaching £700 for a set of four chairs.

Strand Antiques
46 Devonshire Road, W4 2HD (8994 1912). Turnham Green tube. **Open** 10.30am-5.30pm Tue-Sat. **Credit** MC, V.
A showroom for a posse of five friendly antiques dealers, this charmingly crammed little shop is a jumble of (mainly French) treasures, most with a shabby-chic appearance and pleasing price tags. Furniture varies in style and age, but there is a preponderance of art deco and mid 20th-century pieces. On a recent visit, an art deco dressing table was £180, a 1930s Austrian dining chair £65 and a 1900 oak sideboard £750. Strand is known for its mirrors, both overmantel and convex, and early 20th-century French chandeliers (from £110). Of late it has also been diversifying into mid 20th-century heavy art glass, and crystal, amber, glass, jet and Bakelite jewellery. Rummagers can discover all sorts of homewares, such as French linen sheets (£30-£60) and quilts (from £90), picture frames (£8-£25), gramophones and retro clothing. Countless bundles of cutlery, bread bins and ceramic cheese dishes, shellfish and artichoke plates grace the shelves at the back of the store, while the tiny patio beyond has a few well-worn items of garden furniture (chairs are £20 each).

The Vintage Home Store
105 Churchfield Road, W3 6AH (8993 4162). Acton Central rail/bus 70, 207. **Open** 11.30am-5.30pm Mon, Wed-Sat. **Credit** AmEx, MC, V.
Friendly proprietor Sandy Stagg complements her Portobello Road Antique Clothing Shop (*see p58*) with this antiques store dedicated to all that is 'useful and decorative' for the home and garden. The eminently browse-worthy shop is stuffed to the rafters with an eclectic range of goods: garden tables (£50-£75), bathroom cabinets, French café tables, rugs, 1950s curtains (£50-£60), 19th-century patchwork quilts (£100-£350), marble-topped washstands (£150) and hand-thrown terracotta pots (£10). Green-fingered enthusiasts will be charmed by the old-fashioned gardening books; others might be delighted by the quaint kitchenalia (whisks, £10; bread bins £20-£40). Chances are you'll find whatever you're looking for here – even much-loved old teddy bears.

Retro & kitsch

After Noah
121 Upper Street, N1 1QP (7359 4281/ www.afternoah.com). Angel tube/Highbury & Islington tube/rail. **Open** 10am-6pm Mon-Sat; noon-5pm Sun. **Credit** MC, V.
A large part of After Noah's appeal is its retro ambience and charming layout: half of the ground floor is devoted to old-fashioned kids' toys, retro sweets and pocket-money trinkets, the rest is a whimsical array of new gifts and homewares (cards, pill boxes, picture frames, cushions, throws) and reconditioned chrome anglepoise lamps and steel fans (around £99; £145 for floor-standing models), plus some original Arts and Crafts pieces. Nothing is cheap. A Stickley Brothers Mission rocking chair was £1,650, a small glazed 1930s English oak bookcase with original sliding glass doors £475, and a 200 Series Gecko black Bakelite phone £450. For a bargain you might try a rummage in the basement (four oak Arts and Crafts chairs were originally £650

1950s style

After the surreal TV quiz *Shooting Stars* popularised the expression '1950s throwback' as a comedic insult for all people bequiffed and backwards-looking, you'd be forgiven for thinking that the decade had fallen foul of modern fashion. The truth, though, is dramatically different. Take a peep at the stores plying wares from the forefront of 20th-century design, and many take unparalleled delight in the 1950s. No wonder, when you consider that the post-war age of the consumer was all about novelty and innovation. Formica, PVC, rubber, plastics and melamine meant greater versatility. These new materials, combined with the desire to make maximum use of space,

gave rise to stacking furniture, fitted kitchens and the birth of homemaker-style statements.

Today, though, give or take the cutesy retro charms of **Cath Kidston**'s chic wares, you're most likely to be tripping your brothel creepers down one of two avenues: American diner and bar kitsch, or cleverly designed '50s furniture with the kind of slender frame that still looks contemporary. Add a dash of fun and a double measure of frippery to your favourite cocktail by camping it up with animal-print bar stools or a Britvic table lamp (Out of Time at **Stables Market**; *see p178*). Sets of shot glasses, often with stands or trays, and embellished with simple stripes or such

entertainingly random prints as sailing boats, plus retro phones (*pictured*), are available from **Radio Days** (*see below*), while **Flying Duck Enterprises** (*see below*) boasts a truly astonishing range of home bars. For more demure tastes, of course, it's those simple classics in the vein of Eames plywood or mesh chairs (**The Lifestyle Company** and **Back in Time**; for both, *see p177*) that are most desirable, perhaps alongside some vibrant Poole pottery (**Gary Grant Choice Pieces**; *see p176*) or striking Murano glass (*see p177* **Vincenzo Caffarella**). When it comes to enduring 20th-century design, it seems it's those '1950s throwbacks' who are having the last laugh.

Radio Days

for the set, reduced to £95 each), or just content yourself with a spot of kitsch in the shape of a tomato-shaped ketchup dispenser (£2.99). *Mail order.*
For branch see index.

Flying Duck Enterprises
320-322 Creek Road, SE10 9SW (8858 1964/ www.flying-duck.com). Cutty Sark DLR. **Open** 11am-6pm Tue-Fri; 10.30am-6.30pm Sat, Sun. **Credit** AmEx, MC, V.
While proudly proclaiming its infatuation with modern bad-taste gifts (think Elvis and pink flamingo gadgets and, of course, decorative flying ducks), this colourful store also stocks a plethora of reasonably priced original pieces from the 1950s, '60s and '70s. Kitsch '50s bar culture is well represented. There is a range of home bars – padded, rattan, glass and bamboo (upwards of £125) and rarities such as a large '60s L-shaped bar (around £250), plus extras such as glassware, soda syphons, a new neon palm-tree bar sign (£195) or star-print chrome bar stools (£30 each). Vintage fabrics, including pairs of curtains in geometric or pop prints, range from £25 to £100, while groovy wallpaper, usually from the 1960s and '70s, goes from £10 a roll (reaching £35 for something

spectacular). Palm-rich beach scenes are the subject of many murals (door size, £20; full-size, £60). If you were a 1970s kid, you can relive your childhood with a Chopper (up to £750 for a desirable early model) or an array of original board games. *Mail order.*

Radio Days
87 Lower Marsh, SE1 7AB (7928 0800/www.radio daysvintage.co.uk). Waterloo tube/rail. **Open** 10am-6pm Mon-Thur, Sat; 10am-7pm Fri. **Credit** MC, V.
Just swooning along to the sounds of Eartha Kitt or Bessie Smith inspires you to root through the retro rails of this appealingly laid-back shop. Having been here 12 years, it's built up quite a following, so seasoned party-goers and theatre types already know to plunder the extensive post-war clothing collection, while recently the BBC's *Strictly Dance Fever* snapped up some of the period his-and-hers gear. Prices are reasonable, with women's 1940s trousers in coral, bottle green and plain black (£38), full-skirted 1950s halter-neck dresses (£45-£85) and '60s beaded jumpers (around £40). Top sellers for men include fedoras and hip White Stripes-style white-fringed '50s black shirts (£45). Radio Days remains one of the best places for Bakelite telephones (from £65 with a six-month guarantee)

and also specialises in retro collectibles that double as kitsch gifts (1950s shot glasses printed with sailing boats; saucy '70s birthday cards; and powder compacts printed with flying ducks). Of course, there are chunky old-fashioned radios too: all reconditioned and in full working order (from £65). *Mail order.*

Soft furnishings

The Curtain Exchange
129-131 Stephendale Road, SW6 2PS (7731 8316/ www.thecurtainexchange.net). Bus C4, 28, 295. **Open** 10am-5pm Mon-Sat. **Credit** MC, V.
This thriving exchange business is particular about what it buys in, which means only the best second-hand curtains end up on its rails. Fabrics steer clear of tired Laura Ashley florals and William Morris, favouring instead the timeless charms of Nina Campbell, Colefax and Fowler, Andrew Martin, Bennison and Zoffany prints, or classic plain linens and silks. All are top quality, with both interlining and lining, and available on 24-hour home-approval loan. Over 2,000 pairs are stocked (£200-£500), but if you still can't find precisely what you want, the Exchange also offers hand-finished bespoke and 100% cotton new ready-mades.

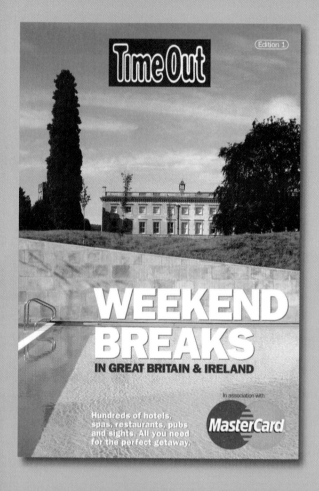

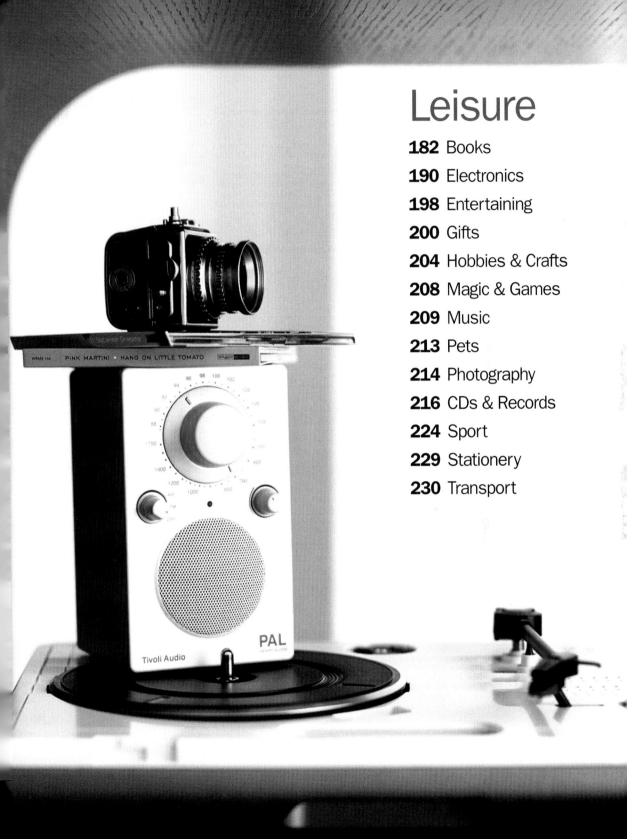

Leisure

Books

Note that many bookstores offer student discounts and a mail-order service.

For book fairs, see p10 **Shopping Diary**.

Departmental bookshops

Blackwell's

100 Charing Cross Road, WC2H 0JG (7292 5100/www.blackwell.co.uk). Tottenham Court Road tube. **Open** 9.30am-8pm Mon-Sat; noon-6pm Sun. **Credit** AmEx, MC, V.
The central London branch of this academic bookselling empire covers the whole spectrum of scholarly subjects, but is particularly strong in history, philosophy, medical sciences and IT. Good fiction and travel sections cater for those less academically orientated. Staff will help to locate the book or section you're after (the store isn't often referred to as 'user-friendly').
Branches: throughout the city.

Books etc

421 Oxford Street, W1C 2PQ (7495 5850/ www.booksetc.co.uk). Bond Street tube. **Open** 9.30am-8pm Mon-Wed, Sat; 9.30am-8.30pm Thur, Fri; 11.30am-6pm Sun. **Credit** AmEx, DC, MC, V.
Run by the US Borders Group – which also owns the UK-based Borders Superstores – Books etc is a pared-down version of its larger sibling. Each of the formulaic stores stocks a healthy selection of general interest material, as well as music, videos and DVDs and greetings cards, and regularly provides offers on current bestsellers.
Branches: throughout the city.

Borders Books & Music

203 Oxford Street, W1D 2LE (7292 1600/www. borders.co.uk). Oxford Circus tube. **Open** 8am-11pm Mon-Sat; noon-6pm Sun. **Credit** AmEx, MC, V.
A browser's paradise over five floors, this US import led the chain bookshop trend of in-house coffee shops, comfortable chairs, late opening hours and large audio-visual sections (with listening stations) that has turned modern bookshops into places to while away entire afternoons or evenings. This branch has an extensive magazine and stationery section on the ground floor.
For branches see index.

Foyles

113-119 Charing Cross Road, WC2H 0EB (7437 5660/www.foyles.co.uk). Tottenham Court Road tube. **Open** 9.30am-9pm Mon-Sat; noon-6pm Sun. **Credit** AmEx, DC, MC, V.
Since the £2 million transformation of this famous, independent store and the opening of a smaller branch at the South Bank Centre (the first new branch for over 70 years), the team here have been feeling more purposeful than ever. New lifts and air-conditioning, along with clear floorplans of the densely filled five storeys, have put an end to the multitude of lost and frustrated-looking customers, while the café area surpasses those of rivals, with organic food and music events organised by Ray's Jazz (incorporated into the store as part of the refurbishment, along with Silver Moon women's bookshop). Author book signings and talks take place throughout the year, with the likes of John Irving and Fay Weldon. There's also a good audio section on the ground floor, and plans for a second-hand section.
For branch see index.

Hatchards

187 Piccadilly, W1J 9LE (7439 9921/www. hatchards.co.uk). Piccadilly Circus tube. **Open** 9.30am-6.30pm Mon, Wed-Sat; 10am-6.30pm Tue; noon-6pm Sun. **Credit** AmEx, DC, MC, V.

Hatchards is the oldest surviving bookstore in London, having been established in 1797, and it has an illustrious roll call of former clients. Spread over five floors, the beautiful premises are bisected by a spiral staircase, and the books themselves are neatly tucked into a maze of comfortable and inviting rooms; Hatchards is a store that clearly likes to take itself seriously. Hardback fiction, biography, history, art and gardening are the largest departments, while other sections include politics and the military. Recent book signings have featured PD James and Alan Bennett.

London Review Bookshop

14 Bury Place, WC1A 2JL (7269 9030/www.lrb. co.uk/lrbshop). Holborn or Tottenham Court Road tube. **Open** 10am-6.30pm Mon-Sat; noon-6pm Sun. **Credit** AmEx MC, V.
This modern, well-run and clearly laid-out shop, owned by the eponymous literary-political journal, is all polished wood, quiet conversations, passionate staff and a seriously informed selection of books. The range is extraordinary, from Alan Bennett's latest offerings and the most recent academic, political and biographical tomes, to up-to-date copies of the *New Yorker*, *Art Review* and *Smoke*, plus a good choice of the best poetry, cookery and gardening titles. Regular readings and talks.

Ottakar's

70 St John's Road, SW11 1PT (7978 5844/ www.ottakars.co.uk). Clapham Junction rail. **Open** 9am-7pm Mon, Wed-Fri; 9am-6pm Tue, Sat; 11am-5pm Sun. **Credit** AmEx, DC, MC, V.
This ever-expanding, general interest chain bucks the impersonal trend of huge, multimedia stores, with an emphasis on helpful staff and features such as reading areas. Clapham Junction's branch is one of the group's most successful; it hosted the SW11 literary festival in autumn 2005 and is particularly strong on literary fiction (it's a haven for reading groups), travel, cookery, health and children's books. An under-fives reading session takes place every Friday, and there are regular author events. As we went to press, Waterstone's had proposed a takeover.
Branches: throughout the city.

Waterstone's

311 Oxford Street, W1C 2HP (7499 6100/www. waterstones.co.uk). Oxford Circus tube. **Open** 9am-8pm Mon-Wed, Fri, Sat; 9am-9pm Thur; noon-6pm Sun. **Credit** AmEx, DC, MC, V.
The latest major branch from Britain's best-known bookselling giant is a celebration of the capital. A London section – on the right as you enter – contains guides, A-Zs and maps, and recommended books (Peter Ackroyd, Iain Sinclair and Monica Ali, among others). Fiction (with good gay interest and black writers sections) and crime novels are also on the ground floor, with arts and children's titles upstairs, and academic and sports books in the basement. Most departments have bays highlighting London titles. Of the other branches in London, the one at 82 Gower Street, WC1 (7636 1577) is the flagship academic outlet.
Branches: throughout the city.

General & local

Blenheim Books

11 Blenheim Crescent, W11 2EE (7792 0777). Notting Hill Gate tube. **Open** 9am-6pm Mon; noon-5pm Sun. **Credit** AmEx, MC, V.
This small, design-led shop provides a good range of titles on interiors, architecture, photography and art, plus a small selection of children's books. The focus, however, is on gardening books, to which the rear of the store is dedicated.

Bolingbroke Bookshop

147 Northcote Road, SW11 6QB (7223 9344). Clapham Junction rail/319 bus. **Open** 9.30am-6pm Mon-Sat; 11am-4pm Sun. **Credit** MC, V.
Bolingbroke (named after a 17th-century Battersea figure) is strong in its selection of children's books, travel and fiction titles (the classics section, in particular, has grown over the past year), but the stock is wide-ranging and includes the full collection of Pevsner architectural guides. There's also a good ordering service, and the shop is committed to local authors, whose works are prominently displayed. Greetings cards are also stocked.

Bookseller Crow on the Hill

50 Westow Street, SE19 3AF (8771 8831/ www.booksellercrow.com). Gypsy Hill rail. **Open** 9am-7.30pm Mon-Fri; 9.30am-6.30pm Sat; 11am-5pm Sun. **Credit** AmEx, MC, V.
While Bookseller Crow is especially strong on contemporary British and American literature, there is plenty here to please all members of the family, including an excellent children's section with chairs and tables for the little 'uns. There are occasional events and signings.

Index Bookcentre

16 Electric Avenue, SW9 8JX (7274 8342/ www.indexbooks.co.uk). Brixton tube/rail. **Open** 10am-6pm Mon-Sat. **Credit** AmEx, MC, V.
Situated next to Brixton market, Index Bookcentre stocks publications with a radical slant, including a broad range of magazines like *Red Pepper* and *International Searchlight*. The store also has general books, plus multi-ethnic children's literature, and works by black authors. Events are held annually during Black History Month, with occasional book signings by locals such as Alex Wheatle. Index also publishes its own titles.

John Sandoe Books

10 Blacklands Terrace, SW3 2SR (7589 9473/ www.johnsandoe.com). Sloane Square tube. **Open** 9.30am-5.30pm Mon, Tue, Thur-Sat; 9.30am-7.30pm Wed. **Credit** AmEx, MC, V.
Still going strong after nearly 50 years, the success of John Sandoe is partly down to the passionate staff, several of whom are writers themselves. Split over three levels, the comfortable and inviting space hasn't seen much change, but houses an impressive quantity of titles. Art and gardening, hardback fiction, history and biographies are on the ground floor; paperback fiction and travel are on the upper, while the basement houses theatre, poetry and kids' books. The Persephone imprint is also stocked.

Kilburn Bookshop

8 Kilburn Bridge, Kilburn High Road, NW6 6HT (7328 7071). Kilburn Park tube. **Open** 10am-6pm Mon-Sat. **Credit** MC, V.
Making efficient use of the rather limited space at its disposal, this popular, independent bookshop stocks a diverse collection on a decent range of subjects. Specialisms include modern fiction, Irish and Caribbean literature and psychology. Staff are friendly, helpful and passionate about their trade. The swift ordering service is another plus.
For branch (Willesden Bookshop) see index.

Metropolitan Books

49 Exmouth Market, EC1R 4QP (7278 6900/ www.metropolitanbooks.co.uk). Farringdon tube/ rail. **Open** 10.30am-6.30pm Mon-Fri; 10.30am-6pm Sat. **Credit** AmEx, MC, V.
With its cheery orange front and carefully chosen stock, this small, fresh space is the antithesis of the traditionally dark and musty local bookshop, and a good spot for recommendations. There's an excellent selection of contemporary and classic fiction, as well as books on design, travel, film, music and history, plus a growing children's section. Cards are also stocked.

Muswell Hill Bookshop

72 Fortis Green Road, N10 3HN (8444 7588/ www.muswellhillbookshop.com). Highgate tube. **Open** 9.30am-6pm Mon-Sat; noon-5pm Sun. **Credit** MC, V.

LEISURE

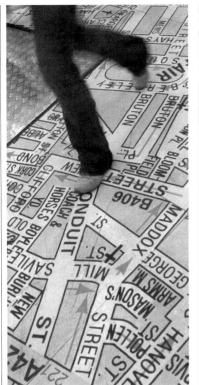

Waterstone's

Bucking the chain trend, this small, independent bookshop is still going strong. Attractions are a good selection of general stock, including all the bestsellers, a strong food and drink section, a cheery local vibe, and a good ordering service. The only thing lacking is a section for juniors. **For branches (Prospero's Books and Palmers Green Books) see index**.

Owl Bookshop
209 Kentish Town Road, NW5 2JU (7485 7793). Kentish Town tube/rail. **Open** 9.30am-6pm Mon-Sat; noon-4.30pm Sun. **Credit** AmEx, MC, V.
A solid all-rounder: as well as practical guides on cookery, travel, gardening and DIY, there's an extensive children's section and an informed choice of literature. Local history is well represented, and there's a very active programme of author events; past poetry readings have included Margaret Atwood and Tobias Hill.

Pan Bookshop
158 Fulham Road, SW10 9PR (7373 4997). South Kensington tube. **Open** 9am-10pm Mon-Fri; 9.30am-10pm Sat; 10am-9pm Sun. **Credit** AmEx, MC, V.
This inviting shop in South Ken (Tara Palmer-Tomkinson is among its myriad loyal locals) is renowned for its strong collection of signed books, and the diverse range of new titles. Over the past year, the mind, body and spirit section has also been refined. On top of this, there's an impressive collection of audio books and BBC radio plays on tape and CD.

Primrose Hill Books
134 Regent's Park Road, NW1 8XL (7586 2022/ www.primrosehillbooks.co.uk). **Open** 9.30am-6pm Mon-Fri; 10am-6pm Sat; 11am-5pm Sun. **Credit** AmEx, MC, V.
A little gem of a bookshop, with a good selection of books covering literature, art, travel, cookery and children's books, over one floor. The second-hand selection is now being sold only through the website. Readings and events are important fixtures here, and local authors such as Martin Amis and Ian McEwan often take part. A good number of signed copies are normally stocked too.

Specialist

Arts

Artwords Bookshop
65A Rivington Street, EC2A 3QQ (7729 2000/ www.artwords.co.uk). Liverpool Street or Old Street tube/rail. **Credit** AmEx, MC, V.
Artwords stocks books, magazines, journals and videos on the contemporary visual arts. All of the latest publications on art, photography, graphics and architecture, from the UK and abroad, are packed into a studio-like space. Knowledgeable staff, plus a huge array of exhibition flyers, help make this a key resource for artists and designers. **For branch see index**.

Cinema Store
4B Orion House, Upper St Martin's Lane, WC2H 9NY (7379 7838/www.the-cinema-store.com). Leicester Square tube. **Open** 10am-6.30pm Mon-Wed, Sat; 10am-7pm Thur, Fri; 11am-5pm Sun. **Credit** AmEx, MC, V.
Books stocked in this friendly shop (which also sells DVDs, posters and soundtracks) cover all aspects of the silver screen. As well as specialist manuals on filmcraft (screenwriting, directing, animation), there's a decent range of screenplays and books on specific films, genres, actors and directors, plus magazines and coffee-table items such as *The Stanley Kubrick Archives*. Shelves of discounted books, plus author events (with signings from the past year including Gene Wilder) are further draws.

Dover Bookshop
18 Earlham Street, WC2H 9LG (7836 2111/ www.doverbooks.co.uk). Covent Garden tube. **Open** 10am-6pm Mon-Wed; 10am-7pm Thur-Sat; 1-5pm Sun. **Credit** AmEx, MC, V.
Dover Bookshop, celebrating its 20th anniversary in 2006, claims to have the world's biggest collection of copyright- and permission-free images, making it a useful resource. Motifs, illustrations, graphics and patterns from subjects as diverse as animals, costumes, ethnic art, poster art and art nouveau are available in book form and on CD.

French's Theatre Bookshop
52 Fitzroy Street, W1T 5JR (7387 9373/www. samuelfrench-london.co.uk). Warren Street tube. **Open** 9.30am-5.30pm Mon-Fri; 11am-5pm Sat. **Credit** AmEx, MC, V.
As well as a selection of over 2,000 playscripts and books on acting, stagecraft and theatre history, French's also stocks audio-visual material, biographies and magazines. Occasionally it hosts festivals and events.

ICA Bookshop
Nash House, The Mall, SW1Y 5AH (7766 1452/ www.ica.org.uk/bookshop). Charing Cross tube/rail. **Open** noon-9pm daily. **Credit** AmEx, DC, MC, V.
Reflecting the ethos of the gallery, the ICA bookshop stocks a selection of cutting-edge material on contemporary art, including critical titles; otherwise hard-to-come-by cult magazines (like *Modern Toss* and *Nice*); quirky little books you can't get elsewhere; limited-edition prints, and a selection of art and film DVDs and videos.

Magma
117-119 Clerkenwell Road, EC1R 5BY (7242 9503/www.magmabooks.com). Farringdon tube/ rail. **Open** 10am-7pm Mon-Sat. **Credit** AmEx, MC, V.
Although Magma stocks plenty of books that are arguably more concerned with style than content, it's still an excellent resource for 'creatives', particularly designers. Books on graphics, book design, illustration, animation, photography, architecture and advertising fill the space, plus there are DVDs, trendy toys, T-shirts and magazines. Customer feedback is encouraged. **For branch see index**.

Nog
182 Brick Lane, E1 6SA (7739 4134). Aldgate East tube. **Open** 10.30am-8pm daily. **Credit** MC, V.
A design bookshop with a sideline in funky products, such as animal motif wallpaper. Literary highlights include *Skateboard Stickers* by Mark Munson and Steve Cardwell, *Twentieth Century Type* by Lewis Blackwell, and Mark Gatter's *Getting It Right in Print*. There's also a vintage vinyl section.

Offstage Theatre & Cinema Bookshop

37 Chalk Farm Road, NW1 8AJ (7485 4996/ www.offstagebooks.com). Chalk Farm tube. **Open** 10am-6pm Mon-Fri; 2-6pm Sat. **Credit** AmEx, MC, V.

As well as a wide-ranging selection of technical and theoretical books on theatre, film and contemporary culture, this charming shop is the place to come for plays and screenplays. Most of the stock is new, but second-hand titles are also available.

Photo Books International

99 Judd Street, WC1H 9NE (7813 7363/www.pbi-books.com). King's Cross tube/rail. **Open** 11am-6pm Wed-Sat. **Credit** AmEx, MC, V.

A plethora of photography books and monographs from all around the world is packed into this small but inviting space. If you can't find what you're after, charming owners Bill and Jasper will be happy to help.

Shipley

70 Charing Cross Road, WC2H 0BQ (7836 4872/ www.artbook.co.uk). Leicester Square tube. **Open** 10am-6pm Mon-Sat. **Credit** AmEx, MC, V.

Shipley continues to fly the flag for traditional booksellers on Charing Cross Road, offering an impressive selection of out-of-print, antiquarian and new, arts and now architecture (moved from Shipley Design next door) titles. The books are neatly arranged, and staff are always on hand to guide you through the stock (which includes a diverse range of monographs, manuscripts and exhibition catalogues).

Shipley Design

72 Charing Cross Road, WC2H 0BE (7240 1559/ www.artbook.co.uk). Leicester Square tube. **Open** 10am-6.30pm Mon-Sat. **Credit** AmEx, MC, V.

This trendy, neatly arranged branch of the arts specialists stocks new and out-of-print titles covering all aspects of graphic and interior design, plus fashion and film. The stock caters for amateurs, professionals and academics, and includes a wide collection of magazines and industry journals. The contents of the now-defunct Shipley Media shop – new and out-of-print titles on photography, photojournalism, cinema, and contemporary art – are now housed here.

Cookery

Books for Cooks

4 Blenheim Crescent, W11 1NN (7221 1992/ www.booksforcooks.com). Ladbroke Grove tube. **Open** 10am-6pm Tue-Sat. **Credit** AmEx, MC, V.

The lovely smells that emanate from this traditional-looking shop ensure its continued popularity: every day, staff cook treats from the limitless recipes to hand in the smart test kitchen/coffee shop at the back. The shop's own publications are worth a look amid the thousands of recipe books covering every type of cuisine. There are titles on nutrition and culinary history, as well as biographies of celebrated chefs. Cookery workshops take place upstairs.

Fashion

RD Franks

Kent House, Market Place, W1W 8HY (7636 1244/www.rdfranks.co.uk). Oxford Circus tube. **Open** 9am-6pm Mon-Fri. **Credit** AmEx, MC, V.

This homage to fashion sells an impressive array of international magazines and trend-forecasting material, plus guides for aspiring designers and fashion photographers, sewing and textile manuals and stylish coffee-table books.

Gambling

High Stakes

21 Great Ormond Street, WC1N 3JB (7430 1021/ www.highstakes.co.uk). Russell Square tube. **Open** noon-6pm Mon-Fri. **Credit** MC, V.

How to Win the Pools and *The Racing Retirement Plan* sit next to less ambitious titles like *Discovering Backgammon* in this small and welcoming store – the only one of its kind in the UK. As well as betting strategy and gambling, stock (some of which is imported) includes books on the concept of 'chance', the history of gambling, sports almanacs and the crime series from No Exit Press.

Gay & lesbian

Gay's the Word

66 Marchmont Street, WC1N 1AB (7278 7654/ www.gaystheword.co.uk). Russell Square tube. **Open** 10am-6.30pm Mon-Sat; 2-6pm Sun. **Credit** AmEx, DC, MC, V.

Whether you're after a practical guide on telling your mother, a more scholarly work on gender studies or politics, or some erotic holiday fiction, you should find what you want among the enormous range of stock (both new and second-hand) available in this homely and colourful shop. Magazines are also sold, and the place hosts events and discussion groups.

Genre fiction & comics

Fantasy Centre

157 Holloway Road, N7 8LX (7607 9433/ www.fantasycentre.demon.co.uk). Holloway Road tube. **Open** 10am-6pm Mon-Sat. **Credit** MC, V.

The oldest surviving shop in the world specialising in books, pulp magazines and digests on sci-fi, fantasy and horror, all for the serious collector. Second-hand publications, including collectable and out-of-print titles, form around 90% of the stock, while the remaining 10% is made up of new books from publishers like Ash-Tree and Tartarus.

Forbidden Planet Megastore

179 Shaftesbury Avenue, WC2H 8JR (7420 3666/www.forbiddenplanet.com). Tottenham Court Road tube. **Open** 10am-7pm Mon-Wed, Fri, Sat; 10am-8pm Thur; noon-6pm Sun. **Credit** AmEx, MC, V.

Heaven for *Star Wars*, Tolkien and Buffy fans, Forbidden Planet is the HMV of the sci-fi, fantasy and cult entertainment world. The colossal selection of books in the megastore's basement covers the spectrum from science fiction and ufology to crime, graphic novels and political and anarchist titles. Manga and anime books and comics are also stocked, and there's a huge range of merchandise and paraphernalia. Frequent book signings have included Christopher Lee.

Gosh!

39 Great Russell Street, WC1B 3NZ (7636 1011/ www.goshlondon.com). Tottenham Court Road tube. **Open** 10am-6pm Mon-Wed, Sat, Sun; 10am-7pm Thur, Fri. **Credit** MC, V.

All your favourite superheroes feature in this orderly shop. On the ground floor, collectable back issues (priced from £5 up to several hundred), new comics and mainstream graphic novels can be found, plus an improved range of children's and illustrated books (of the *Peanuts* and Dr Seuss ilk). Try the basement for underground stuff, like the works of Dan Clowes and Robert Crumb, plus manga books and translated European albums. Staff are knowledgeable and enthusiastic.

Murder One

76-78 Charing Cross Road, WC2H 0BD (7739 8820/www.murderone.co.uk). Leicester Square tube. **Open** 10am-7pm Mon-Wed; 10am-8pm Thur-Sat; noon-6pm Sun. **Credit** AmEx, MC, V.

On moving to smaller premises (across the road) Murder One ditched its horror, fantasy and sci-fi titles, and is now focusing purely on crime (note the life-sized Sherlock Holmes in the window). A modern interior has freshened up the vibe, and the stock is still extensive, with every crime fiction title in print in the UK stocked. A reasonably sized second-hand section sits alongside Jack the Ripper and mafia paperbacks in the basement.

International

Africa Book Centre

38 King Street, WC2E 8JT (7240 6649/www. africabookcentre.com). Covent Garden tube. **Open** 10.30am-6pm Tue-Sat. **Credit** MC, V.

Over 10,000 books both from and on Africa, in English, French and Portuguese (as well as a whole array of African languages), are housed in this neatly laid-out shop. Stock spans popular fiction (including children's), language guides and cookbooks to heavyweight philosophical, political and development titles. Magazines and Caribbean imports are also available.

Arthur Probsthain Oriental & African Bookseller

41 Great Russell Street, WC1B 3PE (7636 1096/ www.oriental-african-books.com). Tottenham Court Road tube. **Open** 9.30am-5.30pm Mon-Fri; 11am-4pm Sat. **Credit** AmEx, DC, MC, V.

Nearly 100 years old, this small, dusty shop near the British Museum continues to act as a magnet for anyone with an academic interest in Asia, Africa and/or the Middle East. As well as historical and political tomes, there are books on art and literature. Members of staff are helpful and have encyclopaedic knowledge.

For branch see index.

European Bookshop

5 Warwick Street, W1B 5LU (7734 5259/www. eurobooks.co.uk). Piccadilly Circus tube. **Open** 9.30am-6pm Mon-Sat. **Credit** AmEx, DC, MC, V.

Owned by the ESB group, this well-used shop stocks a massive range of European-language titles (plus tapes and CDs), including classic and modern continental literature and course books. The German and Spanish sections (the latter with books and materials on Latin American culture and language) are housed in the basement, while the French and Portuguese sections, plus the new Russian department, are on the ground floor.

For branch (Young Europeans Bookstore) see index.

The French Bookshop

28 Bute Street, SW7 3EX (7584 2840/www. frenchbookshop.com). South Kensington tube. **Open** 8.15am-6pm Mon-Fri; 10am-5pm Sat. **Credit** MC, V.

As well as the impressive selection of books by French authors, this established shop also stocks French translations of the latest English titles. The wide range of stock (all in French) also includes literary classics, art, cookery, poetry and sport. If you're not yet ready for the hard stuff, there are children's titles plus books on learning the language. Occasional book signings are held.

Grant & Cutler

55-57 Great Marlborough Street, W1F 7AY (7734 2012/www.grantandcutler.com). Oxford Circus tube. **Open** 9am-6pm Mon-Fri; 9.30am-6pm-Sat; noon-6pm Sun. **Credit** MC, V.

Grant & Cutler is the crème de la crème of foreign-language booksellers, covering more than 200 languages. With over 55,000 books stocked, this is the place to come to for reference books, literature, technical dictionaries and academic titles, plus foreign films on video and DVD, and audio material. The major European languages form the largest departments (with designated country advisers on hand in each section), but there's ample material on less widely spoken languages, including a new oriental catalogue.

Librarie La Page

7 Harrington Road, SW7 3ES (7589 5991). South Kensington tube. **Open** 9.30am-6pm Mon-Fri; 10.30am-5.30pm Sat. **Credit** AmEx, MC, V.

Shoppers at Librarie La Page, the oldest shop of its kind in London, can browse through a superb range of French literature, in light and airy surroundings. The improved children's section is a big plus point (there's even a children's book adviser on hand); also on sale is a small collection of CDs, DVDs and French magazines. A selection of elegant, imported French stationery is housed in the basement.

Maghreb Bookshop

45 Burton Street, WC1H 9AL (7388 1840/www.maghrebreview.com). Euston tube/rail. **Open** by appointment only. **No credit cards.**
Maghreb Bookshop specialises in new, rare and out-of-print books on North Africa, the Arab world and Islam.

Soma Books

38 Kennington Lane, SE11 4LS (7735 2101/ www.somabooks.co.uk). Kennington tube. **Open** 10am-5.30pm Mon-Fri. **Credit** MC, V.
Soma remains a leading importer and distributor of texts (and crafts) from India, stocking an impressive selection of titles, and including dual-language and multicultural children's books. Books are also imported from the US, Africa and the Caribbean on religion, social issues and multiculturalism. As we went to print the store was closing for a huge refurbishment, but will reopen in January 2006 (in the premises next door).

Mind, body & spirit

Atlantis Bookshop

49A Museum Street, WC1A 1LY (7405 2120/ www.theatlantisbookshop.com). Holborn tube. **Open** 10.30am-6pm Mon-Sat. **Credit** AmEx, MC, V.
You may not find the answer to the mystery of the lost continent here (although you're certain to find theories), but at this atmospheric bookseller – the oldest of its kind in London – you will find an extensive selection of new and second-hand books on the occult, from witchcraft to esoteric societies, via Kabbalah and Egyptian gods. There's a good ordering service for hard-to-find titles, a noticeboard packed with flyers, and regular events and workshops.

Mysteries

9-11 Monmouth Street, WC2H 9DA (7240 3688/www.mysteries.co.uk). Covent Garden or Leicester Square tube. **Open** 10am-7pm Mon-Fri; 10am-6pm Sat; noon-6pm Sun. **Credit** AmEx, MC, V.
This popular incense den is made up of three rooms: the first covers self-development, crystal healing, UFOs and astrology; the second focuses on dreams, meditation, yoga and world religions; while the third room at the back concentrates on audio-visual material. Key authors include Deepak Chopra, Louise Hay and Paulo Coelho, and the place boasts a long list of celebrity customers. Daily psychic readings take place upstairs.

Watkins Books

19 Cecil Court, WC2N 4EZ (7836 2182/www. watkinsbooks.co.uk). Leicester Square tube. **Open** 11am-7pm Mon-Sat. **Credit** MC, V.
Specialists in mysticism and spirituality for over a hundred years, Watkins stocks an exceptional selection of books on self-help, alternative therapy, oriental religion, astrology and occultism. There's a large collection of good-quality second-hand titles on the ground floor, plus audio-visual material, healing crystals and even in-house astrologers and tarot readers.
For branch (Watkins Esoteric Centre) see index.

Politics & economics

Bookmarks

1 Bloomsbury Street, WC1B 3QE (7637 1848/ www.bookmarks.uk.com). Tottenham Court Road tube. **Open** noon-7pm Mon; 10am-7pm Tue-Fri; 10am-6pm Sat. **Credit** MC, V.
The interior of this socialist bookshop (official booksellers to the TUC) comes as something of a surprise: with a smart and tidy layout and cheery staff, this isn't your clichéd radical outlet. As well as the abundance of material by the usual suspects – Marx, Trotsky, Marx, Chomsky, Marx, and so forth – there are good sections on film and music (with a left-wing bent, of course), plus second-hand books and lots of journals. Recent events have included a talk by Tariq Ali on US imperialism.

Freedom Press Bookshop

84B Whitechapel High Street (entrance on Angel Alley), E1 7QX (7247 9249/www.freedompress. org.uk). Aldgate East tube. **Open** noon-6pm Mon-Sat. **No credit cards.**
This bare-boards shop may be physically tiny, but stock-wise, it's the largest anarchist bookshop in Britain. It's crammed with radical literature, newspapers, pamphlets, CDs, postcards and posters; books cover titles on anti-fascism and workers' struggles, as well as historical and philosophical works, and include Freedom Press publications as well as second-hand books. A meeting space upstairs aims to get the verbal revolution moving. It's advisable to ring before your visit – opening times can vary.

Housmans

5 Caledonian Road, N1 9DX (7837 4473/ www.housmans.com). King's Cross tube/rail. **Open** 10am-6.30pm Mon-Fri; 10am-6pm Sat. **Credit** AmEx, MC, V.
Open since 1945, and still attracting its fair share of middle-aged men in cords and scruffy shirts, Housmans holds books on progressive politics. Stock features a good range of pacifist writing and titles with a radical interest, and there's also a huge number of left-wing journals, a fiction section, second-hand books in the basement and a stationery department.

The Parliamentary Bookshop

12 Bridge Street, SW1A 2JX (7219 3890/www. bookshop.parliament.uk). Westminster tube. **Open** 9.30am-5.30pm Mon-Thur; 9am-4pm Fri. **Credit** MC, V.
Run and staffed by House of Commons employees, this popular store stocks a good selection of specialist political titles and government publications, including copies of Hansard, acts of parliament and political history books. Note that it closes an hour earlier Monday to Thursday during parliamentary recesses – it's best to ring before making a late-afternoon trip.

Waterstone's Economists' Bookshop

Clare Market, Portugal Street, WC2A 2AB (7405 5531). Temple tube. **Open** 9.30am-7pm Mon, Wed-Fri; 10am-7pm Tue; 9.30am-6pm Sat. **Credit** AmEx, DC, MC, V.
This specialist wing of the Waterstone's chain, appropriately located next to the London School of Economics, provides a robust selection of academic titles with an emphasis on the political, economic, business and law disciplines.

Psychology

H Karnac

118 Finchley Road, NW3 5HT (7431 1075/www. karnacbooks.com). Finchley Road tube. **Open** 9.30am-6pm Mon-Sat. **Credit** AmEx, MC, V.
Now smartened up after a refurbishment in August 2005, H Karnac specialises in texts on psychoanalysis, psychotherapy and related subjects, such as the psychology of organisations, and family, couple, child and adolescent studies. A smaller selection of philosophy and children's literature is also for sale. Karnac also publishes and distributes its own titles.

Sport

Sportspages

Caxton Walk, 94-96 Charing Cross Road, WC2H 0JW (7240 9604/www.sportsbooksdirect.co.uk). Leicester Square tube. **Open** 9.30am-7pm Mon-Sat; noon-5pm Sun. **Credit** AmEx, MC, V.
The cornucopia of sporting literature available in this shop will impress the casual fan and the fanatic. In addition to the excellent selection of books on all the major US and UK sports and fitness methods, you'll find fanzines from football clubs around the UK, and a range of magazines, both British and imported. A section on sports science and a complete collection of FA training guides caters to students and coaches.

Talking books

Audible

0870 890 3773/www.audible.co.uk. **Phone enquiries** 10am-6pm Mon-Fri; 10am-2pm Sat. **Credit** AmEx, MC, V.
With over 10,000 titles on its system, this online service is an excellent audio resource. The broad range of subjects available for download include popular and classic fiction, comedy, drama, personal development, radio programmes and magazines, as well as books in foreign languages. The cost of downloading individual material is much less than buying hard copies of the audiobooks; if you become a member (for £9.49 per month for BasicListener, or £14.99 per month for PremiumListener) savings increase even more.

RNIB Talking Book Service

PO Box 173, Peterborough, Cambs PE2 6WS (0845 762 6843). **Phone enquiries** 8am-6pm Mon-Fri; 9am-4pm Sat. **Credit** MC, V.
For £70 a year, blind and partially sighted people will be loaned a disc player and have access to thousands of books on CD. Ask your local council about receiving this service for free.

The Talking Book Shop

11 Wigmore Street, W1U 1PE (7491 4117/ www.talkingbooks.co.uk). Bond Street tube. **Open** 9.30am-5.30pm Mon-Fri; 10am-5pm Sat; noon-5pm Sun. **Credit** AmEx, MC, V.
TBS has around 6,000 titles on CD and cassette, making this small and friendly store a good place to come to for all your audio needs. Stock covers a broad range of subjects, including comedy, classic and modern literature, drama, popular radio plays, travel, children's and self-help. Bestsellers include *The Hitchhiker's Guide to the Galaxy* and Bill Bryson's *A Short History of Nearly Everything.*

Transport

For **Ian Allan's Transport Bookshop,** *see p205.*

Motor Books

33 & 36 St Martin's Court, WC2N 4AN (7836 5376/6728/3800/www.motorbooks.co.uk). Leicester Square tube/Charing Cross tube/rail. **Open** 9.30am-6pm Mon-Wed, Fri; 9.30am-7pm Thur; 10.30am-5.30pm Sat. **Credit** AmEx, MC, V.
Spread over two separate stores, the specialist stock at Motor Books should get the transport enthusiast's heart racing, with bestsellers including *King of the Nurburgring* and the biography of Didier Pironi. No.33 covers trains and cars, while No.36 focuses on aviation, military and maritime. DVDs and videos are also available.

Travel

Daunt Books

83-84 Marylebone High Street, W1U 4QW (7224 2295/www.dauntbooks.co.uk). Baker Street tube. **Open** 9am-7.30pm Mon-Sat; 11am-6pm Sun. **Credit** MC, V.
A visit to this superb store is worthwhile just to marvel at the Edwardian interior, with its oak galleries and central skylight running the length of the store. The books are uniquely arranged by country, over three levels, with stock boasting a comprehensive selection of specialist travel guides (housed in the galleries, and including second-hand titles), plus literature and maps. There's also a commendable selection of general stock, including the latest quality hardbacks, political biographies and children's books, as well as large sections devoted to gardening, cookery and interior design.
For branches see index.

Stanfords

12-14 Long Acre, WC2E 9LP (7836 1321/www. stanfords.co.uk). Covent Garden or Leicester Square tube. **Open** 9am-7.30pm Mon, Wed, Fri; 9.30am-7.30pm Tue; 9am-8pm Thur; 10am-7pm Sat; noon-6pm Sun. **Credit** MC, V.
With three floors' worth of travel guides, travel writing, road and wall maps (some imported) and

illustrated books covering all continents, plus atlases, globes, magazines and accessories, the flagship branch of Stanfords is an essential stop for anyone planning that big trip (or just a weekend break). European stock is on the ground floor, the rest of the world on the first, while the basement houses guides to London and Britain and the full range of Ordnance Survey maps, plus specialised guides to climbing and cartography.

Travel Bookshop
13-15 Blenheim Crescent, W11 2EE (7229 5260/ www.thetravelbookshop.co.uk). Ladbroke Grove tube. **Open** 10am-6pm Mon-Sat; noon-5pm Sun. **Credit** AmEx, MC, V.
A lovely space in which to while away an hour, this relaxed, local shop inspired Hugh Grant's bookstore in the film *Notting Hill*. Travel guides and classic fiction, categorised by country, are arranged side by side, and there's a superb London and Great Britain section. Despite the healthy range of photographic coffee-table books on display, the emphasis here is definitely on content (with the large range of travel literature supplemented by cabinets with antiquarian and rare books). Maps, atlases, children's travel books and postcards are also for sale.

Women

Persephone Books
59 Lamb's Conduit Street, WC1N 3NB (7242 9292/www.persephonebooks.co.uk). Holborn or Russell Square tube. **Open** 9am-6pm Mon-Fri; noon-5pm Sat. **Credit** AmEx, MC, V.
Persephone Books reprints forgotten or obscure works by 20th-century women writers – mainly novels and short stories, but also diaries and cookery books. All the titles (there are currently 60) are bound with pale grey, softback dust jackets, and make perfect presents (there are gift-wrapped copies for sale). No matter how thick the book, it will cost £10, or £27 for three. Over the past year, a new range of titles – the Persephone 50 – has been introduced, featuring books that Persephone wished they'd published themselves (Elizabeth David's cookbooks, for example). There's also a range of vintage books. Staff are friendly.

Silver Moon
3rd Floor, Foyles, 113-119 Charing Cross Road, WC2H 0EB (7440 1562/www.silvermoon bookshop.co.uk). Tottenham Court Road tube. **Open** 9.30am-9pm Mon-Sat; noon-6pm Sun. **Credit** AmEx, MC, V.
Occupying an annex on the third floor of Foyles, Silver Moon still claims to be Europe's largest women's-interest bookshop. Over the past year, the stock has expanded in the area of sexuality, with the range of gay- and lesbian-interest titles increasing, and a range of DVDs and videos is now also stocked. Other genres include literature, photography, self-help, body and gender issues and sexual politics. There are also sections dedicated to black and Asian authors.

Useful sites for finding books and investigating the stock of book dealers around the world are **www.abebooks.com**, **www.alibris.com**, **www.bibliofind.com** (now an affiliation of Amazon) and **www.ibooknet.co.uk**.

Amwell Book Company
53 Amwell Street, EC1R 1UR (7837 4891). Angel tube/King's Cross tube/rail. **Open** 11am-6pm Mon-Fri; Sat by appointment. **Credit** MC, V.
Amwell specialises in the arts and architecture, and also stocks an impressive range of literature and crime novels (including collectable modern first editions), plus rare and everyday 20th-century children's and illustrated books and manuals. The arts and architecture stock continues to grow and includes well-priced hardback urban- and landscape-design books (a first edition of *City Transformed: Urban Architecture for the 21st century* was on sale for £18) as well as rarer

planning pamphlets, plus a huge range of design and photography coffee-table books. Local interest titles are also stocked. A charming bookshop that's worth going out of your way to visit.

Any Amount of Books
56 Charing Cross Road, WC2H 0QA (7836 3697/www.anyamountofbooks.com). Leicester Square tube. **Open** 10.30am-9.30pm Mon-Sat; 11.30am-8.30pm Sun. **Credit** AmEx, MC, V.
Any Amount of Books is a literary treasure trove with a friendly, laid-back vibe. All subjects are covered, with a large general stock covering modern literature, literary criticism, poetry, biography, art, architecture, gender, history, medicine and religion, and a smaller selection of rare and antiquarian titles. Prices are rarely totally prohibitive, and often very reasonable. Finds from the past year have included an 1853 work on *Legends of Old London*. The trolleys of books outside house paperbacks from £1.

Archive Bookstore
83 Bell Street, NW1 6TB (7402 8212/www. archivebookstore.co.uk). Marylebone tube/rail. **Open** 10.30am-6pm Mon-Sat. **Credit** MC, V.
A visit to this characterful gem is second-hand book shopping in its rawest form – the challenge being to rummage through a plethora of music titles and sheet music hidden away in a two-storey building overflowing with stock, both inside and out. The basement, complete with its own three-quarter-size piano, houses a seemingly endless array of boxes and shelves bursting with scores and texts. Upstairs you'll find a wide range of fiction and general titles on various subjects. Stock is great value for money.

Bernard J Shapero Rare Books
32 St George Street, W1S 2EA (7493 0876/ www.shapero.com). Bond Street or Oxford Circus tube. **Open** 9.30am-6.30pm Mon-Fri; 11am-5pm Sat. **Credit** AmEx, DC, MC, V.
Housed in grand Mayfair premises, Bernard J Shapero's collection of lovingly restored antiquarian and out-of-print texts is finely displayed over four floors. There are specialist titles on travel (with a comprehensive collection of old Baedeker guides – a decent copy of Baedeker's *Great Britain* was selling for £40), natural history, English literature (mainly rare first editions), and continental colour-plate books, plus a good selection of British gardening and landscape books. While the store may not boast the historical pedigree of some of its nearest rivals (it started in 1979 as a stall in Grays Antique market) it is arguably unrivalled in its broad range of subjects, and the specialist staff are very helpful. This store also now houses the Shapero gallery, along with maps, prints and 19th-century photographs.

Bernard Quaritch
8 Lower John Street, W1F 9AU (7734 2983/www. quaritch.com). Piccadilly Circus tube. **Open** 9am-6pm Mon-Fri. **Credit** AmEx, MC, V.
Founded in 1847, this grand store specialises in rare books and manuscripts on architecture and architectural history (up to the mid-19th century). Among its extensive collection are publications on interior decoration and ornament, landscape and garden design, festival and theatre architecture, and books on the fine arts. Other disciplines covered include British literature and history (from the 16th- to the 20th-century), science, medicine, travel and human sciences, plus there's a selection of Middle Eastern books and manuscripts. Stock highlights from 2005 included a first edition of Michelangelo's sonnets (published in 1623) for £2,400, and the only known surviving copy of the first mathematical book printed in English (if you fancy making an offer). A range of catalogues (£5-£10) is available and, what's more, there's an in-house bindery.

Biblion
1-7 Davies Mews, W1K 5AB (7629 1374/www. biblion.com). Bond Street tube. **Open** 10am-6pm Mon-Sat. **Credit** MC, V.
This relative newcomer to the antiquarian book trade opened in 1999. Housed in a berth in Gray's

Antique market, it stocks a fantastic range of over 20,000 antiquarian and modern titles supplied by some of the world's most renowned and respected book dealers. Finely bound tomes rub shoulders with a wonderful collection of illustrated and children's books (on our last visit, we noticed a first edition of Raymond Brigg's *The Snowman* – the pop-up version – on sale for £30), as well as modern first edition literature and texts on art and travel, plus science and medicine and private press publications. There's also a collection of signed copies of modern favourites and Booker Prize winners at reasonable prices. Prices start at around £10, but can run into many thousands.

Book Mongers
439 Coldharbour Lane, SW9 8LN (7738 4225/ http://freespace.virgin.net/book.mongers). Brixton tube/rail. **Open** 10.30am-6.30pm Mon-Sat. **Credit** MC, V.
Book Mongers remains one of the best booksellers south of the river. The seemingly endless store is packed with varied and inexpensive titles covering, in particular, the New Age, occult and spiritualist spectrum, with handbooks on meditation and herbal remedies and guides to yogic peace. For the less ethereal, the shop also has academic titles from geography, sociology and psychology to history, business studies and economics. However, the most exciting thing for the casual shopper – and a reward for making it to the back of the shop – is the range of 50p/£1 books.

Collinge & Clark
13 Leigh Street, WC1H 9EW (7387 7105). Russell Square tube. **Open** 11am-6.30pm Mon-Fri; 11am-3.30pm Sat. **Credit** AmEx, MC, V.
The outside might seem familiar (it was used in the TV series *Black Books*), but the inside will be an intriguing and enjoyable mystery to anyone lacking a knowledge of engraving, printing and typography. The big names of Blake and Morris will resonate with the layman, as might Henry Moore and Eric Gill, but the skill and craft on display in this dusty, two-storey shop are bound to impress any visitor. The informed specialist, meanwhile, will find much to tickle his or her fancy among the various private press editions and 18th- and 19th-century pamphlets (sadly, many aren't for sale), and there's a huge range of illustrated books.

David Drummond at Pleasures of Past Times
11 Cecil Court, WC2N 4EZ (7836 1142). Leicester Square tube. **Open** 11am-2.30pm, 3.30-5.45pm Mon-Fri, 1st Sat of mth; also by appointment. **No credit cards**.
A veritable goldmine of books, scores, playbills, theatre programmes and other ephemera related to the performing arts of bygone eras, and in particular the Victorian Age. Books on the circus, theatre, clowning, conjuring, puppetry and magic are all stocked, as well as historical works like *Penny Theatres of Victorian London*, biographies, and illustrated and children's books (pre-1940). David Drummond himself is always present inside the warren-like, characterful store for advice and guidance. Rent rises, affecting all premises in Cecil Court, were a matter of concern on our last visit.

Fisher & Sperr
46 Highgate High Street, N6 5JB (8340 7244). Archway or Highgate tube. **Open** 10.30am-5pm Mon-Sat. **No credit cards**.
A distinctive four-storey townhouse has been home to this bookshop for over 40 years. The big plus-point here, aside from the enormous amount of stock, is the room dedicated to books on London and London literature, with valuable copies of the works of those distinguished men of the town, Pepys and Johnson, often featuring. The rest of the holdings cover just about any subject you can imagine, with especially strong pickings in the fields of history, literature, travel, art and philosophy. Rarer texts, antiquarian tomes and Greek and Latin classics occupy the back room, while academic books require a trip upstairs. The low ceilings, cramped rooms and rather eccentric owner shouldn't deter the casual browser.

LEISURE

Gekoski

Pied Bull Yard, 15A Bloomsbury Square, WC1A 2LP (7404 6676/www.gekoski.com). Holborn tube. **Open** 10am-5.30pm Mon-Fri; also by appointment. **Credit** MC, V.

Tucked away in a serene courtyard accessed by an alleyway on Bloomsbury Square is Rick Gekoski and Peter Grogan's fascinating shop for the serious-intentioned collector of modern literary firsts and valuable manuscripts. With barely any stock on display, the place feels more like a gallery than a shop; literary artwork and original photos of distinguished authors (all for sale) line the walls. Prices start at a couple of hundred pounds, stretching to tens of thousands for the rarest stock. Rare copies of key works by Auden, Beckett, TS Eliot, Graham Greene and DH Lawrence have all featured over the past year.

Gloucester Road Bookshop

123 Gloucester Road, SW7 4TE (7370 3503). Gloucester Road tube. **Open** 9.30am-10.30pm Mon-Fri; 10.30am-6.30pm Sat, Sun. **Credit** MC, V.

A bright and airy shop that provides a well-ordered and solid range of second-hand titles. In addition to literature, military history, philosophy and architecture, the ground floor holds a small range of antiquarian titles, plus photographic and literary prints. Visit the basement for social studies, performing arts, politics, economics, history and a range of pocket books. The very late opening hours and amicable staff are a bonus. Also open on bank holidays.

Halcyon Books

1 Greenwich South Street, SE10 8NW (8305 2675/ www.halcyonbooks.co.uk). Greenwich rail/DLR. **Open** 10am-6pm daily. **Credit** AmEx, MC, V.

This welcoming store remains one of the best second-hand bookshops in the capital. Its survival (despite rent rises over the last few years) has been secured by its ability to provide an exceptionally diverse range of moderately priced, good-quality editions of texts that cater for almost every conceivable requirement, from history, philosophy and social science titles, to books on cookery, photography, art and travel. There's also a wide range of fiction, plus new books.

Henry Pordes

58-60 Charing Cross Road, WC2H 0BB (7836 9031/www.henrypordesbooks.com). Leicester Square tube. **Open** 10am-7pm Mon-Sat. **Credit** MC, V.

Henry Pordes is always teeming with visitors and bookworms delving through the broad range of books (modern, antiquarian and remainder titles) on offer here. Somewhat of a specialist on Judaica, the shop also has large sections on history and classical literature, as well as natural history, history of science, literary criticism, biography, travel, architecture, art, cinema, crafts, sports, furniture and advertising. Prices are very reasonable, with a 1952 edition of Anne Frank's diary going for £15. What's more, the shop is surprisingly easy to navigate, and the staff are friendly and helpful. Cheaper paperbacks are housed in the basement.

Henry Sotheran

2-5 Sackville Street, W1S 3DP (7439 6151/www. sotherans.co.uk). Green Park or Piccadilly Circus tube. **Open** 9.30am-6pm Mon-Fri; 10am-4pm Sat. **Credit** AmEx, DC, MC, V.

Established in 1815, Sotheran's manages to combine its association with tradition, quality and class (past clients have included King George VI and King Constantine of Greece) with a thoroughly relaxed and friendly vibe. While it's renowned for its collection of antiquarian books on travel, exploration and natural history, the shop also boasts excellent sections on English literature from the 17th to the 20th century, with many important first editions in good condition (such as, on our last visit, Kerouac's *On the Road*, going for £1,200) and children's literature, as well as colour-plate, illustrated and private press books, and titles on sport and pastimes, art and architecture, fine art, economics and Churchill. The print department in the basement sells original antique prints.

PJ Hilton

12 Cecil Court, WC2N 4HE (7379 9825). Leicester Square tube. **Open** 10.30am-5.30pm Mon-Fri; 11am-5pm Sat. **Credit** AmEx, MC, V.

A fixture of Cecil Court for 20 years, this shop sells an excellent range of antiquarian and modern texts. Stock is split over two floors, with cheaper volumes in the basement, and the rarer, more expensive items on the ground floor. After this separation, titles are arranged according to subject, with specialisms including 19th- and 20th-century English literature (with plenty of first editions), theology (including lots of antiquarian bibles) and history. There's also a good selection of 16th-, 17th-, and 18th-century tomes, plus French, German and Latin books; titles on travel and science are also thrown into the mix. Paul Hilton, the unassuming owner, is welcoming, and happy to answer any queries. Prices range from £8 to £1,000.

Jarndyce

46 Great Russell Street, WC1B 3PA (7631 4220/ www.jarndyce.co.uk). Tottenham Court Road tube. **Open** 10.30am-5.30pm Mon-Fri. **Credit** AmEx, MC, V.

Jarndyce is as specialised and dedicated as they come; even the interior of the Georgian building has been redesigned to represent a 19th-century bookshop (with original wooden floors, panelling and a working fireplace). The stock covers 18th-and, in particular, 19th-century English literature, so it's the place to visit for rare and collectable works by Dickens and the Romantics. Also for sale are rare pamphlets and books on social history, theatre and London, and the place is also known for its own-published reference guide to the world's most bizarre and unintentionally funny books, some of which are displayed in the shop window (*Cancer: Is the Dog the Cause?* made us chuckle). Prices start as low as £10, although many items sell for hundreds or even thousands.

Judd Books

82 Marchmont Street, WC1N 1AG (7387 5333). Russell Square tube. **Open** 11am-7pm Mon-Sat; 11am-6pm Sun. **Credit** AmEx, MC, V.

The arts and social sciences are the order of the day at this small, two-storey bookshop, which has floor-to-ceiling shelves full of quality second-hand and remainder books. Outside, crates offer up an assortment of books (and maps) for £2 or under (or three for £4.50), while inside you'll find stacks of books on architecture, art and photography, and a similarly large array of titles on theatre, literature, film, travel, cookery and languages. The basement houses the more weighty history, philosophy, economics, politics and psychology sections. Prices are extremely reasonable (with a 10% discount for students), and the helpful staff and cheery vibe encourage a healthy number of browsers.

Maggs Brothers

50 Berkeley Square, W1J 5BA (7493 7160/ www.maggs.com). Green Park tube. **Open** 9.30am-5pm Mon-Fri. **Credit** MC, V.

This impressive antiquarian and rare book dealer has long provided pre-eminent literary services to libraries and collectors across the world from this beautiful, four-storey Berkeley Square townhouse. An expert, multilingual team of more than 20 span eight specialist departments, which include one focusing on documents and manuscripts of historical significance. Other sections cover travel, natural history, early British (pre-1800), military and continental books, plus first editions by the likes of Jane Austen, Joseph Conrad, Rudyard Kipling, DH Lawrence, Thomas Hardy and Oscar Wilde. Although prices can start at a very manageable £10, they often reach into the thousands (on our last visit, a first edition of Dickens' *A Christmas Carol* was on sale for £6,500) and have been known to reach £500,000. So, rich pickings for, on the whole, rich people yet the atmosphere here is unstuffy.

Marcet Books

4A Nelson Road, SE10 9JB (8853 5408/www. marcetbooks.co.uk). Cutty Sark DLR/Greenwich DLR/rail. **Open** 10am-5.30pm daily. **Credit** AmEx, MC, V.

Housed within a single room off Greenwich market (where the shop has a paperback stall on Thursdays and Fridays), this inviting business is lined floor to ceiling with a diverse range of good-quality books, both antiquarian and modern. While the focus is on maritime texts – with an interesting collection of books on Nelson and Drake – there is also a healthy selection of titles on topography, history, travel, science, art, general literature and mountaineering. Outside is also a set of typical second-hand bookshop offerings for £1 each. *Mail order.*

Marchpane

16 Cecil Court, WC2N 4HE (7836 8661/www. marchpane.com). Leicester Square tube. **Open** 10.30am-6pm Mon-Sat. **Credit** AmEx, MC, V.

Marchpane's decorative window displays always entice passing shoppers in: on our last visit, the theme was the British empire (think Biggles books and classic 1940s aeroplane models). Inside, there's a life-sized original Dalek and a 2,000-strong collection of children's and illustrated books. As well as first editions, with an emphasis on Billy Bunter, Enid Blyton and AA Milne (a first edition, in good nick, of *The House at Pooh Corner* was going for £300) there are always plenty of rare and not-so-rare classics (*The Lion, the Witch and the Wardrobe* and *The Wizard of Oz* included) from the 18th century to the present day, with prices starting from £20. But the real speciality here is Lewis Carroll, and the enormous range of *Alice's Adventures in Wonderland* editions (for which you can pay thousands) won't disappoint aficionados.

Maritime Books

66 Royal Hill, SE10 8RT (8305 1310). Cutty Sark DLR/Greenwich DLR/rail. **Open** 10am-6pm daily. **Credit** MC, V.

Now in new premises, this shop continues to specialise in maritime books, housing an excellent selection of both antiquarian and modern texts covering naval and mercantile history up to the end of World War II. The highlight of the store's collection is its impressive stock of Nelsonalia, but there are diverse offerings aimed at a broad range of interests and wallets, from boys' annuals and hardback academic texts to unique documents and maps. There's also a collection of contemporary and historical naval magazines.

Nigel Williams Rare Books

25 Cecil Court, WC2N 4EZ (7836 7757/www. nigelwilliams.com). Leicester Square tube. **Open** 10am-6pm Mon-Sat. **Credit** AmEx, MC, V.

The ground floor houses the children's and illustrated collection, where you'll often find works by EB White, Raymond Briggs and Ronald Searle, plus good quality copies of Dr Seuss books and Tintin annuals, while the basement is full of well-preserved 19th- and 20th-century literary firsts (with a large range of Agatha Christie novels and works by Tolkien). Draws from the past year have included illustrated first editions of *Watership Down* (signed) and Hemingway's *The Old Man and the Sea*, for £1,450 and £105 respectively, but there are usually plenty of more wallet-friendly options under the £50 mark. PG Wodehouse fans and crime and detective fiction from Arthur Conan Doyle, among others, plus books about Sherlock Holmes, are also available.

Oxfam Books & Music

91 Marylebone High Street, W1U 4RB (7487 3570/www.oxfammarylebone.co.uk). Baker Street or Bond Street tube. **Open** 10am-6pm Mon-Sat; noon-6pm Sun. **Credit** MC, V.

The Marylebone branch of Oxfam Books is all white walls and stripped wooden floorboards, eschewing the traditional image of the charity bookshop. The music section is particularly worth noting, and often features rare finds. The rest of the stock is neatly presented in individual sections such as religion, history, travel, art, economics and science. The shop also organises seasonal poetry readings and other events. And best of all, it's for charity. The Crouch End branch (22 Park Road, 8347 7942) has a good selection of children's books. **Branches**: throughout the city.

Ulysses

jazz). The left-hand side (as you enter) houses ethno-musicological texts and biographies arranged by country, as well as the opera and jazz sections, plus plenty of criticism, and books on dance and performance. The right-hand side is a densely packed wall of sheet music, much of it difficult to find elsewhere. There's also a wide range of new books on all musical subjects, plus periodicals, photos, rare prints and programmes, and an ordering service in the event that the book or score you're after isn't stocked. The more valuable collectors' items are sold on the internet.

Ulysses
40 Museum Street, WC1A 1LU (7831 1600). Holborn tube. **Open** 11am-6pm Mon-Sat. **Credit** AmEx, MC, V.
A first port of call for affordable modern firsts: on our last visit, highlights included the first English editions of Dylan Thomas's *Under Milk Wood* (£155) and Ernest Hemingway's *For Whom the Bell Tolls* (£250). After the rarer finds, there are lots of titles priced between £35 and £100 (books for under £35 are in the basement) and the homely space offers plenty of scope for browsing. There's also a good number of illustrated books for sale.

Unsworths Booksellers
101 Euston Road, NW1 2RA (7436 9836/www. unsworths.com). King's Cross tube/rail. **Open** 10am-6.30pm Mon-Sat. **Credit** AmEx, DC, MC, V.
The place to visit for very affordable used and remainder humanities books (with an emphasis on content rather than collecting), making it a useful resource for nearby University of London students. The antiquarian department (featuring rare Latin and Greek classics, plus works on early printing, law and topography) has moved here from the basement of the old Bloomsbury branch. Books on the ancient, medieval, Renaissance and early modern worlds (including all volumes of the Loeb Classical Library books) are also to be found.

Walden Books
38 Harmood Street, NW1 8DP (7267 8146). Chalk Farm tube. **Open** 10.30am-6.30pm Thur-Sun. **Credit** AmEx, MC, V.
Walden Books is a familiar and popular part of the Camden landscape, thanks largely to owner David Tobin's friendly and dedicated approach. Although it's only open for the latter half of the week, this is possibly the best place in north London for affordable paperbacks, with a large stash of literature (both classic and modern) in the £3 to £5 range. There are also large collections of books on politics, art, philosophy, history and photography, as well as food, travel and film. Rare and antiquarian titles are housed in cabinets inside, while, in contrast, a mad mix of cheap books is for sale on tables outside.

World's End Bookshop
357 King's Road, SW3 5ES (7352 9376). Sloane Square tube then 11, 19, 22 bus. **Open** 10am-6.30pm daily. **Credit** AmEx, MC, V.
Not much seems to change at this friendly, laid-back store (established in the 1960s); it continues to provide a good selection of titles to suit all pockets, from the 50p titles in crates outside to rare, antiquarian titles often costing several hundred pounds. Shelves are crammed with a good selection of titles on art, history, politics, philosophy, astrology, biography, travel, music and drama, as well as literature and fiction. The store operates an active book-buying service and will even collect from your door.

Book search

Twiggers
44 The Strand, Walmer, Deal, Kent CT14 7DX (01304 365 511/www.twiggers.com). **Phone enquiries** 9am-5pm Mon-Fri. **Credit** MC, V.
Twiggers sources books from all over the world, tracking down those elusive out-of-print titles. On finding the requested book, they'll contact you with a no-obligation quote. The initial month-long search is free for up to four books, but can be extended for a further three months for £3 per title.

Pickering & Chatto
36 St George Street, W1S 2FW (7491 2656/www. pickering-chatto.com). Oxford Circus tube. **Open** 9.30am-5.30pm Mon-Fri. **Credit** AmEx, MC, V.
Founded back in 1820 by William Pickering, this established shop is now a well reputed dealer of antiquarian and rare books, stocking (almost) exclusively pre-1900 works. While the store specialises in science and medicine, social, economic, political and legal treatises, texts and collections and also English and Continental literature (the emphasis on which has increased over the past year), it also stocks some books on art. Don't let the buzzer entry system deter you: staff are friendly. Prices range from £50 to the thousands.

Quinto/Francis Edwards
48A Charing Cross Road, WC2H 0BB (7379 7669). Leicester Square tube. **Open** 9am-9pm Mon-Sat; noon-8pm Sun. **Credit** AmEx, DC, MC, V.
Every month this Charing Cross Road institution is closed for two-and-a-half days while the ground-floor stock is taken off the shelves and replaced by new acquisitions, thereby creating a constant stream of interest for regular browsers – and a strong following. The basement stock is mainly out-of-print titles. The branch opposite the British Museum is one of the best-stocked second-hand bookshops in England, and has a more spacious, less ramshackle feel. Both feature large sections on history, culture, religion, psychology, heritage, military history, literature and criticism. Each Quinto is paired with a Francis Edwards antiquarian bookshop, which specialises in bindings, travel, literature and natural history. **For branch see index.**

Ripping Yarns
355 Archway Road, N6 4EJ (8341 6111/www. rippingyarns.co.uk). Highgate tube. **Open** 11am-5pm Tue-Fri; 10am-5pm Sat; 11am-4pm Sun. **Credit** MC, V.
Considering itself to be first and foremost an old-fashioned browsing shop, Ripping Yarns concentrates on collectable children's and illustrated books. Shelves are lined with modern fiction, adventure books from the Blyton school of story telling, and a range of Babars, *Just Williams*, Tintin and *Beano* annuals, plus there's a large number of British comics and football magazines, with plenty of affordable items. We spotted an early edition of *The Tale of Squirrel Nutkin* going for £55, while an illustrated edition of *The Wind in the Willows* was on sale for £25. There are also books for adults, with a particularly good selection of poems and plays.

Simon Finch Rare Books
53 Maddox Street, W1S 2PN (7499 0974/www. simonfinch.com). Oxford Circus tube. **Open** 10am-6pm Mon-Fri. **Credit** AmEx, MC, V.
This recently refurbished six-storey building now stocks the arts, photography and modern English and continental literature (previously housed in the Notting Hill branch, which now holds works of art). Other specialisms among the antiquarian stock include science and medicine, early printing, architecture and design, and the social sciences. Highlights from the past year have included Jane Austen's *Pride and Prejudice* (a rare first edition, over three volumes), on sale for £55,000. There's thankfully plenty more on offer for those with slightly flatter wallets.

Stephen Foster Books
95 Bell Street, NW1 6TL (7724 0876/www.95bell street.com). Edgware Road tube/Marylebone tube/ rail. **Open** 10am-6pm Mon-Sat. **Credit** MC, V.
There are piles of books stacked high in this traditional and friendly store, which offers a decent range of antiquarian and modern titles on a wide range of subjects, including decorative and applied arts, travel, fashion, cinema, photography, natural and ancient history, and children's literature. Outside you'll find shelves stacked with an eclectic mix of bargains.

Tindley & Chapman
4 Cecil Court, WC2N 4HE (7240 2161). Leicester Square tube. **Open** 10am-5.30pm Mon-Fri; 11am-5pm Sat. **Credit** MC, V.
Although the small size and smart presentation make T&C a little more intimidating than some of its neighbours, it should nevertheless be a first port of call for any collector of 20th-century fiction firsts and poetry. Its immaculately preserved stock has a cultish flavour, with works by Paul Auster and Raymond Carver often featuring. And although the shop caters for the collector more than the reader, prices are rarely totally prohibitive. Recent copies of *One Hundred Years of Solitude* and *In Patagonia* were on sale for £500 and £350 respectively. There are also holdings of illustrated books, plus works on photography and architecture.

Travis & Emery
17 Cecil Court, WC2N 4EZ (7240 2129/www. travis-and-emery.com). Leicester Square tube. **Open** 10.30am-6.30pm Mon-Sat; noon-5pm Sun. **Credit** AmEx, MC, V.
One of the finest shops in London for out-of-print, second-hand and antiquarian books on instrumental music (mainly classical, opera and

Electronics

Useful information

Everyone wants a mobile phone, iPod, digital camera, PDA, laptop, hi-fi or all of the above. Yet when you've bought one, it's already been outmoded by a smaller, faster, more powerful, more colourful model. In a fiercely competitive market, manufacturers behave strategically, letting new 'features' trickle out one by one so that the desirability of the brand is continually bolstered. Consequently, it's difficult to keep up, and when it comes to choosing a new device you have to wade through a swamp of jargon and statistics to decide what really counts and what doesn't.

Thankfully, there is no shortage of advice available to help you make decisions. *Which?* magazine, published by the Consumers' Association, is a good starting point – it doesn't only deal with electronics but is very thorough. More specific magazines like *T3*, *Computer Shopper*, *PC Magazine*, *Hi-Fi Choice*, *What Hi-Fi?*, *Total Mobile* and *PCGamer* feature product reviews and round-ups alongside news and other features. You'll be spoilt for choice in most newsagents – though beware of magazines with 'official' in their name, as that usually signifies sponsorship by a manufacturer.

Most magazines have an accompanying website with archived features and reviews – so in reality you probably don't need to leave home to find the information you need. Don't feel restricted to magazine websites, either. **Amazon** (www.amazon.co.uk) has a well-established, reliable review system, often with contributions from consumers. Other useful sites for research are **www.zdnet.co.uk** for computer-related reviews, and **www.imaging-resource.com** for digital cameras. A quick web search will yield numerous others.

Having done the research, there's nothing to stop you buying online too. Prices are frequently cheaper than on the high street, and new devices often available sooner. Of course, you can't try things out first, and after-sales support can be limited, but there's no reason in principle to fear buying online. Common sense is enough to decide whether an online retailer is trustworthy, and as long as you pay with a major credit card you should be covered.

We've had good retail experiences with the following websites: **www.qed-uk.com**, **www.empiredirect.co.uk**, **www.digital-cameras.com**, **www.ebuyer.com**, **www.unbeatable.co.uk**, and, of course, good old Amazon. But this selection is still slightly arbitrary – there are hundreds of equally reputable alternatives. Sites such as **www.kelkoo.co.uk** and now Google's **Froogle UK** (http://froogle.google.co.uk) allow buyers to compare prices directly from different online shops and can point you to retailers you'd otherwise not have come across.

Many retailers tout extended warranties, which outlast the basic protection offered by manufacturers. Our advice is to steer clear. Electronics products are generally reliable, and if they are still in good shape when the manufacturer's warranty runs out, they're likely to carry on working as long as they're treated well. There are a few exceptions to this rule. The long-term durability of plasma screen TVs is still uncertain, and replacing the screen is very costly. Computers – by their very complexity – have a tendency to hiccup occasionally, and care plans offered by the manufacturers (not the retailers) might be worth investigating. Dell and Apple, for example, offer extensions to their basic one-year warranty for a few hundred pounds. Apple offers similar cover for its other products as well. If you are thinking of buying an iPod, consider the extended protection – questions have been raised about the life of the iPod's battery, which is best not replaced at home.

General & audio-visual

HMV and **Virgin Megastore** are the big high-street names for entertainment media – music, videos, DVDs, computer games and accessories. For both, *see chapter* **CDs & Records**.

Ask Electronics
248 Tottenham Court Road, W1T 7QZ (7637 0353/www.askdirect.co.uk). Tottenham Court Road tube. **Open** 10am-7pm Mon-Wed, Fri, Sat; 10am-8pm Thur; noon-6pm Sun. **Credit** AmEx, DC, MC, V.
Ask is one of Tottenham Court Road's smarter inhabitants – it's better looking and much better organised than some of its rather cluttered neighbours. This is partly because it has the luxury of four floors in which to lay out its huge catalogue of products. You'll find a wide range of computers, cameras, MP3 players, hi-fis, gadgets and accessories from reliable mainstream brands like Sony, Pioneer, Fuji, JVC and so on. Prices are competitive and the staff knowledgeable. You can also order on the website, but many of the best deals are only available in store.
Mail order.
For branch see index.

Blue Audio Visual
44 Duncan Street, N1 8BW (7713 6865/www.blue audiovisual.co.uk). Angel tube. **Open** 10am-7pm Mon-Sat; noon-6pm Sun. **Credit** AmEx, MC, V.
Islington stalwart Blue Audio recently moved into bigger premises across the road after 13 years at its original Upper Street address. It owes its continuing success to its passionate, enthusiastic staff and a well-selected, eclectic stock of second-hand equipment. The shop is stuffed with all kinds of recording, studio and DJ gear, hi-fi components, musical instruments, photographic equipment and other assorted gadgetry. For the cine buff, there is a huge range of Super-8 movie cameras, projectors, film and accessories. All used items are thoroughly tested and sold with a three-month guarantee.
Mail order.

Comet
2A Cantium Retail Park, 522 Old Kent Road, SE1 5BA (08705 425 425/www.comet.co.uk). Elephant & Castle tube/rail. **Open** 9am-8pm Mon-Fri; 9am-6pm Sat; 10.30am-4.30pm Sun. **Credit** AmEx, MC, V.
A cornerstone of retail parks from Abergavenny to Yeovil, Comet is many people's only choice for home electronics. The huge stores are packed with budget and mid-range electronics and domestic appliances, from washing machines to Walkmans. It's not the place for connoisseurs, but if you're looking for a straightforward, inexpensive TV, radio, DVD player or stand-alone hi-fi, there are some good deals to be found. Computers are also sold, from a handful of mainstream brands such as Acer, Fujitsu Siemens, Hewlett Packard and Sony. It's not a particularly inspiring retail experience, and don't expect the staff to be especially enthusiastic or knowledgeable, but these are the by-products of an unchanging, reliable formula that is arguably Comet's virtue.
Mail order.
Branches: throughout the city.

Dixons
88 Oxford Street, W1D 1BX (7636 8511/ www.dixons.co.uk). Tottenham Court Road tube. **Open** 10am-7pm Mon-Wed, Fri; 10am-8pm Thur; 9am-6.30pm Sat; noon-6pm Sun. **Credit** AmEx, DC, MC, V.
Dixons is a staple of high streets across the land, which indicates its target market – the general consumer, rather than the expert. It sells a full complement of electronic gear – cameras, camcorders, DVD players, televisions, stereos, MP3 players, video games consoles, games, mobile telephones and more. Whatever device you're after, Dixons is likely to have a few options, at respectable (though not spectacular) prices. A disadvantage of the chain-store template is that staff aren't necessarily too bothered about what they do, so you may be better off doing your research in advance if you're thinking of picking something up here. Dixons is notorious for pushing its 'extended cover' schemes upon customers; as we've said above, we advise against these.
Mail order.
Branches: throughout the city.

Kingsbury Electronics Ltd
421 Kingsbury Road, NW9 9DT (8905 0505/ www.kingsburyelectronics.com). Kingsbury tube. **Open** 9am-6pm Mon-Sat. **Credit** AmEx, MC, V.
A family-owned shop doing valiant battle against the big chains with its more personal approach. It must be doing something right, as it's edging 20 years in the business. Besides kitchen appliances, Kingsbury has hi-fi and video equipment, and its speciality is televisions: there's a wide range from the likes of Panasonic, Philips and Toshiba, at decent prices.

Maplin
166-168 Queensway, W2 6LZ (7229 9301/ www.maplin.co.uk). Bayswater or Queensway tube. **Open** 9am-8pm Mon-Fri; 9am-6pm Sat; 11am-5pm Sun. **Credit** AmEx, MC, V.
It's been over three decades since Roger Allen and Doug Simmons carved out a niche sourcing and selling components to amateur electronics enthusiasts. It's a wonder there were enough people building their own radios and guitar pedals to keep the business afloat, but some 100 stores and well over 1,000 employees in 2005 leave no room for ambiguity. Casual computer builders and electronics experts will be in heaven amid a sea of gizmos, gadgets and components. But, while there are all sorts of things the average consumer's never even heard of, less esoteric items are also stocked – like blank CDs and DVDs, audio-visual cables, MP3 players, headphones and so on. Maplin's approach is thoroughly unpretentious, and its prices reflect this.
Mail order (0870 429 6000).
Branches: throughout the city.

Shasonic
242 Tottenham Court Road, W1T 7QR (0845 634 0333/www.shasonic.co.uk). Tottenham Court Road tube. **Open** 9am-6pm Mon-Wed, Fri, Sat; 9am-7pm Thur; 11am-5pm Sun. **Credit** AmEx, MC, V.
It's hard to draw useful distinctions between the countless electronics shops on Tottenham Court Road: their stock is virtually the same at any given time, the prices broadly similar (and they'll all match each other anyway) and service somewhere between perfunctory and aggressive. The best we can do is say that we've had good experiences with (among others) Shasonic, a veteran of the trade, where the staff's approach has been more tactful than elsewhere. Its comprehensive stock covers precisely what you'd expect: digital cameras, computers, mobiles and all kinds of audio-visual

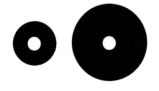

cornflake.co.uk
37 Windmill Street, London W1T 2JU
Telephone +44(0)20 7323 4554
information@cornflake.co.uk

London's best restaurants
all in one guide

Available at bookshops, newsagents
and at www.timeout.com/shop

gear. More respected mainstream brands are favoured. In the basement you'll find all the accessories and extras you'll need to connect, clean, fix, record and store.

Branches: throughout the city.

Rental

Boxclever

08705 546 563/www.boxclever.co.uk. **Phone enquiries** 8am-7pm Mon-Fri; 8am-6pm Sat. **Credit** MC, V.

You might be amazed to learn that there's still a rental market for electronics. After all, Radio Rentals, once a British institution, faded away unceremoniously from our high streets as the price of TVs, VCRs and the like plummeted. However, the company lives on in another guise, having merged with former competitor Granada. Boxclever rents out TVs, DVDs players/VCRs, Sky digital, Sky+ and Freeview boxes (as well as washing machines and dryers). As a price guide, a 43cm flat-panel television can be rented for £29.99 a month; a DVD/VCR combination costs £9.99 a month. It might seem perverse to throw away money like this, but there are certain advantages: all rentals have a free repair and replacement guarantee, and it's very easy to upgrade to newer technology as soon as it becomes available. Boxclever usually delivers within three days of an order being confirmed.

Warehouse shops

Centrax Direct Sales

Unit 17, 193 Garth Road, Morden, Surrey SM4 4LZ (8330 7766/www.clearancelines.co.uk). Morden tube then 93, 293 bus. **Open** 9am-5pm Mon-Sat; 10am-4pm Sun. **Credit** AmEx, DC, MC, V.

Centrax is the public outlet of a company called Clearance Lines, which supplies ex-showroom household goods to market traders. Stuffed with end-of-line, clearance and ex-demonstration TVs, DVDs, freezers, mini hi-fis, fans, hairdryers, irons and toasters, this is the place to kit out a home on a tight budget. You may find that some of the items are cosmetically damaged, but everything is substantially discounted and comes with a one-year guarantee.

Computer games

HMV and Virgin Megastore are major retailers of console and PC games. Many other shops, from **Dixons** (*see p190*) to Woolworths, plus the big supermarkets, stock a smaller selection of titles.

CeX

32 Rathbone Place, W1T 1JJ (0845 345 1664/ www.cex.co.uk). Tottenham Court Road tube. **Open** 10am-7.30pm Mon-Wed, Sat; 10am-8pm Thur, Fri; 11am-7pm Sun. **Credit** MC, V.

A longstanding maxim of video-gaming is that playability is the most important aspect of any game – in other words, the very best games do not tire with the onward march of technology. CeX (or Computer Exchange) is the retail incarnation of this philosophy – a second-hand emporium that catalogues the whole history of video gaming. Here you can buy everything from the original Nintendo LCD Game & Watch hand-helds (around £30) to recent titles for Xbox, GameCube and PlayStation 2, including Japanese and American imports. CeX will also buy your old games.

For branches see index.

Computer Games Exchange

40 Notting Hill Gate, W11 3HX (7460 6716/ www.mveshops.co.uk). Notting Hill Gate tube. **Open** 10am-8pm daily. **Credit** AmEx, MC, V.

There's more gaming nostalgia at this second-hand shop, part of the Notting Hill Music & Video Exchange group. All the old favourites are here for SNES, Atari, Amiga, even the Commodore and Spectrum. Newer machines like the PlayStation 2, Xbox and GameCube are also catered for.

Game

Victoria Plaza, 10 Victoria Place, SW1W 9SJ (7828 9913/www.game.net). Victoria tube/rail. **Open** 8am-8pm Mon-Fri; 9am-7pm Sat; 11am-5pm Sun. **Credit** MC, V.

Part of a pan-European gaming and computer empire, Game is a very big fish, with more video-game stores in this country than anyone else. Selling console units as well as their games, it concentrates on current machines like the PlayStation 2, Xbox, GameCube and Nintendo DS – leaving vintage consoles to the specialists – but it does nevertheless sell second-hand titles alongside new ones. It runs a worthwhile reward scheme – you buy lifetime membership for a £3 one-off fee and receive a discount on all purchases (at a rate of 2.5%, or 5% if you pre-order). Old games and consoles can be turned in for credit.

Mail order.

Branches: throughout the city.

DJ & home studio equipment

We recommend *Sound on Sound* and *DJ* magazines for up-to-date information on the best DJ equipment. For **Turnkey/Soho Soundhouse** and **Digital Village**, which also sell DJ equipment, *see chapter* **Music**.

Sapphires Sound & Light

5-6 Burlington Parade, Edgware Road, NW2 6QG (8450 2426/www.decks.co.uk). Kilburn tube. **Open** noon-7pm Mon-Wed; 11am-7pm Thur, Fri; 10am-7pm Sat. **Credit** AmEx, MC, V.

We don't know how many more DJs the world can handle, but we do know that Sapphires can meet the demand for equipment. Its stock has no gaps – every significant manufacturer is represented, including Technics, Pioneer, Vextax, Allen & Heath, Denon and so on. There are vinyl, CD, MP3 and even new DVD decks, mixing consoles, amps, speakers, needles and record bags. Staff in DJ and record stores are notoriously unhelpful, but in our experience Sapphires breaks the mould.

Mail order (8960 8989).

Westend DJ

10-12 Hanway Street, W1T 1UB (7637 3293/ www.westenddj.co.uk). Tottenham Court Road tube. **Open** 9.30am-6.30pm Mon-Sat; 11am-5pm Sun. **Credit** MC, V.

The six branches of Westend DJ are led from the Hanway Street HQ, where a very impressive range of equipment is flaunted in a deceptively small space. The newest equipment – including vinyl, DVD and CD decks along with amps and mixers – is rigged up in-store ready for demonstration. There's also an excellent range of headphones and other accessories. Westend DJ is another store where expertise is given generously.

Mail order.

Branches: throughout the city.

Hi-fi

Whatever kind of hi-fi equipment you require, London offers unparalleled choice. The first step is to establish a budget and then research the options carefully. The most important part of the research involves, where possible, actually listening to some favourite albums on the systems you are considering. After all, the main requirement is that they sound good. This may seem like stating the obvious, but it's too easy to be seduced by lists of features or mere aesthetics when you start comparing products, forgetting why you're buying a hi-fi in the first place.

If funds are very limited, or if you are buying a smaller second system for somewhere like the kitchen, you are better off looking at stand-alone units (often branded 'mini' or 'micro' systems) rather than hi-fi separates. If you choose wisely, you can find a compact all-in-one with good sound quality at a very reasonable

price. The electronics superstores – **Comet** (*see p190*), **Currys** and **Dixons** (*see p190*) – all stock a respectable range; other places to look are **John Lewis** (*see p13*) and **Argos** (*see p118*). Some shops have all-in-one systems for as little as under £20. However, you get what you pay for, and there's nothing high-fidelity about equipment like this. We'd generally advise you not to bother with any system costing significantly less than £100, which seems to be a watershed price point – at this price level and above we've found several impressive systems.

Stand-alone systems can cost up to about £350. However, if your budget is in this orbit or higher, you should consider getting separates. Mainstream manufacturers sell off-the-shelf packages of separates (including speakers) for around £500 and upwards: this is one option – and the components in these packages are bound to be well matched. The alternative, depending on your budget, is to handpick separates, possibly from different manufacturers. There are plenty of high-end audio specialists who will help you do just that; we've picked our favourites below. Remember that speakers and the amp are the most important components in terms of sound quality.

Hi-fi and home cinema are slowly becoming synonymous, and most of the hi-fi specialists listed below can construct a system that contains visual as well as audio components.

Many of the best-respected shops belong to the **British Audio Dealers Association** (BADA, 0870 126 9137, www.bada.co.uk), which means they offer extended warranties and good exchange/return policies. Membership of the Custom Electronics Design & Installation Association (CEDIA) indicates an installation specialist.

Audio Gold

308-310 Park Road, N8 8LA (8341 9007/ www.audiogold.co.uk). Finsbury Park tube/rail then W7 bus. **Open** 10.30am-6.30pm Mon-Sat. **Credit** MC, V.

Audio Gold is a haven for the enthusiast and collector, but anyone building a serious hi-fi system could well find a very special, one-off component here. The exotic range of second-hand stock comprises vintage amps, turntables, speakers, mics and the like, often from manufacturers we've never heard of. Particularly impressive is the apparently never-ending supply of original 1980s ghetto blasters. Rare, specialist equipment isn't always cheap, but there's a good dose of bargains. Everything sold has been fully overhauled and tested, and comes with a three-month guarantee.

Mail order.

For branch see index.

Audio T

190 West End Lane, NW6 1SG (7794 7848/ www.audio-t.co.uk). West Hampstead tube/rail. **Open** 10am-5.30pm Tue, Wed, Fri, Sat; 10am-7.30pm Thur. **Credit** MC, V.

Now approaching its 40th year, Audio T has cemented its reputation as a quality hi-fi specialist, catering to the middle and top end of the market. The buyers are not prejudiced about brands – they will buy from big companies as well as small ones if they think the equipment is up to it. Expert staff can assemble and install bespoke systems to suit clients' requirements and budgets – from £500 to £50,000; what's more, Audio T insists it will match prices from other retailers – a rare policy at this level. Another advantage is that they will happily transfer items that are being held in their 15 other branches, so the stock is effectively enormous. BADA membership means ten-day exchange and 30-day upgrade policies are offered.

Mail order.

For branch see index.

Audio Venue

*27 Bond Street, W5 5AS (8567 8703/www.
audiovenue.com). Ealing Broadway tube/
rail.* **Open** 10am-6pm Mon-Sat. **Credit** AmEx,
MC, V.
Audio Venue has risen from the ashes of the Audio
Concept hi-fi store, which occupied the same
Ealing premises. The new venue combines a
cutting-edge catalogue with an equally futuristic
shop design. It's a big fan of the phenomenal
Martin Logan speaker range, and also sells music
servers – hard disk-based units that can digitally
store thousands of CDs' worth of music and pipe
audio throughout a whole house. There's a full
range of amplifiers, CD players, tuners, turntables
and home cinema equipment from heavyweight
manufacturers. Be warned: this is not for the
budget-conscious, as the majority of units have
four-figure price tags.
Mail order.

Billy Vee Sound Systems

*248 Lee High Road, SE13 5PL (8318 5755/
www.billyvee.co.uk). Lewisham rail/DLR then 122,
261, 321 bus.* **Open** 10am-6.30pm Mon-Wed, Fri,
Sat. **Credit** AmEx, MC, V.
Like all good hi-fi outlets, Billy Vee was founded
by an enthusiast looking to provide others with a
more satisfying audio experience. Stock is chosen
for its reliability, value, performance and
upgradeability. Systems can be tested out in two
recently refurbished listening rooms (laid out like
domestic sitting rooms for an authentic audio
environment). A BADA member, Billy Vee offers
consultation, finance and installation services, plus
a two-year guarantee, and support for as long as
you own the product.
Mail order.

Cornflake.co.uk

*37 Windmill Street, W1T 2JU (7323 4554/
www.cornflake.co.uk). Goodge Street tube.* **Open**
by appointment only. **Credit** AmEx, MC, V.

The selection of case studies on Cornflake's
website gives you some idea of just what can be
achieved with a top-end hi-fi and home cinema
installation: the premium equipment can be
seamlessly integrated with (and hidden away
within) customised furniture, and sound can be
broadcast to any room in a house and controlled
from anywhere by remote control. Nevertheless,
these five-figure projects represent the most
extravagant end of Cornflake's projects, and
it's just as ready to put together a more humble set-
up. If you're lucky you could escape with a hi-fi bill
of under a grand, although it will be tempting to
blow much more on components by a superb range
of manufacturers such as Rega, Mark Levinson
and Bryston.
Mail order.

Grahams Hi-Fi

*Unit 1, Canonbury Yard, 190A New North Road,
N1 7BS (7226 5500/www.grahams.co.uk).
Highbury & Islington tube/rail.* **Open** 10am-6pm
Tue, Wed; 10am-8pm Thur; 9am-6pm Fri, Sat.
Credit AmEx, DC, MC, V.
In a saturated market, Grahams is in many ways
a cut above its competitors. It's been going since
1929 (although we suspect there were fewer CD
players and power amps in stock then), has a
friendly team of 20 staff, sells a larger range of
equipment than most, and has particularly good
showrooms, tucked away just off the Essex Road
in Islington. If you're looking to invest a good few
zeros in a serious hi-fi system or home cinema,
Grahams is an obvious choice. If you're on a
budget, then you should look elsewhere. After an
initial consultation stage, you can book a
demonstration in the on-site listening rooms –
where any components you have chosen to try
out will have been set up in advance. The service
here is second to none, as you'd expect from one of
the founding members of the British Audio
Dealers Association.
Mail order.

HiFi Experience

*227 Tottenham Court Road, W1T 7HX (7580
3535/www.hifilondon.co.uk). Goodge Street or
Tottenham Court Road tube.* **Open** 10am-6pm
Mon-Sat. **Credit** AmEx, MC, V.
This basement grotto stocks an impressive
selection of mid-range and high-end equipment,
by manufacturers such as Mission, Marantz,
Denon, NAD and Bang & Olufsen. Service is
excellent, the staff know what they're talking
about, and installation and post-sales support are
first-rate. Eight demonstration rooms in which to
listen to equipment mean you should be able to
visit any time.

KJ West One

*26 New Cavendish Street, W1G 8TY (7486
8262/www.kjwestone.com). Baker Street or Bond
Street tube.* **Open** 10am-5.30pm Tue-Fri; 10am-
5pm Sat. **Credit** MC, V.
KJ West One is a veteran of premium hi-fi and
home cinema, with three decades in the trade. All
the finest British and European brands are
represented, as well as some American names
rarely encountered on these shores (McIntosh,
Krell, Audio Research, Martin Logan). Not really a
place for casual browsers, since the rarefied
atmosphere can be intimidating, but staff are
nevertheless friendly and knowledgeable. KJ also
has a range of second-hand and ex-demonstration
equipment, which is listed online.
Mail order.

Martin Kleiser

*109 Chiswick High Road, W4 2ED (8400 5555/
www.martin-kleiser.com). Turnham Green tube.*
Open 9am-5.30pm Tue-Sat. **Credit** MC, V.
A founding member of CEDIA, Martin Kleiser is
renowned for large-scale home installations. If
your tastes run to multi-room hi-fi, earth-shaking
home cinema, high-tech lighting and security
control systems, look no further. Tag McLaren,
Rega, Naim and Linn are among the brands

favoured here. It's the only custom-installation company to be accepted into BIDA (British Interior Designer Association), so you can expect a first-rate service.

Musical Images

18 Monmouth Street, WC2H 9HB (7497 1346/ www.musicalimages.co.uk). Covent Garden or Leicester Square tube. **Open** 10am-6pm Mon-Sat. **Credit** AmEx, MC, V.
Musical Images has a much larger catalogue than some of the more exclusive dealers – it can supply components from over 100 manufacturers. Consequently it's equally good for mid-range and top-end equipment; also, it's worth keeping an eye on special offers (listed online) for real bargains. The company is a member of both BADA and CEDIA, and has plenty of experience with large-scale, multi-room installations.
Mail order.
For branches see index.

Oranges & Lemons

61-63 Webb's Road, SW11 6RX (7924 2040/ www.oandlhifi.co.uk). Clapham Junction rail. **Open** 11am-7pm Mon, Tue, Fri; 11am-9pm Thur; 10am-6pm Sat. **Credit** AmEx, MC, V.
Taking the view that hi-fi and home cinema are ultimately recreational tools, Oranges & Lemons likes to stress that its staff (and general approach) are a bit less aloof than some of the competition. Nevertheless, no corners are cut with the quality of service or goods. Its systems might include speakers from Anthony Gallo or NEAT and components by Naim, Rega or Rotel, among many other possibilities. As usual with high-end retailers, you're advised to book a listening appointment in advance; alternatively, you could start off with a home consultation. Oranges & Lemons is a BADA member.
Mail order.

Richer Sounds

2 London Bridge Walk, SE1 2SX (7403 1201/ www.richersounds.co.uk). London Bridge tube/rail. **Open** 10am-6pm Mon-Wed, Fri; 10am-7pm Thur; 10am-5pm Sat. **Credit** MC, V.
Richer Sounds remains the first choice for audiophiles on a budget, and with branches across the country it's within easy reach for most people. Its shops are small, busy and awash with discounts. Demonstration facilities are limited, but the staff are generally enthusiastic; their advice may not be impartial, though, since some of the brands on sale are either owned or exclusively distributed by Richer Sounds. Stocks of the best deals are often limited to a few items per store, so if you spot a bargain online, call before making the journey.
Branches: throughout the city.

Robert Taussig
Multi-Room Emporium

39 Blandford Street, W1U 7HD (7487 3455). Baker Street tube. **Open** 10am-6pm Mon-Fri; 10am-5pm Sat. **Credit** MC, V.
Robert Taussig's speciality is the design and installation of high-end, multi-room systems, tailored to individual needs and specifications. You could quite easily spend hundreds of thousands of pounds here, but shallower pockets are also catered for, with decent systems starting at around £1,000. Service is top-notch, whatever the chosen price range.
For branch see index.

Sevenoaks Sound & Vision

24 The Green, W5 5DA (8579 8777/ www.sevenoakssoundandvision.co.uk). Ealing Broadway tube. **Open** 10am-6pm Mon, Tue, Fri, Sat; 11am-7pm Thur; noon-5pm Sun. **Credit** MC, V.
Sevenoaks is much more conducive to browsing than many of its high-end competitors – and it is financially more accessible too, stocking more mainstream and mid-range brands like Panasonic and Pioneer alongside connoisseur manufacturers. It concentrates on separates, but a few stand-alone systems are available. Decent listening facilities and helpful staff make this a good place for the

uninitiated to buy a quality first hi-fi. Note that different branches in and around the city carry different product ranges.
For branches see index.

The Studio

28 Aylmer Parade, Aylmer Road, N2 0PE (8348 0990/www.thenaimshop.dsl.pipex.com). Highgate tube/43, 134, 263 bus. **Open** 11am-5pm Sat; other times by appointment only. **Credit** AmEx, MC, V.
Catering to serious audiophiles and generally only open by appointment, the Studio stocks a limited range of carefully selected high-end equipment. Naim is a speciality, but there are also turntables by Project and speakers from Boston Acoustics.

Walrus Systems

11 New Quebec Street, W1H 7RW (7724 7224/ www.walrus.co.uk). Marble Arch tube. **Open** 10.30am-6pm Mon-Sat. **Credit** MC, V.
A haven for vinyl junkies and lovers of analogue sound, Walrus's range includes some of the best vinyl-replay equipment made. There are turntables made by specialists like Michell, Nottingham Analogue and SME, as well as gorgeous valve amps and omni-directional speakers that look like they're from outer space and sound like they're from heaven. It's not for the faint of wallet, but if audio perfection is your goal, this is the place.
Mail order.

Personal computers

If you've so far managed to avoid indoctrination, the first big decision to be made when buying a computer is whether to get a Mac (made only by Apple) or a PC (made by many different manufacturers). In practice, this is really a decision about which software or 'operating system' you will use. Current Macs run Mac OS X, while PCs are usually supplied with Microsoft Windows XP.

There are significant differences between Mac OS and Windows, though in some ways they have got closer over time. Mac OS is designed with user-friendliness as its top priority. For this reason it's generally considered easier for absolute beginners or technophobes, and has traditionally been preferred by graphic designers, music producers and other creative professionals, whose main concern is to get the job done without worrying about the workings of the system.

Windows has become more ergonomic over time (no doubt picking up a trick or two from Mac OS along the way), but Microsoft's priorities have been slightly different. Because PCs are used in many more contexts and by many more people than Macs, Microsoft's chief concern has been to make Windows as flexible and adaptable as possible – so that it can be customised to run everything from databases, spreadsheets and accounts packages to email, web browsers, music production, graphics and games software, accommodating the diverse needs of its hundreds of millions of users. Consequently Windows is more intricate and fiddly, because there are many more options and ways of configuring it. This is what hardened Mac users find irritating.

Our recommendation, therefore, is this: if you are a creative professional, with non-technical needs and no real interest in gaming, get a Mac. Otherwise, get a PC – they're not really that difficult to learn, and in any case, chances are you'll know someone who can fix problems or answer questions about Windows. PCs are also easier to upgrade.

Once you've established which computer's for you, the next decision is how powerful it should be. Apple offers the Mac Mini at entry level (you'll need to buy a screen separately); if you want a bit more kick, get an iMac. Creative

heavyweights use PowerMacs (or PowerBooks). The PC market is naturally more nebulous, but PCs are significantly cheaper than Macs: £500 will buy a system more than capable of any domestic or office tasks. However, as a general rule, pay as much as you can: the more you fork out, the longer the computer will last.

If your eyes glaze over at statistics such as CPU speed, RAM, hard disk, any retailer will be able to help you decide what your requirements are. At the end of the day, every new computer on the market can handle internet, email and office work without trouble.

There's a lot to be said for buying a computer direct from the manufacturer, rather than through a high-street retailer. If something goes wrong (within warranty) it's then the manufacturer's responsibility to resolve it, and this can eliminate the extra hassle of going through the retailer. **Dell** (www.dell.co.uk), despite not having a high-street presence, has rightfully carved out a reputation as the world's most popular PC retailer, with excellent products and service. On the downside, with Dell you won't have the chance to try before you buy. **Evesham** (*see p197*) makes computers that it sells through its own shop outlets, so this is an alternative.

There's nothing intrinsically wrong with buying from a high-street retailer, just make sure you know where you stand on warranties and service, and who will deal with the matter if something goes wrong.

One final caution. Buying PCs from smaller companies is not necessarily wise, as your warranty might not be honoured if the company goes bust. One safety measure is to buy a computer with a credit card: under the Consumer Credit Act 1974, the credit company shares liability with the retailer if the computer is faulty.

Tottenham Court Road

Apple Centre

78 New Oxford Street, WC1A 1HB (7692 9990/ www.squaregroup.co.uk). Tottenham Court Road tube. **Open** 10am-5.30pm Mon, Fri; 10am-7pm Tue-Thur; 10am-5pm Sat. **Credit** MC, V.
The shiny new Apple Store (*see p197*) has stolen the limelight a bit, but the Apple Centre remains a trustworthy supplier of all kinds of Mac hardware, accessories and software. Staff are attentive and will order Mac equipment if it's not in stock. Prices at Apple Centres tend to be higher than elsewhere, so shop around first. Additional services available here include authorised Apple repairs, plus printing and scanning.
Mail order.

CeX

70 Tottenham Court Road, W1T 2HB (0845 345 1664/www.cex.co.uk). Goodge Street tube. **Open** 10am-7.30pm Mon-Wed, Sat; 10am-8pm Thur, Fri; 11am-7.30pm Sun. **Credit** MC, V.
The Tottenham Court Road sibling of the main video-games store (*see p193*) sells second-hand computers, software and accessories at discounted prices. There are also used mobile phones, PDAs, digital cameras, camcorders and DVDs. Much of this equipment is displayed in the shop window, so it's worth having a glance if you're passing to see if you can spot a bargain. IT geeks can buy cheap used parts to build their own machines, trading in their redundant components at the same time.
Mail order.
For branches see index.

Gultronics

264-267 Tottenham Court Road, W1T 7RH (7436 4120/www.gultronics.co.uk). Goodge Street or Tottenham Court Road tube. **Open** 10am-7pm Mon-Sat; 11am-5pm Sun. **Credit** AmEx, DC, MC, V.

Chic tech

HAVING TROUBLE SORTING YOUR MEGABYTES FROM YOUR MEGAPIXELS? HERE'S OUR PICK OF THE SMOOTHEST GADGETS.

LEISURE

Fujifilm FinePix S9500

£499.99

This camera from Fujifilm, a company with a great history in imaging, is likely to remain cutting-edge for a long time, despite the pace of change in electronics. It offers a huge amount of refinements and overrides for people who want to do more than point and shoot, although it will, of course, let you do just that if you prefer. It has a deeply impressive nine million pixels – the dots that make up the picture – so you can be sure of rich, detailed and impressive results. Highly recommended.
Fujifilm (020 7586 5900/ www.fujifilm.co.uk).

Sony PlayStation Portable

£179.99

An irresistibly beautiful portable machine that plays games and movies. Just for gamers, you think? Well, no (however, the games look so good and play so well on the gloriously sharp screen that even hardened Lara Croft-haters will want to have a bash at this). But it's also a stylish, if large, MP3 player and a superb gadget for watching movies – when films come out on DVD they are being released in increasing numbers on UMD (the tiny Mini Disc-like format that the PSP uses) as well. Even action movies play smoothly and impressively, with nary a trace of smear or jumping.
Sony PlayStation (http://uk.playstation.com).

Sony Walkman Bean

£79-£99

The Bean is Sony's coolest MP3 player yet, and in terms of flash players – the smaller capacity, lighter players – may be enough to prise the budget crown away from the iPod Shuffle. The Bean has a bright organic LED screen and comes in two capacities, 512Mb and 1Gb, enough for either 350 or 700 songs. It has fantastic battery life (up to 50 hours between charges) and, best of all, it springs into life after just a three-minute charge, enough to power it for up to three hours. A pop-up connector slots it straight into your PC.
Sony (08705 111 999/ www.sony.co.uk).

Tivoli PAL radio

£129.99

This is a design classic, a neat and gorgeous portable radio that sounds as good as it looks. It comes with a rechargeable battery so you can listen to it in the park and, though the sound is mono, it's very impressive. The tuner inside is stereo, so you can play it in stereo through your hi-fi, or you can connect your MP3 player to play your tunes through the speaker. It comes in a rubberised casing, which is hard to keep your hands off and makes it weatherproof enough to use in the bathroom (carefully, mind). It comes in a range of bright or pastel colours, and in a version styled to match the iPod.
Tivoli Audio (01702 601410/ www.ruark.co.uk).

Motorola PEBL V6 mobile phone

From free with contract

Motorola scored a real hit with the deservedly popular RAZR V3 phone, a slim style phone in aluminium and magnesium. Now it's released the PEBL which, yes, looks like a perfectly smooth pebble. It's deeply tactile: stroke the front of the phone and a gentle mechanism opens the clamshell like an oyster revealing its pearl. Features include Bluetooth (the short-wave radio connection that lets you use a wireless hands-free), a camera that shoots video, as well as still pictures, downloadable games, voice-dialling, MP3 ringtones and more. But in the end you'll buy it for the way it looks.
Motorola (08000 151 151/ www.motorola.com/uk).

Another jam-packed TCR resident, stocked full of the usual cameras, camcorders, DVDs and so on. Gultronics is particularly notable for its range of Toshiba and Sony laptops, plus other computer accessories such as printers and scanners. Prices are competitive, but, as with many of the shops on this street, you can expect staff to pursue a hard sell. As a general rule (both here and in the vicinity), it's worth haggling, and if you can play off different shops against each other's prices, you might well secure a good deal.
Mail order.
For branches see index.

Micro Anvika
245 Tottenham Court Road, W1T 7QT (7467 6000/www.microanvika.co.uk). Goodge Street or Tottenham Court Road tube. **Open** 9.30am-6pm Mon-Wed, Fri, Sat; 9.30am-6.30pm Thur; 11am-5pm Sun. **Credit** AmEx, MC, V.
Micro Anvika has three stores on Tottenham Court Road alone; one just off it in Chenies Street, and another in Selfridges, so you'll have no trouble finding a branch if you decide to take advantage of its large stock of both Macs and PCs. PCs stocked are from mainstream brands like Sony, Toshiba and IBM. Peripherals and software are also available for both platforms. A 90-day technical support policy is a bonus and, though we've heard some mixed reports about after-sales care, our experience has been generally positive. Once again, you've got nothing to lose by haggling on prices.
Mail order (7467 6050).
For branches see index.

Elsewhere

Apple Store
235 Regent Street, W1B 2ET (7153 9000/ www.apple.com). Oxford Circus Tube. **Open** 10am-9pm Mon-Sat; noon-6pm Sun. **Credit** AmEx, MC, V.
Only a giant like Apple could afford to have this much empty space in a huge, premium-location West End shop. Maybe it's supposed to reflect its minimalist design ethic. Then again, perhaps they knew it would be needed to accommodate the hordes of covetous consumers desperate to get their mitts on the newest computers, cinema displays, iPods and other equipment. The Apple Centre opened in 2005 to enormous fanfare, and it's the place to go to see all the new technologies in their full glory. Everything is set out for demonstration and can be tried on the spot, and staff are as passionate as the customers. It's a seductive experience – mind you don't get carried away.

Computer Warehouse
1 Amalgamated Drive, West Cross Centre, Great West Road, Brentford, Middx TW8 9EZ (8400 1234/www.cwonline.co.uk). Boston Manor or Osterley tube/Syon Lane rail. **Open** 9am-5.30pm Mon-Fri; 9am-5pm Sat. **Credit** MC, V.
West Londoners in search of a Mac might prefer to stay out of the centre and visit Computer Warehouse instead, just off the A4. The full range of Mac products (iMacs, PowerBooks, G5s, iPods, printers, scanners and software) is on display, and also available from Computer Warehouse's online store, at competitive prices.
Mail order.

Evesham Technology
4 New Cavendish Street, W1G 8TS (7486 1010/ www.evesham.com). Bond Street tube. **Open** 9.30am-6pm Mon-Sat; 10am-4pm Sun. **Credit** AmEx, MC, V.
Evesham is one of the most reputable PC manufacturers around, having won plentiful customer service and product quality awards during its 20-odd years in business. Its wide range of desktops and notebooks can accommodate any needs. One advantage of buying from Evesham is that you are dealing directly with the manufacturer, with no middleman, so it's easy to get things sorted if something goes wrong later. This set-up also encourages staff to be genuinely helpful, without the hard-sell approach that

characterises other shops. Evesham has a customer helpline, flexible payment plans and lots of upgrade options.
Mail order (0870 160 9500).

Morgan Computer Company
64 New Oxford Street, WC1A 1AX (7255 2115/ www.morgancomputers.co.uk). Tottenham Court Road tube. **Open** 9am-5.30pm Mon-Wed, Fri; 9am-7.30pm Thur; 9am-5pm Sat; 10am-4pm Sun. **Credit** AmEx, MC, V.
The budget-conscious computer buyer with fairly basic needs may find that a refurbished, second-hand or discontinued system is perfectly adequate – and Morgan is probably the best outlet for this kind of merchandise. Prices are extremely low, and you can pick up all sorts of accessories and other digital/AV gear too.
Mail order (0870 120 4930).
For branch see index.

PC World
2 Trojan Way, off Purley Way, Croydon, Surrey CR0 4XL (0870 242 0444/www.pcworld.co.uk). East Croydon or West Croydon rail. **Open** 9am-8pm Mon-Fri; 9am-6pm Sat; 11am-5pm Sun. **Credit** AmEx, MC, V.
PC World needs no introduction, thanks to years of guerrilla marketing and an extraordinarily annoying advertising jingle. It has made itself indispensable as the only nationwide computer superstore chain. Staff are surprisingly well-informed, certainly more so than in the average high-street electronics shop. Its PC packages come from mainstream manufacturers like Packard Bell. The disadvantages are that commercial computers like these aren't so easy to upgrade, and you won't have any direct contact with the manufacturer. PC World comes into its own for supplying accessories – printers, scanners, webcams, special papers and blank CDs. It also sells Macs.
Mail order.
Branches: throughout the city.

Telecommunications

The UK mobile phone market is one of the largest in Europe. Five national networks – **O2, Orange, T-Mobile, Vodafone** and **3** – and a seemingly infinite variety of different tariffs are a recipe for headaches when you are trying to decide what option is best.

In practical terms, there's little to distinguish the networks, except for 3, which uses a new technology called 3G to transmit data much faster, facilitating new services like streamed audio and video. However, 3G is not nearly as widespread as conventional coverage, so currently you can only take advantage of the multimedia extras while within built-up areas; elsewhere 3 reverts to a regular service.

Of the other four networks, some would say that Orange and Vodafone have the upper hand in terms of coverage, but this is debatable – all four occasionally suffer from poor reception in remote areas, and none has any problem whatsoever in London, except underground (and even the tube is set to be kitted out with mobile phone relays by 2008). A sixth network, Virgin Mobile, in fact uses the same network as T-Mobile.

The best way of deciding which phone to get is to compare tariffs and handsets available across all the networks, then work out which suit you best. The first decision to be made is between pre-pay and pay-monthly options. Pre-pay phones are easier to buy, as no paperwork needs to be filled in and there are no monthly bills. You charge up the phone periodically, either by calling an automated hotline and using a credit card, or by visiting a participating shop. The initial cost of buying a phone is higher than with pay-monthly deals, but on the other hand you can't inadvertently run up huge bills. Pre-pay is ideal for infrequent

users, children, students, overseas visitors and those with a poor credit history who may not be able to buy a contract phone.

Pay-monthly deals will suit regular users who need constant, reliable access to a mobile phone. Customers are given an identity and credit check before a contract is drawn up for a minimum service period (usually 12 months). The monthly cost then varies according to the amount of airtime and messages available before usage is charged by individual calls/ texts. The trick when choosing a pay-monthly tariff is to be brutally honest about how much you will use the phone, then add on a margin of error. As many people know from bitter experience, bills start to climb astronomically as soon as the monthly inclusive minutes and messages have been exhausted.

High-street mobile shops fall into two groups – independents and those run by the network operators. The independent dealers sell mobile phones from the full range of network operators, so they're more likely to offer impartial advice. Nevertheless, it's such a fierce business that network-run shops are well aware of competitors' tariffs, and will sometimes match them. Don't expect this information to be volunteered – you'll have to raise the point yourself.

Log on to the phone networks' websites (www.vodafone.co.uk, www.orange.co.uk, www.o2.co.uk, www.tmobile.co.uk, www.three. co.uk and www.virginmobile.co.uk) for details of your nearest network operator-run store. Below is a list of independent dealers.

Carphone Warehouse
146 Marylebone Road, NW1 5PH (0870 168 2002/www.carphonewarehouse.com). Baker Street tube. **Open** 9am-6.30pm Mon-Fri; 10am-6pm Sat; noon-5pm Sun. **Credit** AmEx, MC, V.
The fact that it can hang on to its rather quaint original name (it's called 'The Phone House' in Europe) indicates how well-established the Carphone Warehouse brand is. It's one of the biggest retailers, and offers many products and services, including phones and accessories, insurance, repairs and upgrades. Staff are highly trained, and the chain has a reputation for honest advice. However, the small shops can get very busy, making service frustratingly slow, and staff can be pushy when it comes to closing the deal.
Mail order (0800 424 800).
Branches: throughout the city.

The Link
132 Baker Street, W1M 1FH (7486 4325/www. thelink.co.uk). Baker Street tube. **Open** 9.30am-6.30pm Mon-Fri; 10am-6pm Sat. **Credit** AmEx, DC, MC, V.
Another member of the Dixons Group behemoth, the Link specialises in communications equipment. It sells mobiles, landline phones, fax machines, PDAs and accessories. The staff's enthusiasm can sometimes surpass their expertise, but they can usually manage to explain the high points of each tariff coherently, and as the Link now offers service plans from all networks, there should be an improved chance of getting impartial advice. We still hear stories of the classic Dixons Group hard sell on extended insurance, so be prepared.
Mail order (0500 222 666).
Branches: throughout the city.

Phones 4U
449 Oxford Street, W1C 2PS (7629 2733/ www.phones4u.co.uk). Bond Street tube. **Open** 9.30am-8pm Mon-Fri; 10am-7pm Sat; 11am-5pm Sun. **Credit** AmEx, DC, MC, V.
Another major contender, now with over 350 stores in high streets up and down the country. Phones 4U sells deals on all the mobile networks, so you can expect reasonably impartial advice. In our experience staff are honest and knowledgeable.
Branches: throughout the city.

Entertaining

Balloon, party & joke shops

Balloon & Kite Company
613 Garratt Lane, SW18 4SU (8946 5962/ www.balloonandkite.com). Earlsfield rail. **Open** 9am-6pm Mon-Fri; 9am-5.30pm Sat. **Credit** MC, V.
The sky's the limit at this shop, which sells a fantastic variety of balloons in many colours, shapes and sizes. Everything from sculptures to bouquets made out of the inflatables can be arranged to suit the occasion; the company can even organise your own personal balloon drop. Kites are the other forte, with a colourful selection ranging from simple models for kids to professional stunt kites, alongside a range of party-related accessories.
Mail order.

The Balloon Shop
332 Baker Street, Enfield, Middx EM1 3LH (8363 2670). Gordon Hill rail then W8 bus. **Open** 9.30am-5.30pm Mon-Fri; 9am-6pm Sat; 10am-1pm Sun. **Credit** MC, V.
Personalised and themed balloons are the order of the day here. Hand-painted designs and messages can be added to balloons of all shapes and sizes, and there's also a small range of cards and party-related accessories.

Circus Circus
176 Wandsworth Bridge Road, SW6 2UQ (7731 4128/www.partysource.co.uk). Fulham Broadway tube. **Open** 10am-6pm Mon-Sat. **Credit** AmEx, MC, V.
An extensive and high-quality assortment of accessories to get your party started, from balloons and party poppers to glitter balls and masks. There's also a decent stock of themed costumes for hire (prices start at £25 for three days), plus bubble machines, bouncy castles and a bucking bronco.
Mail order.

Just Balloons
7434 3039/www.justballoons.com. **Credit** AmEx, MC, V.
This mail-order company specialises in multicoloured, helium-filled or gift-wrapped rubber balloons. Teddies, champagne and chocolates can be included if desired, as well as personalised messages and novelty gifts. Just Balloons can also decorate a venue for a special occasion, or arrange a balloon drop for an outdoor event.

Non-Stop Party Shop
214-216 Kensington High Street, W8 7RG (7937 7200/www.nonstopparty.co.uk). High Street Kensington tube. **Open** 9.30am-6pm Mon-Sat; 11am-5pm Sun. **Credit** MC, V.
All your party needs, from hooters (£7.99) to large sparkly 'Happy Birthday' banners (£2.99-£5.99), are sold here. There's also a concise selection of fancy dress masks (75p-£8.99) to complement various costumes (from £10). To mark a special occasion, you can take advantage of the personalised balloon service, and the shop also stocks a range of fireworks all year round.
Mail order.
For branches see index.

Oscar's Den
127-129 Abbey Road, NW6 4SL (7328 6683/ www.oscarsden.com). Swiss Cottage tube/West Hampstead tube/rail. **Open** 9.30am-5.30pm Mon-Sat; 10am-2pm Sun. **Credit** AmEx, MC, V.
Staff at Oscar's Den will take the strain out of organising an event. Considering their clients have included Mick Jagger and the Government (they've twice arranged the traditional children's party at Downing Street), they should know what's what. Everything from the invitations to the entertainment (balloons, bubbles, bouncy castles) can be arranged, including party packs. Fireworks (£5-£100) and costumes are sold too.

Party Party
11 Southampton Road, NW5 4JS (7267 9084/ www.partypartyuk.com). Chalk Farm tube/Gospel Oak rail. **Open** 9.30am-5.30pm Mon-Sat. **Credit** MC, V.
Silly string, party poppers, balloons (including helium hire from £30) and confetti are just a few examples of the myriad party goods sold here. Fancy dress paraphernalia (including wigs, face paints, masks and fairy wings) is also up for grabs alongside gift wrap and cards. A few doors down, the shop at No.3 sells a fine range of fireworks.

Party Superstore
268 Lavender Hill, SW11 1LJ (7924 3210/ www.partysuperstores.co.uk). Clapham Junction rail. **Open** 9am-6pm Mon-Wed, Fri, Sat; 9am-7pm Thur; 10.30am-4.30pm Sun. **Credit** AmEx, MC, V.
Stacked to the ceiling with all manner of party goodies, this shop is useful for anyone organising a bash. Party poppers, bags of 100 balloons (£12.99), pig make-up kits (£2.99) and mermaid sets (£14.99) are among the novelty items. Party bags, piñatas and cake decorations are also sold, and Party Superstore offers a wide choice of costumes for sale and hire alongside bridal shoes and a range of dancewear.
Mail order.

Preposterous Presents
262 Upper Street, N1 2UQ (7226 4166). Highbury & Islington tube/rail. **Open** 10am-6pm Mon-Sat. **Credit** MC, V.
A quirky shop full of all kinds of party goods and funny novelties such as plastic spiders, nodding pigs and a fair few saucy cards. Fancy dress is also a predominant feature here, with stage make-up, latex heads and stick-on wizards' beards (£8.99), plus plenty of wigs and accessories (feather boas, cowboy hats) to try on for size.

Mail order

If the thought of scouring the high street in your search for party gear seems like a fate worse than death, don't fret – help is at hand. The **Party Pieces** (01635 201 844, www.partypieces.co.uk) brochure is filled with tableware, fancy dress costumes and much else besides. Best of all, your chosen products can be delivered directly to your door.

Party organisers

See also above **Oscar's Den**. With over 20 years' experience, **Twizzle** (8789 3232, www. twizzle.co.uk) has a team of party experts who can arrange magicians, jugglers and singers, as well as all the relevant equipment – from party packs and seating to bouncy castles. Catering can also be taken care of, whether you want themed fare or novelty cakes for a children's birthday do or posh canapés for a sophisticated soirée. Phone for prices.

Entertainment

DJs, discos & karaoke

For DJ equipment and PA system hire, *see also* chapter **Music**.

Young's Disco Centre
2 Malden Road, NW5 3HL (7485 1115/ www.youngsdisco.com). Chalk Farm tube. **Open** by appointment only. **Credit** AmEx, MC, V.
Young's showroom has a good choice of disco equipment to hire. Turntables, PA systems, CD players, amplifiers, karaoke machines and coloured lighting are all here. DJs can be hired (from £200) to liven things up with karaoke and dancing competitions.

Entertainment agencies

Cabaret Casino Associates
01932 455 902/www.cabaretcasino.co.uk. **Phone enquiries** 24hrs daily. **No credit cards.**
The guys at Cabaret Casino have previously decked out James Bond film sets (*GoldenEye* and *The World Is Not Enough*) and can likewise transform your venue (whether a lounge or a conference room) into an authentic gambling den. Casino tables, slot machines, professional croupiers and even a Wheel of Fortune can be hired. Scalextric tracks and bingo machines (complete with bingo callers) can also be booked. Phone to check prices and mention you're a *Time Out* reader for 10% discount.

Dark Blues Management
01582 842 226/www.darkblues.co.uk. **Open** 9.30am-5.30pm Mon-Fri. **No credit cards.**
Whether you want a strolling minstrel or a saxophonist, Dark Blues can source and provide just about any entertainment to suit an occasion. Jazz musicians, pianists, tribute bands, DJs and magicians are among the acts on its books. The company's name comes from its ever-popular covers band – the MD is also the bandleader. Phone for a full list of entertainers and quotes.

Jo Peters Management
56 Macready House, 75 Crawford Street, W1H 5LP (7724 6555/www.jopeters.biz). Baker Street tube. **Open** 9am-5pm Mon-Fri. **No credit cards.**
This firm can supply a wide variety of acts – from magicians and cabaret singers to comedians and dancers, as well as after-dinner speakers, for all types of celebration. Big names on the books include Angus Deayton and Jonathan Ross.

Nostalgia Amusements
8398 2141/www.nostalgia-hire.co.uk. **Phone enquiries** 9am-6pm daily. **No credit cards.**
An impressive choice of authentic vintage amusements can be hired from this firm's large stock: pinball tables (from the 1950s), retro games, one-arm bandits and classic jukeboxes. The Victorian amusement parlour boasts a laughing policeman and distorting mirrors, as well as attendants dressed in period costume.

Peter Johnson Entertainments
01580 754 822/www.peterjohnson.co.uk. **Phone enquiries** 9am-5.30pm Mon-Fri. **No credit cards.**
This agency can organise lively entertainment to suit any event, whether it be a small family celebration or a lavish company shindig. As well as comedians and musicians, Peter Johnson Entertainments can provide body-painted human statues, a one-man band (from £240) and a wide choice of fairground rides.

Music

Juke Box Junction
12 Toneborough, Abbey Road, NW8 0BL (7328 6206). St John's Wood tube. **Open** by appointment 9am-5pm Mon-Fri. **No credit cards.**
Michael Flynn has two 1970s Seeburg jukeboxes for hire at £275 a night. Hand over a £50 deposit, choose a playlist of 50 records from his impressive selection of tunes and you're set up for a party.

Latin Touch Entertainments

Fatima Community Centre, Commonwealth Avenue, W12 7QR (8740 9020/www.latintouch. com). **Phone enquiries** 10am-6pm Mon-Fri. **No credit cards.**

For a wide variety of South American music, from Cuban folk to Brazilian salsa and Mexican jazz. Artists are UK-based, but the agency can also book well-known Latin American stars to perform at weddings, private parties and corporate functions.

London Music Agency

01277 633030/www.londonmusicagency.co.uk. **Phone enquiries** 10am-6pm Mon-Fri. **No credit cards.**

LMA can provide all kinds of entertainment. Steel bands, guitarists, vocal ensembles, function bands, banjo players, stilt walkers, male voice choirs, magicians, harpists and casinos are a mere taster of what's offered. Prices start from around £150 for a vocalist.

Music Management

PO Box 1105, SW1X 2DX (7823 1111). **Phone enquiries** 9am-6pm Mon-Fri. **No credit cards.**

With nearly two decades of experience behind them, the people at Music Management (all of whom are professional musicians) cover most tastes. They can organise acts for both large and small functions and budgets.

The Musicians' Union

60-62 Clapham Road, SW9 0JJ (7582 5566/ www.musiciansunion.org.uk). **Phone enquiries** 9.30am-5.30pm Mon-Fri. **Credit** MC, V.

Founded in 1893, the Musicians' Union works to protect the interests of its members up and down the country. Its *London Directory of Acts* provides a diverse list of artists and should be available to the general public by late 2005.

Sacconi String Quartet

07941 053 696/01634 826 359/www.sacconi. com. **Phone enquiries only. No credit cards.**

This talented quartet provides music for occasions ranging from formal concerts and weddings to private parties and corporate functions. The group's flexible repertoire includes work from composers and bands as diverse as Puccini, the Beatles and the Verve. The quartet has even played for the Queen, and at Elton John's White Tie and Tiara ball. Prices start at £450 for the first two hours and £60 for every hour thereafter.

Fancy dress

Other shops in this chapter also sell fancy dress costumes. Vintage fashion stores (*see chapter* **Retro & Second-hand**) are also excellent sources of inspiration.

Angels

119 Shaftesbury Avenue, WC2H 8AE (7836 5678/www.fancydress.com). Leicester Square or Tottenham Court Road tube. **Open** 9am-5.30pm Mon-Fri. **Credit** AmEx, MC, V.

Costumes that look like they're straight out of Hollywood films – from *Star Wars* to *Chicago* – have all found their way to this multi-storey fancy dress den. Elizabethan, Victorian, Georgian and Regency outfits contrast with the frills of the 1970s, and rock-and-roll clobber of the 1950s. Hire prices for a complete outfit start at £82.25 (including VAT), with a £100 refundable deposit required. *Mail order.*

Contemporary Wardrobe

The Horse Hospital, Colonnade, WC1N 1HX (7713 7370/www.thehorsehospital.com). Russell Square tube. **Open** 10am-6pm Mon-Sat; appointment only for hire. **Credit** MC, V.

Roger Burton's collection has been 25 years in the making and exceeds 15,000 garments, from 1940 to the present day. Outfits include vintage Yves Saint Laurent and Givenchy pieces. Contemporary Wardrobe also holds a great choice of shoes, underwear and jewellery. Prices start at £70 plus VAT for three days.

The Costume Studio

Montgomery House, 161 Balls Pond Road, N1 4BG (7388 4481/www.costumestudio.co.uk). Highbury & Islington tube/rail/30, 38, 56, 277 bus. **Open** 9.30am-6pm Mon-Fri; 10am-5pm Sat. **Credit** AmEx, MC, V.

With over 40,000 costumes to choose from, this temple to fancy dress is sure to feed your imagination. Period costumes covering every era and an impressive selection of sci-fi creations are among the most interesting clothing. Hire costs from £65 to £90 (plus VAT) for a week.

Escapade

150 Camden High Street, NW1 0NE (7485 7384/www.escapade.co.uk). Camden Town tube. **Open** 10am-7pm Mon-Fri; 10am-6pm Sat; noon-5pm Sun. **Credit** AmEx, MC, V.

It may be a small shop, but Escapade has over 2,000 costumes for hire, with everything from classic clown outfits to elaborate period designs. The merchandise doesn't stop there – latex heads of Beckham and Prince Charles sit alongside a small selection of fireworks, a huge choice of wigs (from £5) and novelty party buys (plastic jumbo ears or water-squirting bow ties, £2.99 each). Prices for costume hire range from £30 to £50 for four days, with a refundable deposit of £50 required. *Mail order.*

Harlequin

254 Lee High Road, SE13 5PR (8852 0193). Hither Green rail/Lewisham rail/DLR. **Open** 10am-5.30pm Mon, Tue, Thur, Sat; 10am-1pm Wed; 10am-6pm Fri. **Credit** MC, V.

Circus Circus. See p198.

LEISURE

Harlequin has an exciting collection of 1970s outfits and accessories that will kit you out for the most garish of evenings. The collection of 500 costumes includes multicoloured patent knee-high boots, Bay City Roller-style tartan suits and fantastically tasteless Abba-inspired sequinned numbers. Three-day hire starts at £14 (plus £50 deposit). Kids' costumes and a decent choice of party goods are also here.

Knutz
1 Russell Street, WC2B 5JD (7836 3117). Covent Garden tube. **Open** 11am-8pm Mon-Sat. **Credit** MC, V.
Supermodel aprons (£9.99), replica Oscars (£9.99) and pirate beards (£4.50) are just a few examples of what's for sale at this shop. For more diehard fancy dressers, there are not only costumes (mostly priced at around £20 for a full outfit) but a wide variety of hats, wigs (from £8) and rubber masks (Prince Charles and Camilla, both £20), bat capes and fairy wings (both £9.99).

Fireworks

Many of the shops in this chapter sell fireworks, including **Non-stop Party Shop**, **Party Party** and **Oscar's Den**. The following three companies can organise professional fired shows for events and weddings, as well as smaller scale displays: **Dynamic Fireworks** (Unit 18, Peartree Business Centre, Stanway, Colchester, Essex CO3 0JN, 01206 762 123, www.dynamicfireworks.co.uk); **Fantastic Fireworks** (Rocket Park, Pepperstock, Luton, Beds LU1 4LL, 0800 511 511, www.fantastic-fireworks.co.uk); and **Le Maitre** (6 Forval Close, Wandle Way, Mitcham, Surrey CR4 4NE, 8646 2222, www.lemaitreltd.com), whose events start at £1,000 and rocket into the stratosphere.

Marquee hire

The following both offer marquee hire from around £500. Extras such as catering, flooring, lighting and entertainment can also be arranged: **Carrara Quality Marquees** (Iona House, Humber Road, NW2 6EN, 8452 8558, www.carraramarquees.co.uk) and **Field & Lawn Marquees** (Unit 2, Gresham Way, SW19 8ED, 8944 9633, www.fieldandlawn.com).

Special events

There are plenty of companies to help you organise your special event. **Confetti** (*see p63*) is great for invites, tableware and balloons. **Network 7** (PO Box 191, Worcester Park, KT4 7XA, 07000 123 455, www.limousine hireheathrow.com) can arrange stretch limos and people carriers. Singing monks to string quartets are the domain of the **Wedding Music Company & Music For Business** (144 Greenwich High Road, SE10 8NN, 8293 3392, www.weddingmusic.co.uk). **Perrys the Wedding Company** (61C Station Road, Winchmore Hill, N21 3NB, 8360 1144, www.perrys-weddings.com) can deal with everything from the wedding list to ordering the cake and flowers, and booking the entertainment, photographer and venue. **Keith Anderson** (21 Carnarvon Road, Redland, Bristol BS6 7DT, 0800 389 8568, www.crispandcheerful.co.uk) is a professional speech writer who will find the words to suit most occasions, from weddings to social, political or corporate events.

To record the entire event, contact the **Institute of Videographers** (PO Box 625, Loughton, Essex IG10 3GZ, 0845 741 3626, www.iov.co.uk), which can send you a free guide on what to look for when choosing a videographer, and recommend a list of professionals in the field.

Gifts

You will come across other gift ideas throughout the book, particularly in chapters **Jewellery**, **Design**, **Art & Crafts**, **Books**, **Antiques** and **Home Accessories**. Many shops will wrap and send a gift within the UK for an extra charge, though you should allow a few days for it to get there. Most florists will deliver flowers to the rest of the UK (or even abroad); *see chapter* **Gardens & Flowers**. For guidance on where to buy the clichéd – but always appreciated – box of special chocolates, *see chapter* **Food**.

American Retro
35 Old Compton Street, W1D 5JX (7734 3477/ www.americanretro.com). Leicester Square tube. **Open** 10.30am-7pm Mon-Wed, Fri; 10.30am-7.30pm Thur; 10.15am-7pm Sat; 1-6pm Sun. **Credit** AmEx, DC, MC, V.
American Retro is a good source of fun and fashionable gifts, offering a mix of trendy T-shirts, underwear and sunglasses, plus art, design and lifestyle books. Fashion labels include Fred Perry, Seal Kay, Bikkemberg, Dolce & Gabbana and D&G underwear and swimwear, plus there's a wide selection of sought-after watches by the likes of Philippe Starck and U-Boat. Some attractive design items also feature, such as retro clocks and cameras. On the more affordable side are novelty presents such as fairy lights and humorous erotica. *Mail order.*

Anything Left-Handed
57 Brewer Street, W1F 9UL (7437 3910/www. anythingleft-handed.co.uk). Piccadilly Circus tube. **Open** 10am-6pm Mon-Fri; 10am-5.30pm Sat. **Credit** MC, V.
Established in 1968, this diminutive Soho shop is a crusader for lefties. Its broad collection includes practical goods, such as specialist pens, knives and corkscrews, as well as books exploring the medical origins of left-handedness and advice for left-handed children. The extensive internet service ensures all needs are met; left-handed music books, guitars and golf clubs are available to order. Even the shop's brochure opens from the left. *Mail order (8770 3722).*

The Ark
161 Stoke Newington Road, N16 8BP (7275 9311). Rectory Road rail/67, 76, 149, 243 bus. **Open** 11am-6pm Tue-Sat. **Credit** AmEx, MC, V.
The Ark stocks a diverse array of cute, gift-friendly products, including Penguin Books mugs, toiletries from the Celtic Herb Company and Lothantique, and LSA glassware. All pockets are catered for – at the cheaper end are Lily-Flame candles and soft toys from Russ Teddies and Lilydoll, while on the more expensive side, though still good value, are chandeliers, starting from £79.

BBC World Service Shop
Bush House, Strand, WC2B 4PH (7557 2576/ www.bbcshop.com). Temple tube. **Open** 10am-6pm Mon-Fri; 10am-5.30pm Sat; noon-5pm Sun. **Credit** AmEx, MC, V.
Books, recordings and DVDs covering the Beeb's output over the years can all be found in this compact shop. Every genre of TV programme is covered: sitcoms, dramas, documentaries and live performances. More recent comedy hits such as *The Office* and *Little Britain* sit alongside classics such as *Only Fools and Horses*. There are also Alan Bennett audio tapes, Delia Smith cookery bibles, audio tapes of famous political speeches (Churchill, Tony Benn et al) and DVDs of Michael Palin's travel documentaries, plus the accompanying books. *Mail order.*
For branch see index.

Chain Reaction
208 Chalk Farm Road, NW1 8AH (7284 2866). Camden Town tube. **Open** 10am-6pm Mon-Fri; 10am-7pm Sat, Sun. **Credit** AmEx, MC, V.
Kitsch and comedy are the themes of this small shop, which draws the crowds from nearby

Camden Market (*see p15*), so expect Che Guevara doormats, Beatles mugs and the like. Joke items such as 'Irish accent' breath spray and pig-throwing catapults (many under £5) make cheap 'n' cheeky gifts. It's also a student's heaven as fairy lights and funky beaded curtains start at just £9.99. There are humorous cards and wrapping paper, while a selection of Betty Boop figures will satisfy any retro-cartoon connoisseur. *Mail order.*

Dulwich Trader

9-11 Croxted Road, SE21 8SZ (8761 3457). West Dulwich rail. **Open** 9.30am-6pm Mon-Sat; 11am-5pm Sun. **Credit** AmEx, MC, V.
Under the same ownership as Ed (*see below*), Dulwich Trader has an interesting array of furniture, clothing, ceramics and textiles. On our latest trip, we were taken by Cath Kidston make-up bags, tea towels and stationery, Lulu Guinness bags, shoes and perfume, and smellies by L'Occitane, Crabtree & Evelyn and Neal's Yard. There's an excellent range of womenswear, including interesting, well-priced Danish brands such as Day Birger et Mikkelsen, Malene Birger and Jackpot. Furniture adds to the mix – we saw a beautiful French writing desk on our latest visit (£795). Baby clothes and booties are also sold, and jewellery includes the ever-popular Lola Rose label. Prices are fairly high-end, but there are designer key rings and embroidered hand-held mirrors for under £5.
For branch (Tomlinsons) see index.

Eccentrics

3-5 Fortis Green Road, N10 3HP (8883 8030/ www.eccentrics.co.uk). Highgate tube then 34, 134 bus or East Finchley tube then 102, 234 bus. **Open** 10am-6pm Mon-Sat (11am-5pm Sun in Nov & Dec). **Credit** MC, V.
This family-run shop is a showcase for contemporary British design. Stock is constantly changing, but personalised cushions, rattles and keepsake boxes make great christening presents, while photo albums, plates, and the innovative range of lamps and clocks are popular for weddings. *Mail order.*

Ed

41 North Cross Road, SE22 9ET (8299 6938). East Dulwich rail. **Open** 9.30am-6pm Mon-Sat; 11am-5pm Sun. **Credit** AmEx, MC, V.
Beyond the baskets of cheap and cheerful gift toys, this shop has an eclectic range of high-quality gifts, including homeware, clothes for men and women, Umbro photo frames and albums, and a selection of fine beauty products, including Neal's Yard and Cow Shed. Other highlights include Roberts retro radios (£99.95), available in all colours, Jeffrey Fulvimari vanity cases (£15), great for a girlie gift, and funky knitted slippers for £16. The clothing range for both sexes is strong, including labels such as Great Plains, Pink Soda, Noa Noa and Boxfresh.
For branch (Tomlinsons) see index.

Edwards & Todd

25A Museum Street, WC1A 1JU (7636 4650). Holborn tube. **Open** 9.30am-6.30pm Mon-Sat. **Credit** AmEx, MC, V.
This charming shop is a treasure trove of arty gifts, with a Bloomsbury location that draws both tourists and local office workers. The ever-changing stock includes Bath House beauty products, soft toys and scarves, but the beautiful selection of well-priced jewellery (starting from £2.95) is this shop's forte. Vintage glassware, mirrors and oil lamps (from £39) are also sold. *Mail order.*

Family Tree

53 Exmouth Market, EC1R 4QL (7278 1084/ www.familytreeshop.co.uk). Bus 19, 38, 341. **Open** 10am-6pm Mon-Fri; 11am-5pm Sat. **Credit** MC, V.
Former jeweller Takako Copeland owns and runs this little emporium of quirky design, where items of personal adornment jostle for attention with home accessories, which are as likely made by Japanese artists as craftsmen in Clerkenwell. Best known are the washi lampshades (from £19.80), made from tough Japanese rice paper, and printed with patterns from 19th-century kimonos. Then there are stuffed toys – giraffes, say, covered in vintage 1970s fabric; soft leather caterpillar belts (£80) from Morocco; handwoven wool bags, with bamboo handles, by Maria La Rosa (£152); and delicate silver jewellery by Takako herself, often featuring coin pearls and crystal (earrings £26). Best value of all is a range of natural toiletries by Wickle, perfumed with irrestible musk mallow or scented tea leaf (perfume tester bottle, £3.50). Occasional exhibitions by guest artists highlight environmental issues.

Farrago

25-27 Lacy Road, SW15 1NH (8788 0162). Putney Bridge tube/Putney rail. **Open** 10am-6pm Mon-Sat; noon-5pm Sun. **Credit** MC, V.
This friendly neighbourhood shop has an eclectic range of goods, from funky deckchairs to ethnic candles and photo frames. With a wide selection of wedding and baby gifts and some gorgeous gift-wrap, ribbon and cards, this local spot is a godsend when you need to choose and wrap a last-minute present. Alessi goods, glass vases and coffee sets can get pricey, and even an espresso-cup-and-saucer ensemble starts at £8.

Grace & Favour

35 North Cross Road, SE22 9ET (8693 4400). East Dulwich rail/176, 185 bus. **Open** 9.30am-6pm Mon-Sat; 11am-5pm Sun. **Credit** AmEx, MC, V.
Rose Ratcliffe's Aladdin's cave of a shop offers a welcome antidote to the usual mass-produced merchandise – and it's hard to walk out empty-handed. Stock comes from over 200 suppliers, many of them independent designer/makers. A feminine atmosphere prevails ('It's the poor woman's the Cross,' jokes the owner, referring to the girlie boudoir in Notting Hill; *see p36*) and goods range from hand-printed suede photo albums to antique bird cages and unusual women's clothes, such as hand-dyed silk skirts, tops by British-based Sula, or embroidered pieces from London label Salt. This shop is good on kids' stuff too, including adorable hand-knitted baby sweaters. Quilts, cushions, cult Alison van der Lande bags, vintage jewellery, Johnny Loves Rosie hair accessories and moccasin slippers complete the picture. All budgets are covered, from £4.95 for French soaps to £120 for a Salt dress. As we went to press, there were plans for a third shop.
For branch see index.

Huttons

29 Northcote Road, SW11 1NJ (7223 5523). Clapham Junction rail. **Open** 9.30am-6pm Mon-Sat; 11am-5pm Sun. **Credit** AmEx, MC, V.
Huttons stocks a wide range of Alessi goods, plus a selection of sleek Scandinavian homeware – by the likes of Marimekko – that makes such good presents. The front of the shop is attractively arranged to showcase fun gift ideas (we particularly liked the Guardian Angel charms, £7.95), funky jewellery (starting at £9.95) and arty cards and giftwrap, while in the back is the shop's own range of furniture (generally in teak and oak) and clothing by Danish label Saint Tropez. Coffee-table books and Umbro photo frames are also sold. *Mail order.*
For branches see index.

LEISURE

Ian Logan Design Company. See p202.

Ian Logan Design Company

42 Charterhouse Square, EC1M 6EA (7600 9888/ www.ian-logan.co.uk). Barbican tube. **Open** 10am-6.30pm Mon-Fri; 11am-5pm Sat. **Credit** MC, V.
This space started life as Ian Logan's design studio, but is now a chic shop open to the public. The eclectic wares have one thing in common – they'd all look great in one of the area's loft apartments. An Aerolatte coffee maker (£34.95), Moleskine notebooks (from £6.95) or a leather-sheathed hunter's flask – complete with four cups (£52.50) – all make attractive and practical presents. There are also bath products by Côté Bastide, jewellery by independent designers, leather bags by high-profile Dutch designer Hester van Eeghen and some fantastic collectable model aeroplanes by retired Tate & Lyle tinsmith Jim Knubley.
Mail order.

Kiwifruits New Zealand Shop

6-7 Royal Opera Arcade, Pall Mall, SW1Y 4UY (7930 4587/www.kiwifruitsnzshop.com). Piccadilly Circus tube. **Open** 9am-5.30pm Mon-Fri; 10am-4pm Sat. **Credit** MC, V.
A slice of Kiwi country in London, this shop sells a selection of imported comfort foods and newspapers, but it also has a good selection of gifts. There is jewellery crafted from jade, bone, Pacific pearl and paua, and scarves trimmed with ostrich feathers. The book selection ranges from coffee-table collections of stunning New Zealand photography to literature and Maori history. The obligatory All Black paraphernalia, which includes official T-shirts, souvenirs and a tub of All Black face paint, completes this Antipodean tribute.
Mail order.

The Lucky Parrot

2 Bellevue Parade, Bellevue Road, SW17 7EQ (8672 7168/www.lucky-parrot.co.uk). Balham or Tooting Bec tube/Wandsworth Common rail. **Open** *Jan-Nov* 10am-6pm Mon-Sat. *Dec* 10am-8pm Mon-Sat; noon-5pm Sun. **Credit** MC, V.

This down-to-earth shop is named after the real-life resident parrot that welcomes customers in from the front window. Stock includes endearing personal gifts (such as 'Thank you for being my teacher' bookmarks), a good world music CD collection and colourful picnic sets (from £25). We also liked the selection of gifts for men, ranging from silk ties (£35) to office golf sets and cufflinks. Photo albums and Moleskine journals are key gift items, as are the chunky frames and stylish sunglasses.

Map

93 Junction Road, N19 5QX (7687 4005/ www.mapgiftshop.co.uk). Archway tube. **Open** *Sept-Dec* 10am-6.30pm Mon-Fri; 10am-6pm Sat; 11.30am-5.30pm Sun. *Jan-Aug* 10am-6.30pm Mon-Fri; 10am-6pm Sat. **Credit** AmEx, MC, V.
This charming shop shines out on this less-than-lovely stretch of road. Highlights among the hotchpotch of goods include the contemporary silver and crystal jewellery (with a men's selection), smellies from the Croft + Croft range, picture frames, candlesticks and greeting cards designed by local artists. On our latest visit we liked the 'aroma cushion' that warms up and soothes with its scent, and the kit for taking a mould and framing your baby's footprint (£31.95).
Mail order.

Obsessions

2 Hay's Galleria, Tooley Street, SE1 2HD (7403 2374/www.obsessions.co.uk). London Bridge tube/ rail. **Open** 10.30am-6.30pm Mon-Sat. **Credit** MC, V.
The recipient of a present from this stylish shop will probably think you've spent considerably more than you have. There's a plethora of sleek accessories, many in chrome or shiny metal, such as photo frames, cufflinks, perfume atomisers, ashtrays and key rings, all at highly reasonable prices – many under a tenner, some for just a few pounds. Boys' toys such as a mini tool kit and office golf are useful for hard-to-buy-for fathers and brothers. Cheeky cards line the back wall.

Oliver Bonas

137 Northcote Road, SW11 6PX (7223 5223/ www.oliverbonas.com). Clapham Junction rail. **Open** 10am-6.30pm Mon-Fri; 10am-6pm Sat; 11am-5pm Sun. **Credit** MC, V.
As befits its Northcote Road location, Oliver Bonas stocks classy items, yet service is down to earth and welcoming. The shop feels like a cross between a gift store and a boutique, with girlie clothing taking centre stage and gifts arranged around it and in the small back area. Silk-covered photo albums and attractive notebooks make affordable presents, while the irresistible silk kimonos (£49) fall more in the push-the-boat-out range. Cute leather baby booties are £16, while for grown-ups there are fun patterned wellies. In the boudoir-style room at the back, you can browse bedroom accessories or peruse the furniture catalogue from a chaise longue – prices start from £600 for wardrobes, beautiful screens and beds.
Mail order.
Branches: throughout the city.

Rosie Brown

238 St Paul's Road, N1 2LJ (7359 1614). Highbury & Islington tube/rail. **Open** 11am-7pm Mon-Sat; noon-4pm Sun. **Credit** M, V.
With so many pricey interiors shops and boutiques in the vicinity of Upper Street, it's good to see an affordable lifestyle store up past Highbury Corner. Rosie Brown may not have the gloss and polish of some of its N1 competitors, but the mood is refreshingly unpretentious. Stock is fairly evenly split between home and fashion accessories. Exotic domestic trimmings are sourced from around the globe, including exquisite handmade patchwork quilts from India (£185), Vietnamese tea sets (£30), Venetian-style mirrors (from £40) and etched-glass jewellery boxes (from £20). There's also vintage-vibe womenswear by Australian designer Olga de Polga, and bags and jewellery from a stable of independent London-based designers.

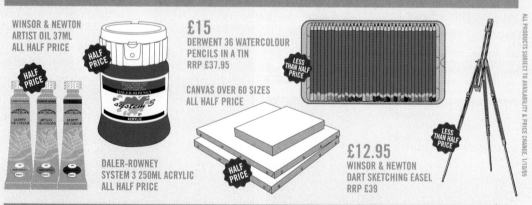

Space EC1

25 Exmouth Market, EC1R 4QL (7837 1344).
Bus 19, 38, 341. **Open** 9.30am-6pm Mon-Fri;
11am-5pm Sat. **Credit** AmEx, MC, V.
A good source of gifts, or treats for yourself, Space
EC1 sells decorative homeware, such as glassware
by Leonardo Joseph Joseph (we liked the glass
place mats and coasters), as well as fun items such
as tea sets (£27), cocktail books and whodunnit
mystery games to liven up a party. Butterfly dip
trays and giant ornamental flamingos provide the
kitsch factor, and smellies come care of London-
based company Croft + Croft.

Tessa Fantoni

73 Abbeville Road, SW4 9JN (8673 1253/
www.tessafantoni.com). Clapham Common or
Clapham South tube. **Open** 10am-6pm Mon-Sat;
10am-2pm Sun. **Credit** MC, V.
Tessa Fantoni is best known for her photograph
albums, box files and desk accessories covered in
beautiful patterned paper, but her shop has a
variety of giftable goods, including frames,
beautiful clocks, novelty 'handbag' lamps,
toiletries by Floris and Neal's Yard, and a wide
range of jewellery, many by independent
designers. Cards and giftwrap are on hand to
complete your offering.
Mail order.

Tintin Shop

34 Floral Street, WC2E 9DJ (7836 1131/www.
thetintinshop.uk.com). Covent Garden tube. **Open**
10am-5.30pm Mon-Sat. **Credit** AmEx, DC, MC, V.
This shop does what is says on the Tintin: here
you'll find a comprehensive range of books
starring the quiffed Belgian boy reporter, plus
cassette and DVD sets (covering all 21 stories) and
posters (available framed). There are also T-shirts
for both kids and adults, plush Snowy toys and
stationery. While those on a pocket-money budget
can find something here (exercise books and
plastic-figure key rings go for a few pounds), resin
collectibles of the 'cast' can shoot up to over £200.
Mail order.

Treehouse

7 Park Road, N8 8TE (8341 4326). Finsbury
Park tube/rail then W7 bus or Highgate tube then
W3 bus. **Open** 10am-6pm Mon-Sat; noon-4.30pm
Sun. **Credit** MC, V.
Treehouse is known for unusual products sourced
from all over the globe. On a recent visit, we saw
silver jewellery from Mexico, embroidered
cushions from India and Venetian glass jewellery,
plus books on a wide range of subjects. Closer to
home, there are Scottish beauty products from the
Arran Aromatics Apothecary range.

Wilde Ones

283 King's Road, SW3 5EW (7376 7982/
www.wildeones.com). Sloane Square tube.
Open 10am-6pm Mon-Fri; 10am-7pm Sat;
noon-6pm Sun. **Credit** AmEx, DC, MC, V.
Chock-full of healing crystals, incense sticks and
essential oils, Wilde Ones is the place to head for the
New Ager on your shopping list. Items are good
quality, from genuine Native American turquoise
and coral jewellery, moccasins and fringed boots to
colourful tie-dyed garments from California. There's
also a wide range of books on such subjects as
astrology and crystal healing, tarot cards, and CDs
across the relaxation and world music spectrum.

Zest

18 Broadwick Street, W1F 8HS (7437 3846/
www.zestessentials.com). Oxford Circus tube.
Open 9.30am-7pm Mon-Fri; 10am-6.30pm Sat.
Credit AmEx, MC, V.
Zest is bursting with novelty items and fun
skincare products. 'Bitch' and 'Slut' body-wash
powders (in dinky retro detergent boxes) are
upfront, but there are more easy-going Elvis alarm
clocks and fur-lined washing-up gloves. There's
also a selection of top-notch toiletries such as
Neal's Yard, I Coloniali and Burt's Bees, as well as
a bona fide pharmacy, which fills prescriptions and
stocks basics such as toothpaste. The combination
is certainly unusual, but seems to work.

Museum shops

No longer just places to grab a boring
old souvenir pencil or rubber, these
days London's museum shops are
a rich resource for original, culturally
interesting gifts. Most have excellent
websites if you want to save yourself
a visit.

The **Design Museum Shop** (Shad
Thames, SE1 2ED, 0870 833 9955,
www.designmuseum.org), the most
cutting-edge of London's museum
shops, has an exciting selection of
items for sale by big names, as well
as up-and-coming designers. Prime
mid-range gift items include Yoshie
Watanabe and Ryosuke Uehara's vinyl
envelopes that, when filled with water,
turn into attractive vases (£12.95 for
two); sculptural toys created by
young British designer Sam
Buxton (for example,
the MIKROgarden
fold-up sculpture,
£25; *pictured*
below); and
colourful
bags (£35)
from leading
Brazilian
talents
Fernando
and Humberto
Campana. Or go
all out on George
Nelson's Ball &
Spoke clock (£155;
pictured right). Wrap it
all up with signature paper
digitally illustrated by designer
Kam Tang.

As you might expect, the **V&A**'s shop
(Cromwell Road, SW7 2RL (7942 2687,
www.vandashop.co.uk) is packed with
thoroughly elegant gifts: there are art

deco notelet sets (£5.95), a 'Fashion
History' silk scarf adorned with
designs from New York fashion
illustrator Ruben Toledo (£20) and
Coalbrookdale jewellery inspired by
Christopher Dresser's iron designs
(from £15). Coffee-table fashion
books abound.

The **Tate Britain** (Mill Bank, SW1P
4RG, 7887 8876, www.tate.org.uk) has
a vast range of art prints and there's
now an easy-to-use online ordering
service. The shop also stocks some
quirky gifts – 'paint-it-yourself' kits for
budding artists or exclusive Terry Frost
mobiles (£25).

Somerset House (The Strand,
WC2R 1LA, 7845 4600, www.somerset-
house.org.uk) has three shops
for its three collections.
The Gilbert Collection
stocks the
eyecatchingly
colourful Pure
Fabrication
range (£15-
£18), which
has some
charming
sparkly
butterfly and
dragonfly
brooches. The
Courtauld and
Hermitage shops
are more geared
towards classic gift
fodder, from impressionist
jigsaws to porcelain tableware.
You're never too old for the gadgets
at the **Science Museum** (Exhibition
Road, SW7 2DD (7942 4499,
www.sciencemuseumstore.com).
Budding Patrick Moores can splash
out on microscopes and
star globes, but the less
scientifically minded will
love the radio-controlled
hovercraft and the
spy calculator.

The **Royal Academy**
(Burlington House,
Piccadilly, W1J 0BD,
7300 5757, www.royal
academy.org.uk) offers
a selection of beautiful
exhibition catalogues
(such as *Matisse: His*
Art and His Textiles,
£21), as well as paint
brushes, ceramics and
jewellery. Fun design-a-
T-shirt kits and modelling
clay are imaginative
treats for the kids, and
prints from the cream
of Britain's artists (David
Hockney, Peter Blake)
make very special –
and correspondingly
expensive – gifts,
from £300.

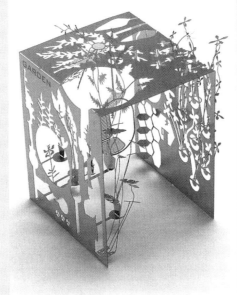

Hobbies & Crafts

Many of the venues listed below, and especially art supply shops, give students a ten per cent discount. For more ideas about workshops and courses, *see chapter* **Design, Art & Crafts**.

Art supplies

Atlantis European

7-9 Plumbers Row, E1 1EQ (7377 8855/www.atlantisart.co.uk). Aldgate East tube. **Open** 9am-6pm Mon-Sat; 10am-5pm Sun. **Credit** AmEx, MC, V.
This enormous warehouse-style shop – among the largest firms of its kind in Europe – specialises in painting equipment. The huge stock encompasses paint, paper, brushes, easels, varnishes, pigments, frames and made-to-measure canvases. Definitely worth the trip east.
Mail order.

Cass Art

13 Charing Cross Road, WC2H 0EP (7930 9940/www.cassart.co.uk). Leicester Square tube. **Open** 9.30am-6.30pm Mon-Sat; 11.30am-5.30pm Sun. **Credit** AmEx, MC, V.
You'll find over 20,000 high-quality art products at each branch of this small central London chain. The walls are lined with paints, card, pastels and pencils in every shade you could possibly require. Cass is also very good for artistic accessories, such as artists' chairs or mini wooden mannequins.
For branches see index.

L Cornelissen & Son

105 Great Russell Street, WC1B 3RY (7636 1045/ www.cornelissen.com). Holborn or Tottenham Court Road tube. **Open** 9.30am-5.30pm Mon-Fri; 9.30am-5pm Sat. **Credit** MC, V.
A delightfully old-fashioned shop, seemingly straight out of a period drama, L Cornelissen celebrated 150 years of trading in 2005. Striking displays of paints and brushes fill the walls, and dark wood shelves store everything from art books to cleaning soap for brushes. You'll also find Mussini resin oils, Horadam watercolours, calligraphy equipment, pastels, gouache and, on the counter, feather quills in glass jars.
Mail order.

Cowling and Wilcox

26-28 Broadwick Street, W1F 8HX (7734 9557/ www.cowlingandwilcox.com). Oxford Circus tube. **Open** 9.30am-6.30pm Mon-Sat. **Credit** AmEx, MC, V.
Portfolio supplies, agency books and presentation portfolios are the fortes here, though there's also a strong line in general art and craft materials, plus a vast range of photo display albums and archival storage equipment.
Mail order.

Handover

Unit 8, Leeds Place, Tollington Park, N4 3RF (7272 9624/www.handover.co.uk). Finsbury Park tube/rail. **Open** 8.30am-5pm Mon-Fri. **Credit** AmEx, MC, V.
Handover is what you might call paintbrush paradise, selling every imaginable size and shape of brushes for artists, sign writers, interior designers and make-up artists. Decorating tools and craft equipment are also available, as well as an excellent range of stencilling products for professional and amateur decorators.
Mail order.

Holloway Art & Stationers

222 Holloway Road, N7 8DA (7607 4738). Holloway Road tube. **Open** 9am-6pm Mon-Fri; 10am-5pm Sat. **Credit** AmEx, MC, V.

An impressive range of art and design supplies is crammed into these small premises. At Holloway, space is found for Rotring pens, oil and acrylic paints, ink-jet cartridges, paper and portfolio cases, plus an extensive range of colour pencils.
Mail order.

London Graphic Centre

16-18 Shelton Street, WC2H 9JL (7240 0095/ www.londongraphics.co.uk). Covent Garden or Leicester Square tube. **Open** 9.30am-6pm Mon-Wed, Fri; 9.30am-7pm Thur; 10.30am-6pm Sat. **Credit** AmEx, MC, V.
The London Graphic Centre, a den of alluring fine art and craft equipment, is the kind of place you pop into for a pencil and come out with a bespoke portfolio. Upstairs is the modelling, craft and fine art goods, and downstairs is the portfolio area, where you can have one made to your requirements.
Mail order.
For branches see index.

Paintworks

99-101 Kingsland Road, E2 8AG (7729 7451/ www.paintworks.biz). Old Street tube/rail/26, 35, 67, 149, 242 bus. **Open** 9.30am-5.30pm Mon-Thur, Sat; 9.30am-6.30pm Fri. **Credit** MC, V.
Paintworks stocks a huge variety of paints and pastels, but is exceptionally good for its framing service. Whatever you need, be it the highest quality frame, or a simple kit frame, you'll find it here. Primed and unprimed canvases are available off the roll, and stretched canvases are sold too.
Mail order.

Russell & Chapple

68 Drury Lane, WC2B 5SP (7836 7521/www. randc.net). Covent Garden or Holborn tube. **Open** 9am-5.30pm Mon-Fri. **Credit** AmEx, MC, V.
This hard-to-find basement shop is London's oldest supplier of canvas products to theatres and artists. Originally specialising in theatre drapes and awnings for Covent Garden's theatres, Russell & Chapple now carries an impressive range of artists' canvas, sourcing and importing materials from all over the world. Various other art supplies are sold. Upstairs, sister shop Brodie & Middleton (7836 3289) specialises in scenic pigments and dyes, glitter, face paints and shoe sprays.
Mail order.

Basketry

Jacobs, Young & Westbury

Bridge Road, Haywards Heath, Sussex RH16 1UA (01444 412 411). **Phone enquiries** 9am-5pm Mon-Fri. **Credit** MC, V.
An importer of bamboo, raw cane, rush, willow, and raffia, this firm sells wholesale and to the public. It also stocks goods for the garden, such as screens made from pine, willow, bamboo and cane. Books about chair restoration, basketry and various other crafts are here too.
Mail order.

Beads

The Bead Shop

21A Tower Street, WC2H 9NS (7240 0931/www. beadshop.co.uk). Covent Garden or Leicester Square tube. **Open** *Main shop* 1-6pm Mon; 10.30am-6pm Tue-Fri; 11.30am-5pm Sat. *Basement* 1-5pm Mon; 10.30am-5pm Tue-Fri; 11.30am-4.30pm Sat. **Credit** MC, V.
All your bead needs are met at this spacious two-floor store, where you could spend hours choosing between, say, Swarovski crystal or Indian glass, Chinese porcelain or bone beads. The shop attracts professional designers, but is just as welcoming to

occasional beaders and curious passers-by. The ground floor sells loose beads and tools, while the basement houses wholesale and pricier beads.
Mail order (8553 3240).

Buffy's Beads

2-3 Kingly Court, London, W1B 5PW (7494 2323/www.buffysbeads.com). Leicester Square tube. **Open** 11am-7pm Mon-Sat; noon-6pm Sunday. **Credit** AmEx, MC, V.
Run by a jewellery designer and her husband, this light, airy shop, with strings of beads hanging from the walls like bunting, sells high-quality beads at reasonable prices. You'll find superior beads from Czech crystal to freshwater pearl and sterling silver on sale, with prices starting at £1.20 each.

Creative Beadcraft

20 Beak Street, W1F 9RE (7629 9964/ www.creativebeadcraft.co.uk). Oxford Circus or Piccadilly Circus tube. **Open** 9am-5.15pm Mon-Fri; 10am-5.15pm Sat. **Credit** AmEx, MC, V.
A long-established treasure trove for bead-related hobbyists, Creative Beadcraft imports a variety of beads, sequins, trimmings, imitation pearls and diamanté from all over the world. View the displays, then select your purchases, Argos-style, from catalogues. Fill out an order form, and pay at the counter while staff bring your goods. Find inspiration from the staff wall displays too, for example, on how to 'bling your thing'.
Mail order (01494 778 818).

London Bead Co/ Delicate Stitches

339 Kentish Town Road, NW5 2TJ (0870 203 2323/www.londonbeadco.co.uk). Kentish Town tube/rail. **Open** 9.30am-5.30pm Mon-Sat; 11am-4pm Sun. **Credit** AmEx, MC, V.
On shared premises, these two firms stock all you need for needlecraft and beading. The London Bead Co is a haven for small beads in several hundred colours, including seed, bugle and hex beads. There are also dozens of books on the subject. Delicate Stitches has an enormous choice of hand-dyed silk ribbon, tapestry and embroidery wools. DIY accessories, such as bag handles and purse frames, are also sold.
Mail order.

Candle-making

Candle Makers Supplies

28 Blythe Road, W14 0HA (7602 4031/www. candlemakers.co.uk). Kensington Olympia tube/rail. **Open** 10.30am-6pm Mon-Fri; 10.30am-5pm Sat. **Credit** AmEx, MC, V.
Established in 1969, Candle Makers Supplies sells kits for novices, plus wicks, moulds, waxes, tools and made-to-measure candles for parties and special events. Equipment for silk painting, batik, resin casting and soap-making is sold here too.
Mail order.

Ceramics & mosaics

Mosaic Workshop

1A Princeton Street, WC1R 4AX (7831 0889/ www.mosaicworkshop.com). Chancery Lane or Holborn tube. **Open** 10am-5.30pm Tue-Fri. **Credit** MC, V.
Just about all you'll need for mosaic making is here: books written by two of the shop's owners (Emma Biggs and Tessa Hunkin), glass tiles, kits, tools and materials. The Mermaid indoor glass starter kit is £40. Classes are run at the Holloway Road site.
Mail order.
For branch see index.

Potterycrafts

8-10 Ingate Place, SW8 3NS (7720 0050/ www.potterycrafts.co.uk). Queenstown Road rail. **Open** 9am-5pm Mon-Sat. **Credit** MC, V.
Catering for the professional, educational and hobby markets, this large firm supplies pottery equipment (kilns, potters' wheels), materials and a firing service. In addition to its own wide choice of glazes, oxides and raw materials, it sells

sculpting materials such as casting resins, plus lots of books. The Mercury Classic range of hobby kilns starts at £590 plus VAT. Glass kilns are now available too.
Mail order.

Eggcraft

John Adlard

Norfolk Geese, Chestnut Farm, Pulham Market, Diss, Norfolk IP21 4XG (01379 676 391). **Phone enquiries** 9am-5pm Mon-Fri. **No credit cards.**
Blown goose eggs are sold for eggcraft from this Norfolk farm. The minimum order is one dozen, at a cost of £21.60.
Mail order.

Enamelling

The Enamel Shop

Trethinna House, Trethinna, Altarnun, Launceston, Cornwall PL15 7SY (01566 880 092). **Phone enquiries** 10am-5pm Mon, Tue, Thur, Fri. **Credit** MC, V.
The Enamel Shop's huge stock is available by mail order. Beginners' kits cost in the region of £200, plus £16 postage.
Mail order.

Feathers

Ostrich Feather Manufacturing Co

11 Northburgh Street, EC1V 0AH (7253 4140). Barbican tube. **Open** by appointment only Mon-Fri. **Credit** MC, V.
Both trade and private buyers beat a path to the OFMC for ostrich, peacock and various other kinds of feathers.
Mail order.

Glass

Lead & Light

35A Hartland Road, NW1 8DB (7485 0997/ www.leadandlight.co.uk). Camden Town tube. **Open** 9am-5.30pm Mon-Fri; 10am-5.30pm Sat. **Credit** AmEx, MC, V.
A working studio that's also a major supplier of tools and materials for decorative stained-glasswork. Plate glass comes in a kaleidoscope of colours; sand-blasting and etching tools are also sold. Courses and workshops covering various aspects of the art are run. Stained-glass artworks can be commissioned or repaired here too.
Mail order.

Hides & leather

Loop Knit Salon. See p207.

Walter Reginald

Unit 6, 100 The Highway, E1W 2BX (7481 2233/ www.walterreginald.com). Shadwell tube/DLR. **Open** 9am-5pm Mon-Fri. **Credit** MC, V.
Finished hides from around the world are sold at competitive prices here. These include lambskin, cowhide, pigskin and sheepskin – but no fur. Hides come in a multitude of colours; there are also textured prints such as mock croc and snake.
Mail order.

Metalworking

Smith's Metal Centres

42-56 Tottenham Road, N1 4BZ (7241 2430/ www.smithmetal.com). Dalston Kingsland rail. **Open** 9.30am-1pm, 2-4.30pm Mon-Fri. **Credit** MC, V.
Non-ferrous metals for decorative art and metalwork are supplied by SMC. The firm undertakes cutting and fabricating work, and there's also a range of plastics such as nylon and PVC suitable for craftwork available.

Models & model-making

See also chapter **Magic & Games.**

Comet Miniatures

44-48 Lavender Hill, SW11 5RH (7228 3702/ www.comet-miniatures.com). Clapham Junction rail. **Open** 9am-5.30pm Mon-Sat. **Credit** MC, V.
Miniature models and toys of film, TV and sci-fi characters are Comet's stock-in-trade. Magazines and model kits are also sold. Collectable *Star Wars* figurines on sale include C3-PO (£100), Darth Vader (£150) and, for die-hard fans, a 25in statue of General Grievous for £380.
Mail order.

Hobby Stores

39 Parkway, NW1 7PN (7485 1818/www.hobby stores.co.uk). Camden Town tube. **Open** 9.30am-5.30pm Mon-Sat. **Credit** MC, V.
Kits for model aircraft, boats, cars, radios and engines are all sold by this small nationwide chain. Tools for the job, and other art and craft accessories, are also supplied. A Trainer 30 radio-controlled aircraft kit costs £54.99.
Mail order.
For branch see index.

Hobby's

Knights Hill Square, SE27 0HH (8761 4244/ www.hobby.uk.com). West Norwood rail. **Open** 9am-5pm Mon-Fri; 9am-1pm Sat. **Credit** AmEx, MC, V.
Dolls' house kits are a major line of this well-established company, though kits for galleons and movements for musical boxes are also sold. Tools and materials for general model-making, plus matchstick kits, books and videos all feature in the firm's bestselling annual catalogue (£2.99).
Mail order.

Model Zone

202 High Holborn, WC1V 7BD (7405 6285). Holborn tube. **Open** 9.30am-6pm Mon-Sat. **Credit** AmEx, MC, V.
Die-cast cars, plastic army kits, model railways and Scalextric are all kept at this central London store, which also stocks all the necessary tools, paints and accessories. Character models from films (James Bond, sci-fi movies and the like) make an appearance too, along with radio-controlled cars and boats.
Mail order.
For branches see index.

My Hobbies

706 High Road, E11 3AJ (8539 9009/www. myhobbies.co.uk). Leytonstone tube. **Open** 9.30am-5.30pm Mon-Sat. **Credit** MC, V.
A specialist in radio-controlled vehicles, My Hobbies is home to monster trucks, rally cars, boats, planes and helicopters. Matchstick kits and radio sets can also be bought here, as can paints and other modelling supplies.
Mail order.

Under Two Flags

4 St Christopher's Place, W1U 1LZ (7935 6934/ www.undertwoflags.com). Bond Street tube. **Open** 10.30am-5pm Tue-Sat. **Credit** MC, V.
Claiming to offer London's best selection of toy and model soldiers, Under Two Flags has been trading from this cosy little shop for 30-odd years. Lines from all the major model manufacturers are stocked, along with military prints, books, paints, bases and brushes.
Mail order.

Railways

See also above **Models & model-making.**

Ian Allan's Transport Bookshop

45-46 Lower Marsh, SE1 7RG (7401 2100/ www.ianallanpub.co.uk). Waterloo tube/rail. **Open** 9am-5.30pm Mon-Fri; 9am-5pm Sat. **Credit** MC, V.
Ian Allan's books, videos and CD-ROMs cover everything from aviation to trams and trolley buses, including military titles. The shop also sells models of buses, aircraft, trains and other vehicles.
Mail order.

LEISURE

The Bead Shop. See p204.

Papercrafts

Blade Rubber Stamps

12 Bury Place, WC1A 2JL (7831 4123/www.blade rubber.co.uk). Holborn tube. **Open** 10.30am-6pm Mon-Sat. **Credit** AmEx, MC, V.
A charming shop selling wooden-backed rubber stamps in hundreds of designs. From Chinese symbols and 'We've Moved' stamps to intricate drawings of motor cars and *Alice In Wonderland* characters, there's a stamp for everyone, as well as stamps made to order. You'll also find goods such as paper, glue, sparkly confetti and sealing wax.
Mail order.

Falkiner Fine Papers

76 Southampton Row, WC1B 4AR (7831 1151). Holborn tube. **Open** 9.30am-5.30pm Mon-Fri; 10.30am-5.30pm Sat. **Credit** MC, V.
From these old timber-floored premises, Falkiner sells a selection of papermaking kits, cards and handmade paper, brightly coloured Japanese notebooks and decorative boxes. There's also exquisite wrapping paper good enough to hang on the wall, books on origami and notepads in every size.
Mail order.

Paperchase

213-215 Tottenham Court Road, W1T 9PS (7467 6200/www.paperchase.co.uk). Goodge Street tube. **Open** 9.30am-7pm Mon-Wed, Fri, Sat; 9.30am-8pm Thur; noon-6pm Sun. **Credit** AmEx, MC, V.
The multi-storey Paperchase flagship is a godsend if you're hunting for birthday cards and patterned Sellotape, but less well known is the second floor's superb range of paper and card in every imaginable colour, and in some interesting, often almost lace-like, textures. The artists' supply area has oil, acrylic, watercolour and fabric paints, plus brushes, pens, pencils and books. *See also chapter* **Stationery**.
Mail order (0161 839 1500).
For branches see index.

Stamps & coins

Stampex stamp fairs are held in London twice a year (in September and February); for more information go to www.stampex.ltd.uk.

Argyll Etkin Gallery

27 Regent Street, SW1Y 4UA (7437 7800/www. argyll-etkin.com). Piccadilly Circus tube. **Open** 9am-5.30pm Mon-Fri. **Credit** MC, V.
Autographs, royal memorabilia, stamps and postal history are the fortes of this Mayfair firm. A signed Christmas card from the Queen will set you back £1,100.
Mail order.

AH Baldwin & Sons

11 Adelphi Terrace, WC2N 6BJ (7930 6879/ www.baldwin.sh). Charing Cross tube/rail. **Open** 9am-5pm Mon-Fri. **Credit** AmEx, MC, V.
Antique coins and commemorative medals are Baldwin's (established 1872) speciality.

Coincraft

44-45 Great Russell Street, WC1B 3LU (7636 1188/www.coincraft.com). Tottenham Court Road tube. **Open** 9.30am-5pm Mon-Fri; 9.45am-2.30pm Sat. **Credit** AmEx, DC, MC, V.
Dealers in antique coins, artefacts, medals, tokens and banknotes.
Mail order.

The Collector's Centre

79 Strand, WC2R 0DE (7836 2579/www.stamp-centre.co.uk/www.scificollector.co.uk). Embankment tube/Charing Cross tube/rail. **Open** 10am-5.30pm Mon-Fri; 10am-5pm Sat. **Credit** AmEx, MC, V.
As well as stamp dealers focusing on first-day covers, royalty collections and pre-1936 stamps, the Centre houses specialists in sci-fi collectibles.
Mail order.
For branch see index.

Simmons Gallery

PO Box 104, London E11 1ND (8989 8097/ www.simmonsgallery.co.uk).
Simmons has no physical shop, but you can buy medals, coins and tokens from its virtual store.

Spink & Son

69 Southampton Row, WC1B 4ET (7563 4000/ www.spink.com). Holborn or Russell Square tube. **Open** 9.30am-5.30pm Mon-Fri. **Credit** AmEx, DC, MC, V.
Boasting three royal warrants, Spink's (established 1666) conducts auctions, online sales and private sales of stamps, coins, banknotes and medals.

Stanley Gibbons/Frasers

399 Strand, WC2R 0LX (7836 8444/ www.stanleygibbons.com). Embankment tube/ Charing Cross tube/rail. **Open** 9am-5.30pm Mon-Fri; 9.30am-5.30pm Sat. **Credit** AmEx, MC, V.
Stamp dealers since 1856, Gibbons claims this to be the world's largest stamp shop. See the website for an online catalogue and details of forthcoming stamp auctions. Sharing the same premises, Frasers specialises in autographs.
Mail order.

Sugar & sweets

Purple Planet

The Greenhouse Garden Centre, Birchen Grove, NW9 8RY (8205 2200/www.purpleplanet.co.uk). Wembley Park tube. **Open** 10am-5pm Mon-Sat; 10am-4.30pm Sun. **Credit** AmEx, MC, V.
Recommended by Nigella Lawson, no less, this firm sells an extensive range of cake-decorating equipment, plus pastry cutters and edible gold leaf.
Mail order.

Textiles

There are two main textile districts in London: **Brick Lane**, E1, which is good for wholesale quantities (ten metres or more); and **Berwick Street**, W1, for top-of-the-range fabrics. Try **Southall Broadway** and **Shepherd's Bush market** for modern and vintage fabrics, and Green Street in **Wembley** and **Brixton market** for a good range of African textiles. Many local markets also have eclectic budget fabric stalls; *see chapter* **Markets**.

Fabrics & trimmings

A1 Fabrics

50 & 52 Goldhawk Road, W12 8DH (8740 7349). Goldhawk tube. **Open** 9am-6pm Mon-Sat. **Credit** MC, V.
Two shops knocked into one, A1 offers a vast array of fabrics, including silk organza, chiffon, polycotton, PVC, lace, linens, lycra, fleece, velvet, suede, silk, denim and cashmere. There's a small selection of trimmings and invisible zips too.
Mail order.

Berwick Street Cloth Shop

*14 Berwick Street, W1F 0PP (7287 2881).
Oxford Circus or Piccadilly Circus tube.* **Open**
9am-6pm Mon-Fri; 9am-5pm Sat. **Credit** AmEx,
DC, MC, V.
With fabrics for everything from mother-of-the-
bride outfits to London Fashion Week designs, this
place stocks a huge range of fabrics, from latex
and luxurious silks to fake furs and chiffons. If
you're unsure what fabric to go for, consult the very
friendly staff who are happy to offer honest advice.
Mail order.

Bhopal Textile

*98 Brick Lane, E1 6RL (7377 1886). Aldgate East
tube.* **Open** 9am-6pm Mon-Fri; 10am-4pm Sat;
9am-4pm Sun. **No credit cards.**
There are plenty of fabric retailers on Brick Lane,
but whereas most are wholesalers who sell a
minimum of ten metres, at Bhopal it's five. Bargain
bolts of fabric – including silk and linen – are
piled around the shop.

Borovick Fabrics

*16 Berwick Street, W1F 0HP (7437 2180/
www.borovickfabricsltd.co.uk). Oxford Circus
tube.* **Open** 8.15am-6pm Mon-Fri; 8.15am-5pm
Sat. **Credit** MC, V.
Trading since 1932, this Soho stalwart is popular
with buyers from the theatre, film and fashion
industries. Look out for flamboyant leopard skin,
fake fur and bright-blue feather fabric in the
enormous range of fabrics and trimmings. There's
a second room called Aladdin's Cave, where your
most exotic fabric fantasies will be met.
Mail order.

Broadwick Silk

*9-11 Broadwick Street, W1F 0DB (7734 3320).
Oxford Circus tube.* **Open** 9am-6pm Mon-Fri;
9am-5pm Sat. **Credit** AmEx, MC, V.
From fabrics for bridal parties to Hollywood
costumes, it's all possible at Broadwick Silk,
purveyors of everything from netting for tutus
(prices range from £1.50 per metre) to encrusted
lace (for £270 per metre). Look out for special off-
cuts from fabrics used in films like *Star Wars* and
Lord of the Rings. Staff are helpful and friendly.
Mail order.

Cloth House

*98 Berwick Street, W1F 0QJ (7287 1555/
www.clothhouse.com). Oxford Circus or
Tottenham Court Road tube.* **Open** 9.30am-6pm
Mon-Fri; 10am-5.30pm Sat. **Credit** MC, V.
Cloth House's two floors hold a vast selection of
velvet, tweed, felt, wools, mohair and PVC, plus,
more recently, leathers in every colour imaginable,
even metallic blue and pink. Opened in 2005, its
sister at No.47 specialises in handwoven,
handprinted cotton and linen, costing anything from
£8.50 to £50 per metre; choose from smooth
naturals and bold print fabrics. It also has an
astounding selection of vintage trimmings
(including Indian sari wedding trim) and ribbons,
and downstairs there are velvets, silks and jerseys.
Mail order.
For branch see index.

The Cloth Shop

*290 Portobello Road, W10 5TE (8968 6001/
www.clothshop.net). Ladbroke Grove tube.* **Open**
10am-6pm Mon-Sat. **Credit** AmEx, MC, V.
The Cloth Shop majors in natural fabrics – cotton,
muslin, wool, linen – all sold by the metre, some of
them Fair Trade. If you're looking for something
extra special, you can also buy antique fabrics.
Mail order.

Fantasy Fayre

*22 Camden Road, NW1 9PD (7916 2100/
www.fantasyfayre.co.uk). Camden Town tube.*
Open 9am-5pm Mon-Sat. **Credit** MC, V.
Vendors of general haberdashery, craft fabrics and
interior fabrics.

Joel & Son Fabrics

*75-83 Church Street, NW8 8EU (7724 6895/
www.joelandsonfabrics.com). Edgware Road tube.*
Open 9am-5pm Mon-Sat. **Credit** AmEx, MC, V.

Four shops rolled into one, this massive store is the
biggest haute-couture fabric store in England.
Priding itself on its knowledgeable and helpful
staff, it's a favourite with big-name designers. Don't
be intimidated, though – the staff are happy to cut
you a metre of whatever you please, be it printed
silks and satins, cottons, denims, men's suiting,
fabric for traditional African dresswear, taffeta or
duchesse satin.
Mail order.

Kleins

*5 Noel Street, W1F 8GD (7437 6162/
www.kleins.co.uk). Oxford Circus tube.* **Open**
10am-5pm Mon-Fri. **Credit** AmEx, MC, V.
Trading since 1936, this specialist haberdashery
boutique sells an enormous variety of trimmings,
from jewel-encrusted to feathered. Ribbons and
buttons occupy a small room at the back of the
shop, and downstairs is craft central, with fabric
paints, dyes and pipe-cleaners aplenty. You'll also
find treats such as peacock feathers, diamanté
accessories, badges, tassels and a large stock of
handbag handles in wood and pyrex. You'll need
to wait outside to be buzzed into the shop, but don't
be put off. Staff are friendly.
Mail order.

MacCulloch & Wallis

*25-26 Dering Street, W1S 1AT (7409 0725/
www.macculloch-wallis.co.uk). Bond Street tube.*
Open 10am-6pm Mon-Wed, Fri; 10am-7pm Thur;
10.30am-5pm Sat. **Credit** AmEx, DC, MC, V.
Founded in 1902, this three-storey shop is the
grande dame of textiles. Vintage flower accessories,
from silk rosebuds to velvet blue wisteria, fill the
ground floor, along with reams of fabric from
organza to beaded lace. On the first floor there's a
rainbow stock of muslin ribbon, buttons and
trimmings, and on the top floor there are feathers,
millinery supplies and a sewing- machine
department, where the famous Bernina machines
are sold and serviced. Look out for the noticeboard
on the ground floor, which is covered with notices
for millinery, lingerie and pattern-cutting courses.
Mail order.

Maple Textiles/US To You

*Unit H, Franklin Industrial Estate, Franklin
Road, SE20 8HW (8778 8049/www.maple
textiles.com).* **Open** by appointment 9am-5pm
Mon-Fri; 10am-4pm 1st Sat of mth. **Credit** MC, V.
Importers of a fabulous range of fabrics – prints,
plains and novelties – that is distributed by mail
order, at needlecraft shows and wholesale.
Mail order.

Nasseri Fabrics

*38 Atlantic Road, SW9 8JW (7274 5627).
Brixton tube/rail.* **Open** 9.30am-5.30pm Mon-Sat.
Credit AmEx, MC, V.
African print hit mainstream fashion in 2005,
making the already very popular Nasseri's even
more crammed with customers. There's a large
selection of bold prints and colour fabrics in here,
available in 11.5m or 5.5m cuts. It's worth going in
the week, to avoid the queues.

Rolls & Rems

*21 Seven Sisters Road, N7 6AN (7263 3272).
Holloway Road tube.* **Open** 9.30am-5.50pm Mon-
Fri; 9am-5.15pm Sat. **Credit** AmEx, MC, V.
Try Rolls & Rems for quality fabric at a fraction
of the price of the West End shops. As well as a
good supply of cotton drill, velvets, PVC, suiting,
cord, polar fleece, Lycra and jersey, there are also
brightly coloured printed fabrics that can't be
found elsewhere. In terms of haberdashery, there's
foam for cushions, plus buttons, threads and
patterns galore.
For branches see index.

The Silk Society

*44 Berwick Street, W1F 8SE (7287 1881).
Oxford Circus tube.* **Open** 9am-6pm Mon-Fri;
9am-5pm Sat. **Credit** AmEx, MC, V.
Fabulous bolts of silk line the walls of this Soho
shop. Though the Silk Society sells primarily to the
theatre and film industries, brides also head here
for its wide selection of ivory silks and chiffons

imported from India and Europe. If you're looking
for beautiful upmarket lace, look no further than
the French handbeaded lace for £80 a metre.
Mail order.

Soho Silks

*22 D'Arblay Street, W1F 8ED (7434 3305).
Oxford Circus or Tottenham Court Road tube.*
Open 9.30am-6pm Mon-Sat. **Credit** MC, V.
Soho Silks' large premises are, as you might expect,
stacked with a fantastic range of silks – crêpe de
chine, taffeta, dupion, duchesse satin and velvet –
but silk is only the tip of the iceberg. Look out also
for buttons, trimmings, lace and wool.
Mail order.

Textile King

*81 Berwick Street, W1F 8TW (7437 7372).
Oxford Circus tube.* **Open** 10am-5pm Mon-Fri;
10am-4pm Sat. **Credit** MC, V.
This busy, friendly shop specialises in fine fabric
for men's clothing. Piled high with wools, cottons,
moleskin, tweed, corduroy, tartans and shirt
fabrics from pinstripe to polka dot, it is indeed the
king of gentlemen's fabrics. New stock is always
coming in, and you can pick up quality woollens
from £25 per metre or splash out on top-of-the-
range cashmere mix for £60 per metre.
Mail order.

Creative Quilting

*32 Bridge Road, Hampton Court, East Molesey,
Surrey KT8 9HA (8941 7075/www.creative
quilting.co.uk). Hampton Court rail.* **Open** 9.30am-
5.30pm Mon-Sat; noon-4pm Sun. **Credit** MC, V.
If you're into quilt-making, this shop is heaven.
Find quilting threads in every colour, American
cotton fabrics, tools including rotary cutters, books
and magazines. Classes and quilting groups are
held on a weekly basis (Wednesday and Saturday)
during the academic term.
Mail order.

Loop Knit Salon

*41 Cross Street, N1 2BB (7288 1160/www.loop.
gb.com). Angel tube.* **Open** 11am-6pm Tue-Sat;
noon-5pm Sun. **Credit** MC, V.
Like NHS spectacles, beige macs and big pants,
knitting is the latest fashion to be ruthlessly
plagiarised from the nation's pensioners. New to
Islington, Loop is a knitting nirvana, selling
needles of all sizes and wool from across the
world, in a rainbow of sherbet shades and
textures ranging from earthy tweeds to luxurious
velvets. There's also an appealing pick 'n' mix
selection of knitted clothing by unusual designers
like Keep & Share, Cast Off and Hiraku Noguchi,
as well as crocheted blankets and knitted toys. A
haberdashery section features an excellent range
of vintage buttons, too. The interior is small and
friendly, with a log pile beside an open fireplace.
For those who want to learn the craft, Loop holds
knitting courses.
Mail order.

WHI Tapestry Shop

*85 Pimlico Road, SW1W 8PH (7730 5366).
Sloane Square tube.* **Open** 9.30am-5pm Mon-Fri.
Credit MC, V.
Create your own design and commission WHI to
make it up as a cushion or wall-hanging for a
personalised gift. Otherwise select from a range of
WHI's own tapestry designs, along with the wool
and supplies to make them.
Mail order.

We know of seven firms selling and servicing
new and second-hand machines: **MacCulloch
& Wallis** (*see p207*), **Chapman Sewing
Machine Co** (80 Parkway, NW1 7AN, 7485
0140), **Chapel Market Sewing Centre**

(17 Chapel Market, N1 9EZ, 7837 5372), **Lewisham & Deptford Sewing Machines** (181 Deptford High Street, SE8 3NT, 8692 1077), **Sewing Centre** (266 Battersea Park Road, SW11 3BP, 7228 3022), **Sew Amazing**, (80 St Stephens Road, E3 5JL, 8980 8898) and **Olympic Sewing Machines** (1B Shepherd's Bush Road, W6 7NA, 8743 6683).

Spinning & weaving

George Weil/Fibrecrafts
Old Portsmouth Road, Peasmarsh, Guildford, Surrey GU3 1LZ (01483 565 800/www.fibre crafts.com). **Phone enquiries** 9am-5pm Mon-Fri. **Credit** MC, V.
An excellent array of supplies for spinning, felting, weaving, paper-making, batik and fabric painting. You'll find all the equipment you need for fibrecrafts too: looms, spinning wheels, beeswax, Kumihimo stands and Europe's leading textile book list.
Mail order.

Handweavers Studio & Gallery
29 Haroldstone Road, E17 7AN (8521 2281/ www.handweaversstudio.co.uk). Blackhorse Road tube/rail. **Open** 10am-5pm Tue-Sat. **Credit** AmEx, MC, V.
This fun, friendly shop sells fibres, fleece, yarns, spinning and weaving equipment, and you can pick up yarns and fibres in any quantity, even as little as 10g. Courses are held in spinning, weaving and felt-making – it costs a very reasonable £45 for a one-day course to learn how to spin and £80 for a two-day course on how to make felt; all materials are included.
Mail order.

Tools, sundries & art materials

Alec Tiranti
27 Warren Street, W1T 5NB (7636 8565/www. tiranti.co.uk). Great Portland Street or Warren Street tube. **Open** 9am-5.30pm Mon-Fri; 9.30am-1pm Sat. **Credit** MC, V.
Tiranti's has been supplying sculptors with materials and tools since 1895. Modelling, carving sculpting and casting equipment is sold, with stock encompassing resins, cement, wax, plaster, a variety of synthetic and earth-based clay, silicone and rubber (for mould-making). You'll also find a small selection of books.
Mail order (0118 930 2775).

4D Model Shop
The Railway Arches, 120 Leman Street, E1 8EU (7264 1288/www.modelshop.co.uk). Aldgate East tube/rail. **Open** 9am-6pm Mon-Fri; 9.30am-6pm Sat. **Credit** AmEx, MC, V.
Though it started by supplying tools and materials for architectural model-making, 4D now sells all kinds of materials and equipment, covering hobbies from jewellery to prop-making. You'll find meshes, plastics, metals, adhesives, moulds, display aids, electrics (for illuminating your creation), resins and scalpel blades among the stock. Hand-built, brass-etched model trees are a particular forte.
Mail order.

Pentonville Rubber
104-106 Pentonville Road, N1 9JB (7837 4582/ www.pentonvillerubber.co.uk). Angel tube. **Open** 9am-5pm Mon-Fri; 10am-3pm Sat. **Credit** AmEx, MC, V.
All your rubber needs are likely to be met here, not to mention any requirements you might have for fire-retardant high-density foam (cut to order, and great as a mattress topper), rubber flooring, acoustic panels, coloured latex sheeting and beanbag filling. The firm supplies businesses from health authorities to theatre companies, but also deals with the public.
Mail order.

Magic & Games

For computer games and consoles, *see chapter* **Electronics**.

Board & fantasy games

BCM Chess Shop/Bridge Shop
44 Baker Street, W1U 7RT (7486 8222/ www.bcmchess.co.uk). Baker Street tube. **Open** 10am-6pm Mon-Sat. **Credit** AmEx, MC, V.
Established in 1881, this is the home to *British Chess* magazine; back issues and bound volumes (going back to 1941) are sold alongside a vast range of chess equipment, computer chess, instruction books and videos. There's also a good selection of dominoes, backgammon, cribbage, mah-jong, Chinese chess, bridge and card games.
Mail order.

Chess & Bridge
369 Euston Road, NW1 3AR (7388 2404/ www.chess.co.uk). Great Portland Street tube. **Open** 10am-6pm Mon-Sat. **Credit** AmEx, MC, V.
This shop offers a staggering array of chess paraphernalia – DVDs, books, computer software – and a huge range of sets, from *Star Wars* figures to chess/backgammon/draughts travel sets. The collection of books on bridge, backgammon and poker is equally extensive.
Mail order.

Compendia
10 Greenwich Market, SE10 9HZ (8293 6616/ www.compendia.co.uk). Cutty Sark Gardens DLR. **Open** 11am-5.30pm Mon-Fri; 10am-5.30pm Sat, Sun. **Credit** MC, V.
Compendia specialises in games from around the world, such as Mexican train dominoes and the Japanese board game Go. It also sells a range of chess and backgammon sets and traditional pub, party and after-dinner games and puzzles.
Mail order.

Games Workshop
The Plaza, 116-128 Oxford Street, W1D 1LT (7436 0839/www.games-workshop.com). Oxford Circus tube. **Open** 10am-7pm Mon-Wed, Fri, Sat; 10am-8pm Thur; noon-6pm Sun. **Credit** AmEx, MC, V.
Introductory sessions are available, giving novices a chance to learn how to play table-top battle games before they buy. *Warhammer* 'artefacts' and *Lord of the Rings* models are popular. **Branches**: throughout the city.

Murray & Brand
8 Heddon Court Parade, EN4 0DB (8449 0827). Cockfosters tube. **Open** 9am-5.30pm Mon-Thur; 9am-6pm Fri, Sat. **Credit** AmEx, MC, V.
An all-purpose toys and games shop stocking action figures, Airfix model planes, toy cars, magic tricks and adult-friendly and traditional board games. The current playground craze, colourful plastic Scoubidou strands used to knot into figures and keychains, is a hot seller.

Orc's Nest
6 Earlham Street, WC2H 9RY (7379 4254/ www.orcsnest.com). Leicester Square tube. **Open** 11am-6.30pm Mon-Wed, Fri; 11am-7pm Thur; 11am-6pm Sat. **Credit** AmEx, MC, V.
Still the UK's largest independent retailer of role-playing games, Orc's Nest also does good business in collectable card games, models and paints, miniatures, magazines and books.
Mail order.

Playin' Games
33 Museum Street, WC1A 1JR (7323 3080). Holborn or Tottenham Court Road tube. **Open** 10am-6pm Mon-Wed, Fri, Sat; 10am-7pm Thur; noon-6pm Sun. **Credit** AmEx, MC, V.

Travel chess and backgammon are popular purchases with tourists wandering in from the British Museum across the road; more serious gamers will be impressed by the comprehensive range of board games, poker sets and accessories, puzzles and jigsaws. The *Star Wars* Saga Edition Monopoly set (£33) is selling by the shedload.
Mail order.

Village Games
65 The West Yard, Camden Lock, NW1 8AF (7485 0653/www.villagegames.com). Camden Town tube. **Open** 10am-6pm Wed-Sun. **Credit** AmEx, MC, V.
An intriguing puzzle shop packed with brain-boggling merchandise, including logic games, 3D jigsaws, mechanical puzzles and traditional toys. During the summer and at Christmas, the shop tends to open seven days a week; phone to check.
Mail order.

Magic

Davenports Magic Shop
7 Charing Cross Underground Shopping Arcade, WC2N 4HZ (7836 0408/www.davenportsmagic.co. uk). Charing Cross tube/rail. **Open** 9.30am-5.30pm Mon-Fri; 10.15am-4pm Sat. **Credit** AmEx, MC, V.
An unlikely location for the world's oldest family magic business, established in 1898. Books, DVDs and tricks for all levels and budgets are sold.
Mail order.

International Magic
89 Clerkenwell Road, EC1R 5BX (7405 7324/ www.internationalmagic.com). Chancery Lane tube. **Open** 11.30am-6pm Mon-Fri; 11.30am-4pm Sat. **Credit** AmEx, MC, V.
A wealth of jokes, novelty items and accessories for card, coin and stage magic, plus instruction videos and manuals for beginners and professionals.
Mail order.

Jugglemania
8390 6855/www.magiccircus.co.uk. **Credit** MC, V.
Clubs, balls, flaming torches, unicycle, stilts and much more. There's also a selection of pocket money-friendly kids' magic.

Kaymar Magic Studio Jokeshop
189 St Mary's Lane, Upminster, Essex RM14 3BU (01708 640557). Upminster tube/rail. **Open** 9.30am-5pm Tue, Wed, Fri; 1-8pm Thur; 9.30am-4pm Sat. **Credit** AmEx, MC, V.
The shop, which also has a section devoted to jokes and novelties, was being sold as we went to press, but it will still supply magic tricks for amateurs and semi-professionals.
Mail order.

Marvin's Magic
Hamleys, 188-196 Regent Street, W1R 6BT (7494 2000/07960 932302). Oxford Circus tube. **Open** 9am-8pm Mon-Wed, Fri, Sat; 9am-9pm Thur; noon-6pm Sun. **Credit** AmEx, DC, MC, V.
At the back of the toy store's hectic ground floor, you'll find Marvin's enticing array of goodies for magicians aged four and up; cup and balls tricks and Dynamic Coins are bestselling favourites.

Table football

Bar Kick
127 Shoreditch High Street, E1 6JE (7739 8700/www.cafekick.co.uk). Old Street tube/rail. **Open** noon-11pm Mon-Wed; noon-midnight Thur-Sat; noon-10.30pm Sun. **Credit** MC, V.
This lively café-bar also sells table-football units, from £699 up to £1,900 for a coin-operated model.
For branch (Café Kick) see index.

Music

Most of the shops in this chapter deal in both new and second-hand equipment. For musical instruments *see also chapter* **Babies & Children**. For DJ and home studio equipment *see chapter* **Electronics**.

General music shops

BEM
395 Coldharbour Lane, SW9 8LQ (7733 6821/www.bem-music.com). Brixton tube/rail. **Open** 10am-6.30pm Mon-Sat. **Credit** AmEx, MC, V.
Instruments sold here include acoustic, electric and bass guitars, keyboards, plus a smaller selection of woodwind and brass. The stock of electronic equipment is especially impressive – musicians will find everything for both studio and live work, from computer hardware to effects boxes and amplification; DJs can pick up CD and vinyl turntables, headphones and more.

Blanks
271-273 Kilburn High Road, NW6 7JR (7624 7777). Kilburn tube. **Open** 10am-5pm Mon, Fri; 10am-5.30pm Tue, Wed; 10am-6pm Thur. **Credit** AmEx, MC, V.
Blanks stocks a range of varied instruments including banjos, harmonicas, flutes, saxophones, clarinets and drums. Guitars are a particular speciality. The focus throughout is on value for money, so the most expensive brands are avoided. Blanks will buy used kit and can also do repairs. *Mail order.*

Chappell of Bond Street
50 New Bond Street, W1S 1RD (7491 2777/ www.chappellofbondstreet.co.uk). Bond Street or Oxford Circus tube. **Open** 9.30am-6pm Mon-Fri; 9.30am-5pm Sat. **Credit** AmEx, MC, V.
One of the oldest music shops in London (established 1811), Chappell sells some of the very newest equipment; it is also the UK's leading Yamaha dealer. Stock (from Yamaha and other manufacturers) includes digital and acoustic pianos, guitars, brass, woodwind and all sorts of electronics. Its collection of sheet music is reputedly the largest in Europe and spans pop, jazz, show tunes, classical and more. *Mail order.*

Foote's
10 Golden Square, W1F 9JA (7734 1822/ www.footesmusic.com). Piccadilly Circus tube. **Open** 9am-6pm Mon-Fri; 9am-5pm Sat. **Credit** AmEx, MC, V.
This veteran Soho shop concentrates on drums and percussion. There are kits and cymbals from top manufacturers such as Yamaha, Ludwig and Zildjian, as well as Latin percussion and high-quality sticks and drumheads. Cases, practice pads and educational materials are also here. Additionally, Foote's has a selection of woodwind, brass and string instruments. *Mail order.*

Gigsounds
86-88 Mitcham Lane, SW16 6NR (8769 3206/ www.gigsounds.co.uk). Tooting Broadway tube, then 57 bus/Streatham Common rail. **Open** 10am-6.30pm Mon-Fri; 10am-6pm Sat. **Credit** AmEx, MC, V.
An amazingly comprehensive stock – ranging from kazoos to studio electronics – is crammed into this two-storey shop. Come to Gigsounds for guitars, amps, PA equipment, effects boxes, DJ gear, even iPods. The special offers are particularly worth investigating. *Mail order.*

World of Music
8, 10, 22, 23 Denmark Street, WC2H 8NJ (7240 7696/www.wom.co.uk). Tottenham Court Road tube. **Open** 10am-6pm Mon-Sat. **Credit** AmEx, MC, V.
World of Music is king of the castle in Denmark Street, owning a good number of its numerous music shops. At No.22 is the well-stocked London Bass Cellar (7240 3483); No.23 is home to the London PA Centre (7497 1178), with its speakers, amps and PA gear. World of Pianos (7240 5555) at No.8 and Rose Morris Specialist Guitars (Basement of No.10, 7240 6896) are the other members of the empire. *Mail order.*

Musical instruments

All Flutes Plus
60-61 Warren Street, W1T 5NZ (7388 8438/ www.allflutesplus.co.uk). Warren Street tube. **Open** 10am-6pm Mon-Fri; 10am-4.30pm Sat. **Credit** MC, V.
Staff at AFP describe themselves as 'players first' and take pride in their impartial advice. Most makes and models are stocked, from basic beginners' flutes to specialist handmade instruments. The shop has an excellent selection of sheet music and undertakes repairs. *Mail order.*

Allodi Accordions Ltd
143-145 Lee High Road, SE13 5PF (8244 3771/ www.accordions.co.uk). Lewisham DLR/rail, then 122, 178, 261, 321 bus. **Open** 2-6pm Mon; 10.30am-6pm Tue, Thur, Fri; 10.30am-5pm Sat. **Credit** AmEx, MC, V.
A family-owned business for more than 50 years, Allodi probably has enough accordions to equip every street musician in Paris and still have a few to spare. The instruments are stacked from floor to ceiling in several rooms and range in price from over £100 to tens of thousands. An on-site workshop can do repairs while you wait. *Mail order.*

Phil Parker
106A Crawford Street, W1H 2HZ (7486 8206/ www.philparker.co.uk). Baker Street tube. **Open** 10am-5.30pm Mon-Fri; 10am-4.30pm Sat. **Credit** AmEx, MC, V.
Parker – a brass specialist selling trombones, tubas, trumpets and other instruments – has basic off-the-shelf models as well as custom-made options. You'll also find mouthpieces, mutes and sheet music. *Mail order.*

TW Howarth
31-35 Chiltern Street, W1U 7PN (7935 2407/ www.howarth.uk.com). Baker Street tube. **Open** 10am-5.30pm Mon-Fri; 10am-4.30pm Sat. **Credit** AmEx, MC, V.
Howarth's oboes are the first choice for many professionals, and its Marylebone shop is the leading London outlet for all woodwind instruments and accessories. Own-brand models are stocked alongside other leading makes. Sheet music is available and there are repair and rental services. *Mail order.*

Drums & percussion

For **Andy's Drum Centre**, *see below* **Andy's Guitar Centre & Workshop**.

Impact Percussion
Unit 7, Goose Green Trading Estate, 47 East Dulwich Road, SE22 9BN (8299 6700). East Dulwich rail. **Open** 10am-6pm Mon-Fri. **Credit** MC, V.

We haven't always found Impact's staff as helpful or polite as we would hope, but the company is a certainly a leader in its field. A full range of kit drums, cymbals, Latin percussion and ethnic instruments can be ordered here, and some is kept in stock, but the real emphasis is on orchestral percussion, including xylophones. Repairs can be carried out on site. *Mail order.*

Professional Percussion
205 Kentish Town Road, NW5 2JU (7485 4434/ www.propercussion.co.uk). Kentish Town tube/rail. **Open** 10am-6pm Mon-Sat. **Credit** MC, V.
Like its Soho sibling Foote's (*see above*), Pro Perc is a percussion specialist, but it is several times bigger, so stock and facilities are much more comprehensive. Kit drums, cymbals, Latin instruments and all the accessories are here and can be tested out in soundproof booths. Call for information about in-store tuition sessions. *Mail order.*

Wembley Drum Centre
Unit 8, Metro Trading Centre, Fifth Way, Wembley, Middx HA9 0YJ (8795 4001/ www.wembleydrumcentre.com). Wembley Park tube. **Open** 10am-6pm Mon-Sat. **Credit** MC, V.
Make a pilgrimage through the badlands of industrial Wembley to reach this veritable drum mecca, which houses a huge range of Pearl, Yamaha, Tama, Sabian, DW and Zildjian kits and equipment. The centre also accommodates the Wembley PA Centre (8902 9070) and the Wembley Guitar Centre (8900 9090). *Mail order.*

Early music & folk

Early Music Shop (London Harpsichord Centre & London Recorder Centre)
34 Chiltern Street, W1U 7QH (7486 9101/ www.e-m-s.com). Baker Street tube. **Open** 10am-6pm Mon-Sat. **Credit** MC, V.
The two departments of the Early Music Shop – the Recorder Centre and the Harpsichord Centre combined – sell a comprehensive selection of medieval, Renaissance and baroque instruments alongside accessories, sheet music and CDs. Other traditional instruments are also available, such as viols, lutes and harps – many of which are made in the Bradford head office/workshop, which has been in business since 1968. *Mail order.*

Hobgoblin
24 Rathbone Place, W1T 1JA (7323 9040/ www.hobgoblin.com). Tottenham Court Road tube. **Open** 10am-6pm Mon-Sat. **Credit** AmEx, MC, V.
Hobgoblin's owners and staff are dedicated to promoting folk music, particularly the traditions of the British Isles. The diverse stock reflects this ethos, covering guitars, mandolins, bagpipes, fiddles, banjos and more. World music is also well represented. Enthusiasts will enjoy the mini museum of folk instruments kept at the shop. *Mail order.*

Paul Hathaway
47 Langley Drive, E11 2LN (8530 4317/ www.paulhathaway.com). Wanstead tube. **Open** by appointment only. **Credit** AmEx, MC, V.
Paul Hathaway is a skilled folk instrument-maker who sells from a fine stock but also undertakes private commissions, lovingly creating mandolins, bouzoukis and lutes, among others. *Mail order.*

Guitars

Andy's Guitar Centre & Workshops
27 Denmark Street, WC2H 8NJ (7916 5080/ www.andysguitarnet.com). Tottenham Court Road tube. **Open** 10am-8pm Mon-Sat; 12.30-6.30pm Sun. **Credit** AmEx, MC, V.

The famous and popular Andy's has been on the same spot for more than a quarter of a century and remains under its original ownership. The whole gamut of guitars and extras is covered on its five floors. Whether you want an acoustic, electric or bass, amplifier, effects box or set of strings, chances are you'll find something suitable here. An expertly chosen mix of vintage and new stock caters to every taste and budget. Next door is Andy's Drum Centre, which repeats the formula with percussion.
Mail order.

The Bass Gallery
142 Royal College Street, NW1 0TA (7267 5458/ www.thebassgallery.com). Camden Town tube. **Open** 11am-6pm Mon-Thur; 11am-5pm Fri, Sat. **Credit** MC, V.
A passion for bass guitars radiates from this shop and from the team of experts who run it. Devoted entirely to basses, the Gallery is lined from wall to wall with good-looking, well-maintained guitars from a dazzling array of different makers. In the workshop, basses can be custom-built or repaired.
Mail order.

Chandler Guitars
300-302 Sandycombe Road, Kew, Surrey TW9 3NG (8940 5874/www.chandlerguitars.co.uk). Kew Gardens tube/rail. **Open** 9.30am-6pm Mon-Sat. **Credit** AmEx, MC, V.
The fact that Chandler has survived so long in its remote, sleepy Kew Gardens locale is a testament to the quality of service and stock here. The catalogue includes all kinds of guitars and accessories; the range of vintage models on sale is invariably superb. Chandler has a range of custom-made guitars in high-end materials from £999.
Mail order.

Hank's Guitars
24 Denmark Street, WC2H 8NJ (7379 1139/ www.hanksguitarshop.com). Tottenham Court Road tube. **Open** 10am-7pm Mon-Sat. **Credit** MC, V.
Leaving electric instruments mainly to its close Denmark Street neighbours, Hank's proudly claims to have the largest selection of acoustic guitars in the country. The bewildering range encompasses everything from connoisseurs' choices from Taylor, Martin and Takamine to entry-level instruments. Stock is both new and second-hand, and also includes folk instruments like mandolins, ukuleles and banjos.
Mail order.

The House of Guitars
2 Tenter Ground, Brune Street, E1 7NH (7247 7847/www.basscentre.com/www.acousticcentre. co.uk). Liverpool Street tube/rail. **Open** 10am-6pm Mon-Sat. **Credit** MC, V.
One of the precious few music shops in the East End, House of Guitars sells a complete selection of acoustic, electric and bass guitars and related accessories. Repairs are also carried out.
Mail order.

Ivor Mairants Musicentre
56 Rathbone Place, W1T 1JT (7636 1481/www. ivormairants.co.uk). Tottenham Court Road tube. **Open** 9.30am-6pm Mon-Sat. **Credit** AmEx, MC, V.
Founded in 1958 by guitar luminary Mairants, whose flamenco instruction book remains a bestseller, this shop claims to be Britain's oldest specialist guitar store. It's also the official London showroom for the American Ovation range. Beginners and experts will find a large selection of electric, acoustic, jazz and classical guitars to suit most budgets, plus accessories. A smattering of other instruments completes the catalogue.
Mail order.

London Guitar Studio/ El Mundo Flamenco
62 Duke Street, W1K 6JT (7493 0033/ www.londonguitarstudio.com/www.elmundoflame nco.co.uk). Bond Street tube. **Open** 9.30am-6pm Mon-Sat; 10am-5pm Sun. **Credit** AmEx, MC, V.
The stock here is exclusively acoustic, and specifically for classical and flamenco playing. Guitars are imported from manufacturers like

Alhambra, Goya and Vicente Sanchis. A flamenco section offers DVDs and videos, books, dance equipment and CDs; if there's not enough here, the sister store Latin Quarter has even more. Repairs and tuition are other services on offer.
Mail order.
For branch (Latin Quarter) see index.

Macari's
92-94 Charing Cross Road, WC2H 0JB (7836 9149/www.macaris.co.uk). Tottenham Court Road tube. **Open** 10.30am-6pm Mon-Sat. **Credit** AmEx, MC, V.
The majority of stock here is guitar-based, with electrics by the dozen upstairs and basses and acoustics just as abundant downstairs. New instruments vie with vintage classics to suit a range of budgets. Macari's also sells a more limited range of other instruments, including saxes, bits of percussion, and even theremins.
Mail order.

Music Ground
25 Denmark Street, WC2H 8LU (7836 5354/ www.musicground.com). Tottenham Court Road tube. **Open** 10am-7pm Mon-Sat. **Credit** MC, V.
Another venerable emporium in the Denmark Street musical epicentre. The phenomenal selection includes left-handed guitars, hard-to-find models and outlandish designs, which can also be viewed on the excellent website. Amps and effects pedals, old and new, are equally well represented. If you are looking for a specific make and model of guitar, Music Ground offers a guitar-finder service.
Mail order.

Rockers
5 Denmark Street, WC2H 8LU (7240 2610). Tottenham Court Road tube. **Open** 10am-7pm Mon-Sat; 11am-5pm Sun. **Credit** AmEx, MC, V.
Owned by the same folk behind Music Ground (*see above*), and with a similar remit, Rockers is especially good for spare parts. It has a vast range of replacement parts alongside guitars and pedals. For repairs, head for the basement workshop.
Mail order.

Spanish Guitar Centre
36 Cranbourn Street, WC2H 7AD (7240 0754/ 0800 371 339/www.spanishguitarcentre.com). Leicester Square tube. **Open** 10.30am-6pm Mon-Sat; 11am-4pm Sun. **Credit** MC, V.
A specialist in handmade guitars by Spanish luthiers, Barry Mason's Spanish Guitar Centre benefits from a wonderfully clean and airy showroom in which to test out the instruments. Prices range from under £100 well into the thousands. There are also models from Germany and Holland, plus instruction books and accessories.
Mail order (0800 371 339).

Vintage & Rare Guitars
6 Denmark Street, WC2H 8LX (7240 7500/ www.vintageandrareguitars.com). Tottenham Court Road tube. **Open** 10am-6pm Mon-Sat; noon-4pm Sun. **Credit** AmEx, MC, V.
It's unusual to see a Denmark Street shop imposing limitations on itself, but V&R admirably aims to be a master of one trade, not a jack of all of them. This wonderfully atmospheric shop is bursting with sought-after collectibles from the likes of Fender, Gibson and Gretsch, and there's also a number of pre-war guitars. Prices are spectacularly variable.
Mail order.

Harps

Holywell Music
58 Hopton Street, SE1 9JH (7928 8451/www.holy wellmusic.co.uk). Blackfriars tube or Southwark tube/rail. **Open** 10am-5pm Mon-Fri. **Credit** MC, V.
Half a century in the business makes Holywell the premier London harp retailer. More than 50 instruments, made by Salvi and Lyon & Healy, are on display in the showroom and available for purchase or rental. Harpists will find everything else they need – strings, sheet music and records – and can have their instruments serviced here too.
Mail order.

Pianos & organs
See also p209 **World of Music**.

Markson Pianos
8 Chester Court, Albany Street, NW1 4BU (7935 8682/www.marksonpianos.com). Great Portland Street or Regent's Park tube. **Open** 9.30am-5.30pm Mon-Sat; 10am-4pm Sun. **Credit** MC, V.
As well as selling pianos, this family-run business has been providing restoration, polishing and tuning services for nearly a century. Uprights, grands and digitals are complemented by a range of designer pianos from manufacturers like Sauter and Pleyel. Markson's hire schemes are well established, with options to purchase – 50% of hire fees will be credited if you decide to buy after a year, or 100% within six months. Markson also owns Phelps Pianos in Kentish Town (49-51 Fortess Road, NW5 1AD, 7485 2042/0800 0748 980).

Piano Warehouse
30 Highgate Road, NW5 1NS (7267 7671/ www.piano-warehouse.co.uk). Kentish Town tube/rail. **Open** 10am-6pm Mon-Sat. **Credit** AmEx, DC, MC, V.
Kentish Town is a historic hotspot for the piano trade, and Piano Warehouse keeps the tradition alive. It sells pianos by the likes of Yamaha, Steinmayer and Weber, plus second-hand and digital instruments. Rental and hire-purchase schemes are promoted.
Mail order.
For branch see index.

Robert Morley & Co
34 Engate Street, SE13 7HA (8318 5838/ www.morleypianos.com). Lewisham rail/DLR. **Open** 9.30am-5pm Mon-Sat. **Credit** MC, V.
As much craftsmen as retailers, staff at Morley's build pianos and early keyboards, such as clavichords, harpsichords, virginals, spinets and celestes. The shop also sells new and second-hand instruments. Prices climb from around £1,500. Repairs and rentals are also available.

Steinway & Sons
Steinway Hall, 44 Marylebone Lane, W1U 2DB (7487 3391/www.steinway.com). Bond Street tube. **Open** 9am-5.30pm Mon-Fri; 11am-5pm Sat. **Credit** MC, V.
Steinway remains the champion piano-maker, with an unassailable prestige and prices to match. Virtually all its pianos cost a five-figure sum, so window shopping might be as far as you get.

Pro audio/ electronics

Digital Village
14 The Broadway, Gunnersbury Lane, W3 8HR (8992 5592/www.dv247.com). Acton Town tube. **Open** 10am-6pm Mon-Sat; 10am-5pm Sun. **Credit** MC, V.
The Acton branch of Digital Village is the most central of its four Greater London outposts. The shop provides for every studio and DJ requirement. There's a full range of Apple G5s for audio use, plus all the additional software and hardware required. There are microphones and monitors, sound cards and sample CDs, and even a few musical instruments.
For branches see index.

Rose Morris Pro Audio Shop
10 Denmark Street, WC2H 8TD (7836 0991/ www.proaudiostore.co.uk). Tottenham Court Road tube. **Open** 10am-7pm Mon-Fri; 10am-6pm Sat. **Credit** MC, V.
In spite of its name and its proximity to all the other World of Music shops in Denmark Street, Rose Morris is an independent store specialising in professional production and recording equipment, from mixers to microphones to software and synthesisers. Major brands like Korg, Roland, Yamaha and Shure are all well represented.
Mail order.

LEISURE

Synthesiser Service Centre

Unit 1, 30 Gorst Road, NW10 6LE (8961 7890/ www.synthservice.com). North Acton tube. **Open** 9am-6.30pm Mon-Fri. **Credit** MC, V.
Take your wounded keyboard, synthesiser or bit of studio kit up to Park Royal and get the expert engineers at the SSC to repair it for you. They're equally at home with more modern, electronic gear and older, weirder mechanical devices. They also keep a retail stock of vintage equipment that can include Rhodes pianos, Hammond organs, original Roland synths and Moog keyboards as well as all kinds of wacky effects boxes.

Turnkey/Soho Soundhouse

114-116 Charing Cross Road, WC2H 0JR (7379 5148/www.turnkey.co.uk). Tottenham Court Road tube. **Open** 10am-6pm Mon-Wed, Fri, Sat; 10am-7pm Thur. **Credit** AmEx, MC, V.
Turnkey's vast catalogue of pro audio equipment includes computer systems and software, keyboards and synthesisers, effects units, multitrack recorders, samplers, monitoring equipment, cables and connectors… the list seems endless. Downstairs there's a wealth of DJ goods from all the major brands, and Loopstation, a sample resource facility for producers. A similarly sizeable range of clearance and ex-display stock means bargains are easily found. Upstairs is Soho Soundhouse, where everything guitar-related can be found.
Mail order.

Strings

Bridgewood & Neitzert

146 Stoke Newington Church Street, N16 0JU (7249 9398/www.londonviolins.com). Stoke Newington rail/73 bus. **Open** 10am-6pm Mon-Fri; 10am-4pm Sat. **Credit** AmEx, MC, V.
The highly respected eponymous duo are experts on both modern and baroque stringed instruments, having started out making lutes, viols and baroque violins. Their reasonably priced retail, repair and restoration services cater to a wide market, from students to professionals.
Mail order.

Ealing Strings

4 Station Parade, Uxbridge Road, W5 3LD (8992 5222/www.ealingstrings.info). Ealing Common tube. **Open** 9.15am-6pm Mon-Sat. **No credit cards.**
Ealing Strings prides itself on its team of passionate experts and craftsmen from across the world. Its large workshop makes brand-new instruments, restores vintage ones and carries out smaller repairs. A varied selection of musical instruments and bows is always kept in stock, and there's a one-hour bow rehairing service (£48 and £38 for students).
Mail order.

Frederick Phelps Ltd

67 Fortess Road, NW5 1AG (7482 0316/ www.phelps-violins.com). Kentish Town tube. **Open** 9.30am-6pm Tue-Fri; 10am-4pm Sat. **Credit** MC, V.
The original Phelps, a piano dealer now owned by Markson (*see p211*), is also still going strong a few doors down, though the shops are under separate management. The strings shop is popular with students and professionals alike. The workshop will take on repairs, adjustments and restorations. A good selection of instruments is kept in stock and can be tried out in spacious rooms upstairs, where masterclasses and recitals are also held. Phelps offers one free rehair on all bows it sells.
Mail order.

J&A Beare

30 Queen Anne Street, W1G 8HX (7307 9666/ www.beares.com). Bond Street tube. **Open** (preferably by appointment) 10am-5pm Mon-Fri. **Credit** MC, V.
Not one for beginners. A 140-year history of dealing Stradivari, Guarneri and other Italian masters has earned Beare an international

Markson Pianos. See p211.

reputation, and its collection of instruments is of the highest calibre. Beare's expert luthiers restore and repair instruments.
Mail order (7307 9650).

JP Guivier

99 Mortimer Street, W1W 7SX (7580 2560/ www.guivier.com). Oxford Circus tube. **Open** 9am-6pm Mon-Fri; 10am-4pm Sat. **Credit** MC, V.
Another long-established, world-renowned string dealer and workshop. Instruments range from under £100 for a beginner's violin to tens of thousands for an antique, handmade French or Italian model. Violins, violas and cellos are all stocked, alongside strings, bows and accessories. Rehairing and repairs are carried out.
Mail order.

Portobello Music

13 All Saints Road, W11 1HA (7221 4040/ www.portobellomusic.co.uk). Westbourne Park tube. **Open** 10.30am-6pm Mon-Sat. **Credit** MC, V.
Portobello Music caters to a more amateur swathe of the market than heavyweights like Beare and Guivier; its orchestral strings are for entry-level and intermediate players. It also sells a selection of new and second-hand guitars, plus amplification and effects units.
Mail order.

World music

See also p209 **Hobgoblin**.

Bina Musicals

31-33 The Green, Southall, Middx UB2 4AN (8574 6992/8571 5904/www.earthvibe music.com). Southall rail. **Open** 10.30am-7pm Mon-Sat; 11am-7pm Sun. **Credit** AmEx, MC, V.
Bina's flagship product is its harmonium, which can be made to order in a wealth of different designs and sizes. Prices start at around £150. But Bina also makes and sells a phenomenal array of ethnic percussion, wind and stringed instruments, most of which you've probably never heard of. Everything from triangles to didgeridoos is here.
Mail order.
For branch see index.

Ray Man

54 Chalk Farm Road, NW1 8AN (7692 6261/ www.raymaneasternmusic.co.uk). Camden Town or Chalk Farm tube. **Open** 10.30am-6pm Tue-Sat; 11am-5pm Sun. **Credit** MC, V.
Set out like a bazaar, Ray Man sells instruments from Asia, Africa, the Middle East and South America. Find chinese zithers and Indian fiddles jostling for shelf space; there are gongs, cymbals, shakers – and some altogether weirder things, such as the Vietnamese frog box and the Indian monkey drum.
Mail order.

Jukeboxes

For jukebox hire, *see p198* **Juke Box Junction**.

Jukebox Services

15 Lion Road, Twickenham, Middx TW1 4JH (8288 1700/www.jukeboxservices.co.uk). Twickenham rail. **Open** 9.30am-5.30pm Mon-Fri; 10am-4pm Sat. **Credit** MC, V.

This Twickenham company sells and repairs jukeboxes for both domestic and commercial customers. Shoppers with a nostalgic impulse and a few grand to spare can visit the showroom to browse through a range of authentic jukeboxes by the likes of Wurlitzer and Seeburg. More mundane CD-only jukeboxes can be rented by hotels, pubs and bars. An on-site workshop does repairs and restorations.
Mail order.

Sheet music

See also p209 **Chappell of Bond Street.**

Argent's

20 Denmark Street, WC2H 8NA (7379 3384). Tottenham Court Road tube. **Open** 9am-6pm Mon-Sat; 11am-5pm Sun. **Credit** AmEx, MC, V.

Argent's selection of printed music is wide-ranging and well balanced, encompassing pop and contemporary, classical, jazz, blues and more. There's also a music theory section, plus instructional videos and DVDs.
Mail order (0800 515814).

Barbican Chimes Music

Cromwell Tower, Silk Street, EC2Y 8DD (7588 9242/www.chimesmusic.com). Barbican tube or Moorgate tube/rail. **Open** 9am-5.30pm Mon-Fri; 9am-4pm Sat. **Credit** AmEx, MC, V.

A classical music specialist, with a second branch in Kensington. There are also rock, jazz and pop sections, instructional books and DVDs.
Mail order.
For branch (Kensington Chimes Music) see index.

Boosey & Hawkes @ Brittens Music

16 Wigmore Street, W1U 2RF (7079 5940/ www.brittensmusic.co.uk). Bond Street tube. **Open** 10am-6pm Mon-Sat. **Credit** AmEx, MC, V.

The shop recently moved down the road from Regent Street but remains a premier retailer of sheet music, mainly classical but with pop and jazz also covered. Music-writing software such as Sibelius can be bought here, and more attention and space is gradually being given to string, woodwind and brass instruments.
Mail order (0808 1000 440).

Equipment hire

Systems etc

Unit 8, Print Village, Chadwick Road, SE15 4PU (7732 3377/www.systemsetc.com). Peckham Rye rail. **Open** 10am-6.30pm Mon-Fri. **Credit** MC, V.

Systems etc has a huge range of equipment for DJs and live gigs for hire. Chances are you'll find what you need in its large South London warehouse.

Peter Webber Hire

110-112 Disraeli Road, SW15 2DX (8870 1335/www.peterwebberhire.com). East Putney tube/Putney rail. **Open** 10am-6pm daily. **Credit** AmEx, MC, V.

This one-stop shop provides musical equipment such as guitars, drum kits and PA systems in premises that also feature two rehearsal studios. Two more are available in Putney's Esmond Street.

Sound Division

Montague House, 389 Liverpool Road, N1 1NP (7609 3999/www.soundivision.co.uk). Highbury & Islington tube/rail. **Open** 9.30am-5.30pm Mon-Fri. **Credit** MC, V.

No show or entertainment project is too big for Sound Division, which hires equipment for some enormous events, but smaller rentals are equally possible. DJ, PA and live gear are all available. Sound Division keeps a stock of the newest equipment and a comprehensive rate card on the website gives daily prices for each item.

Pets

If you want to adopt a pet, **Battersea Dogs & Cats Home** (4 Battersea Park Road, SW8 4AA, 7622 3626, www.dogshome.org) rehomes abandoned animals – you will be interviewed and visited at home first. The £70 charge (dogs; £40 cats) covers a package of useful extras, including a microchip, neutering, health check and vaccinations, among others. The **RSPCA** rehomes around 70,000 animals a year, from mice to horses. It follows a similar procedure and there is a charge of £30 to £70 to cover vaccinations, neutering and other costs. To find your nearest animal centre, call 0870 333 5999 or visit www.rspca.org.uk.

Accessories

As well as grooming, **All Dogs** (*see below*) offers pet accessories. For über-trendy pooches, **Holly & Lil** (www.hollyandlil.co.uk) sells 'couture collars'. **Wowbow** (8995 1761, www.wowbow.co.uk) makes stylish acrylic beds complete with luxurious faux suede cushions (£400-£700). The matching raised 'dining tables' with removable feeding bowls (around £80-£150) are not only civilised, they aid digestion and prevent muscle and joint strain. There are also sculptural acrylic and sisal cat scratching posts (around £100), plus a new range of accessories in collaboration with Bill Amberg.

Mungo & Maud

79 Elizabeth Street, SW1W 9PJ (7952 4570/ www.mungoandmaud.com). Sloane Square tube. **Open** 10am-6pm Mon-Sat. **Credit** AmEx, MC, V.

A chic boutique with everything for the discerning pet (often tested by the owners' English setter, George), from tastefully trimmed bridle-leather collars and leads in a range of colours (from £63) to designer dog beds by Henry Beguelin (from £95) and vintage 1930s cat bowls (£10.50).

Services

Accommodation & pet care

Ask your vet or contact **Pet Care Trust** (0870 062 4400, www.petcare.org.uk) for kennel and cattery recommendations. For information on quarantine and a list of quarantine kennels and carrying agents approved by **DEFRA**, visit www.defra.gov.uk or phone 08459 335 577. Another option is home-sitting – visit any of the following websites: **www.homesitters.co.uk**, **www.home-and-pets.co.uk** or **www.house sittersltd.co.uk**.

Groomers

All Dogs

10 Frognal Parade, 158 Finchley Road, NW3 5HH (7435 9481). Finchley Road tube. **Open** 8am-5pm Tue-Fri; 8am-2pm Sat. **No credit cards.**

A shampoo, brush and trim is from £25 for a Yorkie-sized mutt to £60 for an Old English sheepdog. Accessories, shampoos and treats are also sold.

Primrose Hill Pets

132 Regent's Park Road, NW1 8XL (7483 2023). Chalk Farm tube. **Open** 9am-6pm Mon-Sat; 10am-4pm Sun. **Credit** MC, V.

A brush, shave and claw-clip for your cat (no bathing) costs from £30-£50; the full monty for dogs (bath, groom, nails, ears) costs £25-£80.

Insurance

To avoid high vet's fees and boarding costs at stressful times, it makes sense to take out an insurance policy. The **Blue Cross** (0800 107 7551) has teamed up with Petplan to offer Purely for Pets insurance (around £10/mth for a cat, £20/mth for a dog). Ten per cent of premiums help the Blue Cross.

Animal Friends Insurance

0870 403 0300/www.animalfriends.org.uk.

This company donates 100% of its net profits to animal welfare charities. At £109.97 per year, wherever you live, most breeds of dog (aged over eight years) will be covered for up to £500 per medical condition (to a maximum of £1,500 in any one year) and £1,000,000 for public liability, with additional cover for boarding costs up to £100. For dogs under eight years, the cost is £76.12. Full lifetime options are available for pets with long-term conditions.

Medical services

As well as the clinics listed below, the website **www.any-uk-vet.co.uk** will direct you to your nearest vet. To find your nearest **RSPCA** clinic, call or check website (*see above*). The **People's Dispensary for Sick Animals** is Britain's leading veterinary charity, providing (means-tested) free services to needy pet owners. Call 0800 731 2502 or visit www.pdsa.org.uk to find your nearest PDSA hospital or PetAid practice.

Blue Cross Animals' Hospital

Sheppard House, Hugh Street, SW1V 1QQ (7834 4224/www.thebluecross.org.uk). Victoria tube/rail. **Open** *Appointments* 9.20am-1pm, 2.30-4.20pm Mon, Tue, Thur, Fri; 9.20am-12.20pm Wed. **No credit cards.**

Aimed at low-income pet owners, the hospital treats cats, dogs and other small animals. Appointments are usually required, but there's an emergency unit.
For branches see index.

Elizabeth Street Veterinary Clinic

55 Elizabeth Street, SW1W 9PP (7730 9102/ www.esvc.co.uk). Sloane Square tube/Victoria tube/rail. **Open** 24hrs daily. **Credit** MC, V.

As well as offering pet healthcare within practice hours (ring for details), this private clinic has a 24-hour emergency service (appointments only).

Sponsorship

For those who love the idea of a pet but don't have the room or the time to take one on, sponsorship is an alternative. For £1 a week, sponsor a cat cabin at a **Cats Protection** rescue shelter, and visit its current occupant (www.cats.org.uk); a similar scheme exists at **Dogs Trust** (www.dogstrust.org.uk).

Training

The **Kennel Club** (0870 606 6750, www.the-kennel-club.org.uk),believes that responsible dog ownership is vital for all communities. The Discover Dogs event takes place in November at Earls Court (call 7518 1012 for details). For a list of dog trainers in your area, call the Kennel Club's Good Citizen Dog Scheme (0870 606 6750).

Photography

Tottenham Court Road and its environs have the highest concentration of camera shops in London; in addition to those listed below, there is a rash of cut-price electronic stores stocking cameras and peripherals. Students should enquire about discounts available on purchases of film and equipment, film processing and darkroom hire. *See also chapter* **Electronics**.

General photographic

Calumet

93-103 Drummond Street, NW1 2HJ (7380 1144/ www.calumetphoto.com). Euston tube/rail. **Open** 8.30am-5.30pm Mon-Fri. **Credit** AmEx, MC, V.
Calumet has one of the largest and best stocked photographic showrooms in London, mainly geared towards professionals. It's all here: lights, power packs, gels, tripods, and SLR, digital, medium- and large-format cameras. There are also repair services and an extensive rental section. The clientele ranges from art students to professionals. *Mail order.*
For branches see index.

Gemini

58 High Road, N2 9PM (8883 6152). East Finchley tube/102 bus. **Open** 10am-6pm Tue-Sat. **Credit** AmEx, MC, V.
One of the UK's main Minolta dealers, Gemini also stocks Nikon, Pentax and Canon models. It's a good all-rounder, with telescopes, binoculars, frames, bags and albums, plus a broad selection of digital cameras and accessories. Tripods, video cameras, slide projectors, enlargers and second-hand gear are also sold. Services include camera repairs and overnight film processing (£4.99).

Jacobs Photo, Video & Digital

74 New Oxford Street, WC1A 1EU (7436 5544/ www.jacobsdigital.co.uk). Tottenham Court Road tube. **Open** 9am-6pm Mon-Wed, Fri, Sat; 9am-8pm Thur. **Credit** AmEx, MC, V.
While it's also part of a nationwide chain, Jacobs feels friendlier than the Jessops over the road. The staff are well informed and keen to match customers to the right products. The shop is spacious too, with goods clearly displayed and priced. It stocks an excellent range of compact, digital and SLR cameras and accessories; it also boasts one of the best tripod selections in town. Prices are competitive, with frequent special deals to be had. The second-hand department, encompassing ring flashes and medium-format cameras, is also worth checking out. Next-day colour film processing is £4.99, while the one-hour service is £7.49.
Mail order.

Jessops

63-69 New Oxford Street, WC1A 1DG (7240 6077/www.jessops.com). Tottenham Court Road tube. **Open** 9am-7pm Mon-Wed, Fri; Sat; 9am-8pm Thur; 11am-5pm Sun. **Credit** AmEx, DC, MC, V.
Jessops has nearly 250 stores nationwide; alas, a side effect of its wide reach is patchy staff knowledge and lack of enthusiasm. This, the largest of the chain's 23 London shops, has shifted its stock focus away from the darkroom kit and slide mounts of old towards tourist-friendly displays of camcorders and point-and-shoot digital cameras. There's still a good range of SLR cameras and quality digital stock, but staff seem scared to take them out of their boxes. However,

the excellent second-hand department has clung on to its floor space and is now linked to a nationwide database. Jessops also offers an impressive range of digital and printing services, but these frequently seem to get the better of them: this branch is so busy that there are often long queues.
Mail order (0800 652 6400).
Branches: throughout the city.

Kingsley Photographic

93 Tottenham Court Road, W1T 4HL (7387 6500/www.kingsleyphoto.co.uk). Goodge Street or Warren Street tube. **Open** 9am-5.30pm Mon-Fri; 10am-5.30pm Sat. **Credit** AmEx, MC, V.
For such a tiny place, KP (as it's known to regulars) manages to squeeze in a surprisingly wide range of all things photographic, and if something isn't in stock, it can be ordered. Staff are keen photographers who enjoy introducing products they know and love. Second-hand camera gear is bought and sold too, and repairs are offered. *Mail order.*

London Camera Exchange

98 Strand, WC2R 0EW (7379 0200/www.lce group.co.uk). Charing Cross tube/rail. **Open** 9am-5.30pm Mon-Fri; 11am-5.30pm Sat. **Credit** AmEx, MC, V.
With around 30 stores across the country (all of which are called London Camera Exchange, regardless of the location), this company sells all manner of photographic accessories, including lenses, bags, binoculars, filters, Epson printers and negative/transparency scanners. That's on top of its full range of compact, SLR and digital cameras by all the leading names. Refurbished digital SLR Nikon cameras start from as little as £99. There's also a large second-hand department and a printing service (36 prints cost £3.99 for a five-day service).
Mail order.

Mr Cad

68 Windmill Road, Croydon, Surrey CRO 2XP (8684 8282/www.mrcad.co.uk). East Croydon or West Croydon rail. **Open** 9am-5.30pm Mon-Fri; 9am-5pm Sat. **Credit** AmEx, MC, V.
Mr Cad is Britain's biggest independent photographic store and claims to have the largest stock of used photographic equipment in Europe. It's also an agent for Multiblitz, a German studio flash system, as well as three kinds of Holga 120 camera. There are also cameras from Lomo, the cult camera from Russia. As 90% of stock is second-hand, it's constantly changing, but you can expect to find the likes of Horizon 202 Panoramic cameras and pro Hasselblad lenses, as well as large- and medium-format cameras and rare, collectable brands. Repairs on studio lighting and classic cameras are carried out, too. The shop's location is slightly tricky to find; take a map. *Mail order.*

Nicholas

15 Camden High Street, NW1 7JE (7916 7251/ www.nicholascamera.com). Mornington Crescent tube. **Open** 10am-6pm Mon-Sat. **Credit** AmEx, MC, V.
Run by an eccentric shopkeeper, Nicholas is a good place in which to find second-hand bargains. Instead of browsing the crowded shelves, tell the shopkeeper what you need and he'll reappear from the basement with the item in a couple of minutes. The shop has an extensive range: in addition to large- and medium-format cameras, classic cameras (many by little-known manufacturers), accessories and darkroom kit, there's a growing array of used digital gear.
Mail order.

Percival Cameras

207 Eltham High Street, SE9 1TX (8859 7696/ www.percivalcameras.org.uk). Eltham or New Eltham rail. **Open** 9am-5.30pm Mon-Sat. **Credit** AmEx, DC, MC, V.

The Classic Camera

Percival's stock extends right across the board, from darkroom equipment, paper, filters and lenses to camcorders and telescopes. It's also a Leica binocular specialist and offers expert advice on digital cameras. You'll find all the major camera brands for pros and amateurs alongside an ever-changing line-up of second-hand gear (including manual cameras).
Mail order.
For branch see index.

The Pro Centre
5-6 Mallow Street, EC1Y 8RS (7490 3122/ www.procentre.co.uk). Old Street tube/rail.
Open 8am-6pm Mon-Thur; 9am-7pm Fri.
Credit AmEx, MC, V.
As its name suggests, the Pro Centre caters mainly for professionals. Owned by Hasselblad, the store has new and second-hand stock by the brand, but also rents out equipment by all the other major players. A range of digital cameras – including the Canon EOS-1Ds Mark II, Nikon D2X and Kodak DCS 14n – has been added to the rental department, along with G4 laptops. For orders over £100, there's free delivery throughout London, or you can opt to have your congestion charge refunded.

RG Lewis
9 Southampton Row, WC1B 5HA (7242 2916/ www.rglewis.co.uk). Holborn tube. **Open** 8.30am-6pm Mon-Fri; 9.30am-3.45pm Sat. **Credit** AmEx, DC, MC, V.
This long-established Leica specialist deals in everything from early rangefinder cameras to the latest digital technology. Staff really know their stuff and will happily discuss the relative merits of one camera over another while cleaning a mechanism or replacing a battery. You'll find a good range of used cameras, which all come with a six-month guarantee, as well as new models from all the major brands. There's a decent choice of accessories including tripods, flash guns, light boxes and filters. An overnight printing service is £4.99 (36 exposures); slides are £5.15 for a three-day service.
Mail order.

Teamwork
41-42 Foley Street, W1W 7JN (7323 6455/ www.teamworkphoto.com). Goodge Street tube.
Open 9am-5.30pm Mon-Fri. **Credit** AmEx, DC, MC, V.
Teamwork caters to the professional market, specialising in high-end digital backs and medium-and large-format cameras. It also has a good selection of hire cameras and lighting gear.
Mail order.

York Cameras
18 Bury Place, WC1A 2JL (7242 7182). Holborn tube. **Open** 9am-5pm Mon-Fri.
Credit MC, V.
Staffed by a team of seasoned experts, York Cameras is a Canon Pro Centre, and stocks an impressive range of new and used equipment and accessories by the company. It also sells used Nikon equipment, often rarities. The shop attracts a loyal, discerning clientele, and the service is very attentive. Processing is also offered.

Repairs

Many of the shops listed under the heading **General Photographic** also offer a camera repair service.

Camera City
16 Little Russell Street, WC1A 2HL (7813 2100/ www.cameracity.co.uk). Russell Square tube.
Open 10am-5.30pm Mon-Fri; 10.30am-2pm Sat.
Credit AmEx, DC, MC, V.
Camera City has a wide field of expertise and can repair practically any camera on the premises, so turnaround is faster than at other places. Camera repairs are guaranteed for six months, camcorders for three. The shop's main business is in second-hand equipment, though it stocks a limited array of new digital, SLR and compact cameras.

Picture this

So, you've been to the beach (or the mountains, or Paris), and you've taken your best photos yet. What are you going to do with them? The usual answer is print them, stick them in a book and look at them once a year, but the digital photography revolution is changing more than just our cameras – it's also transforming what we can do with our images. Now you can turn your best photos into snazzy placemats, cute T-shirts, pillowcases, mousepads, bound books or any one of dozens of possibilities – all at the click of a mouse. Most high-street photo printers can turn out T-shirts or mugs, but these days that's just the tip of the iceberg. The line between adorable and tacky is thin here, so tread with caution, but some items are really rather good.

Perhaps the most sophisticated of personalised coasters and placemats come care of **Scarlett Willow** (www.scarlettwillow.co.uk, 8748 7344); coasters start at £29.99 for a set of six. You can either use your own photos or choose from their classy photo library.

If you're thinking bigger – and more original – than that, send a beach scene or abstract photo to **Eyes Wide Digital** (01737 780 789, www.eyeswide digital.com) and have it turned into a one-of-a-kind canvas deck chair (£70). The same company also prints digital images on to canvas (which can be stretched on to a wooden frame) or turns them into trendy pop art prints (*pictured*). If you're seeking to match a photo with your decor, or just a spooky hue, try the free colourising service at **Digital Design Scotland** (0131 477 4524, www.digitaldesign scotland.co.uk), which 'washes' the photo with your chosen tint.

For something a bit more serious, visit **www.fotobook.co.uk**, where you can download software to create bound books filled with your digital photos – you upload your shots, write the captions and choose the colour and texture (faux leather or linen) of the cover; the company then prints it and sends it to you (prices start at £19.99).

Most photo ideas, though, are of the fun and silly variety. **Print a Present** (35 Eastcastle Street, W1W 8DW, 7580 6006, www.printapresent.com) will print photos on just about everything. Mousepads, memo paper blocks, keyrings, bags, puzzles – the list may not be endless, but it's certainly long. You could give personalised canvas bags as party favours; use your best pic for a photo purse (£21.99) or shoulder bag (similar to the Marilyn Monroe versions that were ubiquitous a couple of years back, £49.99); or stretch your creativity choosing an image for the background of a clock (from £19.99). You may, however, want to steer clear of the heart jigsaw (£12.99) and the fridge magnets (£7.99).

The Camera Clinic
26 North End Crescent, W14 8TD (7602 7976/ www.cameraclinic.co.uk). West Kensington tube.
Open 9am-6pm Mon-Fri; 9am-1pm Sat.
Credit AmEx, MC, V.
Authorised repairer of Sony, Panasonic and JVC equipment, the Camera Clinic also deals with most major brands of camcorders and DVD players, as well as compact, APS, 35mm and medium-format cameras and lenses. There's a fee for quotes, but repairs are guaranteed for six months (camcorders for three). The Clinic can also transfer any media, including images and footage, on to a DVD or CD format.
Mail order.
For branch see index.

Sendean
9-12 St Anne's Court, W1F 0BB (7439 8418/ www.sendeancameras.com). Oxford Circus or Tottenham Court Road tube. **Open** 10.30am-6pm Mon-Fri. **Credit** AmEx, MC, V.
The obliging folk here will have a crack at repairing anything, including old and digital cameras. All estimates are free, and there's a six-month guarantee with every repaired item (three months for camcorders). Sendean also sells and repairs cine-cameras, and has a cine-to-video transfer service.
Mail order.

The Classic Camera
2 Pied Bull Yard, off Bury Place, WC1A 2JR (7831 0777/www.theclassiccamera.com). Holborn or Tottenham Court Road tube. **Open** 9.30am-5.30pm Mon-Fri; 10am-4.30pm Sat. **Credit** AmEx, DC, MC, V.
The Classic Camera might not be for those on a tight budget; about 90% of the stock is Leica, both new and used. The remainder is Voigtlander, a similar but more economical brand. To carry your new kit away, there are Peli cases and Billingham bags; books on Leicas are also sold. If your wallet won't stretch, you can always hire a Leica M7 for a daily rate of £35 plus VAT. Call to arrange at least two days in advance.
Mail order.

Jessops Classic
67 Great Russell Street, WC1B 3BN (7831 3640/ www.jessops.com/classic). Holborn tube. **Open** 9am-5.30pm Mon, Tue, Thur-Sat; 9.30am-5.30pm Wed. **Credit** AmEx, DC, MC, V.
This classic camera specialist has a bit of a museum feel to it, with all the goods displayed in dark wood-and-glass cabinets that have to be unlocked before the cameras can be placed on felt mats for closer inspection. There are even

LEISURE

specimens from the early days of photography in the 1860s. The majority of cameras on display here are still 'usable'; only few are merely 'collectable'.

Copying

Denbury Repros
27 John Adam Street, WC2N 6HX (7930 1372). Embankment tube/Charing Cross tube/rail. **Open** 8.30am-5.30pm Mon-Fri. **Credit** MC, V.
This place can copy original photos of any kind, including antiques, and retouching old photos (both colour and black and white) is a speciality. Denbury works mainly with the film and TV industries, but it also prints for the general public.

Darkroom accessories & hire

In addition to **Gemini** (*see p214*), the following have darkrooms for hire: **Arts Factory** (2 Parkhurst Road, N7 0SF, 7607 0561, www.islingtonartsfactory.org.uk); **The Camera Club** (16 Bowden Street, SE11 4DS, 7587 1809, www.thecameraclub.co.uk); **Highgate Newtown Community Centre** (25 Bertram Street, N19 5DQ, 7272 7201, www.hncc.freeuk.com); **Photofusion** (17A Electric Lane, SW9 8LA, 7738 5774, www.photofusion.org); and **Rapid Eye** (79 Leonard Street, EC2A 4QS, 7033 1803, www.rapideye.uk.com).

Silverprint
12 Valentine Place, SE1 8QH (7620 0844/www.silverprint.co.uk). Southwark tube/Waterloo tube/rail. **Open** 9.30am-5.30pm Mon-Fri. **Credit** MC, V.
Everything to do with quality printing, from darkroom to digital equipment, plus Lyson permanent inks, portfolios and photography books. *Mail order.*

Processing & printing

The following offer a professional and/or specialised service.
Ceta Imaging *1-5 Poland Street, W1F 8NA (7434 1235/www.cetaimaging.com). Oxford Circus tube.* **Open** 7am-7pm Mon-Fri. **Credit** AmEx, DC, MC, V.
For branch see index.
Chaudigital *19 Rosebery Avenue, EC1R 4SP (7833 3938/www.chaudigital.com). Bus 19, 38.* **Open** 9am-6pm Mon-Fri. **Credit** AmEx, MC, V. *Mail order.*
Classic Photographic Services *23-55 Great Sutton Street, EC1V 0DN (7250 0007/www.classic-group.info). Farringdon tube/rail.* **Open** 9am-6pm Mon-Fri. **Credit** MC, V. *Mail order.*
Grand Union *49-50 Eagle Wharf Road, N1 7ED (7253 0251/www.grandunionweb.com). Old Street tube/rail.* **Open** 8am-8pm Mon-Fri; 9am-5pm Sat. **Credit** MC, V.
The Image *24-25 Foley Street, W1P 7LA (7580 5020/www.imageblackandwhite.com). Oxford Circus tube.* **Open** 9am-6pm Mon-Fri. **Credit** MC, V. *Mail order.*
Metro Imaging *76 Clerkenwell Road, EC1M 5TN (7865 0000/www.metroimaging.co.uk). Farringdon tube/rail.* **Open** 24hrs daily. **Credit** AmEx, MC, V. *Mail order.*
For branches see index.
Photo Professional *123 Lower Clapton Road, E5 0NP (8986 9621). Hackney Central rail/38 bus.* **Open** 9am-6.30pm Mon-Fri; 10.30am-5.30pm Sat. **Credit** MC, V.
Sky Imaging *Ramillies House, 1-2 Ramillies Street, W1F 7AZ (7434 2266/www.sky-imaging ukltd.co.uk). Oxford Circus tube.* **Open** 9am-6pm Mon-Fri. **Credit** DC, MC, V. *Mail order.*
Team Photographic *37 Endell Street, WC2H 9BA (7240 2902/www.teamphotographic.com). Covent Garden tube.* **Open** 8am-9pm Mon-Fri. **Credit** AmEx, DC, MC, V. *Mail order.*

CDs & Records

Thanks to the download revolution, the past few years have seen the fortunes of London's many CD and record emporia take something of a dive. From the bijou climes of Berwick Street (London's 'music row') to the second-hand shops dotted beyond Zone 1, the future of record-buying is hanging in the balance; and, with constantly improving technology, the trusty CD could be next in a long line of formats cast into the gutter by the emergence of the MP3 player. Not everything combining music and the internet is a bad thing, though. **Gemm** (www.gemm.com) is a handy tool for locating a deleted or hard-to-find disc. CD and record fairs are another way to snap up a bargain (check the weekly *Time Out* for dates). And don't forget: support your local record shops. They need you more than ever.

Megastores

Borders
203 Oxford Street, W1D 2LE (7292 1600/www.borders.co.uk). Oxford Circus tube. **Open** 8am-11pm Mon-Sat; noon-6pm Sun. **Credit** MC, V.
Borders has been recently refurbished, and the CD section has been noticeably streamlined in favour of books and DVDs. It's still pretty good for chart albums though, and the jazz and classical sections remain comprehensive. There are also digital listening posts that enable you to sample most of the albums on sale.
For branches see index.

HMV
150 Oxford Street, W1D 1DJ (7631 3423/www.hmv.co.uk). Oxford Circus tube. **Open** 9am-8pm Mon-Wed, Fri, Sat; 9am-9pm Thur; noon-6pm Sun. **Credit** AmEx, DC, MC, V.
The first and last stop for the record-buying novice in London. With seasonal sales, cut-price box sets and hundreds of rarities and imports, there's little chance you'll leave this world-beating behemoth of a store empty-handed. The vast basement houses broad classical and jazz sections, and staff are always on hand to recommend and locate the discs for you. If they're not currently stocking the CD you're looking for, they can order it in.
Branches: throughout the city.

Virgin Megastore
14-16 Oxford Street, W1D 1AR (7631 1234/www.virgin.com). Tottenham Court Road tube. **Open** 9am-9pm Mon-Sat; noon-6pm Sun. **Credit** AmEx, MC, V.
The long evolution of Virgin's flagship store has seen renovations aplenty and regular furniture shiftings, but lately it seems to have found its feet. Signings and in-store performances happen almost weekly, and the range of rock, pop and dance is vast. As you'd expect from a 'megastore', the world, jazz, classical and folk sections are impressive. It's also big on music merchandise such as T-shirts, posters, musical instruments and amplifiers.
Branches: throughout the city.

Classical

Gramex
25 Lower Marsh, SE1 7RJ (7401 3830). Waterloo tube/rail. **Open** 12.30-7pm Tue-Sat. **Credit** AmEx, MC, V.
Founded in 1898, Gramex is one of the oldest record shops in the world. Mainly stocking second-hand classical CDs, it also has an extensive miscellany of vinyl and sheet music. The stock changes daily.

Harold Moores Records
2 Great Marlborough Street, W1F 7HQ (7437 1576/www.hmrecords.co.uk). Oxford Circus tube. **Open** 10am-6.30pm Mon-Sat; noon-6pm Sun. **Credit** MC, V.
Famous in classical circles for its marvellous used-LP selection, as well as a treasure trove of obscure and hard-to-find oddities. Couple this with a large contemporary and avant-garde section, and Harold Moores is most definitely a place for the hardened music collector. Expect to hear fellow patrons insouciantly discussing the finer points of Stravinsky as you browse.

Les Aldrich
98 Fortis Green Road, N10 3HN (8883 5631/www.lesaldrich.co.uk). Bus 43, 134. **Open** 9.30am-6pm Mon-Fri; 9am-5.30pm Sat. **Credit** MC, V.
Established in 1945, Les Aldrich is a purveyor of all things classical (and for light relief, it also has a small selection of pop and jazz music). An excellent place to pick up new classical releases, as well as curios ranging from show tunes to world music and children's music. There's a wide assortment of sheet music and plenty of musical instruments for children – guitars, violins, percussion instruments and recorders. *Mail order.*

MDC Music & Movies
Level 1, Royal Festival Hall, South Bank, SE1 8XX (7620 0198/www.mdcmusic.co.uk). Waterloo tube/rail. **Open** 10am-10pm daily. **Credit** AmEx, MC, V.
Having moved to premises three times the size of the original, this famed supplier of contemporary classical releases has added jazz and concert DVDs to its splendid range. The website lists a selection of rarities and hard-to-find discs, and MDC is especially good for recordings of West End shows. *Mail order.*
For branch see index.

Second-hand

Beanos
7 Middle Street, Croydon, Surrey CR0 1RE (8680 1202/www.beanos.co.uk). East Croydon rail. **Open** 10am-6pm Mon-Sat; 11am-4pm Sun. **Credit** AmEx, MC, V.
With its garish purple shopfront spanning across two buildings, Beanos's exterior is as colourful as its chatty and knowledgeable staff. The array of second-hand CDs and vinyl in stock is unfathomably huge. There are four floors of 1960s and '70s rock, dance, pop and classical, with prices ranging from £5 to £5,000. There's also a stage where local bands play every Saturday, a mini cinema and a room piled high with used DVDs and videos. When your shopping needs are fulfilled, grab a snack at the 1950s-style café.

Cheapo Cheapo Records
53 Rupert Street, W1A 4WW (7437 8272). Piccadilly Circus tube. **Open** 11.30am-10pm Mon-Sat. **No credit cards.**
From its humble market-stall origins in 1968, it took just two years for Cheapo Cheapo to inhabit its current residence. Filled to the rafters (literally) with cut-price CDs, vinyl, VHS, DVDs and even cassettes, it's a case of dive in, lose yourself for a few hours and come away with whatever you can salvage. The fact that they will sell just about anything you would loosely term as music makes Cheapo Cheapo better for a browse than for picking up new releases and rarities. Prices range from £1 to a maximum of £5: yes, it's cheap(o), but also pretty claustrophobic.

Ray's Jazz at Foyles. See p219.

Flashback
50 Essex Road, N1 8LR (7354 9356/www.flash back.co.uk). Angel tube. **Open** 10am-7pm Mon-Sat; noon-6pm Sun. **Credit** AmEx, MC, V.
This charming Essex Road store has used CDs and vinyl from every genre going. The basement is best, with its well-organised selection of 1960s and '70s rock rarities, hip hop, reggae and ska. The website is also a fine resource for locating rare and deleted items, but don't let that keep you from visiting this small but perfectly formed shop. *Mail order.*

Haggle Vinyl
114-116 Essex Road, N1 8LX (7704 3101/ www.hagglevinyl.com). Angel tube then 38, 56, 73, 341 bus. **Open** 9am-7pm Mon-Sat; 9am-3.30pm Sun. **Credit** MC, V.
Looking for a place to offload a couple of those old Tangerine Dream albums in return for some folding money? Haggle's eccentric shopkeeper will buy almost anything you throw at him. The condition of stock is sometimes variable, but the selection is good. *Mail order.*

Intoxica!
231 Portobello Road, W11 1LT (7229 8010/ www.intoxica.co.uk). Ladbroke Grove tube. **Open** 10.30am-6.30pm Mon-Fri; 10am-6.30pm Sat; noon-5pm Sun. **Credit** AmEx, DC, MC, V.
In an attempt to make the serious act of record-buying into a lighter experience, the decor of Intoxica! comes off as more Disney Store than HMV. Furnishings aside, it stocks an enviable selection of folk, beat and psyche vinyl, as well as a good range of original and reissue vinyl from the 1950s, '60s and '70s. Displacing the retro vibe somewhat, it also sells some of the more highbrow modern indie, such as Tindersticks or Belle and Sebastian, all on vinyl of course. *Mail order.*

Minus Zero Records
2 Blenheim Crescent, W11 1NN (7229 5424/ www.minuszerorecords.com). Ladbroke Grove tube. **Open** 10.30am-6pm Fri, Sat. **Credit** MC, V.
Is that must-have, vinyl test-pressing of Stephen Stills's debut album still eluding you? If these boys don't stock it, they'll know a man who does. Minus excels in rare folk, blues, rock, psychedelia and power pop. Interestingly, the shop also specialises in REM rarities, as well as releasing records for the little-known 1970s West Coast group Skooshny on the house label.

Music & Video Exchange
38 Notting Hill Gate, W11 3HX (7243 8573/ www.mveshops.co.uk). Notting Hill Gate tube. **Open** 10am-8pm daily. **Credit** AmEx, MC, V.
Stockists of second-hand CDs and vinyl, M&VE's selection is sometimes infuriatingly limited (with the same Strokes album cropping up every other CD) and a bit grubby, but that doesn't seem to stop browsers from avidly flicking through the stacks of records on offer. There's a good range of rock and pop, however, and if it's has-been, 1990s indie pop or deleted VHS you're after, the bargain basement is unbeatable.

On the Beat
22 Hanway Street, W1T 1UQ (7637 8934). Tottenham Court Road tube. **Open** 11am-7pm Mon-Sat. **No credit cards**.
Rock and indie heritage is the theme at the laid-back On the Beat, which is reflected in its astonishingly up-to-date selection of seven-inches and LPs. This dimly lit shop can be slightly intimidating at first, but you'll soon be entranced by the old-skool indie trappings and racks of perfectly kept vinyl. The ideal shop for those who like to know about the next big guitar band before everyone else does.

Out on the Floor
10 Inverness Street, NW1 7HJ (7267 5989). Camden Town tube. **Open** 10am-6pm daily. **Credit** AmEx, MC, V.

With the recent closure of the sublime Rhythm Records, non-chain record shops in Camden are in seriously short supply. The decor of this used vinyl shop resembles a Cream album cover, but the collection of ska, reggae, 1960s and '70s rock LPs, grunge, indie and rare seven-inches is very well kept. Venture to the basement, and you'll discover rare singles, as well as a few pieces of grunge, punk and hardcore along the way. Out on the Floor also buys and sells records and CDs.

Promo
47 Church Road, NW4 4EB (8203 8868). Hendon Central tube/Hendon rail. **Open** 11am-5.30pm Tue-Sat. **No credit cards**.
Two rooms jam-packed with 1960s, '70s and '80s rock, soul and funk classics on record, tape and CD. Although the emphasis here is definitely on CDs, there is a nice collection of cheap seven- and 12-inch singles coupled with a multitude of DVDs, videos and games.

Reckless Records
26 & 30 Berwick Street, W1F 8RH (7434 3362/ 7437 4271/www.reckless.co.uk). Oxford Circus tube. **Open** 10am-7pm daily. **Credit** MC, V.
The selection of used CDs and vinyl is cheap, eclectic and always worth a rummage. An incoming section allows regular patrons to keep abreast of what's coming in and if you haven't got the time, the counter staff will gladly search out requests. DVDs and box sets are also starting to take up quite a bit of space, and the basement of No.26 houses a comprehensive collection of 1960s, '70s and '80s rock. Sadly, this branch is the last of the Reckless family to survive a recent cull, which resulted in the closure of shops in Camden and Islington. Sob.

Sounds Familiar
47 North Street, Romford, Essex RM1 1BA (01708 730 737/www.locallife.co.uk/sounds familiar). Romford rail. **Open** 10am-6pm Mon-Sat; noon-4pm Sun. **Credit** MC, V.
The 1960s are alive and well at this shop, where most sounds are covered on vinyl and stock is in fairly good nick. The speciality is deleted items, all of which are listed on the website, but there is no mail order service, so you'll have to take the long road to Romford to pick up anything you want. Upstairs is the silver-screen department, selling videos for next to nothing.

Stand Out Collectors Records
2 Blenheim Crescent, W11 1NN (7727 8406). Ladbroke Grove or Notting Hill Gate tube. **Open** 10am-6.30pm Fri, Sat. **Credit** MC, V.
Those looking to bolster their Scott Walker collection, search no further. Specialising in 1960s CDs and vinyl, with some excellent reissues and remasters, Stand Out is serious about its trade. Whatever you do, don't go throwing the term 'retro' around the place.

Steve's Sounds
20-20A Newport Court, WC2H 7JS (7437 4638). Leicester Square tube. **Open** 10.30am-8pm Mon-Sat; noon-7.30pm Sun. **No credit cards**.
Open-fronted music vendor with honestly priced, new-release CDs and the odd gem nestled away for those prepared to forage. The selection is unashamedly skewed towards the pop end of things, but for £8 an album, who's complaining?

Indie

Rough Trade
130 Talbot Road, W11 1JA (7229 8541/ www.roughtrade.com). Ladbroke Grove tube. **Open** 10am-6.30pm Mon-Sat; noon-5pm Sun. **Credit** AmEx, DC, MC, V.
Arguably London's coolest record shop, Rough Trade stocks some real treasures, but the prices do tend to err on the expensive side. For those nearer central London, you may want to check out the branch in Covent Garden (basement of Slam City Skates, 16 Neal's Yard, WC2H 9DP, 7240 0105), which is similarly decked with indie-rock

obscurities. If there was an award for the friendliest record shop staff in London, Rough Trade would win hands down. Also, their taste is impeccable: recommended buys will rarely miss the spot.
Mail order.

Selectadisc
34-35 Berwick Street, W1V 3RF (7734 3297/ www.selectadisc.co.uk). Oxford Circus or Tottenham Court Road tube. **Open** 9.30am-7pm Mon-Sat; noon-6pm Sun. **Credit** AmEx, MC, V.
For collectors, scenesters and even those inclined towards the casual dalliance, Selectadisc is a record shop nirvana. The new releases are always a few pounds cheaper than the nearby megastores (as they don't jack up the price horrifically on imports) and the selection of American rock and indie is by far the best in London. An hour or so listening to the in-house stereo is a good way to sample the best new sounds on offer.

Sister Ray
94 Berwick Street, W1F 0QF (7287 8385/ www.sisterray.co.uk). Oxford Circus or Piccadilly Circus tube. **Open** 9.30am-8pm Mon-Sat; 11am-5pm Sun. **Credit** AmEx, MC, V.
Despite a pokey exterior, Sister Ray has an almost Tardis-like way of housing a massive selection of alternative CDs and vinyl – from industrial-experimental through to punk and new wave. It's also commended for giving dance and electronica a fair fight against the barrage of rock and indie. With complete back catalogues for big names like Waits, Costello and Zevon, Sister Ray is also good for those trying to track down a bootleg or two.
Mail order.

Sound 323
323 Archway Road, N6 5AA (8348 9595/ www.sound323.com). Highgate tube. **Open** noon-5.30pm Tue-Fri; 10am-5.30pm Sat. **Credit** MC, V.
Owner Mark Wastell and his colleague will track down rare albums (and genuinely relish finding them) and play their recommended tracks to you for hours. The stock consists of mainly deviant genres, ranging from electronica to avant-garde jazz via electro-acoustic improv. Although 70% of its trade is through mail order, the shop itself is well worth visiting – customers make pilgrimages from afar.
Mail order.

Jazz

Honest Jon's
278 Portobello Road, W10 5TE (8969 9822/ www.honestjons.com). Ladbroke Grove tube. **Open** 10am-6pm Mon-Sat; 11am-5pm Sun. **Credit** AmEx, DC, MC, V.
With its own record label and a huge selection of CDs and vinyl, this Damon Albarn-affiliated soul, jazz and hip-hop shop has become something of a London institution. Friendly staff and a laid-back atmosphere complement its enormous spread, which also covers genres from dancehall and ska via dub.

Mole Jazz
2 Great Marlborough Street, W1F 7HQ (7437 8800/www.molejazz.com). Oxford Circus tube. **Open** 10am-6pm Mon-Sat. **Credit** AmEx, MC, V.
With a shop floor that resembles someone's bedroom, Mole Jazz is a friendly establishment with knowledgeable staff. With full ranges of ECM and Blue Note, there are also many second-hand jazz discs on vinyl and CD for about £10 apiece and a neat range of jazz '78s. If Mole Jazz were an album, it would be Coltrane's *A Love Supreme* – small and complex.
Mail order.

Ray's Jazz at Foyles
1st Floor, Foyles Bookshop, 113-119 Charing Cross Road, WC2H 0EB (7440 3205/www. foyles.co.uk). Tottenham Court Road tube. **Open** 9.30am-9pm Mon-Sat; noon-6pm Sun. **Credit** MC, V.

With Ray's Jazz, it seems that everyone who visits instantly becomes a regular. They come for the coffee and stay for the bargain-priced second-hand vinyl and CDs, extensive jazz back catalogues, and the folk, blues and experimental rarities. There is also the added incentive of regular performances by established jazz artists on most Saturday afternoons at 2pm. Has there ever been so much (jazz-related) fun packed into such a small space?

Nostalgia

Discurio
Unit 3, Faraday Way, St Mary Cray, Kent BR5 3QW (01689 879 101/www.discurio.com). Open 9.30am-5pm Mon-Fri. Credit MC, V.
You won't find Britney or Radiohead here, but if it's military, choir and organ music on all formats you're looking for, this is the place to come. Discurio recently moved here from Rochester, and now receives visitors by appointment only, so call before making the trek down there.
Mail order.

The Elvis Shop
400 High Street North, E12 6RH (8552 7551). East Ham tube. **Open** 9.30am-5.30pm Mon-Sat. **Credit** MC, V.
The king is alive and living in East Ham. This emporium dedicated to all things Elvis proves he still has awesome pulling power after 50 years. There's original memorabilia from Colonel Parker's EPE firm, Elvis originals on LP and CD, new releases (coming out all the time) and much more. It's not all expensive, with a good selection for the smaller budget, but a Japanese original ten-inch of *Love Me Tender* can go for £10,000.
Mail order.

Record Detective Agency
492 Green Lanes, N13 5XD (8882 6278). Southgate tube/Palmers Green rail/329, W2, W6 bus. **Open** noon-6pm Mon-Sat. **No credit cards**.
LPs and singles from the 1950s, '60s and '70s are all in good condition here, but most people come for the services of Derek Burbridge, a vinyl-hunter's Sherlock Holmes who uses his sleuthing skills to fill tricky gaps in your record collection.
Mail order.

Sounds Original
169 South Ealing Road, W5 4QP (8560 1155/ www.soundsoriginal.co.uk). South Ealing tube. **Open** 11am-5.30pm Wed-Sat. **Credit** MC, V.
'Condition is king' at this above-average local store, which draws customers wanting to expand or upgrade their record collections. The speciality is antique UK LPs and singles from 1953 to 1968, and expert staff are keen to rise to the challenge of even the most tricky wish list.
Mail order.

Sounds That Swing
46 Inverness Street, NW1 7HB (7267 4682). Camden Town tube. **Open** noon-6pm Wed-Sun. **Credit** AmEx, MC, V.
Break out the pomade for a visit to this stockist of all things 1950s and '60s. It's a repository of vinyl rarities, reissues and compilations dealing mainly in swing, surf and rock 'n' roll.
Mail order.

Reggae

Body Music
261 High Road, N15 4RR (8802 0146). Seven Sisters tube/rail. **Open** 10am-8pm daily. **Credit** DC, MC, V.
Music of black origin in all its forms is supplied here. Body Music boasts friendly staff and a rich selection of CDs and vinyl.

Dub Vendor
274 Lavender Hill, SW11 1LJ (7223 3757/ www.dubvendor.co.uk). Clapham Junction rail. **Open** 10am-7pm Mon-Thur, Sat; 10am-7.30pm Fri; 11am-5pm Sun. **Credit** AmEx, MC, V.

LEISURE

If you think King Tubby is a character from a children's book, this store probably isn't the place for you. If, on the other hand, you enjoy earbleedingly loud bass and chronic dub beats, you'll love it. Dub Vendor boasts an immense selection of pre-release singles and receives more than 600 imports a month.

Hawkeye Record Store

2 Craven Park Road, NW10 4AB (8961 0866). Willesden Junction tube/rail. **Open** 10am-7pm Mon-Fri; 10am-8pm Sat. **Credit** AmEx, MC, V
Hawkeye stocks new reggae releases, rarities and concert videos of the greats. Easily the best resource in the area for those wishing to bolster their CD and vinyl collection, with everything from Lee 'Scratch' Perry to Jimmy Cliff.

Supertone Records, Videos & CDs

110 Acre Lane, SW2 5RA (7737 7761/ www.supertonerecords.co.uk). Brixton tube/rail. **Open** 11am-10pm Mon-Sat; 1-7.30pm Sun. **Credit** MC, V.
In business for 20 years, proprietor Wally B still takes his reggae, revival, soul, soca and gospel very seriously indeed. The website is easy to navigate and lists all the stock, from deluxe CD box sets down to seven-inches.

Wax Unlimited

9 Northwold Road, N16 7HL (7275 7513/ www.waxatax.com). Bus 73. **Open** 10am-8pm Mon-Sat. **Credit** AmEx, MC, V.
Gladdy Wax – aka Mr Wax – owns this Stokey favourite and promises to deliver the heartbeat of Jamaica to your door. He does a roaring trade in reggae, soul, ragga, gospel, jazz and soca, plus plenty of deletions and rarities.

Rock & mainstream

Banquet Records

52 Eden Street, Kingston-upon-Thames, Surrey, KT1 1EE (8549 5871/www.banquetrecords.com). Kingston rail. **Open** 9am-6pm Mon; 10am-6pm Tue, Wed, Sat; 10am-9pm Thur, Fri; noon-5pm Sun. **Credit** MC, V.
Great little independent store with its stock split right down the middle. One half consists of rock and indie (half CDs, half vinyl) and the other is hip hop, soul and funk, with a little bit of techno and house all its forms (soulful, US, deep, tech, electro). If your wallet isn't already feeling the strain, there are also T-shirts, belt buckles, turntable equipment and accessories on offer.
Mail order.

Black Dog Music

69 Berwick Street, W1F 8SZ (7287 6477). Oxford Circus tube. **Open** 10.30am-7pm Mon-Sat. **Credit** MC, V.
Cheap CDs and vinyl are the mainstay of this Berwick Street cornerstone. You can usually pick up new releases for a square tenner; head for the cash-only bargain basement for some rarities if Coldplay and Snow Patrol don't do it for you.

CD City

42 Berwick Street, W1F 8RZ (7287 2272). Oxford Circus tube. **Open** 11am-7pm Mon-Sat; noon-6pm Sun. **Credit** MC, V.
Very similar to nearby Black Dog, cut-price CDs across all genres – on precariously leaning CD shelves – are the stock in trade here. It also stocks some vinyl, including its own BBE label releases.

Clerkenwell Music

27 Exmouth Market, EC1R 4QL (7833 9757). Angel tube/Farringdon tube/rail. **Open** 10.30am-6.30pm Mon-Fri; 10.30am-5.30pm Sat. **Credit** AmEx, MC, V.
A tiny record boutique catering for (nearly) all tastes: classical, folk, country, world, funk, soul and dance, as well as rock and pop. Also a contender for friendliest and best informed staff in a London record shop. If it isn't already in stock, the staff is also perfectly happy to order stuff in for you.

Disque

11 Chapel Market, N1 9EZ (7833 1104/ www.disque.co.uk). Angel tube. **Open** 8am-9pm Mon-Wed; 8am-10pm Thur; 8am-midnight Fri, Sat; 11am-9pm Sun. **Credit** MC, V.
Disque offers two for £20 on most CDs and vinyl. Pop CDs and new dance music sell well here. With the recent closure of Reckless on Upper Street, this is probably the best place for CDs in the area.

Essential Music

16 Greenwich Market, SE10 9HZ (8305 1876). Greenwich rail/DLR. **Open** 10am-6pm daily. **Credit** AmEx, MC, V.
Hidden in the shroud of Greenwich's covered market, Essential is home to a strong selection of CDs: rock, pop, electronica, jazz, blues, soul and 1970s.

Fopp

1 Earlham Street, WC2H 9LL (7379 0883/ www.fopp.co.uk). Covent Garden or Leicester Square tube. **Open** 10am-10pm Mon-Sat; 11am-6pm Sun. **Credit** AmEx, MC, V.
Boasting a delightfully minimalist aesthetic and low, low prices, this burgeoning chain is especially brilliant for those looking to replenish their prog back catalogues on the cheap. Also good for picking up a bit of cult fiction and art-house DVDs at very decent prices.

Mr CD

80 Berwick Street, W1F 8TN (7439 1097/ www.mrcd.co.uk). Oxford Circus tube. **Open** 11.30am-7pm Mon-Fri; 11am-7pm Sat. **Credit** MC, V.
You'll find pop, indie, soul, R&B and hip hop on CD (natch) here at fairly low prices. If you've got the time to spare, the bargain basement also has a few cut-price treasures. There are mainstream DVD releases (especially box sets) for a few quid less than the nearby chainstores.

Vinyl Vault

5 Bradbury Street, N16 8JN (7923 0722). Dalston Kingsland Rail. **Open** 11am-7pm Mon-Sat. **No credit cards.**
Vinyl Vault stocks used vinyl across all genres: rock, reggae, funk, soul, hip hop and dance. Apparently, the shop is sometimes open on Sundays as well, but it all depends on how hard the proprietors were partying the night before. That's the spirit.

Shows & soundtracks

Dress Circle

57-59 Monmouth Street, WC2H 9DG (7240 2227/ www.dresscircle.com). Leicester Square tube. **Open** 10am-6.30pm Mon-Sat. **Credit** AmEx, MC, V.
In business for more than 20 years now, Dress Circle is the London authority on musical theatre. Its rich stock of original Broadway and West End cast recordings is accompanied by a vast selection of books, souvenir programmes, libretti and sheet music. Also of interest is its neat collection of British and American musical scores performed in foreign languages (anyone for Lloyd Webber's *Cats* in Polish?). Musical karaoke backing tracks are also proving popular.
Mail order.

Rare Discs

18 Bloomsbury Street, WC1B 3QA (7580 3516). Holborn or Tottenham Court Road tube. **Open** 10am-6.30pm Mon-Sat. **Credit** AmEx, DC, MC, V.
Rare Discs achieves the almost impossible feat of nurturing the tastes of both the film buff and the music buff in equal parts. Among its collection are kitsch curiosities like the *Arthur* soundtrack, next to bona fide original pressings of early work from Morricone and 1970s schlock horror scores. Both CD and vinyl enthusiasts are catered for. There are also classic movie stills and old magazines like *Picturegoer*, signed photos and original posters.
Mail order.

Soul & dance

Blackmarket

25 D'Arblay Street, W1F 8EJ (7437 0478/ www.blackmarket.co.uk). Oxford Circus tube. **Open** 11am-7pm Mon-Wed, Sat; 11am-8pm Thur, Fri. **Credit** AmEx, MC, V.
Specialising in vinyl house imports, Blackmarket has a reputation for being a focal point of the UK dance scene. Half an hour at the hands of the in-store stereo should have you well versed in all the new beats currently available. The website is comprehensive, and has a mail order service.

City Sounds

5 Kirby Street, EC1N 8TS (7405 5454/www.city-sounds.co.uk). Chancery Lane tube. **Open** 10am-6pm Mon-Wed, Fri, Sat; 10am-6.30pm Thur. **Credit** AmEx, DC, MC, V.
City Sounds is an authority on UK and US dance promos, go for as little as £5.50 a pop. House and garage are specialities, plus techno and drum 'n' bass on vinyl.

Crazy Beat Records

87 Corbets Tey Road, Upminster, Essex RM14 2AH (01708 228 678/www.crazybeat.co.uk). Upminster tube/rail. **Open** 10am-6pm Mon-Sat. **Credit** AmEx, MC, V.
Crazy Beat stocks new and used soul, jazz, hip hop, house and R&B, all with the relevant rarities for those willing to search. Staff accept wish lists by email; just remember you've got to carry it all home unless you want to pay the postage.
Mail order.

Deal Real

3 Marlborough Court, W1F 7EF (7287 7245/ www.dealreal.co.uk). Oxford Circus or Piccadilly Circus tube. **Open** 10.30am-7pm Mon-Sat; noon-6pm Sun. **Credit** AmEx, MC, V.
This centrally located hip-hop shop exudes effortless cool, while also managing to stock new UK and US releases, mix CDs (from £5), plus old soul and rarities. Also check out the in-store performances on the first and third Friday of the month. Recent spots have been filled by the likes of Kanye West, Amy Winehouse and Mos Def.

Eukatech

49 Endell Street, WC2H 9AJ (7240 8060/ www.eukatechrecords.com). Covent Garden tube. **Open** 11am-7pm Mon-Sat. **Credit** AmEx, MC, V.
With ten of its own labels, this Covent Garden shop is still fighting the good fight for techno, house, breaks and lounge music in the capital. An education for those who find dance music as pleasant as listening to a car alarm.
Mail order.

If Music...

3 Greens Court, W1F 0HD (7437 4799/www.if music.co.uk). Oxford Circus tube. **Open** 11am-7.30pm Mon-Sat; by appointment only Sun. **Credit** MC, V.
This little shop caters to 'taste-makers' – in other words, as the beshaded, blazered owner Jean-Claude says, 'A-list DJs'. As well as a mix of nu jazz, nu soul, broken beats and hip hop, If aims to immerse its customer in the world of the music it sells, with original art, Vestex turntables, cameras, vintage trainers and magazines all on offer.
Mail order.

Kinetec

15A Little Portland Street, W1W 8BW (7323 5303/www.bangingtunes.com). Oxford Circus tube. **Open** noon-8pm daily. **Credit** MC, V.
Formerly known as Banging Tunes, these guys are dance specialists with a hard line in trance, nu NRG, techno and acid techno breaks. With titles such as 'Superfast Oz Vs Project Mayhem' and 'Attack of the 50 Foot DJ', a bit of pre-visit dance revision is recommended.

Plastic Fantastic

35 Drury Lane, WC2B 5RH (7240 8055/ www.plasticfantastic.co.uk). Covent Garden tube. **Open** 11.30am-7pm Mon-Sat. **Credit** MC, V.

LEISURE

Opened in 1994 with the aim of giving vinyl (which, at the time, was in a massive slump) the respect it deserves, the bulging record racks of this discreet retailer has managed to attract the likes of Seb Fontaine and Steve Lawler as regulars. Tribal, progressive and tech house are the deal, plus promos and specialist rarities. *Mail order.*

Pure Groove Records

679 Holloway Road, N19 5SE (7281 4877/ www.puregroove.co.uk). Archway tube. **Open** 10am-6pm Mon, Tue, Sat; 10am-7pm Wed-Fri. **Credit** MC, V.

Once entirely vinyl, but now also selling CDs, Pure Groove specialises in UK/US house and garage, as well as promos and remixes. Staff also have a lot of time for more dance-inflected indie, such as bands from DFA to Ninja Tune. Check the website for details of in-store performances. *Mail order.*

Reds

500 Brixton Road, SW9 8EQ (7274 4476). Brixton tube/rail. **Open** 9.30am-8pm Mon-Sat; 11am-6pm Sun. **No credit cards.**

Offers new R&B, reggae, jazz, hip hop and garage on CD and vinyl, plus mixed CDs from £2.99. Staff are generally to be seen singing along – something which is easily done given the volume of the PA placed at the entrance.

Release the Groove

20 Denman Street, W1D 7HR (7734 7712/ www.easyvinyl.com). Piccadilly Circus tube. **Open** 11am-7pm Mon-Wed, Sat; 11am-8pm Thur, Fri. **Credit** MC, V.

A vast selection of breaks, funky house, R&B and drum 'n' bass can be found here. Also, US imports are super-cheap, and there's a nice line in turntable spares and upgrades.

Scenario

12 Ingestre Place, W1F 0JF (7439 0055/ www.scenariorecords.com). Oxford Circus tube. **Open** 11am-7pm Mon-Fri; noon-7pm Sat. **Credit** AmEx, MC, V.

Boasts the best UK and US hip hop, funk and soul, plus mix tapes, DVDs and DJ equipment. It also does a good line in turntablist LPs for those looking to enter the occasional DJ battle.

Selectors Music Emporium

100B Brixton Hill, SW2 1AH (7771 2011). Brixton tube/rail. **Open** 11am-7pm Mon-Sat; 11am-5pm Sun. **No credit cards.**

Selectors Music stock an impressive range of used and new vinyl including soul, two-tone, roots, R&B and garage. Certainly more than just your average reggae shop.

Smallfish

329 Old Street, EC1V 9LE (7739 2252/ www.smallfish.co.uk). Liverpool Street or Old Street tube/rail. **Open** 3-8pm Mon; 11am-8pm Tue-Sat; 11am-5pm Sun. **Credit** MC, V.

Smallfish deals primarily in new vinyl and CDs, with electronica, experimental and mainstream dance being the genres of choice. The number of labels verges on the ridiculous, and staff appear to know every disc intimately. *Mail order.*

Soul Brother Records

1 Keswick Road, SW15 2HL (8875 1018/ www.soulbrother.com). East Putney tube. **Open** 10am-7pm Mon-Sat; 11am-5pm Sun. **Credit** AmEx, MC, V.

If you're a 'soul man', this is the place to let it be known. The store attracts those with a passion for new soul, funk and jazz on vinyl and CD – customers have been known to burst into song to get staff to identify a hook line. There's a huge stock, only a third of which – including an excellent selection of original Blue Note releases and rarities – is kept in the shop. But if it isn't in stock, staff will do their best to find it for you. *Mail order.*

Sounds of the Universe

7 Broadwick Street, W1F 0DA (7494 2004/ www.soundsoftheuniverse.com). Tottenham Court Road tube. **Open** 11.30am-7pm Mon-Fri; noon-6.30pm Sat. **Credit** MC, V.

A vast reggae section, lots of hip hop and dance, plus plenty of classic early house. Unlike most record shops in London, the ambience is boosted immeasurably by tall windows that let in lots of natural light, and nice, clean record racks. The recently opened basement specialises in rare latin, punk and disco, all on vinyl. For impulse buyers, there's a nifty listening post and knowledgeable staff to ease you towards a purchase.

Swag Records

42 Station Road, Croydon, Surrey CR0 2RB (8681 7735/www.swagrecords.com). West Croydon rail. **Open** 11am-7pm Mon-Wed, Fri, Sat; 11am-8pm Thur. **Credit** AmEx, DC, MC, V.

Sounds of the Universe

First opened in 1993, Swag excels in underground UK and US garage, techno, house and breakbeat. It boasts five in-house labels and staff who know the underground scene inside and out.
Mail order.

Trax

55 Greek Street, W1D 3DT (7734 0795/www.trax records.co.uk). Tottenham Court Road tube. **Open** noon-7pm Mon-Thur, Sat; noon-9pm Fri. **Credit** AmEx, MC, V.
If the gay club scene were a shop, then this would be it. Euro dance, funky house and NRG for sale. Alongside some of the more banging house tunes, you can find a camp line in old Eurovision DVDs and Trax's own line in record bags and boxes.
Mail order.

Uptown Records

3 D'Arblay Street, W1 3DF (7434 3639/www.up townrecords.com) Oxford Circus tube. **Open** 10.30am-7pm Mon-Wed, Sat; 10.30am-8pm Thur, Fri. **Credit** AmEx, MC, V.
Independent black dance music is the speciality at this 11-year-old, broom cupboard-sized store. The racks hold plenty of vinyl exclusive to Uptown and there are also soundtracks, DVDs and record bags. The staff are all DJs in their own right, so in terms of recommendations their word is oak.

Vinyl Junkies

9 & 12 Berwick Street, W1F 0PJ (7439 2923/ www.vinyl-junkies.co.uk). Piccadilly Circus tube. **Open** 11am-8pm Mon-Sat; noon-5.30pm Sun. **Credit** AmEx, MC, V.
Compromised slightly by the market stands on Berwick Street that cover its shopfront, VJ

nonetheless carries an exhaustive collection of house music from all over the globe. Checking out the staff choices is also a great shortcut for those looking to increase the hipness of their record collection on the quick.
Mail order.

Wyld Pytch

51 Lexington Street, W1F 9HL (7434 3472/ www.wyldpytch.com). Oxford Circus tube. **Open** 11am-7pm Mon-Sat. **Credit** MC, V.
Founded by the delightfully named Digger Elias, Wyld Pytch features new R&B and hip hop from the US and UK. American promos go for £9.99, and there are how-to-DJ DVDs, compilations and mix tapes too.

World, folk & country

Bud's Country Music Store

184 High Street, SE20 7QB (8676 8801/ www.budscountrymusicstore.com). Kent House rail. **Open** 10.15am-6pm Mon, Tue, Thur-Sat. **Credit** MC, V.
Lovingly laid out with a stock of over 10,000 records – second-hand and new, mainstream and obscure – Bud's is a haven for roots rock, insurgent country and Americana. With everything from Johnny Cash to Kitty Wells, staff can probably even advise you on the right way to wear a bootlace tie.
Mail order.

Mandy's Irish Shop

161 Willesden High Road, NW10 2SG (8459 2842). Willesden Green tube/98 bus. **Open** 8am-6pm Mon-Sat; 8am-3pm Sun. **No credit cards.**

Mandy's stocks a massive range of traditionally played Irish music on CD. Currently the biggest selling folk album is *Notes from the Heart* by Mick, Louise and Michelle Mulcahy. The store also stocks a range of Irish videos and DVDs.
Mail order.
For branch see index.

Musik Dunyasi

58 Green Lanes, N16 9NH (7254 5337/www.turk ishmusicuk.com). Manor House tube/141, 341 bus. **Open** noon-9pm daily. **No credit cards.**
Here you can pick up the latest Tarkan (Turkey's Justin Timberlake) single, as well as a variety of more traditional Turkish music. There are Turkish instruments, football gear and even hookahs too.
Mail order.

Stern's Music

293 Euston Road, NW1 3AD (7387 5550/ www.sternsmusic.com). Warren Street tube. **Open** 10.30am-6.30pm Mon-Sat. **Credit** AmEx, MC, V.
Premier stockists of world music, most notable for the collections from Africa and Latin America.
Mail order.

Trehantiri Greek & Arabic Music

365-367 Green Lanes, N4 1DY (8802 6530/ www.trehantiri.com). Manor House tube. **Open** 10.30am-7pm Mon-Sat; noon-5pm Sun. **Credit** AmEx, DC, MC, V.
With the largest selection of Greek music in the world (outside Greece), this shop has attracted Greek singers looking for copies of their old albums. It also sells Arabic music.
Mail order.

Sport

Department stores generally stock a good range of sports equipment; **John Lewis** has a wide selection of own-brand goods at very competitive prices, while **Selfridges** and **Harrods** house concessions of various London specialist shops, such as the **Cycle Surgery** (*see p230*) and **Speedo**. For ultra-cheap sportswear – tracksuits, T-shirts and the like – **H&M** (*see p44*), **TK Maxx** (57 King Street, W6 9HW, 8563 9200, www.tkmaxx.co.uk) and **Uniqlo** (84-86 Regent Street, W1B 5RR, 7434 9688, www.uniqlo.co.uk) are hard to beat.

All-rounders

British Sports
157 Praed Street, W2 1RL (7402 7511). Paddington tube/rail. **Open** 9am-6pm Mon-Sat. **Credit** AmEx, DC, MC, V.
A good independent sports shop, particularly strong on target sports, including archery, darts, airguns and even paintball guns. There's also a decent selection of second-hand golf clubs. *Mail order.*

Decathlon
Canada Water Retail Park, Surrey Quays Road, SE16 2XU (7394 2000/www.decathlon.co.uk). Canada Water tube. **Open** 10am-7.30pm Mon-Thur; 10am-8pm Fri; 9am-7pm Sat; 11am-5pm Sun. **Credit** MC, V.
A real phenomenon on the Continent, Decathlon is a superstore divided into individually staffed sports sections. It covers almost every activity under the sun but has a particularly good range of camping equipment, plus various specialist products.

JD Sports
268-269 Oxford Street, W1R 1LD (7491 7677/ www.jdsports.co.uk). Oxford Circus tube. **Open** 9am-8pm Mon, Tue, Sat; 9am-9pm Wed-Fri; 11.30am-6pm Sun. **Credit** AmEx, DC, MC, V.
Firmly in the urban youth market, JD has its eye on the bling side of trainers and tracksuits, and even stocks Missy Elliott's new sportswear collection. **Branches**: throughout the city.

Len Smith's
1-15 Heath Road, Twickenham, Middx TW1 4DB (8892 2201/www.lensmiths.co.uk). Twickenham rail. **Open** 9am-5.30pm Mon-Sat. **Credit** MC, V.
This old-style sports shop started out as a school uniform supplier. It still sells uniforms and team strips for local schools, but now also stocks a wide range of sports equipment and clothing for adults and kids. As you might expect, field team sports – cricket, lacrosse and hockey – are well represented. *Mail order.*

Lillywhites
24-36 Lower Regent Street, SW1Y 4QF (0870 333 9600/www.sports-soccer.co.uk). Piccadilly Circus tube. **Open** 10am-9pm Mon-Sat; noon-6pm Sun. **Credit** AmEx, DC, MC, V.
Having been taken over by the Sports Soccer group, Lillywhites has given up on equipment for pricier pursuits – riding, diving and so on – and now focuses on more urban activities, such as football, basketball and running. Sophistication has gone out the window, as bridles have been replaced by pile-'em-high tracksuit deals. Still, it's good for mainstream sports gear.

NikeTown
236 Oxford Street, W1W 8LG (7612 0800/ www.nike.com). Oxford Circus tube. **Open** 10am-7pm Mon-Wed; 10am-8pm Thur-Sat; noon-6pm Sun. **Credit** AmEx, MC, V.

A multi-storey temple to the revered tick, NikeTown combines the layout of a department store with the look of a nightclub. The industrial space is split into different sports (for example, golf and basketball), stocking a lot of trainers and sportswear – some functional, some purely fashionable. Whether you want a golf club or a yoga mat, come here for the choice rather than the bargains – the latter are few and far between. *Mail order.*

Specialists

American sports

English Basketball Enterprises
14A Digby Drive, Melton Mowbray, Leics LE13 0RQ (01664 568 502/www.basketballenter prises.co.uk). **Phone enquiries** 9am-5pm Mon-Fri. **Credit** MC, V.
This subsidiary of the England Basketball sports association supplies team strips, balls, hoops and boots, as well as news of, and tickets for, the NBA. *Mail order.*

First Base International
172 North Gower Street, NW1 2ND (7383 2999/ 0870 241 5193/www.rawlingsdirect.co.uk). **Phone enquiries** 10am-5.30pm Mon-Fri. **Credit** MC, V.
The official UK distributor for classic US baseball and softball brand Rawlings sells mitts, bats, balls, bases and uniforms. Starter kits from £600. *Mail order.*

Trans Atlantic Sports
56 Lightfoot Lane, Fulwood, Preston, Lancs PR2 3LR (0870 0637 466/www.ta-sports.net). **Phone enquiries** 9.30am-4pm Mon-Fri. **Credit** AmEx, MC, V.
A very good online shop for all US and Canadian sports played in Britain, including baseball, ice hockey, American football, softball and basketball.

Archery

Quicks Archery Centre
Apps Court, Hurst Road, Walton-on-Thames, Surrey KT12 2EG (01932 232 211/www.quicks. com). **Open** 9.30am-5pm Mon-Sat. **Credit** MC, V.
This professional supplier is run by archers and provides friendly advice, plus all the gear you need to hit the bullseye. An on-site range is also available. *Mail order (02392 254 114).*

Athletics

For trend-led trainers, *see p53* **Trainerspotting**.

Foot Locker
363-367 Oxford Street, W1R 2BJ (7491 4030/ www.footlocker.com). Oxford Circus tube. **Open** 9am-9pm Mon-Sat; noon-6pm Sun. **Credit** AmEx, MC, V.
Foot Locker is essentially trainer-oriented, though it stocks sportswear too. All the big names are well represented – Nike, Reebok et al – and the stock reflects whatever is de rigueur with the boyz 'n' girlz outside on Oxford Street.
Branches: throughout the city.

Run & Become
42 Palmer Street, SW1H 0PH (7222 1314/ www.runandbecome.com). St James's Park tube. **Open** 9am-6pm Mon-Wed, Fri, Sat; 9am-8pm Thur. **Credit** MC, V.
A specialist in running shoes, with styles for long distance, road running, off-road and track and field events, as well as more basic models. *Mail order.*

Runners Need
34 Parkway, NW1 7AH (7267 7525/ www.runnersneed.co.uk). Camden Town tube. **Open** 10am-6pm Mon, Tue, Thur-Sat; 10am-8pm Wed; 11am-4pm Sun. **Credit** AmEx, DC, MC, V.
Staffed by runners, this shop sells top trainer brands such as Saucony, Sub 4 and Asics, as well as styles for track and field, racing, fell running and cross country, plus more workaday makes. There are also running clothes, books, nutrition and accessories such as injury supports and impact-reducing insoles. There's a concession in the E1 branch of Cycle Surgery (*see p230*).
Mail order (7485 7869).

Triandrun
53 New North Road, Hainault, Essex IG6 2UE (8500 4841/www.triandrun.com). Hainault tube. **Open** 9.30am-5.30pm Mon, Tue, Thur, Fri; 9.30am-6pm Sat. **Credit** MC, V.
This specialist triathlon store is set for a refit in early 2006, which will make more space for its own range of bikes along with running shoes, wetsuits, Speedo and TYR swimwear, plus associated accessories. Race and events news is available too.
Mail order.

Bodybuilding

Workout World
Unit 9, Adam's Walk, Kingston-upon-Thames, Surrey KT1 1DF (8541 4907/www.workout world.net). Kingston-upon-Thames rail. **Open** 10am-6pm Mon-Sat. **Credit** MC, V.
A sizeable store dedicated to sporting nutritional supplements. It also carries a small selection of gym wear and some weightlifting supports.
Mail order.

Bowling

Tenpinshop.com
www.tenpinshop.com. **Credit** MC, V.
An online store selling everything you might need for a day down the alley, from gloves and balls to shoes. It even sells gift vouchers.
Mail order.

Cricket

The Lord's Shop
Lord's Cricket Ground, St John's Wood Road, NW8 8QN (7432 1021/www.shopatlords.com). St John's Wood tube. **Open** *Apr-Sept* 10am-5pm daily (extended hours for test match and finals days). *Oct-Mar* 10am-5pm Mon-Thur; 10am-4.30pm Fri; 11am-4pm Sat, Sun. **Credit** MC, V.
Top-of-the-range cricket gear, covering classic whites, pads, boxes and bats – plus all the extras, including books, prints, souvenirs and a large selection of Oakley sunglasses.
Mail order.

Surrey County Cricket Club Equipment Shop
BRIT Oval Cricket Ground, SE11 5SS (7820 5756/www.surreycricket.com). Oval tube. **Open** *Apr-Oct* 10am-6pm Mon-Fri; 9am-1pm Sat; 10am-end of play Sun (match days only). *Nov-Mar* 10am-9pm Mon-Thur; 10am-7pm Fri; 10am-6pm Sat, Sun. **Credit** MC, V.
There are two shops at the home of the Surrey County Cricket Club. This one stocks equipment and pro-level kit; the other (7820 5714) keeps shorter hours and has more fan-related gear, such as books and logoed memorabilia.
Mail order.

Croquet

The Croquet Association Shop
112 Potters Lane, Send, Woking, Surrey GU23 7AL (01483 776 971/www.croquet.org.uk). **Phone enquiries** 9am-5pm Mon-Sat. **Credit** MC, V.

This mail-order croquet specialist sells garden sets from £120, competition club sets from £730, and mallets, balls and hoops. Call to arrange a visit if you want to see stock before buying.
Mail order.

Cycling

See chapter **Transport**.

Dance

For **Dancia International** and **Freed of London**, *see p72*.

Duo Dance

11 Half Moon Lane, SE24 9JU (7274 4517/ www.duodance.co.uk). Herne Hill rail. **Open** 9.30am-5.30pm Mon, Tue, Thur-Sat. **Credit** AmEx, MC, V.
Duo is undoubtedly the UK's leading supplier of dancing shoes, covering practically every conceivable style for both adults and children. There's also a small range of dance clothing, including leotards and jazz pants, but the emphasis here is really on feet.
Mail order.

Darts

Frank Johnson Sports

189 Ferndale Road, SW9 8BA (7733 1722/ www.frankjohnsonsports.co.uk). Brixton tube/rail. **Open** 9.30am-6pm Mon-Sat. **Credit** MC, V.
Darts enthusiasts should be able to find pretty much everything they need at this store, with its large selection of polyester flights, tips and darts boards. Orders can also be made through the website.
Mail order.

Equestrian

For **Swaine Adeney Brigg**, *see p78*.

Fencing

Leon Paul Equipment

Units 1-2, Cedar Way Industrial Estate, Camley Street, NW1 0PD (7388 8132/www.leonpaul. com). Camden Town tube. **Open** 9am-5pm Mon-Fri; 10am-3pm Sat. **Credit** MC, V.
The official supplier to the British Fencing Team of masks, sabres, breeches and so on, Leon Paul can also advise on where to take up the sport.
Mail order.

Fishing & angling

Bowlers Angling

2-3 Cinema Parade, Whalebone Lane South, Dagenham, Essex RM8 1AA (8592 3273/ www.bowlersangling.co.uk). Dagenham Heathway tube. **Open** 9am-6pm Mon-Thur, Sat; 9am-7pm Fri; 10am-4pm Sun. **Credit** AmEx, MC, V.
A huge range of fishing tackle and accessories by leading brands, from rods and reels to clothing and chairs. There's a repair service too.
Mail order (8948 7533).

Farlows

9 Pall Mall, SW1Y 5LX (7484 1000/www.farlows. co.uk). Piccadilly Circus tube. **Open** 9am-6pm Mon-Wed, Fri; 9am-7pm Thur; 10am-6pm Sat. **Credit** AmEx, DC, MC, V.
It has been around since 1840 and as such knows a thing or two about 'country pursuits'. Farlows is the best place in town to get kitted out for a weekend's shooting or fishing, or even just a smart stroll with one's corgis. The store looks like an art gallery, and the staff, as you might expect, are informed and courteous. Along with the typical Barbour jackets, Hunter boots and fishing rods, it sells slightly less refined brands such as Simms and Patagonia.
Mail order (7484 1000).

Football

All of the capital's professional football clubs have shops at their grounds.

Soccer Scene

56-57 Carnaby Street, W1F 9QF (7439 0778/ www.soccerscene.co.uk). Oxford Circus tube. **Open** 9.30am-7pm Mon-Wed, Fri, Sat; 9.30am-8pm Thur; 11.30am-5.30pm Sun. **Credit** AmEx, MC, V.
A paradise for footie fans seeking celebrity kits – Soccer Scene always has the new replica England and London teams' kits (including kids' sizes) before anyone else. Balls, keepers' gloves, fan scarves, videos and memorabilia are all sold. Rugby Scene (*see p226*) is upstairs.
For branch see index.

Golf

Nevada Bob's

The Rotunda, Broadgate Circle, EC2M 2BN (7628 2333/www.nevadabobsgolf.co.uk). Liverpool Street tube/rail. **Open** 9.30am-6pm Mon-Fri; 10am-4pm Sat. **Credit** AmEx, DC, MC, V.
The UK's leading golfing chain can satisfy almost any customer, including left-handers and juniors. It sells more than 30 brands of club, as well as a whole range of accessories.
For branch see index.

Regent's Park Golf & Tennis School

Outer Circle, Regent's Park, NW1 4RL (7724 0643/www.rpgts.co.uk). Baker Street tube. **Open** 8am-9pm daily. **Credit** AmEx, MC, V.
A good pro shop attached to a driving range, where you can also organise tuition in golf or tennis. Golf clubs can be custom-fitted; tennis racquets can also be bought here, or restrung.

Hockey

The Hockey Centre

151 Maybury Road, Woking, Surrey GU21 5LJ (01483 730 912/www.hockeycentre.com). **Open** 10am-6pm Mon-Fri; 10am-5pm Sat. **Credit** MC, V.
This shop sells good-value gear – including RedHead clothing – for all types and standards of hockey player. Cricket kit is also sold in summer.
Mail order (0845 260 3604).

The Pro Shop

Unit E, 30 Commerce Road, Brentford, Middx TW8 8LE (8568 9929/www.proshopsport.com). Syon Lane rail. **Open** 10am-5.30pm Mon-Fri; 9.30am-5pm Sat. **Credit** MC, V.
Owned by British Olympic bronze and gold medallist Kulbir Bhaura, this shop offers expert advice on which stick to play with. Expect club strips and body protection, along with cricket and rugby equipment.

Kites

Flexifoil kites are stocked by the **Kite Store** (*see below*), **Snow + Rock** (*see p226*) and the Ski and Surf department at **Harrods** (*see p12*).

The Kite Store

48 Neal Street, WC2H 9PA (7836 1666/www.kite store.uk.com). Covent Garden tube. **Open** *Jan-Mar* 10am-6pm Mon-Fri; 10.30am-6pm Sat. *Apr-Nov* 10am-6pm Mon-Wed, Fri; 10am-7pm Thur; 10.30am-6pm Sat. *Dec* 10am-6pm Mon-Wed, Fri; 10am-7pm Thur; 10.30am-6pm Sat; 11am-5pm Sun. **Credit** AmEx, MC, V.
In spite of its fashionable location, the friendly Kite Store has an unpretentious air. No matter what kind of kite you're looking for (kids' toys, power kites, even kite buggies), you're bound to find it here – along with frisbees and boomerangs.
Mail order.

With Flying Colours

9 Wharf Road, Frimley Green, Camberley, Surrey GU16 6LE (01252 836 241/www.withflying colours.co.uk). Frimley Green rail. **Open** 9am-5pm Mon-Fri; 10am-5pm Sat. **Credit** MC, V.
This sports kite specialist sells the full range of harnesses, boards, suits and buggies. Paragliding sails and equipment are also available.

Martial arts

Meijin

141 Goldhawk Road, W12 8EN (8749 9070/ www.meijin.co.uk). Goldhawk Road tube. **Open** 9.30am-5pm Mon-Sat. **Credit** AmEx, MC, V.
Attractive karate clothes, plus mats, belts and training weapons.
Mail order.

Shaolin Way

10 Little Newport Street, WC2H 7JJ (7734 6391/www.shaolinway.com). Leicester Square tube. **Open** 11am-6.30pm Mon-Sat; 11am-5.30pm Sun. **Credit** AmEx, MC, V.
Squeezed into tiny premises, this martial arts discount centre manages to fit in punchbags, pads, sparring mitts, head guards and kung-fu shoes, as well as books such as *The Masters Speak* and details on courses.
Mail order.

Tao Sports

523 Green Lanes, N4 1AN (8348 0870/www.tao sport.co.uk). Turnpike Lane tube. **Open** 10am-6pm Mon-Fri; 10am-4pm Sat. **Credit** MC, V.
A veritable emporium of contact-sports gear, including equipment for karate, judo, kung fu, tae kwon do, ju-jitsu, Thai kick-boxing, regular boxing and boxercise. The relevant footwear, nutrition and weapons are all supplied.
Mail order.

Motorsports

Alex Reade Motorsports

78 Regent Street, W1B 5RW (7434 4324/ www.alexreade.com). Piccadilly Circus tube. **Open** 10am-6.30pm Mon-Sat; noon-6pm Sun. **Credit** AmEx, MC, V.
The shop has relocated and trebled in size, so there's much more room now for the motorsports memorabilia and gallery of prints, photos and paintings. As well as car parts, helmets and suits worn by racers – most of them signed – there's also a good selection of logoed clothing.
Mail order.

Grand Prix Racewear

Power Road, W4 5PY (8987 9999/www.gprdirect.com). Gunnersbury tube. **Open** 9.30am-6pm Mon-Wed, Fri; 9.30am-7.30pm Thur; 9.30am-5pm Sat. **Credit** AmEx, MC, V.
Official racing accessories for Formula 1, rally driving and karting by brands such as Sparco, Alpinestars and Puma.
Mail order (0870 160 0950).

Mountaineering, skiing & outdoor pursuits

Blacks

10-11 Holborn, EC1N 2LE (7404 5681/ www.blacks.co.uk). Chancery Lane tube. **Open** 9.30am-6pm Mon-Wed, Fri; 9.30am-7pm Thur; 9.30am-5.30pm Sat; 11am-5pm Sun. **Credit** AmEx, MC, V.
Full points for brilliant-value camping packages, skiing equipment in winter and lightweight trekking gear in summer. Clothing for all climates – from the likes of Berghaus, North Face and Mountain Hardwear – is sold year-round.
Mail order (0800 056 0127).
Branches: throughout the city.

Cotswold Outdoor

23-26 Piccadilly, W1J 0DJ (7437 7399/www. cotswoldoutdoor.com). Open 10am-6pm Mon-Fri; 10am-6pm Sat; 11am-5pm Sun. **Credit** AmEx, DC, MC, V.
Three storeys of well-organised outdoor, action and travel gear, covering all sorts of useful kit. Walking boots, climbing equipment and camping are particular strengths. Keenly priced mountainwear, good offers year-round and informed, friendly staff are further pluses.
Mail order (0870 442 775).
For branch see index.

Ellis Brigham

Tower House, 3-11 Southampton Street, WC2E 7HA (7395 1010/www.ellis-brigham.com). Covent Garden tube. **Open** 10am-7pm Mon-Wed, Fri; 10am-7.30pm Thur; 9.30am-6.30pm Sat; 11.30am-5.30pm Sun. **Credit** AmEx, MC, V.
Two floors stocked with everything you might need for the outdoors – and decently priced too. There's a lot of camping and trekking equipment from the likes of Berghaus, plus a ski and snowboard section that expands considerably during winter. There's even a two-storey ice wall for urban climbers. Sessions must be booked in advance, and prices range from £20 to £40 per hour, depending on whether you require supervision or equipment hire.
Mail order (0870 444 5555).
For branch see index.

Field & Trek

42 Maiden Lane, WC2E 7LJ (7379 3793/ www.fieldandtrek.com). Covent Garden tube. **Open** 10am-7pm Mon-Wed, Fri; 10am-8pm Thur; 9.30am-6.30pm Sat; 11am-5pm Sun. **Credit** AmEx, MC, V.
This outdoor footwear specialist has been around for more than three decades. Staff are highly trained and offer a 14- or 30-day boot fit guarantee. Climbing, mountaineering and camping gear is also sold, and brands encompass both the well-known and the obscure – Macpac from New Zealand, for instance.
Mail order (0870 777 1071).
For branches see index.

47 Degrees

907-909 Fulham Road, SW6 5HU (7731 5415/ www.47degrees.com). Parsons Green tube. **Open** *Apr-Sept* 10am-6pm Mon-Wed, Fri, Sat; 10am-7pm Thur; 11am-5pm Sun. *Oct-Mar* 10am-7pm Mon-Wed, Fri; 10am-8pm Thur; 10am-6pm Sat; 11am-5pm Sun. **Credit** MC, V.
As well as wide-ranging stock (though no climbing gear), this winter sports hotspot offers expert advice on buying equipment for skiing and boarding. The decent children's selection has a handy trade-in policy.
Mail order.
For branches see index.

The North Face

30-32 Southampton Street, WC2E 7HA (7240 9577/www.thenorthface.com/eu). Covent Garden tube/Charing Cross tube/rail. **Open** 10am-7pm Mon-Wed, Fri; 10am-7.30pm Thur; 9.30am-6.30pm Sat; 11am-5pm Sun. **Credit** AmEx, MC, V.
This handsome flagship store has two floors of clothing and equipment for outdoor activities – everything from walking boots to duffel bags – plus friendly, savvy staff. This American label is both high-quality and hip, a recipe for high prices.
Mail order (0870 444 5555).

Snow + Rock

4 Mercer Street, WC2H 9QA (7420 1444/ www.snowandrock.com). Covent Garden tube. **Open** 10am-7pm Mon-Wed, Fri, Sat; 10am-8pm Thur; 11.30am-5.30pm Sun. **Credit** AmEx, MC, V.
Among the vast quantities of jackets, boots and ropes in this six-storey tribute to the outdoors, there's an injury clinic and a Fairtrade café. What it lacks (ever so slightly) in value for money, it makes up for with choice and charming staff who know what they're on about (annual trips allow them to try out the equipment they sell).
Mail order (0845 100 1000).
For branches see index.

Urban Rock

Westway Sports Centre, 1 Crowthorne Road, W10 6RP (8964 0185/www.urbanrock.com). Latimer Road tube. **Open** noon-10pm Mon-Fri; 10am-8pm Sat, Sun. **Credit** MC, V.
This excellent shop is located at one of the best climbing walls in London. Novices can hire rock boots and harnesses, while experts can kit themselves out with everything they need for indoor and outdoor rock climbing. The personable staff know their stuff. Good for women's gear too.
For branch see index.

Racquet sports

Most good department stores (*see chapter* **Department Stores**) and general sports retailers sell a range of tennis, badminton and squash racquets.

Wigmore Sports

79-83 Wigmore Street, W1U 1QQ (7486 7761/ www.wigmoresports.co.uk). Bond Street tube. **Open** 10am-6pm Mon-Wed, Fri, Sat; 10am-7pm Thur. **Credit** AmEx, MC, V.
London's only racquet-sport specialist – covering tennis, squash, badminton and more – has a 'try before you buy' practice wall. In addition, Wigmore Sports sells whites, shoes for every court surface, balls and accessories; it even offers a restringing service. There are also concessions in Selfridges (*see p14*) and Harrods (*see p12*).
Mail order.

Rugby

Rugby Scene

1st Floor, 56-57 Carnaby Street, W1F 9QF (7287 9628/www.rugbyscene.co.uk). Oxford Circus tube. **Open** 9.30am-7pm Mon-Wed, Fri, Sat; 9.30am-8pm Thur; 11.30am-5.30pm Sun. **Credit** AmEx, MC, V.
Upstairs from Soccer Scene (*see p225*), this shop stocks anything of a rugby nature, including most replica premiership team shirts and major international kits. You'll also find shorts, head-, shin- and gum-shields, plus balls, memorabilia and videos.
For branch see index.

The Rugby Store

15-19 York Street, Twickenham, Middx TW1 3JZ (8892 9250/www.rfu.com). Twickenham rail. **Open** 10am-6pm Mon-Fri; 9am-5pm Sat. **Credit** AmEx, MC, V.
Everything rugby is covered here: replica England and international kits, boots, balls and body protection, plus trophies, scarves, rattles, videos, memorabilia and even tickets to games. The official England shirt is also sold (£70).
Mail order (0870 405 2003).

Skating & skateboarding

Club Blue Room

Marble Arch Tower, W2 2EN (7724 4884/ www.clubblueroom.com). Marble Arch tube. **Open** 10am-8pm Mon-Fri; 10am-6.30pm Sat; 11am-6pm Sun. **Credit** MC, V.
Club Blue Room stocks a large range of in-line skates (mainly recreational and freestyle) and safety equipment, plus some very reasonably priced skateboards (blank decks from £20) and associated accessories. Along with all the hardware is the standard fashion fare, such as Carhartt jeans and Fenchurch caps.
Mail order.

London's Skate Centre

27 Leinster Terrace, W2 3ET (7706 8769/ www.lonskate.com). Lancaster Gate tube. **Open** noon-6.30pm Tue-Fri; 11am-5pm Sat, Sun. **Credit** AmEx, MC, V.
Near to Queens Ice Bowl, this store sells ice skates, ice-hockey and roller-hockey sticks, as well as in-line skates – the latter can also be hired for use in nearby Hyde Park.
Mail order.

Skate Attack

72 Chase Side, N14 5PH (8886 7979/www. skateattack.co.uk). Southgate tube. **Open** 9am-6pm Mon-Sat.
Skate Attack has decades of experience selling ice-hockey skates, team strips, body protection, sticks and pucks; it also sells and repairs in-line skates and hockey gear. Quad skates and a select range of skateboards, including old-skool decks, are stocked too.
Mail order.

Slick Willie's

12 Gloucester Road, SW7 4RB (7225 0004). Gloucester Road tube. **Open** 10am-6.30pm Mon-Sat; noon-5pm Sun. **Credit** AmEx, MC, V.
A long-time favourite for surf gear, snowboard clobber, skateboard and in-line skating equipment, and not far from Hyde Park – the skating hub of London. Skates can be hired for £10 a day.
Mail order.

The Kite Store. See p225.

Snooker & billiards

Thurston
110 High Street, Edgware, Middx HA8 7HF (8952 2002/www.thurston-games.co.uk). Edgware tube. **Open** 8.30am-5.30pm Mon-Fri. **Credit** MC, V.
Established back in 1799, Thurston is a fine place for billiards, snooker and pool tables. The wide-ranging stock includes some antique billiard tables, all manner of cues and overhead shade lights, plus lawn bowls kits and other bar games. A repair service is available.
Mail order.

Surfing & snowboarding

Ocean Leisure (*see below*) stocks a selection of surfboards and bodyboards.

Boardwise
146 Chiswick High Road, W4 1PU (8994 6769/ www.boardwise.com). Turnham Green tube. **Open** 10am-6pm Mon-Wed, Fri, Sat; 10am-7pm Thur; noon-5pm Sun. **Credit** AmEx, MC, V.
With a comprehensive range of equipment and clothing, this is probably the city's best snowboard shop. You can even hire a board for the season. It also sells skateboards, plus surfboards and wetsuits in summer. The end-of-season sales usually yield bargains.
Mail order.

The Snowboard Asylum
Ellis Brigham, Tower House, 3-11 Southampton Street, WC2E 7HA (7395 1010/www.snowboard-asylum.com). Covent Garden tube. **Open** 10am-7pm Mon-Wed, Fri; 10am-7.30pm Thur; 9.30am-6.30pm Sat; 11.30am-5.30pm Sun. **Credit** AmEx, MC, V.
TSA is a shop-within-a-shop, selling snowboards, boots and bindings, as well as cold-weather clothing and all the trimmings. *See also p226* Ellis Brigham.
Mail order (0870 444 5555).
For branches (Ellis Brigham) see index.

Swimming & watersports

Women looking for fashion-conscious bikinis and cossies may want to try one of the new wave of beachwear boutiques, such as **Heidi Klein** (which also stocks men's trunks), **Pistol Panties** and **Biondi** (for all three, *see p75* **Splash out**). Sweaty Betty (*see below*) also stocks swimwear in summer. Diving divas looking for patterned flippers should check out **Funky Fins** (7930 5050, www.funkyfins.com).

Arthur Beale
194 Shaftesbury Avenue, WC2H 8JP (7836 9034). Tottenham Court Road tube. **Open** 9am-6pm Mon-Fri; 9.30am-1pm Sat. **Credit** AmEx, MC, V.
This classic yacht chandler sells everything you might need for any craft, as well as books, accessories and a wonderful collection of ropes.

Mike's Waterfront Warehouse
113 Power Road, W4 5PY (8994 6006/ www.mikeswu.com). Gunnersbury tube. **Open** 10am-6pm Mon-Fri; 10am-5.30pm Sat. **Credit** AmEx, MC, V.
This huge warehouse is full of competitively priced diving gear: BCDs, regulators, masks, maps, wetsuits, drysuits and semi-drys. Tanks can be filled and holidays arranged by the friendly and helpful staff.
For branch see index.

Ocean Leisure
11-14 Northumberland Avenue, WC2N 5AQ (7930 5050/www.oceanleisure.co.uk). Embankment tube. **Open** 9.30am-6pm Mon-Wed, Fri; 9.30am-7pm Thur; 9.30am-5.30pm Sat. **Credit** MC, V.
This impressive watersports emporium is particularly strong on diving, sailing and water-skiing. It also stocks a good selection of surfboards, as well as things to wear on shore, and there's even a special underwater-photography department. Staff are knowledgeable. The Chiswick branch specialises mainly in diving gear and also has a swimming pool for diving lessons.

Speedo
41-43 Neal Street, WC2H 9PJ (7497 0950/ www.speedo.com). Covent Garden tube. **Open** 10am-7pm Mon-Wed, Fri, Sat; 10am-8pm Thur; noon-6pm Sun. **Credit** AmEx, MC, V.

The full range from this classic brand is sold here, from full-length cossies to brightly coloured bikinis. Caps, goggles, fins and training aids also feature. Selfridges has a concession.
Mail order.

Table tennis

Decathlon (*see p224*) stocks a good range of table tennis equipment. **Argos** (*see p118*) stocks some of the cheapest indoor starter tables around.

UK Table Tennis
Unit 8, Riverside Business Park, Lyon Road, SW19 2RL (8540 2500/www.uktabletennis.co.uk). Colliers Wood tube. **Open** 8am-5pm Mon-Thur; 8am-4.30pm Fri. **Credit** MC, V.
An extensive choice of tables is offered here, some at very keen prices (from £285 for a sturdy outdoor model). There are also bats, ping-pong balls, nets and accessories for competitive or home use.
Mail order.

Yoga & Pilates

Calmia (*see p96*) sells designer yoga gear, mats and other accessories.

Pilates Plus
4 Crown Road, St Margarets, Middx TW1 3EE (8892 3403). St Margarets rail. **Open** 10am-5pm Mon-Fri; 10am-4pm Sat. **Credit** MC, V.
A small shop above a Pilates studio selling lots of yoga clothes and stretchwear, as well as all the necessary mats, exercise rings, workout balls, books and videos.

Sweaty Betty
21 Beak Street, W1F 9RR (7287 5128/ www.sweatybetty.com). Oxford Circus or Piccadilly Circus tube. **Open** 11am-7pm Mon-Sat; noon-5pm Sun. **Credit** MC, V.
This brilliant mini chain of women's sports shops is constantly expanding and branching out – it now stocks Stella McCartney's sportswear range for Adidas. Still particularly good for sweats, stretchwear and yoga kit and clothing, it also sells fun bikinis and beachwear in summer, plus ski and snowboard clothes in winter.
For branches see index.

Stationery

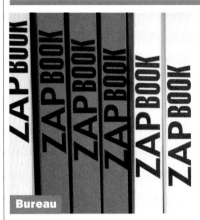

Bureau

Bureau

10 Great Newport Street, WC2H 7JL (7379 8898). Leicester Square tube. **Open** 10.30am-7pm Mon-Sat; noon-6pm Sun. **Credit** AmEx, MC, V.
You'll find everything for your office in this chic shop, from paper clips to envelopes, coloured paper, filing cabinets and furniture, as well as personal items such as photo and wedding albums, a large selection of cards, notepads and laptop cases. Binders and folders come in an array of bright block colours.

Ordning & Reda

186A King's Road, SW3 5XP (7351 1003/www. ordning-reda.com). Sloane Square tube. **Open** 10am-7pm Mon-Sat; noon-6pm Sun. **Credit** MC, V.
Modern, minimalist and stylish stationery is the stock in trade at this Swedish company. There are hundreds of products, including filing and storage systems, photo albums, writing paper and cloth-bound notebooks, gift wrap and bags, available in a veritable rainbow of bright and subdued colours. *Mail order.*

Paperchase

213-215 Tottenham Court Road, W1T 7PS (7467 6200/www.paperchase.co.uk). Goodge Street tube. **Open** 9.30am-7pm Mon, Wed, Fri, Sat; 10am-7pm Tue; 9.30am-8pm Thur; noon-6pm Sun. **Credit** AmEx, MC, V.
The flagship of this stationery superstore is a dream world for stationery addicts, with its eclectic mix of useful, tasteful and fun items. On the ground floor there are diaries, cards, gift wrap, journals, notebooks and desk storage units, while pencils, pens, invitations and coloured notepaper are at the back. More upmarket goods are displayed on the first floor: Lexon accessories, posh pens, clocks, picture frames, Filofaxes and a selection of furniture. The second floor is devoted to artists' materials (board, papers, brushes); *see also p206. Mail order (0161 839 1500).*
Branches: throughout the city.

Papyrus

48 Fulham Road, SW3 6HH (7584 8022/ www.papyrus.uk.com). South Kensington tube. **Open** 10am-6pm Mon-Fri; 10am-5.30pm Sat. **Credit** AmEx, MC, V.
Papyrus sells such elegant writing accoutrements as leather desk accessories, diaries and photo albums bound in leather or marbled paper, correspondence sets, fine notepaper and a range of artists' accessories, such as portfolios and bound sketch books. Prices can be steep, but the quality and craftsmanship are irreproachable. *Mail order.*

Ryman

14-16 Great Portland Street, W1N 5AA (7636 6368/www.ryman.co.uk). Oxford Circus tube. **Open** 8.30am-6pm Mon-Wed, Fri, Sat; 8.30am-7pm Thur. **Credit** AmEx, MC, V.
Good for basic essentials, this nationwide chain sells all manner of everyday stationery and related products, from pens, pencils, notepads and staplers to larger items such as filing cabinets and chairs. *Mail order (0800 801901).*
Branches: throughout the city.

Scribbler

15 Shorts Gardens, WC2H 9AT (7836 9600/ www.scribbler.co.uk). Covent Garden tube. **Open** 9am-7pm Mon-Sat; noon-6pm Sun. **Credit** AmEx, MC, V.
A great spot for fun cards ('You only live once, but if you work it right, once is enough'), cheeky gadgets and games, as well as colourful paper. Notebooks, organisers and diaries are also stocked.
For branches see index.

Smythson

40 New Bond Street, W1S 2DE (7629 8558/ www.smythson.com). Bond Street tube. **Open** 9.30am-6pm Mon-Wed, Fri; 10am-6pm Thur, Sat. **Credit** AmEx, DC, MC, V.
This venerable stationer's, established 1887, holds four royal warrants. Deluxe goods include leather-bound books – everything from diaries and visitors' books to themed notebooks ('Racing Notes', 'Secrets and Wishes') and address books; prices start at around £20. Other classy (and equally pricey) items include impeccable writing paper and bordered cards, which can be personalised, photo albums, desk accessories, manicure sets and leather wallets. *Mail order.*
For branch see index.

The Stationery Department

181 New King's Road, SW6 4SW (7384 1871). Parsons Green tube. **Open** 10am-6pm Mon-Sat. **Credit** MC, V.
A good array of stationery and classy pens is sold, along with paperweights, frames, address books, cards and gift wrap. Personalised letterheads and cards are also sold, as is kids' stuff, such as stickers.

Invitations

For wedding invitations, *see chapter* **Weddings**.

Copyprint

61 Ebury Street, SW1W 0NZ (7730 6282/ www.copyprintshops.co.uk). Victoria tube/rail. **Open** 9am-6pm Mon-Fri. **Credit** MC, V.
Copyprint can work from individual designs; you just supply the text or a logo on disk. In some cases there may be additional artwork charges (for layout or sizing) of £45 per hour. Simple A5 card invitations cost £25 for 100 (plus VAT) and upwards.
For branch see index.

Kall-Kwik

376 King's Road, SW3 5UZ (7351 3133/www. chelsea.kallkwik.co.uk). Bus 11, 19, 22. **Open** 9am-7pm Mon-Fri; 10.30am-1.30pm Sat. **Credit** MC, V.
Kall-Kwik charges from £47 (plus VAT) for 100 black and white A6 cards.
Branches: throughout the city.

Pip Printing

23-24 Denman Street, W1D 7HU (7734 9982/ www.pipuk.co.uk). Piccadilly Circus tube. **Open** 8.30am-5pm Mon-Fri. **Credit** MC, V.
Just £42.50 (plus VAT) buys 100 invitations on high-quality A6 cream card with single-sided black lettering; there's a £25 ink charge for colour.
Branches: throughout the city.

Pens

Penfriend

Bush House Arcade, Strand, WC2B 4PH (7836 9809/www.penfriend.co.uk). Temple tube. **Open** 9.30am-5.15pm Mon-Fri. **Credit** AmEx, DC, MC, V.
Penfriend has over 50 years' experience – reassuring if your pen needs repair or restoration. Leading brands (Swan, Burnham, De La Rue, Stephens, Mentmore), vintage writing instruments and accessories are sold; there's an engraving service too. *Mail order.*
For branch see index.

The Pen Shop

199 Regent Street, W1B 4LZ (7734 4088/ www.penshop.co.uk). Oxford Circus tube. **Open** 9.30am-6pm Mon, Tue, Fri, Sat; 10am-6pm Wed; 9.30am-7pm Thur. **Credit** AmEx, DC, MC, V.
A good range (£6.50-£1,550) of fountain pens, pencils and ballpoints from most big brands is stocked here, as well as gifts (hip flasks, travel clocks) and Filofaxes. The shop also carries out repairs on obsolete pen models. *Mail order.*
For branches see index.

Personal organisers

For **Mulberry**, *see p34*; for **Asprey**, *see p81*.

City Organiser

15 Cabot Place West, E14 4QT (7512 9130/ www.cityorg.co.uk). Canary Wharf tube/DLR. **Open** 9am-7pm Mon-Fri; 10am-6pm Sat; noon-6pm Sun. **Credit** AmEx, MC, V.
Alongside Filofax and Quo Vadis organisers and diaries, CO sells stylish Mulberry leather goods, lavish desktop gifts and accessories, such as Porsche steel pens (from £225) and Leatherman multi-tools (£30-£115). A delectable range of his and hers Paul Smith accessories starts at £18. *Mail order.*
For branch see index.

Filofax

68 Neal Street, WC2H 9PH (7836 1977/www. filofax.co.uk). Covent Garden tube. **Open** 10am-6pm Mon-Wed; 10am-7pm Thur, Fri; 10.30am-6.30pm Sat; noon-5pm Sun. **Credit** AmEx, MC, V.
The full Filofax range can be found here, as well as inserts and accessories, briefcases and wallets. *Mail order.*
For branch see index.

JM Pennifeather

4 Flask Walk, NW3 1HE (7794 0488). Hampstead tube. **Open** 10.30am-5.30pm Mon-Fri; 11am-5.30pm Sat, Sun. **Credit** AmEx, MC, V.
A comprehensive selection of personal organisers and inserts, small leather goods and gifts is stocked here, as well as writing instruments by Mont Blanc, Lamy, Parker and Cross, plus a smart range of silver pens (£40-£300) from Italian firm Lalex. *Mail order.*

LEISURE

Transport

Bikes

The aims of the **London Cycling Campaign** (7928 7220, www.lcc.org.uk) are to promote cycling, by raising its profile with policy-makers and improving conditions for cyclists in London. Membership costs £27.50 (£12 concessions) per year, which entitles members to the bimonthly magazine *London Cyclist*, as well as discounts at selected bike shops around town. For cycling tuition, contact **London School of Cycling** (7249 3779, www.londonschoolofcycling.co.uk).

Giving the 'V' sign to the 'C' sign (congestion charge) are shops like **Ebike Central** (75 Station Approach, South Ruislip, Middx HA4 6SD, 8839 9800, www.ebikecentral.co.uk), which is doing a roaring trade in battery-powered bikes that look like a bicycle but ride like a scooter. The Powabyke Shopper (£595) gets up to 15mph and has to be recharged (at a cost of 8p/charge) every 25 miles. Electric motorcycles (equivalent to a 50CC moped) start at £2,100.

For specialists in children's bikes, *see also* chapter **Babies & Children**.

Action Bikes
23-26 Embankment Place, WC2N 6NN (7930 2525/www.actionbikes.co.uk). Embankment tube. **Open** 9am-6pm Mon-Wed, Fri; 9am-7pm Thur; 9.30am-5.30pm Sat. **Credit** AmEx, MC, V.
This chain's flagship store has an Oakley concession, with the full complement of the brand's kit and clothing. Other names stocked include Trek and Marin, with folding bikes by Mezzo (from £595) and Brompton – check out the lightweight and highly covetable titanium range, which will set you back £900 upwards for a bespoke model. Repairs and servicing are offered too.
For branches see index.

Bikefix
48 Lamb's Conduit Street, WC1N 3LH (7405 1218/www.bikefix.co.uk). Holborn tube. **Open** 8.30am-7pm Mon-Fri; 10am-5pm Sat. **Credit** MC, V.
This highly specialised shop stocks Brompton, Airframe, Birdy, Pashley, plus several recumbents. Quality repairs and maintenance workshop.

Cavendish Cycles
136-138 New Cavendish Street, W1W 6YD (7631 5060). Goodge Street or Oxford Circus tube. **Open** 9am-6pm Mon-Fri; 10am-5pm Sat. **Credit** DC, MC, V.
Formerly the Cycle Centre, this newly acquired shop stocks Trek, Brompton, Scott, Orbea, Giant and some deliciously funky cruisers from Skedaddle. Bike repairs undertaken.
For branch see index.

Condor Cycles
51 Gray's Inn Road, WC1X 8PP (7269 6820/ www.condorcycles.com). Chancery Lane tube. **Open** 9am-6pm Mon, Tue, Thur, Fri; 9am-7.30pm Wed; 10am-5pm Sat. **Credit** AmEx, MC, V.
Condor has been producing racing, touring, commuting, mountain and hybrid bikes for customers all over the world since 1948. The Condor Pista single-speed road bike scored nine out of ten in the latest *Cycling Plus* test. The shop also sells a good range of accessories and clothing.

Cycle Surgery
44 Chalk Farm Road, NW1 8AJ (7485 1000/ www.cyclesurgery.com). Chalk Farm tube. **Open** 9am-6pm Mon, Wed, Fri; 9am-7pm Tue, Thur; 10am-6pm Sat; 11am-5pm Sun. **Credit** AmEx, MC, V.

This highly respectable mountain bike and BMX specialist stocks Trek, Norco, Marin, Orange and Santa Cruz, as well as clothing and accessories by Sugoi, Altura and Pearl Izumi. It also carries out repairs. Selfridges has a concession.
Mail order (7697 2843/0800 298 8898).
Branches: throughout the city.

Evans Cycles
77-81 The Cut, SE1 8LL (7928 4785/www. evanscycles.com). Southwark tube/Waterloo tube/rail. **Open** 8am-8pm Mon-Fri; 9.30am-6pm Sat; 11am-5pm Sun. **Credit** MC, V.
Staff here are experts in supplying tourers and road bikes for city cycling. The wide range includes Bianchi, Specialized, Trek and GT. Also cycling accessories, such as shoes, gloves, saddlebags and helmets. A professional bike-fitting service is available in the Wandsworth branch for £30.
Mail order (0870 600 0908).
Branches: throughout the city.

Herne Hill Bicycles
83 Norwood Road, SE24 9AA (8671 6900). Herne Hill rail. **Open** 9am-6pm Tue-Fri; 10am-5pm Sat. **Credit** MC, V.
This shop majors in commuter bikes such as Ridgeback. Currently generating a lot of interest is the Fuji single-speed track bike for road use (£299). There's an excellent, but very busy, repairs service, so call first. Accessories and clothing are also sold.

London Fields Cycles
281 Mare Street, E8 1PJ (8525 0077/www.london fieldscycles.co.uk). Hackney Central rail. **Open** 8am-6pm Mon-Fri; 10am-5pm Sat. **Credit** AmEx, MC, V.
A recent move to larger premises means more bikes and accessories and a bigger repairs workshop. Stock includes Brompton, Specialized, Trek and Ridgeback. Prices are competitive, and there are special deals to boot. Staff are helpful.

Bikefix

Mosquito Bikes
123 Essex Road, N1 2SN (7226 8765/www. mosquito-bikes.co.uk). Angel tube/Essex Road rail/ 38, 56, 73 bus. **Open** 8.30am-7pm Mon-Fri; 10am-6pm Sat; 11am-4pm Sun. **Credit** AmEx, MC, V.
Home to a large and diverse selection of bikes including Pegoretti, Merlin, Tifosi and Moots, as well as cycling equipment such as child seats (£80-£100) and specialist road and mountain-biking clothes by Spanish company Exte Ondo. Its repairs workshop is highly recommended.
Mail order.

On Your Bike
52-54 Tooley Street, SE1 2SZ (7378 6669/ www.onyourbike.com). London Bridge tube/rail. **Open** 8am-7pm Mon-Fri; 10am-6pm Sat; 11am-5pm Sun. **Credit** MC, V.
Very popular store with bikes from Marin, Whyte, Brompton, Gary Fisher and Cannondale. Repairs and accessories also.

Motorbikes & scooters

For Harley-Davidsons, **Warr's** (611 King's Road, SW6 2EL, 7736 2934, www.warrs.com) stocks a massive range of new and used 'hogs' and Harley-engined Buell racers. **Hein Gericke** (320 Clapham Road, SW9 9AE, 7498 0819, www.heingericke.co.uk) sells a complete collection of apparel and accessories.

Bracken MW
330 St James's Road, SE1 5JX (7232 1814/ www.bracken.co.uk). Bermondsey tube. **Open** 8.30am-6pm Mon, Tue, Thur-Sat. **Credit** MC, V.
Bracken's forte is souped-up Supermoto and high-powered Motocross bikes; it has the largest selection of new and used KTMs in the UK. The newest KTM model is the 950 Supermoto (£7,995), but others start at £4,500. Second-hand BMWs are also sold and repaired, while accessories and apparel from AXO, KTM and Lazer complete the picture.
Mail order.

Jack Nice
129-133 Grove Road, E17 9BU (8520 1920/ www.jacknicemotorcycles.co.uk). Walthamstow Central tube/rail. **Open** 9am-6pm Tue-Fri; 9am-5pm Sat. **Credit** MC, V.
This family business has a good range of bikes, including MZs (from £2,499 for a 125cc), plus meatier Kawasakis (£4,000-plus) and Italian rarities: Benelli and MV Agusta (up to £30,000). New and used scooters (50cc upwards), mainly by Peugeot and MBK, cost from around £1,400, and there's also an assortment of clothing and accessories. MOTs, insurance and tests can be arranged, too.
Mail order.

R Agius
363 Edgware Road, W2 1BS (7723 0995/ www.agiusscooters.com). Edgware Road tube. **Open** 8.30am-7pm Mon-Wed, Fri; 8.30am-6pm Thur; 8.30am-5pm Sat. **Credit** MC, V.
London's oldest Piaggio specialist, Agius opened its doors in 1952 and is loved by scooter fans of all types, from wide boys to City boys. It stocks 18 models (including five models of Vespa), starting at £1,199 for the Piaggio Zip Cat 50.

Reg Allen London
37-41 Grosvenor Road, W7 1HP (8579 1248). Boston Manor tube. **Open** 9.30am-6pm Mon-Sat. **Credit** MC, V.
Reg Allen restores and repairs classic British bikes: Triumphs, Royal Enfields and rare Nortons. Second-hand models start around £1,500 and go up to £8,000 for a fully serviced Triumph Bonneville.
Mail order.

Strada Motorscooters
167 Battersea Park Road, SW8 4BU (7622 5588/ www.stradamotorscooters.com). Battersea Park Rail. **Open** 10am-6pm Tue-Sat. **Credit** MC, V.
For restored Vespas and Lambrettas from the 1950s to the '80s (£800-£2,500). Bike gear (helmets, gloves, jackets) by Tucano Urbano and Momo Design.

Food
& Drink

Food

Food halls

Fortnum & Mason

181 Piccadilly, W1A 1ER (7734 8040/ www.fortnumandmason.co.uk). Green Park or Piccadilly Circus tube. **Open** 10am-6.30pm Mon-Sat; noon-6pm Sun. **Credit** AmEx, DC, MC, V.

A decline in company fortunes has recently led F&M to make its popular food hall a focus of business: there are ambitious plans to expand the entire food range over the next few years. Justly famous for its teas (such as rose pouchong, £7.95/250g, and Russian caravan, £6.75/250g), the store also sells excellent biscuits (such as Lancashire flips) and condiments (picnic pickle, say, or Polish silver fir honey). There are fabulous meat, fish and cheese counters (also offering fresh sevruga and beluga caviars), and confectionery, oils, vinegars, and seasonal fruit and vegetables. Shopping in these lavish surroundings remains a quintessentially English experience.

Harrods

87-135 Brompton Road, SW1X 7XL (7730 1234/www.harrods.com). Knightsbridge tube. **Open** 10am-7pm Mon-Sat; noon-6pm Sun. **Credit** AmEx, DC, MC, V.

Harrods has one of London's most famous, beautiful and spacious food halls. This sumptuous place, with painted tiles and tall columns, incorporates meat, cheese and fish counters, a bakery, a sushi bar, an oyster bar, an ice-cream parlour (where you can place an order for bespoke ice-cream) and, not least, a Krispy Kreme doughnut outlet. Also on offer are coffees (try Colombian San Augustin coffee beans), condiments (like pickled quail's eggs), the Green Cuisine range of herbs and spices, biscuits, cakes, chocolates and a full range of wines, spirits and champagnes. Food orders (including the famous hampers) are particularly popular with British expats.

Harvey Nichols

109-125 Knightsbridge, SW1X 7RJ (7235 5000/ www.harveynichols.com). Knightsbridge tube. **Open** 10am-8pm Mon-Fri; 10am-7pm Sat; noon-6pm Sun. **Credit** AmEx, DC, MC, V.

This bijou food market has a stylish, modern design, and incorporates a lovely wine shop. Also on sale are biscuits (including a delectable blueberry variety); oils, vinegars and dressings (try the wasabi and ginger dressing); confectionery (the espresso chocolate bar is irresistible); teas and coffees; condiments and fresh fruit and veg. There are particularly good ranges of Italian ingredients and American products. Butchers, bakers, greengrocers, fishmongers and cheesemongers are on hand to give specialist advice. Packaging is trendily monochrome. Specialist events such as tastings and cookery book launches also occur from time to time.

Sainsbury's Market at Bluebird

350 King's Road, SW3 5UU (7349 1650). Bus 11, 19, 22, 49, 319. **Open** 8am-9pm Mon-Sat; 11am-5pm Sun. **Credit** AmEx, MC, V.

Housed in a building owned by Conran, this upscale supermarket outlet offers many of the same products as other branches of Sainsbury's. But it stands out for the good selection of traiteur dishes, condiments, fresh pasta and wines. Fish, meat, cheese, freshly baked bread, and fruit and vegetables are all displayed on a variety of attractive deli counters and market stalls. The range of deli-style ready-cooked meals is limited, and prices are a touch high for what is essentially supermarket grub.

For branch (Sainsbury's Market) see index.

Selfridges

400 Oxford Street, W1A 1AB (0870 837 7377/ www.selfridges.com). Bond Street or Marble Arch tube. **Open** 10am-8pm Mon-Fri; 9.30am-8pm Sat; noon-6pm Sun. **Credit** AmEx, DC, MC, V.

Offering an outstanding selection of global ingredients, this popular food hall also sells ready-prepared dishes at its numerous international food counters (Lebanese, Indian, Japanese, Moroccan and kosher). Other sections offer fresh and cooked meat, fish, cheese, freshly baked pretzels, pies from the Square Pie Company, and caviar from Caviar Kaspia. There's a wonderful bakery, a fresh juice counter and a notable selection of unusual fruits and vegetables (including organic varieties). Our favourites are fresh, handmade Machiavelli pasta from Italy and the Oddono's Italian ice-cream parlour (the hazelnut, green apple, and ginger and fig ice-cream flavours are sublime). Look out for demonstrations, tastings, food and wine events, plus food-themed festivals.

Bakeries & pâtisseries

& Clarke's

122 Kensington Church Street, W8 4BU (7229 2190/www.sallyclarke.com). Notting Hill Gate tube. **Open** 8am-8pm Mon-Fri; 8am-4pm Sat. **Credit** AmEx, MC, V.

Located next to her acclaimed restaurant, Sally Clarke's bakery sells a vast range of breads, pastries and cakes, many of which are supplied to restaurants and delis. The range encompasses fig and fennel, and rosemary and raisin breads, jewel-like redcurrant and nectarine tarts, and citrus peel and almond croissants made with unsalted Normandy butter. Also sold are over 40 British and Irish cheeses from Neal's Yard, coffee from Monmouth Coffee House, fresh soups, condiments, olive oils and chocolates. The seasonal fruit, vegetables and herbs include New Forest wild mushrooms, new season Egyptian garlic and pumpkins from Sunnyfields Organic Farm.

Apostrophe

216 Tottenham Court Road, entrance in 20/20 Optical Store or 9 Alfred Place, W1T 7PT (7436 6688/www.apostropheuk.com). Goodge Street or Tottenham Court Road tube. **Open** 7.30am-6pm Mon-Fri; 8.30am-5pm Sat, Sun. **Credit** MC, V.

This modern Parisian-style boulangerie-pâtisserie sells a large variety of breads freshly baked on the premises. The range includes sun-dried tomato, poppy seed, multigrain, wholemeal, walnut, 'farmers' bread', and many flavours of sourdough. Pastries and desserts, savoury tarts, sandwiches and filled baguettes are also available.

For branches see index.

Baker & Spice

75 Salusbury Road, NW6 6NH (7604 3636/ www.bakerandspice.com). Queen's Park tube. **Open** 7am-7pm Mon-Sat; 8.30am-5pm Sun. **Credit** MC, V.

Despite being a chain, Baker & Spice is a byword for quality in breads, pastries, cakes and tarts. Breads include rye, chollah and San Francisco sourdough, and the soft, crumbly croissants have a loyal following. Soups and savouries are also available, and you can eat in or take away.

For branches see index.

Choccywoccydoodah

47 Harrowby Street, W1H 5EA (7724 5465/ www.choccywoccydoodah.com). Marble Arch tube. **Open** 10am-6pm Wed-Sat. **Credit** MC, V.

Choccywoccy who? This fun-sounding shop offering gloriously camp, ostentatiously decorated bespoke cakes is becoming increasingly popular, with many of its designer creations to be found at a wedding or a celebrity event near you. To give an example: miniature cakes are decorated with chocolate orchids, tiny roses and pearly gems. Its speciality is a basic chocolate cake crammed with nuts, dried fruits, whole cherries, spices and French brandy, on which many designs and specialities – from Belgian chocolate wedding cake to 'boudoir flamingo cakes' – can be built.

Mail order.

De Gustibus

53 Blandford Street, W1U 7HL (7486 6608). Baker Street tube. **Open** 7am-4pm Mon-Fri. **No credit cards.**

This multiple award-winning company started life as a home-baking business before becoming one of the most acclaimed artisan bakers in Britain. Set up by Dan and Annette de Gustibus in Oxfordshire in 1990, it now supplies restaurants and offers day courses in bread-making. The bread selection changes regularly, but usually incorporates American varieties (old milwaukee rye, chestnut wholemeal, honey and lavender, and the famous boston brown – the original bread used in baked beans on toast) and British (spelt and Cotswold cobbler). Other varieties include continental (Portuguese cornbread and Swiss cantonese), Mediterranean (porcini, sage and bay) and East European (potato and courgette, cossack sour). All breads are made with natural ingredients, including naturally occurring yeasts.

For branches see index.

Euphorium Bakery

202 Upper Street, N1 1RQ (7704 6905). Highbury & Islington tube/rail. **Open** 7am-11pm Mon-Thur; 7am-midnight; Fri; 8am-midnight Sat; 9am-11pm Sun. **Credit** MC, V.

This contemporary bakery and café sells handcrafted breads made from organic English or unbleached French flour. Focaccia and flavoured breads come in distinctly Mediterranean flavours like pesto, sun-dried tomato, black olive, spinach and feta, rosemary and garlic, and blue cheese. Sourdough and baguettes are also available, and there's a good range of crumbly, buttery croissants, brioches, Danish pastries, strudels, vegetable quiches and savoury pastry rolls (stuffed with cheese, meats or vegetables). Staff are helpful, and the place is popular with local office workers.

For branch see index.

Konditor & Cook

10 Stoney Street, SE1 9AD (7407 5100/www. konditorandcook.com). London Bridge tube/rail. **Open** 7.30am-6pm Mon-Fri; 8.30am-4pm Sat. **Credit** AmEx, MC, V.

Freshly baked cakes made by hand using free-range eggs and pure butter are a speciality here. You'll find it hard to choose from the likes of old-fashioned lemon chiffon, the signature whiskey and orange bombe cake, and miniature coloured fondant cakes. Bespoke options are also available, including tiered and conical wedding and birthday cakes. Flavoured breads, pastries and sandwiches are on sale, too.

For branches see index.

Lighthouse Bakery

64 Northcote Road, SW11 6QL (7228 4537/ www.lighthousebakery.co.uk). Clapham Junction rail. **Open** 8.30am-5pm Tue-Sat. **Credit** MC, V.

Owned by Rachel Duffield (front of house) and Elizabeth Weisberg (one of the few female commercial bakers), this small artisan bakery sells American, British and continental breads, cakes and pastries. The range encompasses speciality breads (Gloucester rye, dark salt-free Tuscan), traditional English wheat breads (Coburg), wholemeal and malted (Geordie brown), seasonal varieties (hot cross buns) and pastries (gingerbread critters, chinois). Breads are baked on the premises in small batches, using Shipton Mill flour. Each loaf is hand-moulded and long fermentation methods are used, resulting in a fuller flavour. The shop also stocks a good selection of American treats (like blueberry cobbler), plus bread crocks and bespoke hand tools for bakers.

Louis' Pâtisserie

32 Heath Street, NW3 6DU (7435 9908).
Hampstead tube. **Open** 9am-6pm daily.
No credit cards.
Set up by Hungarian expat Louis Permayer around 40 years ago, this pâtisserie and café is a favourite haunt of ladies who lunch. The impossibly rich and sumptuous East European specialities (that's the cakes, not the ladies) pre-date Atkins and other dietary fads. They include cream slices, éclairs, meringues, fruit tarts, Florentines, gateaux, macaroons and plump croissants. The chocolate cakes, though, are everybody's favourite.

Maison Blanc

37 St John's Wood High Street, NW8 7NG (7586 1982/www.maisonblanc.co.uk). St John's Wood tube. **Open** 8am-7pm Mon-Sat; 9am-6.30pm Sun. **Credit** MC, V.
Originally set up by Raymond Blanc, this chain has been owned by Lyndale Foods since 1999 and specialises in cakes for big occasions. The seasonal themed cakes are inspired by catwalk colours and designs. Traditional French artisan breads include classics like campaillou and semolina bread, and specialities like sarrazin and seigle noir. Pastries include tarts, chocolate cakes, mousses and danish pastries with prunes and granola topping. Confectionery – such as French chocolates, sugared almonds, amandines, nougat and marzipan – is also sold. Canapés, petits fours and mini sandwiches are available for parties; plus there are savoury brioches, quiches and sandwiches to take away.
Branches: throughout the city.

Old Post Office Bakery

76 Landor Road, SW9 9PH (7326 4408).
Clapham North tube. **Open** 10.30am-7pm Mon, Wed-Fri; 10.30am-5.30pm Tue; 10am-6pm Sat.
No credit cards.
The oldest bakery in south London specialises in organic breads like sunflower, malted grain and wholemeal loaves, plus yeast-free varieties including rye and Californian sourdough. Cakes, such as banana and walnut, carrot, chocolate, apple and almond are made daily and are very popular. There's a non-organic savoury range, which includes pizzas, pasties and filled rolls.

Oliver's Deli on the Hill

56 Fortis Green Road, N10 3HN (8883 0117).
Hornsey rail then 102 bus. **Open** 8am-6pm Mon-Sat; 8am-4pm Sun. **Credit** MC, V.
This lovely deli and café has both indoor and outdoor seating, and stocks a large selection of pastas, meats, olives, preserves, relishes, oils and coffee. There's a good variety of own-baked pastries, bagels and breads – such as sourdough, rye, cereal, walnut, olive, wholemeal, campagna, and golden grain. Also on offer are around 20 speciality and popular cheeses (like brie and dolcelatte) from England, France, Spain, Italy and Switzerland.

Pâtisserie Deux Amis

63 Judd Street, WC1H 9QT (7383 7029). Russell Square tube. **Open** 9am-5.30pm Mon-Sat; 9am-1.30pm Sun. **No credit cards.**
This small bakery and café has pavement tables for alfresco grazing. Choose from pastries (pains au chocolat, croissants, strudel, fruit tarts and meringues) or breads (walnut, sesame, onion, rye, muesli, German). Savoury tarts tend to be vegetarian (onion, mushroom, mixed peppers or spinach), and soups and sandwiches are also sold.

Paul Bakery & Tearoom

115 Marylebone High Street, W1U 4SB (7224 5615/www.paul.fr). Baker Street or Bond Street tube. **Open** 7.30am-8pm Mon-Fri; 8am-8pm Sat, Sun. **Credit** MC, V.
Originating in Lille, this family-run bakery expanded all over France and is now opening up branches in London. The famous breads are made using exacting traditional methods. For instance, over 300 farmers are engaged in growing a special rustic variety of tender winter wheat to the company's specifications; this is then turned into Camp Rémy flour, which is left for a month to mature. Around 140 varieties of bread are offered,
including chapata, polka, benoîtons and bio bread. There's also an enticing range of pastries, such as chouquettes (sugar-coated choux pastry balls), macaroons and cakes, plus sandwiches and flans, which you can eat in the café at the back.
For branch see index.

Pierre Péchon

127 Queensway, W2 4SJ (7229 0746/www. croquembouche.co.uk). Bayswater or Queensway tube. **Open** 7am-7pm Mon-Wed; 7am-8pm Thur-Sat; 8am-7pm Sun. **Credit** MC, V.
This family-run firm of master bakers and confectioners specialises in French and English baked goodies. It is renowned for its cakes and also for croquembouche, an elaborately constructed pyramid of choux balls – variously decorated with nuts, sauces, fresh flowers and spun sugar – served at French celebrations. This is one of the few shops in London where you can buy this famous French confection.

Poilâne

46 Elizabeth Street, SW1W 9PA (7808 4910/ www.poilane.fr). Sloane Square tube/Victoria tube/rail. **Open** 7.30am-7.30pm Mon-Fri; 7.30am-6pm Sat. **Credit** MC, V.
This popular company's sourdoughs are some of the most famous breads in the world – they're ubiquitous in delis, restaurants and at upscale dinner parties. The bread is made using a modernised version of an ancestral recipe. Pesticide-free wheat and spelt flour is mixed with salt from the violet-scented marshes of Guérande in western France; then, after fermentation, the loaves are baked in wood-fired ovens for an hour. The bakery also produces varieties such as rye and walnut, currant and raisin, mixed nut and milk bread.

St John

26 St John Street, EC1M 4AY (7251 0848/ www.stjohnrestaurant.com). Farringdon tube/rail. **Open** noon-3pm, 6-11pm Mon-Fri; 6-11pm Sat. **Credit** AmEx, MC, V.
This internationally renowned restaurant is best known for its concept of 'nose to tail' dining. However, it also sells a daily changing selection of freshly baked breads, such as white, wholemeal, sourdough, rye, soda, raisin and olive. The luscious Eccles cakes (which are also a fixture on the restaurant menu) are renowned.
For branch (St John Bread & Wine) see index.

Cheese shops

Bloomsbury Cheeses

61B Judd Street, WC1H 9QT (7387 7645/ www.bloomsburycheeses.com). Russell Square tube/King's Cross tube/rail. **Open** 10am-7pm Mon-Fri; 10am-5.30pm Sat. **Credit** MC, V.
This beautiful cheesemonger's sells British, Irish, French, Italian and Spanish cheeses. Try the fashionable coolea from County Cork, or more familiar varieties like smoked cheddar, roquefort and buffalo mozzarella. There is a 'weekly special' cheese, and tastings are encouraged. The shop also sells relishes, olive oils and wines.
Mail order.

The Cheese Block

69 Lordship Lane, SE22 8EP (8299 3636). East Dulwich rail. **Open** 9.30am-6.30pm Mon-Fri; 9am-6pm Sat. **Credit** MC, V.
There is a good range of rare and unusual cheeses at this shop, which stocks between 250 and 350 varieties, depending on the season (you'll find more choice at Christmas than midsummer). A selection of goat's, sheep's and cow's milk cheeses are sourced from the UK, Switzerland, Italy, Spain, Holland and France. Pastas, breads, cold meats and olive oils are also on sale.

The Cheeseboard

26 Royal Hill, SE10 8RT (8305 0401/www. cheese-board.co.uk). Greenwich rail/DLR. **Open** 9am-5pm Mon, Wed, Sat; 9am-4.30pm Tue; 9am-1pm Thur; 9am-5.30pm Fri. **Credit** AmEx, MC, V.
Owned by the British Cheese Board – whose aim is to encourage the use of British cheeses and promote their health benefits – this shop sells over 400 varieties of English (as well as French and Italian) cheese. The range includes popular varieties like sage derby, dovedale, buxton blue and cornish yarg. Breads, wine and relishes to go with your cheese are also available, and there are educational leaflets for parents and teachers.
Mail order.

Cheeses

13 Fortis Green Road, N10 3HP (8444 9141).
East Finchley tube. **Open** 9.30am-5.30pm Tue-Fri; 9.30am-6pm Sat. **Credit** MC, V.
Vanessa Wiley's tiny shop is packed with mainly British and French cheeses, plus a few Italian, Spanish and Dutch varieties. The selection includes manchego, emmental, aged gouda and somerset goat's cheese. Also on offer are olives, meats, relishes and organic bread (on Saturdays). Cheeseboards and knives are sold too.

La Fromagerie

2-4 Moxon Street, W1U 4EW (7935 0341/ www.lafromagerie.co.uk). Baker Street or Bond Street tube. **Open** 10.30am-7.30pm Mon; 8am-7.30pm Tue-Fri; 9am-7pm Sat; 10am-6pm Sun. **Credit** AmEx, MC, V.
Located on a street that is not exactly short on fabulous food shops, the seductively laid out Fromagerie still stands out. It has a temperature-controlled cheese room, where up to 120 varieties of hand-picked artisanal French, Italian, Spanish and British cheeses are displayed. There's also a café, and a deli that sells attractively packaged pasta, olive oil, jams, chutneys, wines, and seasonal fruit and veg.
For branch see index.

Hamish Johnston

48 Northcote Road, SW11 1PA (7738 0741).
Clapham Junction rail. **Open** 9am-6pm Mon-Sat.
Credit MC, V.
There is a huge selection of goat's and sheep's milk cheeses at this friendly cheesemonger's, which stocks approximately 150 varieties of cheese. Most of them are British or French, but there are some Spanish and Italian varieties too. You'll also find terrines, preserves, oils and vinegars.
Mail order.

International Cheese Centre

Unit 5, Marylebone Station, NW1 6JJ (7724 1432). Marylebone tube/rail. **Open** 7am-8pm Mon-Wed; 7am-8.30pm Thur, Fri; 11am-7pm Sat. **Credit** AmEx, DC, MC, V.
The company sells around 400 varieties of (mainly populist) cheeses through its outlets at major train stations. Cheddar, goat's cheese, camembert and stilton are always in demand; plus you can pick up pasta, jams, chutneys, sweets and wine. Also on sale are gift packs of honey, chocolate and champagne, plus sandwiches and bagels to take away.
For branches see index.

Jeroboams

96 Holland Park Avenue, W11 3RB (7727 9359/ www.jeroboams.co.uk). Holland Park tube. **Open** 8am-8pm Mon-Fri; 8.30am-7pm Sat; 10am-6pm Sun. **Credit** AmEx, MC, V.
The company owns several food and wine shops, including Mr Christian's deli (*see p238*), and this flagship branch sells mainly British and French cheeses (and a few Swiss and Italian ones), which are individually ripened at their maturing rooms on site. The French selection includes farmhouse cheeses like valençay and chabichou, and the British range has lesser-known types like berkswell and ragstone. Staff are on hand to advise on matching cheese with wine, and dinners and other events are held regularly.
Mail order.
For branches see index.

Jones Dairy

23 Ezra Street, E2 7RH (7739 5372/www.jones dairy.co.uk). Liverpool Street tube/rail then 26, 48 bus/Old Street tube/rail then 55 bus. **Open** 9am-3pm Fri, Sat; 8am-3pm Sun. **No credit cards.**

Established in 1902, this shop and café is one of the originals in a chain of Welsh dairy shops that were ubiquitous across London in the 1900s: what is now the café used to house eight milking cows. Owned by Richard Naylor since the 1980s, the place now sells artisanal farmhouse cheeses from Britain and Holland. The range includes unpasteurised varieties (goat's milk gouda, jersey shield, cotherstone, staffordshire), and pasteurised varieties (young to very old gouda, ewe's milk swaledale, shropshire blue). Other goodies include artisanal breads, pastries, chutneys, preserves, and seasonal fruit and veg.

Neal's Yard Dairy

17 Shorts Gardens, WC2H 9UP (7240 5700).
Covent Garden tube. **Open** 11am-6.30pm Mon-Thur; 10am-6.30pm Fri, Sat. **Credit** MC, V.
Dozens of restaurants and delis in London serve Neal's Yard cheeses, which are, quite simply, shorthand for quality. They're sourced from artisan producers in Britain and Ireland, and matured in the company's own cellars. The range includes coolea, berkswell, extra-mature stilton, goat's cheeses and wash-rind cheeses – depending on season. Staff are exceptionally knowledgeable, and encourage you to taste before buying. Related items like breads and relishes are also on sale.
For branch see index.

Paxton & Whitfield

93 Jermyn Street, SW1Y 6JE (7930 0259/
www.paxtonandwhitfield.co.uk). Green Park tube.
Open 9.30am-6pm Mon-Sat. **Credit** MC, V.
Set up in 1797, Britain's oldest cheesemonger is endorsed by everyone from the royal family and Winston Churchill to Sophie Grigson. Artisan cheeses are sourced from the UK, France and Italy, and allowed to mature. Varieties include British (shires farmhouse), soft (cornish capra) and blue (caradon blue). Biscuits, cakes, relishes, preserves, pâtés, terrines, wines and ales are also available, as are knives, cheeseboards and tableware. There is a monthly cheese club for those who want cheeses delivered to their home in peak condition. The friendly staff's knowledge of their subject is second to none.
Mail order.

The Real Cheese Shop

62 Barnes High Street, SW13 9LF (8878 6676).
Barnes or Barnes Bridge rail. **Open** 9.30am-5pm Tue-Thur; 9am-5.30pm Fri; 9am-5pm Sat. **Credit** (over £10) MC, V.
Owner Robert Handyside stocks a good range of northern cheeses here, such as cheshire and lancashire. There are around 100 varieties in total – an overwhelming majority come from Britain and France, and the rest are from Scandinavia, Spain, Germany and Italy. The selection includes blue goat's cheese, smoked applewood cheddar, old amsterdam, gubbeen, hereford hop (covered in hops) and some unusual ones flavoured with red wine or charcoal. Tastings are encouraged, and oatcakes, honeys and preserves are also sold.

Rippon Cheese Stores

26 Upper Tachbrook Street, SW1V 1SW (7931 0628). Pimlico tube/Victoria tube/rail. **Open** 8am-5.15pm Mon-Sat. **Credit** MC, V.
Around 550 varieties of mainly British and French cheeses are stocked here, including epoisses, roquefort, bleu de cours, beaufort, wensleydale, comté and stilton. Look for regional and seasonal specialities, such as assorted goat's cheeses, stinking bishop and vacherin.
Mail order.

Confectioners

Asian sweets

Ambala Sweet Centre

112-114 Drummond Street, NW1 2HN (7387 3521/www.ambalasweets.com). Euston Square tube/Euston tube/rail. **Open** 9am-8.30pm daily. **Credit** MC, V.
This flagship branch of an expanding chain of Indian confectioners is a must-visit for fans of

Indian sweets, savouries, snacks and pickles. Immaculately displayed pyramids of brightly coloured goodies include anjeer halwa (fig, almond and pistachio), jalebi (sticky sunshine-coloured spirals) and rasmalai (milk dumplings in creamy sauce). Specialities include chamcham (saffron-flavoured sponge dipped in syrup). If you are new to Indian sweets, try the 'variety pack' assortments.
Mail order.
Branches: throughout the city.

Minamoto Kitchoan

44 Piccadilly, W1J ODS (7437 3135/www.kitchoan. com). Piccadilly Circus tube. **Open** 10am-7pm Mon-Fri, Sun; 10am-8pm Sat. **Credit** AmEx, MC, V.
Specialising in wagashi (traditional Japanese confectionery made from rice flour, aduki bean paste and seasonal fruit and nuts), this beguiling confectioner has branches in many major cities. Choose from saisaika (Japanese loquat marzipan), tousenka (white peach stuffed with baby green peach, covered in jelly), oribenishiki (pastry stuffed with red bean and chestnuts), kohakukanume (whole plum encased in plum wine jelly, decorated with gold powder), and honey and green tea sponge cakes.
Mail order.

Royal Sweets

92 The Broadway, Southall, Middx UB1 1QF (8574 0832). Southall rail/207 bus. **Open** 10am-7pm Mon, Tue, Thur-Sat; 10.30am-7pm Sun. **Credit** MC, V.
Indians are divided on the relative merits of Royal and Ambala (*see above*) – each chain has its group of die-hard fans – but it's Royal Sweets that supplies the vast majority of Indian restaurants. There's a good selection of flavoured barfis, laddoos and peras (fudge-like sweets) here, flavoured with almonds, pistachios, coconut or saffron. The company's renowned kulfi (Indian ice-cream) is now also available in many major supermarkets.
For branches see index.

Chocolates

L'Artisan du Chocolat

89 Lower Sloane Street, SW1W 8DA (7824 8365/ www.artisanduchocolat.com). Sloane Square tube.
Open 10am-7pm Mon-Sat. **Credit** MC, V.
This glass-fronted shop with enticing chocolate sculptures is a small-scale, London-based business, set up by Belgium-trained ex-pastry chef Gerard Coleman. He makes small quantities of very fresh chocolates (to be eaten within two weeks), using natural ingredients, judicious quantities of sugar and a variety of ganache. They are highly acclaimed by food writers and Michelin-starred chefs, with flavours that are imaginative and original, including green cardamom, lemon verbena, lapsang souchong, basil and lime, Moroccan mint, Sichuan pepper, banana and thyme, lavender bud, red wine and tobacco. The salt caramels are to die for. Chocolate-tasting evenings are also held.

Charbonnel et Walker

1 The Royal Arcade, 28 Old Bond Street, W1S 4BT (7491 0939/www.charbonnel.co.uk). Green Park tube. **Open** 10am-6pm Mon-Sat. **Credit** AmEx, DC, MC, V.
Established in 1875, this company's sumptuously packaged chocolates will appeal to those who want an old-fashioned treat rather than new-fangled flavours. Individually wrapped chocolates in gold foil are popular, as are fondants with a traditional crystallised finish. Truffles (pink champagne, cappuccino, port and cranberry), and rose and violet creams are particularly lovely.
Mail order.

The Chocolate Society

36 Elizabeth Street, SW1W 9NZ (7259 9222/ www.chocolate.co.uk). Sloane Square tube/Victoria tube/rail. **Open** 9.30am-5.30pm Mon-Fri; 9.30am-4pm Sat. **Credit** MC, V.
Set up to promote the consumption and enjoyment of chocolates, the Society sells mostly own-label, Valrhona and artisan ranges. You'll find fresh

handmade Yorkshire truffles, chocolate bonbons from Alsace and Provence, Eastern Promise bars (with saffron, rose oil and cardamom), Chiman's spice bars (cardamom and blue poppy seed, or allspice and sesame), chocolate honeycombs, nougat, sugared almonds, chocolate dragées, edible gold leaf (essential for Nigella's recipes), and novelty items like chocolate pigs. There's also a small café area with outside seating, where you can enjoy brownies, ice-creams and milkshakes.
For branch see index.

Godiva

17 Russell Street, WC2B 5HP (7836 5706/ www.godiva.com). Covent Garden or Embankment tube/Charing Cross tube/rail. **Open** 10am-7pm Mon-Sat; noon-6pm Sun. **Credit** AmEx, MC, V.
Mochaccino mousse, cinnamon ganache, key lime éclairs, milk chocolate raspberry starfish, Mojito truffles, pecan croquants and a new range of fruity Pop chocolates in glittery boxes for Christmas are some of the delights you'll find at this popular shop. There's a wide selection of truffles, biscuits, bars, nut and caramel assortments, mints, fruit creams, pralines, and ice-cream-based drinks and bars. Sugar-free chocolates and themed collections (such as 'wedding' and 'thank you') are also on sale.
Mail order.
For branches see index.

Leonidas

37 Victoria Street, SW1H 0ED (7222 5399/ www.leonidasbelgianchocolates.co.uk). St James's Park tube. **Open** 8am-6pm Mon-Fri; 10am-5pm Sat. **Credit** AmEx, MC, V.
Founded by a Greek-born Belgian, the company's distinctive blue-and-yellow logo is hard to miss. The chocolates include butter creams, almond and hazelnut gianduja, dark and milk chocolate assortments, marzipan fruits, orangettes, liqueur-centred chocs and the company's famous pralines. A seating area offers coffee and chocolates to eat in.
Mail order.
Branches: throughout the city.

Montezuma's

29 East Street, Chichester, West Sussex PO19 1HS (01243 537 385/www.montezumas.co.uk). **Open** 9am-5.30pm Mon-Sat; 10.30am-4.30pm Sun. **Credit** AmEx, MC, V.
Inspired by their travels in South America, two ex-City lawyers set up this small company making handmade chocolates in Sussex – and in a short time Montezuma's has won several awards and accolades. Espousing fair trade values, the company also sells vegan and organic varieties. Bite-sized chocolate discs in assorted flavours are sold, along with fudge, drinking chocolate, and a child-friendly range in fish and turtle shapes. Bars come in unusual flavour combinations, such as sweet paprika and strawberry or white chocolate with mixed peppercorns. Chocolate fountains are available for hire.
Mail order.

Pierre Marcolini

6 Lancer Square, W8 4EH (7795 6611/ www.pierremarcolini.co.uk). High Street Kensington tube. **Open** 10am-7pm Mon-Sat. **Credit** AmEx, MC, V.
This glamorous chocolate boutique, with smart wooden floors and judiciously placed spotlights, displays chocolates like precious jewellery on handcrafted wooden counters. Pierre Marcolini is one of only four master chocolatiers in Europe. He sources natural ingredients from around the world, and selects his own chocolate beans. The range is stunning – Fabergé-like sculpted eggs at Easter, pretty 'handbags' of chocolates inspired by couture collections, jasmine tea ganache and raspberry hearts packaged in stylish designer boxes. The on-site café serves hot chocolate, coffee and pastries. There's a service offering personalised chocolates, chocolate fountains are available for hire, and chocolate-tasting evenings are held.

Prestat

14 Princes Arcade, SW1Y 6DS (7629 4838/ www.prestat.co.uk). Green Park tube. **Open** 9.30am-6pm Mon-Fri; 10am-5pm Sat. **Credit** AmEx, MC, V.

Lighthouse Bakery. See p232.

Vibrantly coloured packaging is the trademark of this company, which sells handmade English chocolates. Try chocolate-dipped apricots, banoffi truffles or pastel-coloured fruit fondants. Organic chocolate wafers are also sold, in flavours such as cinnamon and earl grey.
Mail order.

Rococo
321 King's Road, SW3 5EP (7352 5857/ www.rococochocolates.com). Sloane Square tube then 11, 19, 22 bus. **Open** 10am-6.30pm Mon-Sat; noon-5pm Sun. **Credit** MC, V.
The beautiful Rococo offers fruit and flower fondants, caramels and gingers. Chocolate bars come in flavours like orange and geranium, rosemary, lavender and Arabic spices. Chilli- and passionfruit-flavoured chocolates are great for adventurous palates, as are saffron and ginger fudge or truffles filled with Islay single malt whisky. Cuban chocolate cigars are another popular choice; sugar-free, dairy-free and organic varieties are also sold. Owner Chantal Coady co-founded the Chocolate Society (*see p234*).
For branch see index.

Theobroma Cacao
43 Turnham Green Terrace, W4 1RG (8996 0431/www.theobroma-cacao.co.uk). Turnham Green tube. **Open** 9am-9pm Mon-Fri; 9am-6pm Sat; 10am-5.30pm Sun. **Credit** AmEx, MC, V.
This delightful little chocolate shop has a loyal local following. Friendly staff will help you choose from a carefully selected range of artisanal truffles, fondants, nuts, bars, creams, fudges and caramels – in all the popular flavours. Try the gorgeous Mexican hot chocolate, which comes in assorted flavours, and which you can sup on site along with a chocolate of choice.
Mail order.

Thorntons
353 Oxford Street, W1C 2JG (7493 7498/www. thorntons.co.uk). Bond Street tube. **Open** 10am-8pm Mon-Sat; noon-6pm Sun. **Credit** AmEx, MC, V.
Possibly the most commercial of the major UK chocolate companies, Thorntons has appointed a master chocolatier to launch individual themed collections, such as Eden (in tropical flavours like guava and passionfruit) and Dessert Gallery (chocs inspired by classic desserts). Truffles, toffees and fudges are still popular, and a sugar-free range is also available.
Mail order (0845 121 1911).
Branches: throughout the city.

Honey

The Hive Honey Shop
93 Northcote Road, SW11 6PL (7924 6233/ www.thehivehoneyshop.co.uk). Clapham Junction rail. **Open** 10am-5pm Mon-Sat. **Credit** MC, V.
Owned by professional beekeeper James Hamill, this specialist shop sells honey, pollen, propolis, beeswax and royal jelly. The wide range of honeys includes single floral varieties like linden blossom, hawthorn and sweet chestnut. Sauces, chocolates, relishes, conserves, mustards, and mead and honey liqueurs are also on offer, along with handmade candles, cosmetics, health products, tableware and Winnie the Pooh giftware. There's a fascinating 5ft-high beehive, cross-sectioned, at the back of the shop, where you can see 20,000 bees in action.
Mail order.

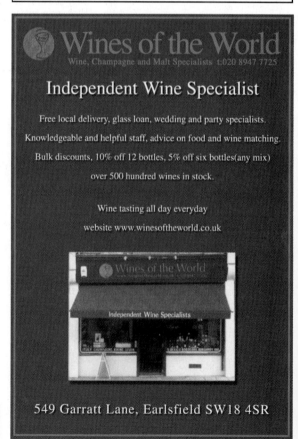

Delicatessens

A&C Continental Groceries
3 Atlantic Road, SW9 8HX (7733 3766). Brixton tube/rail. **Open** 8am-8pm Mon-Sat. **No credit cards.**
Specialising in Mediterranean, Polish, Brazilian and North African products, this lovely deli overlooks Brixton Market. It stocks meats (Milano salami, Napoli salami, chorizo), cheeses, pastas, olives, dips, breads, oils and vinegars. Staff are very helpful.

Belsize Village Delicatessen
39 Belsize Lane, NW3 5AS (7794 4258). Belsize Park tube. **Open** 8.30am-7pm Mon-Fri; 8.30am-6pm Sat; 9am-2pm Sun. **Credit** MC, V.
Located in pretty Belsize Village, this small deli has a very local feel. There is a counter that holds cheeses, charcuterie, pâtés and olives, a chiller cabinet filled with traiteur dishes like Moroccan tagine, and shelves laden with artisan breads, relishes, preserves, oils and vinegars. The deli also caters for the local South African community, and offers a good selection of wind-dried biltong. *Mail order.*

Del'Aziz
24-28 Vanston Place, SW6 1AX (7386 0086). Fulham Broadway tube. **Open** 7am-7pm Mon-Sat; 8am-6pm Sun. **Credit** AmEx, MC, V.
Located next to its own restaurant Aziz, this hip deli with wooden bench seating is especially popular for breakfasts. It specialises in beautifully packaged Moroccan and Middle Eastern ingredients, plus a few Mediterranean items. The range includes pickles and preserves (stuffed cucumber pickle, rose petal jam), pastas, couscous, pestos, nuts, syrups, flower waters and cakes. Freshly baked pastries and breads are also on offer, and there is a counter that sells hot and cold dishes to take away (such as tarts, salads and roast chicken). This is a good place to pick up Moroccan cookware, including colourful tagines and garishly decorated mint tea cups.

The Delicatessen Shop
23 South End Road, NW3 2PT (7435 7315). Hampstead Heath rail. **Open** 9.30am-7pm Mon-Fri; 9am-6pm Sat. **Credit** MC, V.
Popular for its freshly made pesto, roast coffee and delicious chocolates (displayed in a glass cabinet by the entrance), this friendly deli also sells an exquisite range of own-made pasta. Cheeses, charcuterie, breads, cakes, pickles, jams, biscuits, olives, pasta sauces and olive oils are also sold.

East Dulwich Deli
15-17 Lordship Lane, SE22 8EW (8693 2525). East Dulwich rail. **Open** 9am-6pm Mon-Sat; 10am-4pm Sun. **Credit** MC, V.
Specialising in Italian and Spanish artisan products, this welcoming deli sells pastas, olives, cheeses, charcuterie and cooked dishes such as tarts, pies and stuffed vegetables. There is also a selection of Born and Bread breads, including wholemeal, white, ciabatta, black olive and the super-tasty kentish flute.

L'Eau à la Bouche
49 Broadway Market, E8 4PH (7923 0600/ www.labouche.com). London Fields rail/26, 55, 106, 277, 394 bus. **Open** 9am-7pm Mon-Fri; 9am-5pm Sat; 10am-4pm Sun. **Credit** MC, V.
A newcomer to increasingly gentrified Broadway Market, this lovely, mainly French deli has a few tables for eating in. On offer are cold meats, cheeses, coffees and ready-prepared food such as pizza, quiches and sandwiches. A small selection of breads includes sourdough, rye and sunflower.

Elizabeth King
34 New King's Road, SW6 4ST (7736 2826/ www.elizabethking.com). Parsons Green tube. **Open** 9am-8pm Mon-Fri; 9am-6pm Sat; 9am-3.30pm Sun. **Credit** AmEx, MC, V.
Almost like a small specialist supermarket, this spacious deli has a wide range of products from Italy, France and the UK. You'll find over 100 varieties of cheeses, Monmouth House coffee, daily delivered bakery products, Chegworth Valley juices, free-range meat, fresh fish from Cornwall, the Vallebona Sardinian range, fresh pasta, soups, chocolates and wines. There's also a growing organic line, including breads, fruit and vegetables; and own-made frozen food features salmon fishcakes and beef wellington. Prepare to queue at lunchtimes for freshly filled sandwiches, hot meals and salads prepared by the on-site cook.

Felicitous
19 Kensington Park Road, W11 2EU (7243 4050/www.felicitouscatering.co.uk). Ladbroke Grove tube. **Open** 8am-9pm Mon-Fri; 8am-7pm Sat; 9am-5pm Sun. **Credit** MC, V.
This beautiful Mediterranean-looking deli is stylishly cluttered with cakes, breads, biscuits and children's cookery kits. The extensive range of pickles, chutneys, jams and olive oils is impressive. The deli counter displays charcuterie, cheeses, olives and pâtés; and there's a good selection of sandwiches and snacks to take away.

Fields
15 Corsica Street, N5 1JT (7704 1247). Highbury & Islington tube/rail. **Open** 10am-8pm Mon-Fri; 9.30am-6.30pm Sat; 10am-5pm Sun. **Credit** MC, V.
Freshly cooked pies, meatballs and tortilla are a draw at this deli, which also sells cheeses, hams, biscuits, pasta and wines. There is also a notable selection of bread and olive oil. *Mail order.*

Flâneur Food Hall
41 Farringdon Road, EC1M 3JB (7404 4422). Farringdon tube/rail. **Open** 9am-10pm Mon-Sat; 9am-6pm Sun. **Credit** AmEx, DC, MC, V.
Flâneur looks impressive: a large service area in the middle, surrounded by high stools, dominates the space – which is lined with tall shelves that go up to the ceiling. There are a few seats at the front by the window, and there's a restaurant at the back. Every inch of space is crammed with products, which range from the everyday (piccalilli, fresh pasta) to the exotic (fresh Japanese mushrooms, pistachio oil). The sheer variety of groceries, breads, cheeses, wines, pastries and fresh fruit and vegetables is amazing. A daily changing menu of great quality food is available to eat in or take away. Our only complaint is the rather unfriendly service. *Mail order.*

Food Hall
374-378 Old Street, EC1V 9LT (7729 6005). Old Street tube/rail. **Open** 9am-7pm Mon-Fri; 10am-5pm Sat, Sun. **Credit** MC, V.
Housed in a former Victorian dairy, this pretty shop houses breads, pastries, chocolates and deli foods on one side, and a cheese room on the other. The latter offers more than 100 organic, seasonal and regional varieties. The deli selection includes teas, coffees, oils, vinegars, charcuterie, pickles and preserves. Bread varieties include Italian, rye, walnut and raisin and hazelnut. The Food Hall's emphasis is on sourcing products from small independent producers.

Fusebox
12 Stoney Street, SE1 9AD (7407 9888/ www.fuseboxfoods.com). London Bridge tube/ rail. **Open** 11am-5pm Mon-Fri; 9am-4pm Sat. **Credit** MC, V.
Perched on the border of Borough Market, this modern pan-Asian deli stocks oriental sauces, spices, rice, noodles and curry pastes. A daily changing menu of hot and cold global dishes is available to eat in (there is limited seating) or take away. Prepare to tempt your taste buds with dishes such as chorizo and roast vegetable frittata, phanang chicken with pineapple and peanuts, or Cambodian coconut and lemongrass with rice and green leaves.
For branch see index.

George of Greenwich
19 Nelson Road, SE10 9JB (8305 3070/ www.georgeofgreenwich.com). Cutty Sark DLR. **Open** 10am-6pm daily. **Credit** MC, V.
Owned by Greenwich Inc, which also owns a number of restaurants and bars in the area, this gorgeous deli offers fine food and wines from specialist artisan suppliers – many of whom are recipients of the Guild of Fine Food Retailers' Great Taste awards. Cakes and breads (we rate the rocket and olive oil) are baked daily on the premises, and on-site chefs prepare salads and hot meals. The deli counter stocks charcuterie (Tuscan ham, wild boar salami), British cheeses (cropwell bishop, waterloo), antipasti and own-made jams. Shelves are packed with dressings (feta, chilli and lemon thyme), oils (winter truffle oil), preserves (hot banana chutney), Valrhona chocolates, and pastas and sauces. There's also a small wine shop at the back. Staff are knowledgeable and helpful.

Sweet dreams

'It's 1955 in my sweetshop, young man,' announced Miss Hope to an impudent Radio 4 journalist during one of many features on her centre of sweetie excellence, which opened in East Dulwich in 2004. Miss Hope, who runs the shop with Mr Greenwood (no vulgar Christian names here, thank you), had always played sweetshops as a little girl, and this jar-lined retail confection is the realisation of her dreams. It is indeed a shop of dreams, both for children and for those adults who rue the passing of rosy apples, sherbert pips, chewing nuts and cola cubes from the confectionery canon. Hope and Greenwood have proved that the sweets of 20 years ago are still out there, you just have to be a special sort of sweetshop to stock all of them.

It's not just nostalgic adults with mouthfuls of fillings crowding into this most beautiful of shops – children bundle in here daily after school for a fix of liquorice whips and pineapple chunks. They even have sweet tobacco in here (coconut and brown sugar strands once sold alongside chocolate cigarettes, liquorice pipes and candy matches in the bad old 1970s). If the stock sounds a mite too synthetic for sophisticated Londoners of the 21st century, be assured that Hope & Greenwood sell handmade chocolates and quality brands, such as Lindt and Suchard, particularly around Easter and Christmas. To make the shop pay – you can't run a business based on a stream of kids asking for 'two ounces' of Tom Thumb drops – the proprietors also sell sweetie-related goods, such as retro tins and jars, gift wrap, bunting and boxes. Parting is such sweet sorrow – you just know you'll come back again sooner than your dentist would wish.

Hope & Greenwood
20 North Cross Road, East Dulwich, SE22 9EU (8613 1777). East Dulwich rail/12, 40, 176, 185 bus. **Open** 10am-6pm Mon-Sat; 10am-5pm Sun. **Credit** AmEx, MC, V.

The Grocer on Elgin

6 Elgin Crescent, W11 2HX (7221 3844/ www.thegroceron.com). Ladbroke Grove or Notting Hill Gate tube. **Open** 8am-8pm Mon-Fri; 8am-6pm Sat, Sun. **Credit** MC, V.
Owned by Vivienne Hayman and Ashley Sumner, this spacious, trendy shrine to good food is famous for seasonal, handmade ready meals in distinctive vacuum-packed pouches. Saffron and asparagus risotto or rabbit with Bayonne ham are examples of a range of starters, mains, sides and desserts that can be assembled to create a complete meal. A groovy selection of groceries from around the world is also available, among them smoked garlic from Arleux, artisan pasta from Abruzzo, piquillo peppers, sweet chilli sambal, sashimi dressing, slow-roast tamarillos, and spices and dukkahs from the Sugar Club collection.
For branch (The Grocer on Warwick) see index.

Grove Park Deli

22 Fauconberg Road, W4 3JY (8995 8219). Chiswick rail. **Open** 8.30am-5pm Mon-Wed, Sat; 8.30am-7pm Thur, Fri; 9am-2pm Sun. **Credit** MC, V.
This tiny shop has a deli counter on one side that offers cheeses and ready-cooked dishes (a daily changing menu that includes lamb moussaka, fishcakes, Spanish chicken with chickpeas, Thai noodle salad, sausage rolls and cakes), and shelves stacked with a small selection of Mediterranean groceries on the other. The latter includes honeys, chocolates, pastas and pasta sauces. Staff are delightful, and they also run a catering service.

Gusto & Relish

56 White Hart Lane, SW13 0PZ (8878 2005). Barnes Bridge rail. **Open** 10am-6.30pm Mon-Fri; 10am-6pm Sat; 9am-1pm Sun. **Credit** MC, V.
Service is incredibly friendly at this deli, which has a central table piled high with breads, pastries and groceries. Cheeses, charcuterie, wines and ice-creams are also on sale. Daily changing cooked dishes include lamb kebabs, beef fillet, salmon fishcakes and salads.

Korona

30 Streatham High Road, SW16 1DB (8769 6647). Streatham Hill rail. **Open** 9am-7pm Mon-Fri; 9am-6pm Sat; 9.30am-3pm Sun. **Credit** MC, V.
Groceries from around the world (France, Italy, Eastern Europe and South Africa) are stocked at this store. Alongside deli staples such as cheese and charcuterie, there is a notable range of breads (from over a dozen bakeries) and drinks.

Leila's

17 Calvert Avenue, E2 7JP (7729 9789). Liverpool Street or Old Street tube/rail. **Open** 10am-6pm Thu-Sat; 10am-4pm Sun. **Credit** MC, V.
Popular with the Columbia Market crowd on Sundays, this quirky deli stocks cheeses, breads, meats, groceries and kitchenware. Owner Leila McAlister has impeccable taste, and she does short-term projects with different producers (on our visit it was Polish sausage-makers), which result in regularly changing displays.

W Martyn

135 Muswell Hill Broadway, N10 3RS (8883 5642). Highgate tube then 43, 102, 134, 144, W7 bus. **Open** 9.30am-5.30pm Mon-Wed, Fri; 9.30am-1pm Thur; 9am-5.30pm Sat. **Credit** MC, V.
This family-run grocer's was set up in 1897, and majors in old-fashioned hospitality. Fresh coffees (roasted in an ancient roaster) and loose teas are a speciality. Biscuits, nuts, pickles and preserves are also on sale, and the cakes (fruit, date and walnut, 'gypsy') are certainly not run of the mill.

Megan's Delicatessen

571 King's Road, SW6 2EB (7371 7837/ www.megansdeli.com). Bus 11, 14, 22. **Open** 8am-6pm Mon-Fri; 9am-6pm Sat. **Credit** AmEx, DC, MC, V.
Set over two floors with split-level areas, this attractive deli sells Poîlane bread, cheeses, olives, sauces and own-made jams. All the products are

GM- and additive-free, and cakes and muffins are baked on the premises. Home-style dishes, prepared by owner Megan and her chefs, are available for breakfast, lunch and takeaway. These may include salmon coconut curry with rice, or pasta with prosciutto and spinach and peppers in own-made arrabbiata sauce – which can be eaten in the 'secret garden' at the back.

Melrose & Morgan

42 Gloucester Avenue, NW1 8JD (7722 0011/ www.melroseandmorgan.com). Camden Town or Chalk Farm tube. **Open** 9am-8pm Tue-Sat; 10am-6pm Sun. **Credit** AmEx, MC, V.
This beautifully presented deli champions quality produce from small British suppliers and farmers. Standout items include jams and jellies in nostalgic flavours like medlar and crab apple, handmade Madame Oiseau chocolates from a French confectioner based in Canterbury, organic meats, and seasonal fruit and veg. Pâtés, fish pie and even ketchup are made on the premises by the house chefs, and the honey is produced on nearby Hampstead Heath.

Mise-en-Place

53 Battersea Rise, SW11 1HH (7228 4329/ www.thefoodstore.co.uk). Clapham Junction rail. **Open** 8am-8pm daily. **Credit** AmEx, MC, V.
This attractive deli has a small café at the back and outside seating in fine weather. Amazing charcuterie, cheeses, salads, antipasti and freshly cooked dishes are displayed at the counter, and shelves are laden with pickles, chutneys, pasta sauces, oils, vinegars, herbs and spices. Also on offer are a small selection of artisan breads and top-notch ice-creams and frozen desserts.
Mail order.

Mr Christian's

11 Elgin Crescent, W11 2JA (7229 0501/ www.mrchristians.co.uk). Ladbroke Grove tube. **Open** 6am-7pm Mon-Fri; 5.30am-6.30pm Sat; 7am-5pm Sun. **Credit** AmEx, MC, V.
Now part of the Jeroboams group, Mr Christian's opened a wine shop at No.13 in October 2004. Friendly, unpretentious and well-established, the original deli is still busy with local customers taking their pick from the huge variety of cheese (up to 120 varieties), hams, fresh pasta, olives, own-made chutneys and preserves. The range of up to two dozen traiteur dishes changes daily, and might run from chargrilled lamb kebabs to asparagus risotto. Sempre Viva frozen yoghurt has proved a huge hit with the calorie-conscious. On Saturdays and Sundays, a bread stall is set up outside the shop.

Mortimer & Bennett

33 Turnham Green Terrace, W4 1RG (8995 4145/www.mortimerandbennett.com). Turnham Green tube. **Open** 8.30am-6pm Mon-Fri; 8.30am-5.30pm Sat. **Credit** MC, V.
One of London's most acclaimed delis, M&B sources exclusive speciality products from small family suppliers around the world, particularly France. Here you'll find Lebanese fruit syrups, mulberry or wild rose jams, verjuice (very fashionable right now), Terre Exotique brown cane sugar with vanilla, the award-winning Mas Pares Spanish foie gras, barrel-aged feta, New Zealand extra virgin olive oil, Tuscan prosciutto, and mini wild boar and venison salamis in oil. Also on sale are Kama Sutra chocolates (£19.95 per box), unusual fruit and flower vinegars, and fruit dressings from Womersley Foods (golden raspberry dressing with geranium). If you're in an extravagant mood, try La Duchesse, billed as 'the world's most expensive jam' (£12.95/100g).
Mail order.

Myddeltons

25A Lloyd Baker Street, WC1X 9AT (7278 9192). Angel tube. **Open** 7am-6pm Mon-Fri; 7am-5pm Sat. **Credit** MC, V.
This charming deli offers meats (Parma ham, salami, turkey), breads (soda, olive, wholemeal, walnut, focaccia, baguette), cheeses, oils, biscuits, own-label jams, wines, and fresh fruit and veg.

North Street Deli

26 North Street, SW4 0HB (7978 1555). Clapham Common tube. **Open** 10am-6pm Mon-Sat. **Credit** MC, V.
Co-owned by chef Maddalena Bonino and Nathan Middlemiss, this popular deli boasts friendly, knowledgeable staff – it won *Time Out*'s award for Best Food Shop in 2004. It offers top-quality charcuterie, breads from Marcus Miller, carrot gateau and layered chocolate fudge cake, preserves, pickles and oils. Lovely sandwiches and snacks are available to eat in or take away.

Ottolenghi

63 Ledbury Road, W11 2AD (7727 1121). Notting Hill Gate or Westbourne Park tube. **Open** 8am-8pm Mon-Fri; 8am-7pm Sat; 8.30am-6pm Sun. **Credit** AmEx, MC, V.
Looking like a cross between a designer boutique and an art gallery, this strikingly white, hipper-than-thou deli-cum-café is renowned for exceptional, fuss-free cooking influenced by Middle Eastern and Mediterranean flavours. Salads, roast meats, tagines and pastas feature on the savoury food counter, and cakes, tarts, meringues and macaroons make up the range of sweet treats.
For branches see index.

Panzer's

13-19 Circus Road, NW8 6PB (7722 8596/ www.panzers.co.uk). St John's Wood tube. **Open** 8am-7pm Mon-Fri; 8am-6pm Sat; 8am-2pm Sun. **Credit** MC, V.
Established more than 50 years ago, this large, family-run deli is chock-a-block with items from France, Germany, Greece, Italy, Spain, South Africa and the US. Famous for exceptional rare fruits, herbs and vegetables, the shop also has a good kosher range (including cakes and foie gras), more than 50 types of bread, South African dried fruit and nuts, a vast selection of US products (marshmallow fluff, instant grits) and an organic line. The counter at the back stocks charcuterie (bresaola, biltong), cheeses (vacherin, English varieties from Neal's Yard), freshly made salads, olives, smoked salmon and caviar.
Mail order.

Le Pont de la Tour Food Store

Butler's Wharf Building, 36D Shad Thames, SE1 2YE (7403 8403/www.conran.com). Tower Hill tube/London Bridge tube/rail. **Open** 8.30am-8.30pm Mon-Fri; 10am-7.30pm Sat; 10am-6.30pm Sun. **Credit** AmEx, MC, V.
This beautiful store, with its attractive tiled floor, offers gourmet salads and sandwiches to eat in or take away. Groceries include herbs and spices, olive oils and pastas, and the deli sells charcuterie, pâtés and cheeses. Freshly baked breads and cakes are from the Pont bakery, and traiteur dishes include sirloin steak and tuna aspic.

Rosslyn Delicatessen

56 Rosslyn Hill, NW3 1ND (7794 9210/ www.delirosslyn.co.uk). Hampstead tube. **Open** 8.30am-8.30pm Mon-Sat; 8.30am-8pm Sun. **Credit** AmEx, MC, V.
Owned by Helen Sherman, this deli is one of the best loved in London. It's crammed with chocolates (Charbonnel & Walker, Neuhaus) and confectionery (handmade burnt sugar fudge); caviar, including the cheaper trout version; American classics (Froot Loops, Aunt Jemima cornbread mix); biscuits; British, Irish, French, Italian, Swiss, German, Spanish and Danish cheeses; meats (sausages, beef, ham, salami, rillettes, terrines); pastas and sauces; rice and polenta, and oils and vinegars. The range of preserves, condiments, dried herbs and spices is particularly impressive. Other attractions include regular food tastings, picnic hampers and foodie gifts for festivals and special occasions.
Mail order.

Sonny's Food Shop & Café

92 Church Road, SW13 0DQ (8741 8451). Barnes Bridge rail. **Open** 10.30am-5.30pm Mon, Tue; 10.30am-6pm Wed-Fri; 10am-5pm Sat. **Credit** MC, V.

This tiny deli has floor-to-ceiling shelves at the front (stacked with pastas, pickles, preserves, oils, vinegars and chocolates), and a bigger café area at the back. A daily changing menu offers the likes of chicken with sesame seeds, fishcakes, and salads, and breads come in walnut, olive, sesame, sourdough and wholemeal varieties – including a few gluten-free options.

The Store
97 Westbourne Park Villas, W2 5ED (7792 3369). Royal Oak tube. **Open** 8.30am-4pm Mon-Sat. **Credit** MC, V.
There is wooden bench seating in the front yard of this fashionable deli, located near Tom Conran's Cow Dining Rooms. The vibe in this corner of Notting Hill is so relaxed and laid-back that you could spend hours sipping on good coffee and munching on pies, pasties or freshly filled sandwiches, working on that unfinished novel. The range of breads, pastries, confectionery and, in particular, meats is impressive.

Tavola
155 Westbourne Grove, W11 2RS (7229 0571). Notting Hill Gate tube. **Open** 10am-7.30pm Mon-Fri; 9.30am-5pm Sat. **Credit** AmEx, MC, V.
Owned by acclaimed chef Alistair Little, this friendly Mediterranean deli is stunningly laid out, with an elongated central table overflowing with enticingly colourful goodies. A pick 'n' mix range of starters, mains, breads, sides and desserts makes it ideal for a cheat's dinner party. Start with baked blue cheese-stuffed figs wrapped in Parma ham, then move on to beef goulash with sour cream, three-sauce lasagne, Italian meatballs in tomato sauce, or tagine of chicken with chickpeas and vegetables. Then just add friends, wine and music – and watch your popularity soar.

Tom's
226 Westbourne Grove, W11 2RH (7221 8818). Notting Hill Gate tube. **Open** 8am-6pm Mon-Sat; 9am-5pm Sun. **Credit** MC, V.
Enormously popular with local celebrities, Tom's draws you in with colourful baubles of retro-style confectionery, then leads you to the café at the back, which is popular for breakfasts and leisurely lunches. The basement deli stocks jams, chutneys, ice-creams, oils, and fresh fruit and veg, and there's a generous deli counter displaying ready-prepared dishes and olives.
Mail order.

Troubadour Delicatessen
267 Old Brompton Road, SW5 9JA (7341 6341). West Brompton tube. **Open** noon-10pm Mon-Fri; 10am-10pm Sat, Sun. **Credit** MC, V.
Owned by the quirky Troubadour bar-café next door, this deli looks like it could be in New York – a feeling accentuated by the range of deli meats it offers, such as smoked turkey, smoked ham, pastrami, salami and kabanos. No wonder freshly filled lunchtime sandwiches are popular. Breads include ciabatta, granary, wholemeal and focaccia. There's a careful selection of cheeses, condiments, olive oils, pastas and sauces, wines, and fresh fruit and vegetables.

Verde & Co
4 Brushfield Street, E1 6AG (7247 1924). Liverpool Street tube/rail. **Open** 8am-8pm Mon-Fri; 11am-5pm Sat, Sun. **Credit** MC, V.
Next door to A Gold (*see below*), and in an equally lovely restored Georgian building, this exquisite shop is owned by author Jeanette Winterson and run by ex-chef Harvey Cabannis. In contrast to its neighbour's British specialism, many of the goods are Italian, supplied by importer Machiavelli, including fresh pasta flown in twice a week and charcuterie. Pierre Marcolini chocolates are arrayed like trinkets in a jewel case. Fruit and veg are displayed outside with a window dresser's art, alongside a selection of orchids. As well as organic produce, you'll find such delicacies as French white peaches, courgette flowers, and chanterelles from Scotland. Prices reflect the rarefied mood. Sandwiches made on the premises, cakes and coffees are sold to take away.

Villandry
170 Great Portland Street, W1W 5QB (7631 3131/www.villandry.com). Great Portland Street tube. **Open** 7.30am-10pm Mon-Sat; 10am-4pm Sun. **Credit** AmEx, MC, V.
Owned by American businesswoman Martha Greene, this large deli (attached to a restaurant and bar) is one of the most famous in London. Handsome wooden shelves line the sides of the shop, and numerous counters sell deli staples. Cheeses from Britain, France and Italy are sold at three separate counters, and charcuterie (cured continental hams and salamis) has a section of its own. There's a window display of cakes and breads, including prune and Armagnac flan and Mexican wedding cookies, baked in-house using organic flour and French and Cornish butter. Shelves and tables are strewn with gourmet groceries sourced from around the world (including the shop's own product range), and there's a wide range of ready-cooked meals and snacks to take away, such as Lancashire hotpot and Peking duck wraps.

Vivian's
2 Worple Way, Richmond, Surrey TW10 6DF (8940 3600/www.viviansfinefoods.com). Richmond tube/rail. **Open** 9am-7pm Mon-Fri; 9am-6pm Sat; 9am-2pm Sun. **Credit** MC, V.
This lovely deli stocks Bay Tree and Forest Products chutneys (apple and ginger, hot and spicy aubergine, Italian grape, onions in balsamic vinegar), plus all the deli staples. Staff are exceptionally helpful.
Mail order.

International

African & Caribbean

Blue Mountain Peak
2A-8 Craven Park Road, NW10 4AB (8965 3859). Willesden Junction tube. **Open** 7am-6pm Mon, Thur; 7.15am-6pm Tue, Wed; 6.30am-6pm Fri, Sat. **Credit** MC, V.
This large shop is packed with Jamaican and West African groceries. There's a huge variety, encompassing everything from Caribbean hard-dough breads to herbal tonics and root drinks. Other items include spices, seasonings and condiments; beans and flours; dried fish; different types of rice; and tropical fruit and veg, such as African mangoes, purple 'elephant' yam, coo-coo and fresh sugarcane.

Brixton, SW9
Brixton tube/rail.
Inside the bustling Brixton Village indoor market, you'll find everything you need to assemble African and Caribbean meals. **Back Home Foods** sells imported spices, pulses, fruit and veg such as callaloo, yams, breadfruit and mangoes. On nearby Atlantic Road, **First Choice** offers a wide range of Jamaican patties, including lamb and peas, chicken and sweetcorn, salt fish, beef and mixed vegetables.

Dalston, E8
Dalston Kingsland rail.
Dalston's crowded **Ridley Road Market** is immensely popular with the area's African and Caribbean community. Here you'll find everything from specialist hair products to bags of gari (a type of Nigerian grits). Haggling with the good-natured market traders is a must – and part of the experience. There is also a number of West African and Caribbean grocery shops in the area, most of which are family-run places that sell low-priced imported ingredients.

British

A Gold, Traditional Foods of Britain
42 Brushfield Street, E1 6AG (7247 2487/ www.agold.co.uk). Liverpool Street tube/rail. **Open** 11am-8pm Mon-Fri; 10am-6pm Sat; 11am-6pm Sun. **Credit** AmEx, MC, V.

Can you still buy Vimto lollies and Scottish clootie dumplings in the capital? Indeed you can. This charming shop would be at home in a 1950s village, but the nostalgia-inducing ingredients are carefully sourced from artisan producers all over the UK, with regional products a speciality. How about biscuits such as currant Shrewsburys or oat bannocks? Or Cornish saffron cake and ginger brack? Other items include gravy salts, smoked Cornish pilchard fillets, cheeses (cooleeney, cashel blue), teas, preserves, condiments, mustards, cured meats and smoked fish. There's confectionery too. A notable range of soft drinks features dandelion and burdock; the alcoholic drinks run to mead and damson gin.
Mail order.

Chinese

Chinatown, WC2
Leicester Square or Piccadilly Circus tube.
Just off Leicester Square, Chinatown remains the place to buy Chinese and South-east Asian ingredients. You'll find fresh produce such as leafy greens, herbs and exotic fruit, as well as noodles, myriad condiments and other staples. At **Golden Gate Grocers** (100 Shaftesbury Avenue, W1D 5EE, 7437 0014) goods are labelled in English and cover all kinds of exotica, from red date tea to pig maw; there's a greengrocer out back. Loon Fung, once the area's largest Chinese foodstore, has closed, but **New Loon Moon Supermarket** (9 Gerrard Street, W1D 5PN, 7734 3887) remains strong on fresh fruit, vegetables and herbs. Other worthwhile shops are **Good Harvest Fish & Meat** (65 Shaftesbury Avenue, W1B 6LH, 7437 0712), **Golden Gate Hong Supermarket** (700 Shaftesbury Avenue, WC2 7PR, 7437 0014) and **See Woo** (19 Lisle Street, WC2 7P, 7439 8325), which is particularly strong on South-east Asian ingredients. Chinatown is in the process of (controversial) redevelopment, so expect changes.

Wing Yip
395 Edgware Road, NW2 6LN (8450 0422/ www.wingyip.com). Cricklewood rail/16, 32, 316 bus. **Open** 9.30am-7pm Mon-Sat; 11.30am-5pm Sun. **Credit** MC, V.
Highly respected in the Chinese community (its own-label products are a standard-bearer of quality), Wing Yip is the main supplier to Chinese restaurants. There is a vast range of imported Chinese, Malaysian, Thai, Japanese and Indonesian products – many of which come in catering packs. The range includes frozen foods, oriental sauces and marinades (extra hot Maysan curry sauce concentrate, perhaps), herbs and spices (dried angelica root, liquorice powder), snacks, meat, fish, veg, rice, noodles and cooking utensils. Popular staples include Chinese instant cereal, yellow rock sugar, Nago cuttlefish fritters flour, and black sesame dessert mix.
For branch see index.

East European

The Birch
297 Finchley Road, NW3 6DT (7794 0777). Finchley Road tube. **Open** 11am-9pm Mon-Sat; 11am-7pm Sun. **Credit** MC, V.
This small deli is crammed with imported staples from Russia, Poland, Latvia, Lithuania, Estonia and Ukraine. There's a deli counter with fresh meats and sausages, and shelves laden with pickles, jams, grains, biscuits, confectionery and breads (not baked on the premises). A freezer cabinet houses an array of stuffed dumplings, and East European magazines and videos are also sold. It helps if you know what you're looking for as the products are not labelled in English, and service can be hampered by language difficulties.

Filipino

Manila Supermarket
11-12 Hogarth Place, SW5 0QT (7373 8305). Earl's Court tube. **Open** 9am-9pm daily. **Credit** AmEx, MC, V.

FOOD & DRINK

Hamish Johnston. See p233.

This spacious, friendly shop is packed with imported jars, tins, packets and frozen food from the Philippines. There's a wide selection of fresh fruit and vegetables, pickles, seasonings, sauces, instant mixes, pastries and frozen foods. Unless you know what you're looking for, the items may be unfamiliar even to those who are well versed in oriental cuisine; many are based on coconut, yams, tropical fruits, eggs and rice.

French

Comptoir Gascon

61-63 Charterhouse Street, EC1M 6HJ (7608 0851). Farringdon tube/rail. **Open** 8am-11pm Mon-Sat. **Credit** AmEx, MC, V.
This fashionably rustic French deli-café specialises in products from Gascony. There's a lovely selection of own-baked breads (try eight-seed, paysanne, sourdough or walnut), pastries (almond croissants, fruit tarts), imported cheeses, charcuterie (rillettes, terrines, confits, pâtés, cured hams, sausages), and traiteur dishes (such as cassoulet). Olive oil, vinegars, wines and beautifully packaged confectionery complete the picture.

German

German Wurst & Delicatessen

127 Central Street, EC1V 8AP (7250 1322/www. germandeli.co.uk). Barbican tube. **Open** 10am-7pm Mon-Fri; 10am-6pm Sat. **No credit cards**.
Specialising in imported wurst and other meats from Germany, this tiny deli also has cheeses, pickles and groceries. However, it's the meat that's the real draw – you'll find an excellent selection of frankfurters and other sausages, as well as pâtés and hams. Loaves include the fashionable 'bread of Westphalia' – a style of rye bread that's a speciality of Central and Eastern Europe.

Global

Al-Abbas

258-262 Uxbridge Road, W12 7JA (8740 1932). Shepherd's Bush tube. **Open** 7am-midnight daily. **Credit** MC, V.
Endorsed by Nigella, no less, this large supermarket stocks an idiosyncratic selection of everyday and unfamiliar groceries from all over the world. Indian fruit and veg sits alongside Ethiopian injera bread, Lebanese pickles, Nigerian pulses, oriental sauces, Moroccan spices, French confectionery and fresh Turkish lamb kebabs.

Greek

Andreas Michli & Son

405-411 St Ann's Road, N15 3JL (8802 0188). Manor House tube. **Open** 10am-7pm Mon-Sat; 11am-3.30pm Sun. **No credit cards**.
Voluptuous figs flown in from Cyprus and succulent yellow dates are some of the offerings at this large shop; other Greek, Cypriot and Turkish items include cheeses, olives, confectionery, fruit preserves, breads, pulses and dips.

Athenian Grocery

16A Moscow Road, W2 4BT (7229 6280). Bayswater tube. **Open** 8.30am-7pm Mon-Sat; 8.30am-1pm Sun. **No credit cards**.
Imported fresh fruit and vegetables (including fresh nuts in season) are laid out at the entrance of this small, family-run shop. Inside you'll find a counter stacked with cheese, meat, olives and pastries. Oils, pickles, preserves, honeys and (pre-packed) breads line the shelves.

Dulwich Supermarket

18 Lordship Lane, SE22 8HM (8299 2214). East Dulwich rail. **Open** 8am-11pm daily. **Credit** AmEx, MC, V.
The groceries at this Middle Eastern and Mediterranean store are sourced from Greece, Cyprus, Turkey, Italy and Spain. Greek bread, organic bread, pitta and baguettes sit alongside condiments, seasonings, chocolates, rice, oils, and fresh fruit and veg.

FOOD & DRINK

Indian

Brick Lane, E1

Aldgate East tube.

Interspersed with Bangladeshi restaurants, characterful Brick Lane is strewn with small Indian groceries selling rare Bangladeshi veg, fruit and authentic Bengali sweets. The best of the bunch is the huge **Taj Stores** (No.112, E1 0RL, 7377 0061), which has an amazing array of fresh veg and fruit rarely seen outside Bangladesh (and, sadly, rarely seen on Brick Lane menus), plus spices, pickles, rice and snacks. A smaller selection of these items can also be found at **Zaman Brothers** (Nos.17-19, E1 6BU, 7247 1009), which offers a good variety of breads. Don't leave Brick Lane without a box or two of famous Bengali sweets: **Al(l)audin Sweets** (No.72, E1 6RL, 7377 0896) and **Bangladeshi Banoful Mishti** (No.108, E1 6RL, 7247 3465) both offer rosagulla and sondesh (the best-known varieties).

Deepak Cash & Carry

953-959 Garratt Lane, SW17 0LW (8767 7819/ www.asianfood.com). Tooting Broadway tube. **Open** 9am-7.30pm Mon-Sat; 10am-5pm Sun. **Credit** MC, V.

Locals swear by this spicy supermarket, which sells Indian staples like pulses, pickles, rice, chapati flour, instant mixes, frozen food, tinned tropical vegetables, Indian noodles, grains, and fresh fruit and veg. Own-baked breads and pastries are also sold: these include pecan and maple syrup pastries, petit pain, baguettes and poppy seed rolls – but, unusually, no Indian breads.

Drummond Street, NW1

Euston Square tube/Euston tube/rail.

Drummond Street is renowned for its Indian vegetarian eateries. The ever-popular **Ambala** (*see* **Confectionery**, *p234*) and **Gupta** (No.100, NW1 2HH, 7380 1590) are famous for samosas, pakoras, tea-time savouries and fudge-like sweets – try the dense, spicy 'habsi' (aka gypsy) halwa. The sprawling but cramped **Savera Bakery** (No.129, NW1 2HL, 7380 0290) sells a good variety of (packaged) breads, plus mainly Gujarati products in tins and jars. Bangladeshi groceries, vegetables, and meats can be found at **London Oriental Foods** (No.122, NW1 2HN, 7387 3740).

Ealing Road, Wembley

Alperton tube.

After a lull (when affluent Gujaratis and Gujarati businesses moved out to places like Harrow and Kingsbury), Ealing Road seems to be enjoying a renaissance: lots of new Gujarati restaurants and snack shops have opened, alongside Sri Lankan, Tamil and Somali places. **Wembley Exotics** (Nos.133-135, HA0 4BP, 8900 2607) remains iconic: its colourful displays of imported fruit and veg are second to none, and if you get midnight munchies for Alphonso mangoes, it's open until late. The compact **Prashad Sweets** (No.222, HA0 4QL, 8902 1704) is as popular for its sweets and snacks as it is for its rock-bottom prices (most items cost less than £1). Sri Lankan **Bismillah Butchers** (Nos.19 & 33, HA0 4YA, 8903 4922) is perhaps better for tropical fish than meat, and **Ganapathy Cash & Carry** (Nos.34-38, HA0 5YD, 8795 4627) is a treasure trove of Sri Lankan breads, pickles, rice, frozen ready meals, and fruit and vegetables.

Green Street, E7

Upton Park tube.

Disembark from Upton Park tube, and you'd be forgiven for thinking you have arrived at an Indian bazaar. The long, bustling, colourful street is lined with scores of Indian restaurants and food shops (run by Indians of every hue, region and religion), plus a few Afro-Caribbean ones. **Green Street Supermarket** (No. 414-416, E13 9JJ, 8503 4422) is good for groceries, fruit, veg and meat. Pop into **Super Save** (No. 343, 8471 1593) and **Rana Food Store** (No.367, 8471 7523) for low-cost Indian, African and Caribbean spices, grains and pulses. **Bharat Food Store** (No.5, 8472 6393), **Green Village** (No.10A, 8503 4809), and **Variety Foods**

(No.20, 8471 0008) are all located at Carlton Terrace (a part of Green Street), and stock everything from snake-like striped marrows to yam flour. For meatier options, head to **United Halal Meat** (3 Carlton Terrace, 8586 0545), **Iman** (319 Green Street, 8472 3308), **Humza Halal Meat** (No.389, 8470 9093) and **Kaz's Halal Meat** (No.397, 8470 1009). **Green Street Fresh Fish** (No.3, 8472 8918) is an old-fashioned East End operation, where the tuna, salmon and haddock is very fresh.

Southall

Southall rail.

The first things that hit you about Southall, home to Punjabi and Sindhi communities, are the sights (garishly embroidered salwar kameez), sounds (loud Punjabi rap blaring out of shops and car windows) and smells (sizzling samosas or freshly cooked 'naan kebabs'). Having thus whetted your appetite, head to the enormous **Quality Foods** (Witley Gardens Industrial Estate, UB2 4ES, 8571 4893), where you can pick up ingredients to assemble your own Indian meal; the variety of fresh fruit and veg displayed outside is staggering. On the Broadway, family-run **Dokal & Sons** (Nos.133-135, UB1 1LW, 8574 1647) and **Sira Cash & Carry** (No.128, 8574 2280) stock rice, bread, pulses, canned food and imported vegetables like yellow baby aubergines and gigantic marrows.

Tooting, SW17

Tooting Broadway or Tooting Bec tube.

People from all over the Indian subcontinent – Pakistan, Sri Lanka and both north and south India – have made their home in Tooting, making it a great place to eat out or to buy groceries. Try **Deepak** (953-959 Garratt Lane, SW17 0LW, 8767 7819), a good generalist, or **Shiv Darshan** (169 Upper Tooting Road, SW17 7TJ, 8682 5173) and **Pooja** (168 Upper Tooting Road, SW17 7EN, 8682 5148) for Indian sweets. **Nature Fresh** (126-128 Upper Tooting Road, SW17 7EN, 8682 4988) and **Daily Fresh Foods** (152 Upper Tooting Road, SW17 7ER, 8767 7856) stock Asian fruit and veg.

Italian

I Camisa & Son

61 Old Compton Street, W1D 6HS (7437 7610). Leicester Square or Piccadilly Circus tube. **Open** 8.30am-6pm Mon-Sat. **Credit** MC, V.

A great place to pick up fresh pumpkin and sage ravioli, this homely, rustic deli is crammed with an exquisite selection of fresh and dried pastas and olive oils. There's also cured meat, cheese, wild mushrooms, polenta, wine, bread and antipasti.

Carluccio's

28A Neal Street, WC2H 9QT (7240 1487/ www.carluccios.com). Covent Garden tube. **Open** 8am-8pm Mon-Fri; 10am-7pm Sat; noon-6pm Sun. **Credit** AmEx, MC, V.

Beautifully packaged regional Italian products are showcased at Antonio and Priscilla Carluccio's deli, which is located next to their restaurant. You'll find Sardinian olive oil, Calabrian capers, Puglian pasta, risotto rice from Veneto and Piedmont, and regional breads like taralli from Puglia and corn grissini. Pasta (such as truffle tagliolini), spreads and sauces (cuttlefish ink sauce, olive and almond crostini spread), biscuits (fresh amaretti, cantuccini), confectionery, preserved fish, jars of antipasti, herbs and spices, polenta, olive oils, balsamic vinegars, jams, coffees and wines are also sold. The pesto is justly popular, and the shop is famous for one of Carluccio's passions – wild mushrooms in season.
Mail order.
Branches: throughout the city.

Di Lieto Bakery & Delicatessen

175 South Lambeth Road, SW8 1XW (7735 1997). Stockwell tube. **Open** 10.30am-7pm Mon-Sat. **Credit** MC, V.

Regional breads are the big draw at this small shop, which also sells brioches, pastries, focaccia, pizza and tarts. Imported meats (mortadella, speck), cheeses, pastas and marinated vegetables (peppers, artichokes, mushrooms, aubergines, sunblush tomatoes) are also available.

The Grove Deli

6-8 Chepstow Road, W2 5BH (7229 5289). Notting Hill Gate, Queensway or Westbourne Park tube. **Open** 8am-7pm Mon-Sat; 10.30am-4.30pm Sun. **Credit** MC, V.

You'll get service with a smile at this neat little deli, which has a hefty cheese, olive and charcuterie counter on one side, and a café selling breakfasts and hot dishes on the other. A small selection of groceries includes olive oils, pastas, cakes and confectionery.

Lina Stores

18 Brewer Street, W1R 3FS (7437 6482). Piccadilly Circus tube. **Open** 9am-6.30pm Mon-Fri; 9am-5.30pm Sat. **Credit** AmEx, MC, V.

This old-fashioned, long-established deli is crammed with a wide range of pasta (stored in charming wooden crates), rice, polenta, dried mushrooms, beans and lentils, confectionery and preserves. There's also a counter stacked with antipasti, cured meat and fresh pasta. Staff are polite and helpful.

Luigi's Delicatessen

349 Fulham Road, SW10 9TW (7352 7739). Fulham Broadway or South Kensington tube/bus 14. **Open** 9am-9.30pm Mon-Fri; 9am-7pm Sat. **Credit** MC, V.

A large array of wines and spirits lines the shelves of this friendly, scarlet-hued deli, which is popular for its excellent selection of own-cooked dishes. These include salads, fresh pasta, stuffed risotto balls, lasagne, tarts and a tiramisu that's so popular it's sold in three sizes. There is a good variety of biscuits, olive oil, balsamic vinegar, sauces and meat, including the increasingly fashionable lardo di colonnata.

Montes

23 Canonbury Lane, N1 2AS (7354 4335). Highbury & Islington tube/rail. **Open** 10am-7pm Mon-Fri; 10am-6pm Sat; 10.30am-4pm Sun. **Credit** AmEx, MC, V.

Specialising in gourmet products from Italy, this small shop has a good selection of antipasti (grilled artichoke hearts, grilled aubergines, boscaiola olives, preserved garlic cloves), and cheeses from Britain, France and Italy, such as pecorino dolce. Carefully chosen cured meats, sausages and fish include cotto alla brace and finocchiona. You can also pick up home-cooked dishes, perhaps with a bottle of prosecco.

Olga Stores

30 Penton Street, N1 9PS (7837 5467). Angel tube. **Open** 9am-8pm Mon-Fri; 9am-7pm Sat; 10am-2pm Sun. **Credit** MC, V.

Among everyday items like pastas, sauces, olive oils and dressings, this compact but hugely popular neighbourhood deli manages a few surprises – such as bottarga (grey mullet roe) and a unique buffalo milk ice-cream. Somehow space is also found for cheeses, cured meats and traiteur dishes.

I Sapori di Stefano Cavallini

146 Northcote Road, SW11 6RD (7228 2017). Clapham Junction rail. **Open** 9.30am-7pm Mon-Fri; 9.30am-6.30pm Sat. **Credit** MC, V.

Michelin-starred Stefano Cavallini's venture is notable for amazing food cooked on the premises. The fresh pasta (mushroom, asparagus, butternut squash, spinach and ricotta, goat's cheese and mixed pepper ravioli, cuttlefish ink spaghetti) is particularly appealing. Groceries include oils, preserves and antipasti; chocolates are also on sale.

L Terroni & Sons

138-140 Clerkenwell Road, EC1R 5DL (7837 1712). Farringdon tube/rail. **Open** 9am-5.45pm Tue-Fri; 9am-3pm Sat; 9.30am-1.45pm Sun. **Credit** MC, V.

Since being sold to Foodhouse UK at the end of 2003, Terroni & Sons has been able to import an even wider selection of Italian goods – as well as opening a café next door. Charcuterie, cheese, fresh pasta and antipasti sit alongside olive oil, vinegar, pasta sauces, preserves and confectionery.

Japanese

Arigato Japanese Supermarket

48-50 Brewer Street, W1R 3HN (7287 1722). Piccadilly Circus tube. **Open** 10am-9pm Mon-Sat; 11am-8pm Sun. **Credit** MC, V.

This bright shop is neatly stacked with Japanese and Korean staples, such as rice, noodles, sauces, kimchis, miso pastes, Hello Kitty confectionery, drinks such as Blendy and Pulpy, and snacks like rice crackers and wasabi peas. There are chiller cabinets filled with baked wheat balls with octopus or fried fishcakes with green soybean. Sushi and bento boxes are also available, and prices are surprisingly low.
Mail order.

Japan Centre

212 Piccadilly, W1J 9HG (7255 8255/www.japan centre.com). Piccadilly Circus tube. **Open** 10am-7pm Mon-Fri; 10.30am-8pm Sat; 11am-7pm Sun. **Credit** MC, V.

The building houses a restaurant and a food shop that incorporates delicatessen Yoshino. The shop stocks hundreds of items imported from Japan, Korea and the US, among them seaweed, sauces, confectionery, snacks, tofu, edamame, koshihikari rice, fresh Japanese vegetables, organic meats, bento boxes (from the restaurant), freshly baked bread such as an-pan, and teas. The delicatessen sells wonderfully fresh sushi and sashimi, and organic sushi rice milled on-site. Recommended for hard-to-find Japanese items at reasonable prices.

Oriental City

399 Edgware Road, NW9 0JJ (8200 0009). Colindale tube. **Open** 10.30am-9pm Mon-Sat; 10am-8.30pm Sun. **No credit cards.**

Not so much a shopping centre as a great day out for lovers of oriental food, this large complex houses a delightful Japanese confectioner's, a popular Japanese bakery (prepare to queue for the toothsome sweet-savoury confections), a makeshift fruit shop selling prepared durian (a stinky Thai fruit that's considered a delicacy) in season, and a bustling Oriental Food Court that sells everything from okonami-yaki (savoury Japanese pancakes) to roti canai (Malaysian flatbreads with curry sauce). There's also a huge supermarket that sells mainly Japanese ingredients: fresh fruit and veg, instant noodles, saké, sauces, frozen foods and miso pastes are its strong points. A variety of oriental festivals are celebrated throughout the year.
Mail order.

Rice Wine Shop

82 Brewer Street, W1F 9UA (7439 3705/ www.ricewineshop.com). Piccadilly Circus tube. **Open** 10am-10pm Mon-Sat; noon-9pm Sun. **Credit** MC, V.

Bursting with Japanese imports like seaweed, noodles, rice, sauces, snacks and confectionery, this popular shop also sells a good range of vinegars (black vinegar, sushi vinegar) and a variety of saké for cooking and drinking. Service is helpful and knowledgeable, and prices are jaw-droppingly low.

Jewish

Brick Lane Beigel Bake

159 Brick Lane, E1 6SB (7729 0616). Liverpool Street tube/rail. **Open** 24hrs daily. **No credit cards.**

Situated somewhat surreally amid Bangladeshi curry houses and achingly hip bars, this perennial London institution needs no introduction. Prices are shockingly low, and its round-the-clock opening hours make it a popular pit stop for students, cab drivers, clubbers and celebs slumming it for the night. As well as every variety of bagel, the bakery also turns out breads and pastries, like poppy seed chollah and apple pie.

Golders Green Road, NW11

Golders Green tube.

Once home to the Orthodox Jewish community, Golders Green Road has latterly become a melting pot of Indian, Chinese and Eastern European communities. This change is reflected in the area's restaurants: many of them now offer kosher oriental and Mediterranean menus. However, numerous kosher food shops still thrive here. The friendly **Paradise Bakery** (No.109, NW11 1HR, 8201 9694), long-established **M&D Grodzinski** (No.223, NW11 9ES, 8458 3654), and legendary **Carmelli Bakery** (Nos.126-128, NW11 8HB, 8455 2074) are always fragrant with freshly baked biscuits, breads, richly layered cakes, savoury borekas and pizzas. Further along the road is **Kosher Kingdom** (7-9 Russell Parade, NW11 9NN, 8455 1429), a spacious supermarket that sells groceries, meat and fish, breads and pastries, fruit and vegetables, drinks, chocolates and confectionery. Continue walking, and across the road you will find a great range of frozen and chilled foods at the family-run **Kay's** (2 Princes Parade, NW11 9PS, 8458 3756). Chicken is the meat of choice for shoppers at the **Golders Green Kosher Delicatessen & Butcher** (132 Golders Green Road, NW11 8HB, 8381 4450, www.london kosherdeli.com), **Menachems** (15 Russell Parade, NW11 9NN, 8201 8629) and **H Gross & Son** (6 Russell Parade, NW11 9NN, 8455 6662). Note that the latter also sells a good selection of mince and kebabs.

Platters

10 Hallswelle Parade, Finchley Road, NW11 0DL (8455 7345). Golders Green tube then 82, 102, 260 bus. **Open** 8.30am-4.30pm Mon-Fri; 8.30am-4pm Sat; 8.30am-2pm Sun. **Credit** AmEx, MC, V.

This small deli isn't flash, but it does have understated cool: organic spelt flour bagels are sold ('to cater for all these young people on faddy diets', we were told), alongside a great selection of pickles and cold meats that would make a perfect New York-style picnic. Tempting own-cooked dishes, sandwiches, cheeses and grocery items like Israeli couscous are also available.
For branch see index.

Korean

Centre Point Food Store

20-21 St Giles High Street, WC2H 8LN (7836 9860). Tottenham Court Road tube. **Open** 10am-10.30pm Mon-Sat; noon-10pm Sun. **Credit** (over £5) MC, V.

Besides the basics for every Korean meal, such as sushi rice, nori paper, naengmyon (Korean buckwheat noodles) or fresh kimchee (spicy pickled cabbage), this little store also has bucket-loads of cute cookie, cracker and candy packages. To complete the culinary excursion into the world of Korean cuisine there are little gas stoves, Asian crockery and saké glasses on offer.

Latin American

La Bodeguita

Unit 256, Upper Level, Elephant & Castle Shopping Centre, SE1 6TE (7708 5826). Elephant & Castle tube/rail. **Open** 8am-8pm Mon-Sat. **Credit** MC, V.

Who would have thought that the eyesore that is Elephant & Castle shopping centre would house a charming little Colombian food shop? But London is full of such surprises. Here you'll find masa harina flour, a range of Mexican chillies, spices, cakes and drinking chocolate. Tortillas, cheese breads, chilli rellenos and other hot snacks are available to take away.

Middle Eastern

Al Mustapha

132-136 Edgware Road, W2 2HR (7706 7790). Marble Arch tube. **Open** noon-10pm daily. **Credit** AmEx, MC, V.

Excellent halva, baklava, dried fruit and nuts – sold both loose and packaged – are a highlight here. Alongside colourful rugs and sheesha pipes, grains, spices, dips, breads, and a small selection of fresh fruit and veg are sold. There's also a halal meat counter.

Archie Food Store

14 Moscow Road, W2 4BT (7229 2275). Bayswater or Queensway tube. **Open** 8am-7.30pm daily. **No credit cards.**

Fresh green almonds, bunches of baby radishes, plump marrows and verdant fronds of fresh dill are some of the delights you'll find at this Middle Eastern grocery. Also available are cheeses, pickles, breads, confectionery, olives, and dried fruit and nuts.

Green Valley

36-37 Upper Berkeley Street, W1H 5QF (7402 7385). Marble Arch tube. **Open** 8am-midnight daily. **Credit** MC, V.

The splendid array of pastries in the window is a compelling lure to passers-by, but there's far more to be found inside this spacious Lebanese supermarket in Mayfair. Stock is extensive, ranging from store-cupboard staples, fresh fruit and veg to Middle Eastern traiteur dishes and a delectable assortment of nuts. There is a bakery, a halal meat section and an ice-cream counter.

Maroush Deli

45-47 Edgware Road, W2 2HZ (7723 3666). Marble Arch tube. **Open** 8am-midnight daily. **Credit** AmEx, DC, MC, V.

Part of the popular Lebanese restaurant mini-chain, this spacious shop houses Lebanese groceries on two floors. On the ground level you'll find superlative halal meat and fish (some of the best in London), ready-cooked hot dishes to take away, and fresh fruit and veg. The basement is packed with pickles, rice, drinks, pulses and spices, plus there's a deli counter that offers wonderful cheeses and dips.

Naama

384 Uxbridge Road, W12 7LL (8740 0004). Shepherd's Bush tube. **Open** 9am-9pm daily. **Credit** MC, V.

This good-looking Lebanese deli does a brisk trade in flatbread sandwiches at the front, including delicious lamb shawarma. There's a counter that sells halal meat, and a small but carefully chosen selection of groceries includes grains, pulses, packet mixes, preserves, pickles and dairy products. This is the sort of place where thought has gone into choosing the product range; perhaps it's lost in the cacophony of food shops in Uxbridge Road, but in a quieter location it would stand out.

Nut Case

352 Uxbridge Road, W12 7LL (8743 0336). Shepherd's Bush tube then 207 bus. **Open** 10am-9pm Mon-Sat; 10am-5pm Sun. **No credit cards.**

A wonderful variety of plain and flavoured cashews, hazelnuts, pine nuts, almonds and pistachios makes this the best place to buy nuts in west London. Sunflower seeds, melon seeds, dried figs, dried mulberries and dates are also sold. Good news for diabetics and those on diets: this lovely shop stocks boxes of sugar-free sweets, pastries and confectionery.

Reza Pâtisserie

345 Kensington High Street, W8 6NW (7603 0924). High Street Kensington tube. **Open** 9am-10pm daily. **Credit** MC, V.

We can't understand why this aromatic shop isn't better known: the quality and variety of freshly made Iranian sweets, pastries and confectionery is astonishing. Flours, doughs and filo pastry sheets are pummelled into a variety of shapes, dipped in flower waters and honeys, flavoured with saffron, fresh fruit and nuts, and topped with edible gold and silver leaf. The result resembles a cross between Indian and Mediterranean flavours. There's also a small selection of groceries, fresh fruit and veg.

Riteway Supermarket

57 Edgware Road, W2 2HZ (7402 5491). Edgware Road tube. **Open** 24hrs daily. **Credit** MC, V.

If you get late-night munchies for fresh labneh and pickles, or perhaps some baklava, head

Home delivery

The boom in online shopping means that the weekly trudge down the aisles is no longer a necessity. Supermarkets offering online shopping include **Sainsbury's To You** (0845 301 2020, www.sainsburystoyou.com; free delivery on orders over £70 delivered Tue-Thur, otherwise £5), **Tesco** (0845 722 553, www.tesco.com; £3.99 delivery Tue, Wed; £4.99 Mon, Thur; £5.99 Fri-Sun) and, by far the best in terms of customer service and quality, **Waitrose** (www.ocado.com; free delivery over £75, otherwise £5 charge). For organic box schemes and gastronomic treats delivered to your door, try the outfits below.

Abel & Cole
8-15 MGI Estate, Milkwood Road, SE24 0JF (7737 3648/www.abel-cole.co.uk). **Phone enquiries** 9am-7pm Mon-Thur; 9am-6pm Fri. **Credit** MC, V.
From succulent lamb and rosemary sausages to biodynamic pasta and Ecover cleaning products, this environmentally conscious and ethically minded enterprise delivers Soil Association-certified organic fruit and vegetables, meat, fish and dairy goods right to your door.

Food Ferry Co
Units B24-27, New Covent Garden Market, 9 Elms Lane, SW8 5HH (7498 0827/www.foodferry.com). **Phone enquiries** 8am-6pm Mon-Fri. **Credit** AmEx, MC, V.

This long-established, award-winning outfit delivers an impressive range of foodstuffs. Having merged recently with Swaddles Organic Farms, it now deals in a full range of organic produce, including ready meals and wines, as well as bakery-fresh breads, larder essentials and luxurious hampers.

Forman & Field
30A Marshgate Lane, E15 2NH (8221 3939/www.formanandfield.com). **Phone enquiries** 9am-5pm Mon-Fri. **Credit** MC, V.
Britain's oldest salmon smokers (celebrating their centenary in 2005), Forman & Field supplies to top hotels and restaurants around the world, including the Savoy Grill and Nobu. The company also offers a variety of upmarket foodstuffs, from traditional condiments and preserves to rare-breed sausages, game and suckling pigs. Unfortunately, as its factory site has been chosen as the location of the Olympic Stadium, its future is now under threat.

Fresh Food Co
The Orchard, 50 Wormholt Road, W12 0LS (8749 8778/www.freshfood.co.uk). **Phone enquiries** 24hrs daily. **Credit** AmEx, MC, V.
This company lays claim to being Britain's first online organic food retailer, supplying fresh produce direct to customers' doors since 1989. Boxes, delivered weekly or fortnightly, contain fruit, veg and herbs; you can also order meat, farmed or wild fish, plus wine and beer – all of it organic.

straight to this long-established store: it's open 24 hours a day every day and stocks every type of Middle Eastern staple you can imagine. Large loaves of pide bread, pastries and confectionery like sesame halva, fresh and cured halal meats, condiments, rice, olives, and fruit and veg are all present and correct.

Shazia Food Hall
124 Edgware Road, W2 2DZ (7723 4511). Marble Arch tube. **Open** 8am-midnight daily. **No credit cards.**
Fresh halal meat and Lebanese breads and pastries baked on site are the attraction at this well-stocked store, which also offers all the usual Middle Eastern staples, like chickpeas, bulgur wheat, sticky preserves and spreads, large jars of tahini, and bags of nuts.

Super Bahar
349A Kensington High Street, W8 6NW (7603 5083). High Street Kensington tube. **Open** 9am-9pm daily. **Credit** AmEx, MC, V.
Iranian caviar, top-notch nuts and spices, super-sweet confectionery and stacks of prepared, ready-to-eat fresh fruits are the greatest hits at this Iranian shop. Service is helpful and easy-going.

Suroor Market
101-113 Robin Hood Way, Kingston Vale, SW15 3QE (8974 6088). Kingston rail then 85, K3 bus. **Open** 8.30am-9pm daily. **Credit** MC, V.
Large, bustling but friendly (despite language difficulties) this family-run Iraqi store is worth a visit even though it's off the beaten track and hard to get to. It stocks excellent regional specialities that are hard to find in other Middle Eastern shops.

There's a huge variety of prepared meats (great for barbecues), flavoured breads, frozen meals, and unusual herbs and spices. Particularly notable is the vast selection of flower waters – traditionally used in sweets and pastries, they wouldn't look out of place in a cocktail cabinet.

Moroccan

L'Etoile
79 Golborne Road, W10 5NL (8960 9769). Ladbroke Grove or Westbourne Park tube. **Open** 8am-6pm Mon-Sat. **No credit cards.**
Round off your Moroccan meal with a tempting array of fragrant French-influenced pastries from this lovely Moroccan pâtisserie. Cakes, tarts, breads, croissants, confectionery and desserts – fashioned from fresh fruit, nuts, flower waters and sweet spices – are seductive.
For branch see index.

Mahatae
48 Blackstock Road, N4 2DW (7704 6122). Finsbury Park tube/rail. **Open** 9am-11pm daily. **No credit cards.**
Although now under new ownership, this Moroccan shop hasn't changed its stock. You can still buy halal meat and chicken, plus groceries like preserved lemons, olives, couscous and spices. Service is helpful, but somewhat hampered by language barriers.

Le Maroc
94 Golborne Road, W10 5PS (8968 9783). Ladbroke Grove or Westbourne Park tube. **Open** 9am-7pm Mon-Sat. **No credit cards.**

This vibrant shop has a halal butcher who offers prepared meat, kibbeh and merguez sausages. Beans, lentils, cracked wheat, coffee, tea, preserves and pickled fruit are also available.

Ryad Halal Way Butchers & Deli
248 Wandsworth Road, SW8 2JS (7738 8811). Vauxhall tube/rail. **Open** 9am-8pm Mon-Sat; 9am-7pm Sun. **Credit** MC, V.
There's a wonderful selection of halal meat, chicken and sausages here, as well as harissa pastes, various combinations of zataar spice mix, pickles, olives and traditional aged butter.

Polish

Parade Delicatessen
8 Central Buildings, The Broadway, W5 2NT (8567 9066). Ealing Broadway tube/rail. **Open** 10.15am-7pm Mon-Fri; 9.15am-5pm Sat. **Credit** MC, V.
A well-stocked deli counter displays cured meats, sausages and pierogi dumplings, and the shelves are laden with Polish staples such as grains, jams, pickles and chleb breads.

Polish Delicatessen
362 Uxbridge Road, W12 7LL (8932 4487). Shepherd's Bush tube. **Open** 8am-10pm Mon-Sat; 9am-8pm Sun. **No credit cards.**
This tiny shop is packed (there's barely room to move) with lots of instant packet meals at almost throwaway prices: no wonder it's popular with students. A variety of dense rye breads, soft drinks, meats and confectionery are also sold.

Prima Delicatessen
192 North End Road, W14 9MX (7385 2070). West Kensington tube. **Open** 9.30am-7pm Mon-Fri; 9.30am-6pm Sat. **No credit cards.**
This delightful little shop has a wide selection of rye breads, preserves, spices, herbs and grains. The deli counter, crammed with cured meats and flavoured sausages, and the excellent range of pickles (fresh and in jars) are noteworthy.

Portuguese

Ferreira Delicatessen
40 Delancey Street, NW1 7RY (7485 2351). Camden Town tube. **Open** 8am-9pm Mon-Sat; 8am-8pm Sun. **Credit** MC, V.
There's a good selection of cakes, breads and pastries (including custardy pasteis de nata) supplied by Portuguese bakers at this small deli. Staples from Portugal, Spain and Brazil include cheeses, sausages and olives.

Funchal Bakery
141 Stockwell Road, SW9 9TB (7733 3134). Stockwell tube/Brixton tube/rail. **Open** 7am-7pm daily. **No credit cards.**
There's a café for eating in at this friendly Portuguese grocery shop, which also sells soups, rolls, pastries, drinks and ready-prepared meals.

Lisboa
54 Golborne Road, W10 5NR (8969 1052). Ladbroke Grove tube. **Open** 9.30am-7.30pm Mon-Sat; 10am-1pm Sun. **Credit** MC, V.
Owned by Mr and Mrs Gomes (also owners of the pâtisserie opposite) and run by their children, this friendly shop is notable for its meat counter, which houses an enormous range of Portuguese sausages and cured meats, plus a few cheeses. Freshly baked bread is another plus. The interior is charmingly old-fashioned, and the two Lisboa outlets provide a focal point for the local Portuguese community.
For branches (Lisboa Delicatessen; Lisboa Patisserie) see index.

Madeira Pâtisserie
46A-C Albert Embankment, SE1 7TL (7820 1117). Vauxhall tube/rail. **Open** 7am-7pm daily. **Credit** MC, V.
Madeira supplies Portuguese baked goods to many of London's cafés, and the shop on its premises doesn't disappoint. There's a tempting selection of

rich tarts, pastries and cakes, perfumed with vanilla and filled with custard, fresh fruit and almonds.
For branches (Café Bar Madeira; Madeira Café; Pico Bar) see index.

Plender Street, NW1
Mornington Crescent tube.
It would be easy to walk past this tiny, unassuming street off Camden High Street: other than a small market that looks slightly out of place, there doesn't appear to be anything remarkable about it. In recent years, though, a veritable Little Lisbon has sprung up here, with a carefully selected range of Portuguese groceries offered at **Villa Franca** (No.7, NW1 0JT, 7380 0602) – a deli and café that sells good coffee and meaty sandwiches. Although less striking than the Golborne Road original, the branch of **Lisboa Delicatessen** (No.4, NW1 0JT, 7387 1782) is a good place for cakes and breads.

Sintra Delicatessen & Tapas
146A & 148 Stockwell Road, SW9 9TQ (7733 9402). Stockwell tube. **Open** 8.30am-8pm daily. **No credit cards.**
Located next to its popular café, this tiny deli is overflowing with confectionery, cakes, breads, rice, oils, condiments and jars of lupine beans. There's a small counter that offers fresh fish and meat. It helps if you know what you're looking for as the staff don't speak English.

South African

St Marcus Fine Foods
1 Rockingham Close, SW15 5RW (8878 1898/ www.stmarcus.equology.com). Barnes rail/337 bus. **Open** 9am-6pm daily. **Credit** MC, V.
Ever tried monkey gland sauce? It's a spicy fruit sauce that goes well with cheese and coriander-flavoured boerewors. This leading supplier of South African food (to hotels, restaurants, pubs and delis) also sells an award-winning range of droewors, sosaties and biltong. Other products include spicy chakalaka sauce, youngberry jam, guava fruit rolls, spice rubs, cane spirit liqueurs, fruit ales, Rose Kola tonic drink and cooking equipment. Iconic items like Castle Lager and Ouma Muesli Rusk are also available.
Mail order.

Spanish

Brindisa
32 Exmouth Market, EC1R 4QE (7713 1666/ www.brindisa.com). Farringdon tube/rail. **Open** 10am-6pm Mon-Sat. **Credit** MC, V.
Owned by Monika Linton, this importer of top-quality Spanish foods enjoys a cult following among food lovers. Items are sourced from the best-known Spanish producers (including organic ones), and tastings are available. Charcuterie is a strong point – try cecina (cured beef), morcilla (black pudding), lomo (pork loin), Ibérico ham or a dozen varieties of chorizo. Fishy delights include boquerones (marinated fresh white anchovies), bacalao and the ever-popular Ortiz anchovies. Or there are cheeses, such as cabrales (made with a blend of cow's, goat's and sheep's milk), preserves (bitter-sweet green figs), confectionery (turrón, chocolate cigarillos), rice, beans, honey, nuts, herbs and spices, pickles, olives and dried vegetables. You can even buy paella pans and ham-carving sets. Brindisa also runs a stall at Borough Market and a new eaterie nearby, Tapas Brindisa.

P De La Fuente
288 Portobello Road, W10 5TE (8960 5687). Ladbroke Grove tube. **Open** 9am-6pm Mon-Sat. **Credit** MC, V.
Small, neat and well-stocked, this welcoming shop has a good selection of specialist honeys, cakes, confectionery, snacks, pulses, and canned vegetables. Cheeses, meats and preserved fish are also on sale.

R García & Sons
248-250 Portobello Road, W11 1LL (7221 6119). Ladbroke Grove tube. **Open** 9am-6.30pm Mon-Sat; 11am-7pm Sun. **Credit** AmEx, MC, V.
There's a good selection of Spanish bread at this lovely family-run shop, which also sells Spanish pasta, pickles, nuts, saffron, smoked pimentón and other groceries imported from Spain. The owners have recently opened a great tapas bar next door, Café Garcia.

Thai

Sri Thai
56 Shepherd's Bush Road, W6 7PH (7602 0621). Goldhawk Road tube. **Open** 9am-6.30pm Mon-Sat; 10am-5pm Sun. **No credit cards.**
This wonderful family-run shop sells most ingredients required for a Thai meal: seasonings, bottled sauces, canned and frozen meat and fish, and fresh herbs and spices. Rarely seen fruit and vegetables are delivered from Thailand once a week, and the small, daily changing selection of takeaway meals cooked by the owner's wife (such as barbecued pork or sticky rice with jackfruit) is delicious. Fresh, own-made curry pastes are also noteworthy.

Talad Thai
326 Upper Richmond Road, SW15 6TL (8789 8084). Putney rail. **Open** 9am-8pm daily. **Credit** (over £15) MC, V.
Owned by the restaurant of the same name next door, this bustling shop has staff that go out of their way to be helpful. Rice, chilli sauces and curry pastes are its greatest strengths – try Namjai, Sri Racha or Thai Boy products. Thai fruits like mangosteen and toddy palm seed (both fresh and canned) are also available. The Sunday cookery classes (check for timings and availability) are deservedly popular.

Tawana Oriental Supermarket
18-20 Chepstow Road, W2 5BD (7221 6316). Notting Hill Gate tube. **Open** 9.30am-8pm daily. **Credit** MC, V.
For more than two decades, Tawana Oriental Supermarket has been a temple for those after Thai food. Its freezers offer great bulk buys in squid, shrimps, prawns and scallops, alongside bags of purple yam, jute leaves and grated coconut, but you'll also find food from across South-east Asia – frozen dim sum, for example, and wun tun wrappers. Ready-made meals include pad Thai and green and red curries.

Turkish

Green Lanes, N4, N8
Manor House or Turnpike Lane tube.
Best known for pastries, breads and seasonal fruits, vegetables, herbs and fresh nuts of stunning quality, Green Lanes is a mecca for lovers of Turkish and Middle Eastern food. For Syrian confectionery and pastries, aromatic **Nasrullah Pâtisserie** (No.483, N4 1AJ, 8342 9794) is a delight, with helpful staff on hand to help you choose. Turkish staples like pickles, beans, lentils, yoghurt and olives can be found at **Turkish Food Market** (Nos.385-387, N4 1EU, 8340 4547), and halal meat and chicken is sold at **Salah Eddine** (51 Grand Parade, N4 1AG, 8800 4333). The enormous **Yasar Halim** (No.495, N4 1AL, 8340 8090) is packed with nuts, dried fruit, preserves, rice, halal meat, dips, cheese and fresh, own-baked bread, pastries and biscuits.

Turkish Food Centre
89 Ridley Road, E8 2NH (7254 6754). Dalston Kingsland rail/30, 56, 236 bus. **Open** 8am-10pm Mon-Sat; 8.30am-9pm Sun. **Credit** MC, V.
Not only Turkish, but also a wide range of Mediterranean groceries from Greece, Cyprus, Spain and Italy is sold at this busy store. Figs, pomegranates, melons, courgettes, aubergines, coriander and dill are some of the fresh fruit, vegetables and herbs delivered from Turkey and Greece weekly. The on-site bakery turns out beautiful breads and pastries. Staff are jovial bunch, even when busy.
Branches: throughout the city.

Vietnamese

Mare Street, E8
Hackney Central rail.
Hackney has the largest Vietnamese community in London, and among the jewellery stores and beauty salons on Mare Street there are numerous small supermarkets, such as the **Huong-Nam Supermarket** (Nos.185-187, E8 3QE, 8985 8050). This place is especially good for finding a variety of condiments, such as fermented shrimp paste or hoi sin sauce. Rice cookers, crackers and cookies can be found in the nearby **Vietnam Supermarket** (No.193A, E8 3QE, 8525 1655), together with bánh (rice cakes) wrapped in banana leaves. **Lê-Mi** (No.257A, E8 3NS, 8533 1020) offers exotic goodies like succulent dragon fruit or whole durians. For the ultimate Vietnamese experience, the **London Star Night Supermarket & Video** (No.213, E8 3QE, 8985 2949) is the place to go. Not only does it stock fresh seafood, including juicy razor-shell

Verde & Co. See p239.

clams and tender cuttlefish, the shelves are also full of cooking utensils. They even provide miniature Buddhist altars and traditional incense sticks, paper money to burn during the Têt festivities and Vietnamese pop music.

Herbs & spices

The Spice Shop
1 Blenheim Crescent, W11 2EE (7221 4448/ www.thespiceshop.co.uk). Ladbroke Grove tube. **Open** 9.30am-6pm Mon-Sat; 11am-4pm Sun. **Credit** MC, V.
Domestic and professional cooks in the capital would be at a loss without this iconic shop. It is owned by Birgit Erath, who sources hundreds of spices and authentic spice mixes from her travels around the world. The tiny, intensely aromatic space is packed with fresh and dried herbs and spices (from anise myrtle to zedoary medieval ginger), a large variety of dried chillies, curry

blends, condiments, roots and barks, Japanese seasonings, flower waters and essential oils. *Mail order.*

Meat, fish & game

Butchers

A Dove & Son
71 Northcote Road, SW11 6PJ (7223 5191/www. doves.co.uk). Clapham Junction rail. **Open** 8am-4pm Mon; 8am-5.30pm Tue-Sat. **Credit** MC, V.
In business since 1889, Dove's sells prime Scottish beef, grass-fed English lamb, pedigree pork and own-made sausages. Free-range bronze turkeys are available at Christmas.

Allen & Co
117 Mount Street, W1K 3LA (7499 5831). Bond Street or Green Park tube. **Open** 4am-4pm Mon-Fri; 5am-noon Sat. **Credit** (over £20) MC, V.

With its beautifully tiled interior, this venerable Mayfair butcher's is a rare 19th-century survivor. Order a prime cut at restaurants such as Le Gavroche or the Wolseley, and chances are it came from this purveyor of top-class meat, notably beef and game when in season.

Frank Godfrey
7 Highbury Park, N5 1QJ (7226 2425). Highbury & Islington tube/rail. **Open** 8am-6pm Mon-Fri; 8am-5pm Sat. **Credit** MC, V.
This friendly, family-run butcher sells only the best free-range meat and poultry, some of which is organic. Orkney Island Gold beef and lamb are a particular speciality, plus award-winning own-made sausages and bronze turkeys at Christmas.

Ginger Pig
8-10 Moxon Street, W1U 4EW (7935 7788). Baker Street or Bond Street tube/Marylebone tube/rail. **Open** 8.30am-6.30pm Mon-Sat; 9am-3pm Sun. **Credit** MC, V.

A carnivore's paradise, Ginger Pig sells beef, pork and lamb from the owners' Yorkshire Moors farm, which boasts the largest breeding of rare-breed pigs in the country. There is also superb bacon, a range of over 25 bangers, plus pâtés, terrines and pies made on the premises. Ginger Pig also has a stall at Borough Market.

Kingsland, the Edwardian Butchers

140 Portobello Road, W11 2DZ (7727 6067). Notting Hill Gate tube. **Open** 7.30am-6pm Mon-Sat. **Credit** AmEx, MC, V.
Despite the name, this picturesque shop was established in 1848. It's known for its free-range and organic meats: beef is pure-bred Aberdeen Angus, while most of the pork, sausages and bacon come from Old Spot and Tamworth pigs. There's also a good range of deli-style cooked meats, black puddings and own-made pies.

Lidgate

110 Holland Park Avenue, W11 4UA (7727 8243). Holland Park tube. **Open** 7am-6pm Mon-Fri; 7am-5pm Sat. **Credit** MC, V.
For free-range and organic meat and poultry fit for a prince, head to this select butcher; its stock comes from farms including Highgrove Estate, and rare breeds are well represented. Customers flock here at Christmas for free-range bronze and black turkeys and geese, plus award-winning, own-made pies, oven-ready dishes and sausages.

Macken Bros

44 Turnham Green Terrace, W4 1QP (8994 2646). Turnham Green tube. **Open** 7am-6pm Mon-Fri; 7am-5.30pm Sat. **Credit** AmEx, MC, V.
This shop has a loyal local following for its prime Scottish beef, free-range pork, lamb and poultry. Free-range turkeys are available at Christmas, as well as geese and game in season.

M Moen & Sons

24 The Pavement, SW4 0JA (7622 1624/www. moen.co.uk). Clapham Common tube. **Open** 8am-6.30pm Mon-Fri; 8am-5pm Sat. **Credit** MC, V.
Only free-range and additive-free or organic meat is sold at this family butcher's, including prime Scottish beef, lamb and pork. Game, from snipe to wild venison, is available in season. Marinated meats (using own-made marinades) and sausages (more than 20 types) are also popular.

Randalls Butchers

113 Wandsworth Bridge Road, SW6 2TE (7736 3426). Fulham Broadway tube. **Open** 7am-5.30pm Mon-Fri; 7am-4pm Sat. **Credit** MC, V.
In addition to its top-class selection of free-range meat, poultry and rare-breed pork, ever-popular Randalls does a roaring trade in marinated meats such as spiced Moroccan lamb or lemon and coriander chicken kebabs.

Fishmongers

Decent displays of fresh fish can be found at many London food halls (*see p232*); there are also several outstanding stalls at **Borough Market** (*see p18*). The following shops are all reliable.

B&M Seafood *258 Kentish Town Road, NW5 2AA (7485 0346). Kentish Town tube/rail.* **Open** 7.30am-9.30pm Mon-Sat. **Credit** MC, V.
Chalmers & Gray *67 Notting Hill Gate, W11 3JS (7221 6177). Notting Hill Gate tube.* **Open** 8am-5pm Mon-Fri; 8am-4pm Sat. **Credit** MC, V.
Copes Seafood Company *700 Fulham Road, SW6 5SA (7371 7300). Parsons Green tube.* **Open** 10am-8pm Mon-Fri; 9am-6pm Sat. **Credit** AmEx, DC, MC, V.
Covent Garden Fishmongers *37 Turnham Green Terrace, W4 1RG (8995 9273). Turnham Green tube.* **Open** 8am-5pm Tue, Sat; 8am-5.30pm Wed-Fri. **Credit** MC, V.
France Fresh Fish *99 Stroud Green Road, N4 3PX (7263 9767). Finsbury Park tube/rail.* **Open** 9am-6.45pm Mon-Sat; 11am-5pm Sun. **No credit cards.**

Golborne Fisheries *75 Golborne Road, W10 5NP (8960 3100). Ladbroke Grove tube.* **Open** 8am-6pm Mon-Sat. **No credit cards.**
Sandy's *56 King Street, Twickenham, Middx TW1 3SH (8892 5788/www.sandysfish.net). Twickenham rail.* **Open** 8am-6pm Mon-Sat. **Credit** MC, V.
Steve Hatt *88-90 Essex Road, N1 8LU (7226 3963). Angel tube.* **Open** 7am-5pm Tue-Sat. **No credit cards.**
Walter Purkis & Sons *17 The Broadway, N8 8DU (8340 6281/www.purkis4fish.co.uk). Finsbury Park tube/rail then W7 bus.* **Open** 8am-5pm Tue-Sat. **Credit** AmEx, MC, V.

Sausages

See also p240 **German Wurst & Delicatessen**.

Simply Sausages

Harts Corner, 341 Central Markets, EC1A 9NB (7329 3227). Farringdon tube/rail. **Open** 8.30am-6pm Mon-Fri; 9am-2.30pm Sat. **Credit** MC, V.
The name says it all: here you'll find a peerless selection of bangers, from traditional Lincolnshire and Cumberland to more exotic combinations such as Thai chilli and lemongrass; duck, apricot and orange; or the fiery 'Lucifer'.

Alara Wholefoods

58-60 Marchmont Street, WC1N 1AB (7837 1172). Russell Square tube. **Open** 9am-6pm Mon-Wed, Fri; 9am-7pm Thur; 10am-6pm Sat. **Credit** MC, V.
Friendly, family-run and centrally located, Alara combines a shop and a café. The latter serves daily changing hot specials that range from lasagne to the ever-popular sweet curry; dishes can be taken away. Much of the stock, which runs to groceries, grains, pulses, cereals, fruit and vegetables, is organic. Prices are keen.

Bumblebee

30, 32 & 33 Brecknock Road, N7 0DD (7607 1936/www.bumblebee.co.uk). Kentish Town tube/rail/29 bus. **Open** 9am-6.30pm Mon-Wed, Fri, Sat; 9am-7.30pm Thur. **Credit** AmEx, MC, V.
The Bumblebee hive consists of three shops: two adjacent and one opposite. Between them, you'll find deli food (including freshly baked bread), grains, loose nuts and pulses, an impressive range of miso and dried seaweed, and fresh produce, including seasonal organic fruit and veg, eggs and an enticing cheese counter (the only stock that isn't vegetarian, though it is organic). The organic booze selection mainly covers wine, but also features saké, cider and champagne. The shop runs a delivery service throughout London.

Bushwacker Wholefoods

132 King Street, W6 0QU (8748 2061). Hammersmith tube. **Open** 9.30am-6pm Mon, Wed-Sat; 10am-6pm Tue. **Credit** MC, V.
Bushwacker makes a valiant effort to source organic, fair trade and sugar-free goods wherever possible; it's Soil Association-registered, GM-free and even bags its own goods on the premises, thereby creating employment opportunities and reducing waste. The shop itself has an old wooden counter by the door, packed with herbs and spices. Vitamins, supplements and homeopathic remedies are another focus, as well as macrobiotics. Fridges stock organic milk, non-dairy alternatives and vegetarian lunchtime treats.

Don't Panic Go Organic

49 Cavell Sttreet, E1 2BP (7780 9319). Whitechapel tube/Shadwell DLR. **Open** 9.30am-8.30pm Mon-Sat; 10am-6pm Sun. **Credit** MC, V.
Organic shops in the capital may be ten a penny now, but when a tiny corner shop decides it's more lucrative to go organic, you know the trend is unstoppable. Luthfurl Rahman has given his Whitechapel convenience store the once-over and now stocks organic fruit and veg alongside brands such as Go Organic, Suma Organic, Clipper Teas,

Duchy Original, Green & Black's and Ecover. Organic fruit and veg boxes cost £10.99, plus an extra £1 for delivery in the East End on Thursdays.

Fresh & Wild

210 Westbourne Grove, W11 2RH (7229 1063/ www.freshandwild.com). Notting Hill Gate tube. **Open** 8am-9pm Mon-Fri; 8am-8pm Sat; 10am-7pm Sun. **Credit** AmEx, MC, V.
The Fresh & Wild chain, already the biggest organic and natural foods retailer in Britain, joined forces with Whole Food Market, the biggest in the world, in January 2004. Prices may not be the cheapest, but the range is outstanding, with more than 5,000 different products covering organic fruit and veg, supplements, frozen and chilled food and pet care, plus a select library of books. The design cleverly combines an earthy wholefood shop ethic with a supermarket layout for easy navigation. This branch has a café.
For branches see index.

Here

Chelsea Farmers' Market, 125 Sydney Street, SW3 6NR (7351 4321). Sloane Square or South Kensington tube. **Open** 9.30am-8pm Mon-Sat; 10am-6.30pm Sun. **Credit** MC, V.
The concept of supermarket-style health food shops is no longer new, but Here was a pioneer – and it's still slick enough to match its location. Stock is 100% organic, comprising fruit, vegetables, meat and fish, as well as supplements and beauty products. Staff are helpful.

Oliver's Wholefoods Store

5 Station Approach, Kew, Surrey TW9 3QB (8948 3990). Kew Gardens tube/rail. **Open** 9am-7pm Mon-Sat; 10am-7pm Sun. **Credit** MC, V.
Oliver's is a lovely shop with a good local buzz. As well as a great range of groceries (organic poultry, sausages, tofu), there are regular deliveries from quality bakers (Cranks, Authentic Bakery, All Natural Bakery), plus Dr Hauschka products, including make-up. Treatment rooms next door (about to open as we went to press) offer clients a variety of therapies and organic beauty treatments; those looking to cheer themselves up in less healthy ways might be interested in the range of organic wine, beer, cider and spirits.

Planet Organic

42 Westbourne Grove, W2 5SH (7221 7171/ www.planetorganic.com). Bayswater tube. **Open** 9.30am-8.30pm Mon-Sat; noon-6pm Sun. **Credit** AmEx, MC, V.
Established nearly a decade ago, Planet Organic has three branches, all in London, all following the same approach. All produce is organic, and the popular lunchtime takeaway counters follow a simple idea: choose a size of container and staff will fill it up with wholesome tucker until they can barely fit the lid on. This branch has a meat counter and fishmonger, excellent fresh fruit and veg, and a bakery for croissants, pastries, cakes and speciality loaves. The health and beauty section is enhanced by a treatment room (book to see the nutritionist or the homeopath), and it carries a large range of products – Dr Hauschka and REN remain very popular.
For branches see index.

Total Organics

6 Moxon Street, W1U 4ER (7935 8626). Baker Street tube. **Open** 10am-5.30pm Mon, Fri; 10am-6.30pm Tue-Thur; 10am-5pm Sat; 10am-3pm Sun. **Credit** MC, V.
The popularity of their vegetarian stall in Borough Market led the owners – two cousins – to set up shop in the midst of Marylebone. Beans, grains, lentils, cereals, bread and condiments are all sold – along with lots of non-gluten and dairy-free items. Highlights include the Nomato range of tomato-free products (ketchup, baked beans), decently priced fresh fruit and veg, an olive oil refill service, and a juice bar that offers free bags of juice pulp to those who want to make their own compost. Freshly made salads and snacks are available to take away – try the delicious Spanish tortilla if it's on the menu.

FOOD & DRINK

Drink

The best and most interesting wines and spirits can be found at the following shops and wine merchants. Some deliver free within the capital. Some of those listed are wine brokers, able to source rare and fine wines (from châteaux and domaines in France and around the world). *En primeur* wine simply means 'newly produced' – buying before it's been aged is cheaper, but more risky.

Wines & spirits

Wine merchants

Balls Brothers
313 Cambridge Heath Road, E2 9LQ (7739 1642/www.ballsbrothers.co.uk). Bethnal Green tube. **Open** 9am-5.30pm Mon-Fri. **Credit** AmEx, DC, MC, V.
Away from the hubbub of its bars in the City and the West End, the Balls Brothers's cellars sit under railway arches in the East End, where there's enough cellaring space to allow for a fine selection of older Bordeaux and Burgundy, including the velvety, super-fine 1996 Château Haut-Bailly, Pessac-Léognan (£38.50). The extensive lists in classic areas at this quintessentially traditional wine merchant do, however, come at the expense of Spain and Italy, which are poorly represented. The New World needs work too, with only Grant Burge's range from Australia hitting the spot. If you want to try the wines, its bars across town hold occasional tastings, which anyone can attend for a small fee; consult the website for details.
Mail order.

Berry Bros & Rudd
3 St James's Street, SW1A 1EG (7396 9600/ www.bbr.com). Green Park tube. **Open** 10am-6pm Mon-Fri; 10am-4pm Sat. **Credit** AmEx, DC, MC, V.
More like the reception of a country house hotel than a shop, the large wood-panelled main room is gorgeously rickety – and faintly intimidating. Dodge into one of the three rooms showing part of the company's vast selection if you need to get away from the friendly, but slightly pompous staff. Traditional areas rule, with 2002 Premier Cru Chablis, made by Jean-Paul Droin, good value at £16.95, from the excellent Vaillons vineyard. There's a moderate amount of 2004 Bordeaux *en primeur*, plus decent cognac, Armagnac, Calvados and whisky. The fortified selection is one of the best in London, with good sherries, Port and Madeira, especially ten-year-old Sercial from Barbeito (£24.95), with its flavours of Moroccan spice and nuts. The website is an excellent resource.
Mail order.

Bordeaux Index
6th Floor, 159-173 St John Street, EC1V 4QJ (7253 2110/www.bordeauxindex.com). Farringdon tube/rail. **Open** by appointment only. **Credit** AmEx, MC, V.
As the name suggests, Bordeaux is the focus here – though, splitting hairs, it's actually a bit short of the right-bank icon wines Pétrus and Le Pin. The sort of person who buys from Bordeaux Direct wants other classic wines too, so there are vast amounts of Burgundy, including a huge range of Domaine de la Romanée-Conti's wines. Good bottles from the rest of the world include d'Arenburg's Dead Arm from Australia (£295 a case) and 1999 Taurasi Riserva Piano di Montevergine from the excellent Feudi San Gregorio in Italy (£295/case).

Corney & Barrow
194 Kensington Park Road, W11 2ES (7221 5122/www.corneyandbarrow.com). Ladbroke Grove tube. **Open** 10.30am-9pm Mon-Fri; 10.30am-8pm Sat. **Credit** AmEx, MC, V.
This small shop offers a selection of the overall Corney & Barrow range. Bordeaux is passed down piecemeal from the broking division, which explains the fantastic, if erratic, array of older vintages in the mid range, such as 1981 Château Montrose (£45.61). A separate catalogue is devoted to the Burgundy producer Oliver Leflaive – his 2000 Puligny-Montrachet Champ Grain (£14.80) is one of the better wines in a good-to-middling range. Gosset magnum is also good value at £77.07. This isn't bargain territory, but for sophisticated wines that will impress Corney & Barrow is recommended.
Mail order (7265 2400).

Fortnum & Mason
181 Piccadilly, W1A 1ER (7734 8040/ www.fortnumandmason.co.uk). Green Park or Piccadilly Circus tube. **Open** 10am-6.30pm Mon-Sat; noon-6pm Sun. **Credit** AmEx, MC, V.
Tucked in the back corner of the plushly carpeted department store, the wine department at Fortnum & Mason is tweaked to favour its American visitors, with a thorough selection of Domaine de la Romanée-Conti, a large choice of Havana cigars and an array of decent whiskies. There are some more interesting, and less obvious, purchases available too, such as Kevin Arnold's excellent 2002 Boekenhoutskloof cabernet sauvignon from South Africa (£24.50) and 2003 Grüner Veltliner Schutt Smaragd from Emmerich Knoll, in Austria (£21.50). It's good to see St Peter's Ale from Suffolk and ciders from Burrow Hill listed as well.

The Grape Shop
135 Northcote Road, SW11 6PX (7924 3638). Clapham Junction rail. **Open** 10.30am-9pm Mon-Sat; 11.30am-2pm Sun. **Credit** MC, V.
The Grape Shop looks more like an oversized garden shed than a shop, but owner David Potez has long been established on what is now a stretch full of off-licences. Some cracking Loire bottles include the Sancerre taste-alike Menetou-Salon, as well as the real thing from excellent producer Henri Bourgeois – his 2002 Le Bourgeoisie (£14.45) is a beauty. There are decent wines under a tenner, such as the Perrin brothers' (of Château de Beaucastel) 2001 Côtes du Rhône at £7.95, and some fine Australian choices, including the cult classic d'Arenburg Dead Arm, 2002 vintage (£22.50). New Zealand, Spain, Italy and Chile are a bit thinly covered.

Green & Blue
38 Lordship Lane, SE22 8HJ (8693 9250/ www.greenandbluewines.com). East Dulwich rail/ 40, 176, 185 bus. **Open** 11am-11pm Mon-Sat; noon-10.30pm Sun. **Credit** MC, V.
Run by former sommelier Kate Thal, this store boasts a compilation of the unusual and delicious. Even often-dull Muscadet is represented here by the fabulously concentrated Sur Lie, 2002 Semper Excelsior from Pierre Luneau (£12.30). Barrie Smith and Judi Cullam are renowned for their rieslings, made at the Frankland River estate; the 2004 Rocky Gully (£8.40) has gorgeous, exotic honeysuckle flavours. It's definitely worth putting some time aside to browse around this small, minimal store, with a few, well-selected wines laid out on simple metal racks. You can't miss the loud lime-green shopfront, and there's a lovely bar at the back.

Handford Wines
12 Portland Road, W11 4LE (7221 9614/ www.handford.net). Holland Park tube. **Open** 10am-8.30pm Mon-Sat. **Credit** AmEx, MC, V.

The highly personable James Handford has assembled a list of smaller growers in his tiny store, often shipping them direct rather than relying on intermediary importers. His best discoveries include the excellent premier cru champagne producer Brochet-Hervieux, which provides 500 cases a year for the shop. There are also some lovely Bordeaux blends from South Africa, including Sherwood Berriman's 2003 cabernet sauvignon and cabernet franc mix (£12.99).
Mail order.
For branch see index.

Harrods
87-135 Brompton Road, SW1X 7XL (7730 1234/ www.harrods.com). Knightsbridge tube. **Open** 10am-7pm Mon-Sat; noon-6pm Sun. **Credit** AmEx, DC, MC, V.
Beneath the rather tacky sweets and bakery sections, the wine area stands out with its comparatively subtle lighting and – as you might expect – an extensive range of expensive wines. Top names such as 2001 Zinfandel from Turley Cellars, Hayne Vineyard (£75) in the Napa Valley rub shoulders with good Chilean, Argentine and Portuguese selections. Italy and Spain are lightweight by comparison, but there are some excellent whiskies, such as the 40-year-old Bruichladdich at £1,100 and the much cheaper, but still excellent, Compass Box, Vatted Malt, Eleuthera at £37.50 for 70cl.
Mail order.

Haynes Hanson & Clark
25 Eccleston Street, SW1W 9NP (7259 0102/ www.hhandc.co.uk). Victoria tube/rail. **Open** 9am-7pm Mon-Fri. **Credit** AmEx, MC, V.
This small merchant, serving wealthy Pimlico locals, provides friendly service and a good range of Bordeaux *en primeur*. Anthony Barton's 2004 Langoa Barton, for example, is £198 a case. Red Burgundy stands out, with a few wines from the underrated Domaine Chandon de Briailles, producer of long-lived, rich, ripe wines such as 2001 Pernand-Vergelesses 1er Cru Ile de Vergelesses (£20.15). The store delivers cases of 12 free within London, and if you have a second home in the Cotswolds, you're in luck times two, as the main branch is in the idyllic Stow-on-the-Wold.

Jeroboams
6 Pont Street, SW1X 9EL (7235 1612/www.jero boams.co.uk). Knightsbridge or Sloane Square tube. **Open** 10am-8pm Mon-Fri; 10am-7pm Sat. **Credit** AmEx, MC, V.
Jeroboams has become a small chain in the past year, buying the La Reserve shops, which include Milroy's (*see p253*), plus Mr Christian's delis. There's a strong focus on France: Mark Reynier has left the Knightsbridge store, but he still works as a consultant to Jeroboams, maintaining the standard of Burgundy with good, if lesser-known, producers such as Didier Chevillon, at Domaine Dupont-Tisserandot. His 2001 Marsannay Rouge (£13), for example, is a good-value introduction to the region. Look out too for the wines of young, up-and-coming Burgundy producer David Duband.
Mail order.
For branches see index.

Lea & Sandeman
170 Fulham Road, SW10 9PR (7244 0522/ www.londonfinewine.co.uk). Gloucester Road tube. **Open** 10am-8pm Mon-Sat. **Credit** AmEx, MC, V.
Shop assistants in V-neck jumpers and check shirts are helpful and abreast of the medium-to-good range of wines here – a cut above the usual high-street offerings. The store is light and bright, but there's no escaping the fact that it's small. Gruaud Larose (£54.95), from 2000, is stacked in cases across the floor, which makes it hard to get to the decent selection of Burgundy – a shame when there are wines like Jean-Marc Boillot's 2000 Volnay (£21.50) to be had. Italy is well represented too; we particularly like the softly textured 2003 Pinot Grigio from Livio Felluga (£15.95).
Mail order.
For branches see index.

Majestic Wine Warehouses

63 Chalk Farm Road, NW1 8AN (7485 0478/ www.majestic.co.uk). Chalk Farm tube. **Open** 10am-8pm Mon-Fri; 9am-7pm Sat; 10am-5pm Sun. **Credit** AmEx, DC, MC, V.
The minimum sale at Majestic is 12 bottles, and the format is working well – it is one of the few wine merchants on the high street to be showing continually climbing sales. The draw is the decent range of wines – and the very decent prices. There are always deals, such as a recent one whereby if you buy two bottles of the fine 2004 sauvignon blanc Drylands from New Zealand as part of a mixed case, it becomes £7.99, rather than the standard price of £9.99. You can load up your cases of wine into the car in the garage-like forecourt, or have your wine delivered.
Mail order.
Branches: throughout the city.

Nicolas

157 Great Portland Street, W1W 6QR (7580 1622/www.nicolas-wines.com). Great Portland Street or Oxford Circus tube. **Open** 10am-7.30pm Mon-Fri; noon-7pm Sat. **Credit** AmEx, MC, V.
This French-owned store makes a pleasant change. With most high-street chains having gone New World-mad, the sight of shelf after shelf selling wine from France is unusual indeed. Avoid the average selections from classic regions and look to the excellent AC Beaujolais Saint Armour 2004 Domaine des Billards (£9.95) instead. Alternatively, René Muré's 2003 Pinot Noir from Alsace is worth trying for its fruit and refreshing acidity (£11.99), comparable to many a Burgundy at this price. Other pluses are the helpful French staff, and the clean, bright, well-laid out store.
Branches: throughout the city.

Oddbins

41A Farringdon Street, EC4 4AN (7236 7721). Farringdon tube/rail. **Open** 9am-7pm Mon-Fri; 10am-5pm Sat. **Credit** AmEx, MC, V.
Tucked underneath Holborn Viaduct, this branch (one of the first in the chain) is easily missed, but it's worth a peek inside. The takeover of the chain by French company Castel hasn't changed the outfit as much as star buyer Steve Daniel's departure in 2002. The fine wine room is not quite the delight it was, with a little too much 2003 Burgundy. Greece has become less represented over the past two years, and the choice of Italy and Spain, aside from Alejandro Fernandez's wines, also needs some attention. The obsession with winemakers such as Aussie producers d'Arenburg and South African Bruce Jack continues, but there is also a great array of 2004 New Zealand sauvignon blanc, including Villa Maria's Clifford Bay label (£12.09) and those from Hawksbridge (£9.99) and Grove Mill (£8.99).
Mail order (0800 783 2834).
Branches: throughout the city.

Philglas & Swiggot

21 Northcote Road, SW11 1NG (7924 4494/ www.philglas-swiggot.co.uk). Clapham Junction rail. **Open** 11am-7pm Mon-Sat; noon-5pm Sun. **Credit** AmEx, MC, V.
A branch in Marylebone has recently been added to those in Richmond and Battersea, but it hasn't diluted the quality of this outstanding chain, still the place to go for top New World wines. The line-up of Australian rieslings from cool-climate regions in Victoria is exemplary, including Grosset's 2004 Watervale from the Clare Valley (£14.99). There are some crackers from the other side of the country too, such as Cullen's rich Diane Madeline, a cabernet sauvignon/merlot blend from 2001/2 (£36.50). A good range from Italy includes the 2001 Solengo Tenuta di Argiano (£41.99). Wood floors, spare white walls and spotlights provide pleasant surroundings in which to survey some fantastic wines.
For branches see index.

Phillips Newman

28 Northcote Road, SW11 1NZ (7924 7374/ www.phillipsnewman.com). Clapham Junction rail. **Open** 11am-10pm daily. **Credit** AmEx, MC, V.

Part of the Unwins group, this more upmarket division of the chain has recently been given powers to buy wines separately, so expect some more interesting wines. However, instead of being divided by country, the store is split into areas, which have headings like Fruity, Mellow and Chunky, which only serves to ensure that labels like Australia's Rosemount (shiraz, cabernet sauvignon, merlot) and Wolf Blass (chardonnay) crop up repeatedly. The store does at least have the decent Penfolds 2001 Bin 28 Kalimna shiraz (£10.29) and Babich's cabernet sauvignon/merlot blend from the highly rated Gimblett Gravels area of Hawkes Bay.
For branch see index.

Roberson

348 Kensington High Street, W14 8NS (7371 2121/www.robersonwinemerchant.co.uk). Earl's Court or High Street Kensington tube. **Open** 10am-8pm Mon-Sat. **Credit** AmEx, MC, V.
Gaudi-esque twisted plaster walls and shiny metal form the bulk of this ambitious store. Cliff Roberson has built a stellar selection of top wines from Bordeaux, Burgundy, California and Australia, and staff leave you to wander among the enticing rows of great wines in peace. Some cracking examples, like Domaine Arnoux's 1994 Vosne-Romanée Le Suchots (£64) and 1999 Anselma Barolo (£31.95), sit alongside the excellent Alain Graillot's 2002 Crozes-Hermitage from the Rhône (£15.95) and 2003 Kumeu River chardonnay (£18.95). There's also an extra-special room, looking like something out of the London Dungeon, for yet more expensive wines. At Roberson a 2000 Chambolle-Musigny 1er Cru Les Sentiers from Domaine Arlaud – at £41.50 – counts as a bargain.

Uncorked

Exchange Arcade, Broadgate, EC2M 3WA (7638 5998/www.uncorked.co.uk). Liverpool Street tube/ rail. **Open** 10am-6.30pm Mon-Fri. **Credit** AmEx, MC, V.
A ready market of bankers and investors mops up the expensive, idiosyncratic selection of wines here. Bordeaux tends to be popular, as does California – Qupe's Bien Nacido has sold out (but there's a good range of its other wines). You can buy a copy of the seminal Italian wine guide *Gambero Rosso* to help pick through the extensive selection from Italy. The first vintage of La Corte's Il Re Salento Rosso (£23.95), from Puglia, is a cracker. Look out too for a selection of cognacs that doesn't rely on the overpriced, branded norm. Payrault's ten-year-old Petite Fine Champagne (£24.99) is excellent, despite its informal, scribbled label.
Mail order.

Vingt

20 Northcote Road, SW11 1NX (7924 6924/ www.vingt.co.uk). Clapham Junction rail. **Open** 10am-7pm Mon-Sat. **Credit** AmEx, MC, V.
Somehow there's room for a fifth wine merchant on this street serving what must be some very thirsty Battersea locals. There are some lovely examples from small to medium sized producers, such as 2003 La Segreta from the excellent Sicilian winery Planeta (£8.95), or Henri Bourgeois' sauvignon blanc planting in New Zealand, Clos Henri, 2003 (£15.50). Choice is limited, but it is confined to good wines, and prices are keen. The superlative Cirsion from Roda, in Rioja, at £80 is £20 cheaper than in Oddbins next door.
Mail order.

El Vino

47 Fleet Street, EC4Y IBJ (7353 6786/www.el vino.co.uk). Chancery Lane or Temple tube/ Blackfriars tube/rail. **Open** 8.30am-9pm Mon; 8.30am-10pm Tue-Fri. **Credit** AmEx, MC, V.
Timbered, dark and generally populated by solicitors in pin-stripe suits, this wine merchant, founded in 1879, offers reliable white Burgundy, such as Louis Latour's 2000 Corton-Charlemagne (£56.75) and a Mercurey Blanc from Faiveley, 2001 Clos Rochette (£12.75). Port from 2000, which won't be on the retail list for another ten years, is on sale in

bond (you only pay the VAT when these wines leave storage); a recent offer was the restrained and elegant Taylor's (£480/case of 12). You'll also find a great 2004 sauvignon blanc from Chilean Central Valley winemakers Viu Manent (£5.95) on the list – a delicious combination of savoury and fruit flavours.
Mail order.
For branches see index.

Waitrose

98-101 Marylebone High Street, W1U 4SD (7935 4787/www.waitrose.com). Bond Street tube. **Open** 8.30am-9pm Mon-Sat; 11am-5pm Sun. **Credit** AmEx, MC, V.
The Waitrose wine department far exceeds those of its supermarket competitors; all of its buyers have the top MW qualification. The selection wins hands down, specialising in less expensive wines from excellent winemakers. Try Aussie couple Cullen's Ellen Bussell cabernet sauvignon/merlot blend from Margaret River in the west of the country (£9.99), or Vincent Girardin's great 2002 Meursault Le Limozin (£19.99) from Burgundy. The South African brand Spice Route, set up by pioneer Eben Sadie, is represented by a lovely 2003 pinotage (£7.99). There's plenty of wine around the £5 mark, and ample organic choices too.
Branches: throughout the city.

Wapping Food

Wapping Hydraulic Power Station, Wapping Hall, E1W 3ST (7680 2080/www.thewappingproject. com). Wapping tube/Shadwell DLR. **Open** 10am-midnight Mon-Sat. **Credit** AmEx, MC, V
This cavernous restaurant has an unusual setting amid the old turbine hall of a former power station, with clunky equipment dotted around the tables and an art installation at the back. Now, as well as trying the array of interesting Australian wines with a meal – such as 2001 Plantagenet pinot noir (£16) and 2001 The Green Vineyards chardonnay from Yarra Valley, Victoria (£19) – you can order a case too. You will need to wait a week before picking it up.

Wimbledon Wine Cellar

1 Gladstone Road, SW19 1QU (8540 9979/ www.wimbledonwinecellar.com). Wimbledon tube/ rail. **Open** 10am-9pm Mon-Sat. **Credit** AmEx, MC, V.
With highly polished plate-glass bay windows and extensive displays of wine, such as Henri and Paul Jacquesson's 2003 Rully Blanc 1er Cru Gresigny (£175), the feel of this shop is serious, but not overly severe. It's packed with cases of aged Bordeaux and Burgundy jutting out into a couple of aisles and cult New World wines such as 2003 Ares from the Barossa (£68.99). We have come across the occasional unusual find, such as a red 2003 Sancerre from André Dezat (£11.99), or a gem-like Hermann Dönnhoff's 2003 Oberhäuser Brücke riesling Eiswein from the Nahe (£99.99).
Mail order.
For branch see index.

Wine Of Course

216 Archway Road, N6 5AX (8347 9006/ www.easywine.co.uk). Archway tube. **Open** 10am-9pm Mon-Sat; noon-9pm Sun. **Credit** AmEx, MC, V.
This super selection of the world's wines largely avoids Bordeaux and Burgundy, but has a good spread from Australia, Italy, Spain, Germany and New Zealand. Alvaro Espinoza's 2003 Novas Syrah/Mourvèdre (£8.75) represents outstanding value from Chile; the Leitz riesling Rüdesheimer Berg Schlossberg Spätlese 2003 (£17.99) is one of Germany's best at this price.

The Winery

4 Clifton Road, W9 1SS (7286 6475/ www.thewineryuk.com). Warwick Avenue tube. **Open** 11am-9.30pm Mon-Sat; noon-8pm Sun. **Credit** MC, V.
Back in the 1980s, owner David Motion used to manage rock bands (such as Orange Juice), but he now seeks out equally obscure finds from the world's vineyards, sourcing them direct. Excellent Burgundy like 1er Cru Puligny-Montrachet 'Les

Folatières' arrives thanks to longstanding relations with French winemaker Paul Pernot. There's also a fabulous German section, including Andreas Barth's great, virtually chemical-free wines such as 2003 Gäns Spätlese Riesling Trocken (£15.99). A pharmacy in Victorian times, this shop has a gorgeous interior of winding vines and wooden shelves that reach to the ceiling. A Winery outpost has opened in Liberty (see p13).
Mail order.
For branch see index.

Mail order & internet

Many of the places listed above also sell wine by mail order or via their website. The following online merchants tend to sell by the case only (12 bottles), but as they also act as importers to the world's wineries, you'll find some pretty exciting and rare bottles.

Adnams
Adnams Brewery, East Green, Southwold, Suffolk IP18 6JW (01502 727 200/www.adnams.co.uk). **Phone enquiries** 9am-8pm Mon-Fri; 9am-5pm Sat. **Credit** MC, V.
This excellent regional merchant began as a brewery in the 14th century, hence its Adnams ale. It delivers wines anywhere in the UK, whether it's 2003 *en primeur* Port (Dow and Quinto do Noval are good buys, £175 and £190/six-bottle case), the super 2001 chardonnay from Viña Leyda in Chile (£10.83) or 2002 Sur from Bodegas Inurrieta, Navarra, Spain (£5.99). There's also plenty of good southern Burgundy – 'away from the region of *premier cru* egos', as senior buyer Alastair Marshall puts it.

The Australian Wine Club
PO Box 4669, Henley, Oxon, RG9 5XQ (0800 856 2004/www.australianwine.co.uk). **Phone enquiries** 8am-11pm Mon-Fri; 8am-10pm Sat, Sun. **Credit** AmEx, DC, MC, V.

As you'd expect, there is plenty from Australia on show here, demonstrating that the country offers so much more than just Wolf Blass Yellow Label. Try the classic Barossa shiraz, Grant Burge 2002 (£7.50) or The Fergus, a lovely drop from the renowned Tim Adams, using mostly the grenache varietal (£9.99). Knappstein's 2004 riesling vintage wasn't a patch on its previous ones, but they've some cases left of the lovely 1999 (£7.75). Most wines are discounted, and if an order is over £500 there's an additional 5% off.

Bibendum Fine Wine
113 Regent's Park Road, NW1 8UR (7449 4120/ www.bibendum-wine.co.uk). **Phone enquiries** 8am-6pm Mon-Fri. **Credit** MC, V.
Not to be confused with the restaurant of the same name, this Primrose Hill wine merchant's is rather stuffy but has some decent wines. Dodge the supermarket brand Argento, which clogs up the Argentina section, for 2002 Catena Alta Malbec

Corney & Barrow. See p247.

FOOD & DRINK

(£20.71). There's also plenty from Bordeaux, Burgundy, Australia and California. There is a one-case minimum purchase here.

Domaine Direct
6-9 Cynthia Street, N1 9JF (7837 1142/ www.domainedirect.co.uk). **Phone enquiries** 8.30am-6pm Mon-Fri. **Credit** MC, V.
An outstanding selection of wines from Burgundy, as well as a few good buys from the New World, is up for grabs on a well-laid-out website. Jean-Marc Boillot's 1999 1er Cru Montrevenots, Beaune stands out as good value at £19.98 – Boillot is a fine winemaker, and it's a vintage that he made work well. The 2001 Art Series chardonnay from Leeuwin Estate, Margaret River, is another cracking wine, extremely refined and with a finish that lasts (£32.31).

Farr Vintners
220 Queenstown Road, SW8 4LT (7821 2000/ www.farr-vintners.com). **Phone enquiries** 9am-6pm Mon-Fri. **No credit cards.**
These highly renowned Bordeaux specialists also have some fine producers listed from Burgundy and the Rhône and a few more around the globe. There's still plenty of 2000 claret, including the sublime Ausone (£375), which Alain Vauthier has taken to a new, inspired level. At £395 for a case, Beauséjour-Duffau offers superb value – it's a complex and powerful wine, and 2000 is the best for this estate since 1990. Delivery costs £14 in London for fewer than 14 cases, and £25 in the rest of the UK for 14 cases under a value of £1,000. There's a minimum spend of £500.

Fine & Rare Wines
Pall Mall Deposit, 124-128 Barlby Road, W10 6BL (8960 1995/www.frw.co.uk). **Phone enquiries** 9am-6pm Mon-Fri. **Credit** AmEx, MC, V.
If you're looking for a particular wine from a particular year (a 1955 Armagnac for £99, for example), F&RW can source an excellent selection of top names, especially those from Bordeaux and in particular a vast array of the moderately rated 2004 vintage, *en primeur*. There are vintages dating back to 1784 (Lafite Rothschild, £54,105). In a similarly speculative vein, a case of 1990 Pétrus is £14,000 and will only increase in value. But for drinking rather than investment, the 1964 Latour is a good buy (£243, or £88 with a slightly tatty label). It was a strange vintage, poor in Médoc but with Latour producing delicious results.

Goedhuis & Co
6 Rudolf Place, SW8 1RP (7793 7900/www.goed huis.com). **Phone enquiries** 9am-5.30pm Mon-Fri. **Credit** AmEx, MC, V.
These traditional merchants specialise in Bordeaux, Burgundy and the Rhône. They don't have the range of Farr or Fine & Rare, but do list some interesting wines, such as the products of Christian Serafin's winery. There's a good introduction to his style with the 2002 Bourgogne (£119/case of 12). Pierre Gaillard, in the Rhône, makes wine of mixed quality, but his 2003 Condrieu is excellent (£240/case of 12). Those on tighter budgets will usually find some options at around £5 per bottle. The website is attractive and easy to use.

Howard Ripley
25 Dingwall Road, SW18 3AZ (8877 3065/ www.howardripley.com). **Phone enquiries** 9am-8pm daily. **Credit** MC, V.
Specialists in two areas that provide such challenging conditions for growers, Burgundy (from around £7.75) and Germany (from £7), Ripley has the largest selections in the UK of both. The lists are laid out superbly, and there are some outstanding wines. Sylvain Pitiot's 1998 Clos du Tart is superbly nuanced and delicate (£66); the vast improvements in the Paul Pernot estate are clear with the 2001 Puligny-Montrachet (£20.25), which has great mineral character and length.

John Armit Wines
5 Royalty Studios, 105 Lancaster Road, W11 1QF (7908 0600/www.armit.co.uk). **Phone enquiries** 8.45am-5.15pm Mon-Fri. **Credit** MC, V.

Former restaurateur Armit aimed to create an unstuffy wine merchant's. It's so down to earth that, as the website is arranged according to producer, you'll have to read about winemakers' dogs, cats and personal habits before getting to how much each wine costs. From top Côtes du Nuit producer Robert Groffier, 2003 Gevrey-Chambertin (£260/case of 12) is worth buying *en primeur*. Six bottles of Tuscan wine Tenuta dell'Ornellaia are well priced at £313.

Justerini & Brooks
61 St James's Street, SW1A 1LZ (7493 8721/ www.justerinis.com). **Phone enquiries** 9am-5.30pm Mon-Fri. **Credit** AmEx, MC, V.
The focus of this highly traditional wine merchant is mostly on mail order, as the retail outlet is more of an office, restricted to by-the-case sales. There's plenty of Bordeaux *en primeur* for 2004, and a 2003 Port offer, but beware the extensive vintage reports, which can be overly positive in an attempt to sell you the wine. Tasting notes – a 'summer fruit core encircled by bracingly fresh acids' – are also a bit ripe, but the website is easy to use. Great wines include those of the outstanding, maverick Loire producer Didier Dagueneau, who makes the fantastic 2003 Silex, Pouilly-Fumé (£456.46/case of 12). There are also everyday wines at around £5.

Laithwaites
New Aquitaine House, Exeter Way, Theale, Reading, Berks RG7 4PL (0870 444 8383/ www.laithwaites.co.uk). **Phone enquiries** 8am-11pm Mon-Fri; 8am-9pm Sat, Sun. **Credit** AmEx, DC, MC, V.
The emphasis at this large mail-order merchant's is more on bargains and less on fine wine than its rivals. There are significant amounts from Bordeaux and Burgundy, but also plenty from Vin de Pays regions in the rest of France, as well as much from Australia and, unusually among UK wine merchants, Spain. A spicy, silky 1995 Gran Reserva Rioja from Martinez Bujanda (£12.49) is a fine choice. From the grenache-heavy region of the Pyrenees, Haut Cabirou's 2002 version of this varietal, on the French side of the border (£6.67), is a good buy too.

Lay & Wheeler
Holton Park, Holton St Mary, Suffolk CO7 6NN (01206 764 446/www.laywheeler.com). **Phone enquiries** 8.30am-5.30pm Mon-Fri; 9am-1pm Sat. **Credit** MC, V.
This well-respected East Anglian company has recently followed the trend of other wine merchants by opening up wine bars in London, with two new places in the City. The merchant list has admirable amounts of New Zealand, including the decent 2004 Lawson's Dry Hills sauvignon blanc (£8.95), supplemented by lots from Bordeaux and Burgundy. Much is made of the listing of Oliver Leflaive, but look instead to 2001 Aleth Le Royer-Girardin Beaune 1er Cru Clos des Mouches (£21.95) from this north-easterly region. Unfortunately you can't view the full list on the website.

Liberty Wines
Unit D18, The Food Market, New Covent Garden, SW8 5LL (7720 5350/www.libertywine.co.uk). **Phone enquiries** 9am-5.30pm Mon-Fri. **Credit** MC, V.
David Gleave's boutique Italian specialists have an excellent reputation among restaurateurs – and rightly so, with some well-chosen examples of the country's quality and variety. Highlights include the fast-improving Poggio San Polo – its 2000 Brunello di Montalcino (£221.70 for 6 bottles, £36.95 each) is a superb example of winemaking with the sangiovese grape. Saladini Pilastri blends this grape beautifully with montepulciano in his 2004 Rosso Piceno Superiore, Vigna Monteprandone from the Marche (£83.88/case of 12). At the lower end is an 2004 Alpha Zeta soave at £4.75. As we went to press the website was being updated so you may have to call for any details.
Mail order.

Noel Young Wines
56 High Street, Trumpington, Cambridge CB2 2LS (01223 844 744/www.nywines.co.uk). **Open** 10am-8pm Mon-Sat; noon-2pm Sun. **Credit** AmEx, MC, V.
No merchant stocks a better selection of Austrian wines in the UK, with so many from the superb Neusiedlersee-based producer Alois Kracher worth drinking. Try the Trockenbeerenauslese No.9 chardonnay (2002, 33.5cl, £28.49), an outstanding tipple. Noel has a fine selection of Australian wines too. While Charles Melton's shiraz and cabernet sauvignons aren't great, his 2001 Nine Popes, a kind of Australian Châteauneuf-du-Pape is lovely drinking at £19.99. Young and his staff are helpful, down-to-earth and enthusiastic. A mixed six-bottle case of decent Chilean reds can be had for £48.
Mail order.

OW Loeb
3 Archie Street, SE1 3JT (7234 0385/ www.owloeb.com). **Phone enquiries** 8.30am-5.30pm Mon-Fri. **Credit** MC, V.
This off-the-wall merchants is taking its time over a new website, so call instead to discuss the exceptionally good German list – particularly from the country's northwestern region of Mosel – with its friendly staff. From a vast range of excellent rieslings in these parts, the Karthäuserhof's 1996 Eitelsbacher Spätlese (£13.90) stands out as a minerally, tight bottle. Or, for a fuller, fatter version of the grape, drink the Bernkasteler Lay 1997 from Thanisch (£14.10). The Rhône is well-covered by Loeb too, with a lovely 2001 Gigondas by Domaine du Pesquier (£14.49) and there's a good line-up from Burgundy. Listing wines such as Domaine de la Croix Senaillet, Davayé's Saint-Véran (£9.99) shows a good knowledge of less-heralded areas.

Peter Wylie Fine Wines
Plymtree Manor, Plymtree, Cullompton, Devon EX15 2LE (01884 277 555/www.wyliefine wines.co.uk). **Phone enquires** 9am-5.30pm Mon-Fri. **No credit cards.**
Shopping here is like going back to a time when the New World didn't even register with UK buyers. The list comprises classic regions only – Bordeaux, Burgundy, champagne, Port, Madeira, cognac and Armagnac, and all the top properties – Latour, Lafite, Mouton Rothschild, d'Yquem and Pétrus. Look for bargains among labels that are in various states of repair – this brings the price down in certain packages. With most of the 1966 Lafite badly torn, £1,300 for a case of 12 represents excellent value. The Port selection is one of the best in the country, with wines such as 1970 Graham's at £75. Single bottles start at around £15.

Stone, Vine & Sun
13 Humphrey Farms, Hazeley Road, Twyford, Winchester, Hants SO21 1QA (01962 712 351/ www.stonevine.co.uk). **Open** 9am-6pm Mon-Fri; 9.30am-4pm Sat. **Credit** MC, V.
This new merchant's has a name that fashionably suggests an emphasis on the growing rather the making of wine. The inclusion of the lovely 2002 Les Caillerets Chassagne-Montrachet from René Lequin-Colin (£22.50) confirms that individuals and not factories are behind most of the list. Lequin-Colin's has real intensity – it's one to lay down rather than drink now. Credit is due for the extensive range from the Loire, overlooked by so many wine merchants in the UK, and especially for the inclusion of examples from Chinon, such as Joguet's 2000 Clos du Chene Vert (£12.95).

Swig
188 Sutton Court Road, W4 3HR (0800 027 2272/www.swig.co.uk). **Open** 9am-6pm Mon-Fri. **Credit** AmEx, MC, V.
Enjoy this fantastic selection from South Africa, with Thelema and Buitenverwachting among the top names. The latter's 2004 Rhine riesling (£9) is a fine example of the varietal in these parts. South African sauvignon blancs are worth trying too, often with more minerality and complexity than the gooseberry flavours of New Zealand; Vergelegen's 2003 Reserve shows this in spades (£12.75).
Mail order.

Tanners Wines

26 Wyle Cop, Shrewsbury, Salop SY1 1XD (01743 234 500/www.tanners-wines.co.uk). Shrewsbury rail. **Open** 9am-6pm Mon-Sat. **Credit** AmEx, MC, V.

This medium-sized, mid-priced selection of classic regions has good choices all round. Beauties such as 2004 1er cru Domaine des Valery from the lovely Fourchaume vineyard show plenty of ripeness and elegance. Chenin blanc can be dire in some winemakers' hands, but the 2004 Blue White Old Vines from the Coastal Region in South Africa is a top wine (£5.85). From *en primeur* (wines bought before bottling, which are hence cheaper) 2004 Bordeaux, the Sauternes selection stands out. A 12-bottle case of 2me cru Château Doisy-Daëne looks good at £175. Hard by the Welsh borders, Tanners needs a good website to make up for a lack of geographical accessibility and, indeed, it's one of the few with genuinely interesting things written about the winemakers. *Mail order.*

Vinceremos Wines & Spirits

74 Kirkgate, Leeds LS2 7DJ (0113 244 0002/www.vinceremos.co.uk). **Phone enquiries** 9am-5.30pm Mon-Fri. **Credit** AmEx, MC, V.

Many producers coat the vines with sprays, but the 300 wines from across the globe available at Vinceremos have been made by people who, in most cases, take reasonable care of their land. From the US, the Fetzer sub-brand Bonterra is a good starting point. It's a reliable and aromatic, peach-flavoured take on the unusual southern French grape roussanne (£120.36/12 bottles). France has led the way with organics, and it's a shame not to see organic pioneers like Nicolas Joly from the Loire or Jean Meyer from Alsace here because of their deals with other importers, but Huet's 2002 Vouvray Le Haut Lieu Sec is a luscious, honeyed drop. *Mail order.*

Vin du Van Wine Merchants

Colthups, The Street, Appledore, Kent TN26 2BX (01233 758 727). **Phone enquires** 9am-5pm Mon-Fri. **Credit** MC, V.

A one-man band selling the largest range of Australian wines in the UK, Ian Brown should get a medal for his knowledge, service and approach. Brown doesn't have a website, preferring to speak to customers over the phone. And there are some great bottles listed, such as the rich, ripe, delicately balanced 2004 riesling from Ashbrook Estate in Western Australia (£9.95). Because the property isn't as well known as Cape Mentelle or Vasse Felix, this represents exceptional value. Or, for a much drier style with low alcohol – ideal for a pre-lunch aperitif – try the 2002 riesling from Dukes winery (£9.95). Brown also has a range of Penfolds Grange that dates back to 1983 (£175). *Mail order.*

The Vineking

14 Hartington Close, Reigate, Surrey RH2 9NL (08708 508 997/www.thevineking.com). **Phone enquiries** 11am-8pm Mon-Sat. **Credit** AmEx MC, V.

This two-year-old internet merchant majors in France, Australia and Italy. Started by a former Laytons employee, it includes some good wines, including the rich, developed 2002 chardonnay Classico from the excellent Cantina Terlano (£9.50). But there are odd tasting notes too. The 2000 Sasso Tenuta le Querce, Basilicata Aglianico (£7.50) apparently shows 'that lovely freshness you get from so many Italian wines'. They may be well made, but freshness in Italian wines isn't the first thing that springs to mind. The list is ordered, restaurant-style, according to price and you can also search by grape. *Mail order.*

Vintage Roots

Farley Farms, Bridge Farm, Reading Road, Arborfield, Berks RG2 9HT (0118 976 1999/www.vintageroots.co.uk). **Open** 8.30am-5.30pm Mon-Fri. **Credit** MC, V.

The best-known organic wine merchants is owned by Neil Palmer, a man committed to the cause of more naturally made wine. While other merchants stock the wares of top organic winemakers without flagging them up as such, buying from Vintage Roots guarantees you won't be drinking a concoction of chemicals. From the Loire, 2002 Les Progues Pouilly-Fuissé is outstanding drinking by Domaine Jeandeau (£17.99); from the south of Italy, 2003 Salento Rosso from Perrini, IGT (£6.75) is a fruit-bomb of a wine. It's an odd fact that many wines are filtered using gelatine or cow's bladder, but Vintage Roots sells some wines made without either process, making them suitable for both vegetarians and vegans. *Mail order.*

Virginwines

0870 164 9593/www.virginwines.com. **Phone enquiries** 8am-7pm Mon-Fri; 10am-5pm Sat, Sun. **Credit** AmEx, MC, V.

An early entrant to the internet wine market, and one of the few that didn't go bust, this vinous branch of the Richard Branson empire succeeded by reducing the range and concentrating on popular buys. So wine from Alsace tends to be from the large producer Caves de Turckheim, rather than, say Rémy Gresser or Meyer-Fonné. Wines are grouped together by flavour, not the traditional regional ordering. The 2002 Houghton Verdelho (£7.99), an excellent example of the grape from Australia, falls into the 'Fragrant but Dry White' category. You can even listen to Virgin Radio as you order from your laptop. The no-quibbles refund guarantee offers further reassurance.

Wine of the Times

The Observatory, Pinnacle House, 260 Old Oak Common Lane, Park Royal, NW10 6DX (8838 9432/www.wineofthetimes.com). **Phone enquiries** 8.30am-6.30pm Mon-Fri. **Credit** AmEx, MC, V.

Former Leiths employee and Adam Street club consultant Nick Tarayan's new company will deliver quality wines all over the UK. Spain, South Africa, France and Australia are the focus, with the super-concentrated 2003 Angus the Bull cabernet sauvignon, South Australia (£8.95) awarded 89 points by Parker, leading the way. There's also a 2002 Savennières from the young and exciting winemaker Damien Laureau (£11.95).

The Wine Society

Gunnels Wood Road, Stevenage, Herts SG1 2BG (01438 741 177/www.thewinesociety.com). **Phone enquiries** 8.30am-9pm Mon-Fri; 9am-5pm Sat. **Credit** AmEx, MC, V.

'The Society buys direct from suppliers, shipping wine from all over the world to Stevenage,' states the web page. It's hardly the most romantic image, but the storage facilities are extensive, and some of the wines really impress. It seems unreasonable to pay £40 membership just to purchase a bottle of wine, but you do get access to wines like Gaston Huet's Vouvrays dating back to 1921 – yes, white wine can age if it's well-made and there's enough residual sugar. The good-to-average 2004 Burgundy vintage is on offer in bond, so you can buy it without paying VAT, have it stored for you, then pay up when it comes out of the warehouse. Or purchase some lovely 2001 Château d'Armailhac from Bordeaux immediately, which just gets better every year and represents excellent value at £19. *Mail order (01438 740 222).*

Yapp Bros

The Old Brewery, Mere, Wilts BA12 6DY (01747 860 423/www.yapp.co.uk). **Phone enquiries** 9am-6pm Mon-Sat. **Credit** MC, V.

Praise is due to Robin Yapp for majoring in two areas of France that the British wine trade once so neglected – the Loire and the Rhône. The latter has gained in popularity in recent years, but few can match the outstanding selections here from Jean-Louis Chave, including his exceptional 1997 Hermitage, (£80, keep for ten years), as well as the choice of Auguste Clape, with his 2002 Cornas (£28). From the Loire, Domaine du Closel's 2000 La Jalousie, Cuvée Classique is a superb chenin blanc (£10.25) and Domaine Filliatreau's 2003 an excellent Saumur Champigny (£8.50). Despite the quality, prices aren't astronomical. *Mail order.*

Auction houses

Sotheby's and **Christie's** (for both, *see p252*) hold wine auctions approximately once a month. Bordeaux, Burgundy, Port and some cult New World wines make up the bulk of what's on offer. These wines aren't cheap but you can occasionally snag a bargain, compared to what you'd pay for the same wine from a merchant.

Wine accessories & gifts

See also p251 **Autour du Vin**.

Birchgrove Products

Unit 3C, Merrow Business Centre, Merrow Lane, Guildford, Surrey GU4 7WA (01483 533 400/www.birchgrove.co.uk). **Phone enquiries** 9am-5.30pm Mon-Fri. **Credit** MC, V.

A cheesy-looking website depicts a bottle holder in soft focus, as well as leafy vines. But move around to see an extensive range of spittoons, decanters, champagne stoppers, corkscrews, wine buckets, glasses, tasting accessories, cellar equipment and pourers. *Mail order.*

A&W Moore

Merlin Way, Quarry Hill Industrial Park, Ilkeston, Derby DE7 4RA (0115 944 1434/www.wineracks.co.uk). **Phone enquiries** 8am-5.30pm Mon-Fri. **Credit** MC, V.

Primarily a wine-rack supplier that uses cedar, mahogany, redwood, oak, wrought iron or steel to fit a variety of spaces. Avoid the first page of ready-made contraptions, all of which seem more suited to an old people's home. Glasses, chillers and decanters are better-looking examples of stock. *Mail order.*

Tanglewood Wine

Tanglewood House, Mayfield Avenue, New Haw, Addlestone, Surrey KT15 3AG (01932 348 720/www.tanglewoodwine.co.uk). **Phone enquiries** 9am-6pm Mon-Fri; 9am-1pm Sat. **Credit** AmEx, MC, V.

This company specialises in cooling systems that keep wine between the vital temperatures of ten and 16 degrees centigrade. Bottles can be stored either in small cabinets or under air-conditioning if you're looking at regulating a whole cellar. Wine racks in oak or beech can also be made to fit a variety of rooms.

Cellar planning & storage

In addition to the companies listed below, wine merchants **Berry Bros & Rudd**, **Bordeaux Index** (for both, *see p247*), **Justerini & Brooks** (*see p250*) and **Lay & Wheeler** (*see p250*) also offer a cellar-planning service. These companies can advise on which wines to buy when, and often have their own storage space if you don't possess a decent cellar.

Autour du Vin

38-40 New Cavendish Street, W1G 8UD (7935 4679/www.autourduvin.co.uk). Baker Street or Bond Street tube. **Open** 10am-6pm Mon-Fri; by appointment only Sat. **Credit** MC, V.

An extensive range of the excellent EuroCave wine coolers is on offer via these equipment suppliers. EuroCave machines are relatively noise-free and maintain wine at the right storage temperature: around 13 degrees centigrade. Store 75 wines for £1,190, or pay £1,680 to store 210. The company also sells cigar humidors (£2,435) with room for 1,000 cigars. Corkscrews, bottle rests, coolers, decanter driers and glasses by luxury brand Riedel are also sold. *Mail order.*

The Tea & Coffee Plant. See p254.

Smith & Taylor

Chelsea Bridge Cellars, 1C Broughton Street, SW8 3QJ (7627 5070/www.smithandtaylor.com). **Phone enquiries** 9am-5pm Mon-Fri. **No credit cards.**

Like most major wine merchants, Smith & Taylor offers storage for your wine, but the company also builds cellars in the home (corporate clients have included the Square restaurant). There's a range of designs, from a series of diamond-shaped boxes for showing off case by case, to racks built into a tasting table.

Spiral Cellars

Waltham Mead, Old London Road, Coldwaltham, West Sussex RH20 1LF (8834 7371/www.spiral cellars.com). **Phone enquiries** 9am-5.30pm daily. **Credit** MC, V.

As the company name suggests, curving step cellars are a speciality, with space for bottle storage built into the side (up to 1,600 bottles). If you don't have an entire underground cellar, the people at Spiral Cellars will dig a hole and insert the whole construction to a maximum depth of 3m. Or you can have a small wall-fitted storage area, with a stepladder down – neither of these requires planning permission. View all this on an easy-to-use and informative website.

Wine courses & clubs

Plenty of experts, journalists and former buyers offer wine courses to the public. Among the more entertaining are those by Tim Atkins, the *Observer*'s wine critic, at Bank restaurant on Aldwych, with titles like 'One for the vicar' (£45 each; £270 for six weeks; www.bank restaurant.com). Linden Wilkie's Fine Wine Experience offers some great wines as part of the sessions, which explains prices of £795 for his one-off tasting of Domaine de la Romanée-Conti's La Tache. A six-week introductory course costs £195 (www.finewineexperience. com). The Institution of Civil Engineers also runs a vibrant wine club, with regular tastings (www.cecwine.co.uk).

Christie's

153 Great Titchfield Street, W1W 5BD (7665 4350/www.christies.com). Great Portland Street or Warren Street tube. **Open** 9am-5pm Mon-Fri. **Credit** MC, V.

Amid the trading of very expensive wines, this famous auction house runs a five-week wine course (£210). The style of teaching is traditional, with Steven Spurrier and Michael Broadbent among the tutors, but Broadbent in particular has an excellent palate and plenty of experience. One-off lecture events, costing around £80, are also held; the pick of these is Tom Stevenson's talk on Growers' Champagnes (the smaller champagne producers) on 13 December 2005.
For branch see index.

Connoisseur

Radisson Edwardian, The Marlborough Hotel, 9-13 Bloomsbury Street, WC1 3QD (7328 2448/ www.connoisseur.org). Tottenham Court Road tube. **Phone enquiries** 8am-6pm Mon-Sat. **No credit cards.**

Margaret Silbermann of Bacchus wine merchants takes a more informal approach than some of her competitors with her five-session introductory course, six-session intermediate course and one-day lesson, which cost between £50 and £300.

The International Wine & Food Society

IWFS European and African Committee, Gable End, Devonshire Road, Weybridge, Surrey KT13 8HB (01932 701 320/www.iwfs.com). **Phone enquiries** 24hrs. **No credit cards.**

Founded in 1933 by writer and slightly obsessive gourmet André Simon, this international organisation is strongest in North America, where the bulk of its 8,000 members can be found. Local branches in the UK organise tastings and visit vineyards; membership allows you to use the reference library, housed in London's Guildhall. It costs £40 to join – or £20 if you're under 36.

Leiths School of Food & Wine

21 St Albans Grove, W8 5BP (7229 0177/ www.leiths.com). Gloucester Road or High Street Kensington tube. **Phone enquiries** 9am-5pm Mon-Fri. **Credit** AmEx, MC, V.

Helmed by Caroline Waldegrave, Leiths cookery school also offers a five-session Wine Certificate evening class (£320) and a one-off food-and-wine pairing course (£64), tutored by Nancy Gilchrist.

Sotheby's

34-35 New Bond Street, W1A 2AA (7293 5727/www.sothebys.com). Bond Street or Green Park tube. **Open** 9am-5pm Mon-Fri. **Credit** MC, V.

Sotheby's wine courses are held on Monday nights, and six sessions cost £240 (or £450 for two consecutive courses). All the lecturers are Masters of Wine, which guarantees knowledge, if not necessarily communicative ability. In this case, speakers such as Justin Howard-Sneyd, Jonathan Pedley and Sotheby's wine director Serena Sutcliffe who comprise part of the lecture team, are able to impart their vinous wisdom well.

Vinopolis, City of Wine

1 Bank End, SE1 9BU (0870 241 4040/www.vino polis.co.uk). London Bridge tube/rail. **Open** noon-9pm (last tour 7pm) Mon, Fri, Sat; noon-6pm (last tour 4pm) Tue-Thur, Sun. **Credit** MC, V.

London's wine museum offers wine and food pairing courses for both individuals and companies, plus a few cocktail masterclasses, thanks to the recent opening of the Blue bar in the main entrance. Beginners can take a one-day course on Sundays at 3pm (£25). There's an in-depth course for the more knowledgeable on the last Sunday of every month (£35), plus a two-hour pairing of six wines and six dishes (£50). *Mail order.*

Wine Education Service

Vanguard Business Park, Alperton Lane, Western Avenue, Greenford, Middx UB6 8AA (8991 8212/www.wine-education-service.co.uk). **Phone enquiries** 9am-6pm daily. **No credit cards.**

London courses are offered in the City, Hampstead, Holborn, Kensington and Notting Hill at three levels – introductory, intermediate and advanced. There's also a series of whisky sessions, and a one-day workshop. For the introductory level, 48 wines overall are tasted in eight two-hour sessions (£195). At intermediate level, there are six courses (£125-£135 each), each broken up into five two-hour sessions. The advanced level consists of three courses (£145 each), each composed of five two-hour sessions.

Wine & Spirit Education Trust
International Wine & Spirit Centre, 39-45 Bermondsey Street, SE1 3XF (7089 3800/ www.wset.co.uk). **Phone enquiries** 9.30am-5pm Mon-Fri. **Credit** MC, V.
This is the most recognised wine qualification, and one you should pursue if you work in the wine trade – it provides the only wine and spirit qualification recognised by the Government's Qualifications & Curriculum Authority. Most people have sufficient wine knowledge to skip the Foundation certificate and move to the Intermediate level (£265), followed by the Advanced (£489) and the Diploma (£1,323 for the two-year daytime course, £2,590 for the 11-month evening course). There's also a two-day course in spirits, pricey at £295.

Winewise
107 Culford Road, N1 4HL (7254 9734/ www.michaelschusterwine.com). **Phone enquiries** 8.30am-8.30pm Mon-Fri. **No credit cards.**
Renowned taster Michael Schuster runs an entertaining beginners' course, covering most of the world's major wine-producing regions (£175) and a fine-wine course, with some lovely bottles from classic French wine regions (£275). Schuster also runs one-off tastings ranging from £49 to £99.

Wine tours

Arblaster & Clarke Wine Tours
Clarke House, Farnham Road, West Liss, Hants GU33 6JQ (01730 893 344/www.winetours.co.uk). **Phone enquiries** 9am-6pm Mon-Fri; 10am-3pm Sat. **Credit** AmEx, MC, V.
This reliable tour operator takes people to Champagne, Chile, South Africa, New Zealand, the Rhône, Italy, Rioja and the port-growing region of Portugal, among many others.

The Scala School of Wine
PO Box LB740, W1A 9LB (7281 3040). **Phone enquiries** 9am-6pm Mon-Fri. **Credit** AmEx, MC, V.
Tim Hall was previously at the wine merchant's Ehrmanns. Now his wine school, Scala, has evolved into a tour company. Hall takes groups on visits to St Emilion, parts of the Médoc and Sauternes in Bordeaux, or Veuve Clicquot, Ruinart and the smaller but good-quality producers Vilmart, in Champagne.

Winetrails
Greenways, Vann Lake, Ockley, Dorking, Surrey RH5 5NT (01306 712 111/www.winetrails.co.uk). **Phone enquiries** 9.30am-5.30pm Mon-Fri. **Credit** MC, V.
Walk or cycle on wine tours in France, Spain, Italy, Portugal, Bulgaria, Hungary, Cyprus, Madeira, Switzerland and the New World. Winetrails likes to encourage a leisurely approach to visiting wineries, staying in smaller hotels in between visits, but this means it's not the cheapest option.

Spirits specialists

Cadenhead's Covent Garden Whisky Shop
3 Russell Street, WC2B 5JD (7379 4640/ www.coventgardenwhiskyshop.co.uk). Covent *Garden tube.* **Open** 11am-6.30pm Mon, Sat; 11am-7pm Tue-Fri; noon-4.30pm Sun. **Credit** DC, MC, V.
Head to this rickety old shop for undiluted whiskies without the addition of caramel (for colour) or chemicals. These whiskies have been bottled at the level they were when the mixture left

the barrel, known as 'cask strength'. It makes them higher in alcohol, but also more expensive. Instead of Aberlour's 15-year-old at 40% and the normal price of £25.99, it's at 62.1% and £45.50.
Mail order.

Gerry's
74 Old Compton Street, W1D 4UW (7734 4215). Leicester Square tube. **Open** 9am-6.30pm Mon-Fri; 9am-5.30pm Sat. **No credit cards.**
There's an incredible variety of spirits in this quirky shop, and a great range of tequilas that includes Herradura's excellent Blanco (£26.50). Some rarely found rums include J Bally's white version from Martinique (£19.95). But if you don't fancy these, lots of expensive miniatures might encourage some experimentation. Find out what Madeira tastes like with a tiny sample at £1.75 (Blandy's) or how great De Kuyper's Cherry Brandy is in cocktails (£1.75). The wine selection is average on the whole.

Milroy's of Soho
3 Greek Street, W1V 6NX (7437 9311/ www.milroys.co.uk). Tottenham Court Road tube. **Open** 10am-8pm Mon-Fri; 10am-7pm Sat. **Credit** AmEx, MC, V.
Founded in 1964, whisky specialist Milroy's was bought by La Reserve – which in turn was taken over by Jeroboams (*see p247*). There's a fine range of over 700 malts and whiskies from around the world, including rare bottles. Compare 1989 Bruichladdich before the distillery's closure (£39.95) with a present-day style (10-year-old, £11), or take advantage of some deals on wine as Jeroboams sells off old La Reserve stock. Ridge 1999 Montebello from California is one such bargain buy, reduced from £70 to £50. Regular tutored tastings are held in the cellar (see website for details).
Mail order.

Royal Mile Whiskies
3 Bloomsbury Street, WC1B 3QE (7436 4763/ www.royalmilewhiskies.com). Holborn or Tottenham Court Road tube. **Open** 11am-7pm Mon-Sat; noon-5pm Sun. **Credit** MC, V.
Tarted up since its buyout from the Bloomsbury Wine & Spirit Company, RMW is somewhat reminiscent of hotel meeting rooms. Staff could be more knowledgeable about the range of decent whiskies, plus the odd good bourbon, cognac, Armagnac and Scottish beer on offer. Twelve-year-old Lochnagar, the underrated Highland whisky from the royal estate, is well-priced at £25.50, as is a Johnny Drum bourbon at £16.50. There's also an XO from the excellent medium-sized cognac house Château du Plessis (£45.50).
Mail order.

The Vintage House
42 Old Compton Street, W1D 4LR (7437 2592/ www.vintagehouse.co.uk). Leicester Square or Piccadilly Circus tube. **Open** 9am-11pm Mon-Fri; 9.30am-11pm Sat; noon-10pm Sun. **Credit** AmEx DC, MC, V.
Dodge the crowds to enter this refuge from the busy Old Compton Street thoroughfare. It's an independent merchant with over 1,300 malt whiskies, an incredible selection that has 1967 Ardbeg (£500) as one of many good picks from some really old malts. Wines are nothing like as good, with far too many branded bottles at the front of the store. Head to the back for interesting bottles, such as 1997 Wynns John Riddoch cabernet sauvignon, from Coonawarra in Australia.
Mail order.

Beer shops & breweries

The Beer Shop
14 Pitfield Street, N1 6EY (08458 831 492/ www.pitfieldbeershop.co.uk). Old Street tube/ rail. **Open** 11am-7pm Tue-Fri; 10am-4pm Sat. **Credit** MC, V.
A smell of fermenting malt seeps into this store from the organic brewery next door. Those beers go under the Pitfield name, and the IPA here is made to 7%, according to a recipe from 1837. It's quite unlike the much lighter kinds on sale in

British pubs. Owner Martin Kemp has just added the floral, delicate Swiss Appenzeller beers (Naturperle, £1.25/33cl) to his huge range, complementing beers at the other end of the weight spectrum, such as the fantastic, smoky Guinness (£1.15/33cl), brewed in Dublin to 7% for the Belgian market. The shop is packed with beers from England, Scotland and Belgium, as well as a few lovely ciders, such as an apple varietal-named range from Hampshire-based Mr Whitehead's Cider Company – Estival is £1.45 (27.5cl).
Mail order.

Fuller, Smith & Turner
The Griffin Brewery, Chiswick Lane South, W4 2QB (8996 2085/www.fullers.co.uk). Turnham Green tube/94 bus. **Open** 8am-6pm Mon-Thur; 8am-5.30pm Fri; 10am-5pm Sat. **Credit** AmEx, MC, V.
Lovely beers, but the wines aren't so good, so stick to what Fullers knows best at this shop on its brewery site. In a trendy conversion of an old barn, under soaring beams and spotlights, there are rare examples, in 75ml bottles, of what the company does so well in the brewery round the side. London Porter, for example, is a rich chocolate-flavoured brew (£1.80). Or a four-pack combines the lighter IPA, the classic London Pride, the rich, red ESB and the strong, fruitcakey 1845 (£6.69). If you're having a party, 24 bottles of ESB are good value at £16. Or if it's a big one, you might turn to a mini-barrel of ESB (on sale from the middle of November) containing 34 pints of Pride (£45) or 72 pints (£95).
Mail order.

Tea & coffee

Algerian Coffee Stores
52 Old Compton Street, W1D 4PB (7437 2480/ www.algcoffee.co.uk). Leicester Square tube. **Open** 9am-7pm Mon-Sat. **Credit** AmEx, DC, MC, V.
This quaint little Soho store has been selling its aromatic wares since 1887 and still retains its original wooden counter. It manages to pack more than 140 coffees and 200 teas into the small space, including Fairtrade, organic coffees and estate varieties sourced from around the globe. On the tea front, there are Chinese whites, Japanese greens, Indian Darjeelings and Yogi teas – to name but a few. Prices are reasonable (from around £3/250g). There is also a wide range of gadgets for preparing the drinks, including Italian stove-top coffee makers and teapots in all sizes, plus confectionery, including chocolate-covered coffee beans.
Mail order.

Angelucci Coffee Merchants
23B Frith Street, W1D 4RT (7437 5889). Leicester Square or Tottenham Court Road tube. **Open** 9am-5pm Mon-Wed, Fri, Sat; 9am-1pm Thur. **No credit cards.**
An ancient coffee grinder still sits on the counter of this shop, which started life as a café in the 1930s. Still run by the Angelucci family, it now sells 36 coffees (£5-£7.50/500g), from Honduran and Tanzanian varieties to Mokital espresso (blended back in the early days by the Angeluccis) – a favourite with local cafés and restaurants.
Mail order.

Camden Coffee Shop
11 Delancey Street, NW1 7NL (7387 4080). Camden Town tube. **Open** 9.30am-5.30pm Mon-Wed, Fri, Sat; 9.30am-2.30pm Thur. **No credit cards.**
Imagine Camden without the goths and teenage day trippers. The area may have transformed since George Constantinou took over his uncle's business in 1978, but inside this old-fashioned shop, little has changed. The aroma produced by the traditional roasting methods lures passers-by in addition to devoted regulars. The beans on offer are mostly from South America and Africa, and prices are reasonable (£4.40-£6.40/500g).

Drury Tea & Coffee Company
3 New Row, WC2N 4LH (7836 1960/www.drury. uk.com). Leicester Square tube. **Open** 9am-6pm Mon-Fri; 11am-5pm Sat. **Credit** MC, V.

Established in 1936 by three Italian brothers, the DTCC offers a range of more than 100 teas – from classics such as Earl Grey to more exotic leaves from Nepal – and over 30 coffees from Africa and Central and South America, including ethically sourced Colombian Tolima beans (£5.70/500g). Unsurprisingly, given the company's Italian roots, it's especially good for espresso machines, in all shapes and colours, for making the black stuff. There are also tea infusers and flavoured syrups. *Mail order.*

HR Higgins
79 Duke Street, W1K 5AS (7629 3913/www.hrhiggins.co.uk). Bond Street tube. **Open** 9.30am-5.30pm Mon-Fri; 10am-5pm Sat. **Credit** AmEx, MC, V.
When HR Higgins opened his business in an attic on South Molton Street in 1942, he delivered his imported coffees to customers by pushbike and cart. More than 60 years on, the family-run business has a royal warrant under its belt, but its dedication to customer service is still evident. Friendly staff will guide you through the extensive range of original varieties (from such exotic places as the Galapagos and Yemen), speciality blends (from mild Hanover to strong Caffè Roma) and 'very dark roasts', all prepared on the premises. There is also a wide range of teas. Prices aren't cheap (coffee starts at about £15/kg), but you can try before you buy in the café downstairs. *Mail order.*

Markus Coffee Co
13 Connaught Street, W2 2AY (7723 4020/ www.markuscoffee.com). Marble Arch tube. **Open** 9am-5.30pm Mon-Fri; 9am-1pm Sat. **Credit** AmEx, MC, V.
A large antique roaster, together with huge sacks of unroasted coffee beans, confirms the freshness of the product here. Established almost 50 years ago as a supplier to many West End restaurants as well as to the public, Markus stocks a competent range of coffees from around the globe (Brazilian Santos, Ethiopian Mocha and Costa Rican from £6.50/500g) and a small selection of teas (from £3.50/250g). All sorts of coffee makers and accessories are on display and for sale. *Mail order.*

Monmouth Coffee House
27 Monmouth Street, WC2H 9EV (7379 3516/ www.monmouthcoffee.co.uk). Covent Garden tube. **Open** 8am-6.30pm Mon-Sat. **Credit** MC, V.
Connoisseurs will no doubt appreciate the small but discerning selection of predominantly South American and African coffees on display here. There's a small café area at the back, so you can sample before you buy. If you happen to be at Borough market, drop by the stall there, or pop into the second shop, where you can sit at communal tables and sample a good range of pastries, savouries and cakes baked by Villandry (*see p239*). **For branch see index.** *Mail order.*

The Tea & Coffee Plant
180 Portobello Road, W11 2EB (7221 8137/ www.coffee.uk.com). Ladbroke Grove tube. **Open** 8am-6.30pm Mon-Sat; 10am-5pm Sun. **Credit** MC, V.
Dedicated importers of organic and Fairtrade tea and arabica coffee, the TCP has a considerable mail-order service for both the catering industry and the public. Around 30 blends of tea (black, green and herbal) sit alongside a substantial selection of worldwide coffees from as far afield as Peru and Malabar (India). Popular choices include the organic Italian roast and Mexican blend (both £11/kg). Gaggia espresso makers, various cafetières and tea-making accessories are also sold. *Mail order.*

The Tea House
15A Neal Street, WC2H 9PU (7240 7539). Covent Garden tube. **Open** 10am-7pm Mon-Sat; 11am-6pm Sun. **Credit** AmEx, MC, V.
Ignore the novelty teapots, jars of jam and decorated tea strainers, and concentrate on the extensive, reasonably priced selection of teas in this

well-laid-out store. As well as traditional types, there are specialist green teas, classic scented or fruity black Chinese varieties (loose leaf, teabags, and tea 'bricks'). If you prefer caffeine-free infusions, choose from whole-fruit blends (strawberry and kiwi or summer pudding teabags, £1.95/25) and Rooibos (South African teas, believed to have healing properties, from £1.55/25 bags). Organic teas are a further bonus. *Mail order.*

R Twining & Co
216 Strand, WC2R 1AP (7353 3511/www.twinings.com). Temple tube. **Open** 9.30am-4.30pm Mon-Fri. **Credit** AmEx, MC, V.
Twining's is undoubtably the most famous tea company in the world, trading for 300 years and still going strong. It also prides itself on its fair trade policy regarding the purchase of tea. The shop stocks a huge choice of teas, including some that are exclusive to the company, such as Prince of Wales and Lady Grey (both £1.25/125g). Along with the more familiar blends, available loose or in bags, there's a range of green teas, herbal and fruit infusions and organic blends, plus coffees, biscuits and teapots. Limited-edition and speciality teas (such as after-dinner mint) are frequently added to the stock. True aficionados will be interested in the museum at the back of this shop, which displays a neat collection of quirky and unusual tea caddies, along with tea-related paraphernalia. *Mail order.*

Whittard
209 Kensington High Street, W8 6BD (7937 5569/www.whittard.com). High Street Kensington tube. **Open** 9.30am-7pm Mon-Sat; 11am-5pm Sun. **Credit** AmEx, MC, V.
Whittard first retailed its fine teas in 1886 and has proved it can move with the times while maintaining a dedication to producing quality goods. The range includes a selection of coffee, including raw beans for home roasting, and over 50 leaf teas (including Black Dragon Formosa, with a delicate chestnut note, and Rose Petal black tea). New lines are added seasonally and guest coffees are introduced on a regular basis; the adventurous may want to try such exotic flavours as blueberry-and-yoghurt tea (£3.15/125g) or double chocolate-truffle coffee (£3/113g). There's a wide choice of pre-packed house blends, gift packs, biscuits and chocolate drinks, as well as exclusive ceramics, some hand-painted. Tea/coffee machines and equipment from Gaggia, Pavoni and Briel can also be picked up. *Mail order (0800 015 4395).* **Branches:** throughout the city.

Cigars

Chic new cigar bar **La Casa Del Habano** (100 Wardour Street, W1F 0TN, 7314 4001, www.lacasadelhabano.co.uk) has a wide range for sale; special cigar menus offer comprehensive descriptions of the large stock, and sticks can be rolled, cut and lit to order under the expert eye of resident aficionado Juan Carlos Ruiz.

Davidoff of London
35 St James's Street, SW1A 1HD (7930 3079). Green Park tube. **Open** 9am-6pm Mon-Fri; 9.30am-6pm Sat. **Credit** AmEx, DC, MC, V.
Between the chic marble floors and impeccably mannered staff, Davidoff of London is the first port of call for high-rolling dandies looking to augment their cigar-smoking lifestyles. While the range of high-quality, hand-rolled cigars is second to none (you won't pay more than £33 for an Aniversaro No.1, one from Davidoff's own range), it's the accessories that are especially impressive – a rather dapper velvet smoking fez costs £39.95, while the recent introduction of single-malt scotches behind the counter means you can select a dram to complement your favourite cigar. *Mail order.*

JJ Fox (St James's)
19 St James's Street, SW1A 1ES (7930 3787/ www.jjfox.co.uk). Green Park tube. **Open** 9am-6pm Mon-Sat. **Credit** AmEx, DC, MC, V.

Two large wooden American Indians flank the entrance to this prestigious establishment, where staff talk expertly and enthusiastically about their stock to the businessmen of Mayfair. Winston Churchill was a regular patron, and items such as Elie Bleu humidors with a 300-cigar capacity (£2,400) reflect the fact that clients take their cigars very seriously indeed. Cigar- and pipe-smoking literature is available, along with affordably priced ashtrays and Dunhill pipes (from around £30). *Mail order.*

Sautter of Mayfair
106 Mount Street, W1K 2TW (7499 4866). Bond Street tube. **Open** 9am-6pm Mon-Fri; 9am-4.30pm Sat. **Credit** AmEx, DC, MC, V.
Stocking a good number of limited-edition cigars such as the Partagás Serie D No.1 (£20.30 each) and Montecristo Edmundo (£14.30), Sautter is especially popular with American aficionados – the pictures of Jack Nicholson and Bill Cosby sucking on their sticks seem slightly out of place in a shop otherwise full of more traditional motifs. Few smoking needs will be left unmet by the range of tobacco and accessories available here. *Mail order.*

Segar & Snuff Parlour
27A The Market, Covent Garden, WC2E 8RD (7836 8345). Covent Garden tube. **Open** 10.30am-7pm Mon-Wed; 10.30am-8pm Thur-Sat; 11am-5pm Sun. **Credit** AmEx, DC, MC, V.
Boasting over 70 variations of Havana cigar, this tiny shop attracts both tourists and veteran smokers. The manager selects a 'cigar of the week', which is advertised on a blackboard outside the Victorian shopfront, and much of the tobacco comes recommended by the Pipe Club of London. A decorative pipe is competitively priced at £22.95, although you can expect to part with over £600 for a box of large Cuban Cohibas. *Mail order.*

Shervingtons
337-338 High Holborn, WC1V 7PX (7405 2929). Chancery Lane tube. **Open** 9am-6pm Mon-Fri. **Credit** AmEx, DC, MC, V.
Housed in one of the few 15th-century buildings to survive the Great Fire, Shervingtons caters to anyone who considers themselves a smoking all-rounder. Cohibas are the most popular cigars on offer, with prices ranging from £5 to £50, and there are over a dozen varieties of hand-rolling tobacco and 30 blends of pipe tobacco, including chocolate, apple and cherry flavours. *Mail order.*

G Smith & Sons
74 Charing Cross Road, WC2H 0BG (7836 7422). Leicester Square tube. **Open** 9am-6pm Mon-Fri; 9.30am-5.30pm Sat. **Credit** AmEx, DC, MC, V.
Boxes of cigars and display cases of pipes dominate this compact shop. A walk-in humidor houses popular cigar brands from Cuba as well as the Dominican Republic, Brazil and Honduras. Anyone who enjoys a lengthy smoke can equip themselves with an impressively long Santa Clara for £25.50 (as featured in the *Guinness Book of Records*), while pocket tins of specially blended snuff (starting at £2.15) are ideal for ensuring a discreet source of nicotine in an age of public smoking bans. Accessories include lighters, from £2 to £250. *Mail order.*

Tomtom
63 Elizabeth Street, SW1W 9PP (7730 1790/ www.tomtom.co.uk). Sloane Square tube/Victoria tube/rail. **Open** 10am-6pm Mon-Fri; 10am-5pm Sat. **Credit** AmEx, MC, V.
Specialising in Havanas, Tomtom has managed to become one of London's leading cigar merchants since it was founded in 1997. It's a touch more exotic than other stores; you can pick up a 'cheap' Honduran or Nicaraguan smoke for a fiver, but a single Montecristo A is a slightly more prohibitive at £42.50. An excellent website allows customers to browse the extensive stocks of Partagá, Cuaba, Romeo y Julieta and Hoyo de Monterrey. *Mail order.*

Babies & Children

To appreciate London's diverse shopping possibilities for children you need to make full use of your Family Travelcard. It may be tempting to stay in the West End with the big hitters like **Hamley's** (*see p264*) and **Harrods** (*see p12*), but we urge you to explore further afield. Some of the specialist toyshops and crammed clothing exchanges listed below may necessitate close inspection of the *A-Z*, but they're worth it.

All-rounders

The fourth floor of Harrods (*see p12*) is a universe dedicated to children. Each enormous room has its own theme or collection; expect pumping music, wild colours and, in the toy rooms, entertainers. **Selfridges** (*see p14*), meanwhile, calls its third floor Kids' Universe. It's a huge area, so there's plenty of room to swing a toddler. McFly blares on the sound system and white, shiny pods contain the gear (Burberry, Moschino, Caramel, Emilie et Rose). The fourth-floor children's department of **John Lewis** (*see p13*) can be relied on for the most courteous staff, the best-quality nursery equipment, the widest-ranging school uniform selection and some attractive young fashions.

Daisy & Tom

181-183 King's Road, SW3 5EB (7352 5000/ www.daisyandtom.com). Sloane Square tube then 11, 19, 22, 49 bus. **Open** *9.30am-6pm Mon, Tue, Thur, Fri; 10am-7pm Wed, Sat; 11am-5pm Sun.* **Credit** *AmEx, MC, V.*
About as complete as a children's shop could be, Daisy & Tom splits its diverse wares over two bulging levels. On the first floor you'll find nursery equipment and furniture, a toy department and a 'girls' room'. On the second, you'll find clothes and shoes. The biggest thrill is the mini carousel as you walk in (there's no fee, but you may be asked for a small donation to a charity). Another attraction is

the half-hourly puppet re-enactment of *Peter and the Wolf*. As well as the vast selection on sale (everything from sulky-looking Bratz dolls and jolly Lego kits to £2,000-plus handmade rocking horses), there are toys for children to try out. In the book department, there are big beanbags and cushions, so children can read while their parents shop. Shaggy children can be shorn by the resident hairdresser (£8-£16). Among the 12 different brands of pushchair are Boz by Baby Comfort, Silver Cross and the Paltrow-favoured Bugaboo. The clothing department carries Daisy & Tom in abundance, Timberland, Elle, Catimini and more. A programme of events (check the website for details) features in-store face-painting, storytelling and visits from favourite authors.
Buggy access. Catalogue. Disabled access: ramp, toilet. Gift wrapping service. Hairdressing. Mail order. Nappy-changing facilities.

Mothercare

461 Oxford Street, W1C 2EB (7629 6621/ www.mothercare.com). Marble Arch tube. **Open** *9am-8pm Mon-Fri; 9.30am-8pm Sat; noon-6pm Sun.* **Credit** *AmEx, MC, V.*
Retaining its image in the minds of most as the temple for all things infant-related, Mothercare should be your first stop for baby essentials – from breast pads to nursery furniture to car seats. This three-floored branch has everything that'll be on your list for that first mad dash before baby arrives – wipes, muslins and nappies, high chairs and cots – plus most things you'll need for later, not least a decent range of easy-fold, bus-friendly buggies (from £30) and more elaborate travel systems. Pleasant staff and accessible layout are added bonuses at this store, and prices are reasonable. Although it's still a bit pink and blue in the respective girl/boy collections, the styles are far less staid than you would imagine, and the Moda maternity wear is worth a look. The website has articles and advice about coping with life before, during and after birth.
Buggy access. Delivery service. Disabled access: toilet. Mail order. Nappy-changing facilities.
Branches: throughout the city.

Educational

Books

Daunt Books, **Bookseller Crow on the Hill** and **Owl Bookshop** all have excellent children's sections (*see chapter* **Books**).

Bookworm

1177 Finchley Road, NW11 0AA (8201 9811). Golders Green tube. **Open** *9.30am-5.30pm Mon-Sat; 10am-1.30pm Sun.* **Credit** *MC, V.*
This much-loved specialist children's bookshop has a central rotunda full of cushions and beanbags, and a cubby hole with tables and chairs for quiet reading/playing at the back. The stock is exemplary: shelf after shelf of everything from reference books for projects such as *The Victorians* or *The Romans* to the latest fiction. Twice-weekly storytelling sessions take place on Tuesdays and Thursdays (2pm) for under-fives, when badges and stickers are handed out. Writers who have dropped by recently include Joe Craig, Mark Sedgewick, Fiona Dunbar and Morris Gleitzman, from Australia.
Buggy access. Disabled access. Mail order. Play area. Regular author visits.

Children's Book Centre

237 Kensington High Street, W8 6SA (7937 7497). High Street Kensington tube. **Open** *9.30am-6.30pm Mon, Wed, Fri, Sat; 9.30am-6pm Tue; 9.30am-7pm Thur; noon-6pm Sun.* **Credit** *AmEx, MC, V.*
A visit to this two-storey treasure trove will yield far more than books. Downstairs are toys, board games, T-shirts with witty slogans and dressing-up clothes, as well as stationery, accessories, family games and toys at pocket-money prices. There is a PC set up at the back for children to try new computer games, and a large book selection worth browsing on the ground floor. It covers all ages and tastes, from larger picture books and the Dr Seuss titles for new readers to a range for sophisticated consumers of teen literature. This floor also stocks birthday cards, gifts, stationery and jewellery. Visit the website to find out about author visits and other events.
Buggy access. Mail order. Regular author visits.

Children's Bookshop

29 Fortis Green Road, N10 3HP (8444 5500). Highgate tube then 43, 134 bus. **Open** *9.15am-5.45pm Mon-Sat; 11am-4pm Sun.* **Credit** *AmEx, MC, V.*

Catimini. See p258.

Quiet, well-stocked and roomy, this shop provides a famously good atmosphere in which to take in the row upon row of neatly ordered shelves, full of colour and interest, with small themed displays and a children's corner with picture books at floor level. Book-related events are publicised in the quarterly newsletter, which carries helpful, personal reviews of new titles. Books on CD and tape are also available. The staff are happy to order in any title you require if they don't have it already. *Buggy access. Mail order. Regular author visits.*

Golden Treasury

29 Replingham Road, SW18 5LT (8333 0167). Southfields tube. **Open** 9.30am-6pm Mon-Fri; 9.30am-5.30pm Sat; 10.30am-4.30pm Sun. **Credit** MC, V.
An excellent children's bookshop, with a buggy-friendly ramp allowing ease of progress through the store. All phases and crazes are covered, with a fairy and princess section for frothy pink types, a large section devoted to *Horrible Histories*, and a less interesting official educational section with various 'browbeat your child through SATs'-type guides for insecure parents. There's a Dr Seuss tower, a pretty cabinet devoted to Beatrix Potter, mini picture books from Red Fox (just £1.50 each) and a large collection of favourite baby and toddler books. Reads for ages 8-12 and teens take up several shelves and there's a small adult section. *Buggy access. Delivery service. Play area.*

Lion & Unicorn

19 King Street, Richmond, Surrey TW9 1ND (8940 0483/www.lionunicornbooks.co.uk). Richmond tube/rail. **Open** 9.30am-5.30pm Mon-Fri; 9.30am-6pm Sat; noon-5pm Sun. **Credit** MC, V.
We don't believe that many more books can be jammed into this long-established, award-winning bookshop, which counts among its first visiting authors the late, great Roald Dahl. There's a whole wall of signed photos and mementoes from all the children's writers who've visited over the years, and still they come (check the website for details of visits and for the regular Saturday storytelling sections). L&U is owned by Jenny Morris and managed by Tony West, both of whom are clearly keen readers – handwritten reviews of their favourite reads are all over the shop. A regular newsletter, *The Roar*, includes more book reviews and events. Every children's book worth reading is sold here, with displays broken up into current favourites, children's picture books, reads for 8-12s and teen books.
Buggy access. Mail order. Regular author visits.

Tales on Moon Lane

25 Half Moon Lane, SE24 9JU (7274 5759/ www.talesonmoonlane.co.uk). Herne Hill rail. **Open** 9.15am-5.30pm Mon-Sat. **Credit** MC, V.
This bookshop has a warm community feel. It hosts regular events centred around local authors and illustrators, such as Garry Parsons (*Krong!*), Deborah Nash (*Made in China*) and Jennie Walters (*House of Secrets*). Every Tuesday and Thursday a storyteller and playleader run 'Once Upon a Story' for pre-school children (£4 per session). There's also a sofa where children can curl up with a good book. As well as all that, Tales has a very wide range of picture books and tapes, novels and reference for all young readers, from toddlers to teenagers.
Buggy access. Play area. Regular author visits.

Musical instruments

For **Chappell of Bond Street** and additional music shops, *see chapter* **Music**.

Dot's

132 St Pancras Way, NW1 9NB (7482 5424/ www.dotsonline.co.uk). Camden Town tube/ Camden Road rail. **Open** 9am-5.30pm Mon-Sat. **Credit** MC, V.
Run by an experienced music teacher, Dot's has new instruments – mostly stringed and wind – costing from £5 for a recorder, £40 for a guitar and £59 for a violin. There's also a rent-to-buy scheme, with hire costs eventually offsetting the purchase price should a child show consistent interest. The great joy here is receiving unpressured advice in a friendly setting; staff take a genuine interest in children. A noticeboard has adverts for tuition and second-hand instruments, plus there's Dot's own recorder club.
Buggy access. Mail order.

Dulwich Music Shop

2 Croxted Road, SE21 8SW (8766 0202). West Dulwich rail. **Open** 9.30am-5.30pm Mon, Tue, Thur-Sat; 9.30am-7.30pm Wed. **Credit** AmEx, MC, V.
This is a proper community music shop. Staff can help out if you're looking to invest in used or new instruments and sheet music, and there's a range of price lists for wind, brass and stringed instruments, including hire and buy-back prices. Brochures and advertisements for teachers, music groups, concerts and events around the capital are displayed. Reeds, strings and cleaning cloths are also sold, alongside knick-knacks, gifts, CDs and stationery. Recorders, for the early days of parent torture, cost from £4.99.
Buggy access. Mail order.

Northcote Music

155C Northcote Road, SW11 6QB (7228 0074). Clapham Junction rail. **Open** 10.30am-6pm Mon-Sat. **Credit** MC, V.
This is a tiny little shop, so if too many Battersea mums descend at the same time for their darling's first recorder it can be a crush. Northcote squeezes string, percussion and wind instruments into the space, as well as brass and digital equipment for music lovers of all persuasions, and there's an on-site workshop for any instrumental mishaps. Classical sheet music is sold, as well as other musical styles, from show-tune books to Christina Aguilera arranged for vocals, piano and guitar.
Buggy access. Delivery service. Mail order.

Equipment & accessories

Babyworld

239 Munster Road, SW6 6BT (7386 1904/ www.babyworldlondon.com). Fulham Broadway tube then 211, 295 bus. **Open** 10am-6pm Mon-Wed, Fri; 10am-5.30pm Sat. **Credit** AmEx, MC, V.
Friendly staff here can tell you the best transport systems for your precious cargo. Most popular with parents of newborns these days is the latest Bugaboo pram, which comes in a range of colours and its chassis can hold either a carrycot or a buggy seat for older babies and toddlers up to the age of three and a half. Other pram and buggy ranges are by Chicco, Maxi-Cosi and Stokke. There are also toys from Lamaze, plus nursery accessories.
Buggy access. Mail order.

Chic Shack

77 Lower Richmond Road, SW15 1ET (8785 7777/www.chicshack.net). Putney Bridge tube then 14, 22 bus. **Open** 9.30am-6pm Mon-Sat. **Credit** MC, V.
If your tastes for the nursery lean towards vintage bleached cotton, old rose and gingham print, powder blue and pink traditional styles, you'll love Chic Shack. This compact shop on two floors is filled with beautiful things for the whole home, but the stuff for babies' and children's rooms is especially lovely. It's all here, from knitted teddies and snowy bedlinens and shawls to superbly finished nursery furniture. There are delightful wardrobes and cabinets with hand-carved details, bookshelves and clothes baskets, and solid cots that become little beds. The items are inspired by French and Swedish 18th-century design, and can be designed to order. Chic Shack also offers a range of fabrics for curtains and upholstery, as well as nursery gifts, stationery, glassware and lighting. It's not cheap, but prices for furniture reflect its quality.
Buggy access. Delivery service. Mail order.

Dragons of Walton Street

23 Walton Street, SW3 2HX (7589 3795/ www.dragonsofwaltonstreet.com). Knightsbridge or South Kensington tube. **Open** 9.30am-5.30pm Mon-Fri; 10am-5pm Sat. **Credit** AmEx, MC, V.
Veteran hand-painter of nursery furniture Rosie Fisher opened her first Dragons shop in 1979. After nearly 25 years in the business, the name is synonymous with top-quality, exclusive baby rooms. Everything you could ever want in a nursery, including curtains, cots, sofas, chaise longues and tiny chairs, is made to order; you choose your item and your paint or fabric scheme. Favourite themes include fairies, soldiers, animals and flowers, but customers are encouraged to come up with their own ideas. Such hand-picked finery doesn't come cheap: expect to pay £2,000 for a special artwork bed, and between £3,500 and £10,000 for a rocking horse. There are toys as well as furniture: money boxes (£10); doll's houses (£250-£550), wooden toys and teddy bears.
Buggy access. Delivery service. Mail order.

Lilliput

255-259 Queenstown Road, SW8 3NP (7720 5554/www.lilliput.com). Queenstown Road rail. **Open** 9.30am-5.30pm Mon, Tue, Thur, Fri; 9.30am-7pm Wed; 9am-6pm Sat; 11am-4pm Sun. **Credit** MC, V.
A whole world of travel, nursery and entertainment needs for the most demanding of small people met in this cavernous space beneath the railway arches. A rack of product literature and baby services (aromatherapy for children?) just inside the door includes Lilliput's own leaflet entitled 'Equipment you need when having a baby'. A number of young, pink-T-shirted staff are on hand to demonstrate the huge number of prams and buggies (from £30 folding buggies to an £850 Silver Cross carriage pram), cots, cot beds, cabinets and changing tables, bedding, bath equipment, towels and toys. Clothing for babies and toddlers is also sold.
Buggy access. Delivery service. Mail order. Nappy-changing facilities. Play area.
For branch see index.

London Prams

175-179 East India Dock Road, E14 0EA (7537 4117/www.londonprams.co.uk). All Saints DLR. **Open** 10.30am-5.30pm Mon-Sat. **Credit** MC, V.
All infant transport requirements can be addressed at east London's finest, just opposite All Saints DLR station. Brands to conjure with include Bugaboo, Stokke, Mamas & Papas and Silver Cross. It's not just prams, either – there are cots, high chairs, state-of-the-art changing stations, baby carriers, Grobag baby sleeping bags, baby baths and toys. One of the most covetable playthings is the perfectly miniaturised Silver Cross carriage pram in trademark navy or show-off pink, from £250. The excellent Bambino Mio washable nappy range is also sold.
Buggy access. Delivery service. Mail order.

Mini Kin

*22 Broadway Parade, N8 9DE (8341 6898).
Finsbury Park tube then W7 or 41 bus.* **Open**
9.30am-5.30pm Mon-Sat; 11.30am-5pm Sun.
Credit MC, V.

Mini Kin has a children's hairdressing salon, with
animal-themed seats and the possibility of mini
makeovers. Baby haircuts start at £10; or the
special first haircut with lots of fuss, certificate
and samples costs £14.95. Little girlies love the full
princess treatment for £29.95, which involves
glitter, hypoallergenic products, peel-off nail
varnish and goodies, plus photos to take home.
Otherwise there's natural bath and hygiene
products (including the SOS range for eczema),
plus Bugaboo buggies, Baby Björn carriers, potties
and stools, bibs and changers, and Nurtured by
Nature merino wool Babygros. Everyone adores
the Angulus shoes (Itsy Bitsies from £21).
*Buggy access. Disabled access. Hairdressing.
Nappy-changing facilities. Play area.*

Nursery Window

*83 Walton Street, SW3 2HP (7581 3358/
www.nurserywindow.co.uk). South Kensington
tube.* **Open** 10am-6pm Mon-Sat. **Credit** AmEx,
MC, V.

If you want your newborn to snuggle into the finest
cashmere, linen and lambswool, look no further
than Nursery Window. Quality bedlinen in 100%
cotton with pink or blue bunnies, stripes or spots
costs from £14 for pillowcases. There are also
super-soft blankets, towels, cot bumpers and quilts.
As well as the soft stuff, there's a wide selection of
nursery furniture in two ranges; affordable white
painted pine (cot £380) or covetable solid oak (cot
£550). Extras include woollen floor rugs, hanging
nappy stackers and gift sets. The shop also offers
a made-to-measure curtain service; a wide range of
fabric designs includes racing cars, bunnies,
seashells, stripes, sprigs and more.
Buggy access. Delivery service. Mail order.

Rub a Dub Dub

*15 Park Road, N8 8TE (8342 9898). Finsbury
Park tube then W7 or 41 bus.* **Open** 10am-5.30pm
Mon-Fri; 9.30am-5.30pm Sat; 11am-4pm Sun.
Credit MC, V.

Ways of getting babies and children to and fro and
seated comfortably are the strength here. The
knowledgeable owner chooses stock with care –
you'll find the excellent Bugaboo three-in-one
travel system; the posture-reforming Tripp Trapp
high chair (£137); and Nomad travel cots that fold
to backpack size and double as a UV tent (£125).
Also available is Stokke's Xplory baby buggy, an
amazingly space-age, multi-position buggy that
elevates your child above nasty car fumes (£499).
Every conceivable brand of eco-friendly nappy
and bottom cream is stocked.
*Buggy access. Delivery service. Disabled access.
Mail order. Nappy-changing facilities. Play area.*

Fashion

Budget

Adams

*Unit 17, Surrey Quays Centre, Redriff Road,
SE16 7LL (7252 3208/www.adams.co.uk). Surrey
Quays tube.* **Open** 9.30am-6pm Mon-Wed, Fri;
9.30am-8pm Thur; 9am-6pm Sat; 11am-5pm Sun.
Credit AmEx, MC, V.

Rely on Adams for affordable schoolwear: you can
buy packs of two easycare shirts for £8, then
there are skirts, trousers and pinafores, acrylic
jumpers, socks and tights in black, navy and grey,
anoraks and swimming bags, all at very low
prices. Budget babywear is also a boon – packs of
vests, sleepsuits, fleecy outerwear and pyjamas
are all hard-wearing and easily laundered.
Casualwear tends towards the gaudy, particularly
for girls, who get faux-fur gilets and pastel tiered
skirts. For lads, little rugby shirts and combat
trousers look less downmarket. Adams' tights for
girls tend not to bobble or stretch out of shape,
even if the colours and styles are a bit limited.
Buggy access. Disabled access. Play area.
Branches: throughout the city.

H&M

*103-111 Kensington High Street, W8 5SF (7368
3920/www.hm.com). High Street Kensington tube.*
Open 10am-7pm Mon-Wed, Fri, Sat; 10am-8pm
Thur; noon-6pm Sun. **Credit** AmEx, MC, V.

Once you've located the nearest sizing chart (bear
in mind the sizes come up big), you can have fun
selecting a basketload of fashionable gear for boys
and girls in this spacious basement store. You can
afford to be generous here, and the choice is
boggling. There are racks of sweet baby clothes,
with little T-shirts and three-button vests from
£3.99. Hats and socks cost from £1.25 – perfect for
parcelling up and sending to new arrivals. Girls
aged two to ten can find denim in all permutations,
as well as cords, vest tops, pinafores, tiered skirts
and kilts, fashion coats, gilets, cardies and anoraks.
For lads, there are combat trousers, hoodies, jeans,
jackets and puffas. Accessories are brilliant:
jewellery, bags, hair clips and bands, wallets with
chains, key rings and sweatbands.
Buggy access. Disabled access: lift. Play area.
Branches: throughout the city.

Designer

Amaia

*14 Cale Street, SW3 3QU (7590 0999). Sloane
Square or South Kensington tube.* **Open** 10am-
6pm Mon-Sat. **Credit** MC, V.

Amaia is a welcome addition to smart little Chelsea
Green. It's run by friendly Amaia and her partner
Sergolene, whose aim is to dress children to look
their age, rather than in mini versions of adult
street fashions. So there are no combats, hoodies
or fake-fur gilets for pint-sized posers, just rather
beautifully made smart casuals for babies and
children. Prices are reasonable for 100% wool coats
with velvet collars (£125), jackets and pinafores
(from £45), three-quarter length trousers, kilts,
cardigans and polonecks (£25), cords and button-
through shirts.
Buggy access. Disabled access. Mail order.

Barney's

*6 Church Road, SW19 5DL (8944 2915).
Wimbledon tube/rail then 93 bus.* **Open** 10am-
6pm Mon-Sat; noon-5pm Sun. **Credit** MC, V.

As befits jolly Wimbledon Village, Barney's is both
cute and well-to-do. For tiny babies, there are
sleepsuits and light knits from Taille-O, Petit
Bateau and IKKS. Tot 'best' dresses to make an
entrance in are by Graziella and Kenzo; more
sedate cardies and rugby shirts are by Ralph
Lauren. Older children can look perfectly cool in
vibrant wrap knitwear by excellent French label
Eliane et Lena (from £32) and, in the basement,
there are coats, skater jeans and hoodies for
teenagers from Quiksilver, O'Neill and Chipie.
Covetable gifts include Lollipop hair accessories
and jewellery, Gund soft toys and little bags.
Buggy access. Disabled access. Play area.

Bunny London

7627 2318/www.bunnylondon.com. **Phone
enquiries** 10am-6pm Mon-Fri. **Credit** MC, V.

The beautiful hand-sewn dresses that make-up artist
Debbie Bunn used to make for her god-daughter were
noticed by no less a celebrity mum than Madonna.
Pictures of little Lourdes in Bunny London created
a global interest in the girls-only label, whose
distinctive colours, patterns and textures of fabric
make the limited-edition garments must-haves. The
collection continues to expand to include delicately
embroidered pieces, coats in vintage fabrics and
pretty little blousons. Clothes are available in baby
sizes (2-18mths) and child sizes (two-12yrs). The
dresses sell from about £60. As we went to press,
Debbie Bunn had moved out of her South Bank
workshop and boutique and was looking for new
premises. Check the website for up-to-date details.
Her designs can be seen at Harvey Nichols (*see p12*)
and Paul Smith on Westbourne Grove (*see p49*).
Mail order.

Caramel Baby & Child

*291 Brompton Road, SW3 2DY (7589 7001).
South Kensington tube.* **Open** 10am-6.30pm Mon-
Sat; noon-5pm Sun. **Credit** AmEx, MC, V.

Ring the bell to enter this chicer-than-chic designer
outlet for tots whose label-led parents are prepared
to pay through the nose to trendify their offspring.
A stripey cashmere pullover by Baby Caramel
costs £95, while a dusky pink goatskin gilet is
£133. There are little Prada trainers (£90) and
summer collections comprise floaty, hip dresses
and shirts to be worn with teeny Birkenstocks.
Rompers, skirts and trousers for children up to ten,
plus miniature wellies, lambswool-lined papooses
(£220) and a finger puppet set (£40) widen the
store's appeal. The Also Caramel branch stocks
books and toys and has a hairdressing service on
Wednesdays and Saturdays (book in advance).
Buggy access. Hairdressing. Mail order.
For branch see index (Also Caramel).

Catimini

*52 South Molton Street, W1Y 1HF (7629 8099/
www.catimini.com). Bond Street tube.* **Open**
10am-6.30pm Mon-Wed, Fri, Sat; 10am-7pm Thur;
11.30am-5.30pm Sun. **Credit** AmEx, DC, MC, V.

This sophisticated, classic, sometimes kooky French
label is a cheerful provider of outfits to get babies and
children (up to ten) noticed. The everyday range is
strong on stripes, animal and floral patterns, but the
Catimini Atelier line favours more formality: dresses
and skirts for girls in white, yellow, pink and orange,
and suave linen suits for boys. No attention to detail
is spared: girls can have matching socks, tights, shoes
and dresses, light raincoats and headscarves,
adorable cotton knit cardigans, or for *l'hiver*, chunkier
toggle cardigans in vibrant and earthy colours,
tweedy skirts and dresses. Boys get puffa jackets,
sweaters and warm cords. Prices are on the high side
(expect to pay from £60 for the distinctive knitwear).
Buggy access. Disabled access. Mail order. Play area.

Diverse Kids

*46 Cross Street, N1 2BA (7226 6863/
www.diverseclothing.com). Angel tube/Highbury &
Islington tube/rail.* **Open** 10.30am-6.30pm Mon-Sat;
noon-5.30pm Sun. **Credit** AmEx, DC, MC, V.

Designer kiddie clobber in this trendier-than-thou
junior boutique is certainly diverse. If you've got
the cash, you can invest in Agatha Ruiz de la Prada
bottles and bottle warmer, but most parents come for
the clothes. Diesel jeans cost £47 for miniature
sizes – team them with a £63 Quincy jumper and
you're fit for posing down the puppet theatre.
Diverse knitted booties for new arrivals cost £15,
and cute little sandals by Birkenstock are just the
footwear for when baby's steady on their pins.
Other accessories to stock up on include bags,
underwear, hats, socks, tights and trainers.
Buggy access. Delivery service.

Frocks Away

*79-85 Fortis Green Road, N10 3HP (8444 9309).
Highgate tube then 43 or 134 bus.* **Open** 9.30am-
5.30pm Mon-Sat. **Credit** AmEx, MC, V.

Polished floorboards and old-fashioned shop
fittings set the shabby-chic tone in this
independent store. For children up to age 12 there
are flowery tights in wooden hosiery drawers;
church pews are used to seat fidgets while their
feet are measured; and little wooden stands display
adorable headgear. There's a good range of clothes
for women and children, including Petit Bateau,
Ali Bali, Contrevents et Marres and Balu, plus
shoes from Start-rite, Geox, Primigi and Diesel.
Buggy access. Disabled access. Play area.

Jakes

*79 Berwick Street, W1F 8TL (7734 0812/www.
jakesofsoho.com). Tottenham Court Road tube.*
Open 11am-7pm Mon-Sat. **Credit** AmEx, MC, V.

Buy your child a hand-printed T-shirt and help
make a little lad's prospects brighter. Jake is a little
boy with cerebral palsy and a percentage of the
profits made on the clothing range for adults and
children up to age eight go towards his future. The
T-shirts, with the well-known 'Elvis Loves You',
'Lucky Seven' and 'Weapon Of Mass Destruction'
logos are satisfyingly popular, not least in the
celebrity world, and cost £15. Other items for
children include Aran jumpers, sweatshirts,
combat trousers and baseball caps.
Buggy access. Disabled access. Mail order.

Jakss

*463 & 469 Roman Road, E3 5LX (8981 9454/
www.jakss.co.uk). Bethnal Green tube then 8 bus.*
Open 10am-5.30pm Tue-Sat. **Credit** AmEx, DC,
MC, V.
Eat your heart out, Knightsbridge: the Roman
Road has all the labels a toddler never knew he
wanted. Infants as young as three months can be
little fashion victims in pinky purple Burberry
checks (£48 for a skirt, £55 for a little pinafore).
Otherwise, there's a cartload of Oilily, Fornarina,
Timberland, DKNY and D&G. It all continues at
No.469, where there's a full range of Burberry
outerwear for older kids, including black quilted
jackets with the all-important lining (£126). The
Miss Sixty line for girls is bold and eye-catching.
Buggy access. Delivery service. Mail order.

Membery's

*1 Church Road, SW13 9HE (8876 2910). Barnes
Bridge rail.* **Open** 10am-5pm Mon-Sat. **Credit**
AmEx, MC, V.
Idyllically positioned in an old building just
opposite Barnes Pond, Membery's offers the kind
of special occasion wear that warms granny's
cockles. You can bribe small boys into gorgeous
blue or white linen button-on short suits with
double-breasted shirts (from £39). Wee girls look
demure in crisp yellow cotton dresses (from £34).
Christening robes are also sold. Made-to-measure
bridesmaids' dresses are available for all ages.
Christening gifts, such as personalised framed
pictures, are another speciality. Membery's lovely
own label shares space with more relaxed but
pricier casualwear from Catimini, Marèse, IKKS
and Petit Bateau, as well as a selection of baby
toys and accessories.
*Buggy access. Delivery service. Mail order. Play
area.*

Notsobig

*31A Highgate High Street, N6 5JT (8340 4455).
Archway or Highgate tube.* **Open** 9.30am-6pm
Mon-Fri; 10am-6pm Sat; 11am-5pm Sun. **Credit**
MC, V.
The harder you look in this tiny shop, the more
delights you see. Tiny outfits by Quincy, Cacharel,
Braez, Essential Girls, Maharishi, No Angel and
Agatha Ruiz de la Prada hang on the walls; there
is Wright & Teague silver and gold jewellery for
babies, many items with precious stones; and Little
Chums T-shirts sit in organza bags alongside
hand-crocheted monkeys. Halfway down the
winding stairs are tea sets and assorted knick-
knacks, and at the bottom, haphazardly arranged
fancy-dress costumes by Bandicoot Lapin (there
aren't always loads in the shop, but staff can show
you the catalogue, so that you can order the one
you want before the big event; from £60).
*Buggy access. Delivery service. Mail order.
Play area.*

Oilily

*9 Sloane Street, SW1X 9LE (7823
2505/www.oilily-world.com). Knightsbridge tube.*
Open 10am-6pm Mon, Tue, Thur-Sat; 10am-7pm
Wed. **Credit** AmEx, MC, V.
There are Oilily collections in many children's
boutiques, but this is the only London store
dedicated to the Dutch label. Here are clothes to lift
your spirits: exuberant gatherings of orange,
green, pink and blue in inspirational designs on
flounced dresses and skirts; embroidered jeans;
prettily detailed bags, sandals, hats and
accessories. The boys' stuff doesn't shy away from
the prints but hardens up the colours a bit. Expect
to pay about £70 for a girl's dress, with separates
from about £25. Babywear is similarly bold; check
out the sweet little towelling stretch trousers.
Buggy access. Mail order. Play area.

Patrizia Wigan

*19 Walton Street, SW3 2HX (7823
7080/www.patriziawigan.com). Knightsbridge or
South Kensington tube.* **Open** 10.30am-6.30pm
Mon-Fri; 10.30am-6pm Sat. **Credit** AmEx, MC, V.
'Quintessentially English', the PW brand name has
long been favoured by royals and celebrities
(various princesses have been photographed in the

Notsobig

distinctive smocked dresses over the years). The beautifully made, classic styles for children aged up to eight are designed to last beyond fashion fads, which makes the £89 hand-smocked dresses for tiny girls seem reasonably good value; likewise the stunning christening gowns from £195. There are also pressed linen shorts for boys, kilts, velvet dresses for winter parties, and pageboy and bridesmaid outfits made to order. Gifts, baby accessories and furnishings are also sold.
Buggy access. Delivery service. Play area.

Rachel Riley

82 Marylebone High Street, W1U 4QW (7935 7007/www.rachelriley.com). Baker Street or Bond Street tube. **Open** 10am-6pm Mon-Sat. **Credit** AmEx, MC, V.
Riley's unmistakable 1950s retro look is produced from an attic in the Loire Valley, and all the clothes for babies, boys and girls have a rare beauty. Few could resist a smocked floral dress (£79 for baby girls) or the Bishop Neck dress with matching bloomers (£59). Toddler boys look adorable in check H-strap trousers (£49) or a sailor set (£75). It's all built to last, with mother-of-pearl buttons and hand-embroidery. Separates and nightwear are lovely and there are some groovy little character shoes to complete the look. Teenage girls aren't forgotten – they get their hoodies, pea coats and frill skirts in pale blues and heathers.
Buggy access. Delivery service. Mail order.
For branch see index.

Ralph Lauren

143 New Bond Street, W1S 4ES (7535 4600/ www.polo.com). Bond Street tube. **Open** 10am-6pm Mon-Wed, Fri, Sat; 10am-7pm Thur; noon-5pm Sun. **Credit** AmEx, DC, MC, V.
It might look a sight too patrician for some parents' tastes, but the trademark preppy look translates quite distinctively into miniature form. Some items, such as £185 hacking jackets for two-year-olds and £8 bibs for people with more money than sense, induce snorts of derision, but we admired the pretty, bright plaid kilts for little girls (£48); the thick, warm rugby shirts in a rainbow of colours; and the bold lambswool jumpers, pullovers and brightly striped cardigans. The shop is like a film set – all rich wood panelling and gorgeous antique toys with images of idyllic East Coast childhood.
Buggy access. Delivery service. Mail order. Nappy-changing facilities.

Sasti

8 Portobello Green Arcade, 281 Portobello Road, W10 5TZ (8960 1125/www.sasti.co.uk). Ladbroke Grove tube. **Open** 10am-6pm Mon-Sat. **Credit** AmEx, MC, V.
Set up in 1995 by Julie Brown, Sasti is very much the affordable end of individual, British-made, designer clothes for children. Little girls love the frill and flounce skirts in unusual fabrics and prints (strawberries were a big hit last spring). Babies from six months look sweet in the bright-red fleece dinosaur suit (£28) and the Pow! or Zap! tops (£20). Whatever the season, the stock is colourful and pretty unusual. Staff here are young and cool, and endear themselves to the children.
Buggy access. Mail order. Nappy-changing facilities. Play area.

Semmalina

225 Ebury Street, SW1W 8UT (7730 9333). Sloane Square tube. **Open** 9.30am-5.30pm Mon-Sat. **Credit** AmEx, MC, V.
A large fibreglass tree with fairy lights greets you as you step through the door, and a little bridge takes you from the front section (all party-bag toys and trinkets) to the clothes and dressing-up costumes at the back. It's not cheap, but there's no denying the clothes are terribly sweet; we adored the little knits with crystal buttons by the Wool Shed (from £40), the silky sequinned kaftans for little girls and the little logoed T-shirts. Clothes are by the Danish company Miniature, as well as Bob & Blossom and a variety of other designers. Among the toys are vintage items from the 1950s, usually made of tin (a play hospital costs £125, so would be of more interest to nostalgic adults than

children). Semmalina has a party-bag service for parents too busy to concoct their own and, in the basement, there's the Papillon shoe shop.
Buggy access. Delivery service. Nappy-changing facilities. Play area.

Tartine et Chocolat

66 South Molton Street, W1K 5SX (7629 7233). Bond Street tube. **Open** 10am-6pm Mon-Sat. **Credit** AmEx, MC, V.
Blissfully French and posh, the luxury T&C brand dates back to 1977; now there's a whole range of products for babies and under-11s, including clothes, soft toys and gifts. The pink and blue is tempered by snowy-white sleepsuits, little dresses or baby shoes (for under-ones). Prices might make you choke on your tartine: soft and velvety Babygros start at about £40; classic casuals (linen shorts, dresses, wool coats) cost much more.
Delivery service. Mail order.

Their Nibs

214 Kensington Park Road, W11 1NR (7221 4263/www.theirnibs.com). Ladbroke Grove or Notting Hill Gate tube. **Open** 9.30am-6pm Mon-Fri; 10am-6pm Sat; noon-5pm Sun. **Credit** AmEx, MC, V.
A large play area at the back, with blackboard and chalks, books and toys, makes visiting this shop with under-fives a treat. While the subjects play, their minders can rifle through the racks, selecting floaty dresses, fairy dresses, party dresses and baby dresses (£20-£35), cashmere baby cardigans (from £40), and embroidered combats and long-sleeved T-shirts. A sale rail may yield some terrific

bargains, such as handmade gauzy fairy skirts for a tenner. The selection of vintage clothes – ponchos in salmon acrylic, crimplene baby dungarees in sludge brown and psychedelic zip-up polyester tops – starts at about £10. There are wooden baby toys with bells on by Heimess, Nurtured by Nature baby clothes (lovely fine knits) and very distinctive hair accessories. In the hairdressing area, cuts cost from about £7; ring for an appointment.
Buggy access. Disabled access: ramps. Hairdressing. Mail order. Play area.

Tiddlywinks

414 Roman Road, E3 5LU (8981 7000). Bethnal Green tube then 8 bus. **Open** 9.30am-5.30pm Mon-Sat. **Credit** AmEx, MC, V.
Heavyweight designers in miniature mode are represented in this packed little shop, with clothes by Baby Dior, Marèse, Coco, DKNY, Kenzo, Moschino Sulk, Miss Grant and Confetti; there are little trimmed cardigans, all-in-one sleepsuits, pretty dresses and dinky dungas. Fancy little shoes and boots come courtesy of Eli and for boys there are suits, jeans by Diesel and quilted jackets.
Buggy access. Mail order.

Tots

39 Turnham Green Terrace, W4 1RG (8995 0520/www.totschiswick.com). Turnham Green tube. **Open** 10am-6pm Mon-Sat; noon-5pm Sun. **Credit** AmEx, MC, V.
This rather select boutique for babies and children up to about 12 tricks out modish mites in Miniman, Absorba, Berlingot and Catimini, with little leather and fake-fur booties by Robeez to complete the look.

One Small Step One Giant Leap. See p263.

There are sweatshirts, hoodies, shorts and anoraks by Quiksilver, Timberland and O'Neill, while girlie girls can get sticky-out net skirts from Kenzo and zingy designs from Oilily. Brightly patterned and striped tights for girls of all ages are by Kenzo and Country Kids and cost £6-£10.95.
Buggy access. Delivery service. Disabled access. Play area.

Trendys

72 Chapel Market, N1 9ER (7837 9070). Angel tube. **Open** 10am-6pm Mon-Sat; 10am-4pm Sun. **Credit** AmEx, MC, V.
Chapel Market may be a remnant of the 'old Islington' of bargain outlets, but Trendys is very firmly established in the 21st-century world of aspirational and costly fashionwear for tinies. So there's Pringle and Burberry babywear among the more traditional Absorba, Cacharel and Jean de la Lune, Diesel jeans for wee girls, plus Kickers and D&G footwear. The clothes go up to age 14 or so, and regular sales mean that you can pick up some bargains if you're prepared to visit often.
Buggy access. Disabled access. Play area.

Environmentally friendly

If you're thinking of a washable nappy system, the staff at **Green Baby** (*see below*) can offer advice. Go for a shaped nappy that pops into place to avoid wrestling with terry towelling and giant nappy pins. Washable nappies are kinder to your coffers, too. An initial outlay of about £400 sets you up for one or two kids,

saving you over a grand in the long run compared with disposables. **Bambino Mio** (01604 883 777, www.bambinomio.com), the **Ellie Nappie Company** (0151 200 5012, www.elliepants.co.uk) and **Little Green Earthlets** (01435 811 555, www.earthlets.co.uk) also sell real nappies and environmentally friendly cleaning products. Organic cotton babywear and fairly traded cotton casuals for children aged up to ten can be ordered from **People Tree** (7739 0660, www.peopletree.co.uk).

Born

Stoke Newington Church Street, N16 0JL (0845 130 2676/www.borndirect.com). Finsbury Park tube/rail then 106 bus/73, 393, 476 bus. **Open** 9.30am-5.30pm Tue-Sat; noon-5pm Sun. **Credit** AmEx, MC, V .
Born shops specialise in natural, organic, fair trade and practical products, and its staff are trained to dispense sensible advice. Thus, you'll get the lowdown on how your expensive Bugaboo or Stokke pushchairs, prams, Tripp Trapp high chairs and cots work. There's also plenty of opportunity to try on a wide range of baby slings. There are also natural lambskins, cotton sleeping bags, wool baby blankets and natural organic baby bath products and unguents. Breastfeeding mummies with suffering nipples can buy Lansinoh, the purest, safest lanolin ointment for protection. What's more, cotton nappies are a big part of the Born philosophy, so new parents are invited to make an

appointment for a nappy demo at the shop. There are books on all aspects of birth, childcare and healthcare, plus some children's fiction. Toys are by Heimess and other companies that employ only renewable materials in their production.
Buggy access. Disabled access. Mail order. Nappy-changing facilities.

Green Baby

345 Upper Street, N1 0PD (7359 7037/www. greenbaby.co.uk). Angel tube. **Open** 10am-5pm Mon-Fri; 10am-6pm Sat; 11am-4pm Sun. **Credit** MC, V.
If you're about to pop or you've just dropped, make this your first port of call. It has clothing basics for newborns, sheets made from 100% organic cotton, nappy balms and baby lotions based on pure lanolin, sweet almond oil and cocoa butter, and nursery furniture made of beech from sustainable forests. Green Baby clothing is made in South India, as part of a community project that supports the education and employment of young girls.
Buggy access. Delivery service. Mail order (0870 240 6894).
For branch see index.

The Natural Mat Company

99 Talbot Road, W11 2AT (7985 0474/ www.naturalmat.com). Ladbroke Grove, Notting Hill Gate or Westbourne Park tube. **Open** 9am-6pm Mon-Fri; 10am-4pm Sat. **Credit** MC, V.
Infants may safely snooze in the natural organic cotton and wool sheets, blankets, sleeping bags and fleeces sold here. handmade cot mattresses – tufted in wool or mohair on coconut fibre, natural latex or even Chinese horsetail hair cores and wrapped in unbleached cotton – are unique to the company and cost from £65, while the giant machine-washable American fleeces (£68) make fabulous playmats for the nursery. Cots and nursery furniture and pure-cotton baby clothes are also sold.
Buggy access. Delivery service. Disabled access. Mail order. Nappy-changing facilities. Play area.

Mid-range & high street

O'Neill and **Quiksilver** (for both, *see p54*) have skater jeans, sweats, T-shirts, caps and beanies – perfect for school hols. Spanish high-street giant **Zara** (*see p45*) is great for kids.

Biff

41-43 Dulwich Village, SE21 7BN (8299 0911). North Dulwich rail/P4 bus. **Open** 9.30am-5.30pm Mon-Fri; 10am-6pm Sat. **Credit** MC, V.
Dulwich Village's own little children's empire now takes up two shopfronts, which are joined at the back by a Start-rite shoe area. In the baby side of the shop there are little striped togs by Week-end à la Mer, teddy-like fleeces by Seesaw (£32) and Petit Bateau essentials alongside IKKS, Jean Bourget, Berlingot and Catimini rompers, Babygros, vests and cardies, as well as Grobags. For older children up to 16 there's a big Quiksilver and O'Neill presence, as well as shirts by Ben Sherman and shoes by Skechers and Hush Puppies. Accessories include bags, belts and wallets, and plenty of those gorgeous MP tights for little girls. Service is friendly.
Buggy access. Mail order. Nappy-changing facilities. Play area.

Gap Kids

122 King's Road, SW3 4TR (7823 7272/www. gap.com). Sloane Square tube. **Open** 10am-7pm Mon-Wed, Fri, Sat; 10am-8pm Thur; noon-6pm Sun. **Credit** AmEx, MC, V.
Even if you don't want your child to walk around in a fleece hoody that shrieks GAP, the clothes for babies to teens in this ubiquitous chain always score a hit. There are jeans to suit all tastes, from slim-cut bootlegs for the girl to spacious denims for lads who like to have their boxers on display above their trousers. Tiny striped jumpers and summer T-shirts look good on toddlers, anoraks are eminently wearable, and the accessories – including belts, tights, socks, hats and bags – are distinctive.
Buggy access. Delivery service. Disabled access. Nappy-changing facilities.
Branches: throughout the city.

Iana

*186 King's Road, SW3 5XP (7352 0060/
www.iana.it). Sloane Square tube.* **Open** 9am-
6pm Mon, Tue, Thur, Fri; 9am-7pm Wed; 10am-
6.30pm Sat; 11am-6pm Sun. **Credit** AmEx,
DC, MC, V.
Jolly, practical Italian outfits for children up to age
14 include some bargains, such as serviceable
Husky-style quilted jackets from £16 – a bestseller
for the autumn. Other bargains include pretty
white baby vests with crotch poppers (£6 for two)
and light, bright long-sleeved T-shirts from £11.50.
Iana also stocks the distinctive oatmeal-and-rust
uniform for nearby Hill House prep school.
Buggy access. Delivery service. Mail order.
For branch see index.

Igloo

*300 Upper Street, N1 2TU (7354 7300/
www.iglookids.co.uk). Angel tube/Highbury
& Islington tube/rail.* **Open** 10am-6.30pm Mon-
Wed; 9.30am-7pm Thur-Sat. **Credit** MC, V.
This smashing fashion and toy stop for babies and
children under eight holds some unexpected
treasures in both clothing and toy departments. To
wear, there are classics by Petit Bateau, Triple Star
and cheeky shirts by Bob & Blossom, plus
separates by Miniature and macs, souwesters and
gumboots in pastel-pink and powder-blue florals
by Blue Fish. At the back of the shop a Start-rite
shoe shop is ready with the fitting gear and a range
of dear little shoes. In the front are all the toys –
by Lamaze, Galt, Brio and other big hitters, as well
as comic cuddlies from Zooflies. Quirky items, such
as little frying pans that cook your egg into a heart
shape, seem irresistible. Children can also get their
hair cut here (fringe trim £5).
*Buggy access. Delivery service. Disabled access.
Hairdressing. Mail order. Nappy-changing
facilities. Play area.*

Jigsaw Junior

*190-192 Westbourne Grove, W11 2RH (7727
0322/www.jigsaw-online.com). Notting Hill Gate
tube.* **Open** 10.30am-6.30pm Mon; 10am-6.30pm
Tue, Wed, Sat; 10am-7pm Thur, Fri; noon-6pm
Sun. **Credit** AmEx, MC, V.
Children can take a silver slide instead of the stairs
down into the basement level of this beautiful
shop, where all the Jigsaw Junior stuff is. The look
is richly textured but relaxed, which is echoed in
the antique shop fittings. It's still a bit gypsy for
autumn/winter 2005/6, with velvet tiered skirts in
warm colours, pretty long-sleeved T-shirts and
striped jumpers, velvet trimmed cardigans and
sumptuous floppy dresses.
Buggy access. Mail order. Play area.
For branches see index.

JoJo Maman Bébé

*68 Northcote Road, SW11 6QL (7228 0322/
www.jojomamanbebe.co.uk). Clapham Junction
rail.* **Open** 9.30am-5.30pm Mon-Sat; 11am-5pm
Sun. **Credit** MC, V.
This reasonably big branch of the increasingly
popular JoJo brand, but it always seems to be
crammed with double buggies and flutey-voiced
Claphamites. We know why they come: the clothes
for babies, toddlers and infants are a happy
combination of classic (80% wool duffle coats,
£40), essential (two-pack animal-print sleepsuits,
£16) and very pretty (cord flared skirts with velvet
trim, £14). There are lots of brightly striped fleeces
and sweatshirts, plus easy-wash cottons for
comfort. There's also maternity wear, nursery
essentials, all manner of baby furniture, cribs and
cots – available either in store or via the catalogue.
*Buggy access. Delivery service. Disabled access.
Mail order. Nappy-changing facilities.*
For branches see index.

Monsoon Childrenswear

*Unit 25, The Market, WC2H 8AH (7497 9325/
www.monsoon.co.uk). Covent Garden tube.* **Open**
10am-8pm Mon-Sat; 11am-6pm Sun. **Credit**
AmEx, MC, V.
The clothes at this dedicated kids' branch are
extremely pretty for the girls, who look sweet in
tiered skirts with ribbon detail from £30 and 'baby
kitty' ribbon bow cardigans (£24). We're not so
sure about the lurid fake-fur gilets, though. The
baby range (two months and upwards) includes
delicate little dresses (about £26) and cardigans in
beautiful shades. Cords and jeans for older lads are
well priced at £24.
Buggy access. Disabled access. Mail order.
Branches: throughout the city.

Petit Bateau

*106-108 King's Road, SW3 4TZ (7838 0818/
www.petit-bateau.com). Sloane Square tube.* **Open**
10am-6.30pm Mon, Tue, Fri, Sat; 10am-7pm Wed,
Thur; noon-6pm Sun. **Credit** AmEx, MC, V.
The nautical look (sailor stripes in softest cotton,
three-button necklines and jerseys with whales on
them) is as popular as ever in this classic French
chain. This is the largest London branch, with a
drawing table for tots and a full range of baby,
children's and women's wear. We adore the striped
vests (£12), but then stripes are everywhere, from
the gorgeous pastel velour Babygros (£22-£45) to
the cotton sundresses (£30). There are T-shirts for
boys and girls, and boys also get soft denims, logo
T-shirts and padded jackets while girls get
flannelette tops to wear with Prince of Wales pants.
Buggy access. Mail order. Play area.
For branches see index.

Popcorn

*121 Stoke Newington Church Street, N16 0UH,
(7241 1333). Finsbury Park tube/rail then 106
bus/73, 476 bus.* **Open** 10am-6pm Tue-Sat; 11am-
5pm Sun. **Credit** MC, V.
This crowded little addition to a fashionable street
that gets more family-friendly by the month has
clothes for children aged up to six, with the
emphasis on babies and toddlers. There are quirky
tie tops and pants by Duckie Beau, slogan T-shirts
by Toby Tiger and other distinctive fashions from
French Connection for Kids, Eat Your Greens, Ollie,
Uttan and Brightbots. There's a shoe department
with fitting service, and a whole load of baby
accessories, such as Kari Me slings, first shoes in a
gift box, Hippy Chick hip seats and a range of baby
toys that make perfect gifts for new babies.
Buggy access. Disabled access. Play area.

Quackers

*155D Northcote Road, SW11 6QB (7978 4235).
Clapham Junction rail then 319 bus.* **Open**
9.30am-5.30pm Mon-Fri; 10am-5.30pm Sat.
Credit MC, V.
Proprietor Veronica McNaught presides over the
wide range of clothes for children aged up to ten.
Labels for smart babies include the German brand
Kanz, as well as Petit Bateau. There's a good deal of
affordable, individual pieces by Whoopi (vintage-
looking floral pinafore for girls, £24.99), including
cosy coats and cardies for winterwear. Alongside
No Added Sugar T-shirts, there are statement
makers by Toby Tiger, and must-haves for toddlers
include excellent, pretty rainwear by Blue Fish and
Kidorable gumboots that masquerade as ladybirds
or frogs (£13.95).
Buggy access. Play area.

Ideal homes

Children love playing house. It's all
so much more fun when the residents
are well-intentioned Playmobil figures or
Sylvanian Families and there's no nasty
business with rents and mortgages.
Most toyshops sell desirable
residences in miniature, and **Kristin
Baybars**'s shop (*see p266*) is the best
place in London to begin a lifelong
doll's house mania. Ms Baybars's
kingdom is a miniature collector's
paradise, where kits of many varieties
are sold, and where the tiny household
essentials are impressive in their detail.
For basics, however, check out **Soup
Dragon** (*see p266*), a quirky and
traditional toyshop selling pretty
Victorian doll's houses for about £70.

For furnishings, most toy outlets
have a selection, and there are
countless websites where you can
find miniature doll's house accessories
from candlesticks to baby's high chairs
(try www.gillianrichards.co.uk or
www.woodlane.uk.com, where you'll
also find a variety of flat-packed houses
from around £50). For pocket-money
prices, though, the tiny **Never Never
Land** (*see p266*) has a great range of
doll's house kits (from £85), as well
as all the bits and pieces that make
them individual.

If your children prefer the idea of
a playhouse they canu actually enter,
a Wendy house (named after the bossy
little girl in *Peter Pan*, of course) might
be rather more difficult to get home on
the bus. Or there's always a play tent
(the **Early Learning Centre** does them
for around £25; *see p264*). Similarly
affordable options can be found at
Argos (*see p118*), which has a decent
range of playhouses and tents from

a Winnie the Pooh 'pop 'n' fun' version
(£24.99) to a Little Tykes number with
four activity walls (including a grocery
store with ATM machine), made in
durable plastic for £250. If you simply
don't have the space, **Kinderhouse**
(02476 364 414, www.kinderhouse.
co.uk), an online packaging company,
has a flat-packed version that can be
folded away under the bed after use.
It comes in plain white and is designed
to be personalised with paints, pens,
stickers or crayons (£16.99, incl
postage and delivery).

For something a bit fancier, the
Children's Cottage Company (www.play-
houses.com) and **Wood Wizards**
(www.woodwizards.co.uk) are two online
companies that create incredibly
detailed bespoke wooden playhouses.
In the latter case, you can opt for
a pirate's den (complete with treasure
chest and telescope) or a fully furnished
windmill cottage that could potentially
become your child's second home.

Tree houses tend to be a luxury
for those with a big garden and, equally
important, a large tree in it. If you
are one of the fortunate few, it may
be worth looking at **Blue Forest**
(www.blueforest.com), which builds
a range of contemporary tree houses
and 'eco-lodges' costing from £10,000
upwards. What's more, for each
structure sold, the company will
support a Kenyan child through school
for one year (www.assets-kenya.org).
That's commendable, but it could
be argued that a greener way to make
a play home for your child would be
to palm them off with an old washing-
machine box with window- and door-
holes cut into it. Just an idea.

Tomboy Kids

*176 Northcote Road, SW11 1RE (7223 8030/
www.tomboykids.com). Clapham Junction rail.*
Open 10am-5.30pm Mon-Fri; 10am-6pm Sat.
Credit MC, V.
Down the quiet end of Northcote Road, this
spacious shop has fashionable gear for children
and young people of all ages. Nothing is too twee,
although the Fair Isle Choo Choo knits for babies
are cuddly. For older children there's outerwear by
French Connection and Quiksilver, and labels like
IKKS cater for all ages. We love the vibrantly
striped vests and underwear by Molo. During the
summer there's a wide range of cool swimwear and
flip-flops by Reef, and in winter there are plenty of
hoodies and warm jackets from Timberland.
Buggy access. Mail order. Play area.

Trotters

*34 King's Road, SW3 4UD (7259 9620/
www.trotters.co.uk). Sloane Square tube.* **Open**
9am-7pm Mon-Sat; 10.30am-6.30pm Sun. **Credit**
AmEx, MC, V.
A clothes and toy shop that caters for various
peripheral needs. Children can have their hair cut
(£11.50 age three and under; £12.50 older children)
while watching the fish in the massive aquarium.
Those needing new shoes can bounce around in
the Start-rite shoe zone. We like the clothes by
Chelsea Clothing Company for babies and children,
soft little trousers for babies from £14.99, nice
pyjamas and cosy dressing gowns. Other labels
include RiverWoods and Bob & Blossom, while
posh tweedy coats in infant sizes cost from £75.
Toys include favourites from Jellicat and Lollipop
accessories, and there's a small book section.
*Buggy access. Delivery service. Hairdressing.
Nappy-changing facilities. Play area.*
For branch see index.

Second-hand

Boomerang

*69 Blythe Road, W14 0HP (7610 5232). Olympia
tube.* **Open** 10am-6pm Tue-Sat. **Credit** AmEx,
DC, MC, V.
Crammed with babies' and children's clothes and
toys, Boomerang is the sort of place you keep
coming back to. There's a good selection of
Babygros, kids' separates and shoes, and loads of
generally useful baby paraphernalia. You can also
offload your children's hand-me-downs.
Buggy access. Nappy-changing facilities.

Chocolate Crocodile

*39 Morpeth Road, E9 7LV (8985 3330). Bethnal
Green or Mile End tube/277, 388 bus.* **Open**
11am-5pm Mon-Wed, Fri Sat. **Credit** MC, V.
Plumb in the middle of one of Hackney's posh bits
(the Victoria Park area), this small recycling centre
is never short of previously owned, hardly used
baby equipment, toys and clothes – many of which
have a very good pedigree. When we visited there
were new travel cots for £25, a used Leap Pad for
£20, various barely used pushchairs, baby carriers
and slings, and a whole range of well-preserved
children's clothes with labels as diverse as
Monsoon and Adams, all at very reasonable prices.
Turnover is high and space is short.
Buggy access. Play area.

Little Trading Company

*7 Bedford Corner, The Avenue, W4 1LD (8742
3152). Turnham Green tube.* **Open** 9am-5pm
Mon-Fri; 9am-4.30pm Sat. **No credit cards.**
A mark of this area's smartness is the fact that, on
our last visit, alongside the double and single
buggies and high chairs lined up outside the shop,
was a well-preserved navy-blue carriage pram of
the type that sells for £850 new; LTC was offering
it for £350. Items are sold on a profit-share or sale-
or-return basis and include unwanted sports kit,
all sorts of baby accessories and equipment,
including high chairs and car seats, clothes for all
ages and books, toys, DVDs and videos. Children
come in for a haircut on Wednesday and Friday
afternoons, and Saturday mornings (call for an
appointment). New products are also sold.
Buggy access. Hairdressing. Play area.

Merry-Go-Round

*12 Clarence Road, E5 8HB (8985 6308). Hackney
Central rail.* **Open** 10am-5.30pm Mon-Sat; 11am-
5pm Sun. **Credit** AmEx, MC, V.
It may look like a charity shop from the outside, but
once you've stepped inside you realise it's every
green parent's dream (and there are an awful lot of
them living round here). As well as what look like
new and barely used car seats hanging from the
ceiling, there are pushchairs and high chairs, toddler
toys, babywalkers and nursery equipment such as
bottle sterilisers and baby baths all on the ground
floor. Downstairs are clothes and other items for
children aged from two to teenage. Previously
owned clothes are more likely to be Gap than Gucci.
Buggy access. Nappy-changing facilities. Play area.

Pixies

*14 Fauconberg Road, W4 3JY (8995 1568/
www.pixiesonline.co.uk). Chiswick Park or
Turnham Green tube.* **Open** 10am-4.30pm Tue-
Fri; 10am-3pm Sat. During school hols, closed
Tue. **Credit** AmEx, MC, V.
Pixies can furnish you with quality items such as
Stokke high chairs (if you're lucky), various brands
of car seat and pushchair, buggy boards (these are
also sold new), and, for summer, UV bodysuits and
swim shoes. The quality clothing is sensibly
arranged into school uniforms for children aged
from five, then there are racks of babywear, and
items for older children clearly labelled with age
and price. The company also offers panicky new
parents the Babytalk consultation service (£40 per
hour), offering advice on equipment and clothing.
Many new products are also available.
*Buggy access. Delivery service. Disabled access.
Mail order.*

Shoes

Brian's Shoes

*2 Halleswelle Parade, NW11 0DL (8455 7001/
www.briansshoes.com). Finchley Central or
Golders Green tube.* **Open** 9.15am-5.30pm Mon-
Sat; 10.30am-1.30pm Sun. **Credit** MC, V.
This 35-year-old children's shoe shop is conveniently
close to the Bookworm bookshop (see p256) and
offers Start-rite, Ricosta, Skechers, Babybotte, Nike
and Kickers, as well as a range of fancier Italian
designer shoes, in a helpful, calm atmosphere.
Buggy access. Disabled access.

Instep

*45 St John's Wood High Street, NW8 7NJ (7722
7634/www.instepshoes.co.uk). St John's Wood tube.*
Open 9.30am-5.30pm Mon-Sat; 11am-5pm Sun.
Credit AmEx, MC, V.
A one-stop store for children's footwear, offering a
massive range of shoes, sandals, boots and
trainers, as well as all the 'extras' such as football
boots, ballet shoes, plimsolls and gumboots. The
mature, helpful staff are all thoroughly trained
shoe-fitters . Expect to pay around £30 for expertly
fitted baby shoes, £40 for school shoes and from
£50 for the likes of DKNY, D&G, Babybotte,
Mod8, Birkenstock and Ricosta.
Buggy access. Disabled access.
For branches see index.

One Small Step One Giant Leap

*3 Blenheim Crescent, W11 2EE (7243 0535/
www.onesmallsteponegiantleap.com). Ladbroke
Grove or Notting Hill Gate tube.* **Open** 9.30am-
6pm Mon-Sat; 11am-5pm Sun. **Credit** MC, V.
This growing chain of award-winning specialist
children's shoe shops continues to make giant leaps
into parents' good books. Everything is beautifully
set out, and the range of brands, both fashionable
and reliable, is quite astonishing. Babies can have
chubby feet encased in Starchild soft leather
protectors in a wide range of designs, then there
are Start-rites, Skechers, Asters from France,
swanky Roberto Cavalli and Pinco Pallino from
Italy, Puma, Diesel, Birkenstocks, sturdy Geox and
Kickers and many, many more. Prices go from £15
for baby shoes to £34 for sensible Start-rites, and
a bit more for the posh continentals.
Buggy access. Mail order.
For branches see index.

Shoe Station

*3 Station Approach, Kew, Surrey TW9 3QB
(8940 9905/www.theshoestation.co.uk). Kew
Gardens tube.* **Open** 10am-6pm Mon-Sat.
Credit MC, V.
Run by two women who know a thing or two about
small feet – with seven children between them –
this little shop near the station has children's shoes
for every occasion (including football, ballet and
mud) in sizes 18 to 40. Brands include Start-rite,
Ricosta, Aster, Naturino, Babybotte, Giesswein,
Mod8, TTY, Pom d'Api, GEOX, Kenzo, Nike,
Puma, Birkenstock, Primigi, Freed and Daisy
Roots. Staff are trained Start-rite fitters.
Buggy access. Play area.

Stepping Out

*106 Pitshanger Lane, W5 1QX (8810 6141).
Ealing Broadway tube.* **Open** 10am-5.30pm
Mon-Fri; 9am-5.30pm Sat. **Credit** MC, V.
A Start-rite agent first and foremost, Stepping Out
stocks plenty of Ricosta, Mod8 and Kenzo as well.
Experienced assistants specialise in advising on
shoes for children with mobility problems, with
local GPs often referring kids here; lots of styles
provide extra support, but manage to be
fashionable too (Le Loup Blanc, for example, is
perfect for kids with weak ankles). At the back is
a play area with toys and games.
Buggy access. Play area.

Sportswear

Most parents' idea of hell would be to slog down
Oxford Street's sports emporia looking for
child-sized trainers and sports kit. We'd advise
against it and would instead direct you to
pleasant, local sports specialists such as **Ace
Sport & Leisure** (341 Kentish Town Road,
NW5 2TJ, 7485 5367), where there are walls of
footwear for all sports, as well as junior
racquets, footballs, bats and swimming
equipment. Otherwise, the biggest choice for
popular sports would still be **Lillywhites** (*see
p224*), though children's equipment doesn't
seem to be high on the list of priorities in this
West End department store. **Decathlon** (*see
p224*), down at Surrey Quays, does cover
equestrianism. Little footballers can invest in
replica strips at **Soccerscene** (*see p225*); little
fish can find diving, swimming and surfing gear
at **Ocean Leisure** (*see p227*), and tennis
players inspired by youthful Andy Murray can
get junior-sized racquets and a wall to test them
on at **Wigmore Sports** (*see p226*).

Toyshops

Bikes

Chamberlaine & Son

*75-77 Kentish Town Road, NW1 8NY (7485
4488). Camden Town tube.* **Open** 8.30am-6pm
Mon-Sat. **Credit** AmEx, MC, V.
Hundreds of bikes are suspended from the ceiling
and walls at this great shop, including Raleigh
Choppers (£200), which are causing many a parent
to get misty-eyed these days. There are also reclinable
Hamax baby seats (£62.99), Phillips trailer buggies
(from £120) and tag-alongs (£120-£160) for children
who are old enough to pedal behind a parent. A new
child's bike costs about £100; the first service is free.
*Buggy access. Delivery service. Disabled access.
Mail order.*

Edwardes

*221-225 Camberwell Road, SE5 0HG (7703
3676/5720). Elephant & Castle tube/rail then P3,
12, 68, 176 bus.* **Open** 8.30am-6pm Mon-Sat.
Credit AmEx, MC, V.
Bikes for children aged two to 12, including Pro
Bike, Bronx and Giant ranges, are supplemented by
useful accessories such as bike seats, jolly helmets,
trailers and tag-alongs to adult bikes (from £89).
*Buggy access. Delivery service. Disabled access.
Mail order.*

Hills

58 Fortis Green Road, N10 3HN (8883 4644).
Highgate tube then 43, 134 bus. **Open** 9am-
5.30pm Mon-Fri; 9am-5pm Sat. **Credit** MC, V.
Little girls' bikes with gears, streamers and flower
stickers cost £110 (there's a boy's equivalent in
combat colours). Proximity to the Alexandra Palace
ice rink means there's a handy sideline in ice skates
(from £59.99), plus roller skates, unicycles,
skateboards (from £25), crash helmets (£20) and
tag-alongs (by Allycat, £149).
Buggy access. Delivery service. Disabled access.

Two Wheels Good

143 Crouch Hill, N8 9QH (8340 4284/www.two
wheelsgood.co.uk). Finsbury Park tube, then W7
bus. **Open** 8.30am-6pm Mon-Sat; 11am-5pm Sun.
Credit AmEx, MC, V.
Funkier than most bike shops, this one combines
the cool, sporty side of adult biking with a good
range of kids' equipment – the children's versions
of Trek, which cost from about £130, are the
smartest. There are helmets (by Met, £20) with
lovely designs, as well as Trek trailers (£250,
converts to a stroller) and tag-alongs (from £100,
geared and ungeared), plus Bobike child seats (£70).
Buggy access. Disabled access. Mail order.
For branch see index.

Fun & games

Cheeky Monkeys

202 Kensington Park Road, W11 1NR (7792
9022/www.cheekymonkeys.com). Notting Hill Gate
tube, then 52 bus. **Open** 9.30am-5.30pm Mon-Fri;
10am-5.30pm Sat. **Credit** MC, V.
The Notting Hill Monkey opened in 1992 and has,
since then, been joined by four other links to make
a small, independent chain. The shops are strong
on presentation and good at stocking unusual,
attractive and fun products. Pride of place on our
latest visit went to a most impressive ten-in-one
games table (£250), which included a sturdy set-up
for table football, as well as options for air hockey,
ping pong and other games. An enduring bestseller
is the beautiful, shaggy rocking sheep for babies
and toddlers to ride (£49.99). Pocket money toys
along the lines of stickers, fairy accessories and
wooden cars start at £1.99. Fancy-dress outfits are
also sold. There's a bookshop in the basement.
Buggy access. Disabled access. Mail order
(website only).
For branches see index.

Disney Store

360-366 Oxford Street, W1N 9HA (7491 9136/
www.disneystore.co.uk). Bond Street tube. **Open**
10am-8pm Mon-Sat; noon-6pm Sun. **Credit**
AmEx, MC, V.
Selling fast on our last visit were Mr Incredible
dressing-up costumes, with a mask and padded, six-
pack torso. Other dressing-up costumes include
Peter Pan, Snow White, Tinkerbell and Buzz
Lightyear (costumes from £20). There is also
children's underwear, nightwear and casuals
emblazoned with favourite characters. Then there's
the tableware, stationery, lunch bags and boxes and
cuddly toys. Enduring favourites are the character
dolls and, of course, the classic DVDs.
Buggy access. Disabled access. Mail order.
For branches see index.

Early Learning Centre

36 King's Road, SW3 4HD (7581 5764/
www.elc.co.uk). Sloane Square tube. **Open** 9.30am-
7pm Mon-Fri; 9.30am-6pm Sat; 11am-6pm Sun.
Credit AmEx, MC, V.
The huge range of toys, games and art materials is
dedicated to imaginative play for babies and young
children. Everything is sturdy, brightly coloured
and reasonably priced. There are some things ELC
does extremely well, such as simple, soft-bodied
baby dolls, with more sophisticated versions that
suck their dummies and cry. Another bestseller is
the affordable wooden train sets. Then there are the
wonderful art materials, realistic dinosaurs and play
animals and farms, playhouses and pop-up tents,
swings, sandpits, paddling pools, picture books,
science sets and arty-crafty kits. New this season

Traditional Toys. See p266.

was the popular remote-control T-Rex (£25). This
branch holds play sessions for toddlers on Tuesdays
(9.30-11am), except from mid September to early
January, when every inch of space is taken up with
Christmas stock.
Buggy access. Delivery service. Mail order.
Play area.
Branches: throughout the city

Fun Learning

2nd Floor, The Bentall Centre, Clarence Street,
Kingston-upon-Thames, Surrey KT1 1TP (8974
8900). Kingston rail. **Open** 9am-6pm Mon-Wed,
Fri, Sat; 9am-9pm Thur; 11am-5pm Sun. **Credit**
MC, V.
We make no apology for sending you out of town
to one of the best toyshops we know (and while
you're in the Bentall Centre, you can check out the
Lego store, *see p265*). Yes, everything's more or less
educational (though we're not sure how some of the

nuttier outdoor toys, such as Stomp Rockets and
screeching slingshot-type missiles might fit into
that category). There are large sections devoted to
puzzles and number games, art and craft activities,
and science experiments (expect frantic requests for
baking powder and gelatine). Affordable pocket-
money-priced items include balloon-making gunk,
bouncy balls, puzzles, magnifying glasses and other
curiosities. Less affordable are the stunt kites and
the tempting Observer 60 Altaz Refractor
Astronomical Telescope for £99.
Buggy access. Disabled access. Nappy-changing
facilities.
For branch see index.

Hamleys

188-196 Regent Street, W1B 5BT (0870 333
2450/www.hamleys.com). Oxford Circus tube.
Open 10am-8pm Mon-Sat; noon-6pm Sun.
Credit AmEx, DC, MC, V.

This most famous toyshop is a loud, frenetic, exciting experience that can produce tears before bedtime for children who don't understand credit limits. Resting actors demonstrate toys on the ground floor, which also accommodates most of the mayhem and a mountain of soft toys. The basement is the Cyberzone, full of games consoles and high-tech gadgetry. The first floor has items of a scientific bent, plus a lurid sweet factory and a branch of the Bear Factory (from £9.99). The second floor has everything for pre-schoolers. Third is girlie heaven – Barbie World, Sylvanian Families and departments for dressing up, make-up and so on. Fourth has some large and pricey remote-controlled vehicles, plus die-cast models. Fifth is Lego World, which has its own café. Kids can have their birthday party here – typically on a Sunday morning – and Hamleys also arranges Christmas parties and other events.
Buggy access. Café. Delivery service. Disabled access: lift, toilet. Mail order. Nappy-changing facilities. Play areas.

LEGO

Unit 7, The Bentall Centre, Wood Street, Kingston Upon Thames, Surrey KT1 1TR (8546 1280). Kingston rail. **Open** 9.30am-6pm Mon-Wed, Fri; 9.30am-9pm Thur; 9am-6pm Sat. **Credit** MC, V.
Devotees of the knobbly plastic brick and related accessories can find all they need in the Lego line here. There's a huge 'pick-a-brick' wall, which consists of a multitude of perspex containers full of various brick permutations for customers to pick and mix to fill a medium (£6) or large (£11) beaker. Otherwise you can buy special pieces (such as Duplo figures for tots) singly (from 35p) or big presentation boxes of Lego knights and castles, Harry Potter Lego and various other themed sets. Staff sit at the play table and build impressive structures if trade is slack. You can help them.
Buggy access. Disabled access. Mail order. Play areas.

Mystical Fairies

12 Flask Walk, NW3 1HE (7431 1888/www.mysticalfairies.co.uk). Hampstead tube. **Open** 10am-6pm Mon-Sat; 11am-6pm Sun. **Credit** MC, V.
Around 2,000 fairy products find a patch in this amazing shop. Fairy creatures hang from the ceiling on beaded swings, endure being shaken inside glitter-storm bubbles and lend their wings to little girls' rucksacks. Mystical Fairies has realised that no corner of the children's market is untouchable by the fairies. Much energy is going into fairy bedwear now: slippers, dressing gowns, canopies, bed covers and duvet covers. New collections of fairy dresses come from So Fairy Beautiful and Frilly Lilly, in addition to favourite Lucy Lockett and coveted Disney Princess costumes. The Enchanted Garden in the basement is a splendid space for special Mystical Fairies parties; it's also home to Fairy Club and Fairy School.
Buggy access. Mail order.

Toys 'R' Us

760 Old Kent Road, SE15 1NJ (7732 7322/www.toysrus.co.uk). Elephant & Castle tube/rail then 21, 56, 172 bus. **Open** 9am-8pm Mon-Fri; 9am-7pm Sat; 11am-5pm Sun. **Credit** AmEx, MC, V.
The Peckham branch of the chain of spacious toy warehouses is the most central Toys 'R' Us. It stocks industrial quantities of the toy of the moment. Inexpensive bikes (from £39.99), trikes, ride-on tractors and go-karts (£89.99), car seats, baby accessories and buggies are other attractions, and the party paraphernalia is pretty good: themed paperware, silly hats, balloons and party bags with plasticky fillings. Toys 'R' Us, which recently celebrated its 20th birthday, is the best place for large quantities of (good-quality) batteries, and big-name board games, such as new Monopoly editions, Trivial Pursuit and Cluedo, and is a consistently good bet for Action Man, Barbie and My Little Pony.
Buggy access. Car park. Delivery service. Disabled access: toilet. Mail order (website only). Nappy-changing facilities.
Branches: throughout the city.

Local toyshops

Art Stationers/Green's Village Toy Shop

31 Dulwich Village, SE21 7BN (8693 5938). North Dulwich rail. **Open** 9am-5.30pm Mon-Sat. **Credit** MC, V.
If it's art supplies – paint boxes, pastels, crayons, easels, paper, stationery – you want, stay in the front section, where party paperware, cards and craft kits are also sold. Most children canter to the back section, however, where Brio, Sylvanian Families, Playmobil, Crayola, Lego and other giants of the toy kingdom sit. The staff remain cheerful even during the after-school rush for pocket-money-priced must-haves (stickers, stretchy aliens, yo-yos, rings, bubbles) and are happy to advise on toys. Doll's house furniture and dressing-up clothes are also sold.
Buggy access.

Fagin's Toys

84 Fortis Green Road, N10 3HN (8444 0282). East Finchley tube then 102 bus. **Open** 9am-5.30pm Mon-Sat; 10am-3pm Sun. **Credit** MC, V.
This is the sister shop of Word Play in Crouch End (*see p266*) and it has a similar feel: it's a lovely big space and the stock is sensibly chosen. There is almost nothing faddy here: the owner sticks with her favourites (Galt, Orchard, Brio, Lego, Playmobil, Sylvanian Families). Row upon row of games yields to an art corner with paint, art, sewing and henna kits by John Adams and Galt, and the Jellycat stuffed animals are hugely popular too. A large table at the front is chock-a-block with novelties, sweeties, pens and pretty much everything else a child might want to blow their pocket money on, including masks and key rings, kaleidoscopes and gold wands.
Buggy access.

Happy Returns

36 Rosslyn Hill, NW3 1NH (7435 2431). Hampstead tube. **Open** 9.30am-5.30pm Mon-Fri; 10am-6pm Sat; noon-5.30pm Sun. **Credit** MC, V.
A good range of Galt crafts, from Octons and paints to hair art, is complemented by Crayola art equipment. There are cheap and cheerful items like police helmets, swords and feather boas, but otherwise it's all proper boxed toys – Sylvanian Families, bubble machines (£9.99), sailing yachts, Wolfhammer games and action figures. There are some useful products in the way of partywares, and tableware is usually available, from Thomas the Tank Engine to princesses, alongside printed helium balloons or regular balloons. There are also printed banners, cheap party-bag treats and higher-quality mixed packs of presents (good value at £2.50 for four gifts).
Buggy access. Play area.

Patrick's Toys & Models

107-111 Lillie Road, SW6 7SX (7385 9864/www.patrickstoys.co.uk). Fulham Broadway tube. **Open** 9.30am-5.30pm Mon-Sat. **Credit** MC, V.
This recently refurbished shop has something to suit every pocket and, for once, boys get the lion's share of the goods. It's the main service agent for Hornby and Scalextric, so expect lots of tracks and model trains – everything for everyone from novices to adults. Outdoor sports get a look-in with kites, bikes and garden games, while war buffs will find enough to engage in full-scale combat. There's a choice of doll's houses with all the furniture miniature Victorians could wish for, or Barbies, Bratz and Sindies. Cheap party gifts are also sold.
Buggy access. Delivery service (local).

Play

89 Lauriston Road, E9 7HJ (8510 9960/www.playtoyshops.com). Bethnal Green or Mile End tube/277, 388 bus. **Open** 10am-5.30pm Tue-Sat; 11am-4pm Sun. **Credit** MC, V.
The Lauriston Road roundabout area, a hop and a skip from Victoria Park, is a smart little enclave popular with young-ish, wealthy-ish parents. That's why this exciting toyshop on two floors always has customers. There's lots for everyone

to covet: little girls love the flower fairy melamine tableware and sparkly glasses, the Lily Dolls downstairs and the range of Pintoy doll's houses, furniture and people. Everyone wants to cuddle the Gund soft toys and play with the Geomag, Lego, Galt and Playmobil. Downstairs there are books and musical instruments. There's also a whole range of dressing-up stuff and messy play products, alongside trinkets by Jellycat and Lucy Lockett. With space for parking pushchairs and a very well-used community noticeboard, Play is lots of fun to visit, and the charming staff couldn't be more helpful. Look out for monthly themed events.
Buggy access. Play area.

QT Toys

90 Northcote Road, SW11 6QN (7223 8637). Clapham Junction rail. **Open** 9.30am-5.30pm Mon-Sat. **Credit** MC, V.
You can find most stuff at QT, from tacky plastic waterpistols and pocket-money toys to big-brand name items – Barbies, Bratz, Brio and Lego. Then there's a whole wall crowded with craft kits, modelling toys and stationery, plus various educational toys. A huge range of gorgeously detailed Schleich animals includes farm and safari-park livestock, wildlife and cantering horses for knights and soldiers. Small children can find their dollies, buggies, push-along trucks and pull-along dogs, and there's stuff for the garden too, such as paddling pools, sandpits and swings and scooters.
Buggy access. Disabled access.

Route 73 Kids

92 Stoke Newington Church Street, N16 0AP (7923 7873). Finsbury Park tube/rail then 106 bus/73, 393, 476 bus. **Open** 10am-5.30pm Tue-Sun. **Credit** MC, V.
Take the No.73 bendy bus to this brightly coloured, personable shop. Stock includes Brio trains and track, Plan wooden toys, Galt marble runs and art equipment; pocket-money items such as rubber fish, mini pencils, bubbles and mini cars; plus books, puzzles, jigsaws and word games. As for non-toys, there are Daisy Roots soft leather shoes, Lollipop hair accessories and little printed pyjamas in boxes by Bedlam (£20). Route 73 is strong on crafts and also stocks outdoor toys, including play sand and sandpit toys, in summer.
Buggy access. Delivery service (local). Mail order.

Snap Dragon

56 Turnham Green Terrace, W4 1QP (8995 6618). Turnham Green tube. **Open** 9.30am-6pm Mon-Sat; 11am-5pm Sun. **Credit** MC, V.
Playtime looks exceedingly promising at this bright-red shop, where dolls and dolly pushchairs line up against pouty-mouthed Baby and Smoby sit-and-rides. For imaginative play there are doll's houses, accessories and figures by Pintoy and Playmobil. A wide range of family games includes Twister, Buckaroo and the more cerebral Scrabble. Finally there are kits, balls, rockets and remote-control cars for outdoor play.
Buggy access. Delivery service (local). Mail order.

Toy Station

6 Eton Street, Richmond, Surrey TW9 1EE (8940 4896). Richmond tube/rail. **Open** 10am-6pm Mon-Fri; 9.30am-6pm Sat; noon-5pm Sun. **Credit** (over £8) MC, V.
There are so many toys jostling for attention in the window of this old-fashioned, two-storey toyshop that children are saucer-eyed before they even go through the door. Inside, there's a great display of Schleich and Papo farm animals, wild animals, sea creatures, knights and soldiers. Forts and castles are also sold. Elsewhere, there are Nikko remote-control vehicles (Mini Cooper £24.99); doll's houses and traditional wooden toys, fancy-dress costumes and accessories, and party equipment.
Buggy access. Disabled access.

Toystop

80-82 St John's Road, SW11 1PX (7228 9079). Clapham Junction rail. **Open** 9.30am-6pm Mon-Sat; 11am-5pm Sun. **Credit** MC, V.

A spacious toyshop, which devotes a section to Warhammer sets and accessories, a large wall to Sylvanian families sets (from £10.99), Playmobil and Lego. Then there are the dolls, including Bratz and Barbie. Angelina Ballerina also finds favour here. A large table is taken up with party-bag toys (fortune-telling fish, magnetic stones, wobbly ladybirds). There's also a huge sticker tower; outdoor toys including kites, diablos and stomp rockets; board games, puzzles, a small selection of books, make-up cases, novelty stationery, mini racing cars, beads, bangles and baubles.
Buggy access.

Word Play

1 Broadway Parade, N8 9TN (8347 6700). Finsbury Park tube/rail then W7, 41 bus. **Open** 9am-5.30pm Mon-Sat; 11am-5pm Sun. **Credit** MC, V.
A well-loved Crouch End fixture, Word Play is proud of its balance between books and toys, and is very laid-back. A good half of its display space is devoted to children's books, from nursery rhymes to history and reference – Lemony Snicket, unsurprisingly, continues to sell well. Then it has lots of craft supplies, plus popular building toys such as Bionicles or Geomag at sensible prices. New in are those adorably detailed Schleich toys: little figures such as farm animals, knights and soldiers (£1.99-£6.99) and, for £69.99, a great castle. There's only a small collection of wooden toys, but you can buy a nice set of wooden draughts for £7.99. A low '£2 and under' table-top is full of penny dreadfuls, devil bangers and fortune-telling fish for 10p.
Buggy access. Disabled access. Mail order.

Traditional toys

EnglishToys (www.englishtoys.com) focuses on traditional categories of well-crafted toys, including Noah's arks, rocking horses, doll's houses, steam engines and wooden toys.

Benjamin Pollock's Toyshop

44 The Market, WC2E 8RF (7379 7866/www.pollocks-coventgarden.co.uk). Covent Garden tube. **Open** 10.30am-6pm Mon-Sat; 11am-4pm Sun. **Credit** AmEx, MC, V.
Once you've crossed behind the disused shopfront reading 'Pollock's Theatre', dodged the waffle stand, and hiked up some steep stairs, you eventually discover a kooky haven. Best known for its toy theatres, Pollock's is an educational wonderland for young thesps and is hugely enjoyed, on a more superficial level, by all. The most popular paper theatre to assemble is Jackson's (£7.95), with its set and characters for the ballet *Cinderella*. Other items on sale include marionettes, glove and finger puppets, and French music boxes (£37.50). There are quirky pocket-money toys too, such as cardboard masks (£1.40) and pocket compasses (£1.99).
Mail order.

Bob & Blossom

140 Columbia Road, E2 7RG (7739 4737/ www.bobandblossom.com) Old Street tube/rail or 26, 48, 55 bus. **Open** 9am-3pm Sun. **Credit** MC, V.
Not quite a toy shop, Bob & Blossom is probably best described as a 'children's lifestyle shop' (stop sniggering), with beautiful Danish wooden Noah's ark sets, those trademark trendy, tiny T-shirts emblazoned with cheeky mottos, Mexican jumping beans and spinning tops – and prices ranging from £1 to £50. Meanwhile, classic toy cars and wooden musical instruments will induce bouts of nostalgia. Trading hours coincide with the hugely popular Columbia Road Sunday flower market (*see p163*).
Mail order.

Compendia Traditional Games

10 The Market, SE10 9HZ (8293 6616/ www.compendia.co.uk). Cutty Sark DLR/ Greenwich rail. **Open** 11am-5.30pm Mon-Fri; 10am-5.30pm Sat, Sun. **Credit** MC, V.
The ultimate shop for a rainy day, Compendia has the traditionals – chess, backgammon, dominoes

– as well as an appealing range of more obscure games from around the world to suit all ages. If you've had enough, Cluedo, check out Champagne Murders (a murder-mystery game for ages eight to adult). Little ones have fun with Coppit – a wobbly hat game – but the drug-smuggling board game Grass is, of course, for adults only.
Buggy access. Delivery service. Disabled access. Mail order.

Farmyard

63 Barnes High Street, SW13 9LF (8878 7338/ www.thefarmyard.co.uk). Barnes or Barnes Bridge rail. **Open** 10am-5.30pm Mon-Fri; 9.30am-5.30pm Sat. **Credit** MC, V.
Traditional toys and games for newborns to eight-year-olds are corralled into Farmyard, which has its own personalised range of wooden toys, models and kits. As well as the traditional wooden stuff, there are quirky imports, such as Uncle Milton's Ant Farm (a £5.99 plastic 'farm' area into which you release your ants and watch them at work). There are also several shelves of fairy/princess stuff, with Angelina Ballerina very much in evidence. There's a concise collection of dressing-up clothes, including a pretty selection of fairy-princess and ballerina gear (£25-£35). Boys aren't left out: there are also pirates, kings with capes and knights' tabards decorated with chain mail.
Buggy access. Play area.
For branch see index.

Kristin Baybars

7 Mansfield Road, NW3 2JD (7267 0934). Kentish Town tube/Gospel Oak rail/C2, C11 bus. **Open** 11am-6pm Tue-Sat. **No credit cards.**
This miniaturist's paradise is also a fairy tale come true for any child capable of looking without touching. You have to knock to gain entry ('mysterious' is a preferred adjective of Ms Baybars herself), but what you'll see inside is the biggest, most jaw-dropping array of tiny scenes and houses outside a craft fair. Show enough interest and you'll be ushered into the inner sanctum – room after room of amazing little worlds, including a house full of dogs, a macabre execution scenario and an old-fashioned store. The doll's house kits aren't prohibitively expensive (£70 buys you a massive Regency affair, though a few are cheaper), and it's well worth investing a few pounds in tiny accessories; there's plenty at pocket-money prices, though collectors who regularly come here are liable to invest a good deal more.
Buggy access.

Never Never Land

3 Midhurst Parade, N10 3EJ (8883 3997). East Finchley tube. **Open** 10am-5pm Tue, Wed, Fri, Sat. **Credit** MC, V.
This teeny rectangle of a shop is crammed with old-world delights and betrays the love and attention of the devoted owner and assistant. The shop is known for its doll's houses – high-quality structures (from £85) and individually sold bits and pieces that really do fit together. There are modest alternatives to houses, such as shops (£57.50) and conservatories (£20). The owner is adept at sourcing unusual wooden toys (such as dancing musical frogs, £8.99) and also stocks baby-safe toys. Lots of pocket-money potential here too – Russian dolls (£6.99), tiny Chinese cloth purses (99p) and German knights.
Buggy access. Mail order.

Puppet Planet

787 Wandsworth Road (corner of the Chase), SW8 3JQ (7627 0111/www.puppetplanet.co.uk). Clapham Common tube. **Open** 9am-4pm Tue-Sat; also open by appointment. **Credit** AmEx, DC, MC, V.
A specialist shop and hospital for tangled marionettes, Puppet Planet is run by Lesley Butler, whose passion for stringed characters extends to her children's party service. The puppets sold here include classic Pelham characters, traditional Indian and African marionettes, Balinese shadow puppets, and

vintage carved and felt hand-puppets from Germany. Prices go from £1 for a pop-up puppet to quite a bit more for collectors' items. Regular storytelling on Sundays; call to check.
Buggy access. Delivery service. Disabled access. Mail order. Play area.

Rainbow

253 Archway Road, N6 5BS (8340 9700/ www.rainbow-toys.co.uk). Highgate tube. **Open** 10.30am-5.30pm Mon-Sat. **Credit** MC, V.
After 20 years of catering for the play needs of north London's children, Rainbow is more popular than ever. There's a useful website and a nifty little mail-order business to supplement the treasure-stuffed shop. Rainbow's dressing-up costumes are among the best in town: Spiderman and *Star Wars* with light sabre are very popular, as are ballerina outfits and Lucy Lockett fairy dresses. There are lots of wooden Pin and Plan Toys, including plane and car sit-and-rides and tricycles (£30-£50), plus reasonably priced doll's houses (£45-£75) and accessories to go with them.
Buggy access. Delivery service (local). Mail order. Play area.

Soup Dragon

27 Topsfield Parade, Tottenham Lane, N8 8PT (8348 0224/www.soup-dragon.co.uk). Finsbury Park tube/rail then W7 bus. **Open** 9.30am-6pm Mon-Sat; 11am-5pm Sun. **Credit** MC, V.
The north London wing of Soup Dragon was the first to open (in 1989), although the East Dulwich one is bigger. It started out as a market selling unusual kids' clothing, toys and nursery items. These days there are more nursery products, plus some wonderfully colourful baby clothes (fine striped knits, funky tights and bright pinafores). The toys are the mainstay, however, with soft toys for babies, fancy dress, pretty doll's houses (£65 for a contemporary house with flat-screen television and glass walls). Staff are friendly and helpful. Check the website for a list of stock.
Buggy access. Mail order. Play area.
For branch see index.

Traditional Toys

53 Godfrey Street, SW3 3SX (7352 1718/ www.traditionaltoy.com). Sloane Square tube then 11, 19, 22 bus/49 bus. **Open** 10am-5.30pm Mon-Fri; 10am-6pm Sat. **Credit** AmEx, MC, V.
It's a pleasure to visit this terrific little toyshop near Chelsea Green. Every nook and cranny is filled with games, books and toys. There's a wide range of toys at pocket-money prices – such as farm animals, bouncy balls, stickers, skipping ropes and toy soldiers – plus rather more pricey painted ride-on toys for the nursery, a bright-red wooden fire engine (£63) and a handmade wooden marble run of impressive intricacy for £122.99. Shelves hold Breyer model ponies, Brio train sets, doll's houses (and accessories), boats, dolls, teddies by Steiff, Gund and the North American Bear Company, sturdy wooden Noah's arks and much more. Don't miss the fantastic fancy dresses: sheriffs, knights, elves and fairies. There's also a catalogue of costumes that may be ordered from the store.
Buggy access. Delivery service.

Tridias

25 Bute Street, SW7 3EY (7584 2330). South Kensington tube. **Open** 9.30am-5.30pm Mon-Fri; 9am-5.30pm Sat. **Credit** MC, V.
The proximity of Tridias to the big museums manifests itself in shelves stocking intriguing chemistry and science experiment sets (for about £30), but there's also a corner devoted to party equipment. Staff could never hope to get the full Tridias range in here, but anything from the mail order catalogue can be ordered. As well as croquet, cricket and swingball sets, expect to find dressing-up clothes, Brio, tool kits, marble runs and boxed games, garages and cars, doll's houses and accessories, plenty of educational books and board games. The branch in Richmond is a much bigger concern.
Buggy access. Mail order (0870 443 1300).
For branch see index.

Indexes
& Maps

Subject Index

INDEX

INDEX

A-Z Index

INDEX

INDEX

INDEX

INDEX

INDEX

INDEX

INDEX

INDEX

Advertisers Index

Please refer to relevant sections for addresses and /or telephone numbers

INDEX

© Copyright Time Out Group 2006

800 m

800 yds

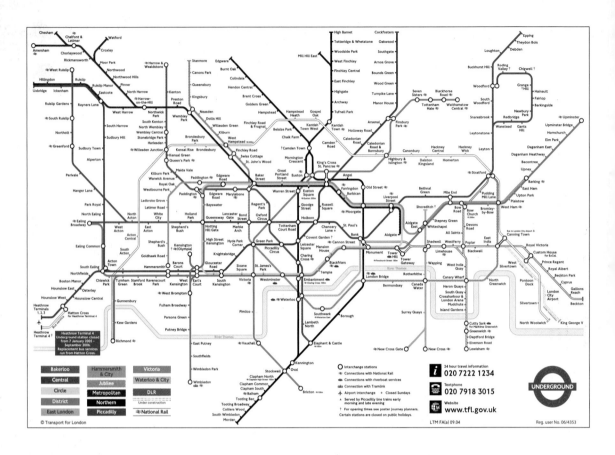